1996

KING'S COLLEGE LONDON

MEDIEVAL STUDIES

XI

King's College London

Centre for Late Antique and Medieval Studies

Director: Janet L. Nelson

KING'S COLLEGE LONDON MEDIEVAL STUDIES

GENERAL EDITOR:

Janet Bately

EXECUTIVE EDITOR:

David Hook

EDITORIAL BOARD:

Roderick Beaton, Janet Cowen, Albinia de la Mare,

Carlotta Dionisotti, Claire Isoz, Martin Jones,

Susan Kruse, Karen Pratt, Jane Roberts, David Yeandle

A THESAURUS OF OLD ENGLISH

in two volumes

Volume I: Introduction and Thesaurus
Volume II: Index

JANE ROBERTS and **CHRISTIAN KAY**

with

LYNNE GRUNDY

Volume II: Index

King's College London
Centre for Late Antique and Medieval Studies
1995

© Jane Roberts, Christian Kay, and Lynne Grundy 1995

ISSN 0953-217X

ISBN: complete work   0 9522119 0 4

ISBN: volume I   0 9522119 2 0

ISBN: volume II   0 9522119 3 9

Typeset by Harold Short at King's College London with the LaTeX Documentation System. LaTeX was developed by Leslie Lamport, and is based on the TeX formatting program of Donald E. Knuth.

Many of the designations used by manufacturers and sellers of computer hardware and software to distinguish their products are claimed as trademarks. Following is a list of trademark designations and their owners relevant to this publication.

Trademark notice

TeX^{TM} is a trademark of the American Mathematical Society.
INGRES^{TM} is a trademark of Ingres Corporation.
UNIX^{TM} is a trademark of AT&T Bell Laboratories.
VAX^{TM} is a trademark of Digital Equipment Corporation.
dBase^{TM} is a trademark of Borland International Inc.
Apricot^{TM} is a trademark of Apricot Computers Ltd.

Printed in England

on 80gsm acid-free recycled paper

by Short Run Press Ltd, Exeter

1995

INDEX

The Index lists all Old English words and phrases in the Thesaurus, together with the lowest numbered headings under which they appear. In the alphabetical order of words *æ* follows *ae*, *þ* follows *t* and the *ge-* prefix is disregarded, as is *(ge)-*. Where variant forms are given, the sort otherwise ignores the presence of parentheses. Preference is given as a rule to normalized forms, but because variation (for example *i*, *ie* and *y*; or *æ* and *ea*) is embedded in the source dictionaries some spelling variation must be negotiated by the reader.

ā 06.01.07.07.02 Impossible; 05.10.05.04.09 Side, quarter, direction; 05.11.09.01 Always; 05.11.01.01.01 Eternity

ā būtan ende 05.11.01.01.01 Eternity

ā forþ ēce 05.11.01.01.01 Eternity

ā on ēcnesse 05.11.01.01.01 Eternity

ā simle 05.11.09.01 Always

ā tīman 05.11.08 A suitable time, opportunity

ā tō wīdan fēore 05.11.09.01 Always

ā woruld 05.11.01.01.01 Eternity

ā worulda woruld 05.11.01.01.01 Eternity

ābacan 04.01.02.02.05.04 Baking

ābacen 04.01.02.02.05.04 Baking

ābǣdan 03.01.16.03 A drop of liquid; 06.02.04.01 Want, need; 12.03.04 A request, prayer; 12.05.06.01 Restraint, check, curb, control

ābǣran 09.05.05 Exposure, revealing, revelation

ābannan 12.03.03.01 Summons, a call, summoning

ābannan ūt 12.03.03.01 Summons, a call, summoning

ābarian 05.10.05.04.13 A removal of that which obscures or conceals; 09.05.05 Exposure, revealing, revelation

abbod 16.02.03.03.01.01 An abbot

abboddōm 16.02.03.03.01.01 An abbot

abbodesse 16.02.03.03.01.02 An abbess

abbodhād 16.02.03.03.01.01 An abbot

abbodlēast 16.02.03.03.01.01 An abbot

abbodrīce 16.02.03.03.01.01 An abbot

ābēatan 05.06.09 Act of striking

ābēcēdē 09.03.07.01 A written character, letter

ābedecian 15.01.06.01 Begging

ābelgan 08.01.03.05.02 Anger; 08.01.03.07.02 Misery, trouble, affliction

ābēodan 09.06.02.01 To tell, make known, declare, relate, announce; 09.06.02.01.05 Proclamation, spreading abroad; 10.03.02 Presenting, offering; 12.03.03 A command, bidding, order

ābeornan 03.01.09.02.01 Fire, burning; 08.01.01.01 Ardour, fervour, strong feeling

āberan 02.01.03.03.02 To bring forth, produce; 05.12.02.02 To carry off, remove; 06.02.04.01.01 Need, distress, straits, difficulty; 08.01.03.07.03 Suffering, torment, pain; 08.01.03.08 Patience; 09.05.05

ābered

Exposure, revealing, revelation; 12.07 An obligation, bounden duty
ābered 11.04.02.01.01 Cunning, craft, craftiness, guile, wile
āberendlic 08.01.03.08 Patience
āberstan 05.08.02 Violence, force
āberstan ūt 05.12.05.03.04.01 To burst forth, break out
ābetēon 14.03.03.01 Accusation
ābīdan 02.01.02.02 To come to life, have life; 05.10.04.03 Presence; 05.12.04 Absence of movement, stillness; 06.01.08 Expectation; 06.01.08.01 Expectation, waiting
ābiddan 10.01.02 Acquisition; 12.03.04.01 Entreaty, solemn appeal; 13.02 War; 16.02.04.08 Prayer
ābiddan æt 12.03.04.01 Entreaty, solemn appeal
ābies 02.07.03.05 Particular trees/shrubs (alphabetical order)
ābifian 05.12.05.05 To shake, quake, wag; 08.01.01 A feeling, what is felt
ābirgan 04 Consumption of food/drink
ābir(g)ing 02.05.07 Faculty of taste
ābisgian 05.10.04.03 Presence; 05.11 A time, period of time; 08.01.03.07.02 Misery, trouble, affliction; 11.02 Occupation, activity, business
ābisgian (in/on/mid/ymb) 11.02 Occupation, activity, business
ābisgian wiþ 12.05.05 Resistance, repulsing
ābisgung 11.02 Occupation, activity, business; 12.05.06.02.03 Trouble, disturbance
ābītan 04 Consumption of food/drink; 05.06.01 Devastation, laying waste; 05.06.06.01 A tearing, laceration

ābit(e)rian 02.05.07.01 Strong taste, acidity, pungency; 07.03.01.03 To loathe, hate, abhor
āblācian 03.01.14.02 Pallor, absence of colour; 05.09 Weakness; 06.01.08.06 Fear
āblǣcan 03.01.14.03 White/whiteness
āblǣst 01.03.01.05 Wind; 02.04.06.07.05 To breathe; 03.01.15.01 Inspiration, inbreathing; 05.08.02 Violence, force
āblāwan 02.08.05.01 Swelling; 03.01.15.01 Inspiration, inbreathing
āblāwan on/ofer 02.04.06.07.05 To breathe
āblāwen 02.08.05.01 Swelling
āblāwnes 02.08.05.01 Swelling
āblāwung 02.08.05.01 Swelling
āblegned 02.08.05.02 Particular inflammation/swelling
āblend 02.05.09.02 Inability to see (because of darkness); 06.01.07.05 Error, being astray
āblendan 02.08.07.02.01 Defective vision; 06.01.07.04.01 Deception, a leading astray
āblendan cancer 02.08.12.02.06 Surgical
āblered 02.04.04.03.04 Bald, shaven
āblīcan 03.01.12.01 Glittering, effulgence
āblindan 02.08.07.02.01 Defective vision
āblindian 02.08.07.02.01 Defective vision
āblinnan 05.07 Ending of existence, end of world; 11.06.04 Abstention, abstaining from
āblinnendlīce 05.11.10.02 End, completion; 05.11.11.01 A not ceasing, persistence, recurrence
āblinnendnes 05.11.10.02 End, completion
āblissian 08.01.01.03.09.03 To make glad

āblycgan 06.01.08.05.01 Amazement, astonishment, wonder, admiration; 06.01.08.06 Fear
āblycge(n)de 06.01.08.05.01 Amazement, astonishment, wonder, admiration
āblysian 07.09.01.01 Reddening with shame, confusion
āblysung 07.09.01.01 Reddening with shame, confusion
ābodian 09.06.02.01.05 Proclamation, spreading abroad
ābogen 07.07 Humility
ābolgennes 08.01.03.05.03 Exasperation, irritation
āborgian 14.03.03.07 Security, pledge, bail
āborgian æt 15.04.01 Lending of money
āborsten 05.06.02 Cleaving, splitting, cutting
ābōtian 17.02.04.01 Repairing, renewing
ābrācian 17.02.05.05.01 Graven, embossed, chased
ābrǣdan 04.01.02.02.05 Cooking; 05.10.05.02.02 Greater, bigger
ābrǣded 05.10.05.02 Extension, stretching
ābraslian 02.05.10.08 A crackling, rustling
ābrecan 02.02.04.03 To kill, slay; 05.06.02.01 A cleft, split; 05.06.03 A dashing together, breaking, shattering; 13.02.03.01 An attack, assault; 14.02 Lawlessness
ābrecan ūp 01.01.03.01.01.07 Spring, fountain, well; 05.10.04.04.01 Dispersion
ābrecan (ūt) 05.12.05.03.04.01 To burst forth, break out; 11.10.05 Escape
ābredwian 02.02.04.03 To kill, slay

ābrēgan 06.01.08.06.03.01 Causing dread, terrifying
ābregdan 02.05.02 Consciousness; 05.10.05.04.14 An opening, aperture; 05.12.02.05 To pull, drag, draw; 05.12.03.01.01 Quick movement or movements; 05.12.05.05 To shake, quake, wag; 10.04.03 To take away, remove; 13.02.08.04.03.02 Armed with a sword; 14.02.01.02.01 Open robbery, rapine, pillage
ābregdan fram 05.12.02.08 To give a different direction to, turn
ābregdan (tō) 05.13.01 Transformation, taking another shape
ābregdan (ūp) 05.06.08 A plucking, taking away; 05.12.02.05 To pull, drag, draw
ābrēotan 02.02.04.03 To kill, slay; 02.08.04 Hurt, injury, damage; 05.06 Destruction, dissolution, loss, breaking
ābrēotnes 02.02.04 Killing, violent death, destruction
ābrēoþan 03.02.01 Decay, decline, corruption; 05.06 Destruction, dissolution, loss, breaking; 11.06.03 Failing, failure; 11.06.03.01 Ill fortune, bad success
ābrocen 04.02.05.02.02 (Of sheep) sore, ulcerous
ābrocen land 04.02.03.02 Arable/ploughed land
ābroþen 12.08.06.01.02 Lacking moral good
ābroþennes 12.08.06.02.06 Deceit, evil, wickedness
ābrūcan 04 Consumption of food/drink
ābrȳtan 05.06 Destruction, dissolution, loss, breaking

ābufan 05.10.05.04.09.01.02 Front, beginning
ābūgan 02.08.04.04 State of being crippled; 05.12.05.03.03 To depart, leave, set out; 05.12.05.13.02 To bow, bend down; 07.04.03 Reverence, respect; 13.02.05.02.01 Surrender, submission
ābūgan fram 05.12 To move, be in motion
ābūgan (fram) 12.08.06.02.05.05 To sin (against), do wrong
ābūgan (tō) 12.05.06.04.02 Submission, subjection, obedience
ābunden 11.12.01 Absence of restraint, freedom
ābūrod 04.02.01 Farmstead; 12.06.03 A site, settlement
ābūtan 03.06 Comparison; 05.10.05.04.02.01 Exterior, outside of; 05.10.05.04.11 A circle, circuit, circumference; 05.13.03 Regular alternation
ābūtan behringan 05.10.05.04.11 A circle, circuit, circumference
ābycgan 11.10.03 Salvation/deliverance from; 12.07 An obligation, bounden duty; 16.02.04.07.02.03 Penance, an act/instance of penance
ābyffan 09.02.03.02 Stammering
ābȳgan 05.10.06.02.02 Curvature, bend, twist; 05.12.02.08 To give a different direction to, turn; 12.05.06 Grasp, power, control, mastery
(ge)ābylgan 08.01.03.05.02 Anger
ābȳwan 04.06.01 Clean
ābȳwed 04.06.01.09 To cleanse, remove impurity from (an object); 12.08.04 Purity, moral cleanness
ac 03.06 Comparison

āc 02.07.03.05 Particular trees/shrubs (alphabetical order); 05.12.01.09.03.01 A ship, boat; 09.03.07.01.01 A runic letter
ācǣglod 04.04.09 A fringe, border, hem
ācalan 02.08.03.02 Itch, irritation; 03.01.11 Coldness, coolness
acan 02.08.03 Pain, bodily discomfort
ācbēam 02.07.03.05 Particular trees/shrubs (alphabetical order)
ācbearo 02.07.03.05 Particular trees/shrubs (alphabetical order)
accent 09.03.07.04.01 To punctuate, divide
āccynn 02.07.03.05 Particular trees/shrubs (alphabetical order)
ācealdian 03.01.11 Coldness, coolness
ācēapian 15.05 Trade, traffic, commerce
ācecg 02.07.03.05 Particular trees/shrubs (alphabetical order)
ācēlan 03.01.11 Coldness, coolness; 04.01.03 Drinking; 08.01.01.02.01 Want of interest or concern, indifference
ācennan 02.01.03.03.02 To bring forth, produce; 05.03 Source, origin; 07.01.01 Choice, election
ācenned 02.01.03.03.03 Birth
ācennedlic 02.03.03.03.01 A native people
ācen(ned)nes 02.01.03.03.03 Birth
ācennend 02.03.02.01 Parent
ācennicge 02.01.03.03.02 To bring forth, produce; 02.03.02.01 Parent
ācenning 02.01.03.03.03 Birth
ācēocian 02.08.07.04.04 Respiratory disease
ācēocung 06.01.01.01.01.01 Consideration, rumination

āceorfan 05.06.02 Cleaving, splitting, cutting
āceorfan fram/of 12.05.07 Casting out, rejection
ācēosan 07.01.01 Choice, election
ācett 02.07.03.05 Particular trees/shrubs (alphabetical order)
āchangra 02.07.03.05 Particular trees/shrubs (alphabetical order)
ācholt 02.07.03.05 Particular trees/shrubs (alphabetical order)
ācīgan 12.03.03.01 Summons, a call, summoning
ācirran 05.12.05 To move and change direction, turn; 05.13 Changeableness, change
āclǣnsian 04.06.01 Clean; 04.06.01.09 To cleanse, remove impurity from (an object)
āclēaf 02.07.03.05 Particular trees/shrubs (alphabetical order)
āclēofan 05.06.02.01 A cleft, split
ācleopian 09.06.02.01 To tell, make known, declare, relate, announce
geāclian 06.01.08.06.03.01 Causing dread, terrifying
āclungen 03.02.01 Decay, decline, corruption
ācmelu 04.01.02.01.03.07 Meal
ācmistel 02.07.03.05 Particular trees/shrubs (alphabetical order)
ācnāwan 06.01.06.01.01.02 To know, recognize
ācnyht 03.03.06.01 A whole formed by joining
ācofrian 02.08.13 Recovery, growing better
ācol 06.01.08.06 Fear

ācōlian 03.01.11 Coldness, coolness; 08.01.01.02.01 Want of interest or concern, indifference
ācolitus 16.02.03.02.12 Cleric in minor orders
ācolmōd 06.01.08.06 Fear
geācolmōdian 06.01.08.06.03.01 Causing dread, terrifying
ācōlod 03.01.11 Coldness, coolness; 08.01.01.02.01 Want of interest or concern, indifference
ācordian 13.01.02 Reconciliation
ācoren 07.02.04.03 Nobleness, excellence, nobility, magnificence
ācorenlic 07.04.04.02 Laudable, praiseworthy
ācostnian 11.03.01.01 Trial, probation
ācræftan 06.02.06.02 A proposal, proposition, suggestion
ācrammian 03.03.06.02 Fullness
ācrēopian 03.03.04.01.02 A great number, multitude
ācrēowed 03.03.04.01.02 A great number, multitude
ācrimman 03.03.06.02 Fullness
ācrind 02.07.03.05 Particular trees/shrubs (alphabetical order)
ācstybb 02.07.03.05 Particular trees/shrubs (alphabetical order)
āctān 02.07.03.05 Particular trees/shrubs (alphabetical order)
āctrēo 02.07.03.05 Particular trees/shrubs (alphabetical order)
ācuman 03.03.04.02 A sufficiency, sufficient supply; 05.12.02.01 To fetch, bring, bear, conduct; 05.12.05.03.04 To come/go out from; 05.12.05.08.01 To go before and guide; 08.01.03.07.03 Suffering, torment, pain
ācumba 17.04.04.01 Oakum, hards, tow

ācumba(-e) 03.01.09.02.01.02 Embers, cinders, ashes; 04.06.02.04 Refuse, litter, rubbish
ācumendlic 06.01.07.07 Possibility; 08.01.03.08 Patience
ācumendlicnes 06.01.07.07 Possibility
ācunnan 14.03.03.01 Accusation
ācunnian 11.03.01 Experience, trial, experiment; 11.03.01.01 Trial, probation; 11.03.01.01.01 Proof, demonstration
ācunnung 11.03.01 Experience, trial, experiment
ācursian 07.05.03.02 Calumny, slander, insult
ācūsan 14.03.03.01 Accusation
ācwacian 05.12.05.05 To shake, quake, wag
ācweccan 05.12.05.05 To shake, quake, wag
ācwelan 02.02.03 To die, perish
ācwellan 02.02.04.03 To kill, slay
ācwellednes 02.02.04 Killing, violent death, destruction
ācwencan 03.01.13.02 A growing dark, darkening; 05.07 Ending of existence, end of world
ācweor(na) 02.06.03.01.13 Rodents
ācweorran 04.01.01.04 Gluttony, overeating, greediness
ācweþan 09.01 To speak, exercise faculty of speech; 09.05.03 An answer, reply
ācwician 02.01.02.02 To come to life, have life; 02.08.13 Recovery, growing better; 08.01.01.03.09.03 To make glad; 16.02.01.12 Spirituality
ācwīnan 03.01.13.02 A growing dark, darkening

ācwincan 03.01.13.02 A growing dark, darkening; 05.07 Ending of existence, end of world
ācwudu 02.07.03.05 Particular trees/shrubs (alphabetical order)
ācwylman 02.02.04.03 To kill, slay
ācwylmian 08.01.03.07.03 Suffering, torment, pain
ācȳþan 09.05.05.01 Showing, manifestation, display
ad te levavi 16.02.05.10.04 Choir books, etc.
ād 02.02.05.01.01 A grave, burial place, sepulchre; 03.01.09.02.01.01 A kind of fire; 03.01.09.02.01.02 Embers, cinders, ashes
ādǣlan 03.03.07.01 Division, partition, separation; 05.12.05.03.01 To part ways, separate from, depart
ādēadian 02.02.03 To die, perish
ādēadod 02.08.04.03 Paralysis; 08.01.01.02 Lacking in feeling, insensitive
ādēafian 02.08.07.03.01 Deafness
ādēafung 02.08.07.03.01 Deafness
ādēaglian 09.05.04.01 Concealment, obscurity
adela 04.05.03.05.02 A privy
adel(a) 04.06.02.02 Foul, filthy, squalid
ādela 02.04.06.06.07 Urine
ādelfan 04.02.04.02.02 To dig up the ground; 05.06.08 A plucking, taking away; 17.02.04.02.02 Digging
adeliht 04.06.02.02 Foul, filthy, squalid
adelsēaþ 04.05.03.05.01 A cess-pool, midden, sewer
ādēman 11.03.01.01 Trial, probation
ādēman fram 12.03.06 Prohibition
ādeorcian 03.01.13 Darkness, obscurity; 03.01.13.02 A growing dark, darkening

āderian 08.01.03.07.02 Misery, trouble, affliction
adesa 17.03.03 A cutting tool
ādfaru 05.12.01.03.01.05 Types of road/path
ādfini 01.01.02.01.04.01 Marsh, bog, swamp
ādfȳr 16.02.04.12 Sacrifice, a sacrifice
ādihtian 09.03.07.07.03 Composition, arrangement, writing
ādīlegian 05.06.01 Devastation, laying waste; 06.01.04.03.01 Forgetfulness, oblivion; 12.08.08.01.02 Unchastity, incontinence; 16.02.04.07.02.03 Penance, an act/instance of penance
ādimmian 02.08.07.02.01 Defective vision; 08.01.03.04 Grief
ādl 02.08.02 Disease, infirmity, sickness
ādlama 16.01.05.02.02 Other terms for devils
ādlberende 02.08.02.01.01 An infectious disease; 04.06.02 Insalubrious, injurious to health
geādled 02.08.02 Disease, infirmity, sickness
ādleg 02.02.05.01.01 A grave, burial place, sepulchre
ādlēg 03.01.09.02.01.01 A kind of fire
ādlian 02.08.02 Disease, infirmity, sickness
(ge)ādlian 05.09.01 Slow, inactive
ādliende 02.08.02 Disease, infirmity, sickness; 02.08.02.01.01 An infectious disease; 04.06.02 Insalubrious, injurious to health
ādlig 02.08.02 Disease, infirmity, sickness; 12.08.06.01.02 Lacking moral good
ādliga 02.08.02.01.04 A sick person, invalid

ādlsēoc 02.08.02.01.01 An infectious disease
ādlþracu 02.08.02 Disease, infirmity, sickness
ādlung 02.08.02.01 An illness, ailment, disorder
ādlwērig 02.05.03.02 Weariness
ādōn 05.06 Destruction, dissolution, loss, breaking; 05.10.04.04.02 Removal, taking away; 05.12.02.01 To fetch, bring, bear, conduct; 05.12.02.04 To cast out, drive away; 05.12.05.08.01 To go before and guide; 05.12.05.12.02 To raise, lift up, elevate
ādōn fram 05.10.04.04.02 Removal, taking away
ādōn of 05.10.04.04.02 Removal, taking away
ādōn (of) 11.10.03 Salvation/deliverance from
ādrǣdan 06.01.08.06.02 Great fear, terror, horror
ādrǣfan 05.12.02.04 To cast out, drive away; 05.12.05.03.04 To come/go out from
ādragan 05.12.02.05 To pull, drag, draw; 13.02.08.04.03.02 Armed with a sword
adreminte 02.07.11 Plants/flowers (alphabetical order)
ādrencan 02.02.04.03 To kill, slay
ādrēogan 05.09.05 Ceasing, decline, fall off; 05.11 A time, period of time; 05.12.02.02 To carry off, remove; 08.01.03.07.03 Suffering, torment, pain; 08.01.03.08 Patience; 11.01.04 A doing, accomplishing (of something)
ādrēopan 03.01.16.03 A drop of liquid

ādrēosan 05.09.05 Ceasing, decline, fall off
ādrīfan 04.05.01.02.07 A fence, hedge; 05.06.07 Pricking, a prick, puncture; 05.12.02.04 To cast out, drive away
ādrīfan (fram/of) 05.12.05.03.04 To come/go out from
ādrīfan spor 05.12.05.10 To go behind, follow
ādrifen 17.02.05.05.01 Graven, embossed, chased
ādrincan 02.02.03 To die, perish; 03.01.13.02 A growing dark, darkening; 05.12.01.09.03.02 Hardship on board
ādrūgian 03.01.18 Dryness (not wetness); 08.01.01.02 Lacking in feeling, insensitive
ādrȳgan 03.01.18 Dryness (not wetness); 08.01.03.07.04.02 Relief, alleviation
ādrȳgan (of) 03.01.18 Dryness (not wetness)
ādrysnian 03.01.13.02 A growing dark, darkening; 12.05.06.01 Restraint, check, curb, control
aduent 16.02.04.04.02.01.01 Around the Nativity
ādumbian 02.05.10.17.01 Dumb, silent; 09.02 Silence, refraining from speech; 09.02.02 Dumbness, lack of speech
ādūn feallan 05.12.05.13.03 To fall
ādūne 05.10.05.04.02.03 Laid below
ādūn(e) 05.10.05.04.02.03 Laid below
ādūne āsettan 05.10.05.04.02.03 Laid below
ādūne (ā)stīgan 05.12.05.13 To go down, descend
ādūnweard 05.10.05.04.02.03 Laid below

ādūstrian 12.07.02.01.01.01 A promise, oath
ādwǣscan 03.01.13.02 A growing dark, darkening; 05.06.01 Devastation, laying waste; 05.07 Ending of existence, end of world
ādwelian 05.12.05.01 To go astray
ādwellan 11.11.02 A hindrance; 12.08.06.01.04.01 To mislead, seduce, lead astray
ādwīnan 05.07 Ending of existence, end of world
ādwolian 03.02.01 Decay, decline, corruption
ādȳdan 05.06.01 Devastation, laying waste; 05.09.01 Slow, inactive; 16.02.04.07.02.03 Penance, an act/instance of penance
ādȳfan 02.05.10.03 Noise, tumult, uproar
ādysgian 06.01.05.03.01.01 Dullness, folly, stupidity
āealdian 02.01.04.03 Aging, growing old
āeargian 11.06.01.01 Negligence, carelessness, heedlessness
āebbian 01.01.03.04 Current, rush of water
āefesian 05.06.06 A scraping, scarifying
āēhtan 12.05.06.02.02 Persecution
āetan 04.01.01 Eating
ǣ 16.02.01.09 The law; 02.05.10.15.01 To raise (the voice), raise up (noise); 12.09 Marriage, state of marriage; 14 Law, custom, covenant; 16.02.04.03.01 A rite, ceremony
ǣbǣre 09.05.05.01 Showing, manifestation, display
ǣbebod 14.01.02 A law, statute
ǣblǣce 02.04.04.01 Having a certain complexion
ǣblǣcnes 03.01.14.02 Pallor, absence of colour

æblǣcung 03.01.14.02 Pallor, absence of colour
æbōc 14.01.02 A law, statute
æbod 14.01.02 A law, statute; 17.02.02 An office, function, employment
æboda 16.02.03.02.10 A preacher, teacher
æbrǣce 12.08.08.01.02.01 Fornication, adultery; 16.02.01.11.02 Impiety, lack of piety
æbrecþ 16.02.04.14 Sacrilege
æbrucol 16.02.04.14 Sacrilege
æbs 02.07.03.05 Particular trees/shrubs (alphabetical order)
æbylg 08.01.03.05.02 Anger
æbylga 08.01.03.05.02 Anger
æbylgnes 08.01.03.05.02 Anger
æbylgþ(u) 08.01.03.05.02 Anger; 08.01.03.07.02.01 Injury, offence
æcelma 02.08.07.08.02 Swelling of the foot
æcelmehte 02.08.07.08.02 Swelling of the foot
æcen 02.07.03.05 Particular trees/shrubs (alphabetical order)
æcer 01.01.02 Land; 04.02.03.01 Plot of land; 04.02.03.03.03 An acre; 04.02.04.03.02 Crop/crops; 05.10.05.03 A measure of distance
æcerceorl 04.02.02 Farmer, cultivator
æcerhege 04.05.01.02.07 A fence, hedge
æcermǣlum 04.02.03.03.03 An acre
æcermann 04.02.02 Farmer, cultivator
æcern 02.07.09.02.01 Nut; 02.07.09.02.01.01 Particular nuts (alphabetical order); 04.01.02.01.04.01 Mast, pig-food
æcernspranca 02.07.03.05 Particular trees/shrubs (alphabetical order)
æcersǣd 04.02.04.03.01 Seed

æcersplott 04.02.03.03.03 An acre
æcertēoþung 16.02.04.20 Church due/requirement
æcertȳning 04.05.01.02.07 A fence, hedge
æcerweg 05.12.01.03.01.05 Types of road/path
æcerweorc 04.02.04.02 Cultivation/tillage
æcin 16.02.01.08.01 The Old Testament
æcnōsle 02.08.02.01.01 An infectious disease
geæcnōsliende 02.08.02.01.01 An infectious disease
æcræft 14.01.02 A law, statute; 16.02.01.09.02 Knowledge of Jewish law
æcræftig 14.01.02 A law, statute; 16.02.01.09.02 Knowledge of Jewish law
æcræftiga 14.01.02 A law, statute; 16.02.01.09.02 Knowledge of Jewish law
æcs 17.03.03 A cutting tool
æcyrf 04.06.02.04 Refuse, litter, rubbish
ædre 01.01.03.01.01.04 Watercourse/channel; 02.04.05.06 Sinew/tendon/ligament; 02.04.06.05.04 Kidney; 02.04.06.08 Heart; 05.11.07.01 Contemporary, coeval
ædreseax 02.08.12.02.06 Surgical
æfdȳne 01.01.02.01.02.02 Hill, mountain
æfelle 05.10.05.04.13 A removal of that which obscures or conceals
æfen 05.11.03.01.05 A day; 05.11.04.02 Night, night time; 16.02.04.05.08 The hour or service of Vespers, evensong

æfencollatio 16.02.04.03.02 Parts of service; 16.02.04.05.09 The hour or service of Compline
æfendrēam 16.02.04.05.08 The hour or service of Vespers, evensong
æfengebed 16.02.04.05.08 The hour or service of Vespers, evensong
æfengereord 04.01.02.04.01.01 Meal at particular time of day
æfengereordian 04.01.02.04.05 Entertainment with food
æfengereordung 04.01.02.04.01.01 Meal at particular time of day
æfengeweorc 17 Work, doings, actions, labour
æfengi(e)fl 04.01.02.04.01.01 Meal at particular time of day
æfenglōm(a) 05.11.04.02.01 Sunset
æfenglōmung 05.11.04.02.01 Sunset
æfengrom 08.01.03.05.02 Anger
æfenlāc 16.02.04.12 Sacrifice, a sacrifice
(ge)æfenlǣcan 05.11.04.02 Night, night time
æfenlēoht 05.11.04.02.01 Sunset
æfenlēoþ 18.02.07.01.01 A song, a poem to be sung or recited
æfenlic 05.11.04.02 Night, night time
æfenlof 16.02.04.05.08 The hour or service of Vespers, evensong
æfenmete 04.01.02.04.01.01 Meal at particular time of day
æfenoffrung 16.02.04.12 Sacrifice, a sacrifice
æfenrǣding 16.02.04.03.02 Parts of service; 16.02.04.05.09 The hour or service of Compline
æfenrepsung 05.11.04.02 Night, night time; 05.11.04.02.01 Sunset
æfenrest 02.05.04 Sleepiness, drowsiness, sleep
æfensang 16.02.04.05.08 The hour or service of Vespers, evensong
æfensceop 09.03.05 Art of poetry
æfenscīma 05.11.04.02.01 Sunset
æfensprǣc 09.01.04 Conversation, discussion
æfensteorra 01.02.01.01.02 Star
æfentīd 05.11.04.02 Night, night time
æfentīma 05.11.04.02 Night, night time
æfenþegnung 04.01.02.04.01.01 Meal at particular time of day; 16.02.04.05.08 The hour or service of Vespers, evensong
æfenþēowdōm 16.02.04.05.08 The hour or service of Vespers, evensong
æferþe 02.07.11.02 Unidentified plants (alphabetical order)
æfesa 02.07.09.02.01 Nut
æfesn 04.01.02.01.04.01 Mast, pig-food; 15.02.04.01 Payment for temporary use, rent, hire
æfest 06.02.05.04.04 Zeal; 08.01.03.09.08 Envy, jealousy
æfestful 08.01.03.09.08 Envy, jealousy
æfestian 08.01.03.09.08 Envy, jealousy
(ge)æfestian 08.01.03.09.08 Envy, jealousy
æfestig 08.01.03.09.08 Envy, jealousy
æfestig (wiþ) 06.02.05.04.04 Zeal
æfestung 08.01.03.09.08 Envy, jealousy
æfgælþ 06.01.07.05 Error, being astray
æfgerēfa 12.01.01.08.01 A servant, attendant
æfgrynde 01.01.02.01.03.02 Abyss, chasm
æfian 08.01.03.07.03 Suffering, torment, pain
æflāst 05.12.01.03 Expanse over which something travels

(ge)æfnan 11.01.05 Accomplishment, fulfilment
geæfnan 05.03.01 A cause (of anything); 05.11.11 Continuity; 08.01.03.07.03 Suffering, torment, pain
(ge)æfnian 05.11.04.02 Night, night time
æfnung 05.11.04.02 Night, night time
æfre 03.06 Comparison; 05.11.01.01.01 Eternity; 05.11.02 A time, particular time, occasion; 05.11.09.01 Always
æfre ǣlc 03.04.03.01 Someone/something
æfre ǣnig 03.06 Comparison
æfre tō ealdre 05.11.01.01.01 Eternity
æfreda 17.04.04.01 Oakum, hards, tow
æfrelīce 05.11.01.01.01 Eternity
æfremmende 16.02.01.11 Firmness in the law, piety, devoutness
æfsecgan 09.07.02 Contradiction
æfsweorc 04.02.03.04.02 Pasture/pasturage
æftan 05.10.05.04.09.02 Hinder part, rear
æftanweard 05.12.05.10 To go behind, follow
æftemest 05.10.05.04.09.02 Hinder part, rear; 05.11.10.02 End, completion
æfter 05.10.05.04.09.02 Hinder part, rear; 05.11.07.04.02 (Of time) later/latter
æfter iernan 13.02.03 To seek with active intent, attack
æfter rīdan 05.12.01.05.01 Modes of riding
æfter rihte 06.01.07 Truth, conformity with absolute standard
æfter rōwan 05.12.01.09.01 To row
æfter sīþfæte 05.11.07.04.02 (Of time) later/latter
æfter þon 05.11.07.04.02 (Of time) later/latter
æfter þȳ 05.11.07.04.02 (Of time) later/latter
æfter/for worulde 11.05 Natural/proper way/manner/mode of action
æfterǣ 16.02.01.08.01.01 Books of the Old Testament
æfterboren 02.01.03.03.03 Birth; 02.03.02.02 Child, offspring
æftercnēoreso 02.03.02.02 Child, offspring
æftercweþan 09.06.02.01.03 Recapitulation; 14.03.03.04 Oath-swearing
æftercweþend 05.11.07.04.02.01 Succession
æftercyning 12.01.01.04.01.01 Kings and queens
æfterealo 04.01.03.05.01.02 Broth
æfterfolgere 05.11.07.04.02.01 Succession
æfterfolgian 05.12.05.10 To go behind, follow
æfterfylgan 05.11.07.04.02.01 Succession
æfterfylgednes 09.03.07.07.02.01.05 Additional material, sequel
æfterfylgend 05.11.07.04.02.01 Succession
æfterfylgende 05.11.07.04.02.01 Succession
æfterfylgendlic 05.11.07.04.02.01 Succession
æfterfylgendlīce 05.11.07.04.02.01 Succession
æfterfylgendnes 05.11.07.04.02.01 Succession
æfterfylgian 05.12.05.10 To go behind, follow
æfterfylgung 05.12.05.10 To go behind, follow; 16.02.01.05 Heresy, error, wrong belief

æftergenga 02.03.02.03.05 Descendant; 05.11.07.04.02.01 Succession; 16.02.01 Faith
æftergengel 05.11.07.04.02.01 Succession
æftergengnes 02.03.02.02 Child, offspring; 05.11.07.04.02.01 Succession; 12.01.01.06.04 Inferiority of status, lowest place
æftergield 15.02.04 Spending, disbursement
æftergildend 10.03.04.01 Restitution, making good, repayment
æfterhǣþa 01.03.01.02 Dry weather
æfterhyrigan 03.06.01.01 Imitation
æfterlēan 10.03.05 Recompense, reward
æfterlic 03.03.03.04.02 Two
æfteronfōnd 10.01.01 Acceptance, receiving
æfterra 03.03.03.04.02 Two; 03.05.02 An arrangement, order, succession; 05.10.05.04.09.02 Hinder part, rear; 05.11.07.04.02 (Of time) later/latter; 05.11.07.04.02.01 Succession
æfterrǣp(e) 04.02.05.06.05.03.07 A tail-harness/crupper
æfterre tā 02.04.03.04.02.05.04 Toe
æfterryne 05.12.01.03 Expanse over which something travels
æftersang 16.02.04.05.02 The hour or service of Matins
æftersingallic 16.02.04.05.02 The hour or service of Matins
æftersingend 16.02.03.02.13 A church singer, singer in choir; 18.02.07.01 Singing, song
æftersōna 05.11.09.06 Frequency, repetition
æftersprǣc 14.03.03 Law, action of the courts

æftersp(r)ecan 14.03.03 Law, action of the courts
æfterspyrian 09.05.01 Inspection, examination
æfterweard 05.10.04.04 Absence
æfterweardnes 02.03.02.02 Child, offspring
æfterwriten 09.03.07 Writing
æfteryld 02.01.04.02 To grow, grow up
æfteryldo 05.11.07.04 Future, time to come
æfteweard 05.10.05.04.09.02 Hinder part, rear; 05.11.07.04.02 (Of time) later/latter; 05.11.10.02 End, completion
æfteweard hēafod 02.04.03.01.02 Back of head
æftewearde 05.10.05.04.09.02 Hinder part, rear
æftresta 05.11.10.02 End, completion
æftum 05.11.07.04.02 (Of time) later/latter
æfþanc 08.01.03.07.02.01 Injury, offence; 08.01.03.09.03 Malevolence, malice
æfweard 05.10.04.04 Absence
æfweardnes 05.10.04.04 Absence
æfwela 10.02.01 Loss, deprivation
æfwyrdelsa 05.06.04 Damage, injury, defect, hurt, loss; 07.03.02 Ill, harm, hurt; 14.02.01.01 Types of crime
æfwyrdla 05.06.04 Damage, injury, defect, hurt, loss; 08.01.03.07.02.01 Injury, offence; 14.05.04 A penalty, punishment
æfwyrþ(u) 07.09.02 Disgrace, shaming, humiliation
ǣfyllende 16.02.01.11.02 Impiety, lack of piety
ǣfyrmþa 04.06.02.04 Refuse, litter, rubbish

æg 02.06.08.01 Part of bird;
    04.01.02.01.02.08 Egg
ægafol 14.01.03.02 Freedom from
    punishment or fine
ægecȳþnes 16.02.01.08 Scripture, the
    scriptures
ægerfelma 02.06.08.01 Part of bird
ægergelu 04.01.02.01.02.08 Egg
ægflota 05.12.01.09.03 A voyage
æg(ge)mang 04.01.02.01.02.08 Egg
æghwā 03.04.03.01 Someone/something
æghwǣr 03.04.03.01
    Someone/something; 05.10.04.03
    Presence
æghwǣr onbūtan 05.10.04.03 Presence
æghwæs 03.03.06.02 Fullness
æghwæt 03.04.03.01 Someone/something
æghwæþer 03.04.03.01
    Someone/something
æghwæþer (ge) ... ge 03.03.06.01 A
    whole formed by joining
æghwanan 05.10.04.03 Presence
æghwanon 03.04.03.01
    Someone/something; 05.10.04.03
    Presence
æghwider 05.10.04.03 Presence
æghwilc 03.04.03.01 Someone/something
æghwilc ān 03.04.03.01
    Someone/something
æghwilces 03.04.03.01
    Someone/something
ægift 10.03.04.01 Restitution, making
    good, repayment; 14.05.04 A penalty,
    punishment
ægilde 14.03.03.09.02 Atonement
æglǣca 02.06.10 Monster, strange
    creature
æglēaw 14.01.02 A law, statute;
    16.02.01.09.02 Knowledge of Jewish
    law
æglīm 09.03.07.07 A book
ægmore 02.04.05.04.02.01 Socket of eye
ægnan 04.02.04.04.05.02 Chaff
ægru lecgan 02.06.08.02 Domestic fowl
ægscill 02.06.08.01 Part of bird
ægþer ... and 03.03.06.01 A whole
    formed by joining
ægweard 11.10.02.02 Watchful care,
    keeping guard
ægwyrt 02.07.11 Plants/flowers
    (alphabetical order)
ægylt 16.02.01.13 Evil-doing,
    transgression, sin
ægylting 16.02.01.13 Evil-doing,
    transgression, sin
ægȳpe 06.01.06.04.02 Ignorance,
    uninstructedness
æhīw 03.01.14.02 Pallor, absence of
    colour
æhīwe 02.08.04.02 Blemish,
    disfigurement; 03.01.14.02 Pallor,
    absence of colour
æhīwnes 03.01.14.02 Pallor, absence of
    colour
æhlȳp 14.02.01.01 Types of crime
æht 02.06.02 Domestic animals,
    livestock; 04.02.05 Livestock; 10
    Having, owning, possession;
    12.01.01.09 Bondage, slavery; 15.01
    Property; 15.01.01 Landed property
æhtboren 12.01.01.09 Bondage, slavery
æhteland 15.01.01 Landed property
æhtemann 04.02.02 Farmer, cultivator;
    12.01.01.09 Bondage, slavery
æhteswān 04.02.05.06.04 A swineherd
æhtgesteald 10 Having, owning,
    possession
æhtgestrēon 15.01.03 Treasure, riches,
    wealth
æhtgeweald 12.01 Power, control, sway

geæhtle 07.04 Consideration, esteem
æhtspēd 15.01.03 Treasure, riches, wealth
æhtspēdig 15.01.05 Possession of wealth
æhtwela 15.01.03 Treasure, riches, wealth
æhtwelig 15.01.05 Possession of wealth
æhwæþer 03.04.03.01 Someone/something
æl 17.03.05 An awl, borer, gimlet, etc.
ǣl 02.06.06.02.01.02 Eel
ǣlǣdend 14.03.02 A legislator
ǣlǣrend 16.02.01.08.01 The Old Testament
ǣlǣte 01.01.02.01.06 Wild/uncultivated land; 06.01.05.03.02.01 Foolishness, lightmindedness; 12.06.03.01 Waste land, deserted place; 12.09.04 Divorce
ǣlagol 14.03.02 A legislator
ǣlan 17.05.04 To kindle, set alight (fire, lamp)
(ge)ǣlan 03.01.09.02.01 Fire, burning; 17.05.04 To kindle, set alight (fire, lamp)
ǣlārēow 16.02.01.08.01 The Old Testament; 16.02.01.09.02 Knowledge of Jewish law
ǣlātēow 14.03.02 A legislator
ǣlc 03.04.03.01 Someone/something
ǣlc ān 03.04.03.01 Someone/something
ǣlc (ān) 03.04.03.01 Someone/something
ǣlc wiht 03.04.03.01 Someone/something
ǣlce þinga 03.04.03.01 Someone/something
ælceald 03.01.11 Coldness, coolness
ǣlces þinges 03.04.03.01 Someone/something
ǣlchwega 03.04.03.01 Someone/something
ælcræftig 16.01.01.01.01.01 Mightiness

geǣld 03.01.09.02.01 Fire, burning
ǣled 03.01.09.02 Fire, flame
ǣled weccan 03.01.09.02.01 Fire, burning
ǣledfȳr 03.01.09.02 Fire, flame
ǣledlēoma 03.01.09.02 Fire, flame
ǣlednes 03.01.09.02.01 Fire, burning
ælegrǣdig 04.01.01.04 Gluttony, overeating, greediness
ælegrēne/eallgrēne 02.07.01 To grow
ælemidde 05.10.05.04.01.01 The middle
ælenge 08.01.03.07.01 Tedium
ælengnes 08.01.03.07.01 Tedium
ælepūte 02.06.06.02.01.01 Burbot
ælere 02.07.10.01 Particular herbs/spices (alphabetical order)
ælf 02.05.04.02 A dream; 16.01.03.04 Elfin race
ælfādl 02.05.04.02 A dream; 16.01.03.04 Elfin race
ælfaru 13.02.10.01.02.02 Armed forces
ælfcynn 16.01.03.04 Elfin race
ælf(en) 16.01.03.04 Elfin race
ælfisc 16.01.03.04 Elfin race
ælfisc 02.06.06.02.01.02 Eel
ælfremed 02.03.02.03.06 Kinship, relationship
ælfremed fram 03.04.01 Singularity, peculiarity
(ge)ælfremedan 12.04.03.01 Estrangement, alienation
ælfremedung 12.04.03.01 Estrangement, alienation
ælfscīene 07.10 Beauty, fairness
ælfsiden 02.05.04.02 A dream; 16.01.03.04 Elfin race
ælfsogoþa 02.08.08.04.02 (Of stomach) disordered
ælfþone 02.07.11 Plants/flowers (alphabetical order)

ælfylce 12.06.05 A foreign country
ælhȳd 02.06.06.02.01.02 Eel
ælic 14.01.02 A law, statute
ælīce 14.01.02 A law, statute
ælīest 14.02 Lawlessness
æling 03.01.09.02 Fire, flame;
    08.01.01.01 Ardour, fervour, strong feeling
ælmesæcer 04.02.04.04.02 Harvesting;
    16.02.04.20 Church due/requirement;
    16.02.05.01 Land
ælmesbæþ 16.02.04.09 Almsgiving, charitableness
ælmesdǣd 16.02.04.09 Almsgiving, charitableness
ælmesdōnd 16.02.04.09 Almsgiving, charitableness
ælmesfeoh 16.02.04.09 Almsgiving, charitableness; 16.02.04.20 Church due/requirement
ælmesful 16.02.04.09 Almsgiving, charitableness
ælmesgedāl 16.02.04.09 Almsgiving, charitableness
ælmesgeorn 16.02.04.09 Almsgiving, charitableness
ælmesgifa 16.02.04.09 Almsgiving, charitableness
ælmeshand 16.02.04.09 Almsgiving, charitableness
ælmeshlāf 04.01.02.01.07.03 Bread
ælmeslāc 16.02.04.09 Almsgiving, charitableness
ælmesland 16.02.05.01 Land
ælmeslēoht 03.01.12.02 A beam of light;
    16.02.04.20 Church due/requirement
ælmeslic 15.01.06 Poverty, indigence;
    16.02.04.09 Almsgiving, charitableness
ælmeslīce 16.02.04.09 Almsgiving, charitableness
ælmesmann 15.01.06 Poverty, indigence
ælmespenig 15.01.04 Coinage, money;
    16.02.04.09 Almsgiving, charitableness
ælmesse 16.02.04.09 Almsgiving, charitableness
ælmesweorc 16.02.04.09 Almsgiving, charitableness
ælmihtig 16.01.01.01.01 The Almighty
ælmihtignes 16.01.01.01.01.01 Mightiness
ælmyrce 12.06.03.03 A neighbour
ælnet 04.03.05 Fishing
ælren 02.07.03.05 Particular trees/shrubs (alphabetical order)
ælsyndrig 03.03.07.01 Division, partition, separation; 03.04.01 Singularity, peculiarity
æltǣwe 02.08.01 Sound physical condition; 02.08.12.02.05 Pharmacy, curing with salves; 03.03.06 Wholeness; 07.02.04.03 Nobleness, excellence, nobility, magnificence
æltǣwlīce 03.03.06 Wholeness
ælwiht 02.06.10 Monster, strange creature
ǣmelle 02.05.07.02 Insipid
ǣmelnes 11.06 Disinclination to act, listlessness
ǣmen 12.06.03.01 Waste land, deserted place
ǣmenne 12.04.04 Solitude
ǣmerge 03.01.09.02.01.02 Embers, cinders, ashes; 04.06.02.05 Dust, powder
ǣmetbed 02.06.01.08 A lair, den
ǣmethwīl 18 Quiet, leisure, rest
ǣmethyll 02.06.01.08 A lair, den
(ge)ǣmetian (tō) 11.02 Occupation, activity, business

æmetla 18 Quiet, leisure, rest
æmetta 18 Quiet, leisure, rest
æmette 02.06.09.02.01 Ant
æmettig 03.03.08 Emptiness; 05.10.04.04 Absence; 12.09.03 Unmarried state; 18 Quiet, leisure, rest
æmettig (fram) 03.04.01 Singularity, peculiarity; 03.03.08 Emptiness
æmōd 08.01.03.01 Despondency
(ge)æmtian 03.03.08 Emptiness; 18 Quiet, leisure, rest
(ge)æmtian (fram) 18.01 Rest, quiet, freedom from toil
geæmtian 18.01 Rest, quiet, freedom from toil
æmtig tīd 18 Quiet, leisure, rest
æmtignes 03.03.08 Emptiness
æmūþa 02.04.06.03.02.04 Intestines
æmynd 08.01.03.09.08 Envy, jealousy
æmyrce 07.02.04.02 Nobleness, nobility, dignity
geǣnan 03.03.06.01 A whole formed by joining
ǣne 03.03.03.04.01 One; 05.11.02 A time, particular time, occasion; 05.11.07.01 Contemporary, coeval; 05.11.07.03 Former times, days of old; 05.11.10.01 A beginning
ǣne sīþa 03.03.03.04.01 One
ǣne sīþe 03.03.03.04.01 One
ǣnes 03.03.03.04.01 One; 05.11.10.01 A beginning
ǣnetlīf 16.02.03.03.04 A solitary (anchorite, hermit)
ǣnetnes 12.04.04 Solitude
ǣnett 12.04.04 Solitude
ǣnga 03.04.01 Singularity, peculiarity
ǣngancundes 03.04.01 Singularity, peculiarity

ǣnge trym 03.03.07 A part, division, portion
ǣnig 03.04.01 Singularity, peculiarity; 03.04.03.01 Someone/something
ǣnig mann 03.04.03.01 Someone/something
ǣnig þing 11.01.04 A doing, accomplishing (of something)
ǣnige þinga 11.01.04 A doing, accomplishing (of something)
ǣnigwiht 05 Aught, anything, something
ǣnlic 03.04.01 Singularity, peculiarity; 07.02.04.03 Nobleness, excellence, nobility, magnificence
ǣnlic/ānlic 12.04.04 Solitude
ǣnlīce 03.04.01 Singularity, peculiarity; 07.02.04.03 Nobleness, excellence, nobility, magnificence
ǣnote 11.08 Uselessness
æpening 02.07.09.02 Particular fruits (alphabetical order)
æppel 02.04.06.01 Sight organ; 02.07.09 Fruit; 02.07.09.02 Particular fruits (alphabetical order); 05.10.06.02 Rotundity, roundness
æppelbǣre 02.07.09.02 Particular fruits (alphabetical order)
æppelbearu 04.02.04.05.02 An orchard
æppelberende 02.07.09.02 Particular fruits (alphabetical order)
æppelcynn 02.07.09 Fruit
æppelcyrnel 02.07.09.02 Particular fruits (alphabetical order)
æppelfæt 04.01.02.02.06.03 Food receptacle, basket
æppelfealu 03.01.14.07 Yellow/yellowness
æppelhūs 04.02.04.04.06 Barn
æppellēaf 02.07.11 Plants/flowers (alphabetical order)

æppelscealu 02.07.09.02 Particular fruits (alphabetical order)
æppelscrēada 04.01.02.02.03 To prepare fruit
æppeltrēow 02.07.09.02 Particular fruits (alphabetical order)
æppeltūn 04.02.04.05.02 An orchard
æppelþorn 02.07.09.02 Particular fruits (alphabetical order)
æppelwīn 04.01.03.05.01.03 Cider
æppled 05.10.06.02 Rotundity, roundness
æpplen 02.07.09.02 Particular fruits (alphabetical order)
æpsen 07.09 Shame, disgrace; 12.08.07.01.04.01 Impropriety, disgrace
æpsenes 07.09 Shame, disgrace
æpsett 02.07.03.05 Particular trees/shrubs (alphabetical order)
ǣr 05.11.07.03.02 Earlier, antecedent; 05.11.08.01.02 (Untimely) earliness; 17.04.02.01 Brass
ǣr and sīþ 05.11.09.01 Always
ǣr dæge and æfter dæge 05.11.11 Continuity
ǣr oþþe sīþ 05.11.02 A time, particular time, occasion
ǣr þissum 05.11.07.03.02 Earlier, antecedent
ǣr þon 05.11.07.03.02 Earlier, antecedent
ǣra 17.03.04 Tools for smoothing/scraping/grinding
ǣrādl 02.08.02.01 An illness, ailment, disorder
ǣrǣt 04.01.01.04 Gluttony, overeating, greediness
ǣrbeþōht 06.01.01.01.01.02 Forethought, consideration
ǣrblǣd 05.12.01.09.03.01.03 Part of ship
ǣrboren 02.03.02.02 Child, offspring

ǣrcwide 06.01.08.04.01 Premonition, prophecy
ǣrdǣd 11.01 Action, doing, performance
ǣrdæg 05.11.04.01 Day (not night)
ǣrdēaþ 02.02.01 Particular mode of death
ǣrēafe 09.05.05.01 Showing, manifestation, display
ǣren 01.01.02.02.03.01 Types of metals/minerals; 02.05.10.11 Clang, sound of metal; 05.12.01.09.03.01.02 Of/concerning a ship, naval; 17.04.02.01 Brass
ǣren screpu 17.03.04 Tools for smoothing/scraping/grinding
ǣrendbōc 09.06.02.01.06 A message, announcement by a messenger
ǣrende 09.06.02.01.06 A message, announcement by a messenger; 17.02.03 A task, service, duty
ǣrendfæst 17.02.03 A task, service, duty
ǣrendgāst 16.01.02.05.01 An angel
ǣrendgewrit 09.03.07.07.03.02.02 A letter; 09.06.02.01.06 A message, announcement by a messenger
ǣrendian 09.06.02.01.01 To make known, cause to know, inform
(ge)ǣrendian 12.02.01 A substitute, representative; 13.01.03 Intercession, pleading, mediation; 17.02.03 A task, service, duty
(ge)ǣrendian (tō) 14.04.04.01 Intercession, mediation
geǣrendian 10.01.02 Acquisition; 11.03.02.01 Efficacy, success
geǣrendian tō 10.01.02 Acquisition
ǣrendraca 09.06.02.01.06.01 A messenger
ǣrendraca/ǣrendwreca 12.02.01 A substitute, representative

ærendscip 05.12.01.09.03.01.01 Kind of ship
ærendsecg 09.06.02.01.06.01 A messenger
ærendspræc 09.06.02.01.06 A message, announcement by a messenger
ærendung 13.01.03 Intercession, pleading, mediation; 14.04.04.01 Intercession, mediation; 17.02.03 A task, service, duty
ærest 05.11.10.01 A beginning
ærest þinga 05.11.10.01 A beginning
ærfæder 02.03.02.03.03 Forefather, ancestor
ærgedōn 05.11.07.03.02 Earlier, antecedent
ærgefremed 05.11.07.03.02 Earlier, antecedent
ærgelǣred 05.11.07.03.02 Earlier, antecedent
ær(ge)nemned 05.11.07.03.02.02 The aforesaid
ærgestrēon 15.01.03 Treasure, riches, wealth
ærgeweorc 04.05.02 A building, edifice, structure
ærgewinn 12.05.04.01 Fighting, contention, warfare, strife
ærgewyrht 11.01 Action, doing, performance
ærglæd 11.05.02.02 Humanity, courtesy, civility
ærgōd 07.02.04 Excellence
ærhwīlum 05.11.07.03 Former times, days of old
æriht 14 Law, custom, covenant
æring 05.11.04.01 Day (not night)
ærist 05.12.05.12 To go up, ascend; 16.01.01.02.09 Resurrection
æristhyht 16.01.01.02.09 Resurrection

ærlic 05.11.04.01 Day (not night)
ærlīce 05.11.04.01 Day (not night); 05.11.08.01.02 (Untimely) earliness
ærmorgen 05.11.04.01 Day (not night)
ærmorgenlic 05.11.04.01 Day (not night)
ærn 04.05.03 A dwelling-place, abode, habitation
(ge)ærnan 05.12.01.05.01 Modes of riding
geærnan 10.01.02 Acquisition
ærnemergenlic 05.11.04.01 Day (not night)
ærneweg 18.02.03.01.02 Racing
ærning 05.12.01.05.01 Modes of riding; 18.02.03.01.02 Racing
ærning/ierning 02.04.06.08.01 Blood; 02.08.08.12 Disease of bowels
ærnþegen 12.01.01.08.01 A servant, attendant
æror 05.11.07.03.02 Earlier, antecedent; 07.01.01.02 To prefer
ærra 05.11.07.03.02 Earlier, antecedent
ærsceaft 04.05.02 A building, edifice, structure
ærwacol 02.05.02 Consciousness
geærwe 12.08.06.01.02 Lacking moral good
ærwela 15.01.03 Treasure, riches, wealth
ærworuld 01 Earth, world
æs 04.01.02.01 Food/sustenance; 04.01.02.01.02.05 Meat; 04.03.02 A snare, trap, noose; 04.03.05 Fishing
æsc 02.07.03.05 Particular trees/shrubs (alphabetical order); 05.12.01.09.03.01 A ship, boat; 09.03.07.01.01 A runic letter; 13.02.08.04.01 A spear
æscǣre 07.10.02 Ugliness
æscan 14.03.03 Law, action of the courts

æscbedd 02.07.03.05 Particular trees/shrubs (alphabetical order)
æscberend 13.02.10.01.02 An armed man
æsce 14.03.03 Law, action of the courts; 14.03.03.02 A search for stolen property
(ge)æsce 09.05.02 A question, inquiry, questioning
æscēada 04.06.02.04 Refuse, litter, rubbish
æsceap 04.04.05.06 To sew, stitch
æscegeswāp 03.01.09.02.01.02 Embers, cinders, ashes
æscen 02.07.03.05 Particular trees/shrubs (alphabetical order); 04.01.03.05.04.03 A bucket, pail
æscett 02.07.03.05 Particular trees/shrubs (alphabetical order)
æscfaru 13.02.01 A military expedition
æscfealu 03.01.14.10 Grey-coated one
æscgrǣg 03.01.14.10 Grey-coated one
æschere 13.02.10.03.01 A fleet
æscholt 13.02.08.04.01 A spear
æscmann 05.12.01.09.03.03 Piracy
æscplega 13.02.02 Battle
æscrind 02.07.03.05 Particular trees/shrubs (alphabetical order)
æscrōf 06.02.07.06 Courage, boldness, valour
æscstede 13.02.02 Battle
æscstederōd 05.10.05.04.11.01.01 Object placed as point to be reached, a mark
æscstybb 02.07.03.05 Particular trees/shrubs (alphabetical order)
æsctīr 07.08.10 Fame of courage, valour
æscþracu 13.02.02 Battle
æscþrote 02.07.11 Plants/flowers (alphabetical order)
æscwiga 13.02.10.01 A man, warrior

æscwyrt 02.07.11 Plants/flowers (alphabetical order)
ǣsellend 14.03.02 A legislator
ǣslītend 14.02 Lawlessness
ǣsmæl 02.08.07.02 Disorders of the eye
ǣsmogu 02.06.07.01.01 Part of snake
æspe 02.07.03.05 Particular trees/shrubs (alphabetical order)
æsphangra 02.07.03.05 Particular trees/shrubs (alphabetical order)
æsprind 02.07.03.05 Particular trees/shrubs (alphabetical order)
æspring 01.01.03.01.01.07 Spring, fountain, well
ǣspryng 05.03 Source, origin; 05.12.05.13 To go down, descend
æstel 09.03.07.07 A book
ǣswǣpa 04.06.02.04 Refuse, litter, rubbish
ǣswic 07.05.01 Censure, reproof, rebuke; 08.01.03.07.02.01 Injury, offence; 11.11.02 A hindrance; 16.02.01.07 Apostasy
ǣswica 12.01.01.12.04 Treachery
ǣswice 14.02 Lawlessness
ǣswician 11.06.06.01 Abandonment (of principle); 16.02.01.07 Apostasy
(ge)ǣswician 07.03.01.03 To loathe, hate, abhor
geǣswician 07.09.02 Disgrace, shaming, humiliation
ǣswicnes 07.05.01 Censure, reproof, rebuke; 11.11.02 A hindrance
geǣswicod 07.09.01 Shame, confusion; 07.09.02 Disgrace, shaming, humiliation
ǣswicung 07.05.01 Censure, reproof, rebuke; 08.01.03.07.02.01 Injury, offence

æswīcung 06.01.07.04.04 Deceitfulness, falseness, duplicity; 12.01.01.12.03 Rebellion, sedition
æswind 11.06 Disinclination to act, listlessness
æt ende 11.01.06 End, completion (of action), fulfilment
æt frumcirre 05.11.07.01 Contemporary, coeval
æt frymþe 05.11.10.01 A beginning
æt hæbbendra handa 14.02.01.02 Wrongful taking, theft
æt hām 04.05.03.02.01 A building, house, hall, palace, etc.
æt handa 05.10.05.01 A little way, no great distance
æt hēafde 03.03.03.04.01 One
æt hilde gedrēosan 02.02.03 To die, perish
æt hūs 04.05.03.02.01 A building, house, hall, palace, etc.
æt nēhstan 05.11.10.02 End, completion
æt gereorde/æt gereordum 04.01.01 Eating
æt sīþemestan 05.11.10.02 End, completion
æt sīþestan 05.11.10.02 End, completion
æt (þām) ende 05.11.10.02 End, completion
æt unlagum 14.02 Lawlessness
ǣt 04.01.02.01 Food/sustenance
ǣt/ete 04.01.01 Eating
ǣt and wǣt 04.01.02.01 Food/sustenance
ǣta 04.01.01 Eating
ætbēon/ætwesan 05.10.04.03 Presence
ætberan 09.05.05.01 Showing, manifestation, display; 10.04.03 To take away, remove
ætberan (ūp/ūt) 05.12.02.02 To carry off, remove

ætberstan 10.02.01 Loss, deprivation; 11.10.05 Escape
ætbrēdendlic 09.03.02.03.01.01.01 Case
ætbregdan 05.07 Ending of existence, end of world; 05.09.05 Ceasing, decline, fall off; 10.03.06 Withholding, keeping back; 10.04.03.01 To take away, deprive of; 11.06.04 Abstention, abstaining from; 11.10.03 Salvation/deliverance from; 12.03.06 Prohibition; 14.02.01.02.01 Open robbery, rapine, pillage
ætclifian 03.01.17 Thickness, viscosity; 06.02.07.03 Perseverance
ætclīpan 06.02.07.03 Perseverance
ætdēman 14.03.03.09 A sentence, judgement, ruling
ætdōn 10.04.03.01 To take away, deprive of
ætdwīnan 02.05.09.14 To vanish, disappear
ǣte healdan 04.01.02.03 To serve (food/drink)
ætēaca 03.03.04.03 Growth, increase
ætealdod 02.01.04.03 Aging, growing old
æteglan 05.06.04 Damage, injury, defect, hurt, loss
ætēowodnes 02.05.09.12 To show
ǣtere/etere 04.01.01 Eating; 04.01.01.04 Gluttony, overeating, greediness
ætfæstan 08.01.03.07.02 Misery, trouble, affliction; 10.03 Giving; 11.10.02.02.01 Care, interest in; 12.09.01 Pledging, betrothal
ætfæstnian 10.03 Giving
ætfaran 11.10.05 Escape
ætfeallan 05.03.02.01.01 An event, occurrence; 05.12.05.13.03 To fall; 11.06.06.01 Abandonment (of

æting/eting

principle); 11.08.04 Vanity, idleness, frivolity; 15.02.01 High/steep price
ætfele 06.01.08.03.01 Belief, trust, faithfulness
ætfeng 14.03.03.02.01 Attaching, distraint of stolen property
ætfeohtan 02.05.06.01 To touch and press; 13.02 War
ætfēolan 02.05.06.01 To touch and press; 03.01.17 Thickness, viscosity; 06.02.07.03 Perseverance; 11.01.01 Practice, exercise, doing; 11.02.01 Energy, vigour, vigorous action
ætfeorrian 10.04.03 To take away, remove; 11.06.06.01 Abandonment (of principle)
ætferian 05.12.02.02 To carry off, remove; 10.04.03 To take away, remove
ætflēon 11.10.04 Flight
ætflōwan 03.03.04.03 Growth, increase
ætfōn 14.03.03.02.01 Attaching, distraint of stolen property
ætforan 05.10.05.04.09.01 Front; 05.10.05.04.09.01.01 Head, front (position); 05.11.07.03.02 Earlier, antecedent; 05.12.05.08 To go before, precede
ætfylgan 06.02.06.03.03 Incitement
ætgædere 03.03.06.01 A whole formed by joining; 05.11.07.01 Contemporary, coeval
ætgæderum 03.03.06.01 A whole formed by joining
ætgǣre 13.02.08.04.01 A spear
ætgangan 05.12.05.02 To go/travel towards, come, approach
ætgār 13.02.08.04.01 A spear
ætgeniman 05.10.04.04.02 Removal, taking away

æt(ge)niman 10.04.03.01 To take away, deprive of
ætgenumen 05.10.04.04.02 Removal, taking away
ætgiefa 04.01.02.04.03 Feeding, nourishing
ætgifan 10.03 Giving
ætglīdan 05.07 Ending of existence, end of world
ætgrǣpe weorþan 10.04.02.02 To seize, take, grasp, lay hold on
æthabban 10 Having, owning, possession
æthealdan 10.03.06 Withholding, keeping back
æthebban 11.06.06.01 Abandonment (of principle)
æthindan 05.12.05.10 To go behind, follow
æthīwian 05.13.01 Transformation, taking another shape
æthlēapan 11.10.05 Escape
æthlȳp 14.02.01.01 Types of crime
æthrīnan 02.05.06 Sense of touch; 05.12.02 To move, set in motion
æthrine 02.05.06 Sense of touch
æthwā 03.04.03.01 Someone/something
æthwāra 03.03.04.04 Littleness, smallness
æthwega 03.03.04.04 Littleness, smallness; 03.04 Form, kind, nature, character
æthweorfan 05.12.05.11.01 To return
æthwōn 03.06 Comparison
ætiernan ūt 11.10.04 Flight
ætīewan 02.05.09.06 Thing seen, sight, vision; 02.05.09.12 To show; 09.05.05.01 Showing, manifestation, display
ǣting 04.02.03.04.02 Pasture/pasturage
ǣting/eting 04.01.01 Eating

737

ætinge 09.02 Silence, refraining from speech
ætlǣdan 05.12.05.08.01 To go before and guide
ætlic/etlic 04.01.02.01.01 Edibility
ætlicgan 11.08.03 Needless, useless, unprofitable
ætlimpan 03.02.01 Decay, decline, corruption
ætlūtian 11.09.01.01 Ambush, lying in wait
ǣtnes 04.01.02.01.01 Edibility
ætreccan 14.05.04 A penalty, punishment
(ge)ǣtred 02.02.04.03 To kill, slay
geǣtred 04.06.02.06 Poison; 07.03.02 Ill, harm, hurt
ǣtren 02.02.04.01 Cause/occasion of death; 04.06.02.06 Poison
ǣtrenmōd 08.01.03.09.03 Malevolence, malice
ǣtrennes 04.06.02.06 Poison
ǣtrian 02.08.05.02.01 Matter, purulence, pus
geǣtrian 02.02.04.03 To kill, slay
ǣtrig 04.06.02.06 Poison; 07.03.02 Ill, harm, hurt
ætrihte 03.06 Comparison
ætrihtes 05.10.05.01 A little way, no great distance
ætsacan 09.07.03.01 A denial; 09.07.03.02 Refusal, denial; 14.03.03.01.01 Defence, reply
ætsamne 03.03.06.01 A whole formed by joining; 05.11.07.01 Contemporary, coeval
ætscēawian 02.05.09.06 Thing seen, sight, vision
ætscēotan 11.10.05 Escape
ætsittan 05.10.04.03 Presence

ætslāpan 02.05.04 Sleepiness, drowsiness, sleep
ætslīdan 05.12.01.04.01.04 To stumble, trip, strike (with the foot); 05.12.05.03 To travel away (from); 11.06.03.01 Ill fortune, bad success
ætslīdende 05.12.01.04.01.04 To stumble, trip, strike (with the foot)
ætspornan 11.04.03 (Of ability) low, mean, of less worth
ætspornan (æt/on) 05.12.01.04.01.04 To stumble, trip, strike (with the foot)
ætsporning 06.01.07.05 Error, being astray
ætspringan 05.12.05.03.04.01 To burst forth, break out
ætspringnes 08.01.03.01 Despondency
ætspurnan 05.12.02.06.01 To push, drive
ætstæppan 05.12.05.02 To go/travel towards, come, approach
ætstandan 03.02.01.05.01 Blight (causing leaves to look burned); 05.11.10.02 End, completion; 05.12.04 Absence of movement, stillness; 05.13.06 Constancy, unchangeableness; 11.06.04 Abstention, abstaining from
ætstandend 02.05.09.05 To watch, observe, survey; 05.10.04.03 Presence
ætstandende 05.10.04.03 Presence
ætsteall 05.10.04.01 Position, stance
ætstillan 05.12.04 Absence of movement, stillness
ætstrengan 10.03.06 Withholding, keeping back
ætstyntan 05.06.05.03 Bruising, crushing; 11.06 Disinclination to act, listlessness
ætswerian 14.03.03.04 Oath-swearing
ætswīgan 02.05.10.17.01 Dumb, silent

æþringan 05.12.02.06 To push, impel, thrust
ætwegan 10.04.03 To take away, remove
ǣtwela 04.01.02.04.02 Feast
ætwenian 06.02.06.03.01 To dissuade (from); 06.02.06.03.04 Allurement
ætwesende 05.11.07.04.01 Nearness, approach, imminence
ætwindan 11.10.05 Escape; 11.10.05.01 Evasion, escape from threat
ætwist 02.01 Existence, life; 05.10.04.03 Presence
ætwītan 07.05.03.03.02 To reproach, revile, abuse
ætwrencan 06.01.07.04.02 Fraud, deceit, trick, trickery; 14.02.01.02.01 Open robbery, rapine, pillage
ætȳcan 03.03.04.03 Growth, increase
ætȳcnes 03.03.04.03 Growth, increase
ætȳwednes 02.05.09.12 To show; 09.05.05.01 Showing, manifestation, display
ætȳw(ed)nes 16.02.01.12.01 Revelation, illumination, inspiration
ætȳwigendlic 09.03.02.02.01.05 Minor parts of speech, etc.
ætȳwnes 02.05.09.12 To show; 06.01.02.01.01 A vision, apparition; 09.03.07.07.03 Composition, arrangement, writing; 09.04.03 Exposition, making clear by explanation; 09.05.05.01 Showing, manifestation, display; 11.03.01.01.01 Proof, demonstration; 16.02.04.04.02.01.01 Around the Nativity
ætȳwung 16.02.01.12.01 Revelation, illumination, inspiration; 16.02.04.04.02.01.01 Around the Nativity

geǣþan 14.03.03.04 Oath-swearing
geǣþed 14.03.03.04 Oath-swearing
æþelboren 05.02.02 Nature, established order of things; 07.02.04.02 Nobleness, nobility, dignity; 12.01.01.06.06 Gentle birth, nobility
æþelborennes 05.02.02 Nature, established order of things; 07.02.04.02 Nobleness, nobility, dignity; 12.01.01.06.06 Gentle birth, nobility
æþelcund 12.01.01.06.06 Gentle birth, nobility
æþelcundnes 07.02.04.03 Nobleness, excellence, nobility, magnificence
æþelcyning 16.01.01.04.02 The Son, Christ
æþelduguþ 12.01.01.07 A follower
æþele 02.05.08.02 Pleasant smell, fragrance, perfume; 05.08.01 Vigour, activity, force; 07.02.04.03 Nobleness, excellence, nobility, magnificence; 12.01.01.06.05 Nobility, noble condition
(ge)æþele 05.02.02 Nature, established order of things
æþelferþingwyrt 02.07.11 Plants/flowers (alphabetical order)
geæþelian 07.08.02 Honour, glory
æþeling 02.03.01.01 Male person, man; 12.01.01.06.08 A person of rank, elder, great man; 16.01.01.04.02 The Son, Christ
æþelinghād 12.01.01.06.07 Royal/princely status/dignity
æþellic 02.05.08.02 Pleasant smell, fragrance, perfume; 07.02.04.03 Nobleness, excellence, nobility, magnificence

æþellīce 07.10.01 Elegance, beauty, comeliness
æþelnes 07.02.04 Excellence; 12.01.01.06.05 Nobility, noble condition
æþelstenc 02.05.08.02 Pleasant smell, fragrance, perfume
æþeltungol 01.02.01.01.02 Star
æþelu 02.03.02.03 Ancestry, descent; 05.02.02 Nature, established order of things; 07.02.04.03 Nobleness, excellence, nobility, magnificence; 12.01.01.06.05 Nobility, noble condition; 12.01.01.06.06 Gentle birth, nobility
æþm 02.04.06.06 Discharge, emanation; 02.04.06.07.03 Breath; 03.01.09.02 Fire, flame; 03.01.15 Vapour, air
æþmian 02.04.06.07.05 To breathe; 02.05.08 Faculty of smell; 08.01.01.01 Ardour, fervour, strong feeling
æþrot 08.01.03.07.01 Tedium
æþryt 08.01.03.07.01 Tedium
geæþryt 08.01.03.07.01 Tedium
æþryt(e) 08.01.03.07.01 Tedium
æþrytnes 08.01.03.07.01 Tedium
(ge)æþryttan 08.01.03.07.01 Tedium
æw 16.02.01 Faith
æwæde 04.04.07.02.01 Nakedness
æwan 07.05.02 Contempt
æwbreca 12.08.08.01.02.01 Fornication, adultery; 16.02.04.13.01 (Of churchman) neglect of chastity
æwbryce 12.08.08.01.02.01 Fornication, adultery; 16.02.04.13.01 (Of churchman) neglect of chastity
æwda 14.03.03.03 Witness, testimony, attestation
æwdamann 14.03.03.03 Witness, testimony, attestation

æwe 12.09 Marriage, state of marriage; 14.01.02 A law, statute
æwelm 01.01.03.01.01.07 Spring, fountain, well
æwenbrōþor 02.03.02.02.05.01 Brother
æwēne 06.01.07.07.03.01 Unknown, uncertain
æwerd 12.08.06.01.02 Lacking moral good
æweweard 16.02.03.02.07 A priest, cleric
æwfæst 12.09 Marriage, state of marriage; 16.02.01.11 Firmness in the law, piety, devoutness
æwfæsten 04.01.01.06.01 Abstinence from food, fast; 16.02.04.04.02.02 A fast, act of fasting
æwfæstlic 14.01.02 A law, statute; 16.02.01 Faith
æwfæstlīce 16.02.01 Faith
æwfæstnes 16.02.01 Faith; 16.02.01.11 Firmness in the law, piety, devoutness
æwicnes 05.11.01.01.01 Eternity
æwielm 05.03 Source, origin
geæwierdlian 02.08.04 Hurt, injury, damage
æwisc 07.09 Shame, disgrace
æwiscberend 02.04.03.04.01.01.01 Finger; 07.09 Shame, disgrace
æwisc(e) 07.09 Shame, disgrace
æwiscfiriniend 12.08.09 Guiltiness, guilt
æwisclic 07.09 Shame, disgrace
æwiscmōd 07.09.01 Shame, confusion
æwiscnes 07.04.03 Reverence, respect; 07.09 Shame, disgrace; 12.08.06.01 Error, wrong conduct, erroneous practice
æwiscod 09.06.02.01.05 Proclamation, spreading abroad

æwita 12.02.02.02 A counsellor, advisor; 16.02.01.09.02 Knowledge of Jewish law
geæwnian 12.09.02 Marriage ceremony
geæw(n)od 12.09 Marriage, state of marriage
æwnung 12.09 Marriage, state of marriage
æwumboren 02.03.02.02 Child, offspring
æwyll 01.01.03.01.01.03 Stream
æwyrp 02.01.03.03.03.01 Child-bearing, childbirth; 04.06.02.04 Refuse, litter, rubbish
āfægan 17.02.05.06 A painting, picture, representation
āfægrian 07.10.03 An adornment, decoration, ornament
āfæman ūt 02.04.06.07.05 To breathe
āfæran 06.01.08.06.03.01 Causing dread, terrifying
āfæstan 04.01.01.06.01 Abstinence from food, fast; 15.01.01.01.01 Hiring, letting out of property/land; 16.02.04.04.02.02 A fast, act of fasting
āfæstlā 06.01.07.07.03 Certainty
āfæstnian 05.06.07 Pricking, a prick, puncture; 05.08 Strength; 05.12.04.01 Stability, firmness; 05.13.06.01 Firm, stable, steady; 09.03.07.07.03.02 To write, state/say in writing; 09.07.04 Assertion, affirmation
āfættian 03.01.17.07.01 An anointing, greasing
āfandian 08.01.01 A feeling, what is felt; 09.07.04 Assertion, affirmation; 11.03.01 Experience, trial, experiment
āfandigendlic 07.04.04.02 Laudable, praiseworthy

āfandod 07.04.04.02 Laudable, praiseworthy
āfandodlic 07.04.04.02 Laudable, praiseworthy
āfandodlīce 07.04.04.02 Laudable, praiseworthy
āfandung 08.01.01 A feeling, what is felt; 11.03.01.01 Trial, probation
āfangennes 05.12.05.12.02 To raise, lift up, elevate
āfaran (of/ūt) 05.12.05.03.03 To depart, leave, set out
āfeallan 02.02.03 To die, perish; 02.08.02 Disease, infirmity, sickness; 05.03.02.01.01 An event, occurrence; 05.06.01 Devastation, laying waste; 05.09.05 Ceasing, decline, fall off; 05.12.05.13.03 To fall; 07.04.03 Reverence, respect; 11.06.03.01 Ill fortune, bad success
āfeallan (on) 12.08.06.01.04 To lead a bad life
āfēd 04.02.04.03 A plant
āfēdan 04.01.01.02 Act/action of sucking; 04.01.02.04.03.01 To feed/nourish; 04.01.02.04.03.02 Bringing-up, fostering; 04.01.02.04.04 To maintain, support, provide for; 05.06.01 Devastation, laying waste; 06.01.06.02.03.04.03 To teach, instruct
āfēgan 03.03.06.01 A whole formed by joining
āfeohtan 13.02 War
āfeormian 02.08.12.02.07.01 Purgative; 04.06.01 Clean; 16.02.04.07.02.03 Penance, an act/instance of penance
āfeormian (of) 02.08.12.02.05.04 To cleanse, clean away
āfeormod 04.06.01 Clean

āfeormung 02.08.12.02.07.01 Purgative; 04.06.01 Clean; 16.02.04.07.02.03 Penance, an act/instance of penance
āfeorsian 05.12.05.03.03 To depart, leave, set out; 05.12.05.03.04 To come/go out from
āfercian 04.01.01 Eating; 04.01.02.04.04 To maintain, support, provide for
āferian 17.02.04.02.03 Carrying, carriage (of materials)
āferscan 03.01.16.02 Water, liquid
affricanisc 02.03.03.06.07.01 African
affricanisc æppel 02.07.09.02 Particular fruits (alphabetical order)
affrice 02.03.03.06.07.01 African
affricisc 02.03.03.06.07.01 African
āfierran 03.03.07.01 Division, partition, separation; 05.12.02.04 To cast out, drive away; 05.12.05.03.03 To depart, leave, set out
āfierrednes 05.12.02.02 To carry off, remove
āfigen 04.01.02.02.05.03 Frying/roasting
āfindan 05.12.05.02.01 To come upon, meet with; 06.01.06 Understanding, knowledge, cognizance; 08.01.01 A feeling, what is felt; 11.03.01.03 Finding, discovery
āflēan 05.06.06.01 A tearing, laceration
āflēon 05.12.05.03.03 To depart, leave, set out
āflēotan of 04.06.01.10 To separate objects already connected, unmix
geaflian 10.01.02 Acquisition
āflīegan 05.12.02.04 To cast out, drive away
āflīeged 16.02.01.07 Apostasy
āflīegung 05.12.02.04 To cast out, drive away

āflīeman 13.02.05.01.01 To overcome, conquer
āflīeman (ūt) 05.12.02.04 To cast out, drive away; 05.12.05.03.04 To come/go out from
āflīemed 12.06.05.01 State of exile, banishment
āflote 05.12.01.08 To move in/on water
āflōwan of/ūt 05.12.05.03.04.02 To flow out, well up, erupt
āflōwan tō 05.13 Changeableness, change
āflōwan ūp 05.12.05.03.04.02 To flow out, well up, erupt
āflygennes 02.08.03.02 Itch, irritation
āfohten 05.06.08 A plucking, taking away
afol 12 Power, might
āfōn 05.10.05.04.02.04.02 Support, maintenance; 08.01 Heart, spirit, mood, disposition; 10.01.01 Acceptance, receiving; 10.01.02 Acquisition; 10.04.02.02 To seize, take, grasp, lay hold on
āfor 02.05.07.01 Strong taste, acidity, pungency; 02.08.12.02.05 Pharmacy, curing with salves; 08.01.03.07.04 Severity, harshness
āforhtian 06.01.08.05.01 Amazement, astonishment, wonder, admiration; 06.01.08.06 Fear
āfrēfr(i)an 08.01.03.07.04.02.01 Comfort, consolation
āfremd(i)an 05.10.04.04.02 Removal, taking away; 12.04.03.01 Estrangement, alienation
āfrēon 11.10.03 Salvation/deliverance from
āfrēoþan 03.01.16.04 Foam, froth
afrisc 02.03.03.06.07.01 African
āfūlian 03.02.01.01 Decay, corruption, rottenness; 07.09.03 Infamy, ignominy, shame

afulic 06.02.07.04.02 Perversity
āfūliende 03.02.01.01 Decay, corruption, rottenness
āfulliend 04.04.01 Fulling
āfunden 10 Having, owning, possession; 11.04 Ability, capacity, power
āfundennes 11.03.01.03.01 Discovery, invention
āfȳlan 04.06.02.02 Foul, filthy, squalid; 12.08.06.01.04.01 To mislead, seduce, lead astray; 12.08.08.01.02 Unchastity, incontinence; 16.02.04.14 Sacrilege
āfȳled 12.08.08.01.02 Unchastity, incontinence
āfylgan 05.12.05.10 To go behind, follow
āfyllan 02.02.04.03 To kill, slay; 03.03.04.02.01 Abundance; 03.03.06.02 Fullness; 05.06.02 Cleaving, splitting, cutting; 05.06.09 Act of striking; 05.07 Ending of existence, end of world; 05.12.05.13.03 To fall; 06.02.05.03 Satisfaction, repletion
āfȳran 02.08.04.02.02 Castrated
āfȳred 02.03.01.03 Eunuch; 02.08.04.02.02 Castrated
āfyrhtan 06.01.08.06.03 Cause of fear, terror, horror
āfyrþan 05.10.04.04.02 Removal, taking away
āfȳsan 05.12.02.04 To cast out, drive away; 05.12.02.06.01 To push, drive; 06.02.05.01 Strong liking for, devotion to
āfȳsed 01.01.03.01.01 Moving water; 01.01.03.04 Current, rush of water
āga 10 Having, owning, possession
āgǣlan 06.01.01.01.01.01 Consideration, rumination; 11.06.01 Neglect;
11.11.02 A hindrance; 16.02.04.14 Sacrilege
āgǣlwan 06.01.08.05.01 Amazement, astonishment, wonder, admiration
āgǣlwed 06.01.08.06.02 Great fear, terror, horror
āgalan 18.02.07.01 Singing, song
āgālian 11.06.01.01 Negligence, carelessness, heedlessness
āgālod 11.06.01.01 Negligence, carelessness, heedlessness
āgan 02.01.03.03 Sex, generation; 10.03.03 Granting; 11.01.05 Accomplishment, fulfilment; 12.03.01 Direction, care, management, supervision; 12.07 An obligation, bounden duty
āgan lof 16.02.04 Worship, honour, praise
āgan sceande 07.09 Shame, disgrace
āgan sige 13.02.05.01 Victory
āgan tō hyhte 06.01.08.02 Hope, expectation
āgan tō geldanne 15.04 A debt, due
āgan þearfe 06.02.04.01 Want, need
āgan wælstōwe geweald 13.02.05.01 Victory
(ge)āgan 10 Having, owning, possession; 10.01.02 Acquisition
āgān 05.03.02.01.01 An event, occurrence; 05.09 Weakness; 05.11 A time, period of time; 05.11.07.03 Former times, days of old; 12.03.04 A request, prayer; 15.01.02.01 Inherited property
āgān ūt 06.01.06.01 Knowledge, cognizance, knowing
āgangan 05.03.02.01.01 An event, occurrence; 05.11 A time, period of time

āgānian 05.10.05.04.14.01 A yawning, gaping opening
āge 15.01 Property
āgēancyme 05.12.05.11.01 To return
āgēancyrding 05.12.05.11.01 To return
āgēanhworfennes 05.12.05.11.01 To return
āgeldan 14.05 Punishment
agen 04.02.04.03.02.01 Grain crops
āgen 03.04.01 Singularity, peculiarity; 12.06.04 Native land; 15.01 Property
āgen nama 09.03.02.02.01.01 A noun; 09.06.02.01.07 A name, appellation
(ge)āgen 10 Having, owning, possession
āgēn bewendan 05.12.05.11.01 To return
āgēn cuman 05.12.05.11.01 To return
āgēn iernan 05.12.05.02.02 To come together, meet
āgēn sendan 05.12.02.03 To send
āgend 10 Having, owning, possession; 16.01.01.01.01 The Almighty
āgendfrēa 10 Having, owning, possession; 16.01.01.01.01 The Almighty
āgendlīce 07.02.01 Right, virtue; 10 Having, owning, possession; 12 Power, might
āgenfrīga 10 Having, owning, possession
āgēn(ge)hweorfan 05.12.05.11.01 To return
āgēnhwyrfan 05.12.05.11.01 To return
āgēnlǣdan 05.12.05.11.01 To return
āgenland 15.01.01 Landed property
āgenlic 10 Having, owning, possession; 14.01.05 Service, obligation, duty
āgennes 05.02.02 Nature, established order of things
āgēnsendan 05.12.05.11.01 To return
āgenslaga 02.02.04.04.02 Suicide

āgēnstandan 12.05.06.03.01 Pressure, compulsion
āgeolwian 03.01.14.07 Yellow/yellowness
āgēomrian 08.01.03.04 Grief
āgeornan 02.05.05.02 Eager desire
āgēotan 03.01.16.01 Moisture; 05.06.01 Devastation, laying waste; 05.12.05.03.04.02 To flow out, well up, erupt; 08.01.01.01 Ardour, fervour, strong feeling; 10.04.03.01 To take away, deprive of; 17.02.04.03.03 Smelting, heating, scorification
āgēotan blōd 02.02.04.03 To kill, slay
āgēotan tēaras 08.01.03.04.02 Shedding of tears
āgiefan 02.08.12 Healing, curing; 10.03.04.01 Restitution, making good, repayment; 11.06.06.01 Abandonment (of principle); 15.02.04 Spending, disbursement
āgiefan andsware 09.05.03 An answer, reply
āgieldan 05.03.02 Event, issue, result; 05.05.02 Productivity, bringing forth; 10.03.04.01 Restitution, making good, repayment; 11.01.04 A doing, accomplishing (of something); 14.03.03.09.02 Atonement; 15.02.04 Spending, disbursement; 16.02.04.12 Sacrifice, a sacrifice
āgīemelēasian 11.06.01 Neglect
āgīemelēasod 11.06.01.01 Negligence, carelessness, heedlessness
āgifian 10.03.03 Granting
āgimmed 17.02.05.01 Ornamental object
āgīta 10.03.08.01 Overliberality, waste of money
āgitan 06.01.06.01 Knowledge, cognizance, knowing; 11.03.01.03 Finding, discovery

āgītan 05.06.01 Devastation, laying waste; 05.06.08 A plucking, taking away
āglāchād 08.01.03.06 Adversity, affliction
āglǣc 08.01.03.07.02 Misery, trouble, affliction
āglǣca 16.01.05.02 Species of devil, hellish race
āglǣccræft 16.01.04 Sorcery, magic, witchcraft
āglǣcwīf 02.06.10 Monster, strange creature
āgleddian 04.06.02.03 Stain, smear
āglīdan 05.09.05 Ceasing, decline, fall off; 05.12.01.04.01.04 To stumble, trip, strike (with the foot)
āgnere 10 Having, owning, possession
āgnes þances 06.02.01 Freewill, own will
āgnett 15.04.01 Lending of money
āgnettan 15.01.01.01 Holding of land
āgnian 15.01.01.01 Holding of land
(ge)āgnian 10 Having, owning, possession; 14.03.03 Law, action of the courts; 15.01.01.01 Holding of land
geāgnian 04.05.03.01 Habitation, sojourn; 10.01.02 Acquisition; 12.06.03.02 Living, dwelling, residence (in)
āgnīdan 05.06.05 A grinding, pounding; 05.06.05.01 A rubbing
āgniden 03.02.01.02 Decay from age
āgniend 10 Having, owning, possession
geāgniendlic 09.03.02.03.01.01.01 Case
geāgnod 02.03.02.04 Adoption
āgnung 15.01 Property; 15.01.01.01 Holding of land
geāgnung 10.01.02 Acquisition

āgoten 03.01.09.01.02 That melts, melting
āgotennes 02.04.06.06 Discharge, emanation
āgrafan 17.02.05.05 A carving, graving; 17.02.05.05.01 Graven, embossed, chased
āgrafen 17.02.05.05 A carving, graving
āgrafenlic 17.02.05.05 A carving, graving
āgrāpian 10.04.02 To grasp, take hold of
āgrētan 13.02.03.01 An attack, assault
āgrimettan 08.01.03.05.02 Anger
agrimonia 02.07.11 Plants/flowers (alphabetical order)
āgrimsian 08.01.03.05.02 Anger
āgrīsan 06.01.08.06.01 A shuddering with fear, nervousness; 06.01.08.06.02 Great fear, terror, horror
āgrōwen 02.07.01 To grow
āgryndan 05.12.05.13 To go down, descend
agu 02.06.08.05 Forest bird, wild-fowl
aguster 02.06.08.05 Forest bird, wild-fowl
agustus 05.11.03.01.03.01 Specific months
āgylpan 07.06.03 Boastfulness, arrogance
āgyltan (wiþ) 12.08.06.02.05.05 To sin (against), do wrong
āgyltend 12.08.06.02.05.02 A sinner, transgressor; 16.02.01.13 Evil-doing, transgression, sin
āgyltnes 12.08.09 Guiltiness, guilt
āgȳman 02.08.12 Healing, curing; 06.01.01.01 Thinking about, minding, heeding
āgȳtan 05.06.01 Devastation, laying waste
āhabban 05.10.05.04.02.04.02 Support, maintenance

āhabban (fram) 11.06.04 Abstention, abstaining from
āhaccian ūt 05.06.08 A plucking, taking away
āhafennes 05.12.05.12.02 To raise, lift up, elevate
āhālsian 12.03.04.01 Entreaty, solemn appeal
āhangian 02.02.04.04.03 Putting to death; 05.12.01.07.01 To hang
āhātan 09.06.02.01.07 A name, appellation
āhātian 03.01.09 Heat; 08.01.01.01 Ardour, fervour, strong feeling
āhealdan 11.06.04 Abstention, abstaining from
āhealtian 02.08.04.04 State of being crippled
āheardian 03.01.03 Hardness, callosity, hard material; 06.02.07.04.01 Obduracy; 08.01.01.02 Lacking in feeling, insensitive; 12.08.06.02.03.02 To do evil
āheardod 03.01.01 Thick, close-textured, dense
āheardung 02.08.08 Internal disease
āhēawan 05.06.02 Cleaving, splitting, cutting; 17.02.04.02.01 Cutting, hewing, shaping
āhēawen 04.05.01.02.01 Boarding, planking, floor; 17.02.04.02.01 Cutting, hewing, shaping
āhebban 04.01.02.02.05.04.01 Preparation of bread; 04.05 Building, construction; 05.03.01 A cause (of anything); 05.12.02.02 To carry off, remove; 06.02.07.01 Strength, fortitude; 07.04.04 Praise, acclamation, applause; 07.06.01.03 To be proud/arrogant; 07.08.06 Exaltation
āhebban handa 11.01.02 An undertaking
āhebban onweg 10.04.03 To take away, remove
āhebban (ūp) 05.12.05.12.02 To raise, lift up, elevate
āhebban wæpen 13.02 War
āhebban (ge)winn 13.02 War
āhefig 08.01.03.07.02 Misery, trouble, affliction
āhefigian 02.05.03.01 Dullness, lack of animation; 08.01.03.07.02 Misery, trouble, affliction
āheled 09.05.04 A secret
āhelian 05.10.05.04.12 The condition of being covered
āhelpan 11.12.02 Aid, help, succour
āhēnan 12.05.06.02 Oppression; 14.03.03.01 Accusation
āheolorian 03.03.02 Measurement by weighing; 06.01.01.01.01 Thought, cogitation, meditation
āheordan 11.10.03 Salvation/deliverance from
āherian 16.02.04 Worship, honour, praise
āhierdan 08.01.03.09.10 Wrath, sternness, displeasure; 17.02.04.03.03 Smelting, heating, scorification
āhierding 08.01.03.09.10 Wrath, sternness, displeasure
āhildan 05.06 Destruction, dissolution, loss, breaking; 05.10.05.04.02.03 Laid below; 05.10.05.04.04 A descent, slope, incline; 05.12.05 To move and change direction, turn; 05.12.05.13 To go down, descend; 06.02.06.03 Persuasion, prompting; 09.03.02.03.01.01 Declension
āhildendlic 09.03.02.03.01.01 Declension
āhīþend 05.06 Destruction, dissolution, loss, breaking

āhladan 05.12.05.03.04 To come/go out from; 05.12.05.08.01 To go before and guide
āhlǣnan 07.06.01.03 To be proud/arrogant
āhlǣnsian 02.04.02.02 Lean, thin, slender; 03.03.04.06 Diminution
āhlēapan (ūp) 05.12.05.12.01 To reach up
āhlēfan 05.06.08 A plucking, taking away; 05.12.02.05 To pull, drag, draw
āhlēoþrian 02.05.10.04 To resound
āhliehhan 07.05.04 Mockery, derision, scorn; 08.01.01.03.07.01 Laughter
āhlocian 05.06.08 A plucking, taking away
āhlōwan 02.05.10.05 Roaring, raging
āhlūttred 04.01.02.02.05.02 To boil
āhlūttrian 04.01.02.02.05.02 To boil; 04.06.01 Clean; 04.06.01.10 To separate objects already connected, unmix; 12.08.04 Purity, moral cleanness
āhlūttrod 04.01.02.01.01.01 Good/palatable food
āhlūttrud 04.01.03.05.01.01 Wine
āhnēapan 05.06.08 A plucking, taking away
āhnescian 05.09 Weakness; 08.01.02.01.02 Gentleness
āhnīgan 05.12.05.13.03 To fall; 07.07 Humility
āhnigen 05.10.05.04.04 A descent, slope, incline
āhogod 06.01.08.06.04 Care, anxiety, solicitude
āholian 17.02.04.02.02 Digging
āholian ūt 05.06.08 A plucking, taking away
āholod 17.02.04.02.02 Digging

āhōn 02.02.04.04.03 Putting to death; 05.12.01.07.01 To hang; 14.05.05.01.01 Crucifixion, death on cross
āhopian tō 06.01.08.03 Trust, faith, confidence
āhrǣcan ūt 02.04.06.06.04 Spittle
āhrǣscian of 05.10.04.04.02 Removal, taking away
āhreddan (æt/on/fram) 11.10.03 Salvation/deliverance from
āhreddan wiþ/fram 11.10.01 Protection, safekeeping
āhredding 16.01.01.02.08 Salvation, redemption
āhrēofian 02.08.06 Skin disease, erysipelas
āhrēosan 05.06.01 Devastation, laying waste; 05.06.03 A dashing together, breaking, shattering; 05.12.05.13.03 To fall
āhrepian 09.06 To take matter for discourse
āhrēran 05.12.05.05 To shake, quake, wag
āhrēred 08.01.01 A feeling, what is felt
āhrīnan 02.05.06 Sense of touch
āhrisian 05.12.05.05 To shake, quake, wag; 08.01.01.01.03 An incitement, cause of strong feeling
āhrisian of 05.10.04.04.02 Removal, taking away
āhrȳran 05.06 Destruction, dissolution, loss, breaking
āhrȳred 05.06 Destruction, dissolution, loss, breaking
āhtes 07.04.01 (Of persons) worth/value, worthiness
āhtlīce 06.02.07.01 Strength, fortitude
āhwā 03.04.03.01 Someone/something

āhwænan 08.01.03.07.02 Misery, trouble, affliction
āhwæned 08.01.03.06 Adversity, affliction
āhwænne 05.11.02 A time, particular time, occasion; 05.11.09.01 Always
āhwǣr 03.04.03.01 Someone/something; 05.10.04.03 Presence
āhwæt 03.04.03.01 Someone/something
āhwǣtan 05.12.05.03.04 To come/go out from
āhwanan 05.10.04.03 Presence
āhwanon 05.10.04.03 Presence
āhweorfan 05.12.02.08 To give a different direction to, turn; 05.13.01 Transformation, taking another shape
āhweorfan fram/of 11.06.06 Turning
āhweorfan in 05.10.05.04.09.01 Front
āhwerfedum sīþe 05.10.05.04.09.03 Reverse, inverted
āhwergen 03.04.03.01 Someone/something; 05.10.04.03 Presence
āhwettan 08.01.01.01.03 An incitement, cause of strong feeling; 10.03.04 Provision, supply
āhwider 05.10.04.03 Presence
āhwierfan 09.05.04.01 Concealment, obscurity
āhwierfan (fram/of) 05.13.01 Transformation, taking another shape
āhwistlian 02.05.10.09 A hissing, whistling
āhwītian 03.01.14.03 White/whiteness; 05.07 Ending of existence, end of world
āhwylfan 05.06 Destruction, dissolution, loss, breaking; 05.12.01.09.03.02 Hardship on board; 05.12.05.04.01 (Of wheel, etc.) to roll, trundle

āhycgan 06.02.06.02 A proposal, proposition, suggestion
āhȳdan 09.05.04.01 Concealment, obscurity
āhyldnes 05.12.05.13 To go down, descend
āhyltan 02.08.04.04 State of being crippled
āhȳran 15.01.01.01.01 Hiring, letting out of property/land
āhȳrian 17.02.01 Management of work
āhyrst 03.01.18 Dryness (not wetness)
āhyrstan 04.01.02.02.05.03 Frying/roasting
āhyscan 08.01.01.03.07.04 Scoffing, mockery
āhyspan 07.05.03.03.02 To reproach, revile, abuse
āhȳþan 05.06.01 Devastation, laying waste
āhȳþende 05.06 Destruction, dissolution, loss, breaking
āīdan 05.12.02.04 To cast out, drive away
āīdl(i)an 02.05.09.14 To vanish, disappear; 03.03.08 Emptiness; 05.07 Ending of existence, end of world; 11.08.04 Vanity, idleness, frivolity; 16.02.04.14 Sacrilege
āiernan 05.07 Ending of existence, end of world; 05.11 A time, period of time
āiernende 01.01.03.03 Flow/flowing
āīeþan 05.06.01 Devastation, laying waste
āl 03.01.09.02 Fire, flame
ālādian 08.01.03.09.07 Threat, threatening, menace; 12.07.03.02 An excuse
ālæccan 10.04.02 To grasp, take hold of
ālǣdan 05.12.02.02 To carry off, remove; 05.12.05.08.01 To go before and

guide; 12.05.06.04 A trampling upon, subjection
ālǣdan (ūt) 05.05.02 Productivity, bringing forth; 11.10.03 Salvation/deliverance from
ālǣnan 10.03 Giving; 15.01.01.01.01 Hiring, letting out of property/land
ālǣran 06.01.06.02.03.04.03 To teach, instruct
ālǣtan 05.12.02.03 To send; 08.01.02.06.02 Forgiveness, remission, clemency; 10.02 Want, lack; 10.02.01 Loss, deprivation; 10.03.03 Granting; 10.03.04.01 Restitution, making good, repayment; 11.06.06.01 Abandonment (of principle); 11.10.03 Salvation/deliverance from; 12.03.05 Permission; 16.02.04.07.02.02 Absolution, forgiveness, remission
ālǣtan ūt 05.12.01.09 To travel on water
ālǣtnes 10.02.01.01 Loss, forfeiture; 16.02.04.07.02.02 Absolution, forgiveness, remission
alamanne 02.03.03.06.02.01 Other peoples
alan 11.12.02.01 Strengthening, confirmation
ālatian 05.09.01 Slow, inactive
ālāþian 07.03.01.03 To loathe, hate, abhor
albe 16.02.05.06.01 Outer garments
aldgeddung 09.06.01.02 A saying, saw, proverb, maxim
ālecgan 02.02.04.03 To kill, slay; 04.05 Building, construction; 05.07 Ending of existence, end of world; 05.09.05 Ceasing, decline, fall off; 05.10.05.04.02.03 Laid below; 11.06.04 Abstention, abstaining from; 12.05.06 Grasp, power, control, mastery
ālecgende word 09.03.02.02.01.02 A verb
ālecgendlic word 09.03.02.02.01.02 A verb
ālēfed/ālēwed 02.08.02 Disease, infirmity, sickness
ālēfednes 02.08.04.04 State of being crippled; 10.03.03 Granting
ālēfian 02.08.04 Hurt, injury, damage; 05.09 Weakness
āleged 02.02.03.02 State of being dead; 05.10.04 Place, room
ālendan 15.01.01.01.01 Hiring, letting out of property/land
ālēodan 02.07.01 To grow
ālēogan 06.01.07.04.03 Untruth, falsehood; 06.01.07.04.04.02 Pretence, feigning, dissimulation; 11.06.01 Neglect; 12.07.02.02.01 To break a promise, vow, etc.
ālēon 15.04.01 Lending of money
ālēoran 05.11 A time, period of time
ālēoran (ūt) 05.12.05.03.03 To depart, leave, set out
alerbedd 02.07.03.05 Particular trees/shrubs (alphabetical order)
alerbrōc 01.01.03.01.01.03 Stream
alerburne 01.01.03.01.01.03 Stream
alerholt 02.07.03.05 Particular trees/shrubs (alphabetical order)
alersceaga 02.07.03.05 Particular trees/shrubs (alphabetical order)
ālesan 07.01.01 Choice, election
ālesan (of) 09.03.07.07.03.02.01 An epitome, short account
alexandre 02.07.11 Plants/flowers (alphabetical order)
alexandrinisc 02.03.03.06.07.01 African

alexand(r)isc 02.03.03.06.07.01 African
ālfæt 04.01.02.02.06.01 Cooking vessel/pot
ālgeweorc 03.01.09.02.01 Fire, burning
ālibban 02.01.02.01 That lives, living; 02.01.02.02.02 Lifetime; 16.01.01.01 Attributes of God
ālicgan 05.07 Ending of existence, end of world
āliefan 10.03.03 Granting; 11.06.06.01 Abandonment (of principle); 12.03.05 Permission
āliefedlic 12.03.05 Permission
āliefedlīce 12.03.05 Permission
āliesan 11.10.03 Salvation/deliverance from; 16.02.04.07.02.03 Penance, an act/instance of penance
āliesan (æt/fram/of) 11.10.03 Salvation/deliverance from
āliesan for/wiþ 11.10.03 Salvation/deliverance from
ālīes(ed)nes 11.10.03 Salvation/deliverance from
āliesend 16.01.01.04.02 The Son, Christ
āliesendlic 05.05.04 That loosens, loosening
āliese(n)dnes 16.01.01.02.08 Salvation, redemption
āliesing 16.01.01.02.08 Salvation, redemption
āliesnes 16.01.01.02.08 Salvation, redemption
ālīf 05.11.01.01.01 Eternity; 16.01.02.03 Reward of heaven
ālīhtan 03.01.12.02 A beam of light; 05.09.03 Mitigation, lightening, alleviation
ālīhtan ... of 05.12.01.05 To ride (on horse, etc.)
ālīhtan (of) 05.12.05.13 To go down, descend
ālīhting 03.01.12.02 A beam of light
ālimpan 05.03.02.01.01 An event, occurrence
āliþian 03.03.07.01 Division, partition, separation
alleluia 16.02.04.03.02 Parts of service
almesgifu 16.02.04.09 Almsgiving, charitableness
almesriht 14.01.04.03 Rights involving money
almessylen 16.02.04.09 Almsgiving, charitableness
āloccian ūt 06.02.06.03.04 Allurement
alor 02.07.03.05 Particular trees/shrubs (alphabetical order)
alordrenc 04.01.03.05 A drink/beverage
alorrind 02.07.03.05 Particular trees/shrubs (alphabetical order)
āloten 05.12.05.13.02 To bow, bend down; 07.04.03 Reverence, respect
alpis (þā muntas) 01.01.02.01.02.02.02 Mountain
alrett 02.07.03.05 Particular trees/shrubs (alphabetical order)
altar(e) 16.02.05.03.04 Part of temple containing altar/idol
ālūcan 03.03.07.01 Division, partition, separation; 05.12.02.05 To pull, drag, draw; 05.12.05.03.02 To keep clear of, stand off from, withdraw
ālūcan (ūt) 05.06.08 A plucking, taking away
ālūtan 05.12.05.13.02 To bow, bend down; 07.04.03 Reverence, respect; 09.03.03 A gesture, action, gesticulation
alwe 02.07.11 Plants/flowers (alphabetical order)

ālȳman 07.08.07 Glory, splendour, magnificence
ālynnan/ālynian 11.10.03 Salvation/deliverance from
ālȳsan of 05.05.04 That loosens, loosening
ālȳþran 03.01.17.07.01 An anointing, greasing; 04.06.01.04 What is used in washing, an ointment
ām 04.04.03 A spinning-house or chamber; 17.03.06 Tools for marking
āmǣran 07.04.04 Praise, acclamation, applause
āmǣstan 04.01.02.04.03.01 To feed/nourish; 04.02.05.01.01 To feed/fatten animals; 08.01.01.03.04 Gladness, cheerfulness
āmǣsted 04.02.05.01.01 To feed/fatten animals
āmǣst(ed) 04.01.02.01.02 Animal(s) for food
āmagian 02.08.13 Recovery, growing better
āmang 05.10.05.04.10 Among; 05.11 A time, period of time
āmang þām 05.11 A time, period of time
āmang þām þe 05.11 A time, period of time
āmanian 14.05.03 Retribution, requital
āmānsian 07.03.01.03 To loathe, hate, abhor
āmānsod 16.02.04.19 Excommunication
āmānsumian 16.02.04.14.02.01 Cursing, imprecation; 16.02.04.19 Excommunication
āmānsumod 16.02.04.19 Excommunication
āmānsumung 16.02.04.19 Excommunication
āmānsung 16.02.04.19 Excommunication

āmasian 06.01.08.05.01 Amazement, astonishment, wonder, admiration
āmāwan 05.06.02 Cleaving, splitting, cutting
ambeht 12.01.01.08 Service; 12.03.03 A command, bidding, order; 17.02.03 A task, service, duty
ambehtnes 17.02.03 A task, service, duty
amber 03.03.01 Specific measures; 04.01.03.05.04 Drinking vessel
amberlīce 08.01.01.03.04 Gladness, cheerfulness
ambiht 06.01.06.02.03.02 Discipleship; 12.01.01.07 A follower; 12.01.01.08.01 A servant, attendant
ambihtere 12.01.01.08.01 A servant, attendant
ambihthēra 12.01.01.08.01 A servant, attendant
ambihthūs 17.02.01 Management of work
ambihtmann 12.01.01.08.01 A servant, attendant
ambihtmecg 12.01.01.08.01 A servant, attendant
ambihtscealc 12.01.01.08.01 A servant, attendant
ambihtsecg 12.01.01.08.01 A servant, attendant
ambihtsmiþ 17.02.04 Trade, calling, craft, aptitude
ambihtsumnes 08.01.02.01 Favour, kindness, grace
ambihtþegn 02.03.03.01 Body of retainers, household
ambrōsie 02.07.02.07 Blossom, flower(s)
ambyr 05.11.08 A suitable time, opportunity
ambyre 01.03.01.05 Wind
āmeallian 02.05.07.02 Insipid

āmeallod 03.03.08 Emptiness
āmearcian 03.06.02 Difference, diversity, dissimilarity; 05.04 Fate, lot, fortune, destiny; 09.03.07.04.01 To punctuate, divide; 09.04.01 Signal, signalling; 09.04.03 Exposition, making clear by explanation; 09.06.02.01.07.02 A categorizing name; 10.03.07.01 To allot, assign
amel 16.02.05.05.06 A vessel for use in services
āmelcan 04.02.05.06.01.02 To milk
āmeldian 09.05.05.01 Showing, manifestation, display; 09.06.02.01 To tell, make known, declare, relate, announce; 09.06.02.01.01 To make known, cause to know, inform; 09.06.02.01.04 A confession, declaration
āmen 16.02.04.03.02 Parts of service
ameos 02.07.11 Plants/flowers (alphabetical order)
amer 04.02.04.03.02.01 Grain crops
āmered 04.01.02.02.05.02 To boil; 04.06.01.09 To cleanse, remove impurity from (an object)
āmerian 11.03.01 Experience, trial, experiment; 11.03.01.01 Trial, probation; 12.08.04 Purity, moral cleanness; 17.02.04.03.03 Smelting, heating, scorification
āmetan 03.03 Measurement, determination of amount; 10.03.07.01 To allot, assign; 17.02.04 Trade, calling, craft, aptitude
āmētan 07.10.03 An adornment, decoration, ornament; 17.02.05.06 A painting, picture, representation
āmetendlic 03.03.03 Number; 05.11.01.02 Shortness/brevity in time

āmetendlīce 09.03.04.04 Discursiveness
āmetsian 04.01.02.04.04.01 Provider/supplier of food
āmīdlian 12.05.06.01 Restraint, check, curb, control
āmidod 06.01.05.03.01.01 Dullness, folly, stupidity
āmierran 02.02.04.03 To kill, slay; 02.08.04 Hurt, injury, damage; 05.06.01 Devastation, laying waste; 05.10.05.04.08 Crookedness, a crooked place; 06.01.07.04.01 Deception, a leading astray; 10.02.01 Loss, deprivation; 11.08.03 Needless, useless, unprofitable; 11.11.02 A hindrance
āmigdal 02.07.09.02.01.01 Particular nuts (alphabetical order)
āmolsnian 02.08.02 Disease, infirmity, sickness
āmolten 03.01.09.01.02 That melts, melting
ampelle 04.01.03.05.04.01 A flask, flagon, bottle
ampre 02.07.11 Plants/flowers (alphabetical order); 02.08.05.01 Swelling; 02.08.07.07 Disorders of the body
āmunan 06.01.04 Faculty of memory
āmundian 11.10.01 Protection, safekeeping
āmylt 04.01.02.02.05.01 Heating, warming
āmyltan 03.01.09.01.02 That melts, melting
āmyrgan 08.01.01.03.09.03 To make glad
āmyrþrian 02.02.04.04 Manslaughter, homicide
ān 03.03.03.04.01 One; 03.04.01 Singularity, peculiarity; 03.06.01.02

Equality; 05.11.10.01 A beginning; 16.01.01.01 Attributes of God; 16.01.01.04 The Trinity
ān and ān 03.03.03.04.01 One
ān flǣsc 12.09 Marriage, state of marriage
ān hwā 03.04.03.01 Someone/something
ān gehwilc 03.04.03.01 Someone/something
ān lǣtan 11.06.04 Abstention, abstaining from
āna 03.04.01 Singularity, peculiarity; 12.04.04 Solitude
ānad 01.01.02.01.06 Wild/uncultivated land
ānægled 17.03.10.02 A pin, peg, nail
ānæglian 17.03.10.02 A pin, peg, nail
ananbēam 02.07.03.05 Particular trees/shrubs (alphabetical order)
anawyrm 02.08.08.04.03 Intestinal worm
anbesettan 12.05.06.02.03 Trouble, disturbance
anbeweorpan 05.12.02.07 To throw, cast, toss
anbid 05.11.08.01.03.01 Delay; 06.01.08 Expectation
(ge)anbidian 05.11.08.01.03.01 Delay; 06.01.08.01 Expectation, waiting
anbidstōw 05.10.04 Place, room
anbidung 05.11.08.01.03.01 Delay
(ge)anbidung 06.01.08 Expectation
ānboren 02.03.02.02 Child, offspring; 16.01.01.04.02 The Son, Christ
anbrucol 01.01.02.01.02.02.05 Crag, rock, stone
ānbūend 16.02.03.03.04 A solitary (anchorite, hermit)
anburge 14.03.03.07 Security, pledge, bail
ānbȳme 05.12.01.09.03.01.02 Of/concerning a ship, naval

geanbyrdan 13.02 War
anbyrdnes 13.02 War
āncenned 02.03.02.02 Child, offspring; 16.01.01.04.02 The Son, Christ
anclēow(e) 02.04.03.04.02.04 Ankle; 02.04.05.04.08 Joint
ancor 05.12.01.09.03.01.03 Part of ship
ancorbend 05.12.01.09.03.01.03 Part of ship
āncor(e)/āncra 16.02.03.03.04 A solitary (anchorite, hermit)
āncorlic 16.02.03.03.04 A solitary (anchorite, hermit)
āncorlīf 16.02.03.03.04 A solitary (anchorite, hermit)
ancormann 05.12.01.09.03 A voyage
ancorrāp 05.12.01.09.03.01.03 Part of ship
ancorsetl 05.12.01.09.03.01.03 Part of ship
āncorsetl 16.02.05.04.02 A hermitage, hermit's cell
āncorsetla 16.02.03.03.04 A solitary (anchorite, hermit)
āncorstōw 16.02.05.04.02 A hermitage, hermit's cell
ancorstrenge 05.12.01.09.03.01.03 Part of ship
āncummum 03.04.01 Singularity, peculiarity
āncummun 03.03.03.04.01 One
āncyn 03.04.01 Singularity, peculiarity
and swā forþ 03.03.04.03 Growth, increase
anda 06.01.08.06 Fear; 08.01.01.01.04 Depth of feeling, zeal; 08.01.03.09.05 Enmity; 08.01.03.09.08 Envy, jealousy
āndæge 05.11.03.01.05 A day

āndaga 05.11.02 A time, particular time, occasion
(ge)āndagian 05.11.02 A time, particular time, occasion
andan (ge)niman 08.01.03.05.04 Irritability
andbēcnian 06.01.08.04.01 Premonition, prophecy
andbeorma 16.02.01.08.04 Jewish seasons/feasts
andbita 16.02.01.08.04 Jewish seasons/feasts
andcwiss 09.05.03 An answer, reply
andcȳþnes 06.01.06.03 Experience
andēaw 07.06.04 Pride, ostentation
andefn 03.03.04 Quantity; 05.02.02.02 (One's) own person
andelbǣre 05.10.05.04.09.03 Reverse, inverted
andergilde 10.03.05 Recompense, reward
andetla 09.06.02.01.04 A confession, declaration
andetnes 16.02.04.02 Thanksgiving, praise
(ge)andetnes 16.02.04.07.02 Confession
andetta bēon/wesan 14.03.03.09 A sentence, judgement, ruling
andetta weorþan 14.03.03.09 A sentence, judgement, ruling
andetta wesan 14.03.03.09 A sentence, judgement, ruling
andettan 12.07.02.01 Covenant, assurance of faith, promise
(ge)andettan 08.01.03.02.01 Compunction, remorse, contrition; 09.06.02.01.04 A confession, declaration; 14.03.03.09 A sentence, judgement, ruling; 16.02.04.02 Thanksgiving, praise; 16.02.04.07.02 Confession
geandettan 06.01.08.03.01 Belief, trust, faithfulness
andettednes 16.02.04.07.02 Confession
andettere 16.02.04.07.02 Confession
andettung 09.06.02.01.04 A confession, declaration
andfang 10.01.01 Acceptance, receiving
andfangol 10.01.01 Acceptance, receiving; 16.01.01.02.04 Protector, defender
andfeax 02.04.04.03.04 Bald, shaven
andfeng 08.01.02.04 Hospitality; 10.01.01 Acceptance, receiving; 10.04.02.02 To seize, take, grasp, lay hold on; 14.02.01.02 Wrongful taking, theft; 15.01.04 Coinage, money; 16.01.01.02.04 Protector, defender
andfenga 10 Having, owning, possession; 16.01.01.02.04 Protector, defender
andfenge 03.06.03 Congruity, fitness, suitability; 10.01.01 Acceptance, receiving; 17.03.12 A receptacle, container
andfengelic 03.06.03 Congruity, fitness, suitability
andfengend 16.01.01.02.04 Protector, defender
andfengnes 06.01.07.06 Mental acceptance, belief; 10.01.01 Acceptance, receiving; 17.03.12 A receptacle, container
andfengstōw 17.03.12 A receptacle, container
andfylstan 11.12.02 Aid, help, succour
and(ge)lōman 17.03 Implements, tools, etc.
andgete 09.05.05.01 Showing, manifestation, display
andgiet 02.05 Sensation, perception, feeling; 06.01.03 Faculty of reason;

06.02.06.02 A proposal, proposition, suggestion; 09.04 Sense, purport, meaning

andgiet(e) 06.01.05 Understanding, intellect; 06.01.06 Understanding, knowledge, cognizance

andgietful 06.01.05.02.01 Intelligent, sensible

andgietfullic 06.01.05.01.01 Clear to the understanding, plain

andgietfullīce 06.01.05.01.01 Clear to the understanding, plain

andgietlēas 06.01.03.03 Absence of reason; 06.01.05.03 Want of understanding

andgietlēast 06.01.05.03 Want of understanding

andgietlic 06.01.05.01.01 Clear to the understanding, plain

andgietlīce 06.01.05.01.01 Clear to the understanding, plain

andgiettācen 06.01.08.04.01 Premonition, prophecy

andgitol 06.01.05.02.01 Intelligent, sensible

andhēafod 04.02.03.02.01 A strip for ploughing

andhweorfan 12.05.05 Resistance, repulsing

andian 03.06.01.01.01 Imitation, emulation; 08.01.03.09.08 Envy, jealousy; 11.02.02.02.01 Attention, cultivation

andiendlīce 08.01.03.09.08 Envy, jealousy

andig 08.01.03.09.08 Envy, jealousy

andlang 05.10.05.04.09 Side, quarter, direction; 05.11.11.01 A not ceasing, persistence, recurrence; 12.04.01.02 A fellow traveller, companion

andlangcempa 13.02.10.01.02.02.02 Branch of army

andlanges 05.10.05.04.09 Side, quarter, direction

andlangne dæg 05.11.03.01.05 A day

andlēan 10.03.05 Recompense, reward; 14.05.03 Retribution, requital

andleofa 04.01.02.01 Food/sustenance

andleofen 04.01.02.01 Food/sustenance; 15.01.04 Coinage, money

andrēas mæsse 16.02.04.04.02.01.04 Other feasts

andribb 02.04.03.03.05 Chest, breast, bosom

andsaca 12.05.04 Strife, hostility; 16.02.01.07 Apostasy

andsacian 14.03.03.04 Oath-swearing

andsæc 09.07.03.01 A denial; 14.03.03.04 Oath-swearing

andsǣte 08.01.03.09.04 Hatred

andsēcan 11.03.01.02 To seek, seek for

andslyht 05.06.09 Act of striking

andspurnan 11.04.03 (Of ability) low, mean, of less worth

(ge)andspurnan 07.03.01.03 To loathe, hate, abhor

andspurnes 07.03.01 Abomination

andsware (ge)sellan 09.05.03 An answer, reply

(ge)andswarian 09.05.03 An answer, reply

geandswarian 11.01 Action, doing, performance

andswaru 09.05.03 An answer, reply

andung 08.01.01.01.04 Depth of feeling, zeal; 08.01.03.09.08 Envy, jealousy

andūstrung 07.03.01 Abomination

andweard 05.10.04.03 Presence; 05.11.07.02 The present (time); 11.02 Occupation, activity, business

geandweard 05.10.04.03 Presence
geandweardian 05.10.04.03 Presence
andweardlīce 05.10.04.03 Presence
andweardnes 05.10.04.03 Presence; 05.11.07.02 The present (time); 11 Action, operation
andweorc 03 Material, matter, substance; 05.03.01 A cause (of anything)
andwerd 09.03.02.03.01.02.03 Tense
andwīg 12.05.05 Resistance, repulsing; 13.02 War
andwīggearo 13.02.04 Defence, guard, protection
andwīs 11.04.02.01.01 Cunning, craft, craftiness, guile, wile
andwīsnes 06.01.06.03 Experience
andwist 04.01.02.01 Food/sustenance
geandwlātod 07.06.01.01 Proud, arrogant
andwlita 02.04.03.01.03 Face; 02.05.09.07 Form, appearance, aspect; 05.10.05.04.02 Face, surface; 05.10.06 Form, shape
andwliteful 08.01.03.05.02 Anger
andwrāþ 08.01.03.09.06 Hostility
andwreþian 05.10.05.04.02.04.02 Support, maintenance
(ge)andwyrdan 09.05.03 An answer, reply
andwyrde 09.05.03 An answer, reply
geandwyrde bēon/wesan munuc 16.02.04.07.05.01.01 Going into a monastery, admission
andwyrding 12.01.01.12.04.02 Conspiracy
ānēage(de) 02.08.07.02.01 Defective vision; 02.04.03.01.03.02 Eye
ānecge 13.02.08.04.03 A sword
geāned 03.03.06.03 Unity/oneness
ānemnan 09.06.02.01 To tell, make known, declare, relate, announce
ānerian 11.10.03 Salvation/deliverance from
ānes wan (þe ...) 10.02 Want, lack
ānfeald 03.03.03.04.01 One; 03.03.06.03 Unity/oneness; 03.04.01 Singularity, peculiarity; 07.07.01 Simplicity, mildness; 07.10.03.01 Unornamented, unadorned; 09.03.04.03 Plain, simple
ānfeald āþ 14.03.03.04 Oath-swearing
ānfeald gerecednes 09.03.06 Prose
ānfealdlīce 03.04.01 Singularity, peculiarity; 09.03.02.03.01.01.02 Number; 09.03.04.03 Plain, simple
ānfealdnes 03.03.06.03 Unity/oneness; 12.08.05 Innocence
ānfēte 02.04.03.04.02.05 Foot; 05.10.06.03 Projection, head, extremity (of anything)
anfilte/anfealt 17.03.02 Item providing support
anfiteatra 18.02.03 A spectacle, display
anfiteatrum 18.02.03 A spectacle, display
ānfloga 12.04.04 Solitude
anforht 06.01.08.06 Fear
ānforlǣtan 10.02 Want, lack; 10.02.01 Loss, deprivation; 10.02.01.01 Loss, forfeiture; 11.06.01 Neglect; 11.12.01 Absence of restraint, freedom
ānforlǣtnes 05.11.11.02 Let up, intermission, cessation; 10.02.01.01 Loss, forfeiture
anga 06.02.06.03.03 Incitement; 08.01.01.01.03 An incitement, cause of strong feeling; 13.02.08.04.04.01 An arrow, dart, bolt
ānga 03.04.01 Singularity, peculiarity
angbrēost 02.08.08.01 Pain in the chest
angel 04.03.05 Fishing; 12.06.01.03 The Continent; 16.01.02.05.01 An angel

angelcyning 12.01.01.04.01.01 Kings and queens
angelcynn 02.03.03.05.01 The English; 02.03.03.05.01.01 Angles
angelcyrice 16.02.03 The church (as temporal/spiritual body)
angelfolc 02.03.03.05.01 The English
angelic 16.01.02.05.01 An angel
angelseaxe 02.03.03.05.01 The English
angeltwicce 04.03.05 Fishing
angelþēod 02.03.03.05.01.01 Angles
angelwita 12.02.02.02 A counsellor, advisor
āngenga 01.02.01.01.02 Star; 02.06 Animal; 12.04.04 Solitude
anger 04.02.03.04 Grassland
āngetrum 13.02.10.01.02.01 An armed force/band
(ge)angian 08.01.03.03 Anxiety
āngilde 14.03.03.09.02 Atonement; 14.05.04.01 A fine; 15.02 Worth, value
āngilde(s) 15.02.04 Spending, disbursement
anginn 05.11.10.01 A beginning; 09.03.03 A gesture, action, gesticulation; 11.01.02 An undertaking; 11.03 Endeavour; 11.05 Natural/proper way/manner/mode of action; 11.05.02 Mode, manner, way, method, fashion, course; 13.02.03.01 An attack, assault
angle 02.03.03.05.01.01 Angles
angmōd 08.01.03 Bad feeling, sadness
angmōdnes 08.01.03 Bad feeling, sadness
angnægl 02.08.07.08.02 Swelling of the foot
angnere 02.04.03.01.03.02 Eye
angnes 02.08.03 Pain, bodily discomfort; 08.01.03.07.02 Misery, trouble, affliction; 08.01.03.07.03 Suffering, torment, pain
angrisla 06.01.08.06.02 Great fear, terror, horror
angrys(en)līce 08.01.03.07.04 Severity, harshness
angset 02.08.06 Skin disease, erysipelas
angsum 08.01.03.07.02 Misery, trouble, affliction
angsume 08.01.03.06 Adversity, affliction
geangsumian 08.01.03.07.02 Misery, trouble, affliction
angsumlic 08.01.03.07.02 Misery, trouble, affliction
angsumlīce 02.08.03 Pain, bodily discomfort
angsumnes 02.08.03 Pain, bodily discomfort; 08.01.03.07.02 Misery, trouble, affliction
ānhaga 12.04.04 Solitude
ānhealfrūh 03.01.05 Roughness; 04.04.07.12 A collar, neck-cloth
anhende 11.02 Occupation, activity, business
ānhende 02.08.04.02 Blemish, disfigurement
ānhīwe 03.04.01 Singularity, peculiarity
ānhoga 12.04.04 Solitude
ānhorn(a) 02.06.10.01.07 Unicorn
ānhundwintre 02.01.04 Age
anhȳdig 06.02.07.01 Strength, fortitude
ānhyrne 02.06.10.01.07 Unicorn
ānhyrne(n)d(e) 02.06.10.01.07 Unicorn
ānīdan 12.05.07 Casting out, rejection
ānīhst 05.11.10.02 End, completion
āniman 10.01.01.01 Receiving, gaining, getting
āniman (of) 10.04.03 To take away, remove

āniþrian 16.01.05.01 Damnation, perdition, reprobation
(ge)ānlǣcan 03.03.06.03 Unity/oneness
geānlǣcan 12.04.02 A crowding together, assembly
ānlaga 12.04.04 Solitude
anlēc 02.05.09.04 To see, look upon, behold
ānlegere 12.09.06 Cohabitation
ānlic 03.04.01 Singularity, peculiarity; 07.02.04.03 Nobleness, excellence, nobility, magnificence; 07.10 Beauty, fairness; 12.01.01.06.02.01 (High) rank, status, degree; 16.02.01.04 Orthodoxy
ānlīce 07.02.04.03 Nobleness, excellence, nobility, magnificence
anlīcnes 16.02.01.06.01.01.01 An image, idol
ānlīepig 03.04.01 Singularity, peculiarity; 12.04.04 Solitude
ānlīpe 03.04.01 Singularity, peculiarity; 18.01 Rest, quiet, freedom from toil
ānlīpi(g) 03.03.03.04.01 One
ānlīpnes 12.04.04 Solitude
ānlīpum 03.04.01 Singularity, peculiarity
geanmēdan 06.02.07.06.01 Emboldening, encouragement
ānmēde 13 Peace, tranquillity
anmēdla 06.02.07.06 Courage, boldness, valour; 07.06.01 Pride, arrogance; 07.08.07 Glory, splendour, magnificence
anmitta 03.03.02 Measurement by weighing
ānmōd 06.02.07.01 Strength, fortitude; 07.06 Pride; 09.07.04.01.03 Unanimity
ānmōdlīce 06.02.07.02 Constancy; 09.07.04.01.03 Unanimity; 11.02.01.03 Unhesitating
ānmōdnes 06.02.07 Will, determination, resolution; 09.07.04.01.03 Unanimity
ānnes 03.03.06.03 Unity/oneness; 09.07.04.01.03 Unanimity; 12.04.04 Solitude; 16.01.01.04 The Trinity
ānnihte 05.11.06.03.01.04 (Of lunar cycle) so many nights old
ānpæþ 05.12.01.03.01 A means of access
ānra gehwilc 03.04.03.01 Someone/something
ānrǣd(e) 03.06.03.01 Compatible
ānrǣd(-e) 06.02.07 Will, determination, resolution
ānrǣd(e) 09.07.04.01.03 Unanimity
ānrǣdlic 06.02.07.02 Constancy
ānrǣdlīce 03.04.01 Singularity, peculiarity; 06.02.07 Will, determination, resolution; 06.02.07.03 Perseverance; 09.07.04.01.03 Unanimity
ānrǣdnes 06.02.07.03 Perseverance; 07 Judgement, forming of opinion; 13 Peace, tranquillity
ānseld/ānsetl 16.02.05.04.02 A hermitage, hermit's cell
ānsetla 16.02.03.03.04 A solitary (anchorite, hermit)
ansīen 02.04.03.01.03 Face; 02.05.09.06 Thing seen, sight, vision; 05.10.05.04.02 Face, surface; 05.10.06 Form, shape
ansīene 02.05.09.09 Visible
anspilde 02.08.12 Healing, curing
ānsprǣce 09.07.04.01.03 Unanimity
ānstandende 12.04.04 Solitude; 16.02.03.03.04 A solitary (anchorite, hermit)
ānstapa 12.04.04 Solitude
ānstelede 02.07.02.03 A stalk, stem

ānstīga 05.12.01.03.01.01 A path, track
ānstonde 16.02.03.03.04 A solitary (anchorite, hermit)
anstōr 16.02.05.09.02 Incense
ānstræc 06.02.07 Will, determination, resolution
ānstreces 05.11.11.01 A not ceasing, persistence, recurrence
ansund 02.08.01 Sound physical condition; 03.01.01 Thick, close-textured, dense; 03.03.06 Wholeness
ansundnes 03.03.06 Wholeness; 12.08.02 Integrity, absence of moral flaw
ānswēge 18.02.07 Music
antecrist 16.01.05.02.01 The devil
antefn 16.02.04.03.03.01 A hymn, song of praise, canticle
antefnere 16.02.05.10.04 Choir books, etc.
āntīd 05.11.02 A time, particular time, occasion
antiphonaria 16.02.05.10.04 Choir books, etc.
antre 02.07.09.02.02.01 Edible root/bulb
ānunga 03.03.06.02 Fullness; 05.11.08.01.01 Suddenness; 05.12.03.01 Swiftness, velocity; 06.02.04 Necessity, inevitability; 09.03.04.05 To put briefly
anweald 12 Power, might
anwealdig 12 Power, might
anwealdu 16.01.02.05.01 An angel
anwedd 14.03.03.07 Security, pledge, bail
anweg āceorfan 05.12.02.08 To give a different direction to, turn
anweg ādōn 05.10.04.04.02 Removal, taking away
ānwīg 13.02.02.01 Single combat
ānwīglīce 13.02.02.01 Single combat

ānwille 06.02.07.04 Obstinacy
ānwillīce 06.02.07.04 Obstinacy
ānwilnes 06.02.07.03 Perseverance; 06.02.07.04 Obstinacy
ānwintre 02.01.04 Age
ānwīte 14.05.04.01 A fine
anwlōh 08.01.01.03.08 Happiness, well-being, prosperity
ānwunung 16.02.03.03.04 A solitary (anchorite, hermit)
geanwyrde bēon/wesan 09.06.02.01.04 A confession, declaration
ānȳdan (āweg/ūt) 05.12.02.04 To cast out, drive away
apa 02.06.04.01.01 Ape
āpǣcan 06.02.06.03.04 Allurement
āparian 11.03.01.03 Finding, discovery
āpinsian 06.01.01.01.01 Thought, cogitation, meditation
āpinsung 03.03.02 Measurement by weighing
āplantian 04.02.04.02.04 Planting; 05.12.05.02.04.01 To insert into (a hole); 05.13.06.01 Firm, stable, steady; 06.02.07 Will, determination, resolution
āplatod 17.02.04.03 Metal worker
āpluccian 05.06.08 A plucking, taking away
apostata 16.02.01.07 Apostasy
apostol 16.02.01.08.03.01 New Testament persons
apostolhād 16.02.01.08.03.01 New Testament persons
apostolic 16.02.01.08.03.01 New Testament persons
aprelis 05.11.03.01.03.01 Specific months
āpriccan 05.06.07 Pricking, a prick, puncture

aprotane 02.07.11 Plants/flowers (alphabetical order)
āpryccan 09.03.07.04.02.01 Marking out, disposition of materials
apuldor 02.07.09.02 Particular fruits (alphabetical order)
apuldorrind 02.07.09.02 Particular fruits (alphabetical order)
apuldortūn 04.02.04.05.02 An orchard
āpyffan 02.04.06.07.05 To breathe
āpyndrian 03.03.02 Measurement by weighing
ār 01.01.02.02.03.01 Types of metals/minerals; 02.03.03.01 Body of retainers, household; 03.03.05.01 Rank, position, degree; 05.12.01.09.03.01.03 Part of ship; 07.04.03 Reverence, respect; 07.08.02 Honour, glory; 08.01.02.01 Favour, kindness, grace; 08.01.02.06 Mercy, pity; 09.06.02.01.06.01 A messenger; 11.07 Use (made of things), service; 15.01 Property; 16.02.01.12.02 Grace
arabisc 02.03.03.06.07.02 Arab
ārǣcan 05.10.05.02 Extension, stretching; 05.12.05.02.03 To arrive; 10.03 Giving
ārǣd 06.01.05.02.01.01 Sagacity; 06.02.07 Will, determination, resolution
ārǣdan 06.01.06.02.03.03.01 An act of reading; 07 Judgement, forming of opinion; 09.04.02.01 A secret, mystery; 11.01.03 Preparation
ārǣdnes 14.04.02 A stipulation
ārǣfan 05.10.05.04.13 A removal of that which obscures or conceals
ārǣfn(i)an 06.01.01.01.01 Thought, cogitation, meditation; 08.01.03.08 Patience; 11.01.04 A doing, accomplishing (of something)
ārǣfniendlic 06.01.07.07 Possibility
ārǣman 05.12.05.12 To go up, ascend; 08.01.01.01.01 Exaltation, elation
ārǣpsan 05.06 Destruction, dissolution, loss, breaking
ārǣpsian 10.04.02 To grasp, take hold of
ārǣran 02.05.10.15.01 To raise (the voice), raise up (noise); 02.08.12 Healing, curing; 04.02.05.01 Care of livestock; 04.05 Building, construction; 05.05.01 An author, source, originator; 05.12.05.12.02 To raise, lift up, elevate; 11.01.05.02 Furtherance, promotion; 12.05.02.01 Lack of peacefulness; 16.02.04 Worship, honour, praise
ārǣran (gild) 15.02.01 High/steep price
ārǣran (on) 05.10.04 Place, room
ārǣred 04.05 Building, construction
ārǣrend 08.01.01.01.03 An incitement, cause of strong feeling
ārǣrnes 05.12.05.12.02 To raise, lift up, elevate
ārāfian 05.05.04 That loosens, loosening
ārāsian 06.01.08.03.02.01 Suspicion; 07.05.01 Censure, reproof, rebuke; 08.01 Heart, spirit, mood, disposition; 11.03.01.01 Trial, probation; 11.03.01.03 Finding, discovery
ārāsod 11.04 Ability, capacity, power
arblast 13.02.08.04.04 A bow
arce 16.02.05.06.02 Garb for neck and shoulders
arcebiscop 16.02.03.02.04 An archbishop
arcebiscopdōm 16.02.03.02.04 An archbishop
arcebiscophād 16.02.03.02.04 An archbishop

arcebiscoprīce 16.02.03.02.04 An archbishop
arcebiscopstōl 16.02.03.02.04 An archbishop
arcedīacon 16.02.03.02.06 An archdeacon
arcehād 16.02.03.02.04 An archbishop
arcerīce 16.02.03.02.04 An archbishop
arcestōl 16.02.03.02.04 An archbishop
ārcræftig 07.04.03 Reverence, respect
ārdǣde 08.01.02.06 Mercy, pity
ārdæg 16.02.04.04.02 A feast-day, holy day
āreafian 05.06.02.02 A tearing apart
āreaht 05.10.05.02 Extension, stretching; 06.01.08.05.01 Amazement, astonishment, wonder, admiration
āreccan 05.12.05.12.02 To raise, lift up, elevate; 07.10.03 An adornment, decoration, ornament; 09.04.03 Exposition, making clear by explanation; 09.04.03.01 A translation; 09.06.01 To relate, recount, tell; 10.03.03 Granting
ārecelēasian 11.06.01.01 Negligence, carelessness, heedlessness
āredian 05.12.05.02 To go/travel towards, come, approach; 06.01.06.03 Experience; 11.01.03 Preparation; 11.01.04 A doing, accomplishing (of something); 11.03.01.03 Finding, discovery
ārendan 05.06.08 A plucking, taking away
āreodian 07.09.01.01 Reddening with shame, confusion
āretan 08.01.01.03.09.03 To make glad
arewe 13.02.08.04.04.01 An arrow, dart, bolt

ārfæst 08.01.02.06 Mercy, pity; 12.07.02 Observance, keeping; 12.08.02.02 Righteousness, rectitude; 16.02.01.11 Firmness in the law, piety, devoutness
ārfæstian 08.01.02.06 Mercy, pity
ārfæstlic 16.02.01.11 Firmness in the law, piety, devoutness
ārfæstlīce 08.01.02.01 Favour, kindness, grace; 16.02.01.11 Firmness in the law, piety, devoutness
ārfæstnes 08.01.02.01 Favour, kindness, grace; 16.02.01.11 Firmness in the law, piety, devoutness
ārfæt 04.01.02.02.06.05 Vessel/utensil/cup
ārful 07.04.03 Reverence, respect; 08.01.02.01 Favour, kindness, grace
ārfullīce 08.01.02.01 Favour, kindness, grace
argentille 02.07.11 Plants/flowers (alphabetical order)
ārgēotere 17.02.04.03.03 Smelting, heating, scorification
ārgesweorf 17.02.04.03.02 Filings
ārgeweorc 17.02.04.03 Metal worker
ārgifa 16.01.01.02.02 A giving (by Deity)
ārhwæt 07.08.01 Nobility (of character, rank, etc.)
(ge)ārian 07.04 Consideration, esteem; 08.01.02.01.02 Gentleness; 08.01.02.06 Mercy, pity; 11.12.02 Aid, help, succour
geārian 15.01 Property
ārīdan ūt of 05.12.01.05.01 Modes of riding
āri(g)end 08.01.02.01 Favour, kindness, grace
āriht 07.02.01 Right, virtue
ārīman 03.03.03 Number; 09.06.01 To relate, recount, tell

ārīsan 01.01.03.01.02.04 State of sea; 02.05.02 Consciousness; 03.03.04.03 Growth, increase; 05.03.02.01.01 An event, occurrence; 05.12.05.12.01 To reach up; 11.02.01 Energy, vigour, vigorous action; 12.07 An obligation, bounden duty; 16.01.01.02.09 Resurrection
ārīsan wiþ 12.05.05 Resistance, repulsing
ārlēas 07.09.03 Infamy, ignominy, shame; 08.01.03.09.12 Pitilessness; 12.08.06.02.03 (Of persons) wicked, evil-doing; 16.02.01.11.02 Impiety, lack of piety
ārlēaslīce 12.08.06.02.03.01 Wickedly; 16.02.01.11.02 Impiety, lack of piety
ārlēasnes 12.08.06.02 Wickedness, evil
ārlēast 07.03.05 Infamy, shame, wickedness
ārlic 02.05.07 Faculty of taste; 03.06.03.04 What is fitting/seemly/appropriate/decent; 07.08.02 Honour, glory
ārlīce 07.08.02 Honour, glory; 08.01.02.03.03 In a friendly manner, kindly; 08.01.02.06 Mercy, pity
ārloc 05.12.01.09.03.01.03 Part of ship
armelu 02.07.11 Plants/flowers (alphabetical order)
ārmidl 05.12.01.09.03.01.03 Part of ship
arod 02.07.11 Plants/flowers (alphabetical order); 05.12.03.01 Swiftness, velocity; 06.02.05.04.03 Promptitude, readiness; 06.02.07.03 Perseverance; 06.02.07.06.02.02 Boldness, daring; 11.02.04.01 Rashness, madness
arodlīce 05.12.03.01 Swiftness, velocity; 11.02.01 Energy, vigour, vigorous action
arodnes 06.02.07 Will, determination, resolution
arodscipe 11.02.01 Energy, vigour, vigorous action
arrianisc 16.02.01.05 Heresy, error, wrong belief
ārsāpe 03.01.14.06 Green/greenness
ārsmiþ 17.02.04.03 Metal worker
ārstæf 08.01.02.01 Favour, kindness, grace
ārþegn 12.01.01.08.01 A servant, attendant
ārþing 15.01.03 Treasure, riches, wealth
ārum/mundum bregdan 05.12.01.09.01 To row
ārung 07.04.03 Reverence, respect; 16.02.04.07.02.02 Absolution, forgiveness, remission
ārweorþ 07.04.03 Reverence, respect
ārweorþe 07.08.02 Honour, glory
ārweorþful 12.08.02.03.01 Honourable conduct, dignity
(ge)ārweorþian 16.02.04 Worship, honour, praise
ārweorþlic 07.04.03 Reverence, respect
ārweorþlīce 07.04.03 Reverence, respect; 08.01.02.01 Favour, kindness, grace
ārweorþnes 07.04.03 Reverence, respect; 07.08.02 Honour, glory
ārweorþung 16.02.04 Worship, honour, praise
ārwesa 07.04.03 Reverence, respect; 16.01.01.01.01 The Almighty
geārwierþan 07.04 Consideration, esteem
ārwiþþe 05.12.01.09.03.01.03 Part of ship
(ge)ārwurþian 07.04.03 Reverence, respect
ārydd(r)an 14.02.01.02.01 Open robbery, rapine, pillage

āryderian 07.09.01.01 Reddening with shame, confusion
ārȳpan 05.10.05.04.13 A removal of that which obscures or conceals
āsadian 06.02.05.03 Satisfaction, repletion
āsǣlan 12.05.06.01 Restraint, check, curb, control
āsānian 05.09.05 Ceasing, decline, fall off
āsāwan 04.02.04.02.03 Sowing
āscamian 07.09 Shame, disgrace
ascbacen 04.01.02.02.05.04 Baking
asce 01.01.02.02 Earth, soil; 03.01.09.02.01.02 Embers, cinders, ashes
āsceacan 05.10.04.04.02 Removal, taking away; 05.12.05.03.03 To depart, leave, set out; 05.12.05.05 To shake, quake, wag
āsceacan fram/of 05.10.04.04.02 Removal, taking away
āscēadan 03.06.02 Difference, diversity, dissimilarity; 05.12.05.03.02 To keep clear of, stand off from, withdraw; 05.12.05.03.04 To come/go out from; 09.04.03 Exposition, making clear by explanation
āsceafan 05.06.06 A scraping, scarifying
āscealian 05.10.05.04.13 A removal of that which obscures or conceals
āscēotan 02.02.04.04.04 To slaughter (an animal); 02.08.12.02.06 Surgical; 05.06.07 Pricking, a prick, puncture; 05.06.08 A plucking, taking away; 05.10.06.03 Projection, head, extremity (of anything); 13.02.08.04.02 A shot, missile, dart, spear, javelin, etc.

āscēotan of 05.12.05.03 To travel away (from)
āscian 09.05.02 A question, inquiry, questioning
(ge)āscian 09.05.02 A question, inquiry, questioning
(ge)āscian (be) 06.01.06.01 Knowledge, cognizance, knowing
geāscian 11.03.01.03 Finding, discovery
āsciendlic 09.03.02.03.01.02.01 Mood
āscieppan 05.05 Constitution, founding (e.g. of world)
āscildan 11.10.01 Protection, safekeeping
āscilian 03.03.07.01 Division, partition, separation
āscīmian 03.01.12.01 Glittering, effulgence
āscīnan 03.01.12 Brightness, light; 07.08.07 Glory, splendour, magnificence
āsciran 05.06.02 Cleaving, splitting, cutting
āscired 05.10.05 A space, span
āscirian 03.03.07.01 Division, partition, separation; 05.10.05 A space, span; 05.12.05.03.04 To come/go out from; 11.06.06 Turning; 14.02.01.02 Wrongful taking, theft; 14.05.04 A penalty, punishment
āscirpan 05.08.02 Violence, force; 11.01.03 Preparation
āscortian 03.03.04.05 Insufficiency, lack, want; 05.11 A time, period of time
āscrencan 11.11.01 A physical difficulty, strait; 12.08.06.01.04.01 To mislead, seduce, lead astray
āscrepan āweg/of 05.06.06 A scraping, scarifying
āscrīfan 16.02.04.07.02 Confession
āscrūtnian 09.05.01 Inspection, examination

āscūfan 05.06 Destruction, dissolution, loss, breaking; 05.06.01 Devastation, laying waste; 05.12.02.04 To cast out, drive away; 05.12.02.06 To push, impel, thrust; 05.12.05.03.04 To come/go out from; 11.06.06.01 Abandonment (of principle)
āscunelic 08.01.03.09.04 Hatred
(ge)āscung 09.05.02 A question, inquiry, questioning
āscyhhan 05.12.02.04 To cast out, drive away; 05.12.05.03.04 To come/go out from
āscyled 09.05.05.01 Showing, manifestation, display
āscylfan 05.06.01 Devastation, laying waste
āscyndan 05.10.04.04.02 Removal, taking away; 05.12.05.03.04 To come/go out from
āscȳran 03.01.12.03 Clear, transparent; 09.04.03 Exposition, making clear by explanation
āscyrigendlic 09.03.02.02.01.03 An adverb
āseārian 03.01.18 Dryness (not wetness)
āsēcan 05.12.05.02.03 To arrive; 05.12.05.02.04 To go in, enter; 06.02.04.01 Want, need; 07.01.01 Choice, election; 11.03.01.02 To seek, seek for
āsēcendlic 09.05.01 Inspection, examination
āsecgan 09.01 To speak, exercise faculty of speech
āsecgan (ymbe) 09.06.01 To relate, recount, tell
āsecgendlic 09.01 To speak, exercise faculty of speech
āsēdan 06.02.05.03 Satisfaction, repletion

āsegendnes 16.02.04.12 Sacrifice, a sacrifice
āsellan 05.12.02.04 To cast out, drive away; 10.03 Giving
āsencan 05.12.05.02.04.03 To plunge (something into something)
āsendan 05.12.02.03 To send; 05.12.05.03.04 To come/go out from; 11.01.02 An undertaking
āsēodan 15.02.04 Spending, disbursement
āseolcan 02.05.03.02 Weariness; 05.09.01 Slow, inactive
āsēon 02.05.09.04 To see, look upon, behold; 04.06.01.10 To separate objects already connected, unmix
āseonod 05.05.04 That loosens, loosening
āsēoþan 11.03.01 Experience, trial, experiment; 12.08.04 Purity, moral cleanness; 17.02.04.03.03 Smelting, heating, scorification
āsēoþan of 04.06.01.09 To cleanse, remove impurity from (an object); 12.08.04 Purity, moral cleanness
āsēowan 04.04.05.06 To sew, stitch
āset 05.11.02 A time, particular time, occasion
āsetnes 14.01.02 A law, statute
āsettan 04.02.04.02.04 Planting; 04.05 Building, construction; 05.03.01 A cause (of anything); 05.04 Fate, lot, fortune, destiny; 05.05.01 An author, source, originator; 05.10.04.04.02 Removal, taking away; 05.12.05.03.03 To depart, leave, set out; 11.10.02.02.01 Care, interest in; 12.02 A public office; 14.02.01.02.01 Open robbery, rapine, pillage; 15.01.05 Possession of wealth

āsettan of 05.12.02.04 To cast out, drive away
āsettan (on) 05.10.04 Place, room
āsettan rǣdels 09.04.02.01 A secret, mystery
āsēþan 09.07.04 Assertion, affirmation
āsīcan 02.04.06.07.06 A sigh; 04.01.01.02 Act/action of sucking
āsiftan 04.06.01.10 To separate objects already connected, unmix
āsīgan 05.06.01 Devastation, laying waste; 05.09.05 Ceasing, decline, fall off; 05.12.05.02.04.03 To plunge (something into something); 05.12.05.13 To go down, descend
āsincan 05.06.01 Devastation, laying waste; 05.12.05.02.04.03 To plunge (something into something)
āsingan 09.01 To speak, exercise faculty of speech; 09.03.05.01.02 Art of verse composition; 18.02.07.01 Singing, song
āsittan 05.12.01.09.03.02 Hardship on board; 06.01.08.06.05 Wariness, carefulness
āsittan on 04.05.03.01 Habitation, sojourn
āslacian 05.09.01 Slow, inactive; 11.06 Disinclination to act, listlessness; 11.06.01.01 Negligence, carelessness, heedlessness
āslacigendlic 09.03.02.02.01.03 An adverb
āslæccan 05.05.04 That loosens, loosening
āslǣpan 02.05.04 Sleepiness, drowsiness, sleep
āslǣwan 11.06 Disinclination to act, listlessness
āslāpen 02.08.04.03 Paralysis

āslāwian 02.08.07.03.01 Deafness; 11.06 Disinclination to act, listlessness
āsleacod 05.05.04 That loosens, loosening
āslēan 05.06.09.01 A slap with the hand, blow; 05.06.09.03 A shower of blows (?hammer on weapon)
āslēan on 17.02.05.05.02 To make a mark/cut by striking
āslegen 02.08.04.03 Paralysis; 05.06.09.03 A shower of blows (?hammer on weapon)
āslīdan 05.12.01.04.01.04 To stumble, trip, strike (with the foot); 05.12.05.03 To travel away (from); 05.12.05.13.03 To fall; 12.08.06.01.04 To lead a bad life
āslīdan on 11.06.03.01 Ill fortune, bad success
āsliden 05.12.05.13.03 To fall
āslīdung 09.03.02.04 A slip of the tongue, solecism
āslītan 05.06 Destruction, dissolution, loss, breaking
āslītan of 11.06.04 Abstention, abstaining from
āslūpan 02.05.09.14 To vanish, disappear; 05.07 Ending of existence, end of world
āsmēad 09.04.03 Exposition, making clear by explanation
āsmēagan 06.01.01.01.01 Thought, cogitation, meditation; 11.03.01.03.01 Discovery, invention; 12.03.04 A request, prayer
āsmēag(i)an 09.05.01 Inspection, examination
āsmēagung 06.01.01.01 Thinking about, minding, heeding

āsmiþian 17.02.04 Trade, calling, craft, aptitude; 17.02.04.03 Metal worker

āsmorian 02.02.04.03 To kill, slay; 02.08.07.04.04 Respiratory disease; 05.06 Destruction, dissolution, loss, breaking

āsmorung 02.02.04.03 To kill, slay; 02.08.07.04.04 Respiratory disease

āsnǣsan 05.06.07 Pricking, a prick, puncture

āsniden 04.02.04.04.02.02 To gather fruits, crops, etc.; 05.06.02 Cleaving, splitting, cutting

āsnīþan (of) 05.06.02 Cleaving, splitting, cutting

āsocen 03.01.18 Dryness (not wetness)

āsoden 04.06.01.09 To cleanse, remove impurity from (an object)

āsolcen 11.06 Disinclination to act, listlessness; 11.06.01.01 Negligence, carelessness, heedlessness

āsolcennes 11.06 Disinclination to act, listlessness

āsolian 04.06.02.01 Dirty, unclean

āspanan 05.12.05.02.04.01 To insert into (a hole); 06.02.06.03.04 Allurement

āspannan 05.05.04 That loosens, loosening

āsparian 03.03.07.02 What is left, remnant, remains

āspēdan 11.10.05 Escape

āspelian 12.02.01 A substitute, representative

āspelian of 12.07.03 Abstinence/exemption (from)

āspendan 05.11 A time, period of time; 10.03.07 Distribution; 10.03.08.01 Overliberality, waste of money; 15.02.04 Spending, disbursement

āspeoft 02.04.06.06.04 Spittle

aspide 02.06.07.01.02.01 Viper, asp

āspillan 05.06 Destruction, dissolution, loss, breaking

āspinnan 04.04.03 A spinning-house or chamber

āspīwan (ūt) 02.08.08.04.02 (Of stomach) disordered

āsplǣtan 05.06.02.01 A cleft, split

āspornen 08.01.03.07.02 Misery, trouble, affliction

āsprēadan 05.10.05.02.01 Diffusion, effusion, spreading

āsprecan 09.01 To speak, exercise faculty of speech

āsprengan 05.12.02.03 To send

āsprindlad 05.06.02.02 A tearing apart

āspringan 05.07 Ending of existence, end of world; 05.10.05.02.01 Diffusion, effusion, spreading; 05.12.05.03.04.01 To burst forth, break out

āspringan of 02.01.03.03.03 Birth; 05.01 Growth, increase, what springs up

āspringan ūp 01.01.03.01.01.07 Spring, fountain, well; 05.12.05.03.04.02 To flow out, well up, erupt

āspringan (ūp) 01.01.03.01.02.06 Surging, rolling, heaving of waves; 05.01 Growth, increase, what springs up

āspringung 03.03.04.05 Insufficiency, lack, want

āsprungen 02.02.03.02 State of being dead

āsprung(en)nes 01.02.01.01.07 An eclipse

āsprungennes 11.06.03 Failing, failure

āsprūtan 02.07.01 To grow

āspryttan 02.07.01 To grow

āspylian 04.06.01.01 Cleansing, washing

āspyrgend 09.05.01 Inspection, examination
āspyrian 05.12.05.10 To go behind, follow; 09.05.01 Inspection, examination; 11.03.01.03 Finding, discovery
assa 02.06.02.01.01 Ass
assedun 03.01.14.09 Dull brown
asse(n) 02.06.02.01.01 Ass
assirisc 02.03.03.06.07.02 Arab
assmyre 02.06.02.01.01 Ass
āst 17.05.02 A hearth, fireplace
āstǣgan 05.12.05.12 To go up, ascend
āstǣgan on scip 05.12.01.09 To travel on water
āstǣlan 14.03.03.01 Accusation
āstǣnan 17.02.05.01 Ornamental object
āstǣned 01.02.01.01.02 Star
āstǣppan 05.12.05.09 To go forward, proceed
āstandan 05.07 Ending of existence, end of world; 05.10.04.01 Position, stance; 05.10.05.04.02.04.01 Uprightness, straightness; 05.12.05.12.01 To reach up; 05.13.06 Constancy, unchangeableness; 06.02.07.03 Perseverance; 08.01.03.07.03 Suffering, torment, pain
āstandende 16.01.01.04 The Trinity
āstandennes 05.11.11 Continuity; 06.02.07.03 Perseverance
āstellan 05.05.01 An author, source, originator; 09.07.04 Assertion, affirmation
āstellan bȳsen 03.06.03.02 Order, decorum, discretion
āstellan of 05.12.05.03 To travel away (from)
āstemnian 04.05 Building, construction; 05.05.01 An author, source, originator

āstemped 17.02.05.05.01 Graven, embossed, chased
āstencan 05.10.04.04.01 Dispersion
āsteorfan 02.02.03 To die, perish
āsteppan 05.12.01.04.01.02 To tread upon, trample
asterion 02.07.11 Plants/flowers (alphabetical order)
āstīfian 02.08.02 Disease, infirmity, sickness; 11.06 Disinclination to act, listlessness
āstīgan ūp 05.10.05.03.03 Height, loftiness, sublimity
āstīgan 03.03.04.03 Growth, increase; 05.12.01 To go, progress, travel (usually on land); 05.12.01.05 To ride (on horse, etc.); 05.12.05.12 To go up, ascend; 05.12.05.13 To go down, descend; 07.06.01.03 To be proud/arrogant
āstīgan ādūne 05.12.05.13 To go down, descend
āstīgan on 05.12.05.13 To go down, descend
āstīgan on scip 05.12.01.09 To travel on water
āstīgan/āstīgian scip 05.12.01.09 To travel on water
āstīgan (ūp) 05.12.05.12 To go up, ascend
āstīgend 05.12.01.05 To ride (on horse, etc.)
āstīgendlic 09.03.02.02.01.03 An adverb
āstigian 05.12.05.12 To go up, ascend
āstīgnes 05.12.05.12 To go up, ascend
āstihtan 14.01.06 A rule, order, precept, tenet, principle
āstihting 06.02.06.03.02 Instigation
āstillian 05.12.04 Absence of movement, stillness

āstingan

āstingan 05.06.08 A plucking, taking away
āstīþian 02.01.04.02 To grow, grow up; 03.01.03 Hardness, callosity, hard material; 03.01.18 Dryness (not wetness); 05.09 Weakness
āstrǣlian 13.02.08.04.02 A shot, missile, dart, spear, javelin, etc.
āstreccan 05.06.01 Devastation, laying waste; 05.10.05.02 Extension, stretching; 05.10.05.04.02.03.02 Reclining, rest
āstregdan 03.01.16.05 A sprinkling
āstregdnes 03.01.16.05 A sprinkling
āstreht 05.10.05.02 Extension, stretching; 05.10.05.04.02.03.02 Reclining, rest
āstrenged 17.02.04.03.01 (Of metal) ductile
āstrīcan 05.06.09 Act of striking
āstrīenan 02.01.03.03.01 To beget
āstrowenes 05.10.05.02.01 Diffusion, effusion, spreading; 05.10.05.03.01 Length
āstundian 12.07 An obligation, bounden duty
āstyfician 05.06.08 A plucking, taking away
āstyltan 06.01.08.05.01 Amazement, astonishment, wonder, admiration
āstyntan 06.01.05.03.01 Mental inertness; 09.07.02 Contradiction; 13.02 War
āstȳpan 10.04.03.01 To take away, deprive of
āstȳp(ed)nes 02.02.05.04 Bereavement
āstȳpt 02.02.05.04 Bereavement
āstȳpte 02.03.02.02 Child, offspring
āstȳran 12.03 Direction, guidance

āstyrfan 02.02.04.03 To kill, slay; 05.06 Destruction, dissolution, loss, breaking
āstyrian 02.08.12.02.07.01 Purgative; 05.03.01 A cause (of anything); 05.12 To move, be in motion; 05.12.02 To move, set in motion; 08.01.01.01.03 An incitement, cause of strong feeling
āstyrian fram 05.10.04.04.02 Removal, taking away
āstyrigend 08.01.01.01.03 An incitement, cause of strong feeling
āstyrred 01.02.01.01.02 Star
āstyrung 02.08.08.04 Pain in stomach; 02.08.12.02.07.01 Purgative; 05.12 To move, be in motion; 05.12.02 To move, set in motion
āsūcan 05.06.04 Damage, injury, defect, hurt, loss
āsūrian 02.05.07.01 Strong taste, acidity, pungency
āswǣman 07.09 Shame, disgrace; 08.01.03.01 Despondency
āswǣtan 02.04.06.06.01 Sweat
āswāmian 05.09.05 Ceasing, decline, fall off
āswāpan 04.06.01 Clean
āswāpan āweg 05.12.02.04 To cast out, drive away
āswārc(i)an 05.09.05 Ceasing, decline, fall off
āswārcian 07.09 Shame, disgrace
āswārcnian 07.09 Shame, disgrace
āswārnian 07.09 Shame, disgrace
āswārnung 07.09.01 Shame, confusion
āswaþian 09.05.01 Inspection, examination
āsweartian 03.01.13.02 A growing dark, darkening; 03.01.14.04 Black/blackness
āsweartod 02.08.04 Hurt, injury, damage; 03.01.14.04 Black/blackness

768

āswebban 02.02.04.03 To kill, slay; 05.09.03 Mitigation, lightening, alleviation; 12.08.06.01.04.01 To mislead, seduce, lead astray
āswefecian 05.06.08 A plucking, taking away
āswellan 02.08.05.01 Swelling
āsweltan 02.02.03 To die, perish
āswencan 12.05.06.02.03 Trouble, disturbance
āswenct 08.01.03.06 Adversity, affliction
āswengan 05.12.02.04 To cast out, drive away
āsweorcan 08.01.03.01 Despondency
āswerian 12.07.02.01.01.01 A promise, oath
āswīcan 11.06.06.01 Abandonment (of principle)
(ge)āswician 08.01.03.07.02 Misery, trouble, affliction
āswīfan 05.12.05.01 To go astray
āswindan 02.02.03 To die, perish; 05.09 Weakness; 05.09.05 Ceasing, decline, fall off; 11.06 Disinclination to act, listlessness
āswingan 14.05.05 Physical punishments
āswōgan 05.10.05.04.12 The condition of being covered
āswollen 02.08.05.01 Swelling
āswōrettan 02.04.06.07.06 A sigh
āsworfen 04.06.01 Clean; 17.02.04.03.02 Filings
āswunden 11.06 Disinclination to act, listlessness
āswundennes 11.06 Disinclination to act, listlessness
āswungennes 14.05.05 Physical punishments
āsynderlic 05.10.05 A space, span

āsyndr(i)an 03.03.07.01 Division, partition, separation; 03.06.02 Difference, diversity, dissimilarity; 04.06.01.10 To separate objects already connected, unmix; 05.10.05 A space, span
āsyndrung 03.03.07.01 Division, partition, separation
āsyngian 16.02.01.13 Evil-doing, transgression, sin
ātǣsan 05.06.04 Damage, injury, defect, hurt, loss; 08.01.03.07.02.01 Injury, offence
āte 04.01.02.01.03.03 Oats; 04.02.04.04 Harvest, crop
ātellan 03.03.03 Number; 03.05.03 A list, tale, series; 09.04.03 Exposition, making clear by explanation; 09.06.01 To relate, recount, tell
ātellan wiþ 07 Judgement, forming of opinion
ātemian 04.02.05.04 To tame, break in (animals); 08.01.01.02.01 Want of interest or concern, indifference
ātendan 03.01.09.02.01 Fire, burning; 03.01.12.02 A beam of light; 08.01.01.01.03 An incitement, cause of strong feeling; 14.05 Punishment
ātendend 08.01.01.01.03 An incitement, cause of strong feeling
ātending 08.01.01.01.03 An incitement, cause of strong feeling
ātendnes 08.01.01.01.03 An incitement, cause of strong feeling
āteon 02.04.06.07.05 To breathe; 05.11.01.01 Long duration, long space; 05.12.01.01 To go on a journey/expedition, travel; 05.12.02.05 To pull, drag, draw; 11.05.02 Mode, manner, way, method,

āteon fram/of

fashion, course; 11.07 Use (made of things), service
āteon fram/of 10.04.03 To take away, remove
āteon of 05.06.08 A plucking, taking away
āteon tō 02.04.06.07.05 To breathe
āteon (ūt) of 05.12.02.05 To pull, drag, draw
āteon ūt of 05.06.08 A plucking, taking away
āteorian 02.05.03 Exhaustion, faintness, weariness; 03.03.04.05 Insufficiency, lack, want; 05.07 Ending of existence, end of world; 09.03.02.03.01.02 A conjugation; 11.06 Disinclination to act, listlessness
āteori(g)endlic 05.09.01 Slow, inactive; 05.11.01.03.01 Mortal state, this life
āteor(ig)endlic 09.03.02.03.01.02 A conjugation
āteorodnes 02.05.03 Exhaustion, faintness, weariness; 05.11.10.02 End, completion
āteorung 02.05.03 Exhaustion, faintness, weariness; 05.09.05 Ceasing, decline, fall off
āteran 05.06.08 A plucking, taking away
ātertān 17.02.05.04 An image, figure
āteshwōn 06.01.07.07.02 Impossible
athēniense 02.03.03.06.03 The Greeks
athēnisc 02.03.03.06.03 The Greeks
ātīdrian 05.09 Weakness
ātīefran 17.02.05.06 A painting, picture, representation
ātihting 06.02.06 Mind, purpose
ātillan 05.12.05.02.03 To arrive
ātimbr(i)an 04.05 Building, construction
ātimplian 05.10.06.03.01 A point, spike, prickle

ātland 04.02.03.02.02.04 Oat land/field
ātlēag 04.02.03.02.02.04 Oat land/field
ātogen 13.02.08.04.03.02 Armed with a sword
atol 06.01.08.06.03 Cause of fear, terror, horror; 06.01.08.06.03.01 Causing dread, terrifying; 07.10.02.01 Deformed, ugly
geatolhīwian 07.10.02.01 Deformed, ugly
(ge)atolian 07.10.02.01 Deformed, ugly
atollic 06.01.08.06.03.01 Causing dread, terrifying; 07.10.02.01 Deformed, ugly
atollīce 06.01.08.06.03.01 Causing dread, terrifying
ātor 02.04.06.05.07.06 Gall/bile; 02.08.02.01.01 An infectious disease; 04.06.02.06 Poison
ātorbǣre 04.06.02.06 Poison
ātorberende 04.06.02.06 Poison
ātorcoppe 02.06.09.02.10 Spider
ātorcræft 02.02.04.03 To kill, slay; 16.01.04.02 Sorcery involving drugs or potions
ātorcyn 04.06.02.06 Poison
ātorgeblǣd 02.08.05.02 Particular inflammation/swelling
ātorlic 02.05.07.01 Strong taste, acidity, pungency
ātorsceaþa 02.02.04.04 Manslaughter, homicide; 05.06 Destruction, dissolution, loss, breaking
ātorspere 02.02.04.03 To kill, slay; 13.02.08.04.01 A spear
ātorþigen 02.02.04.03 To kill, slay; 04.06.02.06 Poison
ātorwyrhta 02.02.04.03 To kill, slay; 16.01.04.02 Sorcery involving drugs or potions

ātrahtnian 09.06 To take matter for discourse
ātredan ūt 05.12.02.05 To pull, drag, draw
ātreddan 09.05.01 Inspection, examination
ātrendlian 05.12.05.04.01 (Of wheel, etc.) to roll, trundle
ātrima 04.01.02.01.03.06 Bran; 04.02.04.03.02.01.03 Oat-bran
atrum 09.03.07.06.02 Ink
ātwēonian 06.01.07.06.02.01 Doubt, uncertainty
ātwiccian 09.03.07.07.03.02.01 An epitome, short account
ātȳdran 02.01.03.03.01 To beget
ātyht 06.01.01.02 Care, attention, observation
ātyhtan 05.10.05.02 Extension, stretching; 05.10.05.02.01 Diffusion, effusion, spreading; 06.01.01.01 Thinking about, minding, heeding; 06.02.06.03.04 Allurement
ātyhting 06.02.06.03.02 Instigation
ātȳnan 05.10.05.04.14 An opening, aperture; 05.12.05.03.04 To come/go out from
āþ 14.03.03.03 Witness, testimony, attestation; 14.03.03.04 Oath-swearing; 14.05.04.01 A fine
āþ sellan 14.03.03.04 Oath-swearing
aþamans 01.01.02.02.02.06 Adamant
āþbryce 14.03.03.06 False witness
āþecgan 04.01.01 Eating
āþegen 03.03.06.02 Fullness; 04.01.02.04.03.01.01 Fed/nourished
āþencan 06.02.06 Mind, purpose; 11.03.01.03.01 Discovery, invention
āþened 02.08.05.01 Swelling

āþenenes 05.10.05.02 Extension, stretching
āþenian 05.06.04 Damage, injury, defect, hurt, loss; 05.10.05.02 Extension, stretching; 05.10.05.02.02 Greater, bigger; 05.11.01.01 Long duration, long space; 05.12.05.13.02 To bow, bend down; 07.04.03 Reverence, respect
āþenian mōd on 06.01.01.02 Care, attention, observation
āþennan 05.10.05.02.01 Diffusion, effusion, spreading
āþenung 02.08.05.01 Swelling
āþēodan 03.03.07.01 Division, partition, separation
āþēostrian 01.03.01.06 Cloud; 03.01.13.02 A growing dark, darkening
āþēotan 18.02.07.02.02.02 A trumpet
āþerscan 05.06.01 Devastation, laying waste
āþexe 02.06.07.03 Lizard, newt
āþfultum 14.03.03.04 Oath-swearing
āþgehāt 12.07.02.01.01.01 A promise, oath
āþiddan 05.12.02.06 To push, impel, thrust
āþierran 04.06.01.01 Cleansing, washing
āþindan 02.08.05.01 Swelling; 07.06.01.03 To be proud/arrogant
āþindung 02.08.05.01 Swelling
āþloga 14.03.03.06 False witness
āþolian 05.13.06 Constancy, unchangeableness; 06.02.07.01 Strength, fortitude; 08.01.03.07.03 Suffering, torment, pain
āþolware 02.03.03.04.05 Populace of a town/city
aþor ōþer 03.06.02.01 Contrariety, diversity

āþracian 06.01.08.06.02 Great fear, terror, horror; 06.01.08.06.03 Cause of fear, terror, horror
āþrǣstan 05.06.08 A plucking, taking away
āþrāwan 05.10.06.02.03 A circular fold, coil; 05.12.02.08 To give a different direction to, turn
āþrāwen 05.10.06.02.03 A circular fold, coil
āþrēatian 06.02.06.03.01 To dissuade (from); 07.05.01 Censure, reproof, rebuke
āþreclic 06.01.08.06.03.01 Causing dread, terrifying
āþrēotan 07.03.01.03 To loathe, hate, abhor; 08.01.03.07.01 Tedium
āþringan 05.12.02.06 To push, impel, thrust; 05.12.03.01 Swiftness, velocity
āþrīstian 07.06.01.03 To be proud/arrogant
āþrotennes 07.03.01 Abomination
āþrotsum 07.03.01.01 Abominable, detestable
āþrōwian 08.01.03.07.03 Suffering, torment, pain
āþrunten 02.08.05.01 Swelling
āþrūten 02.08.05.01 Swelling
āþryccan 12.05.06.02 Oppression
āþrȳn 14.02.01.02.01 Open robbery, rapine, pillage
āþrysmian 02.02.04.03 To kill, slay; 03.01.13.02 A growing dark, darkening
āþrȳtan 08.01.03.07.01 Tedium
āþrȳtnes 02.05.03.02 Weariness
āþstæf 14.03.03.04 Oath-swearing
āþswaru 14.03.03.04 Oath-swearing
āþswerian 12.07.02.01.01.01 A promise, oath

āþswerung 14.03.03.04 Oath-swearing
āþswyrd 14.03.03.04 Oath-swearing
āþum 02.03.02.03.06.02.06 In-law relationships
āþumswēoras 02.03.02.03.06.02.06 In-law relationships
āþunden 01.01.03.01.02.06 Surging, rolling, heaving of waves
āþundennes 02.08.05.01 Swelling; 07.06.01 Pride, arrogance
āþwǣnan 03.03.04.06 Diminution
āþwēan 03.01.17.07.01 An anointing, greasing; 04.06.01.01 Cleansing, washing; 16.02.04.07.01 Baptism, baptizing (and anointing)
āþwēan (fram/of) 12.08.04 Purity, moral cleanness
āþwedd 12.07.02.01.01.01 A promise, oath
āþweran 04.01.02.02.08 Churn
āþwīnan 02.05.09.14 To vanish, disappear
āþwītan 06.01.08.02.02 To disappoint
āþwyrþe 14.01.04 A legal right
āþȳd 05.06.05.03 Bruising, crushing
āþyl(d)gian 08.01.03.08 Patience
āþynnian 05.10.05.02.03 To reduce, make thin(ner)
āþȳwan 05.12.02.06 To push, impel, thrust
āþȳwan on 05.12.02.06 To push, impel, thrust
āurnen 05.11.07.03 Former times, days of old
āwacan 02.01.03.03.03 Birth; 02.05.02 Consciousness
āwacan of 05.01 Growth, increase, what springs up
āwacian 02.05.02 Consciousness

āwācian 05.09 Weakness; 05.09.01 Slow, inactive; 12.08.06.01.04 To lead a bad life; 13.01.02.01 An appeasing, pacifying
āwǣcan 05.09 Weakness
āwæcn(i)an 02.01.03.03.03 Birth; 02.05.02 Consciousness; 16.02.01.12 Spirituality
āwæcn(i)an fram 05.01 Growth, increase, what springs up
āwǣgan 05.07 Ending of existence, end of world; 06.01.07.04 Deception; 11.06.03 Failing, failure
āwǣgnian 11.06.03 Failing, failure
āwǣlan 08.01.03.07.02 Misery, trouble, affliction
āwærlan 11.06.06 Turning
āwandian 11.06.05 Hesitation, scruple
āwanian 03.03.04.06 Diminution
āwannian 03.01.14.04 Black/blackness
āwansian 11.06.01 Neglect
āwārnian 07.09 Shame, disgrace
āwascan 04.06.01.01 Cleansing, washing
āweallan 02.08.10 Fever; 03.01.09 Heat; 03.03.04.01.02 A great number, multitude; 03.03.04.02.01 Abundance; 05.12.05.03.04.02 To flow out, well up, erupt; 08.01.01.01 Ardour, fervour, strong feeling
āweallan (ūt) 01.01.03.01.01.07 Spring, fountain, well
āweardian 11.10.01 Protection, safekeeping
āweaxan 05.01 Growth, increase, what springs up
āweb 04.04.05 Woven material, fabric
āweccan 02.01.03.03.01 To beget; 02.05.02 Consciousness; 02.08.12 Healing, curing; 05.05.01 An author, source, originator; 08.01.01.01.03 An incitement, cause of strong feeling
āweccan tō 06.02.06.03.03 Incitement
āwecenes 08.01.01.01.03 An incitement, cause of strong feeling
āwecgan 05.12.05.05 To shake, quake, wag; 08.01.01 A feeling, what is felt; 11.05.02 Mode, manner, way, method, fashion, course
āwēdan 02.08.11.02.01 Insanity, madness; 05.08.02 Violence, force
āwefan 04.04 Weaving
āweg 05.10.05.04.02.01 Exterior, outside of
āweg ādelfan 05.06.08 A plucking, taking away
āweg ādrīfan 05.12.02.04 To cast out, drive away
āweg āglīdan 05.12.05.03 To travel away (from); 05.12.05.06.01 To travel smoothly, slide, glide
āweg āþȳwan 05.12.05.03.04 To come/go out from
āweg flēon 11.10.04 Flight
āweg gān 05.12.05.03.03 To depart, leave, set out
āweg lǣtan 05.12.02.03 To send; 05.12.05.03.04 To come/go out from; 14.03.03 Law, action of the courts
āweg tengan 11.10.05.01 Evasion, escape from threat
āweg gewītan 05.12.05.03.03 To depart, leave, set out
āwegan 03.03.02 Measurement by weighing; 05.10.04.04.02 Removal, taking away; 07.01 Appraisal, appraising; 12.05.07 Casting out, rejection
āwegan (ūp/ūt) 05.12.02.02 To carry off, remove

āwegāwendan 05.10.04.04.02 Removal, taking away
āwegāworpnes 02.01.03.03.03.01 Child-bearing, childbirth
āweg(e) cuman 11.10.05 Escape
āweggewitenes 02.08.11.02 Mental weakness; 05.12.05.03.03 To depart, leave, set out
āwegweard 05.11.01.02.01 Swift movement of time; 05.11.10.02 End, completion
āwehtnes 08.01.01.01.03 An incitement, cause of strong feeling
āwel 04.01.02.02.06.05.07 Hook for lifting food
āwemman 12.08.08.01.02 Unchastity, incontinence
āwemmed 05.13.01 Transformation, taking another shape
āwemmendnes 12.08.06.01.01 Pollution, impairment
āwēnan 07.01 Appraisal, appraising
āwendan 05.06.01 Devastation, laying waste; 05.07 Ending of existence, end of world; 05.10.04 Place, room; 05.12.02.08 To give a different direction to, turn; 05.12.05 To move and change direction, turn; 05.12.05.03.03 To depart, leave, set out; 05.12.05.11.01 To return; 05.13 Changeableness, change; 05.13.01 Transformation, taking another shape; 05.13.02 A reversal; 05.13.04 Exchange, commutation; 09.04.03.01 A translation; 11.05.02 Mode, manner, way, method, fashion, course; 11.11.03 Impeding of progress, prevention; 12.08.06.01.04.01 To mislead, seduce, lead astray; 13.02.05.01.01 To overcome, conquer; 17.02.05.04 An image, figure
āwendedlicnes 05.11.01.03 Mutability
āwendendlic 05.12.02.08 To give a different direction to, turn .
āwende(n)dlic 05.13.05 Changeability
āwendendnes 05.13 Changeableness, change
āwending 11.11.04 Subversion, change
āwened 04.01.01.02 Act/action of sucking
āwenian 04.01.01.02 Act/action of sucking; 06.02.06.03.01 To dissuade (from)
āwēodian 05.06.08 A plucking, taking away
āweorpan 02.08.08.04.02 (Of stomach) disordered; 05.12.02.07 To throw, cast, toss; 07.05 Disrespect, irreverence; 08.01.03.04 Grief; 12.05.07 Casting out, rejection
āweorpan of 12.05.07 Casting out, rejection
āweorpan (of) 05.12.02.04 To cast out, drive away
āweorpnesse bēc 14.03.03 Law, action of the courts
āweorþan 02.05.07.02 Insipid; 11.08.04 Vanity, idleness, frivolity
āweosung 02.01 Existence, life
āwerde 11.08.04 Vanity, idleness, frivolity
āwerian 03.02.01.02 Decay from age; 07.05 Disrespect, irreverence; 11.10.01.01 Preservation from injury/destruction; 13.02.04 Defence, guard, protection
āwesnis 02.01 Existence, life
āwēstan 05.06.01 Devastation, laying waste

āwēst(ed)nes 05.06.01 Devastation, laying waste
āwēstend 05.06 Destruction, dissolution, loss, breaking
āwēstende 05.06 Destruction, dissolution, loss, breaking
āwīdlian 04.06.02.02 Foul, filthy, squalid; 16.02.04.14 Sacrilege
āwierdan 02.08.04 Hurt, injury, damage; 05.06 Destruction, dissolution, loss, breaking; 08.01.03.07.02 Misery, trouble, affliction; 11.11.02 A hindrance; 12.08.06.01.04.01 To mislead, seduce, lead astray
āwierdend 05.06 Destruction, dissolution, loss, breaking
āwierdnes 02.08.04.02 Blemish, disfigurement; 08.01.03.07.02.01 Injury, offence
āwiergan 02.02.04.03 To kill, slay
āwierg(e)an 07.05 Disrespect, irreverence; 16.02.04.14.02.01 Cursing, imprecation
āwiht 03.06 Comparison; 05 Aught, anything, something; 11.07.03 Use, advantage, profit
āwildian 01.01.02.01.06 Wild/uncultivated land; 05.08.02.01 (Of living creatures) fierceness, roughness
āwillan 04.01.02.02.05.02 To boil
āwilnian 06.02.05.01 Strong liking for, devotion to
āwilwian 05.12.05.04.01 (Of wheel, etc.) to roll, trundle
āwindan 05.09 Weakness
āwindan of 04.04.07 Trappings, equipment, garb; 05.12.05.03 To travel away (from); 05.12.05.04.01 (Of wheel, etc.) to roll, trundle
āwindwian 03.01.15.01 Inspiration, inbreathing
āwinnan 10.01.02 Acquisition; 13.02.05.01.01 To overcome, conquer; 17.01 Strenuous effort, hard work
āwinnan wiþ 12.05.05 Resistance, repulsing
āwisnian 03.01.18 Dryness (not wetness)
āwītegian 06.01.08.04.01 Premonition, prophecy
āwlacian 08.01.01.02.01 Want of interest or concern, indifference
āwlǣtan 07.10.02.01 Deformed, ugly; 12.08.08.01.02 Unchastity, incontinence
āwlǣte 07.10.02.01 Deformed, ugly
āwlancian 07.06.01.03 To be proud/arrogant
āwlenced 07.06.05 Pomp, splendour, magnificence
āwlyspian 09.02.03.03 Lisping
āwoffian 02.08.11.02.01 Insanity, madness; 07.06.01.03 To be proud/arrogant
āwōgian 08.01.02.02.03.01 Wooing
āwōh 12.07.05 Wrong, injustice
āwordennes 05.09.05 Ceasing, decline, fall off
āworpednes 12.05.07 Casting out, rejection
āworpen 12.09.04 Divorce; 16.02.01.07 Apostasy
āworpenlic 12.08.06.01.02 Lacking moral good
āworpenlīce 07.03.04 A wretch, poor creature
āworpennes 05.12.02.04 To cast out, drive away
āworp(en)nes 12.05.07 Casting out, rejection

āwrǣnsan 12.08.08.01 Eager, unseemly desire
āwrǣstan 14.02.01.02.01 Open robbery, rapine, pillage
āwrecan 02.08.12 Healing, curing; 05.12.02.04 To cast out, drive away; 08.01.03.07.02.01 Injury, offence; 09.06.01 To relate, recount, tell; 12.05.04.02 Vengeance, revenge
āwreccan 02.05.02 Consciousness; 08.01.01.01.03 An incitement, cause of strong feeling; 16.01.01.02.09 Resurrection
āwreccend 06.02.06.03.03 Incitement
āwrēon 05.10.05.04.12 The condition of being covered; 09.05.05 Exposure, revealing, revelation
āwreþian 05.10.05.04.02.04.02 Support, maintenance; 11.12.02.01 Strengthening, confirmation
āwrīdian 05.01 Growth, increase, what springs up
āwrigene bōc 16.02.01.08.03 The New Testament
āwrigennes 09.05.05 Exposure, revealing, revelation
āwringan of 03.01.16.03 A drop of liquid
āwrit 09.03.07 Writing
āwrītan 09.03.07.04 To make a symbol, mark; 09.03.07.05 To cover with writing, inscribe; 09.03.07.07.03 Composition, arrangement, writing; 09.03.07.07.03.02 To write, state/say in writing; 09.03.07.07.03.02.02 A letter; 09.03.07.07.03.04.02 A register, catalogue; 17.02.05.05 A carving, graving
āwrītan (be/of) 09.03.07.07.03.01 A description, writing down
āwrīþan 05.05.04 That loosens, loosening; 05.10.06.05 A fold, plait, wrinkle
āwuldrian 16.02.04 Worship, honour, praise
āwunden 05.10.06.02.03 A circular fold, coil; 17.04.04 Fibrous materials
āwundrian 06.01.08.05.01 Amazement, astonishment, wonder, admiration; 16.02.04 Worship, honour, praise
āwunian 05.11.11 Continuity; 05.11.11.01 A not ceasing, persistence, recurrence
āwunigende 05.11.11 Continuity
āwyld 04.01.02.02.05.02 To boil
āwyltan 05.12.05.04.01 (Of wheel, etc.) to roll, trundle; 08.01.03.07.02 Misery, trouble, affliction
āwyrcan 11.01.04 A doing, accomplishing (of something)
āwyrd 02.05.07.01.01 (Of food, etc.) bad, tainted, rancid; 05.06.03 A dashing together, breaking, shattering
āwyrdung 07.09 Shame, disgrace
āwyrgda 16.01.05.02.02 Other terms for devils
āwyrgda wulf 16.01.05.02.02 Other terms for devils
āwyrged 12.08.06.02.03 (Of persons) wicked, evil-doing; 16.01.05.02.02 Other terms for devils
āwyrgedlic 12.08.06.02.03 (Of persons) wicked, evil-doing
āwyrgednes 12.08.06.02 Wickedness, evil; 16.02.04.14.02.01 Cursing, imprecation
āwyrgendlic 07.03.01.01 Abominable, detestable
āwyrigende 12.08.06.02.03 (Of persons) wicked, evil-doing

āwyrigung 16.02.04.14.02.01 Cursing, imprecation
āwyrpan 02.08.13 Recovery, growing better
āwyrttrumian 05.06.08 A plucking, taking away
āwyrtwalian 05.06.08 A plucking, taking away
āwyrtwarian 05.06.08 A plucking, taking away
āyldan 05.11.08.01.03.01 Delay
āyppān 09.05.05 Exposure, revealing, revelation
āȳtan (ūt) 05.12.02.04 To cast out, drive away
bacan 04.01.02.02.05.04 Baking
bacum tōbregdan 12.04.03.01 Estrangement, alienation
bād 06.01.08.01 Expectation, waiting; 14.03.03.07 Security, pledge, bail
bādian 14.03.03.07 Security, pledge, bail
bæc 01.01.03.01.01.03 Stream; 02.04.03.03.01 Back
bæc ... (tō)wendan 05.12.05 To move and change direction, turn
gebæc 04.01.02.01.07 Cooked/cookable food; 04.01.02.02.05.04 Baking
bæcbitol 07.05.03 Calumny, backbiting
bæcbord 05.12.01.09.03.01.03 Part of ship
bæce 02.04.03.03.03 Buttock(s), back parts
bæc(e) 01.01.02.01.03.03 Valley
bæceling 04.01.02.02.06.01 Cooking vessel/pot
bæcere 04.01.02.02.05.04 Baking
bæcering 04.01.02.02.06 Kitchen
bæcern 04.01.02.02.06 Kitchen
bæcestre 04.01.02.02.05.04 Baking
bæcslitol 07.05.03 Calumny, backbiting

bæcstān 04.01.02.02.06 Kitchen
bæcþearm 02.04.06.03.02.04 Intestines
bæcþearmas 02.04.06.03.02.04 Intestines
gebæcu 02.04.03.03.03 Buttock(s), back parts
(ge)bǣdan 06.02.06.03.03 Incitement; 12.03.04 A request, prayer
bæddel 02.01.03.03.06 Sex, kind
bǣdend 06.02.06.03.03 Incitement
bǣdewēg 04.01.03 Drinking
bǣdling 12.08.08.01.02.01.03 Unnatural sexual behaviour
bæftansittende 11.06 Disinclination to act, listlessness
bǣl 02.02.05.01.01 A grave, burial place, sepulchre; 03.01.09.02 Fire, flame
bǣlblǣse 03.01.09.02 Fire, flame
bǣlblȳs(e) 03.01.09.02 Fire, flame
bælc 05.10.05.04.12 The condition of being covered; 07.06 Pride
bǣlegesa 06.01.08.06.03 Cause of fear, terror, horror
bǣlfȳr 02.02.05.01.01 A grave, burial place, sepulchre
bǣlstede 02.02.05.01.01 A grave, burial place, sepulchre
bǣlþracu 03.01.09.02 Fire, flame; 05.08.02 Violence, force
bǣlwudu 02.02.05.01.01 A grave, burial place, sepulchre; 17.05.01 Fuel, tinder
bǣlwylm 02.02.05.01.01 A grave, burial place, sepulchre; 03.01.09.02.01.01 A kind of fire
bǣnen 02.04.05.04.01 Substance of bones
bǣr 04.02.03.02.03 Fallow land; 04.04.07.02 Not dressed, unclothed; 04.04.07.02.01 Nakedness
bǣr 01.01.03.01.02.05 Wave; 02.02.05.02 To prepare for burial; 04.02.03.04.02

Pasture/pasturage; 04.05.04.05 A bed, bedstead
gebǣran 11.05.02 Mode, manner, way, method, fashion, course
bærbǣre 12.06.05 A foreign country
bǣrdisc 04.01.02.02.06.05.02 Tray
gebǣre 05.12 To move, be in motion
bǣrfōt 04.04.07.15 Footwear, covering for the feet
bærlic 04.02.04.03.02.01.01 Barley; 09.05.05.01 Showing, manifestation, display
bǣrlīce 09.05.05.01 Showing, manifestation, display
bǣrman 05.12.02.01 To fetch, bring, bear, conduct
bærnan 02.08.12.02.06 Surgical
(ge)bærnan 03.01.09.01 Warmth, heat; 03.01.09.02.01 Fire, burning; 17.05.04 To kindle, set alight (fire, lamp)
gebǣrnd līm 01.01.02.02.02.03 Limestone, chalk
gebǣrnd stān 01.01.02.02.02.03 Limestone, chalk
bærnelāc 16.02.04.12 Sacrifice, a sacrifice
bærnes 03.01.09.02.01 Fire, burning
gebǣrnes 11.05.02 Mode, manner, way, method, fashion, course
bærnett 02.08.03.02 Itch, irritation; 02.08.12.02.06 Surgical; 03.01.09 Heat; 03.01.09.02.01 Fire, burning; 14.02.01.01 Types of crime
bærning 03.01.09.02.01 Fire, burning; 16.02.04.12 Sacrifice, a sacrifice
bærnīsen 17.03.06 Tools for marking
bærs 02.06.06.02.01.05 Perch
bærsynnig 12.08.09 Guiltiness, guilt

gebǣru 02.05.10.15 Voice, cry (of living creature); 11.05.02 Mode, manner, way, method, fashion, course
bǣst 02.07.03.03.01 Wood (as substance)
bǣsten 17.04.04.01 Oakum, hards, tow
bǣtan 04.03 Hunting, the chase; 05.12.01.09.02 To sail
(ge)bǣtan 04.02.05.06.05.03 Harness, trappings; 12.05.06.01 Restraint, check, curb, control
gebǣte(l) 04.02.05.06.05.03 Harness, trappings
bǣting 05.12.01.09.02 To sail
bæþ 04.06.01.02 A bathing place; 04.06.01.03 A bath; 05.12.05.03.04.02 To flow out, well up, erupt; 14.05.06 Means/implement of torture; 16.02.05.05.03 A font
bæþdæg 16.02.04.04.02.01.01 Around the Nativity
bæþern 04.06.01.02 A bathing place
bæþfæt 04.06.01.03 A bath
bæþhūs 04.06.01.02 A bathing place
bæþsealf 04.06.01.04 What is used in washing, an ointment
bæþstede 04.06.01.02 A bathing place
bæþstōw 04.06.01.02 A bathing place
bæþweg 01.01.03.01.02 Sea/ocean
bæzere 16.02.04.07.01 Baptism, baptizing (and anointing)
balca 14.05.06 Means/implement of torture
balc(a) 04.02.03.02.01 A strip for ploughing; 04.02.03.02.01.01 A furrow
balsalm 02.07.02.03 A stalk, stem; 02.07.03.05 Particular trees/shrubs (alphabetical order)
balsam(um) 02.08.12.02.05.02 Salves, ointments
balsmēþe 02.07.10.01 Particular herbs/spices (alphabetical order)

balsmite 02.07.10.01 Particular herbs/spices (alphabetical order)
bām handum twām 06.02.05.04.04 Zeal
bān 02.04.03.04 Limb; 02.04.05.04.01 Substance of bones; 02.06.01.02 Head; 03.01.03 Hardness, callosity, hard material
bān and fell 02.04.05 Bodily substance
gebān/gebǣne 02.04.05.04 Bone/bones
bana 02.02.04.01 Cause/occasion of death; 02.02.04.03.01 A killer; 16.01.05.02.02 Other terms for devils
bānbryce 02.08.04.04.01 Mutilation/injury to limbs
bāncofa 02.04 Body
bāncoþa 02.08.06 Skin disease, erysipelas
bānece 02.08.07.07 Disorders of the body
bānfæt 02.04 Body
bānfāg 04.05.03.02.02.06.01 A hall building
bangār 13.02.08.04.01 A spear
bān(ge)beorg 13.02.08.03.01.05 Greaves
bāngebrec 02.08.04.04.01 Mutilation/injury to limbs
bānhelm 13.02.08.03.01.02 A helmet
bānhring 02.04.05.04.04 Spine
bānhūs 02.04 Body
baningas 02.03.03.06.02.01.01 Unidentified people
bānlēas 02.04.05.04 Bone/bones; 03.01.04.01 Power of bending, flexibility
bānloca 02.04.05.05 Muscle
gebann 05.11.06 Course/cycle of time; 09.06.02.01.05 Proclamation, spreading abroad; 12.03.03 A command, bidding, order; 12.03.03.01 Summons, a call, summoning;
14.01.06 A rule, order, precept, tenet, principle
bannan ūt 12.03.03.01 Summons, a call, summoning
(ge)bannan (tōsomne) 12.03.03.01 Summons, a call, summoning
gebannan 12.03.03 A command, bidding, order
bannend 09.06.02.01.05 Proclamation, spreading abroad
gebanngēar 05.11.06 Course/cycle of time
bannuc 04.01.02.01.07.04 Cake
bannuccamb 04.04.01 Fulling
bānrift 13.02.08.03.01.05 Greaves
bānsealf 02.08.12.02.07 Remedies for specific parts (head to toe)
bānsele 02.04 Body
bānwærc 02.08.07.05 Pain in bones
banweorc 02.02.04.04 Manslaughter, homicide
bānwyrt 02.07.11.02 Unidentified plants (alphabetical order)
bār 02.06.02.01.07 Pig, swine; 02.06.03.01.05 Boar
barc 02.07.03.03.01 Wood (as substance)
barda 01.01.02.01.02.02.02 Mountain
barda/bar(þ)a 05.12.01.09.03.01.01 Kind of ship
barenian 05.10.05.04.13 A removal of that which obscures or conceals
barian 05.06.01 Devastation, laying waste; 05.10.05.04.13 A removal of that which obscures or conceals
gebarod 16.02.05.11 The cross (as Christian image)
bārspere 04.03 Hunting, the chase
bārsprēot 04.03 Hunting, the chase
basilisca 02.06.10.01.06 Serpent, scorpion, basilisk

basing 04.04.07.07 A long outer garment, covering, cloak, etc.
(ge)bāsnian 06.01.08 Expectation
bāsnung 06.01.08 Expectation
bastard 02.03.02.02.05 Having the same parents
basu 03.01.14.05 Red/redness
basuhǣwen 03.01.14.05 Red/redness
basurēadian 03.01.14.05 Red/redness
baswa stān 17.04.03.04 Gems collectively
gebaswian 03.01.14.05 Red/redness
bāt 05.12.01.09.03.01 A ship, boat
bāt gestīgan 05.12.01.09 To travel on water
batian 02.08.13 Recovery, growing better; 05.08 Strength
(ge)batian 02.08.13 Recovery, growing better
bātswegen 05.12.01.09.03 A voyage
batt 17.03.09 A post, rod, stick, etc.
bātweard 05.12.01.09.03 A voyage
(ge)baþian 04.06.01.01 Cleansing, washing
be ... twēonum 05.10.05.04.10.01 Interposed
be ... wege 05.12.01.03.01 A means of access
be ǣnigum dǣle 03.06 Comparison
be ānfealdum 03.04.01 Singularity, peculiarity
be ānum oþþe twām 03.03.07 A part, division, portion
be āwihte 03.04.03.01 Someone/something
be eallum 03.03.06.02 Fullness
be ēastan 01.01.01.03 East
be ēastsūþan 01.01.01.02.01 South-east
be fullan 03.03.04.02.01 Abundance; 03.03.06 Wholeness
be fullum þingum 03.03.04.02.01 Abundance
be healfe 05.10.05.04.09 Side, quarter, direction
be healfum dǣle 03.03.07 A part, division, portion
be hundfealdum 03.03.03.04.28 Hundred
be hwon 05.03.01.03 Reason, cause
be libban 04.01.01 Eating
be naman 09.06.02.01.07 A name, appellation
be norþan 01.01.01.01 North
be norþanēastan 01.01.01.01.01 North-east
be sōne 02.05.10.02 Noise, din
be sumum dǣle 03.03.04.04 Littleness, smallness; 03.03.07 A part, division, portion
be sūþan 01.01.01.02 South
be twīfealdum 03.03.03.04.02 Two
be þǣm dǣle 03.03.05 Extent, degree
be (þām) mǣstan 03.03.05 Extent, degree
be ungewyrhtum 05.03.01.01 Without need or cause
be ūtan 05.10.05.04.11 A circle, circuit, circumference
be westan 01.01.01.04 West
be westansūþan 01.01.01.02.02 South-west
bēacen 02.05.10.12 An audible signal; 09.04.01 Signal, signalling
gebēacen 09.03.03 A gesture, action, gesticulation
bēacenfȳr 05.12.01.09.03.05 A lighthouse; 11.09.02 A reminder, warning
bēacenstān 05.12.01.09.03.05 A lighthouse; 11.09.02 A reminder, warning

(ge)bēacnian 09.03.03 A gesture, action, gesticulation
gebēacnian 09.04.01 Signal, signalling; 12.03.03 A command, bidding, order
gebēacnung 09.03.04.02.01 A figure
beadorūn 06.01.07.04.02.01 Deception, deceit, snare, wile
beadu 13.02.02 Battle
beaducāf 06.02.07.06 Courage, boldness, valour
beaducræft 13.02.07 War-craft, art of war
beaducræftig 13.02 War
beaducwealm 02.02.04 Killing, violent death, destruction
beadufolm 13.02.02.01 Single combat
beadugrīma 13.02.08.03.01.02 A helmet
beaduhrægl 13.02.08.03.01.04 Coat of mail/corselet
beadulāc 13.02 War
beadulēoma 13.02.08.04.03 A sword
beadumægen 13.02.07 War-craft, art of war
beadumēce 13.02.08.04.03 A sword
beadurǣs 13.02.02 Battle
beadurinc 13.02.10.01 A man, warrior
beadurōf 13.02 War
beaduscearp 13.02.08.04.03 A sword
beaduscrūd 13.02.08.03.01.04 Coat of mail/corselet
beadusearo 13.02.08 Military equipment
beaduserce 13.02.08.03.01.04 Coat of mail/corselet
beaduþrēat 13.02.10.01.02.02 Armed forces
beaduwǣpen 13.02.08.04 Weapons, arms
beaduwang 13.02.02 Battle
beaduweorc 13.02 War
beaduwrǣd 13.02.10.01.02.01 An armed force/band

beæftan 05.10.05.04.09.02 Hinder part, rear; 05.11.07.04.02 (Of time) later/latter
beǣwnod 12.09 Marriage, state of marriage
beaftan 08.01.03.04.01 Complaint, lamentation
bēag 04.04.10.01 A ring (for finger, arm, neck); 05.10.06.02 Rotundity, roundness; 07.08.04 An ornament, honour, glory; 13.02.08.04 Weapons, arms; 13.02.08.04.03 A sword; 15.01.04 Coinage, money
bēaggifa 12.01.01.04 A leader, ruler
bēaggifu 10.03.07 Distribution
bēaghord 15.01.03 Treasure, riches, wealth
bēaghroden 04.04.10.01 A ring (for finger, arm, neck)
gebēagian 07.08.04 An ornament, honour, glory
bēagsele 04.05.03.02.02.06.01 A hall building
bēagþegu 10.01.01 Acceptance, receiving
bēagwriþa 04.04.10.01 A ring (for finger, arm, neck)
beāhsian 12.03.04 A request, prayer
bealcan 09.01.02.01 Excessive fluency, loquacity
bealcettan 02.08.08.04.02 (Of stomach) disordered; 05.12.05.03.04.02 To flow out, well up, erupt; 09.01.02.01 Excessive fluency, loquacity
beald 06.02.07.06.02 Boldness; 07.06.01.01 Proud, arrogant
bealde 05.11.07.07.01 Contemporary, coeval; 06.02.07.06 Courage, boldness, valour
bealdian 06.02.07.06 Courage, boldness, valour

bealdlīce 05.11.07.01 Contemporary, coeval; 06.02.07.06.02 Boldness; 07.06.01.02 Proudly, arrogantly
bealdnes 06.02.07.06 Courage, boldness, valour
bealdor 06.02.07.06 Courage, boldness, valour
bealdwyrde 07.05.03.03.01 Contumelious, scornful
bealg 05.10.06.02 Rotundity, roundness
beall 01.01.02.01.02.02.01 Hill
beallucas 02.04.06.04.01 Male genitalia
bealu 04.06.02.06 Poison; 07.03.02 Ill, harm, hurt; 08.01.03.09.03 Malevolence, malice
bealubend 14.05.07 Binding, fastening with bonds
bealubenn 02.08.04.01 A wound
bealublonden 07.03.02 Ill, harm, hurt
bealuclomm 14.05.07 Binding, fastening with bonds
bealucræft 16.01.04 Sorcery, magic, witchcraft
bealucwealm 02.02.04 Killing, violent death, destruction
bealudǣd 12.08.06.02.05 Misdeed, sin
bealuful 08.01.03.09.11 Hardheartedness, cruelty, severity
bealufūs 12.08.06.02.05.03 Guilty, sinful, criminal
bealuhycgende 08.01.03.09.03 Malevolence, malice
bealuhygdig 08.01.03.09.03 Malevolence, malice
bealuinwit 08.01.03.09.03 Malevolence, malice
bealulēas 12.08.05 Innocence
bealunīþ 12.08.06.02 Wickedness, evil
bealurāp 14.05.07 Binding, fastening with bonds
bealusearu 08.01.03.09.03 Malevolence, malice
bealusīþ 02.02 Death; 08.01.03.06.01 Affliction, misfortune, calamity
bealusorg 08.01.03 Bad feeling, sadness
bealuspell 09.06.02.01.06.03 Ill tidings
bealuþanc 08.01.03.09.03 Malevolence, malice
bēam 02.07.03 A tree; 03.01.12.02 A beam of light; 04.02.04.06.07 Ploughing equipment; 05.12.01.09.03.01 A ship, boat; 16.01.01.02.03 A wonder, miracle; 16.02.05.11 The cross (as Christian image); 17.03.09 A post, rod, stick, etc.
bēamsceadu 03.01.13.03 Overshadowing
bēamtelg 03.01.14.01 Dyeing; 09.03.07.06.02 Ink
bēamweg 05.12.01.03.01.03 A highway
bēamwer 01.01.03.01.03.02 Weir
bēan 02.07.09.02.02.02 Other vegetables (alphabetical order)
bēanbelg 04.02.04.03.02.01 Grain crops
bēanbelgas 02.07.09.02.02.02 Other vegetables (alphabetical order)
bēanbroþ 04.01.02.01.07.01 Soup/pottage
bēancodd 04.02.04.03.02.01 Grain crops
bēancoddas 02.07.09.02.02.02 Other vegetables (alphabetical order)
bēancynn 02.07.09.02.02.02 Other vegetables (alphabetical order)
bēanen 02.07.09.02.02.02 Other vegetables (alphabetical order)
bēanfurlang 04.02.03.02.02.02 Bean land/field
bēanland 04.02.03.02.02.02 Bean land/field

bēanlēag 04.02.03.02.02.02 Bean land/field
bēanmelu 04.01.02.01.03.07 Meal
bēansǣd 02.07.09.02.02.02 Other vegetables (alphabetical order); 04.02.04.03.01 Seed
bēanscealu 02.07.09.02.02.02 Other vegetables (alphabetical order)
bēanset 04.02.03.02.02.02 Bean land/field
bēanstede 04.02.03.02.02.02 Bean land/field
bearce 02.05.10.15.06 A roar, howl, etc.
beard(-as) 02.04.04.03.03.01 Beard, whisker
gebearded 02.04.04.03.03.01 Beard, whisker
beardlēas 02.04.04.03.03.01 Beard, whisker
bearg 02.06.02.01.07 Pig, swine
bearhtm 03.01.12.01 Glittering, effulgence; 05.11.01.02 Shortness/brevity in time
bearhtmhwæt 05.11.01.02 Shortness/brevity in time
bearhtmhwīl 05.11.01.02 Shortness/brevity in time
bearm 01.01.02.01 Ground; 02.04.03.03.05 Chest, breast, bosom; 02.04.03.03.07 Lap; 08.01 Heart, spirit, mood, disposition; 10 Having, owning, possession
bearmclāþ 04.04.07.08 A short garment, skirt, kirtle
bearmhrægl 04.04.07.08 A short garment, skirt, kirtle
bearmtēag 04.01.02.02.06.03 Food receptacle, basket
bearn 02.03.01.04 Child; 02.03.02.02 Child, offspring; 02.03.02.03.05 Descendant; 16.01.01.04.02 The Son, Christ
bearn habban 02.01.03.03.02 To bring forth, produce
bearncennicge 02.01.03.03.02 To bring forth, produce; 02.03.02.01 Parent
bearnēaca 02.01.03.03.01 To beget
bearnēacen 02.01.03.03.01 To beget
bearnēaciende 02.01.03.03.01 To beget
bearnēacnod 02.01.03.03.01 To beget
bearnēacnung 02.01.03.03.01 To beget
bearngebyrda 02.01.03.03.03.01 Child-bearing, childbirth
bearngestrēon 02.01.03.03.01 To beget
bearnlēas 02.01.03.03.01 To beget
bearnlēast 02.01.03.03.01 To beget
bearnlufu 08.01.02.02 Love, affection, care
bearnmyrþra 02.02.04.04 Manslaughter, homicide
bearntēam 02.01.03.03.01 To beget; 02.01.03.03.04 Offspring, race, breed, family, children
bearu 02.07.03.04.01 A small wood, coppice, copse
bearunæs 01.01.02.01.01.03.01 Promontory, headland, cape
bearwe 17.02.04.02.03 Carrying, carriage (of materials)
gebēat 14.05.05 Physical punishments
bēatan 01.01.03.01.01 Moving water; 02.08.04 Hurt, injury, damage; 05.12.01.04.01.02 To tread upon, trample
bēatan (on) 05.08.02 Violence, force; 05.06.09 Act of striking
(ge)bēatan 05.06.05 A grinding, pounding
gebēaten 05.06.05 A grinding, pounding

bēatende 14.05.05 Physical punishments; 17.02.04.03 Metal worker
bēatere 14.05.05 Physical punishments; 18.02.03.01 A combatant, athlete
bēaw 02.06.09.02.07 Fly
bebaþian 04.06.01.01 Cleansing, washing
bebēodan 09.06.02.01.05 Proclamation, spreading abroad; 12.03.03 A command, bidding, order; 16.02.04.12 Sacrifice, a sacrifice
bebēodan in/on 16.02.04.08.01 Kinds of prayer
bebēodend 12.01.01.04.02 A lord, master
bebēodendlic 06.02.04 Necessity, inevitability; 09.03.02.03.01.02.01 Mood
bebeorgan (wiþ) 11.10.01 Protection, safekeeping
beberan 10.03.04 Provision, supply
bebindan 05.05.03 Binding, fastening; 12.05.06.01 Restraint, check, curb, control
bebītan 05.06.06.01 A tearing, laceration
beblāwan 03.01.15.01 Inspiration, inbreathing
bebod 12.03.03 A command, bidding, order
beboddæg 16.02.04.04.02 A feast-day, holy day
beboden 12.09.01 Pledging, betrothal
bebodrǣden 12.03.03 A command, bidding, order
bebrǣdan 05.10.05.04.12.01 To bespread, cover with
bebrecan 05.06.03 A dashing together, breaking, shattering
bebregdan 06.01.07.04.04.02 Pretence, feigning, dissimulation
bebrūcan 04 Consumption of food/drink; 11.01.01 Practice, exercise, doing
bebūgan 05.10.05.02 Extension, stretching; 05.10.05.04.11 A circle, circuit, circumference; 11.06.06 Turning
bebycgan 15.05 Trade, traffic, commerce
bebycgung 15.05 Trade, traffic, commerce
bebyrded 04.04.09 A fringe, border, hem
bebyrgan 02.02.05 A burial, burying
bebyrg(ed)nes 02.02.05 A burial, burying
bebyrgung 02.02.05 A burial, burying
bēc 09.03.07.07 A book
bēc forlǣtennesse 14.03.03 Law, action of the courts
becǣfian 04.04.05.07 Embroidery
(ge)bēcan 15.01.02 Gift, transfer of property
becarcian 08.01.03.03 Anxiety
becca 04.02.04.06.03 A mattock; 17.03.07 Tools for digging/grasping/pulling
bēce 02.07.03.05 Particular trees/shrubs (alphabetical order)
becēapian 15.05 Trade, traffic, commerce
bēcen 02.07.03.05 Particular trees/shrubs (alphabetical order)
beceorfan 02.04.04.03.05 Haircutting, tonsure
beceorian 08.01.03.05 Murmuring, complaint
becēowan 05.06.06.01 A tearing, laceration
becēpan 06.01.01.02 Care, attention, observation
bēcett 02.07.03.05 Particular trees/shrubs (alphabetical order)
becīdan 07.05.03.01 Falseness in speech, detraction
becierran 05.12.05 To move and change direction, turn; 05.13 Changeableness,

change; 06.01.07.04.01 Deception, a leading astray; 11.06.06 Turning
beclǣman 02.08.12.02.05.03 A poultice
beclǣnsian 12.08.04 Purity, moral cleanness
beclemman 14.05.07 Binding, fastening with bonds
beclencan 14.05.07 Binding, fastening with bonds
beclingan 14.05.07 Binding, fastening with bonds
beclypian 14.03.03.01 Accusation
beclyppan 05.10.05.04.01.02 Contents, what is included; 08.01.02.02.02 An embrace
beclypping 08.01.02.02.02 An embrace
beclȳsan 05.07 Ending of existence, end of world; 05.10.05.04.15 Closure, being closed; 14.05.08.01 Prison, confinement, durance
beclȳsan wiþūtan 05.12.05.03.04 To come/go out from
beclȳsed 05.10.05.04.15 Closure, being closed
beclȳsing 05.10.05.04.11 A circle, circuit, circumference; 06.01.03.02 Dialectics, logic
becnāwan 06.01.06.01.01 Knowledge
becneden 04.01.02.02.05.04.01 Preparation of bread; 05.06.05 A grinding, pounding
becneord 06.01.01.02 Care, attention, observation; 11.02.02 Diligence
becnyttan 05.05.03 Binding, fastening
becnyttan on 05.10.05.04.11 A circle, circuit, circumference
becola 16.01.03 A spectre, ghost, demon, goblin
bēcrǣde 06.01.06.02.03.03.01 An act of reading

bēcrǣding 06.01.06.02.03.03.01 An act of reading
becrēopan 05.12.03.02 Slowness; 09.05.04.01 Concealment, obscurity
bēctrēow 02.07.03.05 Particular trees/shrubs (alphabetical order)
becuman 05.03.02.01.01 An event, occurrence; 10.01 Fact of belonging, possession by; 12.07 An obligation, bounden duty
becuman on 11.07 Use (made of things), service; 13.02.03.01 An attack, assault
becuman (on) 05 Aught, anything, something
becuman tō 02.01.02.02.02 Lifetime; 05 Aught, anything, something; 10.01.02 Acquisition
becwelan 02.02.03 To die, perish
becweþan 07.05.01 Censure, reproof, rebuke; 09.01 To speak, exercise faculty of speech; 09.06.02.01 To tell, make known, declare, relate, announce; 15.01.02.01 Inherited property
becweþan (fore) 12.03.04.02 Speech on behalf of, advocacy
becweþere 09.04.03.01 A translation; 09.04.03.03 A commentary, exposition
becwyddod 14.03.03.07 Security, pledge, bail
becwylman 08.01.03.07.02.01 Injury, offence
becyme 05.03.02 Event, issue, result
becȳpan 15.05 Trade, traffic, commerce
(ge)bed 12.03.04 A request, prayer; 16.02.04.08 Prayer
bedǣlan 11.10.03 Salvation/deliverance from
bedǣlan (fram) 10.04.03.01 To take away, deprive of

bedǣlan (of) 10.04.03.01 To take away, deprive of
bedǣrn 16.02.05.02.03 A church, place of worship
bedbǣr 04.05.04.05 A bed, bedstead
gebedbigen 15.02.04 Spending, disbursement; 16.02.04.08 Prayer
bedbolster 04.05.04.05.01 Bedding (e.g. of straw)
bedbūr 04.05.03.04 A closet, chamber, room
bedclāþ 04.05.04.05.01 Bedding (e.g. of straw)
(ge)bedcleofa 02.06.01.08 A lair, den; 04.05.03.04 A closet, chamber, room; 09.05.04.01 Concealment, obscurity
bedcofa 04.05.03.04 A closet, chamber, room
bedd 04.02.04.05.01 A garden-plot; 04.05.04.05 A bed, bedstead; 04.05.04.05.01 Bedding (e.g. of straw); 17.03.02 Item providing support
gebedda 12.04.01 A fellow, companion, associate, comrade; 12.09 Marriage, state of marriage
(ge)beddagas 16.02.04.04.02.01.03 Holy Week
beddclāþas 04.05.04.05.01 Bedding (e.g. of straw)
beddgemāna 02.01.03.03 Sex, generation
beddian 04.05.04.05.01 Bedding (e.g. of straw)
bedding 04.05.04.05 A bed, bedstead; 04.05.04.05.01 Bedding (e.g. of straw)
beddrest 04.05.04.05 A bed, bedstead
beddstōw 04.05.04.05 A bed, bedstead
bedēaglian 09.05.04 A secret
bedecian 15.01.06.01 Begging

bedelfan 02.02.05 A burial, burying; 05.12.05.13.01 To descend beneath, go lower than (a place); 17.02.04.02.02 Digging
bedelfing 17.02.04.02.02 Digging
bedewind 02.07.11 Plants/flowers (alphabetical order)
bedfelt 04.05.04.05.01 Bedding (e.g. of straw)
bedgerid 02.06.01.08 A lair, den
gebedgīht 05.11.04.02 Night, night time
(ge)bedhūs 16.02.05.02.03 A church, place of worship
gebedian 16.02.04.08 Prayer
bedīcian 13.02.06.01 Stronghold, fort/fortified town
bedīglian 09.05.04 A secret; 09.05.04.01 Concealment, obscurity
bedīgling 09.05.04.01 Concealment, obscurity
bedīpan 05.12.05.02.04.03 To plunge (something into something)
bedīpan on 05.12.05.02.04.03 To plunge (something into something)
gebedmann 16.02.04 Worship, honour, praise
bedōn 05.10.05.04.15 Closure, being closed
(ge)bedrǣden 16.02.04.08 Prayer
bedrēaf 04.05.04.05.01 Bedding (e.g. of straw)
bedreda 02.08.02.01.05 Bed of sickness
bedrēosan 06.01.07.04.01 Deception, a leading astray; 10.04.03.01 To take away, deprive of
bedrīfan 01.03.01.03.01 Storm, tempest; 03.01.16.05 A sprinkling; 05.12.02 To move, set in motion; 05.12.02.06.01 To push, drive
bedrīfan tō 06.02.06.03.03 Incitement

bedrīfan trod 05.12.05.10 To go behind, follow
bedrincan 03.01.16.01 Moisture
bedrīp 04.02.04.04.02 Harvesting
bedrōg 06.01.07.05 Error, being astray
bedrūgian 03.01.18 Dryness (not wetness)
bedrȳped 03.01.16.01 Moisture
gebedscipe 12.09.06 Cohabitation
gebedsealm 16.02.04.03.03.02 A psalm
gebedstōw 16.02.05.02.03 A church, place of worship
bedstrēaw 04.05.04.05.01 Bedding (e.g. of straw)
(ge)bedtīd 05.11.04.02 Night, night time
gebedtīd 16.02.04.08 Prayer
bedþegn 12.01.01.08.01 A servant, attendant
bedu 12.03.04 A request, prayer
gebedu ræran 16.02.04.08 Prayer
bedūfan 03.01.16.06 A soaking, steeping
bedul 12.03.04 A request, prayer
bedwāhrift 04.05.04.05.01 Bedding (e.g. of straw)
bedydrian 06.01.07.04.01 Deception, a leading astray
bedydrian ... wiþ 09.05.04.01 Concealment, obscurity
bedȳfan 03.01.16.06 A soaking, steeping
bedȳpan 03.01.16.06 A soaking, steeping
bedȳped 03.01.14.01 Dyeing
bedyppan 03.01.16.06 A soaking, steeping
bedypped 03.01.16.01 Moisture
bedȳpt 03.01.16.01 Moisture
bedyrnan 09.05.04.01 Concealment, obscurity
beecgban 04.02.04.02.02.01 Harrowing

beefesian 02.04.04.03.05 Haircutting, tonsure; 16.02.04.13.03 Tonsure, haircutting, shaving
befæstan 02.02.05 A burial, burying; 05.13.06.01 Firm, stable, steady; 06.01.06.02.03.04.05 Edification, instruction; 06.01.08.03 Trust, faith, confidence; 08.01.01.03.09.03 To make glad; 11.10 Safety, safeness; 11.10.02.02.01 Care, interest in; 14.03.03.07 Security, pledge, bail; 16.02.04.08.01 Kinds of prayer
befæstan tō 17.02.01 Management of work
befæstnian 05.05.03 Binding, fastening; 12.09.01 Pledging, betrothal
befættian 03.01.17.07.01 An anointing, greasing
befæþm(i)an 05.10.05.04.11 A circle, circuit, circumference; 08.01.02.02.02 An embrace
befaran 05.12.05.02.01 To come upon, meet with; 05.12.05.06 To travel over/through/along, traverse; 14.05.08 Captivity
befealdan 05.10.05.04.11 A circle, circuit, circumference; 05.10.05.04.12 The condition of being covered; 05.10.06.02.03 A circular fold, coil; 05.10.06.05 A fold, plait, wrinkle; 14.03.03.01 Accusation
befealdan tō 10.01 Fact of belonging, possession by
befealdian 05.10.06.05 A fold, plait, wrinkle
befeallan 03.04 Form, kind, nature, character; 05.12.05.13.03 To fall
befeallan in/intō/on 11.06.03.01 Ill fortune, bad success
befeallan on 03.03.05.01 Rank, position, degree; 05.03.02.01.01 An event, occurrence

befeallan tō 11.01.02 An undertaking
befeallen (æt) 10.04.03.01 To take away, deprive of
befēgan 03.03.06.01 A whole formed by joining
befeohtan 10.04.02.02 To seize, take, grasp, lay hold on
befēolan 02.02.05 A burial, burying; 06.02.06.03.03 Incitement; 06.02.07.03 Perseverance; 08.01.03.08 Patience; 10.03.03 Granting; 11.01.01 Practice, exercise, doing
befēolan on 06.02.07.03 Perseverance
befēon 14.05.04 A penalty, punishment
befer 02.06.03.01.13 Rodents
beferan 05.12.05.06 To travel over/through/along, traverse; 05.12.05.07 To go beyond, pass; 05.12.05.07.01 To pass by; 11.06.03.01 Ill fortune, bad success
beferian 02.01.02.02.02 Lifetime
befician 06.01.07.04 Deception
beflēan 05.06.06.01 A tearing, laceration; 05.10.05.04.13 A removal of that which obscures or conceals; 14.05.05 Physical punishments
beflēogan 05.12.01.07 To fly (with wings)
beflēon 11.10.04 Flight
beflōwan 01.01.03.03 Flow/flowing
befōn 05.10.04 Place, room; 05.10.05.04.01.02 Contents, what is included; 05.10.05.04.11 A circle, circuit, circumference; 05.12.05.02.01 To come upon, meet with; 09.04.03.03 A commentary, exposition; 10 Having, owning, possession; 10.04.02 To grasp, take hold of; 10.04.02.02 To seize, take, grasp, lay hold on; 12.05.06.01 Restraint, check, curb, control; 14.05.08 Captivity
befōn on 05.02.02.03 A connexion, association; 11.02 Occupation, activity, business
beforan 05.10.04.03 Presence; 05.10.05.04.09.01 Front; 05.11.07.03.02 Earlier, antecedent; 05.12.05.08 To go before, precede; 11.07.04 Superiority, pre-eminence, primacy
beforan (ǣr) 05.11.07.03.02 Earlier, antecedent
beforan gān 05.12.05.08 To go before, precede; 11.07.04 Superiority, pre-eminence, primacy
beforan þissum 05.11.07.03.02 Earlier, antecedent
beforhtian 06.01.08.06.02 Great fear, terror, horror
befōtian 14.05.05 Physical punishments
befrēogan 11.10.03 Salvation/deliverance from
befrignan 09.05.02 A question, inquiry, questioning; 12.03.04 A request, prayer
befrignan (be/of/ymbe) 09.05.02 A question, inquiry, questioning
befrīnung 09.05.02 A question, inquiry, questioning
befȳlan 04.06.02.02 Foul, filthy, squalid; 12.08.06.01.04.01 To mislead, seduce, lead astray
befylgan 06.02.07.03 Perseverance
befyllan 03.03.06.02 Fullness; 05.12.05.13.03 To fall
befylled 10.04.03.01 To take away, deprive of
begalan 16.01.04.01 Sorcery using incantation
begān 04.02.03 Cultivatable land/farmland; 04.02.04.02

Cultivation/tillage; 04.05.03.01 Habitation, sojourn; 05.10.05.04.11 A circle, circuit, circumference; 05.12.05.02 To go/travel towards, come, approach; 05.12.05.02.01 To come upon, meet with; 05.12.05.04 To rotate, turn round, revolve; 05.12.05.06 To travel over/through/along, traverse; 05.12.05.07 To go beyond, pass; 05.12.05.07.01 To pass by; 09.06.02.01.04 A confession, declaration; 10.01.02 Acquisition; 11.01.01 Practice, exercise, doing; 11.05.02 Mode, manner, way, method, fashion, course; 12.07.02 Observance, keeping; 16.02.04 Worship, honour, praise

begān/begangan 07.04.03 Reverence, respect; 11.02.02.02.01 Attention, cultivation

begān (in) 11.02 Occupation, activity, business

begān on borg 15.04 A debt, due

begān tō 05.03.02.01.01 An event, occurrence

begang 04.02.04.02 Cultivation/tillage; 05.12.01.03 Expanse over which something travels; 16.02.04 Worship, honour, praise; 17 Work, doings, actions, labour

begang/bīgeng 11.01.01 Practice, exercise, doing

begangan 05.10.05.04.11 A circle, circuit, circumference; 05.12.05.04 To rotate, turn round, revolve; 05.12.05.07.01 To pass by; 11.01.01 Practice, exercise, doing; 11.02 Occupation, activity, business; 16.02.04 Worship, honour, praise

begangnes 16.02.04.04.02 A feast-day, holy day

begangol 04.02.04.02 Cultivation/tillage; 16.02.04 Worship, honour, praise

begbēam 02.07.03.02 A tree/bush with berries

begeat 10.01.02 Acquisition; 15.01 Property

bēgen 03.03.03.04.02 Two

begenga 04.02.04.02 Cultivation/tillage

begēomerian 08.01.03.04.01 Complaint, lamentation

begeondan 05.10.04.04 Absence; 05.11.07.04.02 (Of time) later/latter

begēotan 03.01.16.05 A sprinkling; 05.10.05.04.12.01 To bespread, cover with

begēotan on 10.03 Giving

beger 02.07.09.01 Berry

begiellan 02.05.10.15.07 Voice, note (of a bird)

begietan 02.01.03.03.01 To beget; 05.03.01 A cause (of anything); 10.01.02 Acquisition; 10.04.02.02 To seize, take, grasp, lay hold on; 11.03.01.03 Finding, discovery

begietan ... hām 05.12.02.01 To fetch, bring, bear, conduct

begietend 10.01.01.01 Receiving, gaining, getting

begietennes 10.01.02 Acquisition

begīman 02.05.09.05 To watch, observe, survey; 02.08.12.02 To tend the sick; 11.10.02.02 Watchful care, keeping guard; 11.10.02.02.01 Care, interest in; 12.07.02 Observance, keeping

begīmen 02.05.09.05 To watch, observe, survey; 06.01.01.02 Care, attention, observation; 12.07.02 Observance, keeping

begīmend 12.03 Direction, guidance
begīming 11.03.01.03.01 Discovery, invention; 12.03.01 Direction, care, management, supervision; 12.07.02 Observance, keeping
begīnan 05.06.01 Devastation, laying waste
beginnan 05.11.10.01 A beginning; 11.01.02 An undertaking; 13.02.03.01 An attack, assault
begleddian 03.01.14.01 Dyeing; 04.06.02.03 Stain, smear
beglīdan 05.12.05.03 To travel away (from)
begnagan 05.06.06.01 A tearing, laceration
begnīdan 05.06.05.01 A rubbing
begnornian 08.01.03.04 Grief; 08.01.03.04.01 Complaint, lamentation
begoten 05.10.05.04.12 The condition of being covered
begrafan 05.12.05.13.01 To descend beneath, go lower than (a place)
begrētan 08.01.03.04.01 Complaint, lamentation
begrindan 04.06.01 Clean; 14.02.01.02 Wrongful taking, theft
begrīpan 07.05.01 Censure, reproof, rebuke; 10.04.02.02 To seize, take, grasp, lay hold on
begripen mid/on 12.08.09 Guiltiness, guilt
begriwen 06.01.06.02 Knowledge, learning, erudition
begroren 08.01.03.06 Adversity, affliction
begrynian 04.03.02 A snare, trap, noose
begyldan 17.02.05.02 Goldsmith's art

begylpan 07.06.03 Boastfulness, arrogance
begyrd 04.04.07 Trappings, equipment, garb
begyrdan 04.04.07 Trappings, equipment, garb; 05.10.05.04.11 A circle, circuit, circumference; 06.02.07.01 Strength, fortitude
behabban 05.10.05.04.01.02 Contents, what is included; 05.10.05.04.11 A circle, circuit, circumference; 10.03.06 Withholding, keeping back; 11.11.03 Impeding of progress, prevention
behādian 16.02.04.07.05.01.02 Unfrocking
behæfednes 12.08.03 Restraint, temperance
behæpsian 05.10.05.04.15.01 A bar, bolt
behǣs 12.07.02.01.01 A promise
behǣttian 02.02.04.04.03 Putting to death; 05.06.06.01 A tearing, laceration
behǣttod 02.04.04.03.04 Bald, shaven
behamelian 02.08.04.02.01 A maimed man
behammen 04.04.07.15 Footwear, covering for the feet
behangen 05.12.01.07.01 To hang
behāt 08.01.03.09.07 Threat, threatening, menace; 12.07.02.01.01 A promise; 16.02.04.15 A vow
behatan 12.09.01 Pledging, betrothal
behātan 08.01.03.09.07 Threat, threatening, menace; 12.07.02.01 Covenant, assurance of faith, promise; 12.07.02.01.01 A promise; 14.04.03 Confirmation, ratification; 16.02.04.15 A vow
behātland 05.10.04.02 A region, zone

behāwian 02.05.09.01 To open the eyes/be awake; 06.01.08.06.05 Wariness, carefulness

behāwian (be) 06.01.01.01.01 Thought, cogitation, meditation

behēafdian 02.02.04.04.03 Putting to death; 14.05.05.01 Capital punishment

behēafdung 02.02.04.04.03 Putting to death; 14.05.05.01 Capital punishment

behēafodlic 14.05.05.01 Capital punishment

behealdan 02.05.09.04 To see, look upon, behold; 02.05.09.05 To watch, observe, survey; 05.10.04.03 Presence; 06.01.01.01 Thinking about, minding, heeding; 09.04 Sense, purport, meaning; 10 Having, owning, possession; 11.07.01 Utility, usefulness; 11.10.01 Protection, safekeeping; 11.10.02.01 Vigilance; 12.05.06.01 Restraint, check, curb, control; 12.07.02 Observance, keeping; 17.02.02 An office, function, employment

behealden 06.01.08.06.05 Wariness, carefulness; 11.02.02.02.01 Attention, cultivation

behealdend 02.05.09.05 To watch, observe, survey

behealdennes 12.07.02 Observance, keeping; 12.08.03.03.01 Continence

behealdnes 02.05.09.04 To see, look upon, behold

behēawan 04.02.04.05.04.01 A forester, woodman; 05.06.02 Cleaving, splitting, cutting; 10.04.03.01 To take away, deprive of

behēfe 06.02.04.01 Want, need; 11.07.01 Utility, usefulness

behēf(e)lic 06.02.04.01 Want, need

behēfnes 11.07.02 Utility, advantage, convenience

behēfþ(u) 06.02.04.01 Want, need

behegian 04.05.01.02.07 A fence, hedge

behelan 09.05.04.01 Concealment, obscurity

behelian 03.01.13.03 Overshadowing; 09.05.04.01 Concealment, obscurity

behelmian 05.10.05.04.12 The condition of being covered

behēofian 08.01.03.04.01 Complaint, lamentation

beheonan 05.10.05.04.01 A little way, no great distance; 05.10.05.04.09 Side, quarter, direction

behildan 05.12.05.03.03 To depart, leave, set out

behindan 05.10.05.04.09.02 Hinder part, rear

behindan lǣtan 05.12.05.07 To go beyond, pass; 11.06.04 Abstention, abstaining from

behīwian 06.01.07.04.04.02 Pretence, feigning, dissimulation

behlǣnan 05.10.05.04.11 A circle, circuit, circumference

behlēapan 05.13.06.01 Firm, stable, steady

behlēapan on 06.02.07 Will, determination, resolution

behlemman 02.05.10.07 A crashing, noise; 05.06.03 A dashing together, breaking, shattering

behleonian 05.10.05.04.12 The condition of being covered

behlēotan 10.03.07.01 To allot, assign

behlīdan 05.10.05.04.12 The condition of being covered

behlīgan 14.03.03.01 Accusation

behlyhhan 07.05.04 Mockery, derision, scorn
behlȳþan 14.02.01.02 Wrongful taking, theft
behōf 06.02.04.01 Want, need; 11.07 Use (made of things), service
behōfian 06.02.04.01 Want, need
behōflic 06.02.04.01 Want, need
behogadnes 11.01.01 Practice, exercise, doing
behogian 06.01.08.06.04 Care, anxiety, solicitude; 11.10.02.02.01 Care, interest in
behogod 11.02.03 Forethought, care
behogodlīce 11.02.02.01 Diligence, studious care
beholen 09.05.04 A secret
behorsod 13.02.10.01.02.02.02 Branch of army
behrēosan 05.12.05.13.03 To fall
behrēowsian 08.01.02.05 Compassion; 12.08.02.02.01 Reform, correction; 16.02.04.07.02.01 Penitence
behrēowsung 08.01.03.02.01 Compunction, remorse, contrition; 16.02.04.07.02.01 Penitence
behrēowsungtīd 16.02.04.04.02.01.02 Lent; 16.02.04.07.02.01 Penitence
behrīman 01.03.01.04.01 Frost
behringan 05.10.05.04.11 A circle, circuit, circumference
behrōpan 12.03.04.03 Importunity, persistence
behroren 05.10.05.04.12 The condition of being covered; 06.02.04.01 Need, distress, straits, difficulty
behrūmian 04.06.02.03 Stain, smear
behrūmig 03.01.13 Darkness, obscurity; 04.06.02.05 Dust, powder
behrūmod 03.01.13 Darkness, obscurity

bēhþ 09.04.01 Signal, signalling
behwearf(t) 05.13.04 Exchange, commutation
behweorfan 02.02.05.02 To prepare for burial; 04.01.02.02.01 To dress animals for food; 11.01.01 Practice, exercise, doing; 11.05.02 Mode, manner, way, method, fashion, course; 11.10.02.02.01 Care, interest in
behwirfan 05.13.04 Exchange, commutation; 06.01.06.02.03.04.03 To teach, instruct
behwirfan (on/tō) 05.13.01 Transformation, taking another shape
behwirfan ūtan 05.10.05.04.11 A circle, circuit, circumference; 05.12.05 To move and change direction, turn
behwīt 03.01.14.03 White/whiteness
behwylfan 05.10.05.04.12 The condition of being covered
behycgan 06.01.01.01.01 Thought, cogitation, meditation
behycgan on 06.01.08.03 Trust, faith, confidence
behȳdan 05.10.05.04.12 The condition of being covered; 09.05.04.01 Concealment, obscurity; 13.02.08.04.03.02 Armed with a sword
behȳdednes 09.05.04.01 Concealment, obscurity
behȳdig 06.01.08.06.04 Care, anxiety, solicitude; 08.01.03.03 Anxiety
behȳdiglīce 06.01.01.02 Care, attention, observation
behȳdignes 06.01.08.06.04 Care, anxiety, solicitude
behȳdnes 09.05.04 A secret
behygdnes 08.01.03.03 Anxiety

behyhtan 06.01.08.03 Trust, faith, confidence
behyldan 05.06.06.01 A tearing, laceration
behylian 04.04.07 Trappings, equipment, garb
behȳpan (on) 03.03.04.01.02.01 A heap, mass, accumulation
behȳran 15.01.01.01.01 Hiring, letting out of property/land
behȳred 15.01.01.01.01 Hiring, letting out of property/land
behȳrung 15.01.01.01.01 Hiring, letting out of property/land
behȳþelīce 07.06.05 Pomp, splendour, magnificence; 15.01.05 Possession of wealth
beiernan 03.01.16.01 Moisture; 05.12.03.01 Swiftness, velocity; 05.12.05.06 To travel over/through/along, traverse
beiernan on 05.03.02 Event, issue, result
beiernan on mōd 06.01 The head (as seat of thought)
beinseglian 14.04.01 A deed, contract, agreement
belācan 05.10.05.04.11 A circle, circuit, circumference
belādian 11.06.06 Turning; 12.07.03.02 An excuse; 14.03.03.08 Justification
belādiendlic 12.07.03.02 An excuse
belādigend 12.07.03.02 An excuse
belādung 12.07.03.02 An excuse
belǣdan 06.01.07.04.01 Deception, a leading astray
belǣfan 03.03.07.02 What is left, remnant, remains; 11.06.04 Abstention, abstaining from
belǣþan 07.03.01.03 To loathe, hate, abhor

belǣwa 06.01.07.04.04.03 Deceit, fraud, treachery
belǣwan 06.01.07.04.04.03 Deceit, fraud, treachery
belǣwend 06.01.07.04.04.03 Deceit, fraud, treachery
belǣwung 06.01.07.04.04.03 Deceit, fraud, treachery
belandian 10.04.03.01 To take away, deprive of
belangian 05.02.02.03 A connexion, association
belcedswēora 07.06.01.01 Proud, arrogant
(ge)beldan 09.03.07.07 A book
belēan 12.03.06 Prohibition; 14.03.03.01 Accusation
belecgan 05.10.05.04.12 The condition of being covered; 08.01.03.07.02 Misery, trouble, affliction; 14.03.03.01 Accusation
belene 02.07.11 Plants/flowers (alphabetical order)
belēogan 06.01.07.04.03 Untruth, falsehood; 06.01.07.05 Error, being astray
belēoran 05.11 A time, period of time
belēorendlic 05.11.07.03 Former times, days of old
belēosan 10.02.01 Loss, deprivation
belflȳs 02.06.02.01.08 Sheep
belg 17.03.12 A receptacle, container; 17.05.02 A hearth, fireplace
gebelg 08.01.03.05.02 Anger
(ge)belgan 08.01.03.05.02 Anger
belgnes 12.07.05 Wrong, injustice
belhring 02.05.10.13.01.01 Stroke/sound of a bell
belhringes bēacn 02.05.10.13.01.01 Stroke/sound of a bell

belicgan 05.10.05.04.11 A circle, circuit, circumference; 05.12.05.04 To rotate, turn round, revolve; 10.01 Fact of belonging, possession by

beliden 02.02.04 Killing, violent death, destruction

belīfan 02.02.03 To die, perish; 03.03.07.02 What is left, remnant, remains; 05.12.04 Absence of movement, stillness

belifen 02.02.03.02 State of being dead

belīfend 11.10.05 Escape

belīfgan 04.01.02.04.04 To maintain, support, provide for

belīfian 02.02.04.03 To kill, slay

belīman 03.03.06.01 A whole formed by joining

belimp 05.02.01 Condition, state of affairs, situation; 05.03.02.01.01 An event, occurrence

belimpan 03.06.03 Congruity, fitness, suitability; 05.02.02 Nature, established order of things; 05.02.02.03 A connexion, association; 05.03.02.01.01 An event, occurrence; 10.01 Fact of belonging, possession by; 12.05.06.04.02 Submission, subjection, obedience

belimpan tō 05.02.02 Nature, established order of things

belisned 06.01.08.05.01 Amazement, astonishment, wonder, admiration

belistnian 02.08.04.02.02 Castrated

belis(t)nod 02.03.01.03 Eunuch; 02.08.04.02.02 Castrated

belīþan 10.04.03.01 To take away, deprive of

bellan 02.05.10.15.06 A roar, howl, etc.

belle 02.05.10.13.01 A bell

bellhūs 16.02.05.03.07 A belfry

bellringestre 02.05.10.13.01.01 Stroke/sound of a bell

belltācen 02.05.10.13.01.01 Stroke/sound of a bell

belltīd 16.02.04.05 Canonical hour, service

belocen 05.10.05.04.15 Closure, being closed

belōcian 02.05.09.04 To see, look upon, behold

beloren 10.04.03.01 To take away, deprive of

belt 04.04.07.13 A girdle, belt

belūcan 05.10.05.04.01.02 Contents, what is included; 05.10.05.04.11 A circle, circuit, circumference; 05.10.05.04.15 Closure, being closed; 05.11.10.02 End, completion; 05.12.05.03.04 To come/go out from; 11.01.06 End, completion (of action), fulfilment; 11.10.01 Protection, safekeeping; 11.11.02 A hindrance; 14.05.08.01 Prison, confinement, durance

belūcan (mid) 05.10.05.04.11 A circle, circuit, circumference

belūtian 11.09.01.01 Ambush, lying in wait

belȳfan 06.01.08.03.01 Belief, trust, faithfulness

belȳfed 06.01.08.03.01 Belief, trust, faithfulness

belyrtan 06.01.07.04 Deception

belytegian 06.02.06.03.04 Allurement

bemǣnan 08.01.02.05 Compassion; 08.01.03.04.01 Complaint, lamentation; 12.08.02.02.01 Reform, correction; 16.02.04.07.02.01 Penitence

bemancian 02.08.04.02.01 A maimed man
bemeldian 09.06.02.01 To tell, make known, declare, relate, announce
bemetan 07.01 Appraisal, appraising
bemīþan 09.05.04.01 Concealment, obscurity; 11.09.01.01 Ambush, lying in wait
bemurcnian 08.01.03.05 Murmuring, complaint
bemurnan 08.01.03.04.01 Complaint, lamentation; 08.01.03.05 Murmuring, complaint
bemūtian on 05.13 Changeableness, change
bemyldan 02.02.05 A burial, burying
bēn 08.01.01.03.08.03 A favour, blessing; 12.01.01.08 Service; 12.03.04 A request, prayer
(ge)bēn 16.02.04.08 Prayer
bēna/bēne 12.03.04 A request, prayer
bēna wesan 12.03.04 A request, prayer
benacian 05.10.05.04.13 A removal of that which obscures or conceals
benǣman 10.04.03.01 To take away, deprive of
benc 04.05.04.01 A bench, seat
bencian 04.05.04.01 A bench, seat
bencsittend 02.03.03.01 Body of retainers, household
bencswēg 18.02 Amusement, revelry, festivity
bencþel 04.05.04.01 A bench, seat
bend 04.04.10 Ornaments, trappings, accoutrements; 05.05.03 Binding, fastening; 14.05.07 Binding, fastening with bonds
gebend 05.10.06.02.02 Curvature, bend, twist
bēndagas 16.02.04.04.02.01.03 Holy Week
(ge)bendan 05.10.06.02.02 Curvature, bend, twist; 14.05.07 Binding, fastening with bonds
bendum belecgan 14.05.07 Binding, fastening with bonds
beneah 06.02.04.01 Want, need; 11.07 Use (made of things), service
benedicite 16.02.04.03.03.01 A hymn, song of praise, canticle
benemnan 09.06.02.01.07 A name, appellation; 09.07.04 Assertion, affirmation; 14.04 Making of terms, agreement, convention
benēotan 10.04.03.01 To take away, deprive of
beneoþan 05.10.05.04.02.02 Under, beneath
bēnfeorm 04.01.02.04.02 Feast
bengeat 02.08.04.01 A wound
benīdan 12.05.06.03 Necessity, constraint
beniman 05.10.05.04.01.02 Contents, what is included; 10.04.03.01 To take away, deprive of; 14.05.08 Captivity
beniming 10.04.03.01 To take away, deprive of
bēnlic 12.03.04.01 Entreaty, solemn appeal
bēnlīce 12.03.04 A request, prayer
benn 02.08.04.01 A wound
gebenn 14.01.06 A rule, order, precept, tenet, principle
benne 02.07.08 Grasses, reeds, etc.
(ge)bennian 02.08.04.01 A wound
benotian 11.07 Use (made of things), service
bēnrīp 04.02.04.04.02 Harvesting
gebēnsende 12.03.04 A request, prayer
bēnsian 12.03.04.01 Entreaty, solemn appeal

bēntīd 16.02.04.04.02.01.03 Holy Week
bēntigþe 08.01.01.03.08.02 Good fortune, success; 08.01.02.01 Favour, kindness, grace
bēnyrþ 04.02.04.02.02.02 Ploughing, tilling
bēo 02.06.09.02.02 Bee, hornet, wasp
bēo/wes þū hāl 11.05.02.02.01 Greetings, courteous terms of address
bēobrēad 04.01.02.01.05.04 Honey
bēoceorl 04.02.05.06.08 A bee-keeper
bēocere 04.02.05.06.08 A bee-keeper
bēod 04.01.02.02.06.05.03 Plate/platter/bowl/dish; 04.01.02.04 Abundance of food; 04.05.04.02 A table
bēodærn 04.01.01.08 Eating place
bēodan gield 15.03 Exaction of tax/tribute
bēodan ūt 12.05.07.01 Separation, dismissal, rejection
(ge)bēodan 10.03 Giving; 10.03.02 Presenting, offering; 11.01 Action, doing, performance; 12.03.03 A command, bidding, order; 12.03.03.01 Summons, a call, summoning
gebēodan 09.06.02.01.05 Proclamation, spreading abroad
bēodbolle 04.01.02.02.06.05.04 Cup/bowl/basin
bēodclāþ 04.04.08 A covering, curtain, veil, garment, etc.
bēoddian 04.05.04.05.01 Bedding (e.g. of straw)
bēodend 06.01.06.02.03.04.02 A teacher
bēodfæt 04.01.02.02.06.05.04 Cup/bowl/basin
bēodfers 16.02.04.03.03.01 A hymn, song of praise, canticle; 16.02.04.08.01 Kinds of prayer

bēodgæst 04.01.01.07 Feasting
bēodgenēat 04.01.01.07 Feasting
bēodgereord 04.01.02.04.02 Feast
bēodhrægl 04.04.08 A covering, curtain, veil, garment, etc.
bēodian 17.02.04.02.01 Cutting, hewing, shaping
bēodlāf 04.01.02.01.01.08 Leftover food
bēodland 16.02.05.01 Land
bēodrēaf 04.04.08 A covering, curtain, veil, garment, etc.
bēodscēat 04.04.08 A covering, curtain, veil, garment, etc.
bēodscȳte 04.04.08 A covering, curtain, veil, garment, etc.
bēodwyst 04.01.02.04 Abundance of food
bēogang 02.06.09.02.02 Bee, hornet, wasp
gebēogol/gebȳgle 12.05.06.04.02 Submission, subjection, obedience
bēohāta 12.01.01.04 A leader, ruler
bēolǣs 04.02.03.04.02.01 Types of pasture
bēomōder 02.06.09.02.02 Bee, hornet, wasp
bēon 05.11.07.04 Future, time to come
bēon/wesan 02 Creation; 02.01 Existence, life; 05 Aught, anything, something; 05.02 State, condition; 05.03.02.01.01 An event, occurrence; 05.10.04.03 Presence
bēon/wesan ābisgod wiþ 12.05.04 Strife, hostility; 13.02 War
bēon/wesan andetta 08.01.03.02.01 Compunction, remorse, contrition
bēon/wesan becnāwe 14.03.03.09 A sentence, judgement, ruling
bēon/wesan forboren 02.08.08.12 Disease of bowels

bēon/wesan hand gemǣne 13.02.02.01 Single combat
bēon/wesan gelōgod on 05.02.02 Nature, established order of things
bēon/wesan gelōgod to his folcum 02.02.03.02 State of being dead
bēon/wesan mann 16.01.01.04.02.01 Incarnation
bēon/wesan genumen 02.08.02.01.01 An infectious disease
bēon/wesan of 05.12.05.03.03 To depart, leave, set out
bēon/wesan on 05.10.05.04.01.02 Contents, what is included
bēon/wesan on ... gemǣnes 11.02 Occupation, activity, business
bēon/wesan on gebyrge 11.10.01 Protection, safekeeping
bēon/wesan gescrifen 16.02.04.07.02 Confession
bēon/wesan gesīene 02.05.09.08 To seem, appear to be
bēon/wesan getrymmed 13.02.07.02 Order (of troops), array
bēon/wesan þurhþȳd 02.08.03 Pain, bodily discomfort
bēon/wesan ūpārehte 16.02.01.12 Spirituality
bēon/wesan ūtweard 05.12.05.03.04 To come/go out from
bēon/wesan yfle gehæft 02.08.04.04.02 (Of limbs) to be diseased
bēon/wesan ymbe 11.02 Occupation, activity, business
beonet 02.07.08 Grasses, reeds, etc.
beoneting 04.02.03.04 Grassland
bēor 04.01.03.05.01.02 Broth; 04.01.03.05.01.04 Mead
gebēor 04.01.01.07 Feasting
bēorbyden 04.01.03.05.04.02 A barrel, tun, vat, cask
beorc 09.03.07.01.01 A runic letter
beorc/byrce 02.07.03.05 Particular trees/shrubs (alphabetical order)
(ge)beorc 02.05.10.15.06 A roar, howl, etc.
beorcan (on) 02.05.10.15.06 A roar, howl, etc.
beorcholt 02.07.03.05 Particular trees/shrubs (alphabetical order)
beorcragu 02.07.06 Lichen
beorcrind 02.07.03.05 Particular trees/shrubs (alphabetical order)
bēordræst(e) 04.01.03.05.01.02 Broth
beorg 01.01.02.01.02.02 Hill, mountain; 02.02.05.01.01 A grave, burial place, sepulchre
(ge)beorg 01.01.02.01.02.02 Mountain
gebeorg 11.10.01 Protection, safekeeping; 11.11.03 Impeding of progress, prevention
beorgælfen 16.01.03.04 Elfin race
beorgan 11.06.04 Abstention, abstaining from
beorgan wiþ 11.06.06 Turning
(ge)beorgan 11.10.01 Protection, safekeeping; 11.10.02.01 Vigilance; 11.11.03 Impeding of progress, prevention
(ge)beorgan wiþ 11.10.01 Protection, safekeeping
beorghleoþ 01.01.02.01.02.02 Mountain
beorghliþ 02.02.05.01.01 A grave, burial place, sepulchre
beorgiht 01.01.02.01.02.02 Mountain
gebeorglic 03.06.03.04 What is fitting/seemly/appropriate/decent; 11.02.03 Forethought, care; 11.10 Safety, safeness

beorgseþel 04.05.03.02.02.01 Dwellings in particular places
beorgstede 01.01.02.01.02.01 Rising ground, eminence
gebeorhnes 11.10.01.02 Refuge, help, shelter
gebeorhstōw 11.10.01.02 Refuge, help, shelter
beorht 02.05.09 Faculty of sight; 02.05.09.01 To open the eyes/be awake; 02.05.10.01 Thing heard; 03.01.12 Brightness, light; 06.01.05.02 Intelligence; 07.08.07 Glory, splendour, magnificence; 16.01.01.01.01.02 Glory
beorhtblōwende 02.07.02.07 Blossom, flower(s)
beorhte 02.05.09.01 To open the eyes/be awake; 03.01.12 Brightness, light; 07.08.07 Glory, splendour, magnificence
beorhthwīl 05.11.01.02 Shortness/brevity in time
beorhtian 02.05.10.01 Thing heard
(ge)beorhtian 02.05.09.03 To give light, restore to sight; 03.01.12 Brightness, light
gebeorhtian 02.08.12 Healing, curing
beorhtlic 03.01.12 Brightness, light
beorhtlīce 02.05.09.01 To open the eyes/be awake; 03.01.12 Brightness, light; 07.08.07 Glory, splendour, magnificence
beorhtnes 02.05.09 Faculty of sight; 02.05.09.01 To open the eyes/be awake
(ge)beorhtnes 03.01.12 Brightness, light; 16.01.01.01.01.02 Glory
beorhtnian 03.01.12 Brightness, light

(ge)beorhtnian 16.01.01.01.01.02 Glory; 16.02.04 Worship, honour, praise
beorhtrodor 01.02 Firmament
beorhtu 16.02.01.12.01 Revelation, illumination, inspiration
beorhtword 02.05.10.15 Voice, cry (of living creature)
bēorhyrde 04.01.01.07 Feasting
beorma 04.01.02.01.06 Leaven/yeast
gebeormad 04.01.02.01.07.03.01 Unleavened bread
beormas 02.03.03.06.02.01 Other peoples
beorn 02.03.01.01 Male person, man; 12.01.01.06.08 A person of rank, elder, great man; 15.01.05 Possession of wealth
beorncyning 12.01.01.04 A leader, ruler
beornice 02.03.03.05.01.09 Northumbrians
beorning/byrning 16.02.05.09.02 Incense
beornþrēat 13.02.10.01.02.01 An armed force/band
beornwiga 06.02.07.06 Courage, boldness, valour
bēorscealc 04.01.01.07 Feasting
(ge)bēorscipe 04.01.02.04.02 Feast
bēorsele 04.01.01.08 Eating place
bēorsetl 04.05.04.01 A bench, seat
bēorþegu 04.01.03 Drinking
beorþor 02.01.03.03.01 To beget
(ge)beorþor 02.01.03.03.03 Birth
beorþorcwelm 02.01.03.03.03.01 Child-bearing, childbirth
beorþorþīnen 02.01.03.03.03.01 Child-bearing, childbirth
beorþþīnenu 02.01.03.03.03.01 Child-bearing, childbirth
bēos 02.07.08 Grasses, reeds, etc.
bēost 04.01.02.01.02.09.04 Beestings (colostrum)

bēosuc 02.07.08 Grasses, reeds, etc.
bēot 11.09 Peril, danger
(ge)bēot 08.01.03.09.07 Threat, threatening, menace; 12.07.02.01.01 A promise
gebēot 07.06.03 Boastfulness, arrogance
bēotian 12.07.02.01.01 A promise
(ge)bēotian 12.07.02.01.01 A promise
(ge)bēotian (tō) 08.01.03.09.07 Threat, threatening, menace
(ge)bēotlic 07.05.03.03.01 Contumelious, scornful
bēotlīce 07.06.03 Boastfulness, arrogance; 08.01.03.09.07 Threat, threatening, menace
bēotmæcg 12.01.01.04 A leader, ruler
bēotung 02.08.02.01.03 A symptom; 08.01.03.09.07 Threat, threatening, menace
gebēotung 07.06.03 Boastfulness, arrogance
bēotword 07.06.03 Boastfulness, arrogance; 08.01.03.09.07 Threat, threatening, menace
bēoþēof 14.02.01.02 Wrongful taking, theft
bēow 04.01.02.01.03.02 Barley; 04.02.04.03.02.01.01 Barley
bēowyrt 02.07.11 Plants/flowers (alphabetical order)
bepǣcan 06.01.07.04.04.02 Pretence, feigning, dissimulation; 06.02.06.03.04 Allurement
bepǣcend 06.01.07.04 Deception; 12.08.08.01.02.01.01 An adulterer/-ess, whore, prostitute
bepǣcestre 12.08.08.01.02.01.01 An adulterer/-ess, whore, prostitute
bepǣcung 06.01.07.04 Deception

beprīwan 02.05.09.01 To open the eyes/be awake
bera 02.06.03.01.03 Bear
berǣdan 06.01.07.04.04.03 Deceit, fraud, treachery; 10.04.03.01 To take away, deprive of; 12.02.02.04 Counsel, deliberation
berǣsan 05.12.03.01.01 Quick movement or movements; 12.05.04.01.01 Fighting, a fight
beran 02.01.03 Fruitfulness, fertility; 04.04.07 Trappings, equipment, garb
beran ūp 11.03.01.01.01 Proof, demonstration
(ge)beran 02.01.03.03.02 To bring forth, produce; 05.10.05.04.02.04.02 Support, maintenance; 05.12.02.01 To fetch, bring, bear, conduct; 06.02.07.01 Strength, fortitude; 10 Having, owning, possession
geberan 02.01.03.03.01 To beget
berascin 02.06.03.01.03 Bear
geberbed 04.04.09 A fringe, border, hem
berbēne 02.07.11 Plants/flowers (alphabetical order)
bere 04.01.02.01.03.02 Barley; 04.02.04.03.02.01.01 Barley
bereærn 04.02.04.04.06 Barn
berēafere 14.02.01.02.01 Open robbery, rapine, pillage
berēafian 10.04.03.01 To take away, deprive of; 14.02.01.02.01 Open robbery, rapine, pillage
berēafigend 14.02.01.02.01 Open robbery, rapine, pillage
berebrytta 04.02.04.04.06 Barn
berēcan 03.01.09.02.01.04 Smoke; 16.02.04.18.02 Burning of incense
bereccan 09.06.02.01 To tell, make known, declare, relate, announce; 12.07.04.01 Justification

berecorn 04.02.04.03.02.01.01 Barley
berecroft 04.02.03.02.02.01 Barley land/field
gebered 05.06.05 A grinding, pounding; 08.01.03.07.02 Misery, trouble, affliction
bereflōr 04.02.04.04.05 To thresh (corn)
beregafol 15.02.04.01 Payment for temporary use, rent, hire
beregræs 04.01.02.01.04 Animal food, fodder
berehalm 04.02.04.03.02.01.01 Barley
bereland 04.02.03.02.02.01 Barley land/field
beren 04.02.04.03.02.01.01 Barley
beren brēad/hlāf 04.01.01.06.01 Abstinence from food, fast
berend 05.12.02.01 To fetch, bring, bear, conduct
berendan 05.10.05.04.13 A removal of that which obscures or conceals
berende 02.01.03 Fruitfulness, fertility
berendlīce 02.01.03 Fruitfulness, fertility
berendnes 02.01.03 Fruitfulness, fertility
berengrytta 04.02.04.03.02.01.01 Barley
berenhulu 04.02.04.03.02.01.01 Barley
berēnian 05.03.01 A cause (of anything)
berēnod 17.02.05.01 Ornamental object
berēocan 03.01.09.02.01.04 Smoke
berēofan 10.04.03.01 To take away, deprive of; 14.02.01.02.01 Open robbery, rapine, pillage
berēotan 08.01.03.04.01 Complaint, lamentation
beresǣd 04.02.04.03.02.01.01 Barley
beretūn 04.02.04.04.05 To thresh (corn); 04.02.04.04.06 Barn
berewæstm 04.02.04.03.02.01.01 Barley
berewīc 04.02 Farm

berewinde 02.07.11 Plants/flowers (alphabetical order)
berge 02.07.09.01 Berry
berian 03.03.08 Emptiness
berīdan 05.12.01.05.01 Modes of riding; 05.12.05.04 To rotate, turn round, revolve; 14.05.08 Captivity
berie 02.07.02.04 Seed, kind of seed; 02.07.09.02 Particular fruits (alphabetical order)
berigdrenc 04.01.03.05 A drink/beverage
berigeblæ 04.02.04.06.02 A fork
berind(r)an 05.10.05.04.13 A removal of that which obscures or conceals
berinnan 03.01.16.01 Moisture
berīsan 03.06.03 Congruity, fitness, suitability
bernhūs 04.02.04.04.06 Barn
berōwan 05.12.01.09.01 To row
geberst 05.12.05.03.04.01 To burst forth, break out
berstan 02.05.10.07 A crashing, noise; 14.02 Lawlessness
berstan (fram) 05.12.05.03.03 To depart, leave, set out
(ge)berstan 05.12.05.03.04.01 To burst forth, break out
berȳfan 14.02.01.02.01 Open robbery, rapine, pillage
berȳpan 14.02.01.02.01 Open robbery, rapine, pillage
besǣged 02.05.04 Sleepiness, drowsiness, sleep
besǣtian 11.09.01.01 Ambush, lying in wait
besārgian 08.01.03.04 Grief; 08.01.03.04.01 Complaint, lamentation; 08.01.03.05 Murmuring, complaint
besārgian (be/for) 08.01.02.05 Compassion

besārgung 08.01.02.05 Compassion
besāwan 04.02.04.02.03 Sowing; 05.12.05.02.04.01 To insert into (a hole)
besāwen 04.02.03.02.02 Sown part of field
bescēad 03.06.02 Difference, diversity, dissimilarity
bescēadan 03.03.07.01 Division, partition, separation; 05.12.02.07.01 To throw, scatter
bescead(uw)ian 05.10.05.04.12 The condition of being covered
besceadwung 05.10.05.04.12 The condition of being covered
besceafan 04.06.01 Clean
besceatwyrpan 12.09.01 Pledging, betrothal
bescēawere 02.05.09.05 To watch, observe, survey
bescēawian 02.05.09.05 To watch, observe, survey; 06.01.01.01.01 Thought, cogitation, meditation; 09.05.01 Inspection, examination; 11.02.02.02 Care, mindfulness, attention
bescēawiendlic 06.01.01.01.01 Thought, cogitation, meditation
bescēawigend 02.05.09.05 To watch, observe, survey
bescēawod 06.01.05.02.01.01 Sagacity
bescēawodnes 02.05.09.06 Thing seen, sight, vision
bescēawung 02.05.09.05 To watch, observe, survey
bescēotan 05.10.05.04.15 Closure, being closed; 05.12.02.07 To throw, cast, toss; 05.12.03.01.01 Quick movement or movements; 05.12.05.02.04.01 To insert into (a hole); 05.12.05.03.04 To come/go out from
bescēotan (on) 05.03.02.01.01 An event, occurrence
bescieran 02.04.04.03.05 Haircutting, tonsure; 03.03.07.01 Division, partition, separation; 16.02.04.13.03 Tonsure, haircutting, shaving
bescierian (fram/of) 10.04.03.01 To take away, deprive of
bescīnan 03.01.12.02 A beam of light
bescītan 04.06.02.02 Foul, filthy, squalid
bescoren 02.04.04.03.05 Haircutting, tonsure; 16.02.04.13.03 Tonsure, haircutting, shaving
bescrēadian 05.06.06 A scraping, scarifying
bescrepan 05.06.06 A scraping, scarifying
bescrȳdan 04.04.07 Trappings, equipment, garb
bescūfan 05.12.02.07 To throw, cast, toss; 12.05.06.03 Necessity, constraint
bescylan 02.05.09.04 To see, look upon, behold
bescyld(i)an 13.02.04 Defence, guard, protection
bescyrednes 09.07.03.01 A denial
bescyrung 16.02.04.07.05.01.02 Unfrocking
besēcan 12.03.04.01 Entreaty, solemn appeal
besecgan 11.05.02.02.01 Greetings, courteous terms of address; 12.07.03.02 An excuse
besecgan on 14.03.03.01 Accusation
besellan 05.10.05.04.11 A circle, circuit, circumference; 10.03 Giving
besencan 05.12.05.02.04.03 To plunge (something into something)
besendan (on) 05.12.02.03 To send

besengan 03.01.09.02.01 Fire, burning
besengd 03.01.09.02.01 Fire, burning
besēon 05.12.02.07.01 To throw, scatter; 05.12.05.02.03 To arrive; 11.02.02.02 Care, mindfulness, attention
besēon on/tō/wiþ 11.02.02.02 Care, mindfulness, attention
besēon (on bæc) 06.01.01.01.01 Thought, cogitation, meditation
besēon (on, tō, wiþ) 02.05.09.04 To see, look upon, behold
besēoþan 03.01.09.01.01 (Of liquids) boiling
besēowian 04.04.05.06 To sew, stitch
besett 03.01.05 Roughness
besettan 05.10.05.04.11 A circle, circuit, circumference; 10 Having, owning, possession; 13.02.03.01.02 To beset, surround; 17.02.05.01 Ornamental object
besettan ēhtnysse on 12.05.06.02.02 Persecution
besettan hiht on 06.01.08.03 Trust, faith, confidence
besettan on 05.10.05.04.01 Inside, interior
besettan tō 06.02.07 Will, determination, resolution
besibb 02.03.02.03.06 Kinship, relationship
besidian 03.05.01 Arranging, ordering, disposition
besierwan 06.01.07.04.02.01 Deception, deceit, snare, wile; 10.04.03.01 To take away, deprive of
besīgan 05.12.03.01.01 Quick movement or movements
besilfran 03.01.14.03 White/whiteness
besilfrian 17.02.05.03 A silversmith

besincan 05.12.05.13 To go down, descend
besingan 08.01.03.04.01 Complaint, lamentation; 16.01.04.01 Sorcery using incantation
besittan 10 Having, owning, possession; 13.02.03.01.02 To beset, surround
beslǣpan 02.05.04 Sleepiness, drowsiness, sleep
beslēan 05.06.02 Cleaving, splitting, cutting; 05.06.02.01 A cleft, split; 05.06.09 Act of striking; 08.01.03.07.02.01 Injury, offence
beslēan in/on 05.12.02.06 To push, impel, thrust
beslēan on 05.06.07 Pricking, a prick, puncture; 05.06.09 Act of striking
beslēpan (on) 05.10.04 Place, room
beslēpt 05.10.05.04.12 The condition of being covered
beslītan 05.06.06.01 A tearing, laceration
besma 04.06.01 Clean; 14.05.06 Means/implement of torture
besmēagan 06.01.01.01.01 Thought, cogitation, meditation
gebēsmed 05.12.01.09.02 To sail
bēsming 05.10.06.02.02 Curvature, bend, twist
besmītan 04.06.02.02 Foul, filthy, squalid; 12.08.08.01.02 Unchastity, incontinence
besmitenes 04.06.02.01 Dirty, unclean; 04.06.02.03 Stain, smear; 12.08.08.01.02 Unchastity, incontinence
besmittian 04.06.02.02 Foul, filthy, squalid; 12.08.08.01.02 Unchastity, incontinence
besmiþian 17.02.04.03 Metal worker

besmocian 02.05.08.02 Pleasant smell, fragrance, perfume; 16.02.04.18.02 Burning of incense
besmyran/besmyrwian 03.01.17.07.01 An anointing, greasing
besnædan 04.02.04.05.04.01.01 Pruning/lopping
besnīwian 01.03.01.06.04 Snow
besnyþþan 03.03.07.01 Division, partition, separation
besolcen 11.06 Disinclination to act, listlessness
besorg 08.01.02.02.01 A favourite, loved one
besorgian 06.01.08.06.02 Great fear, terror, horror; 08.01.03.03 Anxiety
bespǣtan 02.04.06.06.04 Spittle
bespanan 06.02.06.03.04 Allurement
bespanan on 05.03.01 A cause (of anything)
besparrian 05.10.05.04.15.01 A bar, bolt
besprecan 08.01.03.05 Murmuring, complaint; 09.01 To speak, exercise faculty of speech; 14.03.03 Law, action of the courts
besprecende 08.01.03.05 Murmuring, complaint
besprengan 03.01.16.05 A sprinkling
bespyrigan (yrfe) 14.03.03.02 A search for stolen property
bestǣlan (on) 14.03.03.09.01 Unfavourable judgement, condemnation
bestæppan 05.12.01.04 To go, proceed on foot; 05.12.01.04.01.02 To tread upon, trample
bestandan 02.02.05.03 To attend the dead; 08.01.03.07.02.01 Injury, offence; 11.12.02 Aid, help, succour

bestandan (ūtan) 05.10.05.04.11 A circle, circuit, circumference
bestealcian 11.09.01 Stealthiness, a stealthy act
bestefnod 04.04.09 A fringe, border, hem
bestelan 10.04.03.01 To take away, deprive of
bestelan (on) 11.09.01 Stealthiness, a stealthy act
bestelan (on weg) 11.10.05.01 Evasion, escape from threat
bestelan ūp 05.12.01.09 To travel on water; 11.09.01 Stealthiness, a stealthy act
bestingan 05.12.02.06 To push, impel, thrust
bestingan on/in/innan 05.12.02.06 To push, impel, thrust
bestrēdan 05.10.05.04.12.01 To bespread, cover with
bestrēowian 05.10.05.04.12.01 To bespread, cover with
bestreþþan 05.10.05.04.12.01 To bespread, cover with
bestrīcan 05.06.06 A scraping, scarifying
bestrīdan 05.12.01.05 To ride (on horse, etc.)
bestrīpan 14.02.01.02.01 Open robbery, rapine, pillage
bestrūdan 14.02.01.02.01 Open robbery, rapine, pillage
bestuddian 11.02.02.02 Care, mindfulness, attention
bestȳman 03.01.16.01 Moisture
bestȳpan 10.04.03.01 To take away, deprive of
bestyrian 05.10.05.04.12.01 To bespread, cover with
bestyrman 05.12.02 To move, set in motion
besūpan 04 Consumption of food/drink

besūtian 04.06.02.03 Stain, smear
beswǣlan 03.01.09.02.01 Fire, burning
beswǣtan 17.01 Strenuous effort, hard work
beswāpan 04.04.07 Trappings, equipment, garb; 06.02.06.03 Persuasion, prompting
beswelgan 05.06.01 Devastation, laying waste
beswemman 04.06.01.01 Cleansing, washing
beswencan 08.01.03.07.02 Misery, trouble, affliction
besweþþan 05.05.03 Binding, fastening; 05.10.05.04.11 A circle, circuit, circumference
beswic 06.01.07.04.02.01 Deception, deceit, snare, wile
beswica 06.01.07.04 Deception
beswīcan 04.03.04 Fowling; 06.01.07.04.01 Deception, a leading astray; 06.01.07.04.04.03 Deceit, fraud, treachery; 11.06.03 Failing, failure; 12.01.01.12.04.01 Betrayal; 13.02.07.01 A stratagem
beswīcend 06.01.07.04 Deception
beswicennes 06.01.07.04 Deception; 13.02.05.02.01 Surrender, submission
beswician 11.10.05.01 Evasion, escape from threat
beswicol 06.01.07.04 Deception
beswīcung 06.01.07.04 Deception
beswincan 04.02.04.02 Cultivation/tillage; 11.03 Endeavour; 17 Work, doings, actions, labour
beswingan 14.05.05 Physical punishments
beswylian 03.01.16.01 Moisture
besyftan 05.12.02.07.01 To throw, scatter
besylcan 02.05.03.02 Weariness

besylian 04.06.02.02 Foul, filthy, squalid; 04.06.02.03 Stain, smear; 12.08.06.01.04.01 To mislead, seduce, lead astray
bēt 11.12.02.02 Amendment, setting right, reparation
bēt getimbran 17.02.04.01 Repairing, renewing
betācnian 09.04 Sense, purport, meaning
betǣcan 04.03 Hunting, the chase; 10 Having, owning, possession; 10.03.07.01 To allot, assign; 11.10.02.02.01 Care, interest in; 12.01.01.12.04.01 Betrayal; 12.02 A public office; 12.07.02.01 Covenant, assurance of faith, promise; 15.02.04 Spending, disbursement; 16.02.04.12 Sacrifice, a sacrifice
betǣcan tō 12.05.06.04.02 Submission, subjection, obedience
betǣht 10.03.07.01 To allot, assign; 12.09.01 Pledging, betrothal
bētan more 02.07.09.02.02.01 Edible root/bulb
bētan þurst 04.01.03 Drinking
(ge)bētan 02.08.12 Healing, curing; 12.08.02.02.01 Reform, correction; 14.03.03.09.02 Atonement; 16.02.04.07.02.03 Penance, an act/instance of penance; 17.02.04.01 Repairing, renewing; 17.05.04 To kindle, set alight (fire, lamp)
gebētan 02.01.03 Fruitfulness, fertility
betboren 12.01.01.06.06 Gentle birth, nobility
bēte 02.07.09.02.02.01 Edible root/bulb
gebēted 05.11.09.06 Frequency, repetition
beteldan 05.10.05.04.11 A circle, circuit, circumference; 05.10.05.04.12.01 To

bespread, cover with; 05.12.05.04 To rotate, turn round, revolve

betellan 11.03.01.01.01 Proof, demonstration; 12.07.03.02 An excuse; 14.03.03.08 Justification

bētend 17.02.04.01 Repairing, renewing

gebētendnes 11.12.02.02 Amendment, setting right, reparation

betēon 05.10.05.04.12 The condition of being covered; 14.03.03.01 Accusation; 15.01.02 Gift, transfer of property

betera 03.03.05.01.01 Principal/chief (of its class or type)

gebetera 07.02 Goodness

beterian 17.05.04 To kindle, set alight (fire, lamp)

gebeterian 12.08.02.02.01 Reform, correction

(ge)beterung 12.08.02.02.01 Reform, correction

betihtlian 14.03.03.01 Accusation

betimbran 04.05 Building, construction

betlic 07.02.04.03 Nobleness, excellence, nobility, magnificence

bētnes 16.02.04.07.02.03 Penance, an act/instance of penance

betogen 05.10.05.04.12 The condition of being covered

betogennes 14.03.03.01 Accusation

betonice 02.07.11 Plants/flowers (alphabetical order)

betre/furþor dōn 07.01.01.02 To prefer

betredan 05.10.05.04.12 The condition of being covered

betrendan 05.12.05.04.01 (Of wheel, etc.) to roll, trundle

betreppan 04.03.02 A snare, trap, noose

betrymman 13.02.03.01.02 To beset, surround

betst 03.03.05.01.01 Principal/chief (of its class or type)

betstboren 02.03.02.02 Child, offspring; 12.01.01.06.01 Rank, position due to birth; 12.01.01.06.06 Gentle birth, nobility

gebētung 17.02.04.01 Repairing, renewing

betwēoh 03.03.06.01 A whole formed by joining; 05.10.05.04.10 Among; 05.10.05.04.10.01 Interposed; 05.11 A time, period of time

betwēoh þǣm þe 05.11 A time, period of time

betwēohblinnes 05.11.11.02 Let up, intermission, cessation

betwēohceorfan 05.06.02 Cleaving, splitting, cutting

betwēohgangende 03.03.07.01 Division, partition, separation

betwēonan 03.03.06.01 A whole formed by joining; 05.10.05.04.10 Among; 05.10.05.04.10.01 Interposed; 05.11 A time, period of time; 05.13.03 Regular alternation

betwēonanforlǣtnes 05.11.11.02 Let up, intermission, cessation

betwux 03.03.06.01 A whole formed by joining; 05.10.05.04.10 Among; 05.10.05.04.10.01 Interposed; 05.11 A time, period of time

betwux licgan 05.10.05.04.10.01 Interposed

betwuxālegednes 09.03.02.02.01.05 Minor parts of speech, etc.

betwuxāworpennes 09.03.02.02.01.05 Minor parts of speech, etc.

betwuxgesett 05.10.05.04.10.01 Interposed

betyllan 06.02.06.03.04 Allurement

betȳnan 04.05.01.02.07 A fence, hedge; 05.10.05.04.15 Closure, being closed; 05.11.10.02 End, completion; 14.05.08.01 Prison, confinement, durance

betȳnung 09.01.01 A speech, what is said, words

betyran 03.01.14.04 Black/blackness; 03.01.17.06.01 Bitumen, pitch

betyrnan 05.12.05.04 To rotate, turn round, revolve; 07.04.03 Reverence, respect

betyrned 07.04.03 Reverence, respect

beþearfende 15.01.06 Poverty, indigence

beþearflic 11.07.03 Use, advantage, profit

beþearfod 15.01.06 Poverty, indigence

beþeccan 05.10.05.04.12 The condition of being covered

beþencan 06.01.08.03 Trust, faith, confidence

beþencan (ymbe) 06.01.01.01.01 Thought, cogitation, meditation

beþennan 05.10.05.04.12 The condition of being covered

beþēodan 03.03.06.01 A whole formed by joining

beþerscan 13.02.05.01.01 To overcome, conquer

beþettan 02.08.12.02.05.04 To cleanse, clean away

(ge)beþian 02.08.12.02.05.04 To cleanse, clean away; 03.01.09.01 Warmth, heat

beþrāwan 05.10.06.02.03 A circular fold, coil

beþridian 12.05.06.03 Necessity, constraint; 13.02.05.01.01 To overcome, conquer

beþringan 05.10.05.04.11 A circle, circuit, circumference; 05.12.05.04 To rotate, turn round, revolve

beþryccan 05.06.05.03 Bruising, crushing

beþrȳd 05.06.05.03 Bruising, crushing

beþung 02.08.12.02.05.04 To cleanse, clean away

beþurfan 06.02.04.01 Want, need

beþwēan 03.01.16.01 Moisture

beþwȳrian 12.08.08.01.02 Unchastity, incontinence

beþyddan 05.12.02.06 To push, impel, thrust

beþyrfing 10.02 Want, lack

bewacian 11.10.02 Watching, guard, watch

bewadan 05.12.05.02.01 To come upon, meet with

bewǣfan 04.04.07 Trappings, equipment, garb

bewǣgan 06.01.07.04 Deception

bewǣgnan 10.03.02 Presenting, offering

bewǣlan 08.01.03.07.02 Misery, trouble, affliction

bewǣpnian 13.02.08.03.01 Body armour, war gear

bewǣrlan 05.12.05.07.01 To pass by; 11.06.06 Turning

bewarenian 06.01.01.02 Care, attention, observation; 11.10.05.01 Evasion, escape from threat

bewarenian (wiþ) 11.10.01 Protection, safekeeping

bewarian 11.10.01 Protection, safekeeping; 11.10.05.01 Evasion, escape from threat

bewarian wiþ 11.10.02.01 Vigilance

bewāwen 05.06.01 Devastation, laying waste

bewealcan 14.03.03.01 Accusation

beweallan 03.01.09.01.01 (Of liquids) boiling

bewealwian 04.06.02.02 Foul, filthy, squalid
beweardian 06.01.01.02 Care, attention, observation; 11.10.01 Protection, safekeeping
beweaxan 02.07.01 To grow; 05.10.05.04.11 A circle, circuit, circumference
beweddenlic 12.09 Marriage, state of marriage
beweddian 12.09.01 Pledging, betrothal; 14.03.03.07 Security, pledge, bail
beweddod 12.09 Marriage, state of marriage; 12.09.01 Pledging, betrothal
beweddung 12.09.01 Pledging, betrothal
bewefan 05.10.05.04.12 The condition of being covered
bewegan 05.10.05.04.12 The condition of being covered
bewegan ūtan 05.10.05.04.11 A circle, circuit, circumference
bewēled 04.06.02.06 Poison
bewendan 05.12.05 To move and change direction, turn; 11.02.02.02.01 Attention, cultivation
bewenian 08.01.02.04 Hospitality
beweorpan 05.10.05.04.11 A circle, circuit, circumference; 05.10.05.04.12 The condition of being covered; 05.12.02.07 To throw, cast, toss
beweorpan on 05.12.05.02.04.03 To plunge (something into something)
beweorþian 07.08.04 An ornament, honour, glory
bewēpan 08.01.03.04.01 Complaint, lamentation
bewēpendlic 08.01.03.04 Grief
bewerenes 12.03.06 Prohibition
bewerian 11.10.01 Protection, safekeeping; 11.10.05.01 Evasion, escape from threat; 12.03.06 Prohibition
bewerian (fram) 12.05.06.01 Restraint, check, curb, control
bewerian ongēan/wiþ 11.10.01 Protection, safekeeping
bewerigend 11.10.01 Protection, safekeeping
bewerung 11.10.01 Protection, safekeeping
bewīcian 13.02.07.04 A camp, encampment
bewindan 05.10.05.04.11 A circle, circuit, circumference; 05.10.05.04.12 The condition of being covered; 06.01.01.01.01 Thought, cogitation, meditation
bewitan 11.10.02 Watching, guard, watch
bewitian 02.05.09.05 To watch, observe, survey; 11.01.02 An undertaking; 11.02.02.02 Care, mindfulness, attention
bewlātian 02.05.09.04 To see, look upon, behold
bewlītan 02.05.09.04 To see, look upon, behold
bewōpen 08.01.03.04.02 Shedding of tears
bewrecan 05.06.09 Act of striking; 05.12.02.04 To cast out, drive away; 05.12.02.06.01 To push, drive
bewrencan 06.01.07.04 Deception
bewrēon 04.04.07 Trappings, equipment, garb; 05.10.05.04.12 The condition of being covered; 09.05.04.01 Concealment, obscurity; 11.10.01 Protection, safekeeping
bewreþian 05.10.05.04.02.04.02 Support, maintenance

bewrigennes 05.10.05.04.12 The condition of being covered
bewrītan 05.06.06 A scraping, scarifying; 09.03.07.05 To cover with writing, inscribe
bewrīþan 05.10.05.04.11 A circle, circuit, circumference; 05.10.05.04.12 The condition of being covered
bewrixl(i)an 05.13 Changeableness, change; 05.13.04 Exchange, commutation
bewuna 11.05 Natural/proper way/manner/mode of action
bewyllan 03.01.09.01.01 (Of liquids) boiling
bewylwian 05.12.05.13.03 To fall
bewyrcan 05.05 Constitution, founding (e.g. of world); 05.10.05.04.15 Closure, being closed; 13.02.06 A fortification; 14.05.08.01 Prison, confinement, durance
bewyrcan mid 17.02.05.01 Ornamental object
beyrfeweardian 15.01.02.01 Inherited property
bibliopēca 16.02.05.10.05 A bible
bibliopēce 09.03.07.07.01 A library, collection of books; 16.02.01.08 Scripture, the scriptures
bicce 02.06.02.01.04 Dog
(ge)bīcn(i)an 09.03.03 A gesture, action, gesticulation; 09.05.05.01 Showing, manifestation, display; 12.03.03.01 Summons, a call, summoning
gebīcn(i)an 09.03.04.02.01 A figure; 09.03.07.04 To make a symbol, mark
bīcn(ig)end 02.04.03.04.01.01.01 Finger; 09.04.03.03 A commentary, exposition
gebīcn(ig)end 09.03.07.04 To make a symbol, mark

bīcn(ig)endlic 09.03.02.03.01.02.01 Mood
(ge)bīcn(ig)endlic 09.03.04.02.01 A figure
bīcnol 09.03.07.04 To make a symbol, mark
bīcnung 09.04.01 Signal, signalling
(ge)bīcnung 09.03.04.02.01 A figure
gebīcnung 06.01.08.04.01 Premonition, prophecy
bīcwide 09.06.01.02 A saying, saw, proverb, maxim
(ge)bīdan 05.03.02 Event, issue, result; 05.12.04 Absence of movement, stillness; 06.01.08.01 Expectation, waiting; 11.06 Disinclination to act, listlessness
gebīdan 02.01.02.02.02 Lifetime; 10.01.02 Acquisition
gebīdan (mid) 11.12.02.01 Strengthening, confirmation
biddan 12.03.03 A command, bidding, order
(ge)biddan 12.03.04 A request, prayer; 16.02.04.08 Prayer
gebiddan 16.02.04 Worship, honour, praise
biddend 12.03.04 A request, prayer
(ge)biddend 16.02.04.08 Prayer
gebiddend 16.02.04 Worship, honour, praise
biddende 16.02.04.08 Prayer
biddere 12.03.04 A request, prayer
bīdfæst 05.12.04.01 Stability, firmness
bīding 05.11.11.02 Let up, intermission, cessation
bīdsteall gifan 12.05.05 Resistance, repulsing

bīegan 05.10.06.02.02 Curvature, bend, twist; 05.12.05 To move and change direction, turn
bīegan fram 05.12.02.08 To give a different direction to, turn
(ge)bīegan 05.10.06.02.02 Curvature, bend, twist; 05.12.05.13.02 To bow, bend down; 07.09.02 Disgrace, shaming, humiliation; 09.03.02.03.01.01 Declension; 13.02.05.01.01 To overcome, conquer; 16.02.04.10.01 Conversion
(ge)bīegan mōd 06.02.06 Mind, purpose
gebīegan 07.04.03 Reverence, respect; 11.05.02 Mode, manner, way, method, fashion, course
gebīegan tō fulluhte 16.02.04.10.01 Conversion
gebīegan tō gelēafan 16.02.04.10.01 Conversion
gebīeged 05.10.06.02.02 Curvature, bend, twist
(ge)bieldan 06.02.07.06.01 Emboldening, encouragement
bield(o) 06.02.07.02 Constancy
(ge)bield(o) 06.02.07.06 Courage, boldness, valour
bīeme 18.02.07.02.02.02 A trumpet
(ge)bierhtan 03.01.12 Brightness, light; 07.04.04 Praise, acclamation, applause; 07.08.07 Glory, splendour, magnificence
gebierhtan 07.08.05 Glorifying, making great, glorification
bierhtu 03.01.12 Brightness, light
biernan 02.08.03.02 Itch, irritation; 17.05.04 To kindle, set alight (fire, lamp)

(ge)biernan 03.01.09.02 Fire, flame; 03.01.09.02.01 Fire, burning; 05.08.02 Violence, force
biernende 03.01.09 Heat; 03.01.09.02.01 Fire, burning; 05.08.02 Violence, force
bīetl 17.03.08 A hammer, mallet
bīferan 04.01.02.04.04 To maintain, support, provide for
bifian 06.01.08.06.01 A shuddering with fear, nervousness
(ge)bifian 05.12.05.05 To shake, quake, wag
bifigende 06.01.08.06.03.01 Causing dread, terrifying
bifigendlic 06.01.08.06.03.01 Causing dread, terrifying
bifung 06.01.08.06.01 A shuddering with fear, nervousness
bīfylce 12.06.03.03 A neighbour
gebīgan 03.06.03 Congruity, fitness, suitability
bige 15.05 Trade, traffic, commerce
gebīgednes 05.10.06.02.02 Curvature, bend, twist; 09.03.02.03.01.01.01 Case
bīgels 04.05.02.03 An arch, vault; 05.10.06.02.02 Curvature, bend, twist
bīgendlic 02.04.02.04 Flexibility of limbs, suppleness
gebīgendlic 09.03.02.03.01.01 Declension
bīgeng 04.02.04.02 Cultivation/tillage
bigenga 08.01.02.01 Favour, kindness, grace
bīgenga 02.03.03.04 An inhabitant; 04.02.02 Farmer, cultivator; 04.02.04.02 Cultivation/tillage; 04.05.03.01 Habitation, sojourn; 16.02.04 Worship, honour, praise
bigeng(e) 16.02.04 Worship, honour, praise

bīgengere 16.02.04 Worship, honour, praise; 17.02.01 Management of work
bīgengestre 16.02.04 Worship, honour, praise
bīging 05.10.06.02.02 Curvature, bend, twist
bīgnes 03.01.04.01 Power of bending, flexibility; 05.10.06.02.02 Curvature, bend, twist
bigsæc 14.03.03 Law, action of the courts
bigspellbōc 16.02.01.08.01.01 Books of the Old Testament
bigswic 12.01.01.12.04 Treachery
bīgyrdel 15.01.03 Treasure, riches, wealth; 15.01.04 Coinage, money
bile 02.06.01.02 Head; 05.12.01.09.03.01.03 Part of ship
bīleofa 04.01.02 Means of subsistence; 04.01.02.01 Food/sustenance; 15.02.04 Spending, disbursement
bilewit 06.01.07.04.04.02.01 Hypocrisy; 07.07.01 Simplicity, mildness; 12.08.05 Innocence
bilewitlīce 07.07.01 Simplicity, mildness; 08.01.02.01 Favour, kindness, grace; 12.08.02.03.01 Honourable conduct, dignity
bilewitnes 07.07.01 Simplicity, mildness; 12.08.05 Innocence
bill 04.02.04.05.04.01.01 Pruning/lopping; 13.02.08.04.03 A sword; 17.03.03 A cutting tool
billere 02.07.09.02.02.02 Other vegetables (alphabetical order)
billgesliht 13.02.02 Battle
billhete 12.05.04 Strife, hostility
gebilod 02.06.08.01 Part of bird
bilswæþ 02.08.04.01 A wound
bīnama 09.03.02.02.01.01 A noun

gebind 02.08.08.12 Disease of bowels; 03.03.01.02 Dry measures; 05.05.03 Binding, fastening
bindan 17.04.04 Fibrous materials
(ge)bindan 03.03.06.01 A whole formed by joining; 05.05.03 Binding, fastening; 11.11.02 A hindrance; 14.05.07 Binding, fastening with bonds
gebindan 06.02.06.03.04 Allurement; 08.01.03.07.02 Misery, trouble, affliction
binde 04.04.07.11 A headcloth, covering for the head
bindele 02.08.12.02.06.01 A bandage, binding; 14.05.07 Binding, fastening with bonds
bindere 05.05.03 Binding, fastening
binding 05.05.03 Binding, fastening
bing 01.01.02.01.03.03 Valley
binn 04.01.02.02.06.03 Food receptacle, basket; 04.02.05.03.02 A byre, stall, sty, shed
binnan 05.10.05.04.01 Inside, interior; 05.11 A time, period of time
binnan gemǣre 12.06.04 Native land
binnan gemǣrum 12.06.04 Native land
bircen 02.07.03.05 Particular trees/shrubs (alphabetical order)
bircett 02.07.03.05 Particular trees/shrubs (alphabetical order)
biren 02.06.03.01.03 Bear
biren(e)/byrene 02.06.03.01.03 Bear
gebirg 02.05.07 Faculty of taste
(ge)birgan 02.05.07 Faculty of taste
(ge)birging 02.05.07 Faculty of taste
birgnes 02.05.07 Faculty of taste
birihte 05.10.05.04.09 Side, quarter, direction
gebirman 04.01.02.01.07.03.01 Unleavened bread;

04.01.02.02.05.04.01 Preparation of bread; 11.01.03 Preparation
gebirmed 04.01.02.01.07.03.01 Unleavened bread; 07.06.01.01 Proud, arrogant
bīsæc 12.05.01 Rivalry, contest
bīsæcc 15.01.04 Coinage, money
bisceop 16.02.03.02.01 A high priest, chief bishop, etc. (general); 16.02.03.02.05 A bishop
bisceopcynn 16.02.03.02.01 A high priest, chief bishop, etc. (general)
bisceopdōm 16.02.03.02.05 A bishop; 16.02.04.19 Excommunication
bisceopealdor 16.02.03.02.01 A high priest, chief bishop, etc. (general)
bisceopes þegn 16.02.03.02.05 A bishop
bisceopfolgoþ 16.02.03.02.05 A bishop
bisceopgegyrelan 16.02.05.06 Ritual clothing
bisceophād 16.02.03.02.05 A bishop; 16.02.04.07.05.01 Ordination
bisceophādþegnung 16.02.03.02.05 A bishop
bisceophādung 16.02.04.07.05.01 Ordination
bisceophālgung 16.02.04.07.05.01 Ordination
bisceophām 16.02.05.01 Land
bisceophēafodlīn 16.02.05.06.03 Headgear
bisceophīred 16.02.03.02.05 A bishop
(ge)bisceopian 16.02.04.07.03 Confirmation
bisceopland 16.02.05.01 Land
bisceoplic 16.02.03.02.05 A bishop
bisceoplices 16.02.03.02.05 A bishop
bisceoprīce 16.02.03.02.05 A bishop; 16.02.05.01 Land

bisceoprocc 16.02.05.06.01 Outer garments
bisceoprōd 16.02.05.06.02 Garb for neck and shoulders
bisceopscīr 16.02.03.02.05 A bishop
bisceopseld 16.02.03.02.05 A bishop
bisceopseonoþ 16.02.03.01 Ecclesiastical authority
bisceopstæf 16.02.05.05.08 A staff, wand of authority
bisceopstōl 12.06.02.01 A township; 16.02.03.02.05 A bishop; 16.02.05.05.05 A chair
bisceopsunu 02.03.02.05 Spiritual relationships; 16.02.04.07.01 Baptism, baptizing (and anointing)
bisceopþegnung 16.02.03.02.05 A bishop
bisceopung 16.02.04.07.03 Confirmation
bisceopweorod 16.02.03.02.05 A bishop
bisceopwīte 14.05.04.01 A fine
bisceopwyrt 02.07.11 Plants/flowers (alphabetical order)
bisceopwyrtel 02.07.11 Plants/flowers (alphabetical order)
bīsen 09.03.04.02.01 A figure; 09.06.01 To relate, recount, tell; 11.05.02.01 A standard, norm, ethos; 14.01.06 A rule, order, precept, tenet, principle
bīsen (on)stellan 11.05.02.01 A standard, norm, ethos
bisene 02.08.07.02.01 Defective vision
bīsenian 09.03.04.02.01 A figure
(ge)bīsenian 11.05.02.01 A standard, norm, ethos
bises 05.11.06.02.02.01 Adjustment in calculation
(ge)bisgian 08.01.03.07.02 Misery, trouble, affliction; 11.02 Occupation, activity, business

bisgu 08.01.03.07.02 Misery, trouble, affliction; 11.02 Occupation, activity, business
bisgung 11.02 Occupation, activity, business
bisig 11.02 Occupation, activity, business
bisignes 17.02.02 An office, function, employment
bismer 07.03.05 Infamy, shame, wickedness; 07.05.03.03 Scorn, insult, abuse; 07.09 Shame, disgrace; 07.09.03 Infamy, ignominy, shame; 16.02.04.14.01 Blasphemy
bismerful 07.09 Shame, disgrace
bismerglēow 12.08.08.01 Eager, unseemly desire
(ge)bismerian 06.01.07.04.01 Deception, a leading astray; 07.05.04 Mockery, derision, scorn; 16.02.04.14.01 Blasphemy
bismerlēas 12.08.05.01 Blameless
bismerlēoþ 09.03.05.01.01 Poetry
bismerlic 07.09 Shame, disgrace; 08.01.01.03.07.01 Laughter
bismerlīce 07.09 Shame, disgrace; 16.02.04.14.01 Blasphemy
bismernes 07.05.03.03 Scorn, insult, abuse; 12.08.08.01.02 Unchastity, incontinence; 16.02.01.11.02 Impiety, lack of piety
bismersp(r)ǣc 16.02.04.14.01 Blasphemy
bismerung 07.09.03 Infamy, ignominy, shame; 16.02.04.14.01 Blasphemy
(ge)bismerung 07.05.04 Mockery, derision, scorn
bismerword 07.05.03.03 Scorn, insult, abuse
gebīsnere 03.06.01.01 Imitation

bīsnung 11.03.01.01.01 Proof, demonstration; 11.05.02.01 A standard, norm, ethos
bīspell 09.06.01 To relate, recount, tell; 16.02.01.08.03 The New Testament
bissextus 05.11.06.02.02.01 Adjustment in calculation
bita 02.06 Animal; 04.01.02.04 Abundance of food
bītan 02.08.04.01 A wound
bītan tēþ 08.01.03.05.02 Anger
(ge)bītan 05.06.06.01 A tearing, laceration
bite 02.08.02.01.02 Onset, attack of illness; 02.08.03.02 Itch, irritation; 02.08.04 Hurt, injury, damage; 02.08.08 Internal disease; 05.06.01 Devastation, laying waste
bitela 02.06.09.02.03 Beetle
bītende 02.05.07.01 Strong taste, acidity, pungency
biter 02.05.07.01 Strong taste, acidity, pungency; 08.01.03.07.04 Severity, harshness; 08.01.03.09.01.02 Bitterness, acrimony
biterian 08.01.03.09.01.02 Bitterness, acrimony
biterlic 08.01.03.09.01.02 Bitterness, acrimony
biterlīce 08.01.03.04.01 Complaint, lamentation; 08.01.03.07.04 Severity, harshness
biternes 02.05.07.01 Strong taste, acidity, pungency; 08.01.03.09.01.02 Bitterness, acrimony
gebiterod 02.05.07.01 Strong taste, acidity, pungency
biterwyrde 08.01.03.09.01.03 Sharpness (of speech)
bitmǣlum 03.03.07 A part, division, portion

bitol 04.02.05.06.05.03.01 Bridle/halter/curb/muzzle
bitre 03.03.04.01 Much; 08.01.03.07.03 Suffering, torment, pain; 08.01.03.07.04 Severity, harshness; 08.01.03.09.11 Hardheartedness, cruelty, severity
bitrum 08.01.03.07.04 Severity, harshness
bit(t)ernes 08.01.03.04 Grief
biwinþla 02.07.03.04.03 A hedge/border
bīwist 04.01.02.01 Food/sustenance
bīword 09.03.02.02.01.03 An adverb; 09.06.01.02 A saying, saw, proverb, maxim
bīwyrde 09.06.01.02 A saying, saw, proverb, maxim
bizant 15.01.04 Coinage, money
blāc 03.01.12.01 Glittering, effulgence; 03.01.14.02 Pallor, absence of colour
blāchlēor 02.04.04.01 Having a certain complexion
blācian 03.01.14.02 Pallor, absence of colour
blācung 03.01.14.02 Pallor, absence of colour
bladesian 02.05.08 Faculty of smell; 03.01.09.02 Fire, flame
bladesnung 02.05.08 Faculty of smell
bladesung 01.03.01.03.01.02 Lightning
blæc 02.04.04.01 Having a certain complexion; 02.04.04.03.02 Colour of hair; 03.01.14.04 Black/blackness; 09.03.07.06.02 Ink
blæc/blac 03.01.14.04 Black/blackness
blæc gymm 17.04.03.04 Gems collectively
blæc pipor 04.01.02.01.05.05.03 Pepper
blæc 03.01.12 Brightness, light; 03.01.14.02 Pallor, absence of colour

blǣcan 03.01.14.03 White/whiteness
(ge)blǣcan 03.01.14.02 Pallor, absence of colour
geblǣcan 02.08.04.02.01 A maimed man
blæcberie 02.07.09.02 Particular fruits (alphabetical order)
blæcce 03.01.14.04 Black/blackness
blǣce 02.08.06 Skin disease, erysipelas
blǣcern 03.01.12.02 A beam of light; 17.05.03 Sources of fire/light
blǣcernlēoht 03.01.12.02 A beam of light
blæcfexede 02.04.04.03.02 Colour of hair
blæchorn 09.03.07.06.02 Ink
blǣco 03.01.14.02 Pallor, absence of colour
blǣcpytt 04.04.02 A bleaching-pit
blǣcþa 02.08.06 Skin disease, erysipelas
blæcþorn 02.07.03.05 Particular trees/shrubs (alphabetical order)
blǣcþrūstfel 02.08.06 Skin disease, erysipelas
blæd 02.07.02.05 A shoot, sprout, tendril; 05.12.01.09.03.01.03 Part of ship
blǣd 01.03.01.05 Wind; 02.01.01 Life, vital part; 02.04.06.07.03 Breath; 03.01.09.02 Fire, flame; 07.06 Pride; 08.01.01.03.08.02 Good fortune, success
blǣdāgende 07.08.08 Nobleness, honour, glory
geblǣdan 03.01.15.01 Inspiration, inbreathing
blǣdbylig 17.05.02 A hearth, fireplace
blǣddæg 08.01.01.03.08 Happiness, well-being, prosperity
blædderwærc 02.08.08.12 Disease of bowels
(ge)blǣdfæst 08.01.01.03.08.02 Good fortune, success

geblædfæstnes 08.01.01.03.08.02 Good fortune, success
blædgifa 16.01.01.02.02 A giving (by Deity)
blædhorn 18.02.07.02.02.02 A trumpet
blædnes 02.07.02.07 Blossom, flower(s)
blædre 02.04.06.05.05 Bladder; 02.08.05.01 Swelling
blædwela 08.01.01.03.08 Happiness, well-being, prosperity
blæge 02.06.06.02.01.03 Gudgeon, bleak
blægettende 02.05.10.15.01 To raise (the voice), raise up (noise)
blæhæwen 03.01.14.08 A blue dye, woad
blæse 08.01.01.01 Ardour, fervour, strong feeling; 17.05.03 Sources of fire/light
blæsere 14.02.01.01 Types of crime
blæshorn 18.02.07.02.02.02 A trumpet
blæst 01.03.01.05 Wind; 03.01.09.02 Fire, flame
blæstan 05.12.03.01.01 Quick movement or movements
blæstbelg 17.05.02 A hearth, fireplace
blæstm 03.01.09.02 Fire, flame
blætan 02.05.10.15.06 A roar, howl, etc.
blanca 02.06.02.01.06 Horse
(ge)bland 03.03.06.01.01 Mixing, mingling, preparation
gebland 01.01.03.01.02.06 Surging, rolling, heaving of waves
(ge)blandan 03.03.06.01.01 Mixing, mingling, preparation; 11.01.03 Preparation
geblandan 05.12.02 To move, set in motion; 12.08.06.01.04.01 To mislead, seduce, lead astray
geblanden 04.06.02.01 Dirty, unclean
blandenfeax 02.04.04.03.02 Colour of hair
blāt 03.01.14.02 Pallor, absence of colour
blāte 03.01.14.02 Pallor, absence of colour
blātende 03.01.14.02 Pallor, absence of colour
blāwan 02.04.06.07.05 To breathe; 03.01.15.01 Inspiration, inbreathing; 17.02.04.03.03 Smelting, heating, scorification
blāwan ... on 05.12.05.02.04.01 To insert into (a hole)
blāwan mid 18.02.07.02.02.02 A trumpet
(ge)blāwan 01.03.01.05 Wind; 02.01.02.02 To come to life, have life; 02.04.06.07.05 To breathe; 03.01.09.02 Fire, flame; 03.01.15.01 Inspiration, inbreathing; 18.02.07.02.02.02 A trumpet
geblāwan 02.04.06.06.04 Spittle; 06.01.08.02 Hope, expectation; 17.02.04.03.03 Smelting, heating, scorification
blāwend 16.01.01.02.01 Creator
blāwende 01.03.01.05 Wind; 03.01.15.01 Inspiration, inbreathing; 18.02.07.02.02.02 A trumpet
blāwere 17.05.02 A hearth, fireplace
blāwung 01.03.01.05 Wind; 02.08.05.01 Swelling; 18.02.07.02.02.02 A trumpet
blēat 08.01.03.06 Adversity, affliction
blēate 08.01.03.06 Adversity, affliction
blēaþ 06.01.08.06.06 Timidity; 11.06 Disinclination to act, listlessness
blēd 02.07.01 To grow; 02.07.09 Fruit; 04.02.04.04 Harvest, crop
blēdan 02.04.06.08.01 Blood; 02.08.08.12 Disease of bowels
blēdhwæt 02.07.01 To grow
bledu 04.01.02.02.06.05.04 Cup/bowl/basin

blegen 02.08.05.02 Particular inflammation/swelling
geblegenod 02.08.05.02 Particular inflammation/swelling
blencan 06.01.07.04 Deception
(ge)blendan 03.03.06.01.01 Mixing, mingling, preparation
geblendan 06.01.05.03 Want of understanding
(ge)blend(i)an 02.08.07.02.01 Defective vision
blendnes 02.08.07.02.01 Defective vision
blēo 02.05.09.07 Form, appearance, aspect; 05.10.06 Form, shape
(ge)blēo 03.01.14 A colour
blēobord 18.02.02.01 Gaming, playing at dice
blēobrygd 03.01.14.11 Medley/variety of colour
blēocræft 04.04.05.07 Embroidery
geblēod 03.01.14 A colour; 03.01.14.11 Medley/variety of colour; 07.10 Beauty, fairness
bleodu 04.01.02.01.03 Corn; 04.02.04.03.02.01 Grain crops
blēofæstnes 08.01.01.03.05 Pleasure, delight
blēofāg 03.01.14.11 Medley/variety of colour
blēomete 04.01.02.01.07.05 Delicacy/dainty/titbit
blēorēad 03.01.14.05 Red/redness
blēostǣning 04.05.02.10 Flooring, a floor
blere 02.04.04.03.04 Bald, shaven
blerig 02.04.04.03.04 Bald, shaven
blerig pyttel 02.06.08.04 Bird of prey
(ge)bletsian 07.04.04 Praise, acclamation, applause; 10.03.01 Grace, favour; 16.02.01.10 Holiness; 16.02.01.10.02 Consecration; 16.02.01.10.02.01 A blessing, invocation of divine favour; 16.02.04 Worship, honour, praise; 16.02.04.18.01 Sign of the cross
bletsingsealm 16.02.04.03.03.01 A hymn, song of praise, canticle
gebletsod 16.02.01.10 Holiness; 16.02.01.10.02.01 A blessing, invocation of divine favour
bletsung 08.01.01.03.08.03 A favour, blessing; 16.02.04 Worship, honour, praise; 16.02.04.18.01 Sign of the cross
(ge)bletsung 16.02.01.10.02 Consecration; 16.02.01.10.02.01 A blessing, invocation of divine favour
bletsungbōc 16.02.05.10.01 Service books
blīcan 02.05.09.06 Thing seen, sight, vision; 03.01.12.01 Glittering, effulgence
bliccettan 03.01.12.01 Glittering, effulgence; 05.12.05.05 To shake, quake, wag
bliccettung 03.01.12.01 Glittering, effulgence
blice 05.10.05.04.13 A removal of that which obscures or conceals
blic(i)an 03.01.12 Brightness, light
blind 02.07.11 Plants/flowers (alphabetical order); 02.08.07.02.01 Defective vision; 03.01.13 Darkness, obscurity; 03.01.13.01 Not shining, dim; 05.10.05.04.15 Closure, being closed; 06.01.05.03 Want of understanding
blind netel 02.07.11 Plants/flowers (alphabetical order)
blind þearm 02.04.06.03.02.04 Intestines
blind(ā)boren 02.08.07.02.01 Defective vision

blind(e) netel 02.07.11 Plants/flowers (alphabetical order)
geblindfellian 02.05.09.02 Inability to see (because of darkness)
blindlīce 11.02.04.01 Rashness, madness
blindnes 02.05.09.02 Inability to see (because of darkness); 02.08.07.02.01 Defective vision; 03.01.13 Darkness, obscurity; 06.01.05.03 Want of understanding
blinn 05.11.10.02 End, completion
blinnan 10.02.01.01 Loss, forfeiture; 12.02 A public office
(ge)blinnan 05.07 Ending of existence, end of world; 11.06.04 Abstention, abstaining from
blinnes 05.11.11.02 Let up, intermission, cessation
blisful 08.01.01.03.08.03 A favour, blessing
blisgere 14.02.01.01 Types of crime
bliss 08.01.01.03 Good feeling, joy, happiness; 08.01.02.01 Favour, kindness, grace
(ge)blissian 08.01.01.03.06 Exultation, joy; 08.01.01.03.09.03 To make glad
(ge)blissian (be/for/ofer/on) 16.02.04 Worship, honour, praise
geblissian 08.01.01.03.03 Happiness, blessedness
blissig 08.01.01.03 Good feeling, joy, happiness
blissigendlic 08.01.01.03 Good feeling, joy, happiness; 08.01.01.03.06 Exultation, joy
(ge)blissung 08.01.01.03.06 Exultation, joy
blīþe 05.09.02 Mildness, moderate quality; 05.12.04 Absence of movement, stillness; 08.01.01.03 Good feeling, joy, happiness; 08.01.02.03.02 Friendly, amiable; 08.01.02.03.03 In a friendly manner, kindly
(ge)blīþe 08.01.01.03 Good feeling, joy, happiness
blīþelic 05.09.02 Mildness, moderate quality
blīþelīce 06.02.02.01 Will, wish, pleasure; 08.01.01.03 Good feeling, joy, happiness
blīþemōd 08.01.01.03 Good feeling, joy, happiness; 08.01.02.03.02 Friendly, amiable
blīþheort 08.01.01.03 Good feeling, joy, happiness; 08.01.02.01 Favour, kindness, grace
(ge)blīþian 08.01.01.03.06 Exultation, joy; 08.01.01.03.09.03 To make glad
blīþnes 08.01.01.03 Good feeling, joy, happiness
blīþsian 08.01.01.03.06 Exultation, joy
blōd 02.04.06.08.01 Blood
blōd gespillian 02.02.04.03 To kill, slay
blōddolg 02.08.04.01 A wound
blōddrync 02.02.04 Killing, violent death, destruction; 13.02.02 Battle
blōdegesa 06.01.08.06.03 Cause of fear, terror, horror
blōden 02.04.06.08.01 Blood
blōdes flōwnes 02.08.08.12 Disease of bowels
blōdes gyte 02.08.08.12 Disease of bowels
blōdfāg 04.06.02.03 Stain, smear
blōdgemang 02.04.06.08.01 Blood; 03.03.06.01.01 Mixing, mingling, preparation
blōdgēotend 02.02.04.03.01 A killer

blōdgēotende 02.02.04.02 Murderous, bloodthirsty
blōdgian 08.01.03.09.11 Hardheartedness, cruelty, severity
(ge)blōdgian 03.01.14.05 Red/redness; 04.06.02.03 Stain, smear
blōdgyte 02.02.04 Killing, violent death, destruction; 02.08.08.12 Disease of bowels; 13.02.02 Battle
blōdhrǣcung 02.08.08.02 Lung disease
blōdhrēow 08.01.03.09.11 Hardheartedness, cruelty, severity
blōdig 02.04.06.08.01 Blood; 03.01.14.05 Red/redness; 04.06.02.03 Stain, smear; 08.01.03.09.11 Hardheartedness, cruelty, severity; 13.02.02 Battle
blōdig ūtsiht 02.08.08.12 Disease of bowels
(ge)blōdigian 03.01.14.05 Red/redness
blōdigtōþ 08.01.03.09.11 Hardheartedness, cruelty, severity
blōdiorn/blōdryne 02.08.08.12 Disease of bowels
blōdlǣstīd 02.08.12.02.06 Surgical
blōdlǣs(wu) 02.08.12.02.06 Surgical
blōdlǣte 02.08.12.02.06 Surgical
blodlǣtere 02.08.12.02.06 Surgical
blōdlǣting 02.08.12.02.06 Surgical
blōdlēas 02.04.06.08.01 Blood
blōdmenged 03.01.14.05 Red/redness
blōdorc 16.02.05.05.06 A vessel for use in services
blōdrēad 03.01.14.05 Red/redness
blōdryne 02.08.08.03 Heart disease
blōdscēawung 02.04.06.08.01 Blood
blōdseax 02.08.12.02.06 Surgical
blōdseten 02.08.12.02.05 Pharmacy, curing with salves
blōdsihte 02.04.06.08.01 Blood; 02.08.08.12 Disease of bowels
blōdspīwung 02.08.08.02 Lung disease
blōdþigen 02.08.12.02.05 Pharmacy, curing with salves
blōdwīte 14.01.04.03 Rights involving money; 14.05.05 Physical punishments
blōdwracu 12.05.04.02 Vengeance, revenge
blōdyrnende 02.08.08.12 Disease of bowels
blōma 17.04.02 Ore, unwrought metal
blōstm(a) 02.07.02.07 Blossom, flower(s)
blōstmbǣre 02.07.02.07 Blossom, flower(s); 05.08.01 Vigour, activity, force
blōstmberende 02.07.02.07 Blossom, flower(s)
blōstmfrēols 16.02.01.06.01 Belief/practice of heathen people
blōstmgild 16.02.01.06.01 Belief/practice of heathen people
blōstmian 02.07.01 To grow
blōstmiende 02.07.02.07 Blossom, flower(s)
blōstmig 02.07.02.07 Blossom, flower(s)
blōt 02.08.03.02 Itch, irritation
(ge)blōt 16.02.04.12 Sacrifice, a sacrifice
blōtan 16.02.04.12 Sacrifice, a sacrifice
blōtere 16.02.04.12 Sacrifice, a sacrifice
blōtmōnaþ 05.11.03.01.03.01 Specific months
blōtung 16.02.04.12 Sacrifice, a sacrifice
(ge)blōwan 02.07.01 To grow; 05.08.01 Vigour, activity, force
geblōwen 02.07.02.07 Blossom, flower(s); 05.08.01 Vigour, activity, force
blōwende 05.08.01 Vigour, activity, force

blōwendlic 02.07.02.07 Blossom, flower(s)
blȳscan 03.01.12.01 Glittering, effulgence
blyse 17.05.03 Sources of fire/light
blȳsian 03.01.09.02 Fire, flame
bōc 02.07.03.05 Particular trees/shrubs (alphabetical order); 02.07.09.02.01 Nut; 04.01.02.01.04.01 Mast, pig-food; 09.03.07.07 A book; 09.03.07.07.02 A written work, book, treatise; 09.03.07.07.02.01 A main division; 09.03.07.07.03.04.02 A register, catalogue; 14.04.01 A deed, contract, agreement
bōc frēodōmes 14.03.03 Law, action of the courts
bōcæceras 15.01.01 Landed property
bōcblæc 09.03.07.06.02 Ink
bōccest 09.03.07.07.01 A library, collection of books
bōcciste 09.03.07.07.01 A library, collection of books
bōccræft 06.01.06.02.02.01 Learning, science (secular knowledge)
bōccræftig 06.01.06.02 Knowledge, learning, erudition
bōccynn 09.03.07.07.02 A written work, book, treatise
bōcen 02.07.03.05 Particular trees/shrubs (alphabetical order)
bōcere 06.01.06.02.01 A wise man, man of understanding or learning; 09.03.07.03 A scribe, copyist
bōcfell 09.03.07.06.06 Membrane, vellum
bōcfōdder 09.03.07.07.01 A library, collection of books
bōcgesamnung 09.03.07.07.01 A library, collection of books
bōcgestrēon 09.03.07.07.01 A library, collection of books
bōchaga 02.07.03.04.03 A hedge/border
bōcholt 02.07.03.05 Particular trees/shrubs (alphabetical order)
bōchord 09.03.07.07.01 A library, collection of books
bōchūs 09.03.07.07.01 A library, collection of books
(ge)bōcian 15.01.02 Gift, transfer of property
gebōcian 09.03.07.07.01 A library, collection of books
bōclǣden 09.03.01 Particular languages
bōcland 15.01.01 Landed property
bōclār 06.01.06.02.02.01 Learning, science (secular knowledge)
bōclic 06.01.06.02 Knowledge, learning, erudition
bōclic stæf 06.01.06.02.02.01 Learning, science (secular knowledge)
bōcrǣde 06.01.06.02.03.03.01 An act of reading
bōcrǣdere 06.01.06.02.01 A wise man, man of understanding or learning
bōcrǣding 06.01.06.02.03.03.01 An act of reading
bōcrēad 03.01.14.05 Red/redness; 09.03.07.06.02 Ink
bōcriht 14.01.04 A legal right
bōcstæf 09.03.07.01 A written character, letter
bōcstigel 05.10.05.04.14.02 An opening/space in an enclosure
bōctǣcung 06.01.06.02.03.04 Teaching, instruction
bōctalu 06.01.06.02.03.04 Teaching, instruction
bōctrēow 02.07.03.05 Particular trees/shrubs (alphabetical order)
bōcung 15.01.02 Gift, transfer of property

bōcweorc 06.01.06.02.03.03.01 An act of reading
bōcwudu 02.07.03.05 Particular trees/shrubs (alphabetical order)
bod 09.06.02.01.06 A message, announcement by a messenger; 16.02.04.10 Preaching
(ge)bod 14.01.06 A rule, order, precept, tenet, principle
boda 09.06.02.01.06.01 A messenger; 16.02.01.12.01.01 Prophecy
bodere 16.02.03.02.10 A preacher, teacher
bodian 06.01.08.04.01 Premonition, prophecy; 16.02.01.12.01.01 Prophecy; 16.02.04 Worship, honour, praise; 16.02.04.10 Preaching
bodian (be) 07.06.03 Boastfulness, arrogance
(ge)bodian 09.06.02.01.05 Proclamation, spreading abroad
gebodian 14.03.03.01 Accusation
bodiend 09.06.02.01.06.01 A messenger; 16.02.03.02.10 A preacher, teacher
bodig 02.04 Body; 02.04.03.03 Trunk; 17.03 Implements, tools, etc.
bodigendlic 16.01.01.01.01.02 Glory
bodlāc 14.01.06 A rule, order, precept, tenet, principle
(ge)bodscipe 12.03.03 A command, bidding, order
bodung 07.06.03 Boastfulness, arrogance; 09.01 To speak, exercise faculty of speech; 09.04.03 Exposition, making clear by explanation; 09.06.02.01.06 A message, announcement by a messenger; 14.03.03.03 Witness, testimony, attestation; 16.02.04.10 Preaching

bodungdæg 16.02.04.04.02.01.02 Lent
bōg 02.06.01.03 Barrel, body of animal; 02.07.03.03.01 Wood (as substance)
boga 01.03.01.06.02 Rain; 04.05.02.03 An arch, vault; 05.10.06.02.01 A hemisphere; 09.03.07.06.06 Membrane, vellum; 13.02.08.04.04 A bow
bōgan 07.06.03 Boastfulness, arrogance
bogefōdder 13.02.08.04.04 A bow
bogen 02.07.10.01 Particular herbs/spices (alphabetical order)
gebogen 05.10.06.02.02 Curvature, bend, twist; 16.02.04.10.01 Conversion
bogenett 04.03.05 Fishing
bogenstreng 05.12.01.09.03.01.03 Part of ship
bogetung 05.10.06.02.02 Curvature, bend, twist
bogiht 05.10.05.04.08.01 A bend
bōgincel 02.07.03.03.01 Wood (as substance)
bōgung 07.06.03 Boastfulness, arrogance
bōhscyld 13.02.08.03.01.06 A shield
bōhtimber 04.05.01.02 Timber for building
bol 01.01.02.01.02.02.01 Hill; 02.07.03.03.01 Wood (as substance)
bōl 04.04.10.01 A ring (for finger, arm, neck)
bola 02.07.03.03.01 Wood (as substance)
bolca 05.12.01.09.03.01.03 Part of ship
bold 04.05.03 A dwelling-place, abode, habitation; 04.05.03.02.02.06 A royal/noble palace; 12.06.02.01 A township
boldāgend 15.01 Property
boldāgende 04.05.03.02.01 A building, house, hall, palace, etc.
boldgetæl 12.06.02 District, province

boldgetimber/bolttimber 04.05.01.02 Timber for building
boldgetimbru 04.05.02 A building, edifice, structure
boldweard 12.01.01.08.01 A servant, attendant
boldwela 08.01.01.03.08 Happiness, well-being, prosperity; 12.06.02.01 A township; 16.01.02.01 Heavenly dwelling place
bolgenmōd 08.01.03.05.02 Anger
bolla 04.01.02.02.06.05.04 Cup/bowl/basin
bolster 04.05.04.05.01 Bedding (e.g. of straw)
gebolstrod 04.05.04.05.01 Bedding (e.g. of straw)
bolt 13.02.08.04.04.01 An arrow, dart, bolt
bōn 17.02.05.01 Ornamental object
bōnda 02.03.03 A family, household; 04.05.03.02 A human habitation; 12.01.01.10 Freedom, being free; 12.09 Marriage, state of marriage
bōndeland 15.01.01 Landed property
gebōned 17.02.05.01 Ornamental object
bor 01.01.02.01.02.02.01 Hill; 02.08.12.02.06 Surgical
bora 12.01.01.04 A leader, ruler
borcian 02.05.10.15.06 A roar, howl, etc.
bord 04.05.01.02.01 Boarding, planking, floor; 04.05.04.02 A table; 05.12.01.09.03.01 A ship, boat; 05.12.01.09.03.01.03 Part of ship; 13.02.08.03.01.06 A shield
borda 04.04.05.07 Embroidery; 04.04.09 A fringe, border, hem
bordclāþ 04.04.08 A covering, curtain, veil, garment, etc.

bordgelāc 13.02.08.04.04.01 An arrow, dart, bolt
bordhæbbende 13.02.08.03.01.06 A shield
bordhaga 13.02.07.02 Order (of troops), array
bordhrēoþa 13.02.07.02 Order (of troops), array; 13.02.08.03.01.06 A shield
bordrand 13.02.08.03.01.06 A shield
bordrima 04.05.01.02.01 Boarding, planking, floor
bordrīþig 01.01.03.01.01.03 Stream
bordstæþ 05.12.01.09.03.01.03 Part of ship
bordþaca 04.05.02.08 Top of a building; 13.02.07.02 Order (of troops), array
bordweal 13.02.07.02 Order (of troops), array
bordweall 05.12.01.09.03.01.03 Part of ship; 13.02.08.03.01.06 A shield
bordwudu 13.02.08.03.01.06 A shield
boren 12.01.01.06.01 Rank, position due to birth
(ge)boren 05.02.02 Nature, established order of things
geboren 02.01.03.03.03 Birth; 02.03.02.02.05 Having the same parents
geboren brōþor 02.03.02.02.05.01 Brother
borenra 12.01.01.06.06 Gentle birth, nobility
borettan 05.12.05.05 To shake, quake, wag
borg 14.03.03.07 Security, pledge, bail; 15.04 A debt, due; 15.04.01 Lending of money
borgbryce 14.03.03.07 Security, pledge, bail

borggelda 15.04 A debt, due; 15.04.01 Lending of money
borgian 14.03.03.07 Security, pledge, bail; 15.04.01 Lending of money
borgiend 15.04.01 Lending of money
borgsorg 08.01.03.06 Adversity, affliction
borgsteall 04.05.02.01 A foundation
borgwedd 14.03.03.07 Security, pledge, bail
borh 16.02.04.07.01 Baptism, baptizing (and anointing)
borhfæst 14.03.03.07 Security, pledge, bail
(ge)borhfæstan 14.03.03.07 Security, pledge, bail
borhhand 14.03.03.07 Security, pledge, bail
borhlēas 14.03.03.07 Security, pledge, bail
borian on 05.12.05.02.04.01 To insert into (a hole)
borian (on) 05.06.07 Pricking, a prick, puncture
borlīce 07.02.04.03 Nobleness, excellence, nobility, magnificence; 07.08.08 Nobleness, honour, glory
bōs 04.02.05.06.01.01 A cattle pen/cowshed
bōsig 04.02.05.06.01.01 A cattle pen/cowshed
bōsm 02.04.03.03.05 Chest, breast, bosom; 02.04.06.03.01 Cavities of internal organs; 02.04.06.04.02 Female reproductive organs; 05.10.05.03.04 Depth, deepness; 05.12.01.09.03.01.03 Part of ship; 08.01 Heart, spirit, mood, disposition
bōsmig 05.10.05.04.08.01 A bend

bōt 02.08.12.01 Medical care, treatment; 11.12.02 Aid, help, succour; 11.12.02.02 Amendment, setting right, reparation; 12.08.02.02.01 Reform, correction; 14.05.04 A penalty, punishment; 16.02.04.07.02.03 Penance, an act/instance of penance; 17.02.04.01 Repairing, renewing
bōtettan 17.02.04.01 Repairing, renewing
bōtian 17.02.04.01 Repairing, renewing
(ge)bōtian 02.08.13 Recovery, growing better
bōtlēas 14.03.03.09.02 Atonement
botlgestrēon 15.01 Property
botm 01.01.03.01 Body of water; 05.10.05.04.02.03.01 A low position, the bottom; 16.01.05 Hell, lower world, abode of the dead
bōtwyrþe 14.03.03.08 Justification
boþen 02.07.10.01 Particular herbs/spices (alphabetical order)
boþltūn 04.05.03 A dwelling-place, abode, habitation
box 02.07.03.05 Particular trees/shrubs (alphabetical order); 04.05.04.03 A box, case, chest, container; 16.02.05.05.06 A vessel for use in services
boxtrēow 02.07.03.05 Particular trees/shrubs (alphabetical order)
braccas 04.04.07.09 Breeches
brachwīl 05.11.01.02 Shortness/brevity in time
brād 02.04.03.04.01.01 Hand; 03.03.04.01.01 Greatness, bigness, size; 03.03.04.02.01 Abundance; 05.10.01 Amplitude, spaciousness, vastness; 05.10.05.02 Extension, stretching; 05.10.05.03.01.01 Breadth, width across; 05.10.05.04.03 A line, continuous length

brād hand 02.04.03.04.01.01 Hand
brād sweord 13.02.08.04.03 A sword
brād þistel 02.07.11 Plants/flowers (alphabetical order)
brādæx 17.03.03 A cutting tool
brāde 05.10.05 A space, span
brādelēac 02.07.09.02.02.01 Edible root/bulb; 02.07.10.01 Particular herbs/spices (alphabetical order)
brādian 05.10.05.02.02 Greater, bigger
brādian (oþ) 05.10.05.02 Extension, stretching
brādlāstæx 17.03.03 A cutting tool
brādlēaf 02.07.02.06 A leaf
brādlinga 02.04.03.04.01.01 Hand
brādnes 05.10 Space, extent; 05.10.05.04.02 Face, surface; 12.08.01 Magnanimity, greatness of soul
bræc 04.02.03.02.03.01 ?Strip of untilled land
gebræc 02.05.10.07 A crashing, noise
bræc 05.06 Destruction, dissolution, loss, breaking
(ge)bræc 02.08.07.04.04 Respiratory disease
gebræc 01.01.02.01.04.01 Marsh, bog, swamp
bræcce 04.04.07.09 Breeches
bræccoþu 02.08.09.02 Epilepsy
gebræcdrenc 02.08.12.02.07 Remedies for specific parts (head to toe)
bræclian 02.05.10.08 A crackling, rustling
(ge)bræcsēoc 02.08.11.02.01 Insanity, madness
bræd 02.04.05.01 Flesh
(ge)bræd 04.01.02.02.05 Cooking
gebræd 03.01.09.02.01 Fire, burning

brǣdan 02.07.01 To grow; 04.05.03.02.02.09 A tent, pavilion; 05.10.04.04.01 Dispersion
brǣdan (tō) 05.10.05.02 Extension, stretching
(ge)brǣdan 03.01.09.02.01 Fire, burning; 04.01.02.02.05 Cooking; 05.10.05.02.02 Greater, bigger; 09.06.02.01.05.01 To spread, make known, proclaim, celebrate
(ge)brǣdan (on) 05.10.05.04.12 The condition of being covered
brǣd(e) 04.01.02.01.02.05.04 Roasted meat
brǣdepanne/brǣdingpanne 04.01.02.02.06.01 Cooking vessel/pot
brǣding 04.01.02.01.02.05.04 Roasted meat; 04.05.04.05.01 Bedding (e.g. of straw); 05.10.05.02.01 Diffusion, effusion, spreading
brǣd(-u/-o) 05.10.05.03.01.01 Breadth, width across
brægd 06.01.07.04.02 Fraud, deceit, trick, trickery
brægdboga 13.02.08.04.04 A bow
brægde 06.01.07.04.04 Deceitfulness, falseness, duplicity
brægden 06.01.07.04.02 Fraud, deceit, trick, trickery
(ge)brægden 11.04.02.01.01 Cunning, craft, craftiness, guile, wile
gebrægdenlīce 11.04.02.01.01 Cunning, craft, craftiness, guile, wile
gebrægdnes 11.04.02.01.01 Cunning, craft, craftiness, guile, wile
brægdwīs 11.04.02.01.01 Cunning, craft, craftiness, guile, wile
brægen 02.04.06.09 Brain
brægenes hwyrfnes 02.08.11.02 Mental weakness
brægenloca 02.04.05.04.02 Skull
bræg(en)panne 02.04.05.04.02 Skull

brægensēoc 02.08.11.02.01 Insanity, madness
bræs 01.01.02.02.03.01 Types of metals/minerals; 17.04.02.01 Brass
bræsen 01.01.02.02.03.01 Types of metals/minerals; 07.06.01.01 Proud, arrogant; 17.04.02.01 Brass
bræsian 17.02.04.03 Metal worker
bræþ 02.04.06.06 Discharge, emanation; 02.05.08 Faculty of smell; 02.05.08.02 Pleasant smell, fragrance, perfume; 08.01.01.01 Ardour, fervour, strong feeling
bræw 02.04.03.01.03.02 Eye
brand 03.01.09.02.01 Fire, burning; 03.02.01.05.01 Blight (causing leaves to look burned); 13.02.08.04.03 A sword; 17.05.03 Sources of fire/light
brandhāt 08.01.01.01 Ardour, fervour, strong feeling
brandhord 08.01.03.03 Anxiety
brandīren 17.05.02 A hearth, fireplace
brandīsen 17.05.02 A hearth, fireplace
brandrād 17.05.02 A hearth, fireplace
brandrida 17.05.02 A hearth, fireplace
brandstæfn 05.12.01.09.03.01.02 Of/concerning a ship, naval
brant 05.10.05.03.03 Height, loftiness, sublimity; 05.10.05.03.04 Depth, deepness
brassica 02.07.09.02.02.02 Other vegetables (alphabetical order)
gebrastl 02.05.10.08 A crackling, rustling
brastlian 02.05.10.08 A crackling, rustling
brastliende 02.05.10.08 A crackling, rustling
brastlung 02.05.10.08 A crackling, rustling

bratt 04.04.07.07 A long outer garment, covering, cloak, etc.
brēad 04.01.02.01.07.03 Bread; 04.01.02.01.07.03.03 Piece of bread; 16.02.05.09.01 Eucharistic elements
brēad/hlāf and wæter 04.01.01.06.01 Abstinence from food, fast
gebreadian 02.08.12 Healing, curing
breahtm 02.05.10.03 Noise, tumult, uproar
breahtmian 02.05.10.06 Harsh sound
breahtmung 05.12.05.05 To shake, quake, wag
brēaþ 03.01.03.01 Stiffness, hardness
brēawern 04.01.03.05.02 Brewing
brēc 04.04.07.09 Breeches
brecan 02.05.10.07 A crashing, noise; 05.12.05.02.01 To come upon, meet with; 05.12.05.06.02 To force a way through; 06.02.06.03.03 Incitement; 11.03 Endeavour; 14.02 Lawlessness
brecan ādūne 05.06.03 A dashing together, breaking, shattering
brecan gilp 11.06.03 Failing, failure
brecan of 01.01.03.01.01.07 Spring, fountain, well
brecan ofer bæþweg 05.12.01.09 To travel on water
brecan on 05.12.05.06.02 To force a way through
brecan ūp 01.01.03.01.01.07 Spring, fountain, well
(ge)brecan 05.06 Destruction, dissolution, loss, breaking; 05.06.03 A dashing together, breaking, shattering; 12.05.06 Grasp, power, control, mastery
(ge)brecan hlāf 04.01.02.03 To serve (food/drink)
(ge)brecan on/in 05.11.11.02 Let up, intermission, cessation

gebrecan 02.08.04.04 State of being crippled
gebrecan on/in 11.11.02 A hindrance
brēchrægl 04.04.07.09 Breeches
brecþa 08.01.03.03 Anxiety
bred 04.05.01.02.01 Boarding, planking, floor; 05.10.05.04.02 Face, surface; 09.03.07.06.04 A writing-tablet; 09.03.07.07 A book
brēdan 02.01.03.03.01 To beget; 02.06.01.07 Breeding, hatching; 02.06.08.02 Domestic fowl; 11.12.02.01 Strengthening, confirmation
breden 04.05.01.02.01 Boarding, planking, floor
bredīsern 09.03.07.06.01 A writing instrument
bredweall 04.05.01.02.07 A fence, hedge
gebrēfan 09.03.07.07.03.02.01 An epitome, short account
brēgan 06.01.08.05.01 Amazement, astonishment, wonder, admiration
(ge)brēgan 06.01.08.06.03.01 Causing dread, terrifying
gebregd 04.04.05 Woven material, fabric; 05.12.03.01.01 Quick movement or movements; 11.04.02 Skill, skilfulness
bregdan 03.01.12.01 Glittering, effulgence
bregdan hider and geond 05.12.05.05 To shake, quake, wag
bregdan of 05.06.08 A plucking, taking away; 05.12 To move, be in motion
bregdan on 05.13.01 Transformation, taking another shape
bregdan ūp 05.06.08 A plucking, taking away
(ge)bregdan 05.05.03 Binding, fastening; 05.12.02.05 To pull, drag, draw; 05.12.03.01.01 Quick movement or movements; 13.02.08.04.03.02 Armed with a sword; 14.03.03.02.01 Attaching, distraint of stolen property; 17.04.04 Fibrous materials
gebregdan 05.12.05.05 To shake, quake, wag; 06.01.07.04.04.02 Pretence, feigning, dissimulation; 10.04.03 To take away, remove
gebregdan oreþe 02.04.06.07.05 To breathe
gebregden 06.01.07.04.04 Deceitfulness, falseness, duplicity
bregdende 11.04.02.01.01 Cunning, craft, craftiness, guile, wile
gebregdnes 05.11.08.01.01 Suddenness
gebregdstafas 06.01.06.02.02.01 Learning, science (secular knowledge)
brēgendlic 06.01.08.06.03.01 Causing dread, terrifying
brēgnes 06.01.08.06.03 Cause of fear, terror, horror
brego 12.01.01.04 A leader, ruler
brego engla 16.01.01.01.01 The Almighty
brego mancynnes 16.01.01.02.01 Creator
bregorīce 12.06 A province, country, territory
bregorōf 06.02.07.06 Courage, boldness, valour
bregostōl 12.06 A province, country, territory
bregoweard 12.01.01.04 A leader, ruler
brēman 08.01.03.05.02 Anger; 09.06.02.01.05.01 To spread, make known, proclaim, celebrate; 12.07.02 Observance, keeping
(ge)brēman 16.02.04 Worship, honour, praise; 16.02.04.03.01 A rite, ceremony

gebrēman 07.08.02 Honour, glory
brēme 07.08.08 Nobleness, honour, glory
brēmel 02.07.09.02 Particular fruits (alphabetical order)
brēmelæppel 02.07.09.02 Particular fruits (alphabetical order)
brēmelberie 02.07.09.02 Particular fruits (alphabetical order)
brēmelbrǣr 02.07.09.02 Particular fruits (alphabetical order)
brēmelhyrne 01.01.02.01.05 Covered with vegetation
brēmellēaf 02.07.09.02 Particular fruits (alphabetical order)
brēmelrind 02.07.09.02 Particular fruits (alphabetical order)
brēmelþorn 02.07.09.02 Particular fruits (alphabetical order)
brēmelþȳfel 02.07.09.02 Particular fruits (alphabetical order)
brēmelþyrne 02.07.09.02 Particular fruits (alphabetical order)
brēmelwudu 02.07.09.02 Particular fruits (alphabetical order)
brēmen 02.07.03.01 A bush
brēmendlic 07.08 Reputation, fame
brēmerlēah 01.01.02.01.05 Covered with vegetation
brēmling 01.01.02.01.05 Covered with vegetation
bremman 08.01.03.05.02 Anger
bremung 02.05.10.05 Roaring, raging
(ge)brengan 05.05.02 Productivity, bringing forth; 05.12.02.01 To fetch, bring, bear, conduct; 10.03.02 Presenting, offering
(ge)brengan (on) 05.03.01 A cause (of anything)
gebrengnes 16.02.04.12 Sacrifice, a sacrifice

brenting 05.12.01.09.03.01 A ship, boat
breodian 02.05.10.15.01 To raise (the voice), raise up (noise)
breodwian 05.06.09 Act of striking
brēost 02.04.03.03.05 Chest, breast, bosom; 02.04.06.03.02.03 Stomach/belly; 02.04.06.04.02 Female reproductive organs; 02.04.06.05.06 Mammary gland, breast; 06 Spirit, soul, heart; 08.01 Heart, spirit, mood, disposition
brēostbān 02.04.05.04.05.02 Breast-bone
brēostbyden 02.04.03.03.05 Chest, breast, bosom
brēostcearu 08.01.03.03 Anxiety
brēostcofa 02.04.06.05.06 Mammary gland, breast; 08.01 Heart, spirit, mood, disposition
brēost(ge)beorh 13.02.06.01 Stronghold, fort/fortified town
brēostgehygd 06.01.01 Thought, the faculty of thinking, mind
brēostgeþanc 06.01.01 Thought, the faculty of thinking, mind
brēostgewǣdu 13.02.08.03.01.04 Coat of mail/corselet
brēostgyrd 16.02.05.05.08 A staff, wand of authority
brēosthord 06 Spirit, soul, heart; 08.01 Heart, spirit, mood, disposition
brēostlīn 04.04.07.08 A short garment, skirt, kirtle
brēostloca 06 Spirit, soul, heart
brēostnet 13.02.08.03.01.04 Coat of mail/corselet
brēostnyrwet 02.08.08.01 Pain in the chest; 02.08.08.03 Heart disease
brēostrocc 04.04.07.08 A short garment, skirt, kirtle

brēostsefa 06 Spirit, soul, heart; 08.01 Heart, spirit, mood, disposition
brēosttoga 12.01.01.04 A leader, ruler
brēostþing 02.04.03.03.05 Chest, breast, bosom
brēostwærc 02.08.08.01 Pain in the chest
brēostweall 13.02.06.01 Stronghold, fort/fortified town
brēostweorþung 04.04.10.01 A ring (for finger, arm, neck)
brēostwylm 02.04.03.03.05 Chest, breast, bosom; 02.04.06.05.06 Mammary gland, breast; 08.01.01.01 Ardour, fervour, strong feeling
brēotan 05.06.01 Devastation, laying waste
breotenrīce 12.06.01.02 Britain
brēoþan 02.08.08.02 Lung disease
(ge)brēowan 04.01.03.05.02 Brewing
brēowende 04.01.03.05.02 Brewing
brēr 02.07.03.05 Particular trees/shrubs (alphabetical order)
brerd 01.01.02.01.01.03 Shore, bank; 05.10.05.04.02 Face, surface; 05.10.05.04.11.01 A bound, limit
brerdful 03.03.06.02 Fullness
brērhlǣw 01.01.02.01.02.01 Rising ground, eminence
brērig 02.07.03.05 Particular trees/shrubs (alphabetical order)
brērþyrne 02.07.03.05 Particular trees/shrubs (alphabetical order)
bresne 12 Power, might
breting 04.01.02.03 To serve (food/drink)
bretwalda 12.01.01.04.01.01 Kings and queens
brēþel 05.09 Weakness
bridd 02.06.08 Bird
brīdelgym 04.02.05.06.05.03.01 Bridle/halter/curb/muzzle
brīdelhyrst 04.02.05.06.05.03.01 Bridle/halter/curb/muzzle
brīdel(s) 12.05.06.01 Restraint, check, curb, control; 04.02.05.06.05.03.01 Bridle/halter/curb/muzzle
brīdelshring 04.02.05.06.05.03.01 Bridle/halter/curb/muzzle
brīdelþwangas 04.02.05.06.05.03.03 Reins
(ge)brīdlian 12.05.06.01 Restraint, check, curb, control
gebrīdlian 04.02.05.06.05.03.01 Bridle/halter/curb/muzzle
brigd 03.01.14.11 Medley/variety of colour
brim 01.01.02.01.01.03 Shore, bank; 01.01.03.01.02 Sea/ocean
brimceald 03.01.11 Coldness, coolness
brimclif 01.01.02.01.02.02.04 Cliff
brimfaroþ 01.01.02.01.01.03 Shore, bank
brimflōd 01.01.03.01.02 Sea/ocean
brimfugol 02.06.08.06 Water bird
brimgiest 05.12.01.09.03.03 Piracy
brimhengest 05.12.01.09.03.01 A ship, boat
brimhlæst 02.06.06 Fish
brimlād 01.01.03.01.02.01 Region of sea/ocean
brimlīþend 05.12.01.09.03 A voyage
brimmann 05.12.01.09.03 A voyage
brimrād 01.01.03.01.02.01 Region of sea/ocean
brimstæþ 01.01.02.01.01.03 Shore, bank
brimstrēam 01.01.03.01.01.05 Torrent; 01.01.03.01.02 Sea/ocean
brimþyssa 05.12.01.09.03.01 A ship, boat
brimwīsa 05.12.01.09.03 A voyage
brimwudu 05.12.01.09.03.01 A ship, boat
brimwylf 02.06.10.01.05 Sea-monster

brimwylm 01.01.03.01.02.05 Wave
bring 16.02.04.12 Sacrifice, a sacrifice
bringan on gemynde 06.01.04 Faculty of memory
brīw 04.01.02.01.07.01 Soup/pottage; 04.01.02.01.07.02 Porridge
brīwan 11.01.03 Preparation
(ge)brīwan 04.01.02.02 To prepare food
brīwþicce 03.01.17 Thickness, viscosity
broc 02.06.09.02.05 Cricket, grasshopper, locust; 02.08.02 Disease, infirmity, sickness; 11.07.03 Use, advantage, profit; 17.01 Strenuous effort, hard work
(ge)broc 03.03.07 A part, division, portion; 08.01.03.06 Adversity, affliction
gebroc 04.01.02.03 To serve (food/drink)
brōc 01.01.03.01.01.03 Stream; 02.04.03.03.03 Buttock(s), back parts; 04.04.07.09 Breeches
brocc 02.06.03.01.01 Badger
broccen 04.04.06 Undressed condition (of hide)
broccere 18.02.06 Theatricals
brōccerse 02.07.09.02.02.02 Other vegetables (alphabetical order)
brocchol 01.01.02.01.03.01 Cave; 02.06.01.08 A lair, den
broccian 06.01.08.06.01 A shuddering with fear, nervousness
brocen 04.02.03.02 Arable/ploughed land
brocen cyrtel 04.04.07.07 A long outer garment, covering, cloak, etc.
brocenlic 05.09 Weakness
brocian 07.05.01 Censure, reproof, rebuke
(ge)brocian 02.08.04.04 State of being crippled; 08.01.03.07.02 Misery, trouble, affliction

broclic 08.01.03.06 Adversity, affliction
brōcminte 02.07.10.01 Particular herbs/spices (alphabetical order)
brōcrīþ 01.01.03.01.01.02 Tributary
brōcþung 02.07.11 Plants/flowers (alphabetical order)
brocung 02.08.02 Disease, infirmity, sickness
brod 02.07.02.05 A shoot, sprout, tendril
brōd 02.06.01.07 Breeding, hatching
brōdian 03.01.12.01 Glittering, effulgence
brōdig 02.06.08.02 Domestic fowl
brōga 06.01.08.05.01.01.01 An exercise of power, mighty work, miracle; 06.01.08.06.02 Great fear, terror, horror
brogden 17.04.04 Fibrous materials
brogdenmǣl 13.02.08.04.03 A sword
brogdettan 03.01.12.01 Glittering, effulgence; 05.12.05.05 To shake, quake, wag; 06.01.08.06.01 A shuddering with fear, nervousness
brogdettung 05.12.05.05 To shake, quake, wag; 06.01.07.04.04.02 Pretence, feigning, dissimulation
brogen 02.07.03.03.01 Wood (as substance)
(ge)brogna 02.07.02.06 A leaf
gebrōht 05.10.05.04.02.04.02 Support, maintenance
brōhþrēa 08.01.03.06 Adversity, affliction
brōm 02.07.03.01 A bush
brōmfæsten 01.01.02.01.05 Covered with vegetation
brōmig 02.07.03.01 A bush
brord 02.07.02.05 A shoot, sprout, tendril; 02.07.08 Grasses, reeds, etc.;

05.06.07 Pricking, a prick, puncture; 05.10.06.03.01 A point, spike, prickle
(ge)brosnian 05.06.01 Devastation, laying waste; 12.08.06.01.04 To lead a bad life
(ge)brosniende 03.02.01 Decay, decline, corruption
brosniendlic 03.02.01 Decay, decline, corruption
(ge)brosnodlic 03.02.01 Decay, decline, corruption
(ge)brosnung 03.02.01 Decay, decline, corruption
gebrosnung 12.08.06.01.01 Pollution, impairment
gebrot 03.03.07 A part, division, portion
broþ 04.01.02.01.07.01 Soup/pottage
brōþor 02.03.02.02.05.01 Brother; 12.04.01 A fellow, companion, associate, comrade; 16.02.03.03.02 A monk
gebrōþor 02.03.02.02.05.01 Brother; 11.05.02.02.01.01 Courteous forms of address; 16.02.02 Christianity, the Christian faith
gebrōþor þā lēofestan 11.05.02.02.01.01 Courteous forms of address
brōþorbana 02.02.04.04.01 Murder of a relative
brōþorcwealm 02.02.04.04.01 Murder of a relative
brōþordohtor 02.03.02.03.06.02.03 Child of brother/sister
brōþorgyld 12.05.04.02 Vengeance, revenge
brōþorlēas 02.03.02.02.05.01 Brother
brōþorlic 02.03.02.02.05.01 Brother
brōþorlīcnes 08.01.02.03 Friendliness, affection; 16.02.03.03.02 A monk
brōþorlufu 08.01.02.02.04 Love, caritas

brōþorrǣden 12.04 Fellowship, union, association; 16.02.03.03.02 A monk
(ge)brōþorscipe 08.01.02.03 Friendliness, affection
brōþorsibb 02.03.02.02.05.01 Brother; 08.01.02.03 Friendliness, affection
brōþorslaga 02.02.04.04.01 Murder of a relative
brōþorslege 02.02.04.04.01 Murder of a relative
brōþorsliht 02.02.04.04.01 Murder of a relative
brōþorsunu 02.03.02.03.06.02.03 Child of brother/sister
brōþorwīf 02.03.02.03.06.02.06 In-law relationships
brōþorwyrt 02.07.10.01 Particular herbs/spices (alphabetical order)
gebrōþru 16.02.03.03.02 A monk
gebrowen 04.01.03.05.02 Brewing
brū 02.04.03.01.03.02 Eye
brūcan 02.01.03.03 Sex, generation; 04.04.07 Trappings, equipment, garb
(ge)brūcan 04 Consumption of food/drink; 11.07 Use (made of things), service; 17.02.02 An office, function, employment
brūcendlīce 11.07.01 Utility, usefulness
brūcung 11.02 Occupation, activity, business
brūmiddel 02.04.03.01.03.01 Forehead
brūn 03.01.12 Brightness, light; 03.01.13 Darkness, obscurity
brūnbasu 03.01.14.05 Red/redness
brūnecg 03.01.12 Brightness, light
bruneþa 02.08.06 Skin disease, erysipelas
brūn(e)wyrt 02.07.11 Plants/flowers (alphabetical order)
brūnfāg 03.01.12 Brightness, light

brūnian 03.01.13 Darkness, obscurity
brūnwann 03.01.13 Darkness, obscurity
brūnwyrt 02.07.11 Plants/flowers (alphabetical order)
bryce 02.08.04.04.01 Mutilation/injury to limbs; 04.01.02.03 To serve (food/drink); 04.05.01.04 A tile, brick; 05.09 Weakness; 08.01.01.03.05 Pleasure, delight; 11.07 Use (made of things), service; 11.07.03 Use, advantage, profit; 14.02 Lawlessness; 15.01.01.01 Holding of land
bryce healdan 12.01.01.08 Service
(ge)bryce 03.03.07 A part, division, portion
brȳce 11.07.01 Utility, usefulness
brycg 05.12.01.03.03 A fordable place; 05.12.01.03.04 A bridge
brycgbōt 05.12.01.03.04.01 Constructing/repairing bridges
brycggeweorc 05.12.01.03.04.01 Constructing/repairing bridges
(ge)brycgian 05.12.01.03.04.01 Constructing/repairing bridges
gebrycgian 05.12.01.03.01 A means of access
brycgweard 13.02.04 Defence, guard, protection
brȳc(s)ian 11.07.03 Use, advantage, profit
(ge)brȳc(s)ian 11.07 Use (made of things), service
brȳd 12.09 Marriage, state of marriage; 12.09.02 Marriage ceremony
brȳdbedd 12.09.02 Marriage ceremony
brȳdbletsung 12.09.02 Marriage ceremony; 16.02.01.10.02.01 A blessing, invocation of divine favour
brȳdboda 12.09.02 Marriage ceremony
brȳdbūr 04.05.03.04 A closet, chamber, room; 12.09.02 Marriage ceremony
gebryddan 06.01.08.06.03.01 Causing dread, terrifying
brȳdealo(þ) 12.09.02 Marriage ceremony; 04.01.02.04.02 Feast
brȳdgifa 12.09.01 Pledging, betrothal; 12.09.02 Marriage ceremony
brȳdgifta 12.09.01 Pledging, betrothal; 12.09.02 Marriage ceremony
brȳdgifu 12.09.01 Pledging, betrothal
brȳdguma 12.09.01 Pledging, betrothal; 12.09.02 Marriage ceremony
brȳdhlōp 12.09.02 Marriage ceremony
brȳdhūs 12.09.02 Marriage ceremony
brȳdlāc 12.09 Marriage, state of marriage; 12.09.02 Marriage ceremony
brȳdlēoþ 12.09.02 Marriage ceremony
brȳdlic 12.09 Marriage, state of marriage
brȳdlic gewrit 16.02.01.08.01.01 Books of the Old Testament
brȳdloca 12.09.02 Marriage ceremony
brȳdlufu 08.01.02.02.03 A loving relationship
brȳdniht 12.09.02 Marriage ceremony
gebrȳdod 12.09 Marriage, state of marriage
brȳdræst 12.09.02 Marriage ceremony
brȳdrēaf 12.09.02 Marriage ceremony
brȳdsang 12.09.02 Marriage ceremony
brȳdsceamol 12.09.02 Marriage ceremony
brȳdþing 12.09.02 Marriage ceremony
brygd 13.02.08.04.03.02 Armed with a sword
brȳnan 03.01.13 Darkness, obscurity
bryne 02.08.03.02 Itch, irritation; 02.08.05 Inflammation; 03.01.09 Heat; 03.01.09.02 Fire, flame; 03.01.09.02.01 Fire, burning;

brȳne 08.01.01.01 Ardour, fervour, strong feeling; 17.05.03 Sources of fire/light
brȳne 03.01.16.02 Water, liquid
bryneādl 02.08.10 Fever
brynebrōga 06.01.08.06.03 Cause of fear, terror, horror
brynegield 16.02.04.12 Sacrifice, a sacrifice
brynehāt 03.01.09 Heat
bryneléoma 03.01.12.02 A beam of light
brynenes 11.03.01.01 Trial, probation
brynetēar 08.01.03.04.02 Shedding of tears
brynewylm 03.01.09.02 Fire, flame
brynstān 03.01.09.02.01.03 Sulphur, brimstone
bryrdan 06.02.06.03.03 Incitement
bryrdnes 06.02.06.03.03 Incitement
gebryrdnes 08.01.03.02.01 Compunction, remorse, contrition
brȳsan 05.09.03 Mitigation, lightening, alleviation
gebrȳsed 04.01.02.02.04 To season
gebrȳsednes 05.06.05.03 Bruising, crushing
brȳsewyrt 02.07.11 Plants/flowers (alphabetical order)
(ge)brȳs(i)an 07.03.02 Ill, harm, hurt
gebrȳs(i)an 02.08.04.01 A wound
(ge)brȳtan 05.06.05 A grinding, pounding
gebrȳtan 05.06.01 Devastation, laying waste
bryten 05.10.01 Amplitude, spaciousness, vastness; 12.06.01.02 Britain
brytencyning 12.01.01.04.01.01 Kings and queens
brytengrundas 01 Earth, world
brytenland 12.06.01.02 Britain
brytenrīce 12.06 A province, country, territory
brytenwangas 01 Earth, world
brytenwealda 12.01.01.04.01.01 Kings and queens
brytland 12.06.01.02 Britain
brytmǣlum 03.03.07 A part, division, portion
brytnere 10.03.07 Distribution
(ge)brytnian 10.03.07 Distribution
brytnung 10.03.07 Distribution
(ge)brytsen 03.03.07 A part, division, portion
brytsnian 10.03.07 Distribution
gebrytsnian 11.07 Use (made of things), service
brytt 02.03.03.05.02 The British/Welsh/Bretons
brytta 10.03 Giving
bryttas 02.03.03.05.02 The British/Welsh/Bretons; 02.03.03.06.01 Peoples of France
bryttian 11.07 Use (made of things), service
(ge)bryttian 10.03.07 Distribution
bryttisc 02.03.03.05.02 The British/Welsh/Bretons
bryttwealas 02.03.03.05.02 The British/Welsh/Bretons
brytwylisc 02.03.03.05.02 The British/Welsh/Bretons
bryþen 04.01.03.05.01.02 Broth; 04.01.03.05.02 Brewing
brȳwlāc 04.01.03.05.02 Brewing
bū 04.05.03 A dwelling-place, abode, habitation
būan 01.01.02 Land; 05.10.04 Place, room
(ge)būan 04.02.04.01 To occupy and cultivate land; 10 Having, owning, possession

(ge)būan (in/on) 04.05.03.01 Habitation, sojourn
būc 02.04.03.03.06 Belly/abdomen; 02.04.06.03.02.03 Stomach/belly; 04.01.03.05.04.01 A flask, flagon, bottle
bucca 02.06.03.01.06 Deer, hart
bucheort 02.06.03.01.06 Deer, hart
buclic 02.06.02.01.05 Goat
budda 02.06.09.02.03 Beetle
būend 02.03.03.04 An inhabitant; 04.02.02 Farmer, cultivator; 04.02.04.02 Cultivation/tillage; 04.05.03.01 Habitation, sojourn
buf 09.01.03.01 Interjections: Oh!
bufan 05.10.05.04.02 Face, surface; 05.10.05.04.02.04 Above; 05.10.05.04.09.01.02 Front, beginning; 05.11.07.04.02 (Of time) later/latter
bufan(ge)cweden 05.11.07.03.02.02 The aforesaid
bufannemned 05.11.07.03.02.02 The aforesaid
bufansprecen 05.11.07.03.02.02 The aforesaid
būgan 05.12.05.13.03 To fall
būgan on 05.12.05.02.04 To go in, enter
(ge)būgan 05.10.06.02.02 Curvature, bend, twist; 05.12.05.02 To go/travel towards, come, approach; 05.12.05.13.02 To bow, bend down; 11.06.06.01 Abandonment (of principle); 11.10.04 Flight; 12.05.06.04.02 Submission, subjection, obedience; 13.02.05.02.01 Surrender, submission
(ge)būgan (fram/of) 05.12.05.03.03 To depart, leave, set out

(ge)būgan from 05.13 Changeableness, change
(ge)būgan tō 05.13 Changeableness, change
gebūgan 05.12.05.13.02.02 To sit down
būgian 04.05.03.01 Habitation, sojourn
bula 02.06.02.01.03 Cattle
bul(a) 04.04.10.02 A button, brooch
bulberende 04.04.10 Ornaments, trappings, accoutrements
bulentse 02.07.11.02 Unidentified plants (alphabetical order)
bulgarisc 02.03.03.06.02.01 Other peoples
bulloc 02.06.02.01.03 Cattle
bult 03.03.04.01.02.01 A heap, mass, accumulation
bulut 02.07.11 Plants/flowers (alphabetical order)
bund 03.03.04.01.02.01 A heap, mass, accumulation
bunden 05.12.01.09.03.01.02 Of/concerning a ship, naval
(ge)bunden 13.02.08.04.03.01.01 Hilt of sword
gebunden 04.02.05.05.04 Rope, rein; 14.05.07 Binding, fastening with bonds
bundenheord 04.06.01.07 Hair-care
gebundennes 12.05.06.01 Restraint, check, curb, control
bundenstefna 05.12.01.09.03.01.02 Of/concerning a ship, naval
bune 02.07.08 Grasses, reeds, etc.; 04.01.03.05.04 Drinking vessel
gebūnnes 04.05.03 A dwelling-place, abode, habitation
būr 04.01.02.04.05.01.01 Quartering of officials; 04.05.03.02.02.08 A lowly dwelling, cottage, hut; 04.05.03.04 A closet, chamber, room

būr þrȳbeddod 04.05.04.05 A bed, bedstead
(ge)būr 04.02.02 Farmer, cultivator; 12.01.01.11 The common people
būrbyrde 12.01.01.11 The common people
būrcniht 12.01.01.08.01 A servant, attendant
būrcot 04.05.03.04 A closet, chamber, room
burg 04.05.03.02.02 Types of dwelling; 12.06.02.01 A township; 13.02.06.01 Stronghold, fort/fortified town
burgāgend 15.01 Property
burgbryce 14.02.01.01 Types of crime; 14.05.04.01 A fine
burgende 12.06.02.01 A township
būrgeteld 04.05.03.02.02.09 A tent, pavilion
burgfæsten 13.02.06.01 Stronghold, fort/fortified town
burggeat 05.10.05.04.14.02 An opening/space in an enclosure; 13.02.06.01 Stronghold, fort/fortified town
burghege 04.05.01.02.07 A fence, hedge
burglagu 14.01 Law, body of rules
burglēod 02.03.03.04.05 Populace of a town/city
burgloca 05.10.05.04.15.02 A wall
burgræced 04.05.03.02.02.01 Dwellings in particular places
burgrod 04.02.03.01.02 Cleared land
burgrūn(e) 16.01.04.01 Sorcery using incantation
burgsæl 04.05.03.02 A human habitation
burgsǣta 02.03.03.04.05 Populace of a town/city
(ge)burgscipe 12.06.02.01 A township

burgsele 04.05.03.02.02.01 Dwellings in particular places
burgsittend 02.03.03.04.05 Populace of a town/city
burgsittende 02.03.03.04.05 Populace of a town/city
burgstede 04.05.03 A dwelling-place, abode, habitation; 12.06.02.01 A township
burgstrǣt 05.12.01.03.01.03 A highway
burgtūn 12.06.02.01 A township
burgwaran 02.03.03.04.05 Populace of a town/city
burgware 02.03.03.04.05 Populace of a town/city
burgwaru 02.03.03.04.05 Populace of a town/city
burgweall 13.02.06.01 Stronghold, fort/fortified town
burgweg 05.12.01.03.01.03 A highway
burgwīgend 13.02.10.01 A man, warrior
burhbiscop 16.02.03.02.05 A bishop
burhbōt 14.01.05 Service, obligation, duty
burhealdor 12.02.02 An assembly, meeting
burhgeard 04.05.02.12.02 A vestibule, entrance, courtyard; 13.02.06.01 Stronghold, fort/fortified town
burhgemet 03.03.01 Specific measures
burhgemōt 12.02.02 An assembly, meeting
burhgerēfa 12.02.02 An assembly, meeting
burhgeriht 15.03.02 A tax
burh(ge)riht 14.01.01 Law(s) of particular scope
burhgeþingþ 14.03.01 Judicial body, authority
burhmann 02.03.03.04.05 Populace of a town/city

burhrǣden 12.01.01.10 Freedom, being free
burhscipe 12.01.01.10 Freedom, being free
burhscīr 12.06.02.01 A township
burhsprǣc 09.03.04.02.02 Eloquence, elegance in language
burhstaþol 04.05.02.01 A foundation
burhþegn 12.01.01.06.08 A person of rank, elder, great man
burhþelu 04.05.02.10 Flooring, a floor
burhwarumann 02.03.03.04.05 Populace of a town/city
burhwealda 12.02.02 An assembly, meeting
burhweard 11.10.01 Protection, safekeeping
burhwela 15.01.03 Treasure, riches, wealth
burhwelle 01.01.03.01.01.07 Spring, fountain, well
burhwerod 02.03.03.04.05 Populace of a town/city
burhwita 12.02.02 An assembly, meeting
(ge)būrland 15.01.01 Landed property
burn(-a/-e) 01.01.03.01.01.03 Stream; 01.01.03.01.01.07 Spring, fountain, well
burnsele 04.06.01.02 A bathing place
burnstōw 04.06.01.02 A bathing place
būrrēaf 04.04.08.01 Curtain, wall-hanging, etc.
būrrest 04.05.04.05 A bed, bedstead
burse 02.04.06.04.01 Male genitalia
būrþegn 12.01.01.08.01 A servant, attendant
busc 02.07.03.01 A bush
būt 04.01.03.05.04.01 A flask, flagon, bottle

būtan 03.03.04.03 Growth, increase; 03.03.08 Emptiness; 03.04.01 Singularity, peculiarity; 03.06 Comparison; 05.10.05.04.02.01 Exterior, outside of
būtan ǣ 14.02 Lawlessness
būtan fācne 06.01.07.07.03 Certainty
būtan gylte 12.08.05.01 Blameless
būtan intingan 11.08.03 Needless, useless, unprofitable
būtan þām þe 03.03.04.03 Growth, increase
būtan wǣrscipe 11.06.01.01 Negligence, carelessness, heedlessness
būtan gewande 06.02.07.06.02.01 Fearlessness
būtan wīte 12.07.03.01 Impunity
butere 04.01.02.01.02.09.10 Butter
buterflēoge 02.06.09.02.04 Butterfly, moth
butergeþwēor 04.01.02.01.02.09.10 Butter
gebuterod 04.01.02.02.04.08 Dressed with butter
buterstoppa 04.01.02.02.08 Churn
butruc 04.01.03.05.04.01 A flask, flagon, bottle
butsecarl 05.12.01.09.03 A voyage
butt 02.07.03.03.01 Wood (as substance)
buttoc 04.02.03.01 Plot of land
buttucas 01.01.02.01.01 Tract of land
būtū 03.03.03.04.02 Two
byccen 02.06.02.01.05 Goat
(ge)bycgan 15.02.04 Spending, disbursement; 15.05 Trade, traffic, commerce; 16.01.01.02.08 Salvation, redemption
(ge)bycgan wīf 12.09.01 Pledging, betrothal

gebycgan

gebycgan 10.01.02 Acquisition; 14.05.04.01 A fine; 16.02.04.07.02.03 Penance, an act/instance of penance
gebycgan (ūt) 12.01.01.10.01 Freeing, manumission
bycge 01.01.03.01.01.01 River
bycgend 15.05.01 Goods, stock, merchandise
bydel 06.01.08.04.01 Premonition, prophecy; 09.06.02.01.06.01 A messenger; 12.02.01 A substitute, representative; 16.02.03.02.10 A preacher, teacher
bydelæcer 15.01.01 Landed property
bydelland 15.01.01 Landed property
byden 01.01.02.01.03.03 Valley; 03.03.01.02 Dry measures; 04.01.03.05.04.02 A barrel, tun, vat, cask
bydenbotm 05.12.01.09.03.01.03 Part of ship
bydenfæt 04.01.03.05.04.02 A barrel, tun, vat, cask
bȳdla 16.02.04 Worship, honour, praise
byge 05.10.06.02.02 Curvature, bend, twist; 05.10.06.04 A corner, bend, angle; 05.12.05 To move and change direction, turn; 12.01.01.03 Symbols of power
gebyge 05.10.06.02.02 Curvature, bend, twist
gebȳgel 12.01.01.12.01 Obedience, service
bygen 15.05 Trade, traffic, commerce
byht 04.05.03 A dwelling-place, abode, habitation
(ge)byht(e) 05.10.06.02.02 Curvature, bend, twist
byld 04.05.03 A dwelling-place, abode, habitation

bylda/bytla 04.05 Building, construction
byldan 04.05 Building, construction
bȳle 02.08.05.02 Particular inflammation/swelling
bȳl(e) 02.08.05.01 Swelling
byledbrēost 02.04.03.03.05 Chest, breast, bosom
bylgan 02.05.10.15.01 To raise (the voice), raise up (noise)
bȳliht 02.08.05.02 Particular inflammation/swelling
bȳmende 18.02.07.01 Singing, song
bȳmere 18.02.07.02.02.02 A trumpet
bȳmesangere 18.02.07.02.02.02 A trumpet
bȳmian mid/of 18.02.07.02.02.02 A trumpet
bȳne 04.02.01 Farmstead; 04.05.03.01 Habitation, sojourn; 12.06.03 A site, settlement
byrce 02.05.10.15.06 A roar, howl, etc.
byrctrēow 02.07.03.05 Particular trees/shrubs (alphabetical order)
byrd 08.01.03.03 Anxiety; 17.02.04.02.03 Carrying, carriage (of materials)
(ge)byrd 02.01.03.03.03.01 Child-bearing, childbirth; 12.01.01.06.01 Rank, position due to birth
gebyrd 02.01.03.03.03 Birth; 02.03.01.04 Child; 02.03.02.03 Ancestry, descent; 02.04.04.03.03.01 Beard, whisker; 05.02.02 Nature, established order of things; 05.03 Source, origin; 05.04 Fate, lot, fortune, destiny; 05.11.10.01.01 Origin; 08.01.03.07.02 Misery, trouble, affliction; 12.01.01.06.02.01 (High) rank, status, degree

gebyrddæg 05.11.02.01.01 An anniversary
(ge)byrde 12.01.01.06.02.01 (High) rank, status, degree
gebyrde 05.02.02 Nature, established order of things
gebyrded 04.04.09 A fringe, border, hem
(ge)byrdelīce 03.05 Order, arrangement, disposition
byrdestre 04.04.05.07 Embroidery
byrdicge 04.04.05.07 Embroidery
byrding 04.04.05.07 Embroidery
gebyrdlic 03.05 Order, arrangement, disposition
byrdling 02.01.03.03.04 Offspring, race, breed, family, children
byrdscype 02.01.03.03.03.01 Child-bearing, childbirth
gebyrdtīd 05.11.02.01.01 An anniversary; 16.02.04.07.06.03 Commemoration, festival
gebyrdtīma 05.11.02.01.01 An anniversary
gebyrdwiglere 16.01.04.06.01 Astrology
gebyrdwītega 16.01.04.06.01 Astrology
byre 01.03.01.05 Wind; 02.03.02.02 Child, offspring; 02.03.02.03.05 Descendant; 05.11.02 A time, particular time, occasion
(ge)byre 05.11.08 A suitable time, opportunity
bȳre 04.02.05.03.02 A byre, stall, sty, shed
gebȳred 04.02.01 Farmstead; 12.06.03 A site, settlement
gebyredlic 03.06.03.04 What is fitting/seemly/appropriate/decent; 05.11.08 A suitable time, opportunity; 08.01.02.03.02 Friendly, amiable
gebyredlīce 05.11.08 A suitable time, opportunity
byrele 04.01.03.05.03 Tavern; 12.01.01.08.01 A servant, attendant
byrelian 04.01.03 Drinking
byres 17.03.05 An awl, borer, gimlet, etc.
byrga 14.03.03.07 Security, pledge, bail
(ge)byrgan 02.02.05 A burial, burying
byrgels 02.02.05.01.01 A grave, burial place, sepulchre
byrgelslēoþ 02.02.05.03 To attend the dead
byrgelssang 02.02.05.03 To attend the dead
byrgen 02.02.05 A burial, burying
(ge)byrgen 02.02.05.01.01 A grave, burial place, sepulchre
byrgend 02.02.05.01.01 A grave, burial place, sepulchre
byrg(en)lēoþ 02.02.05.03 To attend the dead
byrgennes 02.02.05.01.01 A grave, burial place, sepulchre
byrgensang 02.02.05.03 To attend the dead
byrgenstōw 02.02.05.01 Place of burial
byrgere 02.02.05.02 To prepare for burial
byrging 02.02.05 A burial, burying
byrgland 15.01.01 Landed property
(ge)byrian 03.06.03 Congruity, fitness, suitability; 05.03.02.01.01 An event, occurrence; 10.01 Fact of belonging, possession by; 12.07 An obligation, bounden duty; 14.01.05 Service, obligation, duty
(ge)byrian mid/tō 05.02.02.03 A connexion, association
gebyrian 06.02.04.01 Want, need
byrigberge 02.07.09.02 Particular fruits (alphabetical order)

byrignes 02.02.05 A burial, burying; 02.02.05.01.01 A grave, burial place, sepulchre
byrla 02.06.01.03 Barrel, body of animal
(ge)byrnan 08.01.01.01 Ardour, fervour, strong feeling
byrne 13.02.08.03.01.04 Coat of mail/corselet
byrnete 02.06.08.06 Water bird
byrnham 13.02.08.03.01.04 Coat of mail/corselet
byrnhama 13.02.08.03.01.04 Coat of mail/corselet
byrnig 03.01.09.02.01 Fire, burning
byrnsweord 13.02.08.04.03 A sword
byrnwiga 13.02.10.01.02 An armed man
byrnwīgend 13.02.10.01.02 An armed man
byrnwīgende 13.02.08.03.01.04 Coat of mail/corselet
byrst 02.05.10.07 A crashing, noise; 05.06.01 Devastation, laying waste; 05.06.04 Damage, injury, defect, hurt, loss; 05.10.06.03.01 A point, spike, prickle
gebyrst 05.10.06.03.01 A point, spike, prickle
byrstende 02.05.10.05 Roaring, raging
byrstful 08.01.03.06 Adversity, affliction
byrstig 03.01.05 Roughness; 08.01.03.06 Adversity, affliction
byrþen 08.01.03.03 Anxiety; 14.01.05 Service, obligation, duty; 17.02.04.02.03 Carrying, carriage (of materials)
gebyrþen 02.03.01.04 Child
byrþenmǣlum 03.03.07 A part, division, portion
byrþenmǣte 08.01.03.07.02 Misery, trouble, affliction
byrþenstān 04.01.02.02.09 A mill; 11.11.02 A hindrance
byrþenstrang 05.08 Strength
byrþestre 05.12.02.01 To fetch, bring, bear, conduct
byrþincel 17.02.04.02.03 Carrying, carriage (of materials)
byrþling 05.12.02.01 To fetch, bring, bear, conduct
byrþre 02.01.03.03.02 To bring forth, produce; 02.03.02.01 Parent
(ge)byrþre 05.12.02.01 To fetch, bring, bear, conduct
bysc 02.07.03.04.02 A thicket
bȳsen onstellan 03.06.03.02 Order, decorum, discretion
bysmere healdan 07.05.03.03.02 To reproach, revile, abuse
bysmeriend 07.05.04 Mockery, derision, scorn
(ge)bȳsnian 03.06.03.02 Order, decorum, discretion
bȳsting 04.01.02.01.02.09.04 Beestings (colostrum)
(ge)bytl(i)an 04.05 Building, construction
gebytlu 04.05.02 A building, edifice, structure
(ge)bytlung 04.05.02 A building, edifice, structure
bytme 05.12.01.09.03.01.03 Part of ship
bytming 05.12.01.09.03.01.03 Part of ship
bytn 01.01.02.01.03.03 Valley
bytt 01.01.02.01.01 Tract of land; 04.01.03.05.04.01 A flask, flagon, bottle; 04.01.03.05.04.02 A barrel, tun, vat, cask; 15.01.01 Landed property
bytte hlid 04.01.03.05.04.02 A barrel, tun, vat, cask

byttfylling 03.03.06.02 Fullness
(ge)bȳwan 04.06.01 Clean
byxe 02.07.03.05 Particular trees/shrubs (alphabetical order)
byxen 02.07.03.05 Particular trees/shrubs (alphabetical order); 04.05.01.02 Timber for building
cā 02.06.08.05 Forest bird, wild-fowl
cādac 02.06.08.05 Forest bird, wild-fowl
cæcepol 15.03 Exaction of tax/tribute
cæfester 04.02.05.06.05.03.01 Bridle/halter/curb/muzzle
cæfing 04.04.10 Ornaments, trappings, accoutrements
cæfl 04.02.05.06.05.03.01 Bridle/halter/curb/muzzle
cǣg 09.04.03 Exposition, making clear by explanation; 17.03.10.01 A bolt, lock, bar
cǣgbora 14.05.08.01 Prison, confinement, durance
cǣghiorde 12.01.01.08.01 A servant, attendant
cǣgloca 04.05.04.03 A box, case, chest, container
cæles 04.04.07.15 Footwear, covering for the feet
gecænenes 12.03.03.01 Summons, a call, summoning
cǣpehūs 04.05.03.04 A closet, chamber, room
cæppe 04.04.07.11 A headcloth, covering for the head; 16.02.05.06.01 Outer garments
cæpse 04.05.04.03 A box, case, chest, container
cærse 02.07.09.02.02.02 Other vegetables (alphabetical order)
cærsen 02.07.09.02.02.02 Other vegetables (alphabetical order)
cærsiht 02.07.09.02.02.02 Other vegetables (alphabetical order)
cærsing 04.02.04.05.01 A garden-plot
cærswill 01.01.03.01.01.07 Spring, fountain, well
cāf 05.08 Strength; 05.12.03.01 Swiftness, velocity; 06.02.07.06 Courage, boldness, valour
cāfe 05.12.03.01 Swiftness, velocity
cafertūn 04.05.02.12.02 A vestibule, entrance, courtyard
cāflīce 05.08.01 Vigour, activity, force; 05.12.03.01 Swiftness, velocity; 06.02.07.06.02 Boldness
cāfnes 05.12.03.01 Swiftness, velocity
cafortūn 04.05.03.02.02.06 A royal/noble palace
cāfscipe 05.12.03.01 Swiftness, velocity; 11.02.01 Energy, vigour, vigorous action
gecafstrian 12.05.06.01 Restraint, check, curb, control
calan 03.01.11 Coldness, coolness
calc 04.04.07.15 Footwear, covering for the feet
calcrond 02.06.02.01.06 Horse
caldisc 02.03.03.06.07.07 Other (alphabetical order)
cālend 05.11.03.01.03 A month (lunar or calendar)
cālendcwide 05.11.06.02.02 A calculated space of time
calic 04.01.03.05.04 Drinking vessel; 16.02.05.05.06 A vessel for use in services
calu 01.01.02.01.06 Wild/uncultivated land; 02.04.04.03.04 Bald, shaven
calwerbrīw 04.01.02.01.02.09.07 Buttermilk
calwerclīm 04.01.02.01.02.09.09 Curds

cāma 04.02.05.06.05.03.01 Bridle/halter/curb/muzzle
camb 02.04.04.03.01 Texture of hair; 02.06.08.01 Part of bird; 04.01.02.01.05.04 Honey; 04.04.01 Fulling; 04.06.01.07 Hair-care; 13.02.08.03.01.02.01 Parts of a helmet
cambiht 13.02.08.03.01.02.01 Parts of a helmet
camel 02.06.04.01.02 Camel
cammoc 02.07.11 Plants/flowers (alphabetical order)
camp 01.01.02.01.04 Open (level) land; 14.05.07 Binding, fastening with bonds
(ge)camp 13.02 War
campdōm 13.02.09.01 Military service
campealdor 13.02.10.01.01 A commander, officer
campgefēra 12.04.01 A fellow, companion, associate, comrade
camphād 13.02 War
(ge)campian 13.02 War
camplic 13.02.09 Military style
camprǣden 13.02 War
campstede 13.02.02 Battle
campung 13.02 War
campwǣpen 13.02.08.04 Weapons, arms
campweorod 13.02.10.01.02.02 Armed forces
campwīg 13.02.02 Battle
campwīsa 18.02.03.01 A combatant, athlete
campwudu 13.02.08.03.01.06 A shield
cananisc 02.03.03.06.07.07 Other (alphabetical order)
canc 01.01.02.01.02.02.01 Hill
(ge)canc 07.05.04 Mockery, derision, scorn

canceler 12.01.01.05 A leader, administrator
cancer 02.08.08 Internal disease
cancerādl 02.08.08 Internal disease
cancerwund 02.08.08 Internal disease
cancet(t)an 07.05.04 Mockery, derision, scorn
cancettende 08.01.01.03.07.04 Scoffing, mockery
cancettung 08.01.01.03.07.01 Laughter
candel 17.05.03 Sources of fire/light
candelbora 16.02.03.02.12 Cleric in minor orders
candelbrȳd 17.05.03 Sources of fire/light
candellēoht 03.01.12.02 A beam of light
candelmæsse 16.02.04.04.02.01.01 Around the Nativity
candelmæsseǣfen 16.02.04.04.02.01.01 Around the Nativity
candelmæssedæg 16.02.04.04.02.01.01 Around the Nativity
candelsnȳtels 17.05.03 Sources of fire/light
candelstæf 17.05.03 Sources of fire/light
candelsticca 17.05.03 Sources of fire/light
candeltrēow 17.05.03 Sources of fire/light
candeltwist 17.05.03 Sources of fire/light
candelwēoce 17.05.03 Sources of fire/light
candelwyrt 02.07.11 Plants/flowers (alphabetical order)
cann 14.03.03 Law, action of the courts
canne 04.01.03.05.04 Drinking vessel
cannon 02.07.08 Grasses, reeds, etc.
canon 16.02.01.09.01 Canon law
canonbōc 16.02.05.10.08 A book of canons/decrees
canondōm 16.02.01.09.01 Canon law

canonic 16.02.01.09.01 Canon law; 16.02.03.01 Ecclesiastical authority
canoniclic 16.02.01.09.01 Canon law
canoniclīf 16.02.03.03 A religious
cantel 04.05.02.06 A buttress, support
cantelcāp 16.02.05.06.01 Outer garments
cantelclāþ 16.02.05.06.01 Outer garments
cantercæppe 16.02.05.06.01 Outer garments
cantere 16.02.03.02.13 A church singer, singer in choir
canterstæf 16.02.05.05.08 A staff, wand of authority
cantic 16.02.04.03.03.01 A hymn, song of praise, canticle
canticsang 16.02.04.03.03.01 A hymn, song of praise, canticle
capellan 16.02.03.02.08 A (domestic) chaplain
capian (ūp) 02.05.09.04 To see, look upon, behold
capitelhūs 16.02.05.03.10 A chapter-house
capitol 09.03.07.07.02.01 A main division; 16.02.03.01 Ecclesiastical authority; 16.02.04.03.03.01 A hymn, song of praise, canticle
capitolmæsse 16.02.04.07.04.01 The service of the mass
capitularie 16.02.05.10.04 Choir books, etc.
gecapitulod 09.03.07.07.02.01.01 A heading, title, superscription
cappadonisc 02.03.03.06.07.07 Other (alphabetical order)
capun 02.06.08.02 Domestic fowl
carbunculus 17.04.03.04 Gems collectively
carcern 14.05.08.01 Prison, confinement, durance

carcernþȳstru 03.01.13 Darkness, obscurity
carcernweard 14.05.08.01 Prison, confinement, durance
carcian 11.01 Action, doing, performance
cardinal 16.02.03.02.03 A cardinal
carful 08.01.03.03 Anxiety; 08.01.03.07.04 Severity, harshness; 11.02.02.02 Care, mindfulness, attention
carfullīce 06.01.01.02 Care, attention, observation
carfulnes 08.01.03.03 Anxiety; 11.02.02.02 Care, mindfulness, attention
carfulness 16.02.03.02.07 A priest, cleric
cargealdor 08.01.03.04.01 Complaint, lamentation
cargēst 16.01.03.03 A doomed spirit
carian 08.01.02.02 Love, affection, care; 08.01.03.04 Grief; 11.02.02.02 Care, mindfulness, attention; 11.10.02.02.01 Care, interest in
caric 02.07.09.02 Particular fruits (alphabetical order)
carig 08.01.03.03 Anxiety; 08.01.03.07.04 Severity, harshness
carl 02.03.01.01 Male person, man
carlēas 08.01.01.03.01 Freedom from trouble, comfort, security
carlēasnes 08.01.01.03.01 Freedom from trouble, comfort, security
carlēast 08.01.01.03.01 Freedom from trouble, comfort, security
carles wæn 01.02.01.01.02.01 Constellation
carlfugol 02.06.08.02 Domestic fowl
carlīce 08.01.03.06 Adversity, affliction
carlmann 02.03.01.01 Male person, man

carr 01.01.02.01.02.02.05 Crag, rock, stone; 01.01.02.02.01 Rock, stone
carseld 04.05.03.02.02.03 Disagreeable dwellings
carsīþ 05.12.01.01 To go on a journey/expedition, travel
carsorg 08.01.03.03 Anxiety
carte 09.03.07.06.06 Membrane, vellum; 09.03.07.07.03.02.02 A letter; 09.03.07.07.03.04.01 A document, deed
caru 08.01.03 Bad feeling, sadness; 08.01.03.03 Anxiety; 11.10.02.02.01 Care, interest in
carwylm 08.01.03.04 Grief
cāserdōm 12.01.01 Authority
cāsere 12.01.01.04.01 A royal leader
cāsering 15.01.04 Coinage, money
cāserlic 12.01.01 Authority
cāsern 12.01.01.04.01 A royal leader
cassia 02.07.10.01 Particular herbs/spices (alphabetical order)
cassuc 02.07.08 Grasses, reeds, etc.
cassucen 02.07.08 Grasses, reeds, etc.
cassuclēaf 02.07.08 Grasses, reeds, etc.
castel 05.10.05.04.11 A circle, circuit, circumference; 12.06.02.01 A township; 13.02.06.01 Stronghold, fort/fortified town
castelmann 02.03.03.04.05 Populace of a town/city
castelweall 13.02.06.01 Stronghold, fort/fortified town
castelweorc 04.05 Building, construction
castnere 04.05.04.03 A box, case, chest, container
casul 16.02.05.06.01 Outer garments
cāsum niman 09.03.02.03.01.01 Declension
cāsus 09.03.02.03.01.01.01 Case

catt 02.06.02.01.02 Cat
catte 02.06.02.01.02 Cat
caulic 02.08.12.02.05 Pharmacy, curing with salves; 02.08.12.02.05.01 A herb with medicinal properties
cawellēaf 02.07.09.02.02.02 Other vegetables (alphabetical order)
cawelsǣd 02.07.09.02.02.02 Other vegetables (alphabetical order)
cawelstela 02.07.09.02.02.02 Other vegetables (alphabetical order)
cawelstoc 02.07.09.02.02.02 Other vegetables (alphabetical order)
cawelwurm 02.06.09.02.04 Butterfly, moth
cawl 02.07.09.02.02.02 Other vegetables (alphabetical order); 04.01.02.02.06.03 Food receptacle, basket; 17.03.12.01 A basket
cawlic 02.07.09.02.02.02 Other vegetables (alphabetical order)
cēac 04.01.03.05.04 Drinking vessel; 14.03.03.05 Ordeal
cēacādl 02.08.07.04.03 A disease of the jaws
cēacbān 02.04.05.04.02.02 Cheek/chin bones
cēacbora 04.01.02.03.01 Service in kitchen; 12.01.01.08.01 A servant, attendant
cēace 02.04.03.01.03.05 Cheek; 02.04.03.01.03.07 Jaw(s); 02.04.05.04.02.02 Cheek/chin bones; 02.04.06.03.02.02 Throat/gullet
cēacfull 04.01.03 Drinking
ceacga 02.07.03.01 A bush
ceaf 04.02.04.04.05.02 Chaff
ceaffinc 02.06.08.05 Forest bird, wild-fowl

ceafl 02.04.03.01.03.07 Jaw(s); 02.04.05.04.02.02 Cheek/chin bones; 02.04.06.03.02.02 Throat/gullet
ceaflādl 02.08.07.04.03 A disease of the jaws
ceafor 02.06.09.02.03 Beetle
ceahhe 02.06.08.05 Forest bird, wild-fowl
ceahhetan 08.01.01.03.07.01 Laughter
ceahhetung 08.01.01.03.07.02 Jesting, pleasantry
cealc 01.01.02.02.02.03 Limestone, chalk; 04.05.01.03 Gypsum, chalk
cealccrundel 01.01.02.01.03.03 Valley; 17.04.01 Sources of materials
cealcgraf 17.04.01 Sources of materials
gecealcian 03.01.14.03 White/whiteness
cealcpytt 17.04.01 Sources of materials
cealcsēaþ 17.04.01 Sources of materials
cealcstān 01.01.02.02.02.03 Limestone, chalk
ceald 01.03.01.04 Wintry weather, cold; 03.01.11 Coldness, coolness; 08.01.03.07.04 Severity, harshness
cealde 03.01.11 Coldness, coolness; 08.01.03.07.04 Severity, harshness
cealdheort 08.01.03.09.11 Hardheartedness, cruelty, severity
cealdian 03.01.11 Coldness, coolness
cealdnes 03.01.11 Coldness, coolness
cealer 04.01.02.01.02.09.09 Curds
cealf 02.06.02.01.03 Cattle
gecealfe 02.06.01.07 Breeding, hatching
cealfian 02.06.01.07 Breeding, hatching
cealfloca 04.02.05.06.01.01 A cattle pen/cowshed
cealfwyrt 02.07.11.02 Unidentified plants (alphabetical order)
ceallian 02.05.10.15.01 To raise (the voice), raise up (noise)

cēap 02.06.02 Domestic animals, livestock; 14.03.03.07 Security, pledge, bail; 14.03.03.09.02 Atonement; 15.02 Worth, value; 15.05 Trade, traffic, commerce; 15.05.01 Goods, stock, merchandise
cēap (ge)drīfan 15.05 Trade, traffic, commerce
cēapcniht 12.01.01.09 Bondage, slavery; 15.05 Trade, traffic, commerce
cēapdæg 05.11.03.01.05 A day; 15.05.01 Goods, stock, merchandise
cēapēadig 15.01.05 Possession of wealth
cēapealuþel 04.01.03.05.03 Tavern
cēapgild 15.02 Worth, value
cēapgyld 14.03.03.09.02 Atonement
(ge)cēapian 15.05 Trade, traffic, commerce
gecēapian 10.03.05.01.01 A bribe, gift, payment
cēapland 15.01.01 Landed property
cēapman 15.05.01 Goods, stock, merchandise
cēapsceamul 15.03 Exaction of tax/tribute
cēapscip 05.12.01.09.03.01.01 Kind of ship
cēapsetl 15.03 Exaction of tax/tribute
cēapstow 15.05.01 Goods, stock, merchandise
cēapstrǣt 15.05.01 Goods, stock, merchandise
cēaptoln 15.03.01 Toll
cēapung 15.05 Trade, traffic, commerce
cēapunggemōt 15.05.01 Goods, stock, merchandise
cearcetung 02.05.10.07 A crashing, noise
cearcian 02.05.10.06 Harsh sound
ceare 05.10.06.02.02 Curvature, bend, twist

cearm/cirm 02.05.10.15.01 To raise (the voice), raise up (noise)
cearruce 05.12.01.06 Vehicle
ceart 01.01.02.01.01 Tract of land; 01.01.02.01.06 Wild/uncultivated land
cearwund 02.08.04.01 A wound
cēas 07.05.01 Censure, reproof, rebuke; 12.05.03.01 Quarrel, contentiousness, strife
cēaslunger 12.05.03.01 Quarrel, contentiousness, strife
cēast 07.05.01 Censure, reproof, rebuke; 12.05.03.01 Quarrel, contentiousness, strife
ceaster 12.06.02.01 A township; 13.02.06.01 Stronghold, fort/fortified town; 16.01.02.01 Heavenly dwelling place; 16.01.05.01 Damnation, perdition, reprobation
ceasteræsc 02.07.11 Plants/flowers (alphabetical order)
ceasterbūend 02.03.03.04.05 Populace of a town/city
ceasterherpaþ 05.12.01.03.01.03 A highway
ceasterhlid 05.10.05.04.14.02 An opening/space in an enclosure
ceasterhof 04.05.03.02.02.01 Dwellings in particular places
ceasterlēod(e) 02.03.03.04.05 Populace of a town/city
ceasternisc 12.06.02.01 A township
ceastersǣtan (-e) 02.03.03.04.05 Populace of a town/city
(ge)ceasterwaran (-e/-u) 02.03.03.04.05 Populace of a town/city
ceasterweall 05.10.05.04.15.02 A wall
ceasterwīc 12.06.02.01 A township
ceasterwyrhta 04.04 Weaving
ceasterwyrt 02.07.11 Plants/flowers (alphabetical order)
cēastful 12.05.03.01 Quarrel, contentiousness, strife
cēcel/cycel 04.01.02.01.07.04 Cake
cedelic 02.07.11 Plants/flowers (alphabetical order)
ceder 02.07.03.05 Particular trees/shrubs (alphabetical order)
cederbēam 02.07.03.05 Particular trees/shrubs (alphabetical order)
cedertrēow 02.07.03.05 Particular trees/shrubs (alphabetical order)
cedrisc 02.07.03.05 Particular trees/shrubs (alphabetical order)
ceir 02.05.10.15.01 To raise (the voice), raise up (noise)
(ge)cēlan 03.01.11 Coldness, coolness; 04.01.03 Drinking
celde 01.01.03.01.01.07 Spring, fountain, well
celendre 02.07.10.01 Particular herbs/spices (alphabetical order)
celeþonie 02.07.11 Plants/flowers (alphabetical order)
cēling 03.01.11 Coldness, coolness
celis 04.04.07.15 Footwear, covering for the feet
cella/-e 16.02.05.04.01 Parts of monastery
cellod 13.02.08.03.01.06 A shield; 17.02.05.01 Ornamental object
celmertmonn 12.01.01.08.01 A servant, attendant
cēlnes 01.03.01.05 Wind; 03.01.11 Coldness, coolness
gecēlnes 03.01.11 Coldness, coolness
cemban 04.04.01 Fulling
(ge)cemban 04.06.01.07 Hair-care
cemes 04.04.07.08 A short garment, skirt, kirtle
cempa 13.02.10.01 A man, warrior

cempestre 13.02.10.01 A man, warrior
cēn 09.03.07.01.01 A runic letter; 17.05.03 Sources of fire/light
cēne 06.01.05.02.01.01 Sagacity; 06.02.07.06 Courage, boldness, valour
cenep 02.04.04.03.03.01 Beard, whisker; 04.02.05.06.05.03.02 A bit
cēnlīce 06.02.07.06 Courage, boldness, valour
(ge)cennan 02.01.03.03.02 To bring forth, produce; 02.07.01 To grow; 09.06.02.01 To tell, make known, declare, relate, announce; 09.07.04 Assertion, affirmation; 14.03.03.08 Justification
cennend 02.03.02.01 Parent
cennende 02.04.06.04 Reproductive organs
cennendlic 02.04.06.04 Reproductive organs
cennes 02.01.03.03.02 To bring forth, produce; 02.01.03.03.03 Birth; 02.01.03.03.03.01 Child-bearing, childbirth
cennestre 02.01.03.03.02 To bring forth, produce; 02.03.02.01 Parent
cenning 02.01.03.03.01 To beget; 02.01.03.03.03 Birth; 14.03.03.03 Witness, testimony, attestation
cenningstōw 12.06.04.01 Birthplace
cenningtīd 02.01.03.03.03.01 Child-bearing, childbirth
cent 12.06.01.01 England
centaur 02.06.10.01.03 Half of another kind
centaurie 02.07.11 Plants/flowers (alphabetical order)
centescīr 12.06.01.01 England
centingas 02.03.03.05.01.03 Kentish people
centisc 02.03.03.05.01.03 Kentish people
centland 12.06.01.01 England
centrīce 12.01.01.01 Rule, domination, direction; 12.06.01.01 England
centur(io) 13.02.10.01.01 A commander, officer
centurius 13.02.10.01.01 A commander, officer
centware 02.03.03.05.01.03 Kentish people
cēnþu 06.02.07.06.02 Boldness
cēo 02.06.08.05 Forest bird, wild-fowl
cēod 17.03.12 A receptacle, container
cēol 05.12.01.09.03.01 A ship, boat
cēol gestīgan 05.12.01.09 To travel on water
ceoldre 04.02.05.06.01.02 To milk
ceole 01.01.02.01.03.03 Valley; 01.01.03.01.01.04 Watercourse/channel; 02.04.06.03.02.02 Throat/gullet
ceolor 02.04.06.03.02.02 Throat/gullet
cēolþel 05.12.01.09.03.01.03 Part of ship
ceolwærc 02.08.07.04.04 Respiratory disease
ceorfæx 13.02.08.04 Weapons, arms
ceorfan 05.06.02.02 A tearing apart
(ge)ceorfan 05.06.01 Devastation, laying waste; 05.06.02 Cleaving, splitting, cutting; 17.02.05.05 A carving, graving; 17.02.05.05.01 Graven, embossed, chased
(ge)ceorfan (of) 05.06.02 Cleaving, splitting, cutting
ceorfingīsen 17.03.06 Tools for marking
ceorfsæx 02.08.12.02.06 Surgical
ceorian 08.01.03.05 Murmuring, complaint; 14.03.03 Law, action of the courts
ceorig 08.01.03.05 Murmuring, complaint

ceorl 02.03.01.01 Male person, man; 04.02.02 Farmer, cultivator; 12.01.01.10 Freedom, being free; 12.01.01.11 The common people; 12.08.06.02.06 Deceit, evil, wickedness; 12.09 Marriage, state of marriage; 13.02.10.01 A man, warrior; 16.02.03.03.05 A layman
ceorlæs 12.09.03 Unmarried state
ceorlboren 12.01.01.11 The common people
ceorlfolc 12.01.01.11 The common people
(ge)ceorlian 12.09.02 Marriage ceremony
ceorlic 15.01.01 Landed property
ceorlisc 04.02.02 Farmer, cultivator; 12.01.01.11 The common people
ceorlisce 12.01.01.11 The common people
ceorllīce 03.04.03 Generality
ceorlman 12.01.01.10 Freedom, being free
ceorlstrang 05.08 Strength
ceorran 02.05.10.06 Harsh sound
ceorung 08.01.03.05 Murmuring, complaint
(ge)cēosan 07.01.01 Choice, election
gecēosan 10.01.01.01 Receiving, gaining, getting
gecēosan dōmas 14.03.02 A legislator
ceosel 01.01.02.02.02.01 Sand, gravel
ceoselbǣre 01.01.02.02.02.01 Sand, gravel
ceoselstān 01.01.02.02.02.01 Sand, gravel; 02.08.08 Internal disease
gecēosendlic 07.01.01 Choice, election
ceoslen 01.01.02.02.02.01 Sand, gravel
ceoslig 01.01.02.02.02.01 Sand, gravel
ceosol 02.04.06.03.02.02 Throat/gullet; 02.04.06.03.02.03 Stomach/belly

(ge)cēowan 04.01.01 Eating; 04.01.01.01 Chewing
cēowung 04.01.01.01 Chewing
cēpan 02.05.09.05 To watch, observe, survey; 06.02.05.01 Strong liking for, devotion to; 11.02.02.02 Care, mindfulness, attention; 14.05.08 Captivity; 16.02.04.04.02 A feast-day, holy day
(ge)cēpan 06.01.08.01 Expectation, waiting
cēping 02.05.09.05 To watch, observe, survey
cēpnian 06.01.08.01 Expectation, waiting
ceren 04.01.03.05.01.01 Wine
cerfelle 02.07.11 Plants/flowers (alphabetical order)
cerlic 02.07.11 Plants/flowers (alphabetical order)
certare 05.12.01.06 Vehicle; 13.02.10.01.02.02.02 Branch of army
ceruphīn 16.01.02.05.01 An angel
chor 16.02.03.02.13 A church singer, singer in choir; 16.02.05.03.02 Choir
chorglēo 18.02.04 Dancing; 18.02.07 Music
cīan 02.06.06.01 Part of fish
cicc 05.10.05.04.08.01 A bend
cicen 02.06.08.02 Domestic fowl; 04.01.02.01.02.06 Chicken
cicena mete 02.07.11 Plants/flowers (alphabetical order)
cicropisc 02.03.03.06.07.07 Other (alphabetical order)
(ge)cīd 12.05.03.01 Quarrel, contentiousness, strife
gecīd 07.05.01 Censure, reproof, rebuke
(ge)cīdan 07.05.01 Censure, reproof, rebuke; 12.05.03.01 Quarrel,

contentiousness, strife; 14.03.03.06 False witness
(ge)cīdan (ymb) 07.05.03.01 Falseness in speech, detraction
cīdere 07.05.03.03 Scorn, insult, abuse
cīdung 07.05.01 Censure, reproof, rebuke
(ge)cīegan 02.05.10.15.01 To raise (the voice), raise up (noise); 06.02.06.03.03 Incitement; 09.01.03 To address, speak to; 09.06.02.01.07.02 A categorizing name; 12.03.03.01 Summons, a call, summoning; 16.02.04.08.01 Kinds of prayer
(ge)cīegan tō 08.01.02.04 Hospitality
ciele 01.03.01.04 Wintry weather, cold
cielegicel 01.03.01.04.02 Ice
cielle 17.05.03 Sources of fire/light
cīepeþing 15.05.01 Goods, stock, merchandise
cīeping 15.03.01 Toll; 15.05 Trade, traffic, commerce; 15.05.01 Goods, stock, merchandise
cierr 05.11.02 A time, particular time, occasion; 11.02 Occupation, activity, business
(ge)cierran 05.12.02 To move, set in motion; 05.12.05 To move and change direction, turn; 05.12.05.02 To go/travel towards, come, approach; 05.12.05.11.01 To return; 05.13 Changeableness, change; 05.13.01 Transformation, taking another shape; 11.03 Endeavour; 12.05.06.04.02 Submission, subjection, obedience; 16.02.04.10.01 Conversion
(ge)cierran fram 11.06.04 Abstention, abstaining from
(ge)cierran on/tō 05.13 Changeableness, change

(ge)cierran (on/tō) 05.03.01.02 To work upon, influence
(ge)cierran tō 12.03.05 Permission
(ge)cierran (tō) 08.01.02.01 Favour, kindness, grace; 11.10.02.02.01 Care, interest in
(ge)cierran tō ānum 09.07.04.01 Confirmation, agreement
gecierran 05.10.04 Place, room; 05.12.02.08 To give a different direction to, turn; 06.02.06.03 Persuasion, prompting; 09.04.03.01 A translation
gecierran (tō) 12.05.06.04 A trampling upon, subjection
(ge)cierrednes 16.02.04.10.01 Conversion
gecierrednes 16.02.03.03 A religious
(ge)cierring 16.02.04.10.01 Conversion
gecierring 11.06.06 Turning
cifes 12.08.08.01.02.01.02 Concubinage
cifesboren 02.03.02.02.05 Having the same parents
cifesdōm 12.08.08.01.02.01.02 Concubinage
cifesgemāna 12.08.08.01.02.01.02 Concubinage
cifeshād 12.08.08.01.02.01.02 Concubinage
gecīgednes 09.06.02.01.07 A name, appellation; 12.03.03.01 Summons, a call, summoning
cigel 17.03.09 A post, rod, stick, etc.
gecīgendlic 09.03.02.03.01.01.01 Case
cīgere 02.05.10.15.01 To raise (the voice), raise up (noise)
gecīgnes 09.06.02.01.07 A name, appellation; 12.03.03.01 Summons, a call, summoning; 12.03.04.01 Entreaty, solemn appeal

845

cīgung 12.03.04.01 Entreaty, solemn appeal
cilce 01.01.02.01 Ground; 01.01.02.02.02.03 Limestone, chalk
cild 02.03.01.04 Child; 12.01.01.06.08 A person of rank, elder, great man
cild habban 02.01.03.03.02 To bring forth, produce
cilda trog 04.05.04.05 A bed, bedstead
cildamæssedæg 16.02.04.04.02.01.01 Around the Nativity
cildclāþas 04.04.07.01 Mode of dressing, fashion
cildcradol 04.05.04.05 A bed, bedstead
cildcradul 02.01.04.01 Youth
cildfaru 05.12.01.06 Vehicle
cildfēdende 02.01.03.03.03.02 Nursing, child-feeding
cildfēstre 02.01.03.03.03.02 Nursing, child-feeding
cildfōstre 02.01.03.03.03.02 Nursing, child-feeding
cildgeoguþ 02.01.04.01 Youth
cildgeong 02.01.04.01 Youth
cildhād 02.01.04.01 Youth
cildhama 02.01.03.03.01 To beget; 02.04.06.04.02 Female reproductive organs
cildisc 02.01.04.01 Youth
cildlic 02.01.04.01 Youth
cildsung 06.01.05.03.02.01 Foolishness, lightmindedness
cildyldu 02.01.04.01 Youth
cile bærnett 02.08.03.02 Itch, irritation
cilforlamb 02.06.02.01.08 Sheep
cilic 04.04.05.01 Coarse, rough (of cloth); 04.04.07.01 Mode of dressing, fashion; 16.02.05.06 Ritual clothing
gecilled 03.01.11 Coldness, coolness
cillinesc 02.03.03.06.07.07 Other (alphabetical order)
ciltrog 04.05.04.05 A bed, bedstead
cimbal 18.02.07.02.01 Percussion instruments
cimbalglīwere 18.02.07.02.01 Percussion instruments
cimbing 03.03.06.01 A whole formed by joining
cimbīren 17.03.10 Supports and fastenings
cimbstān 04.05.02.05 A pedestal, socket
cīnan 02.08.05.02.02 Scab, roughness of skin; 05.06.02.01.01 A crack; 05.10.05.04.14.01 A yawning, gaping opening
cinbān 02.04.05.04.02.02 Cheek/chin bones
cinberg 13.02.08.03.01.02.01 Parts of a helmet
cincende 08.01.01.03.07.01 Laughter
cincung 08.01.01.03.07.01 Laughter
cīne 01.01.02.01.03.01 Cave; 05.06.02.01.01 A crack; 09.03.07.06.06 Membrane, vellum
cīneht 05.06.02.01.01 A crack
cinn 02.04.03.01.03.08 Chin
cinnan 05.10.05.04.14.01 A yawning, gaping opening
cintōþ 02.04.06.03.02.01.01 Tooth/teeth
cīpe 02.07.09.02.02.01 Edible root/bulb
cīpelēac 02.07.09.02.02.01 Edible root/bulb
cipp 02.07.03.03.01 Wood (as substance); 04.02.04.06.07 Ploughing equipment; 04.04.03 A spinning-house or chamber; 06.01.05.03 Want of understanding
circian 02.05.10.15.01 To raise (the voice), raise up (noise)
circolwyrde 03.03.03.01 Arithmetic

circul 01.02.01.01.02.01.01 The Zodiac; 03.03.03.01 Arithmetic; 05.11.06.02 Reckoning/computation of time; 05.12.05.04 To rotate, turn round, revolve
circulādl 02.08.06 Skin disease, erysipelas
ciricǣw 16.02.04.07.05 An order (general)
ciricbrǣc 16.02.04.14 Sacrilege
ciricbryce 16.02.04.14 Sacrilege
cirice 16.02.03 The church (as temporal/spiritual body); 16.02.03.03 A religious
ciricend 16.02.03.02 A cleric, clergyman (general)
ciricfultum 15.01.02 Gift, transfer of property
ciricgang 16.02.04.06 Attendance at church, church-going; 16.02.04.13.02 Purificatory rites
ciricgemāna 16.02.03 The church (as temporal/spiritual body)
ciricgeorn 16.02.04.06 Attendance at church, church-going
ciricgriþ 14.05.04 A penalty, punishment
cirichād 16.02.04.07.05 An order (general)
cirichālgung 16.02.01.10.02 Consecration
cirichata 16.02.01.05 Heresy, error, wrong belief
cirichege 02.02.05.01 Place of burial
ciricland 16.02.05.01 Land
ciriclic 16.02.03.01 Ecclesiastical authority
ciricmǣrsung 16.02.01.10.02 Consecration
ciricmangung 16.02.01.13.01 Kinds of sin
ciricnytt 16.02.04.03.01 A rite, ceremony
ciricragu 02.07.06 Lichen
ciricrēna 14.02.01.02 Wrongful taking, theft
ciricsang 16.02.04.03.03 Singing, church singing; 16.02.04.03.03.01 A hymn, song of praise, canticle
ciricsangere 16.02.03.02.13 A church singer, singer in choir
ciricsceatweorc 17 Work, doings, actions, labour
ciricsōcn 16.02.04.06 Attendance at church, church-going
cirictīd 16.02.04.05 Canonical hour, service
ciricþegn 16.02.03.02.07.01 A priest of a church or minster
ciricþēnung 16.02.04.03.01 A rite, ceremony
ciricþingere 16.02.03.02.07 A priest, cleric
ciricwæcce 16.02.04.07.06.02 A vigil
ciricwǣd 16.02.05.06 Ritual clothing
ciricwaru 16.02.03 The church (as temporal/spiritual body)
ciricweard 16.02.03.02.12 Cleric in minor orders
ciricwyrhta 04.05 Building, construction
ciris/cirse 02.07.09.02 Particular fruits (alphabetical order)
cirisbēam 02.07.09.02 Particular fruits (alphabetical order)
cirman 02.05.10.15.01 To raise (the voice), raise up (noise)
cirps 02.04.04.03.01 Texture of hair
(ge)cirpsian 04.06.01.07 Hair-care
cis 01.01.02.02.02.01 Sand, gravel
cīs 07.01.01.01.01 Fastidiousness, daintiness
cisen 01.01.02.02.02.01 Sand, gravel

ciseræppel 02.07.09.02 Particular fruits (alphabetical order)
cīsnes 07.01.01.01.01 Fastidiousness, daintiness
cist 02.02.05.01.01 A grave, burial place, sepulchre; 04.05.04.03 A box, case, chest, container; 17.03.12.01 A basket
cistelett 02.07.03.05 Particular trees/shrubs (alphabetical order)
cistmēlum 06.02.05.04.05 Earnestness
citelflōd 01.01.03.01.01.07 Spring, fountain, well
citelhrūm 03.01.09.02.01.02 Embers, cinders, ashes; 04.06.02.05 Dust, powder
citelian 02.05.06.01 To touch and press
citelung 02.05.06.01 To touch and press
citelwyll 01.01.03.01.01.07 Spring, fountain, well
citere 18.02.07.02.03.01 A harp, lyre
cīþ 02.07.02.04 Seed, kind of seed; 02.07.02.05 A shoot, sprout, tendril; 06.01.05.03 Want of understanding
cīþfæst 02.07.01 To grow; 05.12.04.01 Stability, firmness
clacc 01.01.02.01.02.02.01 Hill
clacu 08.01.03.07.02.01 Injury, offence
cladersticca 04.02.04.06.11 A rattle, clapper
clæclēas 11.10 Safety, safeness; 12.08.05 Innocence
clædur 04.02.04.06.11 A rattle, clapper
clæferwyrt 02.07.11 Plants/flowers (alphabetical order)
clæfre 02.07.11 Plants/flowers (alphabetical order)
clǣg 01.01.02.02.02.02 Clay, loam
clǣig 01.01.02.02.02.02 Clay, loam
(ge)clǣman 02.08.12.02.05.02 Salves, ointments; 04.05.01.03 Gypsum, chalk

clǣming 04.06.02.03 Stain, smear
clǣmman 02.04.03.04.01.01 Hand
clǣmnes 02.08.03.01 Extreme pain, torture, torment
clǣne 03.03.06 Wholeness; 04.01.02.01.01 Edibility; 04.02.03.01.02 Cleared land; 04.06.01 Clean; 04.06.01.09 To cleanse, remove impurity from (an object); 07.02.03 Perfection; 12.08.03.03.01.01 Chastity; 12.08.04 Purity, moral cleanness; 14.01.02 A law, statute; 15.01.01 Landed property; 16.02.04.13 Ceremonial cleanness
clǣne bæc habban 06.01.07.03 Truth of speech or thought, veracity; 12.08.02.03 Goodness, probity; 14.03.03.08 Justification
clǣne legere 02.02.05.01.01 A grave, burial place, sepulchre
clǣngeorn 04.06 Salubrity; 12.08.04 Purity, moral cleanness; 12.09.03.01 Celibacy
clǣnheort 12.08.04 Purity, moral cleanness
clǣnlic 07.02.04.03 Nobleness, excellence, nobility, magnificence; 12.08.04 Purity, moral cleanness; 16.02.04.13 Ceremonial cleanness
clǣnlīce 03.03.06 Wholeness; 06.01.05.01.01 Clear to the understanding, plain; 11.05.02.01 A standard, norm, ethos; 12.08.04 Purity, moral cleanness
clǣnmōd 12.08.04 Purity, moral cleanness
clǣnnes 12.08.03.03.01.01 Chastity; 12.08.04 Purity, moral cleanness; 16.02.04.13 Ceremonial cleanness

clǣnsere 16.02.03.02.07 A priest, cleric; 16.02.03.02.09 A confessor; 16.02.04.07.02.01 Penitence

(ge)clǣnsian 02.08.12.02.07.01 Purgative; 04.06.01 Clean; 04.06.01.09 To cleanse, remove impurity from (an object); 12.08.04 Purity, moral cleanness; 14.03.03.08 Justification; 14.05 Punishment; 16.02.04.13 Ceremonial cleanness

clǣnsung 02.08.12.02.05.04 To cleanse, clean away; 04.06.01 Clean; 12.08.04 Purity, moral cleanness; 16.02.04.13 Ceremonial cleanness

(ge)clǣnsung 16.02.04.07.02.03 Penance, an act/instance of penance

clǣnsungdæg 02.08.12.02.05 Pharmacy, curing with salves; 02.08.12.02.07.01 Purgative

clǣnsungdagas 16.02.04.13 Ceremonial cleanness

clǣnsungdrenc 02.08.12.02.07.01 Purgative

clæppan 05.12.05.05 To shake, quake, wag

clæppettan 02.08.03.02 Itch, irritation; 05.12.05.05 To shake, quake, wag

clæppetung 05.12.05.05 To shake, quake, wag

clām 02.08.12.02.05.03 A poultice; 04.05.01.03 Gypsum, chalk

clamm 10.04.02 To grasp, take hold of; 14.03.03.07 Security, pledge, bail; 14.05.07 Binding, fastening with bonds

clamme belecgan 14.05.07 Binding, fastening with bonds

clangettung 02.05.10.11 Clang, sound of metal

clāte 02.07.11 Plants/flowers (alphabetical order)

clāte crop 02.07.11 Plants/flowers (alphabetical order); 02.07.11 Plants/flowers (alphabetical order)

clater 01.01.02.02.01 Rock, stone

clatrung 02.05.10.10 Clattering, noise

clāþ 04.04.05 Woven material, fabric; 04.04.07 Trappings, equipment, garb; 04.04.08 A covering, curtain, veil, garment, etc.

clāþflyhte 04.04.05.06 To sew, stitch

geclāþian 04.04.07 Trappings, equipment, garb

clāþwēoce 17.05.03 Sources of fire/light

clauster 16.02.05.04 A monastery/convent; 16.02.05.04.01 Parts of monastery

clāwan 05.06.06.01 A tearing, laceration

clāwian 05.06.06.01 A tearing, laceration

clawu 02.04.04.02 Nail; 02.06.01.04 Leg; 02.06.08.01 Part of bird; 17.03.07 Tools for digging/grasping/pulling; 17.03.10 Supports and fastenings

clāwung 02.08.08.04.01 Gripe, colic

cleac 05.12.01.03.03 A fordable place

cleacian 05.12.03.01.02 Haste, hurry

clencan 05.05.03 Binding, fastening

clengan 05.02.02 Nature, established order of things

clent 01.01.02.02.01 Rock, stone

cleofa 01.01.02.01.03.01 Cave; 04.05.03.02.02.01 Dwellings in particular places; 04.05.03.04 A closet, chamber, room; 16.02.05.04.01 Parts of monastery

cleofan 05.06.02.01 A cleft, split

cleofung 05.06.02 Cleaving, splitting, cutting

cleot 17.03.10.02 A pin, peg, nail

cleric 09.03.07.03 A scribe, copyist; 16.02.03.02 A cleric, clergyman (general); 16.02.03.02.12 Cleric in minor orders
clerichād 16.02.03.02 A cleric, clergyman (general)
clericmann 16.02.03.02 A cleric, clergyman (general)
clerus 16.02.03.02.07 A priest, cleric
cleweþa 02.08.03.02 Itch, irritation
clibbor 06.02.07.03 Perseverance
clidren 02.05.10.10 Clattering, noise
clīewen 05.10.06.02 Rotundity, roundness
clif 01.01.02.01.01.03 Shore, bank; 01.01.02.01.02.02.04 Cliff
clīfan 03.01.17 Thickness, viscosity
clife 02.07.11 Plants/flowers (alphabetical order)
clifer 02.06.08.01 Part of bird
cliferfēte 02.06.01.04 Leg
clifhlȳp 05.12.05.13.03 To fall
clifian 05.02.02 Nature, established order of things
(ge)clifian (on) 03.01.17 Thickness, viscosity; 06.02.07.03 Perseverance
clifig 01.01.02.01.02.02.04 Cliff
clifiht 01.01.02.01.02.02.04 Cliff
clifrian 05.06.06.01 A tearing, laceration
clifrung 05.06.06.01 A tearing, laceration
clifstān 01.01.02.02.01 Rock, stone
clifwyrt 02.07.11 Plants/flowers (alphabetical order)
climban 05.12.05.12 To go up, ascend
clinc 01.01.02.01 Ground
clincig 11.11.01 A physical difficulty, strait
clingan 02.01.04.03 Aging, growing old; 03.01.17.01 A coagulating, mixing; 03.01.18 Dryness (not wetness); 05.10.05.02.03 To reduce, make thin(ner)
(ge)clipian 02.05.10.15.01 To raise (the voice), raise up (noise); 09.06.02.01.07.02 A categorizing name; 12.03.03.01 Summons, a call, summoning; 12.03.04.01 Entreaty, solemn appeal
geclipian 09.06.02.01 To tell, make known, declare, relate, announce
clipiende stæf 09 Speech, vocal utterance
clipigendlic 09 Speech, vocal utterance; 09.03.02.03.01.01.01 Case
clipol 09 Speech, vocal utterance
geclips 02.05.10.15.01 To raise (the voice), raise up (noise)
clipung 02.05.10.15.01 To raise (the voice), raise up (noise); 09 Speech, vocal utterance; 09.03.02.02 Vocabulary; 09.06.02.01.07 A name, appellation; 17.02 Work, occupation, employment
(ge)clipung 12.03.04 A request, prayer; 16.02.04.08 Prayer
clipur 02.05.10.13.01 A bell
clite 02.07.11 Plants/flowers (alphabetical order)
cliþa 02.08.12.02.05.03 A poultice
cliþe 02.07.11 Plants/flowers (alphabetical order)
cliþwyrt 02.07.11 Plants/flowers (alphabetical order)
cloccettan 05.12.05.05 To shake, quake, wag
cloccian 02.05.10.15.07 Voice, note (of a bird)
clodd 01.01.02.02 Earth, soil
clodhammer 02.06.08.05 Forest bird, wild-fowl
clōf 01.01.02.01.03.03 Valley
geclofa 03.06.01.01 Imitation

clofe 04.04.10.02 A button, brooch
clōh 01.01.02.01.03.03 Valley
clop 01.01.02.01.02.02.01 Hill
clott 03 Material, matter, substance
clūd 01.01.02.01.02.02.01 Hill;
01.01.02.01.02.02.05 Crag, rock, stone
clūder 01.01.02.01.02.02.05 Crag, rock, stone
clūdig 01.01.02.01 Ground; 01.01.02.01.02.02.01 Hill; 01.01.02.01.02.02.05 Crag, rock, stone
clufeht(e) 02.07.02.02 A clove (bulb, tuber)
clufþung(e) 04.06.02.06 Poison; 02.07.11 Plants/flowers (alphabetical order)
clufu 02.07.02.02 A clove (bulb, tuber); 04.01.02.01.05.05.04 Cloves
clufwyrt 02.07.11 Plants/flowers (alphabetical order)
clugge 02.05.10.13.01 A bell
clum(m)ian 09.02.03.01 Murmur, whispering
clūse 01.01.02.01.03.03 Valley; 14.05.08.01 Prison, confinement, durance; 17.03.10.01 A bolt, lock, bar
clūstor 05.10.05.04.15.01 A bar, bolt; 14.05.08.01 Prison, confinement, durance; 17.03.10.01 A bolt, lock, bar
clūstorcleofa 14.05.08.01 Prison, confinement, durance
clūstorloc 14.05.08.01 Prison, confinement, durance
clūt 03.03.07 A part, division, portion; 04.04.05.06 To sew, stitch; 09.03.07.06.06 Membrane, vellum
geclūtod 04.04.05.06 To sew, stitch
(ge)clyccan 10.04.02 To grasp, take hold of

clȳder 01.01.02.02.01 Rock, stone
geclyft 05.06.02.01 A cleft, split
clymman 05.12.05.12 To go up, ascend
clympre 17.04.02 Ore, unwrought metal
clyne 03 Material, matter, substance
clynnan 02.05.10.04 To resound; 02.05.10.11 Clang, sound of metal
clypnes 10.04.02 To grasp, take hold of
clypp 10.04.02 To grasp, take hold of
clyppan 05.10.05.04.11 A circle, circuit, circumference; 08.01.02.02.02 An embrace; 10.04.02 To grasp, take hold of
geclyppan 07.04 Consideration, esteem
clypping 08.01.02.02.02 An embrace; 10.04.02 To grasp, take hold of
clȳsing 05.10.05.04.15.01 A bar, bolt
(ge)clyster 02.07.02.09 Top of plant, cluster, bunch
(ge)clystre 02.07.09.02 Particular fruits (alphabetical order)
clȳsung 05.10.05.04.11 A circle, circuit, circumference; 09.03.02.01 A period, sentence; 16.02.05.04.01 Parts of monastery
clywen 04.04.04 A thread (of wool, etc.), fibre; 04.04.10 Ornaments, trappings, accoutrements
cnæpling 02.03.01.05 Youth, boy, stripling
cnæpp 01.01.02.01.02.01 Rising ground, eminence; 01.01.02.01.02.02 Hill, mountain; 04.04.10.02 A button, brooch
gecnǣwe 06.01.06.01 Knowledge, cognizance, knowing; 06.01.06.01.01.02 To know, recognize; 09.06.02.01.04 A confession, declaration; 09.07.04.01.01 Acknowledgement

cnafa 02.03.01.05 Youth, boy, stripling
cnapa 02.03.01.05 Youth, boy, stripling; 12.01.01.08.01 A servant, attendant
(ge)cnāwan 06.01.05.01 Understanding; 06.01.06 Understanding, knowledge, cognizance; 06.01.06.01.01 Knowledge; 06.01.06.01.01.01 Acquaintance, knowledge; 06.01.06.01.01.02 To know, recognize; 11.05.02.02.01 Greetings, courteous terms of address
gecnāwan 09.06.02.01 To tell, make known, declare, relate, announce; 15.02.04 Spending, disbursement
cnāwlǣc 09.07.04.01.01 Acknowledgement
cnāwlǣcing 09.07.04.01.01 Acknowledgement
gecnāwnes 09.07.04.01.01 Acknowledgement
cnearr 01.01.02.02.01 Rock, stone; 05.12.01.09.03.01 A ship, boat
cnēatian 09.07.01 Contention, argument, strife of words; 12.05.03.01 Quarrel, contentiousness, strife
gecnēatian 09.04.03 Exposition, making clear by explanation
cnēatung 09.05.02 A question, inquiry, questioning; 09.07 Dispute, debate
(ge)cnedan 04.01.02.02.05.04.01 Preparation of bread
gecneord 06.01.01.02 Care, attention, observation; 06.02.05.04.05 Earnestness
(ge)cneordlǣcan 02.05.09.05 To watch, observe, survey; 06.01.06.02.03.03 To study, apply oneself to learning; 11.03 Endeavour
(ge)cneordlic 11.02.02 Diligence
gecneordlīce 11.02.02 Diligence

(ge)cneordnes 06.02.05.04 Desire, eagerness; 09.05.01 Inspection, examination
gecneordnes 06.01.06.02.02 That which is taught, doctrine or teaching; 11.02.02 Diligence; 11.03 Endeavour
cnēorednes 02.03.03.02 A race, tribe
gecnēorednes 02.03.02.03 Ancestry, descent
gecnēor(e)nes 02.03.02.02 Child, offspring
cnēorisbōc 16.02.01.08.01.01 Books of the Old Testament
cnēorisn 02.03.02.02 Child, offspring; 02.03.03.02 A race, tribe
cnēosār 02.08.07.07 Disorders of the body
cnēow 02.03.02.03 Ancestry, descent; 02.04.03.04.02.02 Knee; 02.04.05.04.08 Joint
cnēowbīgung 05.12.05.13.02.01 To kneel down
cnēowede/-ade 02.04.03.04.02.02 Knee
cnēowgebed 16.02.04.08.01 Kinds of prayer
cnēowholen 02.07.03.01 A bush
(ge)cnēowian 05.12.05.13.02.01 To kneel down; 16.02.04.18.03 Kneeling, bowing, prostration
cnēowiht 02.07.03.03.01 Wood (as substance)
cnēowlian 05.12.05.13.02.01 To kneel down; 16.02.04.18.03 Kneeling, bowing, prostration
cnēowmǣg 02.03.02.03.03 Forefather, ancestor; 02.03.02.03.06.01 Kinsman, relative
cnēowrift 04.06.01.05 ?A cloth for wiping

cnēowrim 02.01.03.03.04 Offspring, race, breed, family, children
cnēowsibb 02.03.03.02 A race, tribe
cnēowung 05.12.05.13.02.01 To kneel down
cnēowwærc 02.08.07.07 Disorders of the body
cnēowwyrst 02.04.05.04.08 Joint
cnīdan 05.06.09 Act of striking
cnīf 17.03.03 A cutting tool
cniht 02.03.01.05 Youth, boy, stripling; 06.01.06.02.03.01 A pupil, disciple, scholar; 12.01.01.07 A follower; 12.02.03 A society, guild, association; 12.09.03 Unmarried state; 13.02.10 The military, soldiers; 13.02.10.01.02.02.02 Branch of army
cnihtcild 02.03.01.04 Child
cnihtgebeorþor 02.01.03.03.03.01 Child-bearing, childbirth
cnihtgeong 02.01.04.01 Youth
cnihthād 02.01.04.01 Youth; 12.09.03 Unmarried state
cnihtiugoþ 02.01.04.01 Youth
cnihtlēas 12.04.04 Solitude
cnihtlic 02.01.04.01 Youth
cnihtþēawas 11.05.02 Mode, manner, way, method, fashion, course
cnihtwesende 02.01.04.01 Youth
cnihtwīse 11.05.02 Mode, manner, way, method, fashion, course
cnōdan 05.03.01.03 Reason, cause
gecnōdan naman 09.06.02.01.07 A name, appellation
cnoll 01.01.02.01.02.01 Rising ground, eminence; 01.01.02.01.02.02 Hill, mountain
cnop 05.10.06.03 Projection, head, extremity (of anything); 17.03.10.02 A pin, peg, nail

gecnos 05.12.02.06.01 To push, drive
cnōsl 02.01.03.03.04 Offspring, race, breed, family, children; 02.03.02.03.06.01 Kinsman, relative
cnossian 05.12.02.06.01 To push, drive
cnotmǣlum 09.03.04.05 To put briefly
cnotta 05.05.03 Binding, fastening; 11.11 Difficulty
cnotted 05.05.03 Binding, fastening
cnucian 05.10.05.04.14 An opening, aperture
(ge)cnucian 05.06.05 A grinding, pounding
(ge)cnucian (æt) 05.12.02.06.01 To push, drive
cnugel 04.02.03.02 Arable/ploughed land
(ge)cnū(w)ian 05.06.05 A grinding, pounding
gecnycc 05.05.03 Binding, fastening
(ge)cnyccan 05.05.03 Binding, fastening
gecnycled 02.08.04.02 Blemish, disfigurement
cnyll 01.01.02.01.02.02.01 Hill; 02.05.10.11 Clang, sound of metal; 02.05.10.13.01.01 Stroke/sound of a bell
cnyllan 02.02.05.03 To attend the dead; 05.10.05.04.14 An opening, aperture
(ge)cnyllan 02.05.10.11 Clang, sound of metal; 02.05.10.13.01.01 Stroke/sound of a bell
(ge)cnyssan 05.12.02.06.01 To push, drive; 08.01.03.07.02 Misery, trouble, affliction; 12.05.06 Grasp, power, control, mastery; 13.02.05.01.01 To overcome, conquer
cnyssung 05.12.02.06.01 To push, drive
(ge)cnyttan 05.05.03 Binding, fastening
gecnyttan 03.03.04.03 Growth, increase

cnyttels 02.04.05.06 Sinew/tendon/ligament
cōc 04.01.02.02.05 Cooking
cocc 02.06.08.02 Domestic fowl; 03.03.04.01.02.01 A heap, mass, accumulation
coccel 04.02.04.04 Harvest, crop
coccscīete 04.03.04 Fowling
cocer 13.02.08.04.03.01.02 Sheath for sword; 13.02.08.04.04.01 An arrow, dart, bolt
cōcerpanne 04.01.02.02.06.01 Cooking vessel/pot
gecōcnian 04.01.02.02.04 To season
cōcnung 04.01.02.01.05 Seasoning/flavouring
cōcormete 04.01.02.01.01.02 Cooked food
cocrodu 04.03.04 Fowling
gecōcsian 04.01.02.02.05 Cooking
codd 02.04.06.04.01 Male genitalia; 02.07.02.04 Seed, kind of seed; 04.02.04.03.02.01 Grain crops; 17.03.12 A receptacle, container
coddæppel 02.07.09.02 Particular fruits (alphabetical order)
cofa 01.01.02.01.03.01 Cave; 04.05.03.04 A closet, chamber, room; 05.12.01.09.03.01.01 Kind of ship
cofgodas 16.02.01.06.01.01.01 An image, idol
cofincel 04.01.02.02.06 Kitchen
cohhetan 02.05.10.15 Voice, cry (of living creature)
coitemǣre 04.01.03.05.01.01 Wine
col 03.01.09.02.01 Fire, burning; 03.01.14.04 Black/blackness; 17.05.01 Fuel, tinder
cōl 01.03.01.01 Hot, fine weather; 01.03.01.04 Wintry weather, cold; 03.01.11 Coldness, coolness; 08.01.01.02.01 Want of interest or concern, indifference
colere 17.05.01 Fuel, tinder
colestre 17.05.01 Fuel, tinder
(ge)cōlian 03.01.11 Coldness, coolness
coliandre 02.07.10.01 Particular herbs/spices (alphabetical order)
colig 17.05.01 Fuel, tinder
collecta 16.02.04.03.02 Parts of service
collectaneum 16.02.05.10.04 Choir books, etc.
gecollenferhtan 06.02.07.06 Courage, boldness, valour
collenferhþ 06.02.07.06.02 Boldness
colloncroh 02.07.11 Plants/flowers (alphabetical order)
colmāse/cummāse 02.06.08.05 Forest bird, wild-fowl
cōlnes 03.01.11 Coldness, coolness
colpytt 17.05.01 Fuel, tinder
colstūc 17.05.01 Fuel, tinder
colsweart 03.01.14.04 Black/blackness
colt 02.06.02.01.06 Horse
coltetræppe 02.07.11 Plants/flowers (alphabetical order)
coltgrǣg 02.07.11 Plants/flowers (alphabetical order)
colþrǣd 17.03.11 Other implements, etc.
columne 04.05.02.04 A column, pillar
comēta 01.02.01.01.05 Comet
comēta se steorra 01.02.01.01.05 Comet
communia 16.02.04.03.03.02 A psalm
concurrentes 05.11.06.02.02 A calculated space of time
consolde 02.07.11 Plants/flowers (alphabetical order)
consul 12.02.02.03 Terms for classical world

coorte 13.02.10.01.02.02.03 Part of an army
cōp 16.02.05.06.01 Outer garments
gecōp 12.07.01 One's due, natural place or position
copel 05.12.04.01.01 Unstable
cōpenere 08.01.02.02.03 A loving relationship
coper 01.01.02.02.03.01 Types of metals/minerals; 17.04.02.02 Copper
copian 14.02.01.02.01 Open robbery, rapine, pillage
gecōplic 12.07.01 One's due, natural place or position
(ge)cōplīce 03.06.03 Congruity, fitness, suitability
copp 01.01.02.01.02.02 Hill, mountain; 04.01.03.05.04 Drinking vessel
copped 02.07.03.03.02 Tree top; 04.02.04.05.04.01.01 Pruning/lopping
gecor 07 Judgement, forming of opinion
gecorded 05.05.03 Binding, fastening
cordewānere 04.04.07.15 Footwear, covering for the feet
(ge)coren 07.01.01 Choice, election
gecoren 07.02.04.03 Nobleness, excellence, nobility, magnificence; 07.04 Consideration, esteem; 08.01.02.02.01 A favourite, loved one; 11.07.04 Superiority, pre-eminence, primacy; 12.08.02.03.01 Honourable conduct, dignity
corenbēg 12.01.01.03 Symbols of power
gecorenlic 09.03.04.02.02 Eloquence, elegance in language
gecorenlīce 07.10.01 Elegance, beauty, comeliness
(ge)corennes 07.01.01 Choice, election
gecorennes 12.08.02.03 Goodness, probity

(ge)corenscipe 07.01.01 Choice, election; 07.02.04 Excellence
corf 05.12.01.03.01.02 A cutting, pass
corflian 05.06.06 A scraping, scarifying
corn 02.07.02.04 Seed, kind of seed; 02.08.07.08.01 Pain in the foot; 03.03.04.04 Littleness, smallness; 04.01.02.01.03 Corn; 04.02.04.03.02.01 Grain crops
cornæppel 02.07.09.02 Particular fruits (alphabetical order)
cornæsceda 04.02.04.04.05.02 Chaff
cornbǣre 02.07.02.04 Seed, kind of seed
cornberende 02.07.02.04 Seed, kind of seed
corncīþ 04.02.04.03.02.01 Grain crops
corngebrot 04.02.04.04.02.02 To gather fruits, crops, etc.
corngesceot 15.02.04 Spending, disbursement
cornhūs 04.02.04.04.06 Barn
cornhwicce 04.01.02.02.06.03 Food receptacle, basket; 04.02.04.04.06 Barn
cornlād 04.02.04.04.02 Harvesting; 17.02.04.02.03 Carrying, carriage (of materials)
cornsǣd 04.02.04.03.02.01 Grain crops
cornsǣlig 15.01.05 Possession of wealth
cornteoþung 16.02.04.20 Church due/requirement
corntrēow 02.07.03.05 Particular trees/shrubs (alphabetical order)
corntrog 04.02.04.06.14.03 A vessel for cleansing corn
cornwurma 03.01.14.05 Red/redness
corōna 12.01.01.03 Symbols of power
gecorōnian 07.08.04 An ornament, honour, glory

corporale 16.02.05.05.09 Cloths; 16.02.05.06.01 Outer garments
corsnæd 14.03.03.05 Ordeal
corþer 04.01.02.02.08 Churn
corþor 12.01.01.07 A follower; 12.04.02 A crowding together, assembly; 13.02.10.01.02.01 An armed force/band
corþr 14.05.06 Means/implement of torture
cosp 14.05.07 Binding, fastening with bonds
(ge)cosped 14.05.07 Binding, fastening with bonds
gecospende 14.05.07 Binding, fastening with bonds
coss 08.01.02.02.02 An embrace; 16.02.04.03.02 Parts of service
cossetung 08.01.02.02.02 An embrace
cossian 08.01.02.02.02 An embrace
cost 02.07.11 Plants/flowers (alphabetical order); 07.01.01 Choice, election; 11.05.02 Mode, manner, way, method, fashion, course; 14.04.02 A stipulation
(ge)cost 12.07.02.02 Truth, faithfulness, good faith, sincerity
gecost 11.04 Ability, capacity, power; 13.02.08.04 Weapons, arms
(ge)costian 06.02.06.03.04.01 Temptation; 08.01.03.07.02 Misery, trouble, affliction; 11.03.01 Experience, trial, experiment; 11.03.01.01.01 Proof, demonstration
costigend 06.02.06.03.04.01 Temptation; 16.01.05.02.02 Other terms for devils
cost(n)ere 06.02.06.03.04.01 Temptation; 16.01.05.02.02 Other terms for devils
gecostnes 11.03.01.01 Trial, probation

cost(n)ung 06.02.06.03.04.01 Temptation; 11.03.01 Experience, trial, experiment
costnung 12.05.06.02.03 Trouble, disturbance
(ge)cost(n)ung 12.05.06.02.03 Trouble, disturbance
costnungstōw 12.05.06.02.03 Trouble, disturbance
cot 04.05.03.04 A closet, chamber, room
cot(e) 04.05.03.02.02.08 A lowly dwelling, cottage, hut
cotlīf 04.05.03.02.02.08 A lowly dwelling, cottage, hut
cotsetla 02.03.03.04.04 Inhabitant(s) of a 'tūn'
cotstōw 04.05.03.02.02.08 A lowly dwelling, cottage, hut
cottere 02.03.03.04.04 Inhabitant(s) of a 'tūn'
cottuc 02.07.09.02.02.02 Other vegetables (alphabetical order); 02.07.11 Plants/flowers (alphabetical order)
coþærn 02.08.12.02.02 An infirmary
coþig 02.08.02 Disease, infirmity, sickness
coþlīce 07.03.04 A wretch, poor creature
coþu 02.08.02 Disease, infirmity, sickness
coþuwyrt 02.07.11.02 Unidentified plants (alphabetical order)
gecow 04.01.02.01.04.03 Prey to be torn or rent
coydic 02.07.11 Plants/flowers (alphabetical order)
crā 02.05.10.15.06 A roar, howl, etc.
crabba 01.02.01.01.02.01.01 The Zodiac; 02.06.06.04.01.02 Crab; 04.01.02.01.02.07 Fish
craca 02.06.08.05 Forest bird, wild-fowl
cracelung 02.05.10.15.07 Voice, note (of a bird)

856

crācettan 02.05.10.15.06 A roar, howl, etc.
cracian 02.05.10.04 To resound
cradol 04.05.04.05 A bed, bedstead
cradolcild 02.03.01.04 Child
cræcetung 02.05.10.15.06 A roar, howl, etc.
cræft 06.01.05 Understanding, intellect; 06.01.06.02 Knowledge, learning, erudition; 06.01.07.04.02 Fraud, deceit, trick, trickery; 07.02.04.01 Excellence, virtue, goodness; 11.04 Ability, capacity, power; 12 Power, might; 17.02.04 Trade, calling, craft, aptitude; 17.02.05 A work/product of art; 17.03 Implements, tools, etc.
cræfta 05.05 Constitution, founding (e.g. of world)
(ge)cræftan 17.02.04 Trade, calling, craft, aptitude
gecræftan 05.03.01 A cause (of anything)
cræftbōc 09.04.03.03 A commentary, exposition
cræft(e)lic 11.04.02 Skill, skilfulness
cræftglēaw 06.01.06.02 Knowledge, learning, erudition
cræftig 05.08 Strength; 06.01.06.02 Knowledge, learning, erudition; 11.04.02.01.01 Cunning, craft, craftiness, guile, wile; 12 Power, might
cræftiga 04.05 Building, construction; 05.05 Constitution, founding (e.g. of world); 17.02.04 Trade, calling, craft, aptitude
cræftigian 12 Power, might
cræftiglīce 11.04.02.01 Art, skill, contrivance, cunning

cræftlēas 11.04.03 (Of ability) low, mean, of less worth; 11.06 Disinclination to act, listlessness
cræftlic 06.01.07.04.04.02 Pretence, feigning, dissimulation
cræftlīce 11.04.02.01.01 Cunning, craft, craftiness, guile, wile
cræftspræc 09.03.02.02 Vocabulary
cræftweorc 17.02.04 Trade, calling, craft, aptitude
cræt 05.12.01.06 Vehicle
crætehors 02.06.02.01.06 Horse
crætwæn 05.12.01.06 Vehicle; 13.02.08.04.06 A chariot
crætwīsa 05.12.01.06 Vehicle; 13.02.10.01.02.02.02 Branch of army
crafian 12.03.04.01 Entreaty, solemn appeal; 14.03.03.01 Accusation
crafing 14.03.03 Law, action of the courts
cramb 01.01.02.01.01.03 Shore, bank
(ge)crammian 03.03.06.02 Fullness
crammingpohha 04.03.04 Fowling
crampul 01.01.03.01.03.01 Pool
cran 02.06.08.06 Water bird
crancstæf 04.04.03 A spinning-house or chamber
cranic 09.03.07.07.03.04 Chronicle, annals, history
cranicwrītere 09.03.07.07.03.03 A writer, author
cranoc 02.06.08.06 Water bird
crāwa 02.06.08.05 Forest bird, wild-fowl
(ge)crāwan 02.05.10.15.06 A roar, howl, etc.
crāw(an)lēac 02.07.09.02.02.01 Edible root/bulb
crāwe 02.06.08.05 Forest bird, wild-fowl
crāwenbēam 02.07.11.02 Unidentified plants (alphabetical order)
crēas 07.10.01 Elegance, beauty, comeliness

créasnes 07.06.01 Pride, arrogance; 07.10.01 Elegance, beauty, comeliness
crécas 02.03.03.06.03 The Greeks
crécisc 02.03.03.06.03 The Greeks
créda 16.02.01.01 Creed, statement of faith; 16.02.04.03.02 Parts of service
credic 04.01.02.02.06.05.03 Plate/platter/bowl/dish
crencestre 04.04 Weaving
créopan 07.07 Humility
(ge)créopan 02.08.04.04 State of being crippled; 05.12.03.02 Slowness; 11.09.01 Stealthiness, a stealthy act
créopere 02.08.04.04 State of being crippled
créopung 11.09.01 Stealthiness, a stealthy act
creowel 01.01.03.01.01.02 Tributary; 05.10.05.04.07 A fork (in river, road, etc.)
cribb 04.02.05.03.02 A byre, stall, sty, shed; 04.05.04.05 A bed, bedstead
crimman 05.12.02.06 To push, impel, thrust
(ge)crimman 03.03.06.02 Fullness
gecrimpan 05.10.06.05 A fold, plait, wrinkle
crinc 07.05.04 Mockery, derision, scorn
cring 02.02.04 Killing, violent death, destruction
(ge)cringan 02.02.03 To die, perish
gecringan 05.09.05 Ceasing, decline, fall off; 05.12.05.13.03 To fall
cringol 05.10.05.04.08.01 A bend
cringwracu 08.01.03.07.03 Suffering, torment, pain
crisma 16.02.04.07.06 Unction, anointing with holy oil; 16.02.05.06 Ritual clothing; 16.02.05.09.03 Holy oil
crismal 16.02.05.06 Ritual clothing

crismcláþ 16.02.05.06 Ritual clothing
crismhálgung 16.02.01.10.02 Consecration; 16.02.04.07.06 Unction, anointing with holy oil
crismlísing 16.02.04.07.03 Confirmation
crismsmyrels 16.02.04.07.06 Unction, anointing with holy oil
crist 16.01.01.04.02 The Son, Christ
cristalla 01.01.02.02.03.01 Types of metals/minerals; 02.07.11 Plants/flowers (alphabetical order)
cristallisc 01.01.02.02.03.01 Types of metals/minerals
cristelmǽl 16.02.04.18.01 Sign of the cross; 16.02.05.11 The cross (as Christian image)
cristelmǽlbéam 16.02.05.11 The cross (as Christian image)
cristen 16.02.01.11 Firmness in the law, piety, devoutness; 16.02.02 Christianity, the Christian faith
cristendóm 16.02.02 Christianity, the Christian faith; 16.02.03 The church (as temporal/spiritual body)
cristene lagu 16.02.01.09 The law
cristenlic 16.02.02 Christianity, the Christian faith
cristenmann 16.02.02 Christianity, the Christian faith
cristennes 16.02.02 Christianity, the Christian faith; 16.02.04.07.01 Baptism, baptizing (and anointing)
cristes ǽ 16.02.01.08.03 The New Testament
cristes bóc 16.02.01.08.03 The New Testament; 16.02.05.10.05 A bible
cristes/drihtnes gebyrdtíd 16.02.04.04.02.01.01 Around the Nativity
cristes lagu 16.02.01.09 The law

cristes līchama 16.02.04.07.04 Communion/eucharist
cristes mǣl 09.03.07.01.02.01 Handwriting, autograph, signature; 16.02.05.11 The cross (as Christian image)
cristes mōdor 02.03.02.05 Spiritual relationships; 16.02.04.07.01 Baptism, baptizing (and anointing)
cristes scīrgerēfa 16.02.03.02.05 A bishop
cristesmæsse 16.02.04.04.02.01.01 Around the Nativity
cristlic 16.02.02 Christianity, the Christian faith
cristnere 16.02.04.07.01 Baptism, baptizing (and anointing)
cristnian 16.02.04.07.01 Baptism, baptizing (and anointing)
(ge)cristnian 16.02.04.07.01 Baptism, baptizing (and anointing)
cristnung 16.02.04.07.01 Baptism, baptizing (and anointing)
crīþan 01.01.03.01.01.07 Spring, fountain, well
crocc/crocca 04.01.02.02.06.04 Pot, vessel, crock
croccere 17.03.12.02 A potter
crocchwer 04.01.02.02.06.04 Pot, vessel, crock
gecrōcod 02.08.04.02 Blemish, disfigurement
crocsceard 17.03.12.02 A potter
crocwyrhta 17.03.12.02 A potter
croft 04.02 Farm; 04.02.03.01.01 Enclosed land/field
crōg 04.01.03.05.04 Drinking vessel
crōgcynn 04.01.03.05.04.01 A flask, flagon, bottle
gecroged 03.01.14.07 Yellow/yellowness

croh 02.07.10.01 Particular herbs/spices (alphabetical order); 03.01.14.07 Yellow/yellowness; 04.01.02.01.05.05.05 Saffron
crōh 02.07.02.05 A shoot, sprout, tendril; 05.10.06.04 A corner, bend, angle
crompeht 04.01.02.01.07.04 Cake
croplēac 02.07.09.02.02.01 Edible root/bulb
cropp 01.01.02.02.02.01 Sand, gravel; 02.04.06.05.04 Kidney; 02.06.08.01 Part of bird; 02.07.02.09 Top of plant, cluster, bunch; 04.02.04.03.02.01 Grain crops
croppa 02.07.02.09 Top of plant, cluster, bunch
croppiht 02.07.02.07 Blossom, flower(s)
cros 16.02.05.11 The cross (as Christian image)
crūc 16.02.04.18.01 Sign of the cross; 16.02.05.11 The cross (as Christian image)
crūce 04.01.02.02.06.04 Pot, vessel, crock; 04.01.02.02.06.05.05 Ladle/scoop; 04.01.03.05.04 Drinking vessel
crucethur 14.05.06 Means/implement of torture
crūdan 05.12.02.06.01 To push, drive; 05.12.05.09 To go forward, proceed
cruft 16.02.05.03.05 Crypt
cruma 04.01.02.01.07.03.03 Piece of bread; 04.01.02.04 Abundance of food
crumb/crump 05.10.05.04.08 Crookedness, a crooked place
crundel 01.01.02.01.03.03 Valley; 17.04.01 Sources of materials
crūse 04.01.03.05.04 Drinking vessel
crūsene 04.04.07.07 A long outer garment, covering, cloak, etc.

crūw 05.10.06.02.02 Curvature, bend, twist
crycc 05.10.05.04.02.04.02 Support, maintenance; 11.12.02.01 Strengthening, confirmation
cryccen 17.03.12.02 A potter
cryde 05.12.05.10 To go behind, follow
crȳde 02.07 A plant
cryfting 04.02 Farm
crymbing 05.10.06.02.02 Curvature, bend, twist
crymel 03.03.07 A part, division, portion
gecrymman 04.01.02.02.05.04.01 Preparation of bread; 05.06.05 A grinding, pounding
gecrympan 04.06.01.07 Hair-care
crype 04.05.03.05 A drain
crypel 02.06.01.08 A lair, den; 02.08.04.04 State of being crippled; 04.05.03.05 A drain
crypelas 04.05.02.13 A window-space
crypelgeat 05.10.05.04.14.02 An opening/space in an enclosure
crypelnes 02.08.04.03 Paralysis
cryppan 02.04.03.04.01.01 Hand
(ge)cryppan 10.04.02 To grasp, take hold of
cū 02.06.02.01.03 Cattle
cū butere 04.01.02.01.02.09.10 Butter
cū ēage 02.06.02.01.03 Cattle
cū meolc 04.01.02.01.02.09.01 Cow's milk
cūbȳre 04.02.05.06.01.01 A cattle pen/cowshed
cūcealf 02.06.02.01.03 Cattle
cucler 04.01.02.02.06.05.05 Ladle/scoop
cuclermǣl 03.03.01 Specific measures
cucumer 02.07.09.02.02.02 Other vegetables (alphabetical order)

cucurbite 02.07.09.02.02.02 Other vegetables (alphabetical order)
cudele 02.06.06.03.01.12 Squid, cuttlefish
cufel 04.04.07.11 A headcloth, covering for the head
cuffie 04.04.07.11 A headcloth, covering for the head
cufle 16.02.05.07 Monastic garb
cugle 16.02.05.07 Monastic garb
cūhorn 02.06.02.01.03 Cattle
cūhyrde 04.02.05.06.01 A cowherd
culfer 02.06.08.02.01.04 Pigeon, dove, culver
culpa 12.08.06.02.05.01 Transgression, trespass
culpian 07.07 Humility
culter 04.02.04.06.07 Ploughing equipment; 17.03.03 A cutting tool
cuma 05.12.05.02.04 To go in, enter; 12.04.03 A stranger
cuman 02.08.13 Recovery, growing better; 05 Aught, anything, something; 05.03.02 Event, issue, result; 05.03.02.01.01 An event, occurrence; 05.12.02.01 To fetch, bring, bear, conduct
cuman āweg 11.10.05 Escape
cuman of 11.10.05 Escape
cuman (of) 05.01 Growth, increase, what springs up
cuman on gemynde 06.01 The head (as seat of thought)
cuman tō 05.02 State, condition
cuman tōgædere 13.02.02 Battle
cuman ūp 02.01.03.03.03 Birth
(ge)cuman 05.12.05.02 To go/travel towards, come, approach
(ge)cuman (fram/of) 05.12.05.03.04 To come/go out from
(ge)cuman ongēan(es)/tōgēan(es) 05.12.05.02.02 To come together, meet

(ge)cuman tō 05.12.05.02.03 To arrive
(ge)cuman (tō) 05.12.05.02.03 To arrive
cumb 01.01.02.01.03.03 Valley;
  03.03.01.01 Liquid measures
cumbol 13.02.08.02 A standard, banner, ensign; 16.02.01.06.01.01.01 An image, idol
cumbolgebrec 13.02.02 Battle
cumbolgehnāst 13.02.02 Battle
cumbolhaga 13.02.07.02 Order (of troops), array
cumbolhete 08.01.03.09.04 Hatred
cumbolwiga 13.02.10.01 A man, warrior
cumena hūs 04.05.03.03 A lodging-house, inn
cumena hūs/wīcung 04.01.02.04.05.01.01 Quartering of officials
cumenhūs 04.01.02.04.05.01.01 Quartering of officials; 04.05.03.03 A lodging-house, inn
cumere 02.03.03.05.01.09 Northumbrians
cumfeorm 04.01.02.04.02 Feast
cūmicge 02.06.02.01.03 Cattle
cūmigoþa 02.06.02.01.03 Cattle
cumlīþe 08.01.02.04 Hospitality
cumlīþian 08.01.02.04.01 Visiting
cumlīþnes 08.01.02.04 Hospitality; 08.01.02.04.01 Visiting
cummǣdre/cumendre 02.03.02.05 Spiritual relationships; 16.02.04.07.01 Baptism, baptizing (and anointing)
cumpæder 02.03.02.05 Spiritual relationships; 16.02.04.07.01 Baptism, baptizing (and anointing)
cumul/cumbl 02.08.05.02 Particular inflammation/swelling
cuneglæsse 02.07.11 Plants/flowers (alphabetical order)
cunele 02.07.10.01 Particular herbs/spices (alphabetical order)
cunnan 02.01.03.03 Sex, generation; 08.01.01 A feeling, what is felt; 09.06.02 A saying, speech, statement; 11.04 Ability, capacity, power
(ge)cunnan 06.01.06.01.01 Knowledge
cunnere 06.02.06.03.04.01 Temptation
cunnian 02.05.09.05 To watch, observe, survey; 11.03 Endeavour
(ge)cunnian 06.02.06.03.04.01 Temptation; 09.05.02 A question, inquiry, questioning; 11.03 Endeavour; 11.03.01 Experience, trial, experiment
gecunnian 06.01.06.03 Experience; 08.01.03.07.02 Misery, trouble, affliction; 11.03.01.01.01 Proof, demonstration
cunning 11.03.01.01 Trial, probation
cunnung 02.01.03.03 Sex, generation; 11.03.01 Experience, trial, experiment
cuopel 05.12.01.09.03.01.01 Kind of ship
cūpe 04.03.05 Fishing
cuppe 04.01.03.05.04 Drinking vessel
curmealle 02.07.11 Plants/flowers (alphabetical order)
curmealle sēo læsse 02.07.11 Plants/flowers (alphabetical order)
curs 16.02.04.14.02.01 Cursing, imprecation; 16.02.04.19 Excommunication
cursian 16.02.04.14.01 Blasphemy; 16.02.04.14.02.01 Cursing, imprecation
cursumbor 16.02.05.09.02 Incense
cursung 08.01.03.07.02 Misery, trouble, affliction; 16.02.04.14.01 Blasphemy; 16.02.04.14.02.01 Cursing, imprecation; 16.02.04.19 Excommunication

curuettrēow 02.07.09.02.02.02 Other vegetables (alphabetical order)
cūsc 12.08.03.03.01.01 Chastity
cūscote 02.06.08.03 Game-bird
cūslyppe 02.07.11 Plants/flowers (alphabetical order)
custure 04.04.05.06 To sew, stitch
cūtægl 02.06.02.01.03 Cattle
cūter 04.01.02.01.07.05.01 Gum
cūþ 02.03.02.03.06 Kinship, relationship; 08.01.02.03.02 Friendly, amiable; 11.05.01 Familiarity
(ge)cūþ 06.01.06.01.01.02 To know, recognize; 07.08 Reputation, fame
cūþa 02.03.02.03.06.01 Kinsman, relative; 08.01.02.03.01 An acquaintance, friend, associate
cūþe 09.05.05.01 Showing, manifestation, display
(ge)cūþian 06.01.06.01 Knowledge, cognizance, knowing
(ge)cūþlǣcan 08.01.02.03.04 To show gladness, be friendly; 11.05.02.02.01 Greetings, courteous terms of address
cūþlic 06.01.07.02 Certainty, truth, what really is
cūþlīce 05.03.01.03 Reason, cause; 08.01.02.03.03 In a friendly manner, kindly; 09.04.03 Exposition, making clear by explanation; 09.05.05.01 Showing, manifestation, display; 11.04.02 Skill, skilfulness
cūþnes 06.01.06.01.01.01 Acquaintance, knowledge
cūþnoma 09.06.02.01.07 A name, appellation
cūwearm 03.01.09.01 Warmth, heat
cwabba 01.01.02.01.04.01 Marsh, bog, swamp

cwacian 02.08.10 Fever; 05.12.05.05 To shake, quake, wag; 06.01.08.06.01 A shuddering with fear, nervousness; 09.03.03 A gesture, action, gesticulation
cwacung 01.01.02.03 Earthquake; 05.12.05.05 To shake, quake, wag; 06.01.08.06.01 A shuddering with fear, nervousness
cwafen 01.01.02.01.04.01 Marsh, bog, swamp
cwalu 02.02.04 Killing, violent death, destruction
cwānian 08.01.03.04.01 Complaint, lamentation
cwānig 08.01.03 Bad feeling, sadness
cwānung 08.01.03.04.01 Complaint, lamentation
cwappa/cwæp 02.06.06.02.01.01 Burbot
cwatern 09.03.07.06.06 Membrane, vellum
cwēad 02.04.06.06.06 Faeces
cwealm 02.02.02 Liability to death, mortality; 02.02.04 Killing, violent death, destruction; 02.08.03.01 Extreme pain, torture, torment; 02.08.10.03.01 Plague, pestilence
gecwealmbǣran 02.02.04.04.03 Putting to death
cwealmbǣre 02.02.04.01 Cause/occasion of death; 02.02.04.02 Murderous, bloodthirsty
cwealmbǣrnes 02.02.04 Killing, violent death, destruction
cwealmbealu 02.02.01 Particular mode of death
cwealmberendlic 02.02.04.01 Cause/occasion of death
cwealmcuma 02.02.04.03.01 A killer
cwealmdrēor 02.04.06.08.01 Blood

cwealmlic 02.02.04.01 Cause/occasion of death
cwealmnes 02.08.03.01 Extreme pain, torture, torment
cwealmstede 02.02.02 Liability to death, mortality; 14.05.05.01 Capital punishment
cwealmstōw 14.05.05.01 Capital punishment
cwealmþrēa 06.01.08.06.02 Great fear, terror, horror
cweartern 14.05.08.01 Prison, confinement, durance
cwearternlic 14.05.08.01 Prison, confinement, durance
cwearternweard 14.05.08.01 Prison, confinement, durance
cweccan ūt 05.12.05.03.04 To come/go out from
(ge)cweccan 05.12.05.05 To shake, quake, wag
gecweccan 10.04.02.01 To pluck, gather
cweccung 05.12.05.05 To shake, quake, wag
cwecesond 01.01.02.01.04.01 Marsh, bog, swamp
gecwed 09.06.02.01.04 A confession, declaration
gecwedfæsten 04.01.01.06.01 Abstinence from food, fast; 16.02.04.04.02.02 A fast, act of fasting
cwedol 09.01.02 Fluency in speech
(ge)cwedrǣden 14.04 Making of terms, agreement, convention
gecwedrǣden 12.01.01.12.04.02 Conspiracy
gecwedrǣdnes 14.04 Making of terms, agreement, convention

gecwedstōw 05.10.04 Place, room; 12.02.02.01 Place of conference or assembly
cwelan 02.02.03 To die, perish
cweldeht 03.02.01.01 Decay, corruption, rottenness
cwelderǣde 02.06.03.01.02 Bat
(ge)cwellan 02.02.04.03 To kill, slay
cwellend 02.02.04.03.01 A killer
cwellere 02.02.04.03.01 A killer; 14.05.05.01 Capital punishment
(ge)cwēman 08.01.01.03.02 Pleasure, satisfaction; 08.01.01.03.09.03 To make glad; 12.01.01.12.01 Obedience, service
(ge)cwēme 03.06.03 Congruity, fitness, suitability
gecwēme 08.01.01.03.09.01 Pleasant, agreeable
gecwēm(ed)lic 03.06.03 Congruity, fitness, suitability
gecwēmedlic 08.01.01.03.09.01 Pleasant, agreeable
(ge)cwēmednes 08.01.01.03.02 Pleasure, satisfaction
gecwēming 08.01.01.03.09 Pleasantness, agreeableness
(ge)cwēmlic 08.01.01.03.09.01 Pleasant, agreeable
cwēmlīce 07.07 Humility
(ge)cwēmlīce 08.01.02.01 Favour, kindness, grace
gecwēmlīce 03.06.03 Congruity, fitness, suitability; 08.01.01.03.09.02 Pleasantly, agreeably
(ge)cwēmnes 08.01.01.03.09 Pleasantness, agreeableness
gecwēmnes 13.01.02.01 An appeasing, pacifying
gecwēmsum 08.01.01.03.09.01 Pleasant, agreeable

cwēn 02.03.01.02 Female person, woman; 12.01.01.04.01 A royal leader; 12.01.01.06.08 A person of rank, elder, great man; 12.09 Marriage, state of marriage; 16.01.02.05.02.01 Mary, queen of heaven

cwēnas 02.03.03.06.05 Scandinavian

cwene 02.03.01.02 Female person, woman; 12.01.01.11 The common people; 12.08.08.01.02.01.01 An adulterer/-ess, whore, prostitute; 12.09 Marriage, state of marriage

cwenfugol 02.06.08.02 Domestic fowl

cwēnhirde 02.03.01.03 Eunuch

cwēnlic 12.01.01.06.07 Royal/princely status/dignity

cweorn 04.01.02.02.09 A mill

cweornbill 17.03.03 A cutting tool

cweornburna 01.01.03.01.01.03 Stream; 04.01.02.02.09 A mill

cweornstān 04.01.02.02.09 A mill

cweorntēþ 02.04.06.03.02.01.01 Tooth/teeth

cweorþ 09.03.07.01.01 A runic letter

cweþan 09.01 To speak, exercise faculty of speech; 09.06.02.01 To tell, make known, declare, relate, announce

(ge)cweþan 09.06.02 A saying, speech, statement; 09.06.02.01.07.02 A categorizing name; 12.03.03 A command, bidding, order; 14.04 Making of terms, agreement, convention

gecweþan 09.07.04.01 Confirmation, agreement; 10.03.02 Presenting, offering; 14.01.06 A rule, order, precept, tenet, principle; 15.01.02 Gift, transfer of property; 15.01.02.01 Inherited property

cwic 02.01.02.01 That lives, living; 03.01.09.02 Fire, flame; 06.01.05.02 Intelligence

cwicǣht 02.06.02 Domestic animals, livestock

cwicælmes 16.02.04.12 Sacrifice, a sacrifice

cwicbēam 02.07.03.05 Particular trees/shrubs (alphabetical order)

cwicbēamen 02.07.03.05 Particular trees/shrubs (alphabetical order)

cwicbēamrind 02.07.03.05 Particular trees/shrubs (alphabetical order)

cwiccliende 05.12.04.01.01 Unstable

cwice 02.07.08 Grasses, reeds, etc.

cwicelmingas 02.03.03.05.01.11 Descendants of Cwicelm

cwicen 02.07.03.05 Particular trees/shrubs (alphabetical order)

cwicfȳr 03.01.09.02.01.03 Sulphur, brimstone

cwichege 02.07.03.04.03 A hedge/border

cwichrērende 02.01.02.01 That lives, living

cwician 02.01.02.02 To come to life, have life; 02.08.13 Recovery, growing better

(ge)cwician 02.01.02 Gift of life; 16.02.01.12 Spirituality

cwiclāc 16.02.04.12 Sacrifice, a sacrifice

cwiclic 02.01.02.01 That lives, living

cwiclīce 05.08.01 Vigour, activity, force

cwiclifigende 02.01.02.01 That lives, living

cwicrind 02.07.03.05 Particular trees/shrubs (alphabetical order)

cwicseolfor 01.01.02.02.03.01 Types of metals/minerals

cwicsūsl 08.01.03.07.03 Suffering, torment, pain; 16.01.05.01 Damnation, perdition, reprobation

cwicsūslen 08.01.03.07.04 Severity, harshness
cwictrēow 02.07.03.05 Particular trees/shrubs (alphabetical order)
cwicu ælmes 16.02.04.12 Sacrifice, a sacrifice
gecwicung 02.08.12 Healing, curing
cwicwelle 01.01.03.03 Flow/flowing
cwidbōc 16.02.01.08.01.01 Books of the Old Testament; 16.02.04.10 Preaching; 16.02.05.10.03 A homiliary
cwiddian 09.06.02 A saying, speech, statement; 14.03.03 Law, action of the courts
cwide 06.02.06.02 A proposal, proposition, suggestion; 07 Judgement, forming of opinion; 09.01.01 A speech, what is said, words; 09.03.02.01 A period, sentence; 09.06.01.02 A saying, saw, proverb, maxim; 14.01.06 A rule, order, precept, tenet, principle; 14.03.03.09 A sentence, judgement, ruling; 16.02.04.03.02 Parts of service; 16.02.04.10 Preaching
cwide oncweþan 09.05.03 An answer, reply
(ge)cwide 14.04 Making of terms, agreement, convention; 14.04.01 A deed, contract, agreement; 15.01.02.01 Inherited property
cwidegiedd 09.01 To speak, exercise faculty of speech
cwidelēas 09.02 Silence, refraining from speech; 15.01.02.01 Inherited property
cwielman 16.02.04.07.02.03 Penance, an act/instance of penance
(ge)cwielman 02.02.04.03 To kill, slay; 16.02.04.16 Martyrdom

cwiferlīce 05.08.01 Vigour, activity, force
cwild 02.08.10.03.01 Plague, pestilence; 04.02.05.02.01 (Of cattle) seized with disease; 05.06 Destruction, dissolution, loss, breaking
cwildbǣre 01.03.01.03.01 Storm, tempest; 02.08.10.03.01 Plague, pestilence
cwildbǣrlīce 05.06 Destruction, dissolution, loss, breaking
cwildberendlic 02.08.10.03.01 Plague, pestilence
cwild(e)flōd 01.01.03.06 Flood
(ge)cwildful 02.02.04.01 Cause/occasion of death
cwildrōf 02.02.04.02 Murderous, bloodthirsty
cwildseten 05.11.04.02.01 Sunset
cwildtīd 05.11.04.02 Night, night time; 05.11.04.02.01 Sunset
cwilm 01.01.03.01.01.07 Spring, fountain, well
gecwis 12.01.01.12.04.02 Conspiracy
cwiss 09 Speech, vocal utterance
cwiþ(a) 02.04.06.04.02 Female reproductive organs
cwīþan 08.01.03.04.01 Complaint, lamentation; 14.03.03.01 Accusation
cwiþenlic 05.02.02 Nature, established order of things
cwīþnes 08.01.03.04.01 Complaint, lamentation
cwīþung 08.01.03.04.01 Complaint, lamentation
cwudu 02.07.02.03 A stalk, stem; 04.01.02.01.04.02 Cud chewed by animals
cwydele 02.08.05.01 Swelling
cwyldbǣre 04.06.02 Insalubrious, injurious to health

cwyldberendlic 04.06.02 Insalubrious, injurious to health
cwylle 01.01.03.01.01.07 Spring, fountain, well
cwylman 08.01.03.07.02.01 Injury, offence
cwylmend 02.02.04.03.01 A killer; 14.05.02 Torment, punishment
cwylmere 02.02.04.03.01 A killer
gecwylmful 02.02.04.01 Cause/occasion of death; 04.06.02 Insalubrious, injurious to health
cwylmian 02.02.04.03 To kill, slay; 08.01.03.07.02.01 Injury, offence; 08.01.03.07.03 Suffering, torment, pain; 16.02.04.07.02.03 Penance, an act/instance of penance
(ge)cwylm(i)an 08.01.03.07.02.01 Injury, offence
(ge)cwylmian 16.02.04.16 Martyrdom
cwylming 02.08.03.01 Extreme pain, torture, torment; 08.01.03.07.03 Suffering, torment, pain; 16.01.01.04.02.02 Events associated with Christ; 16.02.04.07.02.03 Penance, an act/instance of penance; 16.02.04.16 Martyrdom
cwylmnes 08.01.03.07.03 Suffering, torment, pain
cwȳsan 05.06.03 A dashing together, breaking, shattering
gecwȳsan 05.06.05.03 Bruising, crushing
cycene 04.01.02.02.06 Kitchen
cycenþēnung 04.01.02.03.01 Service in kitchen; 12.01.01.08 Service
cycgel 13.02.08.04 Weapons, arms
cȳf 04.01.03.05.04.02 A barrel, tun, vat, cask
cȳfl 04.01.03.05.04.02 A barrel, tun, vat, cask

cylcan 02.08.08.04.02 (Of stomach) disordered
cyldu 03.01.11 Coldness, coolness
cylegicel 01.01.03.02 Ice
cylen 04.01.02.02.06 Kitchen; 17.05.02 A hearth, fireplace
cylewearte 02.08.03.02 Itch, irritation
cylfe 01.01.02.01.02.02.01 Hill
cyll 04.01.02.02.06.01 Cooking vessel/pot; 04.01.03.05.04.01 A flask, flagon, bottle
cyllfylling 03.03.06.02 Fullness
cylu 03.01.14.11 Medley/variety of colour
cymbe 01.01.02.01.03.03 Valley
cyme 05.03.02 Event, issue, result; 05.12.05.02 To go/travel towards, come, approach; 05.12.05.02.03 To arrive; 05.12.05.11.01 To return
cȳme 06.01.08.05.01.01 Wondrous, glorious, marvellous; 07.10 Beauty, fairness
cymed 02.07.11 Plants/flowers (alphabetical order)
cymen 02.07.10.01 Particular herbs/spices (alphabetical order)
cȳmlic 07.10 Beauty, fairness
cymlīce 12.07.01 One's due, natural place or position
cȳmnes 07.01.01.01.01 Fastidiousness, daintiness
cynce 03.03.04.01.02.01 A heap, mass, accumulation
(ge)cynd 02 Creation; 02.01.03.03.06 Sex, kind; 03.04 Form, kind, nature, character; 05.02 State, condition; 12.07.01 One's due, natural place or position
gecynd 02.01.03.03.01 To beget; 02.01.03.03.04 Offspring, race, breed, family, children; 02.03.03.02 A race,

tribe; 02.04.06.04 Reproductive organs; 02.04.06.06.08 Menses; 05.02.01.01 The course of human affairs; 05.02.02 Nature, established order of things; 11.05 Natural/proper way/manner/mode of action

gecyndbōc 16.02.01.08.01.01 Books of the Old Testament

gecynde 02.03.03.03.01 A native people; 05.02.02 Nature, established order of things; 11.05 Natural/proper way/manner/mode of action; 12.07.01 One's due, natural place or position; 15.01.02.01 Inherited property

gecyndelic 02.01.03.03 Sex, generation; 02.03.03.03.01 A native people; 05.02.02 Nature, established order of things; 12.07.01 One's due, natural place or position

gecyndlim 02.04.06.04.02 Female reproductive organs; 12.08.07.01.04 Shamelessness, lasciviousness

gecyndlim(u) 02.04.06.04 Reproductive organs

gecyndnes 02.01.03.03.02 To bring forth, produce; 02.03.03.03 A nation, people

cynebænd 12.01.01.03 Symbols of power

cynebeald 06.02.07.06 Courage, boldness, valour

cynebearn 12.01.01.06.08 A person of rank, elder, great man; 16.01.01.04.02 The Son, Christ

cyneboren 12.01.01.06.07.01 A royal race

cynebōt 14.03.03.09.02 Atonement

cynebotl 04.05.03.02.02.06 A royal/noble palace

cynecynn 12.01.01.06.07.01 A royal race

cynedōm 12.01.01 Authority; 12.01.01.06.07 Royal/princely status/dignity; 12.06 A province, country, territory; 14.01.06 A rule, order, precept, tenet, principle; 14.03.03.09.02 Atonement; 15.01 Property

cynegewǣdu 04.04.07.01 Mode of dressing, fashion

cynegierela 04.04.07.01 Mode of dressing, fashion

cynegild 14.03.03.09.02 Atonement

cynegōd 12.01.01.06.06 Gentle birth, nobility

cynegold 12.01.01.03 Symbols of power

cynegyrd 12.01.01.03 Symbols of power

cynehād 12.01.01.06.07 Royal/princely status/dignity

cynehām 04.05.03.02.02.06 A royal/noble palace

cynehelm 04.04.10 Ornaments, trappings, accoutrements; 12.01.01 Authority; 12.01.01.03 Symbols of power

(ge)cynehelmian 12.01.01.03 Symbols of power

cynehlāford 12.01.01.04.01 A royal leader

cynehof 04.05.03.02.02.06 A royal/noble palace

cynelic 12.01.01.06.07 Royal/princely status/dignity; 15.01.01 Landed property

cynelic ādl 02.08.08.06 Disease of liver

cynelīce 07.02.04.03 Nobleness, excellence, nobility, magnificence

cynelicnes 12.01.01.06.07 Royal/princely status/dignity

cynemann 12.01.01.04.01 A royal leader

cynerēaf 04.04.07.01 Mode of dressing, fashion

cynerīce 12.01.01 Authority; 12.06 A province, country, territory

cyneriht 14.01.04.01 A special right, right peculiar to a class
cynerōf 07.08.08 Nobleness, honour, glory
cynescipe 11.05.02.02.01.01 Courteous forms of address; 12.01.01.06.07 Royal/princely status/dignity; 12.01.01.06.08 A person of rank, elder, great man
cynesetl 12.01.01.02 Seat of authority; 12.06.02.01 A township
cynestōl 04.05.03.02.02.06 A royal/noble palace; 12.01.01.02 Seat of authority; 12.06.02.01 A township
cynestrǣt 05.12.01.03.01.03 A highway
cyneþrymlic 07.08.07 Glory, splendour, magnificence
cyneþrymm 12.01.01 Authority
cynewīse 12.01.01.01 Rule, domination, direction
cynewiþþe 12.01.01.03 Symbols of power
cyneword 09.03.04.01 Mode of speech
cynewyrþe 12.01.01.06.06 Gentle birth, nobility
cyning 12.01.01.04.01 A royal leader; 16.01.01.01.01 The Almighty; 16.01.05.02.01 The devil
cyningǣþe 14.01.04 A legal right
cyninge 12.01.01.04.01 A royal leader
cyninges genēat 12.01.01.08.01 A servant, attendant
cyninges wyrt 02.07.10.01 Particular herbs/spices (alphabetical order)
cyningfeorm 04.01.02.04 Abundance of food; 04.01.02.04.05.01 Hospitality, harbouring, entertaining
cyninggenīþla 08.01.03.09.05 Enmity
cyninggereordu 04.01.02.04.02 Feast
cyningstān 18.02.02.01 Gaming, playing at dice
cyningwīc 04.05.03.02.02.06 A royal/noble palace
cyningwuldor 16.01.01.01.01 The Almighty
cynlic 03.06.03.04 What is fitting/seemly/appropriate/decent
cynlīce 03.06.03.04 What is fitting/seemly/appropriate/decent
cynling 02.03.03.01 Body of retainers, household
cynn 02.01.03.03.04 Offspring, race, breed, family, children; 02.01.03.03.06 Sex, kind; 02.03.02.02 Child, offspring; 02.03.03.02 A race, tribe; 03.04 Form, kind, nature, character; 03.06.03.04 What is fitting/seemly/appropriate/decent; 09.03.02.03.01.01.03 Gender; 11.05.02.01 A standard, norm, ethos
gecynnes 02.03.02.03.05 Descendant
cynnig 12.01.01.06.06 Gentle birth, nobility
cynnreccenes 02.03.02.03 Ancestry, descent
cynren 02.01.03.03.04 Offspring, race, breed, family, children; 02.03.02.02 Child, offspring; 02.03.03.02 A race, tribe; 02.03.03.03 A nation, people; 03.04 Form, kind, nature, character
cynresu 02.03.02.02 Child, offspring
cȳpa 15.05.01 Goods, stock, merchandise
(ge)cȳpan 15.05 Trade, traffic, commerce
cȳpe 15.05 Trade, traffic, commerce; 17.03.12.01 A basket
gecȳpe 15.05 Trade, traffic, commerce
cȳpedæg 05.11.03.01.05 A day; 15.05.01 Goods, stock, merchandise
cȳp(e)mann 15.05.01 Goods, stock, merchandise

cȳpend 15.05.01 Goods, stock, merchandise
cypera 02.06.06.02.01.06 Pike; 02.06.06.03.01.07 Salmon
cypersealf 02.08.12.02.05.02 Salves, ointments; 03.01.17.07 Salves, ointments, etc.
cȳplic 15.05 Trade, traffic, commerce
cypren 01.01.02.02.03.01 Types of metals/minerals; 17.04.02.02 Copper
cypressen 02.07.03.05 Particular trees/shrubs (alphabetical order)
cypressus 02.07.03.05 Particular trees/shrubs (alphabetical order)
cyrcan lād 16.02.04.20 Church due/requirement
cyre 07.01.01 Choice, election
cyreāþ 14.03.03.04 Oath-swearing
cyrelīf 05.02.01.01 The course of human affairs; 12.01.01.10 Freedom, being free
cyrf 05.06.02 Cleaving, splitting, cutting; 09.03.02.01 A period, sentence
cyrfel 17.03.10.02 A pin, peg, nail
cyrfet 02.07.09.02.02.02 Other vegetables (alphabetical order)
cyricǣw underfōn 16.02.04.07.05.01 Ordination
cyricbelle 16.02.05.05.02 A church/monastery bell
cyricbōc 16.02.05.10 A church/monastic book; 16.02.05.10.06 A manual, ritual
cyricbōt 16.02.04.20 Church due/requirement
cyricdor/cyricduru 16.02.05.03.01 Door or gate of church
cyrice 16.02.05.02.01 A temple; 16.02.05.02.03 A church, place of worship

cyricfæt 16.02.05.05.06 A vessel for use in services
cyricfriþ 16.02.04.18.04 Church peace, right of sanctuary
cyricgang 16.02.04.04.02.01.01 Around the Nativity
cyricgeriht 16.02.04.20 Church due/requirement
cyricgriþ 16.02.04.18.04 Church peace, right of sanctuary
cyrichege 16.02.05.01 Land
cyricmitta 03.03.01 Specific measures
cyricnēod 16.02.04.20 Church due/requirement
cyricsceat 16.02.04.20 Church due/requirement
cyricsōcn 16.02.04.18.04 Church peace, right of sanctuary
cyrictūn 16.02.05.01 Land
cyricþing 16.02.05.05 Something holy/belonging to a church
cyricwāg 16.02.05.03.12 A church wall
cyricwyrhta 16.02.05.02.03 A church, place of worship
cyrn 04.01.02.02.08 Churn
cyrnel 02.04.06.05.01 Tonsil; 02.07.02.04 Seed, kind of seed; 02.08.07.06 Disorders of the neck
gecyrnlod 02.07.02.04 Seed, kind of seed
gecyrnod 02.07.03.03.01 Wood (as substance); 03.01.05 Roughness
cyrografum 14.03.03 Law, action of the courts
cyrriol 16.02.04.03.02 Parts of service
cyrstrēow 02.07.09.02 Particular fruits (alphabetical order)
gecyrted 03.03.04.06 Diminution
cyrtel 04.04.07.08 A short garment, skirt, kirtle
cyrten 07.10.01 Elegance, beauty, comeliness; 07.10.03 An adornment,

decoration, ornament;
11.05.02.02.01.01 Courteous forms of address
cyrtenes 07.10.01 Elegance, beauty, comeliness
(ge)cyrtenlǣcan 07.10 Beauty, fairness
gecyrtenlǣcan 09.03.04.02 (Of language) embellished
cyrtenlīce 07.10.01 Elegance, beauty, comeliness; 11.04.02.01 Art, skill, contrivance, cunning
cȳse 04.01.02.01.02.09.11 Cheese
cȳsebrīw 04.01.02.01.02.09.07 Buttermilk
cȳsefæt 04.01.02.02.08.01 Cheese tub/vat
cȳsehwǣg 04.01.02.01.02.09.08 Whey
cȳsgerunn 04.01.02.01.02.09.06 Rennet
cȳslybb 04.01.02.01.02.09.06 Rennet
(ge)cyspan 14.05.07 Binding, fastening with bonds
(ge)cyssan 08.01.02.02.02 An embrace
cȳsstycce 04.01.02.01.02.09.11 Cheese
cyst 07.01.01 Choice, election; 07.02.04 Excellence; 07.02.04.01 Excellence, virtue, goodness; 10.03.08 Bountifulness, munificence; 13.02.10.01.02.01 An armed force/band
cystan 15.05 Trade, traffic, commerce
cyste 09.03.04.01 Mode of speech
cystel(bēam) 02.07.03.05 Particular trees/shrubs (alphabetical order)
cysten 02.07.03.05 Particular trees/shrubs (alphabetical order)
cyst(en)bēam 02.07.03.05 Particular trees/shrubs (alphabetical order)
cystian 02.02.05.01.01 A grave, burial place, sepulchre
cystig 10.03.08 Bountifulness, munificence; 12.08.02.01 Goodness, excellence, virtue
cystiglīce 10.03.08 Bountifulness, munificence
cystignes 03.03.04.02.01 Abundance; 10.03.08 Bountifulness, munificence
cystlēas 12.08.06.01.02 Lacking moral good
cȳswucu 04.01.01.06.01 Abstinence from food, fast; 16.02.04.04.02.01.02 Lent
cȳswyrhte 04.01.02.02.08.01 Cheese tub/vat
cȳta 02.06.08.04 Bird of prey; 02.06.08.06 Water bird
cȳte 04.05.03.02.02.08 A lowly dwelling, cottage, hut; 16.02.05.04.01 Parts of monastery
cytel 04.01.02.02.06.01 Cooking vessel/pot
cytwer 04.03.05 Fishing
cȳþan be dǣle 09.06.02 A saying, speech, statement
(ge)cȳþan 06.01.06.01 Knowledge, cognizance, knowing; 09.05.05.01 Showing, manifestation, display; 09.06.02.01.01 To make known, cause to know, inform; 09.06.02.01.05 Proclamation, spreading abroad; 11.01.01 Practice, exercise, doing; 14.04.03 Confirmation, ratification
gecȳþan 07.08 Reputation, fame
gecȳþednes 14.03.03.03 Witness, testimony, attestation
cȳþere 14.03.03.03 Witness, testimony, attestation; 16.02.04.16 Martyrdom
cȳþig 06.01.06.01.01.02 To know, recognize
gecȳþig 06.01.06.01 Knowledge, cognizance, knowing
cȳþing 09.06.02 A saying, speech, statement

(ge)cȳþlǣcan 06.01.06.01 Knowledge, cognizance, knowing
cȳþnes 06.01.06.01.01.01 Acquaintance, knowledge
(ge)cȳþnes 14.03.03.03 Witness, testimony, attestation; 16.02.01.08 Scripture, the scriptures
cȳþnesse getrymman 14.03.03.03 Witness, testimony, attestation
(ge)cȳþþ 12.06.04 Native land
cȳþþu 02.03.02.03.06 Kinship, relationship; 02.03.02.03.06.01 Kinsman, relative; 02.03.03.03.01 A native people; 06.01.06 Understanding, knowledge, cognizance; 06.01.06.01.01 Knowledge; 06.01.06.01.01.01 Acquaintance, knowledge
cȳþþ(u) 08.01.02.03 Friendliness, affection
dā 02.06.03.01.06 Deer, hart
dǣd 06.02.07.06 Courage, boldness, valour; 11.01 Action, doing, performance
dǣdbana 02.02.04.04 Manslaughter, homicide
dǣdbēta 16.02.04.07.02 Confession; 16.02.04.07.02.01 Penitence
dǣdbētan 08.01.03.04 Grief; 16.02.04.07.02.03 Penance, an act/instance of penance
dǣdbētend 16.02.04.07.02 Confession; 16.02.04.07.02.01 Penitence
dǣdbētende 16.02.04.07.02.01 Penitence
dǣdbētere 16.02.04.07.02 Confession; 16.02.04.07.02.01 Penitence
dǣdbōt 08.01.03.02.01 Compunction, remorse, contrition; 16.02.04.07.02.01 Penitence; 16.02.04.07.02.03 Penance, an act/instance of penance

dǣdbōtlīhtung 16.02.04.07.02.03 Penance, an act/instance of penance
dǣdbōtnes 16.02.04.07.02.01 Penitence
dǣdcēne 06.02.07.06 Courage, boldness, valour
dǣdfrom 11.02.01 Energy, vigour, vigorous action
dǣdfruma 11.01.04 A doing, accomplishing (of something); 13.02.10.01 A man, warrior; 17.02.01 Management of work
dǣdhata 05.06 Destruction, dissolution, loss, breaking
dǣdhwæt 06.02.07.06 Courage, boldness, valour
dǣdlata 11.06 Disinclination to act, listlessness
dǣdlēan 10.03.05 Recompense, reward
dǣdlic 09.03.02.03.01.02.02 Voice
dǣdrōf 07.08.10 Fame of courage, valour
dǣdscūa 16.01.05.02.01 The devil
dǣdweorc 06.01.08.05.01.01.01 An exercise of power, mighty work, miracle
(ge)dǣftan 11.01.03 Preparation
gedǣfte 08.01.02.01.02 Gentleness
gedǣftelīce 03.06.03 Congruity, fitness, suitability; 05.11.08 A suitable time, opportunity; 08.01.02.01.02 Gentleness
gedǣftu 08.01.02.01.02.02 Gentleness, meekness, composure
dæg 02.01.04 Age; 05.11.02 A time, particular time, occasion; 05.11.03 Period of time, era, epoch; 05.11.03.01.05 A day; 05.11.04.01 Day (not night); 09.03.07.01.01 A runic letter
dæg æfter dæg 05.11.11 Continuity

dæg ǣr 05.11.07.03.01 Time within remembrance
dæg gearwunga 16.02.01.08.04 Jewish seasons/feasts
dæg cennesse 05.11.02.01.01 An anniversary
dægbōt 16.02.04.07.02.03 Penance, an act/instance of penance
dægcandel 01.02.01.01.03 Sun
dægcūþ 09.05.05.01 Showing, manifestation, display
dǣge 04.01.02.02.05.04 Baking
dǣgenlic 05.11.03.01.05 A day
dǣges 05.11.03.01.05 A day
dǣges and nihtes 05.11.11 Continuity; 05.11.11.01 A not ceasing, persistence, recurrence
dǣges ēage 02.07.11 Plants/flowers (alphabetical order)
dægfæsten 04.01.01.06.01 Abstinence from food, fast; 16.02.04.04.02.02 A fast, act of fasting
dægfeorm 04.01.02.04 Abundance of food
dæg(ge)hwāmlic 05.11.03.01.05 A day
dæg(ge)hwāmlīce 05.11.03.01.05 A day
dæggehwilc 05.11.03.01.05 A day
dæghlūtre 03.01.12 Brightness, light
dæghwām 05.11.03.01.05 A day
dæghwāmlic 11.05 Natural/proper way/manner/mode of action
dæghwīl 02.01.04 Age
dæglang 05.11.03.01.05 A day
dæglanges 05.11.03.01.05 A day
dægmǣl 05.11.05 A dial, horloge
dægmǣles pīl 17.03.11 Other implements, etc.
dægmǣles pinn 17.03.11 Other implements, etc.
dægmēlscēawere 16.01.04.06.01 Astrology
dægmete 04.01.02.04.01 Meal
dægrēd 05.11.04.01.01 Dawn, daybreak, sunrise; 05.11.04.02.01 Sunset
dægrēdlēoma 05.11.04.01.01 Dawn, daybreak, sunrise
dægrēdlic 05.11.04.01.01 Dawn, daybreak, sunrise
dægrēdoffrung 16.02.04.12 Sacrifice, a sacrifice
dægrēdsang 16.02.04.05.02 The hour or service of Matins
dægrēdwōma 05.11.04.01.01 Dawn, daybreak, sunrise
dægrīm 05.11.06.02.02 A calculated space of time
dægrima 05.11.04.01.01 Dawn, daybreak, sunrise
dægryne 05.11.03.01.05 A day
dægsang 16.02.04.05 Canonical hour, service
dægsceald 01.02.01.01.03 Sun
dægsteorra 01.02.01.01.02 Star
dægswǣsendo 04.01.02.04 Abundance of food
dægtīd 05.11 A time, period of time; 05.11.03.01.05 A day; 05.11.04.01 Day (not night)
dægtīma 05.11.04.01 Day (not night)
dægþerlic 05.11.03.01.05 A day; 11.05 Natural/proper way/manner/mode of action
dægþern 05.11.03.01.05 A day
dægþerne 05.11.03.01.05 A day
dægwæcce 16.02.04.07.06.02 A vigil
dægweard 11.10.02.02 Watchful care, keeping guard
dægweorc 17 Work, doings, actions, labour

dægweorþung 16.02.04.04.02 A feast-day, holy day
dægwilla 05.11.03.01.05 A day; 11.07.03 Use, advantage, profit
dægwine 15.02.04 Spending, disbursement
dægwist 04.01.02.04.01 Meal
dægwōma 05.11.04.01.01 Dawn, daybreak, sunrise
dæl 01.01.02.01.03.03 Valley
dǣl 03.03.03.01 Arithmetic; 03.03.04.01 Much; 03.03.04.02 A sufficiency, sufficient supply; 03.03.07 A part, division, portion; 03.04.01 Singularity, peculiarity; 05.02.01 Condition, state of affairs, situation; 05.10.04.02 A region, zone; 09.03.02.02 Vocabulary; 09.03.02.02.01 A part of speech, form; 10.01.03 A sharing, participation; 10.03.07 Distribution; 11.05.02 Mode, manner, way, method, fashion, course
dǣlan 09.01 To speak, exercise faculty of speech
(ge)dǣlan 03.03.07.01 Division, partition, separation; 05.12.05.03.01 To part ways, separate from, depart; 10.03.03 Granting; 10.03.07 Distribution; 12.04.03.01 Estrangement, alienation; 15.02.04 Spending, disbursement; 16.02.04.09 Almsgiving, charitableness
(ge)dǣlan wiþ 10.01.03 A sharing, participation; 10.03.03 Granting
gedǣlan 03.06.02 Difference, diversity, dissimilarity; 05.06.02.02 A tearing apart; 05.10.04 Place, room; 05.10.04.04.01 Dispersion; 05.10.05.02.01 Diffusion, effusion, spreading; 05.12.05.03.02 To keep clear of, stand off from, withdraw; 10.01.02 Acquisition; 10.01.03 A sharing, participation; 12.09.04 Divorce
gedǣled bēon/wesan 05.06.02.02 A tearing apart
gedǣledlīce 03.03.07.01 Division, partition, separation
dǣlend 14.03.02 A legislator
dǣlere 10.03.07 Distribution; 13.01.03 Intercession, pleading, mediation; 16.02.04.09 Almsgiving, charitableness
dǣllēas 06.01.06.04.02 Ignorance, uninstructedness; 10.02 Want, lack
dǣlmǣlum 03.03.07 A part, division, portion
dǣlnes 04.01.02.03 To serve (food/drink)
dǣlnimend 09.03.02.02.01.02 A verb; 10.01.03 A sharing, participation
dǣlnimendnes 10.01.03 A sharing, participation
dǣlnimung 10.01.03 A sharing, participation
dǣlnumelnes 10.01.03 A sharing, participation
dǣlnumennes 10.01.03 A sharing, participation
dǣlnymendlic 09.03.02.02.01.02 A verb
dǣlung 10.01.03 A sharing, participation
dærst 04.01.02.01.01.08 Leftover food; 04.01.02.01.06 Leaven/yeast; 04.01.03.05.02 Brewing
dærste 04.06.02.04 Refuse, litter, rubbish
gedærsted 04.01.02.01.07.03.01 Unleavened bread
gedafen 03.06.03 Congruity, fitness, suitability; 03.06.03.04 What is fitting/seemly/appropriate/decent
(ge)dafenian 03.06.03 Congruity, fitness, suitability

(ge)dafenlic 03.06.03.04 What is fitting/seemly/appropriate/decent
gedafenlīce 03.06.03 Congruity, fitness, suitability; 03.06.03.04 What is fitting/seemly/appropriate/decent
gedafenlicnes 03.06.03 Congruity, fitness, suitability; 05.11.08 A suitable time, opportunity; 11.07.01.01 Desirability, expediency
gedafennes 03.06.03 Congruity, fitness, suitability
gedafniendlic 03.06.03.04 What is fitting/seemly/appropriate/decent
gedafniendlīce 03.06.03 Congruity, fitness, suitability; 03.06.03.04 What is fitting/seemly/appropriate/decent
gedafni(g)endlic 12.07.01 One's due, natural place or position
dāg 04.01.02.01.07.03 Bread
dagas 02.01.04 Age; 05.11.03 Period of time, era, epoch
(ge)dagian 05.11.04.01.01 Dawn, daybreak, sunrise
dagung 05.11.04.01.01 Dawn, daybreak, sunrise
(ge)dāl 03.06.02 Difference, diversity, dissimilarity; 05.04 Fate, lot, fortune, destiny; 05.12.05.03.01 To part ways, separate from, depart; 10.01.03 A sharing, participation; 10.03.07 Distribution; 16.02.04.09 Almsgiving, charitableness
gedāl 03.03.07.01 Division, partition, separation; 05.06 Destruction, dissolution, loss, breaking
dalc 04.04.10.02 A button, brooch
(ge)dālland 15.01.01 Landed property
dālmǣd 15.01.01 Landed property
dalmatice 16.02.05.06.01 Outer garments
darian 11.09.01.01 Ambush, lying in wait

daroþ 13.02.08.04.01 A spear
daroþa lāf 13.02.10.02.01 Survivors of a battle
daroþhæbbende 13.02.08.04.01 A spear
daroþlācend 13.02.10.01.02 An armed man
daroþsceaft 13.02.08.04.01 A spear
daru 02.08.04 Hurt, injury, damage; 08.01.03.07.02.01 Injury, offence; 10.02.01 Loss, deprivation
datārum 05.11.02.01 A definite point of time, date
dauidisc 16.02.01.08.01.01 Books of the Old Testament
dauidlic 16.02.01.08.01.01 Books of the Old Testament
dauitic 16.02.01.08.01.01 Books of the Old Testament
dēad 01.01.03.01 Body of water; 02.02.03.02 State of being dead; 02.05.01 Without feeling, insensible; 03.01.17.01 A coagulating, mixing; 08.01.03.07.01 Tedium
dēadblōd 02.04.06.08.01 Blood
dēadboren 02.02.03.02 State of being dead
dēadhrægl 02.02.05.02 To prepare for burial
dēadian 02.02.03 To die, perish
gedēadian 02.02.04.03 To kill, slay
dēadlic 02.02.03.01 In process of dying; 02.02.04.01 Cause/occasion of death; 02.05.03.01 Dullness, lack of animation; 05.06 Destruction, dissolution, loss, breaking; 05.11.01.03.01 Mortal state, this life
dēadlīce 02.02.04.01 Cause/occasion of death
dēadlicnes 05.11.01.03.01 Mortal state, this life

dēadspring 02.08.05.01 Swelling
dēadsynnig 14.03.03.09.01 Unfavourable judgement, condemnation
dēadwylle 02.01.03.02 Barrenness, sterility
dēaf 02.01.03.02 Barrenness, sterility; 02.08.07.03.01 Deafness
dēafnes 02.08.07.03.01 Deafness
dēafu 02.08.07.03.01 Deafness
dēag 03.01.14 A colour; 03.01.14.01 Dyeing; 05.08 Strength; 07.02 Goodness; 11.07.03 Use, advantage, profit
dēagan 02.02.03 To die, perish
dēaggede 02.08.07.08 Foot ailments, ?gout
(ge)dēagian 03.01.14.01 Dyeing
dēagung 03.01.14.01 Dyeing
deall 07.06 Pride; 07.06.05 Pomp, splendour, magnificence
dearf 07.06.01.01 Proud, arrogant
dearflic 07.06.01.01 Proud, arrogant
dearfscipe 07.06.01 Pride, arrogance
dearnunga 09.05.04 A secret
dearr 06.02.07.06.02.02 Boldness, daring; 07.06.01.03 To be proud/arrogant; 11.09 Peril, danger
dēaþ 02.02 Death; 02.02.01 Particular mode of death; 02.02.03.02 State of being dead; 02.02.03.04 Spiritual death; 02.02.04.01 Cause/occasion of death; 16.01.03.01 Soul of a deceased person
dēaþbǣre 02.02.04.01 Cause/occasion of death
dēaþbǣrlic 02.02.04.01 Cause/occasion of death
dēaþbǣrnes 02.02.04 Killing, violent death, destruction
dēaþbēacnigende 02.02.04.01 Cause/occasion of death
dēaþbēam 02.02.04.01 Cause/occasion of death
dēaþbedd 02.02.05.01.01 A grave, burial place, sepulchre
dēaþberende 02.02.04.02 Murderous, bloodthirsty; 02.08.10.03.01 Plague, pestilence; 04.06.02 Insalubrious, injurious to health; 07.03.02 Ill, harm, hurt
dēaþcwalu 02.02.01 Particular mode of death
dēaþcwealm 02.02.04 Killing, violent death, destruction
dēaþcwylmende 02.02.04 Killing, violent death, destruction
dēaþdæg 02.02.02 Liability to death, mortality
dēaþdenu 02.02.02 Liability to death, mortality
dēaþdrepe 02.02.04.01 Cause/occasion of death
dēaþfǣge 02.02.03.03 Appointed death, doom
dēaþfiren 12.08.06.02.05 Misdeed, sin
dēaþgedāl 02.02 Death
dēaþgod 16.01.05.02.02 Other terms for devils
dēaþlēg 16.01.05 Hell, lower world, abode of the dead
dēaþlic 02.02.02 Liability to death, mortality; 02.04.01 Dead body; 05.11.01.03.01 Mortal state, this life; 08.01.03.07.04 Severity, harshness
dēaþlicnes 02.01.02.02.01 Condition of life; 02.02.02 Liability to death, mortality; 05.11.01.03.01 Mortal state, this life
dēaþmægen 16.01.05.02 Species of devil, hellish race

dēaþræced 02.02.05.01.01 A grave, burial place, sepulchre
dēaþrǣs 02.02.04 Killing, violent death, destruction
dēaþrēaf 13.02.05.01.02.02 Booty, spoils
dēaþrēow 08.01.03.09.11 Hardheartedness, cruelty, severity
dēaþscūa 02.02.04.03.01 A killer
dēaþscufa 02.02.03.02 State of being dead
dēaþscyld 14.02.01.01 Types of crime
dēaþscyldig 14.03.03.09.01 Unfavourable judgement, condemnation
dēaþsele 16.01.05 Hell, lower world, abode of the dead
dēaþslege 02.02.04.01 Cause/occasion of death
dēaþspere 13.02.08.04.01 A spear
dēaþstede 02.02.02 Liability to death, mortality
dēaþsynnignes 14.03.03.09.01 Unfavourable judgement, condemnation
dēaþþēnung 02.02.05.02 To prepare for burial
dēaþwang 02.02.02 Liability to death, mortality
dēaþwēge 02.02.01 Particular mode of death
dēaþwērig 02.02.03.02 State of being dead
dēaþwīc 02.02.02 Liability to death, mortality
dēaþwyrd 02.02.03.03 Appointed death, doom
dēaw 01.03.01.06.01.01 Dew
gedēaw 01.03.01.06.01.01 Dew
dēawig 01.03.01.06.01.01 Dew; 03.01.16.01 Moisture
dēawigendlic 01.03.01.06.01.01 Dew
dēawigfeþera 02.06.08.01 Part of bird
dēawung 01.03.01.06.01.01 Dew
dēawwyrm 02.08.07.08 Foot ailments, ?gout
dēawwyrmede 02.08.07.08 Foot ailments, ?gout
decan 16.02.03.03.01.04 A dean (in charge of ten religious)
(ge)dēcan 03.01.17.07.01 An anointing, greasing
decanhād 16.02.03.02.11 A deacon, minister of the church
december 05.11.03.01.03.01 Specific months
decembermōnaþ 05.11.03.01.03.01 Specific months
declīnian 09.03.02.03.01.01 Declension
declīnigendlic 09.03.02.03.01.01 Declension
declīnung 09.03.02.03.01.01 Declension
gedēfe 02.05.10.16 Quiet, soft, faint; 03.06.03.04 What is fitting/seemly/appropriate/decent; 06.01.07.01.01 Strictness, exactness; 08.01.01.03.09.01 Pleasant, agreeable; 08.01.02.01.02 Gentleness; 08.01.02.01.02.02 Gentleness, meekness, composure; 12.08.02.02 Righteousness, rectitude
(ge)dēfelic 03.06.03 Congruity, fitness, suitability
gedēfelic 12.08.02.01 Goodness, excellence, virtue
gedēfelīce 03.06.03.04 What is fitting/seemly/appropriate/decent; 06.01.07.01.01 Strictness, exactness
gedēfenes 08.01.02.01.02 Gentleness
gedelf 01.01.02.01.03 Hollow/depression in land; 17.02.04.02.02 Digging

delfan 02.02.05 A burial, burying; 04.02.04.02.02 To dig up the ground
(ge)delfan 05.06.08 A plucking, taking away; 17.02.04.02.02 Digging
delfere 04.02.04.02.02 To dig up the ground
delfīn 02.06.05.01.01 Dolphin
delfīsen 04.02.04.06.01 A spade; 17.03.07 Tools for digging/grasping/pulling
delfung 17.02.04.02.02 Digging
dell 01.01.02.01.03.03 Valley
delu 02.04.03.03.05 Chest, breast, bosom
dēma 12.02.02.02 A counsellor, advisor; 14.03.02 A legislator; 16.01.01.02.06 God as judge
dēman 09.06.02.01 To tell, make known, declare, relate, announce; 16.02.04 Worship, honour, praise
(ge)dēman 06.01.01.01.01 Thought, cogitation, meditation; 07 Judgement, forming of opinion; 07.01 Appraisal, appraising; 10.03.07.01 To allot, assign; 14.01.06 A rule, order, precept, tenet, principle; 14.03.03 Law, action of the courts; 14.03.03.09 A sentence, judgement, ruling; 14.03.03.09.01 Unfavourable judgement, condemnation
(ge)dēman tō 14.03.03.09 A sentence, judgement, ruling
dēmedlic 14.03.03 Law, action of the courts
dēmend 14.03.02 A legislator; 16.01.01.02.06 God as judge
dēmere 14.03.02 A legislator; 16.01.01.02.06 God as judge
demm 07.03.02 Ill, harm, hurt
dēmon 16.01.05.02 Species of devil, hellish race

dena lagu 14.01.01 Law(s) of particular scope
denbǣre 04.02.03.04.02.01.03 Swine pasture
denberende 04.02.03.04.02.01.03 Swine pasture
dene 01.01.02.01.03.03 Valley; 02.03.03.06.05 Scandinavian
deneland 01.01.02.01.03.03 Valley
denemearc 12.06.01.03 The Continent
dengan 05.06.09 Act of striking
denisc 02.03.03.06.05 Scandinavian; 09.03.01 Particular languages
denn 01.01.02.01.03.01 Cave; 02.06.01.08 A lair, den; 04.02.03.04.02.01.03 Swine pasture
dennian 03.01.16.01 Moisture
denstōw 04.02.03.04.02 Pasture/pasturage
dēofles bearn 16.02.01.11.02 Impiety, lack of piety
dēofol 02.08.11.02.01.01 Paroxysm of madness, folly; 07.05.03.03 Scorn, insult, abuse; 12.08.06.02.02 A bad man, inhuman person; 16.01.05.02 Species of devil, hellish race; 16.01.05.02.01 The devil; 16.01.06 A god (of any faith)
dēofolcræft 16.01.04 Sorcery, magic, witchcraft
dēofolcunda 16.01.05.02.02 Other terms for devils
dēofolcynn 16.01.05.02 Species of devil, hellish race
dēofoldǣd 08.01.03.09.03 Malevolence, malice
dēofolgield 16.02.01.06.01.01 Pagan worship, idolatrous practice(s); 16.02.01.06.01.01.01 An image, idol
dēofolgieldhūs 16.02.05.02.01 A temple

dēofolgilda 16.02.01.06 Paganism, a false religion
dēofolgītsung 06.02.05.02 Greed, importunate desire, rapacity; 12.08.07 Immoderation, excess; 16.02.01.13 Evil-doing, transgression, sin
dēofollic 16.01.05.02.02 Other terms for devils
dēofollīce 08.01.03.09.11 Hardheartedness, cruelty, severity; 16.01.05.02.02 Other terms for devils
dēofolscīn 16.01.03.02 A demonic apparition
dēofolscipe 16.02.01.06.01.01 Pagan worship, idolatrous practice(s)
dēofolsēoc 02.08.11.02.01 Insanity, madness
dēofolsēocnes 02.08.11.02.01 Insanity, madness
dēofolwītega 16.01.04.06.04 Prophecy, divine speech
(ge)dēon 04.01.01.02 Act/action of sucking
dēonde 04.01.01.02 Act/action of sucking
dēop 01.01.02.01.03.02 Abyss, chasm; 01.01.03.01 Body of water; 01.01.03.01.02 Sea/ocean; 05.10.05.03.04 Depth, deepness; 06.01.01.01.01.01 Consideration, rumination; 08.01.03.07.04 Severity, harshness; 12.08.06.02.04 Darkness, evil; 14.03.03.04 Oath-swearing; 17.01 Strenuous effort, hard work
dēop cēap 15.02.01 High/steep price
dēope 03.03.06 Wholeness; 05.10.05.03.04 Depth, deepness; 06.01.01.01.01.01 Consideration, rumination; 08.01.01.01.04 Depth of feeling, zeal; 08.01.03.09.10 Wrath, sternness, displeasure; 12.08.06.02.04 Darkness, evil; 14.03.03.04 Oath-swearing
dēophycgende 06.01.01.01.01.01 Consideration, rumination
dēophȳdig 06.01.01.01.01.01 Consideration, rumination
(ge)dēopian 05.10.05.03.04 Depth, deepness
dēoping 01.01.02.01.03 Hollow/depression in land
dēoplic 06.01.01.01.01.01 Consideration, rumination; 08.01.03.07.04 Severity, harshness; 12.08.06.02.04 Darkness, evil
dēoplīce 03.03.06 Wholeness; 05.03.02 Event, issue, result; 06.01.01.01.01.01 Consideration, rumination; 08.01.01.01.04 Depth of feeling, zeal; 11.04.02.01 Art, skill, contrivance, cunning
dēopnes 01.01.02.01.03.02 Abyss, chasm; 05.10.05.03.04 Depth, deepness; 09.04.02 Depth of meaning, mystery; 11.04.02.01.01 Cunning, craft, craftiness, guile, wile
dēopþancenlīce 06.01.01.01.01.01 Consideration, rumination
dēopþancol 06.01.01.01.01.01 Consideration, rumination
dēopþancollīce 06.01.01.01.01.01 Consideration, rumination; 06.01.06.02 Knowledge, learning, erudition
dēor 01.03.01.06.02 Rain; 02.06 Animal; 02.06.03.01.06 Deer, hart; 05.08.02.01 (Of living creatures) fierceness, roughness; 06.02.07.06 Courage, boldness, valour; 08.01.03.09.10 Wrath, sternness, displeasure
dēoran 08.01.02.02 Love, affection, care

(ge)dēoran 07.08.05 Glorifying, making great, glorification
dēorboren 12.01.01.06.06 Gentle birth, nobility
deorc 03.01.13 Darkness, obscurity; 08.01.03.06 Adversity, affliction; 09.04.02.01 A secret, mystery; 12.08.06.02.04 Darkness, evil; 16.01.05 Hell, lower world, abode of the dead
deorce 08.01.03 Bad feeling, sadness
deorcegrǣg 03.01.14.10 Grey-coated one
deorcful 03.01.13 Darkness, obscurity; 12.08.06.02.04 Darkness, evil
deorcian 02.08.07.02.01 Defective vision
deorclīce 08.01.03.07.04 Severity, harshness; 12.08.06.02.04 Darkness, evil
deorcnes 03.01.13 Darkness, obscurity
deorcung 05.11.04.02.01 Sunset
dēorcynn 02.06 Animal
dēore 07.02.04.03 Nobleness, excellence, nobility, magnificence; 08.01.02.03.03 In a friendly manner, kindly; 08.01.03.09.11 Hardheartedness, cruelty, severity; 15.02.01 High/steep price
dēoren 02.06 Animal
gedeorf 08.01.03.06 Adversity, affliction; 17.01 Strenuous effort, hard work
dēorfald 04.02.05.06.09 An enclosure for wild animals
(ge)deorfan 17.01 Strenuous effort, hard work
gedeorfan 02.02.03 To die, perish; 05.12.01.09.03.02 Hardship on board
dēorfellen 04.04.06 Undressed condition (of hide)
gedeorflēas 08.01.01.03.08 Happiness, well-being, prosperity

gedeorfnes 08.01.03.06 Adversity, affliction
dēorfriþ 04.03 Hunting, the chase
gedeorfsum 08.01.03.07.04 Severity, harshness
dēorgeat 04.02.05.03 A park, enclosure for animals
dēorhege 04.02.05.06.09 An enclosure for wild animals
dēorlic 06.02.07.06 Courage, boldness, valour
dēorlīce 07.02.04.03 Nobleness, excellence, nobility, magnificence; 07.04.04.02 Laudable, praiseworthy
dēormōd 06.02.07.01 Strength, fortitude
dēornett 04.03.03 Net, drag-net, hunting net
dēortūn 04.02.03.04.02 Pasture/pasturage; 04.02.05.03 A park, enclosure for animals
dēorwierþe 07.02.04.03 Nobleness, excellence, nobility, magnificence; 07.04.01 (Of persons) worth/value, worthiness; 15.02.01 High/steep price
dēorwierþlic 07.04.01 (Of persons) worth/value, worthiness
dēorwierþlīce 07.04.04.02 Laudable, praiseworthy; 07.06.05 Pomp, splendour, magnificence
dēorwyrþnes 07.08.03 Honour, veneration; 15.01.03 Treasure, riches, wealth
dēra (-e) 02.03.03.05.01.09 Northumbrians
gedered 02.08.04 Hurt, injury, damage
gederednes 02.08.04 Hurt, injury, damage
(ge)derian 07.03.02 Ill, harm, hurt
deriendlic 07.03.02 Ill, harm, hurt
derodine 03.01.14.05 Red/redness
derung 07.03.02 Ill, harm, hurt

gedēþan 02.02.04.03 To kill, slay; 16.02.04.07.02.03 Penance, an act/instance of penance

dēþing 02.02.04.04.03 Putting to death

deþþan 04.01.01.02 Act/action of sucking

deuteronomium 16.02.01.08.01.01 Books of the Old Testament

dīacon 16.02.03.02.11 A deacon, minister of the church

dīacongegyrela 16.02.05.06 Ritual clothing

dīaconhād 16.02.03.02.11 A deacon, minister of the church

dīaconrocc 16.02.05.06.01 Outer garments

dīaconþēnung 16.02.03.02.11 A deacon, minister of the church

dīc 01.01.02.01.03 Hollow/depression in land; 04.02.04.02.01.02 To irrigate (plants, land)/channel (water); 04.05.03.05.03.01 A ditch, dike; 13.02.06.01 Stronghold, fort/fortified town

dīcende 04.05.03.05.03.01 A ditch, dike

dīcere 04.02.04.02.01.02 To irrigate (plants, land)/channel (water)

dīchæg 04.05.03.05.03.01 A ditch, dike

dīchēafod 04.05.03.05.03.01 A ditch, dike

(ge)dīcian 17.02.04.02.02 Digging

dicor 03.03.03.04.10 Ten

dīcsceard 04.05.03.05.03.01 A ditch, dike

dīcsticce 04.05.01.02.06 A log, stake, etc.

dīcung 17.02.04.02.02 Digging

dīcwalu 04.05.03.05.03.01 A ditch, dike

dīcweall 04.05.03.05.03.01 A ditch, dike

dīegle 09.04.02.01 A secret, mystery; 09.05.04 A secret

(ge)dīegl(i)an 09.05.04.01 Concealment, obscurity; 11.09.01.01 Ambush, lying in wait

gedīegl(i)an 16.02.05.04 A monastery/convent

dīegol 02.02.05.01.01 A grave, burial place, sepulchre; 02.05.09.13 Invisible; 06.01.06.04.01 What is uncertain/unknown; 09.04.02.01 A secret, mystery; 09.05.04 A secret; 09.05.04.01 Concealment, obscurity; 12.04.04 Solitude

dīegolful 09.04.02.01 A secret, mystery

dīegollic 09.05.04 A secret

dīegollīce 02.05.10.16 Quiet, soft, faint; 09.05.04 A secret; 11.09.01 Stealthiness, a stealthy act

(ge)dīegollīce 09.05.04 A secret

dīegolnes 09.04.02.01 A secret, mystery; 09.05.04.01 Concealment, obscurity; 12.04.04 Solitude

dīend 02.06 Animal

(ge)diernan 09.05.04 A secret; 09.05.04.01 Concealment, obscurity

dierne 09.05.04 A secret; 12.08.06.02.04 Darkness, evil; 16.01.04 Sorcery, magic, witchcraft

gedīgan 02.01.02.02.02 Lifetime; 02.08.13 Recovery, growing better; 11.10.05 Escape; 13.02.05.01 Victory

diger 03.01.01 Thick, close-textured, dense

diht 03.05 Order, arrangement, disposition; 06.02.06 Mind, purpose; 09.06.01.02 A saying, saw, proverb, maxim; 11.05.02 Mode, manner, way, method, fashion, course; 12.01.01.01 Rule, domination, direction; 12.02 A public office; 12.02.02.04 Counsel, deliberation; 12.03 Direction, guidance; 14.01.06 A rule, order,

precept, tenet, principle;
16.01.01.02.01 Creator
(ge)diht 09.03.07.07.02 A written work, book, treatise; 09.03.07.07.03 Composition, arrangement, writing
gediht 07.10.03 An adornment, decoration, ornament
(ge)dihtan 06.01.06.02.03.03.01 An act of reading; 09.03.07.07.03 Composition, arrangement, writing; 14.01.06 A rule, order, precept, tenet, principle
gedihtan 05.05 Constitution, founding (e.g. of world); 11.01 Action, doing, performance; 16.01.01.02.01 Creator
(ge)dihtan/diht(n)ian 12.03 Direction, guidance
dihtend 12.03 Direction, guidance
dihtere 06.01.06.02.01 A wise man, man of understanding or learning
dihtnere 12.01.01.08.01 A servant, attendant; 12.03 Direction, guidance
(ge)dihtnian 03.05.01 Arranging, ordering, disposition
(ge)dihtnung 03.05.01 Arranging, ordering, disposition
dihtung 03.05.01 Arranging, ordering, disposition
dile 02.07.10.01 Particular herbs/spices (alphabetical order)
(ge)dīlegian 05.06 Destruction, dissolution, loss, breaking
gedīlegian 05.07 Ending of existence, end of world
dīlignes 05.06 Destruction, dissolution, loss, breaking
dilmeng 06.01.07.04.04.02 Pretence, feigning, dissimulation
dimgende 02.08.07.02.01 Defective vision

dimhīw 03.01.14.04 Black/blackness
dimhof 11.09.01.01 Ambush, lying in wait
dimhūs 14.05.08.01 Prison, confinement, durance
dimlic 03.01.13.01 Not shining, dim; 09.05.04 A secret
dimm 02.05.09.13 Invisible; 03.01.13.01 Not shining, dim; 03.01.14.04 Black/blackness; 07.03.04 A wretch, poor creature; 09.05.04.01 Concealment, obscurity; 12.08.06.02.04 Darkness, evil
dimmian 02.08.07.02.01 Defective vision; 03.01.13.01 Not shining, dim
dimnes 02.08.07.02.01 Defective vision; 03.01.13 Darkness, obscurity; 12.08.06.02.04 Darkness, evil
dimscūa 03.01.13.03 Overshadowing
dīnor 15.01.04 Coinage, money
dīpan 03.03.04.03 Growth, increase
(ge)dīpan 05.12.05.02.04.03 To plunge (something into something)
dirige 16.02.04.05.02 The hour or service of Matins
disc 04.01.02.02.06.05.03 Plate/platter/bowl/dish
discberend 04.01.02.03.01 Service in kitchen; 12.01.01.08.01 A servant, attendant
discipul 06.01.06.02.03.02 Discipleship; 06.01.06.02.03.04.02 A teacher; 16.02.01.08.03.01 New Testament persons
discipula 06.01.06.02.03.02 Discipleship
discipulhād 06.01.06.02.03 The action of learning
discþegn 04.01.02.03.01 Service in kitchen; 12.01.01.08.01 A servant, attendant

disma(-e) 02.07.11 Plants/flowers (alphabetical order)
distæf 04.04.03 A spinning-house or chamber
dōc 02.03.02.02.05 Having the same parents
docce 02.07.11 Plants/flowers (alphabetical order)
doccþȳfel 02.07.11 Plants/flowers (alphabetical order)
docga 02.06.02.01.04 Dog; 07.05.03.03 Scorn, insult, abuse
dōcincel 02.03.02.02.05 Having the same parents
dōere 11.01.04 A doing, accomplishing (of something)
dofian 02.08.11.02 Mental weakness
(ge)dofung 06.01.05.03.02.01 Foolishness, lightmindedness
dōgor 02.01.04 Age; 05.11.02 A time, particular time, occasion; 05.11.03.01.05 A day
dōgorrīm 02.01.04 Age
dohtig 06.02.07.06 Courage, boldness, valour
dohtor 02.03.02.02.04 A daughter; 02.03.02.03.05 Descendant
dohtorsunu 02.03.02.03.05 Descendant
gedohtra 02.03.02.02.04 A daughter
dol 06.01.05.03.01.01 Dullness, folly, stupidity; 06.01.05.03.02 Foolish, silly, stupid; 06.02.07.06.02.03 Presumption
dolg 02.08.04.01 A wound; 02.08.05.01 Swelling
dolgbenn 02.08.04.01 A wound
dolgbōt 14.05.04 A penalty, punishment
dolgilp 07.06.03 Boastfulness, arrogance
gedolgod 02.08.04.01 A wound

dolgrūne 02.07.11 Plants/flowers (alphabetical order)
dolgsealf 02.08.12.02.05.02 Salves, ointments
dolgslege 05.06.09 Act of striking
dolgswæþ 02.08.04.01 A wound
dolhdrenc 02.08.12.02.05.02 Salves, ointments
dolhsmelt 02.08.12.02.06.01 A bandage, binding
dolhwund 02.08.04.01 A wound
dollic 06.01.05.03.01.01 Dullness, folly, stupidity; 11.02.04.01 Rashness, madness
dollīce 11.02.04.01 Rashness, madness
dolsceaþa 05.06 Destruction, dissolution, loss, breaking
dolscipe 06.01.07.05 Error, being astray
dolspræc 09.01.02.01 Excessive fluency, loquacity
dolwillen 11.02.04.01 Rashness, madness
dolwīte 02.08.04.01 A wound
dōm 05.02.01.01 The course of human affairs; 07 Judgement, forming of opinion; 07.01 Appraisal, appraising; 07.01.01 Choice, election; 07.08 Reputation, fame; 09.04.03 Exposition, making clear by explanation; 12.01.01 Authority; 14.01.06 A rule, order, precept, tenet, principle; 14.03.01 Judicial body, authority; 14.03.03 Law, action of the courts; 14.03.03.09 A sentence, judgement, ruling; 14.03.03.09.01 Unfavourable judgement, condemnation
dōmærn 14.03.01 Judicial body, authority
dōmbōc 14.01.02 A law, statute
dōmdæg 16.02.01.08.03 The New Testament

dōmēadig 07.08.08 Nobleness, honour, glory
dōmere 14.03.02 A legislator
dōmes belecgan 07.08.02 Honour, glory
dōmes dæg 16.02.01.08.03 The New Testament
dōmfæst 07.08.09 Renown, fame, glory; 12.07.01 One's due, natural place or position; 12.07.04 Truth, righteousness, justice, equity; 16.02.01.12.03 Righteousness
dōmfæstnes 12.07.04 Truth, righteousness, justice, equity
dōmgeorn 06.02.05.04.01 Ambition; 07.08.01 Nobility (of character, rank, etc.); 12.08.02.02 Righteousness, rectitude
dōmhūs 14.03.01 Judicial body, authority
dōmhwæt 16.02.04 Worship, honour, praise
dōmian 16.02.04 Worship, honour, praise
dōmisc 16.02.01.08.03 The New Testament
dōmlēas 07.09.03 Infamy, ignominy, shame
dōmlic 07.08.08 Nobleness, honour, glory; 14.01.02 A law, statute
dōmlic tīd 16.02.04.05 Canonical hour, service
dōmlīce 07.08.07 Glory, splendour, magnificence; 12.07.04 Truth, righteousness, justice, equity
domne 12.01.01.06.08 A person of rank, elder, great man; 16.02.03.03.01.02 An abbess; 16.02.03.03.02 A monk
dōmsetl 14.03.01 Judicial body, authority
dōmsettend 14.03.02 A legislator
dōmstōw 14.03.01 Judicial body, authority
dōmweorþung 07.08.02 Honour, glory

dōn 07.01 Appraisal, appraising; 11 Action, operation
dōn be/of 11.01 Action, doing, performance
dōn dǣdbōte 16.02.04.07.02.03 Penance, an act/instance of penance
dōn edlēan 10.03.05 Recompense, reward
dōn fram 05.12.05.03.03 To depart, leave, set out
dōn nēode 10.03.04 Provision, supply
dōn of 04.04.07 Trappings, equipment, garb
dōn on 04.04.07 Trappings, equipment, garb
dōn to hīerran hāde 11.01.05.02 Furtherance, promotion
dōn tō nāuhte 05.07 Ending of existence, end of world
dōn tō witanne 06.01.05.02.01.01 Sagacity; 09.06.02.01.01 To make known, cause to know, inform
dōn þancas 08.01.02.04.02 Thanks, gratitude
(ge)dōn 05.02.01.01 The course of human affairs; 05.03.01.02 To work upon, influence; 05.05 Constitution, founding (e.g. of world); 05.10.04 Place, room; 05.11 A time, period of time; 06.02.06.03 Persuasion, prompting; 10.03.04 Provision, supply; 11 Action, operation; 11.01 Action, doing, performance; 11.01.06 End, completion (of action), fulfilment; 11.05.02 Mode, manner, way, method, fashion, course
(ge)dōn fram 05.12.02.04 To cast out, drive away; 11.10.03 Salvation/deliverance from
(ge)dōn fram/of 05.10.04.04.02 Removal, taking away

(ge)dōn in/on 05.10.05.04.01 Inside, interior
(ge)dōn tō 11.07 Use (made of things), service; 03.03.03.01 Arithmetic
(ge)dōn (tō) 05.03.01 A cause (of anything)
(ge)dōn ūp 05.12.05.12.02 To raise, lift up, elevate
gedōn 05.03.01 A cause (of anything); 05.11.10.02 End, completion; 11.01.04 A doing, accomplishing (of something); 11.04 Ability, capacity, power; 15.02.04 Spending, disbursement
gedōn æt 05.12.05.02.03 To arrive
gedōn forþ 09.05.05.01 Showing, manifestation, display
gedōn ūp 02.02.05 A burial, burying
gedōn ūt 15.01.02 Gift, transfer of property
dōnlic 11.02 Occupation, activity, business
dopened 02.06.08.06 Water bird
dopfugel 02.06.08.06 Water bird
doppettan 05.12.05.02.04.03 To plunge (something into something)
dor 04.05.02.12 Gate/doorway of a building
dora 02.06.09.02.02 Bee, hornet, wasp
dorweard 12.01.01.08.01 A servant, attendant
dott 02.08.05.02 Particular inflammation/swelling
dox 03.01.14.04 Black/blackness
doxian 03.01.13 Darkness, obscurity; 03.01.14.04 Black/blackness
draca 02.06.10.01.01 Dragon; 02.06.10.01.06 Serpent, scorpion, basilisk; 13.02.08.02 A standard, banner, ensign; 16.01.05.02.01 The devil
drācentse 02.07.11 Plants/flowers (alphabetical order)
dracu 08.01.03.06 Adversity, affliction
drǣdan 06.01.08.06.02 Great fear, terror, horror
drǣfan ūt 05.12.02.04 To cast out, drive away
(ge)drǣfan 05.12.02.06.01 To push, drive
drǣfend 04.03 Hunting, the chase
gedræg 02.05.10.03 Noise, tumult, uproar
drǣge 04.03.03 Net, drag-net, hunting net
drǣgnet 04.03.03 Net, drag-net, hunting net
drǣstig 04.06.02.04 Refuse, litter, rubbish
drāf 02.06 Animal; 03.03.04.01.02.01 A heap, mass, accumulation; 05.12.01.03.01.05 Types of road/path; 05.12.02.04 To cast out, drive away; 05.12.02.06.01 To push, drive; 12.04.02 A crowding together, assembly
dragan 05.11.01.01 Long duration, long space; 05.12.01 To go, progress, travel (usually on land); 08.01.03.07.03 Suffering, torment, pain
(ge)dragan 05.12.02.05 To pull, drag, draw
gedragan 13.02.08.04.03.02 Armed with a sword
drān 02.06.09.02.02 Bee, hornet, wasp
gedreag 12.04.02 A crowding together, assembly
drēahnian 04.06.01.10 To separate objects already connected, unmix
drēam 08.01.01.03 Good feeling, joy, happiness; 08.01.01.03.07 Joyous sound, mirth; 08.01.03.04.01

Complaint, lamentation; 18.02.07 Music
drēamcræft 18.02.07 Music
drēamere 18.02.07.02 A musical instrument
drēamhæbbende 08.01.01.03 Good feeling, joy, happiness
drēamhealdende 08.01.01.03 Good feeling, joy, happiness
drēamlēas 08.01.03 Bad feeling, sadness
drēamlic 18.02.07 Music
drēamnes 18.02.07.01 Singing, song
drēariend 01.01.03.04 Current, rush of water
dreccan 12.08.08.01.02 Unchastity, incontinence
(ge)dreccan 08.01.03.07.02 Misery, trouble, affliction; 12.05.06.02.03 Trouble, disturbance
gedreccan 05.06 Destruction, dissolution, loss, breaking
(ge)dreccednes 02.08.03.01 Extreme pain, torture, torment; 08.01.03.06 Adversity, affliction
gedreccednes 02.08.02.01 An illness, ailment, disorder
dreccing 08.01.03.06 Adversity, affliction
gedrecenes 02.08.03.01 Extreme pain, torture, torment; 08.01.03.06 Adversity, affliction
(ge)drēfan 01.01.03.01.02.04 State of sea; 06.01.08.06.03 Cause of fear, terror, horror; 08.01.03.07.02 Misery, trouble, affliction; 12.05.02.01 Lack of peacefulness
gedrēfedlic 03.01.13 Darkness, obscurity
(ge)drēfednes 05.08.02 Violence, force; 07.09.01 Shame, confusion; 08.01.03.03 Anxiety; 08.01.03.07.02 Misery, trouble, affliction

gedrēfednes 12.05.02.01 Lack of peacefulness
drefela 02.04.06.06.04 Spittle
(ge)drēfend 12.05.02.01 Lack of peacefulness
drēfing 05.12 To move, be in motion
dreflian 02.04.06.06.04 Spittle
(ge)drēfnes 08.01.03.03 Anxiety
gedrēfnes 05.08.02 Violence, force
drēfre 12.05.02.01 Lack of peacefulness
gedrehtnes 08.01.03.06 Adversity, affliction
(ge)drēman 16.02.04.03.03 Singing, church singing
drenc 02.02.04.03 To kill, slay; 02.08.12.02.05 Pharmacy, curing with salves; 04.01.03 Drinking; 04.01.03.05 A drink/beverage
(ge)drenc 04.01.03 Drinking
drencan 04.01.03.02 To drink heavily, get drunk
(ge)drencan 02.02.03 To die, perish; 02.02.04.03 To kill, slay; 03.01.16.06 A soaking, steeping; 04.01.03 Drinking; 05.12.05.02.04.03 To plunge (something into something)
drencecuppe 04.01.03.05.04 Drinking vessel
drenceflōd 01.01.03.06 Flood
drencfæt/dryncfæt 04.01.03.05.04 Drinking vessel
drenchorn/dryncehorn 04.01.03.05.04 Drinking vessel
drenchūs 04.01.03.05.03 Tavern
dreng 13.02.10.01 A man, warrior
gedrēog 03.06.03.04 What is fitting/seemly/appropriate/decent; 04.02.05.04 To tame, break in (animals); 04.04.07.15 Footwear,

drēogan

covering for the feet; 11.05.02.01 A standard, norm, ethos
drēogan 08.01.01.03.05 Pleasure, delight; 12.03.05 Permission
drēogan æfter 11.02 Occupation, activity, business
drēogan unstille/bysig 11.02 Occupation, activity, business; 17.02 Work, occupation, employment
(ge)drēogan 05.11 A time, period of time; 08.01.03.07.03 Suffering, torment, pain; 11 Action, operation; 11.01.04 A doing, accomplishing (of something); 11.01.05 Accomplishment, fulfilment
gedrēoglǣcan 03.05 Order, arrangement, disposition
(ge)drēoglīce 11.05.02.01 A standard, norm, ethos
gedrēoglīce 03.05 Order, arrangement, disposition
(ge)drēopan 03.01.16.03 A drop of liquid
drēopian 01.03.01.06.02 Rain; 05.12.05.13.03 To fall
drēopung 01.03.01.06.02 Rain
drēor 02.04.06.08.01 Blood
drēorfāh 02.04.06.08.01 Blood; 13.02.02 Battle
drēorig 02.04.06.08.01 Blood; 05.12.05.13.03 To fall; 08.01.03 Bad feeling, sadness; 08.01.03.04 Grief
drēorigferþ 08.01.03 Bad feeling, sadness
drēorighlēor 08.01.03 Bad feeling, sadness
drēorigian 08.01.03 Bad feeling, sadness
drēoriglic 08.01.03 Bad feeling, sadness
drēoriglīce 08.01.03 Bad feeling, sadness
drēorigmōd 08.01.03 Bad feeling, sadness
drēorignes 08.01.03 Bad feeling, sadness
drēorlic 08.01.03.04 Grief
drēorsele 04.05.03.02.02.03 Disagreeable dwellings
drēorung 01.03.01.06.02 Rain
(ge)drēosan 01.03.01.06.02 Rain; 02.02.03 To die, perish; 05.07 Ending of existence, end of world; 05.09.05 Ceasing, decline, fall off
drēosende 05.11.01.03.01 Mortal state, this life
drēosendlic 05.11.01.03.01 Mortal state, this life
gedrep 05.06.09 Act of striking
(ge)drepan 05.06.09 Act of striking
drepe 02.02.04.01 Cause/occasion of death
(ge)drif 02.08.10 Fever
gedrif 04.02.04.04.05.02 Chaff
gedrīf 05.12.01.03 Expanse over which something travels
drīfan 05.08.02 Violence, force; 05.12.02.06 To push, impel, thrust; 06.02.06.03.03 Incitement; 08.01.03.07.03 Suffering, torment, pain; 09.01 To speak, exercise faculty of speech; 11.02.01 Energy, vigour, vigorous action; 12.05.06.03 Necessity, constraint
drīfan fram/of/ūt 05.12.02.04 To cast out, drive away
drīfan of 05.05 Constitution, founding (e.g. of world)
drīfan trod 05.12.05.10 To go behind, follow
(ge)drīfan 04.03 Hunting, the chase; 05.12.02.06 To push, impel, thrust; 05.12.02.06.01 To push, drive; 05.12.05.01 To go astray
gedrīfan 05.12.02.04 To cast out, drive away

gedrīhþ 11.05.02.01 A standard, norm, ethos
(ge)drinc 04.01.01.07 Feasting
gedrinca 12.01.01.08.01 A servant, attendant
drincan 02.05.08.02 Pleasant smell, fragrance, perfume
(ge)drincan 04.01.01.07 Feasting; 04.01.03 Drinking; 06.01.06.02.03.03 To study, apply oneself to learning
gedrincan 04.01.03.02 To drink heavily, get drunk
drincere 04.01.03.02 To drink heavily, get drunk
drisne 02.07.02.01 Root
gedrītan 02.04.06.06.06 Faeces
drīting 02.04.06.06.06 Faeces
(ge)drōf 01.01.02.01.04.01 Marsh, bog, swamp; 01.01.03.01.01 Moving water
gedrōf 01.01.03.01.02.04 State of sea
drōfe 08.01.03.03 Anxiety
drōfig 08.01.03.01 Despondency
drōflic 08.01.03.07.04 Severity, harshness
dròge 02.04.06.06.06 Faeces
droht 11.05.02 Mode, manner, way, method, fashion, course
drōht 05.12.01.09.01 To row
drohtaþ 05.02.01.01 The course of human affairs; 12.04 Fellowship, union, association
drohtaþ/drohtnoþ 11.05.02 Mode, manner, way, method, fashion, course
drohtnian 11.01.04 A doing, accomplishing (of something)
droht(n)ian 11.05.02 Mode, manner, way, method, fashion, course
drohtnian mid/betwux 12.04 Fellowship, union, association
droht(n)oþ 12.06.03.02 Living, dwelling, residence (in)
droht(n)ung 11.05 Natural/proper way/manner/mode of action; 12.06.03.02 Living, dwelling, residence (in)
(ge)drohtnung 11.05.02 Mode, manner, way, method, fashion, course
dropa 02.04.06.05.07.01 Humours; 02.08.02 Disease, infirmity, sickness; 02.08.07.08 Foot ailments, ?gout; 03.01.16.03 A drop of liquid
gedropa 02.07.09.02 Particular fruits (alphabetical order)
dropena drēorung 01.03.01.06.02 Rain
dropfāg 02.06.08.05 Forest bird, wild-fowl; 03.01.14.11 Medley/variety of colour
dropian 03.01.16.03 A drop of liquid
dropmǣlum 03.01.16.03 A drop of liquid; 03.03.07 A part, division, portion
droppettan 03.01.16.03 A drop of liquid
droppetung 03.01.16.03 A drop of liquid
dropung 03.01.16.03 A drop of liquid
gedrorenlic 05.11.01.03.01 Mortal state, this life
drōs 02.04.06.05.07.04 Secretions of ear; 04.06.02.04 Refuse, litter, rubbish
drōsna 01.01.02.01.04.01 Marsh, bog, swamp; 04.01.02.01.01.08 Leftover food; 04.01.03.05.02 Brewing; 04.06.02.04 Refuse, litter, rubbish
(ge)drūgian 03.01.18 Dryness (not wetness)
drūgoþ 01.01.02.01.06 Wild/uncultivated land; 01.03.01.02 Dry weather; 03.01.18 Dryness (not wetness)
drūgung 01.01.02.01.06 Wild/uncultivated land; 01.03.01.02 Dry weather; 03.01.18 Dryness (not wetness)

druncen 04.01.01.07 Feasting; 04.01.03.02 To drink heavily, get drunk
druncen gedrincan 04.01.03.02 To drink heavily, get drunk
(ge)druncen 04.01.03.02 To drink heavily, get drunk
druncengeorn 04.01.03.02 To drink heavily, get drunk
druncenhād 04.01.03.02 To drink heavily, get drunk
druncenig 04.01.03.02 To drink heavily, get drunk
druncenlǣwe 04.01.03.02 To drink heavily, get drunk
druncennes 04.01.03.02 To drink heavily, get drunk
druncenscipe 04.01.03.02 To drink heavily, get drunk
druncenwillen 04.01.03.02 To drink heavily, get drunk
druncmennen 04.01.03.02 To drink heavily, get drunk
druncnian 04.01.03 Drinking
(ge)druncnian 04.01.03.02 To drink heavily, get drunk; 05.12.01.09.03.02 Hardship on board
druncning 04.01.03.02 To drink heavily, get drunk
drūpung 08.01.03.01 Despondency
drūsende 02.05.04 Sleepiness, drowsiness, sleep
drūsian 01.01.03.01.02.04 State of sea; 05.12.03.02 Slowness
drūt 08.01.02.02.03 A loving relationship
drȳ 16.01.04 Sorcery, magic, witchcraft
gedrycned 02.08.02 Disease, infirmity, sickness
drȳcræft 16.01.04 Sorcery, magic, witchcraft; 16.01.04.04 A magical apparatus
drȳcræft drīfan 16.01.04 Sorcery, magic, witchcraft
drȳcræfta 16.01.04 Sorcery, magic, witchcraft
drȳcræftig 16.01.04 Sorcery, magic, witchcraft
drȳgan 03.01.18 Dryness (not wetness)
(ge)drȳgan 03.01.18 Dryness (not wetness)
drȳge 01.01.02.01.06 Wild/uncultivated land; 01.03.01.02 Dry weather; 01.03.01.05 Wind; 02.08.04.04.03 Withered; 03.01.18 Dryness (not wetness)
drȳgnes 01.03.01.02 Dry weather; 03.01.18 Dryness (not wetness)
drȳgscēod 04.04.07.15 Footwear, covering for the feet
dryht 02.03.01 People
(ge)dryht 12.04.02 A crowding together, assembly; 13.02.10.01.02.02 Armed forces
gedryht 02.03.03.01 Body of retainers, household; 05.04 Fate, lot, fortune, destiny
gedryhta 13.02.10 The military, soldiers
dryhtbearn 02.03.01.05 Youth, boy, stripling
dryhtcwēn 12.01.01.04.01 A royal leader
dryhtealdor 08.01.02.04 Hospitality; 12.09.02 Marriage ceremony
dryhtealdormann 12.09.02 Marriage ceremony
dryhten 12.01.01.04.01 A royal leader; 16.01.01 God, the Lord
dryhtenbēag 14.05.04.01 A fine
dryhtenbealu 08.01.03.06 Adversity, affliction
dryhtendōm 12.01.01 Authority

dryhtenhold 12.01.01.12 Loyalty
dryhtenlic 16.01.01 God, the Lord
dryhtenlīce 16.01.01 God, the Lord
dryhtenweard 12.01.01.04.01 A royal leader
dryhtfolc 02.03.03.03 A nation, people
dryhtgesīþ 13.02.10 The military, soldiers
dryhtgestrēon 15.01.03 Treasure, riches, wealth
dryhtguma 12.09.02 Marriage ceremony; 13.02.10 The military, soldiers
dryhtguman 02.03.01 People
dryhtlēoþ 16.02.01.08.01.01 Books of the Old Testament; 16.02.04.03.03.02 A psalm; 18.02.07.01.01 A song, a poem to be sung or recited
dryhtlic 07.02.04.03 Nobleness, excellence, nobility, magnificence; 12.01.01.06.05 Nobility, noble condition; 16.01.01 God, the Lord
dryhtlic gebed 16.02.04.08.01 Kinds of prayer
dryhtlīce 12.01.01.06.05 Nobility, noble condition; 16.01 A divine being
dryhtmann 12.09.02 Marriage ceremony
dryhtmāþm 15.01.03 Treasure, riches, wealth
dryhtnē 02.04.01 Dead body
dryhtscipe 12.01.01 Authority
dryhtsele 04.05.03.02.02.06.01 A hall building
dryhtsibb 13.01.01.01 Cessation of hostilities
dryhtwēmend 12.09.02 Marriage ceremony
dryhtwēmere 12.09.02 Marriage ceremony
dryhtwer 12.01.01.04 A leader, ruler

dryhtwuniende 04.05.03.01 Habitation, sojourn
dryhtwurþa 16.02.01.08.03.01 New Testament persons
drȳicge 16.01.04 Sorcery, magic, witchcraft
drȳlāc 16.01.04 Sorcery, magic, witchcraft
drȳlic 16.01.04 Sorcery, magic, witchcraft
drȳman 08.01.03.04.01 Complaint, lamentation; 18.02.07.01 Singing, song
(ge)drȳman 08.01.01.03.07 Joyous sound, mirth
drȳmann 16.01.04 Sorcery, magic, witchcraft
(ge)drȳme 18.02.07 Music
gedrȳme 08.01.01.03.07 Joyous sound, mirth
gedrȳmed 18.02.07 Music
drync 04.01.03.05.01 Intoxicating liquor
(ge)drync 04.01.03 Drinking
gedrync 04.01.03.02 To drink heavily, get drunk
drync(a) 04.01.03 Drinking; 04.01.03.05 A drink/beverage
gedrynca 04.01.03.05.03 Tavern
dryncelēan 04.01.02.04.02 Feast; 04.01.03.05.01 Intoxicating liquor; 15.05 Trade, traffic, commerce; 18.02 Amusement, revelry, festivity
dryncgemett 03.03.01.01 Liquid measures
gedryncnes 16.02.04.07.01 Baptism, baptizing (and anointing)
dryncwērig 04.01.03.02 To drink heavily, get drunk
(ge)drȳpan 03.01.16.03 A drop of liquid
dryppan 03.01.16.03 A drop of liquid
dryre 05.09.05 Ceasing, decline, fall off

drysmian 03.01.13.02 A growing dark, darkening
drysnan 03.01.13.02 A growing dark, darkening
gedrysnian 02.05.09.14 To vanish, disappear
dubb/dybb 01.01.03.01.03.01 Pool
dubbian 12.01.01.03 Symbols of power
dūce 02.06.08.02.01.01 Duck
gedūfan 05.12.05.02.04.03 To plunge (something into something)
gedūfan in/on 05.12.05.02.04.03 To plunge (something into something)
dūfedoppa 02.06.08.07 Exotic bird
dugende 12.08.02.01 Goodness, excellence, virtue
duguþ 02.01.04.02 To grow, grow up; 07.04.01 (Of persons) worth/value, worthiness; 07.08.01 Nobility (of character, rank, etc.); 07.08.07 Glory, splendour, magnificence; 08.01.01.03.08 Happiness, well-being, prosperity; 08.01.02.01 Favour, kindness, grace; 11.05.02.01 A standard, norm, ethos; 12 Power, might; 12.01.01.06.08 A person of rank, elder, great man; 12.04.02 A crowding together, assembly; 16.01.02.05 Inhabitants of heaven
duguþa 07.02.04.03 Nobleness, excellence, nobility, magnificence
duguþgifu 10.03.08 Bountifulness, munificence
duguþlic 07.02.04.02 Nobleness, nobility, dignity
duguþmiht 12.01 Power, control, sway
duguþnǣmere 10.01.01 Acceptance, receiving
dulmunus 05.12.01.09.03.01.01 Kind of ship

dumb 02.05.10.17.01 Dumb, silent; 09 Speech, vocal utterance; 09.02.02 Dumbness, lack of speech
dumba 09.02.02 Dumbness, lack of speech
dumbnes 09.02.02 Dumbness, lack of speech
dumpel/dumbel 01.01.02.01.03.03 Valley
dūn 01.01.02.01.02 High land; 01.01.02.01.02.02 Hill, mountain; 01.01.02.01.02.02.01 Hill
dūnælf(en) 16.01.03.04 Elfin race
dūne 05.10.05.04.02.03 Laid below
dūnestīgende 05.12.05.13 To go down, descend
dunfealu 03.01.14.09 Dull brown
dung 04.02.04.02.01.01 To manure, dung; 14.05.08.01 Prison, confinement, durance
dungrǣg 03.01.14.10 Grey-coated one
dūnhunig 04.01.02.01.05.04 Honey
dūniendlic 05.12.01.04.01.03 To amble, stagger
dūnland 01.01.02.01.04 Open (level) land
dūnlendisc 01.01.02.01.02.02 Hill, mountain
dūnlic 01.01.02.01.02.02 Hill, mountain
dunn 03.01.14.09 Dull brown
dunnian 03.01.13.02 A growing dark, darkening
dūnsǣte 02.03.03.05.02 The British/Welsh/Bretons
dūnscræf 01.01.02.01.03.01 Cave
durhere 04.05.02.12 Gate/doorway of a building
durstodl 04.05.02.12 Gate/doorway of a building
duru 04.05.02.12 Gate/doorway of a building

duruhaldend 12.01.01.08.01 A servant, attendant
durustod 04.05.02.12 Gate/doorway of a building
duruþegn 12.01.01.08.01 A servant, attendant
duruþēowen 12.01.01.08.01 A servant, attendant
duruþīnen 12.01.01.08.01 A servant, attendant
duruweard 12.01.01.08.01 A servant, attendant
dūs 03.03.04.01.02.01 A heap, mass, accumulation
dūst 01.01.02.02 Earth, soil; 02.04.01 Dead body; 04.06.02.05 Dust, powder
dūstdrenc 02.08.12.02.05.01 A herb with medicinal properties
dūstig/dȳstig 04.06.02.05 Dust, powder
dūstscēawung 02.02.05.03 To attend the dead
dūstswearm 01.03.01.02 Dry weather
dūþhamor 02.07.08 Grasses, reeds, etc.
(ge)dwællic 16.02.01.05 Heresy, error, wrong belief
dwǣs 06.01.05.03.02 Foolish, silly, stupid
(ge)dwǣs 06.01.05.03.01.01 Dullness, folly, stupidity
(ge)dwǣscan 03.01.13.02 A growing dark, darkening; 05.07 Ending of existence, end of world
dwǣsian 06.01.05.03.01.01 Dullness, folly, stupidity
dwǣslic 06.01.05.03.01.01 Dullness, folly, stupidity
dwǣslīce 06.01.05.03.01.01 Dullness, folly, stupidity
gedwǣsmann 06.01.05.03.02 Foolish, silly, stupid
(ge)dwǣsnes 06.01.05.03.01.01 Dullness, folly, stupidity
dwelian 02.08.11.02.01 Insanity, madness; 05.12.05.01 To go astray; 06.01.07.05 Error, being astray; 12.08.06.01.04 To lead a bad life
(ge)dwelian 05.12.05.01 To go astray; 06.01.07.04.01 Deception, a leading astray; 06.01.07.05 Error, being astray
dweliende 01.02.01.01.01 Planet
dwellan 04.05.03.01 Habitation, sojourn; 11.11.02 A hindrance
(ge)dwellan 06.01.07.04.01 Deception, a leading astray
gedwellan 05.12.05.01 To go astray; 12.08.06.01.04 To lead a bad life
dwelsian 05.12.05.01 To go astray; 06.01.07.05 Error, being astray
dweorg 02.03.01.10 Dwarf
dweorgedwosle 02.07.10.01 Particular herbs/spices (alphabetical order)
dweorgedwusle 02.07.11 Plants/flowers (alphabetical order)
(ge)dwild 16.02.01.05 Heresy, error, wrong belief
gedwild 05.12.01.02 To wander; 06.01.07.04.01 Deception, a leading astray; 06.01.07.05 Error, being astray
gedwildæfterfylgung 16.02.01.05 Heresy, error, wrong belief
gedwildlic 06.01.07.04.01 Deception, a leading astray
gedwildman 16.02.01.05 Heresy, error, wrong belief
gedwimor 06.01.02.01 An imaginary form, fancy; 06.01.07.04.02 Fraud, deceit, trick, trickery; 06.01.07.04.04 Deceitfulness, falseness, duplicity; 06.01.07.05 Error, being astray
gedwimorlic 06.01.02.01 An imaginary form, fancy

(ge)dwimorlīce 06.01.02.01 An imaginary form, fancy
(ge)dwīnan 05.09.05 Ceasing, decline, fall off
gedwīnan 02.05.09.14 To vanish, disappear
(ge)dwol 16.02.01.05 Heresy, error, wrong belief
(ge)dwola 06.01.07.05 Error, being astray; 12.08.06.01 Error, wrong conduct, erroneous practice
gedwola 02.08.11.02.01 Insanity, madness; 06.01.07.04.02 Fraud, deceit, trick, trickery; 16.02.01.05 Heresy, error, wrong belief
gedwolbiscop 16.02.03.02.05 A bishop
(ge)dwolcræft 16.01.04 Sorcery, magic, witchcraft
gedwolen 06.01.05.03 Want of understanding; 06.01.07.05 Error, being astray
gedwolenlic 06.01.05.03.02 Foolish, silly, stupid
gedwolfær 05.12.05.01 To go astray
gedwolgod 16.01.06 A god (of any faith)
gedwolhring 05.11.06.02 Reckoning/computation of time
dwolian 02.08.11.02.01 Insanity, madness
(ge)dwolian 05.12.05.01 To go astray; 06.01.07.05 Error, being astray
gedwolian 12.08.06.01.04 To lead a bad life
dwoliende 16.02.01.05 Heresy, error, wrong belief
dwoligende 06.01.07.05 Error, being astray
dwoligendlic 16.02.01.05 Heresy, error, wrong belief
(ge)dwollic 16.02.01.05 Heresy, error, wrong belief
(ge)dwollīce 06.01.07.05 Error, being astray
(ge)dwolma 05.08.02 Violence, force
(ge)dwolmann 16.02.01.05 Heresy, error, wrong belief
gedwolmann 06.01.07.05 Error, being astray
gedwolmist 06.01.07.05 Error, being astray
dwolpæþ 05.12.01.03 Expanse over which something travels
dwolscipe 06.01.07.05 Error, being astray
gedwolspræc 16.02.01.05 Heresy, error, wrong belief
gedwolsum 06.01.07.04.01 Deception, a leading astray
(ge)dwolþing 16.01.04 Sorcery, magic, witchcraft
gedwolþing 06.01.07.04.04.02 Pretence, feigning, dissimulation
dwolung 02.08.11.02.01.02 Madness, frenzy, folly
dybbian 06.01.01.02 Care, attention, observation
dȳdan 02.02.04.03 To kill, slay
dydrian 06.01.07.04.01 Deception, a leading astray
dydrin 04.01.02.01.02.08 Egg
dydrung 06.01.02.01 An imaginary form, fancy
(ge)dȳfan 05.12.05.02.04.03 To plunge (something into something)
dyfe 01.01.02.01.03.03 Valley
dyfel 17.03.10.02 A pin, peg, nail
dȳfing 16.02.04.07.01 Baptism, baptizing (and anointing)
gedyhtedum 07.02.04.03 Nobleness, excellence, nobility, magnificence
dyhtig 05.08 Strength

dylf(et) 01.01.02.01.03 Hollow/depression in land
dylsta 02.04.06.05.07.02 Mucus, phlegm, rheum; 02.08.05.02.01 Matter, purulence, pus
dylstiht 02.04.06.05.07.02 Mucus, phlegm, rheum; 02.08.05.02.01 Matter, purulence, pus
dyncge 02.04.06.06.06 Faeces; 04.02.03.02 Arable/ploughed land
dyncg(e) 04.02.04.02.01.01 To manure, dung
(ge)dyne 02.05.10.02 Noise, din
gedyng(i)an 04.02.04.02.01.01 To manure, dung
dyngung 04.02.04.02.01.01 To manure, dung
dynian 02.05.10.01 Thing heard; 02.05.10.04 To resound
dynige 02.07.11.02 Unidentified plants (alphabetical order)
dynt 02.05.10.07 A crashing, noise; 02.08.03 Pain, bodily discomfort; 02.08.04 Hurt, injury, damage; 05.06.09 Act of striking
gedȳpan 03.01.17.07.01 An anointing, greasing; 16.02.04.07.01 Baptism, baptizing (and anointing)
dyple 03.03.03.04.02 Two
dyppan 05.12.05.02.04.03 To plunge (something into something); 16.02.04.07.01 Baptism, baptizing (and anointing)
gedyre 04.05.02.12 Gate/doorway of a building
dȳre 08.01.02.02.01 A favourite, loved one
dyrfan 08.01.03.07.02 Misery, trouble, affliction

gedyrfan 11.09 Peril, danger; 17.01 Strenuous effort, hard work
dyrfing 08.01.03.07.02.01 Injury, offence
dȳrling 08.01.02.02.01 A favourite, loved one
dȳrlingþegn 08.01.02.02.01 A favourite, loved one
dyrne forliger 12.08.08.01.02.01 Fornication, adultery
dyrneceorl 08.01.02.02.03 A loving relationship
dyrneforlegen 12.08.08.01.02.01 Fornication, adultery
dyrneforlege(r)nes 12.08.08.01.02.01 Fornication, adultery
dyrne(ge)legerscipe 12.08.08.01.02.01 Fornication, adultery
dyrne(ge)liger 12.08.08.01.02.01 Fornication, adultery
dyrneleger 12.08.08.01.02.01 Fornication, adultery
dyrnelegere 12.08.08 Carnal nature, sensual appetites
dyrngewrit 16.02.01.08.02 Apocrypha
dyrnhǣmende 12.08.08.01.02.01 Fornication, adultery
dyrnlic 09.05.04 A secret
dyrnlīce 09.05.04 A secret
dyrnlicgan 12.08.08.01.02.01 Fornication, adultery
dyrnmaga 16.02.03.02.07.01 A priest of a church or minster
gedȳrsian 07.08.05 Glorifying, making great, glorification
gedyrst 08.01.03.06 Adversity, affliction
(ge)dyrstig 06.02.07.06.02.03 Presumption
gedyrstig 06.02.07.06.02.02 Boldness, daring; 07.06.01.01 Proud, arrogant
gedyrstigian 06.02.07.06.02.03 Presumption

dyrstiglīce 06.02.07.06.02.02 Boldness, daring
(ge)dyrstiglīce 07.06.01.02 Proudly, arrogantly
(ge)dyrsti(g)nes 06.02.07.06.02.03 Presumption
gedyrstignes 11.01.02 An undertaking
(ge)dyrstlǣcan 06.02.07.06.02.03 Presumption
gedyrstlǣcung 07.06.01 Pride, arrogance
gedyrstlic 07.06.01.01 Proud, arrogant
gedyrstnes 06.02.07.06.02.03 Presumption
dysgung 06.01.05.03.01.01 Dullness, folly, stupidity
dysig 06.01.05.03.01.01 Dullness, folly, stupidity; 06.01.05.03.02 Foolish, silly, stupid
dysigan 16.02.04.14.01 Blasphemy
dysigcræftig 16.01.04.06 Divination, augury
dysigdōm 06.01.05.03.01.01 Dullness, folly, stupidity
gedysigend 06.01.05.03.02 Foolish, silly, stupid
(ge)dysigian 06.01.05.03.02 Foolish, silly, stupid
dysiglic 06.01.05.03.02 Foolish, silly, stupid
dysiglīce 06.01.05.03.02 Foolish, silly, stupid
dysignes 06.01.05.03.01.01 Dullness, folly, stupidity; 06.01.07.05 Error, being astray; 16.02.04.14.01 Blasphemy
dysigu/-o 06.01.05.03.01.01 Dullness, folly, stupidity
dyslic 06.01.05.03.02 Foolish, silly, stupid
dyslīce 06.01.05.03.02 Foolish, silly, stupid

dyttan 05.10.05.04.15 Closure, being closed
dȳþ 17.05.01 Fuel, tinder
dȳþhamor 17.05.01 Fuel, tinder
ēa 01.01.03.01.01.01 River
ēabrycg 05.12.01.03.04 A bridge
ēac 03.03.04.03 Growth, increase
ēac hwæþre 03.06 Comparison
ēac māre tō 03.03.04.03 Growth, increase
ēac ne 09.07.03.01 A denial
ēac sōþ 06.01.07.01 Correct, right, free from error
ēac sōþlīce 06.01.07.01 Correct, right, free from error
ēac swā 03.03.04.03 Growth, increase
ēac swylce 03.03.04.03 Growth, increase
ēaca 03.03.04.02.02 Excess; 03.03.04.03 Growth, increase; 09.03.02.02.01.05 Minor parts of speech, etc.; 09.03.07.07.02.01.05 Additional material, sequel; 10.01.02 Acquisition; 13.02.10.01.02.02.03 Part of an army
ēacan 03.03.04.03 Growth, increase
ēacen 02.01.03.03.01 To beget; 03.03.04.03 Growth, increase; 07.02.04.03 Nobleness, excellence, nobility, magnificence; 10 Having, owning, possession
ēacencræftig 03.03.04.01.01 Greatness, bigness, size
ēacerse 02.07.09.02.02.02 Other vegetables (alphabetical order)
ēacian 03.03.04.03 Growth, increase
ēacnian 03.03.04.03 Growth, increase
(ge)ēacnian 02.01.03.03.02 To bring forth, produce; 03.03.04.03 Growth, increase
(ge)ēacnian tō 03.03.04.03 Growth, increase

geēacnian 02.01.03.03.01 To beget
ēacniende 02.01.03 Fruitfulness, fertility
ēacniendlic 03.03.04.03 Growth, increase
ēacnigende 02.01.03.03.01 To beget
ēacnung 03.03.04.03 Growth, increase
(ge)ēacnung 02.01.03.03.01 To beget; 02.01.03.03.03.01 Child-bearing, childbirth
geēacnung 02.01.03.03.04 Offspring, race, breed, family, children
ēacrop 02.07.11.02 Unidentified plants (alphabetical order)
ēad 08.01.01.03.03 Happiness, blessedness; 08.01.01.03.08 Happiness, well-being, prosperity; 15.01.03 Treasure, riches, wealth; 16.02.01.10.02.01 A blessing, invocation of divine favour
ēaden 05.04.01 Fortune, Fate (personification)
ēadfruma 16.01.01.02.02 A giving (by Deity)
ēadgiefa 16.01.01.02.02 A giving (by Deity)
ēadgiefu 08.01.01.03.03 Happiness, blessedness; 16.01.01.01 Attributes of God
ēadhrēþig 08.01.01.03.03 Happiness, blessedness; 16.02.01.10.02.01 A blessing, invocation of divine favour
ēadig 08.01.01.03.03 Happiness, blessedness; 08.01.01.03.08.02 Good fortune, success; 12.01.01.06.02.01 (High) rank, status, degree; 15.01.05 Possession of wealth; 16.02.01.10.02.01 A blessing, invocation of divine favour
ēadigan 07.04 Consideration, esteem
geēadigan 16.02.01.10.02.01 A blessing, invocation of divine favour
ēadigian 08.01.01.03.03 Happiness, blessedness
(ge)ēadigian 08.01.01.03.09.03 To make glad
ēadiglic 08.01.01.03.03 Happiness, blessedness; 08.01.01.03.08.02 Good fortune, success; 08.01.01.03.08.03 A favour, blessing; 16.02.01.10.02.01 A blessing, invocation of divine favour
ēadiglīce 08.01.01.03 Good feeling, joy, happiness; 08.01.01.03.03 Happiness, blessedness; 16.02.01.10.02.01 A blessing, invocation of divine favour
ēadignes 08.01.01.03.08 Happiness, well-being, prosperity
ēadlufu 08.01.02.02.04 Love, caritas
(ge)ēadmēd(i)an 16.02.04 Worship, honour, praise
ēadocce 02.07.11 Plants/flowers (alphabetical order)
ēadorgeard 02.04 Body
ēadwela 08.01.01.03 Good feeling, joy, happiness; 15.01.03 Treasure, riches, wealth
ēafisc 02.06.06.02 River fish, freshwater fish
eafor 02.06.02.01.06 Horse; 14.01.05 Service, obligation, duty
eafora 02.03.02.02 Child, offspring
eafoþ 12 Power, might
ēagan beorht 05.11.01.02 Shortness/brevity in time
ēagan byrhtm 05.11.01.02 Shortness/brevity in time
ēagbrǣw 02.04.03.01.03.02 Eye
ēagduru 04.05.02.13 A window-space
ēage 02.04.03.01.03.02 Eye; 02.04.06.01 Sight organ; 05.10.05.04.14 An opening, aperture
ēagece 02.08.07.02 Disorders of the eye

ēagegebyrd 02.05.09 Faculty of sight
ēagflēah 02.08.07.02 Disorders of the eye
ēaggemearc 01.01 Surface of the earth
ēaghring 02.04.05.04.02.01 Socket of eye; 02.04.06.01 Sight organ
eāghyll 02.04.03.01.03.04 Nose
ēaghyrne 02.04.03.01.03.02 Eye
ēagmist 02.08.07.02.01 Defective vision
ēagsealf 02.08.12.02.07 Remedies for specific parts (head to toe)
ēagsēoung 02.08.07.02 Disorders of the eye
ēagsȳne 02.05.09.09 Visible
ēagsȳnes 02.05.09.09 Visible
ēagþyrel 04.05.02.13 A window-space
ēagwærc 02.08.07.02 Disorders of the eye
ēagwund 02.08.07.02 Disorders of the eye
ēagwyrt 02.07.11 Plants/flowers (alphabetical order)
eaht 03.03.03 Number; 07.04 Consideration, esteem
eaht besittan 12.02.02 An assembly, meeting
eahta 03.03.03.04.08 Eight
eahta nihta eald 05.11.06.03.01.04 (Of lunar cycle) so many nights old
eahtafeald 03.03.03.04.08 Eight
eahtahyrnede 05.10.06.04 A corner, bend, angle
eahtan 07.01 Appraisal, appraising; 07.04 Consideration, esteem; 12.05.06.02.02 Persecution
eaht(a)tēoþa 03.03.03.04.18 Eighteen
eahtatīene 03.03.03.04.18 Eighteen
eahtatig 03.03.03.04.26 Eighty
eahtatȳnewintre 02.01.04 Age
eahtawintre 02.01.04 Age
eahtend 12.05.06.02.02 Persecution
eahtere 07.01 Appraisal, appraising

eahtian 06.01.01.01.01 Thought, cogitation, meditation; 07.01 Appraisal, appraising; 07.04.04 Praise, acclamation, applause
geeahtian 15.02 Worth, value
eahtnes 12.05.06.02.02 Persecution
eahtnung 07.01 Appraisal, appraising
eahtoþa 03.03.03.04.08 Eight
eahtung 07.01 Appraisal, appraising; 12.02.02.04 Counsel, deliberation
eal gearo 11.01.03 Preparation
ēalā 09.01.03.01 Interjections: Oh!
ēalād 01.01.03.01 Body of water
ēaland 01.01.02.01.01.02 Island; 01.01.02.01.01.03 Shore, bank
ēalandcyning 12.01.01.04.01.01 Kings and queens
eald 02.01.04 Age; 02.01.04.03 Aging, growing old; 02.03.02.03.04 (Of degrees of descent) great-, grand-; 05.11.07.03 Former times, days of old; 05.11.07.03.03 Old, not new; 11.05 Natural/proper way/manner/mode of action; 12.01.01.06.08 A person of rank, elder, great man
eald hrīþer 02.06.02.01.03 Cattle
eald genēat 12.04.01 A fellow, companion, associate, comrade
eald on 11.04 Ability, capacity, power
ealda 02.03.01.08 Adult male; 16.01.05.02.01 The devil
ealda fæder 02.03.02.03.04 (Of degrees of descent) great-, grand-
ealda hālga dæg 16.02.04.04.02.01.02 Lent
ealdbacen 04.01.02.02.05.04 Baking
ealdcȳþþ 12.06.04 Native land
ealdcȳþþu 08.01.02.03 Friendliness, affection

ealddagas 05.11.07.03 Former times, days of old

ealddōm 02.01.04.03 Aging, growing old

ealde mōdor 02.03.02.03.03 Forefather, ancestor; 02.03.02.03.04 (Of degrees of descent) great-, grand-

ealdefæder 02.03.02.03.04 (Of degrees of descent) great-, grand-

ealdewita 16.02.01.09.02 Knowledge of Jewish law

ealdfæder 02.03.02.03.03 Forefather, ancestor

ealdfēond 16.01.05.02.02 Other terms for devils

ealdgecynd 05.02 State, condition

ealdgefā 08.01.03.09.05 Enmity

ealdgefēra 12.04.01 A fellow, companion, associate, comrade

ealdgemǣre 05.10.05.04.11.01 A bound, limit

ealdgenīþla 16.01.05.02.01 The devil

eald(ge)riht 14.01.04.01 A special right, right peculiar to a class

ealdgesegen 09.06.01.01 A tradition, ordinance handed down

ealdgesīþ 12.04.01 A fellow, companion, associate, comrade

ealdgestrēon 15.01.03 Treasure, riches, wealth

ealdgeþungen 02.01.04.03 Aging, growing old; 07.08.01 Nobility (of character, rank, etc.)

ealdgeweorc 01 Earth, world; 02 Creation

ealdgewinn 12.05.04.01 Fighting, contention, warfare, strife

ealdgewinna 08.01.03.09.05 Enmity

ealdgewyrht 11.01 Action, doing, performance

ealdhettend 08.01.03.09.05 Enmity

ealdhlāford 12.01.01.04.01 A royal leader; 12.01.01.04.02 A lord, master

ealdhlāfordcynn 12.01.01.06.07.01 A royal race

ealdhrȳþerflǣsc 04.01.02.01.02.05 Meat

ealdian 02.01.04.03 Aging, growing old

(ge)ealdian 05.11 A time, period of time

ealdigende 02.01.04.03 Aging, growing old

ealdland 04.02.03.02.03 Fallow land

ealdlandrǣden 14.01.01 Law(s) of particular scope

ealdlic 02.01.04.02 To grow, grow up; 02.01.04.03 Aging, growing old; 05.11.07.03 Former times, days of old

ealdnes 02.01.04.03 Aging, growing old

ealdor 02.01.01 Life, vital part; 02.03.02.01 Parent; 03.03.05.01.01 Principal/chief (of its class or type); 05.05.01 An author, source, originator; 05.11.01.01.01 Eternity; 05.11.10.01.01 Origin; 06.01.06.02.01 A wise man, man of understanding or learning; 12.01.01.04 A leader, ruler; 12.01.01.05 A leader, administrator; 12.09 Marriage, state of marriage; 16.02.03.03.01.03 A prior

ealdor geæfnan 05.11 A time, period of time

ealdorapostol 16.02.01.08.03.01 New Testament persons

ealdorbana 02.02.04.03.01 A killer

ealdorbealu 02.02 Death

ealdorbiscop 16.02.03.02.01 A high priest, chief bishop, etc. (general); 16.02.03.02.02 The pope; 16.02.03.02.04 An archbishop

ealdorbold/ealdorbotl 04.05.03.02.02.06 A royal/noble palace

ealdorburg 12.06.02.01 A township

ealdorcearu 08.01.03 Bad feeling, sadness
ealdordæg 02.01.04 Age
ealdordēma 12.01.01.05 A leader, administrator
ealdordēofol 16.01.05.02.01 The devil
ealdordōm 05.11.10.01 A beginning; 11.07.04 Superiority, pre-eminence, primacy; 12.01.01 Authority
ealdordōmlic 03.03.05.01.01 Principal/chief (of its class or type)
ealdordōmlicnes 12.01.01 Authority
ealdordōmscipe 12.02 A public office
ealdorduguþ 12.01.01.06.08 A person of rank, elder, great man
ealdorfrēa 12.01.01.04.01 A royal leader
ealdorgeard 02.04 Body
ealdorgedāl 02.02 Death
ealdorgesceaft 02.01.02.02.01 Condition of life
ealdorgewinna 08.01.03.09.05 Enmity
ealdorlang 05.11.01.01 Long duration, long space
ealdorlēas 02.02.03.02 State of being dead; 02.03.02.02 Child, offspring; 12.04.04 Solitude
ealdorlegu 02.01.02.02.02 Lifetime
ealdorlic 03.03.05.01.01 Principal/chief (of its class or type); 06.01.07 Truth, conformity with absolute standard; 07.02.04.03 Nobleness, excellence, nobility, magnificence; 12.02.02.03 Terms for classical world
ealdorlīce 03.03.05.01.01 Principal/chief (of its class or type); 07.02.04.03 Nobleness, excellence, nobility, magnificence
ealdorlicnes 12.01.01 Authority
ealdormann 12.01.01.04 A leader, ruler; 12.01.01.05 A leader, administrator; 12.01.01.06.08 A person of rank, elder, great man; 12.02.02.03 Terms for classical world; 16.02.03.02.01 A high priest, chief bishop, etc. (general); 17.02.01 Management of work
ealdorneru 11.10 Safety, safeness
ealdorsācerd 16.02.03.02.01 A high priest, chief bishop, etc. (general)
ealdorscipas 16.01.02.05.01 An angel
ealdorscipe 12.01.01 Authority
ealdorsetl 12.01.01.02 Seat of authority
ealdorstōl 12.01.01.02 Seat of authority
ealdorþegn 12.01.01.07 A follower; 16.02.01.08.03.01 New Testament persons
ealdorwīsa 12.01.01.04 A leader, ruler
ealdoþ 01.01.03.01.01.04 Watercourse/channel
ealdre 16.02.03.03.01.02 An abbess
ealdre gedīgan 11.10.05 Escape
ealdseaxe(-an) 02.03.03.06.02 Germany and Low Countries
ealdspell 09.06.01.01 A tradition, ordinance handed down
ealdsprǣc 09.06.01.02 A saying, saw, proverb, maxim
ealdung 02.01.04.03 Aging, growing old
ealdwerig 16.01.05.02.02 Other terms for devils
ealdwīf 02.03.01.09 Old woman
ealdwita 06.01.05.02.01.01 Sagacity
ealdwrītere 09.03.07.07.03.03 A writer, author
ealfara 02.06.02.01.06 Horse
ealfela 03.03.04.01 Much
ealfelo 04.06.02.06 Poison
(ge)ealgian 13.02.04 Defence, guard, protection

ealgodweb 04.04.05.05 Fine woven material from silk, cotton or linen
ealgodwebben 04.04.05.05 Fine woven material from silk, cotton or linen
ealh 16.02.05.02.01 A temple
ealhālgung 16.02.01.10.02 Consecration
ealhstede 16.02.05.02.01 A temple
ēalic 01.01.03.01.01.01 River
ēalifer 02.07.11 Plants/flowers (alphabetical order)
ēalīþend 05.12.01.09.03 A voyage
eall 03.03.06 Wholeness; 03.03.06.02 Fullness; 03.04.03.01 Someone/something
eall efne 03.04.03.01 Someone/something
eall endemes 05.11.07.01 Contemporary, coeval
eall gōd 16.01.01.01 Attributes of God
eall hālig 16.02.01.10 Holiness
eall īren 17.04.02.05 Iron
eall nīwe 05.11.07.04.03 Newness, novelty
eall rihte 06.01.07.01 Correct, right, free from error
eall tela 07.02 Goodness
eall ūtan behȳpan 05.10.05.04.11 A circle, circuit, circumference
eall gewǣpnod 13.02.08 Military equipment
eallbeorht 03.01.12 Brightness, light
ealle 03.03.06.02 Fullness
ealle dagas 05.11.09.01 Always
ealle hālige 16.01.02.05.02 A saint
ealle þrāge 05.11.11 Continuity
eallencten 16.02.04.04.02.01.02 Lent
ealles 03.03.06.02 Fullness; 03.04.01 Singularity, peculiarity
ealles nāuht 05.07 Ending of existence, end of world

eallebern 17.04.04.02 Skin, hide (as material)
eallgelēaflic 16.02.01.04 Orthodoxy
eallgrēne 03.01.14.06 Green/greenness
eallgylden 03.01.14.07 Yellow/yellowness
eallhwīt 03.01.14.03 White/whiteness
eallic 16.01.01.01 Attributes of God; 16.01.01.01.01 The Almighty; 16.02.01.04 Orthodoxy
ealling 05.11.09.01 Always
eallīsig 03.01.11 Coldness, coolness
eallmægen 11.03 Endeavour
eallmiht 16.01.01.01.01.01 Mightiness
eallnacod 04.04.07.02.01 Nakedness
ealloffrung 03.01.09.02.01.01 A kind of fire; 16.02.04.12 Sacrifice, a sacrifice
eallseolcen 04.04.05.05 Fine woven material from silk, cotton or linen
eallswā 03.06.01 Similitude, likeness
eallsweart 03.01.14.04 Black/blackness
eallswilc 03.06.01 Similitude, likeness
eallunga 03.03.06.02 Fullness; 06.01.07.07.03 Certainty
eallwealda 16.01.01.01.01 The Almighty; 16.01.01.01.01.01 Mightiness
eallwealdend 16.01.01.01.01 The Almighty
eallwealdende 16.01.01.01.01.01 Mightiness
eallwiht 02 Creation
eallwriten 09.03.07.01.02.01 Handwriting, autograph, signature
eallwundor 06.01.08.05.01.01.01 An exercise of power, mighty work, miracle
ealne weg 05.11.09.01 Always
ealne wīdan feorh 05.11.01.01.01 Eternity
ealneg 05.11.09.01 Always; 05.11.11 Continuity

ealning(a) 05.11.09.01 Always
ealra 03.03.06.02 Fullness; 03.04.01 Singularity, peculiarity
ealra hālgena mæssedæg 16.02.04.04.02.01.04 Other feasts
ealu 04.01.03.05.01 Intoxicating liquor; 04.01.03.05.01.02 Broth
ealubenc 04.05.04.01 A bench, seat
ealuclyfa 04.01.03.05.03 Tavern
ealufæt 04.01.03.05.04.02 A barrel, tun, vat, cask
ealugafol 15.03.02 A tax
ealugāl 04.01.03.02 To drink heavily, get drunk
ealugālnes 04.01.03.02 To drink heavily, get drunk
ealugeweorc 04.01.03.05.02 Brewing
ealuhūs 04.01.03.05.03 Tavern
ealumealt 04.01.03.05.02 Brewing
ealuscerwen 06.01.08.06.02 Great fear, terror, horror; 08.01.03.06 Adversity, affliction
ealuscop 18.02.05 Buffoonery, speech of buffoon/actor
ealusele 04.01.03.05.03 Tavern
ealuwǣge 04.01.03.05.04 Drinking vessel
ealuwosa 04.01.03.02 To drink heavily, get drunk
ēam 02.03.02.03.06.02.01 Uncle (especially maternal)
geēane 02.06.01.07 Breeding, hatching
ēanian 02.01.03.03.02 To bring forth, produce
ēaōfer 01.01.02.01.01.03 Shore, bank
ear 04.02.04.06.06 Harrowing equipment; 17.03.07 Tools for digging/grasping/pulling
ēar 01.01.02.01 Ground; 01.01.03.01.02 Sea/ocean; 04.02.04.03.02.01 Grain crops; 09.03.07.01.01 A runic letter

ēaracu 01.01.03.01.01.01 River
ēarblǣd 04.02.04.03.02.01 Grain crops
earce 04.05.04.03 A box, case, chest, container; 16.02.05.05.01 Ark of the covenant
earc(e) 05.12.01.09.03.01.01 Kind of ship
ēarclǣnsend 02.04.03.04.01.01.01 Finger
ēarcoþu 02.08.07.03 Disorders of the ear
eard 01.01.02 Land; 04.05.03 A dwelling-place, abode, habitation; 05.02.01.01 The course of human affairs; 12.06 A province, country, territory
eardǣrn 04.05.03 A dwelling-place, abode, habitation
eardbegenga 02.03.03.04 An inhabitant; 04.05.03.01 Habitation, sojourn
eardbegengnes 04.05.03.01 Habitation, sojourn; 12.06.03.02 Living, dwelling, residence (in)
eardere 02.03.03.04 An inhabitant
eardfæst 02.03.03.04 An inhabitant; 04.05.03.01 Habitation, sojourn; 05.13.06.01 Firm, stable, steady
eardgeard 01 Earth, world
eardgyfu 10.03 Giving
(ge)eardian æt/in 05.11 A time, period of time
(ge)eardian (in/on) 04.05.03.01 Habitation, sojourn
eardiend 02.03.03.04 An inhabitant; 04.05.03.01 Habitation, sojourn
eardiendlic 04.05.03.01 Habitation, sojourn; 12.06.03 A site, settlement
eardland 12.06.04 Native land
eardlufu 12.06.04 Native land
eardstapa 05.12.01.02 To wander; 12.06.05.01 State of exile, banishment
eardstede 04.05.03 A dwelling-place, abode, habitation

eardung 04.05.03 A dwelling-place, abode, habitation; 12.06.03.02 Living, dwelling, residence (in)
eardungburg 12.06.02.01 A township
eardunghūs 04.05.03 A dwelling-place, abode, habitation
eardungstōw 04.05.03 A dwelling-place, abode, habitation
eardweall 01.01.02.01.02.01 Rising ground, eminence
eardwīc 04.05.03 A dwelling-place, abode, habitation
eardwrecca 12.06.05.01 State of exile, banishment
eardwunung 12.06.03.02 Living, dwelling, residence (in)
ēare 02.04.03.01.03.03 Ear; 02.04.06.02 Hearing organ; 02.05.10 Faculty of hearing; 06.01.01.02 Care, attention, observation
ēarede 17.03 Implements, tools, etc.
ēarendel 03.01.12.02 A beam of light; 05.11.04.01.01 Dawn, daybreak, sunrise
earfe 02.07.11 Plants/flowers (alphabetical order); 04.02.04.04 Harvest, crop
ēarfinger 02.04.03.04.01.01.01 Finger
earfoþcierre 06.02.07.04 Obstinacy
earfoþcynn 12.08.06.01 Error, wrong conduct, erroneous practice
earfoþdǣde 11.11 Difficulty
earfoþdæg 08.01.03.06 Adversity, affliction
earfoþe 02.08.03 Pain, bodily discomfort; 08.01.03.06 Adversity, affliction; 08.01.03.07.04 Severity, harshness; 11.11 Difficulty; 17 Work, doings, actions, labour; 17.01 Strenuous effort, hard work

earfoþfēre 11.11.01 A physical difficulty, strait
earfoþfynde 02.05.09.13 Invisible
earfoþhāwe 02.05.09.13 Invisible
earfoþhwīl 08.01.03.06 Adversity, affliction
earfoþhylde 08.01.03.02 Discontent
(ge)earfoþian 08.01.03.07.02 Misery, trouble, affliction
earfoþlǣre 06.02.07.04 Obstinacy; 12.05.06.01 Restraint, check, curb, control
earfoþlǣte 02.08.08.12 Disease of bowels
earfoþlic 08.01.03.07.04 Severity, harshness; 11.11 Difficulty
earfoþlīce 08.01.03.07.04 Severity, harshness; 11.11 Difficulty
earfoþlicnes 02.08.03 Pain, bodily discomfort
earfoþmæcg 08.01.03.06 Adversity, affliction
earfoþnes 02.08.03 Pain, bodily discomfort; 08.01.03.06.01 Affliction, misfortune, calamity; 11.11 Difficulty
earfoþrecce 11.11 Difficulty
earfoþrihte 06.02.07.04 Obstinacy
earfoþrīme 03.03.03 Number
earfoþsǣlig 08.01.03.06.01 Affliction, misfortune, calamity
earfoþsīþ 05.12.01.01 To go on a journey/expedition, travel; 08.01.03.06.01 Affliction, misfortune, calamity
earfoþtǣcne 02.05.09.13 Invisible
earfoþþrāg 08.01.03.06 Adversity, affliction
earfoþwylde 05.08.02.01 (Of living creatures) fierceness, roughness

earg 06.02.07.07 Cowardice, pusillanimity; 12.08.06.01.02 Lacking moral good
earge 07.03 Evil
ēargebland 01.01.03.01.02.06 Surging, rolling, heaving of waves
ēargespeca 12.02.02.02 A counsellor, advisor
eargian 06.02.07.07 Cowardice, pusillanimity
earglic 06.02.07.07 Cowardice, pusillanimity
earglīce 06.02.07.07 Cowardice, pusillanimity; 07.09.03 Infamy, ignominy, shame
eargnes 12.08.07.01.01 Wantonness, sensuality, lasciviousness
ēargrund 01.01.03.01.02.01 Region of sea/ocean
eargscipe 06.02.07.07 Cowardice, pusillanimity; 12.08.07.01.01 Wantonness, sensuality, lasciviousness
earh 13.02.08.04.04.01 An arrow, dart, bolt
earhfaru 13.02.08.04.04.01 An arrow, dart, bolt
ēar(h)ring 04.04.10.01 A ring (for finger, arm, neck)
earhwinnende 06.01.08.06.03.01 Causing dread, terrifying
ēarisc 02.07.08 Grasses, reeds, etc.
ēarīþ 01.01.03.01.01.03 Stream
ēarlæppa 02.04.03.01.03.03 Ear
ēarliprica 02.04.03.01.03.03 Ear
ēarlocc 02.04.04.03.03 Hair of head
earm 01.01.02.01.01.03.02 Inlet in river/sea; 02.04.03.04.01 Arm; 02.06.01.04 Leg; 08.01.03.06 Adversity, affliction; 10.02 Want, lack; 15.01.06 Poverty, indigence; 16.02.05.11 The cross (as Christian image)
earmbēag 04.04.10.01 A ring (for finger, arm, neck)
earmboga 02.04.03.04.01 Arm
earmcearig 08.01.03 Bad feeling, sadness
earme 07.03 Evil
earmella 04.04.07.03 Part of garment
earmful 07.07 Humility; 08.01.03.06 Adversity, affliction
earmgegirela 04.04.10.01 A ring (for finger, arm, neck)
earmheort 06.02.07.07 Cowardice, pusillanimity; 08.01.02.06.01 Pity
earmheortnes 08.01.02.06.01 Pity
earmhrēad 04.04.10.01 A ring (for finger, arm, neck)
earmian 08.01.02.06.01 Pity
earming 07.03.04 A wretch, poor creature; 07.09 Shame, disgrace; 08.01.02.05 Compassion; 08.01.03.06 Adversity, affliction
earmlic 07.07 Humility; 08.01.02.06.01 Pity; 08.01.03.04 Grief; 08.01.03.06 Adversity, affliction
earmlīce 07.07 Humility; 08.01.02.06.01 Pity; 08.01.03.06 Adversity, affliction; 08.01.03.07.04 Severity, harshness
earmsceanca 02.04.05.04.06 Bone of arm
earmsceapen 07.03.04 A wretch, poor creature; 08.01.03.06.01 Affliction, misfortune, calamity
earmslīfe 04.04.07.03 Part of garment
earmstoc 04.04.07.03 Part of garment
earmstrang 05.08 Strength
earmswīþ 05.08 Strength
earn 02.06.08.04 Bird of prey
earncynn 02.06.08.04 Bird of prey
earngēap/-gēat 02.06.08.04 Bird of prey
earnian 11.03 Endeavour

(ge)earnian 10.01.02 Acquisition
(ge)earnian (tō) 07.04.02 Merit, desert(s)
geearnian 11.07 Use (made of things), service
earningland 15.01.01 Landed property
earnung 11.03 Endeavour; 15.02.04 Spending, disbursement
(ge)earnung 07.04.02 Merit, desert(s)
geearnung 08.01.02.01 Favour, kindness, grace
earp 03.01.13 Darkness, obscurity
ēarplætt 05.06.09 Act of striking
(ge)ēarplætt(i)gan 05.06.09 Act of striking
ēarprēon 04.04.10.01 A ring (for finger, arm, neck)
ears 02.04.06.03.02.04 Intestines
ēarscripel 02.04.03.04.01.01.01 Finger
ēarsealf 02.08.12.02.07 Remedies for specific parts (head to toe)
earsendu 02.04.03.03.03 Buttock(s), back parts
earsgang 02.04.06.03.02.04 Intestines; 02.04.06.06.06 Faeces; 04.05.03.05.02 A privy
ēarslege 05.06.09 Act of striking
earslȳra 02.04.03.03.03 Buttock(s), back parts
earsode 02.04.03.03.03 Buttock(s), back parts
ēarspinl 04.04.10.01 A ring (for finger, arm, neck)
earsþerl 02.04.06.03.02.04 Intestines
ēarþyrel 02.04.06.02 Hearing organ
ēarwærc 02.08.07.03 Disorders of the ear
ēarwela 01.01.03 Water
ēarwicga 02.06.09.02.06 Earwig
earwunga 05.03.01.01 Without need or cause
ēase 04.01.03.05.04 Drinking vessel

ēast 01.01.01.03 East
ēastæþ 01.01.02.01.01.03 Shore, bank
ēastān 01.01.02.02.01 Rock, stone
ēastan(e) 01.01.01.03 East
ēastannorþan 01.01.01.01.01 North-east
ēastannorþanwind 01.03.01.05.01 Winds from particular points
ēastansūþan 01.01.01.02.01 South-east
ēastansūþanwind 01.03.01.05.01 Winds from particular points
ēast(an)wind 01.03.01.05.01 Winds from particular points
ēastcentingas 02.03.03.05.01.03 Kentish people
ēastcyning 12.01.01.04.01.01 Kings and queens
ēastdǣl 01.01.01.03 East
ēastdene 02.03.03.06.05 Scandinavian
ēastende 01.01.01.03 East
ēastengle 02.03.03.05.01.01 Angles; 12.06.01.01 England
ēasterǣfen 16.02.04.04.02.01.03 Holy Week
ēasterdæg 16.02.01.08.04 Jewish seasons/feasts; 16.02.04.04.02.01.03 Holy Week
ēasterfæsten 16.02.04.04.02.01.02 Lent
ēasterfeorm 04.01.02.04.02 Feast
ēasterfrēolsdæg 16.02.01.08.04 Jewish seasons/feasts
ēastergewuna 16.02.04.04.02.01.03 Holy Week
ēasterlic 01.01.01.03 East; 05.11.03.01.02.01 Spring; 16.02.01.08.04 Jewish seasons/feasts; 16.02.04.04.02.01.03 Holy Week
ēastermōnaþ 05.11.03.01.03.01 Specific months
easterne nute bēam 02.07.09.02.01.01 Particular nuts (alphabetical order)

ēasterne 01.01.01.03 East; 02.03.03.04 An inhabitant
ēasterniht 16.02.04.04.02.01.03 Holy Week
ēastersunnandæg 16.02.04.04.02.01.03 Holy Week
ēastersymbel 16.02.01.08.04 Jewish seasons/feasts
ēastertīd 16.02.01.08.04 Jewish seasons/feasts; 16.02.04.04.02.01.03 Holy Week
ēasterþēnung 16.02.01.08.04 Jewish seasons/feasts
ēasterwucu 16.02.04.04.02.01.03 Holy Week
ēasteweard 01.01.01.03 East
ēastfolc 02.03.03.06.07.03 Eastern/Oriental people
ēastfrancan 02.03.03.06.01 Peoples of France
ēastgārsecg 01.01.03.01.02.03 Sea in particular area
ēastgemǣre 05.10.05.04.11.01 A bound, limit
ēasthealf 01.01.01.03 East
ēastland 01.01.01.03 East; 12.06.01.03 The Continent
ēastlang 01.01.01.03 East
ēastlēode 02.03.03.06.07.03 Eastern/Oriental people
ēastmearc 05.10.05.04.11.01 A bound, limit
ēastnorþ 01.01.01.01.01 North-east
ēastnorþerne 01.01.01.01.01 North-east
ēastnorþwind 01.03.01.05.01 Winds from particular points
ēastorlic regol 16.02.05.10.12 A computus and calendar
ēastportic 16.02.05.03.01 Door or gate of church

ēastre 05.11.03.01.02.01 Spring; 16.02.01.08.04 Jewish seasons/feasts; 16.02.04.04.02.01.03 Holy Week
ēastrēam 01.01.03.01.01.01 River
geēastrian 16.02.04.04.02.01.03 Holy Week
ēastrīce 01.01.01.03 East; 12.06 A province, country, territory
ēastrihte 01.01.01.03 East
ēastrihtes 01.01.01.03 East
ēastrodor 01.02.01 Heaven(s), sky
ēastsǣ 01.01.03.01.02.03 Sea in particular area
ēastseaxe (-an) 02.03.03.05.01.10 Saxons
ēaststæþ 01.01.02.01.01.03 Shore, bank
ēastsūþ 01.01.01.02.01 South-east
ēastsūþdǣl 01.01.01.02.01 South-east
ēastsūþlang 01.01.01.02.01 South-east
ēastþēod 02.03.03.06.07.03 Eastern/Oriental people
ēastþyringas 02.03.03.06.02.01 Other peoples
ēastweard 01.01.01.03 East
ēastweardes 01.01.01.03 East
ēastweg 05.12.01.03.01 A means of access
ēastwegas 01.01.01.03 East
ēastwille 02.03.03.05.01.12 An unknown people
ēaþbede 08.01.02.01 Favour, kindness, grace
ēaþbegēate 11.12 Easiness
ēaþbelg 08.01.03.05.04 Irritability
ēaþbēne 08.01.02.01 Favour, kindness, grace
ēaþbylgnes 08.01.03.05.04 Irritability
ēaþbylige 08.01.03.05.04 Irritability
ēaþcnǣwe 11.12 Easiness
ēaþdǣde 11.12 Easiness

ēaþe 02.05.05.04 Sensual pleasure; 06.01.07.07.01 Likelihood, probability, chance; 06.02.02.01 Will, wish, pleasure; 06.02.07.05.01 Inconstancy; 08.01.02.01 Favour, kindness, grace; 11.12 Easiness
ēaþ(e) 11.12 Easiness; 02.05.05.04 Sensual pleasure
ēaþe mæg 05.03.01.03 Reason, cause; 06.01.07.07.01 Likelihood, probability, chance
ēaþelic 11.08.04 Vanity, idleness, frivolity; 11.12 Easiness
ēaþelīce 02.05.05.04 Sensual pleasure; 06.02.07.05.01 Inconstancy; 11.12 Easiness
ēaþelicnes 11.12 Easiness
ēaþfēre 05.12.01.03.01 A means of access
ēaþfynde 11.03.01.03 Finding, discovery
ēaþgē(a)te 11.12 Easiness
ēaþgeorn 02.05.05.04.01 Luxuries, dainties, good things; 08.01.01.03.02 Pleasure, satisfaction
eāþgesīene 02.05.09.09 Visible
ēaþhylde 08.01.01.03.02 Pleasure, satisfaction
ēaþlǣc(n)e 02.08.12 Healing, curing
ēaþlǣre 06.01.06.02.03.04.04 Under instruction, being taught
ēaþmēde 07.07 Humility
(ge)ēaþmēd(i)an 07.07 Humility; 12.05.06.04.02 Submission, subjection, obedience
geēaþmēd(i)an 05.06.01 Devastation, laying waste; 07.04.03 Reverence, respect; 07.09.02 Disgrace, shaming, humiliation; 12.05.06.04 A trampling upon, subjection
ēaþmēdlīce 07.07 Humility

ēaþmēdu 07.07 Humility; 13.02.05.02.01 Surrender, submission
ēaþmēdum 07.07 Humility
geēaþmettan 07.07 Humility
ēaþmēttu 07.07 Humility
ēaþmōd 07.07 Humility; 12.01.01.12.01 Obedience, service; 16.01.01.01 Attributes of God
ēaþmōdheort 07.07 Humility
(ge)ēaþmōdian 07.07 Humility; 12.01.01.12.01 Obedience, service
geēaþmōdian 07.05.02 Contempt
ēaþmōdlic 07.07 Humility
ēaþmōdlīce 07.07.02 Humility, meekness
ēaþmōdnes 07.07.02 Humility, meekness; 08.01.02.01 Favour, kindness, grace
ēaþmylte 04.01.02.01.01 Edibility
ēaþrǣde 11.12 Easiness
ēaþwylte 05.12.02.08 To give a different direction to, turn
ēawdnes 02.05.09.12 To show; 09.05.05.01 Showing, manifestation, display
ēawisclic 09.05.05.01 Showing, manifestation, display
ēawisclīce 09.05.05.01 Showing, manifestation, display
ēawiscnes 09.05.05.01 Showing, manifestation, display
ēawunga 09.05.05.01 Showing, manifestation, display
ēawyrt 02.07.11 Plants/flowers (alphabetical order)
eax 17.03.02 Item providing support
eaxelgespann 17.03.02 Item providing support
eaxl 02.04.03.03.02 Shoulder
eaxlclāþ 16.02.05.06.02 Garb for neck and shoulders

eaxlgestealla 12.04.01 A fellow, companion, associate, comrade; 12.05.01 Rivalry, contest
ebba 01.01.03.04 Current, rush of water
ebbian 01.01.03.06 Flood
geebbian 01.01.03.04 Current, rush of water
ēbreas 02.03.03.06.07.05 Jews
ebrēisc 02.03.03.06.07.05 Jews
ebrēisclīce 09.03.01 Particular languages
ece 02.08.03 Pain, bodily discomfort
ēce 05.11.01.01.01 Eternity; 05.11.11 Continuity; 05.13.06 Constancy, unchangeableness
ēce līf 05.11.01.01.01 Eternity; 16.01.02.03 Reward of heaven
eced 04.01.02.01.05.02 Vinegar
eceddrenc 02.08.12.02.05 Pharmacy, curing with salves
ecedfæt 04.01.02.02.06.03 Food receptacle, basket
ecedwīn 04.01.03.05.01.01 Wine
ēcelic 05.11.01.01.01 Eternity; 05.11.11 Continuity
ēcelīce 05.11.01.01.01 Eternity; 05.11.11 Continuity
ecg 01.01.02.01.02.02.04 Cliff; 13.02.08.04 Weapons, arms
ecgan 05.10.06.03.01 A point, spike, prickle
(ge)ecgan 04.02.04.02.02.01 Harrowing
ecgbana 02.02.04.03.01 A killer
ecgclif 01.01.02.01.02.02.04 Cliff
ecgheard 13.02.08.04.03 A sword
ecghete 08.01.03.09.04 Hatred
ecglāst 13.02.08.04 Weapons, arms
geecgode 05.10.06.03.01 A point, spike, prickle
ecgplega 13.02.02 Battle
ecgþracu 05.08 Strength

ecgung 04.02.04.02.02.01 Harrowing
ecgwæl 02.02.04 Killing, violent death, destruction
eclinga 05.10.05.04.11.01 A bound, limit
eclypsis 01.02.01.01.07 An eclipse
ēcnes 05.11.01.01.01 Eternity
edblōwan 02.01.03 Fruitfulness, fertility; 02.04.06.07.05 To breathe
geedbyrdan 02.01.03.03.05 Rebirth/regeneration; 16.01.01.02.09 Resurrection
edcēlnes 08.01.01.03.09 Pleasantness, agreeableness
geedcennan 16.02.01.12 Spirituality
edcenned 16.01.01.02.09 Resurrection
edcenning 16.01.01.02.09 Resurrection
geedcīegan 12.03.03.01 Summons, a call, summoning
edcierr 02.08.02.01.02 Onset, attack of illness; 05.12.05.11.01 To return
geedcucod 02.08.12 Healing, curing
edcwic 02.08.12 Healing, curing
(ge)edcwician 16.01.01.02.09 Resurrection
geedcwician 02.08.13 Recovery, growing better
edcwide 09.06.01 To relate, recount, tell
geedfrēolsian 15.01.02 Gift, transfer of property
edgeong 02.01.04.01 Youth
edgift 10.03.04.01 Restitution, making good, repayment; 14.05.04 A penalty, punishment
geedgirnan 11.03.01.02 To seek, seek for
edgrōwung 05.01 Growth, increase, what springs up
geedgunnen 05.11.09.06 Frequency, repetition
edgyldan 10.03.05 Recompense, reward

edgyldend 10.03.05 Recompense, reward; 15.02.04 Spending, disbursement
geedhīwian 05.13.01 Transformation, taking another shape
edhwierfan 05.12.05.11.01 To return
edhwyrft 02.08.13 Recovery, growing better; 05.11.09.06 Frequency, repetition; 05.12.05.11.01 To return
geedhyrtan 16.02.01.12 Spirituality
edisc 04.02.03.04.02 Pasture/pasturage
edischenn 02.06.08.03 Game-bird
ediscweard 04.02.03.04.02 Pasture/pasturage
(ge)edlǣcan 09.06.02.01.03 Recapitulation
geedlǣcan 05.11.09.06 Frequency, repetition; 09.06.02 A saying, speech, statement
edlǣcende 05.11.09.06 Frequency, repetition
edlǣcung 05.11.09.06 Frequency, repetition
(ge)edlǣht 02.08.02.01 An illness, ailment, disorder
geedlǣstan 05.11.09.06 Frequency, repetition
edlēan 10.03.05 Recompense, reward; 14.05.03 Retribution, requital
(ge)edlēanian 10.03.05 Recompense, reward; 14.05.03 Retribution, requital
(ge)edlēan(i)end 10.03.05 Recompense, reward
edlēanung 10.03.05 Recompense, reward; 12.05.04.02.01 Retribution, requital
edlesende 05.13.04 Exchange, commutation
edlesendlic 09.03.02.02.01.05 Minor parts of speech, etc.
edlesendlīce 03.06 Comparison
edlesung 09.03.02.03.01.06 Relation

edmǣle 05.11.02.01.02 A time of celebration; 18.02.01 A festival
edmēldæg 05.11.02.01.02 A time of celebration; 18.02.01 A festival
edmēltīd 05.11.02.01.02 A time of celebration; 18.02.01 A festival
ednīwan 05.11.07.04.03.01 Renewal, restoration; 05.11.09.06 Frequency, repetition
(ge)ednīwan 05.11.07.04.03.01 Renewal, restoration
ednīwe 05.11.07.04.03 Newness, novelty; 05.11.07.04.03.01 Renewal, restoration; 05.11.09.06 Frequency, repetition; 11.12.02.02 Amendment, setting right, reparation; 16.02.01.12 Spirituality
ednīwian 05.11.07.04.03.01 Renewal, restoration
(ge)ednīwian 05.11.09.06 Frequency, repetition
geednīwian 16.02.01.12 Spirituality
ednīwigend 16.01.01.02.01 Creator
ednīwinga 05.11.07.04.03.01 Renewal, restoration; 05.11.09.06 Frequency, repetition
(ge)ednīwung 05.11.07.04.03.01 Renewal, restoration
edreccan/eodorcan 06.01.01.01.01.01 Consideration, rumination
edroc 02.04.06.03.02.02 Throat/gullet; 02.04.06.03.02.03 Stomach/belly; 06.01.01.01.01.01 Consideration, rumination
edryne 05.12.05.11.01 To return
edsceaft 02 Creation; 05.11.07.04.03 Newness, novelty
edsihþ 07.04.03 Reverence, respect
edspellung 09.06.02.01.03 Recapitulation

(ge)edstaþelian 05.05.01 An author, source, originator; 05.11.07.04.03.01 Renewal, restoration
geedstaþelian 02.08.12 Healing, curing; 16.02.01.12 Spirituality
(ge)edstaþeligend 16.01.01.02.01 Creator
(ge)edstaþelung 10.03.04.01 Restitution, making good, repayment; 16.02.01.12 Spirituality
edstaþol 02.08.13 Recovery, growing better
edtelgung 03.01.14.01 Dyeing
edþingung 13.01.02 Reconciliation
geedþrāwen 05.10.06.02.03 A circular fold, coil
edwend 05.13 Changeableness, change
edwendan 05.12.05.11.01 To return
edwenden 05.11.10.02 End, completion; 05.13.02 A reversal
edwielle 01.01.03.05 Whirlpool
edwihte 05 Aught, anything, something
edwinde 01.01.03.05 Whirlpool
edwist 02.01 Existence, life
geedwistan 10.01.03 A sharing, participation
geedwistian 04.01.02.04.03.01 To feed/nourish
edwistlic 09.03.02.02.01.02 A verb
edwīt 07.05.01 Censure, reproof, rebuke; 07.05.03.03 Scorn, insult, abuse; 07.09 Shame, disgrace
edwītful 07.09 Shame, disgrace
edwītfullic 07.09 Shame, disgrace
edwīt(i)an 07.05.03.03.02 To reproach, revile, abuse
edwītlīf 07.09.03 Infamy, ignominy, shame
edwītscipe 07.09 Shame, disgrace
edwītspræc 07.05.03.03 Scorn, insult, abuse
edwītspreca 07.05.03.03 Scorn, insult, abuse
edwītstæf 07.09 Shame, disgrace
edwylm 01.02.01.01.06 Heavenly light
geedwyrpan 02.08.13 Recovery, growing better
edwyrping 02.08.13 Recovery, growing better
geedyppol 09.05.01 Inspection, examination
efen 01.01.02.01.04 Open (level) land; 08.01.02.01.02.02 Gentleness, meekness, composure; 12.01.01.06 Condition, rank, standing; 12.07.04 Truth, righteousness, justice, equity; 18.02.07 Music
efen wel 03.03.04.03 Growth, increase
efenæþele 12.01.01.06.05 Nobility, noble condition
efenāmeten 03.06.01 Similitude, likeness
efenapostol 16.02.01.08.03.01 New Testament persons
efenbehēfe 06.02.04 Necessity, inevitability; 11.07.01 Utility, usefulness
efenbeorht 03.01.12 Brightness, light
efenbisceop 16.02.03.02.05 A bishop
efenblissian 08.01.01.03.06 Exultation, joy
efenblīþe 08.01.01.03.06 Exultation, joy
efenboren 12.01.01.06.01 Rank, position due to birth
efenbrād 05.10.05.02 Extension, stretching
efenbyrde 12.01.01.06.01 Rank, position due to birth
efenceasterwaran 12.06.03.03 A neighbour
efencempa 13.02.10 The military, soldiers

efencristen 16.02.02 Christianity, the Christian faith
efencuman 05.12.05.02.02 To come together, meet; 09.07.04.01 Confirmation, agreement
efendȳre 08.01.02.02.01 A favourite, loved one; 15.02.01 High/steep price
efeneadig 08.01.01.03.03 Happiness, blessedness; 16.01.01.04 The Trinity
efeneald 05.11.07.01 Contemporary, coeval
efenealda 05.11.07.01 Contemporary, coeval
efeneardigende 05.11.07.01 Contemporary, coeval; 16.01.01.04 The Trinity
efenēce 16.01.01.04 The Trinity
efenedwistlic 16.01.01.04 The Trinity
efenēhþ 05.10.05.04.11.01 A bound, limit
efenemn 05.10.05.04.03 A line, continuous length
efenesne 12.01.01.08.01 A servant, attendant
efenetan 04.01.01 Eating
efenēþe 11.12 Easiness
efenfela 03.03.04.01.02 A great number, multitude
efenforþ 05.11.08.01.02 (Untimely) earliness
efenfrēfrian 08.01.03.07.04.02.01 Comfort, consolation
efengedǣlan 10.01.03 A sharing, participation
efengefēon 08.01.01.03.06 Exultation, joy
efen(ge)lic 12.01.01.06 Condition, rank, standing
efen(ge)līca 12.01.01.06 Condition, rank, standing
efengemǣcca 12.01.01.06 Condition, rank, standing

efengemetgian 17.02.04.03.03 Smelting, heating, scorification
efengemynd 06.01.04 Faculty of memory
efengemyndig 06.01.04.02 Living, remembered
efengespittan 02.04.06.06.04 Spittle
efengeþeahtian 09.07.04.01 Confirmation, agreement
efengōd 07.02 Goodness
efenhāda 12.01.01.06 Condition, rank, standing
efenhālig 16.02.01.10 Holiness
efenhēafda 12.04.01 A fellow, companion, associate, comrade
efenhēafodling 12.04.01 A fellow, companion, associate, comrade
efenhēah 12.01.01.06.02.01 (High) rank, status, degree
efenhēap 12.04.01.01 A company of people, fellowship, society
efenheort 13 Peace, tranquillity
efenherenes 16.02.04.01 Shared worship
efenherian 16.02.04.01 Shared worship
efenhlēoþor 18.02.07 Music
efenhlēoþrian 18.02.07 Music
efenhlēoþrung 18.02.07 Music
efenhlȳta 10.01.03 A sharing, participation
efenhlȳte 10.01.03 A sharing, participation
efenhlytta 10.01.03 A sharing, participation
(ge)efenlǣcan 03.06.01.01 Imitation
geefenlǣcan 03.06 Comparison; 03.06.01 Similitude, likeness; 11.05.02.01 A standard, norm, ethos
efenlǣce 03.06.01.01 Imitation
efenlǣcend 03.06.01.01 Imitation
efenlǣcere 03.06.01.01 Imitation
geefenlǣcestre 03.06.01.01 Imitation

(ge)efenlǣcung 03.06.01.01 Imitation
efenlang 05.10.05.02 Extension, stretching
efe(n)lāste 02.07.11 Plants/flowers (alphabetical order)
efenlēof 02.05.05.01 Object of desire; 08.01.02.02.01 A favourite, loved one
efenleornere 06.01.06.02.03.02 Discipleship
efenlic 05.10.05.02 Extension, stretching
(ge)efenlic 12.01.01.06 Condition, rank, standing
efenlīce 03.06.01.02 Equality; 05.10.05.04.03 A line, continuous length; 08.01.02.01.02.02 Gentleness, meekness, composure; 09.07.04.01.03 Unanimity
(ge)efenlīcian 08.01.01.03.09.03 To make glad; 11.05.02.01 A standard, norm, ethos
geefenlīcian 03.06.01.02 Equality
efenlīcnes 03.06.01.02 Equality
efenling 12.04.01 A fellow, companion, associate, comrade
efenmǣre 07.08.09 Renown, fame, glory
efenmǣsseprēost 16.02.03.02.07.01 A priest of a church or minster
efenmedome 07.08.02 Honour, glory
efenmetan 03.06 Comparison
efenmicel 03.03.04.01 Much; 03.06.01.02 Equality
efenmid 05.10.05.04.01.01 The middle
efenmihtig 16.01.01.04 The Trinity
efenmōdlīce 08.01.02.01.02.02 Gentleness, meekness, composure
efennēah 05.10.05.01 A little way, no great distance
efenneahtlic 05.11.06.01 Cycle of the year

efennes 03.06 Comparison; 03.06.01.02 Equality; 12.08.02.02 Righteousness, rectitude
efenniht 05.11.06.01 Cycle of the year
efenrēþe 08.01.03.09.11 Hardheartedness, cruelty, severity
efenrīce 12 Power, might
efensācerd 16.02.03.02.07.01 A priest of a church or minster
efensāre 08.01.03.04.01 Complaint, lamentation
efensārgian 08.01.02.05 Compassion
efensārgung 08.01.02.05 Compassion
efensārig 08.01.02.05 Compassion; 08.01.03.04 Grief
efenscearp 05.10.06.03.01 A point, spike, prickle
efenscōlere 06.01.06.02.03.01 A pupil, disciple, scholar
efenscyldig 12.08.09 Guiltiness, guilt
efensecgan 09.07.04.01 Confirmation, agreement
efensorgian 08.01.02.05 Compassion
efenspēdiglic 16.01.01.04 The Trinity
efensprǣc 12.02.02.04 Counsel, deliberation
efenstālian 11.01.03 Preparation
efentēam 12.01.01.12.04.02 Conspiracy
efenþegn 12.01.01.08.01 A servant, attendant
efenþēow(a) 12.01.01.08.01 A servant, attendant; 12.01.01.06 Condition, rank, standing
efenþēowen 12.01.01.08.01 A servant, attendant
efenþrōwian 08.01.02.05 Compassion
efenþrōwung 08.01.02.05 Compassion
efenþwǣre 03.06.03.01 Compatible
efenunwemme 16.02.04.18.04 Church peace, right of sanctuary

efenwæge 03.03.02 Measurement by weighing
efenweaxan 02.07.01 To grow
efenweorþ 07.08.02 Honour, glory; 12.01.01.06 Condition, rank, standing
efenwerod 12.04.01.01 A company of people, fellowship, society
efenwesende 05.11.07.01 Contemporary, coeval; 16.01.01.04 The Trinity
efenwiht 12.04.01 A fellow, companion, associate, comrade
efenwrītan 09.03.07.07.03 Composition, arrangement, writing
efenwyrcend 12.04.01 A fellow, companion, associate, comrade
efenwyrhta 12.04.01 A fellow, companion, associate, comrade
efenyrfeweard 15.01.02.01 Inherited property
ēfern 05.11.04.02 Night, night time
ēfernlic 05.11.04.02 Night, night time
ēferntīd 05.11.04.02 Night, night time
efes 04.05.02.08 Top of a building; 05.10.05.04.11.01 A bound, limit
(ge)efesian 02.04.04.03.05 Haircutting, tonsure; 04.06.01.07 Hair-care; 16.02.04.13.03 Tonsure, haircutting, shaving
efestan 05.11.01.02.01 Swift movement of time; 05.12.03.01.02 Haste, hurry
(ge)efestan 11.03 Endeavour
geefestan 10.01.02 Acquisition
efestlīce 05.12.03.01.02 Haste, hurry
efestung 05.12.03.01.02 Haste, hurry
efesung 02.04.04.03.05 Haircutting, tonsure; 16.02.04.13.03 Tonsure, haircutting, shaving
efete 02.06.07.03 Lizard, newt
eficisc 02.03.03.06.07.07 Other (alphabetical order)

efnan 05.10.05.04.03 A line, continuous length
(ge)efnan 03.06.01.02 Equality
geefnan 03.06 Comparison
efne 03 Material, matter, substance; 03.03.04.03 Growth, increase; 03.03.06.02 Fullness; 03.04.01 Singularity, peculiarity; 03.06.01.02 Equality; 05.11.09.06 Frequency, repetition; 08.01.02.01.02.02 Gentleness, meekness, composure; 12.07.04 Truth, righteousness, justice, equity
efne/efen 06.01.07.01 Correct, right, free from error
efne nū 05.11.07.01 Contemporary, coeval
efne (nū) 05.11.07.01 Contemporary, coeval; 09.01.03.01 Interjections: Oh!; 02.05.09.04 To see, look upon, behold
efne swā 03.06.01 Similitude, likeness
efne swelce 03.06.01 Similitude, likeness
efne swīþe 03.06.01.02 Equality
efnes 03.03.06.02 Fullness
efnettan 03.06.01.01 Imitation
(ge)efnettan 03.06.01.02 Equality; 05.10.05.04.03 A line, continuous length
geefnettan 03.06 Comparison
efneunrōtnes 08.01.03 Bad feeling, sadness
efneunrōtsad 08.01.03 Bad feeling, sadness
efning 12.04.01 A fellow, companion, associate, comrade
eft 03.03.04.03 Growth, increase; 05.11.07.04 Future, time to come; 05.11.07.04.02 (Of time) later/latter; 05.11.07.04.03.01 Renewal, restoration; 05.11.09.06 Frequency,

repetition; 05.12.05.11 To turn back, retreat; 10.03.04.01 Restitution, making good, repayment
eft āgiefan 10.03.04.01 Restitution, making good, repayment
eft ārīsan 05.12.05.12 To go up, ascend
eft cuman 05.12.05.11.01 To return
eft cyrran 05.12.05.11.01 To return
eft gān 05.12.02.08 To give a different direction to, turn
eft hweorfan 05.12.05.11.01 To return
eft hwirfende 05.12.05.11.01 To return
eft ongēan 05.12.05.11 To turn back, retreat
eft scēogian 04.04.07.15 Footwear, covering for the feet
eft sīþian 05.12.05.11.01 To return
eft sōna 03.03.04.03 Growth, increase
eftācenned 02.01.03.03.05 Rebirth/regeneration
eftācenn(ed)nes 02.01.03.03.05 Rebirth/regeneration
eftǣrist 16.01.01.02.09 Resurrection
eftārīsan 16.01.01.02.09 Resurrection
eftbētung 02.08.13 Recovery, growing better
eftboren 02.01.03.03.05 Rebirth/regeneration
eftbōt 02.08.13 Recovery, growing better
eftcnēoreso 02.01.03.03.05 Rebirth/regeneration
eftcyme 05.12.05.11.01 To return
eftcynn 16.01.01.02.09 Resurrection
eftcyrr 05.12.05.11.01 To return
eftedwītan 07.05.01 Censure, reproof, rebuke
eftflōwan 01.01.03.04 Current, rush of water
eftflōwung 01.01.03.04 Current, rush of water

eftforfunden 07.05.01 Censure, reproof, rebuke
eftforgifnes 16.02.04.07.02.02 Absolution, forgiveness, remission
geeftgadrian 05.11.09.06 Frequency, repetition
eftgeafung 15.02.04 Spending, disbursement
eftgecīgan 12.03.03.01 Summons, a call, summoning
eftgemyndgian 06.01.04 Faculty of memory
eft(ge)myndig 06.01.04 Faculty of memory
eftgewæxen 02.07.01 To grow
eftgian 09.06.02.01.03 Recapitulation
efthwyrfan 05.11.09.06 Frequency, repetition
eftlēan 10.03.05 Recompense, reward
eftlēaniend 10.03.05 Recompense, reward
eftlīesend 16.01.01.04.02 The Son, Christ
eftlīsing 16.01.01.02.08 Salvation, redemption
eftlōcung 07.04.03 Reverence, respect
eftnīwung 16.02.01.12 Spirituality
eftondfōend 10.01.01 Acceptance, receiving
eftryne 05.12.05.11.01 To return
eftscippan 11.12.02.02 Amendment, setting right, reparation
eftsittan 04.05.03.01 Habitation, sojourn
eftsīþ 05.12.05.11.01 To return
eftsōna 05.11.09.06 Frequency, repetition
eftspellung 09.06.02.01.03 Recapitulation
eft(tō)selenes 14.05.03 Retribution, requital
eftþingung 13.01.02 Reconciliation
eftwyrd 16.02.01.08.03 The New Testament

eg lā eg 08.01.03.04.01 Complaint, lamentation
ege 06.01.08.06 Fear
egeful 06.01.08.06 Fear; 06.01.08.06.03 Cause of fear, terror, horror
egefullīce 06.01.08.06.03.01 Causing dread, terrifying
egelēaslīce 06.02.07.06.02.01 Fearlessness
egelēasnes 06.02.07.06.02.01 Fearlessness
egelic/ahwlic 06.01.08.06.03.01 Causing dread, terrifying
egenu 04.02.04.03.02.01 Grain crops
egesa 06.01.08.06 Fear; 06.01.08.06.03 Cause of fear, terror, horror
egesful 06.01.08.05.01.01 Wondrous, glorious, marvellous; 06.01.08.06.03 Cause of fear, terror, horror
egesfullic 06.01.08.06.02 Great fear, terror, horror; 06.01.08.06.03.01 Causing dread, terrifying
egesfullīce 06.01.08.06.03.01 Causing dread, terrifying
egesfulnes 06.01.08.06.03 Cause of fear, terror, horror
egesgrīma 02.05.04.02 A dream; 16.01.03 A spectre, ghost, demon, goblin
(ge)egesian 06.01.08.06.03 Cause of fear, terror, horror; 08.01.03.09.07 Threat, threatening, menace
egesig 06.01.08.06.03.01 Causing dread, terrifying
egeslic 06.01.08.06.03 Cause of fear, terror, horror; 08.01.03.09.07 Threat, threatening, menace
egeslīce 06.01.08.06.03.01 Causing dread, terrifying
egesung 06.01.08.06.03 Cause of fear, terror, horror; 08.01.03.09.07 Threat, threatening, menace
egeswīn 02.06.06.02.01.02 Eel
egeþgetigu 04.02.04.06.06 Harrowing equipment
egewylm 01.01.03.01.02.05 Wave; 06.01.08.06.03 Cause of fear, terror, horror
geeggian 06.02.06.03.03 Incitement
egipte 02.03.03.06.07.01 African
egiptisc 02.03.03.06.07.01 African
egl 03.03.04.04 Littleness, smallness; 04.02.04.03.02.01.01 Barley
egle 08.01.03.07.04 Severity, harshness; 08.01.03.09.04 Hatred
(ge)eglian 08.01.03.07.02 Misery, trouble, affliction
egnes 06.01.08.06 Fear
egnwirht 15.02.04 Spending, disbursement
ēgor 01.01.03.04 Current, rush of water
ēgorhere 01.01.03.06 Flood
ēgorstrēam 01.01.03.01.02 Sea/ocean; 01.01.03.04 Current, rush of water
geegþan 04.02.04.02.02.01 Harrowing
egþe 04.02.04.06.06 Harrowing equipment; 17.03.07 Tools for digging/grasping/pulling
egþere 04.02.04.02.02.01 Harrowing
egþwirf 02.06.02.01.01 Ass
ēht 05.12.05.10 To go behind, follow
ēhtan 04.03 Hunting, the chase; 07.05.03.03.02 To reproach, revile, abuse; 13.02.03.01 An attack, assault
(ge)ēhtan 05.12.05.10 To go behind, follow; 08.01.03.07.02.01 Injury, offence; 12.05.06.02.02 Persecution
geēhtan 10.01.02 Acquisition; 13.02.05.01.01 To overcome, conquer

ēhtend 05.12.05.10 To go behind, follow; 12.05.04.01.01 Fighting, a fight; 12.05.06.02.02 Persecution
ēhtend gestandan 12.05.06.02.02 Persecution
ēhtere 12.05.06.02.02 Persecution
ēhting 12.05.06.02.02 Persecution
ēhtnes 12.05.06.02.02 Persecution
eit 01.01.02.01.01.02 Island
ēl 01.01.02.01.01.02 Island
elcian 05.11.08.01.03.01 Delay
elciend 05.11.08.01.03.01 Delay
elcor 03.03.04.03 Growth, increase; 03.06.02.01 Contrariety, diversity; 05.03.01.03 Reason, cause; 05.10.04.04 Absence; 05.13.04 Exchange, commutation
elc(o)ra 03.06.02.01 Contrariety, diversity
elcran 03.06.02.01 Contrariety, diversity
elcung 05.11.08.01.03.01 Delay
ele 03.01.17.04 Oil; 04.01.02.01.05.03 Oil
elebacen 04.01.02.02.05 Cooking
elebēam 02.07.09.02 Particular fruits (alphabetical order)
elebēamen 02.07.09.02 Particular fruits (alphabetical order)
elebēamstybb 02.07.09.02 Particular fruits (alphabetical order)
elebearu 02.07.09.02 Particular fruits (alphabetical order)
eleberende 03.01.17.04 Oil
eleberge 02.07.09.02 Particular fruits (alphabetical order)
elebytt 16.02.05.05.06 A vessel for use in services
eledrōsna 04.06.02.04 Refuse, litter, rubbish
elefæt 04.01.02.02.06.03 Food receptacle, basket; 16.02.05.05.06 A vessel for use in services

elegrēofa 17.05.01 Fuel, tinder
elehorn 04.01.02.02.06.03 Food receptacle, basket
elehtre 02.07.11 Plants/flowers (alphabetical order)
el(e)land 12.06.05 A foreign country
elelēaf 02.07.09.02 Particular fruits (alphabetical order)
elelēast 04.01.01.03 Hunger
elelendisc 12.06.05 A foreign country
elesealf 03.01.17.07 Salves, ointments, etc.
eleseocche 04.06.01.10 To separate objects already connected, unmix
eletredde 04.01.02.02.07 Press
eletrēow 02.07.09.02 Particular fruits (alphabetical order)
eletrēowen 02.07.09.02 Particular fruits (alphabetical order)
eletwig 02.07.09.02 Particular fruits (alphabetical order)
elewana 04.01.01.03 Hunger
elfremed 12.04.03 A stranger
elhygd 08.01.01.01.02 Alienation of mind, ecstasy, rapture
ell 03.06.02 Difference, diversity, dissimilarity; 09.03.07.01 A written character, letter
elleahtor 09.03.07.02 To make a mistake in writing
ellen 02.07.03.05 Particular trees/shrubs (alphabetical order); 05.08 Strength; 06.02.07.06 Courage, boldness, valour; 08.01.01.01.04 Depth of feeling, zeal; 12.05.01 Rivalry, contest
ellenasce 03.01.09.02.01.02 Embers, cinders, ashes
ellencampian 12.05.01 Rivalry, contest; 12.05.04.01 Fighting, contention, warfare, strife

ellencræft 12 Power, might
ellencropp 02.07.03.05 Particular trees/shrubs (alphabetical order)
ellendǣd 06.02.07.06 Courage, boldness, valour
ellende 12.06.05 A foreign country
ellengǣst 16.01.03.02 A demonic apparition
ellengrāfa 02.07.03.05 Particular trees/shrubs (alphabetical order)
ellenheard 06.02.07.06 Courage, boldness, valour
ellenhete 08.01.03.09.08 Envy, jealousy
ellenlǣca 12.05.01 Rivalry, contest
ellenlēaf 02.07.03.05 Particular trees/shrubs (alphabetical order)
ellenlēas 06.02.07.07 Cowardice, pusillanimity
ellenlic 06.02.07.06 Courage, boldness, valour
ellenlīce 06.02.07.06 Courage, boldness, valour
ellenmǣrþu 07.08.10 Fame of courage, valour
ellenrind 02.07.03.05 Particular trees/shrubs (alphabetical order)
ellenrōf 06.02.07.06 Courage, boldness, valour
ellensēoc 02.02.03.01 In process of dying
ellensprǣc 09.03.04.02.02 Eloquence, elegance in language
ellenstybb 02.07.03.05 Particular trees/shrubs (alphabetical order)
ellentān 02.07.03.05 Particular trees/shrubs (alphabetical order)
ellentrēow 02.07.03.05 Particular trees/shrubs (alphabetical order)
ellenþrīst 06.02.07.06.02 Boldness

ellenweorc 06.02.07.06 Courage, boldness, valour; 12.08.02.02 Righteousness, rectitude
ellenwōd 08.01.01.01.04 Depth of feeling, zeal; 08.01.03.05.02 Anger
ellenwōdian 12.05.01 Rivalry, contest
ellenwōdnes 08.01.01.01 Ardour, fervour, strong feeling
ellenwyrt 02.07.11 Plants/flowers (alphabetical order)
ellenwyrttruma 02.07.03.05 Particular trees/shrubs (alphabetical order)
elles 03.03.04.03 Growth, increase; 03.06.02 Difference, diversity, dissimilarity; 03.06.02.01 Contrariety, diversity; 05.10.04.04 Absence; 05.13.04 Exchange, commutation
elles hū 03.06.02.01 Contrariety, diversity
elles gehwǣr 05.10.04.04 Absence
elles hwanon 05.10.04.04 Absence
elles hwergen 05.10.04.04 Absence
elles hwider 05.10.04.04 Absence
ellor 05.10.04.04 Absence
ellorfūs 05.12.05.03 To travel away (from)
ellorgǣst 16.01.03.02 A demonic apparition
ellorsīþ 02.02 Death
ellret 02.07.03.05 Particular trees/shrubs (alphabetical order)
elm 02.07.03.05 Particular trees/shrubs (alphabetical order)
elmen 02.07.03.05 Particular trees/shrubs (alphabetical order)
elmrind 02.07.03.05 Particular trees/shrubs (alphabetical order)
eln 05.10.05.03 A measure of distance
elnboga 02.04.03.04.01 Arm
elngemet 05.10.05.03 A measure of distance
elnian 05.08 Strength; 06.02.07.01 Strength, fortitude

(ge)elnian 08.01.03.09.08 Envy, jealousy
elnung 06.01.08.02.01 Encouragement, comfort; 06.02.05.04.04 Zeal; 08.01.03.09.08 Envy, jealousy
elpend 02.06.04.01.03 Elephant
elpendbǣnen 02.06.04.01.03 Elephant; 17.04.03.03 Horn
elpendbān 02.06.04.01.03 Elephant; 17.04.03.03 Horn
elpendtōþ 02.06.04.01.03 Elephant
elren 02.07.03.05 Particular trees/shrubs (alphabetical order)
elreord 12.06.05 A foreign country
elreordig 12.06.05 A foreign country
elþēod 12.06.05 A foreign country
elþēode 02.03.03.03 A nation, people
elþēod(g)ian 05.12.01.01 To go on a journey/expedition, travel; 16.02.04.11 Pilgrimage
geelþēod(g)ian 02.08.11.02.01 Insanity, madness
elþēod(g)ung 05.12.01.01 To go on a journey/expedition, travel
elþēodig 12.04.03 A stranger; 12.04.03.01 Estrangement, alienation; 12.06.05 A foreign country; 12.06.05.01 State of exile, banishment
elþēodiga 12.06.05 A foreign country
elþēodige 12.06.05 A foreign country
elþēodiglic 12.06.05 A foreign country
elþēod(ig)līce 12.06.05 A foreign country
elþēodignes 05.12.01.01 To go on a journey/expedition, travel; 12.06.05.01 State of exile, banishment; 16.02.04.11 Pilgrimage
elþēodisc 12.06.05 A foreign country
em 09.03.07.01 A written character, letter
geembiht(i)an 12.01.01.08 Service
emblissian 08.01.01.03.06 Exultation, joy
embren 04.01.03.05.04.03 A bucket, pail
emleahtor 09.03.07.02 To make a mistake in writing
emnet 01.01.02.01.04 Open (level) land
emnihtes dæg 05.11.06.01 Cycle of the year
geendadung 05.11.10.02 End, completion
ende 01.01 Surface of the earth; 02.02 Death; 02.04.06.03.02.04 Intestines; 03.04 Form, kind, nature, character; 05.03.02 Event, issue, result; 05.07 Ending of existence, end of world; 05.10.04.02 A region, zone; 05.10.05.04.11.01 A bound, limit; 05.11.10.02 End, completion; 06.02.06.01 An end, goal; 10.01.03 A sharing, participation; 11.01.06 End, completion (of action), fulfilment; 13.02.10.01.02.02.03 Part of an army
ende habban 05.07 Ending of existence, end of world
endebyrd 03.05 Order, arrangement, disposition
endebyrdend 06.02.06.02.01 To devise a plan, arrange, settle
endebyrdes 03.05 Order, arrangement, disposition
(ge)endebyrd(i)an 03.05 Order, arrangement, disposition; 05.04 Fate, lot, fortune, destiny
geendebyrd(i)an 09.06.01 To relate, recount, tell; 12.02 A public office
endebyrdlic 03.03.03.02 A number (mark/symbol)
endebyrdlīce 03.05.02 An arrangement, order, succession
(ge)endebyrdlīce 03.05 Order, arrangement, disposition
endebyrdnes 02.01.04 Age; 03.03.05.01 Rank, position, degree; 03.05 Order, arrangement, disposition; 03.05.01

Arranging, ordering, disposition; 03.05.02 An arrangement, order, succession; 05.11.11.01 A not ceasing, persistence, recurrence; 09.06.01 To relate, recount, tell; 11.05 Natural/proper way/manner/mode of action; 11.05.02 Mode, manner, way, method, fashion, course; 12.01.01.06 Condition, rank, standing; 14.01.06 A rule, order, precept, tenet, principle; 16.02.04.03.01 A rite, ceremony
endedæg 02.02.02 Liability to death, mortality; 05.07 Ending of existence, end of world
endedēaþ 02.02 Death
endedōgor 02.02.02 Liability to death, mortality
endefæstend 11.01.06 End, completion (of action), fulfilment
endefurh 04.02.03.02.01.01 A furrow
endelāf 11.10.05 Escape
endelēan 14.05.03 Retribution, requital
endelēas 05.11.01.01.01 Eternity
endelēaslic 05.11.01.01.01 Eternity
endelēaslīce 05.11.01.01.01 Eternity; 05.11.11.01 A not ceasing, persistence, recurrence
endelēasnes 05.11.01.01.01 Eternity
endelīf 02.02 Death
endemann 02.03.01 People
endemes 03.03.06 Wholeness; 03.03.06.01 A whole formed by joining; 03.06.01 Similitude, likeness; 05.11.07.01 Contemporary, coeval
endemest 05.11.10.02 End, completion
endemestenes 05.10.05 A space, span
endenēhst 03.05.02 An arrangement, order, succession; 05.10.05 A space, span; 05.11.07.04.03 Newness, novelty; 05.11.10.02 End, completion; 12.01.01.06.04 Inferiority of status, lowest place
enderīm 03.03.03 Number
endesǣte 11.10.02.02 Watchful care, keeping guard
endespǣc 09.03.07.07.02.01.04 A passage in a book
endestæf 02.02.03.03 Appointed death, doom; 05.11.10.02 End, completion
endetīma 02.02.02 Liability to death, mortality
endeþræst 05.06 Destruction, dissolution, loss, breaking
(ge)endian 05.07 Ending of existence, end of world; 11.01.06 End, completion (of action), fulfilment
geendian 02.02.03 To die, perish; 02.02.04.03 To kill, slay; 03.03.06.02 Fullness; 05.06.01 Devastation, laying waste; 07.02.03 Perfection; 11.01.04 A doing, accomplishing (of something); 11.01.05 Accomplishment, fulfilment
endleofan 03.03.03.04.11 Eleven
endleoft(eþ)a 03.03.03.04.11 Eleven
endlifangilde 14.03.03.09.02 Atonement
endlyfenfeald 03.03.03.04.11 Eleven
endlyfte 03.03.03.04.11 Eleven
geendodlic 03.03.03 Number
endung 11.01.06 End, completion (of action), fulfilment
(ge)endung 02.02 Death; 05.07 Ending of existence, end of world; 05.11.10.02 End, completion
geendung 05.10.05 A space, span; 09.03.02.03.01.01.01 Case; 09.03.07.07.02.01.04 A passage in a book
endwerc 02.08.07.07 Disorders of the body

ened 02.06.08.02.01.01 Duck
enge 05.10.02 Narrowness, scantiness of space; 08.01.03.07.04 Severity, harshness
geenged 08.01.03.03 Anxiety
engel 16.01.02.05.01 An angel
engelcund 16.01.02.05.01 An angel
engelcynn 16.01.02.05.01 An angel
engellic 16.01.02.05.01 An angel
engla lagu 14.01.01 Law(s) of particular scope
engla land 12.06.01.01 England
engle 02.03.03.05.01 The English; 02.03.03.05.01.01 Angles
englisc 02.03.03.05.01 The English; 09.03.01 Particular languages
englisc cost 02.07.11 Plants/flowers (alphabetical order)
englisc more 02.07.09.02.02.01 Edible root/bulb
engliscman 02.03.03.05.01 The English
engu 05.10.02 Narrowness, scantiness of space
ent 02.03.01.11 Giant
entcynn 02.03.01.11 Giant
entisc 03.03.04.01.01 Greatness, bigness, size
eodor 01.01 Surface of the earth; 05.10.04.02 A region, zone; 05.10.05.04.11 A circle, circuit, circumference; 12.01.01.04 A leader, ruler
eodorbrecþ 14.02.01.01 Types of crime
eodorbrice 14.02.01.01 Types of crime
eodorgong 15.01.06 Poverty, indigence
eodorwīr 04.05.01.02.07 A fence, hedge
eofole 02.07.11.02 Unidentified plants (alphabetical order)
eofor 02.06.03.01.05 Boar; 13.02.08.03.01.02.01 Parts of a helmet

eoforcumbol 13.02.08.02 A standard, banner, ensign
eoforfearn 02.07.04 Fern
eoforhēafodsegn 13.02.08.02 A standard, banner, ensign
eoforlīc 13.02.08.03.01.02.01 Parts of a helmet
eoforspere 04.03 Hunting, the chase; 13.02.08.04.01 A spear
eoforsprēot 04.03 Hunting, the chase; 13.02.08.04.01 A spear
eoforswīn 02.06.03.01.05 Boar
eoforþring 01.02.01.01.02.01 Constellation
eoforþrote 02.07.11 Plants/flowers (alphabetical order)
(ge)eofot 12.08.06.02.05.01 Transgression, trespass
eoh 02.06.02.01.06 Horse; 09.03.07.01.01 A runic letter; 13.02.08.04.06 A chariot
ēoh 02.07.03.05 Particular trees/shrubs (alphabetical order)
eolet 05.12.01.09.03 A voyage
eolh 02.06.03.01.06 Deer, hart
eolhsand 17.04.03.01 Amber
eolhsecg 02.07.08 Grasses, reeds, etc.; 09.03.07.01.01 A runic letter
eolone 02.07.11 Plants/flowers (alphabetical order)
eorclanstān 17.04.03.04 Gems collectively
eorcnanstān 07.04.01 (Of persons) worth/value, worthiness; 08.01.02.02.01 A favourite, loved one; 17.04.03.04 Gems collectively
ēored 05.12.01.06 Vehicle; 13.02.08.04.06 A chariot; 13.02.10.01.02.01 An armed force/band

ēoredcist 13.02.10.01.02.01 An armed force/band
ēoredgeatwe 13.02.08 Military equipment
ēoredgerīd 13.02.10.01.02.02.02 Branch of army
ēoredhēap 13.02.10.01.02.01 An armed force/band
ēoredmæcg 13.02.10.01.02.02.02 Branch of army
ēoredman 05.12.01.06 Vehicle
ēoredmann 13.02.10.01.02.02.02 Branch of army
ēoredmenigu 13.02.10.01.02.02.03 Part of an army
ēoredþrēat 13.02.10.01.02.01 An armed force/band
ēoredwered 13.02.10.01.02.01 An armed force/band
eorl 06.02.07.06 Courage, boldness, valour; 12.01.01.06.08 A person of rank, elder, great man
eorlcund 12.01.01.06.05 Nobility, noble condition
eorldōm 12.01.01 Authority
eorldōmlic 12.01.01 Authority
eorle 02.03.03.06.02.01 Other peoples
eorlgebyrd 12.01.01.06.06 Gentle birth, nobility
eorlgestrēon 15.01.03 Treasure, riches, wealth
eorlgewæde 13.02.08.03.01 Body armour, war gear
eorlgifu 10.03 Giving
eorlic 12.01.01.06.05 Nobility, noble condition
eorlisc 12.01.01.06.05 Nobility, noble condition
eorlmægen 13.02.10.01.02.01 An armed force/band

eorlriht 14.01.04.01 A special right, right peculiar to a class
eorlscipe 06.02.07.06 Courage, boldness, valour
eorlwerod 13.02.10.01.02.01 An armed force/band
eormencynn 02.03 Humankind
eormengrund 01 Earth, world
eormenlāf 15.01.02.01 Inherited property
eormenstrȳnd 02.01.03.03.04 Offspring, race, breed, family, children
eormenþēod 02.03 Humankind
eornost 06.02.05.04.05 Earnestness
eornoste 06.02.05.04.05 Earnestness
eornostlīce 05.03.01.03 Reason, cause; 06.02.05.04.05 Earnestness; 12.08.03.02 Strictness, austerity, severity
eorþæppel 02.07.09.02.02.02 Other vegetables (alphabetical order)
eorþærn 02.02.05.01.01 A grave, burial place, sepulchre
eorþbeofung 01.01.02.03 Earthquake
eorþberge 02.07.09.02 Particular fruits (alphabetical order)
eorþbīgenga 02.03.01 People; 02.03.03.04 An inhabitant
eorþbīgengnes 04.02.04.02 Cultivation/tillage
eorþbrycg 05.12.01.03.04 A bridge
eorþbūend 02.03.01 People
eorþbyrgen 02.02.05.01.01 A grave, burial place, sepulchre
eorþbyrig 13.02.06.01 Stronghold, fort/fortified town
eorþceafer 02.06.09.02.03 Beetle
eorþcenned 02.03.01 People
eorþcræft 03.03.03.01 Arithmetic
eorþcrop 02.07.11.02 Unidentified plants (alphabetical order)

eorþcryppel 02.08.04.03 Paralysis
eorþcund 01 Earth, world
eorþcundlic 01 Earth, world
eorþcyning 12.01.01.04.01.01 Kings and queens
eorþcynn 02.03 Humankind
eorþdene 01.01.02.01.03.03 Valley
eorþdraca 02.06.10.01.01 Dragon
eorþdyne 01.01.02.03 Earthquake
eorþe 01 Earth, world; 01.01.02 Land; 01.01.02.01 Ground; 01.01.02.02 Earth, soil; 03 Material, matter, substance; 12.06 A province, country, territory
eorþe(r)n 01.01.02.01 Ground
eorþfæst 05.12.04.01 Stability, firmness
eorþfæt 02.04 Body
eorþg(e)alla 02.07.11 Plants/flowers (alphabetical order)
eorþgeberst 01.01.02.01.02.02.05 Crag, rock, stone
eorþgemǣre 05.10.05.04.11.01 A bound, limit
eorþgemet 03.03.03.01 Arithmetic
eorþgesceaft 02 Creation
eorþgestrēon 15.01.03 Treasure, riches, wealth
eorþgræf 01.01.02.01.03 Hollow/depression in land
eorþgrāp 02.02.05.01.01 A grave, burial place, sepulchre
eorþhele 05.10.05.04.12 The condition of being covered
eorþhrērnes 01.01.02.03 Earthquake
eorþhūs 01.01.02.01.03.01 Cave
eorþifig 02.07.03.05 Particular trees/shrubs (alphabetical order)
eorþlic 01 Earth, world; 01.01.02.01 Ground
eorþlīce 01 Earth, world

eorþmægen 12.01 Power, control, sway
eorþmata 02.06.09.02.11 Worm
eorþmistel 02.07.10.01 Particular herbs/spices (alphabetical order)
eorþnafela 02.07.09.02.02.02 Other vegetables (alphabetical order)
eorþnutu 02.07.09.02.02.01 Edible root/bulb
eorþreced 04.05.03.02.02.01 Dwellings in particular places
eorþrest 04.05.04.05 A bed, bedstead
eorþrīce 01 Earth, world; 12.06 A province, country, territory
eorþrima 02.07.11.02 Unidentified plants (alphabetical order)
eorþryne 01.01.02.03 Earthquake
eorþscræf 01.01.02.01.03.01 Cave; 02.02.05.01.01 A grave, burial place, sepulchre; 04.05.03.02.02.03 Disagreeable dwellings
eorþsele 04.05.03.02.02.01 Dwellings in particular places
eorþslihtes 05.10.05.04.03 A line, continuous length
eorþstede 01 Earth, world
eorþstyren 01.01.02.03 Earthquake
eorþstyrennes 01.01.02.03 Earthquake
eorþstyrung 01.01.02.03 Earthquake
eorþtilia 04.02.04.02 Cultivation/tillage
eorþtilþ 04.02.04.02 Cultivation/tillage
eorþtilung 04.02.04 Agriculture
eorþtūdor 02.03 Humankind
eorþtyrwe 03.01.17.06.01 Bitumen, pitch
eorþwæstm 02.07.01.01 Fruit of the earth
eorþware 02.03.01 People
eorþweall 01.01.02.01.02.01 Rising ground, eminence; 13.02.06.01 Stronghold, fort/fortified town
eorþweard 11.10.01 Protection, safekeeping

eorþweg 01 Earth, world
eorþwela 02.01.03.01 Fertility, plenty; 15.01.03 Treasure, riches, wealth
eorþweorc 04.02.04.01 To occupy and cultivate land
eorþwerod 02.03 Humankind
eoten 02.03.01.11 Giant
eotenas 02.03.03.06.02 Germany and Low Countries
eotenisc 03.03.04.01.01 Greatness, bigness, size
eotolware 02.03.03.06.04 Italians
eotonweard 11.10.02.02 Watchful care, keeping guard
ēow 08.01.03.04.01 Complaint, lamentation
ēowberge 02.07.03.05 Particular trees/shrubs (alphabetical order)
ēowde 02.06.02.01.08 Sheep; 04.02.05.06.02.01 A sheepfold
ēowe meoluc 04.01.02.01.02.09.03 Ewe's milk
ēowende 02.04.06.04.01 Male genitalia
ēowerlendisc 02.03.03.03.01 A native people; 12.06.04 Native land
ēowestre 04.02.05.06.02.01 A sheepfold
ēowigendlic 09.03.02.02.01.05 Minor parts of speech, etc.
ēowocig 03.01.17.04 Oil
ēowohumele 02.07.09.02 Particular fruits (alphabetical order)
ēowu 02.06.02.01.08 Sheep
epactas 05.11.06.02.02.01 Adjustment in calculation
epistol(a) 09.03.07.07.03.02.02 A letter
eretic 16.02.01.05 Heresy, error, wrong belief
(ge)erian 04.02.04.02.02.02 Ploughing, tilling
erinaces 02.06.03.01.09 Hedgehog

eringland 04.02.03.02 Arable/ploughed land
eriung 04.02.04.02.02.02 Ploughing, tilling
ern 04.02.04.03.02.01 Grain crops
ernþ 04.02.04.03.02.01 Grain crops
ersc 04.02.03.02.02.06 Stubble field
erscgrāfa 02.07.03.04.01 A small wood, coppice, copse
erschen 02.06.08.03 Game-bird
esne 02.03.01.01 Male person, man; 02.03.01.05 Youth, boy, stripling; 06.01.06.02.01 A wise man, man of understanding or learning; 07.08.01 Nobility (of character, rank, etc.); 12.01.01.08.01 A servant, attendant; 12.01.01.11 The common people
esnecund 12.01.01.11 The common people
esnemann 12.01.01.08.01 A servant, attendant
esnewyrhta 12.01.01.08.01 A servant, attendant
esnlīce 06.02.07.01 Strength, fortitude
esol 02.06.02.01.01 Ass
esole 02.06.02.01.01 Ass
ess 09.03.07.01 A written character, letter
essian 05.09.05 Ceasing, decline, fall off
ēst 02.05.05.04.01 Luxuries, dainties, good things; 04.01.02.01.07.05 Delicacy/dainty/titbit; 08.01.02.01 Favour, kindness, grace; 10.03.01 Grace, favour; 10.03.08 Bountifulness, munificence; 12.03.05 Permission
ēstan 04.01.01.07 Feasting; 04.01.02.04.03.01 To feed/nourish
este 02.03.03.06.02.01 Other peoples
ēste 08.01.02.01 Favour, kindness, grace; 10.03.08 Bountifulness, munificence

ēstēadig 08.01.01.03.08 Happiness, well-being, prosperity
ēst(e)līce 02.05.05.04.01 Luxuries, dainties, good things
ēstelīce 06.02.02.01 Will, wish, pleasure; 08.01.02.01 Favour, kindness, grace
ēstful 02.05.05.04.01 Luxuries, dainties, good things; 16.02.01.11 Firmness in the law, piety, devoutness
ēstfullīce 08.01.02.02 Love, affection, care; 16.02.01.11 Firmness in the law, piety, devoutness
ēstfulnes 02.05.05.04.01 Luxuries, dainties, good things; 16.02.01.11 Firmness in the law, piety, devoutness
ēstgeorn 02.05.05.04.01 Luxuries, dainties, good things
ēstig 10.03.08 Bountifulness, munificence; 16.02.01.11 Firmness in the law, piety, devoutness
ēstines 08.01.02.01 Favour, kindness, grace
ēstlic 02.05.05.04.01 Luxuries, dainties, good things; 08.01.02.01 Favour, kindness, grace; 16.02.01.11 Firmness in the law, piety, devoutness
ēstmete 02.05.05.04.01 Luxuries, dainties, good things; 04.01.02.01.07.05 Delicacy/dainty/titbit
ēstnes 08.01.01.03 Good feeling, joy, happiness
ēstum 06.02.02.01 Will, wish, pleasure
esulcweorn 04.01.02.02.09 A mill
etan 04.01.02.04.04.01 Provider/supplier of food; 05.06.01 Devastation, laying waste
(ge)etan 04.01.01 Eating
eteland 04.02.03.04.02 Pasture/pasturage
etende 05.06 Destruction, dissolution, loss, breaking
etenlǣs 04.02.03.04.02 Pasture/pasturage
etisc(e) 04.02.03.01 Plot of land; 01.01.02.01.01 Tract of land
etol 04.01.01.04 Gluttony, overeating, greediness; 05.06 Destruction, dissolution, loss, breaking
etolnes 04.01.01.04 Gluttony, overeating, greediness
ettan 04.02.03.04.02 Pasture/pasturage; 04.02.05.01.01.01 To put out to pasture
ēþel 01 Earth, world; 09.03.07.01.01 A runic letter; 12.06.04 Native land; 16.01.02.01 Heavenly dwelling place
ēþelboda 16.02.03.02.10 A preacher, teacher
ēþelcyning 12.01.01.04.01 A royal leader
ēþeldrēam 08.01.01.03 Good feeling, joy, happiness
ēþeleard 12.06.04 Native land
ēþelfæsten 13.02.06.01 Stronghold, fort/fortified town
ēþelland 12.06.04 Native land
ēþellēas 12.04.04 Solitude
ēþelmearc 05.10.05.04.11.01 A bound, limit
ēþelrīce 12.06.04 Native land
ēþelriht 14.01.04.01 A special right, right peculiar to a class
ēþelseld 12.06.03 A site, settlement
ēþelstæf 15.01.02.01 Inherited property
ēþelstaþol 12.06.03 A site, settlement
ēþelstōl 04.05.03.02.02.05 A paternal dwelling; 12.06.02.01 A township
ēþelstōw 04.05.03 A dwelling-place, abode, habitation
ēþelturf 12.06.04 Native land
ēþelþrymm 07.08.02 Honour, glory
ēþelweard 12.01.01.04.01 A royal leader

ēþelwynn 12.06.04 Native land;
 15.01.01.01 Holding of land
geēþgian 06.02.05.01 Strong liking for,
 devotion to
ēþ(g)ung 02.04.06.07.04 Breathing;
 02.05.08 Faculty of smell
ēþian 02.05.08 Faculty of smell
ēþian on 02.04.06.07.05 To breathe
(ge)ēþian 02.04.06.07.05 To breathe
euangelista 16.02.01.08.03.01 New
 Testament persons
ēuwā 08.01.03.04.01 Complaint,
 lamentation
ex(e) 02.04.06.09 Brain
exodus 16.02.01.08.01.01 Books of the
 Old Testament
exorcista 16.02.03.02.12 Cleric in minor
 orders
fācen 06.01.07.04.04 Deceitfulness,
 falseness, duplicity; 06.01.07.04.04.03
 Deceit, fraud, treachery;
 12.08.06.02.06 Deceit, evil,
 wickedness; 14.02.01 An offence;
 16.02.01.13 Evil-doing, transgression,
 sin
fācendǣd 16.02.01.13 Evil-doing,
 transgression, sin
fācenful 06.01.07.04 Deception
fācenfullic 06.01.07.04 Deception
fācenfullīce 06.01.07.04 Deception
fācengecwis 12.01.01.12.04.02
 Conspiracy
facenlēas 17.02.05.01 Ornamental object
facenlēas 12.08.05 Innocence
fācenlic 06.01.07.04 Deception
fācenlīce 06.01.07.04.04 Deceitfulness,
 falseness, duplicity
fācennes 06.01.07.04 Deception
fācensearu 12.01.01.12.04 Treachery
fācenstafas 12.01.01.12.04 Treachery

fācentācen 06.01.07.04.04.02 Pretence,
 feigning, dissimulation
facg 02.06.06.03.01.05 Plaice, loach
fācian 05.12.05.02.03 To arrive;
 06.02.05.01 Strong liking for,
 devotion to
fācnesful 06.01.07.04 Deception
(ge)fadian 03.05 Order, arrangement,
 disposition; 03.05.01 Arranging,
 ordering, disposition
gefadian 06.02.06.02.01 To devise a plan,
 arrange, settle; 07.10.03 An
 adornment, decoration, ornament
fadiend 12.01.01.08.01 A servant,
 attendant
gefadod 03.05 Order, arrangement,
 disposition
(ge)fadung 03.05.01 Arranging, ordering,
 disposition; 14.01.06 A rule, order,
 precept, tenet, principle
gefadung 12.01 Power, control, sway
fæc 03.06.02 Difference, diversity,
 dissimilarity; 05.10 Space, extent;
 05.10.05 A space, span; 05.11 A time,
 period of time; 05.11.06 Course/cycle
 of time
fæcan 06.02.05.01 Strong liking for,
 devotion to
fæcele 17.05.03 Sources of fire/light
fæcful 05.10.01 Amplitude, spaciousness,
 vastness
fæcna 16.01.05.02.02 Other terms for
 devils
fæcne 06.01.07.04 Deception;
 06.01.07.04.04 Deceitfulness,
 falseness, duplicity; 12.08.06.02.03.01
 Wickedly; 12.08.06.02.06 Deceit, evil,
 wickedness
fæcnig 11.04.02.01.01 Cunning, craft,
 craftiness, guile, wile

fæcnung 06.01.08.03.02.01 Suspicion
gefæd 03.06.03.02 Order, decorum, discretion; 12.08.02.01 Goodness, excellence, virtue
fæder 02.03.02.01 Parent; 02.03.02.03.03 Forefather, ancestor; 02.03.02.03.06.02.05 Step relationships; 02.03.02.05 Spiritual relationships; 02.03.03 A family, household; 11.10.02.02.01 Care, interest in; 16.01.01.04.01 God the Father; 16.02.01.08.05 One of the church fathers; 16.02.04.07.01 Baptism, baptizing (and anointing)
fæder ēþel 12.06.04 Native land
fæder land 15.01.02.01 Inherited property
fæder rīce 16.01.02.01 Heavenly dwelling place
fædera 02.03.02.03.06.02.01 Uncle (especially maternal)
gefædera 02.03.02.05 Spiritual relationships; 16.02.04.07.01 Baptism, baptizing (and anointing)
fæderæþelo 15.01.02.01 Inherited property
gefædere 02.03.02.05 Spiritual relationships
fæderen 02.03.02.03.01 Ancestry, paternal kinship
gefæderen 02.03.02.02.05 Having the same parents
fæderenbrōþor 02.03.02.02.05.01 Brother
fæd(e)rencnōsl 02.03.02.03.06.01 Kinsman, relative
fæderencynn 02.03.02.03.06.01 Kinsman, relative
fæderenhealf 02.03.02.03.01 Ancestry, paternal kinship

fæderenmæg 02.03.02.03.06.01 Kinsman, relative
fæderenmægþ 02.03.02.03.06.01 Kinsman, relative
fæderfeoh 12.09.01 Pledging, betrothal
fædergeard 04.05.03.02.02.05 A paternal dwelling
fædergestrēon 15.01.02.01 Inherited property
fæderhīwisc 02.03.03 A family, household
fæderlēas 02.03.02.02 Child, offspring
fæderlic 02.03.02.03 Ancestry, descent; 02.03.02.03.01 Ancestry, paternal kinship; 05.11.07.03.03 Old, not new; 08.01.02.03.02 Friendly, amiable; 16.01.01.04.01 God the Father
fæderlīce 08.01.02.03.03 In a friendly manner, kindly
fædernama 09.06.02.01.07 A name, appellation
fæderslaga 02.02.04.04.01 Murder of a relative
fæderswica 06.01.07.04.04.03 Deceit, fraud, treachery; 12.01.01.12.04 Treachery
gefædlic 03.06.03.04 What is fitting/seemly/appropriate/decent
gefædlīce 03.05 Order, arrangement, disposition; 11.04.02.01.01 Cunning, craft, craftiness, guile, wile; 12.08.03 Restraint, temperance
fædrenfeoh 12.09.01 Pledging, betrothal
fægan 17.02.05.06 A painting, picture, representation
fæge 02.02.03.01 In process of dying; 02.02.03.02 State of being dead; 06.01.08.06.06 Timidity; 16.01.05.02.02 Other terms for devils
(ge)fægen 08.01.01.03.06 Exultation, joy

fægennes 08.01.01.03 Good feeling, joy, happiness
fæger 01.03.01.01 Hot, fine weather; 02.05.08.02 Pleasant smell, fragrance, perfume; 07.02.04.03 Nobleness, excellence, nobility, magnificence; 07.10 Beauty, fairness; 08.01.01.03.01 Freedom from trouble, comfort, security; 09.03.04.02.02 Eloquence, elegance in language; 12.08.04 Purity, moral cleanness; 18.02.07 Music
fægere 05.12.04 Absence of movement, stillness; 07.02.03.01 Uninjured, unhurt, unharmed; 07.02.04.03 Nobleness, excellence, nobility, magnificence; 07.10 Beauty, fairness; 09.03.04.02.02 Eloquence, elegance in language; 11.05.02.01 A standard, norm, ethos; 11.05.02.02 Humanity, courtesy, civility; 12.07.04 Truth, righteousness, justice, equity; 18.02.07 Music
fægerlīce 07.02.04.03 Nobleness, excellence, nobility, magnificence
fægernes 07.10.03 An adornment, decoration, ornament; 08.01.01.03.09 Pleasantness, agreeableness; 09.03.04.02.02 Eloquence, elegance in language; 12.08.02 Integrity, absence of moral flaw
(ge)fægernes 07.10 Beauty, fairness
fægerwyrde 11.05.02.02 Humanity, courtesy, civility
fægnian 07.04.04.01 Approbation, applause; 08.01.01.03.07 Joyous sound, mirth; 08.01.02.04 Hospitality
(ge)fægnian 08.01.01.03.06 Exultation, joy
fægnung 07.04.04.01 Approbation, applause
(ge)fægnung 08.01.01.03.06 Exultation, joy
fægrian 07.10 Beauty, fairness
(ge)fægrian 07.10.03 An adornment, decoration, ornament
fǣhþ 08.01.03.09.05 Enmity; 12.05.04.02 Vengeance, revenge
fǣhþbōt 14.03.03.09.02 Atonement
fǣhþe (ge)stǣlan 12.05.03 Disagreement, discord, dissension
fǣle 06.01.07 Truth, conformity with absolute standard; 07.02.03 Perfection; 08.01.02.02.01 A favourite, loved one; 12.01.01.12 Loyalty
(ge)fǣlsian 04.06.01.09 To cleanse, remove impurity from (an object); 12.08.04 Purity, moral cleanness
gefǣlsian 05.12.05.02.04 To go in, enter; 16.02.04.07.02.03 Penance, an act/instance of penance
fǣman 02.08.11.02.01.02 Madness, frenzy, folly; 03.01.16.04 Foam, froth
fǣmende 03.01.16.04 Foam, froth
fǣmne 02.03.01.02 Female person, woman; 02.03.01.07 Girl
fǣmn(en)lic 12.09.03 Unmarried state
fǣmnhād 12.09.03 Unmarried state
fǣmnhādes mann 12.09.03 Unmarried state
fǣmnhādlic 12.09.03 Unmarried state
fær 05.02.01.01 The course of human affairs; 05.11 A time, period of time; 05.12.01 To go, progress, travel (usually on land); 05.12.01.01 To go on a journey/expedition, travel; 05.12.01.03.01 A means of access; 05.12.01.04.01 Manner of going, gait; 05.12.01.09.03 A voyage; 05.12.01.09.03.01 A ship, boat;

fǣr

05.12.05.03.03 To depart, leave, set out; 11.01.02 An undertaking; 12.04.01.01 A company of people, fellowship, society
fǣr 02.08.02.01.02 Onset, attack of illness; 06.01.08.06.03 Cause of fear, terror, horror; 08.01.03.06.01 Affliction, misfortune, calamity
fǣrærning 05.12.01.05.01 Modes of riding
fǣran 06.01.08.06.03.01 Causing dread, terrifying
fǣrbēna 05.12.01.01 To go on a journey/expedition, travel; 12.01.01.11 The common people
fǣrbifongen 08.01.03.06 Adversity, affliction
fǣrblǣd 01.03.01.05 Wind
fǣrbryne 03.01.09 Heat
fǣrclamm 10.04.02 To grasp, take hold of
fǣrcoþu 02.08.09.01 Apoplexy
fǣrcumen 05.11.08.01.01 Suddenness
fǣrcwealm 02.08.10.03.01 Plague, pestilence
fǣrcyle 03.01.11 Coldness, coolness
fǣrdēaþ 02.02.01 Particular mode of death; 02.08.09.01 Apoplexy
fǣrdryre 05.12.05.13.03 To fall
gefǣred 06.01.08.06 Fear
fǣreht 15.02 Worth, value
fǣreld 05.02.01.01 The course of human affairs; 05.12.01 To go, progress, travel (usually on land); 05.12.01.01 To go on a journey/expedition, travel; 05.12.01.03.01 A means of access; 05.12.01.03.01.01 A path, track; 05.12.01.04 To go, proceed on foot; 05.12.01.06 Vehicle; 05.12.05.03.03 To depart, leave, set out; 13.02.01 A military expedition;

13.02.10.01.02.02.01 Types of army; 16.02.01.08.04 Jewish seasons/feasts
fǣreldbōc 05.12.01.01 To go on a journey/expedition, travel
fǣreldfrēols 16.02.01.08.04 Jewish seasons/feasts
fǣrende 06.02.05.02 Greed, importunate desire, rapacity
fǣrfrīge 12.01.01.10 Freedom, being free
fǣrfyll 05.12.05.13 To go down, descend; 05.12.05.13.03 To fall
fǣrgripe 10.04.02 To grasp, take hold of
fǣrgryre 06.01.08.06.03 Cause of fear, terror, horror
fǣrhaga 02.08.02.01.02 Onset, attack of illness
fǣring 08.01.01.01.02 Alienation of mind, ecstasy, rapture; 14.03.03.01 Accusation
fǣringa 05.03.02.01 Chance, hap, event; 05.11.07.01 Contemporary, coeval; 05.11.08.01.01 Suddenness
fǣrlic 04.06.02.06 Poison; 05.03.02.01 Chance, hap, event; 05.11.08.01.01 Suddenness; 05.12.03.01 Swiftness, velocity
fǣrlīce 05.03.02.01 Chance, hap, event; 05.11.07.01 Contemporary, coeval; 05.11.08.01.01 Suddenness; 05.12.03.01 Swiftness, velocity
fǣrnes 05.11.08.01.01 Suddenness
fǣrnīþ 08.01.03.07.02.01 Injury, offence
fǣrrǣs 05.12.03.01.01 Quick movement or movements
fǣrrǣsende 05.12.03.01.01 Quick movement or movements
fǣrsceat/feresceat 15.02 Worth, value
fǣrsceaþa 08.01.03.09.05 Enmity; 13.02.03 To seek with active intent, attack

færscyte 13.02.08.04.02 A shot, missile, dart, spear, javelin, etc.
færsearo 11.04.02.01.01 Cunning, craft, craftiness, guile, wile
færsēaþ 01.01.02.01.03 Hollow/depression in land; 01.01.02.01.03.02 Abyss, chasm
færslide 05.12.05.13.03 To fall
færspell 06.01.08.06.03 Cause of fear, terror, horror
færspryng 02.08.05.02 Particular inflammation/swelling
færsteorfa 04.02.05.02.01 (Of cattle) seized with disease
færstice 02.08.03 Pain, bodily discomfort
færstyltnes 06.01.08.05.01 Amazement, astonishment, wonder, admiration
færswīge 06.01.08.05.01 Amazement, astonishment, wonder, admiration
færswile 02.08.05.02 Particular inflammation/swelling
færuntrymnes 02.08.02.01.02 Onset, attack of illness
færweg 05.12.01.03.01.05 Types of road/path
færwundor 06.01.08.06.03 Cause of fear, terror, horror
fæs 04.04.09 A fringe, border, hem
fæsl 02.01.03.03.04 Offspring, race, breed, family, children
fæst 02.05.04 Sleepiness, drowsiness, sleep; 02.08.08.12 Disease of bowels; 03.03.06.01 A whole formed by joining; 05.05.03 Binding, fastening; 05.10.05.04.15 Closure, being closed; 05.12.01.09.03.01.02 Of/concerning a ship, naval; 05.12.04.01 Stability, firmness; 05.13.06 Constancy, unchangeableness; 05.13.06.01 Firm, stable, steady; 06.01.07.07.03 Certainty; 06.02.07.02 Constancy; 06.02.07.04 Obstinacy; 13.02.06 A fortification
gefæst 06.02.07 Will, determination, resolution
(ge)fæstan 04.01.01.06.01 Abstinence from food, fast; 11.06.04 Abstention, abstaining from; 11.10.02.02.01 Care, interest in; 16.02.04.04.02.02 A fast, act of fasting
(ge)fæstan (fram) 10.02 Want, lack
gefæstan 05.10.04 Place, room; 09.04.03 Exposition, making clear by explanation
fæste 02.05.04 Sleepiness, drowsiness, sleep; 03.03.06.02 Fullness; 05.05.03 Binding, fastening; 05.08.01 Vigour, activity, force; 05.10.05.04.15 Closure, being closed; 05.11.07.01 Contemporary, coeval; 05.12.04.01 Stability, firmness; 06.01.07.07.03 Certainty; 06.02.07 Will, determination, resolution; 09.05.04 A secret; 13.02.06 A fortification
fæsten 01.02 Firmament; 04.01.01.06.01 Abstinence from food, fast; 05.10.05.04.11 A circle, circuit, circumference; 11.10.01.02.01 A naturally secure place, fastness; 12.06.02.01 A township; 13.02.06 A fortification; 13.02.06.01 Stronghold, fort/fortified town; 16.02.04.04.02.02 A fast, act of fasting; 16.02.04.07.06.02 A vigil; 17.03.10.01 A bolt, lock, bar
fæsten drēogan 04.01.01.03 Hunger
fæsten hēowan 16.02.04.04.02.02 A fast, act of fasting
(ge)fæsten 04.01.01.06.01 Abstinence from food, fast

fæstenbryce 16.02.04.04.02.02 A fast, act of fasting
fæstendæg 04.01.01.06.01 Abstinence from food, fast; 16.02.04.04.02.02 A fast, act of fasting
fæstendīc 04.05.03.05.03.01 A ditch, dike; 13.02.06.01 Stronghold, fort/fortified town
fæstengeat 05.10.05.04.14.02 An opening/space in an enclosure
fæstengeweorc 17.02.04.01 Repairing, renewing
fæstenlic 16.02.04.04.02.01.02 Lent
fæstentīd 16.02.04.04.02.02 A fast, act of fasting
fæstenwucu 16.02.04.04.02.01.02 Lent; 16.02.04.04.02.02 A fast, act of fasting
fæstergeat 05.10.05.04.14.02 An opening/space in an enclosure
fæstgangol 06.02.07.02 Constancy
fæsthafol 05.05.03 Binding, fastening; 06.02.07.02 Constancy; 10.03.09.01 Parsimony, niggardliness
fæsthafolnes 10.03.09.01 Parsimony, niggardliness
fæsthaful 06.01.04 Faculty of memory
fæstheald 05.12.04.01 Stability, firmness
fæsthȳdig 06.02.07.02 Constancy
fæsting 04.01.02.04.05.01.01 Quartering of officials; 11.10.02.02.01 Care, interest in
fæstingmann 04.01.02.04.05.01.01 Quartering of officials; 12.01.01.08.01 A servant, attendant
fæstland 05.10.04.02 A region, zone
fæstlic 05.08.01 Vigour, activity, force; 05.12.04.01 Stability, firmness; 05.13.06 Constancy, unchangeableness; 06.02.07 Will, determination, resolution
fæstlīce 03.03.06 Wholeness; 05.08.01 Vigour, activity, force; 05.11.07.01 Contemporary, coeval; 05.11.11 Continuity; 05.13.06.01 Firm, stable, steady; 06.01.04.02 Living, remembered; 06.01.07.01 Correct, right, free from error; 06.02.07.03 Perseverance; 12.08.03.02 Strictness, austerity, severity
(ge)fæstlīce 06.02.07.02 Constancy
gefæstlīce 06.01.07.07.03 Certainty
fæstmōd 06.02.07.02 Constancy
fæstnes 01.02 Firmament; 05.08.01 Vigour, activity, force; 05.12.04.01 Stability, firmness; 10.04.01 To hold, have; 11.10.01.02.01 A naturally secure place, fastness
(ge)fæstnian 03.03.06.01 A whole formed by joining; 06.02.07 Will, determination, resolution; 14.04.03 Confirmation, ratification; 14.05.07 Binding, fastening with bonds
(ge)fæstnian (on/tō) 05.12.04.01 Stability, firmness; 06.02.07 Will, determination, resolution
gefæstnian 05.12.04 Absence of movement, stillness; 05.12.04.01 Stability, firmness; 07 Judgement, forming of opinion; 11.10 Safety, safeness; 11.10.02.02.01 Care, interest in; 13.02.06 A fortification; 14.05.08.01 Prison, confinement, durance
gefæstnian on 12.05.06.02.03 Trouble, disturbance
fæstnod 12.09.01 Pledging, betrothal
fæstnung 05.05.03 Binding, fastening; 05.10.05.04.15 Closure, being closed; 05.12.04.01 Stability, firmness;

06.02.06.03.03.01 Incitement, prompting, exhortation; 11.10.01.02.01 A naturally secure place, fastness; 12.07.02.01 Covenant, assurance of faith, promise; 13.02.06 A fortification; 14.04.01 A deed, contract, agreement; 14.04.03 Confirmation, ratification
fæstrǣd 06.02.07.02 Constancy
fæstrǣdlic 06.02.07.02 Constancy
fæstrǣdlīce 06.02.07.02 Constancy
fæstrǣdnes 05.13.06 Constancy, unchangeableness; 06.02.07.02 Constancy
fæststeall 05.13.06.01 Firm, stable, steady
fæt 03.03.07 A part, division, portion; 04.01.02.02.06.05 Vessel/utensil/cup; 04.05.04.03 A box, case, chest, container; 16.02.01 Faith
(ge)fǣtan 08.01.03.07.02 Misery, trouble, affliction; 12.05.06.02 Oppression; 17.02.04.02.03 Carrying, carriage (of materials)
fǣted 17.02.05.01 Ornamental object
fǣtedhlēor 04.02.05.06.05.03.01 Bridle/halter/curb/muzzle
fǣtedsinc 15.01.03 Treasure, riches, wealth
fætels 16.02.01 Faith; 17.03.12 A receptacle, container
fætelsian 17.03.12 A receptacle, container
fætfyllere 04.01.03.05.03 Tavern; 12.01.01.08.01 A servant, attendant
fǣtnes 03.01.17.03 Fat, grease; 03.03.04.01.01 Greatness, bigness, size; 07.02.04 Excellence
fǣtt 02.04.02.01 Fat/plump; 02.08.01 Sound physical condition; 03.01.17.03 Fat, grease; 03.03.04.01.01 Greatness, bigness, size; 03.03.04.02.01 Abundance; 04.01.02.01.01.01 Good/palatable food; 04.01.02.01.02 Animal(s) for food; 04.01.03.05 A drink/beverage; 04.02.05.01.01 To feed/fatten animals; 17.02.04.03 Metal worker; 17.02.05.01 Ornamental object
(ge)fǣttian 16.02.04.07.06 Unction, anointing with holy oil
gefǣttian 02.04.02.01 Fat/plump
fæþel 18.02.06 Theatricals
fæþm 02.04.03.04.01 Arm; 05.10.01 Amplitude, spaciousness, vastness; 05.10.05.03 A measure of distance; 05.10.05.04.01 Inside, interior; 10.04.02 To grasp, take hold of; 11.10.02.02.01 Care, interest in
fæþmende 05.10.05.04.08.01 A bend
fæþmian 05.06.01 Devastation, laying waste; 05.10.05.04.01.02 Contents, what is included; 05.10.05.04.11 A circle, circuit, circumference
fæþmlic 05.10.05.04.08.01 A bend; 05.10.05.04.11 A circle, circuit, circumference
fæþmrīmes 05.10.05.03 A measure of distance
fæderæþelo 02.03.02.03.01 Ancestry, paternal kinship
fāg 03.01.12 Brightness, light; 03.01.13 Darkness, obscurity; 03.01.14.11 Medley/variety of colour
fāgettan 03.01.13.02 A growing dark, darkening; 03.01.14.11 Medley/variety of colour
fāgettan mid wordum 06.01.06.02.02.01.01 Philosophy

fāgetung 03.01.13.02 A growing dark, darkening; 03.01.14.11 Medley/variety of colour

fāgian 03.01.13.02 A growing dark, darkening; 03.01.14.11 Medley/variety of colour; 05.13 Changeableness, change

fāgnes 02.08.05.02 Particular inflammation/swelling; 03.01.12 Brightness, light; 03.01.14.11 Medley/variety of colour; 12.08.08.01.02 Unchastity, incontinence

gefāgod 03.01.14.11 Medley/variety of colour

fāgung 03.01.14.11 Medley/variety of colour; 03.04.02 A diversity

fāgwyrm 02.06.10.01.06 Serpent, scorpion, basilisk

fāh 08.01.03.09.06 Hostility; 12.08.06.02.03 (Of persons) wicked, evil-doing; 12.08.09 Guiltiness, guilt

(ge)fāh 14.03.03.09.03 Outlawry

fāhmann 14.02 Lawlessness

fālǣcan 08.01.03.09.06 Hostility

fald 04.02.05.03.01 A pen, fold, enclosure

gefalden bōc 09.03.07.07 A book

faldere 04.02.05.03.01 A pen, fold, enclosure

faldgang 04.02.03.04.02.01 Types of pasture

faldhrīþer 02.06.02.01.03 Cattle

faldian 04.02.05.06.02.01 A sheepfold

faldwyrþe 14.01.04.02 Rights involving property

fals 03.03.02 Measurement by weighing; 06.01.07.04.02 Fraud, deceit, trick, trickery; 06.01.07.04.03 Untruth, falsehood; 15.01.04 Coinage, money

fām 01.01.03.01.02 Sea/ocean; 02.04.06.06.04 Spittle; 03.01.16.04 Foam, froth; 06.01.07.04.03 Untruth, falsehood

fāmian 03.01.16.04 Foam, froth

fāmiende 03.01.16.04 Foam, froth

fāmig 01.01.03.01.02.05 Wave; 03.01.16.04 Foam, froth

fāmigbord 05.12.01.09.03.01.02 Of/concerning a ship, naval

fāmigbōsm 01.01.03.01.02.01 Region of sea/ocean; 05.12.01.09.03.01.03 Part of ship

fāmigheals 05.12.01.09.03.01.02 Of/concerning a ship, naval

fana 13.02.08.02 A standard, banner, ensign

fanbyrde 13.02.08.02 A standard, banner, ensign

fandere 11.03.01 Experience, trial, experiment

fandian 06.02.06.03.04.01 Temptation; 08.01.02.04.01 Visiting; 11.03.01.03 Finding, discovery

(ge)fandian 02.05.07 Faculty of taste; 08.01.01 A feeling, what is felt; 08.01.03.05.03 Exasperation, irritation; 09.05.02 A question, inquiry, questioning; 11.03 Endeavour; 11.03.01 Experience, trial, experiment

gefandian 14.02.01.02.01 Open robbery, rapine, pillage

fandung 06.02.06.03.04.01 Temptation; 11.03.01 Experience, trial, experiment; 11.03.01.01.01 Proof, demonstration

(ge)fandung 11.03.01 Experience, trial, experiment

fane 02.07.11 Plants/flowers (alphabetical order)

fang 13.02.05.01.02.02 Booty, spoils
gefangian 03.03.06.01 A whole formed by joining
fann 04.02.04.06.14.01 A winnowing fan
fannian 04.02.04.04.05.01 To winnow
fant 01.01.03.01.01.07 Spring, fountain, well; 16.02.05.05.03 A font
fantbæþ 16.02.04.07.01 Baptism, baptizing (and anointing); 16.02.05.05.03 A font
fantbletsung 16.02.04.07.01 Baptism, baptizing (and anointing)
fantfæt 16.02.05.05.03 A font
fanthālgung 16.02.04.07.01 Baptism, baptizing (and anointing)
fanthālig 16.02.04.07.01 Baptism, baptizing (and anointing)
fantwæter 16.02.05.09.04 Holy Water
gefara 12.04.01 A fellow, companion, associate, comrade
faran 01.01.03.03 Flow/flowing; 05.03.02.01.01 An event, occurrence; 05.07 Ending of existence, end of world; 15.01.04 Coinage, money
faran ... onbūtan 05.12.05 To move and change direction, turn
faran be 03.06.03 Congruity, fitness, suitability
faran mid 11.01.01 Practice, exercise, doing
faran tōgædere 13.02.02 Battle
faran tōsomne 13.02.02 Battle
(ge)faran 05.02.01.01 The course of human affairs; 05.12.01 To go, progress, travel (usually on land); 05.12.05.02 To go/travel towards, come, approach; 05.12.05.03.03 To depart, leave, set out; 11 Action, operation; 13.02.01 A military expedition

(ge)faran ūt 05.12.05.03.04 To come/go out from
gefaran 05.03.02 Event, issue, result; 05.12.05.02.03 To arrive; 11.01.04 A doing, accomplishing (of something); 11.01.05 Accomplishment, fulfilment; 13.02.05.01.02 To gain by fighting
gefaran feorh 11.10.05 Escape
gefāran 02.02.03 To die, perish
gefaren 02.02.03.02 State of being dead; 06.01.06.03 Experience
farende 02.02.03.01 In process of dying; 05.12.01.01 To go on a journey/expedition, travel
farendlic 05.12.05.02.04 To go in, enter
farisēas 02.03.03.06.07.05 Jews
farisēisc 02.03.03.06.07.05 Jews
farnian 08.01.01.03.08 Happiness, well-being, prosperity
faroþ 01.01.02.01.01.03 Shore, bank; 01.01.03.01.02.04 State of sea
faroþhengest 05.12.01.09.03.01 A ship, boat
faroþlācende 05.12.01.08 To move in/on water; 05.12.05.05.01 To wave, undulate
faroþrīdende 05.12.01.09.03 A voyage
faroþstrǣt 01.01.03.01.02.01 Region of sea/ocean
faru 02.03.03.01 Body of retainers, household; 05.02.01.01 The course of human affairs; 05.12.01 To go, progress, travel (usually on land); 05.12.01.01 To go on a journey/expedition, travel; 05.12.01.06 Vehicle; 11.01.01 Practice, exercise, doing; 11.05.02 Mode, manner, way, method, fashion, course; 13.02.01 A military expedition; 15.01 Property

faþu 02.03.02.03.06.02.02 Aunt
faþusunu 02.03.02.03.06.02.04 Cousin
fēa 03.03.04.04.01 Paucity, fewness, scarcity; 03.06 Comparison
gefēa 08.01.01.03 Good feeling, joy, happiness
fealcen 02.06.08.04 Bird of prey
feald 05.10.06.05 A fold, plait, wrinkle
feald/fild 03.03.03.01 Arithmetic
(ge)feald 05.10.05.04.11 A circle, circuit, circumference
(ge)fealdan 05.05.03 Binding, fastening; 05.10.06.05 A fold, plait, wrinkle
gefealdan 05.12.05.04.01 (Of wheel, etc.) to roll, trundle; 11.02 Occupation, activity, business
fealgian 04.02.04.02.02.02 Ploughing, tilling
fealh 04.02.03.02.03 Fallow land; 17.02.04.02.04 Leading/conducting of water
fealh/felg 17.03.01 A wheel
gefēalic 08.01.01.03.09.01 Pleasant, agreeable
gefēalīce 08.01.01.03 Good feeling, joy, happiness
(ge)feall 05.12.05.13.03 To fall
feallan 01.01.03.03 Flow/flowing; 12.05.06.04.02 Submission, subjection, obedience
(ge)feallan 02.02.03 To die, perish; 03.02.01 Decay, decline, corruption; 05.12.01.04.01.04 To stumble, trip, strike (with the foot); 05.12.05.13.03 To fall; 07.04.03 Reverence, respect; 16.02.04.18.03 Kneeling, bowing, prostration
(ge)feallan in/on 05.12.05.02.01 To come upon, meet with

gefeallan 11.02.01 Energy, vigour, vigorous action
gefeallan on lufe 08.01.02.02.03 A loving relationship
fealle 04.03.02 A snare, trap, noose
gefeallen 05.12.05.13.03 To fall
feallende 03.02.01 Decay, decline, corruption; 05.12.05.13.03 To fall
feallende feax 02.08.06 Skin disease, erysipelas
feallendlic 05.11.01.03.01 Mortal state, this life
fealletan 05.12.05.13.03 To fall
gefealnes 05.12.05.13.03 To fall
fēalōg 15.01.06 Poverty, indigence
fealohilte 13.02.08.04.03.01.01 Hilt of sword
fealþing 03.03.02 Measurement by weighing
fealu 02.07.01 To grow; 03.01.13 Darkness, obscurity; 03.01.14.07 Yellow/yellowness; 03.01.18 Dryness (not wetness); 04.02.03.02.03 Fallow land
fealwian 03.02.01.05.01 Blight (causing leaves to look burned); 04.02.04.04.01 To ripen
fēanes 03.03.04.04.01 Paucity, fewness, scarcity
gefēannes 08.01.01.03 Good feeling, joy, happiness
fearh 02.06.02.01.07 Pig, swine
fearhhama 02.06.02.01.07 Pig, swine
fearhrȳþer 02.06.02.01.03 Cattle
gefearhsugu 02.06.02.01.07 Pig, swine
fearlic 02.06.02.01.03 Cattle
fearm 17.02.04.02.03 Carrying, carriage (of materials)
fearn 02.07.04 Fern
fearnbedd 02.07.04 Fern
fearnbracu 02.07.04 Fern

fearnedisc 04.02.03.04.02.01 Types of pasture
fearnhege 04.05.01.02.07 A fence, hedge
fearnig 02.07.04 Fern
fearnlǣs 04.02.03.04.02.01 Types of pasture
fearr 02.06.02.01.03 Cattle
fēasceaft 15.01.06 Poverty, indigence
fēasceaftig 15.01.06 Poverty, indigence
fēasceaftnes 15.01.06 Poverty, indigence
fēawa 03.03.04.04.01 Paucity, fewness, scarcity
fēawlic 03.03.04.04.01 Paucity, fewness, scarcity
(ge)fēawnes 03.03.04.04.01 Paucity, fewness, scarcity
fēawum sīþum 05.11.09.04 Seldom, rarely
feax 02.04.04.03 Hair; 02.04.04.03.03 Hair of head; 02.07.03.01 A bush
feax ēaran 02.04.04.03.03 Hair of head
feaxclāþ 04.04.07.11 A headcloth, covering for the head
feaxede 02.04.04.03 Hair; 02.07.03.01 A bush
gefeax(en) 02.04.04.03 Hair
feaxfang 10.04.02 To grasp, take hold of
feaxfeallung 02.08.06 Skin disease, erysipelas
feaxhār 02.04.04.03.02 Colour of hair
feaxnǣdel 04.06.01.07 Hair-care
feaxnes 02.04.04.03.03 Hair of head
feaxnett 04.04.07.11 A headcloth, covering for the head
feaxprēon 04.04.10 Ornaments, trappings, accoutrements
feaxscēara 04.06.01.07 Hair-care
feaxwund 02.08.07.01 Pain in head/neck
februarius 05.11.03.01.03.01 Specific months

(ge)feccan 10.01.02 Acquisition
gefeccan 05.12.02.01 To fetch, bring, bear, conduct
gefēd 04.01.02.04.03.01.01 Fed/nourished
fēdan 04.02.05.01 Care of livestock; 04.02.05.01.01 To feed/fatten animals; 04.02.05.01.01.01 To put out to pasture; 11.12.02.01 Strengthening, confirmation
fēdan and fōstrian 04.01.02.04.03.01 To feed/nourish
(ge)fēdan 04.01.01.02 Act/action of sucking; 04.01.02.04.03.01 To feed/nourish; 06.01.06.02.03.04.03 To teach, instruct
fēdelfugol 02.06.08.02 Domestic fowl; 04.01.02.01.02.06 Chicken
fēdels 02.06.02 Domestic animals, livestock; 04.01.02.01.02 Animal(s) for food; 04.01.02.04.03 Feeding, nourishing
fēdelsswīn 02.06.02.01.07 Pig, swine; 04.01.02.01.02.03 Pig killed for food
fēdende 04.01.02.01.01.01 Good/palatable food
fēding 04.01.02.04.03 Feeding, nourishing
fēdnes 04.01.02.04.01 Food/sustenance; 11.12.02.01 Strengthening, confirmation
fēfer 02.08.10 Fever
fēferādl 02.08.10 Fever
fēfercyn 02.08.10 Fever
fēferende 02.08.10 Fever
feferfūge 02.07.11 Plants/flowers (alphabetical order)
fēferian 02.08.10 Fever
fēferig 02.08.10 Fever
fēferseoc 02.08.10 Fever

gefēg 03.03.06.01 A whole formed by joining; 09.03.07.04.02 A diagram
fēgan 12.05.06.01 Restraint, check, curb, control
(ge)fēgan 05.05 Constitution, founding (e.g. of world); 12.04 Fellowship, union, association
gefēgan 03.03.06.01 A whole formed by joining; 08.01 Heart, spirit, mood, disposition; 17.02.04 Trade, calling, craft, aptitude
gefēged 03.03.06.01 A whole formed by joining; 03.06.03 Congruity, fitness, suitability
gefēgednes 05.10.06 Form, shape
gefēg(ed)nes 09.03.02.02.01.05 Minor parts of speech, etc.
gefēgednes 09.03.04.02.01 A figure
fēging 09.03.02.03 Composition (inflectional or compounding)
(ge)fēging 03.03.06.01 A whole formed by joining
fēgnes 09.03.02.02.01.05 Minor parts of speech, etc.
gefēgnes 12.04 Fellowship, union, association
feht 02.06.02.01.08 Sheep
fela 03.03.04.01 Much
fela rīce 15.01.05 Possession of wealth
fēla lāf 13.02.08.04.03 A sword
felaǣte 04.01.01.04 Gluttony, overeating, greediness
felafǣcne 12.01.01.12.04 Treachery
felafeald 03.03.04.01.02 A great number, multitude
felafealdnes 03.03.04.01.02 A great number, multitude
felafrēcne 05.08.02.01 (Of living creatures) fierceness, roughness

felafricgende 06.01.06.02 Knowledge, learning, erudition
felagēomor 08.01.03 Bad feeling, sadness
felageong(e) 05.12.01.01 To go on a journey/expedition, travel
felahrōr 06.02.07.06 Courage, boldness, valour
felaīdelsprǣce 09.01.02.01 Excessive fluency, loquacity
felalēof 08.01.02.02.01 A favourite, loved one
felameahtig 16.01.01.01.01.01 Mightiness
felamōdig 06.02.07.06.02 Boldness
(ge)fēlan 02.05 Sensation, perception, feeling; 02.05.06 Sense of touch
felasprǣc 09.01.02.01 Excessive fluency, loquacity
felasprǣce 09.01.02.01 Excessive fluency, loquacity
felasp(r)ecol 09.01.02.01 Excessive fluency, loquacity
felasp(r)ecolnes 09.01.02.01 Excessive fluency, loquacity
felasynnig 12.08.09 Guiltiness, guilt
felawlanc 07.06.05 Pomp, splendour, magnificence
felawyrde 09.01.02.01 Excessive fluency, loquacity
felawyrdnes 09.01.02.01 Excessive fluency, loquacity
felcyrf 02.04.06.04.01 Male genitalia
feld 01.01.02.01.04 Open (level) land; 04.02.03.01.01 Enclosed land/field; 05.02.01.01 The course of human affairs; 13.02.02 Battle
feldǣlfen 16.01.03.04 Elfin race
feldbēo 02.06.09.02.02 Bee, hornet, wasp
feldbisceopwyrt 02.07.11 Plants/flowers (alphabetical order)

feldcyrice 16.02.05.02.03 A church, place of worship
feldfare 02.06.08.05 Forest bird, wild-fowl
feldgangende 02.06 Animal
feldhrīþer 02.06.02.01.03 Cattle
feldhūs 04.05.03.02.02.09 A tent, pavilion
feldlǣs 04.02.03.04.02.01 Types of pasture
feldland 01.01.02.01.04 Open (level) land
feldlic 02.07 A plant; 12.06.02.01.01 Country (not town)
feldmædere 02.07.10.01 Particular herbs/spices (alphabetical order)
feldminte 02.07.10.01 Particular herbs/spices (alphabetical order)
feldmore 02.07.09.02.02.01 Edible root/bulb
feldoxa 02.06.02.01.03 Cattle
feldrūde 02.07.11 Plants/flowers (alphabetical order)
feldsæten 04.02.03.04.02 Pasture/pasturage
feldswamm 02.07.05 Fungus
feldware 02.03.03.04.01 Country people
feldwēsten 01.01.02.01.06 Wild/uncultivated land
feldwōp 02.07.09.02 Particular fruits (alphabetical order)
feldwyrt 02.07.11 Plants/flowers (alphabetical order)
gefēle 02.05 Sensation, perception, feeling
fēlelēas 02.05.01 Without feeling, insensible
fell 02.04.04 Skin; 02.06.01.06 Skin, hide; 04.04.07.01 Mode of dressing, fashion
fellan 05.07 Ending of existence, end of world; 05.12.02.07 To throw, cast, toss

fellen 17.04.04.02 Skin, hide (as material)
fellerēad 03.01.14.05 Red/redness
fellstycce 17.04.04.02 Skin, hide (as material)
felma/filmen 02.04.05.03 Membrane
(ge)fēlnes 02.05 Sensation, perception, feeling
felofe(o)rþ 02.06.01.03 Barrel, body of animal
felofor 02.06.08.06 Water bird
felt 04.04.05.02 Felt
feltere 02.07.11 Plants/flowers (alphabetical order)
feltūn 04.05.03.05.02 A privy
feltūngrēp 04.05.03.05.01 A cess-pool, midden, sewer
feltwurma 02.07.10.01 Particular herbs/spices (alphabetical order)
feltwyrt 02.07.11 Plants/flowers (alphabetical order)
fencerse 02.07.09.02.02.02 Other vegetables (alphabetical order)
fenester 04.05.02.13 A window-space
fenfearn 02.07.04 Fern
fenfisc 02.06.06.02 River fish, freshwater fish
fenfreoþu 11.10.01.02.01 A naturally secure place, fastness
fenfugol 02.06.08.03 Game-bird
feng 08.01.02.02.02 An embrace; 10.04.02 To grasp, take hold of; 13.02.05.01.02.02 Booty, spoils; 14.05.08 Captivity; 17.03.10 Supports and fastenings
(ge)feng 10.04.02.02 To seize, take, grasp, lay hold on
gefeng 14.05.08 Captivity
fengel 12.01.01.04 A leader, ruler
fengelād 01.01.02.01.04.01 Marsh, bog, swamp

fengnett 04.03.03 Net, drag-net, hunting net
fengtōþ 02.04.06.03.02.01.01 Tooth/teeth
fenhleoþu 01.01.02.01.04.01 Marsh, bog, swamp
fenhop 01.01.02.01.04.01 Marsh, bog, swamp
fenix 02.06.10.01.04 Phoenix; 02.07.09.02 Particular fruits (alphabetical order)
fenland 01.01.02.01.04.01 Marsh, bog, swamp
fenlic 01.01.02.01.04.01 Marsh, bog, swamp; 04.06.02.02 Foul, filthy, squalid
fenminte 02.07.10.01 Particular herbs/spices (alphabetical order)
fenn 01.01.02.01.04.01 Marsh, bog, swamp; 04.06.02.02 Foul, filthy, squalid
fennig 01.01.02.01.04.01 Marsh, bog, swamp; 04.06.02.02 Foul, filthy, squalid
fennþæc 04.05.02.08.01 Thatch
fenogrecum 02.07.09.02.02.02 Other vegetables (alphabetical order)
fenompre 02.07.11 Plants/flowers (alphabetical order)
fenȳce 02.06.07.02 Frog, toad
(ge)fēogan 07.03.01.03 To loathe, hate, abhor
feoh 02.06.02 Domestic animals, livestock; 09.03.07.01.01 A runic letter; 15.01 Property; 15.01.03 Treasure, riches, wealth; 15.01.04 Coinage, money; 15.02 Worth, value; 15.02.04 Spending, disbursement
feoh gesettan 15.02.03 An account
feoh (ge)slēan 15.01.04 Coinage, money
feohbehāt 12.07.02.01.01 A promise
feohbīgenga 04.02.05.06.01 A cowherd
feohbōt 14.03.03.09.02 Atonement
feohfang 14.01.04.03 Rights involving money; 14.02.01.01 Types of crime
feohgafol 15.04.01 Lending of money
feohgehāt 12.07.02.01.01 A promise
feohgeorn 10.03.09.01.01 Covetousness, avarice
feohgeornes 10.03.09.01.01 Covetousness, avarice
feohgerēfa 12.01.01.08.01 A servant, attendant
feohgesceot 15.02.04 Spending, disbursement
feohgesteald 15.01.05 Possession of wealth
feohgestrēon 15.01.03 Treasure, riches, wealth
feohgīfre 10.03.09.01.01 Covetousness, avarice
feohgift 10.03.08 Bountifulness, munificence
feohgītsere 10.03.09.01.01 Covetousness, avarice
feohgītsung 10.03.09.01.01 Covetousness, avarice
feohgōd 15.01 Property
feohhord 15.01.03 Treasure, riches, wealth
feohhūs 15.01.03 Treasure, riches, wealth
feohlænung 15.04.01 Lending of money
feohland 04.02.03.04.02 Pasture/pasturage
feohlēas 14.03.03.09.02 Atonement; 15.01.06 Poverty, indigence
feohlēasnes 15.01.06 Poverty, indigence
feohlufu 10.03.09.01.01 Covetousness, avarice
feohsceatt 15.02.04 Spending, disbursement

936

feohspēda 15.01.03 Treasure, riches, wealth
feohspillung 10.03.08.01 Overliberality, waste of money
feohstrang 15.01.05 Possession of wealth
(ge)feoht 12.05.04.01.01 Fighting, a fight; 13.02.02 Battle
gefeoht 12.05.01 Rivalry, contest
gefeoht drēogan 13.02 War
(ge)feohtan 12.05.01 Rivalry, contest; 12.05.04.01 Fighting, contention, warfare, strife; 13.02 War
(ge)feohtan wiþ 13.02 War
gefeohtan 13.02.05.01.02 To gain by fighting
gefeohtan on 14.03.03.05 Ordeal
gefeohtdæg 13.02.02 Battle
feohte 12.05.04.01 Fighting, contention, warfare, strife
feohtegod 16.01.06.02 Classical gods
feohtehorn 13.02.08.01 Battle-horn; 18.02.07.02.02.02 A trumpet
feohtend 13.02.10.01 A man, warrior
feohtere 13.02.10.01 A man, warrior
feohtgegyrela 13.02.08.03 An article of warlike apparel
feohtlāc 12.05.04.01.01 Fighting, a fight
feohtling 13.02.10.01 A man, warrior
gefeohtsumnes 08.01.01.03 Good feeling, joy, happiness
fēol 17.03.04 Tools for smoothing/scraping/grinding
fēolaga 12.04.01 A fellow, companion, associate, comrade
fēolagscipe 12.04 Fellowship, union, association
(ge)fēolan 03.01.17 Thickness, viscosity; 05.12.05.02 To go/travel towards, come, approach

gefēolan 05.12.05.02.04 To go in, enter; 06.02.07.03 Perseverance
fēolheard 03.01.03 Hardness, callosity, hard material; 13.02.08.04.03 A sword
fēolian 17.02.04.03.02 Filings
fēologan 03.01.14.04 Black/blackness
(ge)fēon 08.01.01.03.06 Exultation, joy
gefēon 10.01.02 Acquisition
fēond 02.08.11.02.01.01 Paroxysm of madness, folly; 04.06.02 Insalubrious, injurious to health; 08.01.03.09.05 Enmity; 12.08.06.02.02 A bad man, inhuman person; 16.01.05.02 Species of devil, hellish race
fēondæt 16.02.04.14 Sacrilege
(ge)fēonde 08.01.01.03.06 Exultation, joy
fēondgrāp 10.04.02 To grasp, take hold of
fēondgyld 02.08.11.02.01 Insanity, madness; 16.02.01.06.01.01 Pagan worship, idolatrous practice(s); 16.02.01.06.01.01 An image, idol
fēondlic 08.01.03.05.02 Anger; 08.01.03.09.06 Hostility; 16.01.05.02.02 Other terms for devils
fēondlīce 08.01.03.09.06 Hostility
fēondrǣden 08.01.03.09.05 Enmity
fēondrǣs 13.02.03.01 An attack, assault
fēondsceaþa 08.01.03.09.05 Enmity
fēondscipe 08.01.03.09.05 Enmity
fēondsēoc 02.08.11.02.01 Insanity, madness
fēondulf 14.02 Lawlessness
feor and wīde 05.10.05 A space, span
feorbūend 12.06.05 A foreign country
feorcȳþþ 05.10.04.02 A region, zone
fēore gedīgan 11.10.05 Escape
fēores nēotan 02.01.02.02.02 Lifetime
feorh 02 Creation; 02.01.01 Life, vital part; 02.01.01.01 Soul, spirit; 02.03.01 People; 02.04.01 Dead body

feorh āgiefan 02.02.03 To die, perish
feorh losian 02.02.03 To die, perish
feorh gesellan 02.02.03 To die, perish
feorhādl 02.08.02.01 An illness, ailment, disorder
feorhbana 02.02.04.03.01 A killer
feorhbealu 02.02.04 Killing, violent death, destruction
feorhbenn 02.02.04.01 Cause/occasion of death
feorhberend 02 Creation
feorhbold 02.04 Body
feorhbora 02 Creation
feorhcwalu 02.02 Death
feorhcwealm 02.02 Death
feorhcynn 02 Creation
feorhdagas 02.01.04 Age
feorhdolg 02.02.04.01 Cause/occasion of death
feorhēacen 02.01.02.01 That lives, living
feorhfægen 02.01.02.01 That lives, living; 08.01.01.03.06 Exultation, joy
feorhgebeorh 11.10 Safety, safeness
feorhgedāl 02.02 Death
feorhgener 11.10.01.01 Preservation from injury/destruction
feorhgenīþla 08.01.03.09.05 Enmity
feorhgiefu 02.01.02 Gift of life
feorhgifa 16.01.01.02.02 A giving (by Deity)
feorhgōma 16.01.05 Hell, lower world, abode of the dead
feorhhama 02.04.06.04.02 Female reproductive organs
feorhhord 02.01.01.01 Soul, spirit
feorhhūs 02.04 Body
feorhhyrde 11.10.01 Protection, safekeeping
feorhlāst 05.12.01.03.01.01 A path, track
feorhlēan 10.03.05 Recompense, reward
feorhlegu 02.02 Death
feorhlic 02.01 Existence, life
feorhlīf 02.01.01 Life, vital part
feorhloca 08.01 Heart, spirit, mood, disposition
feorhlyre 02.02 Death
feorhneru 04.01.02.01 Food/sustenance; 11.10.01.02 Refuge, help, shelter; 16.01.01.02.08 Salvation, redemption
feorhnest 04.01.02.01 Food/sustenance
feorhrǣd 11.07.03 Use, advantage, profit
feorhscyldig 14.03.03.09.01 Unfavourable judgement, condemnation
feorhsēoc 02.02.03.01 In process of dying
feorhsweng 05.06.09 Act of striking; 13.02.08.04.03.02.01 Striking/attack with sword
feorhþearf 06.02.04.01 Want, need
feorhweard 11.10.02.02 Watchful care, keeping guard
feorhwund 02.02.04.01 Cause/occasion of death
feorland 05.10.04.02 A region, zone
feorlicor 05.10.05 A space, span
feorm 04.01.02.01 Food/sustenance; 04.01.02.04 Abundance of food; 04.01.02.04.02 Feast; 04.01.02.04.05.01 Hospitality, harbouring, entertaining; 11.07.03 Use, advantage, profit; 15.01 Property; 15.02.04.01 Payment for temporary use, rent, hire
feorme hām 04.02 Farm
feormend 04.01.02.04.04.01 Provider/supplier of food; 04.01.02.04.05.01 Hospitality, harbouring, entertaining; 04.06.01 Clean
feormendlēas 04.06.01 Clean

feormere 04.01.02.04.04.01 Provider/supplier of food
feormfultum 15.01.02 Gift, transfer of property
feormian 04.01.02.04.04 To maintain, support, provide for; 04.06.01 Clean; 11.07.03 Use, advantage, profit; 11.12.02.01 Strengthening, confirmation
(ge)feormian 04.01.02.04.05 Entertainment with food; 04.01.02.04.05.01 Hospitality, harbouring, entertaining; 04.06.01.01 Cleansing, washing; 11.12.02 Aid, help, succour; 12.08.04 Purity, moral cleanness; 14.01.05 Service, obligation, duty; 16.02.04.13 Ceremonial cleanness
gefeormian 04.01.01 Eating; 04.06.01 Clean
feormung 04.01.02.04.05.01 Hospitality, harbouring, entertaining; 04.06.01 Clean; 16.02.04.13 Ceremonial cleanness
feornes 05.10.05 A space, span
feorr 03.03.04.03 Growth, increase; 03.06.02 Difference, diversity, dissimilarity; 05.10.05 A space, span; 05.11.01.01 Long duration, long space; 08.01.01.02.01 Want of interest or concern, indifference; 12.04.03.01 Estrangement, alienation
feorr and nēah 05.10.05 A space, span
feorran 05.10.05 A space, span; 05.11.01.01 Long duration, long space
feorran and nēan 05.10.05 A space, span
feor(ran)cumen 12.06.05 A foreign country
feor(ran)cund 12.06.05 A foreign country

(ge)feorrian 05.12.05.03 To travel away (from); 11.06.06.01 Abandonment (of principle)
feorrung 05.12.02.02 To carry off, remove
feorsian 05.12.05.03 To travel away (from)
feorsibb 02.03.02.03.06.02 Close relationship
feorstuþu 04.05.02.06 A buttress, support
feorting 02.04.06.06.05 Action of breaking wind
fēorþa 03.03.03.03 Fractions; 03.03.03.04.04 Four
fēorþa fæder 02.03.02.03.04 (Of degrees of descent) great-, grand-
fēorþa sunu 02.03.02.03.05 Descendant
fēorþan dǣl 03.03.03.03 Fractions
fēorþe 03.03.03.04.04 Four
fēorþe dohtor 02.03.02.03.05 Descendant
fēorþe healf 03.03.03.04.03.01 Three and a half
fēorþe tā 02.04.03.04.02.05.04 Toe
feorþēod 05.10.04.02 A region, zone
fēorþling 03.03.03.03 Fractions; 15.01.04 Coinage, money
fēorþung 03.03.03.03 Fractions; 15.01.04 Coinage, money
feorweg 05.10.05 A space, span
fēoung 08.01.03.09.04 Hatred
fēower 03.03.03.04.04 Four
fēowerdōgor 05.11.03.01.05 A day
fēowerecg(ed)e 05.10.06.04 A corner, bend, angle
fēowerfeald 03.03.03.04.04 Four
fēowerfealdlīce 03.03.03.04.04 Four
fēowerfēte 02.06 Animal
fēowerfōt(ed)e 02.06 Animal
fēowergǣrede 05.10.06.04 A corner, bend, angle

fēowergild 14.03.03.09.02 Atonement
fēowerhwēolod 05.12.01.06 Vehicle
fēowernihte 05.11.06.03.01.04 (Of lunar cycle) so many nights old
fēowerscȳte 05.10.06.04 A corner, bend, angle
fēowerstrenge 18.02.07.02.03 Stringed instruments
fēowertēoþa 03.03.03.04.14 Fourteen
fēowertīene 03.03.03.04.14 Fourteen
fēowertīenenihte 05.11.06.03.01.04 (Of lunar cycle) so many nights old
fēowertīenewintre 02.01.04 Age
fēowertig 03.03.03.04.22 Forty
fēowertigfeald 03.03.03.04.22 Forty; 16.02.04.04.02.01.02 Lent
fēowertiggēare 05.11.03.01 A year
fēowertiggetel 03.03.03.04.22 Forty
fēowertiglic 03.03.03.04.22 Forty; 16.02.04.04.02.01.02 Lent
fēowertigoþa 03.03.03.04.22 Forty
fēowerþe mōdor 02.03.02.03.04 (Of degrees of descent) great-, grand-
fēowerwintre 02.01.04 Age
fēowung 08.01.01.03.06 Exultation, joy
fēra 12.04.01 A fellow, companion, associate, comrade
(ge)fēra 08.01.02.03.01 An acquaintance, friend, associate
gefēra 02.03.03.01 Body of retainers, household; 10.01.03 A sharing, participation; 11.12.02 Aid, help, succour; 12.01.01.08.01 A servant, attendant; 12.02.03 A society, guild, association; 12.04.01 A fellow, companion, associate, comrade; 12.06.03.03 A neighbour; 12.09 Marriage, state of marriage; 13.02.10 The military, soldiers; 16.02.03.02 A cleric, clergyman (general)

fēran forþ 02.02.03 To die, perish
(ge)fēran 05.02.01.01 The course of human affairs; 05.03.02.01.01 An event, occurrence; 05.12.01.01 To go on a journey/expedition, travel; 05.12.05.06 To travel over/through/along, traverse
gefēran 02.02.03 To die, perish; 05.03.01 A cause (of anything); 05.03.02 Event, issue, result; 05.12.02.01 To fetch, bring, bear, conduct; 05.12.05.02.03 To arrive; 11.05.02 Mode, manner, way, method, fashion, course
fērbedd 04.05.04.05 A bed, bedstead
fercian 05.12.02.01 To fetch, bring, bear, conduct; 05.12.05.02 To go/travel towards, come, approach; 05.12.05.08.01 To go before and guide; 06.01.07.06 Mental acceptance, belief
(ge)fercian 11.12.02.01 Strengthening, confirmation
fercung 04.01.02.01 Food/sustenance
ferdwyrt 02.07.11 Plants/flowers (alphabetical order)
ferdwyrþig 13.02.09.01 Military service
fēre 05.12.01.09.03.01.02 Of/concerning a ship, naval; 13.02.09.01 Military service
gefēre 02.03.03.01 Body of retainers, household; 05.12.01.03.01 A means of access; 12.04.01.01 A company of people, fellowship, society; 16.02.03.03 A religious
gefēred 12.04 Fellowship, union, association
ferele 14.05.06 Means/implement of torture
fērend 05.12.01.09.03 A voyage; 09.06.02.01.06.01 A messenger

fērende 05.12 To move, be in motion; 05.12.01 To go, progress, travel (usually on land)
feresōca 17.03.12 A receptacle, container
fergenbeorg 01.01.02.01.02.02.02 Mountain
ferht 12.08.02.03 Goodness, probity
ferhtlic 12.07.04 Truth, righteousness, justice, equity
ferhþ 06 Spirit, soul, heart
ferhþbana 02.02.04.03.01 A killer
ferhþcearig 08.01.03.01 Despondency
ferhþcleofa 06 Spirit, soul, heart
ferhþcofa 06 Spirit, soul, heart
ferhþe 02.04.04 Skin
ferhþfrec 06.02.07.06 Courage, boldness, valour
ferhþgefēonde 08.01.01.03.06 Exultation, joy
ferhþgenīþla 08.01.03.09.05 Enmity
ferhþgewit 06.01.05.01 Understanding
ferhþglēaw 06.01.05.02.01.01 Sagacity
ferhþgrim 08.01.03.09.01 Fierceness
ferhþloca 06.01 The head (as seat of thought)
ferhþlufu 08.01.02.02 Love, affection, care
ferhþsefa 06.01 The head (as seat of thought)
ferhþweg 02.02 Death
ferhþwērig 08.01.03.01 Despondency
ferian 05.12.01.01 To go on a journey/expedition, travel; 11.01.01 Practice, exercise, doing; 12.03 Direction, guidance
ferian ... ūp 05.12.05.12.02 To raise, lift up, elevate
(ge)ferian 05.12.02.01 To fetch, bring, bear, conduct; 05.12.05.03.03 To depart, leave, set out; 05.12.05.08.01 To go before and guide
fer(i)gend 05.12.02.01 To fetch, bring, bear, conduct
feri(g)end 05.12.05.08.01 To go before and guide
fering 05.12.01.06 Vehicle
fēring 05.12.01.01 To go on a journey/expedition, travel
gefērlǣcan 03.03.06.01 A whole formed by joining; 05.10.05.04.01.02 Contents, what is included; 12.04 Fellowship, union, association
gefērlic 08.01.02.03.02 Friendly, amiable
(ge)fērlīplīce 08.01.02.03.03 In a friendly manner, kindly
ferme land 04.02.03 Cultivatable land/farmland
(ge)fērnes 05.12.05.03.03 To depart, leave, set out
(ge)fērrǣden 12.04 Fellowship, union, association; 16.02.03.03 A religious
gefērrǣden 08.01.02.03 Friendliness, affection
fers 09.01.01 A speech, what is said, words; 09.03.05.01.02 Art of verse composition; 16.02.04.03.02 Parts of service
fersc 03.01.16.02 Water, liquid; 04.01.02.01.01.03 Fresh/not preserved; 04.01.03.04 Water; 04.06 Salubrity
fersceta 01.01.03.01.01.03 Stream
fērscipe 12.09 Marriage, state of marriage
(ge)fērscipe 12.02.03 A society, guild, association; 12.04 Fellowship, union, association; 12.04.01.01 A company of people, fellowship, society
gefērscipe 12.01.01.06 Condition, rank, standing; 12.01.01.07 A follower; 16.02.03.02.07 A priest, cleric

geferscipian 12.04.01.02 A fellow traveller, companion
fersian 09.03.05.01.02 Art of verse composition
ferþfriþende 11.12.02.01 Strengthening, confirmation
fēsterbearn 06.01.06.02.03.01 A pupil, disciple, scholar
fēsterfæder 02.03.02.04.01 Foster relationships; 06.01.06.02.03.04.02 A teacher
fēsterling 06.01.06.02.03.01 A pupil, disciple, scholar
fēstermann 14.03.03.07 Security, pledge, bail
fēstermōdor 02.03.02.04.01 Foster relationships
(ge)fēstrian 04.01.02.04.03.01 To feed/nourish; 11.12.02.01 Strengthening, confirmation
fēt fealdan 05.12.05.13.02.02 To sit down
gefetan 05.12.05.13.03 To fall
fetelhilt 13.02.08.04.03.01.01 Hilt of sword
fetel(s) 13.02.08.04.03.01.01 Hilt of sword
(ge)fetelsod 13.02.08.04.03.01.01 Hilt of sword
gefeterian 14.05.07 Binding, fastening with bonds
(ge)fetian 05.12.02.01 To fetch, bring, bear, conduct; 05.12.05.08.01 To go before and guide; 10.01.02 Acquisition
fetor 04.02.05.05.04 Rope, rein; 14.05.07 Binding, fastening with bonds
fetorwrāsen 14.05.07 Binding, fastening with bonds
gefetred 14.05.08 Captivity

fēþa 05.12.01.04 To go, proceed on foot; 13.02.10.01.02.02 Armed forces; 13.02.10.01.02.02.02 Branch of army
fēþan 05.12.01.04 To go, proceed on foot
fēþe 05.12.01.04 To go, proceed on foot; 05.12.03 Speed, rate of movement
fēþecempa 13.02.10.01.02.02.02 Branch of army
fēþegang 05.12.01.04 To go, proceed on foot
fēþegeorn 06.02.05.04 Desire, eagerness
fēþegest 05.12.01.01 To go on a journey/expedition, travel
fēþehere 13.02.10.01.02.02.02 Branch of army
fēþehwearf 12.04.02 A crowding together, assembly
fēþelāst 05.12.01.04.01 Manner of going, gait
fēþelēas 02.08.04.04 State of being crippled
fēþemann 05.12.01.04 To go, proceed on foot; 13.02.10.01.02.02.02 Branch of army
fēþemund 02.06.01.04 Leg
feþer 02.06.08.01 Part of bird; 09.03.07.06.01 A writing instrument; 13.02.10.01.02.02.03 Part of an army
feþerbǣre 05.12.01.07 To fly (with wings)
feþerbedd 04.05.04.05 A bed, bedstead
feþerberend 02.06.08 Bird
feþercræft 04.04.05.07 Embroidery
gefeþered 02.06.08.01 Part of bird
feþergearwe 13.02.08.04.04.01 An arrow, dart, bolt
feþergeweorc 04.04.05.07 Embroidery
feþerhama 05.12.01.07 To fly (with wings)
feþerswēg 02.05.10.15.07 Voice, note (of a bird)

fēþespēdig 05.12.01.04 To go, proceed on foot; 05.12.03.01 Swiftness, velocity
fēþewīg 13.02.02 Battle
feþorbyrste 03.03.07 A part, division, portion
feþrian 02.06.08 Bird
gefeþrian 17.02.04.02.03 Carrying, carriage (of materials)
feþriht 02.06.08.01 Part of bird
fēþung 05.12.01.04 To go, proceed on foot
gefic 06.01.07.04.02 Fraud, deceit, trick, trickery
fīc 02.07.09.02 Particular fruits (alphabetical order); 02.08.08.09 Piles
fīcādl 02.08.08.09 Piles
fīcæppel 02.07.09.02 Particular fruits (alphabetical order)
fīcbēam 02.07.09.02 Particular fruits (alphabetical order)
fician 07.07.03 Flattery
fīclēaf 02.07.09.02 Particular fruits (alphabetical order)
ficol 06.01.07.04 Deception
fīctrēow 02.07.09.02 Particular fruits (alphabetical order)
ficung 06.01.07.04.02 Fraud, deceit, trick, trickery
fīcwyrm 02.08.08.04.03 Intestinal worm
fīcwyrt 02.07.11 Plants/flowers (alphabetical order)
fiell 02.02.04 Killing, violent death, destruction; 05.06.01 Devastation, laying waste; 09.03.02.03.01.01.01 Case; 12.08.06.01 Error, wrong conduct, erroneous practice
(ge)fiell 05.12.05.13.03 To fall
fīendwīc 13.02.07.04 A camp, encampment

fierd 13.02.01 A military expedition; 13.02.07.04 A camp, encampment; 13.02.09.01 Military service; 13.02.10.01.02.02 Armed forces
fiersn 02.04.03.04.02.05.01 Heel
fīf 03.03.03.04.05 Five
fīfalde 02.06.09.02.04 Butterfly, moth
fīfbēc 16.02.01.08.01.01 Books of the Old Testament
fīfecgede 05.10.06.04 A corner, bend, angle
fīfel 02.06.10.01.05 Sea-monster
fīfela gefeald 05.10.04.02 A region, zone
fīfelcynn 02.06.10.01.05 Sea-monster
fīfeldor 01.01.03.01.01.01 River
fīfele 04.04.10.02 A button, brooch
fīfelstrēam 01.01.03.01.02 Sea/ocean
fīfelwæg 01.01.03.01.02 Sea/ocean
fīffeald 03.03.03.04.05 Five
fīffētede 09.03.05.01.02 Art of verse composition
fīffingre 02.07.11 Plants/flowers (alphabetical order)
fīfflēre 04.05.02 A building, edifice, structure
fīfgēar 05.11.06 Course/cycle of time
fīfhund 03.03.03.04.30 Five hundred
fīfhundred 03.03.03.04.30 Five hundred
fīflæpped 02.04.06.05.03 Liver
fīflēafe 02.07.11 Plants/flowers (alphabetical order)
fīfmægen 16.01.04 Sorcery, magic, witchcraft
fīfnihte 05.11.06.03.01.04 (Of lunar cycle) so many nights old
fīfta 03.03.03.04.05 Five
fīfta fæder 02.03.02.03.04 (Of degrees of descent) great-, grand-
fīfta sunu 02.03.02.03.05 Descendant
fīfte 03.03.03.04.05 Five
fīfte dohtor 02.03.02.03.05 Descendant

fīfte mōdor 02.03.02.03.04 (Of degrees of descent) great-, grand-
fīfteogoþa 03.03.03.04.23 Fifty
fīftēoþa/-tegþa 03.03.03.04.15 Fifteen
fīftīene 03.03.03.04.15 Fifteen
fīftīene nihte 05.11.06.03.01.04 (Of lunar cycle) so many nights old
fīftig 03.03.03.04.23 Fifty; 16.02.01.08.01.01 Books of the Old Testament
fīftigdæg 16.02.04.04.02.01.03 Holy Week
fīfti(g)esman 13.02.10.01.01 A commander, officer
fīftigfeald 03.03.03.04.23 Fifty
fīftigwintre 02.01.04 Age
fīfwintre 02.01.04 Age
fīgende 08.01.03.09.04 Hatred
gefīgo 02.08.08.09 Piles
fihl 04.04.05 Woven material, fabric
fiht 17.04.04.03 Fleece, pelt
fihtwīte 14.05.04.01 A fine
fild 04.02.05.06.01.02 To milk; 05.10.06.05 A fold, plait, wrinkle
fildburne 01.01.03.01.01.03 Stream
fildcump 04.02.05.06.01.02 To milk
filde 01.01.02.01.04 Open (level) land
gefilde 01.01.02.01.04 Open (level) land
fildenu 01.01.02.01.03.03 Valley
fileþe 04.02.04.03.02.03 Hay
filiende 05.06.05.02 A filing, rubbing with file
filiþlēag 04.02.03.04.01 Meadow land/meadow
fille 02.07.10.01 Particular herbs/spices (alphabetical order)
fillen 05.12.05.13.03 To fall
fillet 04.02.03.01.02 Cleared land
filling 04.02.03.01.02 Cleared land

filmen 02.04.06.04.01 Male genitalia; 02.07.02.04 Seed, kind of seed; 05.06.02.01.01 A crack
fīn 03.03.04.01.02.01 A heap, mass, accumulation; 04.02.04.05.04.01 A forester, woodman; 04.05.03.02.02.08 A lowly dwelling, cottage, hut
fīna 02.06.08.05 Forest bird, wild-fowl
finc 02.06.08.05 Forest bird, wild-fowl
findan 03.03.03.01 Arithmetic; 05.03.02 Event, issue, result; 06.01.06.01 Knowledge, cognizance, knowing; 09.03.05 Art of poetry; 10.01.02 Acquisition; 12.02 A public office
findan (æt) 11.01 Action, doing, performance
findan (wer)borh 14.03.03.07 Security, pledge, bail
(ge)findan 05.12.05.02.01 To come upon, meet with; 06.02.06.02.01 To devise a plan, arrange, settle; 10 Having, owning, possession; 10.01.02 Acquisition; 10.03.04 Provision, supply; 11.03.01.03 Finding, discovery; 14.01.06 A rule, order, precept, tenet, principle
findend 11.03.01.03 Finding, discovery
gefindig 11.04 Ability, capacity, power
finding 11.03.01.03.01 Discovery, invention
finger 02.04.03.04.01.01.01 Finger
fingeræppla 02.07.09.02 Particular fruits (alphabetical order)
fingerdocca 02.07.11 Plants/flowers (alphabetical order)
fingerlic 02.04.03.04.01.01.01 Finger
fingerliþ 02.04.05.04.08 Joint
fingermǣl 05.10.05.03 A measure of distance
fīning 04.02.04.05.04.01 A forester, woodman

finn 02.06.06.01 Part of fish
finnas 02.03.03.06.05 Scandinavian
finol 02.07.09.02.02.02 Other vegetables (alphabetical order)
finolsæd 02.07.09.02.02.02 Other vegetables (alphabetical order)
finta 02.06.08.01 Part of bird; 05.03.02 Event, issue, result
firas 02.03.01 People
firel 02.07.03.05 Particular trees/shrubs (alphabetical order)
firen 08.01.03.07.03 Suffering, torment, pain; 16.02.01.13 Evil-doing, transgression, sin
firenbealu 16.02.01.13 Evil-doing, transgression, sin
firencræft 12.08.06.02 Wickedness, evil
firendæd 16.02.01.13 Evil-doing, transgression, sin
firenearfeþe 08.01.03.07.02 Misery, trouble, affliction
firenfremmende 16.02.01.13 Evil-doing, transgression, sin
firenful 16.02.01.13 Evil-doing, transgression, sin
firengeorn 16.02.01.13 Evil-doing, transgression, sin
firenhicge 12.08.08.01.02.01.01 An adulterer/-ess, whore, prostitute
firenhicgend 12.08.08.01.02.01.01 An adulterer/-ess, whore, prostitute
firenian 07.05.03.03.02 To reproach, revile, abuse; 12.08.08.01.02.01 Fornication, adultery
(ge)firenian 16.02.01.13 Evil-doing, transgression, sin
gefirenian 16.02.04.07.02.03 Penance, an act/instance of penance
firenleahter 16.02.01.13.01 Kinds of sin

firenlic 12.08.06.02.03 (Of persons) wicked, evil-doing
firenlīce 11.02.04.01 Rashness, madness; 12.08.06.02.05.04 Sinfully, wickedly
firenligerian 12.08.08.01.02.01 Fornication, adultery
firenlust 12.08.08.01 Eager, unseemly desire
firenlustful 12.08.07.01.01 Wantonness, sensuality, lasciviousness
firenlustgeorn 12.08.08.01 Eager, unseemly desire
firensynn 16.02.01.13.01 Kinds of sin
firensynnig 16.02.01.13 Evil-doing, transgression, sin
firentācnian 16.02.01.13 Evil-doing, transgression, sin
firenþearf 08.01.03.06 Adversity, affliction
firenum 03.03.04.02.02 Excess; 12.08.06.02.03.01 Wickedly
firenweorc 12.08.06.02.05 Misdeed, sin
firenwyrcende 16.02.01.13 Evil-doing, transgression, sin
firenwyrhta 12.08.06.02.05.02 A sinner, transgressor
firgenbēam 02.07.03 A tree
firgenbucca 02.06.04.01.06 Ibex
firgengāt 02.06.04.01.06 Ibex
firgenholt 02.07.03.04 A wood, trees
firgenstrēam 01.01.03.01.01.03 Stream
firmettan 12.03.04 A request, prayer
firnþe 01.01.02.01.05 Covered with vegetation; 02.07.04 Fern
first 04.05.02.08 Top of a building; 04.05.02.08.02 A ceiling, inner roof; 05.11 A time, period of time; 05.11.11.02 Let up, intermission, cessation
first(ge)mearc 05.11 A time, period of time

firsthrōf 04.05.02.08.02 A ceiling, inner roof
firstmearc 05.11.02 A time, particular time, occasion; 05.11.11.02 Let up, intermission, cessation
fisc 02.06.06 Fish; 04.01.02.01.02.07 Fish
fiscbrȳne 04.01.02.01.05.05.06 Sauce for fish
fisccynn 02.06.06 Fish
fiscdēah 03.01.14.05 Red/redness
fiscere 02.06.08.06 Water bird; 04.03.05 Fishing; 09.05.01 Inspection, examination
fisces bæþ 01.01.03.01.01.02 Sea/ocean
fisces ēþel 01.01.03.01.01.02 Sea/ocean
fischūs 04.02.05.06.07 A fish-pond
fiscian 04.03.05 Fishing
gefiscian 11.03.01.02 To seek, seek for
fiscincel 02.06.06 Fish
fisclacu 01.01.03.01.01.03 Stream; 01.01.03.01.03.01 Pool
fiscmere 01.01.03.01.03.01 Pool
fiscnett 04.03.05 Fishing
fiscnoþ 01.01.03.01.01.01 River
fisc(n)oþ 04.03.05 Fishing
fiscoþ 14.01.04.02 Rights involving property
fiscpōl 01.01.03.01.03.01 Pool; 04.02.05.06.07 A fish-pond
fiscþrūt 02.06.06 Fish
fiscwell(e) 04.02.05.06.07 A fish-pond
fiscwer 01.01.03.01.01.01 River; 04.03.05 Fishing
fiscwylle 03.03.04.02.01 Abundance
fīsting 02.04.06.06.05 Action of breaking wind
fitelfōta 02.06.01.04 Leg
fitersticca 04.05.03.02.02.09 A tent, pavilion
fitt 09.03.05.01.01 Poetry; 12.05.04.01 Fighting, contention, warfare, strife
fiþele 18.02.07.02.03.03 A fiddle
fiþelere 18.02.07.02.03.03 A fiddle
fiþelestre 18.02.07.02.03.03 A fiddle
fiþerberende 05.12.01.07 To fly (with wings)
fiþercian 05.12.01.07 To fly (with wings); 05.12.05.05 To shake, quake, wag
fiþerdǣled 05.10.06 Form, shape
fiþere 02.06.08.01 Part of bird; 04.01.02.01.02.06 Chicken
fiþerfeald 03.03.03.04.04 Four
fiþerflēdende 01.01.03.01.01.01 River
fiþerflōwende 01.01.03.01.01.01 River
fiþerfōtnīeten 02.06 Animal
(ge)fiþerhamod 05.12.01.07 To fly (with wings)
fiþerhīwe 03.04.02 A diversity
fiþerian 05.12.01.07 To fly (with wings); 05.12.05.05 To shake, quake, wag
gefiþerian 08.01 Heart, spirit, mood, disposition
fiþerlēas 05.12.01.07 To fly (with wings)
gefiþerod 05.12.01.07 To fly (with wings)
fiþerrīca 12.02.02.03 Terms for classical world
fiþerrīce 12.01.01 Authority; 12.06 A province, country, territory
fiþerscēatas 05.10.04.02 A region, zone
fiþerscīte 05.10.06.04 A corner, bend, angle
fiþersleht 05.12.01.07 To fly (with wings)
fiþertēme 05.12.01.06 Vehicle
fiþertōdǣled 03.03.07 A part, division, portion
flā 13.02.08.04.04.01 An arrow, dart, bolt
flacg 02.08.12.02.05.03 A poultice
flacor 05.12.01.07 To fly (with wings)
flǣre 02.04.03.01.03.03 Ear; 02.04.03.01.03.04 Nose

flæsc 02 Creation; 02.03.02.03.06 Kinship, relationship; 02.04 Body; 02.04.05.01 Flesh; 04.01.02.01.02.05 Meat; 12.08.08 Carnal nature, sensual appetites; 16.01.01.04.02.01 Incarnation; 16.02.04.07.04 Communion/eucharist
flæsc and bān 02.04.05 Bodily substance
flæsc and fell 02.04.05 Bodily substance
flæscæt 04.01.01 Eating
flæscbana 14.05.05.01 Capital punishment
flæscbesmitennes 12.08.08.01.02 Unchastity, incontinence
flæsccofa 02.04 Body
flæsccostnung 06.02.06.03.04.01 Temptation
flæsccwellere 14.05.05.01 Capital punishment
flæsccӯping 15.05.01 Goods, stock, merchandise
flæsceht 02.04.05.01 Flesh
flæscen 02.04.05.01 Flesh
(ge)flæsc(en)nes 16.01.01.04.02.01 Incarnation
flæscgebyrd 16.01.01.04.02.01 Incarnation
flæschama 02.04 Body; 16.02.01.13 Evil-doing, transgression, sin
geflæschamod 16.01.01.04.02.01 Incarnation
flæschord 02.04 Body
flæschūs 15.05.01 Goods, stock, merchandise
flæsclic 02.03 Humankind; 02.03.02.03.06 Kinship, relationship; 02.04 Body; 12.08.08 Carnal nature, sensual appetites; 16.02.01.12.05 The world (i.e. unspirituality, worldliness)

flæsclīce 02.03 Humankind; 02.03.02.03.06 Kinship, relationship; 12.08.08 Carnal nature, sensual appetites
flæsclicnes 02.04 Body; 16.01.01.04.02.01 Incarnation
flæscmangere 04.01.02.02.01 To dress animals for food; 15.05.01 Goods, stock, merchandise
flæscmaþu 02.06.09.02.11 Worm
flæscmete 04.01.02.01.02.05 Meat
flæscniming 16.01.01.04.02.01 Incarnation
geflæscod 16.01.01.04.02.01 Incarnation
flæscsand 04.01.02.04 Abundance of food
flæscstrǣt 15.05.01 Goods, stock, merchandise
flæsctāwere 04.01.02.02.01 To dress animals for food; 15.05.01 Goods, stock, merchandise
flæsctōþ 02.04.06.03.02.01 Mouth
flæscþēnung 04.01.02.04 Abundance of food
flæscwyrm 02.06.09.02.11 Worm
flæþ 17.04.04.03 Fleece, pelt
flæþecamb 04.04.03 A spinning-house or chamber
flāh 06.01.07.04.04.03 Deceit, fraud, treachery
flān 13.02.08.04.04.01 An arrow, dart, bolt
flānboga 13.02.08.04.04 A bow
flanc 02.04.03.03.04 Side
flāngeweorc 13.02.08.04.04.01 An arrow, dart, bolt
flānhred 05.11.01.02.01 Swift movement of time
flāniht 05.10.06.03.01 A point, spike, prickle
flānþracu 13.02.03.01 An attack, assault

flasce 04.01.03.05.04.01 A flask, flagon, bottle
flaxfōte 02.06.08.01 Part of bird
flēa 02.06.09.01 Parasite
flēah 02.08.07.02 Disorders of the eye
flēam 11.10.04 Flight; 13.02.05.02 Defeat
flēama 01.01.03.01.01.03 Stream
flēamdōm 11.10.04 Flight
flēamlāst 16.02.01.07 Apostasy
flēan 05.06.06.01 A tearing, laceration
(ge)fleard 12.08.06.01 Error, wrong conduct, erroneous practice
fleardere 12.08.06.01 Error, wrong conduct, erroneous practice
fleardian 12.08.06.01.04 To lead a bad life
fleaþe/fleoþe 02.07.11 Plants/flowers (alphabetical order)
fleaþorwyrt 02.07.11 Plants/flowers (alphabetical order)
flēawyrt 02.07.11 Plants/flowers (alphabetical order)
fleax 04.02.04.03.02.02 Flax; 04.04.04 A thread (of wool, etc.), fibre
flēd 01.01.03.06 Flood
flēde 01.01.03.06 Flood
flēd(e) 01.01.03.01.01.03 Stream
flēding 03.01.16 Liquid, a liquid
flēge 05.12.01.09.03.01.01 Kind of ship
flemisc 02.03.03.06.02 Germany and Low Countries
flēogan 05.12.03.01 Swiftness, velocity; 05.12.05.03.03 To depart, leave, set out; 11.06.06 Turning; 11.10.04 Flight
(ge)flēogan 05.12.01.07 To fly (with wings)
flēoge 02.06.09.02.07 Fly
flēogenda 02.06.08 Bird
flēogende 05.12.01.07 To fly (with wings)
flēogendlic 05.12.01.07 To fly (with wings)
flēogryft 04.04.08.03 A fly-net, mosquito-net
flēohcynn 02.06.09.02.07 Fly
flēohnet 04.04.08.03 A fly-net, mosquito-net
flēohtan 17.04.04 Fibrous materials
flēon 05.11.01.02.01 Swift movement of time; 05.12.02.04 To cast out, drive away; 05.12.05.03.03 To depart, leave, set out; 09.07.03.02 Refusal, denial; 11.06.06 Turning; 12.06.05.01 State of exile, banishment; 14.03.03.09.03 Outlawry
(ge)flēon 05.12.01.07 To fly (with wings); 05.12.05.03.03 To depart, leave, set out; 11.10.04 Flight
flēonde 05.11.01.02.01 Swift movement of time; 05.12.01.07 To fly (with wings)
flēot 01.01.02.01.01.03.02 Inlet in river/sea
flēotan 01.01.03.03 Flow/flowing; 05.12.01.08 To move in/on water; 05.12.01.09 To travel on water
flēotan (of) 04.06.01.10 To separate objects already connected, unmix
flēot(e)/flīete 05.12.01.09.03.01.01 Kind of ship
flēotend 05.12.01.09.03 A voyage
flēotende 05.12.01.08 To move in/on water; 05.12.01.08.01 To swim
flēotham 01.01.02.01.04.01 Marsh, bog, swamp
flēotig 05.12.03.01 Swiftness, velocity
flēotwyrt 02.07.11.01 Seaweed
flēring 03.03.07 A part, division, portion; 04.05.02.09 A storey
geflerod 04.04.07.07 A long outer garment, covering, cloak, etc.

fleswian 11.01 Action, doing, performance
fletgefeoht 12.05.04.01.01 Fighting, a fight
fletræst 04.05.04.05 A bed, bedstead
fletsittend 02.03.03.01 Body of retainers, household; 08.01.02.04.01 Visiting
flett 04.05.02.10 Flooring, a floor; 04.05.03 A dwelling-place, abode, habitation
flettgesteald 15.01 Property
flettpæþ 04.05.02.10 Flooring, a floor
fletwerod 13.02.10.01.02.01 An armed force/band; 13.02.10.01.02.01.01 Military followers (of household)
flēwsa 02.08.08.12 Disease of bowels
flexæcer 04.02.03.02.02.03 Flax land/field
flexgescot 16.02.04.20 Church due/requirement
flexhamm 04.02.03.02.02.03 Flax land/field
flexlīne 17.03.02 Item providing support
flicce 04.01.02.01.02.05.02 Pork
flicorian 05.12.01.07 To fly (with wings)
flīema 11.08.04 Vanity, idleness, frivolity; 11.10.04 Flight; 12.06.05.01 State of exile, banishment; 16.02.01.07 Apostasy
flīeman feorm 14.02 Lawlessness
flīeman (ge)feormian 14.02 Lawlessness
(ge)flīeman 13.02.05.01.01 To overcome, conquer
(ge)flīeman (ūt) 05.12.02.04 To cast out, drive away
geflīeman 04.03 Hunting, the chase
(ge)flīeme 12.06.05.01 State of exile, banishment

flīemena firmþ 14.01.03 Special law, privilege, law for an individual; 14.01.04.03 Rights involving money
flīemig 12.06.05.01 State of exile, banishment
flīeming 12.06.05.01 State of exile, banishment
flīes 02.06.01.06 Skin, hide; 02.06.02.01.08 Sheep; 02.07.03.03.01 Wood (as substance); 17.04.04.03 Fleece, pelt
flīete 04.01.02.01.02.09.05 Cream
fligel 04.02.04.06.14 A flail for threshing corn
flint 01.01.02.02.01 Rock, stone; 01.01.02.02.02.05 Flint; 17.05.01 Fuel, tinder
flinten 08.01.03.09.10 Wrath, sternness, displeasure
flintgrǣg 03.01.14.10 Grey-coated one
(ge)flit 09.07.01 Contention, argument, strife of words; 12.05.03.01 Quarrel, contentiousness, strife; 12.05.04.01 Fighting, contention, warfare, strife
geflit 13.02.02 Battle; 14.03.03 Law, action of the courts; 18.02.03.01.02 Racing
(ge)flītan 09.07.01 Contention, argument, strife of words; 12.05.01 Rivalry, contest; 12.05.03.01 Quarrel, contentiousness, strife; 12.05.04.01 Fighting, contention, warfare, strife; 13.02 War
(ge)flītan on/wiþ 14.03.03.01 Accusation
flitcræft 06.01.03.02 Dialectics, logic
flitcræftlic 06.01.03.02 Dialectics, logic
gefliten 12.05.03.01 Quarrel, contentiousness, strife
flītende 09.07.01 Contention, argument, strife of words
flītere 12.05.03.01 Quarrel, contentiousness, strife

(ge)flitful 12.05.03.01 Quarrel, contentiousness, strife
flitfullic 12.05.03.01 Quarrel, contentiousness, strife
geflitfulnes 12.05.03.01 Quarrel, contentiousness, strife
flitgāra 18.02.03 A spectacle, display
(ge)flitgeorn 12.05.03.01 Quarrel, contentiousness, strife
geflitlīce 11.02.01 Energy, vigour, vigorous action
(ge)flitmǣlum 11.02.01 Energy, vigour, vigorous action
flōc 02.06.06.03.01.01 Flounder, fluke
flōcan 07.04.04.01.01 Clapping (the hands), applause
flocc 02.06 Animal; 12.04.01.01 A company of people, fellowship, society; 13.02.10.01.02.01 An armed force/band
floccmǣlum 03.03.04.01.02.01 A heap, mass, accumulation
flocgian 05.12.01.09 To travel on water
flocrād 13.02.10.01.02.02.02 Branch of army
flōd 01.01.03 Water; 01.01.03.01.01 Moving water; 01.01.03.01.01.01 River; 01.01.03.01.01.05 Torrent; 01.01.03.04 Current, rush of water; 01.01.03.06 Flood; 03.01.16.03 A drop of liquid; 05.06.01 Devastation, laying waste; 08.01.03.06.01 Affliction, misfortune, calamity
flōd tēara 08.01.03.04.02 Shedding of tears
flōdblāc 03.01.14.02 Pallor, absence of colour
flōde 01.01.03.01.01.04 Watercourse/channel; 01.01.03.06 Flood

flōdegesa 06.01.08.06.03 Cause of fear, terror, horror
flōden 01.01.03.01.01.01 River
flōdgrǣg 03.01.14.10 Grey-coated one
flōdhamm 01.01.02.01.01 Tract of land
flōdlic 01.01.03.01.01.01 River
flōdmǣd 04.02.03.04.01.01 Water meadow
flōdweard 01.01.03.01.02.05 Wave
flōdweg 01.01.03.01.02 Sea/ocean
flōdwudu 05.12.01.09.03.01 A ship, boat
flōdwylm 01.01.03.01.02.05 Wave
flōdȳþ 01.01.03.01.02.05 Wave
geflog 02.08.02.01.01 An infectious disease
flogettan 05.12.01.07 To fly (with wings); 05.12.05.05 To shake, quake, wag; 06.02.07.05 Irresolution
flogoþa 04.06.02.06 Poison
flōh 03.03.07 A part, division, portion
flohtenfōte 02.06.08.01 Part of bird
flōr 04.05.02.10 Flooring, a floor
flōrisc 16.02.01.10.02.01 A blessing, invocation of divine favour
flōrstān 04.05.02.10 Flooring, a floor
flot 01.01.03.01.02 Sea/ocean
flota 05.12.01.09.03 A voyage; 05.12.01.09.03.01 A ship, boat; 05.12.01.09.03.03 Piracy; 13.02.10.03 Crew/men of a ship; 13.02.10.03.01 A fleet
floterian 05.12.01.08 To move in/on water; 05.12.05.05 To shake, quake, wag; 05.12.05.05.01 To wave, undulate
floteriende 05.12 To move, be in motion
flothere 05.12.01.09.03.03 Piracy
flotian 05.12.01.09 To travel on water
flotlic 13.02.10.03.01 A fleet

flotmann 05.12.01.09.03 A voyage; 05.12.01.09.03.03 Piracy
flotscip 05.12.01.09.03.01.01 Kind of ship
flotsmeru 04.01.02.01.02.05.05 Fat/suet/lard; 04.06.02.04 Refuse, litter, rubbish
flotweg 01.01.03.01.02 Sea/ocean
flotwyrt 02.07.11.01 Seaweed
flōwan 01.01.03.03 Flow/flowing; 01.01.03.06 Flood; 02.04.06.08.01 Blood; 02.08.08.12 Disease of bowels; 03.01.16 Liquid, a liquid; 03.01.16.01 Moisture; 03.03.04.02.01 Abundance; 12.04.02 A crowding together, assembly
flōwan ūt 01.01.03.03 Flow/flowing
(ge)flōwan 01.01.03.03 Flow/flowing; 05.12.05.03.04.02 To flow out, well up, erupt
geflōwan 01.01.03.06 Flood
flōwende 01.01.03.03 Flow/flowing; 03.01.16 Liquid, a liquid; 03.02.01.01 Decay, corruption, rottenness
flōwendlic 03.01.16 Liquid, a liquid
flōwing 02.04.06.08.01 Blood; 02.08.08.12 Disease of bowels
flōwnes 02.08.08.12 Disease of bowels; 03.01.16 Liquid, a liquid; 05.12.05.03.04.02 To flow out, well up, erupt
flugol 05.11.01.02.01 Swift movement of time; 05.12.03.01 Swiftness, velocity
flyge 05.12.01.07 To fly (with wings)
flygepīl 13.02.08.04.02 A shot, missile, dart, spear, javelin, etc.
flygerēow 08.01.03.09.01 Fierceness
flyht 05.12.01.07 To fly (with wings)
flyhte 04.04.05.06 To sew, stitch
flyhteclāþ 04.04.05.06 To sew, stitch

flyhthwæt 05.12.01.07 To fly (with wings); 05.12.03.01 Swiftness, velocity
flyne 02.08.12.02.05.03 A poultice; 03.01.17 Thickness, viscosity
flȳtme 02.08.12.02.06 Surgical
(ge)fnæd 04.04.09 A fringe, border, hem
fnǣran 02.05.10.15.06 A roar, howl, etc.
fnǣrettan 02.04.06.07.07 To snore
fnæs 04.04.09 A fringe, border, hem
fnǣst 02.04.06.07.03 Breath; 02.04.06.07.04 Breathing; 03.01.09.02.01.04 Smoke
fnǣstian 02.04.06.07.05 To breathe
fnēosung 02.04.06.05.07.02 Mucus, phlegm, rheum
fnesan 02.04.06.07.05 To breathe
gefnesan 02.04.06.05.07.02 Mucus, phlegm, rheum
fnora 02.04.06.05.07.02 Mucus, phlegm, rheum
foca 04.01.02.01.07.04 Cake
focga 04.02.04.03.02.03 Hay
fōda 04.01.02.01 Food/sustenance; 04.01.02.04 Abundance of food; 04.01.02.04.03 Feeding, nourishing; 11.12.02.01 Strengthening, confirmation; 16.02.01.12 Spirituality
fōdder 04.01.02.01 Food/sustenance; 04.01.02.01.04 Animal food, fodder; 04.05.04.03 A box, case, chest, container
fōdderbill 04.02.04.06.12 A scythe, sickle
fōdderbrytta 04.02.05.01.02 To tend, herd
fōddergifu 04.01.02.01 Food/sustenance
fōdderhec 04.02.05.03.02 A byre, stall, sty, shed
fōddornōþ 04.01.02 Means of subsistence

fōddorþegu 04 Consumption of food/drink; 04.01.02.01 Food/sustenance
fōddorwela 04.01.02.04 Abundance of food
fōddurgifa 11.12.02.01 Strengthening, confirmation
fōdnoþ 04.01.02.04 Abundance of food
fōdnōþ 04.01.02 Means of subsistence
fōdrere 04.01.02.04.04.01 Provider/supplier of food
fōd(r)ing 04.02.03.04.02 Pasture/pasturage
gefōg 03.03.06.01 A whole formed by joining; 03.06.03 Congruity, fitness, suitability
fōgclāþ 04.04.05.06 To sew, stitch
gefōgstān 04.05.01.01 Masonry, building in stone
gefol 02.06 Animal
fola 02.06 Animal
folc 02.03.01 People; 02.03.03.01 Body of retainers, household; 02.03.03.02 A race, tribe; 02.03.03.03 A nation, people; 02.03.03.04.01 Country people; 12.01.01.11 The common people; 12.04.02 A crowding together, assembly; 13.02.10.01.02.01 An armed force/band; 13.02.10.01.02.02 Armed forces; 16.02.03.03.05 A layman
folcāgende 02.03.01.01 Male person, man
folcbealo 08.01.03.06 Adversity, affliction
folcbearn 02.03.01.01 Male person, man
folccū 02.06.02.01.03 Cattle
folccūþ 06.01.06.01.01.02 To know, recognize; 07.08 Reputation, fame; 11.05.01 Familiarity
folccwēn 12.01.01.04.01 A royal leader

folccwide 09.06.01.02 A saying, saw, proverb, maxim
folccyning 12.01.01.04.01 A royal leader
folcdryht 12.04.02 A crowding together, assembly
folcegesa 06.01.08.06.02 Great fear, terror, horror
folcfiren 12.08.06.02.05 Misdeed, sin
folcfrēa 12.01.01.04 A leader, ruler
folcfrēo 12.01.01.10 Freedom, being free
folcgedrēfnes 08.01.03.06 Adversity, affliction
folcgefeoht 13.02 War; 13.02.02 Battle
folc(ge)mōt 12.02.02 An assembly, meeting
folcgerēfa 12.02.02 An assembly, meeting
folcgesīþ 12.01.01.04 A leader, ruler
folcgestealla 12.04.01 A fellow, companion, associate, comrade
folcgestrēon 15.01.03 Treasure, riches, wealth
folcgetæl 03.03.03 Number
folcgetrum 13.02.10.01.02.02 Armed forces
folcgewinn 13.02 War
folcherpaþ 05.12.01.03.01.03 A highway
folcisc 02.03.03.03 A nation, people; 09.03.01 Particular languages; 12.01.01.11 The common people; 16.02.03.02 A cleric, clergyman (general)
folclagu 14.01 Law, body of rules
folcland 12.06 A province, country, territory; 15.01.01 Landed property
folclār 16.02.04.03.02 Parts of service; 16.02.04.10 Preaching
folclēasung 14.02.01.01 Types of crime
folclic 02.03.03.03 A nation, people; 03.04.03 Generality; 09.03.01 Particular languages; 09.05.05.01

Showing, manifestation, display; 12.01.01.11 The common people; 12.06.03 A site, settlement
folcmægen 02.03.03.03 A nation, people
folcmǣgþ 02.03.03.03 A nation, people
folcmǣre 07.08 Reputation, fame
folcnēd 06.02.04.01 Want, need
folcrǣd 11.07.03 Use, advantage, profit
folcrǣden 02.03.03.03 A nation, people; 14.01 Law, body of rules
folcriht 14.01 Law, body of rules; 14.01.02 A law, statute; 15.01 Property
folcsǣl 04.05.03.02.01 A building, house, hall, palace, etc.
folcscearu 02.03.03.03 A nation, people; 15.01.01 Landed property
folcsceaþa 12.08.06.02.02 A bad man, inhuman person
folcscipe 02.03.03.03 A nation, people
folcslite 12.01.01.12.03 Rebellion, sedition
folcsōþ 06.01.07 Truth, conformity with absolute standard
folcstede 04.05.03 A dwelling-place, abode, habitation; 13.02.02 Battle
folcstōw 12.06.02.01.01 Country (not town)
folcswēot 12.04.02 A crowding together, assembly
folctalu 02.03.02.03 Ancestry, descent
folctoga 12.01.01.04 A leader, ruler; 16.02.03.02.07 A priest, cleric
folctruma 02.03.03.03 A nation, people
folcwelig 12.06.03 A site, settlement
folcwer 02.03.01.01 Male person, man
folcwiga 13.02.10.01 A man, warrior
folcwita 12.02.02.02 A counsellor, advisor
folcwōh 14.02.01 An offence

foldærn 02.02.05.01.01 A grave, burial place, sepulchre; 02.04 Body
foldbold 04.05.03.02.01 A building, house, hall, palace, etc.
foldbūend 02.03.03.03.01 A native people
foldbūende 02.03.01 People
folde 01 Earth, world; 01.01.02 Land; 01.01.02.01 Ground; 01.01.02.02.02.02 Clay, loam; 12.06 A province, country, territory
foldgræf 02.02.05.01.01 A grave, burial place, sepulchre
foldhrērende 05.12.01.01 To go on a journey/expedition, travel
foldræst 02.02.05.01.01 A grave, burial place, sepulchre
foldwæstm 02.07.01.01 Fruit of the earth
foldwang 01 Earth, world
foldweg 01 Earth, world; 05.12.01.03.01 A means of access
foldwela 15.01.03 Treasure, riches, wealth
foldwylm 01.01.03.01.01.03 Stream
folgere 05.11.07.04.02.01 Succession; 06.01.06.02.03.02 Discipleship; 12.01.01.07 A follower
folgian 05.11.07.04.02 (Of time) later/latter; 05.12.05.10 To go behind, follow; 11.02 Occupation, activity, business; 12.01.01.12.01 Obedience, service; 12.04.01.02 A fellow traveller, companion; 16.02.03.03 A religious
(ge)folgian 05.02 State, condition; 05.12.05.10 To go behind, follow; 06.01.06.02.03.03 To study, apply oneself to learning; 12.01.01.07 A follower
gefolgian 05.12.05.02.03 To arrive

folgoþ 05.02.01.01 The course of human affairs; 12.01.01 Authority; 12.01.01.08 Service; 12.06.02 District, province
folm 02.04.03.04.01.01 Hand
folm(e) 02.04.03.04.01.01 Hand
fōn 05.03.02 Event, issue, result
fōn on 09.06 To take matter for discourse; 10.04 To take; 13.02.03.01 An attack, assault
fōn on/tō 11.01.02 An undertaking
fōn (on) 05.11.10.01 A beginning
fōn ongēan 12.05.02 Hostility, contention, opposition
fōn tō 11.10.02 Watching, guard, watch; 12.02 A public office; 17.02.02 An office, function, employment; 09.06 To take matter for discourse; 10.01.01.01 Receiving, gaining, getting; 11.05 Natural/proper way/manner/mode of action
fōn (tō) 11.01.02 An undertaking
fōn tō friþe 13.01.01.01 Cessation of hostilities
fōn tō rīce 12.01.01.02 Seat of authority
fōn tō sibbe 13.01.01.01 Cessation of hostilities
fōn tōgædere 12.04 Fellowship, union, association; 13.02.02 Battle
fōn tōgēanes 13.02.03.01 An attack, assault
fōn wiþ 13.02 War
fōn ymb 09.06 To take matter for discourse
(ge)fōn 04.03 Hunting, the chase; 10.01.02 Acquisition; 10.04 To take; 10.04.02 To grasp, take hold of; 14.05.08 Captivity
(ge)fōn tō 10.04 To take
gefōn 05.12.02.01 To fetch, bring, bear, conduct; 06.01.07.04.02.01 Deception, deceit, snare, wile; 10.01.01.01 Receiving, gaining, getting; 10.04.02.02 To seize, take, grasp, lay hold on; 13.02.05.01.02 To gain by fighting
gefōn on 10.04.02 To grasp, take hold of
fonfȳr 03.01.09.02.01 Fire, burning
for ... hand 12.02.01 A substitute, representative
for ... intingan 11.12.02 Aid, help, succour
for ... lufum 11.12.02 Aid, help, succour
for ... þingum 11.12.02 Aid, help, succour
for ... willan 11.12.02 Aid, help, succour
for ān 03.04.01 Singularity, peculiarity
for hwon 05.03.01 A cause (of anything)
for hwȳ 05.03.01 A cause (of anything)
for lange 05.11.07.03 Former times, days of old
for longunge 08.01.03 Bad feeling, sadness
for nāuht dōn 07.03.03.02 To degrade, debase
for nīede 06.02.04 Necessity, inevitability
for þǣm 05.03.01 A cause (of anything)
for þǣm (þe) 05.03.01 A cause (of anything)
for þisum þingum 05.03.01.03 Reason, cause
for þon 05.03.01 A cause (of anything)
for þon (þe) 05.03.01 A cause (of anything)
for þȳ 05.03.01 A cause (of anything); 05.03.01.03 Reason, cause
for þȳ ... for þǣm 05.03.01.03 Reason, cause
for þȳ ... þȳ 05.03.01.03 Reason, cause

for þȳ (þe) 05.03.01 A cause (of anything)
fōr 02.06.02.01.07 Pig, swine; 05.12.01 To go, progress, travel (usually on land); 05.12.01.01 To go on a journey/expedition, travel; 13.02.01 A military expedition
foran 02.05.09.09 Visible; 03.03.05.01.01 Principal/chief (of its class or type); 05.10.04.03 Presence; 05.10.05.04.09.01 Front; 05.11.07.03.02 Earlier, antecedent
foran ongēan 12.05.02 Hostility, contention, opposition
foran tō 05.11.07.03.02 Earlier, antecedent
foranbodig 02.04.03.03.05 Chest, breast, bosom
foranbrēost/forebrēost 02.04.03.03.05 Chest, breast, bosom
forandæg 05.11.04.01 Day (not night)
forane 05.11.07.03.02 Earlier, antecedent
foran(e) 05.10.05.04.09.01 Front
foran(e) (on)gēan 05.10.05.04.09.04 Opposite (av)
forane tōgēanes 12.05.02 Hostility, contention, opposition
foranhēafod 02.04.03.01.03.01 Forehead
foranlencten 05.11.03.01.02.01 Spring
foranniht 05.11.04.02 Night, night time
forannihtsang 16.02.04.05.09 The hour or service of Compline
forbærnan 03.01.09.02.01 Fire, burning
forbærnednes 02.08.03.02 Itch, irritation
forbærning 02.08.05 Inflammation; 03.01.09.02.01 Fire, burning
fōrbed 05.12.01.06 Vehicle
forbelgan 08.01.03.05.02 Anger
forbēn 16.02.04.08 Prayer

forbēodan 11.11.03 Impeding of progress, prevention; 12.03.06 Prohibition; 12.05.06.01 Restraint, check, curb, control
forbēodendlic 09.03.02.02.01.03 An adverb
forbeornan 03.01.09.02.01 Fire, burning
forberan 08.01.03.07.03 Suffering, torment, pain; 08.01.03.08 Patience; 10.02 Want, lack; 11.06.02 Suffering (not acting); 11.06.04 Abstention, abstaining from
forberendlīce 08.01.03.08 Patience
forberstan 05.06.03 A dashing together, breaking, shattering; 05.07 Ending of existence, end of world; 10.03.08.01 Overliberality, waste of money; 14.03.03 Law, action of the courts
forbīgan 07.09.02 Disgrace, shaming, humiliation
forbindan 05.05.03 Binding, fastening
forbītan 05.06.06.01 A tearing, laceration
forblāwan 01.03.01.05 Wind
forblāwen 02.08.05.01 Swelling
forblindian 02.08.07.02.01 Defective vision
forbod 12.03.06 Prohibition
forboden 12.03.06 Prohibition
forboren 16.01.04.02 Sorcery involving drugs or potions
forbrecan 05.06 Destruction, dissolution, loss, breaking; 05.06.03 A dashing together, breaking, shattering; 12.05.06.02 Oppression; 12.07.02.02.01 To break a promise, vow, etc.
forbregdan 05.06.01 Devastation, laying waste; 05.06.04 Damage, injury, defect, hurt, loss; 05.10.05.04.12 The condition of being covered; 05.13.01 Transformation, taking another shape

955

forbrītan 05.06.03 A dashing together, breaking, shattering
forbrocen 03.02.01.02 Decay from age
forbrȳtan 05.06.01 Devastation, laying waste
forbrȳtednes 08.01.03.02.01 Compunction, remorse, contrition
forbrȳtennes 08.01.03.02.01 Compunction, remorse, contrition
forbrȳtnes 08.01.03.02.01 Compunction, remorse, contrition
forbūgan 05.12.02.08 To give a different direction to, turn; 05.12.05.03.02 To keep clear of, stand off from, withdraw; 05.12.05.03.03 To depart, leave, set out; 07.05 Disrespect, irreverence; 11.06.01 Neglect; 11.06.03 Failing, failure; 11.06.04 Abstention, abstaining from; 11.06.06 Turning; 12.01.01.12.02 Disobedience; 12.05.07 Casting out, rejection
forbyrd 06.02.07.01 Strength, fortitude; 08.01.03.08 Patience; 11.06.04 Abstention, abstaining from
forbyrdian 06.01.08.01 Expectation, waiting
forbyrdig 08.01.03.08 Patience
forcampian 13.02.02.01 Single combat
force 17.03.07 Tools for digging/grasping/pulling
forcēap 15.05 Trade, traffic, commerce
forcel 04.02.04.06.02 A fork; 17.03.07 Tools for digging/grasping/pulling
forceorfan 05.06.01 Devastation, laying waste; 05.06.02 Cleaving, splitting, cutting
forcēowan 05.06.06.01 A tearing, laceration

forcierran 05.12.05 To move and change direction, turn; 11.06.06 Turning; 12.08.06.01.04.01 To mislead, seduce, lead astray
forcierred 12.08.06.01.02 Lacking moral good
forcierrednes 06.02.07.04.02 Perversity; 11.06.06 Turning
forcierring 11.06.06 Turning
forcilled 03.01.11 Coldness, coolness
forcinnan 05.06 Destruction, dissolution, loss, breaking
forcippian 05.06.02 Cleaving, splitting, cutting
forclæman 04.05.01.03 Gypsum, chalk
forclingan 03.01.18 Dryness (not wetness)
forclungen 02.07.01 To grow; 03.01.18 Dryness (not wetness)
forclyccan ēaran 02.05.10 Faculty of hearing
forclȳsan 02.08.07.03.01 Deafness
forcnēow 02.01.03.03.04 Offspring, race, breed, family, children
forcorfen 05.06.02 Cleaving, splitting, cutting
forcostian 06.02.06.03.04.01 Temptation
forcrafian 06.02.04.01 Want, need
forcunnian 06.02.06.03.04.01 Temptation
forcūþ 04.06.02.01 Dirty, unclean; 07.03.03.01 Empty, useless, worthless; 07.03.05 Infamy, shame, wickedness; 10.03.09.01 Parsimony, niggardliness
forcūþe 07.03.05 Infamy, shame, wickedness
forcūþlic 07.03.03.01 Empty, useless, worthless; 07.09.03 Infamy, ignominy, shame
forcūþlīce 07.05.02 Contempt; 07.09.03 Infamy, ignominy, shame

forcweþan 07.05.01 Censure, reproof, rebuke; 07.05.03.03.02 To reproach, revile, abuse; 09.07.03.02 Refusal, denial; 11.06.06 Turning; 12.05.07 Casting out, rejection

forcwolstan 04 Consumption of food/drink

forcwȳsan 05.12.05.05 To shake, quake, wag

forcȳþan 07.05.01 Censure, reproof, rebuke

ford 05.12.01.03.03 A fordable place

fordǣlan 15.02.04 Spending, disbursement

fordelfan 05.06.08 A plucking, taking away

fordēman 07 Judgement, forming of opinion; 07.05 Disrespect, irreverence; 14.03.03.09 A sentence, judgement, ruling; 14.03.03.09.01 Unfavourable judgement, condemnation; 14.05.04 A penalty, punishment; 16.01.05.01 Damnation, perdition, reprobation

fordēmed 16.01.05.02.02 Other terms for devils

fordēmedlic 14.03.03.09.01 Unfavourable judgement, condemnation

fordēmedlīce 16.02.04.14.02.01 Cursing, imprecation

fordēmednes 14.03.03.09.01 Unfavourable judgement, condemnation; 16.01.05.01 Damnation, perdition, reprobation

fordēmend 14.03.03.01 Accusation

fordēming 14.05.04 A penalty, punishment

fordemman 05.10.05.04.15 Closure, being closed

fordēn 16.02.01.13.02 Evil, reprobate, damned

fordīcian 11.11.02 A hindrance

fordilemengan 06.01.07.04.04.02 Pretence, feigning, dissimulation

fordīlgian 02.02.04.03 To kill, slay; 05.06 Destruction, dissolution, loss, breaking; 11.06.01 Neglect

fordimmian 02.08.07.02.01 Defective vision; 03.01.13.02 A growing dark, darkening; 06.01.07.05 Error, being astray

fordōn 02.02.04 Killing, violent death, destruction; 02.02.04.03 To kill, slay; 05.06 Destruction, dissolution, loss, breaking; 16.01.05.01 Damnation, perdition, reprobation; 16.01.05.02.02 Other terms for devils; 16.02.01.13.02 Evil, reprobate, damned

fordrǣfan 12.05.06.03 Necessity, constraint

fordrencan 04.01.03.02 To drink heavily, get drunk

fordrīfan 02.05.03.02 Weariness; 05.12.02.04 To cast out, drive away; 05.12.02.06.01 To push, drive; 05.12.05.03.04 To come/go out from

fordrifen 05.12.02.04 To cast out, drive away; 12.06.05.01 State of exile, banishment

fordrifnes 12.05 Contradiction, opposition

fordrūgian 03.01.18 Dryness (not wetness)

fordruncen 04.01.03.02 To drink heavily, get drunk

fordruncnian 04.01.03.02 To drink heavily, get drunk

fordwer 01.01.03.01.03.02 Weir

fordwilman 06.01.07.04.01 Deception, a leading astray

fordwīnan 02.05.09.14 To vanish, disappear; 05.09.05 Ceasing, decline, fall off; 06.01.04.03.01 Forgetfulness, oblivion

fordyslic 06.01.05.03.02 Foolish, silly, stupid

fordytt 05.10.05.04.15 Closure, being closed

fordyttan 05.10.05.04.15 Closure, being closed

fore 05.03.01 A cause (of anything); 05.10.04.03 Presence; 05.10.05.04.09.01 Front; 05.11.07.03.02 Earlier, antecedent; 05.13.04 Exchange, commutation; 07.08.02 Honour, glory; 11.07.04 Superiority, pre-eminence, primacy; 11.12.02 Aid, help, succour

forealdian 02.01.04.03 Aging, growing old; 03.02.01.01 Decay, corruption, rottenness; 03.02.01.02 Decay from age

forealdod 02.01.04.03 Aging, growing old; 03.02.01.02 Decay from age

forealdung 02.01.04.03 Aging, growing old

foreāstreccan 05.06.01 Devastation, laying waste

foreāþ 14.03.03.04 Oath-swearing

foreāþe 11.12 Easiness

foreāþelic 11.12 Easiness

forebēacen 06.01.08.04.01 Premonition, prophecy

forebegān 11.11.03 Impeding of progress, prevention

foreberan 07.01.01.02 To prefer

forebētan 14.03.03.09.02 Atonement

forebīcnung 06.01.08.04.01 Premonition, prophecy

forebiscop 16.02.03.02.01 A high priest, chief bishop, etc. (general)

forebisegian 06.01.01.01.01.01 Consideration, rumination

forebōc 05.12.01.01 To go on a journey/expedition, travel

forebod 16.02.04.10 Preaching

foreboda 09.06.02.01.06.01 A messenger

forebodere 09.06.02.01.06.01 A messenger

forebodian 09.06.02.01.05 Proclamation, spreading abroad; 16.02.04.10 Preaching

forebodung 16.02.04.10 Preaching

forebrǣdan 03.01.13.03 Overshadowing

foreburh 04.05.02.12.02 A vestibule, entrance, courtyard; 13.02.06.01 Stronghold, fort/fortified town

forebȳsen 03.06.03.02 Order, decorum, discretion

forecennednes 02.01.03.03.04 Offspring, race, breed, family, children

foreceorfan 05.06.02 Cleaving, splitting, cutting

foreceorfend 02.04.06.03.02.01.01 Tooth/teeth

forecēosan 07.01.01 Choice, election

foreclipian 09.06.02.01.05 Proclamation, spreading abroad

forecnēowres 02.01.03.03.04 Offspring, race, breed, family, children

forecnyll 02.05.10.13.01.01 Stroke/sound of a bell

forecostian 16.02.04.14 Sacrilege

forecostung 16.02.04.14 Sacrilege

forecuman 05.03.02 Event, issue, result; 05.06 Destruction, dissolution, loss, breaking; 05.11.07.03.02.01 A precursor, one who goes before; 05.12.05.03.04 To come/go out from; 05.12.05.09 To go forward, proceed;

11.03.02 Advancement, progress; 11.11.02 A hindrance
forecweden 05.11.07.03.02.02 The aforesaid
forecweþan 06.01.08.04.01 Premonition, prophecy; 09.06.01 To relate, recount, tell; 16.02.04.10 Preaching
forecwide 06.01.08.04.01 Premonition, prophecy; 09.03.07.07.02.01.01 A heading, title, superscription
forecyme 05.12.05.09 To go forward, proceed
forecymen 02.05.03.02 Weariness
forecynrēd 02.01.03.03.04 Offspring, race, breed, family, children
forecynren 02.01.03.03.04 Offspring, race, breed, family, children
forecȳþan 06.01.08.04.01 Premonition, prophecy; 09.06.02.01 To tell, make known, declare, relate, announce
foredēman 07 Judgement, forming of opinion
foreduru 04.05.02.12.02 A vestibule, entrance, courtyard
foredyre 04.05.02.12.02 A vestibule, entrance, courtyard
foredyrstig 06.02.07.06.02.03 Presumption
foreealdian 05.11.10.02 End, completion
forefeax 02.04.04.03.03 Hair of head
forefengnes 02.07.03.04 A wood, trees
forefeohtend 13.02.04 Defence, guard, protection
foreferan 05.12.05.08 To go before, precede
for(e)flēon (fram) 11.10.04 Flight
forefōn 10.04.02.02 To seize, take, grasp, lay hold on
forefrēfrend 12.02.02.03 Terms for classical world

foregān 05.10.06.03 Projection, head, extremity (of anything)
foregangan 05.12.05.08 To go before, precede; 11.07.04 Superiority, pre-eminence, primacy
foregangende 05.11.07.03.02 Earlier, antecedent
foregearwung 11.01.03 Preparation
foregebiddan 13.01.03 Intercession, pleading, mediation
foregeblind 02.08.07.02.01 Defective vision
fore(ge)blindan 03.01.13.01 Not shining, dim
foregecēosan 07.01.01 Choice, election
fore(ge)gān 05.12.05.08 To go before, precede
foregehāt 12.07.02.01.01 A promise
foregehātan 12.03.03 A command, bidding, order
fore(ge)hātan 12.07.02.01.01 A promise
foregelēoran 05.07 Ending of existence, end of world
foregenga 05.11.07.03.02.01 A precursor, one who goes before; 05.12.05.08 To go before, precede; 12.01.01.04.02 A lord, master; 12.01.01.08.01 A servant, attendant
foregengel 05.11.07.03.02.01 A precursor, one who goes before; 05.12.05.08 To go before, precede
fore(ge)scēawung 06.01.08.04 Foreseeing
foregesecgan 05.04 Fate, lot, fortune, destiny
fore(ge)sellan 15.02.04 Spending, disbursement
foregetihtged 05.04 Fate, lot, fortune, destiny
foregeþīstrod 08.01.03.01 Despondency

fore(ge)þýstred 03.01.13 Darkness, obscurity
fore(ge)þýstrian 03.01.13.02 A growing dark, darkening
foregewīs 06.01.08.04 Foreseeing
foregiedd 09.06.01.02 A saying, saw, proverb, maxim
foregīmnes 02.05.09.05 To watch, observe, survey
foregīsl 13.02.05.01.02.01 State of being a hostage
foreglēaw 06.01.05.02.01.01 Sagacity; 06.01.08.04 Foreseeing; 06.01.08.04.01 Premonition, prophecy
foreglēawlīce 06.01.05.02.01.01.02 Prudence, forethought
forehēafod 02.04.03.01.03.01 Forehead
forehradian 05.12.03.01.02 Haste, hurry
forehūs 04.05.02.12.02 A vestibule, entrance, courtyard
foreiernan 05.12.03.01 Swiftness, velocity
foreiernend 05.12.05.08 To go before, precede
foreiernere 05.11.07.03.02.01 A precursor, one who goes before
forelǣdan 05.12.05.08.01 To go before and guide
forelǣrend 06.01.06.02.03.04.02 A teacher
forelǣtan 12.03.06 Prohibition
forelār 16.02.04.10 Preaching
forelāttēow 12.01.01.04 A leader, ruler
forelcian 05.11.08.01.03.01 Delay
forelēoran 05.12.05.07.01 To pass by; 05.12.05.08 To go before, precede
forelocc 02.04.04.03.03 Hair of head
foremǣre 07.08.09 Renown, fame, glory
foremǣrlic 07.08.01 Nobility (of character, rank, etc.)
foremǣrnes 07.08.09 Renown, fame, glory
foremanian 06.01.08.04 Foreseeing
for(e)manig 03.03.04.01.02 A great number, multitude
foremearcod 05.11.07.03.02.02 The aforesaid
foremearcung 09.03.07.07.02.01.01 A heading, title, superscription
foremihtig 12 Power, might
foremihtiglic 05.08 Strength
foremunt 01.01.02.01.01.03.01 Promontory, headland, cape
forenama 09.06.02.01.07 A name, appellation
forenemned 05.11.07.03.02.02 The aforesaid
forenyme 11.01.02 An undertaking
foreonfong 11.01.02 An undertaking
forerīm 09.03.07.07.02.01.02 A prologue, preface
forerynel 05.11.07.03.02.01 A precursor, one who goes before; 05.12.05.08 To go before, precede
foresacan 12.03.06 Prohibition
foresǣd 05.11.07.03.02.02 The aforesaid
foresǣgdnes 09.03.07.07.02.01.02 A prologue, preface
foresaga 09.03.07.07.02.01.02 A prologue, preface; 09.04.03.01 A translation
forescēawere 16.01.01.02.07 Divine providence
forescēawian 06.01.01.01 Thinking about, minding, heeding; 06.01.08.04 Foreseeing; 10.03.04 Provision, supply; 16.01.01.02.07 Divine providence
forescēawodlīce 06.01.08.04 Foreseeing

forescēawung 06.01.01.01 Thinking about, minding, heeding; 06.01.08.04 Foreseeing; 16.01.01.02.07 Divine providence
for(e)scending 05.06 Destruction, dissolution, loss, breaking
forescieldnes 11.10.01 Protection, safekeeping
forescynian 11.06.06 Turning
forescyttels 05.10.05.04.15.01 A bar, bolt
forescywa 03.01.13.03 Overshadowing
forescywung 03.01.13.03 Overshadowing
foresēcan 14.03.03 Law, action of the courts
foresecgan 05.11.07.03.02.02 The aforesaid; 06.01.08.04 Foreseeing; 06.01.08.04.01 Premonition, prophecy; 09.06.02.01.05 Proclamation, spreading abroad; 12.03.03 A command, bidding, order; 16.02.04.10 Preaching
foreseld 07.08.04 An ornament, honour, glory
foresendan 05.12.02.03 To send
foresēon 06.01.08.04 Foreseeing; 10.03.04 Provision, supply
foresēond 10.03.04 Provision, supply
foresēones 16.01.01.02.07 Divine providence
foreset 05.10.05.04.09.01.02 Front, beginning
foresetnes 06.02.06.02 A proposal, proposition, suggestion; 09.03.02.02.01.05 Minor parts of speech, etc.; 17.02.03 A task, service, duty
foresettan 05.10.05.04.09.01.01 Head, front (position); 06.02.06.02 A proposal, proposition, suggestion; 07.01.01.02 To prefer

foreset(ted)nes 09.01.01 A speech, what is said, words
foresettendlic 09.03.02.02.01.05 Minor parts of speech, etc.
foresingend 16.02.03.02.13 A church singer, singer in choir
foresittan 09.05.05.01 Showing, manifestation, display; 12.01.01.02 Seat of authority
foresmēagan 06.01.01.01.01.02 Forethought, consideration
foresnotor 06.01.05.02.01.01 Sagacity
foresōþscip 06.01.07 Truth, conformity with absolute standard
forespræc 09.03.07.07.02.01.02 A prologue, preface; 09.03.07.07.02.01.03 Contents so far; 09.07.04.01 Confirmation, agreement; 12.03.04.02 Speech on behalf of, advocacy; 12.07.03.02 An excuse; 14.03.02 A legislator; 14.04 Making of terms, agreement, convention; 16.02.04.07.01 Baptism, baptizing (and anointing)
forespreca 13.01.03 Intercession, pleading, mediation
foresp(r)eca 14.03.02 A legislator
forespreca 16.02.04.07.01 Baptism, baptizing (and anointing)
foresprecan 13.01.03 Intercession, pleading, mediation
foresprecen 05.11.07.03.02.02 The aforesaid
forestæppan 05.12.05.02 To go/travel towards, come, approach; 05.12.05.08 To go before, precede; 11.11.03 Impeding of progress, prevention
forestæppend 05.11.07.03.02.01 A precursor, one who goes before; 05.12.05.08 To go before, precede

forestæppende 05.12.05.08 To go before, precede
forestæppung 05.11.08.01.02.01 Anticipation
forestandan 11.03.02 Advancement, progress
forestandend 12.03 Direction, guidance
forestapul 05.12.05.08 To go before, precede
foresteall 04.02.01 Farmstead; 11.11.03 Impeding of progress, prevention; 12.05.05 Resistance, repulsing; 13.02.03.01 An attack, assault; 14.05.04.01 A fine
forestemman 11.11.02 A hindrance; 12.03.06 Prohibition
forestēora 05.12.01.09.03 A voyage
forestīgan 11.03.02 Advancement, progress
forestig(e) 04.05.02.12.02 A vestibule, entrance, courtyard
forestiht 05.04 Fate, lot, fortune, destiny
forestihtian 05.04 Fate, lot, fortune, destiny
forestihtung 05.04 Fate, lot, fortune, destiny
foreswerian 14.03.03.07 Security, pledge, bail
foretācn 06.01.08.04.01 Premonition, prophecy
foretācnian 06.01.08.04.01 Premonition, prophecy
foreteohhian 05.04 Fate, lot, fortune, destiny
foreteohhung 05.04 Fate, lot, fortune, destiny
foretēon 05.04 Fate, lot, fortune, destiny
foretēþ 02.04.06.03.02.01.01 Tooth/teeth
foretīge 04.05.02.12.02 A vestibule, entrance, courtyard

foretimbrigende 11.11.02 A hindrance
foretrymman 14.03.03.03 Witness, testimony, attestation
foretyhtan 06.02.07.06.01 Emboldening, encouragement
foretȳned 11.11.02 A hindrance
foreþanc 06.01 The head (as seat of thought); 06.01.01.01.01.02 Forethought, consideration; 06.01.08.04 Foreseeing
foreþancful 06.01.05.02.01.01.02 Prudence, forethought
foreþanclic 11.02.03 Forethought, care
foreþanclīce 11.02.03 Forethought, care
foreþancol 06.01.05.02.01.01.02 Prudence, forethought
foreþancolnes 06.01.05.02.01.01.02 Prudence, forethought
foreþencan 06.01.01.01.01.02 Forethought, consideration
foreþēon 11.03.02 Advancement, progress
foreþingere 13.01.03 Intercession, pleading, mediation
foreþingian 13.01.03 Intercession, pleading, mediation; 14.03.03 Law, action of the courts
foreþingiend 13.01.03 Intercession, pleading, mediation
foreþingrǣden 13.01.03 Intercession, pleading, mediation
foreþingung 13.01.03 Intercession, pleading, mediation
forewarenian 06.01.08.04 Foreseeing
forewarnian 06.01.08.04 Foreseeing
foreweall 13.02.06.01 Stronghold, fort/fortified town
foreweard 05.10.05.04.09.01 Front; 05.11.04.01 Day (not night); 05.12.05.08 To go before, precede;

09.03.07.07.02.01.02 A prologue, preface; 14.04 Making of terms, agreement, convention; 14.04.02 A stipulation
foreweard hēafod 02.04.03.01.03.01 Forehead
foreweardnes 05.10.05.04.09.01.02 Front, beginning
forewesan 12.01.01.01 Rule, domination, direction
forewīs 06.01.08.04 Foreseeing
forewitan 06.01.08.04 Foreseeing
forewītegian 06.01.08.04.01 Premonition, prophecy
forewītegung 06.01.08.04.01 Premonition, prophecy
forewitig 06.01.05.02.01.01 Sagacity; 06.01.08.04 Foreseeing; 06.01.08.04.01 Premonition, prophecy
forewitol 06.01.08.04 Foreseeing
forewittiendlic 06.01.08.04.01 Premonition, prophecy
for(e)word 14.04.02 A stipulation
foreworden 05.04 Fate, lot, fortune, destiny
geforewrit 09.03.07.07.02.01.02 A prologue, preface
forewriten 05.11.07.03.02.02 The aforesaid
forewritennes 12.06.05.01 State of exile, banishment
forewyrcend 12.01.01.08.01 A servant, attendant
forewyrd 14.04 Making of terms, agreement, convention; 14.04.02 A stipulation
(ge)forewyrdan 14.04.04 An agreement, arrangement of dispute
forfæger 07.10 Beauty, fairness

forfang 14.03.03.02 A search for stolen property
forfangfeoh 14.03.03.02 A search for stolen property
forfaran 02.02.03 To die, perish; 02.02.04.03 To kill, slay; 13.02.03.01.02 To beset, surround
forfaren 05.06 Destruction, dissolution, loss, breaking
forfeallan 05.06.03 A dashing together, breaking, shattering
forfēran 02.02.03 To die, perish
forferian 02.02.04.04 Manslaughter, homicide
forflēon 11.06.04 Abstention, abstaining from; 11.06.06 Turning; 11.10.04 Flight
forflȳgan 05.12.02.04 To cast out, drive away; 05.12.05.03.03 To depart, leave, set out
forfōn 10.04.02 To grasp, take hold of; 10.04.02.02 To seize, take, grasp, lay hold on; 14.05.04 A penalty, punishment; 14.05.08 Captivity
forfōn (forane) 11.11.03 Impeding of progress, prevention
forfyllan 11.11.02 A hindrance
forfyrht 06.01.08.06.02 Great fear, terror, horror
forgǣgan 11.03.02 Advancement, progress; 11.06.01 Neglect
forgǣgednes 12.08.06.02.05.01 Transgression, trespass
forgǣgend 12.08.06.02.05.02 A sinner, transgressor
forgǣgung 12.08.06.02.05.01 Transgression, trespass
forgǣlan 11.06.06 Turning
forgān 05.07 Ending of existence, end of world; 05.12.05.07 To go beyond,

pass; 10.02 Want, lack; 11.06.04 Abstention, abstaining from
forgangan 11.06.04 Abstention, abstaining from
forgeare 09.04.03 Exposition, making clear by explanation
forgebind 02.08.08.12 Disease of bowels
forgeearnung 07.02.04.01 Excellence, virtue, goodness
forgenge 11.11 Difficulty
forgeorne 06.01.01.02 Care, attention, observation
forgiefan 05.03.01 A cause (of anything); 08.01.02.06.02 Forgiveness, remission, clemency; 10.03 Giving; 10.03.03 Granting; 10.03.04.01 Restitution, making good, repayment; 10.03.05 Recompense, reward; 12.03.05 Permission; 12.09.01 Pledging, betrothal; 14.01.03.02 Freedom from punishment or fine; 16.02.04.07.02.02 Absolution, forgiveness, remission
forgiefednes 16.02.04.07.02.02 Absolution, forgiveness, remission
forgiefen 05.10.04 Place, room; 08.01.02.01.02.01 Mildness, leniency, indulgence; 10.03 Giving; 10.03.07 Distribution; 11.05 Natural/proper way/manner/mode of action; 12.09 Marriage, state of marriage; 16.02.04.07.02.02 Absolution, forgiveness, remission
forgiefnes 08.01.02.01.02.01 Mildness, leniency, indulgence; 08.01.02.06.02 Forgiveness, remission, clemency; 11.10.03 Salvation/deliverance from; 12.08.07.01 Laxity, indulgence; 14.01.03.02 Freedom from punishment or fine; 16.02.04.07.02.02 Absolution, forgiveness, remission
forgieldan 10.02.01.01 Loss, forfeiture; 10.03.04.01 Restitution, making good, repayment; 10.03.05 Recompense, reward; 11.01.05 Accomplishment, fulfilment; 11.10.03 Salvation/deliverance from; 14.03.03.09.02 Atonement
forgīeman 07.05 Disrespect, irreverence; 11.06.01 Neglect; 11.06.01.01 Negligence, carelessness, heedlessness
forgīemelēasian 11.06.01.01 Negligence, carelessness, heedlessness
forgietan 06.01.04.03 Forgetfulness
forgifend 10.03.03 Granting
forgifendlic 09.03.02.03.01.01.01 Case
forgifenlic 12.07.03.02 An excuse
forgifestre 10.03 Giving
forgifung 12.09.01 Pledging, betrothal
forgītan 05.06 Destruction, dissolution, loss, breaking
forgitel 06.01.04.03 Forgetfulness
forgitelian 06.01.04.03 Forgetfulness
forgitelnes 06.01.04.03 Forgetfulness
forgiten 06.01.04.03 Forgetfulness
forgiting 06.01.04.03 Forgetfulness
forglendred 04.01.01.04 Gluttony, overeating, greediness
forglendrian 05.06.01 Devastation, laying waste
forgnagan 04.01.01.01 Chewing
forgnīdan 05.06 Destruction, dissolution, loss, breaking; 05.06.01 Devastation, laying waste; 05.06.03 A dashing together, breaking, shattering; 05.06.08 A plucking, taking away
forgniden 07.07 Humility; 08.01.03.02.01 Compunction, remorse, contrition; 16.02.04.07.02.01 Penitence

forgnidennes 08.01.03.02.01 Compunction, remorse, contrition

forgolpen 07.06.03 Boastfulness, arrogance; 09.06.02.01.05 Proclamation, spreading abroad

forgrindan 05.06 Destruction, dissolution, loss, breaking; 05.06.05 A grinding, pounding

forgrīpan 05.06.01 Devastation, laying waste; 10.04.02.01 To pluck, gather; 10.04.02.02 To seize, take, grasp, lay hold on; 12.05.04.01.01 Fighting, a fight

forgriwen 12.08.06.01.02 Lacking moral góod

forgrōwen 03.03.04.02.02 Excess

forgylt 14.03.03.09.01 Unfavourable judgement, condemnation

forgyltan 14.03.03.09.01 Unfavourable judgement, condemnation

forgyrdan 05.10.05.04.11 A circle, circuit, circumference

forhabban 05.10.05.04.15 Closure, being closed; 09.05.04 A secret; 10 Having, owning, possession; 11.06.04 Abstention, abstaining from; 12.03.06 Prohibition; 12.05.06.01 Restraint, check, curb, control; 15.02.04 Spending, disbursement

forhæbbend 12.08.03.01 Abstinence (from); 12.09.03.01 Celibacy

forhæfed 02.08.08.12 Disease of bowels; 12.08.03.01 Abstinence (from)

forhæfednes 10.03.09.01 Parsimony, niggardliness; 12.08.03.03.01 Continence

forhæfendlīce 12.08.03.03.01 Continence

forhǣlan 02.08.04 Hurt, injury, damage

forhǣtan 03.01.09.01 Warmth, heat

forhǣþed 05.06.01 Devastation, laying waste

forhātan 12.07.02.01.01 A promise

forhātene 16.01.05.02.02 Other terms for devils

forhealdan 07.05 Disrespect, irreverence; 10 Having, owning, possession; 11.09 Peril, danger; 12.01.01.12.02 Disobedience; 12.08.08.01.02 Unchastity, incontinence; 14.02 Lawlessness; 15.02.04 Spending, disbursement

forhealden 08.01.03.07.02.01 Injury, offence; 12.08.08.01.02 Unchastity, incontinence

forhealdnes 12.08.08.01.02 Unchastity, incontinence

forheard 03.01.03 Hardness, callosity, hard material; 12.08.03.02 Strictness, austerity, severity

forhearde 03.03.04.01 Much

forheardian 03.01.03 Hardness, callosity, hard material

forheardod 03.01.03 Hardness, callosity, hard material

forhēawan 02.02.04.03 To kill, slay; 05.06.02 Cleaving, splitting, cutting

forhelan 09.05.04.01 Concealment, obscurity

forheled 09.05.04 A secret

forhelian 04.04.07 Trappings, equipment, garb

forhergend 05.06 Destruction, dissolution, loss, breaking

forhergian 05.06.01 Devastation, laying waste; 13.02.05.01.02 To gain by fighting

forhergung 05.06.01 Devastation, laying waste

forhīenan 05.06.01 Devastation, laying waste; 13.02.05.01.01 To overcome, conquer
forhīened 08.01.03.06 Adversity, affliction
forhogian 07.05.02 Contempt; 11.06.01 Neglect; 12.01.01.12.02 Disobedience
forhogiend 07.05.02 Contempt
forhogiendlic 07.05.02 Contempt
forhogod 07.03.03.01 Empty, useless, worthless
forhogodlic 07.05.02 Contempt
forhogodlīce 07.05.04 Mockery, derision, scorn
forhogodnes 07.05.02 Contempt
forhogung 07.05.02 Contempt
forholen 09.05.04 A secret
forhorwade 04.06.02.03 Stain, smear
forhradian 05.11.08.01.02.01 Anticipation; 05.12.03.01.02 Haste, hurry; 06.01.08.04 Foreseeing
forhrædlīce 05.12.03.01 Swiftness, velocity
forhraþe 05.11.07.01 Contemporary, coeval
forhreppan 10.04 To take
forhrēred 05.07 Ending of existence, end of world
forht 06.01.08.06.03 Cause of fear, terror, horror
(ge)forht 06.01.08.06 Fear
forhtferþ 06.01.08.06.02 Great fear, terror, horror
forhtful 06.01.08.06 Fear
forhtian 06.01.08.06 Fear
forhtiende 06.01.08.06 Fear
forhtiendlic 06.01.08.06 Fear; 06.01.08.06.03 Cause of fear, terror, horror
forhtig 06.01.08.06.06 Timidity

forhtlēasnes 06.02.07.06.02.01 Fearlessness
forhtlic 06.01.08.06 Fear; 06.01.08.06.03 Cause of fear, terror, horror
forhtlīce 06.01.08.06 Fear
forhtmōd 06.01.08.06 Fear
forhtnes 06.01.08.06 Fear
forhto 06.01.08.06 Fear
forhtung 06.01.08.06 Fear
forhwega 05.10.04.03 Presence
forhweorfan 05.07 Ending of existence, end of world
forhwierfan 05.10.04.04.02 Removal, taking away; 11.11.04 Subversion, change; 12.08.06.01.04.01 To mislead, seduce, lead astray
forhwierfan (tō) 05.13.01 Transformation, taking another shape
forhwierfed 12.08.06.01.02 Lacking moral good; 16.01.05.02.02 Other terms for devils
forhwierfedlic 12.08.06.01.02 Lacking moral good
forhwierfednes 12.08.06.01 Error, wrong conduct, erroneous practice
forhȳdan 09.05.04.01 Concealment, obscurity
forhygdelic 07.05.02 Contempt
forhylman 12.01.01.12.02 Disobedience
forhyrdan 08.01.03.09.10 Wrath, sternness, displeasure
forieldan 05.11.08.01.03.01 Delay
forierþ 04.02.03.02.01 A strip for ploughing
forildu 02.01.04.03 Aging, growing old
forinlīce 03.03.06 Wholeness
forinweardlīce 03.03.06 Wholeness
forlācan 06.01.07.04.01 Deception, a leading astray; 06.01.07.04.04.03 Deceit, fraud, treachery

forlædan 05.10.05.04.02.01 Exterior, outside of; 05.12.02.01 To fetch, bring, bear, conduct; 05.12.05.08.01 To go before and guide; 06.01.07.04.01 Deception, a leading astray

forlæran 06.01.07.05 Error, being astray; 12.08.06.01.04.01 To mislead, seduce, lead astray

forlæt 05.12.05.03.03 To depart, leave, set out

forlætan 02.02.03 To die, perish; 02.08.12.02.06 Surgical; 03.04.01 Singularity, peculiarity; 05.03.01 A cause (of anything); 05.10.04.04 Absence; 05.12.05.03.01 To part ways, separate from, depart; 08.01.02.06.02 Forgiveness, remission, clemency; 10.02 Want, lack; 10.02.01.01 Loss, forfeiture; 11.06.01 Neglect; 11.06.01.01 Negligence, carelessness, heedlessness; 11.06.04 Abstention, abstaining from; 11.06.06.01 Abandonment (of principle); 11.12.01 Absence of restraint, freedom; 12.03.05 Permission; 12.06.03.01 Waste land, deserted place; 15.01.02.01 Inherited property; 16.02.04.07.02.02 Absolution, forgiveness, remission

forlætan forþ/ūt 09.01 To speak, exercise faculty of speech

forlætan (tō) 10.03.03 Granting

forlætan (ūt) 11.10.03 Salvation/deliverance from

forlæte 08.01.03.06.01 Affliction, misfortune, calamity

forlætednes 05.11.11.02 Let up, intermission, cessation

forlæten wīf 12.09.05 State of woman whose husband has died

forlæt(en)nes 05.06.01 Devastation, laying waste; 05.12.05.03.03 To depart, leave, set out; 16.02.04.07.02.02 Absolution, forgiveness, remission

forlætere 11.06.06.01 Abandonment (of principle); 11.10.04 Flight

forlæting 05.11.11.02 Let up, intermission, cessation; 05.12.05.03.03 To depart, leave, set out

forlætnes 05.11.11.02 Let up, intermission, cessation; 10.02.01.01 Loss, forfeiture; 11.06.01 Neglect; 11.06.06.01 Abandonment (of principle)

forlæþan 07.03.01.03 To loathe, hate, abhor

forlēan 07.05.01 Censure, reproof, rebuke

forlecgan 05.10.05.04.12 The condition of being covered

forlegen 12.08.08.01.01 Rape; 12.08.08.01.02.01 Fornication, adultery

forlegen bēon/wesan 12.08.08.01.02 Unchastity, incontinence

forlegenlic 07.10.02 Ugliness

forleg(en)nes 12.08.08.01.02.01 Fornication, adultery

forlegeswīfa hūs 12.08.08.01.02.01.01 An adulterer/-ess, whore, prostitute

forleg(n)is 12.08.08.01.02.01.01 An adulterer/-ess, whore, prostitute

forlēogan 14.03.03.06 False witness

forlēornes 12.08.06.02.05.01 Transgression, trespass; 16.02.01.13 Evil-doing, transgression, sin

forleornung 06.01.07.05 Error, being astray
forlēosan 05.06 Destruction, dissolution, loss, breaking; 10.02 Want, lack; 12.08.06.01.04.01 To mislead, seduce, lead astray
forlettan 11.11.03 Impeding of progress, prevention
forlicgan 09.05.04.01 Concealment, obscurity; 11.06.01 Neglect; 12.08.08.01.02 Unchastity, incontinence
forlicgan mid/wiþ 12.08.08.01.02.01 Fornication, adultery
forlicgend 12.08.08.01.02.01 Fornication, adultery
forliden 05.12.01.01 To go on a journey/expedition, travel; 05.12.01.09.03.02 Hardship on board
forlidennes 05.12.01.09.03.02 Hardship on board
forliger 12.08.08.01.02.01.01 An adulterer/-ess, whore, prostitute; 12.08.08.01.02.01.03 Unnatural sexual behaviour
forligerbed 12.08.08.01.02.01 Fornication, adultery
forligeren 12.08.08.01.02.01 Fornication, adultery
forligerhūs 12.08.08.01.02.01.01 An adulterer/-ess, whore, prostitute
forligerlic 12.08.08.01.02.01 Fornication, adultery
forligerlīce 12.08.08.01.02.01 Fornication, adultery
forligerwīf 12.08.08.01.02.01.01 An adulterer/-ess, whore, prostitute
forliggang 12.08.08.01.02.01 Fornication, adultery
forligrian 12.08.08.01.02.01 Fornication, adultery
forlīsgleng 04.04.07.01 Mode of dressing, fashion
forlīþan 05.12.01.09.03.02 Hardship on board
forlogen 14.03.03.06 False witness
forlor 05.06 Destruction, dissolution, loss, breaking
forloren 16.02.01.13.02 Evil, reprobate, damned
forloren hēap 13.02.10.01.02.01 An armed force/band
forlorenes 05.06.01 Devastation, laying waste
forlorian 10.02.01 Loss, deprivation
forlosian 05.06.01 Devastation, laying waste
forlustlīce 06.02.02 Will, disposition
forlȳtel 03.03.04.04 Littleness, smallness
forma 05.11.10.01 A beginning
formæl 14.04 Making of terms, agreement, convention
formǣlan 15.05 Trade, traffic, commerce
formala 09.01.01 A speech, what is said, words
formelle 04.05.04.01 A bench, seat
formeltan 03.01.16 Liquid, a liquid
formengan 03.03.06.01.01 Mixing, mingling, preparation
fōrmete 04.01.02.04 Abundance of food
formicel 11.07.04 Superiority, pre-eminence, primacy
formilt 03.01.16 Liquid, a liquid
formogod 03.02.01.01 Decay, corruption, rottenness
formolsnian 03.02.01.01 Decay, corruption, rottenness
formolsnod 03.02.01.01 Decay, corruption, rottenness

formolsung 03.02.01.01 Decay, corruption, rottenness
formyrþrian 02.02.04.04 Manslaughter, homicide
forn 02.06.06.02.01.09 Trout
forn ongēan 05.10.05.04.09.01 Front
fornǣman 08.01.03.07.02 Misery, trouble, affliction
fornēah 03.06 Comparison
fornerwian 03.01.18 Dryness (not wetness)
fornetecle 02.06.06.02.01.09 Trout
fornētes folm 02.07.11 Plants/flowers (alphabetical order)
fornēþan 11.09 Peril, danger
forniman 05.06.01 Devastation, laying waste; 06.01.07.04.02 Fraud, deceit, trick, trickery; 07.10.02.01 Deformed, ugly; 10.04.02.02 To seize, take, grasp, lay hold on; 14.02.01.02.01 Open robbery, rapine, pillage; 14.05.08 Captivity
fornȳdan 12.05.06.03 Necessity, constraint
fornytlīce 11.07.01 Utility, usefulness
forod 02.08.04.04.01 Mutilation/injury to limbs; 05.06.03 A dashing together, breaking, shattering; 07.07 Humility; 07.09.02 Disgrace, shaming, humiliation; 14.02 Lawlessness
forodfōt(e) 02.08.04.04.01 Mutilation/injury to limbs
foroft 05.11.09.02 Frequent, of common occurrence
forpǣran 05.06.01 Devastation, laying waste; 12.08.06.01.04.01 To mislead, seduce, lead astray
forpyndan 05.10.05.04.15 Closure, being closed

forracu 05.12.01.01 To go on a journey/expedition, travel
forrǣda 12.01.01.12.04.02 Conspiracy
forrǣdan 02.08.04 Hurt, injury, damage; 06.01.07.04.04.03 Deceit, fraud, treachery; 12.01.01.12.04.02 Conspiracy; 14.03.03.09.01 Unfavourable judgement, condemnation
forrǣpe 04.02.03.02 Arable/ploughed land
forrēcelēasian 11.06.01 Neglect
forrīdan 05.12.01.05.01 Modes of riding; 11.11.03 Impeding of progress, prevention
forridel 05.12.01.05 To ride (on horse, etc.); 05.12.05.08 To go before, precede; 09.06.02.01.06.01 A messenger
forrotednes 03.02.01.01 Decay, corruption, rottenness
forrotian 03.02.01.01 Decay, corruption, rottenness
forrotod 03.02.01.01 Decay, corruption, rottenness
forsacan 09.07.03.02 Refusal, denial; 12.05.07 Casting out, rejection
forsacennes 09.07.03.01 A denial
forsacung 09.07.03.01 A denial
forsǣtian 11.09.01.01 Ambush, lying in wait
forscamian 07.09 Shame, disgrace
forscamung 12.08.03.03 Moral restraint, modesty, sobriety
forscapung 08.01.03.06.01 Affliction, misfortune, calamity
forscēadan 05.10.04.04.01 Dispersion
forsceap 12.08.06.02.01 Wrong, evil-doing
forsceorfan 05.06.01 Devastation, laying waste

forscēotan 05.11.08.01.02.01 Anticipation; 11.11.03 Impeding of progress, prevention; 15.04.01 Lending of money
forscepen 05.13.01 Transformation, taking another shape
forscieppan 05.13.01 Transformation, taking another shape
forscip 05.12.01.09.03.01.03 Part of ship
forscired 05.10.05 A space, span
forscīt 01.01.03.01.03.02 Weir
forscrencan 05.06 Destruction, dissolution, loss, breaking; 05.06.01 Devastation, laying waste; 13.02.05.01.01 To overcome, conquer
forscrencedness 12.01.01.12.04.01 Betrayal
forscrencend 02.08.02 Disease, infirmity, sickness; 13.02.10.02 A victor/conqueror
forscrenct 12.05.06.02 Oppression
forscrīfan 14.03.03.09.01 Unfavourable judgement, condemnation; 14.03.03.09.03 Outlawry; 16.01.04 Sorcery, magic, witchcraft
forscrincan 03.01.18 Dryness (not wetness)
forscruncen 02.08.02 Disease, infirmity, sickness; 03.01.18 Dryness (not wetness)
forscūfan 05.12.02.04 To cast out, drive away
forscyldgod 14.03.03.09.01 Unfavourable judgement, condemnation
forscyldig 12.08.06.02.03 (Of persons) wicked, evil-doing
forscyldigan 12.08.06.02.03.02 To do evil; 14.03.03.09.01 Unfavourable judgement, condemnation

forscyldigod 12.08.06.02.03 (Of persons) wicked, evil-doing
forscyttan 05.10.05.04.15 Closure, being closed
forsēarian 03.01.18 Dryness (not wetness); 05.09.05 Ceasing, decline, fall off
forsēcan 13.02.03 To seek with active intent, attack
forsecgan 14.03.03.06 False witness
forsellan 10.02.01.01 Loss, forfeiture; 15.05 Trade, traffic, commerce
forsencan 12.05.07 Casting out, rejection
forsendan 05.06.01 Devastation, laying waste; 05.10.04.04.02 Removal, taking away; 05.12.02.04 To cast out, drive away; 05.12.05.03.04 To come/go out from
forsēon 07.05.02 Contempt; 09.07.03.02 Refusal, denial; 12.05.07 Casting out, rejection
forset 11.11.02 A hindrance
forseten 05.10.05.04.15 Closure, being closed
forsetnian 11.09.01.01 Ambush, lying in wait; 13.02.03.01.02 To beset, surround
forsettan 11.11.02 A hindrance; 12.05.06.02 Oppression
forsewen 07.05.02 Contempt
forsewenlic 07.05.02 Contempt
forsewenlīce 07.05.02 Contempt
forsewennes 07.05.02 Contempt
forsewestre 07.05.02 Contempt
forsittan 02.08.08.12 Disease of bowels; 05.07 Ending of existence, end of world; 05.10.04.04 Absence; 05.10.05.04.15 Closure, being closed; 05.11.08.01.03.01 Delay; 11.06.01 Neglect; 11.11.01 A physical difficulty, strait

forsīþian 02.02.03 To die, perish
forslægen 05.11.10.02 End, completion;
　13.02.05.02 Defeat
forslǽwan 05.11.08.01.03.01 Delay
forslāwian 05.12.03.02 Slowness;
　11.06.01.01 Negligence, carelessness,
　heedlessness
forslēan 02.02.04.03 To kill, slay;
　02.08.04.01 A wound; 05.06.01
　Devastation, laying waste;
　13.02.05.01.01 To overcome, conquer;
　14.03.03.09.01 Unfavourable
　judgement, condemnation
forslegen 02.02.04 Killing, violent death,
　destruction
forslegenlic 07.09.03 Infamy, ignominy,
　shame
forsliht 02.02.04 Killing, violent death,
　destruction
forslītan 05.06.01 Devastation, laying
　waste
forsmored 02.02.04.03 To kill, slay
forsmorian 02.02.04.03 To kill, slay
forsoden 03.02.01 Decay, decline,
　corruption
forsogen 02.08.08.04.02 (Of stomach)
　disordered
forsorgian 08.01.03.03 Anxiety
forsōþ 06.01.07.01 Correct, right, free
　from error
forspanan 06.02.06.03.04 Allurement
forspaning 06.02.06.03.04 Allurement
forspecan 06.01.07.04.01 Deception, a
　leading astray; 14.03.03 Law, action
　of the courts
forspēdian 08.01.01.03.08 Happiness,
　well-being, prosperity
forspendan 10.03.08.01 Overliberality,
　waste of money

forspennend 12.08.08.01.02.01.01 An
　adulterer/-ess, whore, prostitute
forspennendlic 06.02.06.03.04
　Allurement
forspennestre 12.08.08.01.02.01.01 An
　adulterer/-ess, whore, prostitute
forspenning 05.06.01 Devastation, laying
　waste; 06.02.06.03.04 Allurement
forspild 05.06 Destruction, dissolution,
　loss, breaking
forspildan 05.06 Destruction, dissolution,
　loss, breaking
forspillan 05.06 Destruction, dissolution,
　loss, breaking; 10.02.01 Loss,
　deprivation; 10.03.08.01
　Overliberality, waste of money
forspillednes 05.06 Destruction,
　dissolution, loss, breaking;
　16.01.05.01 Damnation, perdition,
　reprobation
forspillende 12.08.07.01.01 Wantonness,
　sensuality, lasciviousness
forsp(r)ecan 07.05.03.03.02 To reproach,
　revile, abuse
forspyrcan 03.01.18 Dryness (not
　wetness)
forst 01.01.02.01.02.01 Rising ground,
　eminence; 01.03.01.04.01 Frost
forstalian 11.10.05.01 Evasion, escape
　from threat
forstandan 05.11.10.02 End, completion;
　05.13.04 Exchange, commutation;
　06.01.05.01 Understanding; 11.06.04
　Abstention, abstaining from; 11.07.03
　Use, advantage, profit; 11.11.02 A
　hindrance; 11.11.03 Impeding of
　progress, prevention; 12.05.06 Grasp,
　power, control, mastery; 13.02.04
　Defence, guard, protection

forstandan (fram) 11.10.01 Protection, safekeeping; 13.02.04 Defence, guard, protection
forstelan 14.02.01.02 Wrongful taking, theft
forstig/fyrstig 01.03.01.04.01 Frost
forstlic 01.03.01.04.02 Ice; 03.01.11 Coldness, coolness
forstolen 14.02.01.02 Wrongful taking, theft
forstoppian 05.10.05.04.15 Closure, being closed
forstrang 05.08 Strength
forstregdan 05.06 Destruction, dissolution, loss, breaking
forstrogdnes 05.10.04.04.01 Dispersion
forstyltan 06.01.08.05.01 Amazement, astonishment, wonder, admiration
forstyntan 02.08.07.02.01 Defective vision; 05.06.05.03 Bruising, crushing
forsūcan 04 Consumption of food/drink
forsūgan 02.08.08.04.02 (Of stomach) disordered
forsuncen 03.01.14.02 Pallor, absence of colour
forsuwung 02.05.10.17 Absence of noise or disturbance
forswǣlan 02.08.03.02 Itch, irritation; 03.01.09.02 Fire, flame; 03.01.09.02.01 Fire, burning
forswǣled 05.06.01 Devastation, laying waste
forswǣlednes 03.01.09.02.01 Fire, burning
forswāpan 05.12.02.06 To push, impel, thrust
forswarung 14.03.03.06 False witness
forswealtan 02.02.03 To die, perish
forswefian 02.02.04.03 To kill, slay
forswelan 03.01.09.02.01 Fire, burning
forswelgan 04 Consumption of food/drink
(ge)forswelgan 05.06.01 Devastation, laying waste
forswelgend 05.06 Destruction, dissolution, loss, breaking
forswelgende 01.01.03.04 Current, rush of water
forsweltan 05.07 Ending of existence, end of world
forsweorcan 03.01.13.02 A growing dark, darkening
forsweorced 03.01.13 Darkness, obscurity
forsweorfan 05.06 Destruction, dissolution, loss, breaking
forsweotole 09.05.05.01 Showing, manifestation, display
forswerian 14.03.03.06 False witness; 16.01.04.01 Sorcery using incantation
forswiged 09.05.04 A secret
forswigian 02.05.10.17.01 Dumb, silent; 09.05.04 A secret
forswīþ 12 Power, might
forswīþan 05.12.05.03.04 To come/go out from; 11.03.02 Advancement, progress; 13.02.05.01.01 To overcome, conquer
forswīþe 03.03.06 Wholeness; 05.08 Strength; 05.08.02 Violence, force
forsworcen 03.01.13 Darkness, obscurity
forsworcenlic 03.01.13 Darkness, obscurity
forsworcennes 03.01.13 Darkness, obscurity
forsworen 14.03.03.06 False witness
forsworennes 14.03.03.06 False witness
forsyngian 12.08.06.01.04.01 To mislead, seduce, lead astray

forsyngod 16.02.01.13 Evil-doing, transgression, sin
fortendan 02.08.12.02.06 Surgical
fortēon 02.08.08.04.01 Gripe, colic; 03.01.13.03 Overshadowing; 06.02.06.03.04 Allurement
fortimbran 05.10.05.04.15 Closure, being closed
fortimbrian 11.11.02 A hindrance
fortīn/fertīn 06.01.08.04.01 Premonition, prophecy
fortogen 02.08.08.04.01 Gripe, colic
fortogenes 02.08.08.04.01 Gripe, colic
fortogian 02.08.07.06 Disorders of the neck
fortredan 05.06 Destruction, dissolution, loss, breaking; 05.10.05.04.12 The condition of being covered; 05.12.01.04.01.02 To tread upon, trample; 12.05.06.02 Oppression
fortreddan 05.06.04 Damage, injury, defect, hurt, loss
fortreden 07.07 Humility; 08.01.03.02.01 Compunction, remorse, contrition
fortreding 05.06.01 Devastation, laying waste
fortrendan 05.10.05.04.15 Closure, being closed
fortrūwian 07.06.01.03 To be proud/arrogant
gefortrūwod 07.06.01.01 Proud, arrogant
fortrūwodnes 07.06.01 Pride, arrogance
fortrūwung 07.06.01 Pride, arrogance
fortyhtan 12.08.06.01.04.01 To mislead, seduce, lead astray
fortyhted 02.08.02.01.05 Bed of sickness
fortyhtigend 12.08.08.01.02 Unchastity, incontinence
fortyllan 06.02.06.03.04 Allurement

fortȳnan 02.05.09.01 To open the eyes/be awake; 11.11.02 A hindrance
forþ 05.10.05.04.09.01 Front; 05.10.06.03 Projection, head, extremity (of anything); 05.11.07.04.02 (Of time) later/latter; 05.11.11 Continuity; 05.11.11.01 A not ceasing, persistence, recurrence; 05.12.05.03.04 To come/go out from; 05.12.05.09 To go forward, proceed; 11.01.06 End, completion (of action), fulfilment
forþ āræsan 05.12.05.03.03 To depart, leave, set out
forþ ātēon 02.01.03.03.02 To bring forth, produce
forþ cuman 11.03.02.01 Efficacy, success
forþ flēogan 05.12.01.07 To fly (with wings); 05.12.02.06 To push, impel, thrust; 05.12.03.01.01 Quick movement or movements
forþ forlǣtan 09.01.02.01 Excessive fluency, loquacity
forþ heonan 05.11.07.04 Future, time to come
forþ hlifian fore 03.03.05.01.01 Principal/chief (of its class or type)
forþ mid 03.03.06.01 A whole formed by joining
forþ oferfaran 05.12.05.06 To travel over/through/along, traverse
forþ gerīmed 05.11.11.01 A not ceasing, persistence, recurrence
forþācīgan 12.03.03.01 Summons, a call, summoning
forþādīlgian 05.07 Ending of existence, end of world
forþāgān 05.11.07.03 Former times, days of old
forþāgoten 09.03.04.04 Discursiveness

forþāloten 05.10.05.04.02.03.02 Reclining, rest
forþāsliden 12.08.06.01.02 Lacking moral good
forþātēon 05.05.02 Productivity, bringing forth
forþātȳddrede 02.01.03.03.02 To bring forth, produce
forþātȳdred 02.01.03.03.03 Birth
forþaurnen 05.11.07.03 Former times, days of old
forþbǣro 05.05.02 Productivity, bringing forth
forþbecuman 05.12.05.03.04 To come/go out from
forþberan 05.05 Constitution, founding (e.g. of world); 09.05.05 Exposure, revealing, revelation
forþbesēon 02.05.09.04 To see, look upon, behold
forþbigfērende 05.12.05.07.01 To pass by
forþblǣstan 05.12.05.03.04.01 To burst forth, break out
forþblāwan 05.12.05.03.04.01 To burst forth, break out
forþboren 12.01.01.06.06 Gentle birth, nobility
forþbringan 05.05 Constitution, founding (e.g. of world); 05.10.05.04.02.01 Exterior, outside of; 05.12.02.01 To fetch, bring, bear, conduct; 06.01.06.02.03.04.03 To teach, instruct; 11.01.04 A doing, accomplishing (of something); 11.03.01.01.01 Proof, demonstration
forþbylding 06.02.07.06.01 Emboldening, encouragement
forþcuman 02.01.03.03.03 Birth; 05.03.02.01.01 An event, occurrence; 05.12.05.02.03 To arrive; 05.12.05.03.04 To come/go out from; 05.12.05.09 To go forward, proceed
forþcyme 02.01.03.03.03 Birth
forþcȳþan 09.05.05.01 Showing, manifestation, display
forþdǣd 11.07.03 Use, advantage, profit
forþdōn 05.12.02.01 To fetch, bring, bear, conduct
forþeahting 12.02.02.05 Counsel, advice
forþearle 03.03.04.01 Much
forþearlīce 03.03.06.02 Fullness
forþeccan 05.10.05.04.12 The condition of being covered
forþegide 02.08.03.01 Extreme pain, torture, torment
forþencan 06.01.08.06.07 Despair; 07.05.02 Contempt
forþēofan 14.02.01.02 Wrongful taking, theft
forþerscan 05.06.05.03 Bruising, crushing
forþfæder 02.03.02.03.03 Forefather, ancestor; 16.02.01.08.05 One of the church fathers
forþfæderen 02.03.02.03.01 Ancestry, paternal kinship
forþfaran 05.12.05.03.03 To depart, leave, set out
forþfēran 05.12.05.06 To travel over/through/along, traverse; 05.12.05.09 To go forward, proceed
forþfēred 02.02.03.02 State of being dead
forþfērednes 02.02 Death
forþfērende 02.02.03.01 In process of dying
forþfēring 02.02 Death
forþflōwan 01.01.03.03 Flow/flowing
forþfolgian 05.12.05.10 To go behind, follow

forþfōr 02.02 Death
forþframian 02.01.04.02 To grow, grow up; 11.03.02 Advancement, progress
forþframung 05.12.05.03.03 To depart, leave, set out
forþfyligan 05.03.02.01.01 An event, occurrence
forþgān 02.01.04.03 Aging, growing old; 05.11 A time, period of time; 05.12.05.07.01 To pass by; 05.12.05.09 To go forward, proceed
forþgang 02.04.06.03.02.04 Intestines; 04.05.03.05.02 A privy; 05.12.01 To go, progress, travel (usually on land); 05.12.05.03.04 To come/go out from; 05.12.05.09 To go forward, proceed; 09.03.07.07.03.01 A description, writing down
forþgangan 05.12.05.09 To go forward, proceed
forþgangende 05.11.11 Continuity
forþgebrengan 07.08 Reputation, fame
forþgecīgan 12.03.03.01 Summons, a call, summoning
forþ(ge)clipian 06.02.06.03.03 Incitement
forþ(ge)faran 02.02.03 To die, perish; 05.11 A time, period of time
forþ(ge)faren 02.02.03.02 State of being dead
forþ(ge)fēran 02.02.03 To die, perish
forþgefremman 07.08.06 Exaltation
forþgegyrdu 04.02.05.06.05.03.06 A martingale/fore-girdle
forþ(ge)lǣdan 05.05 Constitution, founding (e.g. of world); 05.12.05.08.01 To go before and guide
forþgelang 05.03.01.03 Reason, cause
forþgelēoran 02.02.03 To die, perish

forþ(ge)lēoran 05.12.05.03.04 To come/go out from
forþgelēored 02.02.03.02 State of being dead
forþgelēorednes 02.02 Death
forþ(ge)lōcian 02.05.09.04 To see, look upon, behold
forþgenge 08.01.01.03.08.02 Good fortune, success; 11.01.05.01 Furtherance, making effectual; 11.03.02 Advancement, progress
forþgeorn 06.02.07.06 Courage, boldness, valour; 11.01.05.02 Furtherance, promotion
forþgesceaft 02 Creation; 05.02 State, condition; 05.11.07.04 Future, time to come
forþgestrangian 05.08 Strength
forþgesȳne 02.05.09.09 Visible
forþgewītan 05.07 Ending of existence, end of world; 05.12.05.03.04 To come/go out from
forþgewiten 05.11.07.03 Former times, days of old
forþgewiten tīd 09.03.02.03.01.02.03 Tense
forþgewiten tīma 09.03.02.03.01.02.03 Tense
forþgewitenes 05.12.05.03.03 To depart, leave, set out
forþgiten 05.11.07.03 Former times, days of old
forþgoten 01.01.03.03 Flow/flowing; 05.12.05.03.04.02 To flow out, well up, erupt
forþgyrd 04.02.05.06.05.03.06 A martingale/fore-girdle
forþheald 05.02.02.01 Inclination; 05.10.05.04.02.03.02 Reclining, rest; 05.10.05.04.04 A descent, slope, incline

forþhealdan 12.07.02 Observance, keeping
forþhebban 11.01.05.02 Furtherance, promotion
forþhere 13.02.10.01.02.02.01 Types of army
forþhlīfian 05.10.06.03 Projection, head, extremity (of anything)
forþhnīgan 05.12.05.13.03 To fall
forþhrēosan 05.12.05.03.04.01 To burst forth, break out
forþian ūt 05.12.05.03.04 To come/go out from
(ge)forþian 11.01.05 Accomplishment, fulfilment; 11.12.02 Aid, help, succour
geforþian 05.10.05.04.02.01 Exterior, outside of; 10.03.02 Presenting, offering
forþindan 02.08.05.01 Swelling
forþlǣdan 05.05 Constitution, founding (e.g. of world); 05.10.05.04.02.01 Exterior, outside of
forþlǣdnes 02.01.03.03.02 To bring forth, produce
forþlǣstan 11.01.05 Accomplishment, fulfilment
forþlǣtan 05.12.02.03 To send; 05.12.05.03.04 To come/go out from
forþlīce 05.11.08.01.02 (Untimely) earliness; 07.02.03 Perfection
forþloten 05.02.02.01 Inclination
forþlūtan 05.02.02.01 Inclination; 05.12.05.13.03 To fall
forþmǣre 07.08.07 Glory, splendour, magnificence
forþman 12.01.01.06.08 A person of rank, elder, great man
forþmest 02.01.04 Age; 03.03.05.01.01 Principal/chief (of its class or type);
05.11.10.01 A beginning; 11.07.04 Superiority, pre-eminence, primacy
forþmid 05.11.07.01 Contemporary, coeval
forþōht 06.01.08.06.07 Despair
forþolian 10.02 Want, lack
forþorlǣtenes 12.08.07.01.01 Wantonness, sensuality, lasciviousness
forþrǣcan 05.10.06.03 Projection, head, extremity (of anything)
forþrǣsan 05.10.06.03 Projection, head, extremity (of anything); 05.12.05.12 To go up, ascend
forþrǣsende 01.01.03.04 Current, rush of water; 05.12.05.12 To go up, ascend
forþrǣst 05.06 Destruction, dissolution, loss, breaking
forþrǣstan 05.06.05.03 Bruising, crushing
forþrǣsted 08.01.03.02.01 Compunction, remorse, contrition; 16.02.04.07.02.01 Penitence
forþrǣst(ed)nes 08.01.03.02.01 Compunction, remorse, contrition; 08.01.03.06 Adversity, affliction; 16.02.04.07.02.01 Penitence
forþriccan 02.08.12.02.06 Surgical
forþriht 09.03.04.03 Plain, simple
forþrihte 05.10.05.04.05 Straight, direct; 09.03.04.03 Plain, simple
forþrihtes 05.11.11.01 A not ceasing, persistence, recurrence
forþringan 05.12.02.06 To push, impel, thrust
forþrocettan 05.12.05.03.04.01 To burst forth, break out
forþryccan 02.08.04 Hurt, injury, damage; 05.10.05.04.15 Closure, being closed; 12.05.06.02 Oppression; 14.05.02 Torment, punishment

forþryccednes 08.01.03.07.02 Misery, trouble, affliction
forþrycnes 08.01.03.07.02 Misery, trouble, affliction; 14.02.01.02.01 Open robbery, rapine, pillage
forþryne 01.01.03.01.01.01 River
forþ(r)ysmed 03.01.13 Darkness, obscurity
forþrysmian 05.06 Destruction, dissolution, loss, breaking
forþscacan 05.07 Ending of existence, end of world
forþscencan 04.01.03 Drinking
forþscipe 08.01.01.03.08.02 Good fortune, success
forþscype 05.12.05.09 To go forward, proceed
forþsecgan 09.06.02.01.05 Proclamation, spreading abroad
forþsendan 05.12.02.03 To send; 05.12.05.03.04 To come/go out from
forþsige 02.02 Death
forþsīþ 02.02 Death; 05.12.05.03.04 To come/go out from
forþsnotter 06.01.05.02.01.01 Sagacity
forþspell 09.06.02 A saying, speech, statement
forþspōwnes 08.01.01.03.08 Happiness, well-being, prosperity
forþstæpe 05.12.05.09 To go forward, proceed
forþstæppan 05.10.06.03 Projection, head, extremity (of anything); 05.12.05.09 To go forward, proceed
forþstæpping 05.12.05.09 To go forward, proceed
forþstapan 05.12.05.07.01 To pass by
forþstefn 05.12.01.09.03.01.03 Part of ship

forþswebban 11.07.03 Use, advantage, profit
forþswebbung 01.03.01.03.01 Storm, tempest
forþsyllan 15.02.04 Spending, disbursement
forþtīge 04.05.02.12.02 A vestibule, entrance, courtyard
forþtihtan 06.02.06.03 Persuasion, prompting
forþtilian 11.03 Endeavour
forþþegn 12.01.01.06.08 A person of rank, elder, great man
forþþēon 11.07.03 Use, advantage, profit
forþung 11.01.05.02 Furtherance, promotion
forþweard 02.02.03.02 State of being dead; 05.10.05.04.04 A descent, slope, incline; 05.10.05.04.09.01.01 Head, front (position); 05.11.07.04 Future, time to come; 05.11.11 Continuity; 05.11.11.01 A not ceasing, persistence, recurrence; 05.12.05.09 To go forward, proceed; 08.01.02.02.03 A loving relationship
forþweard scipes 05.12.01.09.03 A voyage; 11.10.02.02 Watchful care, keeping guard
forþweardes 05.12.05.09 To go forward, proceed
forþweardnes 11.03.02 Advancement, progress
forþweaxan 03.03.04.03 Growth, increase
forþwecgan 05.12.05.09 To go forward, proceed
forþweg 02.02 Death; 05.12.05.03.03 To depart, leave, set out
forþwīf 12.01.01.06.08 A person of rank, elder, great man; 12.09 Marriage, state of marriage

forþwyrft 02.08.04.02.01 A maimed man
forþwyrftan 05.06.02 Cleaving, splitting, cutting
forþyldegung 08.01.03.08 Patience
forþyldian 08.01.03.08 Patience
forþylm(i)an 02.08.07.04.04 Respiratory disease; 05.10.05.04.11 A circle, circuit, circumference
forþyppan 05.12.05.03.04 To come/go out from; 09.05.05 Exposure, revealing, revelation
forþyrnende 05.11.07.03.02.01 A precursor, one who goes before
forþyrrian 03.01.18 Dryness (not wetness)
forūtan 03.03.08 Emptiness; 03.04.01 Singularity, peculiarity
forwana 03.03.04.02.01 Abundance
forwandian 07.04.03 Reverence, respect; 07.09 Shame, disgrace; 11.06.05 Hesitation, scruple
forwandigende 07.04.03 Reverence, respect
forwandung 07.09.01 Shame, confusion
forweallan 03.01.09.01.01 (Of liquids) boiling
forweard 05.11.07.04 Future, time to come
forweard titt 02.04.03.03.05 Chest, breast, bosom; 02.04.06.05.06 Mammary gland, breast
forweardmearcung 09.03.07.07.02.01.01 A heading, title, superscription
forweaxan 02.04.02.01 Fat/plump
forweddod 14.03.03.07 Security, pledge, bail
forwegan 02.02.04.03 To kill, slay
forwel 03.03.04.01 Much; 07.02 Goodness
forwened 07.06.01.01 Proud, arrogant
forwēned 07.03.03.01 Empty, useless, worthless
forwēnednes 07.06.01 Pride, arrogance
forweorennes 02.01.04.03 Aging, growing old
forweornan 09.07.03.02 Refusal, denial
forweornian 03.02.01 Decay, decline, corruption; 03.02.01.01 Decay, corruption, rottenness
forweorpan 05.12.02.04 To cast out, drive away; 05.12.02.07 To throw, cast, toss; 10.03.08.01 Overliberality, waste of money; 12.05.07 Casting out, rejection
forweorpnes 05.12.02.04 To cast out, drive away
forweorþan 02.02.03 To die, perish; 02.05.07.01.01 (Of food, etc.) bad, tainted, rancid; 02.08.02 Disease, infirmity, sickness; 04.01.02.01.01 Edibility; 05.06.04 Damage, injury, defect, hurt, loss; 05.07 Ending of existence, end of world; 07.09.03 Infamy, ignominy, shame; 12.08.06.02.05.05 To sin (against), do wrong
forweorþan (tō) 02.02.03 To die, perish
forweorþende 12.08.06.01.02 Lacking moral good
forweorþenes 03.02.01.05.01 Blight (causing leaves to look burned)
forweorþfullic 07.02.04 Excellence
forwerod 02.01.04.03 Aging, growing old; 02.08.02 Disease, infirmity, sickness; 03.02.01.02 Decay from age
forwerodnes 02.01.04.03 Aging, growing old
forwiernan 11.11.02 A hindrance; 12.03.06 Prohibition

forwiernedlīce 12.08.03.03.01 Continence
forwiernednes 12.08.03.01 Abstinence (from)
forwirnan 09.07.03.02 Refusal, denial
forwisnian 03.02.01 Decay, decline, corruption; 03.02.01.01 Decay, corruption, rottenness
forwitolnes 11.02.02 Diligence
forwlencan 07.06.01.03 To be proud/arrogant
forwlenct 07.06.01.01 Proud, arrogant
forwordenes 03.02.01.05.01 Blight (causing leaves to look burned)
forwordenlic 05.07 Ending of existence, end of world; 12.08.06.01.02 Lacking moral good
forworen 02.01.04.03 Aging, growing old; 03.02.01.02 Decay from age
forworht 12.08.06.01 Error, wrong conduct, erroneous practice; 12.08.06.01.02 Lacking moral good
forworht/forwyrht 12.08.09 Guiltiness, guilt; 14.03.03.09.01 Unfavourable judgement, condemnation
forwost 12.01.01.04 A leader, ruler
forwracned 12.06.05.01 State of exile, banishment
forwrecan 05.12.02.04 To cast out, drive away; 12.05.07.01 Separation, dismissal, rejection
forwrecen 12.06.05.01 State of exile, banishment
forwrēgan 14.03.03.06 False witness
forwrēon 05.10.05.04.12 The condition of being covered
forwrītan 05.06.02 Cleaving, splitting, cutting
forwrīþan 02.08.12.02.06.01 A bandage, binding

forwundian 02.08.04.01 A wound
forwundod 08.01.03.06 Adversity, affliction
forwundorlic 06.01.08.05.01.01 Wondrous, glorious, marvellous
forwynsumian 08.01.01.03.05 Pleasure, delight
forwyrcan 05.03.01 A cause (of anything); 05.06 Destruction, dissolution, loss, breaking; 05.06.01 Devastation, laying waste; 05.07 Ending of existence, end of world; 06.01.07.04.04.03 Deceit, fraud, treachery; 10.02.01.01 Loss, forfeiture; 10.03.08.01 Overliberality, waste of money; 11.11.02 A hindrance; 12.07.02.02.01 To break a promise, vow, etc.; 12.08.09 Guiltiness, guilt; 14.03.03.09.01 Unfavourable judgement, condemnation; 14.05.04 A penalty, punishment
forwyrcan (wiþ) 12.08.06.02.05.05 To sin (against), do wrong; 14.02 Lawlessness
forwyrd 05.06 Destruction, dissolution, loss, breaking
forwyrdende 05.11.01.03.01 Mortal state, this life
forwyrht 05.06 Destruction, dissolution, loss, breaking; 16.02.01.13 Evil-doing, transgression, sin
forwyrhta 12.02.01 A substitute, representative
forwyrpnes 12.05.07 Casting out, rejection
forwyrþendlic 05.11.01.03.01 Mortal state, this life
foryldu 02.05.03.02 Weariness

foryrman 12.05.06.02.03 Trouble, disturbance
foss 01.01.02.01.03 Hollow/depression in land
fōsterbearn 06.01.06.02.03.01 A pupil, disciple, scholar
fostere 17.03.07 Tools for digging/grasping/pulling
fōstor 02.01.03.03.02 To bring forth, produce; 04.01.02 Means of subsistence; 04.01.02.04 Abundance of food; 04.01.02.04.03 Feeding, nourishing; 04.01.02.04.03.02 Bringing-up, fostering; 11.12.02.01 Strengthening, confirmation
fōstorbrōþor 02.03.02.04.01 Foster relationships
fōstorcild 02.03.02.04.01 Foster relationships; 06.01.06.02.03.01 A pupil, disciple, scholar
fōstorfæder 02.03.02.04.01 Foster relationships; 16.01.01.04.02 The Son, Christ
fōstorland 16.02.05.01 Land
fōstorlēan 10.03.05.01 Reward, meed, pay
fōstorling 02.03.02.04.01 Foster relationships
fōstormōdor 02.03.02.04.01 Foster relationships; 05.03 Source, origin
fōstornōþ 04.01.02.04 Abundance of food; 04.02.03.04.02 Pasture/pasturage
fōstraþ 04.01.02.01 Food/sustenance
fōstrian 04.01.02.04.03.01 To feed/nourish
(ge)fōstrian 11.12.02.01 Strengthening, confirmation

fōstring 02.03.02.04.01 Foster relationships; 06.01.06.02.03.01 A pupil, disciple, scholar
fōt 02.04.03.04.02.05 Foot; 02.06.01.04 Leg; 05.10.05.03 A measure of distance; 05.10.05.04.02.03.01 A low position, the bottom
fōtādl 02.08.07.08 Foot ailments, ?gout
fōtādlig 02.08.07.08 Foot ailments, ?gout
fōtbred 04.02.05.06.05.03.08 A stirrup
gefōtcopsed 14.05.07 Binding, fastening with bonds
(ge)fōtcopsian 14.05.07 Binding, fastening with bonds
fōtcosp 14.05.07 Binding, fastening with bonds
fōtcoþu 02.08.07.08 Foot ailments, ?gout
(ge)fōtcypsed 14.05.07 Binding, fastening with bonds
fōtece 02.08.07.08.01 Pain in the foot
fōt(en)sceanca 02.06.01.04 Leg
fōtes trym 05.10.05.03 A measure of distance
fōtfeter 14.05.07 Binding, fastening with bonds
fōtgangende 05.12.01.04 To go, proceed on foot
fōtgangende here 13.02.10.01.02.02.02 Branch of army
fōtgemearces 05.10.05.03 A measure of distance
fōtgemet 05.10.05.03 A measure of distance; 14.05.07 Binding, fastening with bonds
fōt(ge)swell 02.08.07.08.02 Swelling of the foot
fōtgewǣde 04.04.07.15 Footwear, covering for the feet
gefōtian 05.12.03.01.02 Haste, hurry
fōtlǣst 02.04.03.04.02.05.02 Sole; 05.10.05.03 A measure of distance; 05.12.01.04.01 Manner of going, gait

fōtlic 05.12.01.04 To go, proceed on foot; 09.03.04.03 Plain, simple
fōtmǣl 05.10.05.03 A measure of distance; 05.10.05.04.11.01.01 Object placed as point to be reached, a mark
fōtmǣlum 03.03.07 A part, division, portion
fōtrāp 05.12.01.09.03.01.03 Part of ship
fōtsceamol 04.05.04.01 A bench, seat
fōtsetl 04.05.04.01 A bench, seat
fōtsīd 04.04.07.07 A long outer garment, covering, cloak, etc.
fōtspor 05.12.01.04.01 Manner of going, gait
fōtspure 04.05.04.01 A bench, seat
fōtstān 04.05.02.05 A pedestal, socket
fōtstapol 05.12.01.04.01 Manner of going, gait
fōtswæþ 05.12.01.03.01.01 A path, track; 05.12.01.04.01 Manner of going, gait
fōtþwēal 04.06.01.01 Cleansing, washing
fōtwærc 02.08.07.08.01 Pain in the foot
fōtwelm(a) 02.04.03.04.02.05.02 Sole
fōþor 04.01.02.01.04 Animal food, fodder; 04.01.02.02.06.03 Food receptacle, basket; 05.10.05.04.12 The condition of being covered; 17.02.04.02.03 Carrying, carriage (of materials); 17.03.12.01 A basket
fox 02.06.03.01.07 Fox
foxes clāte 02.07.11 Plants/flowers (alphabetical order)
foxes clife 02.07.11 Plants/flowers (alphabetical order)
foxes fōt 02.07.11.02 Unidentified plants (alphabetical order)
foxes glōf(a) 02.07.11 Plants/flowers (alphabetical order)
foxhol 02.06.01.08 A lair, den
foxhyll 01.01.02.01.02.02.01 Hill

foxung 11.04.02.01.01 Cunning, craft, craftiness, guile, wile
fracoþ 07.03.05 Infamy, shame, wickedness; 07.05.03.02 Calumny, slander, insult; 11.08.04 Vanity, idleness, frivolity
fracoþdǣd 12.08.06.02.01 Wrong, evil-doing
fracoþe 07.09 Shame, disgrace
fracoþlic 07.09.03 Infamy, ignominy, shame
fracoþlīce 07.09 Shame, disgrace; 12.08.06.02.06 Deceit, evil, wickedness
fracoþnes 07.03.01 Abomination
fracoþscipe 12.08.06.01 Error, wrong conduct, erroneous practice
fracoþword 07.05.03.03 Scorn, insult, abuse
fræfel 11.04.02.01.01 Cunning, craft, craftiness, guile, wile
fræfelian 11.04.02.01.01 Cunning, craft, craftiness, guile, wile
fræfellīce 06.01.01.02 Care, attention, observation; 11.04.02.01.01 Cunning, craft, craftiness, guile, wile; 12.08.07.01.04 Shamelessness, lasciviousness
fræfelnes 11.04.02.01.01 Cunning, craft, craftiness, guile, wile
gefrǣge 06.01.06.01 Knowledge, cognizance, knowing; 07.08.09 Renown, fame, glory; 07.09.03 Infamy, ignominy, shame
(ge)frægn(i)an 09.05.02 A question, inquiry, questioning
frægning 09.05.02 A question, inquiry, questioning
(ge)fræpgian 07.04.03 Reverence, respect; 14.03.03.01 Accusation

fræte 07.03.05 Infamy, shame, wickedness; 07.06.01.01 Proud, arrogant; 11.04.02.01.01 Cunning, craft, craftiness, guile, wile
frætenes 07.10.03 An adornment, decoration, ornament
frætgenge 16.02.01.07 Apostasy
frætig 12.08.06.02.03 (Of persons) wicked, evil-doing
frætlæppa 02.04.05.01 Flesh
frætwe 07.10.03 An adornment, decoration, ornament; 13.02.08.03.01 Body armour, war gear; 15.01.03 Treasure, riches, wealth
frætwednes 07.10.03 An adornment, decoration, ornament
frætwian 11.01.03 Preparation
(ge)frætwian 07.02.03 Perfection; 07.10.03 An adornment, decoration, ornament
gefrætwian 04.04.07 Trappings, equipment, garb
gefrætwod 05.02.02.02 (One's) own person; 07.10.03 An adornment, decoration, ornament; 09.03.04.02 (Of language) embellished
(ge)frætwung 07.10.03 An adornment, decoration, ornament
gefrāgian 09.05.02 A question, inquiry, questioning
fram 05.10.05.04.02.01 Exterior, outside of; 06.02.07.06 Courage, boldness, valour; 11.02.01 Energy, vigour, vigorous action; 11.07.04 Superiority, pre-eminence, primacy
fram ācyrran 05.12.02.08 To give a different direction to, turn
fram ādrīfan 05.12.02.04 To cast out, drive away
fram āhyldan 05.12.02.08 To give a different direction to, turn
fram ānȳdan 05.12.02.04 To cast out, drive away
fram āsceacan 05.10.04.04.02 Removal, taking away
fram āscūfan 05.12.02.04 To cast out, drive away
fram āteran 05.06.02.02 A tearing apart
fram āwendan 05.12.05 To move and change direction, turn
fram āweorpan 05.12.02.07 To throw, cast, toss
fram (ge)būgan 05.12.05.03.03 To depart, leave, set out
fram dēaþes liþe 02.02.03.01 In process of dying
fram dōn 05.11.11.02 Let up, intermission, cessation
fram lǣtan 05.12.05.03.03 To depart, leave, set out
fram swengan 05.12.02.07 To throw, cast, toss
fram swīcan 11.06.06.01 Abandonment (of principle); 11.10.04 Flight
framācnyslian 03.02.01.01 Decay, corruption, rottenness
framācyrran 10.04.03 To take away, remove
framādōn 10.04.03 To take away, remove
framāstyrian 10.04.03 To take away, remove
framātēon 05.12.05.03 To travel away (from)
framāwælted 05.10.04.04.02 Removal, taking away
frambige 11.06.06 Turning
frambringan 10.04.03 To take away, remove
framcyme 02.03.02.02 Child, offspring

framcynn 02.03.02.02 Child, offspring; 02.03.02.03 Ancestry, descent
framcyrran 05.12.02.08 To give a different direction to, turn
framdōn 06.01.05.03.02.01 Foolishness, lightmindedness
frameald 05.11.07.03.03 Old, not new
framfær 05.12.05.03.03 To depart, leave, set out
framfæreld 05.12.05.03.03 To depart, leave, set out
framfēran 05.12.05.03.03 To depart, leave, set out; 05.12.05.03.04 To come/go out from
framfundung 05.12.05.03.03 To depart, leave, set out
framgān/framgangan 05.12.05.03.03 To depart, leave, set out
framgebēgan 05.12.05.03.03 To depart, leave, set out
fram(ge)niman 10.04.03 To take away, remove
framgewītan 05.12.05.03.03 To depart, leave, set out; 16.02.01.07 Apostasy
framhweorfan 05.12.05.03.03 To depart, leave, set out
framhycgend 12.08.06.02.02 A bad man, inhuman person
framian 11.03.02 Advancement, progress; 11.07.03 Use, advantage, profit; 12.05.06 Grasp, power, control, mastery
frami(g)endlic 11.07.01 Utility, usefulness
framirning 05.12.05.03.04.02 To flow out, well up, erupt
framlād 05.12.05.03.03 To depart, leave, set out
framlēce 05.10.05.04.09.02 Hinder part, rear

framlic 06.02.07.06.02 Boldness
framlīce 05.11.07.01 Contemporary, coeval; 06.02.07.06.02 Boldness; 17.01 Strenuous effort, hard work
framlōcian 11.06.06 Turning
framnes 05.08.01 Vigour, activity, force
framrinc 12.01.01.04 A leader, ruler
framscipe 08.01.01.03.08.02 Good fortune, success; 11.02.01 Energy, vigour, vigorous action
framsīþ 05.10.04.04 Absence
framslītnes 05.06.01 Devastation, laying waste
framsundor 05.10.04.04 Absence
framung 11.07.03 Use, advantage, profit
framweard 02.02.03.01 In process of dying; 05.10.05.04.09.02 Hinder part, rear; 05.12.05.03.03 To depart, leave, set out
framweardes 05.12.05.03 To travel away (from)
framwesende 05.10.04.04 Absence
franca 13.02.08.04.01 A spear
francan 02.03.03.06.01 Peoples of France
francrīce 12.06.01.03 The Continent
frankland 12.06.01.03 The Continent
fräsende 09.05.02 A question, inquiry, questioning
fräsian 06.01.07.06.02 Unbelief
(ge)fräsian 09.05.02 A question, inquiry, questioning
fräsung 06.01.07.06.02 Unbelief; 09.05.02 A question, inquiry, questioning
frēa 12.09 Marriage, state of marriage; 16.01.01 God, the Lord
frēa/frīgea 12.01.01.04 A leader, ruler
frēabeorht 02.05.10.01 Thing heard; 03.01.12 Brightness, light; 07.08.07

Glory, splendour, magnificence; 18.02.07 Music
frēabeorhtian 09.06.02.01.05 Proclamation, spreading abroad
frēabodian 09.06.02.01.05 Proclamation, spreading abroad
frēabregd 11.04.02.01.01 Cunning, craft, craftiness, guile, wile
frēadrēman 08.01.01.03.06 Exultation, joy
frēadrihten 12.01.01.04.01 A royal leader; 16.01.01 God, the Lord
frēafǣt 02.04.02.01 Fat/plump
frēaglēaw 06.01.05.02.01.01 Sagacity
frēahrǣd 05.11.01.02.01 Swift movement of time
frēamǣre 07.08 Reputation, fame
frēamicel 07.08.01 Nobility (of character, rank, etc.)
frēamiht 05.08 Strength
frēaofestlīce 05.11.07.01 Contemporary, coeval
frēareccere 12.01.01.04 A leader, ruler
frēatorht 03.01.12 Brightness, light
frēaþancian 08.01.01.03.06 Exultation, joy
frēawine 12.01.01.04.02 A lord, master
frēawlitig 07.10 Beauty, fairness
frēawrāsn 13.02.08.03.01.02.01 Parts of a helmet
frec 02.05.05.02 Eager desire; 04.01.01.04 Gluttony, overeating, greediness; 06.02.07.06.02.02 Boldness, daring
freca 06.02.07.06 Courage, boldness, valour
frēcedlīce 11.09 Peril, danger
frēcednes 11.09 Peril, danger
frēcelnes 11.09 Peril, danger
frēcelsian 11.09 Peril, danger
frēcendlic 11.09 Peril, danger
frēcenful 11.09 Peril, danger
frēcenlic 11.09 Peril, danger
frēcenlīce 11.09 Peril, danger
frēc(en)nes 11.09 Peril, danger
frecful 04.01.01.04 Gluttony, overeating, greediness
frecian 04.01.01.04 Gluttony, overeating, greediness
freclīce 04.01.01.04 Gluttony, overeating, greediness
frecmāse 02.06.08.05 Forest bird, wild-fowl
frēcne 06.01.08.06.03.01 Causing dread, terrifying; 06.02.07.06.02 Boldness; 06.02.07.06.02.02 Boldness, daring; 08.01.03.06 Adversity, affliction; 08.01.03.09.01.01 Savage; 08.01.03.09.10 Wrath, sternness, displeasure; 11.09 Peril, danger; 12.08.06.02.04 Darkness, evil
frēcnensprǣce 09.01.02.03 Using dangerous speech
frecnes 04.01.01.04 Gluttony, overeating, greediness
(ge)frēcnian 11.09 Peril, danger
gefrēcnod 08.01.03.05.02 Anger
frecwāsend 04.01.01.04 Gluttony, overeating, greediness
gefrēdan 02.05 Sensation, perception, feeling
gefrēdendlic (on) 02.05 Sensation, perception, feeling
gefrēdmǣlum 03.03.07 A part, division, portion
gefrēdnes 02.05 Sensation, perception, feeling
gefrēdra 02.08.03 Pain, bodily discomfort

frēfer 08.01.03.07.04.02.01 Comfort, consolation
frēfernes 08.01.03.07.04.02.01 Comfort, consolation
(ge)frēfrian 08.01.03.07.04.02.01 Comfort, consolation
frēfriend 08.01.03.07.04.02.01 Comfort, consolation; 16.01.01.04.03 The Holy Spirit
frēfriende 08.01.03.07.04.02.01 Comfort, consolation; 16.01.01.04.03 The Holy Spirit
frēfrung 08.01.03.07.04.02.01 Comfort, consolation
fregen 09.05.02 A question, inquiry, questioning
fremde 02.03.02.03.06 Kinship, relationship; 05.02.02 Nature, established order of things; 12.04.03 A stranger; 12.06.05 A foreign country
fremde (fram) 11.06.04 Abstention, abstaining from
fremdian 08.01.01.02.01 Want of interest or concern, indifference; 10.04.03.01 To take away, deprive of
(ge)fremdian 06.01.06.04 Ignorance
freme 07.02 Goodness
gefremed 07.02.03 Perfection; 11.01.04 A doing, accomplishing (of something)
fremedlǣcan 12.04.03.01 Estrangement, alienation
fremedlīce 07.02.03 Perfection
fremednes 11.01.04 A doing, accomplishing (of something)
(ge)fremednes 05.03.02 Event, issue, result
fremful 08.01.02.01 Favour, kindness, grace; 11.07.03 Use, advantage, profit
fremfullic 07.02.02 Good, what is beneficial, advantageous, etc.
fremfullīce 11.07.03 Use, advantage, profit
fremfulnes 08.01.02.01 Favour, kindness, grace; 11.07.01 Utility, usefulness
fremian 11.07.03 Use, advantage, profit
fremi(g)endlic 11.07.03 Use, advantage, profit
fremlic 07.02.02 Good, what is beneficial, advantageous, etc.
fremman tō 06.02.06.03.03 Incitement
(ge)fremman 05.05 Constitution, founding (e.g. of world); 11.01.04 A doing, accomplishing (of something); 11.01.05.02 Furtherance, promotion; 12.05.06 Grasp, power, control, mastery
fremming 05.12.05.09 To go forward, proceed; 11.01.04 A doing, accomplishing (of something)
gefremming 11.01.05 Accomplishment, fulfilment; 11.01.05.01 Furtherance, making effectual; 11.07.01 Utility, usefulness
(ge)fremnes 05.03.02 Event, issue, result
fremsum 08.01.02.01 Favour, kindness, grace
fremsume 08.01.02.01 Favour, kindness, grace
fremsumlic 08.01.02.01 Favour, kindness, grace
fremsumlīce 08.01.02.01 Favour, kindness, grace
fremsumnes 08.01.02.01 Favour, kindness, grace; 11.07.03 Use, advantage, profit
fremu 08.01.02.01 Favour, kindness, grace; 11.07.03 Use, advantage, profit
fremung 11.07.03 Use, advantage, profit

frence 04.04.07.07 A long outer garment, covering, cloak, etc.
frencisc 02.03.03.06.01 Peoples of France; 09.03.01 Particular languages
frēo 02.03.01.02 Female person, woman; 06.01.06.02.02.01 Learning, science (secular knowledge); 06.02.01 Freewill, own will; 08.01.01.03.04 Gladness, cheerfulness; 11.12.01 Absence of restraint, freedom; 12.01.01.06.05 Nobility, noble condition; 12.01.01.10 Freedom, being free; 12.07.03 Abstinence/exemption (from); 12.08.05 Innocence; 14.01.03.02 Freedom from punishment or fine; 16.02.01.10 Holiness; 18.01 Rest, quiet, freedom from toil
frēobearn 02.03.01.04 Child; 16.01.01.04.02 The Son, Christ
frēobrōþor 02.03.02.02.05.01 Brother
frēoburh 12.06.02.01 A township
frēod 08.01.02.02 Love, affection, care; 13.01.01 Peace (not war)
frēodohtor 02.03.02.02.04 A daughter
frēodōm 06.01.07.03 Truth of speech or thought, veracity; 06.02.01 Freewill, own will; 10.03.08 Bountifulness, munificence; 11.10.03 Salvation/deliverance from; 11.12.01 Absence of restraint, freedom; 12.07.03 Abstinence/exemption (from); 14.01.03.02 Freedom from punishment or fine; 14.04.01 A deed, contract, agreement; 16.01.01.02.08 Salvation, redemption
frēodscipe 08.01.02.02 Love, affection, care
frēogan 06.02.02 Will, disposition
(ge)frēogan 08.01.02.02 Love, affection, care; 08.01.02.02.02 An embrace; 11.10.03 Salvation/deliverance from; 12.01.01.10.01 Freeing, manumission; 16.01.01.02.08 Salvation, redemption
gefrēogan 14.01.03.02 Freedom from punishment or fine
gefrēogend 16.01.01.02.08 Salvation, redemption
frēolāc 16.02.04.12 Sacrifice, a sacrifice
frēolǣta 12.01.01.10.01 Freeing, manumission
frēolic 07.02.04.03 Nobleness, excellence, nobility, magnificence; 10.03.08 Bountifulness, munificence; 12.01.01.06.06 Gentle birth, nobility
(ge)frēolic 06.02.01 Freewill, own will
frēolīce 06.01.07.03 Truth of speech or thought, veracity; 06.02.01 Freewill, own will; 11.12.01 Absence of restraint, freedom; 12.07.03.01 Impunity; 15.01.01 Landed property; 16.02.04.04.02 A feast-day, holy day
frēols 12.01.01.10 Freedom, being free; 14.01.03 Special law, privilege, law for an individual; 14.01.03.02 Freedom from punishment or fine; 14.04.01 A deed, contract, agreement; 16.02.04.04.02 A feast-day, holy day; 18.02.01 A festival
frēolsǣfen 16.02.04.04.02 A feast-day, holy day
frēolsbōc 14.04.01 A deed, contract, agreement
frēolsbryce 14.02.01.01 Types of crime; 16.02.04.04.02 A feast-day, holy day
frēolsdæg 16.02.04.04.02 A feast-day, holy day; 18.02.01 A festival
frēolsdōm 14.01.03.02 Freedom from punishment or fine

frēolsgēar 05.11.02.01.02 A time of celebration; 16.02.04.04.02 A feast-day, holy day

frēolsgefa 11.10.03 Salvation/deliverance from

(ge)frēolsian 11.12.01 Absence of restraint, freedom; 16.01.01.02.08 Salvation, redemption; 16.02.01.10.02 Consecration; 16.02.04.04.02 A feast-day, holy day

frēolsiend 16.01.01.02.08 Salvation, redemption

frēolslic 16.02.04.04.02 A feast-day, holy day; 18.02.01 A festival

frēolslīce 11.12.01 Absence of restraint, freedom; 16.02.04.04.02 A feast-day, holy day; 18.02.01 A festival

frēolsmann 12.01.01.10.01 Freeing, manumission

frēolsniht 16.02.04.04.02 A feast-day, holy day; 18.02.01 A festival

frēolsstōw 16.02.05.02 A holy place or sanctuary; 18.02.01 A festival

frēolstīd 16.02.04.04.02 A feast-day, holy day; 18.02.01 A festival

frēolsung 16.02.04.04.02 A feast-day, holy day

frēomǣg 02.03.02.03.06.01 Kinsman, relative

frēomann 02.03.01.01 Male person, man; 12.01.01.10 Freedom, being free

frēonama 09.06.02.01.07 A name, appellation

frēond 02.03.02.03.06.01 Kinsman, relative; 08.01.02.02.03 A loving relationship; 08.01.02.03.01 An acquaintance, friend, associate; 11.12.02 Aid, help, succour; 12.04.01 A fellow, companion, associate, comrade; 14.03.02 A legislator

frēondheald 08.01.02.03.02 Friendly, amiable

frēondhealdlic 02.03.02.03.06 Kinship, relationship

frēondlār 12.02.02.05 Counsel, advice

frēondlaþu 08.01.02.04 Hospitality

frēondlēas 02.03.02.02 Child, offspring; 12.04.04 Solitude

frēondlēas mann 12.06.05.01 State of exile, banishment

frēondlēast 12.04.04 Solitude

frēondlic 08.01.02.03.02 Friendly, amiable

frēondlīce 08.01.02.03.03 In a friendly manner, kindly

frēondlīþe 08.01.02.03.02 Friendly, amiable

frēondlufu 08.01.02.02.03 A loving relationship

frēondmynd 08.01.02.02.03 A loving relationship

frēondrǣden 08.01.02.02.03 A loving relationship; 08.01.02.03 Friendliness, affection; 13 Peace, tranquillity

frēondscipe 08.01.02.02.03 A loving relationship; 08.01.02.03 Friendliness, affection; 13 Peace, tranquillity

frēondspēd 08.01.01.03.08.01 Abundance of friends

frēondspēdig 08.01.01.03.08.01 Abundance of friends

frēorig 03.01.11 Coldness, coolness; 08.01.03 Bad feeling, sadness

frēorigferþ 08.01.03.01 Despondency

frēorigmōd 08.01.03 Bad feeling, sadness

frēoriht 14.01.04.01 A special right, right peculiar to a class

(ge)frēosan 01.03.01.04.02 Ice; 03.01.11 Coldness, coolness

frēosceatt 15.01 Property

frēot

frēot 12.01.01.10 Freedom, being free; 12.01.01.10.01 Freeing, manumission
frēotes þolian 12.01.01.09 Bondage, slavery
frēotgifa 11.10.03 Salvation/deliverance from
frēotgift 12.01.01.10.01 Freeing, manumission
frēotgifta 12.01.01.10.01 Freeing, manumission
frēotmann 12.01.01.10.01 Freeing, manumission
frēowīf 12.01.01.10 Freedom, being free
fresan 02.03.03.06.02 Germany and Low Countries
fresisc 02.03.03.06.02 Germany and Low Countries
fretan 04.01.01.01 Chewing
(ge)fretan 05.06.01 Devastation, laying waste; 10.03.08.01 Overliberality, waste of money
frett 04.01.01.04 Gluttony, overeating, greediness
(ge)frettan 05.06.01 Devastation, laying waste
frettol 04.01.01.04 Gluttony, overeating, greediness
frīandæg 05.11.03.01.05.01 Specific days
fricca 09.06.02.01.06.01 A messenger
(ge)fricgan 09.05.02 A question, inquiry, questioning
gefricgan 06.01.06.01 Knowledge, cognizance, knowing
frician 18.02.04 Dancing
friclan 02.05.05 Desire, appetite
friclo 02.05.05 Desire, appetite
frico 15.04.01 Lending of money
(ge)frīend 08.01.02.03.01 An acquaintance, friend, associate
gefrige 06.01.06.01.01 Knowledge

frīge 08.01.02.02.03 A loving relationship
frīgeǣfen 05.11.03.01.05.01 Specific days
frīgedæg 05.11.03.01.05.01 Specific days
frigedōm 06.01.01.01.01.01 Consideration, rumination
frīgeniht 05.11.03.01.05.01 Specific days
(ge)frignan 09.05.02 A question, inquiry, questioning
gefrignan 06.01.06.01 Knowledge, cognizance, knowing; 11.03.01.03 Finding, discovery
(ge)frignes 09.05.02 A question, inquiry, questioning
frīgnes 11.12.01 Absence of restraint, freedom
frignung 09.05.02 A question, inquiry, questioning
friht 16.01.04.06 Divination, augury
frihtere 16.01.04.06 Divination, augury
frihtrian 16.01.04.06 Divination, augury
frihtrung 16.01.04.06 Divination, augury
frīs 02.03.03.06.02 Germany and Low Countries
frisan 02.03.03.06.02 Germany and Low Countries
frið 13 Peace, tranquillity; 13.01 Peace, state of law and order; 13.01.01 Peace (not war); 13.01.01.01 Cessation of hostilities; 14.01.03.01 Sanctuary; 14.03.03.09.03 Outlawry; 16.02.04.18.04 Church peace, right of sanctuary
frið (ge)fæstnian 13.01.01.01 Cessation of hostilities
frið macian 13.01.01.01 Cessation of hostilities
frið (ge)niman 13.01.01.01 Cessation of hostilities

frīþ 07.10.01 Elegance, beauty, comeliness
friþa 11.10.01 Protection, safekeeping
friþāþ 13.01.01.01 Cessation of hostilities
friþbēna 14.03.03.09.02 Atonement
friþborh 14.03.03.07 Security, pledge, bail
friþbrǣc 14.02.01.01 Types of crime
friþburh 13.01 Peace, state of law and order
friþcandel 01.02.01.01.03 Sun
friþen 11.10.01.02 Refuge, help, shelter
friþgeard 14.01.03.01 Sanctuary; 16.01.02.01 Heavenly dwelling place
friþgedāl 02.02 Death
friþgegilda 12.02.03 A society, guild, association
friþgeorn 13 Peace, tranquillity
friþgewrit 13.01.01.01 Cessation of hostilities
friþgild 12.02.03 A society, guild, association
friþgīsl 13.02.05.01.02.01 State of being a hostage
friþhengest 02.06.02.01.06 Horse
friþherpaþ 05.12.01.03.01.03 A highway
friþhūs 14.01.03.01 Sanctuary
friþian 13.01 Peace, state of law and order; 13.01.01.01 Cessation of hostilities; 14.01.03 Special law, privilege, law for an individual; 16.02.04.04.02 A feast-day, holy day
(ge)friþian 11.10.01 Protection, safekeeping; 11.10.01.01 Preservation from injury/destruction; 14.01.03.01 Sanctuary
gefriþian 11.10.03 Salvation/deliverance from
(ge)friþiend 11.10.01 Protection, safekeeping

friþland 13.01.01 Peace (not war)
friþlēas 14.03.03.09.03 Outlawry
friþlic 08.01.02.01.02.01 Mildness, leniency, indulgence
friþmāl 13.01.01.01 Cessation of hostilities
friþmann 14.01.03.01 Sanctuary
friþobēacen 09.04.01 Signal, signalling
gefriþod 11.10.01.02 Refuge, help, shelter; 14.01.03.01 Sanctuary
friþoscealc 16.01.02.05.01 An angel
friþosibb 13.01.01.01 Cessation of hostilities
friþospēd 08.01.01.03.08 Happiness, well-being, prosperity
friþotācn 09.04.01 Signal, signalling
friþoþēawas 08.01.01.03.08 Happiness, well-being, prosperity
friþowǣr 13.01.01.01 Cessation of hostilities
friþowang 01.01.02.01.04 Open (level) land; 13.01.01 Peace (not war)
friþowaru 11.10.01 Protection, safekeeping
friþowebba 16.01.02.05.01 An angel
friþowebba(-e) 13.01.01.01 Cessation of hostilities
friþscip 05.12.01.09.03.01.01 Kind of ship
friþsōcn 14.01.03.01 Sanctuary
friþsplott 14.01.03.01 Sanctuary; 16.02.05.02 A holy place or sanctuary
friþstōl 14.01.03.01 Sanctuary
friþstōw 11.10.01.02 Refuge, help, shelter; 14.01.03.01 Sanctuary
friþsum 13 Peace, tranquillity
gefriþsum 13.02.06 A fortification
friþsumian 13.01.02 Reconciliation

friþu

friþu 11.10.01 Protection, safekeeping; 13.01.01 Peace (not war); 16.02.04.03.02 Parts of service
frōd 05.11.07.03.03 Old, not new; 06.01.05.02.01.01 Sagacity; 11.04.02 Skill, skilfulness
frōde 06.01.05.02.01.01.01 Reason, sense, discretion, prudence
frōdian 06.01.05.02.01.01 Sagacity
frōfor 08.01.03.07.04.02.01 Comfort, consolation; 11.12.02 Aid, help, succour
(ge)frōfor 08.01.03.07.04.02.01 Comfort, consolation
frōforbōc 16.02.05.10.13 Other books
frōforgāst 16.01.01.04.03 The Holy Spirit
frōforlic 08.01.03.07.04.02.01 Comfort, consolation
frōforlīce 08.01.03.07.04.02.01 Comfort, consolation
frōfornes 08.01.03.07.04.02.01 Comfort, consolation
frōforword 08.01.03.07.04.02.01 Comfort, consolation
frogga 02.06.07.02 Frog, toad
frosc 02.06.07.02 Frog, toad
frōwe 02.03.01.02 Female person, woman
frum 05.11.10.01.01 Origin
fruma 02.03.02.02 Child, offspring; 05.03 Source, origin; 05.05.01 An author, source, originator; 05.11.10.01 A beginning; 12.01.01.04 A leader, ruler
frumācennes 02.01.03.03.03 Birth
frumbearn 02.03.02.02 Child, offspring
frumbyrd 02.01.03.03.03 Birth
frumbyrdling 02.03.01.05 Youth, boy, stripling
frumcenned 02.03.02.02 Child, offspring; 09.03.02.03 Composition (inflectional or compounding)
frumcennende 05.11.07.03 Former times, days of old
frumcenning 02.03.02.02 Child, offspring
frumcnēow 02.03.02.03 Ancestry, descent
frumcyn 02.03.03.02 A race, tribe
frumcynn 02.03.02.03 Ancestry, descent
frumcyrr 05.11.10.01 A beginning
frumdysig 16.02.01.13.01 Kinds of sin
frumgār 12.01.01.04 A leader, ruler
frumgesceap 01 Earth, world; 05.05 Constitution, founding (e.g. of world)
frumgeweorc 04.05 Building, construction
frum(ge)weorc 05.05 Constitution, founding (e.g. of world)
frumgewrit 14.04.01 A deed, contract, agreement
frumgield 15.02.04 Spending, disbursement
frumgifu 14.01.03 Special law, privilege, law for an individual
frumgripa 16.02.04.20 Church due/requirement
frumhēowung 01 Earth, world; 05.05 Constitution, founding (e.g. of world)
frumhrægl 04.04.07.01 Mode of dressing, fashion
frumildo 02.01.04.01 Youth
frumlēoht 05.11.04.01.01 Dawn, daybreak, sunrise
frumlīce 05.11.10.01.01 Origin
frumlida 05.12.01.09.03 A voyage
frumlȳhtan 05.11.04.01.01 Dawn, daybreak, sunrise
frummeoluc 04.01.02.01.02.09.04 Beestings (colostrum)

frummynetslæge 15.01.04 Coinage, money
frumrǣd 16.02.01.09.01 Canon law
frumrǣden 14.01.06 A rule, order, precept, tenet, principle
frumrīpa 04.02.04.04.02 Harvesting; 16.02.04.20 Church due/requirement
frumsceaft 01 Earth, world; 02 Creation; 02.01.03.03.03 Birth; 05.02 State, condition; 05.03 Source, origin; 05.05 Constitution, founding (e.g. of world)
frumsceapen 05.10.06 Form, shape
frumsceatt 04.02.04.04.02 Harvesting; 16.02.04.20 Church due/requirement
frumsceppend 16.01.01.02.01 Creator
frumscyld 16.02.01.13.01 Kinds of sin
frumsetnes 12.01.01 Authority
frumsetnung 01 Earth, world; 05.05 Constitution, founding (e.g. of world)
frumslǣp 02.05.04 Sleepiness, drowsiness, sleep
frumspellung 09.06.01 To relate, recount, tell
frumsprǣc 09.03.07.07.02.01.02 A prologue, preface; 12.07.02.01 Covenant, assurance of faith, promise
frumstaþol 05.10.04.01 Position, stance
frumstemn 05.12.01.09.03.01.03 Part of ship
frumstōl 04.05.03.02.02.05 A paternal dwelling; 05.10.04.01 Position, stance; 16.01.02.04 Paradise
frumtalu 14.03.03.01 Accusation
frumtēam 04.02.05.06 Animals yoked together
frumtīd 05.11.10.01 A beginning
frumtyhtle 14.03.03.01 Accusation
frumþylde 02.01.04.01 Youth
frumwæstm 04.02.04.04.02 Harvesting; 16.02.04.20 Church due/requirement
frumweorc 01 Earth, world
frumwīfung 12.09 Marriage, state of marriage
frumwylm 02.08.02.01.03 A symptom; 08.01.01.01.04 Depth of feeling, zeal
frumwyrhta 05.05.01 An author, source, originator
frymdig bēon/wesan 02.05.05 Desire, appetite; 09.05 Curiosity; 12.03.04.01 Entreaty, solemn appeal
frymetling 02.06.02.01.03 Cattle
frymþ 01 Earth, world; 04.02.04.04.02 Harvesting; 05.03 Source, origin; 05.05 Constitution, founding (e.g. of world); 05.11.10.01 A beginning; 16.01.01.02.01 Creator; 16.02.04.20 Church due/requirement
frymþlic 03.03.05.01.01 Principal/chief (of its class or type); 05.11.07.03 Former times, days of old; 09.03.07.07.03.04.01 A document, deed; 16.02.01.13.01 Kinds of sin
frymþlīce 05.11.10.01.01 Origin
frysca 02.06.08.06 Water bird
fugel 02.06.08 Bird
fugelbana 04.03.04 Fowling
fugelcynn 02.06.08 Bird
fugeldoppe 02.06.08.06 Water bird
fugeles wȳse 02.07.11 Plants/flowers (alphabetical order)
fugelhwata 16.01.04.06 Divination, augury
fugellīm 04.03.04 Fowling
fugelnet 04.03.04 Fowling
fugel(n)oþ 04.03.04 Fowling
fugeltimber 02.06.08 Bird
fugeltrēow 04.03.04 Fowling
fugelweohlere 16.01.04.06 Divination, augury
fugelwylle 03.03.04.02.01 Abundance

fuglere 04.03.04 Fowling
fugles bēan 02.07.11 Plants/flowers (alphabetical order)
fugles lēac 02.07.11.02 Unidentified plants (alphabetical order)
fuglian 04.03.04 Fowling
fuglung 04.03.04 Fowling
fuguldæg 04.01.01.06.01 Abstinence from food, fast
fūht 03.01.16.01 Moisture
fūhtian 03.01.16.01 Moisture
ful 03.03.06.02 Fullness; 04.01.03.05.04 Drinking vessel
ful wērig 02.05.03.02 Weariness
fūl 02.05.08.01 Foul smell, stench, stink; 03.02.01.01 Decay, corruption, rottenness; 04.06.02.01 Dirty, unclean; 04.06.02.02 Foul, filthy, squalid; 07.03.05 Infamy, shame, wickedness; 07.10.02 Ugliness; 12.08.06.02 Wickedness, evil; 14.02 Lawlessness; 14.02.01 An offence; 14.03.03.09.01 Unfavourable judgement, condemnation; 16.02.01.10.02.02 Not blessed, unconsecrated
fūla bēam 02.07.03.05 Particular trees/shrubs (alphabetical order)
fulbeorht 03.01.12 Brightness, light
fulberstan 05.06.03 A dashing together, breaking, shattering
fulbrecan 14.02 Lawlessness
fuldōn 03.05 Order, arrangement, disposition; 11.01.04 A doing, accomplishing (of something); 11.01.05 Accomplishment, fulfilment
fūle 02.05.08.01 Foul smell, stench, stink; 12.08.08.01.02 Unchastity, incontinence
fūletrēo 02.07.03.05 Particular trees/shrubs (alphabetical order)

fulfæstnian 14.04.03 Confirmation, ratification
fulfaran 05.12.01.01 To go on a journey/expedition, travel
fulfealdan 09.04.03 Exposition, making clear by explanation
fulgeare 03.03.06 Wholeness; 09.04.03 Exposition, making clear by explanation
fulgeorne 06.02.05.04 Desire, eagerness
fulgōd 07.02 Goodness
fulhār 02.04.04.03.02 Colour of hair; 03.01.14.10 Grey-coated one
fulhealden 03.03.04.02 A sufficiency, sufficient supply
gefulhtnian/(ge)fulwiht(i)an 16.02.04.07.01 Baptism, baptizing (and anointing)
fūlian 03.02.01.01 Decay, corruption, rottenness
fūliende 03.02.01.01 Decay, corruption, rottenness
full 01.01.03.04 Current, rush of water; 01.02.01.01.04 Moon; 03.03.04.01 Much; 03.03.04.02.01 Abundance; 03.03.06 Wholeness; 06.02.05.03 Satisfaction, repletion; 07.02.03 Perfection; 11.01.06 End, completion (of action), fulfilment; 12 Power, might
full æþele 12.01.01.06.05 Nobility, noble condition
full gearwian 10.03.04 Provision, supply
full clǣne 12.08.04 Purity, moral cleanness
full cūþ 11.05.01 Familiarity
full gedrifen 05.12.02.06 To push, impel, thrust
full grōwan 02.01.04.02 To grow, grow up

full medomlīce 03.03.06 Wholeness
full oft 05.11.09.02 Frequent, of common occurrence
full raþe 05.11.07.01 Contemporary, coeval; 05.12.03.01 Swiftness, velocity
full ricene 05.11.07.01 Contemporary, coeval
full singan 18.02.07.01 Singing, song
full slēan 02.02.04.03 To kill, slay
full welig 15.01.05 Possession of wealth
fulla 07.02.03 Perfection
fullǣst 11.12.02 Aid, help, succour
(ge)fullǣstan 11.12.02 Aid, help, succour
fullbētan 16.02.04.07.02.03 Penance, an act/instance of penance
fullblīþe 08.01.01.03 Good feeling, joy, happiness
fullboren 02.01.03.03.03 Birth; 02.08.01 Sound physical condition; 07.02.03 Perfection; 12.01.01.06.01 Rank, position due to birth
fullbryce 14.02.01.01 Types of crime
fullcuman 05.12.05.02.03 To arrive
fullcūþ 06.01.06.01.01.01 Acquaintance, knowledge; 07.08 Reputation, fame
fullcȳþan 09.06.02.01.05 Proclamation, spreading abroad
fulle 02.07.09.02.02.01 Edible root/bulb
fullendian 11.01.06 End, completion (of action), fulfilment
fullere 04.04.01 Fulling
fullflēon 11.10.04 Flight
fullforþian 11.01.05 Accomplishment, fulfilment
fullfremed 06.01.06.02.03.04.04 Under instruction, being taught; 07.02.03 Perfection; 09.03.02.03.01.02.04 Aspect; 11.01.06 End, completion (of action), fulfilment

fullfremedlic 07.02.03 Perfection
fullfremedlīce 03.03.06 Wholeness; 09.03.02.03.01.02.04 Aspect
fullfremednes 03.03.06 Wholeness; 07.02.03 Perfection
fullfremman 05.03.01 A cause (of anything); 07.02.03 Perfection
(ge)fullfremman 11.01.04 A doing, accomplishing (of something); 11.01.06 End, completion (of action), fulfilment
fullfyligan 05.12.05.10 To go behind, follow; 12.01.01.12.01 Obedience, service
fullfyllan 11.01.05 Accomplishment, fulfilment
fullgān 11.01.05 Accomplishment, fulfilment; 11.12.02 Aid, help, succour; 12.07.02 Observance, keeping
fullgangan 11.01.06 End, completion (of action), fulfilment; 11.02 Occupation, activity, business
fullgearwian 11.01.06 End, completion (of action), fulfilment
fullgedrifen 03.03.06.02 Fullness
full(ge)gān 11.02 Occupation, activity, business
fullgeorne 09.04.03 Exposition, making clear by explanation; 11.02.02 Diligence
fullgewǣpned 13.02.08 Military equipment
fullhāl 02.08.01 Sound physical condition
fullian 03.03.06.02 Fullness; 12.07.02 Observance, keeping
(ge)full(i)an 03.03.06.02 Fullness
(ge)fullian 07.02.03 Perfection
fullic 03.03.06.02 Fullness

fūllic 04.06.02.01 Dirty, unclean; 07.03.01.01 Abominable, detestable; 07.09 Shame, disgrace
fullīce 03.03.04.02.01 Abundance; 03.03.06 Wholeness; 04.01.01.05 Satiety (of food); 09.03.02.03.01.02.04 Aspect
fūllīce 04.06.02.02 Foul, filthy, squalid; 07.09 Shame, disgrace
fullmægen 12.01.01 Authority
fullmannod 12.06.03 A site, settlement
fullnes 03.03.06.02 Fullness; 11.01.05 Accomplishment, fulfilment
fulloc 14.04.04 An agreement, arrangement of dispute
fullrīpod 02.01.04.02 To grow, grow up
fullsecgan (be) 09.06.02.01.01 To make known, cause to know, inform
fullþungen 03.03.06 Wholeness
fullþungennes 03.03.06 Wholeness
fulluht underfōn 16.02.04.07.01 Baptism, baptizing (and anointing)
fulluhtþēaw 16.02.04.07.01 Baptism, baptizing (and anointing)
fulluhtþegnung 16.02.04.07.01 Baptism, baptizing (and anointing)
fullunga 03.03.06 Wholeness
fullwearm 03.01.09.01 Warmth, heat
fullweaxen 02.01.04.02 To grow, grow up
fullwer 16.02.04.07.02.03 Penance, an act/instance of penance
gefullwod 16.02.04.07.01 Baptism, baptizing (and anointing)
fullwyrcan 11.01.06 End, completion (of action), fulfilment
fulnēah 03.06 Comparison; 05.10.05.01 A little way, no great distance
fūlnes 02.05.08.01 Foul smell, stench, stink
fūlstincende 02.05.08.01 Foul smell, stench, stink
fulsumnes 03.03.04.01 Much
fultrūwian 06.01.08.03 Trust, faith, confidence
fultum 02.08.12.01 Medical care, treatment; 11.12.02 Aid, help, succour; 13.02.10.01.02.02 Armed forces
fultum gestandan 11.12.02 Aid, help, succour
gefultuma 11.12.02 Aid, help, succour
fultumgestre 11.12.02 Aid, help, succour; 16.01.02.05.02.01 Mary, queen of heaven
(ge)fultumian 11.12.02 Aid, help, succour
(ge)fultumiend 11.12.02 Aid, help, succour
fultumlēas 11.09 Peril, danger
fulwa 04.04.01 Fulling
fulwere 16.02.04.07.01 Baptism, baptizing (and anointing)
(ge)fulwian 16.02.04.07.01 Baptism, baptizing (and anointing)
fulwiht 16.02.04.07.01 Baptism, baptizing (and anointing)
fulwiht onfōn 16.02.04.07.01 Baptism, baptizing (and anointing)
fulwihtbæþ 16.02.04.07.01 Baptism, baptizing (and anointing)
fulwihtbēna 16.02.04.07.01 Baptism, baptizing (and anointing)
fulwihtele 16.02.05.09.03 Holy oil
fulwihtere 16.02.01.08.03.01 New Testament persons; 16.02.04.07.01 Baptism, baptizing (and anointing)
fulwihtfæder 16.02.04.07.01 Baptism, baptizing (and anointing)
fulwihthād 16.02.04.07.01 Baptism, baptizing (and anointing)

fulwihtnama 09.06.02.01.07 A name, appellation
fulwihtstōw 16.02.05.03.08 A baptistry
fulwihttīd 16.02.04.07.01 Baptism, baptizing (and anointing)
fulwihttīd ēces drihtnes 16.02.04.04.02.01.01 Around the Nativity
fulwihtwæter 16.02.04.07.01 Baptism, baptizing (and anointing)
fulwihtwer 16.02.01.08.03.01 New Testament persons; 16.02.04.07.01 Baptism, baptizing (and anointing)
funden cild 02.03.02.02 Child, offspring; 12.04.04 Solitude
gefunden 03.03.03.01 Arithmetic
fundian 05.12.03.01.02 Haste, hurry; 11.03.01 Experience, trial, experiment
fundian tō 12.05.06.02.03 Trouble, disturbance
fundian (tō) 08.01 Heart, spirit, mood, disposition
fundian (tō)) 06.02.06.01 An end, goal
(ge)fundian 05.12.05.09 To go forward, proceed
(ge)fundian (on/tō) 05.12.05.02 To go/travel towards, come, approach
fundung 05.12.05.03.03 To depart, leave, set out
funta/-e 01.01.03.01.01.03 Stream
funta/fynt 01.01.03.01.01.07 Spring, fountain, well
gefuntian 16.02.04.07.01 Baptism, baptizing (and anointing)
furh 04.02.03.02.01.01 A furrow
furh/fyrh 02.07.03.05 Particular trees/shrubs (alphabetical order)
furhwudu 02.07.03.05 Particular trees/shrubs (alphabetical order)

(ge)fūrian 04.02.04.02.02.02 Ploughing, tilling
furlang 04.02.03.03.04 Area a furrow-long across; 05.10.05.03 A measure of distance
furþor 03.03.04.03 Growth, increase; 03.03.05 Extent, degree; 03.03.06 Wholeness; 05.10.05.04.09.01.01 Head, front (position); 05.11.07.04.02 (Of time) later/latter; 11.01.05.02 Furtherance, promotion; 11.02.01 Energy, vigour, vigorous action
furþor dōn 11.01.05.02 Furtherance, promotion
furþor gemedemian 07.08.03 Honour, veneration
furþorlīce 11.07.03 Use, advantage, profit
furþra 02.06.01.04 Leg; 03.03.05.01.01 Principal/chief (of its class or type); 07.02.04 Excellence
furþum 03.06 Comparison; 05.11.07.02 The present (time); 05.11.10.01 A beginning
furþumlic 12.08.07.01 Laxity, indulgence
fūs 02.02.03.01 In process of dying; 03.01.12.01 Glittering, effulgence; 05.12.03.01 Swiftness, velocity; 06.02.05.04.03 Promptitude, readiness
fūslēoþ 02.02.05.03 To attend the dead
fūslic 07.02.04.03 Nobleness, excellence, nobility, magnificence
fūslīce 06.02.02.01 Will, wish, pleasure
fūsnes 05.12.03.01 Swiftness, velocity
fȳhtan 03.01.16.01 Moisture
(ge)fȳlan 04.06.02.02 Foul, filthy, squalid; 16.02.04.14 Sacrilege
gefylca 12.04.01 A fellow, companion, associate, comrade
gefylce 13.02.10.01.02.01 An armed force/band

(ge)fylcian 13.02.07.02 Order (of troops), array
fyld(e)stōl 04.05.04.01 A bench, seat
gefȳled 12.08.06.01.02 Lacking moral good
fylgan 02.08.12.02 To tend the sick; 05.12.05.10 To go behind, follow; 06.02.06.01 An end, goal; 11.02.02.02.01 Attention, cultivation; 12.04.01.02 A fellow traveller, companion
fylgan swæþ 05.12.05.10 To go behind, follow
(ge)fylgan 05.11.07.04.02 (Of time) later/latter; 11.01.01 Practice, exercise, doing; 12.01.01.07 A follower; 12.01.01.12 Loyalty; 12.05.06.04.02 Submission, subjection, obedience
(ge)fylgan (æfter) 05.12.05.10 To go behind, follow
gefylgan 10.01.02 Acquisition
fylgend 11.01.04 A doing, accomplishing (of something)
fylgestre 11.01.04 A doing, accomplishing (of something)
fylging 02.03.03.01 Body of retainers, household; 04.02.03.02.03 Fallow land; 05.12.05.10 To go behind, follow
fyligendlic 03.06.01.01 Imitation
fylignes 11.01.04 A doing, accomplishing (of something)
fyllan 04.02.04.05.04.01 A forester, woodman; 11.11.01 A physical difficulty, strait
(ge)fyllan 03.03.04.02.01 Abundance; 03.03.06 Wholeness; 03.03.06.02 Fullness; 05.06.01 Devastation, laying waste; 05.10.04.03 Presence; 05.12.05.13.03 To fall; 11.01.04 A doing, accomplishing (of something); 11.01.05 Accomplishment, fulfilment; 11.01.06 End, completion (of action), fulfilment
gefyllan 03.03.04.02 A sufficiency, sufficient supply; 09.07.02 Contradiction
gefylled 10.04.03.01 To take away, deprive of
(ge)fyllednes 03.03.06.02 Fullness
gefyllednes 05.11.10.02 End, completion; 11.01.04 A doing, accomplishing (of something); 11.01.05 Accomplishment, fulfilment
fyllend 11.01.04 A doing, accomplishing (of something)
gefyllendlic 03.03.06 Wholeness; 09.03.02.02.01.03 An adverb
fyllere 04.01.03.05.03 Tavern
fyllesēoc 02.08.09.02 Epilepsy
fyllesēocnes 02.08.09.02 Epilepsy
fylleþflōd 01.01.03.04 Current, rush of water
fyllewærc 02.08.09.02 Epilepsy
fylling 03.03.06 Wholeness; 03.03.06.02 Fullness
(ge)fylling 05.11.10.02 End, completion
gefyllingtīd 16.02.04.05.09 The hour or service of Compline
(ge)fyllnes 03.03.06.02 Fullness; 05.11.10.02 End, completion
gefyllnes 03.03.04.03 Growth, increase; 07.02.03 Perfection; 11.01.04 A doing, accomplishing (of something)
fyll(u) 03.03.04.02.01 Abundance; 02.01.03.03.01 To beget; 04.01.01.05 Satiety (of food); 03.03.06.02 Fullness; 04.01.01.04 Gluttony, overeating, greediness

gefylnes 05.06 Destruction, dissolution, loss, breaking
fȳlnes 02.05.08.01 Foul smell, stench, stink; 12.08.06.01.01 Pollution, impairment
fylst 11.12.02 Aid, help, succour
gefylsta 11.12.02 Aid, help, succour; 17.02.01 Management of work
(ge)fylstan 11.12.02 Aid, help, succour
(ge)fylstend 11.12.02 Aid, help, succour
fȳlþ 04.06.02.02 Foul, filthy, squalid; 12.08.06 Moral evil, depravity
fylwērig 02.02.03.01 In process of dying
fyndel 11.03.01.03.01 Discovery, invention
fyne 03.02.01.05 Mould, moisture
(ge)fynegian 03.02.01.05 Mould, moisture
fynig 01.01.02.01.04.01 Marsh, bog, swamp; 03.02.01.05 Mould, moisture
fyniht 01.01.02.01.04.01 Marsh, bog, swamp
fȳr 01.03.01.03.01.02 Lightning; 03 Material, matter, substance; 03.01.09.02 Fire, flame; 03.01.09.02.01 Fire, burning
fȳran 02.08.04.02.02 Castrated
(ge)fȳran 04.02.04.02.02.02 Ploughing, tilling
fȳrbǣre 03.01.09.02 Fire, flame
fȳrbæþ 16.01.05 Hell, lower world, abode of the dead
fȳrbend 17.03.10.01 A bolt, lock, bar
fȳrbēta 17.05.02 A hearth, fireplace
fȳrbryne 03.01.09.02.01.01 A kind of fire
fȳrclamm 17.03.10.01 A bolt, lock, bar
fyrclian 03.01.12.01 Glittering, effulgence
fȳrcrūce 04.01.02.02.06.01 Cooking vessel/pot

fȳrcynn 03.01.09.02.01.01 A kind of fire
fyrdcræft 13.02.10.01.02.01 An armed force/band
fyrdend 13.02.09.01 Military service
fyrdesne 13.02.10.01 A man, warrior
fyrdfǣreld 13.02.09.01 Military service
fyrdfaru 13.02.09.01 Military service
fyrdfōr 13.02.09.01 Military service
fyrdgeatwe 13.02.08 Military equipment
fyrdgemaca 13.02.10 The military, soldiers
fyrdgestealla 13.02.10 The military, soldiers
fyrdgetrum 13.02.10.01.02.01 An armed force/band
fyrdhom 13.02.08.03.01.04 Coat of mail/corselet
fyrdhrægl 13.02.08.03.01 Body armour, war gear
fyrdhwæt 06.02.07.06 Courage, boldness, valour
fyrdian 13.02.09.01 Military service
fyrding 05.12.05.09 To go forward, proceed; 13.02.01 A military expedition; 13.02.09.01 Military service; 13.02.10.01.02.02 Armed forces; 18.02.03.01.02 Racing
fyrdlāf 13.02.10.02.01 Survivors of a battle
fyrdlēas 11.09 Peril, danger; 13.02.10.01.02.02 Armed forces
fyrdlēoþ 13.02.07.03 A war song
fyrdlic 13.02.09 Military style
fyrdmann 13.02.10 The military, soldiers
fyrdnoþ 13.02.09.01 Military service
fȳrdraca 02.06.10.01.01 Dragon
fyrdrian 13.02.09.01 Military service
fyrdrinc 13.02.10 The military, soldiers
fyrdsceorp 13.02.08.03.01 Body armour, war gear

fyrdscip 13.02.10.03.01 A fleet
fyrdsearu 13.02.08.03.01 Body armour, war gear
fyrdsōcn 13.02.09.01 Military service
fyrdstemn 13.02.10.01.02.02.03 Part of an army
fyrdstrǣt 05.12.01.03.01.03 A highway
fyrdtīber 16.02.04.12 Sacrifice, a sacrifice
fyrdtruma 13.02.10.01.02.02 Armed forces
fyrdwǣn 05.12.01.06 Vehicle
fyrdweard 13.02.10.01.02.02.03 Part of an army
fyrdwerod 13.02.10.01.02.02 Armed forces
fyrdwīc 13.02.07.04 A camp, encampment
fyrdwīsa 13.02.10.01.01 A commander, officer
fyrdwīse 13.02.09 Military style
fyrdwīte 14.05.04.01 A fine
fyrdwyrþe 13.02.09.01 Military service; 13.02.10.01 A man, warrior
gefȳred 04.02.03.02 Arable/ploughed land
fyren topp 01.02.01.01.06 Heavenly light
fȳren 03.01.09.02 Fire, flame; 03.01.09.02.01 Fire, burning; 08.01.01.01 Ardour, fervour, strong feeling
fȳren þecele 03.01.09.02.01 Fire, burning
fȳrencylle 17.05.03 Sources of fire/light
fȳrenful 03.01.09.02 Fire, flame; 08.01.01.01 Ardour, fervour, strong feeling
fyrenhycga 12.08.08.01.02.01 Fornication, adultery

fȳrentācen 06.01.08.05.01.01.01 An exercise of power, mighty work, miracle
fȳrentācnian 12.08.06.01.04.01 To mislead, seduce, lead astray
fȳres and fēole lāf 13.02.08.04.03 A sword
fȳres scotung 01.03.01.03.01.02 Lightning
fȳrfeaxen 02.04.04.03.02 Colour of hair
fȳrfōda 17.05.01 Fuel, tinder
fȳrgearwung 04.01.02.02.05 Cooking
fȳrgebeorh 17.05.02 A hearth, fireplace
fȳrgebræc 03.01.09.02 Fire, flame
fyrgen 01.01.02.01.02.02.02 Mountain
fyrgenhēafod 01.01.02.01.01.03.01 Promontory, headland, cape
fȳrgnāst 03.01.09.02 Fire, flame
fȳrhāt 03.01.09 Heat; 08.01.01.01 Ardour, fervour, strong feeling
fȳrheard 03.01.03 Hardness, callosity, hard material; 13.02.08.04.03 A sword
fyrht 06.01.08.06 Fear
(ge)fyrhtian 06.01.08.06 Fear
gefyrht(i)an 06.01.08.06.03 Cause of fear, terror, horror
fyrhtnes 06.01.08.06 Fear
(ge)fyrhto 06.01.08.06 Fear
(ge)fyrhþ(e) 01.01.02.01.05 Covered with vegetation
fȳrhūs 04.05.03.04 A closet, chamber, room
fȳrian 17.05.04 To kindle, set alight (fire, lamp)
fyrlen 05.10.05 A space, span
fȳrlēoht 03.01.12.02 A beam of light
fȳrlēoma 03.01.12.02 A beam of light
fȳrloca 14.05.08.01 Prison, confinement, durance
fyrl(u) 05.10.05 A space, span
fyrm 04.06.01 Clean
fȳrmǣl 13.02.08.04.03 A sword

fyrmest 03.04.03.01 Someone/something; 05.10.05.04.09.01 Front; 05.10.05.04.09.01.01 Head, front (position); 05.11.10.01 A beginning; 07.02.03 Perfection; 07.02.04 Excellence; 11.07.04 Superiority, pre-eminence, primacy; 12.01.01.06.02.01 (High) rank, status, degree

fyrmþ 04.01.02.04.05.01 Hospitality, harbouring, entertaining; 04.06.01.01 Cleansing, washing

fyrn 05.11.07.03 Former times, days of old

(ge)fyrn 05.11.07.03 Former times, days of old

gefyrn 05.11.07.03.02 Earlier, antecedent

(ge)fyrndagas 05.11.07.03 Former times, days of old

fyrngēar 05.11.07.03 Former times, days of old; 05.11.07.03.01 Time within remembrance

fyrngeflit 12.05.04.01 Fighting, contention, warfare, strife

fyrngeflita 08.01.03.09.05 Enmity

fyrngemynd 06.01.04 Faculty of memory

fyrngesceap 01 Earth, world; 05.05 Constitution, founding (e.g. of world)

fyrngesetu 04.05.03.02.02.04 Former dwellings

fyrngestrēon 15.01.03 Treasure, riches, wealth

fyrngeweorc 04.05.02 A building, edifice, structure

fyrngewinn 12.05.04.01 Fighting, contention, warfare, strife

gefyrngewiten 05.11.07.03 Former times, days of old

fyrngewrit 16.02.01.08 Scripture, the scriptures

fyrngewyrht 11.01 Action, doing, performance

fyrngidd 06.01.08.04.01 Premonition, prophecy

fyrnmann 02.03.01 People

gefyrnnes 05.11.07.03 Former times, days of old

fyrnsægen 05.11.07.03.03 Old, not new; 09.06.01.01 A tradition, ordinance handed down

fyrnsceaþa 16.01.05.02.02 Other terms for devils

fyrnstrēama geflota 02.06.05.01.04 Whale

fyrnstrēamas 01.01.03.01.02 Sea/ocean

fyrnweorc 01 Earth, world; 02 Creation

fyrnwita 06.01.05.02.01.01 Sagacity

fȳrpanne 04.01.02.02.06.01 Cooking vessel/pot; 17.05.02 A hearth, fireplace

fȳrræce 17.05.02 A hearth, fireplace

fyrs 02.07.03.01 A bush

fȳrscofl 17.05.02 A hearth, fireplace

fyrsen 02.07.03.01 A bush

fyrsett 01.01.02.01.05 Covered with vegetation

fyrsgāra 01.01.02.01.05 Covered with vegetation

fyrsīg 01.01.02.01.01.02 Island

fyrslēah 01.01.02.01.05 Covered with vegetation

fȳrsmeortende 02.08.03.02 Itch, irritation

fȳrspearca 03.01.09.02 Fire, flame

fyrspenn 04.02.05.03.01 A pen, fold, enclosure; 05.10.05.04.11 A circle, circuit, circumference

fyrsræw 04.05.01.02.07 A fence, hedge

fyrssceaga 02.07.03.01 A bush

fyrst 05.11.10.01 A beginning; 07.02.04 Excellence; 12.01.01.06.02.01 (High) rank, status, degree
gefyrst 01.03.01.04.01 Frost
fyrstān 17.05.01 Fuel, tinder
fȳrsweart 03.01.13 Darkness, obscurity
fȳrtang 17.05.02 A hearth, fireplace
fȳrtorr 05.12.01.09.03.05 A lighthouse
fȳrþolle 14.05.06 Means/implement of torture
(ge)fyrþrian 08.01.01.03.08 Happiness, well-being, prosperity; 11.12.02 Aid, help, succour
gefyrþrian 10.03.03 Granting
fyrþriend 11.10.02.02.01 Care, interest in
(ge)fyrþring 10.03 Giving
fyrþringnes 11.01.05.02 Furtherance, promotion
fyrþrung 11.01.05.02 Furtherance, promotion
fyrwit 08.01.01.01 Ardour, fervour, strong feeling; 09.05 Curiosity
fyrwitful 06.01.08.06.04 Care, anxiety, solicitude
fyrwitgeorn 09.05 Curiosity
fyrwitgeornes 09.05 Curiosity
fyrwitgeornlīce 11.02.02.02 Care, mindfulness, attention
fyrwitnes 08.01.01.01 Ardour, fervour, strong feeling; 09.05 Curiosity
fȳrwylm 03.01.09.02 Fire, flame
fȳsan 05.12.02.04 To cast out, drive away; 05.12.03.01.02 Haste, hurry
(ge)fȳsan 05.12.02.06.01 To push, drive; 11.01.03 Preparation
gefȳsan 08.01.01.01.03 An incitement, cause of strong feeling
gefȳsed 01.01.03.04 Current, rush of water
fȳsian 05.12.02.04 To cast out, drive away

fȳst 02.04.03.04.01.01 Hand
fȳstgebēat 12.05.04.01.01 Fighting, a fight
gefȳstlian 05.06.09.01 A slap with the hand, blow
fȳstslægen 05.06.09.01 A slap with the hand, blow
gefyxan 06.01.07.04 Deception
fyxe 02.06.03.01.07 Fox
fyxenhȳd 02.06.03.01.07 Fox
gabote 04.01.02.02.06.05.03 Plate/platter/bowl/dish
gād 04.02.05.05.01 A goad; 06.02.04.01 Want, need
gegada 08.01.02.02.03 A loving relationship; 12.04.01 A fellow, companion, associate, comrade
gegadere 03.03.06.01 A whole formed by joining
gegaderednes 02.08.05.02 Particular inflammation/swelling
(ge)gaderscipe 12.09 Marriage, state of marriage
gadertang 05.10.05.01 A little way, no great distance; 05.11.11 Continuity
gadertangnes 05.11.11 Continuity
gaderung 09.06 To take matter for discourse
(ge)gaderung 04.02.04.04.02 Harvesting; 12.04 Fellowship, union, association; 12.04.02 A crowding together, assembly
gegaderung 02.08.05.02 Particular inflammation/swelling; 03.03.04.01.02.01 A heap, mass, accumulation; 03.03.06.01 A whole formed by joining; 05.05.03 Binding, fastening; 12.04.01.01 A company of people, fellowship, society

(ge)gaderwist 12.04 Fellowship, union, association
gegaderwyrhtan 17.02.01 Management of work
gādinca 02.06 Animal
gādīren 04.02.05.05.01 A goad
gādīsen 04.02.05.05.01 A goad
gadrian 04.03.03 Net, drag-net, hunting net; 09.03.07.07.03 Composition, arrangement, writing; 10 Having, owning, possession
(ge)gadrian 03.03.04.01.02.01 A heap, mass, accumulation; 03.03.06.01 A whole formed by joining; 04.02.04.04.02.02 To gather fruits, crops, etc.; 12.02.02 An assembly, meeting; 12.04 Fellowship, union, association; 12.04.02 A crowding together, assembly; 12.09.02 Marriage ceremony
gegadrian 09.07.04.01 Confirmation, agreement
gadrigendlic 09.03.02.03.01.01.02 Number
gæd 12.04 Fellowship, union, association
gædeling 02.03.02.03.06.01 Kinsman, relative
gǣlan 05.11.08.01.03.01 Delay; 06.01.07.04 Deception; 11.11.02 A hindrance
gǣling 05.11.08.01.03.01 Delay
gǣlsa 06.02.05.02 Greed, importunate desire, rapacity; 07.06.01 Pride, arrogance; 08.01.03.03 Anxiety
gǣls(a) 12.08.08.01 Eager, unseemly desire
gǣlslic 12.08.07.01.01 Wantonness, sensuality, lasciviousness
gǣrede 05.10.06.04 A corner, bend, angle

gærs 01.01.02.01.05 Covered with vegetation; 02.07 A plant; 02.07.08 Grasses, reeds, etc.; 04.02.03.04.02 Pasture/pasturage; 04.02.04.03.02.01 Grain crops
gærsbedd 02.02.05.01.01 A grave, burial place, sepulchre
gærscīþ 02.07.08 Grasses, reeds, etc.
gærsen 02.07.08 Grasses, reeds, etc.
gærsgrēne 03.01.14.06 Green/greenness
gærshoppa 02.06.09.02.05 Cricket, grasshopper, locust
gærsing 04.02.03.04.02 Pasture/pasturage
gærstūn 04.02.03.04.01 Meadow land/meadow
gærstūndīc 04.05.03.05.03.01 A ditch, dike
gærsuma 15.01.03 Treasure, riches, wealth
gærsum(a) 15.01.03 Treasure, riches, wealth
gærswyrt 02.07 A plant
gærsyrþ 04.02.03.04.02.01.04 Pasturage in return for ploughing labour; 15.02.04.01 Payment for temporary use, rent, hire
gǣsne 02.01.03.02 Barrenness, sterility; 02.02.03.02 State of being dead; 03.03.08 Emptiness
gǣst ofgiefan 02.02.03 To die, perish
gǣstan 06.01.08.06.03.01 Causing dread, terrifying
gǣstcwalu 08.01.03.07.03 Suffering, torment, pain
gǣstgemynd 06.01.01 Thought, the faculty of thinking, mind
gǣstgenīþla 16.01.05.02.02 Other terms for devils
gǣstgewinn 08.01.03.07.03 Suffering, torment, pain

1001

gæstlic 06.01.08.06.03.01 Causing dread, terrifying
gæstlufu 08.01.02.02.04 Love, caritas
gǣten 02.06.02.01.05 Goat; 04.04.06 Undressed condition (of hide)
gegaf 08.01.01.03.07.03 Buffoonery, scurrility
gafeluc 13.02.08.04.01 A spear
gaffetung 08.01.01.03.07.04 Scoffing, mockery
gafol 04.02.04.06.02 A fork; 15.02.04.01 Payment for temporary use, rent, hire; 15.03 Exaction of tax/tribute; 15.03.02 A tax; 15.04 A debt, due; 15.04.01 Lending of money
gafolbere 15.02.04.01 Payment for temporary use, rent, hire
gafoles andfengend 15.03 Exaction of tax/tribute
gafolfisc 15.02.04.01 Payment for temporary use, rent, hire
gafolfrēo 15.03 Exaction of tax/tribute
gafolgerēfa 15.03 Exaction of tax/tribute
gafolgielda 15.01.01.01 Holding of land; 15.04.01 Lending of money
gafolgyld 15.03.02 A tax
gafolgyldere 15.04 A debt, due
gafolheord 15.02.04.01 Payment for temporary use, rent, hire
gafolhwītel 15.03.02 A tax
gafolian 15.01.01.01.01 Hiring, letting out of property/land
gegafolian 15.03 Exaction of tax/tribute
gafolland 15.01.01 Landed property
gafollic 15.03 Exaction of tax/tribute
gafolmǣd 04.02.03.04.01 Meadow land/meadow; 15.02.04.01 Payment for temporary use, rent, hire
gafolmanung 15.03 Exaction of tax/tribute
gafolpenig 15.03 Exaction of tax/tribute
gafolrǣden 15.02.04.01 Payment for temporary use, rent, hire
gafolrand 03.03.03.01 Arithmetic
gafolswān 04.02.05.06.04 A swineherd
gafoltīning 15.02.04.01 Payment for temporary use, rent, hire
gafolwudu 15.02.04.01 Payment for temporary use, rent, hire
gafolyrþ 04.02.04.02.02.02 Ploughing, tilling; 15.02.04.01 Payment for temporary use, rent, hire
(ge)gafsprǣc 08.01.01.03.07.03 Buffoonery, scurrility
gegafsprǣce 08.01.01.03.07.03 Buffoonery, scurrility
gagātes 17.04.03.04 Gems collectively
gagātstān 17.04.03.04 Gems collectively
gagel 02.07.11 Plants/flowers (alphabetical order)
gagelcroppan 02.07.11 Plants/flowers (alphabetical order)
gagolbǣrnes 12.08.07.01.01 Wantonness, sensuality, lasciviousness
gagolisc 12.08.07.01.01 Wantonness, sensuality, lasciviousness
gāl 07.03 Evil; 07.06 Pride; 12.08.07.01.01 Wantonness, sensuality, lasciviousness; 12.08.07.01.03 Wantonness, levity, frivolity
galan 02.05.10.15.07 Voice, note (of a bird); 18.02.07.02.02.02 A trumpet
(ge)galan 16.01.04.01 Sorcery using incantation; 18.02.07.01 Singing, song
galban(um) 02.07.02.03 A stalk, stem
galdor 09.03.05.01.01 Poetry; 16.01.04.01 Sorcery using incantation; 16.01.04.06 Divination, augury; 18.02.07.01.01 A song, a poem to be

sung or recited; 18.02.07.02.02.02 A trumpet
galdorcræft 16.01.04.01 Sorcery using incantation
galdorcræftiga 16.01.04.01 Sorcery using incantation
galdorcwide 16.01.04.01 Sorcery using incantation
galdorgalend 16.01.04.01 Sorcery using incantation
galdorgalere 16.01.04.01 Sorcery using incantation
galdorlēoþ 16.01.04.01 Sorcery using incantation
galdorsang 16.01.04.01 Sorcery using incantation
galdorword 16.01.04.01 Sorcery using incantation
galdre 16.01.04.01 Sorcery using incantation
galdricge 16.01.04.01 Sorcery using incantation
galend 16.01.04.01 Sorcery using incantation
galere 16.01.04.01 Sorcery using incantation
gālferhþ 12.08.07.01.01 Wantonness, sensuality, lasciviousness
gālfrēols 12.08.07.01 Laxity, indulgence
gālful 12.08.07.01.01 Wantonness, sensuality, lasciviousness
gālfullīce 12.08.07.01.01 Wantonness, sensuality, lasciviousness
gālian 12.08.07.01.01 Wantonness, sensuality, lasciviousness
galilēisc 02.03.03.06.07.07 Other (alphabetical order)
galleas 02.03.03.06.01 Peoples of France
gāllic 12.08.08.01 Eager, unseemly desire
gāllīce 12.08.07.01.01 Wantonness, sensuality, lasciviousness
gallie 02.03.03.06.01 Peoples of France
gallisc 02.03.03.06.01 Peoples of France
galluc 02.07.03.03.01 Wood (as substance); 02.07.11 Plants/flowers (alphabetical order)
gālmōd 12.08.07.01.01 Wantonness, sensuality, lasciviousness
gālnes 12.08.07.01.01 Wantonness, sensuality, lasciviousness
gālscipe 12.08.07.01.01 Wantonness, sensuality, lasciviousness
gālsere 12.08.08.01 Eager, unseemly desire
gālsmǣre 12.08.07.01.03 Wantonness, levity, frivolity
galung 16.01.04.01 Sorcery using incantation
galwalas 02.03.03.06.01 Peoples of France
gamen 08.01.01.03.07 Joyous sound, mirth; 08.01.01.03.07.02 Jesting, pleasantry; 18.02 Amusement, revelry, festivity; 18.02.02 Play, (athletic) sport
gamenian 08.01.01.03.07.02 Jesting, pleasantry; 18.02.02 Play, (athletic) sport
gamenlic 08.01.01.03.07.01 Laughter; 18.02.06 Theatricals
gamenlīce 11.04.02.01.01 Cunning, craft, craftiness, guile, wile
gamenung 08.01.01.03.07.02 Jesting, pleasantry
gamenwāþ 05.12.01.01 To go on a journey/expedition, travel
gamenwudu 18.02.07.02.03.01 A harp, lyre
gamol 02.01.04.03 Aging, growing old; 05.11.07.03.03 Old, not new

gamolfeax 02.04.04.03.02 Colour of hair
gamolferhþ 02.01.04.03 Aging, growing old
gamolian 05.11.07.03.03 Old, not new
gān 05.02 State, condition; 05.10.05.02 Extension, stretching; 05.12.02 To move, set in motion; 10.01 Fact of belonging, possession by; 10.01.01 Acceptance, receiving; 15.01.04 Coinage, money
gān for 15.02.04 Spending, disbursement
gān forþ 05.11 A time, period of time
gān forþ mid 05.05.02 Productivity, bringing forth
gān mid 02.01.03.03.01 To beget
gān of 11.06.06.01 Abandonment (of principle)
gān on scip 05.12.01.09 To travel on water
gān tōgædere 13.02.02 Battle
(ge)gān 04.02.04.02.02.02 Ploughing, tilling; 05.02.01.01 The course of human affairs; 05.03.01 A cause (of anything); 05.11 A time, period of time; 05.12.01 To go, progress, travel (usually on land); 05.12.01.04 To go, proceed on foot; 05.12.05.02 To go/travel towards, come, approach; 05.12.05.03.03 To depart, leave, set out; 05.12.05.06 To travel over/through/along, traverse; 10.01 Fact of belonging, possession by; 11.06.03.01 Ill fortune, bad success
(ge)gān (forþ) 05.03.02.01.01 An event, occurrence
gegān 02.02.03 To die, perish; 05.03.02.01.01 An event, occurrence; 05.12.05.02.03 To arrive; 10.01.02 Acquisition; 10.04.02.02 To seize, take, grasp, lay hold on; 11.01 Action, doing, performance
gandra 02.06.08.02.01.02 Goose
gang 02.04.03.04.02.05.02 Sole; 04.05.02.11 A staircase; 04.05.03.05.02 A privy; 05.11.08 A suitable time, opportunity; 05.12.01 To go, progress, travel (usually on land); 05.12.01.01 To go on a journey/expedition, travel; 05.12.01.03 Expanse over which something travels; 05.12.01.03.01 A means of access; 05.12.01.04 To go, proceed on foot; 05.12.01.04.01 Manner of going, gait; 05.12.01.08 To move in/on water; 05.12.05.03.04.02 To flow out, well up, erupt; 12.04.01.01 A company of people, fellowship, society; 14.03.03 Law, action of the courts
gang/sīþ settan 05.12.01.01 To go on a journey/expedition, travel
(ge)gang 05.11.06 Course/cycle of time
gegang 05.03.02.01 Chance, hap, event
gangan 05 Aught, anything, something; 05.02 State, condition; 05.02.01.01 The course of human affairs; 05.10.05.02 Extension, stretching; 05.12.02.06.01 To push, drive; 15.01.04 Coinage, money
gangan ... gereht 05.10.05.04.05 Straight, direct
gangan forþ 05.12.05.09 To go forward, proceed
(ge)gangan 05.03.02 Event, issue, result; 05.12.01 To go, progress, travel (usually on land); 05.12.01.04 To go, proceed on foot; 05.12.05.03.03 To depart, leave, set out; 05.12.05.06 To travel over/through/along, traverse

(ge)gangan tō 05.12.05.02 To go/travel towards, come, approach
gegangan 04.02.04.02.02.02 Ploughing, tilling; 05.03.01 A cause (of anything); 05.03.02.01.01 An event, occurrence; 05.12.05.02.03 To arrive; 05.12.05.07 To go beyond, pass; 10.01 Fact of belonging, possession by; 10.04.02.02 To seize, take, grasp, lay hold on; 11.01.05 Accomplishment, fulfilment
gangdæg 16.02.04.04.02.01.03 Holy Week
gangehere 13.02.10.01.02.02.02 Branch of army
gangende 02.01.02.01 That lives, living; 05.12.01.04 To go, proceed on foot
gangern 04.05.03.05.02 A privy
gangewifre 02.06.09.02.10 Spider
ganggeteld 04.05.03.02.02.09 A tent, pavilion
gangpytt 04.05.03.05.02 A privy
gangsetl 04.05.03.05.02 A privy
gangstōl 04.05.03.05.02 A privy
gangtūn 04.05.03.05.02 A privy
gangweg 05.12.01.03.01 A means of access
gangwucu 16.02.04.04.02.01.03 Holy Week
gānian 05.10.05.04.14.01 A yawning, gaping opening
gāniende 05.10.05.04.14.01 A yawning, gaping opening
ganot 02.06.08.06 Water bird
ganotes bæþ 01.01.03.01.02 Sea/ocean
gānung 05.10.05.04.14.01 A yawning, gaping opening; 07.05.03.03 Scorn, insult, abuse
gār 02.08.03 Pain, bodily discomfort; 13.02.08.04 Weapons, arms; 13.02.08.04.01 A spear; 13.02.08.04.04.01 An arrow, dart, bolt
gāra 04.04.05 Woven material, fabric
gār(a) 04.02.03.01 Plot of land
gāræcer 04.02.03.01 Plot of land
gārbēam 13.02.08.04.01 A spear
gārberend 13.02.10.01 A man, warrior
gārcēne 06.02.07.06.02 Boldness
gārclife 02.07.11 Plants/flowers (alphabetical order)
gārcwealm 02.02.04 Killing, violent death, destruction
gārdene 02.03.03.06.05 Scandinavian
gārfaru 13.02.01 A military expedition
gārgetrum 13.02.10.01.02.01 An armed force/band
gārgewinn 13.02.02 Battle
gārhēap 13.02.10.01.02.01 An armed force/band
gārholt 13.02.08.04.01 A spear
gārlēac 02.07.09.02.02.01 Edible root/bulb
gārmitting 13.02.02 Battle
gārnīþ 13.02 War
gārrǣs 13.02.02 Battle
gārsecg 01.01.03.01.02 Sea/ocean
gārtorn 08.01.03.05.02 Anger
gārþracu 13.02.02 Battle
gārþrīst 06.02.07.06.02.02 Boldness, daring
gārwiga 13.02.10.01 A man, warrior
gārwīgend 13.02.10.01 A man, warrior
gārwudu 13.02.08.04.01 A spear
gāsrīc 02.06 Animal
gāst 02.01 Existence, life; 02.01.01.01 Soul, spirit; 02.04.06.07.03 Breath; 03 Material, matter, substance; 16.01.01.04.03 The Holy Spirit; 16.01.02.05 Inhabitants of heaven;

16.01.02.05.02 A saint; 16.01.03.01 Soul of a deceased person
gāst āgiefan 02.02.03 To die, perish
gāst onsendan 02.02.03 To die, perish
gāstbana 16.01.05.02.02 Other terms for devils
gāstberend 02.03.01 People
gāstbrūcende 16.02.01.12 Spirituality
gāstcofa 06 Spirit, soul, heart
gāstcund 16.02.01.12 Spirituality
gāstcwalu 16.01.05.01 Damnation, perdition, reprobation
gāstcyning 16.01.01.01.01 The Almighty
gāstedōm 16.02.01.12 Spirituality
gāstgedāl 02.02 Death
gāstgehygd 06.01.01 Thought, the faculty of thinking, mind
gāstgeryne 06.01.01 Thought, the faculty of thinking, mind
gāstgerȳne 16.02.01.12 Spirituality
gǣstgewinn 16.01.05.01 Damnation, perdition, reprobation
gāstgifu 16.02.01.12.02 Grace
gāsthālig 16.02.01.10 Holiness
gāstlēas 02.02.03.02 State of being dead
gāstlic 02.03.02.05 Spiritual relationships; 06 Spirit, soul, heart; 16.01.03.01 Soul of a deceased person; 16.02.01.12 Spirituality
gāstlice ūphefnes 08.01.01.01.02 Alienation of mind, ecstasy, rapture
gāstlīce 06 Spirit, soul, heart; 16.02.01.12 Spirituality
gāstsunu 16.01.01.04.02 The Son, Christ
gāt 02.06.02.01.05 Goat
gāta hūs 04.02.05.06.03.01 A house/pen for goats
gāta loc 04.02.05.06.03.01 A house/pen for goats
gātānstīg 05.12.01.03.01.01 A path, track

gātbucca 02.06.02.01.05 Goat
gāte cȳse 04.01.02.01.02.09.11 Cheese
gāte hǣr 17.04.04.03 Fleece, pelt
gāte meoluc 04.01.02.01.02.09.02 Milk from goats
gātetrēow 02.07.03.05 Particular trees/shrubs (alphabetical order)
gāthyrde 04.02.05.06.03 A goatherd
gēa 09.07.04 Assertion, affirmation
gēa lā gēa 09.07.04 Assertion, affirmation
gēac 02.06.08.05 Forest bird, wild-fowl
gēaces sūre 02.07.11 Plants/flowers (alphabetical order)
geador 03.03.06.01 A whole formed by joining
geaflas 02.04.03.01.03.07 Jaw(s)
gēagl 02.04.03.01.03.07 Jaw(s)
gēaglswile 02.08.07.04.03 A disease of the jaws
gealg 08.01.03 Bad feeling, sadness; 08.01.03.05.02 Anger
gealga 14.05.06 Means/implement of torture
gealgmōd 08.01.03 Bad feeling, sadness; 08.01.03.05.02 Anger
gealg(mōd)nes 08.01.03.01 Despondency
gealgtrēow 14.05.06 Means/implement of torture
gealla 02.04.06.05.07.06 Gall/bile; 04.02.05.02.03 Erysipelas in horses
geallādl 02.08.08.06 Disease of liver
geallede 02.06.02.01.06 Horse; 04.02.05.02.03 Erysipelas in horses
gealpettan 07.06.03 Boastfulness, arrogance
gealpettung 07.06.03 Boastfulness, arrogance
gealt 02.06.02.01.07 Pig, swine
gēanbōc 14.04.01 A deed, contract, agreement

gēancirrendlic 09.03.02.02.01.05 Minor parts of speech, etc.
gēancumende 05.12.05.02.02 To come together, meet
gēancyme 05.12.05.02.02 To come together, meet
gēancyr 05.12.05.02.02 To come together, meet; 05.12.05.11.01 To return
gēancyrnes 05.12.05.02.02 To come together, meet
gēandele 01.01.02.01.02.02.04 Cliff
gēandȳne 11.11.01 A physical difficulty, strait
gēanfær 05.12.05.11.01 To return
gēangang 05.12.05.02.02 To come together, meet; 05.12.05.11.01 To return
gēanhwurf 05.12.05.11.01 To return
gēanhwyrft 05.12.05.11.01 To return
geānlǣcan 12.04 Fellowship, union, association
gēannes 05.12.05.02.02 To come together, meet
gēanoþ 08.01.03.04.01 Complaint, lamentation
gēanryne 05.12.05.02.02 To come together, meet
gēantalu 09.07.02 Contradiction
gēanþingian 09.01.03 To address, speak to
gēanul 05.12.05.02.02 To come together, meet
geānwyrdan 12.04 Fellowship, union, association
gēap 05.10.06.02.01 A hemisphere; 05.10.06.02.02 Curvature, bend, twist; 11.04.02.01.01 Cunning, craft, craftiness, guile, wile

gēaplic 11.04.02.01.01 Cunning, craft, craftiness, guile, wile
gēaplīce 11.04.02.01.01 Cunning, craft, craftiness, guile, wile
gēapneb 13.02.08.03.01.01 Mail, iron-rings
gēapscipe 11.04.02.01.01 Cunning, craft, craftiness, guile, wile
gēar 02.01.04 Age; 05.11.03.01 A year; 05.11.03.01.02.01 Spring; 09.03.07.01.01 A runic letter
gēara 05.11.07.03 Former times, days of old
gēara iū 05.11.07.03 Former times, days of old
gēaras 02.01.04 Age
gēarbōt 16.02.04.07.02.03 Penance, an act/instance of penance
(ge)gearcian 10.03.04 Provision, supply; 11.01.03 Preparation
gegearcian 05.12.01.09.03.01.04 Equipping of ships
gearcung 11.01.03 Preparation
(ge)gearcungdæg 16.02.01.08.04 Jewish seasons/feasts
gēarcyning 12.02.02.03 Terms for classical world
geard 04.05.01.02.07 A fence, hedge; 04.05.03 A dwelling-place, abode, habitation; 05.10.04.02 A region, zone; 05.10.05.04.11 A circle, circuit, circumference
gēardagas 02.01.04 Age; 05.11.07.03 Former times, days of old
gēardagum 05.11.07.03 Former times, days of old
geardsteall 04.02.05.06.01.01 A cattle pen/cowshed
geardung 04.05.03 A dwelling-place, abode, habitation

geardungstōw 04.05.03 A dwelling-place, abode, habitation
gēares dæg 05.11.02.01.02 A time of celebration
gēares gehwyrft 05.11.02.01.01 An anniversary
gēarfæc 05.11.03.01 A year
gēargemearc 05.11.06.02 Reckoning/computation of time
gēargemynd 16.02.04.07.06.03 Commemoration, festival
gēargeriht 15.04 A debt, due
gēar(ge)rīm 05.11.06.02 Reckoning/computation of time
gēargetæl 02.01.04 Age; 05.11.06.02.02 A calculated space of time; 05.11.07.03.03 Old, not new
gēarhwāmlīce 05.11.03.01 A year
gēarlanges 05.11.03.01 A year
gēarlic 05.11.03.01 A year
gēarlīce 05.11.03.01 A year
gēarmǣlum 05.11.03.01 A year
gēarmarket 15.05.01 Goods, stock, merchandise
gearn 04.04.04 A thread (of wool, etc.), fibre
gearnwinde 04.04.03 A spinning-house or chamber
gearo 03.03.06 Wholeness; 04.01.02.02.05 Cooking; 04.04.07 Trappings, equipment, garb; 05.12.01.09.03.01.02 Of/concerning a ship, naval; 06.01.05.02 Intelligence; 06.02.05.04.03 Promptitude, readiness; 11.01.03 Preparation; 11.07.02 Utility, advantage, convenience; 11.10.02.01 Vigilance; 13.02.08 Military equipment
gearobrygd 11.04.01 An aptitude, bodily skill
gearofolm 06.02.05.04.03 Promptitude, readiness
gearolīce 02.05.09.01 To open the eyes/be awake; 09.04.03 Exposition, making clear by explanation
gearosnottor 11.04.02 Skill, skilfulness
gearoþoncol 06.01.05.02.01.01 Sagacity
gearowita 06.01.05 Understanding, intellect
gearowite 06.01.06.01.01.02 To know, recognize
gearowitol 06.01.05.02.01.01 Sagacity
gearowitolnes 06.01.05.02.01.01 Sagacity
gearowyrde 09.01.02 Fluency in speech
gearowyrdig 09.01.02 Fluency in speech
gēarryne 05.11.06.01 Cycle of the year
gēartorht 03.01.12 Brightness, light
gēarþēnunga 16.02.04.03 Ritual, rite, service
gearu gangende 05.12.03.01 Swiftness, velocity
gearufang 13.02.10.03.01 A fleet
gēarwæstm 02.07.01.01 Fruit of the earth
gearwe 02.05.09.01 To open the eyes/be awake; 02.07.11 Plants/flowers (alphabetical order); 03.03.06 Wholeness; 04.02.05.06.05.03 Harness, trappings; 04.04.07 Trappings, equipment, garb; 05.10.05.01 A little way, no great distance; 06.02.02.01 Will, wish, pleasure; 06.02.05.04.03 Promptitude, readiness; 09.04.03 Exposition, making clear by explanation; 11.12 Easiness; 13.02.08.03.01 Body armour, war gear; 17.03 Implements, tools, etc.
gearwian 04.02.04.04.01 To ripen; 04.04.07 Trappings, equipment, garb

(ge)gearwian 04.01.02.02 To prepare food; 04.04.07 Trappings, equipment, garb; 10.03.03 Granting; 10.03.04 Provision, supply; 11.01 Action, doing, performance; 11.01.03 Preparation; 13.02.08 Military equipment
gegearwian 02.08.12 Healing, curing; 05.05 Constitution, founding (e.g. of world); 05.05.01 An author, source, originator; 05.12.01.09.03.01.04 Equipping of ships; 07.02.03 Perfection; 11.12 Easiness
(ge)gearwung 11.01.03 Preparation
gegearwung 11 Action, operation
gearwungdæg 16.02.01.08.04 Jewish seasons/feasts
gegearwungnes 11.01.03 Preparation
geaspis 17.04.03.04 Gems collectively
geat 04.05.02.12 Gate/doorway of a building; 05.10.05.04.14.02 An opening/space in an enclosure; 05.12.01.03.01.02 A cutting, pass
gēatan 06.01.07.03 Truth of speech or thought, veracity; 15.01.02 Gift, transfer of property
gēatas 02.03.03.05.01.03 Kentish people; 02.03.03.06.05 Scandinavian
gēatisc 02.03.03.06.05 Scandinavian
geatolic 07.10 Beauty, fairness
geatwan 11.01.03 Preparation
geatwe 04.04.10 Ornaments, trappings, accoutrements; 13.02.08.03.01 Body armour, war gear
geatweard 12.01.01.08.01 A servant, attendant
gēaþ 06.01.05.03.02.01 Foolishness, lightmindedness; 08.01.01.03.07.04 Scoffing, mockery

gecorenscipe 12.08.02.03 Goodness, probity
gēgan 02.05.10.15.01 To raise (the voice), raise up (noise)
gegncwide 09.05.03 An answer, reply
gegegnian 05.12.05.02.02 To come together, meet
gegnpæþ 05.12.01.03.01 A means of access
gegnslege 12.05.04.01.01 Fighting, a fight
gegnum 05.12.05.09 To go forward, proceed
gegnunga 05.10.05.04.05 Straight, direct; 06.02.06 Mind, purpose
gehþu 08.01.03.03 Anxiety
gelde 02.01.03.02 Barrenness, sterility
gellet 04.01.02.02.06.05.04 Cup/bowl/basin
gemengednes 12.08.06 Moral evil, depravity
gēmung 12.09 Marriage, state of marriage
gēmungian 12.09.02 Marriage ceremony
gēmunglic 12.09 Marriage, state of marriage
gēn 03.03.04.03 Growth, increase; 03.06 Comparison; 05.10.05.04.05 Straight, direct; 05.11.09.06 Frequency, repetition
gēna 03.03.04.03 Growth, increase; 05:11.09.06 Frequency, repetition
gēn(a) 05.11.07.03.02 Earlier, antecedent
geneahlīce 05.11.11 Continuity
genesis 16.02.01.08.01.01 Books of the Old Testament
gegenga 12.04.01.02 A fellow traveller, companion
gengan 05.11.07.02 The present (time); 05.12.01 To go, progress, travel (usually on land); 05.12.01.05.01 Modes of riding

genge 04.01.02.01.01.05 (Of food) in season; 04.05.03.05.02 A privy; 13.02.10.01.02.02 Armed forces
genge bēon/wesan 05.11.07.02 The present (time); 07.02.01 Right, virtue; 07.04 Consideration, esteem
(ge)genge 12.04.01.01 A company of people, fellowship, society
gegenge 03.06.03 Congruity, fitness, suitability
gēnlād 01.01.03.01.01.01 River
gēo 05.11.07.03 Former times, days of old; 05.11.07.03.02 Earlier, antecedent
gēo ǣr 05.11.07.03 Former times, days of old
gēo dagum 05.11.07.03 Former times, days of old
gēo gēara 05.11.07.03 Former times, days of old
gēo hwīlum 05.11.07.03 Former times, days of old
gēoabbod 16.02.03.03.01.01 An abbot
geoc 04.02.03.03 A measure of land; 04.02.05.05.03 A yoke; 12.04 Fellowship, union, association; 12.05.06.01 Restraint, check, curb, control; 12.09 Marriage, state of marriage; 14.05.07 Binding, fastening with bonds
gēoc 08.01.03.07.04.02.01 Comfort, consolation; 11.12.02 Aid, help, succour
geocboga 04.02.05.05.03 A yoke; 05.10.06.02.01 A hemisphere
gēocend 16.01.01.04.02 The Son, Christ
(ge)geocian 04.02.05.05.03 A yoke; 05.05.03 Binding, fastening
gēocian 11.10.01.01 Preservation from injury/destruction
geocled 04.02.03.03 A measure of land

gegeocod 03.03.06.01 A whole formed by joining; 04.02.05.05.03 A yoke; 04.02.05.05.04 Rope, rein
gēocor 08.01.03 Bad feeling, sadness; 08.01.03.07.04 Severity, harshness
gēocre 08.01.03.07.04 Severity, harshness
geocsa 02.08.08.04.02 (Of stomach) disordered; 08.01.03.04.03 Sobbing
(ge)geocsian 08.01.03.04.03 Sobbing
geocstecca 04.02.05.05.03 A yoke
geocsung 08.01.03.04.03 Sobbing
geoctēma 04.02.05.06 Animals yoked together
gēodǣd 11.01 Action, doing, performance
gēodæg 05.11.07.03 Former times, days of old
geofola/giefl 04.01.02.04 Abundance of food
geofon 01.01.03.01.02 Sea/ocean; 01.01.03.06 Flood
geofonflōd 01.01.03.04 Current, rush of water
geofonhūs 05.12.01.09.03.01.01 Kind of ship
gēog(e)lere 16.01.04 Sorcery, magic, witchcraft
geogoþmyrþ 08.01.01.03 Good feeling, joy, happiness
geoguþ 02.01.03.03.02 To bring forth, produce; 02.01.04.01 Youth; 02.03.01.05 Youth, boy, stripling; 05.08.01 Vigour, activity, force; 12.04.02 A crowding together, assembly
geoguþcnōsl 02.01.03.03.02 To bring forth, produce
geoguþfeorh 02.01.04.01 Youth
geoguþhād 02.01.04.01 Youth
geoguþhādnes 02.01.04.01 Youth

geoguþlic 02.01.04.01 Youth
geoguþlust 02.05.05.03 Sexual appetite, lust
geoht 04.02.05.06 Animals yoked together
gēol 05.11.02.01.02 A time of celebration; 16.02.04.04.02.01.01 Around the Nativity
gēola 05.11.03.01.03.01 Specific months
gēoldæg 16.02.04.04.02.01.01 Around the Nativity
gēolēan 10.03.05 Recompense, reward
gēolmōnaþ 05.11.03.01.03.01 Specific months
geolna 02.06.08.05 Forest bird, wild-fowl
geolo 03.01.14.07 Yellow/yellowness; 04.01.02.01.02.08 Egg
geoloca 04.01.02.01.02.08 Egg
geolorand 13.02.08.03.01.06 A shield
geolster/gillister 02.04.06.05.07.02 Mucus, phlegm, rheum
geolstor 02.08.05.02.01 Matter, purulence, pus
geolstrig 02.08.05.02.01 Matter, purulence, pus; 04.06.02.06 Poison
geolu 02.04.04.01 Having a certain complexion
geoluhwīt 03.01.14.07 Yellow/yellowness
geolurēad 03.01.14.07 Yellow/yellowness
geolwe 03.01.14.07 Yellow/yellowness
geolwian 03.01.14.07 Yellow/yellowness
(ge)geolwod 03.01.14.07 Yellow/yellowness
gēomāgister 06.01.06.02.03.04.02 A teacher
gēomann 02.03.01 People
gēomēowle 02.03.01.09 Old woman
gēomor 08.01.03 Bad feeling, sadness; 08.01.03.04 Grief
gēomore 08.01.03.04 Grief
gēomorfrōd 02.01.04.03 Aging, growing old
gēomorgidd 02.02.05.03 To attend the dead
gēomorlic 08.01.03.04 Grief
gēomorlīce 08.01.03.04 Grief
gēomormōd 08.01.03 Bad feeling, sadness; 08.01.03.01 Despondency
gēomornes 08.01.03.07.02 Misery, trouble, affliction
gēomrian 08.01.03.04.01 Complaint, lamentation
gēomrung 08.01.03.04.01 Complaint, lamentation
geon 05.10.04.04 Absence
geon ofer 05.10.04.03 Presence
geond 05.10.04.03 Presence; 05.10.04.04 Absence
geond eall 05.10.04.03 Presence
geondan 05.10.04.04 Absence
geondblāwan 02.04.06.07.05 To breathe; 02.08.05.01 Swelling
geondbrǣdan 05.10.05.02.02 Greater, bigger; 05.10.05.04.12.01 To bespread, cover with
geonddrencan 04.01.03.02 To drink heavily, get drunk
geondeardian 04.05.03.01 Habitation, sojourn
geondfaran 05.12.05.02.04 To go in, enter; 05.12.05.06 To travel over/through/along, traverse
geondfēolan 05.12.05.02.04 To go in, enter
geondfēran 05.12.05.06 To travel over/through/along, traverse; 11.03.02 Advancement, progress
geondflōwan 01.01.03.03 Flow/flowing
geondflōwende 01.01.03.04 Current, rush of water

geondgangan 05.12.01.04 To go, proceed on foot; 05.12.05.06 To travel over/through/along, traverse
geondgēotan 03.01.16.01 Moisture; 03.01.16.06 A soaking, steeping; 05.10.05.02.01 Diffusion, effusion, spreading
geondhweorfan 05.12.05.06 To travel over/through/along, traverse
geondhyrdan 17.02.04.03.03 Smelting, heating, scorification
geondlācan 01.01.03.03 Flow/flowing
geondleccan 03.01.16.06 A soaking, steeping
geondleccung 03.01.16.06 A soaking, steeping
geondlīhtan 03.01.12.02 A beam of light
geondlīhtend 16.01.01.02.01 Creator
geondmengan 06.01.05.03.01.01 Dullness, folly, stupidity
geondrēcan 03.01.09.02.01.04 Smoke
geondsāwan 05.12.02.07.01 To throw, scatter
geondscēawian 02.05.09.05 To watch, observe, survey; 06.01.01.01 Thinking about, minding, heeding
geondscīnan 03.01.12.02 A beam of light
geondscrīþan 05.12.05.06 To travel over/through/along, traverse; 06.01.05.03.01.01 Dullness, folly, stupidity
geondscrīþung 05.12.05.06 To travel over/through/along, traverse
geondsēcan 05.12.05.02.04 To go in, enter; 09.05.01 Inspection, examination
geondsendan 05.10.05.02.01 Diffusion, effusion, spreading
geondsēon 09.05.01 Inspection, examination
geondsmēagan 09.05.01 Inspection, examination
geondspǣtan 03.01.16.06 A soaking, steeping
geondsprengan 05.12.02.07.01 To throw, scatter
geondspringan 05.10.05.02.01 Diffusion, effusion, spreading
geondsprūtan 05.12.05.02.04 To go in, enter
geondstrēdnes 05.10.04.04.01 Dispersion
geondstregdan 03.01.16.05 A sprinkling; 05.10.05.02.01 Diffusion, effusion, spreading; 05.12.02.07.01 To throw, scatter
geondstyrian 05.12.02 To move, set in motion
geondswōgan 05.12.05.02.01 To come upon, meet with
geondþencan 06.01.01.01.01 Thought, cogitation, meditation
geondwadan 06.01.06.01.01 Knowledge
geondwlītan 02.05.09.05 To watch, observe, survey
geondyrnan 05.12.05.06 To travel over/through/along, traverse; 06.01.01.01.01 Thought, cogitation, meditation
geong 02.01.04.01 Youth; 05.11.07.04.03 Newness, novelty
geonga 02.03.01.06 Young man
geongest 05.11.07.04.02 (Of time) later/latter; 12.01.01.06.04 Inferiority of status, lowest place
geonglǣcan 02.01.04.02 To grow, grow up
geonglic 02.01.04.01 Youth; 02.03.01.05 Youth, boy, stripling
geonglicnes 02.01.04.01 Youth

geongling 02.03.01.05 Youth, boy, stripling
geongor 12.01.01.06.04 Inferiority of status, lowest place
geongordōm 12.01.01.12.01 Obedience, service
geongorscipe 12.01.01.12.01 Obedience, service
geongra 02.03.02.03.05 Descendant; 06.01.06.02.03.02 Discipleship; 12.01.01.06.04 Inferiority of status, lowest place; 12.01.01.07 A follower; 12.01.01.08.01 A servant, attendant
geongre 12.01.01.08.01 A servant, attendant
geonsīþ 02.02 Death
gēopan 10.01.01 Acceptance, receiving
geormanlēaf 02.07.11 Plants/flowers (alphabetical order)
geormanletic 02.07.11 Plants/flowers (alphabetical order)
georn 02.05.05.02 Eager desire; 11.02.02 Diligence
georne 05.11.01.02.01 Swift movement of time; 06.01.01.02 Care, attention, observation; 06.01.05.01.01 Clear to the understanding, plain; 06.02.02.01 Will, wish, pleasure; 06.02.05.04.05 Earnestness; 08.01.01.01.04 Depth of feeling, zeal; 08.01.01.03.08 Happiness, well-being, prosperity; 11.02.02 Diligence; 11.02.02.02 Care, mindfulness, attention
geornful 02.05.05.02 Eager desire; 06.01.08.06.04 Care, anxiety, solicitude; 08.01.03.09.10 Wrath, sternness, displeasure; 11.02.02 Diligence
geornfullic 11.02.02.01 Diligence, studious care
geornfullīce 06.01.01.02 Care, attention, observation; 06.01.05.01.01 Clear to the understanding, plain; 06.02.02 Will, disposition; 06.02.05.04.05 Earnestness; 11.02.02 Diligence
geornfulnes 06.02.05.04 Desire, eagerness; 06.02.05.04.05 Earnestness; 11.02.02.01 Diligence, studious care
geornian 12.03.04.01 Entreaty, solemn appeal
geornlic 02.05.05.01 Object of desire; 06.02.05.04.05 Earnestness
geornlīce 06.01.01.02 Care, attention, observation; 06.01.05.01.01 Clear to the understanding, plain; 06.02.02.01 Will, wish, pleasure; 06.02.05.04.05 Earnestness; 11.02.01 Energy, vigour, vigorous action; 11.02.02 Diligence
geornlīcor 07.01.01.02 To prefer
geornnes 06.02.05.01 Strong liking for, devotion to; 11.02.02.01 Diligence, studious care; 12.03.04.03 Importunity, persistence
geornung 02.05.05 Desire, appetite; 11.02.02 Diligence
georstu 09.01.03.01 Interjections: Oh!
gēosceaft 05.04 Fate, lot, fortune, destiny
gēosceaftgāst 16.01.03.03 A doomed spirit
geostra 05.11.07.03.01.01 Yesterday
geostran 05.11.07.03.01.01 Yesterday
gēotan 03.01.16.01 Moisture; 05.08.02 Violence, force; 05.12.05.03.04.02 To flow out, well up, erupt; 11.08.03 Needless, useless, unprofitable
(ge)gēotan 17.02.04.03.03 Smelting, heating, scorification
gēotend 02.04.06.08 Heart
gēotendæder 02.04.06.08 Heart

gēotende 05.12.05.03.04.02 To flow out, well up, erupt
gēotenlic 03.01.09.01.02 That melts, melting
gēotere 17.02.04.03.03 Smelting, heating, scorification
gēowine 02.02.03.02 State of being dead
gērscipe 09.01.04 Conversation, discussion
gegerwed 04.04.07 Trappings, equipment, garb
gescēadwīslīce 03.06.03 Congruity, fitness, suitability
gese 09.07.04 Assertion, affirmation
gētan 02.02.04.03 To kill, slay
gētenwyrde 09.07.04.01 Confirmation, agreement
getynge 11.05.02.02 Humanity, courtesy, civility
getyngelīce 11.05.02.02 Humanity, courtesy, civility
gewitnes 02.05.09.05 To watch, observe, survey
giccan 02.08.03.02 Itch, irritation
gicce 02.08.03.02 Itch, irritation
giccende 02.08.03.02 Itch, irritation
giccig 02.08.03.02 Itch, irritation
gicel(e) 01.01.03.02 Ice; 01.03.01.04.02 Ice
gicelgebland 01.03.01.06.03 Hail, shower of hail
gicelic 01.01.03.02 Ice
gicelig 01.03.01.04.02 Ice
gicelnes 02.08.03.02 Itch, irritation
gicelstān 01.03.01.06.03 Hail, shower of hail
gicer 04.02.03.03 A measure of land
gicþa 02.08.03.02 Itch, irritation; 02.08.08.04.02 (Of stomach) disordered

giedd 09.03.04.02.01 A figure; 09.03.04.02.02 Eloquence, elegance in language; 09.03.05.01.01 Poetry; 09.06.01.02 A saying, saw, proverb, maxim; 16.01.04.06.04 Prophecy, divine speech; 18.02.07.01.01 A song, a poem to be sung or recited
gieddian 09.03.05 Art of poetry
(ge)gieddian 09.01.04 Conversation, discussion
gieddung 09.03.05.01.01 Poetry; 09.04.02.01 A secret, mystery; 09.06.01 To relate, recount, tell; 16.01.04.06.04 Prophecy, divine speech
giefa 10.03 Giving
giefan 05.05.02 Productivity, bringing forth; 09.05.05.01 Showing, manifestation, display; 09.06.02.01.01 To make known, cause to know, inform; 10.02 Want, lack; 15.01.02.01 Inherited property; 15.02.04 Spending, disbursement
(ge)giefan 10.03 Giving; 10.03.03 Granting; 10.03.07.01 To allot, assign; 11.10.02.02.01 Care, interest in; 12.09.01 Pledging, betrothal
giefend 10.03 Giving; 10.03.08 Bountifulness, munificence
giefnes 16.01.01.01 Attributes of God
giefu 08.01.02.06.02 Forgiveness, remission, clemency; 09.03.07.01.01 A runic letter; 10.03 Giving; 10.03.01 Grace, favour; 10.03.05.01.01 A bribe, gift, payment; 10.03.08 Bountifulness, munificence; 12.09.01 Pledging, betrothal; 12.09.02 Marriage ceremony; 15.01.02 Gift, transfer of property; 16.01.01.01 Attributes of God; 16.01.01.02.02 A giving (by

Deity); 16.01.01.02.07 Divine providence; 16.02.04.07.02.02 Absolution, forgiveness, remission; 16.02.04.12 Sacrifice, a sacrifice

gield 05.13.04 Exchange, commutation; 14.03.03.09.02 Atonement; 15.02.04 Spending, disbursement; 15.03 Exaction of tax/tribute; 15.03.02 A tax; 16.01.06 A god (of any faith); 16.02.01.06.01.01.01 An image, idol; 16.02.04.03 Ritual, rite, service; 16.02.04.12 Sacrifice, a sacrifice

(ge)gield 12.02.03 A society, guild, association

gieldan 10.03.05 Recompense, reward; 12.05.04.02 Vengeance, revenge; 12.05.04.02.01 Retribution, requital; 14.03.03.09.02 Atonement; 16.02.04.12 Sacrifice, a sacrifice; 16.02.04.15 A vow

(ge)gieldan 08.01.02.04.02 Thanks, gratitude; 14.03.03.09.02 Atonement; 15.02.04 Spending, disbursement

giellan 02.05.10.05 Roaring, raging

giellende 02.05.10.05 Roaring, raging

gielp 07.06.02 Arrogance, vainglory, vanity; 07.06.03 Boastfulness, arrogance; 07.06.04 Pride, ostentation

gielpan 07.04.04 Praise, acclamation, applause; 07.06.03 Boastfulness, arrogance

gielpan (of) 07.06.03 Boastfulness, arrogance

gielpcwide 07.06.03 Boastfulness, arrogance

gielpen 07.06.03 Boastfulness, arrogance

gielpgeorn 07.06.03 Boastfulness, arrogance; 07.08.01 Nobility (of character, rank, etc.)

gielpgeornes 07.06.02 Arrogance, vainglory, vanity

gielphlæden 09.03.05.01.01 Poetry

gielping 07.06.03 Boastfulness, arrogance

gielplic 07.06.02 Arrogance, vainglory, vanity; 07.06.04.01 Ostentation, showiness

gielplīce 07.06.01.02 Proudly, arrogantly

gielpna 07.06.03 Boastfulness, arrogance

gielpnes 07.06.03 Boastfulness, arrogance

gielpplega 13.02 War

gielpsceaþa 07.06.03 Boastfulness, arrogance

gielpsprḣc 07.06.03 Boastfulness, arrogance

gielpword 07.06.03 Boastfulness, arrogance

gīeman 06.01.01.01 Thinking about, minding, heeding; 06.02.05.01 Strong liking for, devotion to; 07.05.01 Censure, reproof, rebuke; 08.01.03.03 Anxiety; 10 Having, owning, possession; 10.03.04 Provision, supply; 11.02.02.02 Care, mindfulness, attention; 11.10.02.02 Watchful care, keeping guard; 11.10.02.02.01 Care, interest in; 12.01.01.01 Rule, domination, direction; 12.01.01.12.01 Obedience, service

(ge)gīeman 02.08.12 Healing, curing; 06.01.01.02 Care, attention, observation; 12.08.02.02.01 Reform, correction

gīeme 11.02.02.02 Care, mindfulness, attention

gīemelēas 02.08.12 Healing, curing; 04.02.05.06.01 A cowherd; 08.01.01.03.01 Freedom from trouble, comfort, security; 11.06.01.01 Negligence, carelessness,

heedlessness; 11.09 Peril, danger; 16.02.01.12.05 The world (i.e. unspirituality, worldliness)
gīemelēasian 16.02.01.12.06 Unfaithfulness, undutifulness
gīemelēaslic 11.06.01.01 Negligence, carelessness, heedlessness
gīemelēaslīce 11.06.01 Neglect; 11.06.01.01 Negligence, carelessness, heedlessness; 16.02.01.12.05 The world (i.e. unspirituality, worldliness)
gīemelēasnes 11.06.01.01 Negligence, carelessness, heedlessness
gīemelēast 06.02.07.06.02.03 Presumption; 08.01.01.02.01 Want of interest or concern, indifference; 08.01.01.03.01 Freedom from trouble, comfort, security; 11.06.01.01 Negligence, carelessness, heedlessness
gīemen 02.08.12 Healing, curing; 06.01.01.01 Thinking about, minding, heeding; 08.01.02.02 Love, affection, care; 08.01.03.03 Anxiety; 11.02.02.02 Care, mindfulness, attention; 11.10.02.02.01 Care, interest in; 12.03.01 Direction, care, management, supervision
gīemen dōn 11.02.02.02 Care, mindfulness, attention
gīemend 02.05.09.05 To watch, observe, survey; 11.10.02.02 Watchful care, keeping guard; 12.01.01.05 A leader, administrator
gīemenes 02.08.12 Healing, curing
gīem(e)nes 07.05.01 Censure, reproof, rebuke; 08.01.03.03 Anxiety; 11.10.02.02.01 Care, interest in
gīeming 08.01.03.03 Anxiety; 11.10.02.02.01 Care, interest in;

12.01.01.01 Rule, domination, direction; 12.03.01 Direction, care, management, supervision; 12.09.02 Marriage ceremony
gīemlēast 11.06.01.01 Negligence, carelessness, heedlessness
gīemnes 06.02.05.01 Strong liking for, devotion to
gierd 02.07.03.03.01 Wood (as substance); 04.02.03.03.02 A hide; 04.02.05.05.01 A goad; 05.10.05.03 A measure of distance; 09.03.07.04.01 To punctuate, divide; 14.05.06 Means/implement of torture; 17.03.09 A post, rod, stick, etc.
gierdweg 05.12.01.03.01.03 A highway
gierdwīte 14.05.02 Torment, punishment
(ge)gierela 04.04.07 Trappings, equipment, garb
gegierela 04.04.10 Ornaments, trappings, accoutrements; 13.02.08.02 A standard, banner, ensign
gegier(e)lad 04.04.07 Trappings, equipment, garb
gegierelic 04.04.07 Trappings, equipment, garb
giernan 12.03.04.01 Entreaty, solemn appeal; 15.01.06.01 Begging; 16.02.04.14.02 Imprecation
giernan on/tō 06.02.05.01 Strong liking for, devotion to
(ge)giernan 02.05.05 Desire, appetite; 06.02.04.01 Want, need; 12.03.04 A request, prayer
(ge)giernendlic 02.05.05.01 Object of desire
giernes 12.03.04 A request, prayer
gierwan 04.04.07 Trappings, equipment, garb

(ge)gierwan 13.02.08.03.01 Body armour, war gear
gegierwan 04.04.07 Trappings, equipment, garb
giest 08.01.02.04.01 Visiting; 12.04.03 A stranger
giestærn 04.01.02.04.05.01.01 Quartering of officials; 04.05.03.03 A lodging-house, inn; 11.10.01.02 Refuge, help, shelter
giesternlic 05.11.07.03.01.01 Yesterday
giesthof 04.01.02.04.05.01.01 Quartering of officials; 04.05.03.03 A lodging-house, inn
giesthūs 04.01.02.04.05.01.01 Quartering of officials; 04.05.03 A dwelling-place, abode, habitation; 04.05.03.03 A lodging-house, inn
giestian 04.05.03.03 A lodging-house, inn; 08.01.02.04.01 Visiting
giestig 12.04.03 A stranger
giesting 12.06.05.01 State of exile, banishment
giestlic 08.01.02.04 Hospitality
giestlīþe 08.01.02.04 Hospitality
giestlīþnes 08.01.02.04 Hospitality
giestning 08.01.02.04 Hospitality
giestran 05.11.07.03.01.01 Yesterday
giestranǣfenne 05.11.07.03.01.01 Yesterday
giestsele 04.01.02.04.05.01.01 Quartering of officials; 04.05.03.03 A lodging-house, inn
gīet 03.03.04.03 Growth, increase; 03.06 Comparison; 05.11.07.04 Future, time to come
gīeta 03.03.04.03 Growth, increase; 03.06 Comparison
gīet(-a) 05.11.07.04 Future, time to come
gīet(a) 05.11.07.03.02 Earlier, antecedent

gietan 10.01.02 Acquisition
gif 16.01.01.01 Attributes of God
gīfer 04.01.01.04 Gluttony, overeating, greediness
gīferlīce 06.02.05.02 Greed, importunate desire, rapacity
gīfernes 04.01.01.04 Gluttony, overeating, greediness; 10.03.09.01.01 Covetousness, avarice
gifestre 10.03 Giving
gifeþe 05.04 Fate, lot, fortune, destiny; 05.04.01 Fortune, Fate (personification)
giffæst 11.04 Ability, capacity, power
gifheall 04.05.03.02.02.06.01 A hall building
gifian 16.02.04 Worship, honour, praise
(ge)gifian 10.03 Giving
gifig 15.01.05 Possession of wealth
gifnes 10.03.01 Grace, favour
gifol 10.03.08 Bountifulness, munificence; 11.05.02.02 Humanity, courtesy, civility
gifola 10.03 Giving
gifolnes 10.03.08 Bountifulness, munificence
gifre 11.07.01 Utility, usefulness
gīfre 02.05.05.02 Eager desire; 04.01.01.04 Gluttony, overeating, greediness; 05.06 Destruction, dissolution, loss, breaking; 06.02.05.02 Greed, importunate desire, rapacity; 10.03.09.01.01 Covetousness, avarice
gifsceatt 10.03 Giving
gifstōl 12.01.01.02 Seat of authority
gift 10.03 Giving; 12.09 Marriage, state of marriage; 12.09.02 Marriage ceremony
gifta dōn 12.09.02 Marriage ceremony

giftbūr 12.09.02 Marriage ceremony
giftfeorm 12.09.02 Marriage ceremony
gifthūs 12.09.02 Marriage ceremony
giftian 12.09.01 Pledging, betrothal
giftlēoþ 12.09.02 Marriage ceremony
giftlic 12.09 Marriage, state of marriage
gifu 16.02.01.12.02 Grace
gifum 10.03.08 Bountifulness, munificence
gifung 09.07.04.01.02 Consent
gīgant 02.03.01.11 Giant
gīgantmæcg 02.03.01.11 Giant
(ge)gilda 12.02.03 A society, guild, association
gegilda 02.03.02.03.06.01 Kinsman, relative
gilddagas 05.11.02.01.02 A time of celebration; 16.02.04.04.02 A feast-day, holy day
gegilde 12.02.03 A society, guild, association
gildet 02.06.02.01.03 Cattle
gildfrēo 15.03 Exaction of tax/tribute
gegildheall 12.02.03 A society, guild, association
gildlic 16.02.04.04.02 A feast-day, holy day; 18.02.01 A festival
gildrǣden 12.02.03 A society, guild, association
(ge)gildscipe 12.02.03 A society, guild, association
gildselen 15.03.02 A tax
gildsester 03.03.01 Specific measures
gildsetl 12.02.03 A society, guild, association
gilm 03.03.04.01.02.01 A heap, mass, accumulation; 04.02.04.04.04 Stack, rick
gilp 04.06.02.05 Dust, powder
gilte 02.06.02.01.07 Pig, swine

gim 01.02.01.01.02 Star
gimbǣre 17.02.05.01 Ornamental object
gimcynn 17.04.03.04 Gems collectively
gimm 17.04.03.04 Gems collectively
gimmian 07.10 Beauty, fairness
gimmisc 17.02.05.01 Ornamental object
gegimmod 17.02.05.01 Ornamental object
gimreced 04.05.03.02.02.06 A royal/noble palace
gimrodor 03.01.12 Brightness, light
gimstān 17.04.03.04 Gems collectively
gimwyrhta 17.02.05.01 Ornamental object
gin 01.01.02.01.03.02 Abyss, chasm
gīnan ongēan 05.12.02.06.01 To push, drive
ginfæst 10.03.08 Bountifulness, munificence
gingest 02.01.04 Age
gingifer 04.01.02.01.05.05.01 Ginger
gingra 02.01.04 Age
ginian 02.04.03.01.03.06 Mouth; 02.05.10.15 Voice, cry (of living creature); 05.10.05.04.14 An opening, aperture; 05.10.05.04.14.01 A yawning, gaping opening
giniend 05.10.05.04.14.01 A yawning, gaping opening
ginnan 05.11.10.01 A beginning
ginne 03.03.04.02 A sufficiency, sufficient supply; 05.10.01 Amplitude, spaciousness, vastness
ginnes 05.11.11.02 Let up, intermission, cessation
ginnwīsed 06.01.06.02 Knowledge, learning, erudition
ginung 02.05.10.15 Voice, cry (of living creature); 05.10.05.04.14.01 A yawning, gaping opening

(ge)girnung 12.03.04 A request, prayer
(ge)girwan 10.03.03 Granting; 13.02.08 Military equipment
gegirwan 04.01.02.02 To prepare food; 04.04.07 Trappings, equipment, garb; 05.12.02 To move, set in motion
gegirwed 04.04.07 Trappings, equipment, garb
gīsl 13.02.05.01.02.01 State of being a hostage
gīsldu 13.02.05.01.02.01 State of being a hostage
gīslhād 13.02.05.01.02.01 State of being a hostage
gīslian 13.02.05.01.02.01 State of being a hostage
gist 04.01.02.01.06 Leaven/yeast
gisterdæg 05.11.07.03.01.01 Yesterday
gistlīþiend 08.01.02.04 Hospitality
gistmægen 08.01.02.04.01 Visiting
gistran dæg 05.11.07.03.01.01 Yesterday
gegite 02.05.02 Consciousness
gegītsan 14.02.01.02.01 Open robbery, rapine, pillage
gītsere 10.03.09.01.01 Covetousness, avarice
(ge)gītsian 06.02.05.01 Strong liking for, devotion to; 10.03.09.01.01 Covetousness, avarice
gītsiend 10.03.09.01.01 Covetousness, avarice
gītsiende 06.02.05.03 Satisfaction, repletion; 10.03.09.01.01 Covetousness, avarice
gītsiendlic 06.02.05.03 Satisfaction, repletion
gītsiendnes 10.03.09.01.01 Covetousness, avarice
gītsung 06.02.05.01 Strong liking for, devotion to; 10.03.09.01.01 Covetousness, avarice
gīþcorn 02.07.11.02 Unidentified plants (alphabetical order)
giþrife 04.02.04.04 Harvest, crop
gīululing 05.11.03.01.03.01 Specific months
gīw 02.06.10.01.02 Griffin
(ge)giwian 12.03.04 A request, prayer
giwung 12.03.04 A request, prayer
glad/glæd 01.01.02.01.03.03 Valley
(ge)gladdian 08.01.01.03.09.03 To make glad
gegladdian 16.02.04.12 Sacrifice, a sacrifice
(ge)gladdung 08.01.01.03.09 Pleasantness, agreeableness
glade 08.01.01.03.04 Gladness, cheerfulness
gladian 03.01.12 Brightness, light
(ge)gladian 08.01.01.03.06 Exultation, joy; 13.01.02.01 An appeasing, pacifying
gegladod 08.01.01.03.04 Gladness, cheerfulness
gladung 08.01.01.03.07 Joyous sound, mirth; 13.01.02.01 An appeasing, pacifying
glæd 01.03.01.01 Hot, fine weather; 03.01.12 Brightness, light; 08.01.01.03.04 Gladness, cheerfulness; 08.01.01.03.06 Exultation, joy; 08.01.01.03.09.01 Pleasant, agreeable
glæd (wiþ) 08.01.02.01 Favour, kindness, grace
glædene 02.07.11 Plants/flowers (alphabetical order)
glædlic 03.01.12 Brightness, light; 08.01.01.03.09.01 Pleasant, agreeable; 08.01.02.01 Favour, kindness, grace

glædlīce 06.02.02.01 Will, wish, pleasure; 08.01.01.03.04 Gladness, cheerfulness
glædman 11.05.02.02 Humanity, courtesy, civility
glædmōd 06.02.05.04.03 Promptitude, readiness; 08.01.01.03.04 Gladness, cheerfulness; 08.01.02.01 Favour, kindness, grace
glædmōdnes 08.01.02.01 Favour, kindness, grace
glædnes 06.02.02.01 Will, wish, pleasure
(ge)glædnes 08.01.01.03 Good feeling, joy, happiness; 08.01.02.01 Favour, kindness, grace
glædscipe 08.01.01.03 Good feeling, joy, happiness
glǣm 03.01.12 Brightness, light; 07.10 Beauty, fairness
glæppe 02.07.09.02.02.02 Other vegetables (alphabetical order)
glær 17.04.03.01 Amber
glæren 17.04.03.02 Glass
glæs 04.01.03.05.04 Drinking vessel; 17.04.03.02 Glass
glæsen 03.01.14 A colour; 17.04.03.02 Glass
glæsen fæt 04.01.03.05.04 Drinking vessel
glæsenēage 02.04.03.01.03.02 Eye
glæsfæt 04.01.03.05.04 Drinking vessel; 04.01.03.05.04.01 A flask, flagon, bottle; 17.05.03 Sources of fire/light
glæsful 04.01.03 Drinking
glæsgegot 17.04.03.02 Glass
glæshlūtor 03.01.12.03 Clear, transparent
glæteriende 03.01.12.01 Glittering, effulgence
glæterung 03.01.12.01 Glittering, effulgence

glēaw 02.05.09.01 To open the eyes/be awake; 06.01.05.02 Intelligence; 06.01.05.02.01.01 Sagacity; 07.02 Goodness; 11.04.02 Skill, skilfulness
glēawe 06.01.05.02.01.01.01 Reason, sense, discretion, prudence; 07.02 Goodness; 11.04.02 Skill, skilfulness
glēawferhþ 06.01.05.02.01.01 Sagacity
glēawhycgende 06.01.01.01.01.01 Consideration, rumination
glēawhȳdig 06.01.05.02.01.01 Sagacity
glēawlic 06.01.05.02.01.01 Sagacity
glēawlīce 06.01.05.02 Intelligence; 06.01.05.02.01.01.01 Reason, sense, discretion, prudence; 11.04.02 Skill, skilfulness
glēawmōd 06.01.05.02.01.01 Sagacity
glēawnes 06.01.03.02 Dialectics, logic; 06.01.05.02 Intelligence; 06.01.05.02.01.01 Sagacity; 09.03.04.02.02 Eloquence, elegance in language; 09.04.01 Signal, signalling; 11.02.02 Diligence; 11.04 Ability, capacity, power
glēawscipe 06.01.05.02.01.01 Sagacity; 11.02.02 Diligence
glēawstōl 04.05.03.02.02.02 Agreeable dwellings
glēd 03.01.09.02 Fire, flame; 03.01.09.02.01 Fire, burning; 14.05.06 Means/implement of torture
geglēdan 03.01.09.02.01 Fire, burning
gleddian 05.12.02.07.01 To throw, scatter
glēde 03.01.09.02.01 Fire, burning
glēdegesa 06.01.08.06.03 Cause of fear, terror, horror
glēdfæt 04.01.02.02.06.01 Cooking vessel/pot; 16.02.05.05.07 A thurible, censer
glēdscofl 17.05.02 A hearth, fireplace

glēdstede 16.02.05.03.04 Part of temple containing altar/idol
glemm 02.08.04.02 Blemish, disfigurement
glendran 04 Consumption of food/drink
(ge)glendrian 05.06.01 Devastation, laying waste
gleng 07.06.05 Pomp, splendour, magnificence; 07.08.04 An ornament, honour, glory; 07.10.03 An adornment, decoration, ornament
glengan 04.06.01.07 Hair-care; 09.03.04 Rhetoric, art of exposition; 17.05.04 To kindle, set alight (fire, lamp)
(ge)glengan 03.05 Order, arrangement, disposition; 07.08.04 An ornament, honour, glory; 07.10.03 An adornment, decoration, ornament
glenge 07.10.03 An adornment, decoration, ornament
geglenged 07.10.03 An adornment, decoration, ornament
(ge)glengendlīce 09.03.04.02.02 Eloquence, elegance in language
glengful 07.10.03 An adornment, decoration, ornament
glenglic 07.06.05 Pomp, splendour, magnificence
glengnes 07.10.03 An adornment, decoration, ornament
glēodǣd 18.02.02 Play, (athletic) sport
glēodrēam 08.01.01.03.07 Joyous sound, mirth
gleomu 03.01.12 Brightness, light
glēsan 09.04.03.02 Glossing
glēsing 09.04.03.02 Glossing
glid 03.01.06 Smoothness
glida 02.06.08.04 Bird of prey

glīdan 02.02.03 To die, perish; 05.12.05.06.01 To travel smoothly, slide, glide
(ge)glīdan 05.12.05.03 To travel away (from)
glid(d)er 03.01.06 Smoothness; 12.08.07.01.01 Wantonness, sensuality, lasciviousness
gliddrian 05.12.04.01.01 Unstable
gliderung 05.07 Ending of existence, end of world
glind 04.05.01.02.07 A fence, hedge; 05.10.05.04.11 A circle, circuit, circumference
glisigende 03.01.12.01 Glittering, effulgence
glisnian 03.01.12.01 Glittering, effulgence
glitenian 03.01.12.01 Glittering, effulgence; 07.08.07 Glory, splendour, magnificence
gliteniende 03.01.12.01 Glittering, effulgence
glitenung 01.03.01.03.01.02 Lightning; 03.01.12.01 Glittering, effulgence
glīw 07.05.04 Mockery, derision, scorn; 08.01.01.03.07.02 Jesting, pleasantry; 18.02.02 Play, (athletic) sport; 18.02.07 Music
glīwbēam 18.02.07.02 A musical instrument
glīwbydenestre 18.02.07.02 A musical instrument
glīwcræft 18.02.07.02 A musical instrument
glīwcynn 18.02.07 Music
glīwdrēam 18.02.07 Music
glīwere 07.07.03 Flattery; 08.01.01.03.07.03 Buffoonery, scurrility; 18.02.05 Buffoonery, speech of buffoon/actor
glīwgamen 18.02.07 Music

glīwgeorn 18.02 Amusement, revelry, festivity
glīwhlēoþriendlic 18.02.07 Music
glīwian 02.05.10.11 Clang, sound of metal; 08.01.01.03.07.02 Jesting, pleasantry; 09.03.05 Art of poetry; 18.02.05 Buffoonery, speech of buffoon/actor; 18.02.07.02 A musical instrument
glīwiend 18.02.07.02 A musical instrument
glīwingman 07.05.04 Mockery, derision, scorn
glīwlic 08.01.01.03.07.02 Jesting, pleasantry
glīwmæden 18.02.07.02 A musical instrument
glīwman 07.07.03 Flattery; 09.03.05 Art of poetry; 18.02.07.02 A musical instrument
glīwstæf 08.01.01.03 Good feeling, joy, happiness
glīwstōl 08.01.01.03.08 Happiness, well-being, prosperity
glīwung 08.01.01.03.07.04 Scoffing, mockery
glīwword 09.03.05.01 Poetical language
glōf 04.04.07.14 A glove
geglōfed 04.04.07.14 A glove
glōfung 04.04.07.14 A glove
glōfwyrt 02.07.11 Plants/flowers (alphabetical order)
glōm 05.11.04.02.01 Sunset
glōmung 05.11.04.02.01 Sunset
gloria 16.02.04.03.02 Parts of service
glōwan 03.01.09.02 Fire, flame
glōwende 03.01.09.02 Fire, flame
gluto 04.01.01.04 Gluttony, overeating, greediness

glyrende 02.05.09.04 To see, look upon, behold
gnæt 02.06.09.02.08 Gnat, midge
gnagan 04.01.01.01 Chewing
gnēadnes 10.03.09.01 Parsimony, niggardliness
gnēaþ 10.03.09.01 Parsimony, niggardliness
gnēaþ/gnēad 12.08.03 Restraint, temperance
gnēaþlicnes 10.03.09.01 Parsimony, niggardliness
gnēaþnes 03.03.04.05 Insufficiency, lack, want; 12.08.03 Restraint, temperance
gnēþe 10.03.09 Moderation in expenditure
gnēþe/gnīþe 03.03.04.05 Insufficiency, lack, want
gnēþelīce 10.03.09 Moderation in expenditure
gnīdan 05.06.05.01 A rubbing
(ge)gnīdan 05.06.05 A grinding, pounding; 05.06.05.01 A rubbing
gnidil 17.03.04 Tools for smoothing/scraping/grinding
gnīding 05.06.05.01 A rubbing
gnorn 08.01.03 Bad feeling, sadness
gnorncearig 08.01.03.03 Anxiety
gnornhof 14.05.08.01 Prison, confinement, durance
gnornian 08.01.03.04 Grief; 08.01.03.04.01 Complaint, lamentation; 08.01.03.05 Murmuring, complaint
gnornscendende 08.01.03 Bad feeling, sadness
gnornsorg 08.01.03 Bad feeling, sadness
gnornung 08.01.03 Bad feeling, sadness; 08.01.03.04.01 Complaint, lamentation; 08.01.03.05.01 A grudge

gnornword 08.01.03.04.01 Complaint, lamentation
gnuddian 05.06.05.01 A rubbing
gegnunga 05.11.07.01 Contemporary, coeval
gnyrn 08.01.03 Bad feeling, sadness; 16.02.01.13 Evil-doing, transgression, sin
gnyrnwracu 12.05.04.02 Vengeance, revenge
gnyrran 02.05.10.15.04 Gnashing of teeth
god 16.01.01 God, the Lord; 16.01.06 A god (of any faith); 16.02.01.06.01.01.01 An image, idol; 16.02.01.12 Spirituality
gōd 02.01.03 Fruitfulness, fertility; 02.05.07 Faculty of taste; 02.05.08.02 Pleasant smell, fragrance, perfume; 03.03.04.01 Much; 03.03.04.02 A sufficiency, sufficient supply; 04.06 Salubrity; 06.02.07.06 Courage, boldness, valour; 07.02 Goodness; 07.02.01 Right, virtue; 07.02.02 Good, what is beneficial, advantageous, etc.; 07.02.03 Perfection; 07.04 Consideration, esteem; 07.04.04.02 Laudable, praiseworthy; 08.01.01.03.08 Happiness, well-being, prosperity; 08.01.01.03.08.03 A favour, blessing; 08.01.02.01 Favour, kindness, grace; 10.03.08 Bountifulness, munificence; 11.02.02.02 Care, mindfulness, attention; 11.04.02 Skill, skilfulness; 11.05.02.02 Humanity, courtesy, civility; 11.07.02 Utility, advantage, convenience; 11.07.03 Use, advantage, profit; 12.07.02.02 Truth, faithfulness, good faith, sincerity; 12.08.02.01 Goodness, excellence, virtue; 12.08.02.02 Righteousness, rectitude; 15.01 Property; 16.01.01.01 Attributes of God; 16.02.01.11 Firmness in the law, piety, devoutness; 16.02.03.01 Ecclesiastical authority
gōd dǣd 16.02.04.09 Almsgiving, charitableness
gōd lār 06.01.06.02.03.04 Teaching, instruction
gōd līf 12.08.02.01 Goodness, excellence, virtue
gōd weorc 16.02.04.09 Almsgiving, charitableness
godæppel 02.07.09.02 Particular fruits (alphabetical order)
godbearn 02.03.02.05 Spiritual relationships; 16.01.01.04.02 The Son, Christ; 16.02.04.07.01 Baptism, baptizing (and anointing)
godborg 14.03.03.07 Security, pledge, bail
godbōt 14.03.03.09.02 Atonement
godcund 16.01 A divine being; 16.01.01 God, the Lord; 16.01.02 The heavens, sky; 16.02.01.01 Creed, statement of faith; 16.02.01.06.01 Belief/practice of heathen people; 16.02.01.11 Firmness in the law, piety, devoutness; 16.02.01.12 Spirituality
godcundlic 16.01 A divine being; 16.01.01 God, the Lord; 16.01.02 The heavens, sky; 16.02.01.11 Firmness in the law, piety, devoutness; 16.02.01.12 Spirituality
godcundlīce 16.01 A divine being; 16.02.01.09.01 Canon law
godcundlicnes 16.01 A divine being
godcundmæht 16.01.01.01.01.01 Mightiness

godcundnes 05.02.02 Nature, established order of things; 16.01 A divine being; 16.02.04.03 Ritual, rite, service; 16.02.04.07.02.03 Penance, an act/instance of penance
godcundspēd 16.01 A divine being
gōddǣd 11.07.03 Use, advantage, profit; 12.08.02.02 Righteousness, rectitude
gōddōend 12.08.02.02 Righteousness, rectitude
goddohtor 02.03.02.05 Spiritual relationships; 16.02.04.07.01 Baptism, baptizing (and anointing)
gōddōnd 08.01.02.01 Favour, kindness, grace
goddrēam 16.01.02.02 Glory/majesty of heaven
gode (ge)sellan 16.02.01.10.02 Consecration
godes bearn 16.02.01.11 Firmness in the law, piety, devoutness
godes bōc 16.02.01.08 Scripture, the scriptures
godes boda 16.01.02.05.01 An angel
godes est 16.02.01.12.02 Grace
godes frēond 16.02.01.11 Firmness in the law, piety, devoutness
godes gifu 16.02.01.12.02 Grace
godes hūs 16.02.05.02.03 A church, place of worship
godes lagu 16.02.01.01 Creed, statement of faith; 16.02.01.08.01 The Old Testament; 16.02.01.09 The law
godes lamb(or) 16.01.01.04.02 The Son, Christ
godes līchama 16.02.04.07.04 Communion/eucharist
godes þegn 16.02.03.02 A cleric, clergyman (general)
godes þēow 16.02.03.02 A cleric, clergyman (general)
godfæder 02.03.02.05 Spiritual relationships; 16.01.01.04.01 God the Father; 16.02.04.07.01 Baptism, baptizing (and anointing)
godforgifnes 16.02.04.07.02.02 Absolution, forgiveness, remission
gōdfremmend 12.08.02.02 Righteousness, rectitude
godfyrht 16.02.01.11 Firmness in the law, piety, devoutness
godgesprǣce 16.02.01.12.01 Revelation, illumination, inspiration
god(ge)sprǣce 06.01.08.04 Foreseeing
godgield 16.02.01.06.01 Belief/practice of heathen people; 16.02.01.06.01.01.01 An image, idol
godgildlic 16.02.01.06.01.01 Pagan worship, idolatrous practice(s)
godgim 01.02.01.01 Heavenly body
godhād 16.01 A divine being
gōdian 03.03.04.01 Much; 08.01.01.03.08 Happiness, well-being, prosperity; 12.07.04.01 Justification; 12.08.02.02 Righteousness, rectitude
(ge)gōdian 10.03.04 Provision, supply; 12.08.02.02.01 Reform, correction; 15.01.02 Gift, transfer of property
gegōdian 02.08.12.01 Medical care, treatment; 07.08.03 Honour, veneration
goding 16.01.01.04.02 The Son, Christ
gōdlēas 08.01.03.06 Adversity, affliction
godlic 16.01.01 God, the Lord
gōdlic 07.10.01 Elegance, beauty, comeliness
godmægen 16.01 A divine being
godmōdor 02.03.02.05 Spiritual relationships; 16.02.04.07.01 Baptism, baptizing (and anointing)

gōdnes 07.02 Goodness; 08.01.01.03.08 Happiness, well-being, prosperity; 08.01.02.01 Favour, kindness, grace; 11.07.03 Use, advantage, profit; 12.08.02.02 Righteousness, rectitude; 16.01.01.01 Attributes of God

gegōdod 10 Having, owning, possession

gōdsǣd 12.01.01.06.08 A person of rank, elder, great man

gōdscipe 08.01.02.01 Favour, kindness, grace

godscyld 16.02.01.11.02 Impiety, lack of piety

godscyldig 16.02.01.11.02 Impiety, lack of piety

godsibb 02.03.02.05 Spiritual relationships; 16.02.04.07.01 Baptism, baptizing (and anointing)

godsibbrǣden 16.02.04.07.01 Baptism, baptizing (and anointing)

gōdspēdig 16.01.01.01.01.01 Mightiness

godspel 16.02.01.08.03 The New Testament; 16.02.02 Christianity, the Christian faith; 16.02.04.03.02 Parts of service; 16.02.05.10.05 A bible

godspelbodung 05.11.03 Period of time, era, epoch

godspellbōc 16.02.01.08.03 The New Testament; 16.02.05.10.05 A bible

godspellere 16.02.01.08.03.01 New Testament persons; 16.02.03.02.10 A preacher, teacher

godspellian 09.06.02.01.06.02 Good tidings; 16.02.04.10 Preaching

godspellic 05.11.03 Period of time, era, epoch; 16.02.01.08.03 The New Testament

godspellisc 16.02.01.08.03 The New Testament

godspelltraht 16.02.04.03.02 Parts of service; 16.02.04.10 Preaching

godsprǣce 16.01.04.06.04 Prophecy, divine speech

godsunu 02.03.02.05 Spiritual relationships; 16.02.04.07.01 Baptism, baptizing (and anointing)

godþrymm 16.01.01.01.01.01 Mightiness

godþrymnes 16.01.01.01.01.02 Glory

godwebb 04.04.05.05 Fine woven material from silk, cotton or linen; 04.04.07.01 Mode of dressing, fashion; 04.04.08.01 Curtain, wall-hanging, etc.; 16.02.05.05.09 Cloths

godwebbcyn 04.04.07.07 A long outer garment, covering, cloak, etc.

godwebb(en) 04.04.05.05 Fine woven material from silk, cotton or linen

godwebgyrla 04.04.07.07 A long outer garment, covering, cloak, etc.

godwebwyrhta 04.04 Weaving

gōdwillende 06.02.02.01 Will, wish, pleasure

godwrǣc 16.02.01.11.02 Impiety, lack of piety

godwrǣclic 16.02.04.14 Sacrilege

godwrecnes 16.02.01.11.02 Impiety, lack of piety

goffian 07.06.02 Arrogance, vainglory, vanity

gōian 08.01.03.04.01 Complaint, lamentation

gold 01.01.02.02.03.01 Types of metals/minerals; 15.01.03 Treasure, riches, wealth; 15.01.04 Coinage, money; 17.04.02.03 Gold

goldǣht 15.01.03 Treasure, riches, wealth

goldbeorht 03.01.12 Brightness, light

goldblēoh 03.01.14.07 Yellow/yellowness

goldblōma 02.07.11 Plants/flowers (alphabetical order)
goldburg 12.06.02.01 A township
golde 02.07.11 Plants/flowers (alphabetical order)
goldfæt 04.01.02.02.06.05 Vessel/utensil/cup
goldfǣted 17.02.05.02 Goldsmith's art
goldfāg 17.02.05.02 Goldsmith's art
goldfell 17.02.05.02 Goldsmith's art
goldfellen 17.04.04.02 Skin, hide (as material)
goldfinc 02.06.08.05 Forest bird, wild-fowl
goldfinger 02.04.03.04.01.01.01 Finger
goldfrætwe 17.02.05.02 Goldsmith's art
goldfyld 17.02.05.02 Goldsmith's art
goldgearwe 17.02.05.02 Goldsmith's art
goldgewefen 04.04.05.05 Fine woven material from silk, cotton or linen
goldgeweorc 17.02.05.02 Goldsmith's art
goldgiefa 12.01.01.04 A leader, ruler
goldhama 13.02.08.03.01.04 Coat of mail/corselet
goldhilted 13.02.08.04.03.01.01 Hilt of sword
goldhladen 04.04.10 Ornaments, trappings, accoutrements
goldhord 15.01.03 Treasure, riches, wealth
goldhordhūs 15.01.03 Treasure, riches, wealth
goldhordian 15.01.05 Possession of wealth
goldhroden 04.04.10 Ornaments, trappings, accoutrements
goldhwæt 03.03.04.02.01 Abundance
goldlǣfer 17.02.05.02 Goldsmith's art
goldlēaf 17.02.05.02 Goldsmith's art

goldmæstling 01.01.02.02.03.01 Types of metals/minerals; 17.04.02.01 Brass
goldmāþm 15.01.03 Treasure, riches, wealth
goldōra 01.01.02.02.03.01 Types of metals/minerals
goldsele 04.05.03.02.02.06.01 A hall building
goldsmiþ 17.02.04.03 Metal worker; 17.02.05.02 Goldsmith's art
goldspēdig 15.01.05 Possession of wealth
goldtorht 03.01.12 Brightness, light
goldþēof 14.02.01.02 Wrongful taking, theft
goldþrǣd 04.04.04 A thread (of wool, etc.), fibre
goldweard 11.10.02.02 Watchful care, keeping guard
goldwecg 01.01.02.02.03.01 Types of metals/minerals; 17.04.02.03 Gold
goldwine 12.01.01.04 A leader, ruler
goldwlanc 04.04.10 Ornaments, trappings, accoutrements; 07.06.04.01 Ostentation, showiness
goldwlencu 07.06.05 Pomp, splendour, magnificence
goldwreken 17.02.05.02 Goldsmith's art
goldwyrt 02.07.11 Plants/flowers (alphabetical order)
gōma 02.04.03.01.03.07 Jaw(s); 02.04.06.03.02.01 Mouth; 16.01.05 Hell, lower world, abode of the dead
gombe 15.03 Exaction of tax/tribute
gomelian 02.01.04.03 Aging, growing old
gomor 03.03.01 Specific measures
gong 02.08.02.01.02 Onset, attack of illness
gōp 12.01.01.09 Bondage, slavery
gor 02.04.06.06.06 Faeces; 03.01.17 Thickness, viscosity; 04.06.02.02 Foul, filthy, squalid

gorettan 02.05.09.04 To see, look upon, behold
gorettung 02.05.09.04 To see, look upon, behold
gorgrǣfe 02.07.03.04.01 A small wood, coppice, copse
gorian 02.05.09.04 To see, look upon, behold
gorst 02.07.03.05 Particular trees/shrubs (alphabetical order)
gors(t) 02.07.03.01 A bush
gorstbēam 02.07.03.01 A bush
gorsten 02.07.03.01 A bush
gorstig 02.07.03.01 A bush
gōs 02.06.08.02.01.02 Goose
gōsfugol 02.06.08.02.01.02 Goose
gōshafoc 02.06.08.04 Bird of prey
gota 01.01.03.01.01.04 Watercourse/channel; 02.03.03.06.05 Scandinavian
gotisc 02.03.03.06.05 Scandinavian
gotonisc 02.03.03.06.05 Scandinavian
gōtwoþe 02.07.11 Plants/flowers (alphabetical order)
gōung 08.01.03.04.01 Complaint, lamentation
grād 03.03.05.01 Rank, position, degree; 16.02.05.03.04 Part of temple containing altar/idol
grǣd 02.07.08 Grasses, reeds, etc.
grǣdan 02.05.10.15.01 To raise (the voice), raise up (noise); 02.05.10.15.06 A roar, howl, etc.
grǣde 02.07.08 Grasses, reeds, etc.; 04.02.03.04 Grassland
grǣdig 02.05.05.02 Eager desire; 04.01.01.04 Gluttony, overeating, greediness; 05.06 Destruction, dissolution, loss, breaking; 06.02.05.04 Desire, eagerness; 10.03.09.01.01 Covetousness, avarice; 12.08.08.01 Eager, unseemly desire
grǣdiglice 02.05.05.02 Eager desire
grǣdiglīce 04.01.01.04 Gluttony, overeating, greediness
grǣdignes 02.05.05.02 Eager desire; 10.03.09.01.01 Covetousness, avarice; 12.08.08.01 Eager, unseemly desire
grǣdtūn 04.02.03.02.02.06 Stubble field
grǣdum 04.01.01.04 Gluttony, overeating, greediness
græf 01.01.02.01.03 Hollow/depression in land; 02.02.05.01.01 A grave, burial place, sepulchre; 09.03.07.06.01 A writing instrument
grǣfe 02.07.03.04.01 A small wood, coppice, copse; 17.05.01 Fuel, tinder
(ge)græfen 17.02.05.05 A carving, graving
græfhūs 02.02.05.01.01 A grave, burial place, sepulchre
græfsex 17.03.03 A cutting tool
græft 16.02.01.06.01.01.01 An image, idol; 17.02.05.05 A carving, graving
græftgeweorc 16.02.01.06.01.01.01 An image, idol; 17.02.05.05 A carving, graving
grǣg 03.01.12 Brightness, light; 03.01.14.10 Grey-coated one
grǣggōs 02.06.08.06 Water bird
grǣghama 03.01.14.10 Grey-coated one
grǣgmǣl 03.01.14.10 Grey-coated one; 13.02.08.04.03 A sword
(ge)græppian 10.04.02.02 To seize, take, grasp, lay hold on
græsmolde 04.02.03.04 Grassland
græswang 01.01.02.01.04 Open (level) land; 04.02.03.04 Grassland
grāf 02.07.03.04.01 A small wood, coppice, copse

grāfa 02.07.03.04.01 A small wood, coppice, copse
grafan 17.02.05.05 A carving, graving
grafere 17.02.05.05 A carving, graving
grafet 01.01.02.01.03 Hollow/depression in land
grafian 17.02.04.02.02 Digging
grafu 01.01.02.01.03.01 Cave
gram 08.01.03.05.02 Anger; 08.01.03.09.05 Enmity; 08.01.03.09.06 Hostility
grama 08.01.03.05.02 Anger; 08.01.03.06 Adversity, affliction; 16.01.05.02 Species of devil, hellish race
graman niman 08.01.03.05.04 Irritability
grambǣre 08.01.03.05.02 Anger
grame 08.01.03.05.02 Anger; 08.01.03.09.10 Wrath, sternness, displeasure
gramfǣrnes 08.01.03.05.02 Anger
gramheort 08.01.03.09.06 Hostility
gramhycgende 08.01.03.09.06 Hostility
gramhygdig 08.01.03.09.06 Hostility
gramian 08.01.03.05.03 Exasperation, irritation
gramigende 08.01.03.05.02 Anger
gramlic 08.01.03.07.04 Severity, harshness; 08.01.03.09.10 Wrath, sternness, displeasure
gramlīce 08.01.03.09.10 Wrath, sternness, displeasure
grammatic 09.03.02 Art of grammar
grammatican cræft 09.03.02 Art of grammar
grammaticcræft 09.03.02 Art of grammar
grammaticere 09.03.02 Art of grammar
grammōd 08.01.03.09.11 Hardheartedness, cruelty, severity

gramword 08.01.03.09.01.03 Sharpness (of speech)
grandorlēas 12.08.05 Innocence
grānian 08.01.03.04.01 Complaint, lamentation
granu 02.04.04.03.03.01 Beard, whisker
grānung 08.01.03.04.01 Complaint, lamentation
granwisc 04.02.04.04.05.02 Chaff
grāp 10.04.02 To grasp, take hold of
(ge)grāpan 10.04.02.02 To seize, take, grasp, lay hold on
grāpian 11.04.03 (Of ability) low, mean, of less worth
(ge)grāpian 02.05.06 Sense of touch; 05.10.05.01 A little way, no great distance
gegrāpian 05.12.05.02.03 To arrive
grāpigendlic 02.05.06 Sense of touch
grāpung 02.05.06 Sense of touch
grāscinnen 04.04.06 Undressed condition (of hide); 17.04.04.02 Skin, hide (as material)
grasian 04.02.05.01.01.01 To put out to pasture
graþul 16.02.04.03.02 Parts of service
grēada 02.04.03.03.05 Chest, breast, bosom; 02.04.03.03.07 Lap; 08.01 Heart, spirit, mood, disposition; 11.10.02.02.01 Care, interest in
grēat 02.04.02.01 Fat/plump; 02.04.02.03.01 Tall; 03.01.05 Roughness; 03.03.04.01.01 Greatness, bigness, size; 05.10.05.03.03 Height, loftiness, sublimity; 11.07.04 Superiority, pre-eminence, primacy
grēat sealt 01.01.02.02.03.01 Types of metals/minerals
grēate wyrt 02.07.11 Plants/flowers (alphabetical order)

(ge)grēatian 05.10.05.02.02 Greater, bigger
grēatnes 02.04.02 Bodily shape/physique; 03.01.07 Weight, heaviness; 03.03.04.01.01 Greatness, bigness, size; 04.04.05.01 Coarse, rough (of cloth); 05.10.05.03.01.01 Breadth, width across
gegrēatod 02.04.02.03.01 Tall
grēcas 02.03.03.06.03 The Greeks
grēcisc 02.03.03.06.03 The Greeks
grēcisc/grēgisc 09.03.01 Particular languages
gregg 06.02.07.07 Cowardice, pusillanimity; 13.02.10.02.02 A coward, deserter
gremian 07.05.03.02 Calumny, slander, insult
(ge)gremian 06.02.06.03.03 Incitement; 08.01.01.01.03 An incitement, cause of strong feeling; 08.01.03.05.02 Anger; 08.01.03.09.06 Hostility
gegremian 02.08.12.02.07.01 Purgative
gegremid 08.01.03.05.02 Anger
gremming 08.01.03.05.03 Exasperation, irritation
grēne 01.01.02.01.05 Covered with vegetation; 02.07.01 To grow; 02.07.03 A tree; 03.01.14.06 Green/greenness; 04.01.02.02.05 Cooking; 04.04.06 Undressed condition (of hide)
grēne ār 01.01.02.02.03.01 Types of metals/minerals; 17.04.02.01 Brass
grēn(e)hæwen 03.01.14.06 Green/greenness
grēnian 02.07.01 To grow
grēnnes 02.07 A plant; 02.07.01 To grow; 03.01.14.06 Green/greenness;
04.02.04.05.04.01 A forester, woodman
grennian 02.08.03 Pain, bodily discomfort
grenniende 02.08.03.01 Extreme pain, torture, torment
grennung 02.08.03 Pain, bodily discomfort
grēofa 04.01.02.02.06.04 Pot, vessel, crock
grēon 01.01.02.02.02.01 Sand, gravel
grēosn 01.01.02.02.02.01 Sand, gravel
grēot 01.01.02 Land; 01.01.02.02 Earth, soil
grēotan 08.01.03.04.01 Complaint, lamentation
grēoten 01.01.02.02.02.01 Sand, gravel
grēothord 02.04 Body
grēp 04.05.03.05 A drain
grēp/grȳpe 04.05.03.05.02 A privy
grētan 02.01.03.03 Sex, generation; 02.08.04 Hurt, injury, damage; 02.08.12.01 Medical care, treatment; 08.01.03.04.01 Complaint, lamentation; 09.01.04 Conversation, discussion; 09.06 To take matter for discourse; 11.01.02 An undertaking; 11.05.02.02.01 Greetings, courteous terms of address; 14.03.03.01.01 Defence, reply; 18.02.07.02.03.01 A harp, lyre
(ge)grētan 05.10.05.01 A little way, no great distance; 08.01.03.07.02 Misery, trouble, affliction; 08.01.03.07.02.01 Injury, offence; 09.01.03 To address, speak to; 11.05.02.02.01.03 To bid farewell; 13.02.03.01 An attack, assault
gegrētan 05.12.05.02 To go/travel towards, come, approach

grēting 09.06.02.01.07.02 A categorizing name; 10.03.05 Recompense, reward; 11.05.02.02.01 Greetings, courteous terms of address; 16.02.04 Worship, honour, praise
grētinghūs 04.05.03.04 A closet, chamber, room
grētingword 11.05.02.02.01 Greetings, courteous terms of address
gegrētlic 11.05.02.02.01 Greetings, courteous terms of address
greþe 12.04.01 A fellow, companion, associate, comrade
griffus 02.06.10.01.02 Griffin
grīghund 02.06.02.01.04 Dog; 04.03.01 Tracking
grillan 02.05.10.05 Roaring, raging; 07.03.01.03 To loathe, hate, abhor; 08.01.03.05.02 Anger
grīma 13.02.08.03.01.02 A helmet; 13.02.08.03.01.02.01 Parts of a helmet; 16.01.03 A spectre, ghost, demon, goblin
grimena 02.06.09 Insect/small creature
grimful 08.01.03.09.01 Fierceness
grīmhelm 13.02.08.03.01.02 A helmet
grimhȳdig 08.01.03.09.06 Hostility
grīming 16.01.03 A spectre, ghost, demon, goblin
grimlic 05.06 Destruction, dissolution, loss, breaking; 05.08.02.01 (Of living creatures) fierceness, roughness; 08.01.03.07.04 Severity, harshness; 08.01.03.09.01 Fierceness; 08.01.03.09.10 Wrath, sternness, displeasure
grimlīce 05.08.02 Violence, force; 08.01.03.09.01 Fierceness; 08.01.03.09.10 Wrath, sternness, displeasure
grimm 05.06 Destruction, dissolution, loss, breaking; 05.08.02.01 (Of living creatures) fierceness, roughness; 07.03.02 Ill, harm, hurt; 08.01.03.07.04 Severity, harshness; 08.01.03.09.11 Hardheartedness, cruelty, severity
grimman 02.05.10.15.01 To raise (the voice), raise up (noise); 08.01.03.05.02 Anger; 08.01.03.09.01 Fierceness
grimmān 16.02.01.13.01 Kinds of sin
grimme 01.03.01.03 Bad weather; 08.01.03.07.04 Severity, harshness; 08.01.03.09.01 Fierceness; 08.01.03.09.10 Wrath, sternness, displeasure
grimnes 05.08.02.01 (Of living creatures) fierceness, roughness; 08.01.03.07.04 Severity, harshness; 08.01.03.09.01 Fierceness; 08.01.03.09.11 Hardheartedness, cruelty, severity
grimsian 05.08.02 Violence, force
grimsung 05.08.02.01 (Of living creatures) fierceness, roughness
grin 02.04.03.03.08 Groin/crotch
grīn 06.02.06.03.04 Allurement; 14.05.06 Means/implement of torture
(ge)grīn 04.03.02 A snare, trap, noose
gegrind 05.12 To move, be in motion
grindan 02.05.10.05 Roaring, raging; 02.05.10.15.04 Gnashing of teeth; 04.01.02.02.09 A mill; 12.05.06.02 Oppression
(ge)grindan 05.06.05 A grinding, pounding
grinde 01.01.02.02.02.01 Sand, gravel
grindel 05.10.05.04.15.01 A bar, bolt
grindende 04.01.02.02.09 A mill; 05.06.05 A grinding, pounding

grindere 04.01.02.02.09 A mill
grindingtōþ 02.04.06.03.02.01.01 Tooth/teeth
grindle 02.06.06.03.01.02 Herring
gegrindswile 02.08.05.02 Particular inflammation/swelling
gegrīnian 06.01.07.04.02.01 Deception, deceit, snare, wile
gripa 03.03.04.01.02.01 A heap, mass, accumulation; 04.02.04.04.04 Stack, rick
grīpan 04.03.02 A snare, trap, noose; 10.04.03 To take away, remove
grīpan (on) 13.02.03.01 An attack, assault
grīpan tōgēanes 10.04.02 To grasp, take hold of
(ge)grīpan 10.01.02 Acquisition
(ge)grīpan (on) 10.04.02 To grasp, take hold of; 10.04.02.02 To seize, take, grasp, lay hold on
gegrīpan 04.03 Hunting, the chase; 14.02.01.02.01 Open robbery, rapine, pillage; 14.05.08 Captivity
gripe 10.04.02 To grasp, take hold of; 12.05.06 Grasp, power, control, mastery; 13.02.03.01 An attack, assault
grīpend 14.02.01.02 Wrongful taking, theft
gegrip(en)nes 10.04.02 To grasp, take hold of
(ge)grippan 10.04.02.02 To seize, take, grasp, lay hold on
gegrippan 10.01.02 Acquisition
gripu 04.01.02.02.06.01 Cooking vessel/pot; 04.01.02.02.06.04 Pot, vessel, crock
gripul 06.01.05.02 Intelligence

grisla 06.01.08.06.02 Great fear, terror, horror
grislic 06.01.08.06.03.01 Causing dread, terrifying
grislīce 06.01.08.06.03.01 Causing dread, terrifying
grīst 04.01.02.01.03 Corn; 05.06.05 A grinding, pounding
gristan 02.05.10.15.04 Gnashing of teeth
gristbātian 02.05.10.15.04 Gnashing of teeth; 08.01.03.05.02 Anger
gristbātung 02.05.10.15.04 Gnashing of teeth
gristbite 02.05.10.15.04 Gnashing of teeth
gristbitian 02.05.10.15.04 Gnashing of teeth; 08.01.03.05.02 Anger
gristbītung 02.05.10.15.04 Gnashing of teeth; 08.01.03.03 Anxiety
gristle 02.04.05.07 Cartilage, gristle
gristlung 02.05.10.15.04 Gnashing of teeth
grīstra 04.01.02.02.09 A mill
griþ 11.10.01 Protection, safekeeping; 13.01.01.01 Cessation of hostilities; 14 Law, custom, covenant; 14.03.03.07 Security, pledge, bail
griþbryce 14.02.01.01 Types of crime; 14.05.04.01 A fine
griþian 13.01.01.01 Cessation of hostilities
(ge)griþian 11.10.01 Protection, safekeeping
griþlagu 14.01.01 Law(s) of particular scope
griþlēas 11.09 Peril, danger; 14.01.03 Special law, privilege, law for an individual
grōf 04.05.03.05.02 A privy
gromtorn 08.01.03 Bad feeling, sadness
grōp 04.05.03.05.03.01 A ditch, dike

gropa 04.01.03.05.04 Drinking vessel
grorn 08.01.03 Bad feeling, sadness; 08.01.03.03 Anxiety
grorne 08.01.03.04 Grief
grornhof 16.01.05 Hell, lower world, abode of the dead
grornian 08.01.03.04 Grief
grorntorn 08.01.03 Bad feeling, sadness
grornung 08.01.03.04.01 Complaint, lamentation
grost 02.04.05.07 Cartilage, gristle
grot 03.03.04.04 Littleness, smallness; 04.01.02.01.03.07 Meal
grotan 04.01.02.01.03.07 Meal
grotig 01.01.02.02.02.01 Sand, gravel
grōwan 02.01.03.01 Fertility, plenty; 02.01.04.02 To grow, grow up; 02.07.01 To grow; 02.07.02.04 Seed, kind of seed; 03.03.04.03 Growth, increase; 05.01 Growth, increase, what springs up; 05.03 Source, origin; 16.02.01.12 Spirituality
(ge)grōwan 01.01.02.01.05 Covered with vegetation; 02.07.01 To grow; 04.02.03 Cultivatable land/farmland; 05.01 Growth, increase, what springs up
gegrōwan 03.03.06.01 A whole formed by joining; 04.02.04.03 A plant
grōwende 02.07.01 To grow
grōwnes 05.01 Growth, increase, what springs up; 08.01.01.03.08 Happiness, well-being, prosperity
gruncian 02.05.05.02 Eager desire
grund 01 Earth, world; 01.01.02 Land; 01.01.02.01 Ground; 01.01.02.01.03.02 Abyss, chasm; 01.01.03.01 Body of water; 01.01.03.01.02.01 Region of sea/ocean; 01.01.03.01.03 Lake; 04.02.03.01 Plot of land; 04.05.02.01 A foundation; 05.10.05.04.02.03.01 A low position, the bottom; 12.06 A province, country, territory; 16.01.05 Hell, lower world, abode of the dead
grundbedd 01.01.02.01 Ground
grundbūend 02.03.01 People
gegrunden 05.06.05 A grinding, pounding; 05.10.06.03.01 A point, spike, prickle
g(r)undeswelge 02.07.11 Plants/flowers (alphabetical order)
grundfūs 12.08.06.02.03 (Of persons) wicked, evil-doing; 16.01.05.01 Damnation, perdition, reprobation
grundhyrde 11.10.02.02 Watchful care, keeping guard
grundinga 03.03.06 Wholeness
grundlēas 03.03.04.01.03 An immense quantity, immensity, immense number; 05.10.05.03.04 Depth, deepness; 16.01.05 Hell, lower world, abode of the dead
grundlēaslic 03.03.04.01.03 An immense quantity, immensity, immense number
grundling 02.06.06.02.01.02 Eel
grundlinga 03.03.06 Wholeness; 05.10.05.04.03 A line, continuous length
grundscēat 01.01 Surface of the earth; 05.10.04.02 A region, zone
grundsele 04.05.03.02.02.01 Dwellings in particular places
grundsopa 02.04.05.07 Cartilage, gristle
grundstān 04.05.02.01 A foundation
gegrundstaþelian 04.05 Building, construction; 05.13.06.01 Firm, stable, steady
grundwæg 01 Earth, world

grundwang 01 Earth, world; 01.01.03.01.03 Lake
grundweall 01.01.02.01.02.02.02 Mountain; 04.05.02.01 A foundation; 05.13.06.01 Firm, stable, steady
(ge)grundweallian 05.13.06.01 Firm, stable, steady
grundwela 15.01.03 Treasure, riches, wealth
grundwiergen 02.06.10.01.05 Sea-monster
grunnettan 02.05.10.15.02 Grunting, bellowing
grun(n)ian 02.05.10.15.02 Grunting, bellowing; 06.01.01.01.01.01 Consideration, rumination
grun(n)ung 02.05.10.15.02 Grunting, bellowing
grut 01.01.03.05 Whirlpool; 05.08.02 Violence, force
grūt 04.01.02.01.03.07 Meal; 04.01.03.05.02 Brewing
grutt 01.01.02.01.03.02 Abyss, chasm
grymet(t)an 02.05.10.05 Roaring, raging
(ge)grymet(t)an 08.01.03.05.02 Anger
grymet(t)ung 02.05.10.05 Roaring, raging
gegrynd 04.02.03.01 Plot of land
gryndan 05.12.05.13 To go down, descend
gegryndan 04.05 Building, construction; 04.05.03.02.01 A building, house, hall, palace, etc.
grynde 01.01.02.01.03.02 Abyss, chasm
grynsmiþ 12.08.06.02.02 A bad man, inhuman person
grȳpe 02.02.05.01.01 A grave, burial place, sepulchre

gryre 06.01.08.06.02 Great fear, terror, horror; 06.01.08.06.03 Cause of fear, terror, horror
gryrebrōga 06.01.08.06.02 Great fear, terror, horror
gryrefæst 06.01.08.06.03.01 Causing dread, terrifying
gryrefāh 03.01.14.11 Medley/variety of colour; 06.01.08.06.03.01 Causing dread, terrifying
gryregeatwe 06.01.08.06.03 Cause of fear, terror, horror; 13.02.08 Military equipment
gryregiest 06.01.08.06.03 Cause of fear, terror, horror
gryrehwīl 08.01.03.06 Adversity, affliction
gryrelēoþ 06.01.08.06.03 Cause of fear, terror, horror; 18.02.07.01.01 A song, a poem to be sung or recited
gryrelic 06.01.08.06.03.01 Causing dread, terrifying
gryremiht 06.01.08.06.03 Cause of fear, terror, horror
gryresīþ 06.01.08.06.03 Cause of fear, terror, horror
gryrran 02.05.10.10 Clattering, noise
grȳtan 03.03.04.03 Growth, increase
grȳto 03.03.04.01.01 Greatness, bigness, size
grytt 04.01.02.01.03.07 Meal; 04.06.02.05 Dust, powder
grytta 04.01.02.01.03.07 Meal
grytte 02.06.09.02.10 Spider
gullisc 17.02.05.02 Goldsmith's art
guma 02.03.01 People
gumcynn 02.03 Humankind; 02.03.03.03 A nation, people
gumcyst 12.08.02.01 Goodness, excellence, virtue
gumdrēam 08.01.01.03 Good feeling, joy, happiness

gumdryhten 12.01.01.04.01 A royal leader
gumfēþa 13.02.10.01.02.01 An armed force/band
gummann 12.01.01.06.08 A person of rank, elder, great man
gumrīce 01 Earth, world; 12.06 A province, country, territory
gumrinc 02.03.01.01 Male person, man
gumstōl 12.01.01.02 Seat of authority
gumþegen 02.03.01.01 Male person, man
gumþēod 02.03 Humankind
gund 02.08.05.02.01 Matter, purulence, pus
gundig 02.08.05.02.01 Matter, purulence, pus; 03.02.01.01 Decay, corruption, rottenness
gupan 02.04.03.03.03 Buttock(s), back parts
gurgullion 02.04.06.03.02.02 Throat/gullet
gutt 01.01.03.01.01.04 Watercourse/channel
guttas 02.04.06.03 Internal organs, innards; 02.04.06.03.02.04 Intestines
gūþ 13.02 War
gūþbeorn 13.02.10.01 A man, warrior
gūþbill 13.02.08.04.03 A sword
gūþbilla gripe 13.02.08.03.01.06 A shield
gūþbord 13.02.08.03.01.06 A shield
gūþbyrne 13.02.08.03.01.04 Coat of mail/corselet
gūþcearu 08.01.03.03 Anxiety
gūþcræft 13.02.07 War-craft, art of war
gūþcwēn 12.01.01.04.01.01 Kings and queens
gūþcyning 12.01.01.04.01.01 Kings and queens
gūþcyst 06.02.07.06 Courage, boldness, valour
gūþdēaþ 02.02.01 Particular mode of death
gūþfana 13.02.08.02 A standard, banner, ensign
gūþflā 13.02.08.04.04.01 An arrow, dart, bolt
gūþfloga 02.06.10.01.01 Dragon
gūþfrec 05.08.02.01 (Of living creatures) fierceness, roughness; 13.02 War
gūþfreca 13.02.10.01 A man, warrior
gūþfremmend 13.02.10.01 A man, warrior
gūþfugol 02.06.08.04 Bird of prey
gūþgeatwe 13.02.08.03.01 Body armour, war gear
gūþgelǣca 13.02.10.01 A man, warrior
gūþgemōt 13.02.02 Battle
gūþgeorn 12.05.03.01 Quarrel, contentiousness, strife
gūþgeþingu 13.02.02 Battle
gūþgewǣde 13.02.08.03.01 Body armour, war gear
gūþ(ge)weorc 13.02 War
gūþgewinn 13.02.02 Battle
gūþhafoc 02.06.08.04 Bird of prey
gūþheard 06.02.07.06.02 Boldness
gūþhelm 13.02.08.03.01.02 A helmet
gūþhere 13.02.10.01.02.02 Armed forces
gūþhorn 13.02.08.01 Battle-horn; 18.02.07.02.02.02 A trumpet
gūþhrēþ 07.08.10 Fame of courage, valour
gūþhwæt 06.02.07.06 Courage, boldness, valour
gūþlēoþ 13.02.07.03 A war song
gūþmæcg 13.02.10.01 A man, warrior
gūþmaga 13.02.10.01 A man, warrior
gūþmōd 06.02.07.06 Courage, boldness, valour

gūþmyrce 12.06.03.03 A neighbour
gūþplega 13.02.02 Battle
gūþrǣs 13.02.02 Battle
gūþrēaf 13.02.08.03.01 Body armour, war gear
gūþrēow 08.01.03.09.01 Fierceness
gūþrinc 13.02.10.01 A man, warrior
gūþrōf 06.02.07.06 Courage, boldness, valour
gūþscearu 02.02.04 Killing, violent death, destruction
gūþsceaþa 02.06.10.01.01 Dragon
gūþsceorp 13.02.08.03.01 Body armour, war gear
gūþscrūd 13.02.08.03.01 Body armour, war gear
gūþsearo 13.02.08.03.01 Body armour, war gear
gūþsele 04.05.03.02.02.06.01 A hall building
gūþspell 09.06.02.01.06.03 Ill tidings
gūþsweord 13.02.08.04.03 A sword
gūþþracu 13.02.03 To seek with active intent, attack
gūþþrēat 13.02.10.01.02.01 An armed force/band
gūþweard 12.01.01.04.01.01 Kings and queens
gūþwērig 02.05.03.02 Weariness
gūþwiga 13.02.10.01 A man, warrior
gūþwine 13.02.08.04.03 A sword
gūþwudu 13.02.08.04.01 A spear
gyden 16.01.06 A god (of any faith)
gydenlic 16.01.06.02 Classical gods
gydig 02.08.11.02.01 Insanity, madness
gegyld 17.02.05.02 Goldsmith's art
(ge)gyldan 17.02.05.02 Goldsmith's art
gylde 02.07.11.02 Unidentified plants (alphabetical order)

gylden 03.01.14.07 Yellow/yellowness; 17.04.02.03 Gold
gyldenbend 12.01.01.03 Symbols of power
gyldenfeax 02.04.04.03.02 Colour of hair
gyldenhilte 13.02.08.04.03.01.01 Hilt of sword
gyldenhīwe 03.01.14.07 Yellow/yellowness
gyldenwecg 17.04.01 Sources of materials
gylece 16.02.05.07 Monastic garb
gylian 02.05.10.05 Roaring, raging
gyliende 02.05.10.05 Roaring, raging; 09.01.02.01 Excessive fluency, loquacity
gyll 01.01.02.01.03.03 Valley
gylt 12.08.06.02.05.01 Transgression, trespass; 12.08.09 Guiltiness, guilt; 14.05.04.01 A fine; 15.04 A debt, due; 16.02.01.13 Evil-doing, transgression, sin
(ge)gyltan 12.08.06.02.05.05 To sin (against), do wrong
gegyltan 12.08.09 Guiltiness, guilt
gyltend 12.08.09 Guiltiness, guilt
gyltig 12.08.09 Guiltiness, guilt
gylting 16.02.01.13 Evil-doing, transgression, sin
gyltlic 16.02.01.13 Evil-doing, transgression, sin
gyltlīce 12.08.06.02.05.04 Sinfully, wickedly
gyltwīte 14.05.04.01 A fine
gylung 09.01.02.01 Excessive fluency, loquacity
(ge)gymmian 02.08.04.01 A wound
gypigend 05.10.05.04.14.01 A yawning, gaping opening
gypung 05.10.05.04.14.01 A yawning, gaping opening

gyr 02.07.03.05 Particular trees/shrubs (alphabetical order)
gyrdan 04.04.07.13 A girdle, belt
(ge)gyrdan 04.04.07 Trappings, equipment, garb; 05.10.05.04.11 A circle, circuit, circumference
gegyrdan 05.02.02 Nature, established order of things
(ge)gyrd(ed) 04.04.07.13 A girdle, belt
gyrdel 17.03.12 A receptacle, container
gyrdelbred 09.03.07.06.04 A writing-tablet
gyrdel(s) 01.01 Surface of the earth; 04.04.07.13 A girdle, belt
gyrdel(s)hring 04.04.10.02 A button, brooch
gyrlgyden 16.01.06.02 Classical gods
gyrman 08.01.03.04 Grief
gyrn 08.01.03 Bad feeling, sadness; 08.01.03.07.02 Misery, trouble, affliction
gyrnstafas 08.01.03.07.02 Misery, trouble, affliction
gyrnwracu 12.05.04.02 Vengeance, revenge
gyrran 02.05.10.06 Harsh sound; 09.01.02.01 Excessive fluency, loquacity
gyrretan 02.05.10.15.06 A roar, howl, etc.
gyrst 08.01.03.05.02 Anger
gyrstan ǣfen 05.11.07.03.01.01 Yesterday
gyrs(t)andæg 05.11.07.03.01.01 Yesterday
gyrtrēow 02.07.03.05 Particular trees/shrubs (alphabetical order)
gyru 01.01.02.01.04.01 Marsh, bog, swamp
gyr(u) 01.01.02.01.04.01 Marsh, bog, swamp
gyrwas 02.03.03.05.01.02 Gyrwe
gyrwefenn 01.01.02.01.04.01 Marsh, bog, swamp
gyse 01.01.03.01.01.05 Torrent
gystran niht 05.11.07.03.01.01 Yesterday
gyte 01.03.01.06.02 Rain
gyte blōdes 02.02.04 Killing, violent death, destruction
gytesǣl 04.01.01.07 Feasting; 04.01.03.05.03 Tavern
gytestrēam 01.01.03.01.01.03 Stream
gytfeorm 04.01.02.04.02 Feast; 04.02.04.02.02.02 Ploughing, tilling
ha ha/hē hē 08.01.01.03.07.01 Laughter
hā 05.12.01.09.03.01.03 Part of ship
habban 02.03.01 People; 05.10.04 Place, room; 05.10.05.04.01.02 Contents, what is included; 10.01.02 Acquisition; 10.04.02.02 To seize, take, grasp, lay hold on; 11.03.01.01.01 Proof, demonstration; 11.05.02 Mode, manner, way, method, fashion, course; 11.10.02.02 Watchful care, keeping guard; 12.03.05 Permission; 12.07 An obligation, bounden duty; 15.01.01.01 Holding of land
habban ... on 02.05.06.01 To touch and press
habban and healdan 10 Having, owning, possession
habban be handa/in handum 10.04.01 To hold, have
habban (for) 07.01 Appraisal, appraising
habban (forþ/ūp/of) 05.12.02.01 To fetch, bring, bear, conduct
habban/āgan gemǣne 10.01.03 A sharing, participation

1036

habban gemǣne wiþ 14.04.04 An agreement, arrangement of dispute
habban genōg 03.03.04.02 A sufficiency, sufficient supply
habban on 07.04 Consideration, esteem
habban on gemynde/in mōde/in gemyndum 06.01.04 Faculty of memory
habban tō 06.02.06.03.03 Incitement; 02.05 Sensation, perception, feeling
habban wiþ … gemǣne 11.02 Occupation, activity, business
(ge)habban 05.02.02 Nature, established order of things; 05.03.01 A cause (of anything); 08.01.01 A feeling, what is felt; 10 Having, owning, possession; 11.02 Occupation, activity, business; 14.05.08 Captivity
gehabban geþyld on 08.01.03.08 Patience
haca 17.03.10.01 A bolt, lock, bar
hacele 04.04.07.07 A long outer garment, covering, cloak, etc.; 16.02.05.06.01 Outer garments
hacod 02.06.06.02.01.06 Pike
hād 02.01.03.03.06 Sex, kind; 02.03.01 People; 02.03.02.03.06 Kinship, relationship; 02.04 Body; 03.04 Form, kind, nature, character; 05.02.02.02 (One's) own person; 09.03.02.03.01.01.04 Person; 12.01.01.06 Condition, rank, standing; 16.01.01.04 The Trinity; 16.02.03.02.07 A priest, cleric; 16.02.04.07.05 An order (general); 18.02.06 Theatricals
hād on settan 16.02.04.07.05.01.01 Going into a monastery, admission
hād onfōn 07.04 Consideration, esteem; 16.02.04.07.05.01 Ordination

hād underfōn 16.02.04.07.05.01 Ordination
gehāda 16.02.03.03 A religious; 16.02.03.03.02 A monk
hādārung 14.03.03.09 A sentence, judgement, ruling
hādbōt 14.03.03.09.02 Atonement
hādbreca 07.03.02 Ill, harm, hurt
hādbryce 14.02.01.01 Types of crime
hād(e)līce 05.02.02.02 (One's) own person
hādesmann 16.02.03.03 A religious
hādgriþ 14.01.03 Special law, privilege, law for an individual
(ge)hādian 16.02.04.07.05.01 Ordination
hādnotu 16.02.03.02.07 A priest, cleric
(ge)hādod 16.02.04.07.05.01 Ordination
gehādod 16.02.03.02 A cleric, clergyman (general)
hādor 02.05.10.01 Thing heard; 03.01.12 Brightness, light
hādre 02.05.10.01 Thing heard; 03.01.12 Brightness, light
hādswǣpe 12.09.02 Marriage ceremony
hādtima 16.02.04.07.05.01 Ordination
hādung 16.02.04.07.05.01 Ordination
hādungdæg 16.02.04.07.05.01 Ordination
hādunge underfōn 16.02.04.07.05.01.01 Going into a monastery, admission
hæbbednes 12.08.03.03.01 Continence
hæbbende 14.02.01.02 Wrongful taking, theft
hæbbendlic 10.04.01 To hold, have
hæbbung 12.08.03.03.01 Continence
hæc(c) 04.03.05 Fishing
gehæcca 04.01.02.01.02.05.03 Sausage meat/sausage
hæcce 04.05.01.02.07 A fence, hedge
hæcc(e) 16.02.05.03.13 A screen, frontal

hæcceleas 04.05.01.02.07 A fence, hedge
hæcgeat 04.05.01.02.07 A fence, hedge
hæcging 05.10.05.04.11 A circle, circuit, circumference
hæcine 04.01.03.05.01.01 Wine
hæcwer 01.01.03.01.03.02 Weir
hædre 08.01.03.03 Anxiety
hæf 01.01.03.01.02 Sea/ocean
hæf(e) 04.01.02.01.06 Leaven/yeast
(ge)hæfed 10 Having, owning, possession
hæfen 05.12.01.09.03.04 A harbour; 10 Having, owning, possession; 15.01 Property
hæfer 02.06.02.01.05 Goat
hæferblæte 02.06.08.03 Game-bird; 02.06.08.06 Water bird
hæfern 02.06.06.04.01.02 Crab
hæfernbite 02.08.08 Internal disease
hæft 10 Having, owning, possession; 12.01.01.09 Bondage, slavery; 14.05.07 Binding, fastening with bonds; 14.05.08 Captivity; 17.03 Implements, tools, etc.
(ge)hæft 10.04.02.02 To seize, take, grasp, lay hold on; 14.05.08 Captivity
(ge)hæftan 12.01.01.09 Bondage, slavery; 14.05.07 Binding, fastening with bonds; 14.05.08 Captivity
gehæftan 03.03.06.01 A whole formed by joining; 12.05.06.01 Restraint, check, curb, control; 12.05.06.04 A trampling upon, subjection
hæfteclomm 14.05.07 Binding, fastening with bonds
gehæftednes 06.01.07.04.02.01 Deception, deceit, snare, wile; 14.05.08 Captivity
hæftedōm 12.01.01.09 Bondage, slavery
hæften 14.05.08 Captivity
gehæftend 14.05.08 Captivity

hæftincel 12.01.01.09 Bondage, slavery
hæfting 17.03.10.01 A bolt, lock, bar
hæftlic 06.01.06.02.02.01.01 Philosophy
hæftling 14.05.08 Captivity
hæftmēce 13.02.08.04.03 A sword
(ge)hæftnes 14.05.08 Captivity
gehæftnian 14.05.08 Captivity
hæftnīed 14.05.07 Binding, fastening with bonds; 14.05.08 Captivity
gehæftnīedan 14.05.08 Captivity
hæftnīedling 14.05.08 Captivity
hæftnīednes 14.05.08 Captivity
hæftnoþ 14.05.08 Captivity
hæftnung 14.05.08 Captivity
hæftung 14.05.07 Binding, fastening with bonds
gehæftworld 01 Earth, world
gehæg 04.02.03.04.01 Meadow land/meadow
hægen/hagen 05.10.05.04.11 A circle, circuit, circumference
hæghāl 11.10 Safety, safeness
gehægholt 02.07.03.04.01 A small wood, coppice, copse
hægsugga/hegesugge 02.06.08.05 Forest bird, wild-fowl
hægtes(se) 16.01.04 Sorcery, magic, witchcraft; 16.01.04.01 Sorcery using incantation
hægþorn 02.07.09.02 Particular fruits (alphabetical order)
hægweard 04.02.05.06.01 A cowherd
hǣl 16.01.04.06.04 Prophecy, divine speech
hǣl ābēodan 11.05.02.02.01 Greetings, courteous terms of address
gehǣl 08.01.01.03.07 Joyous sound, mirth

(ge)hǣlan 02.08.12 Healing, curing; 11.10.03 Salvation/deliverance from; 16.01.01.02.08 Salvation, redemption
gehǣlan 11.05.02.02.01 Greetings, courteous terms of address
hæle 06.02.07.06 Courage, boldness, valour
hǣle 02.08.01 Sound physical condition
(ge)hǣle 11.10 Safety, safeness
gehǣled 04.06 Salubrity
gehǣlednes 02.08.12 Healing, curing
hǣlend 16.01.01.04.02 The Son, Christ
hǣlende 16.01.01.02.08 Salvation, redemption
hǣlendlic 16.01.01.02.08 Salvation, redemption
hǣlestre 16.01.02.05.02.01 Mary, queen of heaven
hæleþ 06.02.07.06 Courage, boldness, valour
hælfter 04.02.05.06.05.03.01 Bridle/halter/curb/muzzle
hælgere 16.02.01.10.02 Consecration
hǣlig 12.08.07.01.03 Wantonness, levity, frivolity
hǣling 02.08.12 Healing, curing
hǣlnes 16.01.01.02.08 Salvation, redemption; 16.02.05.02 A holy place or sanctuary
hǣlnesgriþ 14.01.03 Special law, privilege, law for an individual
hǣlotīd 08.01.01.03.08 Happiness, well-being, prosperity
hǣlþ 02.08 Mental/spiritual health; 02.08.12 Healing, curing; 16.01.01.02.08 Salvation, redemption
hǣlu 02.08 Mental/spiritual health; 02.08.12 Healing, curing
hǣl(u) 08.01.01.03.08 Happiness, well-being, prosperity; 02.08.01 Sound physical condition; 11.10.03 Salvation/deliverance from; 16.01.01.02.08 Salvation, redemption; 16.02.01.12 Spirituality; 11.05.02.02.01 Greetings, courteous terms of address
hǣlubearn 16.01.01.04.02 The Son, Christ
hǣluwyrt 02.07.10.01 Particular herbs/spices (alphabetical order)
hǣman 02.01.03.03 Sex, generation
(ge)hǣman 12.08.08.01.02.01 Fornication, adultery; 12.08.08.01.02.01.02 Concubinage; 12.09.02 Marriage ceremony
gehǣme 11.05.01 Familiarity
hǣmed 02.01.03.03 Sex, generation; 12.08.08.01.02.01 Fornication, adultery; 12.09 Marriage, state of marriage
hǣmedceorl 12.09 Marriage, state of marriage
hǣmedgemāna 12.09 Marriage, state of marriage
hǣmedlāc 02.01.03.03 Sex, generation
hǣmedlāces plegian 12.08.08 Carnal nature, sensual appetites
hǣmedrīm 12.08.08.01.02.01 Fornication, adultery
hǣmedscipe 12.08.08.01.02.01 Fornication, adultery; 12.09 Marriage, state of marriage
hǣmedþing 02.01.03.03 Sex, generation; 12.08.08.01.02.01 Fornication, adultery
hǣmedwīf 12.09 Marriage, state of marriage
hǣmend 12.08.08.01.02.01 Fornication, adultery
hǣmere 12.09 Marriage, state of marriage

(ge)hǣnan 05.06.09.04 Stoning, casting of stones
hænep 04.02.04.03.02.04 Hemp
gehǣp 03.06.03 Congruity, fitness, suitability
gehǣplic 03.06.03 Congruity, fitness, suitability
gehǣplicnes 03.06.03 Congruity, fitness, suitability
hæppan 05.12.01.04.01.04 To stumble, trip, strike (with the foot)
hæpsian 05.10.05.04.15.01 A bar, bolt
hær 01.01.02.01.02.02.01 Hill
hǣr 02.04.04.03 Hair; 02.04.04.03.03 Hair of head
hǣre 04.04.05.01 Coarse, rough (of cloth); 04.04.07.01 Mode of dressing, fashion; 16.02.05.06 Ritual clothing
gehǣr(e) 02.04.04.03 Hair
gehǣrede 02.04.04.03 Hair
hǣren 02.04.04.03 Hair
hærenfagol/hattefagol 02.06.03.01.09 Hedgehog
hærfest 04.02.04.04.02 Harvesting; 05.11.03.01.02.03 Autumn; 05.11.03.01.03.01 Specific months
hærfesthandful 15.04 A debt, due
hærfestlic 04.02.04.04.02 Harvesting; 05.11.03.01.02.03 Autumn
hærfestmōnaþ 05.11.03.01.02.03 Autumn; 05.11.03.01.03.01 Specific months
hærfesttīd 05.11.03.01.02.03 Autumn
hærfesttīma 05.11.03.01.02.03 Autumn
hærfestwǣta 01.03.01.06.02 Rain
hǣrgripa 10.04.02 To grasp, take hold of
hǣriht 02.04.04.03 Hair
hǣring 02.06.06.03.01.02 Herring; 04.01.02.01.02.07 Fish

hǣringtīma 04.03.05 Fishing; 05.11.03.01.02 A season of the year
hǣrloccas 02.04.04.03.03 Hair of head
hærn 01.01.03.01.02 Sea/ocean; 01.01.03.01.02.05 Wave; 02.04.06.09 Brain
hǣrnǣdl 04.06.01.07 Hair-care
hǣrnflota 05.12.01.09.03.01 A ship, boat
hǣrsceard 02.08.04.02 Blemish, disfigurement
hǣrsyfe 04.06.01.10 To separate objects already connected, unmix
hǣru 05.11.07.03 Former times, days of old
hǣs 08.01.02.04 Hospitality; 12.03.03 A command, bidding, order; 17.02.03 A task, service, duty
hæsel 02.07.03.05 Particular trees/shrubs (alphabetical order)
hæselhnutu 02.07.09.02.01.01 Particular nuts (alphabetical order)
hæselrǣw 02.07.03.05 Particular trees/shrubs (alphabetical order)
hæselwrīd 02.07.03.05 Particular trees/shrubs (alphabetical order)
hǣsere 12.01.01.04.02 A lord, master
hæslen 02.07.03.05 Particular trees/shrubs (alphabetical order)
hæsler 02.07.03.05 Particular trees/shrubs (alphabetical order)
hæslett 02.07.03.05 Particular trees/shrubs (alphabetical order)
hæsling 02.07.03.05 Particular trees/shrubs (alphabetical order)
hæspe 17.03.10.01 A bolt, lock, bar
hǣst 05.08.02 Violence, force; 05.08.02.01 (Of living creatures) fierceness, roughness
hǣs(t) 02.07.03.01 A bush
hæt 04.04.07.11 A headcloth, covering for the head

(ge)hætan 03.01.09.01 Warmth, heat
gehætan 08.01.01.01.03 An incitement, cause of strong feeling
hæte 01.03.01.01 Hot, fine weather; 02.08.10 Fever; 03.01.09 Heat; 08.01.01.01 Ardour, fervour, strong feeling
hæte/-u 03 Material, matter, substance
hæteru 04.04.07 Trappings, equipment, garb
hæting 04.01.02.02.05.01 Heating, warming
hættian 05.06.06.01 A tearing, laceration
hætu 01.03.01.01 Hot, fine weather; 02.05.05.03 Sexual appetite, lust; 03.01.09 Heat; 08.01.01.01 Ardour, fervour, strong feeling
hæþ 01.01.02.01.06 Wild/uncultivated land; 02.01.03.02.01 Barrenness, aridity; 02.07.03.05 Particular trees/shrubs (alphabetical order)
hæþa 01.03.01.02 Dry weather
hæþberie 02.07.09.02 Particular fruits (alphabetical order)
hæþcole 02.07.11.02 Unidentified plants (alphabetical order)
hæþen 02.03.03.05.06 Viking(s); 08.01.03.09.01.01 Savage; 16.02.01.06 Paganism, a false religion; 16.02.01.11.02 Impiety, lack of piety; 16.02.01.12.05 The world (i.e. unspirituality, worldliness); 16.02.04.07.01 Baptism, baptizing (and anointing)
hæþena 16.02.01.06 Paganism, a false religion
hæþencyning 12.01.01.04.01.01 Kings and queens; 16.02.01.06 Paganism, a false religion
hæþendom 16.02.01.06.01 Belief/practice of heathen people
hæþendōm 16.02.01.06 Paganism, a false religion
hæþenfolc 16.02.01.06 Paganism, a false religion
hæþengield 16.02.01.06.01.01 Pagan worship, idolatrous practice(s); 16.02.01.06.01.01.01 An image, idol
hæþengilda 16.02.01.06 Paganism, a false religion
hæþenhere 13.02.10.01.02.02.01 Types of army
hæþenisc 16.02.01.06 Paganism, a false religion
hæþennes 16.02.01.06 Paganism, a false religion
hæþenscipe 16.02.01.06 Paganism, a false religion; 16.02.01.06.01 Belief/practice of heathen people; 16.02.01.06.01.01 Pagan worship, idolatrous practice(s)
hæþenstyrc 16.02.01.06.01.01.01 An image, idol
hæþenwēoh 16.02.01.06.01.01.01 An image, idol
hæþfeld 01.01.02.01.06 Wild/uncultivated land
hæþfeldland 01.01.02.01.06 Wild/uncultivated land
hæþiht(e) 01.01.02.01.06 Wild/uncultivated land
hæþstapa 02.06 Animal
hæþung 01.03.01.02 Dry weather
hæwe 03.01.14.08 A blue dye, woad
hæwen 03.01.14.08 A blue dye, woad
hæwengrēne 03.01.14.06 Green/greenness
hæwenhydele 02.07.11.02 Unidentified plants (alphabetical order)
hæwmænged 03.01.14.05 Red/redness

hafela 02.04.03.01 Head
gehafen 04.01.02.01.07.03.01 Unleavened bread
hafenian 05.12.05.12.02 To raise, lift up, elevate
hafenlēas 15.01.06 Poverty, indigence
hafenlēast 15.01.06 Poverty, indigence
hafetian 05.12.05.05 To shake, quake, wag; 07.04.04.01.01 Clapping (the hands), applause
hafoc 02.06.08.04 Bird of prey
hafoccynn 02.06.08.04 Bird of prey
hafocere 04.03.04 Fowling
hafocfugel 02.06.08.04 Bird of prey
hafocung 04.03.04 Fowling
hafocwyrt 02.07.11.02 Unidentified plants (alphabetical order)
haga 02.07.09.02 Particular fruits (alphabetical order); 04.05.01.02.07 A fence, hedge; 04.05.03.02.02 Types of dwelling; 05.10.05.04.11 A circle, circuit, circumference; 11.08.04 Vanity, idleness, frivolity
gehagian 03.06.03 Congruity, fitness, suitability
haging 05.10.05.04.11 A circle, circuit, circumference
hagol 01.03.01.06.03 Hail, shower of hail
hagolberende 01.03.01.06.03 Hail, shower of hail
hagolfaru 01.03.01.06.03 Hail, shower of hail
hagolian 01.03.01.06.03 Hail, shower of hail
hagolscūr 01.03.01.06.03 Hail, shower of hail
hagolstān 01.03.01.06.03 Hail, shower of hail
hagospind 02.04.03.01.03.05 Cheek
hagosteald 12.09.03 Unmarried state; 12.09.03.01 Celibacy; 13.02.10.01 A man, warrior
hagostealdhād 12.09.03 Unmarried state
hagostealdlic 12.09.03 Unmarried state
hagostealdman 12.09.03 Unmarried state; 13.02.10.01 A man, warrior
hagostealdnes 12.09.03 Unmarried state
hagul 09.03.07.01.01 A runic letter
haguþorn 02.07.09.02 Particular fruits (alphabetical order)
hal 09.05.04.01 Concealment, obscurity
hāl 02.08.01 Sound physical condition; 02.08.11.01 Sound mind; 07.02.03.01 Uninjured, unhurt, unharmed; 09.03.04.03 Plain, simple; 11.05.02.02.01 Greetings, courteous terms of address; 12.08.04 Purity, moral cleanness
hāl wes þū 11.05.02.02.01 Greetings, courteous terms of address
(ge)hāl 02.08.13 Recovery, growing better; 03.03.06 Wholeness; 11.10 Safety, safeness; 16.02.01.12 Spirituality
hala 02.01.03.03.01 To beget
gehala 08.01.02.03.01 An acquaintance, friend, associate
hālbǣre 07.02.02 Good, what is beneficial, advantageous, etc.; 11.12.02 Aid, help, succour
hāle līf 02.08.01 Sound physical condition
gehālettan 11.05.02.02.01 Greetings, courteous terms of address
hālettend 02.04.03.04.01.01.01 Finger
hālewǣge 16.02.05.05.06 A vessel for use in services
hālfæst 12.08.04 Purity, moral cleanness
hālga 16.01.02.05.02 A saint
hālga dæg 16.02.04.04.02.01.02 Lent

(ge)hālgan 11.10.03
Salvation/deliverance from
gehālgan 02.08.12 Healing, curing
hālgawaras 16.01.02.05.02 A saint
(ge)hālgian 16.02.01.10 Holiness;
16.02.01.10.02 Consecration;
16.02.01.10.02.01 A blessing,
invocation of divine favour;
16.02.04.04.02 A feast-day, holy day
(ge)hālgian (tō) 16.02.04.07.05.01
Ordination
(ge)hālgigend 16.02.01.10.02
Consecration
(ge)hālgod 16.02.01.10 Holiness
gehālgod 16.02.04.07.04
Communion/eucharist
hālgung 16.02.01.10 Holiness
(ge)hālgung 16.02.01.10.02
Consecration; 16.02.01.10.02.01 A
blessing, invocation of divine favour
hālgungbōc 16.02.05.10.01 Service
books
hālgungram 16.02.04.12 Sacrifice, a
sacrifice
hālig 04.02.05.04 To tame, break in
(animals); 16.01 A divine being;
16.01.01 God, the Lord; 16.01f.01.01
Attributes of God; 16.01.02.05.02 A
saint; 16.02.01.10 Holiness;
16.02.01.10.02.01 A blessing,
invocation of divine favour;
16.02.01.11 Firmness in the law, piety,
devoutness; 16.02.04.03.01 A rite,
ceremony
hālig rōde tācen 16.02.04.18.01 Sign of
the cross
hālig wæter 16.02.05.09.04 Holy Water
hālig wiell 16.02.05.01 Land
hālig gewrit 16.02.01.08 Scripture, the
scriptures

hāligdæg 16.02.01.08.04 Jewish
seasons/feasts; 16.02.04.04.01 The
day of rest, sabbath
hāligdōm 16.01.01.01 Attributes of God;
16.02.01.01 Creed, statement of faith;
16.02.01.10 Holiness; 16.02.04.07 A
sacrament; 16.02.05.02 A holy place
or sanctuary; 16.02.05.05 Something
holy/belonging to a church;
16.02.05.05.10 Relics, a collection of
relics
hāligdōmhūs 16.02.05.03.09 A
vestry/sacristy
hāligern 16.02.05.02 A holy place or
sanctuary
hāliglīce 16.02.01.10 Holiness
hāligmōnaþ 05.11.03.01.03.01 Specific
months
hālignes 16.01.01.01 Attributes of God;
16.02.01.10 Holiness; 16.02.04.03
Ritual, rite, service; 16.02.05.02 A
holy place or sanctuary;
16.02.05.05.10 Relics, a collection of
relics
hāligportic 16.02.05.02 A holy place or
sanctuary
hāligryft 04.04.07.10 A veil; 16.02.05.07
Monastic garb
hāligwæcca 16.02.04.07.06.02 A vigil
hāligware 16.01.02.05.02 A saint
hāligweorc 16.02.05.02 A holy place or
sanctuary
hālnes 03.03.06 Wholeness
hālor 16.01.01.02.08 Salvation,
redemption
hāls 16.01.01.02.08 Salvation, redemption
hālsere 16.01.04.06 Divination, augury
hālsian 16.01.04.06 Divination, augury
(ge)hālsian 12.03.04.01 Entreaty, solemn
appeal; 14.03.03.04 Oath-swearing

(ge)hālsian/healsian 16.02.04.14.02 Imprecation; 16.02.04.17 Exorcism
hālsigend/healsigend 16.02.03.02.12 Cleric in minor orders
hālsigendlic 16.02.04.08.01 Kinds of prayer
hālsung 12.03.04.01 Entreaty, solemn appeal; 14.03.03.04 Oath-swearing; 16.01.04.06 Divination, augury; 16.02.04.03.02 Parts of service; 16.02.04.14.02 Imprecation; 16.02.04.17 Exorcism
hālsungbōc 16.02.05.10.01 Service books
hālsunggebed 16.02.04.08.01 Kinds of prayer
hālsungtīma 12.03.04.01 Entreaty, solemn appeal; 16.02.04.08.01 Kinds of prayer
halswurþing 04.04.10.01 A ring (for finger, arm, neck)
hālwenda 16.01.01.04.02 The Son, Christ
hālwende 02.08.12 Healing, curing; 08.01.01.03.08.03 A favour, blessing; 11.10 Safety, safeness; 12.08.02 Integrity, absence of moral flaw; 16.01.01.02.08 Salvation, redemption; 16.02.01.12 Spirituality
hālwendlic 11.12.02 Aid, help, succour; 16.01.01.02.08 Salvation, redemption; 16.02.01.12 Spirituality
hālwendlica 16.01.01.02.08 Salvation, redemption
hālwendlīce 02.08.12 Healing, curing; 16.01.01.02.08 Salvation, redemption; 16.02.01.12 Spirituality
hālwendnes 04.06 Salubrity; 16.01.01.02.08 Salvation, redemption
ham 04.04.07.04 An undergarment; 15.01.01 Landed property

hām 04.02 Farm; 04.05.03 A dwelling-place, abode, habitation; 04.05.03.02.01 A building, house, hall, palace, etc.; 05.10.04.02 A region, zone; 12.06.04 Native land; 16.01.02.01 Heavenly dwelling place
hām ... sīþian 05.12.05.11.01 To return
hāma 02.06.09.02.05 Cricket, grasshopper, locust
hāmcūþ 06.01.06.01.01.01 Acquaintance, knowledge
hāmcyme 05.12.05.02.03 To arrive
hamel 01.01.02.01.02.02.05 Crag, rock, stone
hamele 05.12.01.09.03.01.03 Part of ship
hamelian 02.08.04.04 State of being crippled
hamera lāf 13.02.08.04.03 A sword
(ge)hāmettan 04.05.03.02.01 A building, house, hall, palace, etc.
hāmfǣreld 05.12.05.11.01 To return
hāmfæst 04.05.03.02.01 A building, house, hall, palace, etc.
hāmfaru 14.02.01.01 Types of crime
hāmhenn 02.06.08.02 Domestic fowl
gehāmian 04.05.03.02.01 A building, house, hall, palace, etc.
hamland 04.02.03.04.02 Pasture/pasturage
hāmlēas 04.05.03.02.01 A building, house, hall, palace, etc.
hamm 02.04.03.04.02.01 Thigh; 02.04.03.04.02.02 Knee; 04.02.03.01.01 Enclosed land/field
gehammen 04.04.07.15 Footwear, covering for the feet
hamola 02.08.04.02.01 A maimed man
hamor 05.12.01.09.03.01.03 Part of ship; 17.03.08 A hammer, mallet
hamorsecg 02.07.08 Grasses, reeds, etc.

hamorwyrt 02.07.11 Plants/flowers (alphabetical order)
hāmscīr 12.02.02.03 Terms for classical world
hāmsittende 04.05.03.02.01 A building, house, hall, palace, etc.
hāmsīþ 05.12.05.11.01 To return
hāmsīþian 05.12.05.11.01 To return
hāmsōcn 14.02.01.01 Types of crime; 14.05.04.01 A fine
hāmsteall 04.05.03 A dwelling-place, abode, habitation
hāmstede 04.05.03 A dwelling-place, abode, habitation
hamstra 02.06.09.02.03 Beetle
hāmweard 04.05.03.02.01 A building, house, hall, palace, etc.
hāmweardes 04.05.03.02.01 A building, house, hall, palace, etc.
hāmweard(es) 12.06.04 Native land
hāmweorþung 07.08.04 An ornament, honour, glory
hāmwerod 02.03.03 A family, household; 04.05.03.02 A human habitation
hāmwyrt 02.07.09.02.02.01 Edible root/bulb
hān 05.10.05.04.11.01 A bound, limit; 05.12.01.09.03.01.03 Part of ship
hana 02.06.08.02 Domestic fowl
hanasang 02.05.10.15.07 Voice, note (of a bird); 05.11.04.02.03 Last hour of the night, just before daybreak
hancrēd 02.05.10.15.07 Voice, note (of a bird); 05.11.04.02.03 Last hour of the night, just before daybreak
hancrēdtīd 05.11.04.02.03 Last hour of the night, just before daybreak
hand 02.03.02.03 Ancestry, descent; 02.04.03.04.01.01 Hand; 03.06 Comparison; 05.10.05.03 A measure of distance; 05.10.05.04.09 Side, quarter, direction; 11.04.01 An aptitude, bodily skill; 11.10.02.02 Watchful care, keeping guard; 12.02.01 A substitute, representative; 12.04.01.01 A company of people, fellowship, society; 15.01.02.01 Inherited property
handæx 17.03.03 A cutting tool
handbæftian 08.01.03.04.01 Complaint, lamentation
handbana 02.02.04.03.01 A killer
handbelle 02.05.10.13.01 A bell
handbōc 09.03.07.07.02 A written work, book, treatise; 16.02.05.10.06 A manual, ritual
handbred 02.04.03.04.01.01 Hand; 05.10.05.03 A measure of distance
handclāþ 04.06.01.05 ?A cloth for wiping
handcops 14.05.07 Binding, fastening with bonds
handcræft 11.04.02 Skill, skilfulness
handcwyrn 04.01.02.02.09 A mill
handdǣda 11.01.04 A doing, accomplishing (of something)
hande brād 05.10.05.03 A measure of distance
gehandfæstan 12.09.01 Pledging, betrothal
handfæstnung 14.03.03.07 Security, pledge, bail
handful 03.03.04.01.02.01 A heap, mass, accumulation
handgang 13.02.05.02.01 Surrender, submission
handgemaca 12.04.01 A fellow, companion, associate, comrade
handgemōt 13.02.02 Battle
handgesceaft 17.02.04 Trade, calling, craft, aptitude

handgesella 12.04.01 A fellow, companion, associate, comrade
handgestealla 12.04.01 A fellow, companion, associate, comrade
handgeswing 05.06.09.01 A slap with the hand, blow
handgeweald 12.05.06 Grasp, power, control, mastery
handgeweorc 11.01 Action, doing, performance; 17.02.04 Trade, calling, craft, aptitude
hand(ge)weorc 16.01.01.02.01 Creator; 17 Work, doings, actions, labour
handgewinn 13.02.02 Battle; 17 Work, doings, actions, labour
handgewrit 09.03.07.01.02.01 Handwriting, autograph, signature; 09.03.07.07.03.04.01 A document, deed; 14.04.01 A deed, contract, agreement
handgewriþen 04.04.05 Woven material, fabric
handgift 12.09.01 Pledging, betrothal
handgripe 10.04.02 To grasp, take hold of
handgriþ 14.01.03.01 Sanctuary
handhæbbende 14.02.01.02 Wrongful taking, theft
handhæf 17.02.04.02.03 Carrying, carriage (of materials)
handhamur 17.03.08 A hammer, mallet
handhrægl 04.06.01.05 ?A cloth for wiping
handhrine 02.05.06 Sense of touch
handhwīl 05.11.01.02 Shortness/brevity in time
handle 17.03 Implements, tools, etc.
handlēan 10.03.05 Recompense, reward
handleng(u) 05.10.05.03 A measure of distance

handlian 02.05.06 Sense of touch
(ge)handlian 09.06 To take matter for discourse
handlīn 04.06.01.05 ?A cloth for wiping; 16.02.05.06.01 Outer garments
handlinga 13.02.02.01 Single combat
handlinga/-lunga 02.04.03.04.01.01 Hand
handlocen 13.02.08.03.01.01 Mail, iron-rings
handlung 02.05.06 Sense of touch
handmægen 05.08 Strength
handnægl 02.04.04.02 Nail
handplega 13.02.02 Battle
handprēost 16.02.03.02.08 A (domestic) chaplain
handrǣs 13.02.03.01 An attack, assault
handrōf 05.08 Strength
handscolu 02.03.03.01 Body of retainers, household
handscyldig 14.03.03.09.01 Unfavourable judgement, condemnation
handseald 10.03 Giving
handseax 13.02.08.04.03 A sword
handselen 10.03 Giving
handseten 09.03.07.01.02.01 Handwriting, autograph, signature; 14.04.01 A deed, contract, agreement
handsmæl 05.06.09.01 A slap with the hand, blow
handspitel 17.03.07 Tools for digging/grasping/pulling
handstoc 04.04.07.03 Part of garment
handswyle 02.08.07.07 Disorders of the body
handtam 04.02.05.04 To tame, break in (animals)
handþegn 12.01.01.07 A follower

(ge)hātan

handþwēal 04.06.01.01 Cleansing, washing
handweorc 17.02.04 Trade, calling, craft, aptitude
handworht 17.02.04 Trade, calling, craft, aptitude
handwundor 06.01.08.05.01.01.01 An exercise of power, mighty work, miracle
handwyrm 02.06.09.01 Parasite
handwyrst 02.04.03.04.01 Arm
gehange 05.02.02.01 Inclination
hangelle 05.12.01.07.01 To hang
hangian 02.02.04.04.03 Putting to death; 05.10.05.04.12 The condition of being covered; 05.12.01.07.01 To hang; 06.02.07.03 Perseverance; 11.03.01.01.01 Proof, demonstration
hangian on 05.02.02.03 A connexion, association
(ge)hangian 02.02.04.04.03 Putting to death; 14.05.05.01.01 Crucifixion, death on cross
hangra 02.07.03.04 A wood, trees
hangwīte 14.05.04 A penalty, punishment
hār 02.04.04.03.02 Colour of hair; 03.01.14.03 White/whiteness; 05.11.07.03.03 Old, not new
hara 02.06.03.01.13 Rodents
haranhige 02.07.11 Plants/flowers (alphabetical order)
haransprecel 02.07.11 Plants/flowers (alphabetical order)
haraþ 02.07.03.04 A wood, trees
hāredagas 01.03.01.01 Hot, fine weather
hāreminte 02.07.10.01 Particular herbs/spices (alphabetical order)
hārewyrt/hāranwyrt 02.07.11.02 Unidentified plants (alphabetical order)

hārhūne 02.07.11 Plants/flowers (alphabetical order)
hārian 02.04.04.03.02 Colour of hair
hārnes 02.04.04.03.02 Colour of hair
hārung 02.04.04.03.02 Colour of hair
hārwelle 05.11.07.03.03 Old, not new
hārwenge 02.04.04.03.02 Colour of hair
hārwengnes 02.04.04.03.02 Colour of hair
hās 02.05.10.15.05 Hoarseness
hāsæta 05.12.01.09.03 A voyage
hāsgrumel 02.05.10.15.05 Hoarseness
hāshrīman 02.05.10.15.05 Hoarseness
hāsian 02.05.10.15.05 Hoarseness
hāsnes 02.05.10.15.05 Hoarseness
hāsrūnigende 02.05.10.15.05 Hoarseness
hassuc 02.07.08 Grasses, reeds, etc.
hāsswēge 02.05.10.15.05 Hoarseness
hasu 03.01.14.10 Grey-coated one
hasufāg 03.01.14.10 Grey-coated one
hasupād 03.01.14.10 Grey-coated one
haswe 03.01.14.10 Grey-coated one
haswig 03.01.14.10 Grey-coated one
haswigfeþre 02.06.08.01 Part of bird
hāt 02.08.10 Fever; 03.01.09 Heat; 08.01.01.01 Ardour, fervour, strong feeling; 08.01.02.02.03 A loving relationship; 08.01.03.05.02 Anger; 14.01.02 A law, statute
hāt bæþ 01.01.03.01.01.07 Spring, fountain, well
gehāt 12.07.02.01.01 A promise; 14.04.02 A stipulation; 16.02.04.15 A vow
gehata 12.05.01 Rivalry, contest
hātan 09.06.02.01.07 A name, appellation
(ge)hātan 09.06.02.01.07 A name, appellation; 09.06.02.01.07.02 A categorizing name; 12.03.03 A command, bidding, order; 12.03.03.01

Summons, a call, summoning;
12.07.02.01.01 A promise
(ge)hātan (tō) 16.02.04.15 A vow
gehātan 08.01.02.04 Hospitality;
08.01.03.09.07 Threat, threatening,
menace; 09.07.04 Assertion,
affirmation; 12.09.01 Pledging,
betrothal
hāte 03.01.09 Heat; 05.08.02 Violence,
force; 08.01.01.01 Ardour, fervour,
strong feeling
hātheort 08.01.01.01 Ardour, fervour,
strong feeling
(ge)hātheort 08.01.03.05.02 Anger
hātheort(e) 08.01.03.05.02 Anger
hātheortlīce 08.01.01.01 Ardour, fervour,
strong feeling; 08.01.03.05.02 Anger
hātheortnes 08.01.01.01.04 Depth of
feeling, zeal; 08.01.03.05.02 Anger
gehāthiert 08.01.03.05.02 Anger
gehāthiertan 08.01.03.05.02 Anger
hāthige 08.01.03.05.02 Anger
hātian 03.01.09 Heat
(ge)hātian 08.01.01.01 Ardour, fervour,
strong feeling; 08.01.03.07.02.01
Injury, offence
(ge)hati(g)an 07.03.01.03 To loathe, hate,
abhor; 08.01.03.09.03 Malevolence,
malice
hatigend 08.01.03.09.05 Enmity
hātigende 03.01.09 Heat;
08.01.03.07.04.01 Unbearableness
hatigendlic 08.01.03.09.04 Hatred
gehātland 05.10.04.02 A region, zone
hātlīce 08.01.01.01 Ardour, fervour,
strong feeling
hātnes 03.01.09 Heat
hatol 08.01.03.09.04 Hatred
hatung 08.01.03.09.03 Malevolence,
malice; 08.01.03.09.04 Hatred

hātung 02.08.05 Inflammation
hātwende 03.01.09 Heat
haþoliþa 02.04.03.04.01 Arm
hāwere 02.05.09.05 To watch, observe,
survey
hāwian 08.01.02.01 Favour, kindness,
grace; 11.02.02.02 Care, mindfulness,
attention; 11.10.02.02 Watchful care,
keeping guard
hāwian æfter 06.02.06.01 An end, goal
(ge)hāwian 06.01.01.02 Care, attention,
observation
(ge)hāwian (on, tō) 02.05.09.04 To see,
look upon, behold
hāwung 02.05.09 Faculty of sight;
02.05.09.05 To watch, observe, survey
hēaf 08.01.03.04.01 Complaint,
lamentation
hēafde beceorfan 02.02.04.04.03 Putting
to death
hēafdes gim 02.04.03.01.03.02 Eye
hēafdes þolian 02.02.03 To die, perish
hēafdian 02.02.04.04.03 Putting to death
gehēafdod 05.10.06.03 Projection, head,
extremity (of anything)
hēafdu ūp āhebban 06.02.07.06
Courage, boldness, valour
hēafe bewindan 08.01.03.04.01
Complaint, lamentation
hēaflic 08.01.03.04 Grief
hēafod 01.01.02.01.02.02 Hill, mountain;
01.01.02.01.02.02.03 Slope;
01.01.03.01.01.01 River; 02.04.03.01
Head; 02.07.02.08 Head, rounded part
of plant; 03.03.03.02 A number
(mark/symbol); 04.02.05 Livestock;
04.05.02.08 Top of a building;
04.05.04.05 A bed, bedstead; 05.03
Source, origin; 05.10.05.04.11.01 A
bound, limit; 05.10.06.03 Projection,

head, extremity (of anything); 05.11.10.01 A beginning; 05.12.01.09.03.01.03 Part of ship; 06.01 The head (as seat of thought); 12.01.01.04 A leader, ruler; 12.06.02.01 A township
hēafod brecan 02.02.04.03 To kill, slay
hēafod hebban 07.06 Pride; 12.05.05 Resistance, repulsing
hēafod lenctenes fæstenes 16.02.04.04.02.01.02 Lent
hēafod niman 12.01.01.09 Bondage, slavery
hēafodæcer 04.02.03.03.03 An acre
hēafodædre 02.04.06.08 Heart
hēafodbæþ 02.08.12.02.07 Remedies for specific parts (head to toe)
hēafodbald 07.06.01.01 Proud, arrogant
hēafodbān 02.04.05.04.02 Skull
hēafodbēag 12.01.01.03 Symbols of power
hēafodbend 12.01.01.03 Symbols of power; 14.05.06 Means/implement of torture
hēafodbeorg 01.01.02.01.02.02 Hill, mountain; 13.02.08.03.01.02 A helmet
hēafodbeorht 02.04.03.01 Head
hēafodbiscop 16.02.03.02.01 A high priest, chief bishop, etc. (general)
hēafodbolla 02.04.05.04.02 Skull
hēafodbolster 04.05.04.05.01 Bedding (e.g. of straw)
hēafodbotl 04.05.03.02.02.05 A paternal dwelling
hēafodbryce 02.08.07.01 Pain in head/neck
hēafodburh 12.06.02.01 A township
hēafodclāþ 02.02.05.02 To prepare for burial; 04.04.07.11 A headcloth, covering for the head

hēafodcwide 09.03.07.07.02.01 A main division; 09.06.01.02 A saying, saw, proverb, maxim
hēafodcyrice 16.02.05.02.02 A cathedral, minster
hēafodece 02.08.07.01 Pain in head/neck
hēafodfrætennes 04.04.10 Ornaments, trappings, accoutrements
hēafodgemæcca 12.04.01 A fellow, companion, associate, comrade
hēafodgerīm 12.04.02 A crowding together, assembly
hēafodgetel 03.03.03.02 A number (mark/symbol)
hēafodgewæde 04.04.07.10 A veil
hēafodgilt 16.02.01.13.01 Kinds of sin
hēafodgimm 02.04.03.01.03.02 Eye
hēafodgold 12.01.01.03 Symbols of power
hēafodhǣr 02.04.04.03.03 Hair of head
hēafodhebba 05.05.01 An author, source, originator; 05.11.10.01 A beginning
hēafodhrægl 04.04.07.11 A headcloth, covering for the head; 04.05.04.05.01 Bedding (e.g. of straw)
hēafodhrīefþo 02.08.06 Skin disease, erysipelas
hēafodiht 02.07.02.08 Head, rounded part of plant
hēafodland 04.02.03.02.01 A strip for ploughing
hēafodleahter 16.02.01.13.01 Kinds of sin
hēafodlēas 02.04.03.01 Head
hēafodlic 05.10.05.03.03 Height, loftiness, sublimity; 11.07.04 Superiority, pre-eminence, primacy; 16.02.01.13.01 Kinds of sin
hēafodling 12.04.01 A fellow, companion, associate, comrade

hēafodloca 02.04.05.04.02 Skull
hēafodmǣg 02.03.02.03.06.02 Close relationship
hēafodmǣgen 16.02.01.12.04 A cardinal virtue
hēafodmāga 02.03.02.03.06.02 Close relationship
hēafodmann 12.01.01.05 A leader, administrator
hēafodmynster 16.02.05.02.02 A cathedral, minster
hēafodpanne 02.04.05.04.02 Skull
hēafodport 12.06.02.01 A township
hēafodrīce 12.06 A province, country, territory
hēafodsār 02.08.07.01 Pain in head/neck
hēafodsealf 02.08.12.02.07 Remedies for specific parts (head to toe)
hēafodsegn 13.02.08.02 A standard, banner, ensign
hēafodsīen 02.04.03.01.03.02 Eye
hēafodslæge 02.02.04.04.03 Putting to death
hēafodsmæl 04.04.07.03 Part of garment
hēafodstede 16.02.05.02 A holy place or sanctuary
hēafodstocc 14.05.06 Means/implement of torture
hēafodstōl 12.06.02.01 A township
hēafodstōw 04.05.04.05 A bed, bedstead
hēafodswīma 02.08.07.01 Pain in head/neck
hēafodsynn 16.02.01.13.01 Kinds of sin
hēafodþwēal 04.06.01.01 Cleansing, washing
hēafodwærc 02.08.07.01 Pain in head/neck
hēafodweard 02.02.05.03 To attend the dead; 09.03.07.07.02.01.01 A heading, title, superscription; 11.10.02.02 Watchful care, keeping guard; 12.01.01.05 A leader, administrator; 12.01.01.07 A follower
hēafodweg 05.12.01.03.01.05 Types of road/path
hēafodwind 01.03.01.05.01 Winds from particular points
hēafodwīsa 12.01.01.04 A leader, ruler
hēafodwōþ 09 Speech, vocal utterance
hēafodwund 02.08.07.01 Pain in head/neck
hēafodwylm 02.08.07.01 Pain in head/neck; 08.01.03.04.02 Shedding of tears
hēafodwyrhta 17.02.01 Management of work
hēafsang 02.02.05.03 To attend the dead
heagorūn 16.01.04.01 Sorcery using incantation
hēah 01.01.02.01.02 High land; 01.01.03.01 Body of water; 01.01.03.01.02 Sea/ocean; 05.10.05.03.03 Height, loftiness, sublimity; 05.10.05.03.04 Depth, deepness; 05.11.04.01.03 Mid-day, noon; 05.12.05.12.02 To raise, lift up, elevate; 06.01.01.01.01.01 Consideration, rumination; 07.02.04 Excellence; 07.06.01.02 Proudly, arrogantly; 07.08.01 Nobility (of character, rank, etc.); 07.08.06 Exaltation; 11.07.04 Superiority, pre-eminence, primacy; 11.11.01 A physical difficulty, strait
hēah cāsere 16.01.01.01.01 The Almighty
hēah nama 16.01.01.03 The divine name
hēah strengþu 05.08 Strength
hēah geþring 01.01.03.01.02.05 Wave

hēahaltare 16.02.05.03.04 Part of temple containing altar/idol
hēahbeorg 01.01.02.01.02.02.02 Mountain
hēahbiscop 16.02.03.02.01 A high priest, chief bishop, etc. (general); 16.02.03.02.04 An archbishop
hēahbliss 08.01.01.03.06 Exultation, joy
hēahboda 16.01.02.05.01 An angel
hēahburg 12.06.02.01 A township
hēahcleofa 04.05.03.04 A closet, chamber, room
hēahclif 01.01.02.01.02.02.04 Cliff
hēahcræft 11.04.02 Skill, skilfulness
hēahcræftiga 17.02.04 Trade, calling, craft, aptitude
hēahcyning 12.01.01.04.01 A royal leader; 16.01.01.01.01 The Almighty
hēahdēma 16.01.01.02.06 God as judge
hēahdēor 02.06.03.01.06 Deer, hart
hēahdēorhund 02.06.02.01.04 Dog; 04.03.01 Tracking
hēahdēorhunta 04.03.01 Tracking
hēahdīacon 16.02.03.02.06 An archdeacon
hēaheald 07.08.01 Nobility (of character, rank, etc.)
hēahealdor 12.01.01.04 A leader, ruler; 12.01.01.05 A leader, administrator
hēahealdormann 12.01.01.05 A leader, administrator
hēahengel 16.01.02.05.01 An angel
hēahfæder 16.01.01.04.01 God the Father; 16.02.01.08.05 One of the church fathers; 16.02.03.02.01 A high priest, chief bishop, etc. (general); 16.02.03.03.01.01 An abbot
hēahfæst 05.13.06 Constancy, unchangeableness
hēahfæsten 13.02.06.01 Stronghold, fort/fortified town
hēahfeaxede 03.01.12.02 A beam of light
hēahflōd 01.01.03.04 Current, rush of water
hēahfore 02.06.02.01.03 Cattle
hēahfrēa 16.01.01 God, the Lord
hēahfrēols 05.11.02.01.02 A time of celebration; 16.02.04.04.02 A feast-day, holy day; 16.02.04.07.04.01 The service of the mass
hēahfrēolsdæg 05.11.02.01.02 A time of celebration; 16.02.04.04.02 A feast-day, holy day; 16.02.04.07.04.01 The service of the mass
hēahfrēolstīd 05.11.02.01.02 A time of celebration; 16.02.04.04.02 A feast-day, holy day; 16.02.04.07.04.01 The service of the mass
hēahfȳr 03.01.09.02 Fire, flame
hēahgǣst 16.01.01.04.03 The Holy Spirit
hēahgealdor 16.01.04.01 Sorcery using incantation
hēahgerēfa 12.01.01.05 A leader, administrator
hēah(ge)samnung 16.02.05.02.03 A church, place of worship
hēahgesceaft 02 Creation
hēahgesceap 05.04 Fate, lot, fortune, destiny
hēahgestrēon 15.01.03 Treasure, riches, wealth
hēahgetimbrad 04.05.02 A building, edifice, structure
hēahgetimbru 04.05.02 A building, edifice, structure
hēah(ge)þungen 07.08.01 Nobility (of character, rank, etc.)
hēah(ge)weorc 17.02.04 Trade, calling, craft, aptitude
hēahgnornung 08.01.03.04 Grief

hēahgod 16.01.01 God, the Lord
hēahgræft 17.02.05.05 A carving, graving
hēahhād 16.02.04.07.05 An order (general)
hēahhæf 01.01.03.01.02 Sea/ocean
hēahhelm 03.01.12.02 A beam of light
hēahheoloþe 02.07.11 Plants/flowers (alphabetical order)
hēahheort 07.06 Pride
hēahhliþ 01.01.02.01.02.02.01 Hill
hēahhlūtor 12.08.04 Purity, moral cleanness
hēahholt 02.07.03.04 A wood, trees
hēahhwīolod 05.12.01.06 Vehicle
hēahhylte 02.07.03.04 A wood, trees
hēahhymele 02.07.11 Plants/flowers (alphabetical order)
hēahhyrde 16.02.03.03.01.01 An abbot
hēahlǣce 02.08.12.02.01 A physician
hēahland 01.01.02.01.02 High land
hēahlārēow 06.01.06.02.03.04.02 A teacher
hēahleornere 06.01.06.02.01 A wise man, man of understanding or learning
hēahlufu 08.01.02.02 Love, affection, care
hēahmægen 16.01.01.01.01.01 Mightiness; 16.02.01.12.04 A cardinal virtue
hēahmæsse 16.02.04.07.04.01 The service of the mass
hēahmæssedæg 16.02.04.04.02 A feast-day, holy day; 16.02.04.07.04.01 The service of the mass
hēahmiht 16.01.01.01.01 The Almighty; 16.01.01.01.01.01 Mightiness
hēahmōd 07.06 Pride; 08.01.01.03.06 Exultation, joy; 12.08.01 Magnanimity, greatness of soul

hēahmōdnes 07.06 Pride
hēahmōr 01.01.02.01.06 Wild/uncultivated land
hēahnes 12.01.01.06.05 Nobility, noble condition
hēahost 16.01.01 God, the Lord
hēahra 05.10.05.03.03 Height, loftiness, sublimity
hēahreced 16.01.02.01 Heavenly dwelling place; 16.02.05.02.01 A temple
hēahrodor 16.01.02 The heavens, sky
hēahrūn 16.01.04.01 Sorcery using incantation
hēahsacerd 16.02.03.02.01 A high priest, chief bishop, etc. (general)
hēahsacerdhād 16.02.03.02.01 A high priest, chief bishop, etc. (general)
hēahsǣl 08.01.01.03 Good feeling, joy, happiness
hēahsǣþēof 05.12.01.09.03.03 Piracy
hēahsangere 16.02.03.02.13 A church singer, singer in choir
hēahsceaþa 05.12.01.09.03.03 Piracy
hēahscēawere 17.02.01 Management of work
hēahscīreman 12.02.02.03 Terms for classical world
hēahseld/-setl 06.01.06.02.03.04.01 A school; 12.01.01.02 Seat of authority
hēahsele 04.05.03.02.02.06.01 A hall building
hēahsetl 07.08.04 An ornament, honour, glory; 14.03.01 Judicial body, authority
hēahsittende 05.10.05.03.03 Height, loftiness, sublimity
hēahstēap 05.10.05.03.03 Height, loftiness, sublimity
hēahstede 01.01.02.01.02 High land

hēahstefn 05.12.01.09.03.01.02 Of/concerning a ship, naval
hēahstrǣt 05.12.01.03.01.03 A highway
hēahsunne 16.02.01.13 Evil-doing, transgression, sin
hēahsynn 16.02.01.13.01 Kinds of sin
hēahtīd 16.02.04.04.02 A feast-day, holy day; 16.02.04.07.04.01 The service of the mass
hēahtimber 04.05.02 A building, edifice, structure
hēahtorr 01.01.02.01.02.02.02 Mountain
hēahtrēow 12.07.02.01 Covenant, assurance of faith, promise
hēahþearf 08.01.03.06 Adversity, affliction
hēahþegn 12.01.01.05 A leader, administrator
hēahþegnung 16.01.01.04.03 The Holy Spirit
hēahþēod 02.03.03.03 A nation, people
hēahþrēa 08.01.03.06 Adversity, affliction
hēahþrymm 16.01.01.01.01.02 Glory
hēahþrymnes 16.01.01.01.01.02 Glory
hēahþungen 05.12.05.12.02 To raise, lift up, elevate; 07.02.04 Excellence
hēahweg 05.12.01.03.01.03 A highway
hēahwēofod 16.02.05.03.04 Part of temple containing altar/idol
hēahwita 12.02.02.02 A counsellor, advisor
hēala 02.08.08.11 Rupture
heald 05.10.05.04.04 A descent, slope, incline; 05.12.01.09.03.01.03 Part of ship
geheald 06.01.01.02 Care, attention, observation; 11.10 Safety, safeness; 11.10.01 Protection, safekeeping; 11.10.02.02 Watchful care, keeping guard; 12.07.02 Observance, keeping
gehealdagas 05.11.06.01 Cycle of the year
healdan 03.01.03.02 Strength, power; 05.10.05.04.01.02 Contents, what is included; 05.10.05.04.11.01 A bound, limit; 05.12.04 Absence of movement, stillness; 07.04 Consideration, esteem; 08.01.01 A feeling, what is felt; 10.04 To take; 11.02 Occupation, activity, business; 11.05.02 Mode, manner, way, method, fashion, course; 11.10.02 Watching, guard, watch; 13.02.04 Defence, guard, protection; 14.05.08 Captivity; 16.02.04 Worship, honour, praise; 17.02.02 An office, function, employment
healdan forþ 11.02.01 Energy, vigour, vigorous action
healdan on/tō 05.12.05.02 To go/travel towards, come, approach
healdan (on/tō) 05.12.05.09 To go forward, proceed
(ge)healdan 04.01.02.04.04 To maintain, support, provide for; 04.02.05.01.02 To tend, herd; 05.10.05.04.02.04.02 Support, maintenance; 05.12.05.09 To go forward, proceed; 06.01.04 Faculty of memory; 06.01.07.06 Mental acceptance, belief; 10 Having, owning, possession; 10.04.01 To hold, have; 11.05.02 Mode, manner, way, method, fashion, course; 11.10.01 Protection, safekeeping; 11.10.02.02 Watchful care, keeping guard; 11.10.02.02.01 Care, interest in; 11.11.02 A hindrance; 12.01.01.01 Rule, domination, direction; 12.03.01 Direction, care, management, supervision; 12.05.06.03 Necessity,

(ge)healdan (wiþ)

constraint; 12.07.02 Observance, keeping; 14.05.08 Captivity; 14.05.08.01 Prison, confinement, durance; 15.01.01.01 Holding of land; 16.02.04.04.02 A feast-day, holy day
(ge)healdan (wiþ) 11.06.04 Abstention, abstaining from
gehealdan 03.05.01 Arranging, ordering, disposition; 09.05.04 A secret; 15.02.04 Spending, disbursement
gehealde 08.01.01.03.02 Pleasure, satisfaction
gehealden 11.10 Safety, safeness; 12.08.03 Restraint, temperance; 12.08.03.03.01 Continence; 16.02.04.04.02 A feast-day, holy day
gehealden (on) 08.01.01.03.02 Pleasure, satisfaction
healdend 11.10.01 Protection, safekeeping; 12.01.01.04 A leader, ruler; 16.01.01.02.04 Protector, defender
gehealdend 10.03.09 Moderation in expenditure
gehealdendgeorn 12.08.03.03.01 Continence
gehealdfæst 11.10 Safety, safeness
healding 12.07.02 Observance, keeping
healdnes 12.07.02 Observance, keeping; 16.02.03.02.05 A bishop
gehealdnes 11.10.02.02.01 Care, interest in
(ge)healdsum 11.10.02.02.01 Care, interest in
gehealdsum 10.03.09 Moderation in expenditure; 12.08.03.03 Moral restraint, modesty, sobriety; 12.08.03.03.01 Continence; 12.08.04 Purity, moral cleanness

(ge)healdsumnes 11.10.01.01 Preservation from injury/destruction; 12.07.02 Observance, keeping
gehealdsumnes 11.10.02 Watching, guard, watch; 12.08.03.03 Moral restraint, modesty, sobriety; 12.08.03.03.01 Continence; 16.02.04.04.02 A feast-day, holy day
hēalede 02.08.08.11 Rupture
healf 03.03.03.03 Fractions; 05.10.05.04.09 Side, quarter, direction; 12.04.01.01 A company of people, fellowship, society
healf dǣl 03.03.03.03 Fractions
healfæcer 04.02.03.03.03 An acre
healfbrocen 05.06.03 A dashing together, breaking, shattering
healfclǣmed 04.05.01.03 Gypsum, chalk
healfclungen 03.01.17.01 A coagulating, mixing
healfclypigende 09 Speech, vocal utterance
healfcwic 02.01.02.01 That lives, living; 02.02.03.01 In process of dying
healfdēad 02.02.03.01 In process of dying
healfe 03.03.03.03 Fractions
healfeald 02.06.02.01.07 Pig, swine
healfes hēafdes ece 02.08.07.01 Pain in head/neck
healffers 09.03.05.01.02 Art of verse composition
healffēþe 02.08.04.04 State of being crippled
healffrēo 12.01.01.10 Freedom, being free
healfgemet 09.03.05.01.02 Art of verse composition
healfgewriten 09.03.07 Writing
healfhār 02.04.04.03.02 Colour of hair
healfhēafod 02.04.03.01.03.01 Forehead

healfhruh 03.01.05 Roughness
healfhunding 02.06.10.01.03 Half of another kind
healfhundisc 02.06.10.01.03 Half of another kind
healfhwīt 03.01.14.03 White/whiteness
healfhȳd 04.02.03.03.02 A hide
healfmann 02.06.10.01.03 Half of another kind
healfmearc 15.01.04 Coinage, money
healfnacod 04.04.07.02.01 Nakedness
healfpenigwurþ 15.02 Worth, value
healfrēad 03.01.14.05 Red/redness
healfsester 03.03.01 Specific measures
healfsinewealt 05.10.06.02.01 A hemisphere
healfslæpende 02.05.04 Sleepiness, drowsiness, sleep
healfsoden 04.01.02.02.05 Cooking
healfsynnig 12.08.09 Guiltiness, guilt
healftryndel 05.10.06.02.01 A hemisphere
healfunga 03.03.05 Extent, degree; 03.03.07 A part, division, portion; 05.10.05.04.09 Side, quarter, direction
healfweg 05.10.05.04.01.01 The middle
healfwudu 02.07.11 Plants/flowers (alphabetical order)
healgamen 18.02 Amusement, revelry, festivity
healh 01.01.02.01.01.03.02 Inlet in river/sea; 01.01.02.01.02.02.03 Slope; 05.10.06.04 A corner, bend, angle; 09.05.04.01 Concealment, obscurity
hēalhālgung 07.06.05 Pomp, splendour, magnificence
healhiht 05.10.06.04 A corner, bend, angle
hēalic 02.05.10.15.01 To raise (the voice), raise up (noise); 03.01.12.02 A beam of light; 05.10.05.03.03 Height, loftiness, sublimity; 07.02.04 Excellence; 07.02.04.02 Nobleness, nobility, dignity; 07.02.04.03 Nobleness, excellence, nobility, magnificence; 07.06.01.01 Proud, arrogant; 08.01.01.01 Ardour, fervour, strong feeling; 12.01.01.06.02.01 (High) rank, status, degree; 12.01.01.06.05 Nobility, noble condition; 12.08.06.02.04 Darkness, evil; 15.02.01 High/steep price
hēalic boda 16.01.02.05.01 An angel
hēalīce 02.05.10.15.01 To raise (the voice), raise up (noise); 03.03.05 Extent, degree; 03.03.05.01.01 Principal/chief (of its class or type); 05.10.05.03.03 Height, loftiness, sublimity; 11.04.02.01 Art, skill, contrivance, cunning; 12.01.01.06.05 Nobility, noble condition
hēalicnes 01.01.02.01.02 High land; 12.01.01.06.02.01 (High) rank, status, degree
hēalīcor 05.10.05.03.03 Height, loftiness, sublimity
heall 01.01.02.02.01 Rock, stone; 04.05.03.02.02.06.01 A hall building; 14.03.01 Judicial body, authority; 16.02.05.02.01 A temple
heallærn 04.05.03.02.02.06.01 A hall building
heallic 04.05.03.02.02.06.01 A hall building
heallrēaf 04.04.08.01 Curtain, wall-hanging, etc.
heallreced 04.05.03.02.02.06.01 A hall building
heallsittend 02.03.03.01 Body of retainers, household

heallþegn 12.01.01.07 A follower
heallwāhrift 04.04.08.01 Curtain, wall-hanging, etc.
heallwudu 04.05.03.02.02.06.01 A hall building
healm 04.02.03.02.02.06 Stubble field; 04.02.04.03.02.01 Grain crops; 04.02.04.04.03 Stubble, straw
healmstrēaw 04.02.04.04.03 Stubble, straw
healoc 01.01.02.01.03 Hollow/depression in land
hēalor 01.01.02.01.02.02.01 Hill
heals 02.04.03.02 Neck; 05.10.06.03 Projection, head, extremity (of anything); 05.12.01.09.03.01.03 Part of ship
healsbēag 04.04.10.01 A ring (for finger, arm, neck)
healsbeorg 13.02.08.03.01.03 Neck armour
healsbeorggold 04.04.10.01 A ring (for finger, arm, neck)
healsbōc 16.01.04.04 A magical apparatus
healsbrynige 13.02.08.03.01.03 Neck armour
healsed 04.04.07.03 Part of garment; 04.04.07.11 A headcloth, covering for the head
healseta 04.04.07.03 Part of garment
healsfæst 07.06.01.01 Proud, arrogant
healsfang 15.02 Worth, value
healsgang 02.08.07.06 Disorders of the neck
healsgebedda 12.09 Marriage, state of marriage
healsgund 02.08.07.06 Disorders of the neck
healsiendlic 12.03.04.01 Entreaty, solemn appeal
healsleþer 04.02.05.06.05.03.03 Reins
healsmægeþ 02.03.01.07 Girl
healsmyne 04.04.10.01 A ring (for finger, arm, neck)
healsōme 02.08.07.06 Disorders of the neck
healsrefeþer 04.05.04.05.01 Bedding (e.g. of straw)
healstān 04.01.02.01.07.04 Cake
healswærc 02.08.07.06 Disorders of the neck
healswriþa 04.04.10.01 A ring (for finger, arm, neck)
healswyrt 02.07.11.02 Unidentified plants (alphabetical order)
healt 02.08.04.04 State of being crippled
healtian 02.08.04.04 State of being crippled; 05.12.03.02 Slowness; 06.01.07.05 Error, being astray; 11.06.05 Hesitation, scruple
hēamol 10.03.09.01 Parsimony, niggardliness
hēamolscipe 10.03.09.01 Parsimony, niggardliness
hēan 07.09.02 Disgrace, shaming, humiliation; 07.09.03 Infamy, ignominy, shame; 08.01.03.01 Despondency; 08.01.03.06.01 Affliction, misfortune, calamity; 11.03.02 Advancement, progress; 11.08.04 Vanity, idleness, frivolity; 12.01.01.11 The common people; 15.01.06 Poverty, indigence; 16.02.04 Worship, honour, praise
(ge)hēan 05.12.05.12.02 To raise, lift up, elevate
hēandōm 08.01.03.06 Adversity, affliction
hēane 07.09 Shame, disgrace

hēanes 05.10.05.03.03 Height, loftiness, sublimity; 05.10.05.03.04 Depth, deepness; 07.08.01 Nobility (of character, rank, etc.); 11.07.04 Superiority, pre-eminence, primacy; 16.01.02 The heavens, sky
hēanlic 07.09.03 Infamy, ignominy, shame; 11.08.04 Vanity, idleness, frivolity
hēanlīce 07.09.02 Disgrace, shaming, humiliation
hēanmōd 08.01.03.01 Despondency
hēannes 05.12.01.04.01.02 To tread upon, trample; 08.01.01.01.01 Exaltation, elation
hēanspēdig 15.01.06 Poverty, indigence
hēap 03.03.04.01.02.01 A heap, mass, accumulation; 12.01.01.07 A follower; 13.02.10.01.02.02 Armed forces; 13.02.10.01.02.02.03 Part of an army; 13.02.10.03 Crew/men of a ship; 16.02.03.02.07 A priest, cleric
gehēapan 10.01.02 Acquisition
(ge)hēapian 03.03.04.01 Much; 03.03.04.01.02.01 A heap, mass, accumulation
gehēapian 12.04.02 A crowding together, assembly
hēapmǣlum 03.03.04.01.02.01 A heap, mass, accumulation
hēapum 03.03.04.01.02.01 A heap, mass, accumulation
hēapung 03.03.04.01.02.01 A heap, mass, accumulation
heard 02.05.07.01 Strong taste, acidity, pungency; 02.07.03.05 Particular trees/shrubs (alphabetical order); 03.01.03 Hardness, callosity, hard material; 03.01.03.02 Strength, power; 05.08.02.01 (Of living creatures) fierceness, roughness; 06.02.07 Will, determination, resolution; 06.02.07.04.01 Obduracy; 06.02.07.06.02 Boldness; 08.01.03.07.04 Severity, harshness; 08.01.03.07.04.01 Unbearableness; 08.01.03.09.10 Wrath, sternness, displeasure; 12.08.03.02 Strictness, austerity, severity
heardcwide 07.05.03.03 Scorn, insult, abuse
hearde 03.03.05 Extent, degree; 05.05.03 Binding, fastening; 08.01.03.07.04 Severity, harshness
heardecg 13.02.08.04.03 A sword
heardhara 02.06.06.03.01.04 Mullet
heardhēaw 17.03.03 A cutting tool
heardheort 06.02.07.04 Obstinacy; 08.01.03.09.10 Wrath, sternness, displeasure
heardheortnes 08.01.03.09.11 Hardheartedness, cruelty, severity
heardhicgende 06.02.07.01 Strength, fortitude
heardhīpende 05.06 Destruction, dissolution, loss, breaking
heardian 02.08.08 Internal disease; 03.01.03 Hardness, callosity, hard material
hearding 06.02.07.06 Courage, boldness, valour
heardlic 06.02.07 Will, determination, resolution; 06.02.07.06.02 Boldness; 08.01.03.07.04.01 Unbearableness; 08.01.03.09.12 Pitilessness
heardlīce 03.03.04.02.02 Excess; 05.08.02 Violence, force; 06.02.07.06.02 Boldness; 08.01.03.07.04 Severity, harshness; 08.01.03.09.12 Pitilessness; 11.11

Difficulty; 12.08.03.02 Strictness, austerity, severity
heardlicnes 12.08.03.02 Strictness, austerity, severity
heardmōd 06.02.07.01 Strength, fortitude; 06.02.07.04 Obstinacy
heardmōdnes 06.02.07.04 Obstinacy
heardnebba 02.06.08.05 Forest bird, wild-fowl
heardnes 03.01.03 Hardness, callosity, hard material; 06.02.07.04.01 Obduracy; 12.08.03.02 Strictness, austerity, severity
heardrǣd 06.02.07 Will, determination, resolution
heardsǣlig 08.01.03.06.01 Affliction, misfortune, calamity
heardsǣlnes 08.01.03.06.01 Affliction, misfortune, calamity
heardsǣlþ 08.01.03.06.01 Affliction, misfortune, calamity; 12.08.06.01 Error, wrong conduct, erroneous practice
heardung 02.08.08 Internal disease
heardwendlīce 08.01.03.09.10 Wrath, sternness, displeasure
hearg 16.02.01.06.01.01.01 An image, idol; 16.02.05.02 A holy place or sanctuary; 16.02.05.02.01 A temple; 16.02.05.03.04 Part of temple containing altar/idol
heargeard 04.05.03.02.02.01 Dwellings in particular places
hearglic 16.02.01.06 Paganism, a false religion
heargtræf 16.02.05.02.01 A temple
hearm 07.03.02 Ill, harm, hurt; 07.05.03.02 Calumny, slander, insult; 08.01.03.06.01 Affliction, misfortune, calamity; 08.01.03.07.02 Misery, trouble, affliction
hearma 02.06.03.01.13 Rodents
hearmascinnen 17.04.04.02 Skin, hide (as material)
hearmberg 08.01.03.06.01 Affliction, misfortune, calamity
hearmcwala 08.01.03.07.03 Suffering, torment, pain
hearmcweodelian 07.05.03.02 Calumny, slander, insult
hearmcweþan 07.05.03.02 Calumny, slander, insult
hearmcweþend 07.05.03.02 Calumny, slander, insult
hearmcwiddian 07.05.03.02 Calumny, slander, insult
hearmcwide 07.05.03.02 Calumny, slander, insult; 16.02.04.14.01 Blasphemy
hearmcwidol 07.05.03.02 Calumny, slander, insult
hearmcwidolnes 07.05.03.02 Calumny, slander, insult
hearmedwīt 07.05.03.03 Scorn, insult, abuse
hearmful 08.01.03.07.02 Misery, trouble, affliction
(ge)hearmian 05.06.04 Damage, injury, defect, hurt, loss
hearmlēoþ 08.01.03.04.01 Complaint, lamentation
hearmlic 08.01.03.06 Adversity, affliction; 08.01.03.07.04 Severity, harshness
hearmloca 14.05.08.01 Prison, confinement, durance
hearmplega 12.05.04.01 Fighting, contention, warfare, strife
hearmscaþa 08.01.03.09.05 Enmity
hearmscearu 14.05 Punishment

hearmslege 05.06.09 Act of striking
hearmspræc 07.05.03.02 Calumny, slander, insult
hearmstæf 08.01.03.07.02 Misery, trouble, affliction
hearmtān 08.01.03 Bad feeling, sadness
hearpan stalu 18.02.07.02.03 Stringed instruments
hearpe 18.02.07.02.03.01 A harp, lyre
hearpenægel 18.02.07.02.03 Stringed instruments
hearpere 18.02.07.02.03.01 A harp, lyre
hearpestre 18.02.07.02.03.01 A harp, lyre
hearpestreng 18.02.07.02.03 Stringed instruments
hearpian 18.02.07.02.03.01 A harp, lyre
hearplic 18.02.07.02.03 Stringed instruments
hearpsang 16.02.01.08.01.01 Books of the Old Testament; 16.02.04.03.03.02 A psalm
hearpslege 18.02.07.02.03 Stringed instruments; 18.02.07.02.03.01 A harp, lyre
hearpswēg 18.02.07.02.03.01 A harp, lyre
hearpung 18.02.07.02.03.01 A harp, lyre
hearra 12.01.01.04 A leader, ruler
heaþor 14.05.08 Captivity
(ge)heaþorian 14.05.08 Captivity
heaþosēoc 02.08.04 Hurt, injury, damage
heaþubyrne 13.02.08.03.01.04 Coat of mail/corselet
heaþudēor 06.02.07.06 Courage, boldness, valour
heaþufremmende 13.02.02 Battle
heaþufȳr 03.01.09.02.01.01 A kind of fire
heaþugeong 13.02.10.01 A man, warrior
heaþuglemm 02.08.04.01 A wound
heaþugrim 08.01.03.09.11 Hardheartedness, cruelty, severity
heaþulāc 13.02.02 Battle
heaþulind 13.02.08.03.01.06 A shield
heaþulīþende 13.02.10.03 Crew/men of a ship
heaþumǣre 07.08.10 Fame of courage, valour
heaþurǣs 13.02.03 To seek with active intent, attack
heaþurēaf 13.02.08.03.01 Body armour, war gear
heaþurinc 13.02.10.01 A man, warrior
heaþurōf 06.02.07.06 Courage, boldness, valour
heaþusceard 13.02.08.04.03 A sword
heaþusigel 01.02.01.01.03 Sun
heaþustēap 13.02.08.03.01.02.01 Parts of a helmet
heaþuswāt 02.02.04 Killing, violent death, destruction; 13.02.02 Battle
heaþusweng 13.02.08.04.03.02.01 Striking/attack with sword
heaþutorht 02.05.10.01 Thing heard
heaþuwǣd 13.02.08.03.01 Body armour, war gear
heaþuweorc 13.02.02 Battle
heaþuwērig 02.05.03.02 Weariness
heaþuwylm 03.01.09.02 Fire, flame
hēawan 13.02.08.04.03.02.01 Striking/attack with sword
(ge)hēawan 04.02.04.05.04.01 A forester, woodman; 05.06.02 Cleaving, splitting, cutting; 13.02.08.04.03.02.01 Striking/attack with sword; 17.02.04.02.01 Cutting, hewing, shaping
hebban 02.05.10.15.01 To raise (the voice), raise up (noise); 05.05.01 An author, source, originator; 05.12.02.01

To fetch, bring, bear, conduct;
06.01.01.01.01.01 Consideration,
rumination; 16.02.04 Worship,
honour, praise
hebban mōd tō 06.01.01.02 Care,
attention, observation
hebban ūp 11.03.01.01.01 Proof,
demonstration
hebban (ūp) 05.10.05.04.02.04 Above
(ge)hebban 07.08.06 Exaltation
(ge)hebban (ūp) 05.12.05.12.02 To raise,
lift up, elevate
heccing 04.02.03.02.02 Sown part of field
hēcen 02.06.02.01.05 Goat
hecge 05.10.05.04.11 A circle, circuit,
circumference
hecg(e) 04.05.01.02.07 A fence, hedge
hēdan 06.01.01.02 Care, attention,
observation; 11.02.02.02 Care,
mindfulness, attention
gehēdan 10 Having, owning, possession
hedclāþ 04.04.07.07 A long outer
garment, covering, cloak, etc.
hēddern 04.05.03.04 A closet, chamber,
room
heden 16.02.05.06.01 Outer garments
hedendlic 06.01.06.02.02.01.01
Philosophy
hedendlīce 06.01.06.02.02.01.01
Philosophy
hefe 03.01.07 Weight, heaviness;
03.03.02 Measurement by weighing;
05.03.01.02.01 A destructive
influence; 11.07.04 Superiority,
pre-eminence, primacy; 11.11.02 A
hindrance
gehefed 08.01.03.07.02 Misery, trouble,
affliction
hefeful 08.01.03.07.04 Severity,
harshness

hefeld 04.04.04 A thread (of wool, etc.),
fibre
(ge)hefeldian 04.04 Weaving
hefelgyrd 04.04.03 A spinning-house or
chamber
hefelic 02.05.04 Sleepiness, drowsiness,
sleep; 08.01.03.07.01 Tedium;
08.01.03.07.04 Severity, harshness;
08.01.03.07.04.01 Unbearableness;
17.01 Strenuous effort, hard work
hefelīce 08.01.03.04 Grief;
08.01.03.07.04 Severity, harshness;
12.08.06.02.04 Darkness, evil
hefelīce/hefiglīce 02.05.03.01 Dullness,
lack of animation
hefelþrǣd 04.04.04 A thread (of wool,
etc.), fibre
hefen 11.11.02 A hindrance
hefig 02.05.03.01 Dullness, lack of
animation; 02.05.04 Sleepiness,
drowsiness, sleep; 02.05.08 Faculty of
smell; 03.01.01 Thick, close-textured,
dense; 03.01.07 Weight, heaviness;
08.01.03.03 Anxiety; 08.01.03.04.01
Complaint, lamentation;
08.01.03.07.04.01 Unbearableness;
08.01.03.09.06 Hostility; 11.06
Disinclination to act, listlessness;
11.07.04 Superiority, pre-eminence,
primacy; 12.05.06.02.03 Trouble,
disturbance; 12.08.06.02.04 Darkness,
evil; 13.02.02 Battle; 17.01 Strenuous
effort, hard work
hefige 02.05.03.01 Dullness, lack of
animation; 08.01.03.07.04 Severity,
harshness; 11.11 Difficulty
hefigian 02.05.03.01 Dullness, lack of
animation; 02.05.04.01 To make
heavy with weariness/sleep;

02.08.02.01.01 An infectious disease; 03.01.07 Weight, heaviness
(ge)hefigian 08.01.03 Bad feeling, sadness; 12.05.06.02 Oppression
gehefigian 02.05.03.01 Dullness, lack of animation; 08.01.03.07.04 Severity, harshness; 11.07.04 Superiority, pre-eminence, primacy
hefiglic 13.02.02 Battle
hefiglic/hefelic 12.08.06.02.04 Darkness, evil
hefiglīce 08.01.01.01.04 Depth of feeling, zeal; 08.01.03.05.02 Anger
hefigmōd 08.01.03 Bad feeling, sadness; 12.05.06.02.03 Trouble, disturbance
hefignes 02.05.03.01 Dullness, lack of animation; 02.08.02 Disease, infirmity, sickness; 03.01.07 Weight, heaviness; 08.01.03.07.02 Misery, trouble, affliction; 12.05.06.02 Oppression; 12.05.06.02.03 Trouble, disturbance
hefigtȳme 08.01.03.07.01 Tedium; 08.01.03.07.02 Misery, trouble, affliction; 08.01.03.07.04.01 Unbearableness; 11.07.04 Superiority, pre-eminence, primacy; 12.05.06.02.03 Trouble, disturbance; 12.08.06.02.04 Darkness, evil; 17.01 Strenuous effort, hard work
hefigtȳmnes 08.01.03.07.02 Misery, trouble, affliction
hege 02.07.03.04.03 A hedge/border
hegeclife 02.07.11 Plants/flowers (alphabetical order)
hegehymele 02.07.09.02 Particular fruits (alphabetical order)
hegeræw 02.07.03.04.03 A hedge/border
hegerife 02.07.11 Plants/flowers (alphabetical order)
hegesāhl 04.02.04.05.04 A detached area of woodland
hegesteall 04.02.04.05.04 A detached area of woodland
hegestōw 04.02.04.05.04 A detached area of woodland
hegeweg 05.12.01.03.01.03 A highway
(ge)hegian 04.02.04.01 To occupy and cultivate land
hegstæf 04.05.01.02.07 A fence, hedge; 05.10.05.04.15.01 A bar, bolt
hēla 02.04.03.04.02.05.01 Heel
hēlade 02.04.03.04.02.05.01 Heel
helan 09.05.04 A secret
(ge)helan 09.05.04 A secret; 09.05.04.01 Concealment, obscurity
(ge)helan wiþ/fram 09.05.04.01 Concealment, obscurity
hēlan 07.05.03.02 Calumny, slander, insult
gehēlan 14.03.03.06 False witness
helcniht 16.01.05.02 Species of devil, hellish race
helde 02.07.11 Plants/flowers (alphabetical order)
helfan 03.03.03.03 Fractions
helgod 16.01.05.02.02 Other terms for devils
(ge)helian 05.10.05.04.12 The condition of being covered; 09.05.04.01 Concealment, obscurity
hell 16.01.05.01 Damnation, perdition, reprobation
hellbend 14.05.06 Means/implement of torture
hellcræft 16.01.04 Sorcery, magic, witchcraft
hellcund 16.01.05 Hell, lower world, abode of the dead

hellcwalu 08.01.03.07.03 Suffering, torment, pain; 16.01.05.01 Damnation, perdition, reprobation
helldor 16.01.05 Hell, lower world, abode of the dead
hell(e) 16.01.05 Hell, lower world, abode of the dead
helle cǣgan 16.01.05 Hell, lower world, abode of the dead
helle clamm 14.05.06 Means/implement of torture
helle flōras 16.01.05 Hell, lower world, abode of the dead
helle god 16.01.05.02.02 Other terms for devils
helle hæft(a) 16.01.05.02.02 Other terms for devils
helle hæftling 16.01.05.02.02 Other terms for devils
hellebealu 08.01.03.07.03 Suffering, torment, pain; 16.01.05.01 Damnation, perdition, reprobation
hellebroga 16.01.05.01 Damnation, perdition, reprobation
hellebryne 16.01.05 Hell, lower world, abode of the dead
helleceafl 16.01.05 Hell, lower world, abode of the dead
hellecinn 16.01.05.02 Species of devil, hellish race
helledēofol 16.01.05.02 Species of devil, hellish race
helledor 16.01.05 Hell, lower world, abode of the dead
helleduru 16.01.05 Hell, lower world, abode of the dead
hellefȳr 16.01.05 Hell, lower world, abode of the dead
hellegāst 16.01.05.02 Species of devil, hellish race
hellegeat 16.01.05 Hell, lower world, abode of the dead
hellegeþwing 16.01.05.01 Damnation, perdition, reprobation
hellegrund 16.01.05 Hell, lower world, abode of the dead
hellegrut 16.01.05 Hell, lower world, abode of the dead
hellegryre 16.01.05.01 Damnation, perdition, reprobation
hellehēaf 16.01.05.01 Damnation, perdition, reprobation
hellehinca 16.01.05.02.02 Other terms for devils
hellehund 12.08.06.02.02 A bad man, inhuman person; 16.01.05 Hell, lower world, abode of the dead
hellehūs 16.01.05 Hell, lower world, abode of the dead
hellelic 16.01.05 Hell, lower world, abode of the dead
helleloc 16.01.05.01 Damnation, perdition, reprobation
hellemægen 16.01.05.02 Species of devil, hellish race
hellemere 16.01.05 Hell, lower world, abode of the dead
hellemūþ 16.01.05 Hell, lower world, abode of the dead
hellenīþ 16.01.05.01 Damnation, perdition, reprobation
hellepīn 16.01.05.01 Damnation, perdition, reprobation
hellerūne 16.01.04.01 Sorcery using incantation
hellescealc 16.01.05.02 Species of devil, hellish race
hellesēaþ 16.01.05 Hell, lower world, abode of the dead

hellestōw 16.01.05 Hell, lower world, abode of the dead
hellesūsl 16.01.05.01 Damnation, perdition, reprobation
helletintreg(a) 16.01.05.01 Damnation, perdition, reprobation
helleþegn 16.01.05.02 Species of devil, hellish race
hellewaran 16.01.05.02 Species of devil, hellish race
hellewīte 16.01.05.01 Damnation, perdition, reprobation
hellewītebrōga 06.01.08.06.03 Cause of fear, terror, horror
hellfenlic 16.01.05 Hell, lower world, abode of the dead
hellfiren 12.08.06.02.05 Misdeed, sin
hellfūs 12.08.06.02.03 (Of persons) wicked, evil-doing; 16.01.05.01 Damnation, perdition, reprobation
hellheoþu 16.01.05 Hell, lower world, abode of the dead
hellic 12.08.06.02.03 (Of persons) wicked, evil-doing; 16.01.05 Hell, lower world, abode of the dead
hellsceaþa 16.01.05 Hell, lower world, abode of the dead; 16.01.05.02 Species of devil, hellish race
helltræf 16.02.05.02.01 A temple
helltrega 16.01.05.01 Damnation, perdition, reprobation
hellwerod 16.01.05.02 Species of devil, hellish race
hellwiht 16.01.05.02 Species of devil, hellish race
helm 02.07.02.06 A leaf; 05.10.05.04.12 The condition of being covered; 09.05.04.01 Concealment, obscurity; 11.10.01 Protection, safekeeping; 12.01.01.03 Symbols of power; 13.02.08.03.01.02 A helmet
helma 05.12.01.09.03.01.03 Part of ship; 12.03 Direction, guidance
helmbǣre 02.07.02.06 A leaf
helmberend 13.02.10.01 A man, warrior
helmberende 02.07.02.06 A leaf
(ge)helmian 05.10.05.04.12 The condition of being covered
gehelmian 07.08.04 An ornament, honour, glory
helmiht 02.07.02.06 A leaf
gehelmod/gehilmed 13.02.08.03.01.02 A helmet
help 02.08.12.01 Medical care, treatment; 11.10.01.02 Refuge, help, shelter; 11.12.02 Aid, help, succour
helpan 02.08.12.01 Medical care, treatment
(ge)helpan 11.07.01 Utility, usefulness; 11.07.03 Use, advantage, profit; 11.12.02 Aid, help, succour
gehelpan 05.09.03 Mitigation, lightening, alleviation
helpend 11.12.02 Aid, help, succour
helpendlic 11.10.03 Salvation/deliverance from
helpendrāp 17.03.10 Supports and fastenings
helrūna 16.01.03.02 A demonic apparition
helrȳnegu 16.01.04.01 Sorcery using incantation
hēlspure 02.04.03.04.02.05.01 Heel
helung 05.10.05.04.12 The condition of being covered
hem 04.04.09 A fringe, border, hem
hemeþe 04.04.07.04 An undergarment
hemming 04.04.07.15 Footwear, covering for the feet

gehendan 10.04.01 To hold, have; 10.04.02.02 To seize, take, grasp, lay hold on
hende 03.06.01 Similitude, likeness
gehende 02.03.02.03.06.02 Close relationship; 03.06.01 Similitude, likeness; 05.10.05.01 A little way, no great distance; 05.11.07.04.01 Nearness, approach, imminence; 06.01.01.02 Care, attention, observation
gehendnes 02.03.02.03.06.02 Close relationship; 05.10.05.01 A little way, no great distance
heng 01.01.02.01.02.02 Hill, mountain
hengeclif 01.01.02.01.02.02.04 Cliff
hengen 02.02.04.04.03 Putting to death; 14.05.05 Physical punishments; 14.05.06 Means/implement of torture; 14.05.08.01 Prison, confinement, durance
hengenwītung 14.05.08.01 Prison, confinement, durance
hengest 02.06.02.01.06 Horse
hengetrēow 14.05.06 Means/implement of torture
hengwīte 14.05.04.01 A fine
henn 02.06.08.02 Domestic fowl
henna 02.06.08.02 Domestic fowl
henne ǣg 04.01.02.01.02.08 Egg
henne broþ 04.01.02.01.07.01 Soup/pottage
henne flǣsc 04.01.02.01.02.06 Chicken
hennebelle 02.07.11 Plants/flowers (alphabetical order)
hennescill 02.06.08.01 Part of bird
hennfugol 02.06.08.02 Domestic fowl
hentan 05.06.09 Act of striking; 10.04.02.02 To seize, take, grasp, lay hold on; 10.04.03 To take away, remove; 14.05.08 Captivity
hentan æfter 11.03 Endeavour
hēodæg 05.11.03.01.05 A day
hēof 08.01.03 Bad feeling, sadness; 08.01.03.04.01 Complaint, lamentation
hēofan 08.01.03.04 Grief; 08.01.03.04.01 Complaint, lamentation
hēofendlic 08.01.03.04.01 Complaint, lamentation
heofenes gim 01.02.01.01.03 Sun
heofenes hlāf 04.01.02.01.07.03.04 (Biblical) manna/bread of heaven
hēofian 08.01.03.04.01 Complaint, lamentation
hēofiend 08.01.03.04.01 Complaint, lamentation
hēofigendlic 08.01.03.04.01 Complaint, lamentation
heofon 01.02 Firmament; 16.01.02.01 Heavenly dwelling place; 16.01.02.02 Glory/majesty of heaven
heofona gehlidu 01.02.01 Heaven(s), sky
heofon(as) 01.02.01 Heaven(s), sky
heofonbēacen 16.01.01.02.03 A wonder, miracle
heofonbeorht 03.01.12 Brightness, light
heofonbig(g)ende 12.08.03.03.01.01 Chastity
heofonbūende 01.02.01 Heaven(s), sky; 16.01.02.05 Inhabitants of heaven
heofonbȳme 18.02.07.02.02.02 A trumpet
heofoncandel 01.02.01.01 Heavenly body; 01.02.01.01.06 Heavenly light
heofoncenned 01.02.01 Heaven(s), sky
heofoncolu 03.01.09 Heat
heofoncund 01.02.01 Heaven(s), sky
heofoncundlic 01.02.01 Heaven(s), sky
heofoncyning 16.01.01.01.01 The Almighty

heofondēma 16.01.01.02.06 God as judge
heofondrēam 16.01.02.02 Glory/majesty of heaven
heofondugoþ 16.01.02.05 Inhabitants of heaven
heofonengel 16.01.02.05.01 An angel
heofonflēogende 05.12.01.07 To fly (with wings)
heofonflōd 01.03.01.06.02 Rain
heofonfugol 02.06.08 Bird
heofonfȳr 01.03.01.03.01.02 Lightning
heofonhæbbend 16.01.01.01.01 The Almighty
heofonhālig 16.01.01.01 Attributes of God
heofonhām 16.01.02.01 Heavenly dwelling place
heofonhēah 05.10.05.03.03 Height, loftiness, sublimity
heofonheall 16.01.02.01 Heavenly dwelling place
heofonhlāf 04.01.02.01.07.03.04 (Biblical) manna/bread of heaven
heofonhrōf 04.05.02.08.02 A ceiling, inner roof; 16.01.02.01 Heavenly dwelling place
heofonhūs 04.05.02.08.02 A ceiling, inner roof
heofonhwealf 16.01.02.01 Heavenly dwelling place
heofonisc 01.02.01 Heaven(s), sky
heofonlēoht 01.02.01.01.06 Heavenly light
heofonlēoma 01.02.01.01.03 Sun
heofonlic 12.08.04 Purity, moral cleanness; 16.01.01 God, the Lord; 16.01.02 The heavens, sky; 16.01.02.01 Heavenly dwelling place
heofonlīce 01.02.01 Heaven(s), sky; 16.01.02 The heavens, sky

heofonmægen 16.01 A divine being; 16.01.01.01.01.01 Mightiness
heofonrīce 16.01.02.01 Heavenly dwelling place
heofonsetl 16.01.02.01 Heavenly dwelling place
heofonsteorra 01.02.01.01.02 Star
heofonstōl 16.01.02.01 Heavenly dwelling place
heofontimber 16.01.02.01 Heavenly dwelling place
heofontorht 03.01.12 Brightness, light
heofontungol 01.02.01.01 Heavenly body; 01.02.01.01.06 Heavenly light
heofonþrēat 16.01.02.05 Inhabitants of heaven
heofonþrymm 16.01.02.02 Glory/majesty of heaven
heofonware(-u) 16.01.02.05 Inhabitants of heaven; 16.01.02.01 Heavenly dwelling place
heofonwealdend 16.01.01.01.01 The Almighty
heofonweard 16.01.01.01.01 The Almighty
heofonwerod 16.01.02.05 Inhabitants of heaven
heofonwlitig 07.10 Beauty, fairness
heofonwolcen 01.03.01.06 Cloud
heofonwōma 02.05.10.03 Noise, tumult, uproar
heofonwuldor 16.01.02.02 Glory/majesty of heaven
hēofsīþ 08.01.03.06 Adversity, affliction
hēofung 08.01.03.04.01 Complaint, lamentation
hēofungdæg 02.02.05.03 To attend the dead; 08.01.03.04 Grief; 16.02.04.07.02.01 Penitence
hēofungtīd 16.02.04.07.02.01 Penitence

heolca 01.03.01.04.01 Frost
heolfor 02.04.06.08.01 Blood
heolfrig 02.04.06.08.01 Blood
heolor 03.03.02 Measurement by weighing
heolorbledu 03.03.02 Measurement by weighing
heolorian 03.03.02 Measurement by weighing; 06.01.01.01.01 Thought, cogitation, meditation
heoloþcynn 16.01.05.02 Species of devil, hellish race
heoloþhelm 13.02.08.03.01.02 A helmet
heolstor 03.01.13 Darkness, obscurity; 04.04.08 A covering, curtain, veil, garment, etc.; 04.05.03.05.02 A privy; 09.05.04.01 Concealment, obscurity
heolstorcofa 02.02.05.01.01 A grave, burial place, sepulchre
heolstorhof 16.01.05.01 Damnation, perdition, reprobation
heolstorloca 14.05.08.01 Prison, confinement, durance
heolstorsceadu 03.01.13.03 Overshadowing
heolstorscuwa 03.01.13.03 Overshadowing
heolstrig 09.05.04.01 Concealment, obscurity
heolstrung 03.01.13 Darkness, obscurity
heolurung 03.03.02 Measurement by weighing
heonan 02.02.03.01 In process of dying; 05.03 Source, origin; 05.10.04.03 Presence; 05.11.07.04 Future, time to come
heonan forþ 05.11.07.04 Future, time to come
heonansīþ 02.02 Death

heonanweard 05.11.01.02.01 Swift movement of time
heonu 02.05.09.04 To see, look upon, behold
hēopbremel 02.07.09.02 Particular fruits (alphabetical order)
hēope 02.07.09.02 Particular fruits (alphabetical order)
(ge)heorcnian 02.05.10 Faculty of hearing
heorcnung 02.05.10 Faculty of hearing
heord 02.03.03 A family, household; 02.06.02 Domestic animals, livestock; 02.07.03.05 Particular trees/shrubs (alphabetical order); 11.10.02.02.01 Care, interest in; 16.02.03.03.05 A layman
heordan 04.04.04 A thread (of wool, etc.), fibre
heordnes 05.11 A time, period of time; 11.10.01.01 Preservation from injury/destruction; 11.10.02.02 Watchful care, keeping guard
(ge)heordnes 11.10.02.02 Watchful care, keeping guard
heordrǣden 04.02.05.01 Care of livestock; 11.10.01.01 Preservation from injury/destruction; 11.10.02 Watching, guard, watch; 11.10.02.02 Watchful care, keeping guard
geheordung 11.10.02.02 Watchful care, keeping guard
hēore 08.01.01.03.09.01 Pleasant, agreeable
heorogeong 13.02.10.01 A man, warrior
heorot 02.06.03.01.06 Deer, hart
heorotberge 02.07.03.05 Particular trees/shrubs (alphabetical order)
heorotbrem(b)el 02.07.03.05 Particular trees/shrubs (alphabetical order)

heorotbrembellēaf 02.07.03.05 Particular trees/shrubs (alphabetical order)
heorotbrēr 02.07.03.05 Particular trees/shrubs (alphabetical order)
heorotclǣfre 02.07.11 Plants/flowers (alphabetical order)
heorotcrop 02.07.03.05 Particular trees/shrubs (alphabetical order)
heorotsmeoru 03.01.17.07 Salves, ointments, etc.
heorotsol 01.01.02.01.04.01 Marsh, bog, swamp
heorr 17.03.10 Supports and fastenings
heorre 04.05.02.12 Gate/doorway of a building
heorr(e) 05.10.04.02 A region, zone
geheort 06.02.07.01 Strength, fortitude
heortan cnys 02.08.08.03 Heart disease
heortan tō besettan 06.02.05.01 Strong liking for, devotion to
heortcoþa/-u 02.08.08.03 Heart disease
heorte 02.04.06.08 Heart; 05.02.02.02 (One's) own person; 05.10.05.04.01.01 The middle; 06 Spirit, soul, heart; 06.01 The head (as seat of thought); 06.02.02 Will, disposition; 08.01 Heart, spirit, mood, disposition
heortece 02.08.08.03 Heart disease
heorten 02.06.03.01.06 Deer, hart
heortgesida 02.04.06.03.02.04 Intestines
heortgryre 06.01.08.06.02 Great fear, terror, horror
heorthama 02.04.05.02 Fat
heorthogu 08.01.03.03 Anxiety
heortlēas 06.01.08.06.06 Timidity
geheortlīce 06.02.07.06.02.02 Boldness, daring
heortlufu 08.01.02.02 Love, affection, care

heortsārnes 08.01.03 Bad feeling, sadness
heortscræf 06 Spirit, soul, heart
heortwærc 02.08.08.03 Heart disease
heorþ 04.05.03.02.01 A building, house, hall, palace, etc.; 17.05.02 A hearth, fireplace
heorþa 02.06.03.01.06 Deer, hart
heorþbacen 04.01.02.02.05.04 Baking
heorþcniht 12.01.01.07 A follower
heorþfæst 12.06.03.02 Living, dwelling, residence (in)
heorþgenēat 12.01.01.07 A follower
heorþpening 16.02.04.20 Church due/requirement
heorþswǣpe 12.09.02 Marriage ceremony
heorþwerod 02.03.03 A family, household; 02.03.03.01 Body of retainers, household
heoru 13.02.08.04.03 A sword
heorublāc 02.08.04.01 A wound
heorubunden 13.02.08.04.03.01.01 Hilt of sword
heorucumbol 13.02.08.02 A standard, banner, ensign
heorudolg 02.08.04.01 A wound
heorudrēor 02.04.06.08.01 Blood
heorudrēorig 02.04.06.08.01 Blood; 08.01.03 Bad feeling, sadness
heorudrync 02.08.04.01 A wound
heorufæþm 02.02.04.01 Cause/occasion of death
heoruflā 13.02.08.04.04.01 An arrow, dart, bolt
heorugīfre 02.02.04.02 Murderous, bloodthirsty
heorugrǣdig 02.02.04.02 Murderous, bloodthirsty; 04.01.01.03 Hunger

heorugrimm 08.01.03.09.11 Hardheartedness, cruelty, severity
heoruhōciht 05.10.06.03.01 A point, spike, prickle
heoruscearp 05.10.06.03.01 A point, spike, prickle
heorusceorp 13.02.08 Military equipment
heoruserce 13.02.08.03.01.04 Coat of mail/corselet
heoruswealwe 02.06.08.04 Bird of prey
heorusweng 05.06.09 Act of striking; 13.02.08.04.03.02.01 Striking/attack with sword
heoruwǣpen 13.02.08.04.03 A sword
heoruweallende 05.08.02 Violence, force
heoruwearg 08.01.03.09.05 Enmity
heoruword 08.01.03.09.01.03 Sharpness (of speech)
heoruwulf 13.02.10.01 A man, warrior
hēr 01 Earth, world; 05.10.04.03 Presence; 05.11.07.02 The present (time)
hēr bæftan 05.11.07.04 Future, time to come
hēr beufan 05.11.07.03.02.02 The aforesaid
hēr rihte 05.10.04.03 Presence
hēr tō ēacan 03.03.04.03 Growth, increase
hēr ymbūtan 05.10.04.03 Presence
hēr(...)inne 05.10.04.03 Presence
hēræfter 05.11.07.04 Future, time to come
hērbeforan 05.11.07.03.02.02 The aforesaid
hērbūende 02.03.01 People
hērbufan 05.10.05.04.09.01.02 Front, beginning
hērcyme 16.01.01.04.02.02 Events associated with Christ

here 05.06.01 Devastation, laying waste; 12.04.02 A crowding together, assembly; 13.02.10.01.02.01 An armed force/band; 13.02.10.01.02.02 Armed forces; 13.02.10.01.02.02.03 Part of an army; 14.02.01.02.01 Open robbery, rapine, pillage
hēre 11.07.04 Superiority, pre-eminence, primacy
herebēacen 05.12.01.09.03.05 A lighthouse; 13.02.08.02 A standard, banner, ensign
herebeorg 04.05.03.03.01 Lodgings, quarters
herebeorgian 04.05.03.03.01 Lodgings, quarters
hereblēaþ 06.02.07.07 Cowardice, pusillanimity
herebrōga 06.01.08.06.03 Cause of fear, terror, horror
herebȳme 13.02.08.01 Battle-horn; 18.02.07.02.02.02 A trumpet
herebyrne 13.02.08.03.01.04 Coat of mail/corselet
herecirm 02.05.10.15.01 To raise (the voice), raise up (noise)
herecombol 13.02.08.02 A standard, banner, ensign
herecyst 13.02.10.01.02.01 An armed force/band
herefeld 13.02.02 Battle
herefeoh 13.02.05.01.02.02 Booty, spoils
herefēþa 13.02.10.01.02.01 An armed force/band
hereflȳme 06.02.07.07 Cowardice, pusillanimity; 13.02.10.02.02 A coward, deserter
herefolc 13.02.10.01.02.02 Armed forces
herefong 02.06.08.04 Bird of prey
hereford 05.12.01.03.03 A fordable place

herefugol 02.06.08.04 Bird of prey
heregang 13.02.03 To seek with active intent, attack; 13.02.03.01 An attack, assault
heregeatland 15.01.02.01 Inherited property
heregeatu 13.02.08 Military equipment; 15.01.02.01 Inherited property
heregild 15.03 Exaction of tax/tribute
heregrīma 13.02.08.03.01.02 A helmet
herehand 13.02.07 War-craft, art of war
herehlōþ 13.02.10.01.02.01 An armed force/band
herehorn 13.02.08.01 Battle-horn; 18.02.07.02.02.02 A trumpet
herehūþ 13.02.05.01.02.02 Booty, spoils
herelāf 13.02.05.01.02.02 Booty, spoils; 13.02.10.02.01 Survivors of a battle
herelic 13.02.09 Military style
herelof 07.08.10 Fame of courage, valour; 13.02.05.01 Victory
heremæcg 13.02.10.01 A man, warrior
heremægen 13.02.10.01.02.02 Armed forces
heremann 13.02.10 The military, soldiers
heremeþel 12.02.02 An assembly, meeting
herenes 07.04.04 Praise, acclamation, applause
herenett 13.02.08.03.01.04 Coat of mail/corselet
herenīþ 13.02 War
herenuma 13.02.05.02.01 Surrender, submission
herepād 13.02.08.03.01.04 Coat of mail/corselet
her(e)pæþ 05.12.01.03.01.03 A highway
herepæþford 05.12.01.03.03 A fordable place
hererǣs 13.02.01 A military expedition

hererǣswa 13.02.10.01.01 A commander, officer
hererēaf 13.02.05.01.02.02 Booty, spoils
hererinc 13.02.10.01 A man, warrior
heresceaft 13.02.08.04.01 A spear
heresceorp 13.02.08.03.01 Body armour, war gear
herescipe 13.02.10.01.02.01 An armed force/band
heresīþ 13.02.01 A military expedition
herespēd 13.02.05.01 Victory
herespel 18.02.07.01.01 A song, a poem to be sung or recited
herestrǣl 13.02.08.04.04.01 An arrow, dart, bolt
herestrǣt 05.12.01.03.01.03 A highway
hereswēg 02.05.10.03 Noise, tumult, uproar; 13.02.02 Battle
heresyrce 13.02.08.03.01.04 Coat of mail/corselet
heretēam 13.02.05.01.02.02 Booty, spoils; 14.02.01.02.01 Open robbery, rapine, pillage
heretēma 13.02.10.01.01 A commander, officer
heretoga 12.01.01.04 A leader, ruler; 12.01.01.05 A leader, administrator; 13.02.10.01.01 A commander, officer
hereþ 13.02.05.01.02.02 Booty, spoils
hereþrēat 13.02.10.01.02.01 An armed force/band
hereþrym 13.02.07.02 Order (of troops), array
herewǣd 13.02.08.03.01 Body armour, war gear
herewǣpen 13.02.08.04 Weapons, arms
herewǣsm 06.02.07.06 Courage, boldness, valour
herewǣþa 13.02.10.01 A man, warrior
hereweg 05.12.01.03.01.03 A highway

hereweorc 13.02 War
herewīc 04.05.03 A dwelling-place, abode, habitation; 13.02.07.04 A camp, encampment
herewīsa 13.02.10.01.01 A commander, officer
herewōp 02.05.10.15.01 To raise (the voice), raise up (noise)
hereword 07.04.04 Praise, acclamation, applause
herewōsa 13.02.10.01 A man, warrior
herewulf 13.02.10.01 A man, warrior
hergaþ 13.02.05.01.02.02 Booty, spoils; 14.02.01.02.01 Open robbery, rapine, pillage
hergendlic 07.04.04 Praise, acclamation, applause
hergere 07.04.04 Praise, acclamation, applause; 14.02.01.02.01 Open robbery, rapine, pillage
(ge)hergian (on) 13.02.03 To seek with active intent, attack
gehergian 13.02.05.01.02 To gain by fighting
hergiend 14.02.01.02.01 Open robbery, rapine, pillage
gehergod 14.05.08 Captivity
hergung 13.02.03 To seek with active intent, attack; 13.02.03.01 An attack, assault; 13.02.05.01.02.02 Booty, spoils; 14.02.01.02.01 Open robbery, rapine, pillage; 16.01.01.04.02.02 Events associated with Christ
(ge)herian 07.04.04 Praise, acclamation, applause; 16.02.04 Worship, honour, praise
herigend 07.07.03 Flattery
herigendlic 07.08.08 Nobleness, honour, glory
(ge)herigendlic 07.04.04.02 Laudable, praiseworthy
herigendlīce 07.04.04.02 Laudable, praiseworthy
herigendsang 18.02.07.01.01 A song, a poem to be sung or recited
herigweard 16.02.03.02.07.01 A priest of a church or minster
gehēring 02.05.10 Faculty of hearing
herlic 07.08.08 Nobleness, honour, glory
hērof 05.03 Source, origin
hēron 05.10.04.03 Presence
hērongēan 03.06.02.01 Contrariety, diversity
hērongemang 05.03 Source, origin; 05.11 A time, period of time
hērongemong 05.10.05.04.10 Among
hērtō 05.10.05 A space, span
herþan 02.04.06.04.01 Male genitalia
herþbelig 02.04.06.04.01 Male genitalia
herung 07.04.04 Praise, acclamation, applause; 16.02.04 Worship, honour, praise; 16.02.04.05.03 The hour or service of Lauds; 18.02.07.01.01 A song, a poem to be sung or recited
hērwiþ 05.11.07.02 The present (time)
hetan 13.02.03.01 An attack, assault
hete 08.01.03.09.03 Malevolence, malice; 08.01.03.09.04 Hatred; 14.05 Punishment
hetegrim 08.01.03.09.11 Hardheartedness, cruelty, severity
hetelic 08.01.03.09.03 Malevolence, malice; 08.01.03.09.10 Wrath, sternness, displeasure
hetelīce 05.08.02 Violence, force; 08.01.03.09.03 Malevolence, malice
heteniþ 08.01.03.09.03 Malevolence, malice
heterōf 08.01.03.09.04 Hatred

1070

heterūn 16.01.04.01 Sorcery using incantation
hetespræc 08.01.03.09.04 Hatred
hetesweng 05.06.09 Act of striking
heteþanc 08.01.03.09.03 Malevolence, malice
heteþancol 08.01.03.09.03 Malevolence, malice
hetlen 08.01.03.09.03 Malevolence, malice
hetol 05.08.02.01 (Of living creatures) fierceness, roughness; 08.01.03.07.04 Severity, harshness; 08.01.03.09.03 Malevolence, malice
hetollīce 05.08.02 Violence, force; 08.01.03.09.10 Wrath, sternness, displeasure
hetolnes 05.08.02.01 (Of living creatures) fierceness, roughness; 08.01.03.09.11 Hardheartedness, cruelty, severity
hettend 08.01.03.09.05 Enmity
heyning 05.10.05.04.11 A circle, circuit, circumference
hī geweorþan him betwēonum 14.04.04 An agreement, arrangement of dispute
hīce 02.06.08.07 Exotic bird
hīcemāse 02.06.08.05 Forest bird, wild-fowl
hicol 02.06.08.05 Forest bird, wild-fowl
hīd 04.02.03.03.02 A hide
hider 01 Earth, world; 05.10.04.03 Presence; 05.10.05.04.09 Side, quarter, direction
hider and geond 05.10.04.03 Presence
hider and þider 05.10.04.03 Presence
hidercyme 05.12.05.02.03 To arrive; 16.01.01.04.02.02 Events associated with Christ
hidere 05.10.04.03 Presence
hidergeond 05.10.04.03 Presence

hideror 05.10.05.01 A little way, no great distance
hiderryne 02.03.03.03.01 A native people
hidertōcyme 05.12.05.02.03 To arrive
hiderweard 05.10.04.03 Presence
hīdgild 15.03.02 A tax
hīdmǣlum 04.02.03.03.02 A hide
hidres þædres 05.10.04.03 Presence
hidres þidres 05.10.04.03 Presence
hīeg 04.01.02.01.04 Animal food, fodder; 04.02.04.03.02.03 Hay
hīeghūs 04.02.04.04.06 Barn
hīegsīþe 04.02.04.06.12 A scythe, sickle
hīehþu 05.10.05.03.03 Height, loftiness, sublimity; 16.01.02.02 Glory/majesty of heaven
hīehþ(u) 16.01.02 The heavens, sky; 11.07.04 Superiority, pre-eminence, primacy
(ge)hield 11.10.01.01 Preservation from injury/destruction; 11.10.02.02.01 Care, interest in
gehield 05.11 A time, period of time; 11.10.02.02 Watchful care, keeping guard; 12.07.02 Observance, keeping; 13.02.04 Defence, guard, protection
(ge)hieldan 05.10.05.04.04 A descent, slope, incline; 05.12.05.13.02 To bow, bend down
gehieldelic 11.10 Safety, safeness
gehieldnes 12.07.02 Observance, keeping
hielfe 17.03 Implements, tools, etc.
hielfling 15.01.04 Coinage, money
hielto 02.08.04.04 State of being crippled
hīenan 07.09.02 Disgrace, shaming, humiliation
(ge)hīenan 05.06 Destruction, dissolution, loss, breaking; 07.09.03 Infamy, ignominy, shame; 12.05.06.02.03 Trouble, disturbance;

12.05.06.04 A trampling upon, subjection; 13.02.05.01.01 To overcome, conquer; 14.03.03.01 Accusation
gehīenan 07.09.02 Disgrace, shaming, humiliation; 14.03.03.09.01 Unfavourable judgement, condemnation
gehīene 05.09 Weakness
hīenend 14.03.03.01 Accusation
hīennes 05.06.01 Devastation, laying waste; 12.05.06.04 A trampling upon, subjection
hīenþ(o) 02.02.04.04.03 Putting to death; 02.08.04 Hurt, injury, damage; 07.09 Shame, disgrace; 15.01.06 Poverty, indigence
hīeran tō 10.01 Fact of belonging, possession by; 12.05.06.04.02 Submission, subjection, obedience; 14.01.05 Service, obligation, duty
(ge)hīeran 02.05.10 Faculty of hearing; 06.01.06.01 Knowledge, cognizance, knowing; 09.07.04.01 Confirmation, agreement; 12.01.01.08 Service; 12.01.01.12.01 Obedience, service
gehīeran 14.03.03 Law, action of the courts
gehīeran Godes drēamas 16.02.04.07.04.01 The service of the mass
(ge)hierdan 06.02.07.01 Strength, fortitude
gehierdan 06.02.07.04.01 Obduracy; 17.02.04.03.03 Smelting, heating, scorification
hierde 04.02.05.01.02 To tend, herd; 10 Having, owning, possession; 11.10.01 Protection, safekeeping; 12.01.01.04 A leader, ruler; 16.01.01.01.01 The Almighty; 16.02.03.02.07 A priest, cleric
hierdebelig 04.02.05.06.02 A shepherd
hierdebōc 16.02.05.10.13 Other books
hierdecnapa 04.02.05.06.02 A shepherd
hierdelēas 04.02.05.06.01 A cowherd; 16.02.03.02.07 A priest, cleric
hierdelic 16.02.03.02.07 A priest, cleric
hierdeman 04.02.05.01.02 To tend, herd; 04.02.05.06.02 A shepherd
hierdewyrt 02.07.11 Plants/flowers (alphabetical order)
hierdnes 05.11 A time, period of time
(ge)hierdnes 11.10.02.02 Watchful care, keeping guard; 11.10.02.02.01 Care, interest in
hīereman/hīeringmann 16.02.03.03.05 A layman
hīeremann 12.01.01.07 A follower; 12.01.01.08.01 A servant, attendant
hīerend 12.05.06.04 A trampling upon, subjection
(ge)hīerend 02.05.10 Faculty of hearing
gehīerendlic 02.05.10.01 Thing heard
hīerigmann 12.01.01.08.01 A servant, attendant
hīeringmann 12.01.01.07 A follower
hīernes 12.01.01.12.01 Obedience, service; 12.06.02 District, province; 14.01.05 Service, obligation, duty
(ge)hīernes 02.05.10 Faculty of hearing
gehīernes 02.05.10.01 Thing heard
hierstan 03.01.09.02.01 Fire, burning
(ge)hierstan 04.01.02.02.05.03 Frying/roasting; 08.01.01.01.03 An incitement, cause of strong feeling
hierste 04.01.02.02.06 Kitchen; 04.01.02.02.06.01 Cooking vessel/pot
hierstepanne/hierstingpanne 04.01.02.02.06.01 Cooking vessel/pot

hiersting 03.01.09.02.01 Fire, burning; 04.01.02.02.05.03 Frying/roasting; 04.01.02.02.06.01 Cooking vessel/pot
hierstinghlāf 04.01.02.01.07.03.02 Loaf
(ge)hīersum 12.01.01.12.01 Obedience, service
hīersumian 16.02.01 Faith
(ge)hīersumian 12.01.01.08 Service; 12.01.01.12.01 Obedience, service; 12.05.06.04 A trampling upon, subjection
hīersumlic 12.01.01.12.01 Obedience, service
hīersumnes 07.07 Humility; 12.01.01.12.01 Obedience, service; 12.05.06.04.02 Submission, subjection, obedience; 16.02.03.03 A religious
(ge)hiertan 06.02.07.06.01 Emboldening, encouragement
gehiertan 02.01.03.03.05 Rebirth/regeneration; 02.08.12 Healing, curing; 11.10.02.02.01 Care, interest in; 16.02.01.12 Spirituality
hierting 02.08.12.01 Medical care, treatment
hierwan 07.05 Disrespect, irreverence; 07.05.03.02 Calumny, slander, insult
(ge)hierwan 07.05.02 Contempt; 08.01.03.07.02 Misery, trouble, affliction; 16.02.04.14.01 Blasphemy
hierwend 16.02.04.14.01 Blasphemy
hierwendlic 07.05.02 Contempt
hierwing 16.02.04.14.01 Blasphemy
hierwnes 07.05.02 Contempt; 16.02.04.14.01 Blasphemy
hīeþ(u) 01.01.02.01.02.02 Hill, mountain
hīewestān 04.05.01.01 Masonry, building in stone
hīewet 04.05.01.01 Masonry, building in stone; 17.02.04.02.01 Cutting, hewing, shaping
hig 06.01.08.05.01 Amazement, astonishment, wonder, admiration
hīgendlīce 05.11.07.01 Contemporary, coeval
higera 02.06.08.05 Forest bird, wild-fowl
hīgian (æfter/tō) 11.03 Endeavour
hīglā 08.01.03.04.01 Complaint, lamentation
hī(g)na ealdor 02.03.03 A family, household
hīgþ 11.03 Endeavour
hīgung 11.03 Endeavour
hild 13.02 War; 13.02.02 Battle
hildbedd 02.02.02 Liability to death, mortality
hildcyst 06.02.07.06 Courage, boldness, valour
hilde dǣlan 13.02 War
hildebil 13.02.08.04.03 A sword
hildeblāc 02.02.03.01 In process of dying
hildebord 13.02.08.03.01.06 A shield
hildecalla 13.02.10 The military, soldiers
hildecorþor 13.02.10.01.02.01 An armed force/band
hildedēofol 16.01.05.02.02 Other terms for devils
hildedēor 06.02.07.06 Courage, boldness, valour
hild(e)freca 13.02.10.01 A man, warrior
hildefrōfor 13.02.08.04 Weapons, arms
hildegeatwe 13.02.08.03.01 Body armour, war gear
hildegesa 06.01.08.06.03 Cause of fear, terror, horror
hildegicel 02.02.04.01 Cause/occasion of death
hildegiest 08.01.03.09.05 Enmity
hildegrāp 10.04.02 To grasp, take hold of

hildeheard 06.02.07.06.02 Boldness
hildehlemm 13.02.02 Battle
hildelēoma 03.01.09.02.01.01 A kind of fire; 13.02.08.04.03 A sword
hildeleoþ 13.02.07.03 A war song
hildemēce 13.02.08.04.03 A sword
hildemecg 13.02.10.01 A man, warrior
hildenǣdre 13.02.08.04.04.01 An arrow, dart, bolt
hildepīl 13.02.08.04.01 A spear
hilderǣs 13.02.03 To seek with active intent, attack
hilderand 13.02.08.03.01.06 A shield
hilderinc 13.02.10.01 A man, warrior
hildesǣd 02.05.03.02 Weariness
hildesceorp 13.02.08.03.01 Body armour, war gear
hildescūr 02.08.03 Pain, bodily discomfort
hildeserce 13.02.08.03.01.04 Coat of mail/corselet
hildesetl 04.02.05.06.05.03.04 Saddle
hildespell 13.02.07.03 A war song
hildestapa 13.02.10.01 A man, warrior
hildestrengo 13.02.07 War-craft, art of war
hildeswāt 03.01.15 Vapour, air
hildeswēg 02.05.10.03 Noise, tumult, uproar; 13.02.02 Battle
hildetorht 03.01.12 Brightness, light
hildetux 02.06.01.02 Head
hildeþremma 13.02.10.01 A man, warrior
hildeþrymm 06.02.07.06 Courage, boldness, valour
hildeþrȳþ 06.02.07.06 Courage, boldness, valour
hildewǣpen 13.02.08.04 Weapons, arms
hildewīsa 13.02.10.01.01 A commander, officer
hildewōma 02.05.10.03 Noise, tumult, uproar; 13.02.02 Battle
hildewrǣsn 14.05.07 Binding, fastening with bonds
hildewulf 06.02.07.06 Courage, boldness, valour; 13.02.10.01 A man, warrior
hildfrom 06.02.07.06 Courage, boldness, valour
hildfruma 13.02.10.01.01 A commander, officer
hildlata 06.02.07.07 Cowardice, pusillanimity; 13.02.10.02.02 A coward, deserter
hildþracu 13.02.02 Battle
gehilmed 02.07.02.06 A leaf
hilt 13.02.08.04.03.01.01 Hilt of sword
(ge)hilte 13.02.08.04.03.01.01 Hilt of sword
hiltecumbor 12.01.01.03 Symbols of power
hilted 13.02.08.04.03.01.01 Hilt of sword
hilting 13.02.08.04.03 A sword
hiltlēas 13.02.08.04.03.01.01 Hilt of sword
hiltsweord 13.02.08.04.03 A sword
hind 02.06.03.01.06 Deer, hart
hindan 05.10.05.04.09.02 Hinder part, rear; 05.12.05.10 To go behind, follow
hindan offaran 05.12.05.07 To go beyond, pass
hindanweard 05.10.05.04.09.02 Hinder part, rear
hindberge 02.07.09.02 Particular fruits (alphabetical order)
hindbrēr 02.07.09.02 Particular fruits (alphabetical order)
hindcealf 02.06.03.01.06 Deer, hart
hindema 05.11.07.04.02 (Of time) later/latter

hinder 05.10.05.04.02.03 Laid below; 05.10.05.04.09.02 Hinder part, rear; 12.08.06.02.03 (Of persons) wicked, evil-doing
hindergēap 11.04.02.01.01 Cunning, craft, craftiness, guile, wile
hindergenga 02.06.06.04.01.02 Crab; 16.02.01.07 Apostasy
hinderhōc 06.01.07.04.02 Fraud, deceit, trick, trickery
hinderling 07.03.04 A wretch, poor creature
hindernes 12.08.06.02 Wickedness, evil
hinderscipe 12.08.06.02 Wickedness, evil
hinderþēostru 16.01.05 Hell, lower world, abode of the dead
hinderweard 05.12.03.02 Slowness
hindeweard 05.10.05.04.09.02 Hinder part, rear
hindfald 04.02.05.06.09 An enclosure for wild animals
hindhæleþe 02.07.11 Plants/flowers (alphabetical order)
(ge)hindrian 11.11.02 A hindrance
hinfūs 02.02.03.01 In process of dying
hingang 02.02 Death
hinsīþ 02.02 Death
hinsīþgryre 06.01.08.06.03 Cause of fear, terror, horror
hīon 02.04.06.09 Brain
hīred 02.03.02 Family/household; 02.03.03 A family, household; 04.05.03.02 A human habitation; 12.04.01.01 A company of people, fellowship, society; 16.02.03.03 A religious
hīredcniht 12.01.01.08.01 A servant, attendant; 12.02.02 An assembly, meeting
hīredcūþ 11.05.01 Familiarity

hīredgerēfa 12.02.02 An assembly, meeting
hīredlēof 08.01.02.02.01 A favourite, loved one
hīredlic 11.05.01 Familiarity
hīredmann 02.03.03.01 Body of retainers, household; 12.01.01.07 A follower
hīredprēost 16.02.03.02.07.01 A priest of a church or minster; 16.02.03.02.08 A (domestic) chaplain
hīredwīfmann 02.03.03 A family, household
hīredwist 11.05.01 Familiarity
hislic 03.06.03 Congruity, fitness, suitability
(ge)hittan 05.12.05.02.01 To come upon, meet with
hiþful 08.01.03.09.04 Hatred
hīw 02.05.09.07 Form, appearance, aspect; 03.01.14 A colour; 03.04 Form, kind, nature, character; 05.04 Fate, lot, fortune, destiny; 05.10.06 Form, shape; 06.01.02.01 An imaginary form, fancy; 06.01.07.04.04.02 Pretence, feigning, dissimulation; 07.10 Beauty, fairness; 09.01.01 A speech, what is said, words; 09.03.02.02.01 A part of speech, form
hīwan 02.03.03 A family, household; 12.01.01.08.01 A servant, attendant; 16.02.03.03 A religious
hīwbeorht 07.10 Beauty, fairness
hīwcund 11.05.01 Familiarity
hīwcūþ 06.01.06.01.01.01 Acquaintance, knowledge; 12.01.01.08 Service
hīwcūþa 02.03.03 A family, household

hīwcūþlic 06.01.06.01.01.01
  Acquaintance, knowledge; 11.05.01
  Familiarity
hīwcūþlīce 08.01.02.03.03 In a friendly
  manner, kindly
gehīwcūþlician 06.01.06.01.01.01
  Acquaintance, knowledge; 11.05.01
  Familiarity
hīwcūþnes 06.01.06.01.01.01
  Acquaintance, knowledge; 11.05.01
  Familiarity
hīwcūþrǣdnes 06.01.06.01.01.01
  Acquaintance, knowledge; 11.05.01
  Familiarity
gehīwed 02.04.04.01 Having a certain
  complexion; 06.01.07.04.04.02
  Pretence, feigning, dissimulation;
  09.03.04.02.01 A figure
gehīwendlic 09.03.04.02.01 A figure
hīwere 06.01.07.04 Deception;
  06.01.07.04.03 Untruth, falsehood;
  06.01.07.04.04.02 Pretence, feigning,
  dissimulation
hīwfæger 07.10.01 Elegance, beauty,
  comeliness
hīwfæst 07.10.01 Elegance, beauty,
  comeliness
hīwgedāl 12.09.04 Divorce
hīwgedāles bōc 14.03.03 Law, action of
  the courts
hīwian 06.01.07.04.04.02 Pretence,
  feigning, dissimulation
hīwian on 05.13.01 Transformation,
  taking another shape
(ge)hīwian 05.13.01 Transformation,
  taking another shape;
  06.01.07.04.04.02 Pretence, feigning,
  dissimulation; 12.09.02 Marriage
  ceremony; 17.02.04 Trade, calling,
  craft, aptitude
gehīwian 03.01.14 A colour
hīwiend 17.02.04 Trade, calling, craft,
  aptitude
hīwisc 02.03.03 A family, household;
  04.02.03.03.02 A hide
hīwisclīce 16.02.03.03 A religious
gehīwlǣcan 03.01.14 A colour; 17.02.04
  Trade, calling, craft, aptitude
hīwlēas 03.01.14.02 Pallor, absence of
  colour; 05.10.06.01 Not formed,
  without form
hīwlic 07.10 Beauty, fairness;
  09.03.04.02.01 A figure; 12.09
  Marriage, state of marriage
hīwnes 07.10 Beauty, fairness
gehīwodlīce 09.03.02.03.01.01.01 Case
hīwrǣden 02.03.03 A family, household;
  02.03.03.02 A race, tribe; 16.02.03.03
  A religious
hīwscipe 02.03.03 A family, household;
  04.02.03.03.02 A hide
hīwsprǣc 09.01.02.02 Dissembling
  speech
hīwung 05.10.06 Form, shape; 05.13.01
  Transformation, taking another shape;
  06.01.02.01 An imaginary form,
  fancy; 06.01.07.04.02 Fraud, deceit,
  trick, trickery; 06.01.07.04.03
  Untruth, falsehood; 06.01.07.04.04.02
  Pretence, feigning, dissimulation;
  09.03.04.02.01 A figure; 09.06.01 To
  relate, recount, tell; 12.09 Marriage,
  state of marriage; 16.02.01.11.01
  Pretence of goodness or piety
(ge)hīwung 05.05 Constitution, founding
  (e.g. of world)
gehīwung 17.02.04.02.01 Cutting,
  hewing, shaping; 17.02.05.04 An
  image, figure

hlacerian 07.05.04 Mockery, derision, scorn
hlacerung 07.05.04 Mockery, derision, scorn
hladan 04.05 Building, construction; 05.10.06.03.02 Hollow; 10.01.02 Acquisition
hladan oroþ 02.04.06.07.05 To breathe
(ge)hladan 03.03.06.02 Fullness; 17.02.04.02.03 Carrying, carriage (of materials); 17.02.04.02.04 Leading/conducting of water
gehladen 03.03.06.02 Fullness
hladung 04.01.03 Drinking; 05.12.02.05 To pull, drag, draw
hlæd 17.02.04.02.03 Carrying, carriage (of materials)
hlæddisc 04.01.02.02.06.05.01 Dish for food/serving-dish
hlædel 04.01.02.02.06.05.05 Ladle/scoop
hlæden 04.01.03.05.04.03 A bucket, pail; 17.02.04.02.04 Leading/conducting of water
hlæder 04.05.02.11 A staircase; 04.05.04.04 A ladder, set of steps
hlæderstæf 04.05.04.04 A ladder, set of steps
hlæderwyrt 02.07.11 Plants/flowers (alphabetical order)
hlædfæt 04.01.03.05.04.03 A bucket, pail; 17.02.04.02.04 Leading/conducting of water
hlædhweogl 17.03.01 A wheel
hlædrede 04.05.04.04 A ladder, set of steps
hlædtrendel 17.03.01 A wheel
hlæfdige 02.03.03 A family, household; 11.05.02.02.01.01 Courteous forms of address; 12.01.01.04.01 A royal leader; 12.01.01.06.08 A person of rank, elder, great man; 16.01.02.05.02.01 Mary, queen of heaven; 16.02.03.03.01.02 An abbess
(ge)hlæg 07.05.04 Mockery, derision, scorn
hlænan 05.10.05.04.04 A descent, slope, incline
hlæne 02.04.02.02 Lean, thin, slender
gehlæned 02.04.02.02 Lean, thin, slender
(ge)hlænian 02.04.02.02 Lean, thin, slender
hlænnes 02.04.02.02 Lean, thin, slender; 06.01.05.03.02.01 Foolishness, lightmindedness
gehlænsed 02.04.02.02 Lean, thin, slender
(ge)hlænsian 02.04.02.02 Lean, thin, slender
gehlænsian 12.08.06.01.04.01 To mislead, seduce, lead astray
hlæst 17.02.04.02.03 Carrying, carriage (of materials)
gehlæst 07.10.03 An adornment, decoration, ornament
(ge)hlæstan 17.02.04.02.03 Carrying, carriage (of materials)
hlæsting 15.03.01 Toll
hlæstscip 05.12.01.09.03.01.01 Kind of ship
hlæw 01.01.02.01.02.02.01 Hill; 01.01.02.01.03.01 Cave; 02.02.05.01.01 A grave, burial place, sepulchre; 04.05.03.02.02.01 Dwellings in particular places; 16.02.01.06.01 Belief/practice of heathen people
hlāf 03 Material, matter, substance; 04.01.02.01 Food/sustenance; 04.01.02.01.07.03 Bread; 04.01.02.01.07.03.02 Loaf;

04.01.02.01.07.03.03 Piece of bread; 04.01.02.04.01 Meal; 16.02.01.12 Spirituality; 16.02.05.09.01 Eucharistic elements
hlāf forþsetenisse 16.02.01.08.04 Jewish seasons/feasts
hlāfǣta 12.01.01.08.01 A servant, attendant
hlāfas forsetne 16.02.01.08.04 Jewish seasons/feasts
hlāfas getemeseda 16.02.01.08.04 Jewish seasons/feasts
hlāfbrytta 04.01.02.03.01 Service in kitchen; 12.01.01.08.01 A servant, attendant
hlāfgang 04.01.01 Eating; 16.02.04.07.04 Communion/eucharist
hlāfgebrece/-gebroc 04.01.02.01.07.03.03 Piece of bread
hlāfhwǣte 04.01.02.01.03.01 Wheat
hlāflēast 04.01.01.03 Hunger
hlāfmæssan dæg 16.02.04.04.02.01.04 Other feasts
hlāfmæsse 16.02.04.04.02.01.04 Other feasts
hlāfmæssedæg 16.02.04.04.02.01.04 Other feasts
hlāfmæssetīd 05.11.02.01.02 A time of celebration; 16.02.04.04.02.01.04 Other feasts
hlāfofen 04.01.02.02.06 Kitchen
hlāford 02.03.03 A family, household; 10 Having, owning, possession; 11.05.02.02.01.01 Courteous forms of address; 12.01.01.04 A leader, ruler; 12.01.01.04.01.01 Kings and queens; 12.01.01.04.02 A lord, master; 12.01.01.05 A leader, administrator; 12.01.01.06.08 A person of rank, elder, great man; 12.09 Marriage, state of marriage; 13.02.10.01.01 A commander, officer; 16.01.01 God, the Lord; 16.02.03.02.01 A high priest, chief bishop, etc. (general); 16.02.03.02.07 A priest, cleric; 17.02.01 Management of work
hlāforddōm 12.01 Power, control, sway; 12.01.01 Authority
hlāfordgift 15.01.02 Gift, transfer of property
hlāfordhold 12.01.01.12 Loyalty
hlāfordhyldo 12.01.01.12 Loyalty
hlāfording 12.01.01.04.01 A royal leader; 12.01.01.06.08 A person of rank, elder, great man
hlāfordlēas 08.01.03.06 Adversity, affliction; 12.04.04 Solitude
hlāfordlic 12.01.01.06.05 Nobility, noble condition
hlāfordscipas 16.01.02.05.01 An angel
hlāfordscipe 12.01.01 Authority
hlāfordsearu 12.01.01.12.04 Treachery
hlāfordsōcn 14.01.03.01 Sanctuary
hlāfordswice 12.01.01.12.04 Treachery
hlāfordswīcung 12.01.01.12.04.01 Betrayal
hlāfordsyrwung 12.01.01.12.04.01 Betrayal
hlāfordþrimm 12.01 Power, control, sway
hlāfrǣce 04.01.02.02.06 Kitchen
hlāfsēnung 16.02.01.10.02.01 A blessing, invocation of divine favour
hlāfweard 12.01.01.05 A leader, administrator
hlagol 08.01.01.03.07.01 Laughter
hlagolende 02.05.10.04 To resound
hlammgeat 05.10.05.04.14.02 An opening/space in an enclosure

hlanc 02.04.02.02 Lean, thin, slender; 03.03.08 Emptiness
hland 02.04.06.06.07 Urine
hleahterful 07.05.04 Mockery, derision, scorn
hleahterlic 08.01.01.03.07.01 Laughter
hleahtor 07.05.04 Mockery, derision, scorn; 08.01.01.03.07.01 Laughter
hleahtorbǣre 08.01.01.03.07.01 Laughter
hleahtorsmiþ 08.01.01.03.07.01 Laughter
hleahtrian 07.05.04 Mockery, derision, scorn
hlēapan 03.03.04.03 Growth, increase; 05.12.05.12.01 To reach up; 18.02.04 Dancing
(ge)hlēapan 05.12.03.01.01 Quick movement or movements
(ge)hlēapan (ūp on) 05.12.01.05 To ride (on horse, etc.)
gehlēapan 01.01.03.03 Flow/flowing; 05.12.05.12.01 To reach up
hlēapende 18.02.04 Dancing
hlēapere 05.12.01.05 To ride (on horse, etc.); 09.06.02.01.06.01 A messenger; 12.06.05.01 State of exile, banishment; 13.02.10.01.02.02.02 Branch of army; 18.02.04 Dancing
hlēapestre 18.02.04 Dancing
hlēapettan 05.12.05.12.01 To reach up
hlēapung 18.02.04 Dancing
hlec 05.06.02.01.01 A crack
hlecan 03.03.06.01 A whole formed by joining
hlēda 04.05.04.01 A bench, seat
hleglende 02.05.10.04 To resound
hlem 02.05.10.01 Thing heard
hlemman 02.05.10.07 A crashing, noise
hlenc 01.01.02.01.02.02 Hill, mountain

gehlencan 05.10.05.04.08.01 A bend
hlence 13.02.08.04.01 A spear
hlenortēar 02.07.11 Plants/flowers (alphabetical order)
hlēo 05.10.05.04.12 The condition of being covered; 11.10.01 Protection, safekeeping; 11.10.01.02 Refuge, help, shelter
hlēobord 09.03.07.07 A book
hlēoburh 12.06.02.01 A township
hlēohræscnes 05.06.01 Devastation, laying waste
hleomoc(-e) 02.07.11 Plants/flowers (alphabetical order)
hlēonaþ 11.10.01.02 Refuge, help, shelter
hlēor 02.04.03.01.03 Face; 02.04.03.01.03.05 Cheek
hlēorbān 02.04.05.04.02.02 Cheek/chin bones
hlēorberg 13.02.08.03.01.02.01 Parts of a helmet
hlēorbolster 04.05.04.05.01 Bedding (e.g. of straw)
hlēordropa 08.01.03.04.02 Shedding of tears
hlēorræscnes 05.06.09 Act of striking
hlēorsceamu 07.09.01.01 Reddening with shame, confusion
hlēorslæge 05.06.09 Act of striking
hlēortorht 07.10 Beauty, fairness
hlēosceorp 04.04.07.01 Mode of dressing, fashion
hlēotan 12.02 A public office; 16.01.04.06.02 Prognostication by casting lots
(ge)hlēotan 10.01.01.01 Receiving, gaining, getting
gehlēotan 10.01 Fact of belonging, possession by; 10.01.02 Acquisition

hlēotend 10.01.01.01 Receiving, gaining, getting
hlēoþere 09.03.04 Rhetoric, art of exposition
hlēoþor 02.05.10 Faculty of hearing; 02.05.10.01 Thing heard; 02.05.10.13 Sound of bell/musical instrument; 02.05.10.15 Voice, cry (of living creature); 02.05.10.15.07 Voice, note (of a bird); 09 Speech, vocal utterance; 18.02.07.01 Singing, song
gehlēoþor 18.02.07 Music
hlēoþorcwide 09 Speech, vocal utterance; 09.03.05.01.01 Poetry; 18.02.07.01.01 A song, a poem to be sung or recited
hlēoþorcyme 13.02.01 A military expedition
hlēoþorstede 12.02.02.01 Place of conference or assembly
hlēoþrian 02.05.10.01 Thing heard; 02.05.10.04 To resound; 09.01 To speak, exercise faculty of speech
hlēoþriende 02.05.10.01 Thing heard
hlēoþrung 07.05.01 Censure, reproof, rebuke; 18.02.07.01.01 A song, a poem to be sung or recited; 18.02.07.02.02.02 A trumpet
(ge)hlēow 03.01.09.01 Warmth, heat
hlēowan 03.01.09.01 Warmth, heat
gehlēowan 02.08.12 Healing, curing; 16.02.01.12 Spirituality
hlēowdrihten 11.10.02.02.01 Care, interest in
hlēowe 03.01.09.01 Warmth, heat
hlēowfæst 03.01.09.01 Warmth, heat; 11.10.01.02 Refuge, help, shelter
hlēowfeþre 11.10.02.02.01 Care, interest in
hlēowlora 11.10.02.02.01 Care, interest in

hlēowmǣg 02.03.02.03.06.01 Kinsman, relative
hlēownes 01.03.01.01 Hot, fine weather
hlēowstede 11.10.01.02 Refuge, help, shelter
hlēowstōl 11.10.01.02 Refuge, help, shelter
hlēowþ 01.03.01.01 Hot, fine weather; 03.01.09.01 Warmth, heat; 11.10.01 Protection, safekeeping; 11.10.01.02 Refuge, help, shelter
hlēowung 11.10.01.02 Refuge, help, shelter
gehlēþa 12.04.01 A fellow, companion, associate, comrade
hlid 05.10.05.04.12 The condition of being covered; 05.10.05.04.14.02 An opening/space in an enclosure
hlidfæst 05.10.05.04.15 Closure, being closed
hlidgeat 04.02.05.03 A park, enclosure for animals; 05.10.05.04.14.02 An opening/space in an enclosure
gehlidod 05.10.05.04.15 Closure, being closed
hliehhan 08.01.01.03.07 Joyous sound, mirth; 08.01.01.03.07.01 Laughter
hliehhan tō bismere/on bismer 07.05.04 Mockery, derision, scorn
(ge)hliehhan 07.05.04 Mockery, derision, scorn
hliehhende 08.01.01.03.07.01 Laughter
hlīep 05.12.05.12.01 To reach up
hlīep(e) 01.01.03.01.01.06 Waterfall; 05.12.01.03.03 A fordable place
hlīepgeat 05.10.05.04.14.02 An opening/space in an enclosure
hlīet 05.04 Fate, lot, fortune, destiny; 10.03.07 Distribution; 16.01.04.06.02 Prognostication by casting lots

hlīf 04.04.10.01 A ring (for finger, arm, neck)
hlifende 05.10.05.03.03 Height, loftiness, sublimity
hlifian 05.10.05.03.03 Height, loftiness, sublimity
hlīgan 05.03.01.03 Reason, cause
hlimman 02.05.10.04 To resound
hlimme 01.01.03.01.01.05 Torrent
hlin 02.07.03.05 Particular trees/shrubs (alphabetical order)
hlinbed 04.05.04.05 A bed, bedstead
hlinc 01.01.02.01.02.01 Rising ground, eminence; 04.02.03.02.01 A strip for ploughing; 05.10.05.04.11.01 A bound, limit
hlincræw 05.10.05.04.11.01 A bound, limit
hlīnduru 04.05.02.12 Gate/doorway of a building
hlinian 05.10.05.04.02.03.02 Reclining, rest; 08.01.02.01 Favour, kindness, grace
(ge)hlinian 04.01.01 Eating; 05.10.05.04.02.03.02 Reclining, rest
hliniend 05.10.05.04.02.03.02 Reclining, rest
hliniende 05.10.05.04.02.03.02 Reclining, rest
hlīnreced 14.05.08.01 Prison, confinement, durance
hlīnscu(w)a 03.01.13 Darkness, obscurity
gehlinung 05.10.05.04.02.03.02 Reclining, rest
(ge)hlīowan 11.10.01.02 Refuge, help, shelter
hlīowsian 11.10.01.02 Refuge, help, shelter
hlīpcumb 01.01.02.01.03.03 Valley
hlīpe 05.12.01.05 To ride (on horse, etc.)

hlīsa 07.04.04.01 Approbation, applause; 07.08 Reputation, fame; 07.08.09 Renown, fame, glory; 09.06.02.01.05.01 To spread, make known, proclaim, celebrate; 16.01.01.01.01.02 Glory
hlīsbǣre 07.08.09 Renown, fame, glory
hlīsēadig 07.08.09 Renown, fame, glory
hlīsēadignes 07.08.09 Renown, fame, glory
hlīsful 07.04.01 (Of persons) worth/value, worthiness; 07.08.09 Renown, fame, glory; 12.08.02.02 Righteousness, rectitude
hlīsfullīce 07.02.04.03 Nobleness, excellence, nobility, magnificence
hlīsig 07.08.09 Renown, fame, glory
hlīþ 01.01.02.01.02.02 Hill, mountain; 01.01.02.01.02.02.03 Slope
hlīwe/hlīg 11.10.01.02 Refuge, help, shelter
hloccetung 08.01.03.04.04.01 Sighing, groaning
hlocettan 08.01.03.04.04.01 Sighing, groaning
hlōse 04.02.05.06.04.01 A piggery
hlosnere 02.05.10 Faculty of hearing; 06.01.06.02.03.02 Discipleship
hlosnian 02.05.10 Faculty of hearing; 06.01.08.05.01 Amazement, astonishment, wonder, admiration
hlosniende 02.05.10 Faculty of hearing; 06.01.08.05.01 Amazement, astonishment, wonder, admiration; 09.05 Curiosity
hlōsstede 04.02.05.06.04.01 A piggery
hlot 05.04 Fate, lot, fortune, destiny; 10.01.03 A sharing, participation; 15.03 Exaction of tax/tribute;

16.01.04.06.02 Prognostication by casting lots
hlot/hlyte sendan 16.01.04.06.02 Prognostication by casting lots
hlot weorpan 16.01.04.06.02 Prognostication by casting lots
(ge)hlot 16.01.04.06.02 Prognostication by casting lots
gehlot 07 Judgement, forming of opinion; 10.03.07 Distribution; 14.03.03.09 A sentence, judgement, ruling
(ge)hlotland 15.01.02.01 Inherited property
hlōþ 12.04.01.01 A company of people, fellowship, society; 13.02.05.01.02.02 Booty, spoils; 14.02.01.02 Wrongful taking, theft
hlōþbōt 14.05.04 A penalty, punishment
hlōþere 14.02.01.02 Wrongful taking, theft
hlōþgecrod 01.03.01.06 Cloud
hlōþian 14.02.01.02.01 Open robbery, rapine, pillage
hlōþsliht 02.02.04.04 Manslaughter, homicide; 14.02.01.01 Types of crime
gehlōw 02.05.10.05 Roaring, raging
hlōwan 02.05.10.01 Thing heard; 02.05.10.15.06 A roar, howl, etc.
hlōwung 02.05.10.05 Roaring, raging
hlūd 02.05.10.02 Noise, din; 09.01.02.01 Excessive fluency, loquacity
hlūdclipol 02.05.10.03 Noise, tumult, uproar
hlūde 02.05.10.02 Noise, din
hlūdnes 02.05.10.02 Noise, din
hlūdstefne 18.02.07.02.02.02 A trumpet
hlūdswēge 02.05.10.02 Noise, din
hlūtor 01.03.01.01 Hot, fine weather; 03.01.12 Brightness, light; 04.06.01.09 To cleanse, remove impurity from (an object); 06.01.05.01.01 Clear to the understanding, plain; 06.01.05.02 Intelligence; 07.02.04.03 Nobleness, excellence, nobility, magnificence; 07.08.07 Glory, splendour, magnificence; 08.01.01.03.01 Freedom from trouble, comfort, security; 12.08.04 Purity, moral cleanness
hlūtorlīce 06.01.05.01.01 Clear to the understanding, plain; 12.08.04 Purity, moral cleanness
hlūtorlicnes 12.08.04 Purity, moral cleanness
hlūtornes 12.08.04 Purity, moral cleanness
hlūtre 03.01.12 Brightness, light; 06.01.05.02 Intelligence; 08.01.01.03.01 Freedom from trouble, comfort, security
hlūtrost 03.01.12 Brightness, light
hlūttor ǣg 04.01.02.01.02.08 Egg
hlūttor dæg 05.11.04.01 Day (not night)
hlūttor pic 03.01.17.06 Resin, tar, gum
hlūttrian 04.06.01.10 To separate objects already connected, unmix; 06.01.05.01.01 Clear to the understanding, plain
(ge)hlūttrian 04.06.01.09 To cleanse, remove impurity from (an object)
gehlūttrod 04.01.02.02.05.02 To boil; 04.01.03.05.01.01 Wine; 04.06.01.09 To cleanse, remove impurity from (an object)
hlȳd 09.06.02.01.05.01 To spread, make known, proclaim, celebrate
(ge)hlȳd 02.05.10.03 Noise, tumult, uproar

gehlȳd 02.05.10.15 Voice, cry (of living creature); 02.05.10.15.01 To raise (the voice), raise up (noise); 11.05.02.03 Indecorum, impropriety, unseemliness; 12.05.02.01 Lack of peacefulness

hlȳda 05.11.03.01.03.01 Specific months

hlȳdan 02.05.10.02 Noise, din; 02.05.10.15.01 To raise (the voice), raise up (noise); 02.05.10.15.06 A roar, howl, etc.

hlȳde 01.01.03.01.01.05 Torrent

hlȳdende 02.05.10.03 Noise, tumult, uproar; 09.01.02.01 Excessive fluency, loquacity; 12.05.02.01 Lack of peacefulness

hlȳdig 09.01.02.01 Excessive fluency, loquacity

hlȳding 02.05.10.03 Noise, tumult, uproar

hlynn 01.01.03.01.01.05 Torrent; 01.01.03.01.01.06 Waterfall

(ge)hlynn 02.05.10.02 Noise, din

hlynnan 02.05.10.04 To resound

hlynsian 02.05.10.04 To resound

hlȳrian 02.04.06.07.05 To breathe

hlysnan 02.05.10 Faculty of hearing

hlysnende 02.05.10 Faculty of hearing; 06.01.08.05.01 Amazement, astonishment, wonder, admiration

hlysnere 02.05.10 Faculty of hearing

(ge)hlyst 02.05.10 Faculty of hearing

hlystan 06.01.06.02.03.03 To study, apply oneself to learning; 06.02.06.03 Persuasion, prompting

(ge)hlystan 02.05.10 Faculty of hearing; 12.01.01.12.01 Obedience, service; 12.07.02 Observance, keeping

gehlyste 02.05.10.01 Thing heard

hlystend 02.05.10 Faculty of hearing; 06.01.06.02.03.01 A pupil, disciple, scholar

hlystere 02.05.10 Faculty of hearing

(ge)hlystful 08.01.02.01 Favour, kindness, grace

hlysting 02.05.10 Faculty of hearing

hlyt 05.04 Fate, lot, fortune, destiny

hlyte 10.03.07 Distribution; 16.01.04.06.02 Prognostication by casting lots

hlytere 16.01.04.06.02 Prognostication by casting lots

hlytm 16.01.04.06.02 Prognostication by casting lots

hlytman 10.03.07.01 To allot, assign

hlytta 16.01.04.06.02 Prognostication by casting lots

gehlytta 07.01.01 Choice, election

gehlyt(t)a 12.04.01 A fellow, companion, associate, comrade

gehlytto 12.04 Fellowship, union, association; 16.01.04.06.02 Prognostication by casting lots

(ge)hlȳttrian 04.06.01.09 To cleanse, remove impurity from (an object)

gehlȳttrod 04.06.01.09 To cleanse, remove impurity from (an object)

hlȳttrung 04.06.01.09 To cleanse, remove impurity from (an object)

(ge)hnæcan 05.06.05.03 Bruising, crushing

gehnæcan 11.11.02 A hindrance

hnægan 02.05.10.15.06 A roar, howl, etc.

(ge)hnægan 07.09.02 Disgrace, shaming, humiliation; 13.02.05.01.01 To overcome, conquer

gehnægan 05.06.01 Devastation, laying waste

hnægung 02.05.10.15.06 A roar, howl, etc.

hnæpp 04.01.02.02.06.05.04 Cup/bowl/basin
hnæppan 05.06.09 Act of striking
gehnǣst 13.02.02 Battle
gehnǣstan 12.05.04.01 Fighting, contention, warfare, strife
hnāg 07.07 Humility; 08.01.03.06 Adversity, affliction; 10.03.09.01 Parsimony, niggardliness; 11.04.03 (Of ability) low, mean, of less worth
hnappian 02.05.04 Sleepiness, drowsiness, sleep
hnappung 02.05.04 Sleepiness, drowsiness, sleep
hnēaw 10.03.09.01 Parsimony, niggardliness
hnēawlīce 10.03.09.01 Parsimony, niggardliness
hnēawnes 10.03.09.01 Parsimony, niggardliness
hnecca 02.04.03.02 Neck
hnesce 02.05.05.04.01 Luxuries, dainties, good things; 02.07.01 To grow; 03.01.03.01 Stiffness, hardness; 03.01.04 Softness; 05.09 Weakness; 05.09.02 Mildness, moderate quality; 05.12.04 Absence of movement, stillness; 06.02.07.05.02 Moral weakness; 08.01.01.03.08 Happiness, well-being, prosperity; 08.01.02.01.02 Gentleness
hnesc(i)an 03.01.04 Softness; 08.01.02.01.02 Gentleness
(ge)hnesc(i)an 05.09 Weakness; 05.09.02 Mildness, moderate quality; 08.01.02.01.02 Gentleness; 08.01.03.07.04.02 Relief, alleviation
gehnesc(i)an 03.01.04 Softness; 12.08.07.01 Laxity, indulgence
hnesclic 02.05.05.04.01 Luxuries, dainties, good things; 12.08.07.01 Laxity, indulgence
hnesclīce 02.05.05.04.01 Luxuries, dainties, good things; 05.09.02 Mildness, moderate quality; 08.01.02.01.02 Gentleness
hnescnes 03.01.04 Softness; 05.09 Weakness; 12.08.07.01 Laxity, indulgence
hnifol 02.04.03.01.03.01 Forehead
hnifolcrumb 07.04.03 Reverence, respect
(ge)hnīgan 05.10.05.04.04 A descent, slope, incline; 05.12.05.13 To go down, descend; 07.04.03 Reverence, respect
hnigian 07.04.03 Reverence, respect
gehnigian 07.04.03 Reverence, respect
hnīpan 07.04.03 Reverence, respect
gehnipen 05.12.05.13.02 To bow, bend down
hnipian 05.12.05.13.02 To bow, bend down; 08.01.03.01 Despondency
hnip(i)ende 07.04.03 Reverence, respect
hnītan 05.06.07 Pricking, a prick, puncture; 05.06.09 Act of striking; 05.12.02.06.01 To push, drive
hnitol 02.06.02.01.03 Cattle
hnitu 02.06.09.01 Parasite
hnoll 02.04.03.01.01 Top of head
hnoppian 05.10.05.04.13 A removal of that which obscures or conceals
hnor 02.04.06.05.07.02 Mucus, phlegm, rheum
hnossian 05.06.09 Act of striking
hnot 02.04.04.03.04 Bald, shaven; 02.06.01.02 Head; 02.07.03.03.02 Tree top; 04.02.03.01.02 Cleared land; 04.02.04.05.04.01.01 Pruning/lopping
hnutbēam 02.07.09.02.01 Nut

hnutcyrnel 02.07.02.04 Seed, kind of seed; 02.07.09.02.01 Nut
hnutscill 02.07.02.04 Seed, kind of seed
hnutu 02.07.02.04 Seed, kind of seed; 02.07.09.02.01 Nut
gehnycned 02.04.04 Skin
hnygelan 03.03.07 A part, division, portion
gehnyscan 05.06.05.03 Bruising, crushing
gehnyst 08.01.03.02.01 Compunction, remorse, contrition
hōbanca 04.05.04.05 A bed, bedstead
hobb 01.01.02.01.02.01 Rising ground, eminence
hōc 04.03.02 A snare, trap, noose; 04.03.05 Fishing; 05.10.06.04 A corner, bend, angle; 05.12.01.09.03.01.04 Equipping of ships; 06.01.07.04.02.01 Deception, deceit, snare, wile; 17.03 Implements, tools, etc.; 17.03.10 Supports and fastenings
hoc(c) 02.07.11 Plants/flowers (alphabetical order)
hōced 05.10.06.02.02 Curvature, bend, twist
hocer 01.01.02.01.02.02.01 Hill
hōciht(e) 05.10.06.04 A corner, bend, angle
hōcīsern 04.02.04.06.12 A scythe, sickle
hoclēaf 02.07.11 Plants/flowers (alphabetical order)
hocor 07.05.04 Mockery, derision, scorn
hocorwyrde 07.05.04 Mockery, derision, scorn
hōd 04.04.07.11 A headcloth, covering for the head
hof 04.05.03 A dwelling-place, abode, habitation; 16.02.05.02.01 A temple
hōf 02.06.01.04 Leg
hofding 12.01.01.04 A leader, ruler
hōfe 02.07.11 Plants/flowers (alphabetical order)
hofer 02.08.04.02 Blemish, disfigurement
(ge)hof(e)rede 02.08.04.02 Blemish, disfigurement
hoflic 02.03.03 A family, household
gehōfod 02.06.01.04 Leg
hōfrec 05.12.01.04.01 Manner of going, gait
hofrede 02.08.02.01.05 Bed of sickness
hōfring 05.12.01.04.01 Manner of going, gait
hofweard 12.01.01.08.01 A servant, attendant
hoga 11.02.03 Forethought, care; 11.03 Endeavour
hogascipe 11.02.03 Forethought, care
hogelēas 08.01.01.03.01 Freedom from trouble, comfort, security
hogg/hocg 02.06.02.01.07 Pig, swine
hogian 06.01.01.01 Thinking about, minding, heeding; 06.01.05.02.01.01 Sagacity; 08.01.03.03 Anxiety; 11.02 Occupation, activity, business; 11.02.02.02 Care, mindfulness, attention
(ge)hogian 06.01.01 Thought, the faculty of thinking, mind; 06.02.06 Mind, purpose
gehogian 06.01.08.02 Hope, expectation
gehogod 06.01.01 Thought, the faculty of thinking, mind
hogu 06.01.08.06.04 Care, anxiety, solicitude
hogung 11.03 Endeavour
hōh 01.01.02.01.01.03.01 Promontory, headland, cape; 01.01.02.01.02.01

Rising ground, eminence;
02.04.03.04.02.05.01 Heel
hōh niþeweard 02.04.03.04.02.05.01
Heel
hohfæst 06.01.05.02.01.01 Sagacity
hōhfōt 02.04.03.04.02.05.01 Heel
hohful 06.01.05.02.01.01 Sagacity;
06.02.07.03 Perseverance; 08.01.03.03
Anxiety; 11.02.02.02 Care,
mindfulness, attention
hohfullīce 06.01.01.02 Care, attention,
observation
hohfulnes 06.01.08.06.04 Care, anxiety,
solicitude; 08.01.03.03 Anxiety
hōhhwyrfing 05.12.05.04 To rotate, turn
round, revolve
hōhing 02.02.04.04.03 Putting to death
hohlīce 06.01.05.02.01.01.01 Reason,
sense, discretion, prudence
hohmōd 08.01.03 Bad feeling, sadness
hōhscanca 02.04.03.04.02.03 Lower leg
hōhsinu 02.04.05.06
Sinew/tendon/ligament
hōhspor 02.04.03.04.02.05.01 Heel
hol 01.01.02.01.03 Hollow/depression in
land; 01.01.02.01.03.03 Valley;
01.01.03.01.03 Lake; 02.06.01.08 A
lair, den; 04.02.05.03 A park,
enclosure for animals; 04.05.02.08
Top of a building; 05.10.05.04.14 An
opening, aperture; 05.10.06.03.02
Hollow; 17.02.04.02.02 Digging
hōl 07.05.03.02 Calumny, slander, insult;
08.01.03.09.03 Malevolence, malice
hōl/hēl 14.03.03.06 False witness
gehola 08.01.02.03.01 An acquaintance,
friend, associate
gehola/gehala 11.10.01 Protection,
safekeeping

holc 01.01.02.01.03 Hollow/depression in
land; 02.08.08 Internal disease
hold 02.04.01 Dead body;
08.01.01.03.09.01 Pleasant, agreeable;
08.01.02.03.02 Friendly, amiable;
12.01.01.06.08 A person of rank,
elder, great man; 12.01.01.12 Loyalty;
12.02.02.03 Terms for classical world;
16.02.01.11 Firmness in the law, piety,
devoutness
hold hlāford 12.01.01.04.02 A lord,
master
holdāþ 12.01.01.12 Loyalty
holde 08.01.02.01 Favour, kindness,
grace; 16.02.01.11 Firmness in the
law, piety, devoutness
holdian 02.02.04.04.04 To slaughter (an
animal)
holdingstōw 02.02.04.04.04 To slaughter
(an animal)
holdlic 08.01.02.03.02 Friendly, amiable
holdlīce 08.01.02.01 Favour, kindness,
grace; 08.01.02.03.03 In a friendly
manner, kindly; 12.01.01.12 Loyalty;
16.02.01.11 Firmness in the law, piety,
devoutness
holdrǣden 12.01.01.12 Loyalty
holdscipe 12.01.01.12 Loyalty
holecerse 02.07.11.02 Unidentified plants
(alphabetical order)
holen 02.07.03.05 Particular trees/shrubs
(alphabetical order)
holenlēaf 02.07.03.05 Particular
trees/shrubs (alphabetical order)
holenrind 02.07.03.05 Particular
trees/shrubs (alphabetical order)
holenstybb 02.07.03.05 Particular
trees/shrubs (alphabetical order)
holh 01.01.02.01.03 Hollow/depression in
land; 01.01.02.01.03.03 Valley

holhnes 01.01.02.01.03 Hollow/depression in land
holian 05.10.06.03.02 Hollow
(ge)holian 17.02.04.02.02 Digging
geholian 10.01.02 Acquisition
hōlian 12.05.06.02 Oppression
holing 17.02.04.02.02 Digging
hollēac 02.07.09.02.02.01 Edible root/bulb
holm 01.01.02.01.01.01 Tract of land; 01.01.02.01.01.02 Island; 01.01.03 Water; 01.01.03.01.02 Sea/ocean
holmærn 05.12.01.09.03.01.01 Kind of ship
holmclif 01.01.02.01.02.02.04 Cliff
holmeg 01.01.03.01.02 Sea/ocean
holmes hlæst 02.06.06 Fish
holmmægen 01.01.03.01.02 Sea/ocean
holmþracu 01.01.03.01.02.04 State of sea
holmweall 01.01.03.01.02.05 Wave
holmweard 05.12.01.09.03 A voyage
holmweg 01.01.03.01.02.01 Region of sea/ocean
holmwudu 02.07.03.04 A wood, trees
holmwylm 01.01.03.01.02.05 Wave
holocaustum 16.02.04.12 Sacrifice, a sacrifice
geholod 05.10.06.03.02 Hollow
holt 02.07.03.04 A wood, trees; 04.02.04.05.04.01 A forester, woodman; 13.02.08.04 Weapons, arms
holthana 02.06.08.03 Game-bird
hōltihte 07.05.03.02 Calumny, slander, insult
holtwudu 04.02.04.05.04.01 A forester, woodman; 17.02.04 Trade, calling, craft, aptitude
hōlunga 11.08.03 Needless, useless, unprofitable

hōn 04.04.07 Trappings, equipment, garb; 05.12.05.13.02 To bow, bend down
(ge)hōn 02.02.04.04.03 Putting to death; 05.12.01.07.01 To hang; 14.05.05.01.01 Crucifixion, death on cross
hōnede 02.04.03.04.02.05.01 Heel
gehongen 07.10.03 An adornment, decoration, ornament
hop 01.01.02.01.04.01 Marsh, bog, swamp; 04.02.03.01.01 Enclosed land/field
hopa 06.01.08.02 Hope, expectation; 06.01.08.03 Trust, faith, confidence
hōpere 17.02.04.02.01 Cutting, hewing, shaping
hōpgehnāst 01.01.03.01.02.06 Surging, rolling, heaving of waves
hopian 06.01.08.02 Hope, expectation
hopian (tō) 06.01.08.03 Trust, faith, confidence
(ge)hopian (tō) 06.01.08.02 Hope, expectation
hōpig 01.01.03.01.02.06 Surging, rolling, heaving of waves
gehopp 02.07.02.04 Seed, kind of seed
hoppāda 04.04.07.07 A long outer garment, covering, cloak, etc.; 16.02.05.06.01 Outer garments
hoppe 04.02.05.06.06 An attendant on dogs; 04.04.10 Ornaments, trappings, accoutrements; 05.10.06.02 Rotundity, roundness
hoppere 18.02.04 Dancing
hoppestre 18.02.04 Dancing
hoppettan 02.08.03.02 Itch, irritation; 05.12.03.01.01 Quick movement or movements; 08.01.01.03.07 Joyous sound, mirth
hoppian 05.12.03.01.01 Quick movement or movements; 05.12.03.02 Slowness

hopping 04.02.04.05.02 An orchard
hopscȳte 04.05.04.05.01 Bedding (e.g. of straw)
hōpsteort 04.04.07.03 Part of garment
hōr 12.08.08.01.02.01 Fornication, adultery
hōrcwene 12.08.08.01.02.01.01 An adulterer/-ess, whore, prostitute
hord 03.03.04.01.02.01 A heap, mass, accumulation; 04.05.03.04 A closet, chamber, room; 07.04.01 (Of persons) worth/value, worthiness; 15.01.03 Treasure, riches, wealth
hordburg 12.06.02.01 A township
hordcleofa 04.05.03.04 A closet, chamber, room
hordcofa 04.05.03.04 A closet, chamber, room; 06 Spirit, soul, heart
hordere 12.01.01.08.01 A servant, attendant; 15.01.03 Treasure, riches, wealth
hordern 04.05.03.04 A closet, chamber, room
horderwȳce 17.02.02 An office, function, employment
hordestre 12.01.01.08.01 A servant, attendant
hordfæt 15.01.03 Treasure, riches, wealth
hordgeat 04.05.02.12 Gate/doorway of a building
hordgestrēon 15.01.03 Treasure, riches, wealth
hordgeþanc 06.01 The head (as seat of thought)
hordian 15.01.05 Possession of wealth
hordloca 06.01 The head (as seat of thought); 15.01.03 Treasure, riches, wealth
hordmægen 15.01.03 Treasure, riches, wealth
hordmāþm 15.01.03 Treasure, riches, wealth
hordweard 11.10.02.02 Watchful care, keeping guard; 12.01.01.04.01 A royal leader; 15.01.02.01 Inherited property
hordwela 15.01.03 Treasure, riches, wealth
hordweorþung 07.08.04 An ornament, honour, glory
hordwynn 15.01.03 Treasure, riches, wealth
hordwyrþe 07.04.01 (Of persons) worth/value, worthiness
hōre 12.08.08.01.02.01.01 An adulterer/-ess, whore, prostitute
hor(g)ian 02.04.06.06.04 Spittle
(ge)horgian 12.08.08.01.02 Unchastity, incontinence
horh 04.06.02.02 Foul, filthy, squalid
horh/hrog 02.04.06.05.07.02 Mucus, phlegm, rheum
horig 04.06.02.02 Foul, filthy, squalid
horines 04.06.02.02 Foul, filthy, squalid
hōring 12.08.08.01.02.01 Fornication, adultery
horn 01.01.02.01.01 Tract of land; 01.02.01.01.04 Moon; 02.06.01.02 Head; 04.01.03.05.04 Drinking vessel; 04.05.02.08 Top of a building; 12.01.01.03 Symbols of power; 13.02.08.04.04 A bow; 16.02.05.03.04 Part of temple containing altar/idol; 17.04.03.03 Horn; 18.02.07.02.02.02 A trumpet
hornādl 02.08.08.10 Disease of penis
hornbǣre 02.06.01.02 Head
hornblāwere 18.02.07.02.02.02 A trumpet
hornboga 13.02.08.04.04 A bow
hornbora 18.02.07.02.02.02 A trumpet

hornede 02.06.01.02 Head
hornfisc 02.06.06.02.01.06 Pike
hornfōtod 02.06.01.04 Leg
horngēap 04.05.02.08 Top of a building
horngestrēon 04.05.02.08 Top of a building
gehornian 07.05.03.03.02 To reproach, revile, abuse
hornlēas 02.06.01.02 Head
hornpīc 04.05.02.08 Top of a building
hornreced 04.05.03.02.02.06.01 A hall building
hornscēaþ 04.05.02.08 Top of a building
hornscip 05.12.01.09.03.01.01 Kind of ship
hornsele 04.05.03.02.02.06.01 A hall building
hornungbrōþor 02.03.02.02.05 Having the same parents
hornungsunu 02.03.02.02.05 Having the same parents
horpytt 01.01.02.01.03 Hollow/depression in land
hors 02.06.02.01.06 Horse
horsbǣr 05.12.01.06 Vehicle
horsc 04.06.02.02 Foul, filthy, squalid; 06.01.05.02 Intelligence; 06.02.07.06.02.02 Boldness, daring
horscamb 04.02.05.06.05.03.10 A curry-comb
horschwæl 02.06.05.01.03 Walrus
horsclic 04.06.02.02 Foul, filthy, squalid
horsclīce 06.01.05.02.01.01.01 Reason, sense, discretion, prudence; 06.02.07.06.02.02 Boldness, daring
horscniht 04.02.05.06.05.01 Care of horses
horscræt 05.12.01.06 Vehicle
horselene 02.07.11 Plants/flowers (alphabetical order)

horsern 04.02.05.06.05.02.01 A stable
horsgærstūn 04.02.03.04.02.01.01 Horse pasture
horshere 13.02.10.01.02.02.02 Branch of army
horshierde 04.02.05.06.05.01 Care of horses
(ge)horsian 13.02.10.01.02.02.02 Branch of army
horsminte 02.07.10.01 Particular herbs/spices (alphabetical order)
gehorsod 05.12.01.05 To ride (on horse, etc.); 13.02.10.01.02.02.02 Branch of army
horsōman 04.02.05.02.03 Erysipelas in horses
horspæþ 05.12.01.03.01.05 Types of road/path
horsþegn 04.02.05.06.05.01 Care of horses; 12.01.01.05 A leader, administrator; 12.01.01.08.01 A servant, attendant
horswǣn 05.12.01.06 Vehicle
horswealh 04.02.05.06.05.01 Care of horses
horsweard 04.02.05.06.05.01 Care of horses
horsweg 05.12.01.03.01.05 Types of road/path
horte 02.07.09.02 Particular fruits (alphabetical order)
horusēaþ 04.05.03.05.01 A cess-pool, midden, sewer
horweg 05.12.01.03.01.04 A lane, street
horweht(e) 04.06.02.02 Foul, filthy, squalid
(ge)horwiende 12.08.08.01.02 Unchastity, incontinence
horwyll 01.01.03.01.01.03 Stream
hos 02.07.02.05 A shoot, sprout, tendril

hōs 12.01.01.07 A follower
hosebend 04.04.07.09 Breeches
hosp 07.05.03.03 Scorn, insult, abuse; 16.02.04.14.01 Blasphemy
hospan 07.05.03.03.02 To reproach, revile, abuse
hospcwide 07.05.03.03 Scorn, insult, abuse
hospettan 07.05.04 Mockery, derision, scorn
hosplic 07.05.03.03.01 Contumelious, scornful
hospspræc 07.05.03.03 Scorn, insult, abuse
hospul 07.09.03 Infamy, ignominy, shame
hospword 07.05.03.03 Scorn, insult, abuse
hosu 04.02.04.03.02.01 Grain crops; 04.04.07.09 Breeches
hraca 02.04.03.01.03.07 Jaw(s)
hrāca 02.04.06.05.07.02 Mucus, phlegm, rheum
hrace 01.01.02.01.03.03 Valley
hrace/-u 02.04.06.03.02.02 Throat/gullet
hradian 09.03.04.05 To put briefly
(ge)hradian 05.11.01.02.01 Swift movement of time; 05.12.03.01.02 Haste, hurry
gehradian 05.11.08.01.02 (Untimely) earliness; 08.01.01.03.08.03 A favour, blessing
gehradod 05.12.03.01 Swiftness, velocity
hradung 05.12.03.01 Swiftness, velocity
hrǣcan 02.04.06.06.04 Spittle; 02.08.08.04.02 (Of stomach) disordered
hrǣcea 02.04.06.05.07.02 Mucus, phlegm, rheum
hrǣcetan 02.04.06.06.04 Spittle
hrǣcetung 02.04.06.06.04 Spittle

hrǣcgebrǣc 02.08.07.04.04 Respiratory disease
hrǣctunge 02.04.06.03.02.01 Mouth
hrǣcung 02.04.06.05.07.02 Mucus, phlegm, rheum
hrǣd 05.11.01.02.01 Swift movement of time; 05.12.03.01 Swiftness, velocity; 05.12.03.01.02 Haste, hurry; 06.01.05.02 Intelligence; 11.02.01 Energy, vigour, vigorous action
hrǣdbita 02.06.09.02.03 Beetle
hrǣdd 05.11.03.01.03.01 Specific months
hrǣdfērnes 05.12.03.01 Swiftness, velocity
hrǣdhȳdig 05.12.03.01.02 Haste, hurry
hrǣdhȳdignes 05.12.03.01.02 Haste, hurry
hrǣding 05.12.03.01.02 Haste, hurry
hrǣdlic 05.11.01.02.01 Swift movement of time; 05.11.08.01.01 Suddenness; 05.11.08.01.02 (Untimely) earliness; 05.12.03.01 Swiftness, velocity
hrǣdlīce 05.11.01.02.01 Swift movement of time; 05.11.07.01 Contemporary, coeval; 05.11.07.04.01 Nearness, approach, imminence; 05.11.08.01.01 Suddenness; 05.12.03.01 Swiftness, velocity; 06.02.05.04.03 Promptitude, readiness
hrǣdlicnes 05.11.08.01.02 (Untimely) earliness
hrǣd(lic)nes 05.12.03.01 Swiftness, velocity
hrǣdmōd 08.01.03.05.04 Irritability
hrǣdnes 05.11.01.02 Shortness/brevity in time; 05.11.01.02.01 Swift movement of time; 06.02.05.04.03 Promptitude, readiness
hrǣdrīpe 05.11.08.01.02 (Untimely) earliness

hrædtæfle 18.02.02.01 Gaming, playing at dice
hrædwǣn 05.12.01.06 Vehicle
hrædwilnes 05.12.03.01.02 Haste, hurry
hrædwyrde 08.01.03.09.01.03 Sharpness (of speech)
hræfn 02.06.08.05 Forest bird, wild-fowl; 13.02.08.02 A standard, banner, ensign
hræfncynn 02.06.08.05 Forest bird, wild-fowl
hræfnes fōt 02.07.11 Plants/flowers (alphabetical order)
hræfnes lēac 02.07.11 Plants/flowers (alphabetical order)
hræfnsweart 03.01.14.04 Black/blackness
hrægelgefrætwodnes 04.04.07.01 Mode of dressing, fashion
hrægelþegn 12.01.01.08.01 A servant, attendant
hrægl 04.04.05 Woven material, fabric; 04.04.07 Trappings, equipment, garb; 04.04.08 A covering, curtain, veil, garment, etc.; 05.12.01.09.03.01.03 Part of ship; 13.02.08.03.01 Body armour, war gear
hræglcyst 04.04.07 Trappings, equipment, garb
hræglgewǣde 04.04.07 Trappings, equipment, garb
hræglhūs 16.02.05.03.09 A vestry/sacristy
hræglscēar 04.04.05.06 To sew, stitch; 17.03.03 A cutting tool
hrægltalu 16.02.05.07 Monastic garb
hræglþegn 16.02.03.03.02.01 Monastic functionaries
hræglþēnestre 12.01.01.08.01 A servant, attendant

hræglung 04.04.07 Trappings, equipment, garb
hræglweard 16.02.03.03.02.01 Monastic functionaries
hrætelwyrt 02.07.11 Plants/flowers (alphabetical order)
hrǣw 02.03.01 People; 02.04 Body; 02.04.01 Dead body
hrǣwīc 02.02.04 Killing, violent death, destruction
hrāfyll 02.02.04 Killing, violent death, destruction
hrāgīfre 02.02.04.02 Murderous, bloodthirsty
hrāgra 02.06.08.06 Water bird
hrama 04.05.01.02.07 A fence, hedge; 11.11.01 A physical difficulty, strait
hramma 02.08.08.04.01 Gripe, colic
hramsa 02.07.09.02.02.01 Edible root/bulb
hramsa(n)crop 02.07.09.02.02.01 Edible root/bulb
hran 02.06.05.01.01 Dolphin; 02.06.05.01.04 Whale
hrān 02.06.03.01.06 Deer, hart
hrandsparwa 02.06.08.05 Forest bird, wild-fowl
hranfix 02.06.05.01.04 Whale
hrānhund 02.06.02.01.04 Dog; 04.03.01 Tracking
hranmere 01.01.03.01.02 Sea/ocean
hranrād 01.01.03.01.02 Sea/ocean
hratele 02.07.11 Plants/flowers (alphabetical order)
hratian 05.12.03.01.02 Haste, hurry
hraþe 05.11.01.02.01 Swift movement of time; 05.11.07.01 Contemporary, coeval; 05.11.07.04.01 Nearness, approach, imminence; 05.12.03.01

Swiftness, velocity; 06.02.02.01 Will, wish, pleasure
hrāwĕrig 02.05.03.02 Weariness
hrāwlic 02.02.05 A burial, burying
hrēa 02.08.08.04.02 (Of stomach) disordered
hrēacc 04.02.04.04.04 Stack, rick
hrēaccopp 04.01.02.04 Abundance of food
hrēacmete 04.01.02.04 Abundance of food
hrēam 02.05.10.03 Noise, tumult, uproar; 02.05.10.15 Voice, cry (of living creature); 08.01.03.04.01 Complaint, lamentation; 09.01 To speak, exercise faculty of speech
hreaþemūs 02.06.03.01.02 Bat
hrēaw 04.01.02.02.05 Cooking; 04.04.06 Undressed condition (of hide)
hrēawan 04.01.02.02.05 Cooking
hrēawnes 04.04.06 Undressed condition (of hide)
hreddan 10.04.03 To take away, remove; 11.10.03 Salvation/deliverance from
hreddere 11.10.01 Protection, safekeeping
hreddung 11.10.03 Salvation/deliverance from; 16.01.01.02.08 Salvation, redemption
(ge)hrēfan 04.05.02.08 Top of a building
hregresi 02.04.03.03.08 Groin/crotch
hrēmig 02.05.10.03 Noise, tumult, uproar; 02.05.10.15.01 To raise (the voice), raise up (noise); 07.06.03 Boastfulness, arrogance
(ge)hremman 11.11.02 A hindrance; 11.11.03 Impeding of progress, prevention
gehremman fram 11.11.03 Impeding of progress, prevention

hremming 11.11.02 A hindrance
hrenian 02.05.08 Faculty of smell
hrēod 01.01.02.01.05 Covered with vegetation; 02.07.08 Grasses, reeds, etc.; 09.03.07.06.01 A writing instrument
hrēodbedd 02.07.08 Grasses, reeds, etc.
hrēodcynn 02.07.08 Grasses, reeds, etc.
hrēoden 02.07.08 Grasses, reeds, etc.
hrēodet 02.07.08 Grasses, reeds, etc.
hrēodgyrd 04.03.05 Fishing
hrēodig 02.07.08 Grasses, reeds, etc.
hrēodiht 02.07.08 Grasses, reeds, etc.
hrēodihtig 02.07.08 Grasses, reeds, etc.
hrēodpīpere 18.02.07.02.02.01 Pipe/flute
hrēodwæter 01.01.02.01.04.01 Marsh, bog, swamp
hrēof 02.08.06 Skin disease, erysipelas; 03.01.05 Roughness
hrēofl 02.08.06 Skin disease, erysipelas
hrēofla 02.08.06 Skin disease, erysipelas; 04.02.05.02 Animal diseases
hrēoflic 02.08.06 Skin disease, erysipelas
hrēoflig 02.08.06 Skin disease, erysipelas
hrēofnes 02.08.06 Skin disease, erysipelas
hrēogan 01.03.01.03 Bad weather
hrēoh 01.03.01.03 Bad weather; 01.03.01.03.01 Storm, tempest; 08.01.03.03 Anxiety; 08.01.03.06 Adversity, affliction; 08.01.03.09.01 Fierceness; 08.01.03.09.10 Wrath, sternness, displeasure
hrēohful 01.03.01.03.01 Storm, tempest
hrēohlic 08.01.03.06 Adversity, affliction
hrēohmōd 08.01.03 Bad feeling, sadness; 08.01.03.09.01 Fierceness
hrēohnes 01.01.02.01.06 Wild/uncultivated land;

01.03.01.03.01 Storm, tempest; 08.01.03.06 Adversity, affliction
hrēol 04.04.03 A spinning-house or chamber
hrēorig 05.06.01 Devastation, laying waste
(ge)hrēosan 02.08.02 Disease, infirmity, sickness; 05.06.01 Devastation, laying waste; 05.12.05.13.03 To fall; 11.06.03.01 Ill fortune, bad success
gehrēosan 02.02.03 To die, perish; 05.12.05.02.01 To come upon, meet with
gehrēosan on 11.02.04 Heedlessness
hrēosende 05.11.01.03.01 Mortal state, this life; 05.12.05.13.03 To fall
hrēosendlic 02.08.02 Disease, infirmity, sickness; 05.11.01.03.01 Mortal state, this life; 13.02.03.01 An attack, assault
(ge)hrēosendlic 05.12.05.13.03 To fall
hrēoung 02.04.06.07.04 Breathing
hrēow 04.01.02.02.05 Cooking; 08.01.03.02.01 Compunction, remorse, contrition; 16.02.04.07.02.01 Penitence
(ge)hrēow 08.01.03.02.01 Compunction, remorse, contrition
hrēowan 12.08.02.02.01 Reform, correction; 16.02.04.07.02.01 Penitence
(ge)hrēowan 08.01.02.06.01 Pity; 08.01.03.02.01 Compunction, remorse, contrition; 08.01.03.04 Grief; 12.08.02.02.01 Reform, correction; 16.02.04.07.02.03 Penance, an act/instance of penance
hrēowcearig 08.01.03.03 Anxiety
hrēowende 08.01.03.02.01 Compunction, remorse, contrition; 16.02.04.07.02.01 Penitence
hrēowig 08.01.03 Bad feeling, sadness
hrēowigmōd 08.01.03.01 Despondency
hrēowlic 08.01.02.06.01 Pity; 08.01.03.06 Adversity, affliction
hrēowlīce 08.01.02.06.01 Pity; 08.01.03.04 Grief; 08.01.03.06.01 Affliction, misfortune, calamity; 08.01.03.07.03 Suffering, torment, pain; 08.01.03.09.11 Hardheartedness, cruelty, severity
(ge)hrēownes 08.01.03.02.01 Compunction, remorse, contrition; 16.02.04.07.02.01 Penitence
hrēowsian 08.01.03.04.01 Complaint, lamentation
(ge)hrēowsian 12.08.02.02.01 Reform, correction; 16.02.04.07.02.01 Penitence; 16.02.04.07.02.03 Penance, an act/instance of penance
hrēowsung 08.01.03.02.01 Compunction, remorse, contrition; 08.01.03.04.01 Complaint, lamentation; 16.02.04.07.02.01 Penitence; 16.02.04.07.02.03 Penance, an act/instance of penance
hrēpan 02.05.10.15.01 To raise (the voice), raise up (noise)
hrepian 02.08.04.01 A wound
hrepian/hreppan 02.08.04 Hurt, injury, damage; 05.06.04 Damage, injury, defect, hurt, loss; 07.05.01 Censure, reproof, rebuke; 11.07 Use (made of things), service
(ge)hrepian 02.05.06 Sense of touch; 13.02.03.01 An attack, assault
(ge)hrepian/hreppan 08.01 Heart, spirit, mood, disposition
(ge)hrepian (ymbe) 09.06 To take matter for discourse

hrepung 02.01.03.03 Sex, generation; 02.05.06 Sense of touch; 11.03.01 Experience, trial, experiment
hrēr 04.01.02.02.05 Cooking
hrēran mid hondum 05.12.01.09.01 To row
(ge)hrēran 03.03.06.01.01 Mixing, mingling, preparation; 05.12.02 To move, set in motion
hrēre 04.01.02.02.05 Cooking
hrērednes 05.12.03.01.02 Haste, hurry
hrēremūs 02.06.03.01.02 Bat
hrērenbrǣden 04.01.02.02.05 Cooking
hrēr(e)nes 05.12 To move, be in motion; 05.12.02 To move, set in motion
gehresp 14.02.01.02.01 Open robbery, rapine, pillage
gehrespan 05.06.02.02 A tearing apart; 14.02.01.02.01 Open robbery, rapine, pillage
hrēþ 07.08.09 Renown, fame, glory; 13.02.05.01 Victory
hrēþa 04.04.07.07 A long outer garment, covering, cloak, etc.
hrēþan 07.06.03 Boastfulness, arrogance
hrēþēadig 07.02.04.03 Nobleness, excellence, nobility, magnificence; 07.08.09 Renown, fame, glory
hreþer 02.04.03.03.05 Chest, breast, bosom; 06 Spirit, soul, heart; 08.01 Heart, spirit, mood, disposition
hreþerbealu 08.01.03 Bad feeling, sadness
hreþercofa 06 Spirit, soul, heart; 08.01 Heart, spirit, mood, disposition
hreþerglēaw 06.01.05.02.01.01 Sagacity
hreþerloca 06 Spirit, soul, heart; 08.01 Heart, spirit, mood, disposition
hrēþlēas 07.09.03 Infamy, ignominy, shame; 13.02.05.02 Defeat
hrēþmann 13.02.10.01 A man, warrior
hrēþmōnaþ 05.11.03.01.03.01 Specific months
hrēþsecg 13.02.10.01 A man, warrior
hrēþsigor 13.02.05.01 Victory
hrīcian 04.02.04.02.02.02 Ploughing, tilling; 05.06.02 Cleaving, splitting, cutting
hriddel 04.02.04.06.14.02 A winnowing sieve
hridder 04.02.04.06.14.02 A winnowing sieve
(ge)hrīdrian 04.02.04.04.05.01 To winnow
hrīeman 02.05.10.15.01 To raise (the voice), raise up (noise)
hrīeman/hrēman 07.06.03 Boastfulness, arrogance
(ge)hrīeman 08.01.03.04.01 Complaint, lamentation
gehrīered 05.06 Destruction, dissolution, loss, breaking
hrif 02.04.06.03.02.03 Stomach/belly; 05.10.05.04.01 Inside, interior
(ge)hrif 02.04.06.04.02 Female reproductive organs
hrifādl 02.08.08.12 Disease of bowels
gehrifian 02.01.03.03.02 To bring forth, produce
(ge)hrīfnian 08.01.03.09.08 Envy, jealousy
hriftēung 02.08.08.04 Pain in stomach
hrīfþo 02.08.05.02.02 Scab, roughness of skin
hrifwerc 02.08.08.04 Pain in stomach
hrifwund 02.08.04.01 A wound
hrīm 01.03.01.04.01 Frost
hrīmceald 01.03.01.04 Wintry weather, cold; 03.01.11 Coldness, coolness
hrīmes dryre 01.03.01.04.01 Frost

hrīmforst 01.03.01.04.01 Frost
hrīmgicel 01.01.03.02 Ice;
 01.03.01.04.02 Ice
hrīmig 01.03.01.04.01 Frost
hrīmigheard 01.03.01.04.02 Ice;
 03.01.11 Coldness, coolness
(ge)hrimpan 05.10.05.02.03 To reduce, make thin(ner)
gehrimpan 05.10.06.02.03 A circular fold, coil
hrīnan 02.05.06 Sense of touch; 05.06.04 Damage, injury, defect, hurt, loss
(ge)hrīnan 02.05.06 Sense of touch; 05.06.09 Act of striking; 05.12.05.02.03 To arrive; 08.01 Heart, spirit, mood, disposition; 08.01.03.07.02 Misery, trouble, affliction
hrindan 05.12.02.06 To push, impel, thrust
hrinde 01.03.01.04.01 Frost
hrine 02.05.06 Sense of touch
(ge)hrinenes 02.05.06 Sense of touch
hring 01.01 Surface of the earth; 03.01.12.02 A beam of light; 04.04.10.01 A ring (for finger, arm, neck); 05.10.05.04.11.01 A bound, limit; 05.10.06.02 Rotundity, roundness; 05.10.06.02.03 A circular fold, coil; 05.11.06 Course/cycle of time; 05.12.01.03 Expanse over which something travels; 07.08.04 An ornament, honour, glory; 12.04.02 A crowding together, assembly; 12.05.06 Grasp, power, control, mastery; 13.02.08.03.01.01 Mail, iron-rings; 17.03.10 Supports and fastenings
hringādl 02.08.06 Skin disease, erysipelas
hringan 02.05.10.13.01.01 Stroke/sound of a bell
(ge)hringan 02.05.10.11 Clang, sound of metal; 02.05.10.13 Sound of bell/musical instrument; 02.05.10.13.01.01 Stroke/sound of a bell
hringbān 02.04.05.04.02.01 Socket of eye
hringboga 02.06.10.01.01 Dragon
hringe 04.04.10.02 A button, brooch
hringed 13.02.08.03.01.01 Mail, iron-rings
hringedstefna 05.12.01.09.03.01.01 Kind of ship
hringel 05.10.06.02 Rotundity, roundness
hringfāg 03.01.14.11 Medley/variety of colour
hringfinger 02.04.03.04.01.01.01 Finger
hringgeat 05.10.05.04.14.02 An opening/space in an enclosure
hringgewindla 02.06.10.01.01 Dragon
hringīren 13.02.08.03.01.01 Mail, iron-rings
hringloca 13.02.08.03.01.04 Coat of mail/corselet
hringmǣl 13.02.08.04.03 A sword
hringmǣled 13.02.08.04.03 A sword
hringmere 01.01.03.01.03.01 Pool
hringnaca 05.12.01.09.03.01.01 Kind of ship
hringnett 13.02.08.03.01.04 Coat of mail/corselet
hringpytt 01.01.02.01.03 Hollow/depression in land; 17.02.04.02.04 Leading/conducting of water
hringsele 04.05.03.02.02.06.01 A hall building
hringsetl/-set 18.02.03 A spectacle, display

hringsittend 02.05.09.05 To watch, observe, survey
hringstān 04.05.02.04 A column, pillar
hringþegu 10.01.01 Acceptance, receiving
hringweorþung 04.04.10.01 A ring (for finger, arm, neck)
hringwyll 17.02.04.02.04 Leading/conducting of water
hrīning 02.05.06 Sense of touch
hrīs 02.07.03.01 A bush
hrisc 02.08.07.07 Disorders of the body
hrīscung 02.05.10.10 Clattering, noise
hrīseht 02.04.04.03 Hair; 02.07.03.01 A bush
hrīsel 02.04.05.04.06 Bone of arm; 04.04.03 A spinning-house or chamber
hrīsen 02.07.03.01 A bush
hrisian 02.05.10.11 Clang, sound of metal; 05.12.05.05 To shake, quake, wag
gehrisian 02.05.10.11 Clang, sound of metal
hrīsig 02.07.03.01 A bush
hrīstle 02.05.10.10 Clattering, noise
hrīstlende 02.05.10.06 Harsh sound
hriþ 02.08.10 Fever
hrīþ 01.03.01.03.01 Storm, tempest
hriþādl 02.08.10 Fever
hrīþer 02.06.02.01.03 Cattle
hrīþeren 02.06.02.01.03 Cattle
hrīþerfrēols 16.02.04.12 Sacrifice, a sacrifice
hrīþerhēawere 04.01.02.02.01 To dress animals for food
hrīþerheord 02.06.02.01.03 Cattle
hrīþerhyrde 04.02.05.06.01 A cowherd
hriþian 02.08.09.02 Epilepsy
hriþing 02.08.10 Fever

hrīþra fald 04.02.05.06.01.01 A cattle pen/cowshed
hrōc 02.06.08.05 Forest bird, wild-fowl
gehroden 07.10.03 An adornment, decoration, ornament
hrōf 01.02.01 Heaven(s), sky; 04.05.02.08 Top of a building; 05.10.05.03.03 Height, loftiness, sublimity; 05.10.05.04.12 The condition of being covered; 09.05.04.01 Concealment, obscurity; 09.06.02.01.05 Proclamation, spreading abroad
hrōffæst 04.05.02.08 Top of a building; 04.05.03.02.02.06.01 A hall building
hrōflēas 04.05.02.08 Top of a building; 15.01.01 Landed property
hrōfsele 04.05.03.02.02.06.01 A hall building
hrōfstān 04.05.02.08 Top of a building
hrōftigel 04.05.01.04 A tile, brick
hrōftimber 04.05.02.08 Top of a building
hrōfwyrhta 04.05.01.04 A tile, brick
hrohian 02.04.06.06.04 Spittle
hrohung 02.04.06.06.04 Spittle
hrōp 02.05.10.15.01 To raise (the voice), raise up (noise)
hrōpan 02.05.10.02 Noise, din
gehror 02.02 Death
hrōr 06.02.07.06 Courage, boldness, valour; 11.02.01.01 Active, nimble; 12 Power, might
gehroren 05.06.01 Devastation, laying waste
gehrorenes 08.01.03.06 Adversity, affliction
gehrorenlic 05.11.01.03.01 Mortal state, this life
hrōst 04.02.05.03.02 A byre, stall, sty, shed; 04.05.02.08 Top of a building

1096

hrōstbēag 04.05.02.08 Top of a building
hrot 03.01.16.04 Foam, froth
hrōþgirela 12.01.01.03 Symbols of power
hrōþor 08.01.03.07.04.02.01 Comfort, consolation; 11.07.03 Use, advantage, profit
hrucge 02.06.08.03 Game-bird
hrūm 03.01.09.02.01.02 Embers, cinders, ashes; 04.06.02.05 Dust, powder
hrūmig 03.01.13 Darkness, obscurity; 04.06.02.05 Dust, powder
hruna 02.07.03 A tree
hrung 17.03.09 A post, rod, stick, etc.
hrurol 02.07.03 A tree
hrūse 01 Earth, world; 01.01.02 Land; 01.01.02.01 Ground; 01.01.02.02 Earth, soil; 01.01.03.01 Body of water; 03 Material, matter, substance; 04.02.03 Cultivatable land/farmland; 05.05.02 Productivity, bringing forth
hrūt/hrȳte 03.01.13 Darkness, obscurity
hrūtan 02.04.06.07.07 To snore; 02.05.10.10 Clattering, noise
gehrūxl 02.05.10.03 Noise, tumult, uproar
hrūxlian 02.05.10.02 Noise, din
hrycg 01.01.02.01.02.01 Rising ground, eminence; 01.01.03.01.02.05 Wave; 02.04.03.03.01 Back; 02.04.05.04.04 Spine; 04.05.02.08 Top of a building
hrycgbān 02.04.05.04.04 Spine
hrycgbrǣdan 02.04.05.01 Flesh
hrycghǣr 02.06.01.06 Skin, hide
hrycghrægl 04.04.07.07 A long outer garment, covering, cloak, etc.
hrycgmearg 02.04.05.04.04 Spine
hrycgmergliþ 02.04.05.04.04 Spine
hrycgrib 02.04.05.04.05.03 Rib
hrycgweg 05.12.01.03.01.05 Types of road/path

hrycriple/ricgrible 02.04.05.01 Flesh
hryding 04.02.03.01.02 Cleared land
hrȳfing 02.08.05.02.02 Scab, roughness of skin
hrympel 02.04.04 Skin; 05.10.06.05.01 A wrinkle
hrȳmþe 02.05.10.02 Noise, din
hryre 01.03.01.06.02 Rain; 02.02 Death; 02.02.04 Killing, violent death, destruction; 02.08.02 Disease, infirmity, sickness; 05.06 Destruction, dissolution, loss, breaking; 05.06.01 Devastation, laying waste; 05.06.09.04 Stoning, casting of stones; 05.09 Weakness; 05.12.05.13.03 To fall; 08.01.03.06.01 Affliction, misfortune, calamity; 12.08.06.01 Error, wrong conduct, erroneous practice; 13.02.05.02 Defeat
hrȳsc 05.06.09 Act of striking
hrȳscan 02.05.10.06 Harsh sound
hrȳscende 02.05.10.06 Harsh sound
hrȳþig 05.06.01 Devastation, laying waste
hū 05.03.01 A cause (of anything)
hū lā 09.01.03.01 Interjections: Oh!
hū gerād 03.04 Form, kind, nature, character
hūfe 04.04.07.11 A headcloth, covering for the head
(ge)hūfian 04.04.07.11 A headcloth, covering for the head
gehūfod 16.02.05.06.03 Headgear
gehugod 06.02.06 Mind, purpose
hūhwega (swā) 03.06 Comparison
hulc 04.05.03.02.02.08 A lowly dwelling, cottage, hut; 05.12.01.09.03.01.01 Kind of ship
hulfere 02.07.03.05 Particular trees/shrubs (alphabetical order)

hulfestre 02.06.08.06 Water bird
hūlic 03.04 Form, kind, nature, character
hulu 04.02.04.03.02.01 Grain crops
humbre 02.03.03.05.01.09 Northumbrians
humbre strēames gemǣre 12.06.01.01 England
hūmeta 05.03.01 A cause (of anything)
huncettan 02.08.04.04 State of being crippled
hund 02.06.02.01.04 Dog; 03.03.03.04.10 Ten; 03.03.03.04.28 Hundred; 04.03.01 Tracking; 07.05.03.03 Scorn, insult, abuse
hundælleftigoþa 03.03.03.04.28.01 One hundred and ten
hundeahtatigoþa 03.03.03.04.26 Eighty
hundeahtatigwintre 02.01.04 Age
hundeahtig 03.03.03.04.26 Eighty
hunden 02.06.02.01.04 Dog
hundendleftig 03.03.03.04.28.01 One hundred and ten
hundes hēafod 02.07.11 Plants/flowers (alphabetical order)
hundes micge 02.07.11 Plants/flowers (alphabetical order)
hundes tunge 02.07.11 Plants/flowers (alphabetical order)
hundesberie 02.07.11 Plants/flowers (alphabetical order)
hundescwelcan 02.07.09.02 Particular fruits (alphabetical order)
hundesflēoge 02.06.09.01 Parasite
hundeslūs 02.06.09.01 Parasite
hundespēo 02.06.09.01 Parasite
hundeswyrm 04.02.05.02.04 Dog's worm
hundfeald 03.03.03.04.28 Hundred
hundfealdgetel 03.03.03.04.28 Hundred
hundfealdlic 03.03.03.04.28 Hundred
hundfrēa 13.02.10.01.01 A commander, officer
hundlic 02.06.02.01.04 Dog
hundnigontēoþa 03.03.03.04.27 Ninety
hundnigontig 03.03.03.04.27 Ninety
hundnigontiggēare 02.01.04 Age
hundnigontigwintre 02.01.04 Age
hundraþ 03.03.03.04.28 Hundred
hundred 03.03.03.04.28 Hundred; 12.02.02 An assembly, meeting; 12.06.02 District, province
hundred healdan 12.02.02 An assembly, meeting
hundredes ealdor 12.02.02 An assembly, meeting; 13.02.10.01.01 A commander, officer
hundredgemōt 12.02.02 An assembly, meeting
hundredmann 12.02.02 An assembly, meeting; 13.02.10.01.01 A commander, officer
hundredpenig 15.03.02 A tax
hundredseten 14.01.01 Law(s) of particular scope
hundredsōcn 12.02.02 An assembly, meeting; 14.05.04.01 A fine
hundseofontig 03.03.03.04.25 Seventy
hundseofontigfeald 03.03.03.04.25 Seventy
hundseofontiggēare 02.01.04 Age
hundseofontigoþa 03.03.03.04.25 Seventy
hundseofontigseofon 03.03.03.04.25 Seventy
hundseofontigseofonfeald 03.03.03.04.25 Seventy
hundseofontigwintre 02.01.04 Age
hundtēontig 03.03.03.04.28 Hundred
hundtēontigfealde 03.03.03.04.28 Hundred

hundtēontigfeald(lic) 03.03.03.04.28 Hundred
hundtēontiggēare 02.01.04 Age
hundtēontigoþa 03.03.03.04.28 Hundred
hundtēontigwintre 02.01.04 Age
hundtwelftig 03.03.03.04.28.02 One hundred and twenty
hundtwelftigwintre 02.01.04 Age
hundtwentig 03.03.03.04.28.02 One hundred and twenty
hundtwēntigwintre 02.01.04 Age
hundwealh 04.02.05.06.06 An attendant on dogs; 12.01.01.08.01 A servant, attendant
hundwelle 03.03.03.04.28 Hundred
hundwintre 02.01.04 Age
hūne 02.07.11 Plants/flowers (alphabetical order)
hungerbiten 04.01.01.03 Hunger
hungergēar 04.01.01.03 Hunger
hungerlǣwe 04.01.01.03 Hunger
hungerlic 03.03.04.05 Insufficiency, lack, want; 04.01.01.03 Hunger
hungor 02.05.05 Desire, appetite; 04.01.01.03 Hunger; 06.02.05 Will, desire, wish
(ge)hungred 04.01.01.03 Hunger
hungrig 03.03.04.05 Insufficiency, lack, want; 04.01.01.03 Hunger
hunig 04.01.02.01.05.04 Honey
hunigæppel 04.01.02.01.07.04 Cake
hunigbǣre 02.07.02.07 Blossom, flower(s); 04.01.02.01.05.04 Honey; 09.03.04.02.02 Eloquence, elegance in language
hunigbinn 04.01.02.02.06.03 Food receptacle, basket
hunigcamb 04.01.02.01.05.04 Honey
hunig(dēaw) 04.01.02.01.05.04 Honey

hunigflōwende 02.07.02.07 Blossom, flower(s); 04.01.02.01.05.04 Honey; 08.01.01.03.09.01 Pleasant, agreeable
huniggafol 15.02.04.01 Payment for temporary use, rent, hire
hunigsmæc 04.01.02.01.05.04 Honey; 08.01.01.03.09 Pleasantness, agreeableness
hunigsūge 02.07.03.05 Particular trees/shrubs (alphabetical order)
hunigswēte 04.01.02.01.05.04 Honey; 08.01.01.03.09.01 Pleasant, agreeable
hunigtēar 04.01.02.01.05.04 Honey
hunigtēaren 04.01.02.01.05.04 Honey
hunigtēarlic 04.01.02.01.05.04 Honey
hūnsporu 05.12.01.09.03.01.03 Part of ship
hunta 02.06.09.02.10 Spider; 04.03 Hunting, the chase
huntaþ 04.01.02.01.02.04 Game
huntaþ dōn 04.03 Hunting, the chase
huntaþfaru 04.03 Hunting, the chase
huntere 04.03 Hunting, the chase
(ge)huntian 04.03 Hunting, the chase
hunticge 04.03 Hunting, the chase
huntigspere 04.03 Hunting, the chase
huntigystre 04.03 Hunting, the chase
hunt(n)aþ 04.03 Hunting, the chase
hunt(n)oþ/huntnold 04.03 Hunting, the chase
huntung 04.01.02.01.02.04 Game; 04.03 Hunting, the chase
hūnþyrlu 05.12.01.09.03.01.03 Part of ship
hupseax 13.02.08.04.03 A sword
hurþ 04.05.01.02.05 A hurdle
hūru 03.03.05.01.01 Principal/chief (of its class or type); 03.04.03.01 Someone/something; 03.06 Comparison; 05.11.10.02 End,

completion; 06.01.07.01 Correct, right, free from error
hūru swīþost 03.03.05 Extent, degree
hūs 02.03.03 A family, household; 02.03.03.02 A race, tribe; 04.05.02 A building, edifice, structure; 04.05.03 A dwelling-place, abode, habitation; 16.02.05.02 A holy place or sanctuary; 16.02.05.02.01 A temple
hūs be wege 04.01.02.04.05.01.01 Quartering of officials; 04.05.03.03 A lodging-house, inn
(ge)hūsa 12.01.01.08.01 A servant, attendant
hūsærn 04.05.03.02.01 A building, house, hall, palace, etc.
hūsbonda 02.03.03 A family, household
hūsbonde 02.03.03 A family, household
hūsbōt 17.02.04.01 Repairing, renewing
hūsbryce 14.02.01.02 Wrongful taking, theft
hūsbrycel 14.02.01.02 Wrongful taking, theft
hūsbryne 03.01.09.02.01.01 A kind of fire
hūscarl 12.01.01.08.01 A servant, attendant
gehūsed 02.06.09.02.09 Snail
hūsel 16.02.04.12 Sacrifice, a sacrifice; 16.02.05.09.01 Eucharistic elements
hūselbearn 16.02.04.07.04 Communion/eucharist
hūselbox 16.02.05.05.06 A vessel for use in services
hūseldisc 16.02.05.05.06 A vessel for use in services
hūselfæt 16.02.05.05.06 A vessel for use in services
hūselgang 16.02.04.07.04 Communion/eucharist

hūselgenga 16.02.04.07.04 Communion/eucharist
hūselhālgung 16.02.04.07.04 Communion/eucharist
hūsellāf 16.02.05.09.01 Eucharistic elements
hūselportic 16.02.05.03.09 A vestry/sacristy
hūselþegn 16.02.03.02.12 Cleric in minor orders
hūsfæst 04.05.03.02.01 A building, house, hall, palace, etc.
hūshefen 04.05.02.08.02 A ceiling, inner roof
hūshlāford 02.03.03 A family, household
hūshlēow 04.05.03.02.01 A building, house, hall, palace, etc.; 11.10.01.02 Refuge, help, shelter
hūsian 04.05.03.02.01 A building, house, hall, palace, etc.; 11.10.01.02 Refuge, help, shelter
hūsincel 04.05.03.02.02 Types of dwelling
hūsl 16.02.04.07.04 Communion/eucharist; 16.02.04.07.04.01 The service of the mass
hūsl ābirgan 16.02.04.07.04 Communion/eucharist
hūsl gehālgian 16.02.04.07.04 Communion/eucharist
hūsl gemǣnsumian 16.02.04.07.04 Communion/eucharist
hūsl tōbrecan 16.02.04.07.04 Communion/eucharist
hūsl þicgan 16.02.04.07.04 Communion/eucharist
hūsles onbyrgan 16.02.04.07.04 Communion/eucharist

hwætemelu

hūsles wirþe 16.02.04.07.04
  Communion/eucharist
(ge)hūslian 16.02.04.07.04
  Communion/eucharist
hūslung 16.02.04.07.04
  Communion/eucharist
hūslwer 16.02.04.07.04
  Communion/eucharist
hūsræden 02.03.03.02 A race, tribe
(ge)hūsscipe 02.03.03.02 A race, tribe
hūsstede 04.05.03.02.01 A building,
  house, hall, palace, etc.
hūsting 12.02.02 An assembly, meeting
hūswist 04.05.03.02.01 A building,
  house, hall, palace, etc.
hūþ 13.02.05.01.02.02 Booty, spoils
hux 07.05.04 Mockery, derision, scorn;
  08.01.01.03.07.04 Scoffing, mockery
huxlic 07.09.03 Infamy, ignominy, shame;
  11.08.02 Inconvenience, unfitness
huxlīce 07.03.05 Infamy, shame,
  wickedness; 07.09.03 Infamy,
  ignominy, shame
huxword 07.05.03.03 Scorn, insult, abuse
hwā 03.04.03.01 Someone/something
gehwā 03.04.03.01 Someone/something
hwǣde 03.03.04.04 Littleness, smallness
(ge)hwǣde 11.08.04 Vanity, idleness,
  frivolity
gehwǣde 02.05.10.16 Quiet, soft, faint;
  05.11.01.02 Shortness/brevity in time
gehwǣdnes 03.03.04.04 Littleness,
  smallness; 03.03.04.04.01 Paucity,
  fewness, scarcity; 12.01.01.06.04
  Inferiority of status, lowest place
hwǣg 04.01.02.01.02.09.08 Whey
hwæl 02.06.05.01.04 Whale
hwælen 02.06.05.01.04 Whale
hwæles ēþel 01.01.03.01.02 Sea/ocean
hwælhunta 04.03.05 Fishing

hwælhuntaþ 04.03.05 Fishing
hwælmere 01.01.03.01.02 Sea/ocean
hwælweg 01.01.03.01.02 Sea/ocean
gehwǣmlic 03.04.03.01
  Someone/something
hwǣr 05.10.04.03 Presence
hwǣr ... hwǣr 05.10.04.03 Presence
hwǣr ... swā 05.10.04.03 Presence
(ge)hwǣr 05.10.04.03 Presence
gehwǣr 05.11.09.01 Always
gehwǣr and þǣr 05.10.04.03 Presence
hwǣrhwega/-hwuga 05.10.04.03
  Presence
hwæs 05.10.06.03.01 A point, spike,
  prickle
hwǣst 02.04.06.07.04 Breathing
hwǣstrian 08.01.03.05 Murmuring,
  complaint; 09.02.03.01 Murmur,
  whispering
hwǣstrung 09.02.03.01 Murmur,
  whispering
hwæt 05.03.01 A cause (of anything);
  05.12.03.01 Swiftness, velocity;
  06.02.07.06.02 Boldness; 11.02.01.01
  Active, nimble
hwæt lā 09.01.03.01 Interjections: Oh!
hwǣte 04.01.02.01.03 Corn;
  04.01.02.01.03.01 Wheat;
  04.02.04.03.02.01.05 Wheat
hwǣteadig 06.02.07.06 Courage,
  boldness, valour
hwǣtecorn 04.01.02.01.03.01 Wheat
hwǣtecroft 04.02.03.02.02.05 Wheat
  land/field
hwǣtecynn 04.02.04.03.02.01.05 Wheat
hwǣtegryttan 04.01.02.01.03.07 Meal
hwǣtehealm 04.02.04.03.02.01.05 Wheat
hwǣteland 04.02.03.02.02.05 Wheat
  land/field
hwǣtemelu 04.01.02.01.03.07 Meal

hwæten 04.01.02.01.03.01 Wheat
hwætesmedma 04.01.02.01.03.07 Meal
hwætewæstm 04.02.04.03.02.01.05 Wheat
hwæthwāra 03.03.04.04 Littleness, smallness
hwæthwega 03.06 Comparison; 05.11.01 Length/duration in time
hwæthwugu 03.03.04.04 Littleness, smallness
hwæthwugununges 03.03.04.04 Littleness, smallness
hwætlīce 05.11.01.02.01 Swift movement of time; 05.12.03.01 Swiftness, velocity; 11.02.01.01 Active, nimble
hwætmōd 06.02.07.06.02 Boldness
gehwætnes 05.11.01.02 Shortness/brevity in time
hwætrēd 06.02.07 Will, determination, resolution
hwætscipe 05.08.01 Vigour, activity, force; 06.02.07.06 Courage, boldness, valour
hwæþer 05.03.01.03 Reason, cause
hwæþer ... þe 05.03.01.03 Reason, cause
hwæþer þe ... þe 05.03.01.03 Reason, cause
(ge)hwæþer 03.04.03.01 Someone/something; 07.01.01 Choice, election
(ge)hwæþere 03.06 Comparison
hwall 07.06.01.01 Proud, arrogant
hwamm 05.10.06.04 A corner, bend, angle
hwamstān 04.05.02.01 A foundation
gehwanon 05.10.04.03 Presence
hwanon(e) 05.03.01 A cause (of anything); 05.03.01.03 Reason, cause
hwanonhwegu 05.10.04.03 Presence
hwasta 02.03.01.03 Eunuch

hwata 16.01.04.06 Divination, augury
hwatend 02.07.11 Plants/flowers (alphabetical order)
hwatu 16.01.04.06 Divination, augury; 16.01.04.06.04 Prophecy, divine speech
hwatung 16.01.04.06 Divination, augury
hwealf 05.10.06.02.01 A hemisphere
hwearf 01.01.02.01.01.03 Shore, bank; 05.12.01.03 Expanse over which something travels; 05.12.01.09.03.04 A harbour; 12.04.02 A crowding together, assembly
(ge)hwearf 05.13.04 Exchange, commutation; 15.01.02 Gift, transfer of property
hwearfian 05.12 To move, be in motion; 05.12.01.02 To wander; 05.12.05 To move and change direction, turn; 05.12.05.04 To rotate, turn round, revolve; 05.12.05.04.01 (Of wheel, etc.) to roll, trundle; 05.12.05.05 To shake, quake, wag; 05.12.05.05.01 To wave, undulate; 05.13 Changeableness, change
hwearfiende 05.12.05.04 To rotate, turn round, revolve
hwearflic 05.11.01.02.01 Swift movement of time
gehwearfnes 16.02.04.10.01 Conversion
hwearft 01.02.01 Heaven(s), sky; 05.11.06 Course/cycle of time
hwearftlian 05.12.01.02 To wander; 05.12.05.04 To rotate, turn round, revolve; 05.12.05.05.01 To wave, undulate
hwearfung 05.13 Changeableness, change; 15.05 Trade, traffic, commerce

hwega 03.03.04.04 Littleness, smallness; 03.06 Comparison
hwelan 02.05.10.05 Roaring, raging
hwelian 02.08.02 Disease, infirmity, sickness; 02.08.05.02.01 Matter, purulence, pus
gehwelian 02.08.12.02.06 Surgical
hwelp(a) 02.06.02.01.04 Dog
hwelpian 02.01.03.03.02 To bring forth, produce
hwelung 02.05.10.02 Noise, din
hwemdragen 05.10.05.04.04 A descent, slope, incline
hwemm 05.10.06.04 A corner, bend, angle
hwemman 05.12.01.09 To travel on water
gehwemman 05.10.05.04.04 A descent, slope, incline
hwēne 03.03.04.04 Littleness, smallness
hwēol 03.03.03.01 Arithmetic; 05.10.06.02 Rotundity, roundness; 14.05.06 Means/implement of torture; 17.03.01 A wheel
hwēolfāg 04.04.09 A fringe, border, hem
hwēolgodweb 04.04.07.07 A long outer garment, covering, cloak, etc.
hwēollāst 05.12.05.04 To rotate, turn round, revolve
hwēolrād 05.12.05.04 To rotate, turn round, revolve
hwēolrīþig 01.01.03.01.01.03 Stream; 04.01.02.02.09 A mill
hwēolweg 05.12.01.03.01.05 Types of road/path
gehweorf 05.10.06.04 A corner, bend, angle; 05.13.01 Transformation, taking another shape; 11.05.02.01 A standard, norm, ethos
hweorfa 02.04.05.04.04 Spine; 02.04.05.04.08 Joint; 04.04.03 A spinning-house or chamber
hweorfan 02.02.03 To die, perish; 05.02.01.01 The course of human affairs; 05.12.01.02 To wander; 05.12.05 To move and change direction, turn; 05.13 Changeableness, change
hweorfan (æfter/be) 05.12.05.06 To travel over/through/along, traverse
(ge)hweorfan 05.12.01 To go, progress, travel (usually on land); 05.12.05.02 To go/travel towards, come, approach; 05.12.05.03.03 To depart, leave, set out; 05.12.05.11.01 To return; 06.01.01.01 Thinking about, minding, heeding; 11.02.01 Energy, vigour, vigorous action; 11.10.02.02.01 Care, interest in; 15.01.02 Gift, transfer of property
(ge)hweorfan (fram/of) 05.12.05.03 To travel away (from)
gehweorfan 05.12.02.08 To give a different direction to, turn; 05.13.04 Exchange, commutation
hweorfbān 02.04.05.04.07 Bone of leg; 02.04.05.04.08 Joint
hweorfende 05.13 Changeableness, change
hwer 04.01.02.02.06.01 Cooking vessel/pot
hwerhwette 02.07.09.02.02.02 Other vegetables (alphabetical order)
hwet(e)stān 17.03.04 Tools for smoothing/scraping/grinding
hwettan 17.02.04.03.02 Filings
(ge)hwettan 08.01.01.01.03 An incitement, cause of strong feeling
hwicce 04.05.04.03 A box, case, chest, container
hwicung 02.05.10.15.06 A roar, howl, etc.

hwider 05.10.04.03 Presence
hwider/hwidre 05.10.04.03 Presence
hwider swā/swā hwider (swā) 05.10.04.03 Presence
gehwider 05.10.04.03 Presence
hwiderhwega 05.10.04.03 Presence
hwiderryne 05.12.05 To move and change direction, turn
hwielfan 05.10.06.02.02 Curvature, bend, twist
hwierfan 05.02.01.01 The course of human affairs; 05.12.01 To go, progress, travel (usually on land); 05.12.05.04 To rotate, turn round, revolve; 06.01.01.01 Thinking about, minding, heeding
(ge)hwierfan 05.12.02.08 To give a different direction to, turn; 05.12.05 To move and change direction, turn; 05.12.05.04 To rotate, turn round, revolve; 05.12.05.11.01 To return; 05.13.01 Transformation, taking another shape
gehwierfan 05.03.01.02 To work upon, influence; 05.06 Destruction, dissolution, loss, breaking; 05.10.04 Place, room; 05.12.02 To move, set in motion; 05.13 Changeableness, change; 06.01.04 Faculty of memory; 09.04.03.01 A translation; 12.08.06.01.04.01 To mislead, seduce, lead astray; 15.01.02 Gift, transfer of property
gehwierfan on 05.13 Changeableness, change
gehwierfan tō/on 11.05.02 Mode, manner, way, method, fashion, course
hwierflīce 05.13.03 Regular alternation
hwīl 05.11 A time, period of time; 05.11.02 A time, particular time, occasion; 05.11.03.01.05 A day; 05.11.03.01.06 An hour
hwilc 03.04.03.01 Someone/something
gehwilc 03.04 Form, kind, nature, character; 03.04.01 Singularity, peculiarity; 03.04.03.01 Someone/something
hwilchwene 03.04.03.01 Someone/something
hwilchwugu 03.04.03.01 Someone/something
(ge)hwilcnes 03.04 Form, kind, nature, character
hwīle 05.11.01 Length/duration in time
hwīlen 05.11.01.02 Shortness/brevity in time; 16.02.03.03.05 A layman
hwīlfæc 05.11 A time, period of time
hwilpe 02.06.08.06 Water bird
hwīlsticce 05.11.01.02 Shortness/brevity in time
hwīltīdum 05.11.09.03 At times, sometimes; 05.11.11.02 Let up, intermission, cessation
hwīltīdum ... hwīltīdum 05.11.09.03 At times, sometimes
hwīlþrāg 05.11 A time, period of time
hwīlum 05.11.02 A time, particular time, occasion; 05.11.09.03 At times, sometimes
hwīlum ... hwīlum 05.11.09.03 At times, sometimes
hwīl(w)ende 05.11.01.02 Shortness/brevity in time; 05.11.01.03 Mutability
hwīlwendlic 05.11.01.02 Shortness/brevity in time
hwīl(w)endlic 05.11.01.03 Mutability; 16.02.03.03.05 A layman
hwīlwendlīce 05.11.01.02 Shortness/brevity in time

hwīnan 02.05.10.09 A hissing, whistling
hwinsian 02.05.10.15.06 A roar, howl, etc.
hwinsung 02.05.10.15.06 A roar, howl, etc.
hwiscettung 02.05.10.15.06 A roar, howl, etc.
hwisprian 02.05.10.16 Quiet, soft, faint
hwisprung 02.05.10.16 Quiet, soft, faint
hwistle 18.02.07.02.02.01 Pipe/flute
hwistlere 18.02.07.02.02.01 Pipe/flute
hwistlian 02.05.10.09 A hissing, whistling
hwistlung 02.05.10.09 A hissing, whistling; 18.02.07.02.02.01 Pipe/flute
hwīt 02.04.04.01 Having a certain complexion; 03.01.12 Brightness, light; 03.01.14.02 Pallor, absence of colour; 03.01.14.03 White/whiteness; 04.01.02.01.01.06 Lenten/fast-day food; 04.01.02.01.02.08 Egg; 04.04.07.06 White clothing; 04.06.01.09 To cleanse, remove impurity from (an object); 12.08.04 Purity, moral cleanness
hwīta sunnandæg 16.02.04.04.02.01.03 Holy Week
(ge)hwītan 03.01.14.03 White/whiteness; 04.06.01 Clean
hwītcorn 04.01.02.01.07.03.04 (Biblical) manna/bread of heaven
hwītcwidu/-cudu 04.01.02.01.07.05.01 Gum
hwīte 03.01.14.03 White/whiteness
hwīte clǣfre 02.07.11 Plants/flowers (alphabetical order)
hwītecylle 17.03.12 A receptacle, container
hwītegōs 02.06.08.02.01.02 Goose
hwītehlāf 04.01.02.01.07.03 Bread
hwītel 04.04.08 A covering, curtain, veil, garment, etc.
hwītfōt 02.06.01.04 Leg
(ge)hwītian 03.01.14.03 White/whiteness
hwītingmelu 03.01.14.03 White/whiteness
hwītingtrēow 02.07.03.05 Particular trees/shrubs (alphabetical order)
hwītlēac 02.07.09.02.02.01 Edible root/bulb
hwītlēadtēafor 02.08.12.02.05.02 Salves, ointments
hwītling 02.06.06.03.01.14 Whiting
hwītloc 02.04.04.03.02 Colour of hair
hwītloccede 02.04.04.03.02 Colour of hair
hwītnes 03.01.14.03 White/whiteness
hwiþa 01.03.01.05 Wind
hwōn 03.03.04.04 Littleness, smallness; 03.03.04.04.01 Paucity, fewness, scarcity; 05.10.05.01 A little way, no great distance; 05.11.01.02 Shortness/brevity in time
hwōnlic 03.03.04.04 Littleness, smallness
hwōnlīce 03.03.04.04 Littleness, smallness; 05.11.01.02 Shortness/brevity in time; 09.03.04.05 To put briefly
hwōnlotum 03.03.07 A part, division, portion
hwonne 05.11.02 A time, particular time, occasion; 05.11.07.03.02 Earlier, antecedent
hwonne ǣr 05.11.02 A time, particular time, occasion
hwōpan 08.01.03.09.07 Threat, threatening, menace
hwōsan 02.04.06.05.07.02 Mucus, phlegm, rheum

hwōsta 02.04.06.05.07.02 Mucus, phlegm, rheum
hwoþerian 02.05.10.05 Roaring, raging
hwoþrung 02.05.10.06 Harsh sound
hwugudǽl 03.03.04.04 Littleness, smallness
hwurful 05.13.05 Changeability
hwurfulnes 05.13.05 Changeability
hwȳ 06.01.08.05.01 Amazement, astonishment, wonder, admiration; 05.03.01 A cause (of anything)
hwylca 02.08.05.02 Particular inflammation/swelling
hwyorf 02.06.02.01.03 Cattle
gehwyrfednes 05.02.02.01 Inclination
gehwyrf(ed)nes 16.02.04.10.01 Conversion
hwyrfel 05.10.06 Form, shape; 05.11.06 Course/cycle of time
hwyrfepōl 01.01.03.05 Whirlpool
hwyrflede 05.10.06.02 Rotundity, roundness
hwyrfling 05.10.06.02 Rotundity, roundness
hwyrflung 08.01.03.06.01 Affliction, misfortune, calamity; 12.08.06.01 Error, wrong conduct, erroneous practice
hwyrfnes 02.08.11.02 Mental weakness
hwyrfolung 05.11.06 Course/cycle of time
hwyrft 05.12.01 To go, progress, travel (usually on land); 05.12.01.03 Expanse over which something travels; 05.12.05 To move and change direction, turn; 05.12.05.04 To rotate, turn round, revolve; 05.12.05.11.01 To return
gehwyrftnes 05.12.05.11.01 To return
hwyrftweg 11.10.05 Escape

hycgan (on/tō) 06.01.08.02 Hope, expectation
(ge)hycgan 06.01.01 Thought, the faculty of thinking, mind; 06.01.01.01 Thinking about, minding, heeding; 06.01.04 Faculty of memory; 06.01.05.01 Understanding; 06.02.06 Mind, purpose
gehycglic 03.03.04.01.01 Greatness, bigness, size
hȳd 02.04.04 Skin; 02.06.01.06 Skin, hide; 14.05.05 Physical punishments; 17.04.04.02 Skin, hide (as material)
gehȳd 02.04.04 Skin
(ge)hȳdan 09.05.04.01 Concealment, obscurity
gehȳdan 09.05.04 A secret; 11.10.01.02 Refuge, help, shelter
hȳdels 09.05.04.01 Concealment, obscurity
hȳdgild 14.05.04.01 A fine
hȳdig 17.04.04.02 Skin, hide (as material)
gehȳdnes 08.01.01.03.01 Freedom from trouble, comfort, security
hȳdsacc 17.03.12 A receptacle, container
hȳdscip 05.12.01.09.03.01.01 Kind of ship
hȳf 04.02.05.06.08.01 A beehive
(ge)hygd 06.01.01.01.01 Thought, cogitation, meditation
gehygd 11.02.03 Forethought, care
hygdig 12.08.03.03.01.01 Chastity
hygdiglīce 12.08.03.03.01.01 Chastity
hygdignes 12.08.03.03.01.01 Chastity
hyge 06.01 The head (as seat of thought); 06.02.07.06 Courage, boldness, valour; 07.06 Pride
hȳge 02.04.06.03.02.02 Throat/gullet
hygebend 08.01 Heart, spirit, mood, disposition

hygeblind 06.01.05.03 Want of understanding
hygeblīþe 08.01.01.03 Good feeling, joy, happiness
hygeclǣne 12.08.04 Purity, moral cleanness
hygecræft 06.01.05.02 Intelligence
hygecræftig 06.01.05.02.01.01 Sagacity
hȳgedriht 12.01.01.07 A follower
hygefæst 06.01.05.02.01.01 Sagacity
hygefrōd 06.01.05.02.01.01 Sagacity
hygefrōfor 08.01.03.07.04.02.01 Comfort, consolation
hygegǣlsa 05.12.03.02 Slowness
hygegāl 12.08.07.01.01 Wantonness, sensuality, lasciviousness
hygegār 11.04.02.01.01 Cunning, craft, craftiness, guile, wile
hygegēomor 08.01.03 Bad feeling, sadness
hygeglēaw 06.01.05.02.01.01 Sagacity
hygegrim 08.01.03.09.11 Hardheartedness, cruelty, severity
hygel 01.01.02.01.02.01 Rising ground, eminence
hygelēas 06.01.05.03.02.01 Foolishness, lightmindedness; 06.02.07.07 Cowardice, pusillanimity; 07.06.04.02 Extravagance
hygelēaslic 06.01.05.03.02.01 Foolishness, lightmindedness
hygelēaslīce 06.01.05.03.02.01 Foolishness, lightmindedness
hygelēast 06.01.05.03.02.01 Foolishness, lightmindedness
hygemǣþum 07.04.03 Reverence, respect
hygemēþe 08.01.03 Bad feeling, sadness
hygerōf 06.02.07.01 Strength, fortitude
hygerūn 09.05.04 A secret

hygesceaft 06 Spirit, soul, heart; 08.01 Heart, spirit, mood, disposition
hygesnottor 06.01.05.02.01.01 Sagacity
hygesorg 08.01.03 Bad feeling, sadness
hygestrang 06.02.07.01 Strength, fortitude
hygetēona 08.01.03.07.02.01 Injury, offence
hygetrēow 12.01.01.12 Loyalty
hygeþanc 06.01.01 Thought, the faculty of thinking, mind
hygeþancol 06.01.05.02.01.01 Sagacity
hygeþihtig 06.02.07.01 Strength, fortitude
hygeþrymm 06.02.07.06 Courage, boldness, valour
hygeþrȳþ 07.06.01 Pride, arrogance
hygewælm 08.01.01.01 Ardour, fervour, strong feeling
hygewlanc 07.06 Pride
hyht 06.01.08.02 Hope, expectation; 06.01.08.03 Trust, faith, confidence; 06.02.06 Mind, purpose; 08.01.01.03.06 Exultation, joy
(ge)hyht 11.10.01.02 Refuge, help, shelter
hyhtan 06.01.08 Expectation; 06.01.08.02 Hope, expectation
(ge)hyhtan 06.01.08.02 Hope, expectation; 08.01.01.03.06 Exultation, joy
(ge)hyhtan (on/tō) 06.01.08.03 Trust, faith, confidence
hyhtende 08.01.01.03.06 Exultation, joy
gehyhtendlic 06.01.08.02 Hope, expectation
hyhtful 06.01.08.02.01 Encouragement, comfort; 08.01.01.03.04 Gladness, cheerfulness; 08.01.01.03.09.01 Pleasant, agreeable
hyhtgiefu 10.03 Giving

hyhtgifa 16.01.01.04.02 The Son, Christ
hyhting 08.01.01.03.06 Exultation, joy
hyhtlēas 06.01.08.06.07 Despair
hyhtlic 06.01.08.02.01 Encouragement, comfort; 08.01.01.03.06 Exultation, joy; 08.01.01.03.09.01 Pleasant, agreeable
hyhtlīce 08.01.01.03.09.02 Pleasantly, agreeably
gehyhtlīce 03.06.03 Congruity, fitness, suitability
hyhtplega 18.02.02 Play, (athletic) sport
hyhtwilla 06.01.08.02 Hope, expectation
hyhtwynn 08.01.01.03 Good feeling, joy, happiness
hylc 01.01.02.01.02.01 Rising ground, eminence; 05.10.05.04.08.01 A bend
gehylced 02.08.04.02 Blemish, disfigurement
hyldan 05.06.06.01 A tearing, laceration
hyldāþ 14.03.03.04 Oath-swearing
hylde 01.01.02.01.02.02 Hill, mountain
hyldemǣg 02.03.02.03.06.02 Close relationship
hyldere 14.05.05 Physical punishments
hylding 05.10.06.02.02 Curvature, bend, twist
hyldo 08.01.02.01 Favour, kindness, grace; 08.01.02.03 Friendliness, affection; 08.01.02.04.02 Thanks, gratitude; 12.01.01.12 Loyalty
hyldrǣden 12.01.01.12 Loyalty
hyll 01.01.02.01.02.02 Hill, mountain; 01.01.02.01.02.02.01 Hill
hyllehāma 02.06.09.02.05 Cricket, grasshopper, locust
hyllic 01.01.02.01.02.02.01 Hill
hylloc 01.01.02.01.02.01 Rising ground, eminence
hylsten 04.01.02.02.05.04 Baking

hylsung 18.02.07.02.01 Percussion instruments
hylu 01.01.02.01.03 Hollow/depression in land
hylwyrt 02.07.10.01 Particular herbs/spices (alphabetical order); 02.07.11 Plants/flowers (alphabetical order)
hymele 02.07.09.02 Particular fruits (alphabetical order)
hymlic/-līce 02.07.11 Plants/flowers (alphabetical order)
hynden 12.04.01.01 A company of people, fellowship, society
hyndenmann 12.02.02 An assembly, meeting
(ge)hyngr(i)an 04.01.01.03 Hunger
hype 02.04.03.03.04 Side
hȳpe 01.01.02.01.02.01 Rising ground, eminence
hypebān 02.04.05.04.05.04 Hip-bone
hypebānece 02.08.07.07 Disorders of the body
hȳpel 01.01.02.01.02.01 Rising ground, eminence; 03.03.04.01.02.01 A heap, mass, accumulation
hypeseax 13.02.08.04.03 A sword
hyppels 05.12.01.03.03 A fordable place
hypping 05.12.01.03.03 A fordable place
hypsār 02.08.07.07 Disorders of the body
hypwærc 02.08.07.07 Disorders of the body
hȳr 15.02.04 Spending, disbursement; 15.02.04.01 Payment for temporary use, rent, hire; 15.04.01 Lending of money
hȳra 12.01.01.07 A follower; 12.01.01.08.01 A servant, attendant; 15.01.01.01 Holding of land
hyran 02.04.06.06.04 Spittle

hyrd 02.06.01.06 Skin, hide; 09.03.07.06.06 Membrane, vellum
hyrdel 02.06.01.03 Barrel, body of animal; 04.05.01.02.05 A hurdle
hyrden 03.01.03 Hardness, callosity, hard material
hyrdung 05.08 Strength
hȳreborg 15.04.01 Lending of money
gehȳred 15.01.01.01.01 Hiring, letting out of property/land
hȳregilda 15.02.04 Spending, disbursement
hȳrgeoht 04.02.05.06 Animals yoked together
hyrian 03.06.01.01 Imitation
(ge)hȳrian 17.02.01 Management of work
hyring 03.06.01.01.01 Imitation, emulation
hȳrling 12.01.01.08.01 A servant, attendant
hyrnan 05.10.05.04.07 A fork (in river, road, etc.)
hyrne 05.10.06.04 A corner, bend, angle
hyrned 05.12.01.09.03.01.02 Of/concerning a ship, naval
gehyrned 02.06.01.02 Head
hyrnednebba 02.06.08.01 Part of bird
hyrnen 05.10.06.04 A corner, bend, angle; 17.04.03.03 Horn
hyrnet(u) 02.06.09.02.07 Fly; 02.06.09.02.02 Bee, hornet, wasp
hyrnful 05.10.06.04 A corner, bend, angle
hyrnig 05.10.06.04 A corner, bend, angle
hyrnstān 04.05.02.01 A foundation; 11.07.04 Superiority, pre-eminence, primacy
hȳroxa 04.02.05.06 Animals yoked together
hyrse 02.06.02.01.06 Horse

hyrst 01.01.02.01.02.01 Rising ground, eminence; 02.07.03.04.01 A small wood, coppice, copse; 04.04.07 Trappings, equipment, garb; 13.02.08.03.01 Body armour, war gear
(ge)hyrst 07.10.03 An adornment, decoration, ornament
gehyrst hlāf 04.01.02.01.07.03.03 Piece of bread
gehyrstan 07.05.03.01 Falseness in speech, detraction; 07.10.03 An adornment, decoration, ornament
(ge)hyrsted 07.10.03 An adornment, decoration, ornament
gehȳrung 15.01.01.01.01 Hiring, letting out of property/land
(ge)hyscan 07.05.04 Mockery, derision, scorn
hȳscen 04.05.03.02.02 Types of dwelling
hyscend 07.05.04 Mockery, derision, scorn
hyscende 07.05.04 Mockery, derision, scorn
hyse 02.03.01.06 Young man; 02.03.02.03.05 Descendant; 13.02.10.01 A man, warrior
hysebeorþor 02.01.03.03.03.01 Child-bearing, childbirth; 02.03.01.05 Youth, boy, stripling
hyseberþling 02.01.03.03.03.01 Child-bearing, childbirth
hyseberþre 02.01.03.03.03.01 Child-bearing, childbirth; 02.03.02.01 Parent
hysebyrding 02.01.03.03.03.01 Child-bearing, childbirth
hysecild 02.03.01.04 Child
hyserinc 02.03.01.06 Young man
hysewīse 02.03.01.06 Young man

gehyspan 07.05.03.03.02 To reproach, revile, abuse; 07.05.04 Mockery, derision, scorn
hyspend 07.05.03.02 Calumny, slander, insult
gehyspendlic 07.05.02 Contempt
hyspful 07.05.03.03.01 Contumelious, scornful
hyspnes 07.05.03.03 Scorn, insult, abuse
hyspung 07.05.03.03 Scorn, insult, abuse
hyt 03.01.09 Heat
hȳþ 05.12.01.09.03.04 A harbour
(ge)hȳþan 05.06.01 Devastation, laying waste; 14.02.01.02.01 Open robbery, rapine, pillage
gehȳþe 03.06.03 Congruity, fitness, suitability
(ge)hȳþegian 11.12.01 Absence of restraint, freedom
hȳþegung 11.07.03 Use, advantage, profit
gehȳþelic 11.07.02 Utility, advantage, convenience
gehȳþelīce 11.07.02 Utility, advantage, convenience
gehȳþelicnes 11.07.03 Use, advantage, profit
hȳþende 05.06 Destruction, dissolution, loss, breaking
hȳþgild 16.02.01.06.01 Belief/practice of heathen people
hȳþlic 05.12.01.09.03.04 A harbour
(ge)hȳþlic 11.07.02 Utility, advantage, convenience
gehȳþnes 11.07.02 Utility, advantage, convenience
hȳþscip 05.12.01.09.03.01.01 Kind of ship
hȳþþ(o) 11.07.03 Use, advantage, profit
gehȳþþo 11.07.02 Utility, advantage, convenience
hȳþweard 05.12.01.09.03.04 A harbour; 11.10.02.02 Watchful care, keeping guard
ī 09.03.07.01 A written character, letter
īacin(c)tus 17.04.03.04 Gems collectively
ianuarius 05.11.03.01.03.01 Specific months
ic 03.04.01 Singularity, peculiarity
īcels 15.01.01 Landed property
īcend 03.03.04.03 Growth, increase
īcestre 03.03.04.03 Growth, increase
icgegold 15.01.03 Treasure, riches, wealth
īdæges 05.11.03.01.05 A day
īdel 03.03.04.05 Insufficiency, lack, want; 03.03.08 Emptiness; 06.01.05.03 Want of understanding; 10.02 Want, lack; 11.06 Disinclination to act, listlessness; 11.08 Uselessness; 11.08.01 Uselessness, unserviceableness; 11.08.04 Vanity, idleness, frivolity
īdel lust 06.02.05.01 Strong liking for, devotion to
īdelbliss 08.01.01.03 Good feeling, joy, happiness
īdelgeorn 11.06 Disinclination to act, listlessness; 11.08.04 Vanity, idleness, frivolity
īdelgield 16.02.01.06.01.01 Pagan worship, idolatrous practice(s)
īdelgielp 07.06.02 Arrogance, vainglory, vanity
īdelgildoffrung 16.02.04.12 Sacrifice, a sacrifice
īdelhende 03.03.04.05 Insufficiency, lack, want; 10.02 Want, lack
īdeling 11.08.04 Vanity, idleness, frivolity
īdellic 11.08.04 Vanity, idleness, frivolity

īdellīce 05.03.01.01 Without need or cause; 11.08.03 Needless, useless, unprofitable
īdelnes 03.03.08 Emptiness; 11.06 Disinclination to act, listlessness; 11.08.01 Uselessness, unserviceableness; 11.08.04 Vanity, idleness, frivolity; 16.02.01.06 Paganism, a false religion
ides 02.03.01.02 Female person, woman
īdig 05.10.06.03.01 A point, spike, prickle
(ge)īdlian 03.03.08 Emptiness; 11.08.03 Needless, useless, unprofitable; 16.02.04.14 Sacrilege
īdol 16.02.01.06.01.01.01 An image, idol
idus 05.11.06.01 Cycle of the year
(ge)īecan 03.03.04.03 Growth, increase
geīecan 11.01.05 Accomplishment, fulfilment
īeg 01.01.02.01.01.02 Island
īegbūend 02.03.03.04.02 Dwellers by the sea
īegland 01.01.02.01.01.02 Island
ieldan 02.08.02 Disease, infirmity, sickness; 03.02.01.02 Decay from age; 06.01.07.04.04.02 Pretence, feigning, dissimulation
(ge)ieldan 05.11.08.01.03.01 Delay
ielde 02.03.01 People
ielden 05.11.08.01.03.01 Delay
ieldendlic 05.11.08.01.03.01 Delay
ieldest 02.01.04 Age; 11.07.04 Superiority, pre-eminence, primacy; 12.01.01.06.08 A person of rank, elder, great man
ieldful 05.11.08.01.03.01 Delay
ieldian 05.11.08.01.03.01 Delay
ielding 05.11.08.01.03.01 Delay; 06.01.07.04.04.02 Pretence, feigning, dissimulation

ieldo 02.01.04.03 Aging, growing old; 03.02.01.02 Decay from age; 05.11.03 Period of time, era, epoch
īeldo 02.01.04 Age
ieldra 02.01.04 Age; 02.03.02.01 Parent; 02.03.02.03.03 Forefather, ancestor; 12.01.01.06.08 A person of rank, elder, great man
ieldra fæder 02.03.02.03.04 (Of degrees of descent) great-, grand-
ierfa 15.01.02.01 Inherited property
ierfe 02.06.02 Domestic animals, livestock; 04.02.05 Livestock; 15.01 Property; 15.01.02.01 Inherited property
(ge)ierfian 10.03.04 Provision, supply
geierfian 04.02.03.04.02 Pasture/pasturage
geiergan 06.01.08.06.03.01 Causing dread, terrifying
iergþ(u) 06.02.07.07 Cowardice, pusillanimity
ierlic 08.01.03.05.02 Anger
ierlīce 08.01.03.05.02 Anger
(ge)ierman 12.05.06.02.03 Trouble, disturbance
geierman 15.01.06 Poverty, indigence
ierming 08.01.03.06 Adversity, affliction
iermþ 08.01.03.06 Adversity, affliction; 12.08.06 Moral evil, depravity; 15.01.06 Poverty, indigence
iernan 02.04.06.08.01 Blood; 02.08.08.12 Disease of bowels; 05.12.03.01 Swiftness, velocity; 05.12.05 To move and change direction, turn; 05.12.05.04 To rotate, turn round, revolve; 09.06.02.01.05.01 To spread, make known, proclaim, celebrate; 11.10.02.02.01 Care, interest in; 18.02.03.01.02 Racing

iernan on gemynde 06.01 The head (as seat of thought)
iernan (ūt, of) 01.01.03.03 Flow/flowing
(ge)iernan 05.11 A time, period of time; 05.12.05.02 To go/travel towards, come, approach; 11.06.03.01 Ill fortune, bad success
(ge)iernan on mōd 06.01 The head (as seat of thought)
(ge)iernan/rinnan (tō) 05.12.03.01 Swiftness, velocity
geiernan 05.12 To move, be in motion; 05.12.05.02.03 To arrive; 10.01.02 Acquisition; 11.02.01 Energy, vigour, vigorous action
geiernan/gerinnan 03.01.17.01 A coagulating, mixing; 05.12.05.02.02 To come together, meet
geiernan in 05.12.05.02.01 To come upon, meet with
geiernan tō 13.02.03 To seek with active intent, attack
iernende 01.01.03.03 Flow/flowing
iernes 08.01.03.05.02 Anger
ierning 05.12.05.04 To rotate, turn round, revolve
ierre 02.08.11.02.01.02 Madness, frenzy, folly; 08.01.03.05.02 Anger; 12.08.06.01.02 Lacking moral good
ierremōd 08.01.03.05.02 Anger
ierreþweorh 08.01.03.05.02 Anger
ierringa 08.01.03.05.02 Anger
ierscipe 08.01.03.05.02 Anger
(ge)iersian 08.01.03.05.02 Anger
(ge)iersian wiþ (on/ongean) 08.01.03.05.02 Anger
iersigende 08.01.03.05.02 Anger
iersigendlic 08.01.03.05.02 Anger
iersung 08.01.03.05.02 Anger
iesend(e)/gesen 02.04.06.03.02.04 Intestines
īeþ 11.12 Easiness
īeþan 05.06.01 Devastation, laying waste
geīeþan 08.01.02.01.02 Gentleness; 08.01.03.07.04.02 Relief, alleviation
īeþbilge 08.01.03.05.04 Irritability
īeþe 01.01.02.01.06 Wild/uncultivated land; 08.01.01.03.09.01 Pleasant, agreeable; 08.01.02.01.02.01 Mildness, leniency, indulgence; 11.12 Easiness
īeþelic 03.03.04.04 Littleness, smallness; 11.12 Easiness
īeþelīce 11.12 Easiness
īeþnes 08.01.01.03.01 Freedom from trouble, comfort, security; 08.01.02.01.02 Gentleness; 11.12 Easiness
īeþost 11.12 Easiness
geīeþrian 02.08.13 Recovery, growing better; 08.01.03.07.04.02 Relief, alleviation
īeþrung 11.12.02.02 Amendment, setting right, reparation
īeþtogen 11.12 Easiness
(ge)īewan 09.05.05.01 Showing, manifestation, display
geīewan 10.03 Giving
īfe 02.07.11.02 Unidentified plants (alphabetical order)
īfed 02.07.03.05 Particular trees/shrubs (alphabetical order)
īfig 02.07.03.05 Particular trees/shrubs (alphabetical order)
īfigbearo 02.07.03.05 Particular trees/shrubs (alphabetical order)
īfigcrop(pa) 02.07.03.05 Particular trees/shrubs (alphabetical order)
īfiglēaf 02.07.03.05 Particular trees/shrubs (alphabetical order)

īfigrind 02.07.03.05 Particular trees/shrubs (alphabetical order)
īfigtearo 03.01.17.06 Resin, tar, gum
īfigtwig 02.07.03.05 Particular trees/shrubs (alphabetical order)
īfiht(e) 02.07.03.05 Particular trees/shrubs (alphabetical order)
iggaþ 01.01.02.01.01.02 Island
geiht 03.03.06.01 A whole formed by joining
īl 02.06.03.01.09 Hedgehog
(ge)ilca 03.06.01.02 Equality
ile 02.04.03.04.02.05.02 Sole; 02.08.07.08.02 Swelling of the foot
ilfetu 02.06.08.06 Water bird
illeracu 04.01.01.05 Satiety (of food)
geillerocad 04.01.03.02 To drink heavily, get drunk
ilme 02.07.03.05 Particular trees/shrubs (alphabetical order)
impa 04.02.04.03 A plant
impian 04.02.04.03 A plant
geimpian 11.02 Occupation, activity, business
imping 04.02.04.05.04 A detached area of woodland
in (...) steall 05.13.04 Exchange, commutation
in āberan 05.12.02.01 To fetch, bring, bear, conduct
in anweald gereccan 12.05.06.04 A trampling upon, subjection
in āsendan 05.12.02.03 To send
in beran 05.12.02.01 To fetch, bring, bear, conduct
in brengan 05.12.02.01 To fetch, bring, bear, conduct
in (ge)bringan 05.12.02.01 To fetch, bring, bear, conduct
in gebūgan 05.12.05.02.04 To go in, enter

in eallum þingum 03.04.03.01 Someone/something
in/on ēawunge 09.05.05.01 Showing, manifestation, display
in ēcnesse 05.11.01.01.01 Eternity
in ende 05.11.11 Continuity
in feccan 05.12.02.01 To fetch, bring, bear, conduct
in fȳre wesan 03.01.09.02.01 Fire, burning
in heortan and heortan 06.01.07.04.04 Deceitfulness, falseness, duplicity
in/on (ge)hrēosan 13.02.03.01 An attack, assault
in (ge)lǣdan 05.12.02.01 To fetch, bring, bear, conduct
in lǣtan 05.12.05.02.04 To go in, enter
in gemǣnnesse 03.04.03 Generality
in sendan 05.12.02.03 To send
in gesincan 02.08.03 Pain, bodily discomfort
in stæpe 05.11.07.01 Contemporary, coeval
in swaþum 02.08.12.02.06.01 A bandage, binding
in þryccan 05.12.05.02.01 To come upon, meet with
in weorcan 05.03.01.02 To work upon, influence
in werþēode 01 Earth, world
inādl 02.08.08 Internal disease
ināwritting 09.03.07.05 To cover with writing, inscribe
inbærnednes 16.02.05.09.02 Incense
inbærnes 16.02.05.09.02 Incense
inbecweþan 06.01.06.02.03.04.05 Edification, instruction; 06.02.06.03.03 Incitement
inbegietan 11.03.01.03 Finding, discovery

inbelǣdan 05.12.05.08.01 To go before and guide
inbelūcan 05.10.05.04.15 Closure, being closed
inbend 02.08.08 Internal disease
inbeslēan 05.06.04 Damage, injury, defect, hurt, loss
inbestingan 05.06.07 Pricking, a prick, puncture
inbetȳnednes 16.02.03.03.04 A solitary (anchorite, hermit)
inbewindan 05.10.05.04.12 The condition of being covered
inbīecnan 06.01.06.02.03.04.05 Edification, instruction
inbirgan 02.05.07 Faculty of taste
inblāwan 02.04.06.07.05 To breathe; 03.01.15.01 Inspiration, inbreathing; 07.06.01.03 To be proud/arrogant
inblāwing 02.04.06.07.04 Breathing
inboden 09.06.02.01.05 Proclamation, spreading abroad
inbolgen 08.01.03.05.02 Anger
inborena 02.03.03.03.01 A native people
inborh 14.03.03.07 Security, pledge, bail
inbrecan 05.12.05.02.01 To come upon, meet with
inbrōht 05.10.04.03 Presence
inbryne 03.01.09.02.01 Fire, burning
inbryrd 08.01.01.01 Ardour, fervour, strong feeling
inbryrdnes 08.01.03.02.01 Compunction, remorse, contrition
(ge)inbūan 04.05.03.01 Habitation, sojourn
inbūend 02.03.03.03.01 A native people; 04.05.03.01 Habitation, sojourn
inburh 04.05.02.12.01 A porch, covered entrance

inbyrde 02.03.03.04.04 Inhabitant(s) of a 'tūn'
inbyrdling 02.03.03.03.01 A native people; 12.01.01.09 Bondage, slavery
inca 05.11.08 A suitable time, opportunity; 06.01.07.06.02 Unbelief; 08.01.03.05.01 A grudge
incan witan 08.01.03.05.01 A grudge
incēgung 16.02.04.08.01 Kinds of prayer
incempa 13.02.10 The military, soldiers
geincfullian 08.01.03.07.02.01 Injury, offence
incleofe 02.06.01.08 A lair, den; 04.05.03.04 A closet, chamber, room; 09.05.04.01 Concealment, obscurity
incniht 12.01.01.08.01 A servant, attendant
incofa 04.05.03.04 A closet, chamber, room; 06 Spirit, soul, heart
incoþu 02.08.08 Internal disease
incuman 05.12.05.02.04 To go in, enter
incund 05.10.05.04.01 Inside, interior; 06 Spirit, soul, heart; 08.01.01.01.04 Depth of feeling, zeal
incundlīce 08.01.01.01.04 Depth of feeling, zeal
incundnes 05.10.05.04.01 Inside, interior; 08.01.01.01 Ardour, fervour, strong feeling
incūþ 12.04.03 A stranger; 12.08.06.02.03 (Of persons) wicked, evil-doing
incūþlīce 08.01.03.07.04 Severity, harshness
incyme 05.12.05.02.04 To go in, enter
indǣlan 05.12.05.02.04.01 To insert into (a hole)
(ge)indēpan 05.12.05.02.04.03 To plunge (something into something)
indīegelnes 09.05.04.01 Concealment, obscurity

indisc 02.03.03.06.07.04 Indian; 09.03.01 Particular languages
indrencan 08.01.01.01.03 An incitement, cause of strong feeling
(ge)indrencan 04.01.03.02 To drink heavily, get drunk
indrincan 04.01.03 Drinking
indruncen 04.01.03.02 To drink heavily, get drunk
indryhten 07.08.08 Nobleness, honour, glory
indryhto 07.08.08 Nobleness, honour, glory
ineardian 04.05.03.01 Habitation, sojourn
ineardiend 02.03.03.04 An inhabitant
ineddisc 15.01 Property
inēþung 02.04.06.07.04 Breathing
infær 04.05.02.12.02 A vestibule, entrance, courtyard; 05.12.05.02.04 To go in, enter; 14.01.04.02 Rights involving property
infæreld 04.05.02.12.02 A vestibule, entrance, courtyard; 14.01.04.02 Rights involving property
infangeneþēof 14.03 Right of holding court, jurisdiction
infaran 05.12.05.02.04 To go in, enter
infarende 05.12.05.02.04 To go in, enter
infaru 13.02.03 To seek with active intent, attack
infeallan 05.12.05.13.03 To fall
infēran 05.12.05.02.04 To go in, enter
infiht 12.05.04.01.01 Fighting, a fight
infindan 11.03.01.03 Finding, discovery
inflǣscnes 16.01.01.04.02.01 Incarnation
inflēde 01.01.03.06 Flood
inflēon 11.10.04 Flight
in(for)lǣtan 05.12.05.02.04 To go in, enter
infōster 04.02.05.01 Care of livestock
infrignan 09.05.02 A question, inquiry, questioning
infrōd 02.01.04.03 Aging, growing old; 06.01.05.02.01.01 Sagacity
ing 09.03.07.01.01 A runic letter
ingān 05.12.05.02.04 To go in, enter
ingang 04.05.02.12.02 A vestibule, entrance, courtyard; 05.11.10.01 A beginning; 05.12.05.02.04 To go in, enter; 14.01.04.02 Rights involving property; 15.02 Worth, value; 16.02.04.07.05.01.01 Going into a monastery, admission
ingangan 05.05.01 An author, source, originator; 05.12.05.02.04 To go in, enter
in(ge)birgan 04 Consumption of food/drink
in(ge)būgan 05.12.05.02.04 To go in, enter
in(ge)cēgan 16.02.04.08.01 Kinds of prayer
ingecīgan 09.01.03 To address, speak to
ingedōn 05.10.05.04.01 Inside, interior
ingedrincan 03.01.16.01 Moisture
ingefeoht 13.02 War
ingefolc 02.03.03.03.01 A native people
ingehrif 02.04.06.04.02 Female reproductive organs
ingehygd 06.01.01 Thought, the faculty of thinking, mind; 06.01.06.01.01 Knowledge; 09.04 Sense, purport, meaning; 11.05.02 Mode, manner, way, method, fashion, course; 12.07 An obligation, bounden duty
ingehygdnes 06.02.06 Mind, purpose
ing(el) 01.01.02.01.02.02.05 Crag, rock, stone
in(ge)laþian 08.01.02.04 Hospitality

ingemen 02.03.03.03.01 A native people
ingemynd 06.01.01 Thought, the faculty of thinking, mind; 06.01.04 Faculty of memory
ingemynde 06.01.04.02 Living, remembered
ingenga 05.12.05.02.04 To go in, enter
ingēotan 05.12.05.02.01 To come upon, meet with; 05.12.05.02.04 To go in, enter
ingēoting 05.12.05.02.04.02 To pour in
ingerǣcan 10.03 Giving
ingeseted 05.12.05.02.04.01 To insert into (a hole)
ingesteald 15.01 Property
ingeswel 02.08.08 Internal disease
ingeþanc 06 Spirit, soul, heart; 06.01.01 Thought, the faculty of thinking, mind; 06.02.06 Mind, purpose; 08.01 Heart, spirit, mood, disposition; 12.07 An obligation, bounden duty
ingeþēod 02.03.03.03.01 A native people
ingeþōht 12.07 An obligation, bounden duty
ingeweaxen 05.12.05.02.04.01 To insert into (a hole)
ingewinn 13.02 War
ingewitnes 06.01.06.01 Knowledge, cognizance, knowing; 12.07 An obligation, bounden duty
inginnan 05.11.10.01 A beginning
ingyte 05.12.05.02.04.02 To pour in
inhǣtan 02.08.10 Fever
inheald 17.02.05.05 A carving, graving
inheord 02.06.02.01.06 Horse
inhildan 05.12.05.13.02 To bow, bend down
inhīred 02.03.03 A family, household

inhīwan 02.03.03 A family, household; 12.01.01.08.01 A servant, attendant; 16.02.03.03 A religious
inhlihhan 07.05.04 Mockery, derision, scorn
inhold 12.01.01.12 Loyalty
inhrēran 05.06.03 A dashing together, breaking, shattering
inhȳrnes 10.01 Fact of belonging, possession by
inlād 15.02 Worth, value; 15.03.01 Toll
(ge)inlagian 14.03.03.09.03 Outlawry
inland 15.01.01 Landed property
inlaþigend 08.01.02.04 Hospitality
inlenda 02.03.03.03.01 A native people
inlende 02.03.03.03.01 A native people
inlendisc 02.03.03.03.01 A native people
inlendiscnes 04.05.03.01 Habitation, sojourn
inlic 05.10.05.04.01 Inside, interior; 08.01.02.03.02 Friendly, amiable
inlīce 05.10.05.04.01 Inside, interior; 08.01.01.01.04 Depth of feeling, zeal
inlīchomung 16.01.01.04.02.01 Incarnation
(ge)inlīhtan 06.01.02 The imaginative faculty
inlīhtend 16.01.01.02.01 Creator
inlīhtian 03.01.12.02 A beam of light
inlīhtnes 03.01.12.02 A beam of light; 16.02.01.12.01 Revelation, illumination, inspiration
inlīxan 05.11.04.01.01 Dawn, daybreak, sunrise
inmang 05.10.05.04.10 Among
inmēde 08.01.01.01.04 Depth of feeling, zeal
inn 04.01.02.04.05.01.01 Quartering of officials; 04.05.03.03 A lodging-house, inn; 04.05.03.04 A closet, chamber, room
in(n) 05.12.05.02.04 To go in, enter

innan 05.10.05.04.01 Inside, interior; 05.11 A time, period of time
innan bordes 12.06.04 Native land
innan landes 12.06.04 Native land
innanburhware 02.03.03.04.05 Populace of a town/city
innancund 05.10.05.04.01 Inside, interior; 08.01.01.01.04 Depth of feeling, zeal
innanearm 02.04.03.04.01 Arm
innanfortog 02.08.08.04.01 Gripe, colic
innanonfeal 02.08.08 Internal disease
innantīdernes 02.08.08 Internal disease
innanweard 05.10.05.04.01 Inside, interior
innanwund 02.08.08 Internal disease
innanwyrm 02.08.08.04.03 Intestinal worm
inne 05.10.05.04.01 Inside, interior
inne mid 03.03.06.01 A whole formed by joining
inne on 05.10.05.04.01 Inside, interior
innecund 05.10.05.04.01 Inside, interior
innefaran 02.04.06.03.02.04 Intestines
innefeoh 15.01 Property
innemest 05.10.05.04.01 Inside, interior; 08.01.01.01.04 Depth of feeling, zeal
innera 05.10.05.04.01 Inside, interior; 06 Spirit, soul, heart
inneweard 02.04.06.03 Internal organs, innards; 05.10.05.04.01 Inside, interior; 08.01.01.01.04 Depth of feeling, zeal
inneweard þeoh 02.04.03.04.02.01 Thigh
innheardmann 13.02.10.01.02.01.01 Military followers (of household)
innhere 13.02.10.01.02.02.01 Types of army
innian 05.12.05.02.04 To go in, enter

(ge)innian 04.05.03.03 A lodging-house, inn
geinnian 03.03.06.02 Fullness; 05.10.05.04.01.02 Contents, what is included; 05.11.07.04.03.01 Renewal, restoration
innierfe 15.01 Property
(ge)innīwian 16.02.01.12 Spirituality
innor 03.03.05.01.01 Principal/chief (of its class or type); 05.10.05.04.01 Inside, interior
innoþ 02.04.06.03 Internal organs, innards; 02.04.06.03.02.03 Stomach/belly; 02.04.06.04.02 Female reproductive organs; 08.01 Heart, spirit, mood, disposition
innoþmægen 05.08 Strength
innoþtȳdernes 02.08.08.12 Disease of bowels
innoþwund 02.08.08 Internal disease
innung 04.05.03 A dwelling-place, abode, habitation; 05.10.05.04.01.02 Contents, what is included; 15.05 Trade, traffic, commerce
innweorud 02.03.03.01 Body of retainers, household
innylfe 02.04.06.03 Internal organs, innards
inorf 15.01 Property
inrǣsan 05.08.02 Violence, force
inrēcels 16.02.05.09.02 Incense
insacian 09.07.03.02 Refusal, denial
(ge)insæglian 14.04.01 A deed, contract, agreement
insǣtehūs 11.09.01.01 Ambush, lying in wait
insceaft 02.01.03.03 Sex, generation
inscēawere 02.05.09.05 To watch, observe, survey
inscēawung 02.05.09.05 To watch, observe, survey

inscūfan 05.12.02.06 To push, impel, thrust
insecgan 06.01.03.02 Dialectics, logic
inseg(e)l 12.02.01.01 A distinguishing mark, stamp; 14.04.01 A deed, contract, agreement; 17.03.10.01 A bolt, lock, bar
(ge)inseglian 12.02.01.01 A distinguishing mark, stamp
geinseglian 05.10.05.04.15 Closure, being closed
inseglung 14.04.01 A deed, contract, agreement
inseten 14.01.02 A law, statute
insetnis 14.01.02 A law, statute
(ge)insettan 14.01.06 A rule, order, precept, tenet, principle
insigle 12.02.01.01 A distinguishing mark, stamp
insiht 09.06 To take matter for discourse
insittend 02.03.03.04 An inhabitant
insmoh 02.06.07.01.01 Part of snake
insnǣd 15.01.01 Landed property
insōcn 12.05.04.01.01 Fighting, a fight
inspīderwiht 02.06.09.02.10 Spider
inspinn 04.04.03 A spinning-house or chamber
instæpe 04.05.02.12.02 A vestibule, entrance, courtyard
instæpe(s) 05.11.07.01 Contemporary, coeval
instandan 05.10.04.03 Presence
instandendlic 06.02.04.01 Want, need
instede 05.11.07.01 Contemporary, coeval
insteppan 05.12.05.02.04 To go in, enter
instice 02.08.08 Internal disease
instīgan 05.12.05.12 To go up, ascend
instihtian 14.01.06 A rule, order, precept, tenet, principle
inswān 04.02.05.06.04 A swineherd

inswōgan 05.12.05.02.01 To come upon, meet with
inswōgennes 05.12.05.02.01 To come upon, meet with
intimbr(i)an 06.01.06.02.03.04.05 Edification, instruction
intinga 05.03.01 A cause (of anything); 05.03.01.03 Reason, cause; 05.11.08 A suitable time, opportunity; 11.02 Occupation, activity, business
intrahtnung 09.04.03 Exposition, making clear by explanation
intrepettan 18.02.04 Dancing
inþīnen 12.01.01.08.01 A servant, attendant
inwærc 02.08.08 Internal disease
inwǣte 02.04.06.05.07.01 Humours
inwaru 14.01.05 Service, obligation, duty
inweard 05.10.05.04.01 Inside, interior; 08.01.01.01.04 Depth of feeling, zeal
inweardlic 05.10.05.04.01 Inside, interior; 08.01.01.01.04 Depth of feeling, zeal
inweardlīce 03.03.06 Wholeness; 05.10.05.04.01 Inside, interior; 08.01.01.01.04 Depth of feeling, zeal
inwecgan 03.01.12.02 A beam of light
inwendan 05.13 Changeableness, change
inweorc 17 Work, doings, actions, labour
inwerdre heortan 08.01.01.01.04 Depth of feeling, zeal
inwidda 12.08.06.02.02 A bad man, inhuman person
inwīse 04.01.02.01.05.05 Spice
inwit 12.08.06.02.06 Deceit, evil, wickedness
inwitfeng 10.04.02 To grasp, take hold of
inwitflān 13.02.08.04.04.01 An arrow, dart, bolt

inwitful 12.08.06.02.06 Deceit, evil, wickedness
inwitgæst 02.06.10.01.01 Dragon
inwitgecynd 12.08.06.01 Error, wrong conduct, erroneous practice
inwitgyren 06.01.07.04.02.01 Deception, deceit, snare, wile
inwithlemm 05.06.09 Act of striking
inwithrōf 04.05.03.02.02.03 Disagreeable dwellings
inwitnet 06.01.07.04.02.01 Deception, deceit, snare, wile
inwitnīþ 08.01.03.09.05 Enmity
inwitrūn 12.02.02.05 Counsel, advice
inwitscear 02.02.04 Killing, violent death, destruction
inwitsearo 06.01.07.04.02.01 Deception, deceit, snare, wile
inwitsorh 08.01.03 Bad feeling, sadness
inwitspell 09.06.01 To relate, recount, tell
inwitstæf 12.08.06.02 Wickedness, evil
inwitþanc 08.01.03.09.06 Hostility
inwitweorc 12.08.06.02.01 Wrong, evil-doing
inwitwrāsn 14.05.07 Binding, fastening with bonds
inwrītere 09.03.07.03 A scribe, copyist
inwrittung 09.03.07.05 To cover with writing, inscribe
inwudu 15.01.01 Landed property
inwund 02.08.08 Internal disease
inwunennes 06.02.07.03 Perseverance
inwunung 04.05.03.01 Habitation, sojourn
inwyrm 02.08.08.04.03 Intestinal worm
īor 02.06.06.02.01.02 Eel; 09.03.07.01.01 A runic letter
iotas 02.03.03.06.02 Germany and Low Countries
ipnalis 02.06.07.01.02.01 Viper, asp

īren 17.03 Implements, tools, etc.; 17.04.02.05 Iron
īrenbend 14.05.07 Binding, fastening with bonds
īrenbyrne 13.02.08.03.01.04 Coat of mail/corselet
īrengelōma 17.03 Implements, tools, etc.
īrenheard 03.01.03 Hardness, callosity, hard material; 17.04.02.05 Iron
īrensmiþ 17.02.04.03 Metal worker
īrenþrēat 13.02.10.01.02.01 An armed force/band
iringes weg 01.02.01.01.02.01 Constellation
is nēod 06.02.05.04 Desire, eagerness
īs 01.01.03.02 Ice; 01.03.01.04.02 Ice; 09.03.07.01.01 A runic letter
īsceald 03.01.11 Coldness, coolness
īsearn 02.06.08.06 Water bird
īsen 13.02.08.04.03 A sword; 14.03.03.05 Ordeal; 17.03 Implements, tools, etc.
īsen clūt 17.02.04.03 Metal worker
īsen þel 17.02.04.03 Metal worker
īsengræf 17.04.01 Sources of materials
īsengræg 02.04.04.03.02 Colour of hair
īsenhearde 02.07.11 Plants/flowers (alphabetical order)
īsenhelm 13.02.08.03.01.02 A helmet
īsenhyrst 17.03.10.01 A bolt, lock, bar
īsenordāl 14.03.03.05 Ordeal
īsenpanne 04.01.02.02.06.01 Cooking vessel/pot
īsensmiþ 17.02.04.03 Metal worker
īsenswāt 17.04.02.06 Dross, slag
īsentange 17.05.03 Sources of fire/light
īse(r)n 01.01.02.02.03.01 Types of metals/minerals; 14.05.07 Binding, fastening with bonds; 17.04.02.05 Iron
īsernbyrne 13.02.08.03.01.04 Coat of mail/corselet

īse(r)nfetor 14.05.07 Binding, fastening with bonds
īserngelōma 17.03 Implements, tools, etc.
īse(r)ngrǣg 03.01.14.10 Grey-coated one
īsernhere 13.02.10.01.02.02.01 Types of army
īsernōre 17.04.01 Sources of materials
īsernscērure 17.03.03 A cutting tool
īsernscofl 17.03.07 Tools for digging/grasping/pulling
īsernscūr 13.02.08.04.04.01 An arrow, dart, bolt
īse(r)nwyrhta 17.02.04.03 Metal worker
īses gicel 01.01.03.02 Ice; 01.03.01.04.02 Ice
īsgebind 01.03.01.04.02 Ice
īsgeblǣd 02.08.07.08.02 Swelling of the foot
īsig 01.01.03.02 Ice; 01.03.01.04.02 Ice; 03.01.11 Coldness, coolness
īsigfeþera 03.01.11 Coldness, coolness
īsiht 01.01.03.02 Ice; 01.03.01.04.02 Ice
īsiht(e) 03.01.11 Coldness, coolness
īsīþes 05.11.07.01 Contemporary, coeval
īsmere 01.01.03.01.03 Lake
(ge)īsned 13.02.08.03.01 Body armour, war gear
ispanisc 02.03.03.06.06 Spanish
istoria 09.06.01.01 A tradition, ordinance handed down
īþung 05.06.01 Devastation, laying waste
iūdēas 02.03.03.06.07.05 Jews
iūdēisc 02.03.03.06.07.05 Jews
iūlius 05.11.03.01.03.01 Specific months
īw 02.07.03.05 Particular trees/shrubs (alphabetical order)
lā 06.01.07.01 Correct, right, free from error; 06.01.08.05.01 Amazement, astonishment, wonder, admiration
lā hū 09.01.03.01 Interjections: Oh!

lāc 09.06.02.01.06 A message, announcement by a messenger; 10.03 Giving; 13.02.05.01.02.02 Booty, spoils; 16.02.04.12 Sacrifice, a sacrifice
lāc onsendan 16.02.04.12 Sacrifice, a sacrifice
(ge)lāc 12.05.04.01 Fighting, contention, warfare, strife
gelāc 05.04 Fate, lot, fortune, destiny; 05.12 To move, be in motion; 12.04.02 A crowding together, assembly
lācan 05.12 To move, be in motion; 05.12.05.05 To shake, quake, wag; 13.02 War; 18.02.07.02 A musical instrument
(ge)lācan 06.01.07.04 Deception
lācdǣd 10.03.08 Bountifulness, munificence
lacen 04.04.07.07 A long outer garment, covering, cloak, etc.
lācende 05.12 To move, be in motion
lācfæsten 16.02.04.04.02.02 A fast, act of fasting
lācgeofa 10.03.08 Bountifulness, munificence
gelācian 10.03 Giving
(ge)lācnian 02.08.12.01 Medical care, treatment; 02.08.12.02.05.02 Salves, ointments
lācniende 02.08.12 Healing, curing
lācnigendlic 02.08.12.02.06 Surgical
lācnimende 10.03.05 Recompense, reward
lācnung 02.08.12.01 Medical care, treatment
(ge)lācnung 02.08.12.01 Medical care, treatment
lācnystre 02.08.12.02.01 A physician
gelācod 10.03 Giving

lācsang 16.02.04.03.03.01 A hymn, song of praise, canticle
lactūce 02.07.09.02.02.02 Other vegetables (alphabetical order)
lacu 01.01.03.01.01.01 River; 01.01.03.01.01.03 Stream; 01.01.03.01.03.01 Pool
lācweg 05.12.01.03.01.05 Types of road/path
lād 01.01.03.01.01.04 Watercourse/channel; 04.01.02 Means of subsistence; 05.12.01 To go, progress, travel (usually on land); 05.12.01.08 To move in/on water; 05.12.02.01 To fetch, bring, bear, conduct; 12.03 Direction, guidance; 14.03.03.01 Accusation; 14.03.03.01.01 Defence, reply; 14.03.03.08 Justification; 17.02.04.02.03 Carrying, carriage (of materials)
(ge)lādian 14.03.03.08 Justification
lādiendlic 12.07.03.02 An excuse
lādmann 12.03 Direction, guidance
lādrinc 12.03 Direction, guidance
lādscipe 12.01.01 Authority
lādung 14.03.03.08 Justification
læ 02.04.04.03.03 Hair of head
gelæca 12.05.01 Rivalry, contest
læcan 05.12 To move, be in motion
gelæcan 12.04 Fellowship, union, association; 18.02.03.01 A combatant, athlete
(ge)læccan 04.01.01 Eating; 13.02.05.01.02 To gain by fighting
(ge)læccan (mid) 14.02.01.02.01 Open robbery, rapine, pillage
gelæccan 02.08.02.01.01 An infectious disease; 04.03 Hunting, the chase; 06.01.05.01 Understanding; 10.01.02 Acquisition; 10.04.02 To grasp, take hold of
gelæccan of 11.10.03 Salvation/deliverance from
gelæccan (of) 10.04.02.02 To seize, take, grasp, lay hold on
læccung 07.05.01 Censure, reproof, rebuke
læc(e) 01.01.03.01.01.03 Lake; 01.01.02.01.04.01 Marsh, bog, swamp
læce 02.06.09.01 Parasite; 02.08.12.02.01 A physician
læcebōc 02.08.12.02.03 A medicine, prescription
læcecræft 02.08.12 Healing, curing; 02.08.12.01 Medical care, treatment; 02.08.12.02.03 A medicine, prescription
læcecræftig 02.08.12.02.01 A physician
læcecyn 02.08.12.02.01 A physician
læcecyst 02.08.12.02.04 Medical apparatus
læcedōm 02.08.12 Healing, curing; 02.08.12.01 Medical care, treatment; 16.01.01.02.08 Salvation, redemption
læcedōmlic 16.01.01.02.08 Salvation, redemption
læcedōmnes 02.08.12.02.05.03 A poultice
læcefeoh 15.02 Worth, value
læcefinger 02.04.03.04.01.01.01 Finger
læcegeatwa 02.08.12.02.04 Medical apparatus
læcehūs 02.08.12.02.02 An infirmary
læceīren 02.08.12.02.06 Surgical
læcesealf 02.08.12.02.05.02 Salves, ointments
læceseax 02.08.12.02.06 Surgical
læcewyrht 02.08.12.01 Medical care, treatment

lǣcewyrt 02.07.11 Plants/flowers (alphabetical order); 02.08.12.02.05.01 A herb with medicinal properties

lǣdan 05.10.04 Place, room; 05.10.05.04.11.01 A bound, limit; 05.12.01.09 To travel on water; 05.12.05.08.01 To go before and guide; 11.01.02 An undertaking; 11.05.02 Mode, manner, way, method, fashion, course; 12.04.01.02 A fellow traveller, companion; 18.02.07.01 Singing, song

lǣdan tō 05.10.04 Place, room

(ge)lǣdan 05.03.01.02 To work upon, influence; 05.05 Constitution, founding (e.g. of world); 05.12.02.01 To fetch, bring, bear, conduct; 05.12.05.08.01 To go before and guide; 12.03 Direction, guidance; 13.02.10.01.01 A commander, officer; 14.03.03 Law, action of the courts

lǣden 09.03 A language; 09.03.01 Particular languages

lǣdenbōc 09.03.07.07.02 A written work, book, treatise

lǣdend 05.12.02.01 To fetch, bring, bear, conduct; 05.12.05.08.01 To go before and guide; 12.07.03.02 An excuse

(ge)lǣdendlic 17.02.04.03.01 (Of metal) ductile

lǣdengereord 09.03.01 Particular languages

lǣdengeþēode 09.03.01 Particular languages

lǣdenisc 09.03.01 Particular languages

lǣdenlār 06.01.06.02.02.01 Learning, science (secular knowledge); 09.03.01 Particular languages

lǣdenlic 09.03.01 Particular languages

lǣdennama 09.03.02.02.01.01 A noun

lǣdensprǣc 09.03.01 Particular languages

lǣdenstæfum 09.03.01 Particular languages

lǣdenware 02.03.03.06.04 Italians

lǣdenword 09.03.01 Particular languages

lǣdere 12.01.01.04 A leader, ruler

lǣdnes 02.01.03.03.02 To bring forth, produce

lǣfan 03.03.07.02 What is left, remnant, remains; 11.06.04 Abstention, abstaining from; 15.01.02.01 Inherited property

(ge)lǣfan 03.03.07.02 What is left, remnant, remains; 11.06.04 Abstention, abstaining from

læfel 04.01.02.02.06.05.04 Cup/bowl/basin

læfer 02.07.08 Grasses, reeds, etc.; 17.02.04.03 Metal worker

læferbedd 02.07.08 Grasses, reeds, etc.

lǣgæcer 04.02.03.02.03 Fallow land

lǣghrycg 04.02.03.02.03 Fallow land

lǣl 02.08.04 Hurt, injury, damage; 03.01.14.04 Black/blackness; 14.05.06 Means/implement of torture

lǣlian 02.08.04 Hurt, injury, damage; 13.02.08.04.02 A shot, missile, dart, spear, javelin, etc.

lǣmen 17.03.12.02 A potter

lǣn 10.03 Giving; 15.01.01.01 Holding of land; 15.04.01 Lending of money

lǣnan 15.04.01 Lending of money

(ge)lǣnan 10.03 Giving; 15.01.01.01.01 Hiring, letting out of property/land; 15.01.02 Gift, transfer of property

lǣndagas 05.11.01.03.01 Mortal state, this life

læne 05.09 Weakness; 05.11.01.02 Shortness/brevity in time; 16.02.01.13 Evil-doing, transgression, sin

lænelic 05.11.01.02 Shortness/brevity in time

lænend 15.04.01 Lending of money

lænendlic 05.11.01.02 Shortness/brevity in time

lænere 15.04.01 Lending of money

lænland 15.01.01 Landed property

læpeldre 04.01.02.02.06.05.03 Plate/platter/bowl/dish

læpewince 02.06.08.05 Forest bird, wild-fowl

læppa 02.04.03.01.03.03 Ear; 02.04.06.05.03 Liver; 04.04.07.03 Part of garment; 05.10.04.02 A region, zone

gelǣr 03.03.04.05 Insufficiency, lack, want; 03.03.08 Emptiness

lǣran 05.12.05.08.01 To go before and guide; 06.01.04 Faculty of memory; 09.06.02.01.05 Proclamation, spreading abroad; 12.03 Direction, guidance; 14.01.06 A rule, order, precept, tenet, principle

lǣran forþ 15.01.02.01 Inherited property

(ge)lǣran 05.12.05.08.01 To go before and guide; 06.01.06.02.03.04.03 To teach, instruct; 12.03 Direction, guidance; 12.03.02 Advice, admonition

gelǣran 04.02.05.04 To tame, break in (animals); 05.13.01 Transformation, taking another shape; 06.02.06.03 Persuasion, prompting

gelǣred 06.01.05.02.01.01 Sagacity; 06.01.06.02 Knowledge, learning, erudition; 11.04.02 Skill, skilfulness

gelǣrednes 06.01.06.02 Knowledge, learning, erudition

lǣrend 06.01.06.02.03.04.02 A teacher; 06.02.06.03.03 Incitement

lǣrestre 06.01.06.02.03.04.02 A teacher

lǣrgedēfe 06.01.06.02.02 That which is taught, doctrine or teaching

lærig 13.02.08.03.01.06 A shield

lǣringmæden 06.01.06.02.03.01 A pupil, disciple, scholar

lǣringmann 06.01.06.02.03.02 Discipleship

lǣrnes 03.03.08 Emptiness

lǣs 02.08.12.02.06 Surgical; 03.03.03.01 Arithmetic; 03.03.04.06 Diminution; 04.02.03.04.02 Pasture/pasturage; 12.01.01.06.04 Inferiority of status, lowest place

lǣsboren 12.01.01.11 The common people

lǣssa 03.03.04.04.01 Paucity, fewness, scarcity; 03.03.04.06 Diminution; 11.08.04 Vanity, idleness, frivolity; 12.01.01.06.04 Inferiority of status, lowest place; 12.01.01.11 The common people

læst 16.02.01.13 Evil-doing, transgression, sin

lǣst 03.03.04.04 Littleness, smallness; 03.03.05.01.03 Inferior; 07.05.02 Contempt; 11.01.04 A doing, accomplishing (of something); 12.01.01.11 The common people

(ge)lǣstan 05.11.01.01.01 Eternity; 11.01.04 A doing, accomplishing (of something); 12.01.01.07 A follower; 12.01.01.12 Loyalty; 12.04.01.02 A fellow traveller, companion; 12.07 An obligation, bounden duty

gelǣstan 03.03.04.02 A sufficiency, sufficient supply; 10.03 Giving; 11.01

læste

Action, doing, performance; 11.01.01 Practice, exercise, doing
læste 04.04.07.15 Footwear, covering for the feet
læstend 11.01.04 A doing, accomplishing (of something)
gelæstende 05.11.11 Continuity
gelæstfullian 14.03.03.03 Witness, testimony, attestation
læstwyrhta 04.04.07.15 Footwear, covering for the feet
læswende 04.02.05.01.01.01 To put out to pasture
læswian 04.02.05.01.01.01 To put out to pasture
(ge)læswian 04.02.05.01.01.01 To put out to pasture; 11.12.02.01 Strengthening, confirmation
læt 05.09.01 Slow, inactive; 05.11.07.04.02 (Of time) later/latter; 05.11.08.01.03 Late; 05.12.03.02 Slowness; 12.01.01.10 Freedom, being free
lætan 02.08.12.02.06 Surgical; 05.03.01 A cause (of anything); 05.12.05.03.04.02 To flow out, well up, erupt; 07.01 Appraisal, appraising; 07.04 Consideration, esteem; 10.04.01 To hold, have; 11.05.02 Mode, manner, way, method, fashion, course; 11.06.04 Abstention, abstaining from; 11.06.06.01 Abandonment (of principle); 12.02.01 A substitute, representative; 15.01.02.01 Inherited property
lætan ... flēogan 05.12.02.06 To push, impel, thrust
lætan bēon/wesan 11.06.04 Abstention, abstaining from
lætan (fram/of) 11.06.04 Abstention, abstaining from
lætan of 12.03.05 Permission
lætan ofdūne 05.12.05.13 To go down, descend
(ge)lætan 05.12.02.03 To send; 10.03.03 Granting; 12.03.05 Permission
(ge)lætan (tō) 15.01.01.01.01 Hiring, letting out of property/land
gelætan nēah 05.12.01.09 To travel on water
lætbyrd 02.01.03.03.03.01 Child-bearing, childbirth
lætcumen 05.11.08.01.03 Late
gelæte 11.05.02 Mode, manner, way, method, fashion, course
lætemest 05.11.07.04.02 (Of time) later/latter
læt(e)mest 05.11.10.02 End, completion
lætest 05.11.10.02 End, completion
læthȳdig 02.05.03.01 Dullness, lack of animation
lætlic 05.11.08.01.03 Late
lætlīce 05.12.03.02 Slowness
lætnes 02.05.03.01 Dullness, lack of animation; 05.12.03.02 Slowness
lætræde 11.02.03 Forethought, care
lætsum 05.11.08.01.03 Late
lætt 04.05.02.07 A beam, rafter
lættend 11.11.02 A hindrance
læTTewestre 05.12.05.08.01 To go before and guide
læþ 12.06.02 District, province; 15.01.01 Landed property
læþan 07.03.01.03 To loathe, hate, abhor; 07.05.03.03.02 To reproach, revile, abuse
læþþ(o) 08.01.03.09.04 Hatred; 08.01.03.07.02.01 Injury, offence
læw 06.01.07.04.04.03 Deceit, fraud, treachery

læwa 06.01.07.04.04.03 Deceit, fraud, treachery; 12.01.01.12.04.01 Betrayal
læwan 06.01.07.04.04.03 Deceit, fraud, treachery
læwede 06.01.06.04.02 Ignorance, uninstructedness; 16.02.03.03.05 A layman
læwedmann 16.02.03.03.05 A layman
læwend 06.01.07.04.04.03 Deceit, fraud, treachery
læwung 12.01.01.12.04.01 Betrayal
lāf 03.03.07.02 What is left, remnant, remains; 12.09.05 State of woman whose husband has died; 13.02.08 Military equipment
(ge)lafian 04.06.01.01 Cleansing, washing
lafor 02.06.04.01.08 Leopard
gelagian 14.01.06 A rule, order, precept, tenet, principle
lagu 01.01.03 Water; 01.01.03.01.02 Sea/ocean; 01.01.03.01.03 Lake; 06.01.06.02.02 That which is taught, doctrine or teaching; 09.03.07.01.01 A runic letter; 11.05 Natural/proper way/manner/mode of action; 14 Law, custom, covenant; 14.01 Law, body of rules; 14.01.01 Law(s) of particular scope; 14.01.02 A law, statute; 14.01.06 A rule, order, precept, tenet, principle; 14.03.03 Law, action of the courts; 16.02.01.08.01 The Old Testament; 16.02.01.09 The law
gelagu 01.01.03.01 Body of water
lagucræftig 05.12.01.09.03 A voyage
lagufæsten 01.01.03.01.02 Sea/ocean
lagufæþm 01.01.03 Water
laguflōd 01.01.03 Water; 01.01.03.01.02 Sea/ocean

lagulād 01.01.03.01.02.01 Region of sea/ocean
lagumearg 05.12.01.09.03.01 A ship, boat
lagusiþ 05.12.01.09.03 A voyage
lagustrǣt 01.01.03.01.02.01 Region of sea/ocean
lagustrēam 01.01.03 Water; 01.01.03.01.01.01 River
lagustrēama ful 01.03.01.06 Cloud
laguswimmend 02.06.06 Fish
lahbreca 16.02.01.11.02 Impiety, lack of piety
lahbrecende 16.02.01.11.02 Impiety, lack of piety
lahbryce 14.02 Lawlessness
lahcēap 14.03.03.09.03 Outlawry
lahgewrit 14.01.02 A law, statute
lahlic 14.01.02 A law, statute
lahlīce 14.01.02 A law, statute
lahmann 14.03.02 A legislator
lahriht 14.01.04 A legal right
lahslitt 14.05.04.01 A fine
lahwita 14.03.02 A legislator
lām 01.01.02.02.02.02 Clay, loam; 04.06.02.02 Foul, filthy, squalid
lama 02.08.04.04 State of being crippled
laman legeres ādl 02.08.04.03 Paralysis
lamb 12.08.05 Innocence
lambes cerse 02.07.09.02.02.02 Other vegetables (alphabetical order)
lamb(or) 02.06.02.01.08 Sheep
lambyrd 02.01.03.03.03.01 Child-bearing, childbirth
lāmfæt 02.04 Body
lamprede 02.06.06.03.01.03 Lamprey; 04.01.02.01.02.07 Fish
lāmpytt 17.04.01 Sources of materials
lāmsceall 04.05.01.04 A tile, brick
lāmsēaþ 17.04.01 Sources of materials
lāmwyrhta 17.03.12.02 A potter

land 01.01.02 Land; 01.01.02.01 Ground; 01.01.02.02 Earth, soil; 04.02 Farm; 04.02.03 Cultivatable land/farmland; 04.02.03.02.01.01 A furrow; 11.01.01 Practice, exercise, doing; 12.06 A province, country, territory; 12.06.02.01.01 Country (not town); 15.01.01 Landed property
land āwerian/(ge)werian 14.01.05 Service, obligation, duty
land gesēcan 05.12.01.09 To travel on water
land gewerian 04.02.03.04.02 Pasture/pasturage
gelanda 02.03.02.03.06.01 Kinsman, relative; 02.03.03.03.01 A native people
landælf 16.01.03.04 Elfin race
landāgend 02.03.03.03.01 A native people
landāgende 15.01.01.01 Holding of land
landār 15.01.01 Landed property
landbegang 12.06.03.02 Living, dwelling, residence (in)
landbegenga 02.03.03.03.01 A native people; 04.02.02 Farmer, cultivator
landbegengnes 12.06.03.02 Living, dwelling, residence (in)
landbōc 14.04.01 A deed, contract, agreement
landbrǣce 04.02.04.02.02.02 Ploughing, tilling
landbūend 02.03.03.03.01 A native people; 04.02.02 Farmer, cultivator; 12.06.03 A site, settlement
landbūendas 02.03.01 People
landbūende 02.03.01 People
landbūnes 12.06.03 A site, settlement
landcēap 14.05.04.01 A fine

landcofa 12.06 A province, country, territory
landefne 15.01.01 Landed property
landesmann 02.03.03.03.01 A native people
landfæsten 13.02.06.01 Stronghold, fort/fortified town
landfeoh 15.02.04.01 Payment for temporary use, rent, hire
landfolc 02.03.03.03.01 A native people
landfruma 12.01.01.04.01 A royal leader
landfyrd 13.02.10.01.02.02 Armed forces
landfyrding 13.02 War
landgafol 15.03.02 A tax
landgehwearf 15.01.02 Gift, transfer of property
landgemaca 12.06.03.03 A neighbour
landgemǣre 05.10.05.04.11.01 A bound, limit
landgemirce 01.01.02.01.01.03 Shore, bank; 05.10.05.04.11.01 A bound, limit
landgesceaft 01 Earth, world; 02 Creation
landgeweorc 13.02.06.01 Stronghold, fort/fortified town
landgewyrpe 01.01.02.01.02.01 Rising ground, eminence
landhæbbende 12.01.01.01 Rule, domination, direction; 15.01.01.01 Holding of land
landhæfen 15.01.01 Landed property
landhere 13.02.10.01.02.02 Armed forces; 13.02.10.01.02.02.01 Types of army
landhlāford 12.01.01.04.01 A royal leader; 15.01.01.01 Holding of land
landhredding 15.04.01 Lending of money
landlagu 14.01.01 Law(s) of particular scope
landlēas 15.01.01.01 Holding of land

landlēod 02.03.03.03 A nation, people
landlēod(-a) 02.03.03.03.01 A native people
landlyre 10.02.01 Loss, deprivation
landman 02.03.03.03.01 A native people
landmearc 05.10.05.04.11.01 A bound, limit
landmearca 12.06 A province, country, territory
gelandod 15.01.01.01 Holding of land
landopenung 04.02.04.01 To occupy and cultivate land
landperan 05.12.01.03.04 A bridge
landrest 02.02.05.01.01 A grave, burial place, sepulchre
landrīca 15.01.01.01 Holding of land
landrīce 12.06 A province, country, territory
landriht 14.01 Law, body of rules; 15.04 A debt, due
landscearu 01.01.02.01.01 Tract of land; 05.10.05.04.11.01 A bound, limit
landscipe 05.10.04.02 A region, zone
landsēta 12.06.03 A site, settlement
landseten 15.01.01 Landed property; 15.01.01.01 Holding of land
landseþla 15.01.01.01 Holding of land
landsidu 11.05 Natural/proper way/manner/mode of action
landsittende 15.01.01.01 Holding of land
landsōcn 12.06.03 A site, settlement
landspēd 15.01.01 Landed property
lāndspēdig 15.01.05 Possession of wealth
landsplott 01.01.02.01.01 Tract of land
landstede 12.06 A province, country, territory
landstycce 01.01.02.01.01 Tract of land
landwaru 02.03.03.03.01 A native people
landweard 11.10.02.02 Watchful care, keeping guard

landwela 15.01.03 Treasure, riches, wealth
lang 02.04.02.03.01 Tall; 05.10.05.03.01 Length; 05.10.05.03.03 Height, loftiness, sublimity; 05.11.01.01 Long duration, long space; 09 Speech, vocal utterance
lang ... siþþan 05.11.07.04.02 (Of time) later/latter
lang ǣr 05.11.07.03.02 Earlier, antecedent
lang gyrd 09.03.07.04.01 To punctuate, divide
lang hām 16.01.02.01 Heavenly dwelling place
lang pipor 04.01.02.01.05.05.03 Pepper
gelang 05.03.01.03 Reason, cause; 05.10.04.03 Presence
langa frīgedæg 16.02.04.04.02.01.03 Holy Week
langbolster 04.05.04.05 A bed, bedstead
lange 05.10.05 A space, span; 05.11.01.01 Long duration, long space
lange hwīle 05.11.01.01 Long duration, long space
lange on dæg 05.11.04.02 Night, night time
lange þrāge 05.11.01.01 Long duration, long space
langfǣre 02.01.04.03 Aging, growing old; 05.11.11 Continuity
langfērnes 05.11.01.01 Long duration, long space
langfirst 05.11.01.01 Long duration, long space
langgestrēon 15.01.03 Treasure, riches, wealth
langian 05.11.01.01 Long duration, long space; 06.02.05.01 Strong liking for,

(ge)langian

devotion to; 08.01.03.02 Discontent;
10.01 Fact of belonging, possession by
(ge)langian 12.03.03.01 Summons, a call, summoning
gelangian 10.04.02.02 To seize, take, grasp, lay hold on; 11.10.03 Salvation/deliverance from
langieldo 02.01.04.03 Aging, growing old
langiende 05.11.03.01.05 A day
langlīce 05.11.01.01 Long duration, long space
langlīfe 02.01.04.03 Aging, growing old
langmōd 08.01.03.08 Patience
langmōdig 08.01.03.08 Patience
langmōdlīce 08.01.03.08 Patience
langmōdnes 08.01.03.08 Patience
langne fyrst 05.11.01.01 Long duration, long space
langnes 05.10.05.03.01 Length; 05.11.01 Length/duration in time
langoþ 02.05.05 Desire, appetite; 08.01.03.02 Discontent
langsceaft 13.02.08.04.01 A spear
langscip 13.02.10.03.01 A fleet
langstrang 08.01.03.08 Patience
langsum 05.10.05.03.01 Length; 05.11.01.01 Long duration, long space; 05.11.08.01.03.01 Delay; 08.01.03.08 Patience
langsumlic 08.01.03.07.01 Tedium
langsumlīce 05.11.01.01 Long duration, long space; 08.01.03.08 Patience
langsumnes 05.10.05.03.01 Length; 05.10.05.03.03 Height, loftiness, sublimity; 05.11.01 Length/duration in time; 08.01.03.08 Patience
langswēored 02.06.01.02 Head
langtoh 05.11.01.01 Long duration, long space

langtwīdig 05.11.01.01 Long duration, long space
langung 05.11.08.01.03.01 Delay; 06.02.05.01 Strong liking for, devotion to; 08.01.03.04 Grief
langunge 06.02.05.01 Strong liking for, devotion to
langunghwīl 08.01.03.06 Adversity, affliction
langweb 04.04.05 Woven material, fabric
langweg 05.12.01.01 To go on a journey/expedition, travel
langwyrpe 05.10.06.04 A corner, bend, angle
lann 14.05.07 Binding, fastening with bonds
lanu 05.12.01.03.01.04 A lane, street
lapian 04.01.03 Drinking
lappe 02.07.11 Plants/flowers (alphabetical order)
lār 06.01.06.02 Knowledge, learning, erudition; 06.01.06.02.02 That which is taught, doctrine or teaching; 06.01.06.02.03 The action of learning; 06.01.06.02.03.04 Teaching, instruction; 09.06.01.01 A tradition, ordinance handed down; 11.04.02.01.01 Cunning, craft, craftiness, guile, wile; 12.01.01.12.04.02 Conspiracy; 12.02.02.05 Counsel, advice; 12.03.03 A command, bidding, order; 14.01.06 A rule, order, precept, tenet, principle; 16.02.01.01 Creed, statement of faith; 16.02.04.03.02 Parts of service; 16.02.04.10 Preaching
lārbōc 16.02.04.10 Preaching; 16.02.05.10.13 Other books
lārbodung 16.02.04.10 Preaching
lārbȳsn 16.02.01.08.03 The New Testament

lārcniht 06.01.06.02.03.02 Discipleship
lārcræft 06.01.06.01.01 Knowledge; 06.01.06.02 Knowledge, learning, erudition
lārcwide 14.01.06 A rule, order, precept, tenet, principle
lārdōm 06.01.06.02.03.04 Teaching, instruction
lārēow 06.01.06.02.01 A wise man, man of understanding or learning; 06.01.06.02.03.04.02 A teacher; 16.02.03.02.07 A priest, cleric; 16.02.03.02.10 A preacher, teacher
lārēowdōm 06.01.06.02.02 That which is taught, doctrine or teaching; 06.01.06.02.03.04 Teaching, instruction; 16.02.03.01 Ecclesiastical authority
lārēowlic 06.01.06.02.03.04.02 A teacher
lārēowsetl 06.01.06.02.03.04.01 A school
lārfæsten 04.01.01.06.01 Abstinence from food, fast; 16.02.04.04.02.02 A fast, act of fasting
lārhlystend 16.02.04.07.01 Baptism, baptizing (and anointing)
lārhūs 06.01.06.02.03.04.01 A school
lārlēast 06.01.06.04.02 Ignorance, uninstructedness
lārlic 06.01.06.02.03 The action of learning; 06.01.06.02.03.04.04 Under instruction, being taught; 06.02.06.03 Persuasion, prompting; 16.02.01.01 Creed, statement of faith
lārsmiþ 12.02.02.02 A counsellor, advisor
lārspell 09.06.01 To relate, recount, tell; 16.02.04.03.02 Parts of service; 16.02.04.10 Preaching
lārsum 06.01.06.02.03.04.04 Under instruction, being taught

lārswice 06.01.07.04.02 Fraud, deceit, trick, trickery
lārþegn 06.01.06.02.03.04.02 A teacher
lārwita 06.01.06.02.01 A wise man, man of understanding or learning
lāser 04.02.04.04 Harvest, crop
lāst 02.04.03.04.02.05.02 Sole; 05.12.01.03.01.01 A path, track; 05.12.01.04.01 Manner of going, gait
lāst weardian 05.10.05.04.09.02 Hinder part, rear; 05.12.05.10 To go behind, follow
gelāst 12.07 An obligation, bounden duty
lāstas lecgan 05.12.01.01 To go on a journey/expedition, travel; 05.12.01.02 To wander
gelāstful 11.12.02 Aid, help, succour
lāstweard 02.03.02.03.05 Descendant; 05.12.05.10 To go behind, follow
lāstword 07.08.11 Fame after death
lata 05.12.03.02 Slowness
late 05.12.03.02 Slowness
(ge)latian 05.11.08.01.03.01 Delay; 05.12.03.02 Slowness
latimer 09.04.03.03 A commentary, exposition
lāttēah 04.02.05.06.05.03.03 Reins
lāttēow 05.12.05.08.01 To go before and guide; 12.03 Direction, guidance; 13.02.10.01.01 A commander, officer; 16.01.01.02.05 Guide
lāttēowdōm 05.12.05.08.01 To go before and guide; 06.01.06.02.03.04 Teaching, instruction; 12.01.01 Authority
latu 05.11.08.01.03.01 Delay
gelatu 11.11.02 A hindrance
latung 05.11.08.01.03.01 Delay
lāþ 06.02.03 Unwilling, loath; 07.03 Evil; 07.03.01 Abomination; 08.01.03.06

gelāþ

Adversity, affliction; 08.01.03.07
Unpleasantness; 08.01.03.07.02.01
Injury, offence; 08.01.03.07.04
Severity, harshness; 08.01.03.09.04
Hatred; 08.01.03.09.05 Enmity;
12.08.07.01.01 Wantonness,
sensuality, lasciviousness
gelāþ 08.01.03.09.06 Hostility
lāþbite 02.08.04.01 A wound
lāþe 07.03.01.02 With hatred or enmity
lāþettan 07.03.01.03 To loathe, hate, abhor
lāþgenīþla 08.01.03.09.05 Enmity
lāþgetēona 08.01.03.09.05 Enmity
lāþgewinna 08.01.03.09.05 Enmity
gelaþian 08.01.02.04 Hospitality;
12.03.03.01 Summons, a call, summoning; 12.03.04 A request, prayer
lāþian 07.03.01.03 To loathe, hate, abhor
lāþlēas 12.08.05 Innocence
lāþlic 08.01.03.07 Unpleasantness; 08.01.03.09.04 Hatred
lāþlīce 07.03.01.02 With hatred or enmity; 08.01.03.06 Adversity, affliction
lāþscipe 08.01.03.06 Adversity, affliction
lāþsearu 08.01.03.09.04 Hatred
lāþsīþ 02.02 Death
lāþspell 09.06.02.01.06.03 Ill tidings
laþung 12.03.03.01 Summons, a call, summoning
(ge)laþung 16.01.02.05 Inhabitants of heaven; 16.02.03 The church (as temporal/spiritual body)
lāþwende 07.03 Evil; 08.01.03.09.04 Hatred
lāþwendemōd 08.01.03.09.04 Hatred
lāþwendnes 08.01.03.09.04 Hatred
lāþweorc 12.08.06.02.01 Wrong, evil-doing
laur 02.07.03.05 Particular trees/shrubs (alphabetical order); 07.08.04 An ornament, honour, glory
laurbēam 02.07.03.05 Particular trees/shrubs (alphabetical order)
laurberige 02.07.03.05 Particular trees/shrubs (alphabetical order)
gelaured 04.01.02.02.04.05 Flavoured with laurel
laurisc 02.07.03.05 Particular trees/shrubs (alphabetical order)
laurtrēow 02.07.03.05 Particular trees/shrubs (alphabetical order)
lāwerce 02.06.08.05 Forest bird, wild-fowl
lawernbēam 02.07.03.05 Particular trees/shrubs (alphabetical order)
lēac 02.07.09.02.02.01 Edible root/bulb
lēacblæd 02.07.09.02.02.01 Edible root/bulb
lēaccærse 02.07.09.02.02.02 Other vegetables (alphabetical order)
lēactrog 04.01.02.02.06.03 Food receptacle, basket
lēactūn 04.02.04.05 Garden
lēactūnweard 04.02.04.05 Garden
lēacweard 04.02.04.05 Garden
lēad 01.01.02.02.03.01 Types of metals/minerals; 04.01.02.02.06.01 Cooking vessel/pot; 14.05.06 Means/implement of torture; 17.04.02.07 Lead
lēaden 01.01.02.02.03.01 Types of metals/minerals; 17.04.02.07 Lead
lēadgedelf 17.04.01 Sources of materials
lēadgewiht 03.03.02 Measurement by weighing
lēadgota 17.02.04.03.03 Smelting, heating, scorification

lēadstæf 14.05.06 Means/implement of torture
lēaf 02.07.02.06 A leaf; 09.03.07.06.02 Ink; 09.03.07.07 A book; 12.03.05 Permission
gelēaf 02.07.02.06 A leaf
(ge)lēafa 12.03.05 Permission; 16.02.01 Faith; 16.02.02 Christianity, the Christian faith
gelēafa 06.01.07.06 Mental acceptance, belief; 06.01.08.03 Trust, faith, confidence; 16.02.01.01 Creed, statement of faith
(ge)lēafful 16.02.01 Faith
gelēafful 06.01.08.03 Trust, faith, confidence; 16.02.01.04 Orthodoxy; 16.02.02 Christianity, the Christian faith
gelēaffulle 16.02.03.02.07 A priest, cleric
gelēaffullīce 06.01.08.03 Trust, faith, confidence; 06.01.08.03.01 Belief, trust, faithfulness; 16.02.02 Christianity, the Christian faith
gelēaffulnes 06.01.08.03.01 Belief, trust, faithfulness
lēafhelmig 02.07.02.06 A leaf
(ge)lēafhlystend 16.02.04.07.01 Baptism, baptizing (and anointing)
(ge)lēaflēas 16.02.01.03 Unbelief, want of belief
gelēaflēasnes 16.02.01.03 Unbelief, want of belief
gelēaflēast 16.02.01.12.06 Unfaithfulness, undutifulness
gelēaflēast/gelēaflȳst 16.02.01.03 Unbelief, want of belief
lēaflēoht 06.01.07.06 Mental acceptance, belief; 06.01.07.07.01 Likelihood, probability, chance

gelēaflic 06.01.07.07.01 Likelihood, probability, chance; 16.02.01.04 Orthodoxy
gelēaflīce 06.01.07.07.01 Likelihood, probability, chance; 16.02.02 Christianity, the Christian faith
lēafnes 12.03.05 Permission
(ge)lēafnes 12.03.05 Permission
lēafnesword 12.03.05 Permission
lēafscead 03.01.13.03 Overshadowing
lēafsele 03.01.13.03 Overshadowing
(ge)lēafsum 16.02.01 Faith
gelēafsum 06.01.07.07.01 Likelihood, probability, chance
lēafwyrm 02.06.09.02.04 Butterfly, moth
lēag 02.08.12.02.05 Pharmacy, curing with salves
lēah 04.02.03.04.01 Meadow land/meadow
leahtor 02.08.02.01 An illness, ailment, disorder; 07.09 Shame, disgrace; 16.02.01.13 Evil-doing, transgression, sin
leahtorcwide 16.02.04.14.01 Blasphemy
leahtorfull 12.08.06.01.02 Lacking moral good
leahtorlēas 07.02.03 Perfection; 12.08.04 Purity, moral cleanness; 14.03.03.08 Justification
leahtorlic 09.03.02.04 A slip of the tongue, solecism
leahtorlīce 07.03.01.02 With hatred or enmity
leahtrian 14.03.03.01 Accusation
(ge)leahtrian 12.08.06.01.04.01 To mislead, seduce, lead astray
geleahtrian 07.05.01 Censure, reproof, rebuke
leahtric 02.07.09.02.02.02 Other vegetables (alphabetical order)

leahtrung 07.05.01 Censure, reproof, rebuke; 07.09 Shame, disgrace
lēan 06.02.06.03.01 To dissuade (from); 07.05.01 Censure, reproof, rebuke; 10.03.05 Recompense, reward; 12.05.04.02.01 Retribution, requital; 15.02.04 Spending, disbursement
lēan forgyldan 10.03.05 Recompense, reward
lēan sellan 10.03.05 Recompense, reward
lēangyfa 16.01.01.02.02 A giving (by Deity)
(ge)lēanian 10.03.05 Recompense, reward; 10.03.05.01 Reward, meed, pay; 12.05.04.02.01 Retribution, requital; 15.04 A debt, due
lēap 02.04.03.03 Trunk; 03.03.01 Specific measures; 04.03.05 Fishing; 17.03.12.01 A basket
lēas 03.03.08 Emptiness; 06.01.07.04.03 Untruth, falsehood; 06.01.07.04.04 Deceitfulness, falseness, duplicity; 06.01.07.04.04.02 Pretence, feigning, dissimulation; 06.01.07.05 Error, being astray; 12.01.01.12.04 Treachery; 12.08.07.01.01 Wantonness, sensuality, lasciviousness
lēasbrēd 06.01.07.04.02 Fraud, deceit, trick, trickery; 06.01.07.04.03 Untruth, falsehood
lēasbrēda 06.01.07.04 Deception
lēasbrēden 06.01.07.04.03 Untruth, falsehood
lēasbrēdende 06.01.07.04 Deception
lēasbrēdnes 06.01.07.04.03 Untruth, falsehood
lēascræft 06.01.07.04 Deception
lēase 06.01.07.04.03 Untruth, falsehood

lēasere 06.01.07.04.04.02.01 Hypocrisy; 18.02.05 Buffoonery, speech of buffoon/actor
lēasettan 06.01.07.04.04.02 Pretence, feigning, dissimulation
lēasferhþ 06.01.07.04.04.01 Inconstancy, folly, falseness
lēasferþnes 06.01.07.04.04.01 Inconstancy, folly, falseness
lēasgespeca 06.01.07.04.03 Untruth, falsehood
lēasgewita 14.03.03.06 False witness
lēasgewitnes 14.03.03.06 False witness
lēasgielp 07.06.02 Arrogance, vainglory, vanity
lēasian 06.01.07.04.03 Untruth, falsehood
lēasing 06.01.07.04 Deception
lēaslic 06.01.07.04.03 Untruth, falsehood; 06.01.07.04.04.02 Pretence, feigning, dissimulation
lēaslīce 06.01.07.04 Deception; 06.01.07.05 Error, being astray
lēaslīcettan 06.01.07.04.04.02 Pretence, feigning, dissimulation
lēaslīcettung 06.01.07.04.04.02 Pretence, feigning, dissimulation
lēasmōdnes 12.08.07.01.03 Wantonness, levity, frivolity
lēasnes 06.01.07.04.03 Untruth, falsehood; 12.08.07.01.03 Wantonness, levity, frivolity
lēasōlæccere 07.07.03 Flattery
lēasōleccend 07.07.03 Flattery
lēasōleccung 07.07.03 Flattery
lēassagol 06.01.07.04.03 Untruth, falsehood
lēasscēawere 11.09.01 Stealthiness, a stealthy act
lēasspell 06.01.07.04.03 Untruth, falsehood
lēasspellung 06.01.07.04.03 Untruth, falsehood

lēassponung 06.02.06.03.04 Allurement
lēastyhtende 07.07.03 Flattery
lēastyhtung 07.07.03 Flattery
lēasuht 06.02.06.03.04 Allurement
lēasung 06.01.07.04.02 Fraud, deceit, trick, trickery; 06.01.07.04.03 Untruth, falsehood; 12.08.07.01.03 Wantonness, levity, frivolity; 14.03.03.06 False witness; 16.02.04.07.02.03 Penance, an act/instance of penance
lēasungspell 06.01.07.04.03 Untruth, falsehood
lēaswyrcend 06.01.07.04 Deception
lēaþor 04.06.01.04 What is used in washing, an ointment
lēaþorwyrt 02.07.11 Plants/flowers (alphabetical order)
lēawfinger 02.04.03.04.01.01.01 Finger
leax 02.06.06.03.01.07 Salmon; 04.01.02.01.02.07 Fish
lēc 02.05.09.04 To see, look upon, behold
(ge)leccan 03.01.16.01 Moisture
leccung 03.01.16.06 A soaking, steeping
lecg 13.02.08.04.03.01.02 Sheath for sword
lecgan 02.02.04.03 To kill, slay; 02.02.05 A burial, burying
lecgan beforan 09.05.05 Exposure, revealing, revelation
lecgan fȳr on 03.01.09.02.01 Fire, burning
lecgan in 10.03.07.01 To allot, assign
lecgan on 05.10.05.04.12 The condition of being covered
lecgan tō ēacan 03.03.06.01 A whole formed by joining
lecgan þone mæst 05.12.01.09 To travel on water
lecgan wedd 14.03.03.07 Security, pledge, bail
(ge)lecgan 05.10.04 Place, room; 12.05.06.03 Necessity, constraint; 14.01.06 A rule, order, precept, tenet, principle
(ge)lecgan on 03.05 Order, arrangement, disposition
(ge)lecgan (on) 14.03.03.01 Accusation
lecþa 05.12.01.09.03.01.03 Part of ship
lēf 02.08.02 Disease, infirmity, sickness
gelēfed 02.01.04.03 Aging, growing old; 02.08.02 Disease, infirmity, sickness; 02.08.04 Hurt, injury, damage; 12.08.06.01.02 Lacking moral good
gelēfenscipe 12.07.04.01 Justification
lēfmon 02.08.02.01.04 A sick person, invalid
lēfung 02.08.04.03 Paralysis
lēgelēoht 03.01.12.02 A beam of light
leger 02.02.03.02 State of being dead; 02.02.05.01.01 A grave, burial place, sepulchre; 02.02.05.02 To prepare for burial; 02.08.02 Disease, infirmity, sickness; 04.05.04.05 A bed, bedstead
leger weardian 02.08.02.01.05 Bed of sickness
legerbǣre 02.08.02 Disease, infirmity, sickness
legerbedd 02.02.05.01.01 A grave, burial place, sepulchre; 02.08.02.01.05 Bed of sickness
gelegered 02.08.02.01.05 Bed of sickness
legerfæst 02.08.02 Disease, infirmity, sickness
gelegergield 18.02.02 Play, (athletic) sport
legerstōw 02.02.05.01 Place of burial
legertēam 02.01.03.03 Sex, generation
legerwīte 14.05.04.01 A fine

legie 13.02.10.01.02.02.03 Part of an army
gelegu 01.01.02.01.01 Tract of land
leloþre 02.07.11 Plants/flowers (alphabetical order)
lemian 02.08.04.04 State of being crippled; 08.01.03.07.02 Misery, trouble, affliction
lempedu 02.06.06.03.01.03 Lamprey
lemphealt 02.08.04.04 State of being crippled
lempit 04.01.02.02.06.05.03 Plate/platter/bowl/dish
len(c)ten 05.11.03.01.02.01 Spring; 16.02.04.04.02.01.02 Lent
lenctenādl 02.08.10.01 Malaria
lenctenbere 04.02.04.03.02.01.01 Barley
lenctenbryce 16.02.04.04.02.01.02 A fast, act of fasting
lenctendæg 16.02.04.04.02.01.02 Lent
lenctenerþe 04.02.03.02 Arable/ploughed land
lenctenfæsten 16.02.04.04.02.01.02 Lent
lenctenhǣto 03.01.09 Heat
lenctenlic 05.11.03.01.02.01 Spring; 16.02.04.04.02.01.02 Lent
lenctenlifen 04.01.02.01.01.06 Lenten/fast-day food
lenctenmōnaþ 05.11.03.01.02.01 Spring
lenctentīd 05.11.03.01.02.01 Spring; 16.02.04.04.02.01.02 Lent
lenctentīma 05.11.03.01.02.01 Spring; 16.02.04.04.02.01.02 Lent
lenctenwucu 16.02.04.04.02.01.02 Lent
gelend 15.01.01.01 Holding of land
gelenda 15.01.01.01 Holding of land
(ge)lendan 05.12.01.09 To travel on water
gelendan 05.12.05.09 To go forward, proceed; 15.01.02 Gift, transfer of property

lendenādl 02.08.08.08 Disease of loins
lendenbān 02.04.05.04.04 Spine; 02.04.05.04.05.04 Hip-bone
lendenbrǣde 02.04.03.03.04 Side
lendenece 02.08.08.08 Disease of loins
lendensēoc 02.08.08.08 Disease of loins
lendensīd 04.04.07.07 A long outer garment, covering, cloak, etc.
lendenu 02.04.03.03.04 Side
lendenwyrc 02.08.08.07 Disease of kidneys
lending 05.12.01.09.03.04 A harbour
leng 05.11.01.01 Long duration, long space; 05.11.07.04.02 (Of time) later/latter
(ge)lengan 05.10.05.02.02 Greater, bigger; 05.11.01.01 Long duration, long space; 05.11.08.01.03.01 Delay; 05.12.03.02 Slowness
lenge 05.02.02 Nature, established order of things
gelenge 02.03.02.03.06 Kinship, relationship; 11.05 Natural/proper way/manner/mode of action
gelenged 12.03.04 A request, prayer
lengtogra 05.11.01.01 Long duration, long space
lengþu 05.10.05.03.03 Height, loftiness, sublimity
leng(u) 02.04.02.03 Height, stature or form; 05.10.05.03.01 Length; 05.10.05.03.03 Height, loftiness, sublimity; 05.11.01.01 Long duration, long space
lent 02.07.09.02.02.02 Other vegetables (alphabetical order)
lenticulas 02.07.09.02.02.02 Other vegetables (alphabetical order)
lēo 02.06.04.01.09 Lion

léod 02.03.01.01 Male person, man; 02.03.03.03.01 A native people; 12.01.01.04.01 A royal leader; 14.05.04.01 A fine
geléod 02.03.03.03.01 A native people
(ge)léodan 02.01.03.03.02 To bring forth, produce; 02.07.01 To grow
léodbealu 08.01.03.06 Adversity, affliction
léodbisceop 16.02.03.02.05 A bishop
léodburg 12.06.02.01 A township
léodbygen 15.05 Trade, traffic, commerce
léodcyning 12.01.01.04.01 A royal leader
léode 02.03.01 People; 02.03.03.03.01 A native people
léodfruma 02.03.02.03.03 Forefather, ancestor; 12.01.01.04.01 A royal leader
léodgeard 12.06 A province, country, territory
léodgebyrga 12.01.01.04.01 A royal leader
léodgeld 14.05.04.01 A fine
léodgeþincþ 03.03.05.01 Rank, position, degree
léodgewinn 12.05.04 Strife, hostility
léodgryre 06.01.08.06.02 Great fear, terror, horror
léodhata 12.05.06.02.01 Tyranny
léodhete 08.01.03.09.04 Hatred
léodhryre 08.01.03.06.01 Affliction, misfortune, calamity
léodhwæt 06.02.07.06 Courage, boldness, valour
léodmæg 02.03.03.03.01 A native people
léodmægen 13.02.10.01.02.02 Armed forces
léodmearc 12.06 A province, country, territory
léodrǽden 02.03.03.03 A nation, people
léodriht 14.01 Law, body of rules
léodrúne 16.01.04.01 Sorcery using incantation
léodscearu 02.03.03.03 A nation, people
léodsceaþa 08.01.03.09.05 Enmity
léodscipe 02.03.03.03 A nation, people; 12.06 A province, country, territory
léodstefn 12.02.02 An assembly, meeting
léodþéaw 11.05 Natural/proper way/manner/mode of action
léodweard 12.01.01.01 Rule, domination, direction
léodweras 02.03.03.03.01 A native people
léodwerod 12.04.02 A crowding together, assembly
léodwita 12.02.02.02 A counsellor, advisor
léodwynn 08.01.01.03 Good feeling, joy, happiness
léof 08.01.01.03.05 Pleasure, delight; 08.01.01.03.09 Pleasantness, agreeableness; 08.01.02.02.01 A favourite, loved one; 08.01.02.02.03 A loving relationship; 16.01.03.04 Elfin race
(ge)léof 08.01.02.02 Love, affection, care
léofa 11.05.02.02.01.01 Courteous forms of address
léofan men 11.05.02.02.01.01 Courteous forms of address
léoffæst 08.01.02.02.01 A favourite, loved one
léoflic 07.04.04.02 Laudable, praiseworthy; 07.10.01 Elegance, beauty, comeliness; 08.01.01.03.09.01 Pleasant, agreeable; 08.01.02.02.01 A favourite, loved one; 15.02.01 High/steep price

lēoflīce 06.02.02.01 Will, wish, pleasure; 08.01.02.02 Love, affection, care; 16.01.01.01 Attributes of God
lēofre 07.01.01.02 To prefer
lēofspell 09.06.02.01.06.02 Good tidings
lēoftǣl 07.04.04.02 Laudable, praiseworthy; 08.01.01.03.09.01 Pleasant, agreeable; 16.01.01.01 Attributes of God
lēofwende 08.01.01.03.09.01 Pleasant, agreeable; 08.01.02.02 Love, affection, care; 15.02.01 High/steep price
lēofwendum 08.01.02.02 Love, affection, care
lēogan 06.01.07.04.04.03 Deceit, fraud, treachery; 06.01.07.05 Error, being astray
lēogan on 14.03.03.06 False witness
(ge)lēogan 06.01.07.04 Deception; 06.01.07.04.03 Untruth, falsehood
lēogere 06.01.07.04.03 Untruth, falsehood; 06.01.07.04.04.02.01 Hypocrisy
lēoht 01 Earth, world; 02 Creation; 02.05.04 Sleepiness, drowsiness, sleep; 02.05.05.04 Sensual pleasure; 02.05.09 Faculty of sight; 03.01.08 Light, of little weight; 03.01.12 Brightness, light; 03.01.12.02 A beam of light; 04.01.02.01.01 Edibility; 04.01.03.05.01 Intoxicating liquor; 05.12.03.01 Swiftness, velocity; 06.01.05.02 Intelligence; 07.08.07 Glory, splendour, magnificence; 07.10.01 Elegance, beauty, comeliness; 08.01.01.03.01 Freedom from trouble, comfort, security; 08.01.03.08 Patience; 09.04.03 Exposition, making clear by explanation; 11.08.04 Vanity, idleness, frivolity; 11.12 Easiness; 12.08.07.01.01 Wantonness, sensuality, lasciviousness; 17.02.04.02.03 Carrying, carriage (of materials)
lēoht dæg 05.11.04.01 Day (not night)
lēoht sellan 03.01.12.02 A beam of light
lēohtbǣre 03.01.12 Brightness, light; 07.02.04.03 Nobleness, excellence, nobility, magnificence
lēohtbēamede 03.01.12.02 A beam of light
lēohtberend 16.01.05.02.01 The devil
lēohtberende 03.01.12 Brightness, light
lēohtbora 12.01.01.08.01 A servant, attendant
lēohtbrǣdnes 12.08.07.01.03 Wantonness, levity, frivolity
lēohte 03.01.12 Brightness, light; 05.12.04 Absence of movement, stillness; 06.01.05.02 Intelligence; 08.01.01.03.01 Freedom from trouble, comfort, security
lēohtfæt 17.05.03 Sources of fire/light
lēohtfætels 17.05.03 Sources of fire/light
lēohtflōwende 03.01.12.02 A beam of light
lēohtfruma 16.01.01.02.01 Creator
lēohtgescēot 16.02.04.20 Church due/requirement
lēohtian 02.08.13 Recovery, growing better; 03.01.12.02 A beam of light; 05.11.04.01.01 Dawn, daybreak, sunrise
lēohtīsern 17.05.03 Sources of fire/light
lēohtlēas 03.01.13 Darkness, obscurity
lēohtlic 03.01.12 Brightness, light; 11.08.04 Vanity, idleness, frivolity; 16.02.01.13.01 Kinds of sin

lēohtlīce 02.05.04 Sleepiness, drowsiness, sleep; 03.01.08 Light, of little weight; 03.03.04.04 Littleness, smallness; 05.09.02 Mildness, moderate quality; 05.12.03.01 Swiftness, velocity; 06.01.05.03.03 Indiscretion; 08.01.02.01.02.01 Mildness, leniency, indulgence; 09.03.04.03 Plain, simple; 11.06.01.01 Negligence, carelessness, heedlessness; 11.12 Easiness

lēohtmōd 12.08.07.01.03 Wantonness, levity, frivolity

lēohtmōdnes 12.08.07.01.03 Wantonness, levity, frivolity

lēohtsāwend 16.01.01.02.01 Creator

lēohtscēawigend 02.05.09 Faculty of sight

lēohtstān 17.05.03 Sources of fire/light

lēoma 01.03.01.03.01.02 Lightning; 02.05.09 Faculty of sight; 03.01.12 Brightness, light; 03.01.12.02 A beam of light

gelēomod 03.01.12.02 A beam of light

lēon 10.03 Giving; 15.01.01.01.01 Hiring, letting out of property/land

lēona/-e 02.06.04.01.09 Lion

lēona sēaþ 14.05.06 Means/implement of torture

lēones 12.04 Fellowship, union, association

lēonflǣsc 02.06.04.01.09 Lion

lēonfōt 02.07.11 Plants/flowers (alphabetical order)

lēonhwelp 02.06.04.01.09 Lion

lēopard 02.06.04.01.08 Leopard

lēoran 02.02.03 To die, perish

(ge)lēoran 05.07 Ending of existence, end of world; 05.12.05.03.03 To depart, leave, set out

gelēoran 02.04.06.06 Discharge, emanation

(ge)lēor(ed)nes 05.12.05.03.04 To come/go out from

(ge)lēorednes 08.01.01.01.02 Alienation of mind, ecstasy, rapture

gelēor(ed)nes 02.02 Death; 05.11.02.01.01 An anniversary; 16.02.04.07.06.03 Commemoration, festival

gelēoren 02.02.03.02 State of being dead

lēorende 05.11.01.02 Shortness/brevity in time

gelēorendlic 05.11.01.02 Shortness/brevity in time

leornend 06.01.06.02.03.03.01 An act of reading

leornere 06.01.06.02.01 A wise man, man of understanding or learning; 06.01.06.02.03.02 Discipleship; 06.01.06.02.03.03.01 An act of reading

leornes 06.01.06.02 Knowledge, learning, erudition

leornestre 06.01.06.02.03.01 A pupil, disciple, scholar

leornian 06.01.06.02.03.03 To study, apply oneself to learning; 06.01.06.02.03.03.01 An act of reading

(ge)leornian 06.01.06.01 Knowledge, cognizance, knowing

leorningcild 06.01.06.02.03.01 A pupil, disciple, scholar

leorningcniht 06.01.06.02.03.01 A pupil, disciple, scholar; 06.01.06.02.03.02 Discipleship; 16.02.01.08.03.01 New Testament persons

leorni(n)gende 06.01.06.02.03.04.04 Under instruction, being taught

leorninghūs 06.01.06.02.03.04.01 A school
leornung 06.01.06.02.03 The action of learning; 06.01.06.02.03.02 Discipleship; 06.01.06.02.03.03.01 An act of reading; 06.01.06.02.03.04 Teaching, instruction
leornungcræft 06.01.06.02 Knowledge, learning, erudition
leornungmann 06.01.06.02.01 A wise man, man of understanding or learning; 06.01.06.02.03.01 A pupil, disciple, scholar; 06.01.06.02.03.02 Discipleship
leornungscōl 06.01.06.02.03.04.01 A school
lēosan 10.02.01.01 Loss, forfeiture
lēoþ 09.03.05.01.01 Poetry; 09.03.05.01.02 Art of verse composition; 18.02.07.01.01 A song, a poem to be sung or recited
lēoþcræft 09.03.05 Art of poetry; 09.03.05.01.02 Art of verse composition; 18.02.07.01 Singing, song
lēoþcræftig 06.01.06.02.02.01 Learning, science (secular knowledge)
lēoþcwide 09.03.05.01.01 Poetry
lēoþgidding 09.03.05.01.01 Poetry; 18.02.07.01.01 A song, a poem to be sung or recited
lēoþlic 09.03.05.01.01 Poetry
lēoþsang 18.02.07.01 Singing, song
leoþu 12.01.01.07 A follower
leoþubend 14.05.07 Binding, fastening with bonds
leoþubīg 02.04.02.04 Flexibility of limbs, suppleness
leoþubīge 07.07 Humility
leoþubīgnes 02.04.02.04 Flexibility of limbs, suppleness
leoþucræft 06.01.06.02 Knowledge, learning, erudition; 11.04.01 An aptitude, bodily skill
leoþucræftig 02.04.02.04 Flexibility of limbs, suppleness; 02.04.03.04 Limb
leoþufæst 06.01.05.02.01 Intelligent, sensible
leoþulic 02.04.03.04 Limb
lēoþurūn 12.02.02.05 Counsel, advice; 18.02.07.01.01 A song, a poem to be sung or recited
leoþusār 02.08.07.07 Disorders of the body
leoþusyrce 13.02.08.03.01.04 Coat of mail/corselet
leoþuwāc 02.04.02.04 Flexibility of limbs, suppleness; 03.01.04.01 Power of bending, flexibility
leoþuwācunga 05.09.03 Mitigation, lightening, alleviation
(ge)leoþuwǣcan 03.01.04.01 Power of bending, flexibility; 05.12.04 Absence of movement, stillness
geleoþuwǣcan 08.01.02.01.02 Gentleness
leoþuwyrt/liþwyrt 02.07.11 Plants/flowers (alphabetical order)
lēoþweorc 09.03.05.01.01 Poetry
lēoþwīs 09.03.05.01.01 Poetry
lēoþword 09.03.05.01.01 Poetry
lēoþwrenc 06.01.07.04.04.02 Pretence, feigning, dissimulation; 09.03.05.01.01 Poetry
lēoþwyrhta 09.03.05 Art of poetry
lēow 02.04.03.04.02.01 Thigh; 04.01.02.01.02.05.01 Edible part of animal
lēowe 05.10.05.03 A measure of distance
lēpene 17.03.12.01 A basket

leppan 04.03.04 Fowling
geles 16.02.04.03.02 Parts of service
lesan 03.03.04.01.02.01 A heap, mass, accumulation
lesca 02.04.03.03.08 Groin/crotch
lētania 16.02.04.03.02 Parts of service; 16.02.04.08.01 Kinds of prayer
lettan on gemynde 06.01.04 Faculty of memory
(ge)lettan 05.11.08.01.03.01 Delay; 05.12.04 Absence of movement, stillness; 11.11.02 A hindrance; 11.11.03 Impeding of progress, prevention
gelettan 08.01.03.07.02.01 Injury, offence
letting 05.12.03.02 Slowness
(ge)letting 11.11.02 A hindrance
leþer 17.04.04.02 Skin, hide (as material)
leþercodd 17.03.12 A receptacle, container
leþerhelm 13.02.08.03.01.02 A helmet
leþerhosu 04.04.07.09 Breeches
leþerwyrhta 04.04.06 Undressed condition (of hide)
leþren 17.04.04.02 Skin, hide (as material)
leuiticus 16.02.01.08.01.01 Books of the Old Testament
lēwsa 02.08.07.02 Disorders of the eye; 08.01.03.07.02 Misery, trouble, affliction
libanisc 02.03.03.06.07.01 African
libban 13.02.05.01.01 To overcome, conquer; 16.01.02.03 Reward of heaven
(ge)libban 02.01.02.01 That lives, living; 02.01.02.02 To come to life, have life; 02.01.02.02.02 Lifetime; 04.05.03.01 Habitation, sojourn; 08.01.01 A feeling, what is felt
gelibban 16.02.01.12 Spirituality
libbende 02.01.02.01 That lives, living; 06.01.04.02 Living, remembered
libbende/lifigende 16.01.01.04.02.01 Incarnation
līc 02.03 Humankind; 02.04 Body; 02.04.01 Dead body; 02.04.03.03 Trunk; 16.02.01.13 Evil-doing, transgression, sin
(ge)līc 03.06.01 Similitude, likeness
gelīc 03.06.01.02 Equality; 06.01.07.07.01 Likelihood, probability, chance; 09.06.01 To relate, recount, tell; 12.07.01 One's due, natural place or position
gelīca 03.06.01 Similitude, likeness; 12.01.01.06 Condition, rank, standing
līcbeorg 02.02.05.01.01 A grave, burial place, sepulchre
gelīcbīsen 03.06.01.01 Imitation
gelīcbīsnung 03.06.01.01 Imitation
līcburg 02.02.05.01 Place of burial
liccian 03.01.16.01 Moisture; 04.01.03 Drinking
liccian eorþan 13.02.05.02 Defeat
(ge)liccian 02.05.06.03 Licking
liccung 02.05.06.03 Licking
gelīce ... swā 03.06.01 Similitude, likeness
gelīce 03.06.01 Similitude, likeness; 03.06.01.02 Equality
gelīce and ... 03.06.01 Similitude, likeness
līcettan 06.01.07.04.04.02 Pretence, feigning, dissimulation; 06.01.07.04.04.02.01 Hypocrisy; 07.07.03 Flattery; 14.03.03.06 False witness; 16.01.04.03 Sorcery involving deceptive appearances

gelīcettan 03.06.01.01 Imitation; 06.01.07.04.04.02 Pretence, feigning, dissimulation; 10.01.02 Acquisition
gelīcettan tō 03.06.01.01.01 Imitation, emulation
līcettere 06.01.07.04.04.02.01 Hypocrisy
līcettung 03.06.01.01 Imitation; 06.01.07.04.04.02.01 Hypocrisy; 07.07.03 Flattery; 14.03.03.06 False witness
līcfæt 02.04 Body
licgan 01.01.02 Land; 02.01.03.02 Barrenness, sterility; 02.02.03 To die, perish; 02.02.03.02 State of being dead; 02.02.05 A burial, burying; 02.05.04 Sleepiness, drowsiness, sleep; 04.05.03.03.01 Lodgings, quarters; 05.02 State, condition; 05.02.02.01 Inclination; 05.10.04 Place, room; 09.05.04.01 Concealment, obscurity; 11.06 Disinclination to act, listlessness
licgan (in/on/under) 12.05.06.04.02 Submission, subjection, obedience
licgan on 06.02.06.01 An end, goal
licgan on/ymbe 04.04.07 Trappings, equipment, garb
licgan on cnēowum 05.12.05.13.02.01 To kneel down
licgan ongēan 12.05.05 Resistance, repulsing
licgan (tō) 05.10.05.02 Extension, stretching
(ge)licgan 02.08.02.01.05 Bed of sickness; 05.07 Ending of existence, end of world; 05.10.04 Place, room; 05.10.05.04.02.03.02 Reclining, rest; 05.12.04 Absence of movement, stillness
(ge)licgan tō/intō 15.01 Property

(ge)licgan (wiþ, mid) 02.01.03.03 Sex, generation
gelicgan 05.04.01 Fortune, Fate (personification); 06.01.08.06 Fear
licgende feoh 15.01.04 Coinage, money
līchama 02.03 Humankind; 02.04 Body; 02.04.01 Dead body; 02.04.03.03 Trunk; 02.07.03.03.01 Wood (as substance)
līchamlēas 16.01.02.05.01 An angel
līchamlic 02.04 Body; 12.08.08 Carnal nature, sensual appetites
līchamlice geþēodnes 02.01.03.03 Sex, generation
līchamlīce 02.04 Body; 12.08.08 Carnal nature, sensual appetites
gelīchamod 16.01.01.04.02.01 Incarnation
līchanga 14.05.06 Means/implement of torture
līchord 06 Spirit, soul, heart
līchrægl 02.02.05.02 To prepare for burial
līchryre 02.02 Death
līcian 03.03.04.02 A sufficiency, sufficient supply
(ge)līcian 08.01.01.03.09.03 To make glad; 11.07.03 Use, advantage, profit
gelīcian 03.06 Comparison; 03.06.01.01 Imitation; 06.01.07.07.01 Likelihood, probability, chance
līc(i)endlic 08.01.01.03.09.01 Pleasant, agreeable
(ge)līcigende 08.01.01.03.09.01 Pleasant, agreeable
gelīclǣtan 03.06 Comparison
līclāf 16.02.05.05.10 Relics, a collection of relics
līclēoþ 02.02.05.03 To attend the dead
līclic 02.02.05 A burial, burying

(ge)līclic 12.07.01 One's due, natural place or position
gelīclīce 03.06.01.02 Equality
līcmann 02.02.05.02 To prepare for burial
(ge)līcnes 02.04.02 Bodily shape/physique; 03.06.01 Similitude, likeness; 05.10.06 Form, shape; 17.02.05.04 An image, figure
gelīcnes 03.06.01.02 Equality; 11.05.02.01 A standard, norm, ethos
līcrest 02.02.05.01 Place of burial; 02.02.05.01.01 A grave, burial place, sepulchre; 02.02.05.02 To prepare for burial
līcsang 02.02.05.03 To attend the dead
līcsār 02.08.04.01 A wound
līcstōw 02.02.05.01 Place of burial
līcsyrce 13.02.08.03.01.04 Coat of mail/corselet
līctūn 02.02.05.01 Place of burial
līcþēnung 02.02.05.02 To prepare for burial
līcþēote 02.04.04 Skin
līcþrōwere 02.08.06 Skin disease, erysipelas
līcþrūh 02.02.05.01.01 A grave, burial place, sepulchre
gelīcung 08.01.01.03.09 Pleasantness, agreeableness
līcwiglung 16.01.04.05 Necromancy
līcwund 02.08.04.01 A wound
līcwyrþe 07.04.04.02 Laudable, praiseworthy; 15.01.04 Coinage, money
(ge)līcwyrþe 08.01.01.03.09.01 Pleasant, agreeable
līcwyrþlīce 07.04.04.02 Laudable, praiseworthy
līcwyrþnes 08.01.01.03.09 Pleasantness, agreeableness

lid 05.12.01.09.03.01 A ship, boat
lida 05.12.01.09.03 A voyage
lidmann 05.12.01.09.03 A voyage
lidweard 05.12.01.09.03 A voyage
lidwērig 02.05.03.02 Weariness
līefan hām 12.03.05 Permission
līefan (tō) 06.01.08.03 Trust, faith, confidence
(ge)līefan 06.01.08.03.01 Belief, trust, faithfulness; 10.03.03 Granting; 12.03.05 Permission
(ge)līefan (on) 06.01.08.03.01 Belief, trust, faithfulness
gelīefan 06.01.07.06 Mental acceptance, belief; 16.02.01 Faith
gelīefan (tō) 07.01 Appraisal, appraising; 06.01.08.03 Trust, faith, confidence
gelīefed 06.01.07.07.01 Likelihood, probability, chance; 06.01.08.03.01 Belief, trust, faithfulness; 08.01.02.02.01 A favourite, loved one; 16.02.01 Faith
gelīefedlic 12.03.05 Permission
gelīefedlīce 06.01.08.03 Trust, faith, confidence; 12.03.05 Permission
gelīefen 12.03.05 Permission
gelīefend 06.01.07.06 Mental acceptance, belief
(ge)līesan 05.05.04 That loosens, loosening; 16.01.01.02.08 Salvation, redemption
(ge)līesan (of) 11.10.03 Salvation/deliverance from
līesend 16.01.01.02.08 Salvation, redemption
līesing 12.01.01.10.01 Freeing, manumission; 16.01.01.02.08 Salvation, redemption
(ge)līesnes 16.01.01.02.08 Salvation, redemption

līf

līf 02.01 Existence, life; 02.01.01 Life, vital part; 02.01.02.02.01 Condition of life; 02.01.02.02.02 Lifetime; 02.03.01 People; 05.11.01.01.01 Eternity; 09.03.07.07.02 A written work, book, treatise; 11.01.01 Practice, exercise, doing; 16.01.02.03 Reward of heaven; 16.02.05.04 A monastery/convent; 16.02.05.10.11 A vita; 17.02 Work, occupation, employment
līf geendian 02.02.03 To die, perish
līf gelōgian 11.05.02 Mode, manner, way, method, fashion, course
līfbrycgung 17.02 Work, occupation, employment
līfbysig 02.02.03.01 In process of dying
līfcearu 08.01.03.03 Anxiety
līfdæg 02.01.02.02.02 Lifetime
lifen 02.01.02.02.01 Condition of life; 04.01.02 Means of subsistence
lifer 02.04.06.05.03 Liver; 03.03.02.01 A weight, definite amount; 04.01.02.01.02.05.01 Edible part of animal
liferādl 02.08.08.06 Disease of liver
liferbȳl 02.08.08.06 Disease of liver
liferhol 02.08.08.06 Disease of liver
liferlæppa 02.04.06.05.03 Liver
liferseoc 02.08.08.06 Disease of liver
liferseocnes 02.08.08.06 Disease of liver
liferwærc 02.08.08.06 Disease of liver
liferwyrt 02.07.11 Plants/flowers (alphabetical order)
līfes 02.01.02.01 That lives, living
līfes nēotan 02.01.02.02.02 Lifetime
līffadung 11.05.02 Mode, manner, way, method, fashion, course
līffæc 02.01.02.02.02 Lifetime

līffæst 02.01.02 Gift of life; 02.01.02.01 That lives, living; 04.05.03.01 Habitation, sojourn; 05.08.01 Vigour, activity, force
gelīffæst 16.02.05.11 The cross (as Christian image)
(ge)līffæstan 02.01.02 Gift of life; 08.01 Heart, spirit, mood, disposition; 16.02.01.12 Spirituality
gelīffæstan 02.01.02.02 To come to life, have life
gelīffæsted 16.02.01.12 Spirituality
līffæstende 16.01.01.04.02.01 Incarnation
gelīffæstnian 16.02.01.12 Spirituality
līffrēa 16.01.01.02.02 A giving (by Deity)
līffruma 16.01.01.02.02 A giving (by Deity)
līfgedāl 02.02 Death
līfgesceaft 02.01.02.02.02 Lifetime
līfgetwinnan 02.03.02.02.01 Twins
lifiende 02.01.02.01 That lives, living
līflād 02.01.02.02.02 Lifetime; 11.05.02 Mode, manner, way, method, fashion, course
līflēas 02.02.03.02 State of being dead; 02.07 A plant; 16.02.01.06.01 Belief/practice of heathen people
līflēast 02.02 Death
līflic 02.01 Existence, life; 02.01.02.01 That lives, living; 02.01.04.03 Aging, growing old; 06.01.05.02 Intelligence; 16.02.01.12 Spirituality
līflīce 02.01.02 Gift of life
līflyre 02.02 Death
līfneru 04.01.02.01 Food/sustenance
lifrig 03.01.17.01 A coagulating, mixing
līfweard 16.01.01.04.02 The Son, Christ
līfweg 05.02.01.01 The course of human affairs; 11.05.02 Mode, manner, way, method, fashion, course
līfwela 15.01.03 Treasure, riches, wealth

līfwelle 02.01.02 Gift of life
līfwraþu 11.10.01.01 Preservation from injury/destruction
līfwynn 08.01.01.03 Good feeling, joy, happiness
līg 03.01.09.02 Fire, flame; 08.01.01.01 Ardour, fervour, strong feeling
līgbǣre 03.01.09.02 Fire, flame
līgberende 03.01.09.02 Fire, flame
līgbryne 03.01.09.02 Fire, flame
līgbysig 03.01.09.02 Fire, flame
līgcwalu 14.05.05 Physical punishments
līgdraca 02.06.10.01.01 Dragon
līgegesa 06.01.08.06.03 Cause of fear, terror, horror
līgen 03.01.09.02 Fire, flame
līger 03.01.09.02 Fire, flame
geligere 12.08.08.01.02.01 Fornication, adultery
geligernes 12.08.08.01.02.01 Fornication, adultery
līget 01.03.01.03.01.02 Lightning
līgetræsc 01.03.01.03.01.02 Lightning
līgetsleht 01.03.01.03.01.02 Lightning
līgetung 01.03.01.03.01.02 Lightning
līgfǣmende 03.01.09.02 Fire, flame
līgfāmblāwende 03.01.09.02 Fire, flame
līgfȳr 03.01.09.02 Fire, flame
līgfȳrberende 03.01.09.02 Fire, flame
līglic 03.01.09.02 Fire, flame
līglocc(ed) 03.01.09.02 Fire, flame
līgnan 09.07.03.01 A denial
līgrægel 04.04.07.01 Mode of dressing, fashion
līgræsc 01.03.01.03.01.02 Lightning
līgræsc(et)ung 01.03.01.03.01.02 Lightning
līgspīwel 03.01.09.02 Fire, flame
līgþracu 03.01.09.02 Fire, flame
līgȳþ 03.01.09.02 Fire, flame

līhtan 03.01.09.02.01 Fire, burning; 12.01.01.10.01 Freeing, manumission
(ge)līhtan 02.05.09.03 To give light, restore to sight; 03.01.12 Brightness, light; 03.01.12.02 A beam of light; 05.09.03 Mitigation, lightening, alleviation; 05.11.04.01.01 Dawn, daybreak, sunrise; 05.12.05.13 To go down, descend; 08.01.03.07.04.02 Relief, alleviation
(ge)līhtan (of) 05.12.01.05 To ride (on horse, etc.)
gelīhtan 02.08.12.01 Medical care, treatment; 05.12.05.02 To go/travel towards, come, approach; 07.05 Disrespect, irreverence; 17.05.04 To kindle, set alight (fire, lamp)
līhtende 03.01.12 Brightness, light
līhting 01.03.01.03.01.02 Lightning; 03.01.12 Brightness, light; 03.01.12.02 A beam of light; 05.09.03 Mitigation, lightening, alleviation; 05.11.04.01.01 Dawn, daybreak, sunrise; 06.01.02 The imaginative faculty; 08.01.02.06.02 Forgiveness, remission, clemency; 08.01.03.07.04.02 Relief, alleviation; 16.02.04.07.02.02 Absolution, forgiveness, remission
līhtnes 03.01.12 Brightness, light
lilie 02.07.11 Plants/flowers (alphabetical order)
lim 02.04.03 Part of body; 02.04.03.04 Limb; 02.04.03.04.02 Leg; 02.04.06.04.01 Male genitalia; 02.07.03.03.01 Wood (as substance); 09.03.02.01 A period, sentence; 12.08.06.02.02 A bad man, inhuman person; 16.02.02 Christianity, the Christian faith

līm

līm 04.03.04 Fowling; 04.05.01.03 Gypsum, chalk
gelīman 03.03.06.01 A whole formed by joining
līmfīn 17.04.01 Sources of materials
limgelecg 02.04.02.03 Height, stature or form
limgesīþ 02.04 Body
limhāl 02.08.01 Sound physical condition
līming 04.05.01.03 Gypsum, chalk
limlæw 02.08.04.04.01 Mutilation/injury to limbs
limlæweo 02.08.04.02.01 A maimed man
limlēas 02.08.04.04 State of being crippled
limmælum 03.03.07 A part, division, portion
limmlama 02.08.04.04 State of being crippled
limnacod 04.04.07.02.01 Nakedness
gelimp 05.03.02 Event, issue, result; 05.03.02.01.01 An event, occurrence; 05.04 Fate, lot, fortune, destiny; 08.01.01.03.08.02 Good fortune, success; 09.03.02.03.01 Accidence
limpan 10.01 Fact of belonging, possession by
(ge)limpan 03.04 Form, kind, nature, character; 03.06.03 Congruity, fitness, suitability; 05.03.02.01.01 An event, occurrence
gelimpan 03.03.05.01 Rank, position, degree; 05 Aught, anything, something; 05.03.02 Event, issue, result
gelimpe 05.03.02.01 Chance, hap, event
gelimpful 03.06.03 Congruity, fitness, suitability
gelimplæcan 03.06.03 Congruity, fitness, suitability

gelimplic 03.06.03 Congruity, fitness, suitability; 05.03.02.01.01 An event, occurrence; 05.11.08 A suitable time, opportunity; 09.03.02.03.01 Accidence; 11.04 Ability, capacity, power
(ge)limplīce 03.06.03 Congruity, fitness, suitability
gelimplīce 11.05.02.01 A standard, norm, ethos; 12.07.01 One's due, natural place or position
gelimplicnes 05.11.08 A suitable time, opportunity
limrǣden 05.10.06 Form, shape
limsēoc 02.08.04.04 State of being crippled
limwǣde 04.04.07 Trappings, equipment, garb
limwæstm 02.04.02.03 Height, stature or form
limwērig 02.02.03.02 State of being dead
līn 04.02.04.03.02.02 Flax; 04.04.05.04 Linen, linen cloth
līnacer 04.02.03.02.02.03 Flax land/field
lind 02.07.03.05 Particular trees/shrubs (alphabetical order); 13.02.08.03.01.06 A shield
lindcroda 13.02.02 Battle
linden 02.07.03.05 Particular trees/shrubs (alphabetical order)
lindgecrod 13.02.10.01.02 An armed man
lindgelāc 13.02.02 Battle
lindgestealla 12.04.01 A fellow, companion, associate, comrade
lindhæbbend 13.02.10.01 A man, warrior
lindplega 13.02.02 Battle
lindrycg 01.01.02.01.02.01 Rising ground, eminence
lindwered 13.02.10.01.02 An armed man
lindwiga 13.02.10.01 A man, warrior

lindwīg(g)end 13.02.10.01.02 An armed man
līne 03.05.02 An arrangement, order, succession; 05.10.05.04.03 A line, continuous length; 09.03.07 Writing; 16.02.01.09.01 Canon law; 17.03.10 Supports and fastenings
līnen 04.04.05.04 Linen, linen cloth
līnenhrægl 04.04.05.04 Linen, linen cloth
līnete 02.06.08.05 Forest bird, wild-fowl
līneweard 04.04.07.01 Mode of dressing, fashion
līnhǣwen 03.01.14.03 White/whiteness
līnland 04.02.03.02.02.03 Flax land/field
līnlēag 04.02.03.02.02.03 Flax land/field
linnan 11.06.04 Abstention, abstaining from
linnan ealdre 02.02.03 To die, perish
līnsǣd 04.02.04.03.02.02 Flax
līnsētcorn 04.02.04.03.02.02 Flax
līntwig(l)e 02.06.08.05 Forest bird, wild-fowl
līnwǣd 04.04.07.01 Mode of dressing, fashion
līnwyrt 04.02.04.03.02.02 Flax
lioþucǣga 12.09.03 Unmarried state
lippa 02.04.03.01.03.06 Mouth
līra 02.04.05.01 Flesh; 02.04.05.05 Muscle; 04.01.02.01.02.05.01 Edible part of animal
līreht 02.04.05.01 Flesh
lisc 02.07.08 Grasses, reeds, etc.
gelise 06.01.06.02.02.01 Learning, science (secular knowledge)
gelīsian 05.12.01.04.01.04 To stumble, trip, strike (with the foot)
liss 05.09.03 Mitigation, lightening, alleviation; 08.01.01.03 Good feeling, joy, happiness; 08.01.01.03.05 Pleasure, delight; 08.01.02.01 Favour, kindness, grace; 08.01.02.06 Mercy, pity; 11.05.02.02 Humanity, courtesy, civility; 16.02.04.07.02.02 Absolution, forgiveness, remission
lissan 05.09.03 Mitigation, lightening, alleviation
lissian 08.01.02.06.01 Pity
lissum 08.01.02.01 Favour, kindness, grace
list 11.04.02 Skill, skilfulness; 11.04.02.01.01 Cunning, craft, craftiness, guile, wile
liste 04.04.09 A fringe, border, hem
listelīce 06.01.01.02 Care, attention, observation
listhendig 11.04.01 An aptitude, bodily skill
listum 11.04.02.01 Art, skill, contrivance, cunning
listwrenc 11.04.02.01.01 Cunning, craft, craftiness, guile, wile
lit 03.01.14.01 Dyeing
lītan 05.12.05.13.02 To bow, bend down
litigere 03.01.14.01 Dyeing
liþ 02.04.03.04 Limb; 02.04.03.04.01.01.01 Finger; 02.04.05.04.08 Joint; 05.10.06.03 Projection, head, extremity (of anything); 13.02.10.03.01 A fleet
līþ 04.01.03 Drinking; 04.01.03.05.01 Intoxicating liquor; 08.01.02.06 Mercy, pity
līþa 02.08.07.08 Foot ailments, ?gout; 05.11.03.01.03.01 Specific months
līþamōnaþ 05.11.03.01.03.01 Specific months
līþan 10.02.01 Loss, deprivation
(ge)līþan 05.12.01 To go, progress, travel (usually on land); 05.12.01.09 To travel on water

gelīþan 05.11 A time, period of time
līþe 02.05.07.03 Sweetness;
04.01.03.05.01 Intoxicating liquor;
05.09.02 Mildness, moderate quality;
05.12.04 Absence of movement,
stillness; 07.07.03 Flattery;
08.01.01.03 Good feeling, joy,
happiness; 08.01.01.03.09.01
Pleasant, agreeable; 08.01.02.01
Favour, kindness, grace;
08.01.02.01.02 Gentleness;
11.05.02.02 Humanity, courtesy,
civility; 14.01.02 A law, statute
līþelēaf 02.07.10.01 Particular
herbs/spices (alphabetical order)
līþelic 07.07.03 Flattery; 11.05.02.02
Humanity, courtesy, civility
līþelīce 05.09.02 Mildness, moderate
quality; 07.07.03 Flattery; 08.01.02.01
Favour, kindness, grace;
08.01.02.01.02.01 Mildness, leniency,
indulgence; 11.05.02.02 Humanity,
courtesy, civility
gelīþen 05.12.01.01 To go on a
journey/expedition, travel
līþercian 07.07.03 Flattery
līþere 13.02.08.04.05 A warlike engine
līþerlic 02.05.10.07 A crashing, noise
gelīþewācian 05.09.03 Mitigation,
lightening, alleviation; 13.01.02.01 An
appeasing, pacifying
(ge)līþewǣcan 05.09.03 Mitigation,
lightening, alleviation
gelīþewǣcan 03.06.03 Congruity, fitness,
suitability; 13.01.02.01 An appeasing,
pacifying; 16.02.01.12 Spirituality
gelīþewǣht 02.08.13 Recovery, growing
better
(ge)līþian 11.12.01 Absence of restraint,
freedom
līþian 05.09.03 Mitigation, lightening,
alleviation; 08.01.02.01 Favour,
kindness, grace
līþig 02.04.02.04 Flexibility of limbs,
suppleness; 03.01.04.01 Power of
bending, flexibility; 06.02.07.05.02
Moral weakness
gelīþigan 13.01.02.01 An appeasing,
pacifying
līþigian 05.12.04 Absence of movement,
stillness; 08.01.02.01.02 Gentleness
(ge)līþigian 05.09.03 Mitigation,
lightening, alleviation;
08.01.01.03.09.03 To make glad
līþincel 02.04.05.04.08 Joint
līþnes 02.08.12.02.05 Pharmacy, curing
with salves; 05.09.02 Mildness,
moderate quality; 07.07.03 Flattery;
08.01.02.01.02 Gentleness
gelīþran 04.06.01.04 What is used in
washing, an ointment
līþsēaw 02.04.06.05.07.03 Synovia, oily
matter between joints
līþsmann 05.12.01.09.03 A voyage
līþsmenn 13.02.10.01.02.01.01 Military
followers (of household); 13.02.10.03
Crew/men of a ship
līþule 02.04.06.05.07.03 Synovia, oily
matter between joints
līþung 08.01.03.07.04.02 Relief,
alleviation; 16.02.04.07.02.02
Absolution, forgiveness, remission
līþwǣge 04.01.03.05.04 Drinking vessel
līþwǣrc 02.08.07.07 Disorders of the
body
līþwyrde 11.05.02.02 Humanity,
courtesy, civility
(ge)līxan 03.01.12.01 Glittering,
effulgence

līxende 01.03.01.03.01.02 Lightning; 03.01.12 Brightness, light; 07.02.04.03 Nobleness, excellence, nobility, magnificence
līxung 03.01.12 Brightness, light
lobbe 02.06.09.02.10 Spider
loc 04.02.05.06.02.01 A sheepfold; 06.01.03.02 Dialectics, logic; 09.03.02.01 A period, sentence; 14.04.04 An agreement, arrangement of dispute; 17.03.10.01 A bolt, lock, bar
lōc 02.05.09.04 To see, look upon, behold
lōc hweþer 07.01.01 Choice, election
lōc nū 02.05.09.04 To see, look upon, behold
loca 04.04.04 A thread (of wool, etc.), fibre; 05.10.05.04.11 A circle, circuit, circumference
lōc(a) hwā 03.04 Form, kind, nature, character
lōc(a) hwylce 03.04 Form, kind, nature, character
lōca hū 03.06 Comparison
lōca hwǣr 05.10.04.03 Presence
lōca hwonne/hwænne 05.11.02 A time, particular time, occasion
lōca nū hū 03.06 Comparison
locbore 12.01.01.10 Freedom, being free
locc 02.04.04.03.03 Hair of head; 02.04.04.03.03.01 Beard, whisker
geloccian 06.02.06.03.04 Allurement
loccod 02.04.04.03.03 Hair of head
locen 03.03.06.01 A whole formed by joining
gelocen 04.04.05 Woven material, fabric
lōcere 04.02.05.06.02 A shepherd
locettan 09.01.02.01 Excessive fluency, loquacity
locfeax 02.04.04.03.03 Hair of head

locgewind 02.04.04.03.03 Hair of head
lochyrdel 04.02.05.06.02.01 A sheepfold; 04.05.01.02.05 A hurdle
lōcian 06.01.01.01 Thinking about, minding, heeding; 06.01.06.01.01.02 To know, recognize; 09.05.01 Inspection, examination; 11.02.02.02 Care, mindfulness, attention; 11.10.02 Watching, guard, watch; 12.07.02 Observance, keeping
lōcian (in) tō 10.01 Fact of belonging, possession by
lōcian on 07.04 Consideration, esteem
lōcian tō 11.02.02.02.01 Attention, cultivation; 06.01.01.01 Thinking about, minding, heeding; 12.01.01.07 A follower
(ge)lōcian 02.05.09 Faculty of sight
(ge)lōcian (on, tō) 02.05.09.04 To see, look upon, behold
locor 17.03.04 Tools for smoothing/scraping/grinding
locstān 05.10.05.04.15.01 A bar, bolt
geloda 02.04.05.04.08 Joint
loddere 15.01.06 Poverty, indigence
gelodr 02.04.05.04.04 Spine
lodrung 11.08.04 Vanity, idleness, frivolity
gelodwyrt 02.07.11 Plants/flowers (alphabetical order)
lof 07.04.04 Praise, acclamation, applause; 07.08 Reputation, fame; 16.02.04 Worship, honour, praise; 16.02.04.03.03.01 A hymn, song of praise, canticle
lof beran 16.02.04 Worship, honour, praise
lof hebban 16.02.04 Worship, honour, praise

lof reccan and rǣran 16.02.04 Worship, honour, praise
lof wyrcan 16.02.04 Worship, honour, praise
lōf 04.04.07.11 A headcloth, covering for the head
lofbǣre 16.02.04 Worship, honour, praise
lofdǣd 11.01 Action, doing, performance
lofgeorn 06.02.05.04.01 Ambition; 07.06.03 Boastfulness, arrogance; 07.08.01 Nobility (of character, rank, etc.)
lofherung 16.02.04 Worship, honour, praise
(ge)lofian 07.01 Appraisal, appraising; 16.02.04 Worship, honour, praise
loflāc 16.02.04.12 Sacrifice, a sacrifice
loflǣcan 16.02.04 Worship, honour, praise
loflic 07.04.04.02 Laudable, praiseworthy
loflīce 07.04 Consideration, esteem
lofmægen 16.02.04 Worship, honour, praise
lofsang 16.02.04.03.03.01 A hymn, song of praise, canticle; 16.02.04.05 Canonical hour, service; 16.02.04.05.03 The hour or service of Lauds; 18.02.07.01.01 A song, a poem to be sung or recited
lofsealm 16.02.04.03.03.02 A psalm
lofsingende 16.02.04.03.03 Singing, church singing
lofsum 07.04.04.02 Laudable, praiseworthy
lofu 16.02.04.03.03.02 A psalm
lofung 07.01 Appraisal, appraising; 16.02.04 Worship, honour, praise
gelōgendlic 03.05 Order, arrangement, disposition

lōgian 09.03.07.07.03.02 To write, state/say in writing
(ge)lōgian 03.05 Order, arrangement, disposition; 03.05.01 Arranging, ordering, disposition; 05.10.04 Place, room; 10 Having, owning, possession; 12.06.03 A site, settlement
gelōgian 02.02.05 A burial, burying; 03.03.04.01.02.01 A heap, mass, accumulation; 03.03.06.01 A whole formed by joining; 04.01.02.02.04 To season; 04.05.03.03.01 Lodgings, quarters; 06.02.06.03 Persuasion, prompting; 09.03.04.01 Mode of speech; 15.01.05 Possession of wealth
logþer 11.04.02.01.01 Cunning, craft, craftiness, guile, wile
gelōgung 03.05 Order, arrangement, disposition
lōh 05.10.04 Place, room
lōhsceaft 17.03.10.01 A bolt, lock, bar
gelōm 05.11.09.02 Frequent, of common occurrence
gelōma 17.03 Implements, tools, etc.
(ge)lōme 05.11.09.02 Frequent, of common occurrence
gelōme 05.11.11 Continuity; 11.02.02.01 Diligence, studious care
(ge)lōmlǣcan 08.01.02.04.01 Visiting
gelōmlǣcan 05.11.09.02 Frequent, of common occurrence; 05.11.09.06 Frequency, repetition; 12.04.02 A crowding together, assembly
gelōmlǣcende 09.03.02.02.01.03 An adverb
gelōmlǣcing 05.11.09.06 Frequency, repetition; 12.04.02 A crowding together, assembly
gelōmlǣcnes 12.04.02 A crowding together, assembly

(ge)lōmlic 05.11.09.02 Frequent, of common occurrence
gelōmlic 03.03.04.01.02 A great number, multitude; 05.10.04.03.01 Visiting/seeking of a place; 06.02.07.03 Perseverance; 12.04.02 A crowding together, assembly
(ge)lōmlīce 05.11.09.02 Frequent, of common occurrence
gelōmlīcian 05.11.09.02 Frequent, of common occurrence
gelōmlicnes 05.11.09.06 Frequency, repetition; 12.04.02 A crowding together, assembly
gelōmrǣde 05.11.09.02 Frequent, of common occurrence
londādl 02.08.08.12 Disease of bowels
longbeardas 02.03.03.06.04 Italians
lopost 02.06.06.04.01.03 Lobster
loppe 02.06.09.02.10 Spider
loppestre 02.06.06.04.01.03 Lobster; 02.06.09.02.05 Cricket, grasshopper, locust; 04.01.02.01.02.07 Fish
lorg 04.04.03 A spinning-house or chamber
lorte 01.01.02.01.04.01 Marsh, bog, swamp
losian 02.02.03.04 Spiritual death; 02.08.02 Disease, infirmity, sickness; 08.01.03.06.01 Affliction, misfortune, calamity; 10.02 Want, lack; 10.02.01 Loss, deprivation; 11.08.03 Needless, useless, unprofitable; 12.08.06.01.04 To lead a bad life
(ge)losian 02.02.03 To die, perish; 03.02.01 Decay, decline, corruption; 05.06 Destruction, dissolution, loss, breaking; 10.02.01 Loss, deprivation; 12.08.06.01.04.01 To mislead, seduce, lead astray

losigendlic 08.01.03.06.01 Affliction, misfortune, calamity
losing 05.06.01 Devastation, laying waste
loswist 05.06.01 Devastation, laying waste
lot 06.01.07.04.02 Fraud, deceit, trick, trickery
geloten dæg 05.11.04.01.03 Mid-day, noon
lotwrenc 06.01.07.04.02 Fraud, deceit, trick, trickery
loþa 04.04.07.07 A long outer garment, covering, cloak, etc.
loþrung 06.01.02.01 An imaginary form, fancy
lox 02.06.04.01.10 Lynx
lūcan 05.06.08 A plucking, taking away; 05.11.10.02 End, completion; 05.12.05.02.02 To come together, meet
(ge)lūcan 05.10.05.04.15 Closure, being closed; 05.10.05.04.15.01 A bar, bolt
ludgæt 05.10.05.04.14.02 An opening/space in an enclosure
lufe niman tō 08.01.02.02.03 A loving relationship
lufen 04.05.03.02.02.02 Agreeable dwellings
lufestice 02.07.11 Plants/flowers (alphabetical order)
lufestre 08.01.02.02.03 A loving relationship; 12.08.08.01.02.01.01 An adulterer/-ess, whore, prostitute
luffeorm 04.01.02.04.05.01 Hospitality, harbouring, entertaining
lufian 06.02.05.01 Strong liking for, devotion to; 07.04 Consideration, esteem; 08.01.02.02 Love, affection, care; 11.05 Natural/proper way/manner/mode of action

1149

lufian (on) 08.01.02.02 Love, affection, care
(ge)lufian 06.02.05.01 Strong liking for, devotion to; 08.01.01.03.05 Pleasure, delight; 08.01.02.02 Love, affection, care; 08.01.02.02.02 An embrace
lufiend 08.01.02.02 Love, affection, care; 08.01.02.02.03 A loving relationship; 11.10.02.02.01 Care, interest in
lufiende 08.01.02.02 Love, affection, care
lufi(g)endlic 08.01.01.03.09.01 Pleasant, agreeable; 08.01.02.02.01 A favourite, loved one
luflic 08.01.01.03.09.01 Pleasant, agreeable; 08.01.02.02 Love, affection, care
luflīce 06.02.02.01 Will, wish, pleasure; 08.01.02.02 Love, affection, care; 11.05.02.02 Humanity, courtesy, civility
lufrǣden 08.01.02.02 Love, affection, care
lufsum 08.01.01.03.09.01 Pleasant, agreeable
lufsumlic 08.01.01.03.09.01 Pleasant, agreeable
lufsumlīce 08.01.02.03.03 In a friendly manner, kindly
lufsumnes 08.01.02.02 Love, affection, care
luftācen 08.01.02.02.02 An embrace
luftȳme 08.01.01.03.09.01 Pleasant, agreeable
luftȳmlic 08.01.01.03.09.01 Pleasant, agreeable
lufu 02.05.05.01 Object of desire; 02.05.05.03 Sexual appetite, lust; 06.02.05.01 Strong liking for, devotion to; 08.01.02.02 Love, affection, care; 08.01.02.02.03 A loving relationship; 08.01.02.02.04 Love, caritas; 11.05.02.02 Humanity, courtesy, civility; 14.03.03 Law, action of the courts
lufu/þancas gereccan 16.02.04.02 Thanksgiving, praise
lufung 08.01.02.02.03 A loving relationship
lufwende 08.01.01.03.09.01 Pleasant, agreeable; 08.01.02.02.03 A loving relationship
lufwendlic 08.01.02.03.02 Friendly, amiable
lufwendlīce 08.01.02.03.03 In a friendly manner, kindly
luh 01.01.03.01.03 Lake
lumm 01.01.03.01.03.01 Pool
gelumpenlic 03.06.03 Congruity, fitness, suitability; 05.03.02.01 Chance, hap, event; 05.11.02 A time, particular time, occasion
lunares 05.11.06.02.02 A calculated space of time
luncian 02.08.04.04 State of being crippled
lundlaga 02.04.06.05.04 Kidney
lundonisc 02.03.03.05.01.05 Belonging to London
lungen 02.04.06.07.02 Lungs
lungenādl 02.08.08.02 Lung disease
lungenǣder 02.04.06.08 Heart
lungencoþu 02.08.08.02 Lung disease
lungensealf 02.08.12.02.07 Remedies for specific parts (head to toe)
lungenwyrt 02.07.11.02 Unidentified plants (alphabetical order)
lungor 05.12.03.01 Swiftness, velocity
lungre 03.03.06.02 Fullness; 05.08.02 Violence, force; 05.11.07.01 Contemporary, coeval

lūs 02.06.09.01 Parasite
lust 02.05.05 Desire, appetite; 02.05.05.02 Eager desire; 02.05.05.03 Sexual appetite, lust; 05.08.01 Vigour, activity, force; 06.02.05 Will, desire, wish; 06.02.05.01 Strong liking for, devotion to; 08.01.01.03.05 Pleasure, delight; 12.08.08.01 Eager, unseemly desire
lustbǣre 02.05.05 Desire, appetite; 06.02.02.01 Will, wish, pleasure; 08.01.01.03.09.01 Pleasant, agreeable
lustbǣrlic 08.01.01.03.09.01 Pleasant, agreeable
lustbǣrlīce 08.01.01.03.05 Pleasure, delight
lustbǣrnes 02.05.05.02 Eager desire; 08.01.01.03.05 Pleasure, delight
lustful 02.05.05 Desire, appetite; 02.05.05.02 Eager desire
(ge)lustful 02.05.05.01 Object of desire
(ge)lustfullian 08.01.01.03.05 Pleasure, delight; 08.01.01.03.06 Exultation, joy; 08.01.01.03.09.03 To make glad
lustfullīce 08.01.01.03 Good feeling, joy, happiness
(ge)lustfullīce 06.02.05.04.05 Earnestness; 08.01.01.03.02 Pleasure, satisfaction
(ge)lustfullung 08.01.01.03.05 Pleasure, delight
gelustfullung 08.01.01.03.09 Pleasantness, agreeableness
(ge)lustfulnes 08.01.01.03.05 Pleasure, delight
lustgeornnes 12.08.08.01 Eager, unseemly desire
lustgryn 12.08.07.01 Laxity, indulgence
gelustian 08.01.01.03.05 Pleasure, delight
lustlīce 06.02.02.01 Will, wish, pleasure

lustmoce 02.07.11 Plants/flowers (alphabetical order)
lustsumlic 08.01.01.03.09.01 Pleasant, agreeable
lustsumlīce 06.02.02 Will, disposition
lustum 06.02.02.01 Will, wish, pleasure
lūsþorn 02.07.03.05 Particular trees/shrubs (alphabetical order)
lūtan 07.04.03 Reverence, respect
(ge)lūtan 05.11.10.02 End, completion; 05.12.05.13 To go down, descend; 05.12.05.13.02 To bow, bend down
gelūtan 05.12.05.13.02.02 To sit down
lutegār 04.03 Hunting, the chase
(ge)lūtian 11.09.01.01 Ambush, lying in wait
lūtiend 11.09.01.01 Ambush, lying in wait
lybb 02.08.12.02.05 Pharmacy, curing with salves
lybbestre 16.01.04 Sorcery, magic, witchcraft
lybcorn 02.08.12.02.07.01 Purgative
lybcræft 16.01.04 Sorcery, magic, witchcraft
lybesn 16.01.04.04 A magical apparatus
lyblāc 16.01.04.02 Sorcery involving drugs or potions
lyblǣca 16.01.04 Sorcery, magic, witchcraft
lycce 05.10.05.04.11 A circle, circuit, circumference
lycettan 07.05.03.01 Falseness in speech, detraction
lyffetere 07.07.03 Flattery
lyffettende 07.07.03 Flattery
lyffett(i)an 07.07.03 Flattery
lyffetung 07.07.03 Flattery
lyft 01.02.01 Heaven(s), sky; 01.03 Air surrounding earth, atmosphere;

01.03.01.05 Wind; 01.03.01.06 Cloud; 03 Material, matter, substance; 03.01.15 Vapour, air
lyftādl 02.08.04.03 Paralysis
lyftedor 01.03.01.06 Cloud
lyften 01.03 Air surrounding earth, atmosphere
lyftfæt 01.02.01.01.04 Moon
lyftflēogend 02.06.08 Bird
lyftfloga 02.06.10.01.01 Dragon
lyftgelāc 05.12.01.07 To fly (with wings)
lyftgeswenced 05.12.02.06.01 To push, drive
lyfthelm 01.03.01.06 Cloud
lyftlācende 05.12.01.07 To fly (with wings)
lyftlic 01.03 Air surrounding earth, atmosphere
lyftsceaþa 02.06.08.05 Forest bird, wild-fowl
lyftwundor 06.01.08.05.01.01.01 An exercise of power, mighty work, miracle
lyftwynn 08.01.01.03 Good feeling, joy, happiness; 08.01.01.03.05 Pleasure, delight
lyge 06.01.07.04.03 Untruth, falsehood
lygen 06.01.07.04.03 Untruth, falsehood
lygesearu 06.01.07.04.02.01 Deception, deceit, snare, wile
lygespell 06.01.07.04.03 Untruth, falsehood
lygesynnig 06.01.07.04.03 Untruth, falsehood
lygetorn 08.01.03.07.02.01 Injury, offence
lygeword 06.01.07.04.03 Untruth, falsehood
lygewyrhta 06.01.07.04.03 Untruth, falsehood
lygnes 06.01.02.01 An imaginary form, fancy; 06.01.07.04.04 Deceitfulness, falseness, duplicity
(ge)lygnian 14.03.03.06 False witness
lȳman 03.01.12 Brightness, light
(ge)lynd(e) 03.01.17.03 Fat, grease
gelynde 04.01.02.01.02.05.05 Fat/suet/lard
gelyndu 02.04.05.04.08 Joint
lynibor 17.03.05 An awl, borer, gimlet, etc.
lynis 17.03.10.02 A pin, peg, nail
lȳpenwyrhta 17.03.12.01 A basket
lyre 02.02 Death; 05.06 Destruction, dissolution, loss, breaking; 05.06.04 Damage, injury, defect, hurt, loss; 10.02.01 Loss, deprivation
lyrewrenc 06.01.07.04.02 Fraud, deceit, trick, trickery; 10.02.01 Loss, deprivation
lystan 02.05.05 Desire, appetite; 06.02.05.04.03 Promptitude, readiness; 08.01.01.03.09.03 To make glad
(ge)lystan 02.05.05 Desire, appetite
gelysted 02.05.05 Desire, appetite
lysu 12.08.06.01 Error, wrong conduct, erroneous practice; 12.08.06.01.02 Lacking moral good; 12.08.06.02.01 Wrong, evil-doing; 12.08.06.02.06 Deceit, evil, wickedness
lyswen 02.08.05.02.01 Matter, purulence, pus; 03.02.01.01 Decay, corruption, rottenness
lȳt 03.03.04.04 Littleness, smallness; 03.03.04.04.01 Paucity, fewness, scarcity
lȳtel 02.01.04.01 Youth; 02.04.02.03.02 Short; 03.03.04.04 Littleness, smallness; 03.03.04.04.01 Paucity,

fewness, scarcity; 03.03.05.01.03 Inferior; 05.10.05.01 A little way, no great distance; 05.11.01.02 Shortness/brevity in time; 07.03.04 A wretch, poor creature; 11.08.04 Vanity, idleness, frivolity; 12.01.01.06.04 Inferiority of status, lowest place
lȳtel forca 17.03.07 Tools for digging/grasping/pulling
lȳtelhȳdig 06.02.07.07 Cowardice, pusillanimity
lȳtelmōd 06.02.07.07 Cowardice, pusillanimity
lȳtelnes 03.03.04.04 Littleness, smallness
lȳtes(t)ne 03.06 Comparison
lȳthwōn 03.03.04.04 Littleness, smallness; 03.03.04.04.01 Paucity, fewness, scarcity; 03.06 Comparison; 05.10.05.01 A little way, no great distance; 05.11.01.02 Shortness/brevity in time; 05.12.03.02 Slowness
lytig 06.01.05.02.01.01 Sagacity; 11.04.02.01.01 Cunning, craft, craftiness, guile, wile
lytigian 11.04.02.01.01 Cunning, craft, craftiness, guile, wile
lytiglic 11.04.02.01.01 Cunning, craft, craftiness, guile, wile
lytiglīce 11.04.02.01.01 Cunning, craft, craftiness, guile, wile
lytignes 11.04.02.01.01 Cunning, craft, craftiness, guile, wile
lȳtle 03.03.04.04 Littleness, smallness; 12.01.01.09 Bondage, slavery
lȳtle tā 02.04.03.04.02.05.04 Toe
lȳtlian 05.09 Weakness; 05.11.01.02 Shortness/brevity in time

(ge)lȳtlian 03.03.04.06 Diminution; 03.03.05.01.03 Inferior
gelȳtlian 07.03.03.02 To degrade, debase
lȳtling 02.03.01.04 Child; 11.08.04 Vanity, idleness, frivolity
lȳtlum 03.03.04.04 Littleness, smallness; 05.12.03.02 Slowness
lȳtlum and lȳtlum 05.12.03.02 Slowness
lȳtlung 03.03.04.05 Insufficiency, lack, want
(ge)lȳtlung 03.03.04.06 Diminution
lyttuc 03.03.04.04 Littleness, smallness
lytwist 06.01.07.04 Deception
lȳþa 05.11.03.01.03.01 Specific months
lȳþerful 12.08.06.01.02 Lacking moral good
lȳþerlic 07.03.04 A wretch, poor creature
lȳþerlīce 07.03.04 A wretch, poor creature
lȳþernes 12.08.06.02 Wickedness, evil
(ge)lȳþran 03.01.17.07.01 An anointing, greasing
lȳþre 07.03 Evil; 07.03.02 Ill, harm, hurt; 07.03.04 A wretch, poor creature; 07.03.05 Infamy, shame, wickedness
mā 03.03.05 Extent, degree; 03.03.04.03 Growth, increase; 05.11.01.01 Long duration, long space; 03.03.04.01.02 A great number, multitude; 05.10.05.02.02 Greater, bigger
mā and mā 03.03.05 Extent, degree
(ge)maca 03.06.01.02 Equality; 12.09 Marriage, state of marriage
gemaca 02.06.01.07 Breeding, hatching; 12.04.01 A fellow, companion, associate, comrade
macalic 03.06.03 Congruity, fitness, suitability
macian 03.03.03.01 Arithmetic; 04.01.02.02 To prepare food; 04.01.02.04.04.01 Provider/supplier of

food; 09.03.02.03.01.01 Declension; 11.05.02 Mode, manner, way, method, fashion, course
macian loc 14.04 Making of terms, agreement, convention
macian ūp 05.12.01.07.01 To hang
(ge)macian 05.03.01 A cause (of anything); 11.01 Action, doing, performance; 11.07 Use (made of things), service; 17.02.04 Trade, calling, craft, aptitude
(ge)macian seht(e) 13.01.02 Reconciliation
(ge)macian (tō) 05.03.01 A cause (of anything)
gemacian 03.06 Comparison; 06.02.06.02.01 To devise a plan, arrange, settle
macung 11.01 Action, doing, performance
gemād 02.08.11.02.01.02 Madness, frenzy, folly
gemæc 03.06.01.02 Equality; 03.06.03 Congruity, fitness, suitability
(ge)mæcca 12.09 Marriage, state of marriage
gemæcca 03.06.01.02 Equality; 12.01.01.06 Condition, rank, standing
gemæccan 12.09 Marriage, state of marriage
mæcg 02.03.01.01 Male person, man; 06.01.06.02.03.02 Discipleship
mæcga 02.03.01.01 Male person, man
gemæclic 12.09 Marriage, state of marriage
gemæcnes 02.01.03.03 Sex, generation
gemæcscipe 02.01.03.03 Sex, generation; 12.09.06 Cohabitation
mǣd 04.02.03.04.01 Meadow land/meadow

gemǣd 02.08.11.02.01 Insanity, madness; 06.01.05.03.01.01 Dullness, folly, stupidity
mǣdæcer 04.02.03.04.01 Meadow land/meadow
mǣddīc 04.05.03.05.03.01 A ditch, dike
mæddre 02.07.11 Plants/flowers (alphabetical order); 03.01.14.05 Red/redness
mǣdencild 02.03.01.04 Child
mǣdenhēap 12.09.03 Unmarried state
mǣdenlic 12.09.03 Unmarried state
mǣdercīþ 02.07.11 Plants/flowers (alphabetical order)
gemǣdla 02.08.11.02.01.02 Madness, frenzy, folly
mǣdlacu 01.01.03.01.01.03 Stream
mǣdmǣwect 04.02.04.04.02.03 Mowing
mǣdmann 04.02.04.04.02.01 Reaper, mower
mǣdmēd 15.02.04 Spending, disbursement
mǣdmōnaþ 05.11.03.01.03.01 Specific months
mǣdrǣden 04.02.04.03.02.03 Hay; 04.02.04.04.02.03 Mowing
mǣdsplott 04.02.03.04.01 Meadow land/meadow
mǣdwe 04.02.03.04.01 Meadow land/meadow
mǣd(we)land 04.02.03.04.01 Meadow land/meadow
mæg 02.08.01 Sound physical condition; 06.01.07.07.01 Likelihood, probability, chance; 06.02.04 Necessity, inevitability; 11.07.03 Use, advantage, profit; 12.03.05 Permission
mæg tō 11.07.01 Utility, usefulness
mæg wiþ 02.08.12.01 Medical care, treatment

mæg 02.03.02.03.06.01 Kinsman, relative; 02.03.03.03.01 A native people
mæg tō 05.03.01 A cause (of anything)
mǣgbana 02.02.04.04.01 Murder of a relative
mǣgbōt 14.03.03.09.02 Atonement
mǣgburg 02.03.02.03 Ancestry, descent; 02.03.02.03.06.01 Kinsman, relative
mǣgburh 02.03.03.02 A race, tribe
mǣgcild 02.03.02.03.06.01 Kinsman, relative
mǣgcnafa 02.03.02.03.06.01 Kinsman, relative
mǣgcūþ 02.03.02.03.06 Kinship, relationship
mǣgcwalm 02.02.04.04.01 Murder of a relative
mægden 02.03.01.07 Girl; 12.01.01.08.01 A servant, attendant; 12.09.03 Unmarried state
mægdenǣw 12.09 Marriage, state of marriage
mægdeneorþe 01.01.02.02 Earth, soil
mægdenhād 12.09.03 Unmarried state
mægdenmann 12.09.03 Unmarried state
mægen 02.08.12.02.05 Pharmacy, curing with salves; 06.01.08.05.01.01.01 An exercise of power, mighty work, miracle; 11.04 Ability, capacity, power; 12.04.02 A crowding together, assembly; 12.08.02.02 Righteousness, rectitude; 13.02.10.01.02.02 Armed forces; 16.01.01.02.03 A wonder, miracle
mægenāgende 12 Power, might
mægenbyrþen 17.02.04.02.03 Carrying, carriage (of materials)
mægencorþor 13.02.10.01.02.01 An armed force/band

mægencræft 12 Power, might
mægencyning 12.01.01.04.01.01 Kings and queens
mægendǣd 11.01 Action, doing, performance
mægenēaca 11.12.02 Aid, help, succour
mægenēacen 12 Power, might
mægenearfeþe 08.01.03.06 Adversity, affliction
mægenellen 06.02.07.06 Courage, boldness, valour
mægenfæst 05.08.01 Vigour, activity, force; 05.12.04.01 Stability, firmness
mægenfolc 12.04.02 A crowding together, assembly
mægenfultum 11.12.02 Aid, help, succour
mægenhēap 12.04.02 A crowding together, assembly
mægenheard 12 Power, might
mæg(e)nian 12 Power, might
gemæg(e)nian 12 Power, might
mægenig 05.08 Strength
mægenlēas 05.09 Weakness
mægenlēaslīce 05.09 Weakness
mægenlēast 05.09 Weakness
mægenrǣs 13.02.03.01 An attack, assault
mægenrōf 16.01.01.01.01.01 Mightiness
mægenscype 12 Power, might
mægensibb 08.01.02.02 Love, affection, care
mægenspēd 12 Power, might
mægenstān 01.01.02.02.01 Rock, stone
mægenstrang 12 Power, might; 16.01.01.01.01.01 Mightiness
mægenstrengu 05.08 Strength
mægenþegen 16.01.02.05.01 An angel
mægenþise 05.08.02 Violence, force
mægenþrēat 12.04.02 A crowding together, assembly

mægenþrymm 16.01.01.01.01.01
Mightiness; 16.01.01.01.01.02 Glory;
16.01.01.04.02 The Son, Christ;
16.01.02.02 Glory/majesty of heaven;
16.01.02.05.01 An angel
mægenþrymnes 16.01.01.01.01.02 Glory
mægenweorc 16.01.01.02.03 A wonder,
miracle
mægenwīsa 13.02.10.01.01 A
commander, officer
mægenwudu 13.02.08.04.01 A spear
mægenwundor 06.01.08.05.01.01.01 An
exercise of power, mighty work,
miracle
mæger 02.04.02.02 Lean, thin, slender
mægerian 02.04.02.02 Lean, thin, slender
mæggemōt 12.02.02 An assembly,
meeting
mæggewracu 12.05.04.02 Vengeance,
revenge
mæggewrit 02.03.02.03 Ancestry,
descent
mæggieldan 14.03.03.09.02 Atonement
mæghæmed 12.08.08.01.02.01.03
Unnatural sexual behaviour
mæghand 02.03.02.03.06.01 Kinsman,
relative
mæglagu 14.01.01 Law(s) of particular
scope
mæglēas 02.03.02.02 Child, offspring
mæglic 02.03.02.03.06 Kinship,
relationship
mæglufu 08.01.02.02 Love, affection,
care
mægmann 02.03.02.03.06.01 Kinsman,
relative
mægmorþor 02.02.04.04.01 Murder of a
relative
mægmyrþra 02.02.04.04.01 Murder of a
relative

mægracu 02.03.02.03 Ancestry, descent
mægræden 02.03.02.03.06 Kinship,
relationship
mægræs 13.02.03.01 An attack, assault
mægscīr 02.03.03.03.01 A native people
mægsibb 02.03.02.03.06 Kinship,
relationship; 08.01.02.02 Love,
affection, care
mægsibbung 13.01.02 Reconciliation
mægsiblic 02.03.02.03.06 Kinship,
relationship
mægslaga 02.02.04.04.01 Murder of a
relative
mægsliht 02.02.04.04.01 Murder of a
relative
mægþ 02.03.01.07 Girl; 12.09.03
Unmarried state
mægþ 02.03.02.03.05 Descendant;
02.03.02.03.06.01 Kinsman, relative;
02.03.03.01 Body of retainers,
household; 12.06 A province, country,
territory
(ge)mægþ 02.03.03.02 A race, tribe;
02.03.03.03 A nation, people
gemægþ 06.02.05.02 Greed, importunate
desire, rapacity
mægþa/mageþa 02.07.11 Plants/flowers
(alphabetical order)
mægþblǣd 12.09.03 Unmarried state
mægþbōt 14.05.04.01 A fine
mægþegsan wyn 05.12.01.09.03.01 A
ship, boat
mægþhād 12.04.02 A crowding together,
assembly; 12.09.03 Unmarried state
mægþhād 02.03.02.03.06 Kinship,
relationship
mægþlēas 12.01.01.11 The common
people
mægþmann 12.09.03 Unmarried state

mægþmorþor 02.02.04.04.01 Murder of a relative
mægþmyrþra 02.02.04.04.01 Murder of a relative
mægþræden 02.03.02.03.06 Kinship, relationship
mægþsibb 02.03.02.03.06.01 Kinsman, relative
mægwine 08.01.02.03.01 An acquaintance, friend, associate
mægwlite 03.04 Form, kind, nature, character; 05.10.06 Form, shape
mægwlitian 17.02.04 Trade, calling, craft, aptitude
mægwlitlīce 09.03.04.02.01 A figure
mæl 03.03 Measurement, determination of amount; 04.01.02.04.01 Meal; 04.01.02.04.01.01.01 Meal time; 05.11.02 A time, particular time, occasion; 09.01.04 Conversation, discussion; 12.05.04.01 Fighting, contention, warfare, strife
gemæl 04.06.02.03 Stain, smear
(ge)mælan 04.06.02.03 Stain, smear; 09.01 To speak, exercise faculty of speech
mælcearu 08.01.03.06 Adversity, affliction
mældæg 05.11.02.01 A definite point of time, date
mældropa 02.04.06.05.07.02 Mucus, phlegm, rheum; 02.04.06.05.07.05 Saliva
mældropiende 02.04.06.05.07.02 Mucus, phlegm, rheum
mæle 04.01.02.02.06.05.04 Cup/bowl/basin; 04.06.02.03 Stain, smear
mælgesceaft 05.04 Fate, lot, fortune, destiny

mælsceafa 02.06.09.02.04 Butterfly, moth; 02.08.06 Skin disease, erysipelas
mæltange 03.03.03.01 Arithmetic
mæltīd 04.01.02.04.01.01.01 Meal time
mæltīma 04.01.02.04.01.01.01 Meal time
mænan 06.02.06.02 A proposal, proposition, suggestion; 09.04 Sense, purport, meaning; 09.04.01 Signal, signalling
(ge)mænan 08.01.03.04.01 Complaint, lamentation; 08.01.03.05.01 A grudge; 09.01 To speak, exercise faculty of speech; 09.04 Sense, purport, meaning
gemænan 06.01.01.01.01 Thought, cogitation, meditation; 09.03 A language
mæne 12.08.06.02.06 Deceit, evil, wickedness; 14.03.03.06 False witness
(ge)mæne 10.01.03 A sharing, participation; 15.01.01 Landed property
gemæne 02.03.02.02.05 Having the same parents; 03.03.06.01 A whole formed by joining; 03.06.01.02.01 Mutual; 05.09.01 Slow, inactive; 12.04 Fellowship, union, association; 16.02.01.04 Orthodoxy; 16.02.03.02.12 Cleric in minor orders
gemænelic 02.03 Humankind; 04.06.02.01 Dirty, unclean; 09.03.02.02.01.01 A noun; 09.05.05.01 Showing, manifestation, display; 11.05 Natural/proper way/manner/mode of action; 12.01.01.11 The common people; 12.04 Fellowship, union, association
gemænelīce 02.03 Humankind; 03.04.03 Generality; 03.06.01.02.01 Mutual; 12.04 Fellowship, union, association

gemǣnelicnes 03.04.03 Generality
mænibrǣde 03.04.02 A diversity
mænigtȳwe 11.04.01 An aptitude, bodily skill
mænihīwe 03.04.02 A diversity
gemǣnlic 16.02.04.13 Ceremonial cleanness
gemǣnnes 08.01.02.03 Friendliness, affection; 10.01.03 A sharing, participation; 12.04 Fellowship, union, association; 12.06.03.02 Living, dwelling, residence (in); 15.01.01.01 Holding of land
gemǣnscipe 03.03.06.01 A whole formed by joining; 10.01.03 A sharing, participation; 12.04 Fellowship, union, association; 16.02.01.02 Communion, fellowship
(ge)mǣnsumian 03.03.06.01 A whole formed by joining; 10.01.03 A sharing, participation; 12.04 Fellowship, union, association; 12.09.02 Marriage ceremony
(ge)mǣnsumian drihtnes līchaman and blōde 16.02.04.07.04 Communion/eucharist
gemǣnsumian 09.01.03 To address, speak to; 09.06.02.01.01 To make known, cause to know, inform; 12.08.06.01.04.01 To mislead, seduce, lead astray
gemǣnsumnes 10.01.03 A sharing, participation; 12.04 Fellowship, union, association; 16.02.04.07.04 Communion/eucharist
mǣnsumung 10.01.03 A sharing, participation
gemǣnsumung 16.02.04.07.04 Communion/eucharist
gemǣnung 12.09.02 Marriage ceremony

mǣrāc 02.07.03.05 Particular trees/shrubs (alphabetical order); 05.10.05.04.11.01 A bound, limit
mǣran 05.10.05.04.11.01 A bound, limit
(ge)mǣran 07.08.02 Honour, glory; 09.06.02.01.05.01 To spread, make known, proclaim, celebrate
mǣrapeldre 02.07.09.02 Particular fruits (alphabetical order)
(ge)mǣrbrōc 01.01.03.01.01.03 Stream
mǣrccnoll 01.01.02.01.02.02.01 Hill
mǣrcumb 01.01.02.01.03.03 Valley
mǣrdīc 04.05.03.05.03.01 A ditch, dike
mǣre/mare 02.05.04.02 A dream
mǣre 04.06.01.09 To cleanse, remove impurity from (an object); 07.02.04.03 Nobleness, excellence, nobility, magnificence; 07.08.09 Renown, fame, glory; 07.09.03 Infamy, ignominy, shame; 09.06.02.01.04 A confession, declaration; 15.01.04 Coinage, money; 16.01.01.01.01.02 Glory
(ge)mǣre 05.10.05.04.11.01 A bound, limit
gemǣre 01.01.02.01.01.03 Shore, bank; 05.10.05 A space, span; 05.11.10.02 End, completion; 12.06.01.01 England; 12.06.01.02 Britain; 12.06.03.03 A neighbour
mǣrehwīt 03.01.14.03 White/whiteness
mǣrelsrāp 05.12.01.09.03.01.03 Part of ship
mǣretorht 03.01.12 Brightness, light
mǣrflōde 01.01.03.01.01.03 Stream
mǣrford 05.12.01.03.03 A fordable place
mǣrfurh 04.02.03.02.01.01 A furrow
mǣrgeard 04.05.01.02.07 A fence, hedge
gemǣrhaga 04.05.01.02.07 A fence, hedge

mærhege 04.05.01.02.07 A fence, hedge
mærhlinc 01.01.02.01.02.01 Rising ground, eminence
mærhlīsa 07.09.03 Infamy, ignominy, shame
mǣrian 07.08.08 Nobleness, honour, glory
gemǣrian 05.10.05.04.11.01 A bound, limit
mæringcwudu 04.01.02.01.07.05.01 Gum
(ge)mǣrlacu 01.01.03.01.01.03 Stream
mǣrlic 07.02.04.03 Nobleness, excellence, nobility, magnificence; 07.08.07 Glory, splendour, magnificence; 16.01.01.01.01.02 Glory
mǣrlīce 07.02.04.03 Nobleness, excellence, nobility, magnificence
mǣrnes 07.08.08 Nobleness, honour, glory
mǣrpōl 01.01.03.01.03.01 Pool
mǣrpull 01.01.03.01.03.01 Pool
mǣrpytt 01.01.02.01.03 Hollow/depression in land
mǣrsere 09.06.02.01.06.01 A messenger
mǣrsian 05.10.05.02.02 Greater, bigger; 07.08.04 An ornament, honour, glory
(ge)mǣrsian 07.08.05 Glorifying, making great, glorification; 09.06.02.01.05.01 To spread, make known, proclaim, celebrate; 16.02.04.03.01 A rite, ceremony; 16.02.04.04.02 A feast-day, holy day
gemǣrsian 05.10.05.04.11.01 A bound, limit
mǣrsīc 01.01.03.01.01.03 Stream
mǣrstān 05.10.05.04.11.01 A bound, limit

mǣrsung 07.08.05 Glorifying, making great, glorification; 07.08.09 Renown, fame, glory; 09.06.02.01.05.01 To spread, make known, proclaim, celebrate; 16.02.04.04.02 A feast-day, holy day
(ge)mǣrsung 07.08.08 Nobleness, honour, glory
mǣrsungtīma 05.11.02.01.02 A time of celebration; 16.02.04.04.02 A feast-day, holy day
gemǣrtrēow 02.07.03 A tree; 05.10.05.04.11.01 A bound, limit
mǣrþorn 02.07.03.05 Particular trees/shrubs (alphabetical order); 05.10.05.04.11.01 A bound, limit
mǣrþ(u) 06.01.08.05.01.01.01 An exercise of power, mighty work, miracle
mǣrþ(-u) 07.08.09 Renown, fame, glory
mǣrþyrne 02.07.03.05 Particular trees/shrubs (alphabetical order); 05.10.05.04.11.01 A bound, limit
gemǣrung 05.11.10.02 End, completion
(ge)mǣrweg 05.12.01.03.01.05 Types of road/path
mǣrweorc 06.01.08.05.01.01.01 An exercise of power, mighty work, miracle
(ge)mǣrwyll 01.01.03.01.01.03 Stream
mæscre 17.04.04 Fibrous materials
mæsen 02.07.03.05 Particular trees/shrubs (alphabetical order)
mæslere 16.02.03.02.12 Cleric in minor orders
mæsse 16.02.04.04.02 A feast-day, holy day; 16.02.04.07.04.01 The service of the mass
mæsseǣfen 16.02.04.04.02 A feast-day, holy day
mæssebōc 16.02.05.10.01 Service books

mæssecapitel 16.02.04.07.04.01 The service of the mass
mæssecrēda 16.02.04.03.02 Parts of service
mæssedæg 16.02.04.04.02 A feast-day, holy day
mæssegierela 16.02.05.06.01 Outer garments
mæssehacele 16.02.05.06.01 Outer garments
mæssehrægl 16.02.05.06.01 Outer garments
mæsselāc 16.02.04.07.04 Communion/eucharist
mæsseniht 16.02.04.04.02 A feast-day, holy day
mæsseprēost 16.02.03.02.07.01 A priest of a church or minster
mæsseprēosthād 16.02.03.02.07.01 A priest of a church or minster
mæsseprēostscīr 16.02.03.02.07.01 A priest of a church or minster
mæsserbana 02.02.04.04 Manslaughter, homicide
mæssere 16.02.03.02.07.01 A priest of a church or minster
mæsserēaf 16.02.05.06 Ritual clothing
mæssesang 16.02.04.07.04.01 The service of the mass
mæssesteall 16.02.05.03.04 Part of temple containing altar/idol
mæssetīd 16.02.04.07.04.01 The service of the mass
mæsseþegn 16.02.03.02.07.01 A priest of a church or minster
mæsseþēnung 16.02.04.07.04.01 The service of the mass
mæsseūhta 16.02.04.05.02 The hour or service of Matins

mæssewīn 16.02.05.09.01 Eucharistic elements
(ge)mæssian 16.02.04.07.04.01 The service of the mass
mæssung 16.02.04.07.04.01 The service of the mass
mæst 02.07.09.02.01 Nut; 04.01.02.01.04.01 Mast, pig-food; 05.12.01.09.03.01.03 Part of ship; 16.02.04.07.06 Unction, anointing with holy oil
gemæst 03.01.17.07.01 An anointing, greasing; 04.02.05.01.01 To feed/fatten animals
mǣst 03.03.04.01 Much; 03.03.05.01.01 Principal/chief (of its class or type)
mǣst ǣlc 03.04.03.01 Someone/something
mǣst eall 03.06 Comparison
mæstan 04.02.05.01.01 To feed/fatten animals
mæstcyst 05.12.01.09.03.01.03 Part of ship
mæstelberg 02.06.02.01.07 Pig, swine
mæsten 02.07.09.02.01 Nut; 04.02.03.04.02.01.03 Swine pasture
mæst(en)rǣden 14.01.04.02 Rights involving property
mæstentrēow 02.07.09.02.01 Nut
mæstland 04.02.03.04.02.01.03 Swine pasture
mǣstlicost 03.03.05.01.01 Principal/chief (of its class or type)
mæstling 01.01.02.02.03.01 Types of metals/minerals; 04.01.02.01.02 Animal(s) for food; 04.01.02.02.06.05 Vessel/utensil/cup; 17.04.02.01 Brass
mæstlingsmiþ 17.02.04.03 Metal worker
mæstlōn 05.12.01.09.03.01.03 Part of ship

mæstrāp 05.12.01.09.03.01.03 Part of ship
mæsttwist 05.12.01.09.03.01.03 Part of ship
(ge)mǣtan 02.05.04.02 A dream
mǣte 03.03.04.04 Littleness, smallness; 07.03 Evil
(ge)mǣte 03.06.03 Congruity, fitness, suitability
gemǣte 03.06.03.03 Measure, degree, proportion
mǣting 02.05.04.02 A dream
mǣtra 12.01.01.11 The common people
mǣtre 03.03.05.01.03 Inferior
mǣþ 03.06.03.03 Measure, degree, proportion; 04.02.04.04.02.03 Mowing; 05.02.01.01 The course of human affairs; 07.04.03 Reverence, respect; 11.04 Ability, capacity, power; 12.07.01 One's due, natural place or position
gemǣþ(eg)ian 07.08.04 An ornament, honour, glory
mæþel 12.02.02 An assembly, meeting
(ge)mæþel 09.01.04 Conversation, discussion
mæþelærn 12.02.02.03 Terms for classical world
mæþelcwide 09.01.01 A speech, what is said, words
mæþelfriþ 13.01 Peace, state of law and order
mæþelhēgende 12.02.02.04 Counsel, deliberation
mæþelhergende 07.04.04 Praise, acclamation, applause
mæþelstede 12.02.02.01 Place of conference or assembly
mæþelword 09.01.01 A speech, what is said, words

mǣþere 04.02.04.04.02.01 Reaper, mower
mǣþful 08.01.02.01.01 Humaneness, humane behaviour
mǣþhādlic 12.09.03 Unmarried state
mǣþian 07.04 Consideration, esteem
mǣþlēas 04.01.01.03 Hunger
mǣþlic 12.07.01 One's due, natural place or position
mǣþlīce 08.01.02.01.01 Humaneness, humane behaviour
(ge)mǣþrian/gemēþrian 07.08.02 Honour, glory
mǣþung 07.01 Appraisal, appraising
mǣw 02.06.08.06 Water bird
mǣwes ēþel 01.01.03.01.02 Sea/ocean
mǣwpul 01.01.03.01.03.01 Pool
maffian 12.08.07.01.01 Wantonness, sensuality, lasciviousness
maffiend 12.08.07.01.01 Wantonness, sensuality, lasciviousness
maga 02.04.06.03.02.03 Stomach/belly; 11.04 Ability, capacity, power; 12 Power, might; 15.01.05 Possession of wealth
māga 02.03.01.01 Male person, man; 02.03.02.02.03 A son; 02.03.02.03.06.01 Kinsman, relative
magan ādl 02.08.08.04 Pain in stomach
magan untrumnes 02.08.08.04 Pain in stomach
māgatoga 06.01.06.02.03.04.02 A teacher
magaþiht 02.08.01 Sound physical condition
magdalatrēow 02.07.09.02.01.01 Particular nuts (alphabetical order)
māgeēct 03.03.04.03 Growth, increase
mageþe 02.07.10.01 Particular herbs/spices (alphabetical order);

02.08.12.02.05.01 A herb with medicinal properties
magian 12.05.06 Grasp, power, control, mastery
magister 12.01.01.04.02 A lord, master
magister ciriclices sanges 16.02.03.02.13 A church singer, singer in choir
māgister 04.02.05.04 To tame, break in (animals); 06.01.06.02.03.02 Discipleship; 06.01.06.02.03.04.02 A teacher; 12.03 Direction, guidance
māgisterdōm 06.01.06.02.03.04.02 A teacher
māgling 02.03.02.01 Parent
magnificat 16.02.04.03.03.01 A hymn, song of praise, canticle
mago 02.03.01.04 Child; 12.01.01.07 A follower
magodryht 13.02.10.01.02.01 An armed force/band
magogeoguþ 02.01.04.01 Youth
magorǣdend 12.02.02.02 A counsellor, advisor
magorǣswa 12.01.01.04 A leader, ruler
magorinc 02.03.01.05 Youth, boy, stripling; 13.02.10.01 A man, warrior
magotimber 02.01.03.03.04 Offspring, race, breed, family, children; 02.03.01.04 Child
magotūdor 02.01.03.03.04 Offspring, race, breed, family, children
magoþegn 12.01.01.07 A follower
(ge)māh 12.03.04.03 Importunity, persistence; 12.08.07.01.04 Shamelessness, lasciviousness
gemāh 07.06.01.01 Proud, arrogant; 12.08.06.02.06 Deceit, evil, wickedness; 16.01.05.02.02 Other terms for devils

gemāhlic 07.06.01.01 Proud, arrogant; 12.03.04.03 Importunity, persistence; 12.08.07.01.04 Shamelessness, lasciviousness
gemāhlīce 07.06.01.02 Proudly, arrogantly; 11.05.02.03 Indecorum, impropriety, unseemliness; 12.03.04.03 Importunity, persistence
gemāhlicnes 08.01.03.06 Adversity, affliction; 12.03.04.03 Importunity, persistence
gemāhnes 06.02.07.06.02.03 Presumption; 07.06.01 Pride, arrogance; 12.03.04.03 Importunity, persistence
mailrosisc 02.03.03.05.01.09 Northumbrians
māius 05.11.03.01.03.01 Specific months
māl 03.02.01 Decay, decline, corruption; 14.03.03 Law, action of the courts; 14.04 Making of terms, agreement, convention
malscrung 16.01.04 Sorcery, magic, witchcraft
mālswyrd 13.02.08.04.03 A sword
mamme 02.04.03.03.05 Chest, breast, bosom; 02.04.06.05.06 Mammary gland, breast
mamor 02.05.04 Sleepiness, drowsiness, sleep
mamrian 06.02.06.02 A proposal, proposition, suggestion
man 03.04.03 Generality
mān 12.08.06.02 Wickedness, evil; 12.08.06.02.01 Wrong, evil-doing; 12.08.06.02.05.01 Transgression, trespass; 12.08.06.02.06 Deceit, evil, wickedness; 14.03.03.06 False witness
gemāna 02.01.03.03 Sex, generation; 10.01.03 A sharing, participation; 12.04 Fellowship, union, association;

12.04.01.01 A company of people, fellowship, society; 15.01 Property; 16.02.01.02 Communion, fellowship; 16.02.04.07.04 Communion/eucharist
mānāþ 14.03.03.06 False witness
mānāþswaru 14.03.03.06 False witness
mānbealu 08.01.03.09.11 Hardheartedness, cruelty, severity
manbōt 14.05.04.01 A fine
mānbryne 03.01.09.02.01.01 A kind of fire
mancus 15.01.04 Coinage, money
mancwealm 02.02.04 Killing, violent death, destruction; 02.08.10.03.01 Plague, pestilence
mancwealmnes 02.02.04.04 Manslaughter, homicide
mancwyld 02.08.10.03.01 Plague, pestilence
mancynn 02.03 Humankind; 02.03.03.03 A nation, people
māncynn 12.08.06.01 Error, wrong conduct, erroneous practice
mancyst 12.08.02.01 Goodness, excellence, virtue
mand 17.03.12.01 A basket
māndǣda 12.08.06.02.02 A bad man, inhuman person
māndǣde 12.08.06.02.03 (Of persons) wicked, evil-doing
māndēad 12.08.06.02.05 Misdeed, sin
māndeorf 12.08.06.02.03 (Of persons) wicked, evil-doing
mandragora 02.08.12.02.05.01 A herb with medicinal properties
mandrēam 18.02 Amusement, revelry, festivity
māndrinc 04.06.02.06 Poison
mandryhten 12.01.01.04.01 A royal leader

gemane 02.06.01.06 Skin, hide
mānfǣhþu 12.08.06.02 Wickedness, evil
manfaru 12.04.02 A crowding together, assembly
mānfeld 02.02.04 Killing, violent death, destruction
mānfolm 16.02.01.13 Evil-doing, transgression, sin
mānfordǣdla 12.08.06.02.02 A bad man, inhuman person
mānforwyrht 12.08.06.02.01 Wrong, evil-doing
mānfrēa 16.01.05.02.01 The devil
mānfremmende 12.08.06.02.03 (Of persons) wicked, evil-doing
mānful 04.06.02.06 Poison; 12.08.06.02.03 (Of persons) wicked, evil-doing; 16.01.05.02.02 Other terms for devils
mānfullic 12.08.06.02.03 (Of persons) wicked, evil-doing
mānfullīce 12.08.06.02.03.01 Wickedly
mānfulnes 12.08.06.02 Wickedness, evil
manfultum 13.02.10.01.02.02 Armed forces
gemang 02.01.03.03 Sex, generation; 03.01.17.01 A coagulating, mixing; 03.03.04.01.02 A great number, multitude; 03.03.06.01.01 Mixing, mingling, preparation; 05.10.05.04.10 Among; 05.11 A time, period of time; 12.02.02 An assembly, meeting; 12.04.02 A crowding together, assembly; 17.02.02 An office, function, employment
gemang þǣm þe 05.11 A time, period of time
māngenga 12.08.06.02.02 A bad man, inhuman person

māngenīþla 12.08.06.02.02 A bad man, inhuman person
gemang(en)nes 03.03.06.01.01 Mixing, mingling, preparation
mangere 15.05.01 Goods, stock, merchandise
māngewyrhta 12.08.06.02.05.02 A sinner, transgressor; 16.02.01.13 Evil-doing, transgression, sin
mangian 15.05 Trade, traffic, commerce
gemangian 15.05 Trade, traffic, commerce
mangung 15.05 Trade, traffic, commerce
mangunge drīfan 15.05 Trade, traffic, commerce
mangunghūs 15.05.01 Goods, stock, merchandise
mangyld 15.02 Worth, value
mānhūs 16.01.05 Hell, lower world, abode of the dead
(ge)manian 06.02.06.03.02 Instigation; 12.03.02 Advice, admonition; 12.03.04 A request, prayer
gemanian 02.08.13 Recovery, growing better; 06.01.04.01 To remind, bring to the notice of; 15.02.03 An account
mānīdel 12.08.06.01.02 Lacking moral good
maniend 12.03.02 Advice, admonition; 15.04.01 Lending of money
manig 03.03.04.01.02 A great number, multitude
manigfeald 03.03.04.01.02 A great number, multitude; 03.04.02 A diversity; 09.03.02.03.01.01.02 Number
(ge)manigfealdan/(ge)manigfildan 03.03.04.03 Growth, increase
(ge)manigfealdan 03.03.04.01 Much
gemanigfealdan 03.03.04.03 Growth, increase; 10.03.05 Recompense, reward
manigfealde 03.03.04.01.02 A great number, multitude
manigfealdian/manigfildan 03.03.04.01.02 A great number, multitude
gemanigfealdian 03.03.04.01 Much
manigfealdlic 03.03.04.01.02 A great number, multitude; 03.04.02 A diversity
manigfealdlīce 03.03.04.01.02 A great number, multitude; 03.04.02 A diversity; 09.03.02.03.01.01.02 Number
manigfealdnes 03.03.04.01 Much; 03.04.02 A diversity
manigfealdsumnes 03.03.04.01 Much
gemanigfildan 03.03.03.01 Arithmetic
manighēowlic 03.04.02 A diversity
manigsīþes 05.11.09.02 Frequent, of common occurrence
manigtēaw 11.04.01 An aptitude, bodily skill
manigtēawnes 11.04.01 An aptitude, bodily skill
manlēas 12.06.03.01 Waste land, deserted place
mānlic 07.03.05 Infamy, shame, wickedness
manlīce 07.02.04.03 Nobleness, excellence, nobility, magnificence
mānlīce 12.08.06.02.06 Deceit, evil, wickedness
manlufu 08.01.02.02 Love, affection, care
mann 02 Creation; 02.03.01 People; 02.03.01.01 Male person, man; 02.03.01.04 Child; 02.03.01.08 Adult male; 09.03.07.01.01 A runic letter;

1164

12.01.01.07 A follower; 12.01.01.09 Bondage, slavery; 13.02.10.01 A man, warrior; 16.02.03.03.05 A layman
manna 02.03.01 People; 04.01.02.01.07.03.04 (Biblical) manna/bread of heaven
mannbǣre 02.01.03.01 Fertility, plenty
mannēaca 02.01.03.03.04 Offspring, race, breed, family, children
mannes eln 05.10.05.03 A measure of distance
mannhata 08.01.03.09.05 Enmity
(ge)mannian 13.02.04 Defence, guard, protection
mannlāf 15.05 Trade, traffic, commerce
mannlīca 17.02.05.04 An image, figure
mannmǣgen 13.02.10.01.02.02 Armed forces
mannmenigu 12.04.02 A crowding together, assembly
mannmyrring 02.02.04 Killing, violent death, destruction; 05.06.01 Devastation, laying waste
mannmyrþra 02.02.04.04 Manslaughter, homicide
mannrǣden 12.01.01.12 Loyalty; 15.02.04.01 Payment for temporary use, rent, hire
mannslege 02.02.04.04 Manslaughter, homicide
mannsylen 15.05 Trade, traffic, commerce
mannþwǣre 11.05.02.02 Humanity, courtesy, civility
mannweorod 12.04.02 A crowding together, assembly
manrīm 12.04.02 A crowding together, assembly
mānsceatt 15.04.01 Lending of money

mānsceaþa 12.08.06.02.02 A bad man, inhuman person; 12.08.06.02.05.02 A sinner, transgressor; 16.02.01.13 Evil-doing, transgression, sin
mānscild 12.08.06.02.05 Misdeed, sin
manscipe 11.05.02.02 Humanity, courtesy, civility
mānscyldig 12.08.09 Guiltiness, guilt
manslaga 02.02.04.04 Manslaughter, homicide
mānslagu 05.06.09 Act of striking
manslēan 02.02.04.04 Manslaughter, homicide
manslieht 02.02.04.04 Manslaughter, homicide
manslot 15.01.01 Landed property
mānsumung 16.02.04.19 Excommunication
mānsung 16.02.04.19 Excommunication
manswǣs 07.07.02 Humility, meekness
mānswara 14.03.03.06 False witness
mānswaru 14.03.03.06 False witness
mānswerian 14.03.03.06 False witness
mānswica 06.01.07.04.04.03 Deceit, fraud, treachery
manþēaw 11.05 Natural/proper way/manner/mode of action
manþēof 14.02.01.02 Wrongful taking, theft
manþrymm 13.02.10.01.02.01 An armed force/band
gemanþwǣrian 08.01.02.01.02 Gentleness
manþwǣrnes 11.05.02.02 Humanity, courtesy, civility
manu 02.06.01.06 Skin, hide
manung 02.03.03.04.03 People of a shire; 12.03.02 Advice, admonition; 12.06.02 District, province; 15.03 Exaction of tax/tribute

mānwamm 12.08.06.01.01 Pollution, impairment
mānweorc 12.08.06.02.03 (Of persons) wicked, evil-doing; 12.08.06.02.05 Misdeed, sin
manweorþung 16.02.01.06.01 Belief/practice of heathen people
manwīse 11.05 Natural/proper way/manner/mode of action
mānword 07.03.02 Ill, harm, hurt
mānwrǣce 12.08.06.02.03 (Of persons) wicked, evil-doing
mānwyrhta 12.08.06.02.05.02 A sinner, transgressor; 16.02.01.13 Evil-doing, transgression, sin
mapulder 02.07.03.05 Particular trees/shrubs (alphabetical order)
mapuldern 02.07.03.05 Particular trees/shrubs (alphabetical order)
mapuldorgeat 02.07.03.05 Particular trees/shrubs (alphabetical order); 04.02.03.01.02 Cleared land; 05.10.03 A gap, cleft
mapultrēow 02.07.03.05 Particular trees/shrubs (alphabetical order)
marc 03.03.02.01 A weight, definite amount; 15.01.04 Coinage, money
mārels 05.12.01.09.03.01.03 Part of ship; 17.03.10 Supports and fastenings
gemārian 03.03.04.03 Growth, increase
market 14.01.04.03 Rights involving money; 15.05.01 Goods, stock, merchandise
marma 01.01.02.02.02.04 Marble
marmanstān 01.01.02.02.02.04 Marble
marmelstān 01.01.02.02.02.04 Marble
marmorstān 01.01.02.02.02.04 Marble
marmstān 01.01.02.02.02.04 Marble
marmstāngedelf 17.02.04.02.02 Digging
martir 16.02.04.16 Martyrdom
martirologium 16.02.05.10.10 A legendary
martius 05.11.03.01.03.01 Specific months
martyrcynn 16.02.04.16 Martyrdom
martyrdōm 08.01.03.07.03 Suffering, torment, pain; 16.02.04.16 Martyrdom
martyrhād 08.01.03.07.03 Suffering, torment, pain; 16.02.04.16 Martyrdom
(ge)martyrian 16.02.04.16 Martyrdom
gemart(y)rian 02.02.04.03 To kill, slay; 14.05.02 Torment, punishment
martyrlīua 16.02.05.10.10 A legendary
martyrracu 16.02.04.16 Martyrdom
martyrung 08.01.03.07.03 Suffering, torment, pain; 16.02.04.16 Martyrdom
masc 04.01.03.05.02 Brewing
māse 02.06.08.05 Forest bird, wild-fowl
massere 15.01.04 Coinage, money; 15.05.01 Goods, stock, merchandise
mattuc 04.02.04.06.03 A mattock; 17.03.03 A cutting tool; 17.03.07 Tools for digging/grasping/pulling
maþa 02.06.09.02.11 Worm
gemaþel 09 Speech, vocal utterance
maþelere 09.01 To speak, exercise faculty of speech
maþelian 09.01 To speak, exercise faculty of speech
maþeliend 09.01 To speak, exercise faculty of speech
maþelig 09.01.02.01 Excessive fluency, loquacity
maþelung 09.01.02.01 Excessive fluency, loquacity
māþmǣht 15.01.03 Treasure, riches, wealth
māþmcleofa 15.01.03 Treasure, riches, wealth

māþmcyst 15.01.03 Treasure, riches, wealth
māþmgestrēon 15.01.03 Treasure, riches, wealth
māþmhord 15.01.03 Treasure, riches, wealth
māþmhūs 15.01.03 Treasure, riches, wealth
māþmhyrde 15.01.03 Treasure, riches, wealth
māþþum 15.01.03 Treasure, riches, wealth
māþþumfæt 04.01.02.02.06.05 Vessel/utensil/cup
māþþumgesteald 15.01.03 Treasure, riches, wealth
māþþumgifu 10.03 Giving
māþþumgyfa 12.01.01.04 A leader, ruler
māþþumsele 04.05.03.02.02.06.01 A hall building
māþþumsigle 17.04.03.04 Gems collectively
māþþumsweord 13.02.08.04.03 A sword
māþþumwela 15.01.03 Treasure, riches, wealth
māþum 15.01.03 Treasure, riches, wealth
(ge)māwan 04.02.04.04.02.03 Mowing
māwe 04.02.03.04.01 Meadow land/meadow
māwen 02.07.03.04.03 A hedge/border
max 17.04.04 Fibrous materials
maxwyrt 04.01.03.05.02 Brewing
meagol 06.02.07 Will, determination, resolution; 08.01.01.01.04 Depth of feeling, zeal
meagollīce 08.01.01.01.04 Depth of feeling, zeal
meagolmōd 06.02.05.04.05 Earnestness
meagolmōdnes 06.02.05.04.05 Earnestness

meagolnes 06.02.05.04.05 Earnestness
mealmeht 01.01.02.02.02.01 Sand, gravel
mealmstān 01.01.02.02.02.03 Limestone, chalk
mealt 02.05.07.01 Strong taste, acidity, pungency; 04.01.03.05.02 Brewing
mealtealoþ 04.01.03.05.01.02 Broth
mealtgesceot 15.02.04 Spending, disbursement
mealthūs 04.01.03.05.02 Brewing
mealtwyrt 02.07.09.02 Particular fruits (alphabetical order); 04.01.03.05.02 Brewing
mealu 01.01.02.01.02.01 Rising ground, eminence
mealwe 02.07.11 Plants/flowers (alphabetical order)
mearc 05.10.05.04.11.01 A bound, limit; 05.10.05.04.11.01.01 Object placed as point to be reached, a mark; 05.11.10.02 End, completion; 09.03.07 Writing; 09.03.07.01.02.01 Handwriting, autograph, signature; 09.04.01 Signal, signalling; 12.02.01.01 A distinguishing mark, stamp; 12.06 A province, country, territory; 13.02.08.02 A standard, banner, ensign
mearca 09.03.07 Writing
mearcdīc 04.05.03.05.03.01 A ditch, dike
mearcere 09.03.07.03 A scribe, copyist
mearcford 05.12.01.03.03 A fordable place
mearcgemōt 14.03.01 Judicial body, authority
mearcgræfa 02.07.03.04.02 A thicket; 05.10.05.04.11.01 A bound, limit
mearchlinc 01.01.02.01.02.01 Rising ground, eminence

mearchof 04.05.03.02.02.01 Dwellings in particular places

mearcian 05.10.05.04.11.01 A bound, limit; 06.01.01.02 Care, attention, observation

(ge)mearcian 03.03 Measurement, determination of amount; 05.10.05.04.11.01 A bound, limit; 09.03.07 Writing; 09.03.07.04.01 To punctuate, divide; 09.03.07.07.03.02 To write, state/say in writing; 09.04.01 Signal, signalling

(ge)mearcian mid ... rōde 16.02.04.18.01 Sign of the cross

gemearcian 05.10.05.04.11.01.01 Object placed as point to be reached, a mark; 10.03.07.01 To allot, assign

mearcīse(r)n 17.03.06 Tools for marking

mearcland 01.01.02.01.01.03 Shore, bank; 01.01.02.01.06 Wild/uncultivated land; 12.06 A province, country, territory

gemearcod 09.03.07.04 To make a symbol, mark; 09.04.01 Signal, signalling; 16.02.04.07.01 Baptism, baptizing (and anointing)

mearcpæþ 05.12.01.03.01 A means of access

mearcstapa 05.12.01.02 To wander; 12.06.05.01 State of exile, banishment

mearcstede 01.01.02.01.06 Wild/uncultivated land

mearctrēow 02.07.03 A tree; 05.10.05.04.11.01 A bound, limit

mearcþrēat 13.02.10.01.02.02.01 Types of army

mearcung 01.02.01.01.02.01 Constellation; 09.03.07 Writing; 09.03.07.07.02.01.01 A heading, title, superscription; 09.04.01 Signal, signalling

(ge)mearcung 09.03.07.04.02.01 Marking out, disposition of materials

mearcweard 02.06.03.01.15 Wolf

mearcweg 05.12.01.03.01.05 Types of road/path

mearcwill 01.01.03.01.01.07 Spring, fountain, well

mearg 02.04.05.04.01 Substance of bones; 04.01.02.01.02.05.01 Edible part of animal; 04.01.02.01.02.05.03 Sausage meat/sausage

meargealla 02.07.11 Plants/flowers (alphabetical order)

mearglic 03.01.17.03 Fat, grease

gemeargod 02.04.05.04.01 Substance of bones; 03.01.17.03 Fat, grease

mearh 02.06.02.01.06 Horse

mearhæccel 04.01.02.01.02.05.03 Sausage meat/sausage

mearhcofa 02.04.05.04 Bone/bones

mearhgehæc 04.01.02.01.02.05.03 Sausage meat/sausage

gemearr 06.01.05.03.02.01 Foolishness, lightmindedness; 11.11.02 A hindrance; 12.08.06.01 Error, wrong conduct, erroneous practice; 12.08.06.02.06 Deceit, evil, wickedness

mearrian 12.08.06.01.04 To lead a bad life

mearþ 02.06.03.01.10 Marten

mearu 02.01.04.01 Youth; 02.08.01 Sound physical condition; 03.01.04 Softness

mearulic 12.08.07.01 Laxity, indulgence

mearulīce 05.09 Weakness; 08.01.02.01.02 Gentleness

mearuwnes 08.01.02.01.02 Gentleness

meatte 04.04.08.02 Figured cloth, tapestry, carpet
mēce 13.02.08.04.03 A sword
mēcefisc 02.06.06.03.01.04 Mullet
mechanisc 17.02.04 Trade, calling, craft, aptitude
mēd 10.03.05 Recompense, reward
mēdan on 06.02.07.06.01 Emboldening, encouragement
meddrōsna 04.01.03.05.01.04 Mead
gemēde 06.02.02.01 Will, wish, pleasure; 07.10.01 Elegance, beauty, comeliness; 12.07.01 One's due, natural place or position
medema 04.04.03 A spinning-house or chamber
medeme 03.03.04.04 Littleness, smallness; 03.03.05.01.02 Of middle rank, in the middle; 03.03.05.01.03 Inferior; 07.03.03 Mediocrity, insignificance; 11.04 Ability, capacity, power; 12.07.01 One's due, natural place or position
medemest 07.02.04 Excellence
medemian 10.03.07.01 To allot, assign
(ge)medemian 07.01 Appraisal, appraising; 07.04 Consideration, esteem
gemedemian 03.05.01 Arranging, ordering, disposition; 07.09.02 Disgrace, shaming, humiliation; 12.03.05 Permission
medemlic 03.03.04.04 Littleness, smallness; 03.03.05.01.02 Of middle rank, in the middle; 07.08.02 Honour, glory
medemlīce 03.03.04.04 Littleness, smallness; 03.03.05.01.02 Of middle rank, in the middle; 03.06.03.04 What is fitting/seemly/appropriate/decent; 08.01.02.01 Favour, kindness, grace
gemedemlīce 07.08.02 Honour, glory
medemlicnes 07.03.03 Mediocrity, insignificance
medemmicel 05.11.01.02 Shortness/brevity in time
medemnes 07.08.02 Honour, glory; 08.01.02.01 Favour, kindness, grace
medemung 07.01 Appraisal, appraising
mēdgilda 12.01.01.08.01 A servant, attendant
mēdian 10.03.05 Recompense, reward
medmicel 03.03.04.04 Littleness, smallness; 11.08.04 Vanity, idleness, frivolity; 12.01.01.11 The common people; 16.02.01.13.01 Kinds of sin
medmicelnes 06.01.05.03.02.01 Foolishness, lightmindedness
medmicle 12.01.01.11 The common people
gemēdred/gemēdren 02.03.02.02.05 Having the same parents
mēdrencynn 02.03.02.03.06.01 Kinsman, relative
mēdrengecynd 05.02.02.02 (One's) own person
mēdrenmǣg 02.03.02.03.06.01 Kinsman, relative
mēdrenmǣgþ 02.03.02.03.06.01 Kinsman, relative
medrīce 12.01.01.11 The common people
mēdsceatt 10.03.05.01.01 A bribe, gift, payment; 15.02.04 Spending, disbursement
medsēlþ 08.01.03.06.01 Affliction, misfortune, calamity; 11.06.03.01 Ill fortune, bad success
medspēdig 15.01.06 Poverty, indigence
medstrang 12.01.01.06.03 Of middle rank

medtrum 02.08.02 Disease, infirmity, sickness; 12.01.01.11 The common people
medtrumnes 02.08.02 Disease, infirmity, sickness
medu 04.01.03.05.01.04 Mead
meduærn 04.01.01.08 Eating place
medubenc 04.05.04.01 A bench, seat
meduburg 04.01.03.05.03 Tavern; 12.06.02.01 A township
medudrēam 04.01.01.07 Feasting; 04.01.03.05.03 Tavern
medudrenc 04.01.03.05.01.04 Mead
medudrinc 04.01.03 Drinking
meduful 04.01.03.05.04 Drinking vessel
medugāl 04.01.03.02 To drink heavily, get drunk
meduheall 04.01.01.08 Eating place
medumlic 07.10.03.01 Unornamented, unadorned
medurǣden 04.01.03 Drinking
meduscenc 04.01.03.05.04 Drinking vessel
meduseld 04.01.01.08 Eating place
medustīg 05.12.01.03.01.05 Types of road/path
meduwērig 04.01.03.02 To drink heavily, get drunk
meduwong 04.01.01.08 Eating place
meduwyrhta 04.01.03.05.02 Brewing
meduwyrt 02.07.11 Plants/flowers (alphabetical order)
medwīs 06.01.05.03.01.01 Dullness, folly, stupidity
mēdwyrhta 12.01.01.08.01 A servant, attendant
melc 02.04.06.05.06 Mammary gland, breast
(ge)melcan 04.02.05.06.01.02 To milk
melcebrēost 02.04.06.05.06 Mammary gland, breast
meld 09.06.02.01.05 Proclamation, spreading abroad
melda 09.06.02.01.01 To make known, cause to know, inform; 12.01.01.12.04.01 Betrayal
melde 02.07.11 Plants/flowers (alphabetical order)
meldfeoh 14.03.03.02 A search for stolen property
meld(i)an 09.06.02.01.05 Proclamation, spreading abroad
(ge)meld(i)an 09.06.02.01 To tell, make known, declare, relate, announce
(ge)meldian 14.03.03.01 Accusation
meldung 14.03.03.01 Accusation
meledēaw 02.07.02.07 Blossom, flower(s); 04.01.02.01.05.04 Honey
mell 04.01.02.01.05.04 Honey
(ge)meltan 03.01.09.01.02 That melts, melting; 04.01 Digestion
gemeltan tōgædere 03.01.09.01.02.01 Fusible
meltende 04.01.02.01.01 Edibility
(ge)meltende 03.01.09.01.02 That melts, melting; 03.01.16 Liquid, a liquid
meltung 04.01 Digestion
melu 04.01.02.01.03.07 Meal; 04.01.02.01.07.03.04 (Biblical) manna/bread of heaven
melugescot 15.02.04 Spending, disbursement
meluhūdern 04.02.04.04.06 Barn
meluhūs 04.02.04.04.06 Barn
memfitisc 02.03.03.06.07.07 Other (alphabetical order)
mene 04.04.10.01 A ring (for finger, arm, neck)
menescilling 04.04.10.01 A ring (for finger, arm, neck)

(ge)mengan 07.01.01.03 Confusion; 12.04 Fellowship, union, association
(ge)mengan (mid) 03.03.06.01.01 Mixing, mingling, preparation
(ge)mengan wiþ 03.03.06.01.01 Mixing, mingling, preparation
gemengan 03.03.06.01 A whole formed by joining; 11.01.03 Preparation; 12.08.06.01.04.01 To mislead, seduce, lead astray
gemengan on þǣm hǣmede 02.01.03.03 Sex, generation
gemengan tō 03.03.06.01.01 Mixing, mingling, preparation
gemenged 03.03.06.01.01 Mixing, mingling, preparation; 04.01.03.05 A drink/beverage; 06.01.05.03.01.01 Dullness, folly, stupidity; 07.01.01.03 Confusion
gemengedlic 03.03.06.01.01 Mixing, mingling, preparation
gemengedlīce 03.03.06.01.01 Mixing, mingling, preparation
gemeng(ed)nes 02.01.03.03 Sex, generation
gemengednes 03.03.06.01.01 Mixing, mingling, preparation
mengung 03.03.06.01.01 Mixing, mingling, preparation; 12.04.02 A crowding together, assembly
gemengung 07.01.01.03 Confusion
menigdu 12.04.02 A crowding together, assembly
menigu 12.04.02 A crowding together, assembly
menn 02.03.01 People
mennen 12.01.01.09 Bondage, slavery
mennisc 02.03 Humankind; 02.03.01 People; 02.03.03.02 A race, tribe

mennisclic 02.03 Humankind; 08.01.02.01.01 Humaneness, humane behaviour
mennisclīce 02.03 Humankind
mennisclicnes 02.03 Humankind; 08.01.02.01.01 Humaneness, humane behaviour
menniscnes 16.01.01.04.02.01 Incarnation
menniscu 02.03 Humankind
mentel 04.04.07.07 A long outer garment, covering, cloak, etc.
mentelprēon 04.04.10.02 A button, brooch
mēo 04.04.07.15 Footwear, covering for the feet
meodudrenc 04.01.03 Drinking
meoduscerwen 06.01.08.06.02 Great fear, terror, horror; 08.01.03.06 Adversity, affliction
meolc 02.04.06.05.07.08 Milk; 02.06 Animal; 02.07.02.03 A stalk, stem; 04.01.02.01.02.09 Milk
meolcdēond 02.06 Animal
meolcen 04.01.02.01.02.09 Milk
meolcfæt 04.02.05.06.01.02 To milk
meolchwīt 03.01.14.03 White/whiteness
meolcian 02.04.06.05.07.08 Milk; 04.02.05.06.01.02 To milk
(ge)meolcian 04.01.01.02 Act/action of sucking
meolclīþe 08.01.02.01.02 Gentleness
meolcsūcend 02.06 Animal
meord 10.03.05.01 Reward, meed, pay
meoring 11.11.01 A physical difficulty, strait
mēos 02.07.07 Moss
meotudwang 13.02.02 Battle
mēowle 02.03.01.02 Female person, woman; 12.09.03 Unmarried state

meox 02.04.06.06.06 Faeces; 04.02.04.02.01.01 To manure, dung
meoxbearwe 04.02.04.06.10 A dung-barrow
meoxforce 04.02.04.06.02 A fork
meoxscofl 04.02.04.06.01 A spade
meoxwille 04.02.04.06.10 A dung-barrow
mera 16.01.03.04 Elfin race
mere 01.01.03.01.02 Sea/ocean; 01.01.03.01.03 Lake; 01.01.03.01.03.01 Pool; 17.02.04.02.04 Leading/conducting of water
merebāt 05.12.01.09.03.01 A ship, boat
merecandel 01.02.01.01.03 Sun
merece 02.07.11 Plants/flowers (alphabetical order)
mereciest 05.12.01.09.03.01.01 Kind of ship
gemered 04.01.02.02.05.02 To boil; 04.06.01.09 To cleanse, remove impurity from (an object)
meredēaþ 02.02.01 Particular mode of death
meredēor 02.06.10.01.05 Sea-monster
merefara 05.12.01.09.03 A voyage
merefaroþ 01.01.03.01.02.06 Surging, rolling, heaving of waves
merefix 02.06.10.01.05 Sea-monster
mereflōd 01.01.03.01 Body of water; 01.01.03.01.02 Sea/ocean; 01.01.03.06 Flood
meregrot 08.01.02.02.01 A favourite, loved one
meregrot(a) 17.04.03.04 Gems collectively
meregrund 01.01.03.01.03 Lake
merehengest 05.12.01.09.03.01 A ship, boat

merehrægl 05.12.01.09.03.01.03 Part of ship
merehūs 05.12.01.09.03.01.01 Kind of ship
merehwearf 01.01.02.01.01.03 Shore, bank
mērehwīt 15.01.04 Coinage, money
merelād 01.01.03.01.02.01 Region of sea/ocean
merelīþende 05.12.01.09.03 A voyage
merememn(en) 02.06.10.01.03 Half of another kind
merenǣddra 02.06.06.03.01.03 Lamprey
meresmylte 01.01.03.01 Body of water; 01.03.01.01 Hot, fine weather
meresteall 01.01.03.01 Body of water; 01.01.03.01.03.01 Pool
merestrǣt 01.01.03.01.02.01 Region of sea/ocean
merestrēam 01.01.03.01.02.02 Sea-channel; 01.01.03.04 Current, rush of water
merestrengu 05.12.01.08.01 To swim
mereswīn 02.06.05.01.01 Dolphin
meretorht 03.01.12 Brightness, light
meretorr 01.01.03.01.02.05 Wave
mereþyssa 05.12.01.09.03.01 A ship, boat
mereweard 11.10.02.02 Watchful care, keeping guard
merewērig 02.05.03.02 Weariness
merewīf 02.06.10 Monster, strange creature
merewīoing 02.03.03.06.01 Peoples of France
mergendæg 05.11.04.01.02 Morning
mergenlic 05.11.04.01.02 Morning
mergentīd 05.11.04.01.02 Morning
merian 12.08.04 Purity, moral cleanness
(ge)merian 04.06.01.09 To cleanse, remove impurity from (an object)

mersc 01.01.02.01.04.01 Marsh, bog, swamp
merschōfe 02.07.11 Plants/flowers (alphabetical order)
merschop 01.01.02.01.02.01 Rising ground, eminence; 01.01.02.01.04.01 Marsh, bog, swamp
merscland 01.01.02.01.04.01 Marsh, bog, swamp
merscmealwe 02.07.11 Plants/flowers (alphabetical order)
merscmeargealla 02.07.11 Plants/flowers (alphabetical order)
merscmylen 04.01.02.02.09 A mill
merscware 02.03.03.04.01 Country people; 02.03.03.05.01.03 Kentish people
mertze 15.03.01 Toll; 15.05.01 Goods, stock, merchandise
merþern 04.04.06 Undressed condition (of hide); 17.04.04.02 Skin, hide (as material)
mesa 02.04.06.06.06 Faeces
mēsan 04.01.01 Eating
mēse 04.01.02.04 Abundance of food; 04.05.04.02 A table
mēshrægl 04.06.01.05 ?A cloth for wiping
(ge)met 03.03 Measurement, determination of amount
gemet 03.03.03.01 Arithmetic; 03.03.04.02 A sufficiency, sufficient supply; 03.06.03.02 Order, decorum, discretion; 03.06.03.03 Measure, degree, proportion; 03.06.03.04 What is fitting/seemly/appropriate/decent; 05.10.05.03 A measure of distance; 09.03.02.03.01.02.01 Mood; 10.03.07 Distribution; 11.04 Ability, capacity, power; 11.05.02 Mode, manner, way, method, fashion, course; 12.07.01 One's due, natural place or position; 14.01.02 A law, statute
gemēt 17.02.05.06 A painting, picture, representation
metan 03.06 Comparison
(ge)metan 03.03 Measurement, determination of amount; 05.10.05.04.11.01 A bound, limit; 05.12.05.06 To travel over/through/along, traverse
(ge)mētan 05.03.02 Event, issue, result; 05.12.05.02.01 To come upon, meet with; 05.12.05.02.02 To come together, meet; 11.03.01.03 Finding, discovery; 17.02.05.06 A painting, picture, representation
gemētan 06.01.06.03 Experience; 10.01.02 Acquisition; 12.05.02 Hostility, contention, opposition; 12.05.04 Strife, hostility
metbælg 04.01.02.02.06.03 Food receptacle, basket
metcund 09.03.05.01.02 Art of verse composition
metcundlic 09.03.05.01.02 Art of verse composition
mete 04.01.02.01 Food/sustenance; 04.01.02.04 Abundance of food; 04.01.02.04.01 Meal
gemete 03.06.03 Congruity, fitness, suitability
meteærn 04.01.01.08 Eating place
meteāflīung 02.08.08.12 Disease of bowels
meteāwel 04.01.02.02.06.05.07 Hook for lifting food
meteclyfa 04.01.02.02.06.02 Larder, pantry
metecorn 04.01.02.04 Abundance of food

metecū 04.01.02.01.02.01 Cattle for slaughter; 02.06.02.01.03 Cattle; 04.01.02.04 Abundance of food
metecweorra 02.08.08.04.02 (Of stomach) disordered
(ge)mētednes 11.03.01.03 Finding, discovery
gemētednes 11.03.01.03.01 Discovery, invention
metefæt 04.01.02.02.06.05.03 Plate/platter/bowl/dish
metefætels 04.01.02.02.06.03 Food receptacle, basket
metegafol 15.03.02 A tax
metegearwa 04.01.02.04 Abundance of food
metelāf 04.01.02.01.01.08 Leftover food
metelēas 04.01.01.03 Hunger; 04.01.01.06.01 Abstinence from food, fast
metelīest 04.01.01.03 Hunger
metend 03.03 Measurement, determination of amount; 16.01.01.02.01 Creator
gemētend 11.03.01.03 Finding, discovery
metenēad 04.01.02.04 Abundance of food
metenīþung 10.03.09.01 Parsimony, niggardliness
mēter 09.03.05.01.02 Art of verse composition
meterǣdere 16.02.03.03.02.01 Monastic functionaries
mētercræft 09.03.05.01.02 Art of verse composition
mētercund 09.03.05.01.02 Art of verse composition
mētere 17.02.05.06 A painting, picture, representation
mēterfers 09.03.05.01.02 Art of verse composition
mētergeweorc 09.03.05.01.02 Art of verse composition
mēterlic 09.03.05.01.02 Art of verse composition
mēterwyrhta 09.03.05.01.02 Art of verse composition
metesōcn 04.01.01.03 Hunger
metesticca 04.01.02.02.06.05.05 Ladle/scoop
meteswamm 02.07.05 Fungus
metetīd 04.01.02.04.01.01.01 Meal time
meteþearfende 04.01.01.03 Hunger
meteþegn 12.01.01.08.01 A servant, attendant
meteþiht 04.01.02.04.03.01.01 Fed/nourished
meteþing 04.01.02.02.05 Cooking
meteþistel 02.07.09.02.02.02 Other vegetables (alphabetical order)
meteūtsiht 02.08.08.12 Disease of bowels
gemetfæst 08.01.02.01 Favour, kindness, grace; 08.01.02.01.02 Gentleness; 10.03.09 Moderation in expenditure; 12.08.03.03 Moral restraint, modesty, sobriety
gemetfæstan 03.06 Comparison
gemetfæstlic 08.01.02.01.02 Gentleness; 12.08.03.03 Moral restraint, modesty, sobriety
(ge)metfæstlīce 08.01.02.01.02 Gentleness
gemetfæstlīce 12.08.03.03 Moral restraint, modesty, sobriety
gemetfæstnes 04.01.01.06 Moderation in eating; 08.01.02.01.02 Gentleness; 12.08.03.03 Moral restraint, modesty, sobriety
gemetfæt 03.03 Measurement, determination of amount

metgeard 03.03.03.01 Arithmetic; 05.10.05.03 A measure of distance

metgian 06.01.01.01.01 Thought, cogitation, meditation

(ge)metgian 03.05.01 Arranging, ordering, disposition; 10.03.07.01 To allot, assign

gemetgian 03.03 Measurement, determination of amount; 03.03.06.01.01 Mixing, mingling, preparation; 05.09.03 Mitigation, lightening, alleviation

gemetgiend 12.01.01.05 A leader, administrator

metgung 06.01.01.01.01 Thought, cogitation, meditation

(ge)metgung 05.09.02 Mildness, moderate quality

gemetgung 03.03 Measurement, determination of amount; 03.05.01 Arranging, ordering, disposition; 10.03.09 Moderation in expenditure; 12.03.01.01 Control, direction, regulation; 12.08.03 Restraint, temperance

gemethāt 03.01.10 Tepidity, lukewarmness

metian 04.01.02.04.04.01 Provider/supplier of food

mēting 17.02.05.06 A painting, picture, representation

(ge)mēting 05.12.05.02.02 To come together, meet; 12.04.02 A crowding together, assembly

gemēting 11.03.01.03.01 Discovery, invention; 12.05.04 Strife, hostility; 14.04 Making of terms, agreement, convention

gemetlǣcan 05.09.03 Mitigation, lightening, alleviation

gemetlic 03.03 Measurement, determination of amount; 03.03.03 Number; 03.03.04.02 A sufficiency, sufficient supply; 08.01.02.01.02 Gentleness; 12.07.01 One's due, natural place or position; 12.08.03 Restraint, temperance; 12.08.03.03 Moral restraint, modesty, sobriety

(ge)metlīce 03.06.03.03 Measure, degree, proportion

gemetlīce 03.05 Order, arrangement, disposition; 03.06.03.04 What is fitting/seemly/appropriate/decent; 05.09.02 Mildness, moderate quality; 05.11.08 A suitable time, opportunity; 12.08.03 Restraint, temperance

gemetlicung 02.08.12 Healing, curing

gemetnes 05.09.02 Mildness, moderate quality

gemētnes 11.03.01.03.01 Discovery, invention

metod 16.01.01.02.01 Creator

gemetodlīce 06.02.04 Necessity, inevitability

metodsceaft 02.02.03.03 Appointed death, doom

metrāp 05.12.01.09.03.01.03 Part of ship

metscipe 04.01.02.04.01 Meal

metseax 04.01.02.02.06.05.06 Knife

metsian 04.01.02.04.03.01 To feed/nourish

(ge)metsian 04.01.02.04.04.01 Provider/supplier of food

metsung 04.01.02.01 Food/sustenance

gemetta 04.01.01.07 Feasting

metten 05.04.01 Fortune, Fate (personification)

gemetu 09.03.05.01.02 Art of verse composition

mēþe 02.02.03.01 In process of dying; 02.05.03.02 Weariness; 08.01.03.01 Despondency; 08.01.03.07.04 Severity, harshness
meþelstede 13.02.02 Battle
(ge)mēþgian 02.05.03.02 Weariness
mēþig 02.05.03.02 Weariness
mēþnes 02.05.03 Exhaustion, faintness, weariness
micclum 03.03.04.01 Much
(ge)micclung 16.01.01.01 Attributes of God
micel 02.05.10.02 Noise, din; 03.03.04.01 Much; 03.03.04.01.01 Greatness, bigness, size; 05.11.01.01 Long duration, long space; 07.02.04.03 Nobleness, excellence, nobility, magnificence; 11.07.04 Superiority, pre-eminence, primacy; 12 Power, might; 13.02.02 Battle
micel līc 02.08.05.01 Swelling
micelǣte 04.01.01.04 Gluttony, overeating, greediness
miceldōend 06.01.08.05.01.01.01 An exercise of power, mighty work, miracle
micelhēafdede 02.04.03.01 Head
micellic 07.02.04.03 Nobleness, excellence, nobility, magnificence
micellīce 03.03.05 Extent, degree; 07.02.04.03 Nobleness, excellence, nobility, magnificence
micelmōd 12.08.01 Magnanimity, greatness of soul
micelnes 03.03.04.01 Much; 03.03.04.01.01 Greatness, bigness, size
(ge)micelnes 07.02.04.03 Nobleness, excellence, nobility, magnificence

micelsprecende 07.06.03 Boastfulness, arrogance
micelu 03.03.04.01.01 Greatness, bigness, size
micga 02.04.06.06.07 Urine
micgern 02.04.05.02 Fat
micle tā 02.04.03.04.02.05.04 Toe
micles 03.03.04.01 Much; 03.03.05 Extent, degree
miclian 03.03.04.03 Growth, increase; 07.08.05 Glorifying, making great, glorification
(ge)miclian 03.03.04.03 Growth, increase; 07.04.04 Praise, acclamation, applause; 16.02.04 Worship, honour, praise
(ge)miclung 07.02.04.01 Excellence, virtue, goodness
gemiclung 11.01 Action, doing, performance
mid 03.03.06.01 A whole formed by joining; 05.10.05.04.10 Among; 05.11.02 A time, particular time, occasion; 05.11.07.01 Contemporary, coeval; 05.12.05.02 To go/travel towards, come, approach; 11.01.04 A doing, accomplishing (of something); 11.12.02 Aid, help, succour
mid ... twīh 07.01.01.01 Discrimination, faculty of distinguishing
mid/of ānum mūþe 09.07.04.01.03 Unanimity
mid ānwilnesse 06.02.07.04 Obstinacy
mid bearne 02.01.03.03.01 To beget
mid ealle 03.03.06.01 A whole formed by joining; 03.03.06.02 Fullness
mid eallum 03.03.06.01 A whole formed by joining; 03.03.06.02 Fullness
mid gefōge 03.06.03 Congruity, fitness, suitability

mid gān 12.04.01.02 A fellow traveller, companion
mid him selfum 03.04.01 Singularity, peculiarity
mid inseglum beclȳsan 17.03.10.01 A bolt, lock, bar
mid inwerdre heortan 08.01.01.01.04 Depth of feeling, zeal
mid līfe gedīgan 11.10.05 Escape
mid gemete 03.06.03 Congruity, fitness, suitability; 05.08 Strength
mid nānum þingum 03.06 Comparison
mid rihtan þingum 12.07.04 Truth, righteousness, justice, equity
mid sōþum þingce 06.01.07.01 Correct, right, free from error
mid standan 11.12.02 Aid, help, succour
mid þām 05.11.02 A time, particular time, occasion
mid þȳ 03.06 Comparison; 05.11.02 A time, particular time, occasion; 05.03.02 Event, issue, result
mid þȳ þe 05.11 A time, period of time
mid þȳ (þe) 05.11 A time, period of time
mid ungemete 03.03.04.02.02 Excess
mid unrihte 12.07.05 Wrong, injustice
mid unrihtum þingum 06.01.07.04.02 Fraud, deceit, trick, trickery
mid wēas 05.03.02.01 Chance, hap, event
mid wihte 06.01.07.07.02 Impossible
mid gewisse 06.01.07.01 Correct, right, free from error; 06.01.07.07.03 Certainty; 06.02.06.01 An end, goal
mid/be gewyrhtum 07.04.02 Merit, desert(s)
midblissian 08.01.01.03.06 Exultation, joy
midd 05.10.05.04.01.01 The middle

middæg 05.11.04.01.03 Mid-day, noon; 16.02.04.05.06 The hour or service of Sext
middæglic 05.11.04.01.03 Mid-day, noon
middægsang 16.02.04.05.06 The hour or service of Sext
middægtīd 05.11.04.01.03 Mid-day, noon
middægþēnung 04.01.02.04.01.01 Meal at particular time of day
middandæglic 05.11.04.01.03 Mid-day, noon
middangeard 01 Earth, world; 02.03 Humankind
middangearden 11.02 Occupation, activity, business
middangeardlic 01 Earth, world; 11.02 Occupation, activity, business
middangeardtōdǣlend 01.02 Firmament
middansumer 05.11.03.01.02.02 Summer
middanwinter 05.11.03.01.02.04 Winter
middel 02.04.03.03 Trunk; 05.10.05.04.01.01 The middle
middelǣdr 02.04.06.08 Heart
middeldæg 05.11.04.01.03 Mid-day, noon
middeldǣl 05.10.05.04.01.01 The middle
middelfinger 02.04.03.04.01.01.01 Finger
middelflēra 02.04.03.01.03.04 Nose
middelfōt 02.04.03.04.02.05.03 Instep
middelgemǣru 05.10.05.04.01.01 The middle
middelgesculdru 02.04.03.03.02 Shoulder
middelhrycg 01.01.02.01.02.01 Rising ground, eminence
middelniht 05.11.04.02.02 Midnight
middelrīce 12.06 A province, country, territory
middelsǣ 01.01.03.01.02.02 Sea-channel
midde(r)niht 05.11.04.02.02 Midnight

middeweard 05.10.05.04.01.01 The middle
middewintres tīd 16.02.04.04.02.01.01 Around the Nativity
midfæsten 16.02.04.04.02.01.02 Lent
midfeorh 02.01.04.02 To grow, grow up
midfeorwe 02.01.04.02 To grow, grow up
midferh(þ) 02.01.04.02 To grow, grow up
midfyrhtnes 02.01.04.02 To grow, grow up
midgearwung 11.01.03 Preparation
midgehlytto 12.04 Fellowship, union, association
midgetellan 03.05.03 A list, tale, series
midhelp 11.12.02 Aid, help, succour
midhlȳt 12.04 Fellowship, union, association
midhrif 02.04.06.03.01.01 Diaphragm; 02.04.06.03.02.04 Intestines
midhriþre 02.04.06.03.01 Cavities of internal organs; 02.04.06.03.01.01 Diaphragm
midl 05.12.01.09.03.01.03 Part of ship
mīdl 04.02.05.06.05.03.02 A bit
gemidleahtrian 07.05.01 Censure, reproof, rebuke
midlen 05.10.05.04.01.01 The middle
midlencten 16.02.04.04.02.01.02 Lent
midlest 05.10.05.04.01.01 The middle
midleste tā 02.04.03.04.02.05.04 Toe
mīdlhring 04.02.05.06.05.03.02 A bit
gemidlian 03.03.03.03 Fractions
(ge)mīdlian 12.05.06.01 Restraint, check, curb, control
midligend 13.01.03 Intercession, pleading, mediation
gemīdlod 04.02.05.06.05.03.01 Bridle/halter/curb/muzzle
midlung 05.10.05.04.01.01 The middle
midlunga 03.03.05.01.02 Of middle rank, in the middle
midmest 05.10.05.04.01.01 The middle
midne dæg 05.11.04.01.03 Mid-day, noon
midnes 05.10.05.04.01.01 The middle
midniht 05.11.04.02.02 Midnight
midrād 05.12.01.05 To ride (on horse, etc.); 12.04.01.02 A fellow traveller, companion
midsingend 16.02.03.02.13 A church singer, singer in choir; 18.02.07.01 Singing, song
(ge)midsīþ(eg)ian 12.04.01.02 A fellow traveller, companion
midsp(r)eca 12.07.03.02 An excuse; 14.03.02 A legislator
midsp(r)ecend 12.03.04.02 Speech on behalf of, advocacy
midsprecend 14.03.02 A legislator
midstrēam 01.01.03.01.01.01 River
midsumer 05.11.03.01.02.02 Summer
midsumermōnaþ 05.11.03.01.03.01 Specific months
midþeahtian 09.07.04.01.02 Consent
midþolian 08.01.02.05 Compassion
midþrōwung 08.01.02.05 Compassion
midþwǣrian 09.07.04.01.02 Consent
midweg 05.10.05.04.01.01 The middle
midwinter 05.11.03.01.02.04 Winter; 16.02.04.04.02.01.01 Around the Nativity
midwintermōnaþ 05.11.03.01.03.01 Specific months
midwist 05.10.04.03 Presence; 12.04 Fellowship, union, association
midwunung 12.04 Fellowship, union, association
midwyrcan 11 Action, operation
midwyrhta 12.04.01 A fellow, companion, associate, comrade

midyrfenuma 15.01.02.01 Inherited property
mieltan 04.06.01.09 To cleanse, remove impurity from (an object)
(ge)mieltan 03.01.16 Liquid, a liquid; 04.01 Digestion
gemieltan 05.09.04 Abatement, reduction, checking; 08.01.02.06.01 Pity
(ge)mielt(ed) 03.01.16 Liquid, a liquid
mierce 02.03.03.05.01.06 Mercians; 12.06.01.01 England
gemierce 05.10.05.04.11.01 A bound, limit; 09.04.01 Signal, signalling
miercisc 02.03.03.05.01.06 Mercians
miere 02.06.02.01.06 Horse
mierra 06.01.07.04 Deception
mierran 10.03.08.01 Overliberality, waste of money; 12.08.06.01.04 To lead a bad life
(ge)mierran 11.11.02 A hindrance
gemierran 06.01.07.04.01 Deception, a leading astray
gemierred 06.01.07.05 Error, being astray
mierrelse 11.11.02 A hindrance
mierrend 10.03.08.01 Overliberality, waste of money
mierring 06.01.07.04.01 Deception, a leading astray
mierrung 10.03.08.01 Overliberality, waste of money
(ge)mīgan 02.04.06.06.07 Urine
miggung 02.04.06.06.07 Urine
migol 02.08.12.02.07.01 Purgative
migoþa 02.04.06.06.07 Urine
miht 05.08 Strength; 06.01.07.07 Possibility; 06.01.08.05.01.01.01 An exercise of power, mighty work, miracle; 11.04 Ability, capacity, power; 12 Power, might; 12.01 Power, control, sway; 12.01.01 Authority; 12.03.03 A command, bidding, order; 12.08.02.01 Goodness, excellence, virtue; 16.01.01.01.01.01 Mightiness; 16.01.06 A god (of any faith)
mihta 16.01.02.05.01 An angel
mihtelic 06.01.07.07 Possibility
mihtelīce 06.01.08.05.01.01 Wondrous, glorious, marvellous
mihtelīce/mihtiglīce 12 Power, might
mihtesetl 12.01.01.02 Seat of authority
mihtful 16.01.01.01.01.01 Mightiness
mihtig 02.08.12.02.05 Pharmacy, curing with salves; 06.01.07.07 Possibility; 16.01.01.01.01.01 Mightiness
mihtlēas 05.09 Weakness
mihtloc 17.03.10.01 A bolt, lock, bar
mihtmōd 08.01.03.05.02 Anger
mīl 04.01.02.01.03.05 Millet; 04.02.04.03.02.01.02 A kind of millet; 05.10.05.03 A measure of distance
mīla stān 05.10.05.03 A measure of distance
milde 08.01.02.01 Favour, kindness, grace; 08.01.02.06 Mercy, pity
mildelic 08.01.02.06 Mercy, pity
mildelīce 08.01.02.06 Mercy, pity
(ge)mild(g)ian 05.12.04 Absence of movement, stillness
mildheort 08.01.02.01.02 Gentleness; 08.01.02.05 Compassion
mildheortlic 08.01.02.06 Mercy, pity
mildheortlīce 08.01.02.05 Compassion
mildheortnes 08.01.02.06 Mercy, pity
gemildian 08.01.02.01.02 Gentleness
mildnes 08.01.02.01.02 Gentleness
milenfeld 04.01.02.02.09 A mill
mīlgemearces 05.10.05.03 A measure of distance

mīlgemet 05.10.05.03 A measure of distance
mīlgetæl 05.10.05.03 A measure of distance
milisc 04.01.02.01.05.04 Honey; 04.01.03.05.01.01 Wine
miliscian 04.01.02.02.04.06 To sweeten
mīlite 13.02.10 The military, soldiers
mīlitisc 13.02.09 Military style
mīlpæþ 05.12.01.03.01.03 A highway
gemilscad 04.01.02.01.05.04 Honey
milscapuldor 02.07.09.02 Particular fruits (alphabetical order)
mīlstān 05.10.05.03 A measure of distance
miltcoþe 02.08.08.05 Disease of spleen
milte 02.04.06.05.02 Spleen
miltende 03.01.09.01.02.01 Fusible
milteseoc 02.08.08.05 Disease of spleen
miltewærc 02.08.08.05 Disease of spleen
milts 08.01.02.06 Mercy, pity
(ge)miltsian 08.01.02.06.01 Pity
gemiltsian 08.01.02.01.02 Gentleness; 08.01.02.05 Compassion
(ge)miltsi(g)end 08.01.02.06.01 Pity
miltsigendlic 16.02.01.13.01 Kinds of sin
miltsum 08.01.01.03.06 Exultation, joy
miltsung 08.01.03.07.04.02 Relief, alleviation; 16.02.04.07.02.03 Penance, an act/instance of penance
(ge)miltsung 08.01.02.05 Compassion
mīma 18.02.06 Theatricals
gemimor 06.01.06.01.01 Knowledge
mimorian 06.01.04 Faculty of memory
gemimorlīce 06.01.06.01.01 Knowledge
min 07.03.02 Ill, harm, hurt
mind 12.01.01.03 Symbols of power
mindōm 06.01.05.03.02.01 Foolishness, lightmindedness; 06.02.07.07 Cowardice, pusillanimity

mines þances 06.02.02 Will, disposition
minlic 03.03.05.01.03 Inferior
mīnlīce 11.05.02 Mode, manner, way, method, fashion, course
(ge)minsian 03.03.04.06 Diminution
geminsian 07.05 Disrespect, irreverence
minsung 10.03.09.01 Parsimony, niggardliness
minte 02.07.10.01 Particular herbs/spices (alphabetical order)
mintfeld 04.02.04.05.01 A garden-plot
minthamm 04.02.04.05.01 A garden-plot
mintlēag 04.02.04.05.01 A garden-plot
mircapuldor 02.07.09.02 Particular fruits (alphabetical order)
mirce 03.01.13 Darkness, obscurity; 12.08.06.02.04 Darkness, evil
mircels 06.02.06.01 An end, goal; 09.04.01 Signal, signalling; 12.02.01.01 A distinguishing mark, stamp; 13.02.05.01 Victory
mircna land/rīce 12.06.01.01 England
misbegān 07.10.02.01 Deformed, ugly
mis(be)hworfen 12.08.06.01.02 Lacking moral good
misbēodan 08.01.03.07.02.01 Injury, offence; 09.03.02.04 A slip of the tongue, solecism
misboren 02.08.04.02 Blemish, disfigurement; 12.08.06.01.02 Lacking moral good
misbregdan 05.13.01 Transformation, taking another shape
misbyrd 02.01.03.03.03.01 Child-bearing, childbirth
misbyrdo 02.08.04.02 Blemish, disfigurement
misbȳsnian 06.01.06.02.03.04.03 To teach, instruct

miscealfian 02.06.01.07 Breeding, hatching
miscenning 14.03.03 Law, action of the courts; 14.05.04.01 A fine
miscian 03.03.06.01.01 Mixing, mingling, preparation
miscrōced 02.08.04.02 Blemish, disfigurement
miscrōcettan 02.05.10.15.06 A roar, howl, etc.
miscweden 09.03.02.04 A slip of the tongue, solecism
miscwēman 08.01.03.07 Unpleasantness
miscweþan 16.02.04.14.02.01 Cursing, imprecation
miscyrran 12.08.06.01.04.01 To mislead, seduce, lead astray
misdǣd 12.08.06.02.05.01 Transgression, trespass
misdōn 12.08.06.02.03.02 To do evil
misefesian 16.02.04.13.03 Tonsure, haircutting, shaving
misendebyrdan 03.05 Order, arrangement, disposition
misfadian (līf) 12.08.06.01.04 To lead a bad life
misfadung 12.08.06.01 Error, wrong conduct, erroneous practice
misfaran 11.06.03.01 Ill fortune, bad success; 12.08.06.01.04 To lead a bad life
misfēdan 04.01.02.04.03.01 To feed/nourish
misfeng 12.08.06.02.05 Misdeed, sin
misfēran 12.08.06.01.04 To lead a bad life
misfōn 06.01.07.05 Error, being astray; 11.04.03 (Of ability) low, mean, of less worth

misgedwield 12.08.06.01 Error, wrong conduct, erroneous practice
misgehygd 12.08.06.02 Wickedness, evil
mis(ge)limp 08.01.03.06.01 Affliction, misfortune, calamity
misgemynd 06.01.04.02 Living, remembered
mis(ge)widere 01.03.01.03 Bad weather
misgrētan 11.05.02.02.01.02 To greet amiss, insult
misgȳman 11.06.01.01 Negligence, carelessness, heedlessness
mishæbbende 02.08.02 Disease, infirmity, sickness
mishealdan 11.06.01 Neglect
mishealdennes 11.06.01 Neglect
mishealdsumnes 11.06.01 Neglect
mishērnes 12.01.01.12.02 Disobedience
mishweorfed 12.08.06.01.02 Lacking moral good
mishȳran 12.01.01.12.02 Disobedience
mislǣdan 06.01.07.04.01 Deception, a leading astray
mislǣran 06.01.06.02.03.04.03 To teach, instruct
mislār 06.01.06.02.03.04 Teaching, instruction
mislic 03.06.02 Difference, diversity, dissimilarity; 05.12.05.01 To go astray
mislīce 03.06.02 Difference, diversity, dissimilarity; 05.12.05.01 To go astray
mislīcian 08.01.03.07 Unpleasantness
mislīcnes 03.06.02 Difference, diversity, dissimilarity
mislīcum 03.06.02 Difference, diversity, dissimilarity
mislimpan 05.03.02 Event, issue, result
mislybban 12.08.06.01.04 To lead a bad life
mismacian 05.06.04 Damage, injury, defect, hurt, loss

mismicel 03.03.04.01.01 Greatness, bigness, size
mispeler 02.07.09.02 Particular fruits (alphabetical order)
misrǣcan 07.05.03.03.02 To reproach, revile, abuse
misrǣd 12.01.01.01 Rule, domination, direction; 12.08.06.01 Error, wrong conduct, erroneous practice
misrǣdan 09.04.02.01 A secret, mystery; 12.03.02 Advice, admonition
miss 05.10.04.04 Absence; 10.02.01 Loss, deprivation
missan 05.12.02.07 To throw, cast, toss; 11.06.01 Neglect
misscrence 02.08.04.04.03 Withered; 03.01.18 Dryness (not wetness)
misscrȳden 04.04.07.01 Mode of dressing, fashion
missenlic 03.06.02 Difference, diversity, dissimilarity
missenlīce 03.06.02 Difference, diversity, dissimilarity
missenlicnes 05.02.02 Nature, established order of things
missenlīcnes 03.06.02 Difference, diversity, dissimilarity
missere 05.11.03.01 A year; 05.11.03.01.01 A half-year
misspōwan 11.06.03.01 Ill fortune, bad success
missprecan 08.01.03.05 Murmuring, complaint
misstīgan 05.12.05.13 To go down, descend
mist 01.03.01.06.01 Cloud, mist; 02.08.07.02.01 Defective vision; 03.01.15 Vapour, air; 06.01.05.03 Want of understanding

mistǣcan 06.01.06.02.03.04.03 To teach, instruct
mistel 02.07.03.05 Particular trees/shrubs (alphabetical order); 02.07.10.01 Particular herbs/spices (alphabetical order)
mistellām 04.03.04 Fowling
misteltān 02.07.03.05 Particular trees/shrubs (alphabetical order)
mistglōm 01.03.01.06.01 Cloud, mist; 03.01.13 Darkness, obscurity
misthelm 01.03.01.06.01 Cloud, mist; 06.01.07.05 Error, being astray
misthliþ 01.01.02.01.02.02.04 Cliff; 01.03.01.06.01 Cloud, mist
mistian 01.03.01.06.01 Cloud, mist; 02.08.07.02.01 Defective vision
mistīd 08.01.03.06 Adversity, affliction
mistīdan 05.03.02 Event, issue, result
mistig 01.03.01.06.01 Cloud, mist
mistihtan 06.02.06.03.04 Allurement
mistihtendlic 09.03.02.02.01.03 An adverb
mistīmian 05.03.02.01.01 An event, occurrence
mistran 02.08.07.02.01 Defective vision
mistrīwan 06.01.08.03.02 Distrust, want of faith or confidence
mistūcian 12.05.06.02.03 Trouble, disturbance
misþēon 12.08.06.01.04 To lead a bad life
misþyncan 06.01.07.05 Error, being astray
misweaxende 02.08.04.02 Blemish, disfigurement
miswendan 11.08.03 Needless, useless, unprofitable; 12.08.06.01.04 To lead a bad life
miswende 12.08.06.01.02 Lacking moral good

miswenian 11.08.03 Needless, useless, unprofitable
misweorc 12.08.06.02.01 Wrong, evil-doing
misweorþan 08.01.03.06.01 Affliction, misfortune, calamity
miswissian 06.01.07.04.01 Deception, a leading astray
miswrītan 09.03.07.02 To make a mistake in writing
miswurþian 16.02.04.14 Sacrilege
miswyrcan 05.05 Constitution, founding (e.g. of world)
mīte 02.06.09 Insect/small creature
mitta 03.03.01 Specific measures
(ge)mittan 11.03.01.03 Finding, discovery
gemittan 05.03.02 Event, issue, result; 05.12.05.02.02 To come together, meet; 12.04 Fellowship, union, association; 12.05.04 Strife, hostility
(ge)mitting 12.04.02 A crowding together, assembly
gemitting 05.12.05.02.02 To come together, meet
mīþan 06.01.07.04.04.02 Pretence, feigning, dissimulation; 09.05.04.01 Concealment, obscurity; 11.06.04 Abstention, abstaining from
miþgian 09.05.04.01 Concealment, obscurity
miþnumen 05.06.08 A plucking, taking away
mixen 02.04.06.06.06 Faeces; 04.02.04.02.01.01 To manure, dung
mixendynge 02.04.06.06.06 Faeces
mixenplante 02.07.11 Plants/flowers (alphabetical order)
mōd 06 Spirit, soul, heart; 06.02.07.06 Courage, boldness, valour; 07.02.04.03 Nobleness, excellence, nobility, magnificence; 07.06.01 Pride, arrogance; 08.01 Heart, spirit, mood, disposition
mōd niman 06.02.07.06 Courage, boldness, valour
(ge)mōd 06 Spirit, soul, heart; 06.01 The head (as seat of thought)
gemōd 09.07.04.01 Confirmation, agreement; 13 Peace, tranquillity
mōdblind 06.01.05.03 Want of understanding
mōdblissiende 08.01.01.03.06 Exultation, joy
mōdbysgung 08.01.03.03 Anxiety
mōdcearig 08.01.03 Bad feeling, sadness
mōdcearu 08.01.03 Bad feeling, sadness
mōdcræft 06.01.05.02 Intelligence
mōdcræftig 06.01.05.02.01 Intelligent, sensible
mōddren 02.03.02.03.02 Maternal descent
mōdearfoþ 08.01.03.03 Anxiety
mōdes elhygd 02.08.11.02 Mental weakness
mōdes geswæþrung 02.08.11.02 Mental weakness
mōdewǣg 01.01.03.01.02.05 Wave
mōdful 07.06 Pride
mōdgehygd 06.01.01 Thought, the faculty of thinking, mind
mōdgemynd 06.01 The head (as seat of thought)
mōdgēomor 08.01.03 Bad feeling, sadness
mōdgeþanc 06.01 The head (as seat of thought); 06.01.01 Thought, the faculty of thinking, mind
mōdgeþōht 06.01 The head (as seat of thought)

mōdgeþyldig 08.01.03.08 Patience
mōdgewinna 08.01.03.03 Anxiety
mōdglæd 08.01.01.03 Good feeling, joy, happiness
mōdglēaw 06.01.05.02.01.01 Sagacity
mōdhēap 13.02.10.01.02.02.01 Types of army
mōdhete 08.01.03.09.04 Hatred
mōdhord 06.01 The head (as seat of thought)
mōdhwæt 06.02.07.01 Strength, fortitude
mōdig 01.01.03.01.01.01 River; 05.08.02.01 (Of living creatures) fierceness, roughness; 06.02.07.04.02 Perversity; 06.02.07.06 Courage, boldness, valour; 07.06.01.01 Proud, arrogant; 08.01.01.01.04 Depth of feeling, zeal; 12.08.01 Magnanimity, greatness of soul
mōdig(i)an 01.01.03.01.02.06 Surging, rolling, heaving of waves; 07.06.01.03 To be proud/arrogant; 07.06.03 Boastfulness, arrogance; 07.06.05 Pomp, splendour, magnificence; 08.01.01.03.06 Exultation, joy; 08.01.03.05.04 Irritability
mōdiglēas 06.01.05.03.01.01 Dullness, folly, stupidity
mōdiglic 06.02.07.06 Courage, boldness, valour; 07.06.05 Pomp, splendour, magnificence
mōdiglīce 06.02.07.06 Courage, boldness, valour
mōdignes 07.06.01 Pride, arrogance; 12.08.01 Magnanimity, greatness of soul
mōdlēast 06.02.07.07 Cowardice, pusillanimity
mōdlēof 08.01.02.02.01 A favourite, loved one

mōdlufu 08.01.02.02 Love, affection, care
gemōdod 06.02.06 Mind, purpose
mōdor 02.01.03.03.02 To bring forth, produce; 02.03.02.01 Parent; 02.03.02.03.03 Forefather, ancestor; 02.06 Animal; 11.12.02 Aid, help, succour; 16.02.03.03.01.02 An abbess
mōdor bōsm 02.04.06.04.02 Female reproductive organs
mōdor hrif 02.04.06.04.02 Female reproductive organs
mōdor innoþ 02.04.06.04.02 Female reproductive organs
mōdorcild 02.03.02.02.05 Having the same parents
mōdorcynn 02.03.02.03.02 Maternal descent
mōdorhealf 02.03.02.03.02 Maternal descent
mōdorlēas 02.03.02.02 Child, offspring
mōdorlic 02.03.02.03.02 Maternal descent
mōdorlīce 08.01.02.03.03 In a friendly manner, kindly
mōdorlufu 08.01.02.02 Love, affection, care
mōdorslaga 02.02.04.04.01 Murder of a relative
mōdri(g)e 02.03.02.03.06.02.02 Aunt; 02.03.02.03.06.02.04 Cousin
mōdrōf 06.02.07.06 Courage, boldness, valour
mōdsefa 06 Spirit, soul, heart; 06.01.01 Thought, the faculty of thinking, mind; 06.02.07.06 Courage, boldness, valour
mōdsēoc 08.01.03.01 Despondency
mōdsēocnes 06.01.08.06.01 A shuddering with fear, nervousness

mōdsnotor 06.01.05.02.01.01 Sagacity
mōdsorg 08.01.03 Bad feeling, sadness
mōdstaþol 12.08 Principle, character
mōdstaþolnes 12.08.02.03 Goodness, probity
gemōdsum 09.07.04.01 Confirmation, agreement; 13 Peace, tranquillity
gemōdsumian 09.07.04.01 Confirmation, agreement
gemōdsumnes 09.07.04.01 Confirmation, agreement; 13 Peace, tranquillity
mōdswīþ 06.02.07 Will, determination, resolution
mōdþracu 06.02.07.06 Courage, boldness, valour
mōdþrēa 08.01.03.03 Anxiety
mōdþwǣre 08.01.02.01.02 Gentleness
mōdþwǣrnes 08.01.03.08 Patience
mōdwelig 11.04 Ability, capacity, power
mōdwlanc 06.02.07.06 Courage, boldness, valour; 07.06 Pride
mōdwyn 15.01.03 Treasure, riches, wealth
molcen 04.01.02.01.02.09.09 Curds
(ge)molcen 04.02.05.06.01.02 To milk
molda 02.04.03.01.01 Top of head
moldærn 02.02.05.01.01 A grave, burial place, sepulchre
moldcorn 02.07.11 Plants/flowers (alphabetical order)
molde 01 Earth, world; 01.01.02.01 Ground; 01.01.02.02 Earth, soil
moldgewind 02.04.03.01.01 Top of head
moldgræf 02.02.05.01.01 A grave, burial place, sepulchre
moldhrērende 05.12.01.01 To go on a journey/expedition, travel
moldhȳpe 04.06.02.05 Dust, powder
moldstōw 02.02.05.01.01 A grave, burial place, sepulchre

moldweg 01 Earth, world
moldwyrm 02.06.09.02.11 Worm
molegn 04.01.02.01.02.09.09 Curds
molegnstycce 04.01.02.01.02.09.09 Curds
molsn 03.02.01.01 Decay, corruption, rottenness
(ge)molsnian 03.02.01.01 Decay, corruption, rottenness
gemolsnod 03.02.01.01 Decay, corruption, rottenness
mōna 01.02.01.01.04 Moon; 05.11.06.03.01 Time/period of the moon
mōnan ieldo 05.11.06.03.01 Time/period of the moon
mōnanǣfen 05.11.03.01.05.01 Specific days
mōnandæg 05.11.03.01.05.01 Specific days
mōnanniht 05.11.03.01.05.01 Specific days
mōnaþ 05.11.03.01.03 A month (lunar or calendar)
mōnaþādl 02.04.06.06.08 Menses
mōnaþādlig 02.04.06.06.08 Menses
mōnaþblōd 02.04.06.06.08 Menses
mōnaþbōt 16.02.04.07.02.03 Penance, an act/instance of penance
mōnaþfylen 05.11.06.03.01.01 Time of full moon
mōnaþgecynd 02.04.06.06.08 Menses
mōnaþlic 02.04.06.06.08 Menses; 05.11.03.01.03 A month (lunar or calendar); 05.11.06.03 Lunar cycle of nineteen years
mōnaþsēoc 02.04.06.06.08 Menses; 02.08.11.02.01 Insanity, madness
mōnaþsēocnes 02.08.11.02.01 Insanity, madness

mōnelic 01.02.01.01.04 Moon; 05.11.03.01.03 A month (lunar or calendar); 05.11.06.03 Lunar cycle of nineteen years
mōnsēoc 02.08.11.02.01 Insanity, madness
mōr 01.01.02.01.02 High land; 01.01.02.01.04.01 Marsh, bog, swamp; 01.01.02.01.06 Wild/uncultivated land
moraþ 04.01.03.05.01.01 Wine
mōrbēam 02.07.09.02 Particular fruits (alphabetical order)
mōrberie 02.07.09.02 Particular fruits (alphabetical order)
more 02.07.09.02.02.01 Edible root/bulb
mōrfæsten 11.10.01.02.01 A naturally secure place, fastness
mōrflēoge 02.06.09.02.07 Fly
morgen 05.11.04.01.01 Dawn, daybreak, sunrise; 05.11.04.01.02 Morning; 05.11.07.04.01.01 (To)morrow
morgenceald 01.03.01.04 Wintry weather, cold
morgencolla 06.01.08.06.03 Cause of fear, terror, horror
morgendæg 05.11.04.01.02 Morning; 05.11.07.04.01.01 (To)morrow
morgendrenc 02.08.12.02.05 Pharmacy, curing with salves
morgengebedtīd 16.02.04.05.02 The hour or service of Matins
morgengifu 12.09.02 Marriage ceremony
morgenlēoht 05.11.04.01.01 Dawn, daybreak, sunrise
morgenlic 05.11.04.01.02 Morning; 05.11.07.04.01.01 (To)morrow
morgenlong 05.11.03.01.05 A day
morgenmæsse 16.02.04.07.04.01 The service of the mass

morgenmete 04.01.02.04.01.01 Meal at particular time of day
morgenrēn 01.03.01.06.02 Rain
morgensēoc 08.01.03 Bad feeling, sadness
morgenspǣc 12.02.03 A society, guild, association
morgenspell 09.06.02.01.06 A message, announcement by a messenger
morgensteorra 01.02.01.01.02 Star
morgenswēg 08.01.03.04.01 Complaint, lamentation
morgentīd 05.11.04.01.02 Morning
morgentīdlic 05.11.04.01.02 Morning
morgentorht 03.01.12 Brightness, light
morgenwacian 02.05.02 Consciousness; 05.11.08.01.02 (Untimely) earliness
morgenwlǣtung 02.08.08.04.02 (Of stomach) disordered
mōrhǣþ 01.01.02.01.02 High land; 01.01.02.01.06 Wild/uncultivated land
mōrhana 02.06.08.03 Game-bird
mōrhēald 01.01.02.01.04.01 Marsh, bog, swamp
mōrhop 01.01.02.01.04.01 Marsh, bog, swamp
mōrig 01.01.02.01.04.01 Marsh, bog, swamp
mōrlǣs 04.02.03.04.02.01 Types of pasture
mōrland 01.01.02.01.06 Wild/uncultivated land
mōrsceaþa 14.02.01.02 Wrongful taking, theft
mōrsecg 02.07.08 Grasses, reeds, etc.
mōrseohtre 04.05.03.05.03.01 A ditch, dike
mōrslæd 01.01.02.01.03.03 Valley
mōrstapa 02.06 Animal

mortere 17.03.04 Tools for smoothing/scraping/grinding
morþ 02.02.02 Liability to death, mortality; 02.02.04.04 Manslaughter, homicide; 14.02.01.01 Types of crime; 16.01.04.04 A magical apparatus; 16.02.01.13.01 Kinds of sin
morþcrundel 02.02.05.01.01 A grave, burial place, sepulchre
morþcwalu 02.02.04.04 Manslaughter, homicide
morþdǣd 02.02.04.04 Manslaughter, homicide; 12.08.06.02.05 Misdeed, sin
morþor 02.02.04.04 Manslaughter, homicide; 08.01.03.07.03 Suffering, torment, pain; 16.02.01.13.01 Kinds of sin
morþorbealu 02.02.04.04 Manslaughter, homicide
morþorbedd 02.02.02 Liability to death, mortality
morþorcofa 14.05.08.01 Prison, confinement, durance
morþorcræft 16.01.04 Sorcery, magic, witchcraft
morþorcwalu 02.02.04.04 Manslaughter, homicide
morþorcwealm 02.02.04.04 Manslaughter, homicide
morþorhete 08.01.03.09.04 Hatred
morþorhof 16.01.05.01 Damnation, perdition, reprobation
morþorhūs 16.01.05.01 Damnation, perdition, reprobation
morþorhycgende 02.02.04.02 Murderous, bloodthirsty
morþorlēan 14.05.03 Retribution, requital
morþorscyldig 12.08.09 Guiltiness, guilt
morþ(or)slaga 02.02.04.04 Manslaughter, homicide
morþorslagu 02.02.04.04 Manslaughter, homicide
morþorslege 02.02.04.04 Manslaughter, homicide
morþ(or)sliht 02.02.04.04 Manslaughter, homicide
morþ(or)wyrhta 02.02.04.04 Manslaughter, homicide
morþweorc 16.01.04.02 Sorcery involving drugs or potions
mōrwyrt 02.07.11 Plants/flowers (alphabetical order)
mos 01.01.02.01.04.01 Marsh, bog, swamp
mōs 04.01.02.01 Food/sustenance
mot 03.03.04.04 Littleness, smallness
mōt 06.01.07.07.01 Likelihood, probability, chance; 06.02.04 Necessity, inevitability; 12.03.05 Permission; 15.03.01 Toll
(ge)mōt 12.04.02 A crowding together, assembly
gemōt 05.12.01.03.01 A means of access; 05.12.05.02.02 To come together, meet; 12.02.02 An assembly, meeting; 12.05.04 Strife, hostility; 14.03.01 Judicial body, authority; 14.03.03 Law, action of the courts; 16.02.01.08.03 The New Testament; 16.02.03.01 Ecclesiastical authority
gemōt wyrcan 12.02.02.04 Counsel, deliberation
(ge)mōtærn 14.03.01 Judicial body, authority
mōtbell 02.05.10.13.01.01 Stroke/sound of a bell
(ge)mōtbeorh 12.02.02.01 Place of conference or assembly

mōtere 09.01.02 Fluency in speech
mōtgerēfa 12.02.02 An assembly, meeting
(ge)mōthūs 12.02.02.01 Place of conference or assembly
(ge)mōtian 09.07.01 Contention, argument, strife of words
(ge)mōtian (ymb/be) 12.02.02.04 Counsel, deliberation
mōtlǣþu 12.02.02 An assembly, meeting
gemōtlēah 12.02.02.01 Place of conference or assembly
gemōtmann 09.01.02 Fluency in speech; 12.02.02 An assembly, meeting; 15.02.03 An account
gemōtstede 12.02.02.01 Place of conference or assembly
(ge)mōtstōw 12.02.02.01 Place of conference or assembly; 14.03.01 Judicial body, authority
mōtung 09.01.04 Conversation, discussion
mōtweorþ 12.02.02 An assembly, meeting
moþfreten 03.02.01.03 Worm-eaten state
moþþe 02.06.09.02.04 Butterfly, moth
mōyses lagu 16.02.01.08.01 The Old Testament
mucgwyrt 02.07.11 Plants/flowers (alphabetical order)
muddig 01.01.02.01.04.01 Marsh, bog, swamp
mūga 04.02.04.04.04 Stack, rick
mūl 02.06.02.01.01 Ass
mūlhyrde 04.02.05.06.05.01 Care of horses
gemun 06.01.04 Faculty of memory
munan 07.01 Appraisal, appraising; 11.02.02.02 Care, mindfulness, attention

gemunan 06.01.01.01 Thinking about, minding, heeding; 06.01.01.01.01 Thought, cogitation, meditation; 06.01.04 Faculty of memory; 06.01.04.01 To remind, bring to the notice of; 09.03.07.07.03.02 To write, state/say in writing
mund 02.04.03.04.01.01 Hand; 05.10.05.03 A measure of distance; 11.10.01 Protection, safekeeping; 11.10.02.02.01 Care, interest in; 12.05.06 Grasp, power, control, mastery; 14 Law, custom, covenant; 14.05.04.01 A fine
mundbeorg 01.01.02.01.02.02 Hill, mountain; 13.02.06.01 Stronghold, fort/fortified town
mundbora 11.10.01 Protection, safekeeping; 11.10.02.02 Watchful care, keeping guard
mundbryce 14.02.01.01 Types of crime; 14.05.04.01 A fine
mundbyrd 11.10.01 Protection, safekeeping; 14.05.04.01 A fine
mundbyrdan 11.10.01 Protection, safekeeping
(ge)mundbyrdan 11.10.01 Protection, safekeeping; 13.02.04 Defence, guard, protection
mundbyrdnes 11.10.01 Protection, safekeeping; 14.04.01 A deed, contract, agreement
mundcræft 11.10.01 Protection, safekeeping
mundgripe 02.05.06 Sense of touch
mundhēals 11.10.01 Protection, safekeeping
mundian 11.10.02.02.01 Care, interest in
(ge)mundian 11.10.01 Protection, safekeeping

mundiend 11.10.01 Protection, safekeeping
mundlēow 04.06.01.03 A bath
mundrōf 05.08 Strength
mundwist 11.10.02.02.01 Care, interest in
gemuning 06.01.04 Faculty of memory
munt 01.01.02.01.02.02 Hill, mountain; 01.01.02.01.02.02.02 Mountain
muntælfen 16.01.03.04 Elfin race
muntclȳse 01.01.02.01.03 Hollow/depression in land
muntgīu 01.01.02.01.02.02.02 Mountain
muntland 01.01.02.01.02 High land
munuc 16.02.03.03 A religious; 16.02.03.03.02 A monk; 16.02.03.03.03 A nun
munucbehāt 16.02.03.03 A religious
munuccild 02.03.01.04 Child; 16.02.04.07.05.01.01 Going into a monastery, admission
munuccnapa 16.02.03.03.02 A monk
munucgegyrela 16.02.05.07 Monastic garb
munuchād 16.02.03.03 A religious
munuchēap 16.02.03.03.02 A monk
munucian 16.02.04.07.05.01.01 Going into a monastery, admission
munuclic 16.02.03.03 A religious
munuclīce 16.02.03.03 A religious
munuclīf 16.02.03.03 A religious; 16.02.05.04 A monastery/convent
munuclīf dōn/lǣdan 16.02.03.03 A religious
munucrēaf 16.02.05.07 Monastic garb
munucregol 16.02.03.03 A religious
munucscrūd 16.02.05.07 Monastic garb
munucstōw 16.02.05.04 A monastery/convent
munucþēaw 16.02.03.03 A religious

mūr 04.05.02.02 A wall; 05.10.05.04.15.02 A wall
murcen 08.01.03.04 Grief
murcian 08.01.03.04.01 Complaint, lamentation
murciende 08.01.03.05 Murmuring, complaint
murcnere 08.01.03.04 Grief
murcnian 08.01.03.05 Murmuring, complaint
murcung 08.01.03.04 Grief; 08.01.03.05 Murmuring, complaint
murnan 06.01.08.06 Fear
murnan æfter 06.02.05.01 Strong liking for, devotion to
murnan (æfter/for) 08.01.03.04.01 Complaint, lamentation
murnende 08.01.03.04 Grief
murnung 08.01.03.04 Grief
mūs 02.04.05.05 Muscle; 02.06.03.01.13 Rodents
muscelle 04.01.02.01.02.07 Fish
muscel(le) 02.06.06.04.01.04 Mussel
mūsepise 02.07.11 Plants/flowers (alphabetical order)
mūsere 02.06.08.04 Bird of prey
mūsfealle 04.06.02.02 Foul, filthy, squalid
mūsfealu 03.01.14.09 Dull brown
mūshafoc 02.06.08.04 Bird of prey
must 04.01.03.05.01.01 Wine
mustflēote 02.06.09.02.07 Fly
mustwyrm 02.06.09 Insect/small creature
mūsþēof 02.06.03.01.13 Rodents
mūtung 15.04.01 Lending of money
mūþ 02.04.03.01.03 Face; 02.04.03.01.03.06 Mouth; 02.04.06.03.02.01 Mouth; 05.10.05.04.14 An opening, aperture

mūþ belūcan 09.02 Silence, refraining from speech
mūþa 04.05.02.12 Gate/doorway of a building
mūþ(a) 01.01.03.01.01.01 River
mūþādl 02.08.07.04.01 Mouth disease
mūþberstung 02.08.07.04.01 Mouth disease
mūþbona 02.02.04.03.01 A killer
mūþcoþu 02.08.07.04.01 Mouth disease
mūþes hrōf 02.04.06.03.02.01 Mouth
mūþettan 09.06.02.01 To tell, make known, declare, relate, announce
mūþfrēo 11.12.01 Absence of restraint, freedom
mūþhǣl 09.06.02.01.06.02 Good tidings
mūþhrōf 02.04.06.03.02.01 Mouth
mūþlēas 02.04.03.01.03.06 Mouth; 05.10.05.04.15 Closure, being closed
mūþsār 02.08.07.04.01 Mouth disease
mūþsealf 02.08.12.02.07 Remedies for specific parts (head to toe)
mycg 02.06.09.02.08 Gnat, midge
mycgnet 04.04.08.03 A fly-net, mosquito-net
mydd 03.03.01.02 Dry measures
mȳderce 15.01.04 Coinage, money
myl 04.06.02.05 Dust, powder
mylde 01.01.02.02 Earth, soil
mylen 04.01.02.02.09 A mill
mylenbrōc 01.01.03.01.01.03 Stream; 04.01.02.02.09 A mill
mylenburna 01.01.03.01.01.03 Stream; 04.01.02.02.09 A mill
mylendīc 04.01.02.02.09 A mill
mylenfeld 04.02.03.01 Plot of land
mylengafol 04.01.02.02.09 A mill; 15.03.02 A tax
mylengear 01.01.03.01.03.01 Pool; 04.03.05 Fishing
mylengear/mylenwer/myller 04.01.02.02.09 A mill
mylenhwēol 04.01.02.02.09 A mill
mylenoxa 02.06.02.01.03 Cattle
mylenpull 01.01.03.01.03.01 Pool; 04.01.02.02.09 A mill
mylenscearp 05.10.06.03.01 A point, spike, prickle
mylenstān 04.01.02.02.09 A mill
mylensteall 04.01.02.02.09 A mill
mylenstede 04.01.02.02.09 A mill
mylenstīg 04.01.02.02.09 A mill; 05.12.01.03.01.05 Types of road/path
mylentroh 01.01.03.01.01.03 Stream; 04.01.02.02.09 A mill
mylenweard/mylenwyrd 04.01.02.02.09 A mill
mylenweg 04.01.02.02.09 A mill; 05.12.01.03.01.05 Types of road/path
mylestrēam 01.01.03.01.01.03 Stream; 04.01.02.02.09 A mill
mylnere 04.01.02.02.09 A mill
gemylt(ed) 04.01.02.02.05.01 Heating, warming
myltenhūs 12.08.08.01.02.01.01 An adulterer/-ess, whore, prostitute
myltestre 12.08.08.01.02.01.01 An adulterer/-ess, whore, prostitute
myltestrehūs 12.08.08.01.02.01.01 An adulterer/-ess, whore, prostitute
myltestrern 12.08.08.01.02.01.01 An adulterer/-ess, whore, prostitute
gemynd 02.05.02 Consciousness; 02.08.11.01 Sound mind; 05.11.02.01.01 An anniversary; 05.11.07.03.01 Time within remembrance; 06.01 The head (as seat of thought); 06.01.01.01 Thinking about, minding, heeding; 06.01.04 Faculty of memory; 06.01.04.02

Living, remembered; 06.02.06 Mind, purpose; 07.08.11 Fame after death; 09.03.07.07.03.02 To write, state/say in writing; 11.09.02 A reminder, warning; 12.08 Principle, character; 16.02.04.07.06.03 Commemoration, festival; 16.02.05.05.10 Relics, a collection of relics

gemynddæg 05.11.02.01.01 An anniversary; 16.02.04.04.02 A feast-day, holy day; 16.02.04.07.06.03 Commemoration, festival

gemynde 01.01.03.01.01.01 River; 06.01.04 Faculty of memory

gemynd(e) habban 06.02.06 Mind, purpose

(ge)myndegian 06.01.04.01 To remind, bring to the notice of

gemyndelic 06.01.04.02 Living, remembered

gemyndewyrþe 06.01.04.02 Living, remembered

gemyndful 06.01.04 Faculty of memory

(ge)myndgian/(ge)mynegian 11.09.02.01 An admonition, warning, exhortation

myndgian 12.03.02 Advice, admonition; 15.02.03 An account

myndgian/mynegian 06.02.06 Mind, purpose; 06.02.06.03.03.01 Incitement, prompting, exhortation

gemyndgian 06.01.01.01 Thinking about, minding, heeding; 06.01.04 Faculty of memory; 08.01.02.05 Compassion; 09.06.02.01.01 To make known, cause to know, inform

myndgiend 06.01.04.01 To remind, bring to the notice of

gemyndgod 05.11.07.03.02.02 The aforesaid

myndgung 15.02.03 An account; 16.02.05.05.10 Relics, a collection of relics

myndgung/mynegung 06.01.04.01 To remind, bring to the notice of; 11.09.02.01 An admonition, warning, exhortation

gemyndgung 06.01.04 Faculty of memory

gemyndig 06.01.01.01 Thinking about, minding, heeding; 06.01.04 Faculty of memory; 06.01.05.02 Intelligence; 06.01.08.06.04 Care, anxiety, solicitude; 06.02.06 Mind, purpose; 07.08 Reputation, fame; 11.02.03 Forethought, care; 11.10.02.02.01 Care, interest in; 12.01.01.12.01 Obedience, service; 16.02.04.08.01 Kinds of prayer

gemyndiglic 11.09.02 A reminder, warning

gemyndig(lic) 06.01.04.02 Living, remembered

gemyndiglīce 06.01.01.01 Thinking about, minding, heeding; 06.01.04 Faculty of memory

gemyndiglicnes 06.01.04 Faculty of memory

gemyndlēas 02.08.11.02 Mental weakness

gemyndlȳst 02.08.11.02.01.02 Madness, frenzy, folly

gemyndstōw 16.02.05.05.10 Relics, a collection of relics

myne 02.05.05 Desire, appetite; 02.06.06.02.01.04 Minnow; 06.01 The head (as seat of thought); 06.01.04 Faculty of memory; 08.01.02.02 Love, affection, care; 16.02.05.05.10 Relics, a collection of relics

gemyne 06.01.04 Faculty of memory

mynecen(u) 16.02.03.03.03 A nun
(ge)mynegian 06.01.04 Faculty of memory
gemynegian 06.01.04.01 To remind, bring to the notice of; 09.06.02.01.01 To make known, cause to know, inform
mynegiendlic 11.09.02.01 An admonition, warning, exhortation
mynelic 02.05.05.01 Object of desire
mynet 15.01.04 Coinage, money
mynetcȳpa 15.01.04 Coinage, money
mynetere 15.01.04 Coinage, money
(ge)mynetian 15.01.04 Coinage, money
mynetīsen 15.01.04 Coinage, money
mynetslege 15.01.04 Coinage, money
mynetsmiþþe 15.01.04 Coinage, money
mynian 06.02.06.01 An end, goal; 12.03.02 Advice, admonition
mynle 06.02.05.01 Strong liking for, devotion to
mynna 06.02.06 Mind, purpose
mynster 16.02.05.02.02 A cathedral, minster; 16.02.05.04 A monastery/convent
mynsterbōc 16.02.05.10 A church/monastic book
mynsterclǣnsung 16.02.04.13.02 Purificatory rites
mynsterclūse 16.02.05.04 A monastery/convent
mynsterfæder 16.02.03.03.01.01 An abbot
mynsterfǣmne 16.02.03.03 A nun
mynstergang 16.02.04.07.05.01.01 Going into a monastery, admission
mynstergeat 16.02.05.04.01 Parts of monastery
mynsterhām 16.02.05.04 A monastery/convent

mynsterhata 16.02.03.03 A religious
mynsterland 16.02.05.01 Land
mynsterlic 16.02.03.03 A religious
mynsterlīce 16.02.03.03 A religious
mynsterlīf 16.02.03.03 A religious; 16.02.05.04 A monastery/convent
mynstermann 16.02.03.03 A religious; 16.02.03.03.02 A monk
mynstermunuc 16.02.03.03.02 A monk
mynsterprafost 16.02.03.03.01.03 A prior
mynsterprēost 16.02.03.02.07.01 A priest of a church or minster
mynsterscīr 16.02.03.03 A religious
mynsterstede 16.02.05.04 A monastery/convent
mynsterstōw 12.06.02.01 A township
mynstertimbrung 04.05 Building, construction
mynsterþēaw 16.02.03.03 A religious
mynsterþegnung 16.02.03.03 A religious
mynsterþing 16.02.05.01 Land
mynsterwīse 16.02.03.03 A religious
gemynt 06.02.06 Mind, purpose
myntan 05.04.01 Fortune, Fate (personification); 06.01.07.06.01 To accept as the result of enquiry, suppose; 10.03 Giving
(ge)myntan 06.02.06.02 A proposal, proposition, suggestion
gemyntan (tō) 05.04 Fate, lot, fortune, destiny
myrgan 08.01.01.03.06 Exultation, joy
myrge 08.01.01.03.09.01 Pleasant, agreeable; 18.02.07 Music
myrgelēoþ 02.02.05.03 To attend the dead
myrgen 08.01.01.03.05 Pleasure, delight
myrgnes 18.02.07 Music
myrgþ 08.01.01.03.09 Pleasantness, agreeableness; 18.02.07 Music

myrige 18.02.07 Music
myriglīce 18.02.07 Music
myrra 02.05.08.02 Pleasant smell, fragrance, perfume
myrten 02.02.03.02 State of being dead; 02.06.01.01 Flesh of dead animal
myrþra 02.02.04.04 Manslaughter, homicide
myrþrung 02.02.04.04 Manslaughter, homicide
myrþu 02.02.04.02 Murderous, bloodthirsty; 08.01.03.06 Adversity, affliction
myscan 08.01.03.07.02.01 Injury, offence
(ge)myscan 08.01.03.07.02.01 Injury, offence
mysci 02.06.09.02.07 Fly
(ge)mȳþe 01.01.02.01.03.03 Valley; 01.01.03.01.01.01 River
gemȳþe 05.10.05.04.14.02 An opening/space in an enclosure
gemȳþ(e) 01.01.03.01.01.01 River
nā 05.11.09.05 Never; 09.07.03.01 A denial
nā lǣs þonne 03.03.04.01.02 A great number, multitude
nā mā 05.07 Ending of existence, end of world
nā māre 05.07 Ending of existence, end of world
nā on līfe 05.11.09.05 Never
nā þæt ān þæt ... ac ēac swylce 03.04.01 Singularity, peculiarity
nā þȳ lǣs 03.06 Comparison
nabban 10.02 Want, lack
naca 05.12.01.09.03.01 A ship, boat
nacod 04.02.05.06.05.03.04 Saddle; 04.04.07.02.01 Nakedness; 05.10.05.04.13 A removal of that which obscures or conceals; 09.03.04.03 Plain, simple; 11.08.03 Needless, useless, unprofitable; 13.02.08.04.03.02 Armed with a sword; 15.01.06 Poverty, indigence
genacodian 05.10.05.04.13 A removal of that which obscures or conceals
nacodplegere 18.02.03.01 A combatant, athlete
nacudwraxlere 18.02.03.01 A combatant, athlete
nǣcednes 04.04.07.02.01 Nakedness
nǣced(u) 04.04.07.02.01 Nakedness
nǣdderfāh 03.01.14.11 Medley/variety of colour
nǣdderwinde 02.07.11 Plants/flowers (alphabetical order)
nǣderbita 02.06.04.01.07 Ichneumon
nǣdercynn 02.06.07.01 Reptile (serpent, snake)
nǣdl 04.04.05.06 To sew, stitch
nǣdre 02.06.07.01 Reptile (serpent, snake)
nǣdrewyrt 02.07.11 Plants/flowers (alphabetical order)
nǣfd 10.02 Want, lack
nǣfebor 17.03.05 An awl, borer, gimlet, etc.
nǣfre 05.11.09.05 Never
nǣft 15.01.06 Poverty, indigence
nǣftig 15.01.06 Poverty, indigence
(ge)nǣgan 09.01.03 To address, speak to
genǣgan 05.12.05.02 To go/travel towards, come, approach; 08.01.03.07.02 Misery, trouble, affliction
nǣgelīsern 17.03.10.02 A pin, peg, nail
nǣgl 02.04.04.02 Nail; 17.03.10.02 A pin, peg, nail; 18.02.07.02.03 Stringed instruments
(ge)nǣgled 17.03.10.02 A pin, peg, nail

nægledbord 05.12.01.09.03.01.02 Of/concerning a ship, naval
nægledcnearr 05.12.01.09.03.01.01 Kind of ship
nægledcræt 05.12.01.06 Vehicle
nægledsinc 04.01.03.05.04 Drinking vessel
(ge)næglian 17.03.10.02 A pin, peg, nail
(ge)næglian on rōde 02.02.04.04.03 Putting to death; 14.05.05.01.01 Crucifixion, death on cross
genæglian 04.05 Building, construction
næglsex 17.03.03 A cutting tool
næm 14.03.03.02.01 Attaching, distraint of stolen property
genǣman on 10.04.03 To take away, remove
nǣmel 06.01.06.02.03.04.04 Under instruction, being taught
nǣming 14.04 Making of terms, agreement, convention
nǣnig 05.07 Ending of existence, end of world
nǣnig þing 03.06 Comparison
nǣnig þinga 03.06 Comparison
nǣnig wiht 03.06 Comparison
nǣnigdǣl 03.06 Comparison
nǣp 02.07.09.02.02.01 Edible root/bulb
nǣpsǣd 02.07.09.02.02.01 Edible root/bulb
nǣrende 05.07 Ending of existence, end of world
næsc 02.06.03.01.06 Deer, hart
næsgristle 02.04.03.01.03.04 Nose; 02.04.05.07 Cartilage, gristle
næshliþ 01.01.02.01.02.02.03 Slope
næss 01.01.02.01 Ground; 01.01.02.01.03.02 Abyss, chasm; 16.01.05 Hell, lower world, abode of the dead

næss(e) 01.01.02.01.01.03.01 Promontory, headland, cape
næster 04.01.03.05.04 Drinking vessel
næsþyrl 02.04.03.01.03.04 Nose
næt 03.01.16.01 Moisture
nǣtan 07.05.01 Censure, reproof, rebuke
(ge)nǣtan 08.01.03.07.02 Misery, trouble, affliction
genǣtan 12.08.06.01.04.01 To mislead, seduce, lead astray
nǣting 07.05.01 Censure, reproof, rebuke
nafela 02.04.03.03.06 Belly/abdomen
nafeþa 17.03.01 A wheel
nafogār 17.03.05 An awl, borer, gimlet, etc.
nafu 17.03.01 A wheel
nafulsceaft 02.04.03.03.06 Belly/abdomen
nāh 10.02 Want, lack; 12.03.06 Prohibition; 12.07.03 Abstinence/exemption (from)
nāht 03.06 Comparison; 05.07 Ending of existence, end of world; 11.08.04 Vanity, idleness, frivolity; 12.08.06.02.01 Wrong, evil-doing
nāht elles 05.07 Ending of existence, end of world
nāhte 05.07 Ending of existence, end of world
nāhtes 11.08.04 Vanity, idleness, frivolity
nāhtfremmend 12.08.06.02.02 A bad man, inhuman person
nāhtgītsung 10.03.09.01.01 Covetousness, avarice
nāhtlic 07.03.03.01 Empty, useless, worthless; 11.08.03 Needless, useless, unprofitable
nāhtlīce 06.02.07.07 Cowardice, pusillanimity; 12.08.06.02.03.01 Wickedly

nāhtnes 06.02.07.07 Cowardice, pusillanimity
nāhtscipe 06.02.07.07 Cowardice, pusillanimity
nāhtwela 11.08.04 Vanity, idleness, frivolity
nāhwǣr 03.06 Comparison; 05.10.04.04 Absence; 05.11.09.05 Never
nāhwǣr eorþan hū 05.03.01 A cause (of anything)
nāhwǣrn 05.10.04.04 Absence
nāhwæþer 05.07 Ending of existence, end of world; 09.03.02.03.01.01.03 Gender
nāhwæþer ne ... ne 03.06 Comparison
nāhwanon 03.06 Comparison; 05.10.04.04 Absence
nāhwider 05.10.04.04 Absence
nām 14.03.03.02.01 Attaching, distraint of stolen property
nama 07.08 Reputation, fame; 09.03.02.02.01.01 A noun; 09.06.02.01.07 A name, appellation; 09.06.02.01.07.02 A categorizing name; 12.01.01.06.08 A person of rank, elder, great man; 16.01.01.03 The divine name
naman/tō naman (ge)scieppan 09.06.02.01.07 A name, appellation
nambōc 09.03.07.07.03.04.02 A register, catalogue
nambred 09.03.07.07.03.04.02 A register, catalogue
namcūþ 06.01.06.01.01.01 Acquaintance, knowledge; 07.08.09 Renown, fame, glory
namcūþlīce 09.06.02.01.07.02 A categorizing name
namcȳging 09.06.02.01.07.02 A categorizing name

(ge)namian 09.06.02.01.01 To make known, cause to know, inform; 09.06.02.01.07 A name, appellation; 09.06.02.01.07.01 A title, label; 09.06.02.01.07.03 To mention by name, name
(ge)namian (tō) 12.02 A public office
genamian 10.03.07.01 To allot, assign
nammǣlum 09.06.02.01.07 A name, appellation
genamna 12.04.01 A fellow, companion, associate, comrade
namnian 09.06.02.01.07.02 A categorizing name
namrǣden 09.06.02.01.07.02 A categorizing name
nān 05.07 Ending of existence, end of world
nān rīm 03.03.04.01.03 An immense quantity, immensity, immense number
nān þing 03.06 Comparison
nān wiht 03.06 Comparison
nāne 03.06 Comparison
nānes þinges 03.06 Comparison
nānwiht 05.07 Ending of existence, end of world
nard 02.07.11 Plants/flowers (alphabetical order); 02.08.12.02.05.02 Salves, ointments
nasu 02.04.03.01.03.04 Nose
nāt 06.01.06.04 Ignorance
nāteshwōn 03.06 Comparison
nāteþæshwōn 03.06 Comparison
nāthwā 03.04.03.01 Someone/something
nāthwǣr 05.10.04.03 Presence
nāthwæt 03 Material, matter, substance
nāthwilc 03.04.03.01 Someone/something
nāþing 05.07 Ending of existence, end of world

nāwa 05.11.09.05 Never
nazarenisc 02.03.03.06.07.07 Other (alphabetical order)
ne 05.11.09.05 Never; 09.07.03.01 A denial
ne ... ǣngum eahta 09.07.03.01 A denial
ne ǣr ne sīþ 05.11.09.05 Never
ne hwarne 03.06 Comparison
ne lȳthwōn 03.03.04.01 Much
ne nā 09.07.03.01 A denial
ne standan tō āhte 11.08.04 Vanity, idleness, frivolity
ne tō wuhte 06.01.07.07.02 Impossible
ne wēnan 06.01.08.06.07 Despair
ne wihte 06.01.07.07.02 Impossible
nēadclam 08.01.03.06 Adversity, affliction
nēadcofa 14.05.08.01 Prison, confinement, durance
nēadgafol 15.03.02 A tax
nēadgewuna 11.05 Natural/proper way/manner/mode of action
nēadgyld 15.03.02 A tax
nēadgylda 15.04 A debt, due
nēadhād 12.05.06.03 Necessity, constraint
nēadhǣs 12.03.03 A command, bidding, order
(ge)nēadian 12.05.06.03 Necessity, constraint
nēadignes 12.07 An obligation, bounden duty
nēadlunga 12.05.06.03 Necessity, constraint
nēadnēod 06.02.04 Necessity, inevitability
nēadprin 10.03.04 Provision, supply
nēadung 06.02.04 Necessity, inevitability; 12.05.06.03 Necessity, constraint
nēadunga 06.02.04 Necessity, inevitability; 12.05.06.03 Necessity, constraint
nēadwīs 06.02.04 Necessity, inevitability; 12.07.01 One's due, natural place or position
nēadwīslīce 06.02.04 Necessity, inevitability
nēadwīsnes 06.02.04 Necessity, inevitability
nēadwraca 12.05.04.02 Vengeance, revenge
geneah 11.04 Ability, capacity, power
nēah 03.06 Comparison; 05.10.05.01 A little way, no great distance; 05.11.07.04.01 Nearness, approach, imminence; 05.11.07.04.03 Newness, novelty
genēah 03.03.04.02 A sufficiency, sufficient supply; 03.03.04.02.01 Abundance
nēahbūend 12.06.03.03 A neighbour
nēahceaster 12.06.02.01 A township
nēahcyrice 16.02.05.02.03 A church, place of worship
nēahdǣl 05.10.05.01 A little way, no great distance
nēahdūn 01.01.02.01.02.02.01 Hill
nēahēa 01.01.03.01.01.01 River
nēahēalond 01.01.02.01.01.02 Island
nēahfæder 16.02.03.02.07.01 A priest of a church or minster
nēahfeald 08.01.02.03.02 Friendly, amiable
nēahfealdlic 08.01.02.03.02 Friendly, amiable
nēahfrēond 02.03.02.03.06.02 Close relationship
nēahgangol 05.10.05.01 A little way, no great distance

nēahgebūr 12.06.03.03 A neighbour
nēahgebȳren 12.06.03.03 A neighbour
nēahgebȳrild 12.06.03.03 A neighbour
nēahgehūsa 12.06.03.03 A neighbour
(ge)neahhe 05.11.09.02 Frequent, of common occurrence
geneahhe 03.03.04.02 A sufficiency, sufficient supply; 03.03.06.02 Fullness; 05.11.11 Continuity; 06.02.07.03 Perseverance
nēahhēahland 05.10.05.01 A little way, no great distance
geneahhelīce 05.11.11 Continuity
nēahhergung 13.02.03 To seek with active intent, attack
genēahhian 05.12.05.02 To go/travel towards, come, approach
nēahland 05.10.05.01 A little way, no great distance
nēahmǣg 02.03.02.03.06.02 Close relationship
nēahmǣgþ 12.06.03.03 A neighbour
nēahmann 12.06.03.03 A neighbour
nēahmunt 01.01.02.01.02.02.02 Mountain
nēahmynster 16.02.05.04 A monastery/convent
nēahnes 05.10.05.01 A little way, no great distance
nēahnunmynster 16.02.05.04 A monastery/convent
nēahsibb 02.03.02.03.06.02 Close relationship
nēahstōw 05.10.05.01 A little way, no great distance
nēahtīd 05.11.07.04.01 Nearness, approach, imminence
nēahtūn 05.10.05.01 A little way, no great distance
nēahþēod 12.06.03.03 A neighbour

nēahwæter 01.01.03.01 Body of water
genēahwian 05.12.05.02 To go/travel towards, come, approach; 06.02.07.03 Perseverance
nēahwudu 02.07.03.04 A wood, trees
(ge)nēalǣcan 05.12.05.02 To go/travel towards, come, approach
nēalǣcan 09.07.04.01 Confirmation, agreement
(ge)nēalǣcan 05.11.07.04.01 Nearness, approach, imminence; 12.04 Fellowship, union, association
genēalǣcan 02.01.03.03 Sex, generation; 03.06.01 Similitude, likeness; 06.02.07.03 Perseverance
nēalǣcung 05.11.07.04.01 Nearness, approach, imminence; 05.12.05.02 To go/travel towards, come, approach
(ge)nēalǣcung 05.11.10.01 A beginning
nēalic 05.10.05.01 A little way, no great distance
nēalīce 03.06 Comparison; 05.10.05.01 A little way, no great distance; 11.11 Difficulty
genēalīce 06.02.07.03 Perseverance; 11.05 Natural/proper way/manner/mode of action
nealles 03.06 Comparison
nēan 05.10.05.01 A little way, no great distance; 05.11.07.04.01 Nearness, approach, imminence
nēar 05.11.07.04.02 (Of time) later/latter
nēar and nēar 05.10.05.01 A little way, no great distance
nearobregd 11.04.02.01.01 Cunning, craft, craftiness, guile, wile
nearocræft 11.04.01 An aptitude, bodily skill; 11.11.01 A physical difficulty, strait
nearofāh 08.01.03.09.04 Hatred

nearogrāp 10.04.02 To grasp, take hold of
nearolic 08.01.03.07.02 Misery, trouble, affliction
nearolīce 05.10.02 Narrowness, scantiness of space; 06.01.07.01.01 Strictness, exactness; 08.01.03.07.04 Severity, harshness; 09.03.04.05 To put briefly; 12.08.06.02.03.01 Wickedly
nearonēd 08.01.03.06 Adversity, affliction
nearones 02.08.03 Pain, bodily discomfort; 05.10.02 Narrowness, scantiness of space; 08.01.03.03 Anxiety; 11.11.01 A physical difficulty, strait; 15.01.06 Poverty, indigence
nearosearu 11.04.02.01.01 Cunning, craft, craftiness, guile, wile
nearosorg 08.01.03.06 Adversity, affliction
nearoþanc 12.08.06.02 Wickedness, evil
nearoþancnes 12.08.06.02 Wickedness, evil
nearoþearf 08.01.03.07.02 Misery, trouble, affliction
nearowrenc 11.04.02.01.01 Cunning, craft, craftiness, guile, wile
nearu 02.08.08.01 Pain in the chest; 05.10.02 Narrowness, scantiness of space; 07.03.04 A wretch, poor creature; 08.01.03.07.04 Severity, harshness; 09.05.04.01 Concealment, obscurity; 11.11.01 A physical difficulty, strait; 12.08.03.02 Strictness, austerity, severity; 14.05.08.01 Prison, confinement, durance
nearu þrōwian 11.11.01 A physical difficulty, strait
genearwad 08.01.03.07.02 Misery, trouble, affliction
nearwe 06.01.07.01.01 Strictness, exactness; 08.01.03.07.04 Severity, harshness; 12.05.06.02 Oppression; 14.05.08.01 Prison, confinement, durance
(ge)nearwian 05.10.05.02.03 To reduce, make thin(ner); 14.05.08 Captivity
nēat 02.06 Animal; 02.06.02.01.03 Cattle
(ge)nēat 15.01.01.01 Holding of land
genēat 02.03.03.01 Body of retainers, household
genēatland 15.01.01 Landed property
genēatmann 15.01.01.01 Holding of land
genēatriht 14.01.01 Law(s) of particular scope
genēatscolu 02.03.03.01 Body of retainers, household
nēawest 05.10.04.03 Presence; 05.10.05.01 A little way, no great distance; 12.04 Fellowship, union, association; 12.09.06 Cohabitation
genēawian 02.01.03.03 Sex, generation
nēawung 05.11.07.04.01 Nearness, approach, imminence
neb(b) 05.10.06.03 Projection, head, extremity (of anything); 02.04.03.01.03.04 Nose; 02.04.03.01.03 Face; 02.06.08.01 Part of bird; 05.12.01.09.03.01.03 Part of ship
nebbian 07.05.03.03.02 To reproach, revile, abuse
nebcorn 02.08.05.02 Particular inflammation/swelling
nebgebræc 02.04.06.05.07.02 Mucus, phlegm, rheum
nebsealf 04.06.01.08 Face powder

nebwlātful 07.06.01.01 Proud, arrogant
nebwlātung 07.06.01 Pride, arrogance
nebwlite 02.04.03.01.03 Face
nefa 02.03.02.03.05 Descendant; 02.03.02.03.06.02.05 Step relationships
(ge)nefa 02.03.02.03.06.02.03 Child of brother/sister
genefa 02.03.02.03.06.02.04 Cousin
nefe 02.03.02.03.05 Descendant
nefene 02.03.02.03.06.02.03 Child of brother/sister
nefte 02.07.11 Plants/flowers (alphabetical order)
nēfugol 02.06.08.04 Bird of prey
nemnan 09.01.03 To address, speak to; 12.02 A public office
(ge)nemnan 09.06.02.01.01 To make known, cause to know, inform; 09.06.02.01.07 A name, appellation; 09.06.02.01.07.03 To mention by name, name; 16.02.04.08.01 Kinds of prayer
genemnan 09.06.02.01.07.01 A title, label
genemnan tō 09.06.02.01.07.03 To mention by name, name
nemne 03.04.01 Singularity, peculiarity
(ge)nemne 03.04.01 Singularity, peculiarity
nemni(g)endlic 09.03.02.03.01.01.01 Case
nemning 09.06.02.01.07 A name, appellation
nēobedd 02.02.02 Liability to death, mortality
nēod 06.02.05.01 Strong liking for, devotion to; 08.01.01.03.05 Pleasure, delight; 11.02.02 Diligence

nēode 06.02.05.04 Desire, eagerness; 11.02.02 Diligence
nēodfræce 02.05.05.02 Eager desire
nēodfrēond 02.03.02.03.06.01 Kinsman, relative
nēodful 06.02.05.04.04 Zeal
(ge)nēodian 06.02.04.01 Want, need
nēodlaþu 12.03.03.01 Summons, a call, summoning
nēodlīce 03.03.04.01 Much; 06.02.05.04.05 Earnestness; 11.02.02 Diligence
nēodlof 16.02.04 Worship, honour, praise
nēodspearuwa 02.06.08.05 Forest bird, wild-fowl
nēodweorþung 07.08.03 Honour, veneration
genēopan 05.06.01 Devastation, laying waste
neorxnawang 16.01.02.01 Heavenly dwelling place; 16.01.02.04 Paradise
neorxnawanglic 16.01.02 The heavens, sky; 16.01.02.01 Heavenly dwelling place
nēosian 05.12.05.10 To go behind, follow; 09.05.02 A question, inquiry, questioning; 11.03.01.02 To seek, seek for
(ge)nēosian 05.10.04.03.01 Visiting/seeking of a place; 05.12.05.02.03 To arrive; 08.01.02.04.01 Visiting
genēosian 06.01.02.01.01 A vision, apparition
nēosīþ 02.02 Death
(ge)nēosung 06.01.02.01.01 A vision, apparition; 08.01.02.04.01 Visiting
genēosung 08.01.02.04 Hospitality
nēotan 11.07 Use (made of things), service
neoþan 05.10.05.04.02.02 Under, beneath

neoþan(e) 05.10.05.04.02.02 Under, beneath
neoþanweard 05.10.05.04.02.03.01 A low position, the bottom
nēowe wīn 04.01.03.05.01.01 Wine
neowelnes 01.01.02.01.03.02 Abyss, chasm; 16.01.05 Hell, lower world, abode of the dead
neowol 01.01.02.01.02.02.04 Cliff; 01.01.02.01.03.02 Abyss, chasm; 01.03.01.06 Cloud; 05.10.05.03.04 Depth, deepness; 05.10.05.04.02.03.02 Reclining, rest; 05.12.05.13.03 To fall
neowollic 05.10.05.03.04 Depth, deepness
nēp 03.03.08 Emptiness
nēpflōd 01.01.03.04 Current, rush of water
(ge)ner 11.10.01 Protection, safekeeping; 11.10.01.02 Refuge, help, shelter
generednes 11.10.03 Salvation/deliverance from
generenes 11.10.03 Salvation/deliverance from
nergend 16.01.01.04.02 The Son, Christ
nergendlic 16.01.01.02.08 Salvation, redemption
(ge)nerian 11.10.01.01 Preservation from injury/destruction; 11.10.03 Salvation/deliverance from
generian 11.10 Safety, safeness
generian (wiþ) 11.10.01 Protection, safekeeping
neriende 16.01.01.02.08 Salvation, redemption
nering 11.10.01 Protection, safekeeping
generstede 11.10.01.02 Refuge, help, shelter; 14.01.03.01 Sanctuary
(ge)nesan 11.10.05 Escape
genesan 11.06.06 Turning

nese 09.07.03.01 A denial
nest 02.06.01.08 A lair, den; 02.06.08 Bird; 04.01.02.01 Food/sustenance; 04.01.02.04 Abundance of food
nestan 04.04.03 A spinning-house or chamber
nestlian 02.06.01.08 A lair, den
nestpohha 04.01.02.02.06.03 Food receptacle, basket
neta/nette 02.04.06.03.01 Cavities of internal organs
netel(e) 02.07.11 Plants/flowers (alphabetical order)
nett 02.06.09.02.10 Spider; 04.03.03 Net, drag-net, hunting net; 04.04.08.03 A fly-net, mosquito-net; 17.04.04 Fibrous materials
nettgern 17.04.04 Fibrous materials
genettian 04.03.03 Net, drag-net, hunting net
nettrāp 04.03.02 A snare, trap, noose
(ge)nēþan 06.02.07.06.02.02 Boldness, daring; 07.06.01.03 To be proud/arrogant
nēþing 06.02.07.06.02.02 Boldness, daring
neurisn 02.08.04.03 Paralysis
newesēoþa 02.04.03.03.06 Belly/abdomen
nic 09.07.03.01 A denial
niccan 09.07.03.02 Refusal, denial
nicēnisc 16.02.04.03.02 Parts of service
nicor 02.06.04.01.04 Hippopotamus; 02.06.10.01.05 Sea-monster
nicorhūs 02.06.01.08 A lair, den
nīdfaru 02.02 Death
nīed 06.02.04 Necessity, inevitability; 06.02.04.01 Want, need; 08.01.03.06 Adversity, affliction; 09.03.07.01.01 A runic letter; 12.05.06.03 Necessity,

constraint; 12.07 An obligation, bounden duty; 14.05.08 Captivity
nīed habban 06.02.04 Necessity, inevitability; 06.02.04.01 Want, need; 15.01.06 Poverty, indigence
nīed is 06.02.04 Necessity, inevitability
nīedan tō leornunge 06.01.06.02.03.04.03 To teach, instruct
(ge)nīedan 12.05.06.03 Necessity, constraint
genīedan tō 05.12.05.02.01 To come upon, meet with
genīedan tō nīedhǣmde 12.08.08.01.01 Rape
nīedbād 02.08.03.01 Extreme pain, torture, torment; 15.03.02 A tax
nīedbādere 15.03 Exaction of tax/tribute
nīedbehǣfdlic 06.02.04.01 Want, need
nīedbehǣfednes 06.02.04.01 Want, need
nīedbehǣfnes 06.02.04.01 Want, need
nīedbehēfe 06.02.04 Necessity, inevitability; 06.02.04.01 Want, need
nīedbehōf 06.02.04.01 Want, need
nīedbehōflic 06.02.04.01 Want, need
nīedbeþearf 06.02.04.01 Want, need
nīede 06.02.04 Necessity, inevitability; 12.05.06.03 Necessity, constraint; 12.07 An obligation, bounden duty
genīedelic 12.05.06.03 Necessity, constraint
nīedes 06.02.04 Necessity, inevitability
nīedful 06.02.04.01 Want, need
nīedhǣmed 12.08.08.01.01 Rape
nīedhīernes 12.01.01.09 Bondage, slavery
nīedhūs 04.05.03.05.02 A privy
nīedinga 12.05.06.03 Necessity, constraint

nīedling 05.12.01.09.03 A voyage; 12.01.01.09 Bondage, slavery; 14.05.08 Captivity
nīedmicel 11.07.04 Superiority, pre-eminence, primacy
nīednǣm 14.02.01.02.01 Open robbery, rapine, pillage
nīedscyld 12.07 An obligation, bounden duty
nīedsibb 02.03.02.03.06 Kinship, relationship
nīedþearf 06.02.04 Necessity, inevitability; 06.02.04.01 Want, need; 08.01.03.06 Adversity, affliction; 12.05.06.03 Necessity, constraint; 12.07 An obligation, bounden duty
nīedþearflic 06.02.04.01 Want, need; 11.07.01 Utility, usefulness
nīedþearflīce 06.02.04 Necessity, inevitability; 11.07.01 Utility, usefulness
nīedþearfnes 06.02.04.01 Want, need; 12.05.06.03 Necessity, constraint
nīedþēow 12.01.01.09 Bondage, slavery
nīedþing 06.02.04.01 Want, need
nīedþrafung 07.05.01 Censure, reproof, rebuke
nīedwǣdla 15.01.06 Poverty, indigence
nīehsta 02.03.02.03.06.01 Kinsman, relative; 08.01.02.03.01 An acquaintance, friend, associate
(ge)nīehsta 12.06.03.03 A neighbour
nīehstan 05.11.10.02 End, completion
nierwan 07.05.01 Censure, reproof, rebuke
(ge)nierwan 08.01.03.07.02 Misery, trouble, affliction; 11.11.01 A physical difficulty, strait; 14.05.08.01 Prison, confinement, durance
genierwan 03.03.04.01.02 A great number, multitude; 05.10.05.02.03 To reduce, make thin(ner)

nīeten 02.06 Animal; 02.06.02.01.03 Cattle
nīetencynn 02.06.02.01.03 Cattle
nīetenlic 12.08.07.01.02 Brutishness
nīetenlīce 12.08.07.01.02 Brutishness
nīetennes 12.08.07.01.02 Brutishness
nift 02.03.02.03.05 Descendant; 02.03.02.03.06.02.03 Child of brother/sister; 02.03.02.03.06.02.05 Step relationships
nīgecyrre 16.02.04.10.01 Conversion
nīgehālgod 16.02.04.07.05.01 Ordination
nī(ge)hwurfed 16.02.04.10.01 Conversion
nī(ge)hwyrfed 16.02.04.10.01 Conversion
nigend healf 03.03.03.04.08.01 Eight and a half
nigende 03.03.03.04.09 Nine
nīghworfen 16.02.04.10.01 Conversion
nigon 03.03.03.04.09 Nine
nigonfeald 03.03.03.04.09 Nine
nigongilde 14.03.03.09.02 Atonement
nigongylde 14.03.03.09.02 Atonement
nigonnihte 05.11.06.03.01.04 (Of lunar cycle) so many nights old
nigontēoþa 03.03.03.04.19 Nineteen; 03.03.03.04.27 Ninety
nigontīene 03.03.03.04.19 Nineteen
nigontig 03.03.03.04.27 Ninety
nigontȳnlic 03.03.03.04.19 Nineteen; 05.11.06.02.02.01 Adjustment in calculation
nigonwintre 02.01.04 Age
nigoþa 03.03.03.04.09 Nine
nigoþe 03.03.03.04.09 Nine
nīgslȳcod 03.01.12 Brightness, light
nihstig 04.01.01.06.01 Abstinence from food, fast

niht 05.11.02 A time, particular time, occasion; 05.11.03.01.05 A day; 05.11.04.02 Night, night time; 05.11.04.02.01 Sunset
nihtbealu 02.02.04 Killing, violent death, destruction; 05.06.01 Devastation, laying waste
nihtbutorflēoge 02.06.09.02.04 Butterfly, moth
nihtēage 02.05.09 Faculty of sight; 02.08.07.02.01 Defective vision
nihteald 05.11.07.03.01.01 Yesterday
nihtegale 02.06.08.05 Forest bird, wild-fowl
nihtegesa 06.01.08.06.03 Cause of fear, terror, horror
nihterne 05.11.04.02 Night, night time
nihternes 05.11.04.02 Night, night time
nihternum 05.11.04.02 Night, night time
nihtes 05.11.04.02 Night, night time
nihtfeormung 04.01.02.04.05.01 Hospitality, harbouring, entertaining
nihtgenga 16.01.03 A spectre, ghost, demon, goblin
nihtgenge 02.06.04.01.05 Hyena
niht(ge)rīm 05.11.06.02 Reckoning/computation of time
nihtgild 16.02.04.12 Sacrifice, a sacrifice
nihtglōm 05.11.04.02.01 Sunset
nihthelm 05.11.04.02.01 Sunset
nihthræfn 02.06.08.05 Forest bird, wild-fowl
nihthrōc 02.06.08.05 Forest bird, wild-fowl
nihthwīl 05.11.03.01.05 A day
genihtian 05.11.04.02.01 Sunset
nihtlang 05.11.04.02 Night, night time
nihtlic 05.11.04.02 Night, night time
nihtnihstig 04.01.01.06.01 Abstinence from food, fast

nihtrest 02.05.04 Sleepiness, drowsiness, sleep; 04.05.04.05 A bed, bedstead
nihtsang 16.02.04.05.09 The hour or service of Compline; 16.02.05.10.04 Choir books, etc.
nihtsangbōc 16.02.05.10.04 Choir books, etc.
nihtscada 02.07.11 Plants/flowers (alphabetical order)
nihtscūa 05.11.04.02.01 Sunset
nihtslǣp 02.05.04 Sleepiness, drowsiness, sleep
genihtsumian 06.02.05.03 Satisfaction, repletion
nihtwacu 05.11 A time, period of time
nihtwæcce 05.11 A time, period of time
nihtwaru 04.04.07.05 Night-wear
nihtweard 11.10.02.02 Watchful care, keeping guard
nihtweorc 11.01 Action, doing, performance
nīlǣred 16.02.04.10.01 Conversion
niman 04 Consumption of food/drink; 06.01.03.02 Dialectics, logic; 06.01.07.06 Mental acceptance, belief; 07.01.01 Choice, election
niman in 05.02.02 Nature, established order of things
niman on gemynde 06.01.04 Faculty of memory
niman tō 02.07.01 To grow
niman tō þām miclan hāde 11.01.05.02 Furtherance, promotion
niman ūp 02.02.05 A burial, burying
(ge)niman 03.03.07.01 Division, partition, separation; 04.03 Hunting, the chase; 04.05.03.03.01 Lodgings, quarters; 05.10.05.04.01.02 Contents, what is included; 05.12.01 To go, progress, travel (usually on land); 05.12.02.01 To fetch, bring, bear, conduct; 05.12.02.02 To carry off, remove; 06.01.04 Faculty of memory; 06.01.05.01 Understanding; 10.01.01.01 Receiving, gaining, getting; 10.03.04 Provision, supply; 10.04 To take; 10.04.01 To hold, have; 10.04.02.01 To pluck, gather; 10.04.02.02 To seize, take, grasp, lay hold on; 10.04.03 To take away, remove; 11.01.01 Practice, exercise, doing; 13.02.05.01.02 To gain by fighting; 14.02.01.02 Wrongful taking, theft; 14.02.01.02.01 Open robbery, rapine, pillage; 15.01.01.01 Holding of land
(ge)niman lāre 06.01.06.02.03.03 To study, apply oneself to learning
(ge)niman tō 10.01.01.01 Receiving, gaining, getting
geniman 06.01.01.01.01 Thought, cogitation, meditation; 10 Having, owning, possession; 11.03.01.03 Finding, discovery; 11.07 Use (made of things), service; 12.05.06.01 Restraint, check, curb, control; 13.02.03.01.03 To occupy a conquered land
geniman æfest tō 07.03.01.03 To loathe, hate, abhor
nimung 10.04.02.01 To pluck, gather
niomian 18.02.07.02.03 Stringed instruments
genip 01.03.01.06 Cloud; 02.08.07.02.01 Defective vision; 03.01.13 Darkness, obscurity; 08.01.03.06 Adversity, affliction
(ge)nīpan 03.01.13.02 A growing dark, darkening
genipfull 01.03.01.06 Cloud

genipu 03.01.13.03 Overshadowing
nirewett 02.08.08.01 Pain in the chest; 05.10.02 Narrowness, scantiness of space; 05.12.01.03.01.02 A cutting, pass; 14.05.08.01 Prison, confinement, durance
nirwþ 14.05.08.01 Prison, confinement, durance
nīsoden 04.01.02.02.05.02 To boil
nist(i)an 02.06.01.08 A lair, den
nistl(i)an 02.06.01.08 A lair, den
nīþ 08.01.03.06 Adversity, affliction; 08.01.03.09.05 Enmity; 08.01.03.09.08 Envy, jealousy; 12.05.04 Strife, hostility; 12.08.06.02 Wickedness, evil; 12.08.06.02.01 Wrong, evil-doing; 13.02.02 Battle; 16.01.05 Hell, lower world, abode of the dead
nīþan 08.01.03.09.08 Envy, jealousy
nīþcwalu 05.06 Destruction, dissolution, loss, breaking
nīþcwealm 05.06 Destruction, dissolution, loss, breaking
nīþdraca 02.06.10.01.01 Dragon
niþemest 03.03.05.01.03 Inferior; 05.10.05.04.02.03.01 A low position, the bottom; 12.08.06.02.04 Darkness, evil
niþer 03.03.05.01.03 Inferior
niþer āscūfan 05.12.02.06 To push, impel, thrust
niþer āsīgan 05.12.01.04.01.04 To stumble, trip, strike (with the foot)
niþer āstīgan 05.12.05.13 To go down, descend
niþer gān 05.12.05.13 To go down, descend
niþera 03.03.05.01.03 Inferior; 05.10.05.04.02.03.01 A low position, the bottom
niþer(a) 05.10.05.04.02.03 Laid below
niþera lippa 02.04.03.01.03.06 Mouth
niþerāsettan 05.10.05.04.02.03 Laid below
niþerāstīgende 05.12.05.13 To go down, descend
niþerāstreht 05.10.05.04.02.03.02 Reclining, rest
niþerāworpen 13.02.05.02 Defeat
niþerbogen 05.10.06.02.02 Curvature, bend, twist
niþerdǣl 05.10.05.04.02.03.01 A low position, the bottom
niþer(e) 05.10.05.04.02.02 Under, beneath
niþerecg 05.10.05.04.11.01 A bound, limit
niþerfaran 05.12.05.13 To go down, descend
niþerflōre 04.05.02.09 A storey
niþergang 05.12.05.13 To go down, descend
niþergewend 05.10.06.02.02 Curvature, bend, twist
niþerheald 05.10.05.04.02.03 Laid below
niþerhrēosende 05.12.05.13.03 To fall
niþerhryre 05.12.05.13.03 To fall
(ge)niþerian 07.09.02 Disgrace, shaming, humiliation; 12.05.06.02 Oppression; 14.03.03.01 Accusation; 14.03.03.09.01 Unfavourable judgement, condemnation
(ge)niþerian tō 14.03.03.09 A sentence, judgement, ruling
(ge)niþerigendlic 14.03.03.09.01 Unfavourable judgement, condemnation
niþerlǣtan 06.01.08.06.07 Despair

niþerlang 05.10.05.04.04 A descent, slope, incline
niþerlecgung 02.02.05 A burial, burying
niþerlic 01.01.02.01.03.03 Valley; 03.03.05.01.03 Inferior; 07.07 Humility
niþernes 05.10.05.04.02.03.01 A low position, the bottom
geniþerod 14.03.03.09 A sentence, judgement, ruling
niþeronwend 05.10.05.04.04 A descent, slope, incline
niþersceotende 05.12.05.13 To go down, descend
niþerscyfe 05.12.05.13 To go down, descend
niþersige 05.12.05.13 To go down, descend
niþerstige 05.12.05.13 To go down, descend
niþerstigende 05.12.05.13 To go down, descend
niþertorfian 07.09.02 Disgrace, shaming, humiliation
(ge)niþerung 16.01.05.01 Damnation, perdition, reprobation
geniþerung 07.09.02 Disgrace, shaming, humiliation
niþerweard(es) 05.10.05.04.02.03 Laid below
niþeweard 05.10.05.04.02.02 Under, beneath; 05.10.05.04.02.03.01 A low position, the bottom
niþeweard fōt 02.04.03.04.02.05.02 Sole
nīþful 08.01.03.09.03 Malevolence, malice; 08.01.03.09.08 Envy, jealousy
nīþfullīce 08.01.03.09.03 Malevolence, malice
nīþgæst 08.01.03.09.05 Enmity
nīþgetēon 13.02.03.01 An attack, assault

nīþ(ge)weorc 08.01.03.09.03 Malevolence, malice
nīþgrama 08.01.03.09.03 Malevolence, malice
nīþgrim 08.01.03.09.11 Hardheartedness, cruelty, severity
nīþhata 08.01.03.09.05 Enmity
nīþheard 06.02.07.06 Courage, boldness, valour
nīþhell 16.01.05 Hell, lower world, abode of the dead
nīþhete 08.01.03.07.02 Misery, trouble, affliction; 08.01.03.09.03 Malevolence, malice; 08.01.03.09.04 Hatred
nīþhycgende 08.01.03.09.03 Malevolence, malice
nīþhygdig 08.01.03.09.06 Hostility
nīþhygdig 08.01.03.09.03 Malevolence, malice
nīþig 08.01.03.09.08 Envy, jealousy
nīþing 14.02 Lawlessness
genīþla 05.08.02 Violence, force; 08.01.03.09.05 Enmity
nīþlīce 06.02.07.07 Cowardice, pusillanimity
nīþloca 14.05.08.01 Prison, confinement, durance
nīþplega 13.02.02 Battle
(ge)niþrad 16.01.05.02.02 Other terms for devils
nīþsceaþa 08.01.03.09.05 Enmity
nīþscipe 12.08.06.02 Wickedness, evil
nīþsele 04.05.03.02.02.03 Disagreeable dwellings
nīþsynn 12.08.06.02.05 Misdeed, sin; 16.02.01.13 Evil-doing, transgression, sin
niþþas 02.03.01 People
nīþweorc 13.02.02 Battle

nīþwracu 14.05 Punishment
nīþwundor 06.01.08.04.01 Premonition, prophecy
nīwan 05.11.07.04.03 Newness, novelty
nīwan stefne 05.11.09.06 Frequency, repetition
nīwanācenned 02.01.04.01 Youth
nīw(an)bacen 04.01.02.02.05.04 Baking
nīwcend 02.01.04.01 Youth
nīwcilct 03.01.14.03 White/whiteness
nīwcumen 05.12.05.02.03 To arrive; 16.02.04.07.05.01.01 Going into a monastery, admission; 16.02.04.10.01 Conversion
nīwe 03.06.02 Difference, diversity, dissimilarity; 05.11.06.03.01.03 Newness/crescent phase; 05.11.07.04.03 Newness, novelty; 05.11.09.06 Frequency, repetition; 06.01.06.04.01 What is uncertain/unknown; 11.04.03 (Of ability) low, mean, of less worth; 11.12.02.02 Amendment, setting right, reparation; 16.02.04.10.01 Conversion
nīwerne 02.01.04.01 Youth
nīwfyllan 10.03.04.01 Restitution, making good, repayment
nīw(ge)fara 12.04.03 A stranger
(ge)nīwian 05.11.07.04.03.01 Renewal, restoration; 05.11.09.06 Frequency, repetition; 17.02.04.01 Repairing, renewing
genīwian 05.11.06.03.01.03 Newness/crescent phase
nīwlic 02.07.01 To grow
nīwlīce 05.11.07.04.03 Newness, novelty
nīwlinga 05.11.09.06 Frequency, repetition
nīwnes 02.01.04.01 Youth; 05.11.06.03.01.03 Newness/crescent phase; 05.11.07.04.03 Newness, novelty
nīwtyrwed 05.12.01.09.03.01.02 Of/concerning a ship, naval
(ge)nīwung 05.11.10.01.01 Origin
nīwunga 05.11.07.04.03.01 Renewal, restoration
nō þon lange 05.11.07.04 Future, time to come
noctern 16.02.04.05.01 The hour or service of Nocturns
(ge)nōg bēon/wesan 03.03.04.02 A sufficiency, sufficient supply
genōg 03.03.04.02 A sufficiency, sufficient supply; 03.03.04.02.01 Abundance; 03.03.06.02 Fullness
genōgian 03.03.04.02.01 Abundance
nōht(e) þon lǣs 03.06 Comparison
nōhte þȳ lǣs 03.06 Comparison
non 16.02.03.03.02 A monk
nōn 05.11.04.01.03 Mid-day, noon; 16.02.04.05.07 The hour or service of Nones
nōnas 05.11.06.01 Cycle of the year
nōnbelle 16.02.05.05.02 A church/monastery bell
nōngereord 04.01.02.04.01.01 Meal at particular time of day
nōnhring 02.05.10.13.01.01 Stroke/sound of a bell
nōnmete 04.01.02.04.01.01 Meal at particular time of day
nōnsang 16.02.04.05.07 The hour or service of Nones
nōntīd 05.11.04.01.03 Mid-day, noon
nōntūma 05.11.04.01.03 Mid-day, noon
normandig 12.06.01.03 The Continent
norþ 01.01.01.01 North
norþan 01.01.01.01 North
norþanēastan 01.01.01.01.01 North-east

norþanēastanwind 01.03.01.05.01 Winds from particular points
norþ(an)hymbre 02.03.03.05.01.09 Northumbrians; 12.06.01.01 England
norþanweard 01.01.01.01 North
norþanwestan 01.01.01.01.02 North-west
norþanwestanwind 01.03.01.05.01 Winds from particular points
norþ(an)wind 01.03.01.05.01 Winds from particular points
norþcroft 04.02 Farm
norþdǣl 01.01.01.01 North
norþdene 02.03.03.06.05 Scandinavian
norþduru 04.05.02.12 Gate/doorway of a building
norþēast 01.01.01.01.01 North-east
norþēastende 01.01.01.01.01 North-east
norþēasterne 01.01.01.01.01 North-east
norþēasthyrne 01.01.01.01.01 North-east
norþēastlang 01.01.01.01.01 North-east
norþēastrodor 01.02.01 Heaven(s), sky
norþefes 05.10.05.04.11.01 A bound, limit
norþende 01.01.01.01 North
norþerne 01.01.01.01 North; 02.03.03.04 An inhabitant; 02.03.03.06.02 Germany and Low Countries; 02.03.03.06.05 Scandinavian
norþerra 01.01.01.01 North
norþeweard 01.01.01.01 North
norþfolc 02.03.03.05.01.08 People of Norfolk; 02.03.03.05.01.09 Northumbrians; 12.06.01.01 England
norþfresan 02.03.03.06.02 Germany and Low Countries
norþgārsecg 01.01.03.01.02.03 Sea in particular area
norþgemǣre 05.10.05.04.11.01 A bound, limit

norþgyrwas 02.03.03.05.01.02 Gyrwe
norþheald 01.01.01.01 North
norþhealf 01.01.01.01 North
norþhere 13.02.10.01.02.02.01 Types of army
norþhylde 01.01.02.01.02.02.03 Slope
norþhymbre 02.03.03.05.01.09 Northumbrians
norþhymbrisc 02.03.03.05.01.09 Northumbrians
norþhyrne 01.01.01.01 North
norþland 01.01.01.01 North
norþlang 01.01.01.01 North
norþlanu 05.12.01.03.01.04 A lane, street
norþlēode 02.03.03.05.01.01 Angles
norþlic 01.01.01.01 North
norþmandisc 02.03.03.06.01 Peoples of France
norþmann 02.03.03.04 An inhabitant; 02.03.03.05.05 A northern people; 02.03.03.06.05 Scandinavian
norþmearc 05.10.05.04.11.01 A bound, limit
norþmest 01.01.01.01 North
norþmirce 02.03.03.05.01.06 Mercians
norþor 01.01.01.01 North
norþportic 04.05.02.12.01 A porch, covered entrance
norþrihte(s) 01.01.01.01 North
norþrodor 01.02.01 Heaven(s), sky
norþsǣ 01.01.03.01.02.02 Sea-channel; 01.01.03.01.02.03 Sea in particular area
norþscēata 01.01.01.01 North; 01.01.02.01.01.03.01 Promontory, headland, cape
norþsciphere 13.02.10.03.01 A fleet
norþscottas 02.03.03.05.03 The Scots
norþþēod 02.03.03.05.05 A northern people

norþþunor 01.03.01.03.01.01
Thundering, thunder
norþwēalas 02.03.03.05.02 The
British/Welsh/Bretons; 12.06.01.02
Britain
norþwēalcynn 02.03.03.05.02 The
British/Welsh/Bretons
norþweall 04.05.02.02 A wall
norþweard 01.01.01.01 North
norþweardes 01.01.01.01 North
norþweg 05.12.01.03.01 A means of
access; 12.06.01.03 The Continent
norþwest 01.01.01.01.02 North-west
norþwestende 01.01.01.01.02 North-west
norþwestgemǣre 05.10.05.04.11.01 A
bound, limit
norweg 12.06.01.03 The Continent
nōse 01.01.02.01.01.03.01 Promontory,
headland, cape
nostle 04.04.07.11 A headcloth, covering
for the head
nosþirl 02.04.03.01.03.04 Nose
nosu 02.04.03.01.03.04 Nose
nos(u)gris(t)le 02.04.03.01.03.04 Nose;
02.04.05.07 Cartilage, gristle
nōt 09.03.07 Writing
notere 09.03.07.03 A scribe, copyist
notgeorn 17 Work, doings, actions,
labour
notian 17.02.02 An office, function,
employment
(ge)notian 04 Consumption of food/drink
genotian 11.07 Use (made of things),
service
genotod 09.03.07.04 To make a symbol,
mark
notu 11.07 Use (made of things), service;
11.07.03 Use, advantage, profit; 12.02
A public office; 17.02.02 An office,
function, employment

notwierþe 11.07.01 Utility, usefulness
notwrītere 09.03.07.03 A scribe, copyist
noþ 02.08.05.01 Swelling
nōþ 06.02.07.06.02.02 Boldness, daring
nouember 05.11.03.01.03.01 Specific
months
nouembermōnaþ 05.11.03.01.03.01
Specific months
nōw 05.12.01.09.03.01 A ship, boat
nōwend 05.12.01.09.03 A voyage
nū 05.11.07.01 Contemporary, coeval;
06.01.08.05.01 Amazement,
astonishment, wonder, admiration;
05.11.07.02 The present (time);
05.11.02 A time, particular time,
occasion
nū gīet 03.03.04.03 Growth, increase;
05.11.07.03.02 Earlier, antecedent
nū hwænne 05.11.07.01 Contemporary,
coeval
nū hwīlum 05.11.07.02 The present
(time)
nū hwonne 05.11.07.02 The present
(time)
nū lā 06.01.08.05.01 Amazement,
astonishment, wonder, admiration
nū gēn 05.11.07.03.02 Earlier, antecedent
nū gēo 05.11.07.03.02 Earlier, antecedent
nū rihte 05.11.07.01 Contemporary,
coeval
nū tō gēare 05.11.03.01 A year
nū þā 05.11.07.02 The present (time)
nū (þonne) 05.03.01.03 Reason, cause
genumen 02.05.07.01.01 (Of food, etc.)
bad, tainted, rancid
numol 05.06 Destruction, dissolution,
loss, breaking; 06.01.05.02
Intelligence
nūna 05.11.07.02 The present (time)
nunfǣmne 16.02.03.03.03 A nun

nunhīred 16.02.05.04 A monastery/convent
nunlīf 16.02.03.03.03 A nun
nun(nan)mynster 16.02.05.04 A monastery/convent
nunne 16.02.03.02.07.01 A priest of a church or minster; 16.02.03.03.03 A nun
nunscrūd 16.02.05.07 Monastic garb
nȳdbebod 12.03.03 A command, bidding, order
nȳdboda 09.06.02.01.06.03 Ill tidings
nȳdbrice 11.07 Use (made of things), service
nȳdbysgu 08.01.03.06 Adversity, affliction
nȳdbysig 08.01.03.06 Adversity, affliction
nȳdcleofa 14.05.08.01 Prison, confinement, durance
nȳdcosting 08.01.03.07.02 Misery, trouble, affliction
nȳddǣda 06.02.04 Necessity, inevitability
genȳdenlic 12.05.06.03 Necessity, constraint
nȳdfara 12.06.05.01 State of exile, banishment
nȳdgedāl 02.02 Death
nȳdgefēra 12.04.01 A fellow, companion, associate, comrade
nȳdgenga 12.06.05.01 State of exile, banishment
nȳdgestealla 12.04.01 A fellow, companion, associate, comrade
genȳdgewald 12.05.06.02.01 Tyranny
nȳdgrāp 10.04.02 To grasp, take hold of
nȳdgripe 10.04.02 To grasp, take hold of
nȳdgylta 15.04 A debt, due

nȳdhǣmedre 12.08.08.01.02.01 Fornication, adultery
nȳdhǣmestre 12.08.08.01.02.01.01 An adulterer/-ess, whore, prostitute
nȳdhelp 11.12.02 Aid, help, succour
nȳdlic 06.02.04 Necessity, inevitability
(ge)nȳdmǣg 02.03.02.03.06.02 Close relationship
nȳdmægen 12.05.06.03 Necessity, constraint
nȳdmāge 02.03.02.03.06.02 Close relationship
nȳdnǣman 12.08.08.01.01 Rape
nȳdnes 06.02.04 Necessity, inevitability
nȳdnima 12.05.06.02 Oppression
nȳdniman 10.04.02.02 To seize, take, grasp, lay hold on; 12.08.08.01.01 Rape
nȳdnimend 14.02.01.02.01 Open robbery, rapine, pillage
nȳdnimu 14.02.01.02.01 Open robbery, rapine, pillage
nȳdnimung 12.08.08.01.01 Rape; 14.02.01.02.01 Open robbery, rapine, pillage
nȳdriht 14.01.05 Service, obligation, duty; 15.04 A debt, due
nȳdsyndrig 05.10.05 A space, span
nȳdþēowetling 12.01.01.09 Bondage, slavery
nȳdþēowigan 12.05.06.03 Necessity, constraint
nȳdwracu 08.01.03.06 Adversity, affliction
nȳdwrǣclīce 05.08.02 Violence, force
nȳdwyrhta 06.02.04 Necessity, inevitability
genyht 03.03.04.02 A sufficiency, sufficient supply; 03.03.04.02.01 Abundance
genyhtful 03.03.04.02.01 Abundance

genyhtlīce 03.03.04.02.01 Abundance
(ge)nyhtsum 03.03.04.02.01 Abundance
(ge)nyhtsumian 03.03.04.02 A sufficiency, sufficient supply; 03.03.04.02.01 Abundance
(ge)nyhtsumiende 03.03.04.02.01 Abundance
genyhtsumlīce 03.03.04.02 A sufficiency, sufficient supply; 03.03.04.02.01 Abundance
(ge)nyhtsumnes 03.03.04.02 A sufficiency, sufficient supply
genyhtsumnes 08.01.01.03.08 Happiness, well-being, prosperity
genyhtsumung 03.03.04.02.01 Abundance
nymþe 03.04.01 Singularity, peculiarity; 09.07.03.01 A denial
nypel 02.06.01.02 Head
nyten 06.01.06.04 Ignorance
nytende 06.01.06.04 Ignorance
nytenlic 06.01.06.04 Ignorance
nytennes 06.01.06.04 Ignorance; 06.01.06.04.02 Ignorance, uninstructedness; 07.09.03 Infamy, ignominy, shame; 12.04.03 A stranger
nytlic 11.07.01 Utility, usefulness; 11.07.03 Use, advantage, profit
nytlīce 11.07.01 Utility, usefulness
nytlicnes 11.07.01 Utility, usefulness; 11.07.03 Use, advantage, profit
nytnes 11.07.01 Utility, usefulness; 11.07.03 Use, advantage, profit; 15.05 Trade, traffic, commerce
nytt 11.07.01 Utility, usefulness; 11.07.03 Use, advantage, profit
(ge)nyttian 11.07 Use (made of things), service
nytt(o) 11.07.01 Utility, usefulness; 12.03.01 Direction, care, management, supervision; 17.02.02 An office, function, employment
nyttol 11.07.01 Utility, usefulness
nyttung 11.07.03 Use, advantage, profit
nytþearflic 11.07.01 Utility, usefulness
nytweorþlicnes 11.07.01 Utility, usefulness
nytwierþe 11.07.01 Utility, usefulness; 11.07.03 Use, advantage, profit
nytwierþlic 11.07.01 Utility, usefulness
nytwierþlīce 11.07.01 Utility, usefulness
nytwierþnes 11.07.01 Utility, usefulness
nyþer āsīgan 05.12.05.13.03 To fall
october 05.11.03.01.03.01 Specific months
octobermōnaþ 05.11.03.01.03.01 Specific months
ōcusta 02.04.03.04.01 Arm
ōden 04.02.04.04.05 To thresh (corn)
ōdencolc 04.02.04.04.05 To thresh (corn)
oemseten wīngeardes 02.07.09.02 Particular fruits (alphabetical order); 04.02.04.05.03 A wine-growing country
of āceorfan 04.02.04.05.04.01.01 Pruning/lopping; 05.06.02 Cleaving, splitting, cutting
of ādōn 03.04.01 Singularity, peculiarity; 05.06.08 A plucking, taking away
of ādrīfan 05.12.05.03.04 To come/go out from
of ādrincan 04.01.03 Drinking
of āgān 05.12.05.03.03 To depart, leave, set out
of āhēawan 05.06.02 Cleaving, splitting, cutting
of āpluccian 05.06.08 A plucking, taking away
of āpullian 05.06.08 A plucking, taking away

of āsciran 05.06.02 Cleaving, splitting, cutting
of āscrēadian 04.02.04.05.04.01.01 Pruning/lopping
of āslēan 05.06.02 Cleaving, splitting, cutting
of āsnīþan 05.06.02 Cleaving, splitting, cutting
of āstingan 02.02.04.03 To kill, slay
of ātēon 05.06.08 A plucking, taking away; 05.12.02.05 To pull, drag, draw
of āweorpan 05.10.04.04.02 Removal, taking away
of āwyrtrumad 05.06.08 A plucking, taking away
of belimpe 05.03.02.01 Chance, hap, event
of dōn 05.06.08 A plucking, taking away; 05.12.02.05 To pull, drag, draw
of drincan 04.01.03.02 To drink heavily, get drunk
of druncnian 04.01.03.02 To drink heavily, get drunk
of feorrian 05.12.05.03.04 To come/go out from
of gān 05.12.05.03.04 To come/go out from
of gemynde 06.01.04.03 Forgetfulness
of nīede 06.02.04 Necessity, inevitability
of stede 05.11.07.01 Contemporary, coeval
of strīcan 04.06.01 Clean
ofācēapian 14.05.04.01 A fine
ofācennan 02.01.03.03.02 To bring forth, produce
ofācsian 06.01.06.01 Knowledge, cognizance, knowing
ofādræfed 12.06.05.01 State of exile, banishment

ofādrȳgan 03.01.18 Dryness (not wetness)
ofærnan 05.12.01.05.01 Modes of riding; 05.12.05.07 To go beyond, pass
ofǣte 04.01.02.01 Food/sustenance
ofǣte/ofeten 02.04.02.01 Fat/plump
ofāniman 10.04.03 To take away, remove
ofāsceacan 05.10.04.04.02 Removal, taking away
ofāslēan 02.02.04.03 To kill, slay
ofāstīgan 05.12.05.13 To go down, descend
ofbēatan 02.02.04.04.03 Putting to death
ofblindian 02.08.07.02.01 Defective vision
ofcalen 03.01.11 Coldness, coolness
ofcirran 05.06.01 Devastation, laying waste; 05.12.05.03.04 To come/go out from
ofclipian 02.05.10.15.01 To raise (the voice), raise up (noise); 12.03.04 A request, prayer
ofcuman 05.12.05.03.04 To come/go out from
ofcumende 09.03.02.03 Composition (inflectional or compounding)
ofcyrf 02.08.12.02.06 Surgical; 03.03.07 A part, division, portion; 05.06.02 Cleaving, splitting, cutting
ofdǣle 05.10.05.04.02.03 Laid below; 05.10.05.04.04 A descent, slope, incline
ofdelfan 05.06.08 A plucking, taking away
ofdēman 07.01 Appraisal, appraising
ofdōn 04.04.07 Trappings, equipment, garb
ofdrǣdd 06.01.08.06.02 Great fear, terror, horror
ofdūne 05.10.05.04.02.03 Laid below

ofdūne āstīgan 05.12.05.13 To go down, descend
ofdūneheald 05.10.05.04.02.03 Laid below
ofdūneonwend 05.10.05.04.02.03 Laid below
ofdūnesettan 05.10.05.04.02.03 Laid below
ofdūneweard(es) 05.10.05.04.02.03 Laid below
ofdūnrihte 05.10.05.04.02.03 Laid below
ofearmian 08.01.02.05 Compassion
ofearmung 08.01.02.05 Compassion
ofēhtan 12.05.06.02.02 Persecution
ofen 17.05.02 A hearth, fireplace
ofenbacen 04.01.02.02.05.04 Baking
ofenraca 17.05.02 A hearth, fireplace
ofenraca/-u 04.01.02.02.06 Kitchen
ofer (…) hēafod 05.10.05.04.02.04 Above
ofer ǣlc gerīm 03.03.04.01.03 An immense quantity, immensity, immense number
ofer bæc 05.12.05.11 To turn back, retreat
ofer bæc būgan 11.10.04 Flight
ofer bēon/wesan 12.01.01.01 Rule, domination, direction
ofer dēop gedræg 01.01.03.01.02.06 Surging, rolling, heaving of waves
ofer eall 05.10.04.03 Presence
ofer gemet 03.03.04.01.03 An immense quantity, immensity, immense number
ofer midne dæg 05.11.04.01.03 Mid-day, noon
ōfer 01.01.02.01.01.03 Shore, bank; 05.10.05.04.11.01 A bound, limit
oferǣt 04.01.01.04 Gluttony, overeating, greediness; 04.01.02.04.02 Feast
oferǣte 04.01.01.04 Gluttony, overeating, greediness

oferbæcgetēung 02.08.07.06 Disorders of the neck
oferbebēodan 12.01.01.01 Rule, domination, direction
oferbecuman 05.03.02.01.01 An event, occurrence
oferberan 05.12.02 To move, set in motion
oferbīdan 02.01.02.02.02 Lifetime
oferbiternes 08.01.03.09.01.02 Bitterness, acrimony
oferblica 05.10.05.04.02 Face, surface
oferblissian 16.02.04 Worship, honour, praise
oferblīþe 08.01.01.03 Good feeling, joy, happiness
oferbrǣdan 05.10.05.04.12 The condition of being covered; 05.10.05.04.12.01 To bespread, cover with
oferbrǣdels 02.02.05.02 To prepare for burial; 04.04.08 A covering, curtain, veil, garment, etc.
oferbrāw 02.04.03.01.03.02 Eye
oferbrecan 14.02 Lawlessness
oferbregdan 05.10.05.04.12.01 To bespread, cover with
oferbrū(wa) 02.04.03.01.03.02 Eye
oferbrycg(i)an 05.12.01.03.04.01 Constructing/repairing bridges
ofercæfed 17.02.05.01 Ornamental object
oferceald 03.01.11 Coldness, coolness
ofercīdan 07.05.01 Censure, reproof, rebuke
ofercīdung 07.05.01 Censure, reproof, rebuke
ofercierr 05.12.05.06 To travel over/through/along, traverse
ofercierran 05.12.05.06 To travel over/through/along, traverse

oferclimban 05.12.05.12 To go up, ascend
oferclipian 02.05.10.15.01 To raise (the voice), raise up (noise)
ofercostung 12.05.06.02.03 Trouble, disturbance
ofercræft 06.01.07.04.02 Fraud, deceit, trick, trickery
ofercuman 05.03.02 Event, issue, result; 05.12.05.02.01 To come upon, meet with; 09.07.02 Contradiction; 10.01.02 Acquisition; 12.05.06 Grasp, power, control, mastery; 13.02.05.01.01 To overcome, conquer
ofercwealm 02.02 Death
ofercweþan 09.06.02.01.03 Recapitulation
ofercyme 05.12.05.02.03 To arrive
ofercymend 12.05.04.01.01 Fighting, a fight
ofercȳþan 14.03.03.03 Witness, testimony, attestation
oferdæg 05.11.06.02.02.01 Adjustment in calculation
oferdōn 12.08.07 Immoderation, excess
oferdōne þing 12.08.07 Immoderation, excess
oferdrenc/oferdrync 04.01.03.02 To drink heavily, get drunk
oferdrencan 04.01.03.02 To drink heavily, get drunk
oferdrenct 04.01.03.02 To drink heavily, get drunk
oferdrīfan 05.10.05.04.12 The condition of being covered; 09.07.02 Contradiction; 13.02.05.01.01 To overcome, conquer
oferdrincan 04.01.03.02 To drink heavily, get drunk
oferdrincere 04.01.03.02 To drink heavily, get drunk
oferdruncen 04.01.03.02 To drink heavily, get drunk
oferdruncennes 04.01.03.02 To drink heavily, get drunk
oferdruncolnes 04.01.03.02 To drink heavily, get drunk
oferēaca 03.03.04.03 Growth, increase; 03.03.07.02 What is left, remnant, remains
ofereald 02.01.04.03 Aging, growing old
oferealdormann 12.02.02 An assembly, meeting
oferetol 04.01.01.04 Gluttony, overeating, greediness
oferetolnes 04.01.01.04 Gluttony, overeating, greediness
oferfær 05.12.05.06 To travel over/through/along, traverse
oferfæreld 05.12.05.06 To travel over/through/along, traverse
oferfæst 05.12.04.01 Stability, firmness
oferfǣt 02.04.02.01 Fat/plump
oferfæþman 05.10.05.04.11 A circle, circuit, circumference
oferfaran 02.01.02.02.02 Lifetime; 05.11 A time, period of time; 05.12.01 To go, progress, travel (usually on land); 05.12.05.02.01 To come upon, meet with; 05.12.05.02.04 To go in, enter; 05.12.05.06 To travel over/through/along, traverse; 11.10.05 Escape
oferfeallan 05.12.05.13.03 To fall; 13.02.03.01 An attack, assault
oferfeng 04.04.10.02 A button, brooch
oferfeohtan 13.02.05.01.01 To overcome, conquer
oferfēran 05.12.05.02.01 To come upon, meet with; 05.12.05.03.03 To depart,

leave, set out; 05.12.05.06 To travel over/through/along, traverse; 05.12.05.07.01 To pass by
oferferian 05.12.02 To move, set in motion
oferfērnes 05.12.01.03.03 A fordable place
oferfēþre 17.02.04.02.03 Carrying, carriage (of materials)
oferfindan 11.03.01.01 Trial, probation
oferflēde 01.01.03.06 Flood
oferflēon 05.12.01.07 To fly (with wings); 11.10.04 Flight
oferflēwednes 03.03.04.02.02.01 Superabundance, excess
oferflītan 09.07.02 Contradiction; 13.02.05.01.01 To overcome, conquer
oferflōwan 01.01.03.06 Flood; 03.03.04.02.02.01 Superabundance, excess; 03.03.06.02 Fullness
oferflōwedlicnes 03.03.04.02.02.01 Superabundance, excess
oferflōwend 03.03.04.02.02.01 Superabundance, excess; 12.08.07 Immoderation, excess
oferflōwe(n)dlic 03.03.04.02.02.01 Superabundance, excess; 12.08.07 Immoderation, excess
oferflōwendlīce 03.03.04.02.02.01 Superabundance, excess; 12.08.07 Immoderation, excess
oferflōwe(n)dnes 03.03.04.02.02.01 Superabundance, excess; 12.08.07 Immoderation, excess
oferflōwnes 03.03.04.02.02.01 Superabundance, excess; 07.06.04.01 Ostentation, showiness
oferfōn 14.05.08 Captivity
oferfrecednes 12.05.06.02 Oppression
oferfroren 03.01.11 Coldness, coolness

oferfull 03.03.06.02 Fullness
oferfundennes 11.03.01 Experience, trial, experiment
oferfylgan 05.12.05.10 To go behind, follow
oferfyllan 04.01.01.05 Satiety (of food)
oferfyllo 04.01.03.05 A drink/beverage
oferfyll(o) 04.01.01.04 Gluttony, overeating, greediness; 04.01.01.05 Satiety (of food)
oferfylnes 04.01.01.05 Satiety (of food)
oferfyr 05.10.05 A space, span
ofergǣgan 12.08.06.02.05.05 To sin (against), do wrong
ofergǣgednes 16.02.01.13 Evil-doing, transgression, sin
ofergǣgend 12.08.06.02.05.02 A sinner, transgressor
ofergān 05.07 Ending of existence, end of world; 05.10.05.04.12 The condition of being covered; 05.12.05.02.01 To come upon, meet with; 05.12.05.06 To travel over/through/along, traverse; 05.12.05.07 To go beyond, pass; 11.03.02 Advancement, progress; 12.05.06 Grasp, power, control, mastery; 12.08.06.02.05.05 To sin (against), do wrong; 13.02.05.01.01 To overcome, conquer
ofergangan 05.07 Ending of existence, end of world; 05.12.05.02.01 To come upon, meet with; 05.12.05.06 To travel over/through/along, traverse; 05.12.05.07 To go beyond, pass; 12.05.06 Grasp, power, control, mastery; 13.02.05.01.01 To overcome, conquer
ofergapian 11.06.01.01 Negligence, carelessness, heedlessness

ofergēare 02.01.04.03 Aging, growing old
ofergeatu 06.01.04.03.01 Forgetfulness, oblivion
ofer(ge)drync 04.01.03.02 To drink heavily, get drunk
ofer(ge)dyre 04.05.02.12 Gate/doorway of a building
ofergemet 12.08.07 Immoderation, excess
ofergēmnes 02.05.09.05 To watch, observe, survey
ofergenga 05.12.01.01 To go on a journey/expedition, travel
ofergenihtsumian 03.03.04.02.02.01 Superabundance, excess
ofergeong 05.12.05.06 To travel over/through/along, traverse
ofergēotan 03.01.12.02 A beam of light; 03.01.16.01 Moisture
ofergeotende 06.01.04.03 Forgetfulness
ofer(ge)set 12.01.01.05 A leader, administrator; 12.01.01.06.02 Superior
ofergeseted 05.10.04 Place, room
ofer(ge)standan 05.10.05.04.02.04 Above
ofergeswincfull 01.03.01.03 Bad weather
ofergetilian 12.05.06 Grasp, power, control, mastery
ofergetimbran 04.05 Building, construction
ofergeþyld 08.01.03.06 Adversity, affliction
ofer(ge)weorc 02.02.05.01.01 A grave, burial place, sepulchre; 04.05.02.08.02 A ceiling, inner roof
ofergewrit 09.03.07.07.02.01.01 A heading, title, superscription
ofergīeman 11.06.01 Neglect

ofergietan 06.01.04.03 Forgetfulness; 11.06.01.01 Negligence, carelessness, heedlessness
ofergīfre 04.01.01.04 Gluttony, overeating, greediness
ofergitolian 06.01.04.03 Forgetfulness
ofergitolnes 06.01.04.03 Forgetfulness
ofergittol 06.01.04.03 Forgetfulness
oferglenged 07.06.04.02 Extravagance
oferglēsan 09.04.03.02 Glossing
oferglīdan 05.12.05.06.01 To travel smoothly, slide, glide
ofergrǣdig 10.03.09.01.01 Covetousness, avarice
ofergrōwan 02.07.01 To grow
ofergumian 11.06.01.01 Negligence, carelessness, heedlessness
ofergyld 17.02.05.02 Goldsmith's art
ofergyldan 17.02.05.02 Goldsmith's art
ofergylden 17.02.05.02 Goldsmith's art
ofergyrd 04.04.07.01 Mode of dressing, fashion
ofergytnes 06.01.04.03.01 Forgetfulness, oblivion
oferhacele 04.04.07.07 A long outer garment, covering, cloak, etc.
oferhangen 05.10.05.04.12 The condition of being covered
oferhāt 03.01.09 Heat
oferhēafod 03.04.03 Generality
oferhēah 05.10.05.03.03 Height, loftiness, sublimity
oferhealdan 08.01.03.07.02 Misery, trouble, affliction; 11.06.01 Neglect
oferhealfhēafod 02.04.03.01.01 Top of head
oferhebban 11.06.01 Neglect
oferhebbendlic 16.01.01.01.01.02 Glory
oferhelian 03.01.13.03 Overshadowing; 05.10.05.04.12 The condition of being

1215

oferheling

covered; 09.05.04.01 Concealment, obscurity
oferheling 05.10.05.04.12 The condition of being covered
oferhelmian 05.10.05.04.12 The condition of being covered
oferhelung 04.04.07 Trappings, equipment, garb
oferheortnes 08.01.01.01 Ardour, fervour, strong feeling
oferhergian 13.02.03 To seek with active intent, attack
oferhīeran 02.05.10 Faculty of hearing; 12.01.01.12.02 Disobedience
oferhīernes 12.01.01.12.02 Disobedience; 14.02 Lawlessness
oferhige 07.06 Pride
oferhigendlīce 06.02.07.06.02.03 Presumption
oferhīgian 13.02.05.01.01 To overcome, conquer
oferhīrnes 14.05.04.01 A fine
oferhīwian 03.01.14 A colour; 05.13.01 Transformation, taking another shape
oferhlæstan 17.02.04.02.03 Carrying, carriage (of materials)
oferhlēapan 05.12.05.07 To go beyond, pass; 05.12.05.12.01 To reach up
oferhlēapend 05.12.05.12.01 To reach up
oferhlēoþrian 02.05.10.03 Noise, tumult, uproar; 05.12.05.07 To go beyond, pass
oferhlēoþur 02.05.10 Faculty of hearing
oferhlīfian 03.03.05.01.01 Principal/chief (of its class or type); 05.10.05.03.03 Height, loftiness, sublimity; 06.01.08.06.03.01 Causing dread, terrifying; 11.03.02 Advancement, progress

oferhlīfung 05.10.05.03.03 Height, loftiness, sublimity
oferhlūd 02.05.10.03 Noise, tumult, uproar
oferhlūde 02.05.10.03 Noise, tumult, uproar
oferhlȳde 02.05.10.03 Noise, tumult, uproar
oferhlȳp 05.12.05.12.01 To reach up
oferhlȳttrian 04.06.01.10 To separate objects already connected, unmix
oferhoga 07.06.01 Pride, arrogance
oferhogian 07.05.02 Contempt
oferhogiend 07.05.02 Contempt
oferhogodnes 07.06 Pride
oferholt 13.02.07.02 Order (of troops), array
oferhrēfan 04.05.02.08 Top of a building
oferhrēosan 05.12.05.13.03 To fall
oferhrops 04.01.01.04 Gluttony, overeating, greediness
oferhrȳred 05.06 Destruction, dissolution, loss, breaking
oferhwīt 03.01.14.03 White/whiteness
oferhycgan 07.05.02 Contempt
oferhygd 07.06 Pride; 07.06.01 Pride, arrogance; 12.08.01 Magnanimity, greatness of soul
oferhygdian 07.06 Pride
oferhygdig 07.06 Pride; 07.06.01.01 Proud, arrogant
oferhygdiglīce 07.06.01.02 Proudly, arrogantly
oferhygdlic 07.06.01.01 Proud, arrogant
oferhygdlīce 07.06.01.02 Proudly, arrogantly
oferhygdnes 07.06.01 Pride, arrogance
oferhylmend 06.01.07.04.04.02 Pretence, feigning, dissimulation
oferhȳre 11.06.01.01 Negligence, carelessness, heedlessness

oferhyrned 05.10.06.03 Projection, head, extremity (of anything)
oferīdellīce 11.08.03 Needless, useless, unprofitable
ofering 03.03.04.02.02.01 Superabundance, excess
oferlād 16.02.05.05.10 Relics, a collection of relics
oferlǣdan 05.10.05.04.12.01 To bespread, cover with; 09.04.03.01 A translation
oferlǣfan 03.03.07.02 What is left, remnant, remains
oferlagu 04.04.07.07 A long outer garment, covering, cloak, etc.
oferlecgan 04.01.01.05 Satiety (of food); 05.10.05.04.12 The condition of being covered; 05.10.05.04.12.01 To bespread, cover with
oferlēof 08.01.02.02.01 A favourite, loved one
oferlēoran 05.12.05.07 To go beyond, pass; 11.06.06.01 Abandonment (of principle); 12.08.06.02.05.05 To sin (against), do wrong
oferlēornes 12.08.06.02.05.01 Transgression, trespass; 16.02.01.13 Evil-doing, transgression, sin
oferlibban 02.01.02.02.02 Lifetime
oferlīce 03.03.04.02.02 Excess
oferlifa 04.01.01.04 Gluttony, overeating, greediness
oferlīhtan 03.01.12 Brightness, light; 05.12.05.13 To go down, descend
oferlīþan 05.12.01.09 To travel on water
oferlufu 08.01.02.02 Love, affection, care
oferlyftlic 01.02.01 Heaven(s), sky
ofermæcga 07.08.09 Renown, fame, glory
ofermæg 13.02.05.01 Victory

ofermægen 12 Power, might
ofermǣnan 09.07.02 Contradiction
ofermǣstan 04.01.02.04.03.01 To feed/nourish
ofermǣte 03.03.04.01.03 An immense quantity, immensity, immense number
ofermǣtlic 03.03.04.01.03 An immense quantity, immensity, immense number
ofermǣto/ofermētto 07.06.01 Pride, arrogance
ofermāþum 15.01.03 Treasure, riches, wealth
ofermearcung 09.03.07.05 To cover with writing, inscribe
ofermēde 07.06 Pride; 07.06.01.01 Proud, arrogant
ofermēdla 07.06.01 Pride, arrogance
ofermete 04.01.01.04 Gluttony, overeating, greediness
ofermicel 03.03.04.02.02 Excess
ofermicelnes 03.03.04.02.02 Excess
ofermistian 01.03.01.06.01 Cloud, mist; 06.01.07.05 Error, being astray
ofermōd 07.06.01 Pride, arrogance; 07.06.01.01 Proud, arrogant
ofermōdgung 07.06 Pride
ofermōdig 07.06.01.01 Proud, arrogant
ofermōd(ig)ian 07.06.01.03 To be proud/arrogant
ofermōdiglīce 07.06.01.02 Proudly, arrogantly
ofermōd(ig)nes 07.06.01 Pride, arrogance
ofermōdlic 07.06.01.01 Proud, arrogant
ofermōdlīce 07.06.01.02 Proudly, arrogantly
ofernēod 06.02.04.01 Want, need
oferniman 05.12.05.07 To go beyond, pass; 10.04.03 To take away, remove; 12.08.08.01.01 Rape
ofernōn 05.11.04.01.03 Mid-day, noon

oferplantian 04.02.04.02.04 Planting
oferprūt 07.06.01 Pride, arrogance; 07.06.01.01 Proud, arrogant
oferrǣdan 06.01.01.01.01 Thought, cogitation, meditation; 06.01.06.02.03.03.01 An act of reading
oferrǣdlīce 05.11.09.02 Frequent, of common occurrence
oferranc 07.06.04.02 Extravagance
oferreccan 06.02.06.03 Persuasion, prompting; 09.07.02 Contradiction; 11.03.01.01.01 Proof, demonstration
oferrencu 07.06.04.02 Extravagance
oferrīcsian 12.01.01.01 Rule, domination, direction
oferrīdan 05.12.01.05.01 Modes of riding
oferrōwan 05.12.01.09.01 To row
ofersǣlic 12.06.05 A foreign country
ofersǣlig 08.01.01.03.08.02 Good fortune, success
ofersǣlþ 08.01.01.03.05 Pleasure, delight
ofersǣwisc 12.06.05 A foreign country
ofersāwan 04.02.04.02.03 Sowing
oferscēadan 05.12.02.07.01 To throw, scatter
oferscead(ew)ian 03.01.13.03 Overshadowing
ofersceatt 15.04.01 Lending of money
oferscēawian 12.03.01 Direction, care, management, supervision
oferscēawigend 17.02.01 Management of work
oferscīnan 03.01.12 Brightness, light; 03.01.12.02 A beam of light
oferscrūd 04.04.07.07 A long outer garment, covering, cloak, etc.
oferscuwian 03.01.13.03 Overshadowing
ofersēam 17.03.12 A receptacle, container

ofersēcan 12.05.06.02 Oppression
ofersegl 05.12.01.09.03.01.01.03 Part of ship
oferseglian 05.12.01.09 To travel on water
ofersendan 05.12.02.03 To send
ofersēocnes 02.08.02 Disease, infirmity, sickness
oferseolfrad 17.02.05.03 A silversmith
oferseolfrian 17.02.05.03 A silversmith
ofersēon 02.05.09.04 To see, look upon, behold; 02.05.09.05 To watch, observe, survey; 11.06.01 Neglect
ofersettan 12.05.06 Grasp, power, control, mastery
ofersewenlic 07.05.02 Contempt
ofersewennes 14.05.04.01 A fine
ofersittan 05.10.04.03 Presence; 11.06.04 Abstention, abstaining from
oferslǣp 02.05.04 Sleepiness, drowsiness, sleep
oferslēan 05.09.04 Abatement, reduction, checking
oferslege 04.05.02.12 Gate/doorway of a building
oferslop 04.04.07.07 A long outer garment, covering, cloak, etc.; 16.02.05.06.01 Outer garments
oferslype 04.04.07.07 A long outer garment, covering, cloak, etc.; 16.02.05.06.01 Outer garments
ofersmēaung 09.05.01 Inspection, examination
ofersmītan 03.01.17.07.01 An anointing, greasing
ofersprǣc 09.01.02.01 Excessive fluency, loquacity
ofersprǣce 07.05.03.03.01 Contumelious, scornful; 09.01.02.01 Excessive fluency, loquacity

ofersprǣdan 04.05.04.05.01 Bedding (e.g. of straw)
oferspreca 07.05.03.03 Scorn, insult, abuse
ofersprecan 07.05.03.03.02 To reproach, revile, abuse
ofersprecen 09.01.02.01 Excessive fluency, loquacity
ofersprecol 07.05.03.03.01 Contumelious, scornful; 09.01.02.01 Excessive fluency, loquacity
ofersprecolnes 09.01.02.01 Excessive fluency, loquacity
oferspyrian 05.12.05.06 To travel over/through/along, traverse
oferstǣlan 06.02.06.03 Persuasion, prompting; 09.07.02 Contradiction; 14.03.03.09.01 Unfavourable judgement, condemnation
oferstæppan 05.12.05.07 To go beyond, pass
ofersteall 12.05.05 Resistance, repulsing
oferstealla 11.10.05 Escape
oferstellan 05.12.05.07 To go beyond, pass; 05.12.05.12.01 To reach up
oferstīgan 03.03.05.01.01 Principal/chief (of its class or type); 05.12.05.07 To go beyond, pass; 05.12.05.12 To go up, ascend; 11.03.02 Advancement, progress; 11.12.01 Absence of restraint, freedom; 13.02.05.01.01 To overcome, conquer
oferstige 06.01.08.05.01 Amazement, astonishment, wonder, admiration
oferstīgendlic 09.03.02.03.01.01.05 Comparative
oferstigennes 08.01.01.01.02 Alienation of mind, ecstasy, rapture
oferswicol 06.01.07.04 Deception
oferswimman 05.12.01.08.01 To swim

oferswingan 05.06.09 Act of striking
oferswīþan 13.02.05.01.01 To overcome, conquer
oferswīþe 03.03.04.01.03 An immense quantity, immensity, immense number
oferswīþend 13.02.10.02 A victor/conqueror
oferswīþestre 13.02.10.02 A victor/conqueror
oferswīþnes 08.01.03.07.02 Misery, trouble, affliction
oferswīþrian 13.02.05.01.01 To overcome, conquer
oferswīþung 08.01.03.07.02 Misery, trouble, affliction
oferswōgan 05.10.05.04.12 The condition of being covered
ofersylfran 03.01.14.03 White/whiteness
ofersȳman 08.01.03.07.02 Misery, trouble, affliction
ofertæl 03.03.03.02 A number (mark/symbol)
ofertǣle 06.01.07.05 Error, being astray
oferteldan 05.10.05.04.12 The condition of being covered
ofertēon 05.07 Ending of existence, end of world; 05.10.05.04.12.01 To bespread, cover with
ofertogennes 05.10.05.04.12 The condition of being covered
ofertrahtnian 09.04.03 Exposition, making clear by explanation
ofertredan 12.05.06.02 Oppression
ofertrūwa 06.02.07.06.02.04 Overconfidence
ofertrūwian 06.02.07.06.02.04 Overconfidence
ofertrūwod 06.02.07.06.02.04 Overconfidence
oferþearf 15.01.06 Poverty, indigence

oferþearfa 15.01.06 Poverty, indigence
oferþeccan 05.10.05.04.12 The condition of being covered
oferþencan 06.01.01.01.01 Thought, cogitation, meditation
oferþēon 11.03.02 Advancement, progress
oferþryccednes 08.01.03.07.02 Misery, trouble, affliction
oferþrymm 12 Power, might
oferufa 05.10.05.04.02 Face, surface
oferwacian 11.10.02.02 Watchful care, keeping guard
oferwadan 05.12.01.04 To go, proceed on foot
oferwandian 05.11.08.01.03.01 Delay
oferwealdan 12.05.06 Grasp, power, control, mastery
oferwealdend 16.01.01.01.01 The Almighty
oferweaxan 02.07.01 To grow; 05.10.05.02.01 Diffusion, effusion, spreading
oferweder 01.03.01.03.01 Storm, tempest
oferwelig 15.01.05 Possession of wealth
oferwenian 07.06.01.03 To be proud/arrogant
oferweorpan 05.06.01 Devastation, laying waste; 05.12.01.04.01.04 To stumble, trip, strike (with the foot); 05.12.02.07.01 To throw, scatter; 12.05.04.01.01 Fighting, a fight
oferwēsnes 04.01.01.04 Gluttony, overeating, greediness
oferwīgan 13.02.05.01.01 To overcome, conquer
oferwillan 03.01.09.01.01 (Of liquids) boiling; 04.01.02.02.05.02 To boil
oferwinnan 13.02.05.01.01 To overcome, conquer

oferwintran 05.11 A time, period of time
oferwist 04.01.01.04 Gluttony, overeating, greediness
oferwlenced 07.06.05 Pomp, splendour, magnificence
oferwlencu 07.06.04.02 Extravagance
oferwrecan 13.02.05.01.01 To overcome, conquer
oferwrēon 04.04.07 Trappings, equipment, garb; 05.10.05.04.12 The condition of being covered
oferwrigels 05.10.05.04.12 The condition of being covered
oferwrit 09.03.07.05 To cover with writing, inscribe; 16.02.01.08.03 The New Testament
oferwriten 09.03.07.05 To cover with writing, inscribe
oferwrīþan 05.10.05.04.12 The condition of being covered
oferwunnen 13.02.05.02 Defeat
oferwyllan 04.01.02.02.05.02 To boil
oferwyrcan 04.05 Building, construction; 05.10.05.04.12 The condition of being covered
oferyldu 02.01.04.03 Aging, growing old
oferymbwoendnisse 05.13.01 Transformation, taking another shape
oferyrnan 01.01.03.03 Flow/flowing; 05.12.05.02.01 To come upon, meet with; 05.12.05.06 To travel over/through/along, traverse; 09.04.03 Exposition, making clear by explanation
oferȳþ 01.01.03.01.02.05 Wave
ofes(c) 05.10.05.04.11.01 A bound, limit
ofestan 05.12.03.01.02 Haste, hurry
ofett 02.07.09 Fruit
offaran 05.12.05.07 To go beyond, pass

offeallan 02.02.04.03 To kill, slay; 02.02.04.04.02 Suicide; 05.12.05.13.03 To fall; 13.02.05.01.01 To overcome, conquer
offēran 05.12.05.07 To go beyond, pass
offerenda 16.02.04.03.03.01 A hymn, song of praise, canticle
offerian 05.12.02.02 To carry off, remove
offēstre 02.03.02.04.01 Foster relationships
offrettan 04.01.01 Eating; 05.06.01 Devastation, laying waste
(ge)offrian 16.02.04.12 Sacrifice, a sacrifice
offringclāþ 16.02.05.05.09 Cloths
offringdagas 16.02.01.08.04 Jewish seasons/feasts
offringdisc 16.02.05.05.06 A vessel for use in services
offringhlāf 16.02.01.08.04 Jewish seasons/feasts
offringsang 16.02.04.03.03.01 A hymn, song of praise, canticle
offringsceatt 16.02.05.05.09 Cloths
offrung 16.02.04.12 Sacrifice, a sacrifice; 16.02.05.09.01 Eucharistic elements
offrunghūs 16.02.05.02.03 A church, place of worship
offrungspic 16.02.01.06.01 Belief/practice of heathen people
offyligan 05.12.05.07 To go beyond, pass
offyllan 02.02.04.03 To kill, slay
ofgān 05.03 Source, origin; 12.03.04 A request, prayer; 14.02.01.02.01 Open robbery, rapine, pillage; 15.01.01.01 Holding of land
ofgangan 10.01.02 Acquisition; 12.03.04 A request, prayer; 14.02.01.02.01 Open robbery, rapine, pillage

ofgangende 09.03.02.03 Composition (inflectional or compounding)
ofgangendlic 09.03.02.03 Composition (inflectional or compounding)
ofgebīged 05.11.07.03 Former times, days of old
of(ge)niman 10.04.03 To take away, remove
ofgeorn 08.01.01.01.01 Exaltation, elation
ofgēotan 03.01.13.02 A growing dark, darkening; 03.01.16.01 Moisture; 03.01.16.06 A soaking, steeping
ofgestīgnes 05.12.05.13 To go down, descend
ofgiefan 10.02 Want, lack; 11.06.06.01 Abandonment (of principle)
ofgoten 03.01.16.06 A soaking, steeping
ofhabban 10.03.06 Withholding, keeping back
ofhæccan 05.06.02 Cleaving, splitting, cutting
ofhagian 11.08.02 Inconvenience, unfitness
ofhealdan 10.03.06 Withholding, keeping back
ofhearmian 08.01.03.04 Grief
ofhende 10.02.01 Loss, deprivation
ofhīeran 02.05.10 Faculty of hearing
ofhilde 05.12.05.13 To go down, descend
ofhingrian 04.01.01.03 Hunger
ofhingrod 02.05.05.02 Eager desire
ofhnītan 02.02.04.04.03 Putting to death
ofhrēosan 05.06.05.03 Bruising, crushing; 05.12.05.13.03 To fall
ofhrēowan 08.01.02.06.01 Pity; 08.01.03.04 Grief
ofhrēran 05.12.02 To move, set in motion
ofhroren 05.06.05.03 Bruising, crushing
ofhwylfan 05.12.05.04.01 (Of wheel, etc.) to roll, trundle

ofhyrian 03.06.01.01 Imitation
ofirnan 02.05.03.02 Weariness; 05.12.03.01 Swiftness, velocity; 05.12.05.07 To go beyond, pass
oflǣtan 02.08.12.02.06 Surgical; 11.06.06.01 Abandonment (of principle)
oflǣte 04.01.02.01.07.03.03 Piece of bread; 16.02.04.12 Sacrifice, a sacrifice; 16.02.05.09.01 Eucharistic elements
oflǣthlāf 16.02.05.09.01 Eucharistic elements
oflangod 02.05.05.02 Eager desire
oflecgan 05.10.05.04.12 The condition of being covered
ofleged 05.10.04 Place, room
ofleogan 06.01.07.04.03 Untruth, falsehood
oflicgan 02.02.04.03 To kill, slay
oflīcian 08.01.03.07 Unpleasantness
oflinnan 11.06.04 Abstention, abstaining from
oflysted 02.05.05 Desire, appetite; 06.02.05.01 Strong liking for, devotion to
ofmanian 15.03 Exaction of tax/tribute
ofmunan 06.01.04 Faculty of memory
ofmyrþrian 02.02.04.04 Manslaughter, homicide
ofnēadian 14.02.01.02.01 Open robbery, rapine, pillage
ofniman 05.09.05 Ceasing, decline, fall off
ofost 05.12.03.01.02 Haste, hurry
ofostlīce 05.12.03.01 Swiftness, velocity; 05.12.03.01.02 Haste, hurry
ofrǣcan 10.01.02 Acquisition
ofrīdan 05.12.01.05.01 Modes of riding
ofsacan 14.03.03.01.01 Defence, reply

ofscacan 06.01.08.06.01 A shuddering with fear, nervousness
ofsceamian 07.09 Shame, disgrace
ofsceamod 07.09.01 Shame, confusion
ofscēotan 02.02.04.03 To kill, slay; 02.08.04.01 A wound
ofscoten 04.02.05.02.01 (Of cattle) seized with disease
ofscotian 02.08.04.01 A wound
ofsendan 12.03.03.01 Summons, a call, summoning
ofsēon 02.05.09.04 To see, look upon, behold
ofset 02.08.11.02.01 Insanity, madness
ofseten 02.08.11.02.01 Insanity, madness; 12.05.06.01 Restraint, check, curb, control
ofsetenes 05.12.05.13.02.02 To sit down; 13.02.03.01.02 To beset, surround
ofsetnian 13.02.03.01.02 To beset, surround
ofsettan 02.05.06.01 To touch and press; 02.08.04 Hurt, injury, damage; 05.06.05.03 Bruising, crushing; 08.01.03.07.02 Misery, trouble, affliction; 12.05.06.02 Oppression
ofsittan 05.12.05.13.02.02 To sit down; 06.01 The head (as seat of thought); 08.01.03.07.02 Misery, trouble, affliction; 11.11.02 A hindrance; 12.05.06.02 Oppression; 13.02.03.01.02 To beset, surround
ofslēan 02.02.04.03 To kill, slay; 05.06 Destruction, dissolution, loss, breaking; 05.12.05.03.04 To come/go out from
ofslege 05.06.09 Act of striking
ofslegen 02.02.04 Killing, violent death, destruction; 02.08.02 Disease, infirmity, sickness

ofslegennes 02.02.04.04.04 To slaughter (an animal)
ofslītan 02.08.03.02 Itch, irritation
ofsmorian 02.02.04.03 To kill, slay
ofsnīþan 02.02.04.04.04 To slaughter (an animal); 05.06.02 Cleaving, splitting, cutting
ofspring 02.03.02.02 Child, offspring
ofspyrian 11.03.01.03 Finding, discovery
ofstǣnan 02.02.04.04.03 Putting to death
ofstæppan 05.06.04 Damage, injury, defect, hurt, loss; 05.12.01.04.01.02 To tread upon, trample
ofstandan 05.11.11 Continuity; 05.12.05.12 To go up, ascend; 10.03.04.01 Restitution, making good, repayment; 15.04 A debt, due
ofstanden 05.12.04.01 Stability, firmness
ofstende 05.12.03.01.02 Haste, hurry
ofstician 02.02.04.03 To kill, slay; 05.06.07 Pricking, a prick, puncture
ofsticod 02.02.04.04.04 To slaughter (an animal)
ofstig 05.12.03.01 Swiftness, velocity
ofstīgan 05.12.05.03.03 To depart, leave, set out; 05.12.05.12 To go up, ascend; 05.12.05.13 To go down, descend
ofstingan 02.02.04.03 To kill, slay; 05.06.07 Pricking, a prick, puncture
ofstofen 05.12.02.06.01 To push, drive
ofstum 05.12.03.01.02 Haste, hurry
ofswelgan 05.06.01 Devastation, laying waste
ofswerian 14.03.03.04 Oath-swearing
ofswingan 02.02.04.04.03 Putting to death
ofswȳþan 13.02.05.01.01 To overcome, conquer
ofsyndrige 05.10.04.04 Absence

oft 05.11.09.02 Frequent, of common occurrence
oft ... gelōme 05.11.09.02 Frequent, of common occurrence
oft and gelōme 05.11.09.02 Frequent, of common occurrence
oftacan 05.12.05.07 To go beyond, pass
oftalu 14.03.03.09 A sentence, judgement, ruling
oftēon 05.12.05.11 To turn back, retreat; 10.03.06 Withholding, keeping back; 10.04.03.01 To take away, deprive of
oftfēþre 17.02.04.02.03 Carrying, carriage (of materials)
oftige 10.03.06 Withholding, keeping back
oftor micle 05.11.09.02 Frequent, of common occurrence
oftorfian 02.02.04.04.03 Putting to death; 05.06.09.04 Stoning, casting of stones
oftost 05.11.09.02 Frequent, of common occurrence
oftost symle 05.11.11 Continuity
oftrǣde 05.11.09.02 Frequent, of common occurrence; 06.02.05.04.03 Promptitude, readiness
oftrǣdlic 05.11.09.02 Frequent, of common occurrence
oftrǣdlīce 05.11.09.02 Frequent, of common occurrence
oftredan 02.02.04.04.03 Putting to death; 05.06.04 Damage, injury, defect, hurt, loss; 05.12.01.04.01.02 To tread upon, trample
oftsīþum 05.11.09.02 Frequent, of common occurrence
oftþwēal 04.06.01.01 Cleansing, washing
oftyrfan 05.06.09.04 Stoning, casting of stones
ofþǣnan 03.01.16.01 Moisture
ofþǣned 03.01.16.01 Moisture

ofþanc 08.01.03.09.08 Envy, jealousy
ofþecgan 05.06.01 Devastation, laying waste
ofþefian 03.01.09.01 Warmth, heat
ofþencan 06.01.04 Faculty of memory
ofþinen 03.01.16.01 Moisture
ofþringan 03.03.04.01.02 A great number, multitude
ofþryccan 05.06.05.03 Bruising, crushing; 05.09.04 Abatement, reduction, checking; 08.01.03.07.02.01 Injury, offence; 12.05.06.02 Oppression; 13.02.03.01.03 To occupy a conquered land; 13.02.05.01.01 To overcome, conquer
ofþryccednes 08.01.03.07.02 Misery, trouble, affliction
ofþrycnes 12.05.06.02 Oppression
ofþryscan 05.09.04 Abatement, reduction, checking
ofþrysm(i)an 05.06 Destruction, dissolution, loss, breaking
ofþylman 02.02.04.03 To kill, slay
ofþyncan 08.01.03.04 Grief; 08.01.03.07.02 Misery, trouble, affliction
ofþyrst(ed) 04.01.03.01 Thirst; 02.05.05 Desire, appetite
ofþȳstrian 02.08.07.02.01 Defective vision; 03.01.13.02 A growing dark, darkening; 06.01.07.05 Error, being astray
ofunnan 06.02.03 Unwilling, loath; 10.03.06 Withholding, keeping back
ofweard 05.10.04.04 Absence
ofweorpan 02.02.04.04.03 Putting to death
ofworpian 02.02.04.04.03 Putting to death
ofwundrian 06.01.08.05.01 Amazement, astonishment, wonder, admiration
ofwundrod 06.01.08.05.01 Amazement, astonishment, wonder, admiration
ofwyrtrumian 05.06.08 A plucking, taking away
ōga 06.01.08.06 Fear; 06.01.08.06.03 Cause of fear, terror, horror
ōgengel 17.03.10.01 A bolt, lock, bar
ōhilde/ōheald 05.10.05.04.04 A descent, slope, incline
ōht 06.01.08.06 Fear
ōhte grettan 16.02.04.14 Sacrilege
ōhtrīp 04.02.04.04.02 Harvesting
ōlǣcung 12.01.01.12.04.02 Conspiracy
ōleccan 07.07.03 Flattery; 08.01.01.03.09 Pleasantness, agreeableness
(ge)ōleccan 05.09.02 Mildness, moderate quality; 08.01.01.03.09.03 To make glad
ōleccere 07.07.03 Flattery
ōleccung 05.09.02 Mildness, moderate quality; 07.07.03 Flattery; 08.01.01.03.09 Pleasantness, agreeableness
ōlectend 07.07.03 Flattery
ōlehtung 07.07.03 Flattery; 08.01.01.03.09 Pleasantness, agreeableness; 12.08.07.01 Laxity, indulgence
olfenda/-e 02.06.04.01.02 Camel
olfendmyre 02.06.04.01.02 Camel
oll 07.05.02 Contempt
ōlþwong 14.05.06 Means/implement of torture
ōlyhtword 07.07.03 Flattery
ōm 03.02.01.04 Rust
oma 03.03.01.01 Liquid measures
ōman 02.08.06 Skin disease, erysipelas

ōmcynn 02.08.02 Disease, infirmity, sickness
omer 02.06.08.05 Forest bird, wild-fowl
ōmian 03.02.01 Decay, decline, corruption
ōmig 03.02.01.04 Rust
ōmig/ōmihte 02.08.05 Inflammation
on ... foran 05.10.05.04.09.01 Front
on ... healfe 12.02.01 A substitute, representative
on (...) middan 05.10.05.04.10 Among
on (...) stale 05.13.04 Exchange, commutation
on (...) stede 05.13.04 Exchange, commutation
on (...) gewrixle 05.13.04 Exchange, commutation
on ǣnne sīþ 03.03.03.04.01 One
on ǣr 05.11.07.03 Former times, days of old; 05.11.07.03.02 Earlier, antecedent
on ǣrdagum 05.11.07.03 Former times, days of old
on ǣrran dæge 05.11.07.03.01 Time within remembrance
on ǣwiscnesse 09.05.05.01 Showing, manifestation, display
on āhōn 14.05.05.01.01 Crucifixion, death on cross
on ān 05.11.11.01 A not ceasing, persistence, recurrence
on andan 08.01.03.05.03 Exasperation, irritation; 08.01.03.09.06 Hostility
on andlang 05.10.05.04.09 Side, quarter, direction
on andlanges 05.10.05.04.09 Side, quarter, direction
on ānne sīþ 05.11.07.01 Contemporary, coeval
on ānum 05.11.11.01 A not ceasing, persistence, recurrence

on bæc 05.12.05.11 To turn back, retreat
on bæc lǣtan 11.06.01 Neglect
on bæc settan 11.06.01 Neglect
on bæcling gewend 05.10.05.04.09.02 Hinder part, rear
on bæcling(a) 05.12.05.11 To turn back, retreat
on bēagwīsan 05.10.06.02 Rotundity, roundness
on beblāwan 03.01.15.01 Inspiration, inbreathing
on bid wrecan 11.11.03 Impeding of progress, prevention
on gebyrd 05.11.11.01 A not ceasing, persistence, recurrence
on cnēow(um) sittan 05.12.05.13.02.01 To kneel down
on dæg 05.11.03.01.05 A day
on dagunge 05.11.04.01 Day (not night)
on dene lage 12.06.02 District, province
on dīglum 09.05.04 A secret
on drȳgum 01.01.02 Land
on dūn(e) 05.10.05.04.02.03 Laid below
on ēage beran 02.05.09.12 To show; 09.05.05.01 Showing, manifestation, display
on ealdre 05.11.01.01.01 Eternity
on ealne ǣrnemergen 05.11.04.01 Day (not night)
on earsling 05.12.05.11 To turn back, retreat
on ēce yrfe 15.01.02.01 Inherited property
on ēcnesse 05.11.01.01.01 Eternity
on ēcum þingum 05.11.01.01.01 Eternity
on efentwā 03.03.03.03 Fractions
on elne 06.02.07.06.02 Boldness
on elþēode 12.06.05.01 State of exile, banishment

on elþēodige 12.06.05.01 State of exile, banishment
on emne 03.06.01.02 Equality
on ende 05.11.11.01 A not ceasing, persistence, recurrence
on engla lage 12.06.02 District, province
on eornost 06.02.05.04.05 Earnestness
on eornost(e) 06.01.07.01 Correct, right, free from error
on fēþe 05.12.01.04 To go, proceed on foot
on firste 05.11.07.04 Future, time to come
on flēame weorþan 11.10.04 Flight
on flot(e) 05.12.01.08 To move in/on water
on foreweardum 05.10.05.04.09.01.02 Front, beginning
on foreweard(um) 05.10.05.04.09.01 Front
on frymþe 05.11.10.01 A beginning
on fūlan lecgan 02.02.05 A burial, burying
on fultum gestandan 11.12.02 Aid, help, succour
on gistlīþnesse 08.01.02.04.01 Visiting
on grunde 01 Earth, world
on hālre tungan 11.03.01.01.01 Proof, demonstration
on gehālum þingum 02.08.01 Sound physical condition
on hand gān 12.05.06.04.02 Submission, subjection, obedience; 13.02.05.02.01 Surrender, submission
on hand sellan 14.03.03.07 Security, pledge, bail
on hand (ge)sellan 10.03 Giving
on hand(a) 10 Having, owning, possession
on handa habban 11.02 Occupation, activity, business
on/under handa habban 10 Having, owning, possession
on handa standan 08.01.03.07.02 Misery, trouble, affliction; 10.01 Fact of belonging, possession by
on hēape 03.03.04.01.02.01 A heap, mass, accumulation
on hīehþu(m) 07.08.06 Exaltation; 11.07.04 Superiority, pre-eminence, primacy
on hindan 05.10.05.04.09.02 Hinder part, rear; 05.12.05.10 To go behind, follow
on hinder 05.12.05.11 To turn back, retreat
on hinderling 05.12.05.11 To turn back, retreat
on his dæge 05.11 A time, period of time
on hōh 05.10.05.04.09.02 Hinder part, rear
on hrædinge 05.12.03.01.02 Haste, hurry
on hringwīsan 05.10.06.02 Rotundity, roundness
on hwearfte 05.10.05.04.11 A circle, circuit, circumference
on īdel 05.03.01.01 Without need or cause; 11.08.03 Needless, useless, unprofitable
on īdelnesse 11.08.03 Needless, useless, unprofitable
on in 05.10.05.04.01 Inside, interior
on indisc 09.03.01 Particular languages
on lāst 05.11.10.02 End, completion
on lāst faran 05.12.05.11.01 To return
on lāst lecgan 05.12.05.10 To go behind, follow
on lāste 05.11.07.04.02.01 Succession
on lāst(e) 05.10.05.04.09.02 Hinder part, rear
on lengþe 05.11.10.02 End, completion
on lēoþwīsan 09.03.05.01.01 Poetry

on/tō līfe 02.01.02.01 That lives, living
on lofte 05.10.05.04.02.04 Above
on lufan 11.12.02 Aid, help, succour
on lust(e) 06.02.02.01 Will, wish, pleasure
on lyfte 05.10.05.04.02.04 Above
on/in gemange 05.10.05.04.10 Among
on mergen 05.11.04.01.02 Morning
on middan 05.10.05.04.01.01 The middle
on mōd geniman 06.02.06 Mind, purpose
on morgen 05.11.04.01.02 Morning
on morg(en)ne 05.11.07.04.01.01 (To)morrow
on munucwīsan 16.02.03.03 A religious
on nēod 06.02.05.04 Desire, eagerness
on niman 02.08.12.01 Medical care, treatment
on norþan 01.01.01.01 North
on ofoste 05.12.03.01.02 Haste, hurry
on ofstum 05.12.03.01.02 Haste, hurry
on oftsīþas 05.11.09.02 Frequent, of common occurrence
on oll 11.08.03 Needless, useless, unprofitable
on rǣwe 03.05.02 An arrangement, order, succession
on (ge)rǣwe 03.05.02 An arrangement, order, succession
on rihte 07.02.01 Right, virtue
on gerihte 05.10.05.04.05 Straight, direct
on rīme 03.03.03 Number
on rīsan 12.01.01.12.03 Rebellion, sedition
on gerūm 05.10.04.04 Absence; 11.12.01 Absence of restraint, freedom
on sǣlum 08.01.01.03 Good feeling, joy, happiness
on scipwīsan 05.12.01.09.03.01.02 Of/concerning a ship, naval
on simbel 11.05 Natural/proper way/manner/mode of action
on sittan 05.11 A time, period of time
on (ge)sittan 12.05.06.02 Oppression
on spēd 09.01.02 Fluency in speech
on stale bēon/wesan 11.12.02 Aid, help, succour
on styde 05.11.07.01 Contemporary, coeval
on swāpan 05.12.05.03.04 To come/go out from
on symbel 05.11.11 Continuity
on syndrige 05.10.04.04 Absence
on tēon 05.12.02.05 To pull, drag, draw
on/tō getēon 05.03.01 A cause (of anything)
on tīde 05.11.08 A suitable time, opportunity
on trēowe gelǣtan 11.10.02.02.01 Care, interest in; 12.02 A public office
on tūn gān 09.05.05.01 Showing, manifestation, display
on tyhte 05.12.01.01 To go on a journey/expedition, travel
on þā/þǣre gelīcnesse 03.06.01 Similitude, likeness
on þā gerād þæt 06.02.06.01 An end, goal
on þā wrace 12.05.04.02.01 Retribution, requital
on (þǣm) ǣrran dæge 05.11.07.03.01 Time within remembrance
on þæt gerād 05.03.01.03 Reason, cause
on (þām) ende 05.11.10.02 End, completion
on þance 08.01.02.04.02 Thanks, gratitude
on þance/to þances/to þance 08.01.01.03.09.02 Pleasantly, agreeably
on þrēo 03.03.03.04.03 Three

on þweorh 12.08.06.01.03 Evilly, badly
on ufan 03.03.05 Extent, degree
on ūhtan 05.11.04.01 Day (not night)
on under 05.10.05.04.02.02 Under, beneath
on ungearwe 06.01.08.05 Unexpected
on unwær 06.01.08.05 Unexpected
on unwaran 06.01.08.05 Unexpected
on uppan 03.03.05 Extent, degree
on ūteweardum 05.10.04.03 Presence
on gewædian 05.10.05.04.12 The condition of being covered
on wæl 13.02.02 Battle
on wang stīgan 05.12.01.09 To travel on water
on wealcan 01.01.03.01.02.06 Surging, rolling, heaving of waves
on wedde (ge)sellan 14.03.03.07 Security, pledge, bail
on wega gehwām 05.11.09.01 Always
on wega gehwylcum 05.11.09.01 Always
on westwēalas 12.06.01.02 Britain
on westwēalum 12.06.01.02 Britain
on wīdan fēore 05.11.01.01.01 Eternity
on gewil 06.02.02.01 Will, wish, pleasure
on wōh dōn 12.08.06.01.04.01 To mislead, seduce, lead astray
on wōn 12.07.05 Wrong, injustice
on woruld 03.06 Comparison
on gewunan bringan 11.01.01 Practice, exercise, doing
on gewunan habban 11.01.01 Practice, exercise, doing
on ymbegang 05.10.05.04.11 A circle, circuit, circumference
on/in ymbhwyrfte 05.10.05.04.11 A circle, circuit, circumference
on ymbhwyrfte 05.10.05.04.10 Among
on ȳtmestum sīþe 02.02.03.01 In process of dying

onǣlan 03.01.09.02.01 Fire, burning; 06.01.02 The imaginative faculty; 06.02.06.03.03 Incitement; 08.01.01.01.03 An incitement, cause of strong feeling; 17.05.04 To kindle, set alight (fire, lamp)
onǣlet 01.03.01.03.01.02 Lightning
onāfæstnian 05.05.03 Binding, fastening
on(ā)gēotan 05.12.05.02.04.01 To insert into (a hole)
onāgēotan 05.12.05.02.04.02 To pour in
onāhebban 07.08.06 Exaltation
onāhōn 05.12.01.07.01 To hang
onāl 03.01.09.02.01 Fire, burning; 16.02.05.09.02 Incense
onārīsende 12.05.04.01.01 Fighting, a fight
onāsāwan 05.12.05.02.04.01 To insert into (a hole)
onāsendan 05.12.05.02.04.01 To insert into (a hole)
onāsendednes 05.12.02.03 To send
onāsetednes 02.05.06.01 To touch and press; 16.02.01.10.02.01 A blessing, invocation of divine favour
onāslagen 17.02.04.03 Metal worker
onāslīdan 05.09.05 Ceasing, decline, fall off
on(ā)swēgan 02.05.10.02 Noise, din
onāwinnan 13.02 War
onbæc 05.10.05.04.09.02 Hinder part, rear
onbæcling 05.10.05.04.09.02 Hinder part, rear; 05.11.09.06 Frequency, repetition
onbærnan 03.01.09.01 Warmth, heat; 03.01.09.02.01 Fire, burning; 06.02.06.03.03 Incitement; 08.01.01.01.03 An incitement, cause of strong feeling

onbærning 16.02.05.09.02 Incense
onbærnnes 16.02.05.09.02 Incense
onbæru 12.08.03 Restraint, temperance
onbāsnung 06.01.08 Expectation
onbecyme 05.12.05.02 To go/travel towards, come, approach
onbefeallan 05.12.05.13.03 To fall
onbeflōwan 01.01.03.03 Flow/flowing
onbēgnes 05.10.06.02.02 Curvature, bend, twist
onbehrēosan 05.12.05.13.03 To fall
onbelǣdan 12.05.06.02.03 Trouble, disturbance
onbelgan 08.01.03.05.02 Anger
onbēn 16.02.04.14.02 Imprecation
onbēodan 09.06.02.01.05 Proclamation, spreading abroad; 12.03.03 A command, bidding, order
onbeornan 02.08.10 Fever; 03.01.09.02.01 Fire, burning; 08.01.01.01.03 An incitement, cause of strong feeling
onbēotend 05.11.07.04.01 Nearness, approach, imminence
onberan 02.08.02 Disease, infirmity, sickness; 14.02.01.02.01 Open robbery, rapine, pillage
onbescēawung 09.05.01 Inspection, examination
onbescūfan 05.12.05.03.04 To come/go out from
onbesendan 05.12.02.03 To send
onbesettan 05.12.05.02.04.03 To plunge (something into something)
onbeslagen 02.08.04 Hurt, injury, damage; 05.06.09 Act of striking
onbesmītan 04.06.02.02 Foul, filthy, squalid
onbestǣlan 14.03.03.09.01 Unfavourable judgement, condemnation

onbestingan 05.12.02.06 To push, impel, thrust
onbīdan 06.01.08 Expectation; 06.01.08.01 Expectation, waiting; 12.01.01.08 Service
onbīgan 12.05.06.04 A trampling upon, subjection
onbindan 05.05.03 Binding, fastening; 05.05.04 That loosens, loosening
onbirgan 02.05.07 Faculty of taste
onbītan 04 Consumption of food/drink
onblǣst 13.02.03.01 An attack, assault
onblǣstan 05.12.05.02.01 To come upon, meet with
onblanden 03.03.06.01.01 Mixing, mingling, preparation
onblāwan 02.04.06.07.05 To breathe; 03.01.15.01 Inspiration, inbreathing; 07.06.01.03 To be proud/arrogant
onblāwnes 16.02.01.12.01 Revelation, illumination, inspiration
onblōtan 16.02.04.12 Sacrifice, a sacrifice
onbolgen 08.01.03.05.02 Anger
onborgian 15.04.01 Lending of money
onbrǣdan 05.10.05.04.12 The condition of being covered
onbregdan 05.10.05.04.14 An opening, aperture; 05.12.02.05 To pull, drag, draw; 05.12.03.01.01 Quick movement or movements; 05.12.05.05 To shake, quake, wag
onbring 06.02.06.03.02 Instigation
onbringelle 06.02.06.03.02 Instigation
onbrūcan 04 Consumption of food/drink
onbryce 13.02.03.01.01 Inroad, attack
onbryrd 08.01.01.01 Ardour, fervour, strong feeling
(ge)onbryrd 08.01.03.02.01 Compunction, remorse, contrition; 16.02.04.07.02.01 Penitence

onbryrdan 06.02.06.03 Persuasion, prompting; 08.01 Heart, spirit, mood, disposition

onbryrdan mid/tō 08.01.01.01.03 An incitement, cause of strong feeling

onbryrded 08.01.03.02.01 Compunction, remorse, contrition; 16.02.04.07.02.01 Penitence

onbryrding 06.02.06.03.03 Incitement

onbryrdnes 06.02.06.03.03.01 Incitement, prompting, exhortation; 08.01.01.01 Ardour, fervour, strong feeling; 08.01.01.01.03 An incitement, cause of strong feeling; 08.01.03.02.01 Compunction, remorse, contrition; 16.02.01.12.01 Revelation, illumination, inspiration

onbūgan 05.10.05.04.04 A descent, slope, incline; 07.04.03 Reverence, respect; 12.05.06.04.02 Submission, subjection, obedience

onbūgan of 11.06.06 Turning

onbūtan 05.10.05.04.11 A circle, circuit, circumference

onbūtān 05.11.07.02 The present (time)

onbyrgan 14.03.03.07 Security, pledge, bail

onbyrging 04.01.01 Eating

onbyrhtan 06.01.06.02.03.04.05 Edification, instruction

onbyrignes 02.05.07 Faculty of taste; 04 Consumption of food/drink

oncennan 02.01.03.03.02 To bring forth, produce

oncierran 05.12.01 To go, progress, travel (usually on land); 05.12.05 To move and change direction, turn; 05.13 Changeableness, change; 11.05.02 Mode, manner, way, method, fashion, course; 12.08.06.01.04.01 To mislead, seduce, lead astray

oncierran cwide 14.03.03.09 A sentence, judgement, ruling

oncierran fram 11.06.06 Turning

oncierran (on) 05.13.01 Transformation, taking another shape

oncīgnes 16.02.04.08.01 Kinds of prayer

oncīgung 16.02.04.08.01 Kinds of prayer

onclifian 03.01.17 Thickness, viscosity; 05.02.02 Nature, established order of things; 06.02.07.03 Perseverance; 10.04.01 To hold, have

onclyfiende 06.02.07.03 Perseverance

onclypian 16.02.04.08.01 Kinds of prayer

oncnǣwe 06.01.06.01.01.02 To know, recognize

oncnāwan 06.01.06 Understanding, knowledge, cognizance; 06.01.06.01.01.02 To know, recognize; 09.06.02.01.04 A confession, declaration; 11.05.02.02.01 Greetings, courteous terms of address

oncnāwend 06.01.06.01.01 Knowledge

oncnāw(en)nes 06.01.06.01 Knowledge, cognizance, knowing

oncnāwennes 09.07.04.01.01 Acknowledgement

oncnāwung 06.01.06.01.01 Knowledge

oncnyssan 08.01.03.07.02 Misery, trouble, affliction

oncunnan 06.01.06.01.01 Knowledge; 14.03.03.01 Accusation

oncunnes 14.03.03.01 Accusation

oncunning 14.03.03.01 Accusation

oncwealdan 02.02.04.03 To kill, slay

oncweþan 02.05.10.04 To resound; 09.05.03 An answer, reply

oncȳþan 09.06.02.01.05 Proclamation, spreading abroad

oncȳþdǣd 02.08.04 Hurt, injury, damage
oncȳþig 06.01.06.01.01.02 To know, recognize; 09.05.05 Exposure, revealing, revelation
oncȳþþ 08.01.03.03 Anxiety
ondǣlan 05.12.05.02.04.01 To insert into (a hole); 05.12.05.02.04.02 To pour in
ondǣlend 10.03 Giving
ondegslic 06.01.08.06.03.01 Causing dread, terrifying
ondesn(es) 06.01.08.06 Fear
ondlēanian 10.03.03 Granting
ondōn 04.04.07 Trappings, equipment, garb; 05.10.05.04.14 An opening, aperture
ondōung 02.08.12.02.05.04 To cleanse, clean away
ondrǣdan 06.01.08.06.02 Great fear, terror, horror
ondrǣdendlic 06.01.08.06.02 Great fear, terror, horror; 06.01.08.06.03.01 Causing dread, terrifying
ondrǣding 06.01.08.06.02 Great fear, terror, horror
ondrencan 04.01.03.02 To drink heavily, get drunk
ondrincan 03.01.16.06 A soaking, steeping; 04.01.03 Drinking
ondruncnian 04.01.03.02 To drink heavily, get drunk
ondrys(e)nlic 06.01.08.06.03.01 Causing dread, terrifying
ondrysenlīce 07.04.03 Reverence, respect
ondrys(e)nlīce 08.01.03.07.04 Severity, harshness
ondrysne 06.01.08.06.03.01 Causing dread, terrifying; 07.03.01.01 Abominable, detestable; 07.04.03 Reverence, respect
ondrysnu 06.01.08.06 Fear; 07.04.03 Reverence, respect; 11.05.02.01 A standard, norm, ethos
onealdian 02.01.04.03 Aging, growing old; 05.11.07.03.03 Old, not new
oneardian 04.05.03.01 Habitation, sojourn
oneardiend 04.05.03.01 Habitation, sojourn
onēgan 06.01.08.06.02 Great fear, terror, horror
onēhting 12.05.06.02.02 Persecution
onemn 05.10.05.01 A little way, no great distance
onemnþrōwigan 08.01.02.05 Compassion
onerian 04.02.04.02.02.02 Ploughing, tilling
onerning 13.02.03.01 An attack, assault
ōnettan 05.11.08.01.02.01 Anticipation; 05.12.03.01 Swiftness, velocity; 05.12.03.01.02 Haste, hurry; 11.02.01.01 Active, nimble; 11.03 Endeavour
ōnettan (forþ) 05.12.05.09 To go forward, proceed
geōnettan 10.04.02.02 To seize, take, grasp, lay hold on
ōnettung 05.12.03.01.02 Haste, hurry
onēþgung 02.04.06.07.04 Breathing
onfægnian 08.01.02.03.04 To show gladness, be friendly
onfǣreld 05.12.01.01 To go on a journey/expedition, travel; 13.02.03.01 An attack, assault
onfǣstan 05.05.03 Binding, fastening
onfǣstnian 05.06.07 Pricking, a prick, puncture
onfæþmnes 11.10.02.02.01 Care, interest in
onfangen 11.01.02 An undertaking

onfangend 10.01.01 Acceptance, receiving
onfangennes 08.01.02.04 Hospitality; 10.01.01.01 Receiving, gaining, getting; 16.02.04.07.04 Communion/eucharist
onfealdan 05.10.05.04.13 A removal of that which obscures or conceals; 05.10.06.05 A fold, plait, wrinkle
onfeall 02.08.05.01 Swelling
onfeallende 05.08.02 Violence, force
onfeng 10.04.02.02 To seize, take, grasp, lay hold on; 13.02.03.01 An attack, assault
onfeohtan 13.02.03.01 An attack, assault
onfeohtende 13.02.03.01 An attack, assault
onfindan 05.03.02 Event, issue, result; 06.01.06.02.03.03 To study, apply oneself to learning; 08.01.01 A feeling, what is felt; 10.01.02 Acquisition; 11.03.01.03 Finding, discovery
onfindend 11.03.01.03 Finding, discovery
onflæscnes 16.01.01.04.02.01 Incarnation
onflyge(n) 02.08.02.01.01 An infectious disease
onfōn 02.01.03.03.01 To beget; 04.05.02.01 A foundation; 05.11.10.01 A beginning; 08.01.02.04 Hospitality; 09.07.04.01 Confirmation, agreement; 10.01.01 Acceptance, receiving; 10.01.01.01 Receiving, gaining, getting; 10.04 To take; 10.04.02.02 To seize, take, grasp, lay hold on; 11.01.02 An undertaking; 11.12.02 Aid, help, succour; 12.03.05 Permission; 16.02.04.07.04 Communion/eucharist

onfōn æt fulluhte 16.02.04.07.01 Baptism, baptizing (and anointing)
onfōnd 11.12.02 Aid, help, succour
onfōndlic 10.01.01 Acceptance, receiving
onforan 05.10.05.04.09.01 Front; 05.11.07.03.02 Earlier, antecedent
onfordōn 05.06 Destruction, dissolution, loss, breaking
onforhtian 06.01.08.06 Fear
onforwyrd 05.06 Destruction, dissolution, loss, breaking
onfundelnes 11.03.01.01 Trial, probation
onfunden 06.01.06.03 Experience
onfundennes 11.03.01 Experience, trial, experiment; 11.03.01.03 Finding, discovery
ongalan 16.01.04.01 Sorcery using incantation
ongalend 16.01.04.01 Sorcery using incantation
ongalnes 18.02.07.01 Singing, song
ongān 05.03.02.01.01 An event, occurrence; 05.12.05.02.04 To go in, enter
ongang 05.12.05.02.01 To come upon, meet with; 05.12.05.02.04 To go in, enter; 13.02.03.01 An attack, assault; 16.02.04 Worship, honour, praise
ongeador 03.03.06.01 A whole formed by joining
ongēan 03.06.02.01 Contrariety, diversity; 05.10.05.04.09.04 Opposite (av); 05.11.07.04 Future, time to come; 05.11.09.06 Frequency, repetition; 05.12.05.02 To go/travel towards, come, approach; 05.12.05.11 To turn back, retreat; 05.13.04 Exchange, commutation; 09.05.03 An answer, reply; 12.05.02 Hostility, contention, opposition
ongēan fēran 05.12.05.11.01 To return

ongēan (ge)healdan 12.05.05 Resistance, repulsing
ongēan hwyrfan 05.12.05.11.01 To return
ongēan (ge)lǣdan 05.12.05.11.01 To return
ongēan þæt 03.06.02.01 Contrariety, diversity
ongēan þæt(te) 11.01.03 Preparation
ongēan werian 07.05.03.03.02 To reproach, revile, abuse
ongēan wiþerian 12.05.02 Hostility, contention, opposition
ongēancīgan 12.03.03.01 Summons, a call, summoning
ongēancyme 05.12.05.11.01 To return
ongēancyrrendlic 09.03.02.02.01.05 Minor parts of speech, etc.
ongēanfær 05.12.05.11.01 To return
ongēanfealdan 05.10.05.04.13 A removal of that which obscures or conceals
ongēanflōwende 01.01.03.04 Current, rush of water
ongēangang 05.12.05.04 To rotate, turn round, revolve
ongēangeclipod 12.03.03.01 Summons, a call, summoning
ongēan(ge)clypian 12.03.03.01 Summons, a call, summoning
ongēanhwirfende 05.12.05.11.01 To return
ongēanhworfennes 11.11.02 A hindrance
ongēanhwyrft 05.12.05.11.01 To return
ongēanlecgan 15.01.05 Possession of wealth
ongēanryne 05.12.05.04 To rotate, turn round, revolve; 05.12.05.11.01 To return
ongēansp(r)ecan 09.07.02 Contradiction
ongēansprecend 07.05.03.03 Scorn, insult, abuse
ongēanweard 05.12.05 To move and change direction, turn
ongēanweardes 05.12.05.02 To go/travel towards, come, approach
ongēanweardlic 09.03.02.02.01.03 An adverb
ongēanweardlīce 09.03.02.02.01.03 An adverb
ongēanwinnende 12.05.05 Resistance, repulsing
ongēanwyrdnes 11.11.02 A hindrance
ongeboren 05.02.02 Nature, established order of things
ongebrōht 14.03.03.03 Witness, testimony, attestation
on(ge)byrgan 04 Consumption of food/drink
on(ge)cīgan 16.02.04.08.01 Kinds of prayer
ongefealdan 05.10.05.04.12 The condition of being covered
ongefeht 13.02.03.01 An attack, assault
ongeflogen 02.08.02.01.01 An infectious disease
ongefōn 11.03 Endeavour
on(ge)hrēosan 05.06.03 A dashing together, breaking, shattering
ongehȳþnes 11.07.03 Use, advantage, profit
ongelīc 17.02.05.04 An image, figure
on(ge)līc 03.06.01 Similitude, likeness
ongelīc(e) 03.06.01 Similitude, likeness
ongelīcnes 09.06.01 To relate, recount, tell
on(ge)līcnes 05.10.06 Form, shape; 17.02.05.04 An image, figure
on(ge)mang 05.10.05.04.10 Among
on(ge)mētan 11.03.01.03 Finding, discovery

ongemong 05.11 A time, period of time
ongemong þisum/þǣm 05.11 A time, period of time
ongemong þisum/þǣm þe 05.11 A time, period of time
ongenǣman 10.04.03 To take away, remove
ongeniman 10.04.03 To take away, remove
ongēotan 05.12.05.02.04 To go in, enter
ongēotung 05.12.05.02.04.02 To pour in
on(ge)sendan 05.12.02.03 To send
ongesetenes 06.01.06.01.01 Knowledge
ongeslēan 02.02.04.03 To kill, slay
ongespanan 06.02.06.03.04 Allurement
ongetǣcan 06.01.06.02.03.04.05 Edification, instruction
ongetimbran 04.05 Building, construction
ongewinn 13.02.03.01 An attack, assault
on(ge)wrig(en)nes 16.02.01.12.01 Revelation, illumination, inspiration
ongiefan 10.03.04.01 Restitution, making good, repayment
ongieldan 14.05 Punishment; 15.02.04 Spending, disbursement; 16.02.04.07.02.03 Penance, an act/instance of penance; 16.02.04.12 Sacrifice, a sacrifice
ongierwan 04.04.07 Trappings, equipment, garb; 05.10.05.04.13 A removal of that which obscures or conceals
ongietan 02.01.03.03 Sex, generation; 02.05.09.04 To see, look upon, behold; 02.05.10 Faculty of hearing; 06.01.01.01.01 Thought, cogitation, meditation; 06.01.05.01 Understanding; 06.01.06.01.01 Knowledge; 06.01.06.01.01.02 To know, recognize; 07 Judgement, forming of opinion; 08.01.01 A feeling, what is felt; 10.04.02.02 To seize, take, grasp, lay hold on
ongietenes 06.01.06 Understanding, knowledge, cognizance; 09.04 Sense, purport, meaning
ongifan 16.02.04.07.02.02 Absolution, forgiveness, remission
onginnan 05.11.10.01 A beginning; 11.03 Endeavour; 13.02.03.01 An attack, assault
onginnendlic 09.03.02.03.01.02.04 Aspect
onginnes 11.01.02 An undertaking
ongrataþ 08.01.01.03.07.01 Laughter
ongrisla 06.01.08.06.02 Great fear, terror, horror
ongrislic 06.01.08.06.03.01 Causing dread, terrifying
ongrynt 08.01.01.03.07.01 Laughter
ongrype 13.02.03.01 An attack, assault
ongryrelic 06.01.08.06.03.01 Causing dread, terrifying
ongyrdan 04.04.07 Trappings, equipment, garb
ongyte 05.12.05.02.04.02 To pour in
onhǣle 09.05.04 A secret
onhǣtan 03.01.09.01 Warmth, heat; 08.01.01.01.03 An incitement, cause of strong feeling
onhafen 04.01.02.01.07.03.01 Unleavened bread
onhagian 08.01.01.03.09.03 To make glad; 11.04 Ability, capacity, power; 11.07.02 Utility, advantage, convenience
onhangen 02.02.04.04.03 Putting to death
onhātan 12.07.02.01.01 A promise
onhātian 03.01.09 Heat

onhāwian 02.05.09.04 To see, look upon, behold
onhealdan 12.07.02 Observance, keeping
onhēaw 17.03.02 Item providing support
onhebban 02.05.10.15.01 To raise (the voice), raise up (noise); 04.01.02.02.05.04.01 Preparation of bread; 05.12.02.02 To carry off, remove; 07.06.01.03 To be proud/arrogant; 07.08.06 Exaltation; 11.01.02 An undertaking
onhebban (ongēan) 12.01.01.12.03 Rebellion, sedition
onhebban (ūp) 05.12.05.12.02 To raise, lift up, elevate
onhefednes 05.12.05.12.02 To raise, lift up, elevate
onhergian 08.01.03.07.02 Misery, trouble, affliction
onhetting 08.01.03.07.02 Misery, trouble, affliction
onhieldan 05.12.05.13 To go down, descend; 05.12.05.13.02 To bow, bend down; 12.05.06 Grasp, power, control, mastery; 12.05.06.04.02 Submission, subjection, obedience
onhield(ed) 05.10.05.04.02.04.02 Support, maintenance
onhield(ed)nes 05.12.05.13 To go down, descend
onhīgian 05.03.02.01.01 An event, occurrence; 13.02.03.01 An attack, assault
onhiscend 07.05.04 Mockery, derision, scorn
onhladan 05.10.05.04.01.02 Contents, what is included; 17.02.04.02.03 Carrying, carriage (of materials)
onhlīdan 02.05.09.06 Thing seen, sight, vision; 05.10.05.04.14 An opening, aperture
onhlinian 05.10.05.04.02.03.02 Reclining, rest
onhnīgan 05.12.05.13.02 To bow, bend down; 07.04.03 Reverence, respect
onhnigenes 07.04.03 Reverence, respect
onhōhsnian 05.07 Ending of existence, end of world
onhōn 02.02.04.04.03 Putting to death; 05.12.01.07.01 To hang; 14.05.05.01.01 Crucifixion, death on cross
onhrēodan 07.10.03 An adornment, decoration, ornament
onhrēosan 13.02.03.01 An attack, assault
onhrēosende 05.08.02 Violence, force
onhrēran 05.12.02 To move, set in motion; 08.01.01.01.03 An incitement, cause of strong feeling; 08.01.03.07.02 Misery, trouble, affliction
onhrīnan 10.04.02 To grasp, take hold of
onhrine 02.05.06 Sense of touch
onhrōp 02.05.10.15.01 To raise (the voice), raise up (noise); 07.05.03.03 Scorn, insult, abuse
onhryre 13.02.03.01 An attack, assault
onhupian 11.06.06 Turning
onhwelan 02.05.10.04 To resound
onhweorfan 05.13.02 A reversal
onhwerfan 05.10.05.04.09.03 Reverse, inverted; 05.12.05 To move and change direction, turn; 05.12.05.04 To rotate, turn round, revolve; 05.13 Changeableness, change
onhwerfednes 05.13 Changeableness, change
onhycgan 06.01.01.01.01 Thought, cogitation, meditation

onhyrdan 06.02.07.06.01 Emboldening, encouragement
onhyrenes 03.06.01.01 Imitation
onhyrian 03.06.01.01.01 Imitation, emulation
onhyr(i)gend 03.06.01.01.01 Imitation, emulation
onhyring 03.06.01.01.01 Imitation, emulation
onhȳrsumian 11.02 Occupation, activity, business
onhyscan 07.03.01.03 To loathe, hate, abhor; 07.05.03.03.02 To reproach, revile, abuse; 08.01.01.03.07.04 Scoffing, mockery
onhyscend 08.01.01.03.07.04 Scoffing, mockery
onīdlian 03.03.08 Emptiness
oniernan 05.10.05.04.14 An opening, aperture
oninnan 05.10.05.04.01 Inside, interior
onlæccan 07.05.03.03.02 To reproach, revile, abuse
onlǣdan 05.12.02.01 To fetch, bring, bear, conduct
onlǣnan 10.03 Giving; 15.01.01.01.01 Hiring, letting out of property/land
onlǣran 06.01.06.02.03.04.03 To teach, instruct
onlǣtan 05.05.04 That loosens, loosening; 12.03.05 Permission
onlecgende 02.08.12.02.05.03 A poultice
onlegen 02.08.12.02.05.03 A poultice
onlēon 10.03 Giving; 10.03.03 Granting
onlīce 03.06.01 Similitude, likeness
geonlīcian 03.06 Comparison
geonlīc(i)an tō 03.06.01.01.01 Imitation, emulation

onlīcnes 02.04.02.03 Height, stature or form; 03.06.01 Similitude, likeness; 09.03.04.02.01 A figure
onlīcung 03.06.01 Similitude, likeness
onlīesan 11.10.03 Salvation/deliverance from
onlīesednes 16.02.04.07.02.02 Absolution, forgiveness, remission
onlīesend 16.01.01.04.02 The Son, Christ
onlīesendlic 16.02.04.07.02.02 Absolution, forgiveness, remission
onlīesnes 16.01.01.02.08 Salvation, redemption
onlīg(i)an 08.01.01.01.03 An incitement, cause of strong feeling
onlīhtan 02.05.09.03 To give light, restore to sight; 03.01.12 Brightness, light; 03.01.12.02 A beam of light; 05.09.03 Mitigation, lightening, alleviation; 06.01.02 The imaginative faculty; 06.01.06.02.03.04.05 Edification, instruction
onlīhtend 16.01.01.02.01 Creator
onlīhting 16.02.01.12.01 Revelation, illumination, inspiration
onlīhtnes 16.02.01.12.01 Revelation, illumination, inspiration
onlīþian 05.05.04 That loosens, loosening
onlīþian 05.09.03 Mitigation, lightening, alleviation
onlīþigan 09.07.04.01 Confirmation, agreement
onlōcian 02.05.09.04 To see, look upon, behold
onlōciend 02.05.09.05 To watch, observe, survey
onlūcan 05.03.01 A cause (of anything); 05.10.05.04.14 An opening, aperture; 09.05.05 Exposure, revealing, revelation
onlūtan 05.12.05.13.02 To bow, bend down

onlūtung 11.09.01.01 Ambush, lying in wait
onlȳsan 05.05.04 That loosens, loosening
onmǣlan 09.01.03 To address, speak to
onmearca 09.03.07.05 To cover with writing, inscribe
onmearcung 09.03.07.05 To cover with writing, inscribe
onmētan mid sceame 07.09.01.01 Reddening with shame, confusion
onmunan 07.04 Consideration, esteem
onmyrran 11.11.02 A hindrance
onnēan 05.12.05.02 To go/travel towards, come, approach
onnīed 12.05.06.02 Oppression
onniman 10.04 To take
ono 02.05.09.04 To see, look upon, behold
onopenian 05.10.05.04.14 An opening, aperture
onorþian 02.04.06.07.05 To breathe; 03.01.15.01 Inspiration, inbreathing
onorþung 02.04.06.07.04 Breathing; 03.01.15.01 Inspiration, inbreathing
onpenn(i)an 05.10.05.04.14 An opening, aperture
onrād 05.12.01.05 To ride (on horse, etc.)
onrǣs 05.12.05.02.01 To come upon, meet with; 13.02.03.01 An attack, assault; 13.02.03.01.01 Inroad, attack
onrǣsan 05.08.02 Violence, force; 13.02.03.01 An attack, assault
onrǣsend 12.05.04.01.01 Fighting, a fight
onrēafian 13.02.05.01.02.02 Booty, spoils
onred 02.07.11.02 Unidentified plants (alphabetical order)
onrid 02.06.02.01.06 Horse
onrīdan 05.12.01.05 To ride (on horse, etc.)

onriht 07.02.01 Right, virtue; 12.07.01 One's due, natural place or position
onrihtlīce 07.02.01 Right, virtue
onrīptīd 05.11.03.01.02.03 Autumn
onryne 05.12.05.02.01 To come upon, meet with; 05.12.05.04 To rotate, turn round, revolve
onsacan 09.07.02 Contradiction; 09.07.03.02 Refusal, denial; 12.05.04.01.01 Fighting, a fight; 12.05.07 Casting out, rejection; 12.07.03.02 An excuse; 14.03.03.01.01 Defence, reply
onsæc 09.07.03.01 A denial; 09.07.03.02 Refusal, denial; 12.07.03 Abstinence/exemption (from)
onsǣgan 05.10.05.04.02.03.02 Reclining, rest
onsǣge 02.02.04 Killing, violent death, destruction; 05.03.02.01.01 An event, occurrence; 13.02.03.01 An attack, assault
onsægednes 16.02.04.12 Sacrifice, a sacrifice
onsægnes 16.02.04.12 Sacrifice, a sacrifice
onsægung 16.02.04.12 Sacrifice, a sacrifice
onsǣlan 05.05.04 That loosens, loosening
onsǣtnes 06.01.07.04.02.01 Deception, deceit, snare, wile
onsǣtnung 06.01.07.04.02.01 Deception, deceit, snare, wile
onsagu 14.03.03.01 Accusation
onsand 05.12.02.03 To send
onsang 16.01.04.01 Sorcery using incantation
onsāwan 04.02.04.02.03 Sowing; 05.12.05.02.04.01 To insert into (a hole)

onscægan 07.05.04 Mockery, derision, scorn
onsceacan 05.10.04.04.02 Removal, taking away; 05.12.05.05 To shake, quake, wag
onscendan 07.09 Shame, disgrace
onsceortian 05.11.03.01.05 A day
onscēotan 02.02.04.04.04 To slaughter (an animal); 05.06.08 A plucking, taking away
onscillan 02.05.10.04 To resound
onscōgan 04.04.07.15 Footwear, covering for the feet
onscrȳdan 04.04.07 Trappings, equipment, garb
onscunian 06.01.08.06 Fear; 07.03.01.03 To loathe, hate, abhor; 08.01.03.05.03 Exasperation, irritation; 09.07.03.02 Refusal, denial; 11.06.06 Turning
onscuniend 08.01.03.09.04 Hatred
onscuniendlic 08.01.03.09.04 Hatred
onscunodlic 08.01.03.09.04 Hatred
onscunung 08.01.03.05.03 Exasperation, irritation; 08.01.03.09.04 Hatred
onscyte 05.12.05.02.01 To come upon, meet with; 07.05.03 Calumny, backbiting
onsēcan 12.03.04 A request, prayer
onsecgan 14.03.03.04 Oath-swearing; 16.02.04.12 Sacrifice, a sacrifice
onsecgend 16.02.04.12 Sacrifice, a sacrifice
onsendan 02.02.04.03 To kill, slay; 05.12.02.03 To send; 05.12.05.03.04 To come/go out from; 05.12.05.03.04.02 To flow out, well up, erupt; 09.01 To speak, exercise faculty of speech; 13.02.08.04.02 A shot, missile, dart, spear, javelin, etc.

onsēon 02.05.09.04 To see, look upon, behold
onset(e)nes 02.05.06.01 To touch and press; 05.05 Constitution, founding (e.g. of world); 16.02.01.10.02.01 A blessing, invocation of divine favour
onsetl 05.12.01.05 To ride (on horse, etc.)
onsettan 05.10.05.04.12 The condition of being covered; 12.05.06.02 Oppression
onsīcan 02.05.10.15.03 Groaning
onsīen 03.03.04.05 Insufficiency, lack, want
onsīgan 05.12.05.02.01 To come upon, meet with; 05.12.05.13 To go down, descend
onsīgende 02.01.04.03 Aging, growing old; 05.12.05.02.01 To come upon, meet with
onsittan 04.05.03.01 Habitation, sojourn; 06.01.08.06.02 Great fear, terror, horror; 12.05.04.01.01 Fighting, a fight; 12.05.06.02 Oppression
onsittend 05.12.01.05 To ride (on horse, etc.)
onslæge 05.06.09 Act of striking
onslǣpan 02.05.04 Sleepiness, drowsiness, sleep
onslīdan 05.09.05 Ceasing, decline, fall off
onslūpan 05.05.04 That loosens, loosening
onsmyrung 16.02.04.07.06 Unction, anointing with holy oil
onsnīþan 05.06.02 Cleaving, splitting, cutting
onsongbōc 16.02.05.10.04 Choir books, etc.
onspǣc 14.03.03 Law, action of the courts
onspǣtan 02.04.06.06.04 Spittle

onspannan 05.05.04 That loosens, loosening; 09.06.02 A saying, speech, statement
onspeca 14.03.03.01 Accusation
onspecend 14.03.03.01 Accusation
onspillend 18.02.05 Buffoonery, speech of buffoon/actor
onspræc 09.01.04 Conversation, discussion
onsprecan 02.01.02 Gift of life
onsprengan 03.01.16.05 A sprinkling
onspringan 01.01.03.01.01.01 River; 01.01.03.01.01.07 Spring, fountain, well; 05.06.03 A dashing together, breaking, shattering
onsprungennes 01.02.01.01.07 An eclipse
onspurnan 11.04.03 (Of ability) low, mean, of less worth
onstæl 03.05 Order, arrangement, disposition
onstælan 14.03.03.01 Accusation
onstæpe 05.12.05.02.04 To go in, enter
onstæppan 05.12.01.04 To go, proceed on foot
onstal 10.03.04 Provision, supply
onstāl 14.03.03.01 Accusation
onstandan 05 Aught, anything, something; 05.11.07.04.01 Nearness, approach, imminence; 05.11.11.01 A not ceasing, persistence, recurrence; 11.02 Occupation, activity, business
onstandende 05.11.11.01 A not ceasing, persistence, recurrence
onstellan 05.04 Fate, lot, fortune, destiny; 05.05.01 An author, source, originator
onstēpan 05.12.05.12.02 To raise, lift up, elevate
onstīgend 05.12.01.05 To ride (on horse, etc.)

onsting 12.01.01 Authority
onstingan 08.01.03.05.02 Anger
onstīþian 08.01.03.09.10 Wrath, sternness, displeasure
onstregdan 03.01.16.05 A sprinkling
onstydfullnes 05.13.05 Changeability
onstȳran 12.03 Direction, guidance
onstyre(d)nes 05.12 To move, be in motion; 05.12.02 To move, set in motion
onstyrian 05.12 To move, be in motion; 08.01.01.01.03 An incitement, cause of strong feeling; 08.01.03.07.02 Misery, trouble, affliction
onsundran 03.03.05.01.01 Principal/chief (of its class or type); 03.03.07.01 Division, partition, separation; 05.10.04.04 Absence
onswāpan 03.01.15.01 Inspiration, inbreathing
onswebban 02.02.04.03 To kill, slay; 02.02.05 A burial, burying
onswīfan 05.12.02.08 To give a different direction to, turn; 05.12.05 To move and change direction, turn
onswiþlic 02.05.10.02 Noise, din
onswōgan 05.12.05.02.01 To come upon, meet with
onswornod 06.01.08.06.01 A shuddering with fear, nervousness
onsymbelnes 16.02.04.07.04.01 The service of the mass
ontalu 14.03.03 Law, action of the courts
ontendan 03.01.09.02.01 Fire, burning; 03.01.12.02 A beam of light; 08.01.01.01.03 An incitement, cause of strong feeling; 17.05.04 To kindle, set alight (fire, lamp)
ontendnes 02.05.05.03 Sexual appetite, lust; 02.08.05 Inflammation;

onteon

03.01.09.02.01 Fire, burning; 08.01.01.01 Ardour, fervour, strong feeling
onteon 05.05.04 That loosens, loosening; 05.06.08 A plucking, taking away
onteona 08.01.03.07.02 Misery, trouble, affliction
ontīgan 05.05.04 That loosens, loosening
ontige 11.01.02 An undertaking
ontihting 06.02.06 Mind, purpose
ontimber 03 Material, matter, substance; 04.04.05 Woven material, fabric; 05.03.01.03 Reason, cause
ontimbernes 03 Material, matter, substance; 06.01.06.02.03.04 Teaching, instruction
ontimbr(i)an 06.01.06.02.03.04.05 Edification, instruction
ontrēowan 06.01.08.03 Trust, faith, confidence
ontȳdran 11.12.02.01 Strengthening, confirmation
ontȳdre 05.09 Weakness
ontygnes 14.03.03.01 Accusation
ontyhtan 06.02.06 Mind, purpose; 06.02.06.03.03 Incitement
ontyhting 06.02.06.03.02 Instigation
ontȳnan 05.10.05.04.14 An opening, aperture; 09.05.05.01 Showing, manifestation, display
ontȳnan ēagan 02.05.09.03 To give light, restore to sight
ontȳnan ēaran 02.05.10 Faculty of hearing
ontȳnan hand 10.03.08 Bountifulness, munificence
ontȳnan mūþ/weoloras 09.01 To speak, exercise faculty of speech
ontȳnnes 05.10.05.04.14 An opening, aperture

onþenian 05.10.05.02 Extension, stretching
onþēon 08.01.01.03.08 Happiness, well-being, prosperity; 11.07.01 Utility, usefulness
onþēowigan 12.01.01.08 Service
onþicgan 04.01.01 Eating
(ge)onþracian 06.01.08.06.02 Great fear, terror, horror
onþracung 06.01.08.06 Fear
onþræce 06.01.08.06.03.01 Causing dread, terrifying
onþræclic 06.01.08.06.03.01 Causing dread, terrifying
onþrēagung 07.05.03.03 Scorn, insult, abuse
onþrecan 06.01.08.06.02 Great fear, terror, horror
onþringan 05.12.05.09 To go forward, proceed
onþwægennes 04.06.01.01 Cleansing, washing
onþwēan 04.06.01.01 Cleansing, washing
onufan 05.10.05.04.02 Face, surface; 05.11.07.04.02 (Of time) later/latter
onufan (ge)sittan 12.05.06.02 Oppression
onuppan 05.10.05.04.02 Face, surface
onūtan 05.10.05.04.02.01 Exterior, outside of
onwacan 02.01.03.03.03 Birth; 02.05.02 Consciousness
onwaccan 06.02.06.03.03 Incitement
onwadan 05.12.05.02.01 To come upon, meet with
onwǣcan 05.09.03 Mitigation, lightening, alleviation
onwæcenes 08.01.01.01.03 An incitement, cause of strong feeling
onwæcnan 06.02.06.03.03 Incitement

1240

onwæcn(i)an 02.01.03.03.03 Birth
onwæstm 02.07.03.03.01 Wood (as substance); 03.03.04.03 Growth, increase
onwarian 11.10.02.01 Vigilance
onwealcan 05.10.06.05 A fold, plait, wrinkle; 05.12.05.04.01 (Of wheel, etc.) to roll, trundle
onweald 12.01 Power, control, sway; 12.01.01.01 Rule, domination, direction; 12.06 A province, country, territory
onwealda 12.01.01.04 A leader, ruler; 16.01.01.01.01 The Almighty
onwealdan 12.01.01.01 Rule, domination, direction
onwealdend 12.01.01.04 A leader, ruler
geonwealdian 12.01.01.01 Rule, domination, direction
onwealdnes 12.01 Power, control, sway
onwealg 03.03.06 Wholeness; 05.11.11.01 A not ceasing, persistence, recurrence; 07.02.03.01 Uninjured, unhurt, unharmed; 12.08.02 Integrity, absence of moral flaw
onwealglīce 03.03.06.02 Fullness
onwealhnes 03.03.06 Wholeness; 12.08.02 Integrity, absence of moral flaw
onweard 08.01.03.09.06 Hostility
onwece 06.02.06.03.03 Incitement
onweg 05.10.04.04 Absence
onweg ādrīfan 05.12.02.04 To cast out, drive away
onweg āfirran 05.12.05.03.04 To come/go out from
onweg āscūfan 05.12.02.06 To push, impel, thrust
onweg drīfan 05.12.02.04 To cast out, drive away
onweg losian 11.10.05 Escape
onwegācyr(red)nes 16.02.01.07 Apostasy
onwegādrifennes 05.12.02.04 To cast out, drive away
onwegālædnes 05.10.04.04.02 Removal, taking away
onwegāwendan 05.10.04.04.02 Removal, taking away
onwegfæreld 05.12.05.03.03 To depart, leave, set out
onweggewite 05.12.05.03.03 To depart, leave, set out
onweggewitenes 05.12.05.03.03 To depart, leave, set out
onwegpullian 05.06.02.02 A tearing apart; 05.12.02.05 To pull, drag, draw
onwendan 05.06 Destruction, dissolution, loss, breaking; 05.10.05.04.09.03 Reverse, inverted; 05.12.02 To move, set in motion; 05.12.05.11.01 To return; 05.13 Changeableness, change; 05.13.04 Exchange, commutation; 08.01.03.07.02 Misery, trouble, affliction; 12.08.06.01.04.01 To mislead, seduce, lead astray; 14.01.06 A rule, order, precept, tenet, principle
onwendan āweg 05.12.05 To move and change direction, turn
onwendan fram/of 11.06.06 Turning
onwendan of 05.12.02.08 To give a different direction to, turn
onwended 05.10.05.04.09.03 Reverse, inverted
onwendedlic 05.13.05 Changeability
onwendedlicnes 05.13.05 Changeability
onwend(ed)nes 05.12.02 To move, set in motion; 05.12.05 To move and change

direction, turn; 05.13 Changeableness, change
onweorpan fram 05.12.02.08 To give a different direction to, turn
onweorpnes 05.12.02.07 To throw, cast, toss
onwīcan 05.12.05.11 To turn back, retreat
onwille 08.01.01.03.09.01 Pleasant, agreeable
onwindan 05.05.04 That loosens, loosening; 05.12.05.11 To turn back, retreat
onwinnan 13.02.03.01 An attack, assault
onwinnende 13.02.03.01 An attack, assault
onwist 12.06.03.02 Living, dwelling, residence (in)
onworpennes 08.01.01.01 Ardour, fervour, strong feeling
onwrecscip 04.05.03.01 Habitation, sojourn
onwrēon 05.10.05.04.13 A removal of that which obscures or conceals; 06.01.06.02.03.03 To study, apply oneself to learning; 09.04.02.01 A secret, mystery; 09.05.05 Exposure, revealing, revelation; 09.05.05.01 Showing, manifestation, display; 16.02.01.12.01 Revelation, illumination, inspiration
onwrigennes 05.10.05.04.13 A removal of that which obscures or conceals; 09.04.03 Exposition, making clear by explanation; 09.05.05 Exposure, revealing, revelation
onwrītung 09.03.07.05 To cover with writing, inscribe
onwrīþan 05.10.05.04.13 A removal of that which obscures or conceals

onwrīþod 05.10.05.04.02.04.02 Support, maintenance
onwrīþung 02.08.12.02.06.01 A bandage, binding
onwunian 04.05.03.01 Habitation, sojourn; 05.11.07.04.01 Nearness, approach, imminence; 11.01.01 Practice, exercise, doing
onwunung 04.05.03 A dwelling-place, abode, habitation; 06.02.07.03 Perseverance; 12.06.03.02 Living, dwelling, residence (in)
onwyllan 08.01.01.01.03 An incitement, cause of strong feeling
onwylwan 05.10.06.05 A fold, plait, wrinkle
onȳþan 05.12.05.02.04.02 To pour in
onȳwan 03.06.01 Similitude, likeness; 09.05.05.01 Showing, manifestation, display
open 03.04.03 Generality; 05.10.05.04.13 A removal of that which obscures or conceals; 05.10.05.04.14 An opening, aperture; 05.12.01.03.01 A means of access; 06.01.05.01.01 Clear to the understanding, plain; 09 Speech, vocal utterance; 09.05.05.01 Showing, manifestation, display; 09.06.02.01.05 Proclamation, spreading abroad; 11.09 Peril, danger; 11.12.01 Absence of restraint, freedom; 13.02.02 Battle; 14.03.03 Law, action of the courts
open sott 06.01.05.03.02 Foolish, silly, stupid
openærs 02.07.09.02 Particular fruits (alphabetical order)
openere 05.10.05.04.14 An opening, aperture
openian 05.10.05.04.14 An opening, aperture

(ge)openian 05.06.02.02 A tearing apart; 05.10.05.04.14 An opening, aperture; 05.10.05.04.14.01 A yawning, gaping opening; 09.05.05.01 Showing, manifestation, display; 09.06.02.01 To tell, make known, declare, relate, announce

geopenian 09.04.03 Exposition, making clear by explanation; 09.06.02.01.05.01 To spread, make known, proclaim, celebrate; 11.12.01 Absence of restraint, freedom

openlic 09.05.05.01 Showing, manifestation, display

openlīce 02.05.10.01 Thing heard; 06.01.05.01.01 Clear to the understanding, plain; 09.05.05.01 Showing, manifestation, display; 09.06.02.01.05 Proclamation, spreading abroad; 11.12.01 Absence of restraint, freedom

opennes 09.05.05 Exposure, revealing, revelation; 09.05.05.01 Showing, manifestation, display

openung 09.05.05 Exposure, revealing, revelation

(ge)openung 05.10.05.04.14 An opening, aperture

ōr 05.10.05.04.09.01.01 Head, front (position); 05.11.10.01.01 Origin

ōra 01.01.02.02.03 Minerals and metals; 05.10.05.04.11.01 A bound, limit; 15.01.04 Coinage, money; 17.04.02 Ore, unwrought metal

orc 04.01.02.02.06.05.04 Cup/bowl/basin; 16.01.03 A spectre, ghost, demon, goblin

orcēape(s) 15.02.02 Cheap

orcēapunga 15.02.02 Cheap

orcēapungum 15.02.02 Cheap

orcēas 12.08.04 Purity, moral cleanness

orcēasnes 12.08.04 Purity, moral cleanness

orcerdlēh 04.02.04.05.02 An orchard

orcerdweard 04.02.04.05 Garden

orcnǣwe 09.05.05.01 Showing, manifestation, display

orcnēas 16.01.03.03 A doomed spirit

ord 05.03 Source, origin; 05.10.05.03.03 Height, loftiness, sublimity; 05.10.05.04.09.01.01 Head, front (position); 05.10.06.03 Projection, head, extremity (of anything); 05.10.06.03.01 A point, spike, prickle; 12.01.01.04 A leader, ruler; 12.01.01.06.08 A person of rank, elder, great man; 13.02.08.04 Weapons, arms; 13.02.08.04.01 A spear; 13.02.10.01.02.02.03 Part of an army

ordǣle 11.06.04 Abstention, abstaining from

ordāl 14.03.03.05 Ordeal

ordālīsen 14.03.03.05 Ordeal

ordbana 02.02.04.03.01 A killer

ordfruma 05.03 Source, origin; 05.11.10.01 A beginning; 12.01.01.04 A leader, ruler; 16.01.01.02.01 Creator

ordfrymm 05.11.10.01.01 Origin

ordstæpe 02.08.04.01 A wound

ordwiga 13.02.10.01 A man, warrior

oreald 02.01.04.03 Aging, growing old

ōreblāwere 17.02.04.03.03 Smelting, heating, scorification

orel 04.04.07 Trappings, equipment, garb

orenlīcost 12.08.07 Immoderation, excess

ōret 12.05.04.01 Fighting, contention, warfare, strife

ōretfeld 18.02.03 A spectacle, display

ōretla 07.05.03.03 Scorn, insult, abuse

ōretlof 16.01.01.02.09 Resurrection; 18.02.03 A spectacle, display
ōretmæcg 13.02.10.01 A man, warrior
ōretmæcga 18.02.03.01 A combatant, athlete
ōretstōw 18.02.03 A spectacle, display
ōretta 13.02.10.01 A man, warrior
orf 02.06.02.01.03 Cattle
orfcwealm 04.02.05.02.01 (Of cattle) seized with disease
orfcynn 02.06.02.01.03 Cattle
orfeorme 04.06.02.02 Foul, filthy, squalid; 06.02.04.01.01 Need, distress, straits, difficulty; 07.03.03.01 Empty, useless, worthless
orfeormnes 04.06.02.02 Foul, filthy, squalid
orfgebitt 04.01.02.01.04 Animal food, fodder
orfiermu 04.06.02.02 Foul, filthy, squalid
orfyrmþ 04.06.02.04 Refuse, litter, rubbish
organ 18.02.07.01.01 A song, a poem to be sung or recited
organdrēam 18.02.07.02 A musical instrument
organe 02.07.10.01 Particular herbs/spices (alphabetical order)
organe(-a) 18.02.07.02 A musical instrument
organystre 18.02.07.02 A musical instrument
orgel 07.06.05 Pomp, splendour, magnificence
orgeldrēam 18.02.07.02 A musical instrument
orgele 18.02.07.02 A musical instrument
orgellic 07.09.03 Infamy, ignominy, shame
orgellīce 07.06.01.02 Proudly, arrogantly
orgello 07.06 Pride
orgelnes 07.06 Pride
orgelword 07.06.03 Boastfulness, arrogance
orgilde 14.03.03.09.02 Atonement
orgnian 18.02.07.01 Singing, song
orgyte 09.05.05.01 Showing, manifestation, display
orhlyte 06.02.04.01.01 Need, distress, straits, difficulty
orīege 02.05.09.13 Invisible
orlæg 05.04 Fate, lot, fortune, destiny
orleahter 11.09 Peril, danger; 12.08.04 Purity, moral cleanness
orleahtre 12.08.05.01 Blameless
orlegcēap 13.02.05.01.02.02 Booty, spoils
orlege 12.05.04 Strife, hostility; 13.02 War
orlegfrom 06.02.07.06.02 Boldness
orleggīfre 12.05.03.01 Quarrel, contentiousness, strife
orleghwīl 13.02 War
orlegnīþ 12.05.04 Strife, hostility
orlegstund 08.01.03.06 Adversity, affliction
orlegweorc 13.02 War
ormǣdum 06.01.08.05.01.01 Wondrous, glorious, marvellous
ormǣte 03.03.04.01.01 Greatness, bigness, size; 03.03.04.01.03 An immense quantity, immensity, immense number; 03.03.04.02.02 Excess
ormǣtlic 03.03.04.01.01 Greatness, bigness, size; 03.03.04.01.03 An immense quantity, immensity, immense number

ormǣtlīce 03.03.04.01.03 An immense quantity, immensity, immense number; 03.03.04.02.02 Excess
ormǣtnes 03.03.04.01.03 An immense quantity, immensity, immense number; 05.10.01 Amplitude, spaciousness, vastness
ormōd 06.01.08.06.07 Despair
ormōdnes 06.01.08.06.07 Despair
orne 02.08.04 Hurt, injury, damage; 03.03.04.01.03 An immense quantity, immensity, immense number; 12.08.07 Immoderation, excess
ornest 14.03.03.05 Ordeal
oroþ 02.04.06.07.03 Breath; 02.04.06.07.04 Breathing
orped 05.08 Strength
orpedlīce 09.05.05.01 Showing, manifestation, display
orrest 14.03.03.05 Ordeal
orretscipe 07.09.03 Infamy, ignominy, shame
(ge)orrettan 07.09 Shame, disgrace
orsāwle 02.02.03.02 State of being dead
orsceattinga 15.02.02 Cheap
orscylde 12.08.05 Innocence
orsorg 08.01.01.03.01 Freedom from trouble, comfort, security; 11.10 Safety, safeness
orsorglēas 08.01.03.03 Anxiety
orsorglic 11.10 Safety, safeness
orsorglīce 08.01.01.03.01 Freedom from trouble, comfort, security; 11.06.01.01 Negligence, carelessness, heedlessness; 11.10 Safety, safeness
orsorgnes 08.01.01.03.01 Freedom from trouble, comfort, security; 08.01.01.03.08 Happiness, well-being, prosperity; 11.06.01.01 Negligence, carelessness, heedlessness

ortgeard 04.02.04.05.02 An orchard
ortrēowe 06.01.08.03.02 Distrust, want of faith or confidence
ortrēowe/ortrīewe 12.01.01.12.04 Treachery
ortrēownes 06.01.08.03.02 Distrust, want of faith or confidence
ortrēowþ 06.01.08.06.07 Despair
geortrīewan 06.01.07.06.02.01 Doubt, uncertainty; 06.01.08.03.02 Distrust, want of faith or confidence; 06.01.08.06.07 Despair
ortrīewe 06.01.08.03.02 Distrust, want of faith or confidence; 06.01.08.06.07 Despair
geortrūwian 06.01.07.06.02.01 Doubt, uncertainty; 06.01.08.06.07 Despair
geortrūwod 06.01.08.06.07 Despair
ortrūwung 06.01.08.06.07 Despair
ortȳdre 02.01.03.02 Barrenness, sterility
orþanc 06.01.05 Understanding, intellect; 11.04 Ability, capacity, power; 11.04.02.01 Art, skill, contrivance, cunning; 17.02.04 Trade, calling, craft, aptitude
orþancbend 17.03.10 Supports and fastenings
orþances 11.06.01.01 Negligence, carelessness, heedlessness
orþanclic 11.04.02 Skill, skilfulness
orþancpīl 04.02.04.06.07 Ploughing equipment; 05.10.06.03.01 A point, spike, prickle
orþancscipe 17.02.04 Trade, calling, craft, aptitude
orþancum 11.04.02 Skill, skilfulness
orþian 02.01.02.02 To come to life, have life; 02.04.06.07.05 To breathe
orþian (tō) 06.02.05.02 Greed, importunate desire, rapacity

orþung 02.01.01.01 Soul, spirit; 02.04.04 Skin; 02.04.06.07.03 Breath; 02.04.06.07.04 Breathing; 03.01.15.01 Inspiration, inbreathing
orwearde 11.09 Peril, danger
orweg 11.11.01 A physical difficulty, strait
orwegnes 05.10.05 A space, span
orwegstīg 05.12.01.03.01.01 A path, track
georwēnan 06.01.08.06.07 Despair
orwēne 06.01.08.06.07 Despair
orwēnnes 06.01.08.06.07 Despair
orwīge 13.02.04.01 Defenceless, unwarlike; 14.01.03.02 Freedom from punishment or fine
orwirþe 13.02.05.02 Defeat
orwīte 12.07.03.01 Impunity
orwurþ 07.09.03 Infamy, ignominy, shame
georwyrþan 07.09.02 Disgrace, shaming, humiliation
(ge)orwyrþed 07.09.02 Disgrace, shaming, humiliation
orwyrþlic 07.09.03 Infamy, ignominy, shame
orwyrþu 07.05.03.03 Scorn, insult, abuse
orwyrþ(u) 07.09 Shame, disgrace
oryldu 02.01.04.03 Aging, growing old
ōs 09.03.07.01.01 A runic letter; 16.01.06.01 Northern gods
oser 02.07.03.05 Particular trees/shrubs (alphabetical order)
ōsle 02.06.08.05 Forest bird, wild-fowl
ōst 02.07.03.03.01 Wood (as substance)
osterhlāf 04.01.02.01.02.07 Fish
osterscyll 02.06.06.04.01.05 Oyster
ōstig/ōstiht 03.01.05 Roughness
ostre 02.06.06.04.01.05 Oyster; 04.01.02.01.02.07 Fish
oterhola 02.06.01.08 A lair, den

otor 02.06.03.01.12 Otter
oþ 03.03.05 Extent, degree; 05.11.07.03.02 Earlier, antecedent; 05.12.05.02 To go/travel towards, come, approach
oþ nū 05.11.07.02 The present (time)
oþ on worulde 05.11.01.01.01 Eternity
oþ þæt (þe) 05.11.07.03.02 Earlier, antecedent
oþ þisum 05.11.07.02 The present (time)
oþberan 05.12.02.02 To carry off, remove; 13.02.08.03.01 Body armour, war gear
oþberstan (ūt) 11.10.05 Escape
oþbregdan 05.12.02.02 To carry off, remove; 10.04.03.01 To take away, deprive of
oþclīfan 05.02.02 Nature, established order of things
oþcwelan 02.02.03 To die, perish
oþcyrran 12.08.06.01.04 To lead a bad life
oþdōn 05.06.08 A plucking, taking away
oþēcan 03.03.04.03 Growth, increase
oþēhtian 05.12.02.04 To cast out, drive away
ōþer 03.03.03.04.02 Two; 03.03.07.02 What is left, remnant, remains; 03.05.02 An arrangement, order, succession; 03.06.02 Difference, diversity, dissimilarity
ōþer ... ōþer 03.03.03.04.02 Two; 03.06.02 Difference, diversity, dissimilarity
ōþer gēara 05.11.07.04.01 Nearness, approach, imminence
ōþer ēasterdæg 16.02.04.04.02.01.03 Holy Week
ōþer healf 03.03.03.04.01.01 One and a half

ōþer līf 02.01.02.02.01 Condition of life; 05.11.07.04 Future, time to come
ōþer oþþe ... oþþe 07.01.01 Choice, election
ōþer swilc 03.06.01 Similitude, likeness
ōþer twēga oþþe ... oþþe 07.01.01 Choice, election
ōþerhwīle 05.11.09.03 At times, sometimes
ōþerhwīlen 05.11.09.03.01 Occasional
ōþerlicor 03.06.02.01 Contrariety, diversity
oþfæstan 10.03 Giving; 11.10.02.02.01 Care, interest in; 12.05.06.02.03 Trouble, disturbance
oþfaran 11.10.04 Flight
oþfeallan 03.02.01 Decay, decline, corruption; 11.06.04 Abstention, abstaining from
oþfēolan 03.01.17 Thickness, viscosity
oþfeorrian 05.10.04.04.02 Removal, taking away
oþferian 05.12.02.02 To carry off, remove; 14.02.01.02.01 Open robbery, rapine, pillage
oþflēogan 05.12.01.07 To fly (with wings)
oþflēon 11.10.04 Flight
oþflītan 14.03.03 Law, action of the courts
oþgān 11.10.05 Escape
oþglīdan 05.12.05.03 To travel away (from); 05.12.05.06.01 To travel smoothly, slide, glide
oþgrīpan 10.04.03 To take away, remove
oþhealdan 10.03.06 Withholding, keeping back
oþhebban 07.04.04 Praise, acclamation, applause
oþhlēapan 11.10.05 Escape

oþhrīnan 02.05.06 Sense of touch; 05.10.05.01 A little way, no great distance; 08.01 Heart, spirit, mood, disposition
oþhȳdan 09.05.04.01 Concealment, obscurity
oþiernan/oþrinnan 11.10.05 Escape
oþīewan 02.05.09.06 Thing seen, sight, vision; 02.05.09.12 To show; 09.05.05.01 Showing, manifestation, display
oþlǣdan 05.12.02.02 To carry off, remove; 05.12.05.08.01 To go before and guide
oþlengan 05.02.02 Nature, established order of things
ōþre dæg 05.11.02 A time, particular time, occasion
ōþre sīþe ... ōþre sīþe 05.11.09.03.01 Occasional
oþrīdan 05.12.01.05.01 Modes of riding
oþrōwan 11.10.05 Escape
oþsacan 09.07.03.01 A denial; 11.06.01 Neglect
oþscacan 11.10.05 Escape
oþscēotan 05.12.05.03 To travel away (from); 11.06.06 Turning; 11.10.05 Escape; 11.10.05.01 Evasion, escape from threat
oþscūfan 05.12.05.03 To travel away (from)
oþsperning 11.11.02 A hindrance
oþspurnan 11.04.03 (Of ability) low, mean, of less worth
oþstandan 05.12.04 Absence of movement, stillness; 05.13.06 Constancy, unchangeableness; 06.01.05.03.01.01 Dullness, folly, stupidity

oþstillan 05.07 Ending of existence, end of world; 11.11.03 Impeding of progress, prevention
oþswerian 14.03.03.04 Oath-swearing
oþswīgan 02.05.10.17.01 Dumb, silent
oþswimman 11.10.05 Escape
oþtēon 10.04.03.01 To take away, deprive of
oþþe 05.13.04 Exchange, commutation
oþþe … oþþe 07.01.01 Choice, election
oþþēodan 05.06.02.01 A cleft, split
oþþicgan 10.04.03.01 To take away, deprive of
oþþingian 15.01.01.01 Holding of land
oþþringan 10.04.03 To take away, remove
oþþringan feorh/līf 02.02.04.03 To kill, slay
oþwendan 10.04.03.01 To take away, deprive of
oþwindan 11.10.05 Escape
oþwītan 07.05.03.03.02 To reproach, revile, abuse; 14.03.03.01 Accusation
oþwyrcan 05.06.04 Damage, injury, defect, hurt, loss
ōwæstm 02.07.03.03.01 Wood (as substance)
ōweb 04.04.05 Woven material, fabric
ōwef 04.04.05 Woven material, fabric
ōwisc 05.10.05.04.11.01 A bound, limit
oxa 02.06.02.01.03 Cattle
oxancealf 02.06.02.01.03 Cattle
oxangang 04.02.03.03.02 A hide
oxanhyrde 04.02.05.06.01 A cowherd
oxanslippe 02.07.11 Plants/flowers (alphabetical order)
oxantunge 02.07.11.02 Unidentified plants (alphabetical order)
ōxn 02.04.03.04.01 Arm

oxna lybb 02.07.11 Plants/flowers (alphabetical order)
pād 04.04.07.07 A long outer garment, covering, cloak, etc.
paddanīeg 01.01.02.01.01.02 Island
padde 02.06.07.02 Frog, toad
pǣca 06.01.07.04 Deception
pǣcan 06.01.07.04 Deception
pǣcung 06.01.07.04 Deception
pægel 03.03.01.01 Liquid measures
pǣl 13.02.08.04.01 A spear
pæll 03.01.14.05 Red/redness; 04.04.05.05 Fine woven material from silk, cotton or linen; 04.04.07.07 A long outer garment, covering, cloak, etc.; 04.04.08.01 Curtain, wall-hanging, etc.; 16.02.05.05.09 Cloths
pællen 03.01.14.05 Red/redness; 04.04.05.05 Fine woven material from silk, cotton or linen
pærl 17.04.03.04 Gems collectively
pæþ 01.01.02.01.03.03 Valley; 01.01.03.01.01.01 River; 05.12.01.03.01.01 A path, track
pæþþan 05.12.05.06 To travel over/through/along, traverse
pāl 04.02.04.06.01 A spade; 17.03.07 Tools for digging/grasping/pulling; 17.03.09 A post, rod, stick, etc.
palendse/palent(s)e 04.05.03.02.02.06 A royal/noble palace
palentlic 04.05.03.02.02.06.01 A hall building
pallium 04.04.07.01 Mode of dressing, fashion; 16.02.05.06.02 Garb for neck and shoulders
palm(a) 02.07.09.02 Particular fruits (alphabetical order)
palmæppel 02.07.09.02 Particular fruits (alphabetical order)

palmbearu 02.07.09.02 Particular fruits (alphabetical order)
palmdæg 16.02.04.04.02.01.03 Holy Week
palmsunnandæg 16.02.04.04.02.01.03 Holy Week
palmtrēow 02.07.09.02 Particular fruits (alphabetical order)
palmtwig 02.07.09.02 Particular fruits (alphabetical order)
gepalmtwigian 16.02.04.04.02.01.03 Holy Week
palmwucu 16.02.04.04.02.01.03 Holy Week
palstr 05.10.06.03.01 A point, spike, prickle
palþer 02.06.04.01.11 Panther
pamp 01.01.02.01.02.02.01 Hill
pandher 02.06.04.01.11 Panther
panic 04.01.02.01.03.05 Millet; 04.02.04.03.02.01.02 A kind of millet
panmete 04.01.02.01.07 Cooked/cookable food
panne 04.01.02.02.06.01 Cooking vessel/pot
pāpa 16.02.03.02.02 The pope
pāpan hād 16.02.03.02.02 The pope
pāpdōm 16.02.03.02.02 The pope
paper 09.03.07.06.05 Papyrus
papolstān 01.01.02.02.01 Rock, stone
pāpseld 16.02.03.02.02 The pope
pāpseld/-setl 12.01.01.02 Seat of authority; 16.02.05.05.05 A chair
pāpseld/pāpsetl 16.02.03.02.02 The pope
paradīs 16.01.02.01 Heavenly dwelling place; 16.01.02.04 Paradise
paralisin 02.08.04.03 Paralysis
pardus 02.06.04.01.08 Leopard
part 03.03.07 A part, division, portion

passion 16.02.01.08.03 The New Testament
paternoster 16.02.04.08.01 Kinds of prayer
patte 01.01.02.01.04.01 Marsh, bog, swamp
pāwa 02.06.08.02.01.03 Peacock
pāwe 02.06.08.02.01.03 Peacock
pēa 02.06.08.02.01.03 Peacock
pēac 01.01.02.01.02.02.01 Hill
pēaclond 01.01.02.01.02 High land
peall 01.01.02.01.02.02.04 Cliff; 04.01.03.05.01 Intoxicating liquor
pearr 05.10.05.04.11 A circle, circuit, circumference
pearroc 04.02.03.01.01 Enclosed land/field; 05.10.05.04.11 A circle, circuit, circumference; 13.02.06.01 Stronghold, fort/fortified town
pearroc/-uc 04.05.01.02.07 A fence, hedge
pecg 02.06.02.01.07 Pig, swine
pellican 02.06.08.07 Exotic bird
pening 03.03.02.01 A weight, definite amount; 15.01.04 Coinage, money
peningas 15.01.04 Coinage, money
peninghwyrfere 15.01.04 Coinage, money
peningmangere 15.01.04 Coinage, money
peningslæht 15.01.04 Coinage, money
peningwǣg 03.03.02.01 A weight, definite amount
peningweorþ 15.02 Worth, value
penitentialem 16.02.05.10.09 A penitential
penn 04.02.05.03.01 A pen, fold, enclosure
pentecosten 16.02.04.04.02.01.03 Holy Week

peonie 02.07.11 Plants/flowers (alphabetical order)
peorþ 09.03.07.01.01 A runic letter
peren 02.07.09.02 Particular fruits (alphabetical order)
pērēnei (þā beorgas) 01.01.02.01.02.02.02 Mountain
perewōs 04.01.03.05 A drink/beverage
pernex 02.06.08.03 Game-bird
persic 02.07.09.02 Particular fruits (alphabetical order)
persisc 02.03.03.06.07.06 Persian
persoctrēow 02.07.09.02 Particular fruits (alphabetical order)
peru 02.07.09.02 Particular fruits (alphabetical order)
perwince 02.07.11 Plants/flowers (alphabetical order)
petermæsse 16.02.04.04.02.01.04 Other feasts
petersilie 02.07.10.01 Particular herbs/spices (alphabetical order)
philosoph 06.01.06.02.02.01.01 Philosophy
pic 03.01.17.06.01 Bitumen, pitch
pīc 05.10.06.03.01 A point, spike, prickle; 13.02.08.04 Weapons, arms
pīced 05.10.06.03.01 A point, spike, prickle
picen 03.01.17.06.01 Bitumen, pitch
picga 02.06.02.01.07 Pig, swine
picgbrēad 02.07.09.02.01 Nut; 04.01.02.01.04.01 Mast, pig-food
gepīcod 17.03.12.02 A potter
pīcung 05.06.07 Pricking, a prick, puncture
pidu 01.01.02.01.04.01 Marsh, bog, swamp
pīe 02.06.09.01 Parasite

pierisc 02.03.03.06.07.07 Other (alphabetical order)
pigment 02.08.12.02.05 Pharmacy, curing with salves
pihten 04.04.03 A spinning-house or chamber
pīl 02.07.02.05 A shoot, sprout, tendril; 05.10.06.03.01 A point, spike, prickle
pīle 04.01.02.02.07.01 Mortar; 17.03.04 Tools for smoothing/scraping/grinding
gepīled 05.10.06.03.01 A point, spike, prickle
pīlere 17.03.04 Tools for smoothing/scraping/grinding
pilian 05.10.05.04.13 A removal of that which obscures or conceals
(ge)pīlian 17.03.04 Tools for smoothing/scraping/grinding
pillsāpe 04.06.01.04 What is used in washing, an ointment
pīlstæf 17.03.04 Tools for smoothing/scraping/grinding
pīlstampe 17.03.04 Tools for smoothing/scraping/grinding
pīlstocc 17.03.04 Tools for smoothing/scraping/grinding
pīn 08.01.03.07.03 Suffering, torment, pain
pīnbēam 02.07.03.05 Particular trees/shrubs (alphabetical order)
pīnecwalu 02.02.01 Particular mode of death
pīnere 14.05.02 Torment, punishment
pīnhnutu 02.07.03.05 Particular trees/shrubs (alphabetical order)
(ge)pīnian 14.05.02 Torment, punishment
pinn 09.03.07.06.01 A writing instrument; 17.03.10.02 A pin, peg, nail
pinne 04.01.03.05.04.01 A flask, flagon, bottle

pīnnes 08.01.03.07.03 Suffering, torment, pain
pinsian 06.01.01.01.01 Thought, cogitation, meditation; 07.01 Appraisal, appraising
pintel 02.04.06.04.01 Male genitalia
pīntrēow 02.07.03.05 Particular trees/shrubs (alphabetical order)
pīntrēowen 02.07.03.05 Particular trees/shrubs (alphabetical order)
pīnung 14.05.02 Torment, punishment
pīnungtōl 14.05.06 Means/implement of torture
pīpdrēam 18.02.07.02.02.01 Pipe/flute
pīpe 01.01.03.01.01.04 Watercourse/channel; 16.02.05.05.06 A vessel for use in services; 17.03.11 Other implements, etc.; 18.02.07.02.02.01 Pipe/flute
pīpere 18.02.07.02.02.01 Pipe/flute
(ge)pip(e)rian 04.01.02.02.04.02 To pepper
pīpian 18.02.07.02.02.01 Pipe/flute
pipineale 02.07.11 Plants/flowers (alphabetical order)
piplian 02.08.05.02 Particular inflammation/swelling
pīplic 18.02.07.02 A musical instrument
pipor 04.01.02.01.05.05.03 Pepper
piporcorn 04.01.02.01.05.05.03 Pepper
piporcwyrn 04.01.02.02.09 A mill
piporhorn 04.01.02.02.06.03 Food receptacle, basket
pīrēni 01.01.02.01.02.02.02 Mountain
pirenisc 02.03.03.06.07.07 Other (alphabetical order)
pirgrāf 04.02.04.05.02 An orchard
pirie 02.07.09.02 Particular fruits (alphabetical order)
pīs 03.01.07 Weight, heaviness

pise 02.07.09.02.02.02 Other vegetables (alphabetical order)
pisen 02.07.09.02.02.02 Other vegetables (alphabetical order); 04.02.03.02.02.02 Bean land/field
pisle 04.05.03.04 A closet, chamber, room
pīslic 08.01.03.07.02 Misery, trouble, affliction
pīslīce 08.01.03.07.02 Misery, trouble, affliction
pistelari 16.02.01.08.03 The New Testament; 16.02.05.10.05 A bible
pistol 09.03.07.07.03.02.02 A letter; 16.02.01.08.03 The New Testament
pistolbōc 16.02.01.08.03 The New Testament; 16.02.05.10.05 A bible
pistolclāþ 16.02.05.06 Ritual clothing
pistolrǣdere 16.02.03.02.11 A deacon, minister of the church
pistolrǣding 16.02.04.03.02 Parts of service
pistolrocc 16.02.05.06 Ritual clothing
piþa 02.07.02.03 A stalk, stem
plæce 12.06.02.01 A township
plæsc 01.01.03.01.03.01 Pool
plætt 02.05.10.07 A crashing, noise
plættan 14.05.05 Physical punishments
planēta 16.02.05.06.01 Outer garments
plante 02.07 A plant
plantian 05.13.06.01 Firm, stable, steady; 06.02.07 Will, determination, resolution
(ge)plantian 04.02.04.02.04 Planting
plantsticca 04.02.04.06.08 A dibble
plantung 02.07 A plant; 04.02.04.02.04 Planting; 04.02.04.03 A plant
plaster 02.08.12.02.05.03 A poultice
geplatod 17.02.04.03 Metal worker
platung 17.02.04.03 Metal worker

plega 05.12.03.01.01 Quick movement or movements; 07.04.04.01.01 Clapping (the hands), applause; 09.03.03 A gesture, action, gesticulation; 13.02.02 Battle; 18.02 Amusement, revelry, festivity; 18.02.02 Play, (athletic) sport; 18.02.04 Dancing; 18.02.06 Theatricals
plegan for 11.03 Endeavour
plegdīc 04.05.03.05.03.01 A ditch, dike
plegende 18.02.02 Play, (athletic) sport
plegere 18.02.03.01 A combatant, athlete
plegestre 18.02.03.01 A combatant, athlete
pleghūs 18.02.06 Theatricals
pleg(i)an 05.12.03.01 Swiftness, velocity; 05.12.03.01.01 Quick movement or movements; 06.01.06.02.02.01.01 Philosophy; 07.04.04.01.01 Clapping (the hands), applause; 08.01.01.03.07.04 Scoffing, mockery; 11.02 Occupation, activity, business; 18.02.02 Play, (athletic) sport; 18.02.06 Theatricals; 18.02.07.02 A musical instrument
pleg(i)an (mid) 18.02.02 Play, (athletic) sport
(ge)pleg(i)an 18.02.04 Dancing
pleglic 08.01.01.03.07.01 Laughter; 18.02.03.01 A combatant, athlete; 18.02.06 Theatricals
plegmann 18.02.03.01 A combatant, athlete
plegol 08.01.01.03.07.02 Jesting, pleasantry; 12.08.07.01.01 Wantonness, sensuality, lasciviousness
plegscip 05.12.01.09.03.01.01 Kind of ship
plegscyld 13.02.08.03.01.06 A shield
plegstall 18.02.03 A spectacle, display
plegstede 18.02.03 A spectacle, display
plegstōw 18.02.03 A spectacle, display
pleoh 11.09 Peril, danger; 12.07 An obligation, bounden duty; 12.08.06 Moral evil, depravity; 14.01.05 Service, obligation, duty
plēolic 11.09 Peril, danger; 12.08.06.01.02 Lacking moral good
plēon 11.09 Peril, danger
plett 04.02.05.03.01 A pen, fold, enclosure
pliht 11.09 Peril, danger; 12.08.06 Moral evil, depravity
plihtan 11.09 Peril, danger; 14.05.04 A penalty, punishment
plihtere 05.12.01.09.03 A voyage
plihtlic 11.09 Peril, danger
plōg 04.02.03.03.01 A ploughland
plōges land 04.02.03.03.01 A ploughland
plot 01.01.02.01.01 Tract of land; 04.02.03.01 Plot of land
pluccian 05.06.08 A plucking, taking away; 07.01.01 Choice, election
plūmblǣd 02.07.09.02 Particular fruits (alphabetical order)
plūme 02.07.09.02 Particular fruits (alphabetical order)
plūmfeþer 04.05.04.05.01 Bedding (e.g. of straw)
plūmsēaw 04.01.03.05 A drink/beverage
plūmslā 02.07.09.02 Particular fruits (alphabetical order)
plūmtrēow 02.07.09.02 Particular fruits (alphabetical order)
plūn 02.07.09.02 Particular fruits (alphabetical order)
plyccan 02.05.05 Desire, appetite; 05.06.08 A plucking, taking away
plȳme 02.07.09.02 Particular fruits (alphabetical order)

pocādl 02.08.06 Skin disease, erysipelas
pocc 02.08.05.02 Particular inflammation/swelling
pocca/pohha 02.04.03.01.03.04 Nose
pohha 17.03.12 A receptacle, container
pohhede 04.04.07.01 Mode of dressing, fashion
pōl 01.01.03.01.01.01 River; 01.01.03.01.03.01 Pool
pōlbǣr 04.02.03.04.02.01 Types of pasture
polente 04.01.02.01.03.09 Parched corn (biblical); 04.02.04.03.02.01 Grain crops
pollegie 02.07.10.01 Particular herbs/spices (alphabetical order)
pollup 14.05.06 Means/implement of torture
polra 01.01.02.01.04.01 Marsh, bog, swamp
popig 02.05.04.01 To make heavy with weariness/sleep; 02.07.11 Plants/flowers (alphabetical order)
popul 02.07.03.05 Particular trees/shrubs (alphabetical order)
porlēac 02.07.09.02.02.01 Edible root/bulb
porr 02.07.09.02.02.01 Edible root/bulb
port 04.05.02.12 Gate/doorway of a building; 05.12.01.09.03.04 A harbour; 12.06.02.01 A township
portcwene 12.08.08.01.02.01.01 An adulterer/-ess, whore, prostitute
portgeat 05.10.05.04.14.02 An opening/space in an enclosure
portgerēfa 12.02.02 An assembly, meeting
portgeriht 15.03.02 A tax
portherpaþ 05.12.01.03.01.03 A highway

(ge)portian 17.03.04 Tools for smoothing/scraping/grinding
portic 04.05.02.12.01 A porch, covered entrance; 04.05.03.02.02 Types of dwelling; 05.10.05.04.11 A circle, circuit, circumference; 16.02.05.03.01 Door or gate of church; 16.02.05.03.11 A niche, arched recess
portmann 02.03.03.04.05 Populace of a town/city
portstrǣt 05.12.01.03.01.03 A highway
portwara 02.03.03.04.05 Populace of a town/city
portweall 05.10.05.04.15.02 A wall
portweg 05.12.01.03.01.03 A highway
portwer 02.03.03.04.05 Populace of a town/city
(ge)pos 02.08.07.04.04 Respiratory disease
poshlīwe 04.05.03.02.02.08 A lowly dwelling, cottage, hut; 11.10.01.02 Refuge, help, shelter
posl 02.08.12.02.05 Pharmacy, curing with salves
post 04.05.02.04 A column, pillar; 17.03.09 A post, rod, stick, etc.
postling 02.08.12.02.05 Pharmacy, curing with salves
postol 16.02.01.08.03.01 New Testament persons
potian 05.06.09 Act of striking
pott 04.01.02.02.06.04 Pot, vessel, crock
pottere 17.03.12.02 A potter
prætt 11.04.02.01.01 Cunning, craft, craftiness, guile, wile
prættig 11.04.02.01.01 Cunning, craft, craftiness, guile, wile
prafost 12.01.01.05 A leader, administrator; 16.02.03.03.01.03 A prior
prafostfolgoþ 16.02.03.03.01.03 A prior

prafostscīr 16.02.03.03.01.03 A prior
prass 02.05.10.03 Noise, tumult, uproar; 07.06.05 Pomp, splendour, magnificence
prāw 02.05.09.10 Look-out place
prēdicere 16.02.03.02.10 A preacher, teacher
prēdician 16.02.04.10 Preaching
prēdicung 16.02.04.10 Preaching
preg 05.10.06.03.01 A point, spike, prickle
prēon 04.04.10.02 A button, brooch
prēost 16.02.03.02 A cleric, clergyman (general); 16.02.03.02.07 A priest, cleric; 16.02.03.02.07.01 A priest of a church or minster; 16.02.03.02.08 A (domestic) chaplain
prēostgesamnung 16.02.03.02.07 A priest, cleric
prēostgyrd 16.02.05.05.08 A staff, wand of authority
prēosthād 16.02.03.02.07 A priest, cleric
prēosthēap 16.02.03.02.07 A priest, cleric
prēosthīred 16.02.03.02.07 A priest, cleric
prēostlagu 16.02.01.09.01 Canon law
prēostlic 16.02.01.09.01 Canon law
prēostlīf 16.02.05.04.03 Priests' quarters
prēostrēaf 16.02.05.06 Ritual clothing
prēostregol 16.02.01.09.01 Canon law
prēostscīr 16.02.03.02.07.01 A priest of a church or minster
prēowthwīl 05.11.01.02 Shortness/brevity in time
press 04.05.04.03 A box, case, chest, container
prica 03.03.04.04 Littleness, smallness; 05.10.02 Narrowness, scantiness of space; 05.10.06.03.01 A point, spike, prickle; 05.11.01.02 Shortness/brevity in time; 09.03.07.04.01 To punctuate, divide; 09.03.07.04.02.01 Marking out, disposition of materials
pricel 05.10.06.03.01 A point, spike, prickle; 09.03.07.06.01 A writing instrument
pricele 03.03.04.04 Littleness, smallness; 15.01.04 Coinage, money
pricels 05.10.06.03.01 A point, spike, prickle
prician 02.08.03.02 Itch, irritation
(ge)prician 05.06.07 Pricking, a prick, puncture; 06.02.06.03.03 Incitement
geprician 09.03.07.04 To make a symbol, mark; 09.03.07.04.01 To punctuate, divide; 09.03.07.04.02.01 Marking out, disposition of materials
pricmǣlum 05.11.09.06 Frequency, repetition; 05.11.11.02 Let up, intermission, cessation
pricþorn 02.07.03.05 Particular trees/shrubs (alphabetical order)
pricung 08.01.03.02.01 Compunction, remorse, contrition
prīm 05.11.04.01 Day (not night); 16.02.04.05.04 The hour or service of Prime
prīmsang 16.02.04.05.04 The hour or service of Prime
princ 05.11.01.02 Shortness/brevity in time
prior 16.02.03.03.01.03 A prior
pritol 09.01.02.01 Excessive fluency, loquacity
prodbor 17.03.05 An awl, borer, gimlet, etc.
prōfian 11.03.01.01.01 Proof, demonstration

prologa 09.03.07.07.02.01.02 A prologue, preface
prūd 07.06.01.01 Proud, arrogant
prutene 02.07.11 Plants/flowers (alphabetical order)
prūtian 07.06 Pride
prūtlic 07.06.01.01 Proud, arrogant
prūtlīce 06.01.08.03 Trust, faith, confidence; 07.06.01.02 Proudly, arrogantly; 07.06.05 Pomp, splendour, magnificence
prūtscipe 07.06.01 Pride, arrogance
prūtswongor 07.06.01.01 Proud, arrogant
prūtung 07.06.01 Pride, arrogance
pryfet 02.07.03.05 Particular trees/shrubs (alphabetical order)
prȳt(e) 07.06.01 Pride, arrogance
prȳtu(-o) 07.06.05 Pomp, splendour, magnificence
pūca 16.01.03.04 Elfin race
pūcel 16.01.03.04 Elfin race
pucian 05.06.09 Act of striking
pudd 02.08.05.02 Particular inflammation/swelling
puddel 01.01.03.01.03.01 Pool
puduc 02.08.05.02 Particular inflammation/swelling
pull 01.01.02.01.01.03.02 Inlet in river/sea; 01.01.03.01.03.01 Pool
pullian 04.02.05.06.02.03 Sheep-shearing; 05.06.08 A plucking, taking away; 05.10.05.04.13 A removal of that which obscures or conceals
pūlsper 02.07.08 Grasses, reeds, etc.
pumic 04.06.01.04 What is used in washing, an ointment
pumicstān 04.06.01.04 What is used in washing, an ointment

pund 03.03.01.01 Liquid measures; 03.03.02.01 A weight, definite amount; 04.02.05.03.01 A pen, fold, enclosure; 05.10.05.04.11 A circle, circuit, circumference; 11.11.02 A hindrance; 15.01.04 Coinage, money
pundere 06.01.06.02.01 A wise man, man of understanding or learning
pundern 17.03.11 Other implements, etc.
punderngend 06.01.01.01.01.01 Consideration, rumination
pundfald 04.02.05.03.01 A pen, fold, enclosure
pundmǣte 03.03.02.01 A weight, definite amount
pundur 03.03.02 Measurement by weighing; 17.03.11 Other implements, etc.
pundwǣg 03.03.02.01 A weight, definite amount
pūnere 17.03.04 Tools for smoothing/scraping/grinding
pung 17.03.12 A receptacle, container
pungetung 02.08.03 Pain, bodily discomfort
(ge)pūnian 17.03.04 Tools for smoothing/scraping/grinding
punt 05.12.01.09.03.01.01 Kind of ship
pūr 02.06.08.06 Water bird
purlamb 02.06.02.01.08 Sheep
purpul 03.01.14.05 Red/redness
purpure 03.01.14.05 Red/redness; 04.04.05.05 Fine woven material from silk, cotton or linen; 04.04.07.01 Mode of dressing, fashion
purpuren 03.01.14.05 Red/redness
purs 17.03.12 A receptacle, container
pusa 17.03.12 A receptacle, container
puslian 07.01.01 Choice, election
putta 02.06.08.04 Bird of prey
puttoc 02.06.08.04 Bird of prey

pūtung 06.02.06.03.02 Instigation
pȳcan 05.06.08 A plucking, taking away
pyff 01.03.01.05 Wind
pyfian 03.01.15.01 Inspiration, inbreathing
pyle 04.05.04.05.01 Bedding (e.g. of straw)
pylece 04.04.07.07 A long outer garment, covering, cloak, etc.
pylewer 04.05.04.05.01 Bedding (e.g. of straw)
pynca 05.10.06.03.01 A point, spike, prickle
gepyndan 04.02.04.02.01.02 To irrigate (plants, land)/channel (water); 12.05.06.01 Restraint, check, curb, control
pynding 01.01.03.01.03.02 Weir
pyngan 05.06.07 Pricking, a prick, puncture; 06.02.06.03.03 Incitement; 09.03.07.04.01 To punctuate, divide
pyretre 02.07.11 Plants/flowers (alphabetical order)
pysecynn 02.07.09.02.02.02 Other vegetables (alphabetical order)
pȳtan (ūt) 05.06.08 A plucking, taking away
pytt 01.01.02.01.03 Hollow/depression in land; 01.01.03.01.01.07 Spring, fountain, well; 02.02.05.01.01 A grave, burial place, sepulchre; 02.06.01.08 A lair, den; 02.08.05.02 Particular inflammation/swelling; 07.06 Pride
pytted 05.06.04 Damage, injury, defect, hurt, loss
pyttel 02.06.08.04 Bird of prey
rā 02.06.03.01.06 Deer, hart
rabbi 16.02.01.09.02 Knowledge of Jewish law

rabbian 08.01.03.05.02 Anger
raca 04.02.04.06.04 A rake
racca 05.12.01.09.03.01.03 Part of ship
racente 14.05.07 Binding, fastening with bonds
geracentēagian 14.05.07 Binding, fastening with bonds
racentēah 14.05.07 Binding, fastening with bonds
racian 05.12.03.01 Swiftness, velocity; 05.12.03.01.02 Haste, hurry; 05.12.05.09 To go forward, proceed; 12.01.01.01 Rule, domination, direction
raciend 09.01.02 Fluency in speech
racu 06.01.03 Faculty of reason; 06.01.03.01 Argument, reasoning; 09.03.04 Rhetoric, art of exposition; 09.04.03 Exposition, making clear by explanation; 09.06.01 To relate, recount, tell; 15.02.03 An account; 18.02.06 Theatricals
rād 05.12.01.05 To ride (on horse, etc.); 05.12.01.09.03 A voyage; 09.03.07.01.01 A runic letter; 13.02.01 A military expedition; 18.02.07.01 Singing, song
gerād 03.05 Order, arrangement, disposition; 05.02 State, condition; 05.02.01 Condition, state of affairs, situation; 05.10.05.04.05 Straight, direct; 06.01.03 Faculty of reason; 06.01.05.02.01.01.01 Reason, sense, discretion, prudence; 06.02.06.02 A proposal, proposition, suggestion; 11.04.02 Skill, skilfulness; 14.04.02 A stipulation
gerāde sprǣc 09.03.06 Prose
rād(e)cniht 12.01.01.06.08 A person of rank, elder, great man

1256

radelod 02.07.03.03.01 Wood (as substance)
rādhors 02.06.02.01.06 Horse
gerādian 03.03.03 Number; 06.01.06.02.03.04.03 To teach, instruct; 06.02.06.02.01 To devise a plan, arrange, settle
(ge)rādlic 03.06.03.04 What is fitting/seemly/appropriate/decent
gerādlīce 06.01.05.02 Intelligence
gerādod 06.01.05 Understanding, intellect
rādpytt 17.02.04.02.04 Leading/conducting of water
gerādscipe 06.01.05 Understanding, intellect
rādstefn 09.06.02.01.06 A message, announcement by a messenger
rādwērig 02.05.03.02 Weariness
(ge)rǣcan 05.10.05.02 Extension, stretching; 05.12.05.02.03 To arrive; 09.03.03 A gesture, action, gesticulation; 10.03 Giving; 10.03.02 Presenting, offering
gerǣcan 02.08.04.01 A wound; 05.02 State, condition; 05.12.01 To go, progress, travel (usually on land); 05.12.05.02.01 To come upon, meet with; 09.01.03 To address, speak to; 10.01.02 Acquisition; 10.04.02.02 To seize, take, grasp, lay hold on; 13.02.05.01.02 To gain by fighting
gerǣcan on 10.04.03 To take away, remove
rǣcc 02.06.02.01.04 Dog; 04.03.01 Tracking
rǣcing 09.03.03 A gesture, action, gesticulation; 10.03.02 Presenting, offering; 10.04.02.02 To seize, take, grasp, lay hold on

rǣd 06.01.05.02 Intelligence; 06.01.05.02.01.01.01 Reason, sense, discretion, prudence; 06.01.06.02.03.03.01 An act of reading; 06.02.06.02 A proposal, proposition, suggestion; 11.07.03 Use, advantage, profit; 11.12.02 Aid, help, succour; 12.01.01.01 Rule, domination, direction; 12.01.01.12.04.02 Conspiracy; 12.02.02 An assembly, meeting; 12.02.02.04 Counsel, deliberation; 12.02.02.05 Counsel, advice; 14.01.06 A rule, order, precept, tenet, principle
rǣd gelǣran 12.02.02.05 Counsel, advice
rǣdan 04.02.04.02.01 To prepare land/soil; 06.01.03.02 Dialectics, logic; 06.01.06.02.03.03 To study, apply oneself to learning; 06.01.06.02.03.03.01 An act of reading; 06.01.07.06.01 To accept as the result of enquiry, suppose; 09.04.02.01 A secret, mystery; 10 Having, owning, possession; 12.01.01.01 Rule, domination, direction; 12.02.02 An assembly, meeting; 12.02.02.05 Counsel, advice; 17.05.04 To kindle, set alight (fire, lamp)
rǣdan on 14.03.03 Law, action of the courts
rǣdan (wiþ) 12.02.02.04 Counsel, deliberation
(ge)rǣdan 06.01.06.02.03.03.01 An act of reading; 12.02.02.05 Counsel, advice
gerǣdan 07 Judgement, forming of opinion; 10.03.04 Provision, supply; 14.01.06 A rule, order, precept, tenet, principle

rǣdbana 14.02 Lawlessness
rǣdbora 12.02.02.02 A counsellor, advisor; 12.02.02.03 Terms for classical world
rǣdda 02.06.08.05 Forest bird, wild-fowl
rǣde 05.12.01.05 To ride (on horse, etc.); 13.02.10.01.02.02.02 Branch of army; 16.02.04.03.02 Parts of service
gerǣde 03.05 Order, arrangement, disposition; 04.02.05.06.05.03 Harness, trappings; 04.04.07 Trappings, equipment, garb; 04.04.10 Ornaments, trappings, accoutrements; 09.03.04.03 Plain, simple; 11.04.02 Skill, skilfulness; 13.02.08.03.01 Body armour, war gear
rǣdebōc 16.02.05.10.02 A lectionary
rǣdecempa 13.02.10.01.02.02.02 Branch of army
rǣdefæsting 04.01.02.04.05.01.01 Quartering of officials
rǣdegafol 15.02.04.01 Payment for temporary use, rent, hire
rǣdehere 13.02.10.01.02.02.02 Branch of army
rǣdels 06.01.01.01 Thinking about, minding, heeding; 06.01.02 The imaginative faculty; 06.01.03.02 Dialectics, logic; 09.04.02.01 A secret, mystery; 09.04.03 Exposition, making clear by explanation; 12.02.02.04 Counsel, deliberation
rǣdemann 05.12.01.05 To ride (on horse, etc.)
rǣden 03.03.03 Number; 12.01.01.01 Rule, domination, direction
(ge)rǣden 14.04.02 A stipulation
rǣdend 06.01.06.02.03.03.01 An act of reading; 12.01.01.04 A leader, ruler; 16.01.04.06 Divination, augury

rǣdende 12.02.02.04 Counsel, deliberation
rǣdendlic 14.01.02 A law, statute
rǣdengewrit 14.04.01 A deed, contract, agreement
rǣdere 06.01.06.02.01 A wise man, man of understanding or learning; 06.01.06.02.03.03.01 An act of reading; 16.01.04.06 Divination, augury; 16.02.03.02.12 Cleric in minor orders
rǣdescamol 16.02.05.05.04 A lectern
rǣdesmann 12.01.01.08.01 A servant, attendant; 12.02.02.02 A counsellor, advisor
rǣdewiga 13.02.10.01.02.02.02 Branch of army
rǣdfæst 06.01.05.02.01.01 Sagacity; 06.02.07 Will, determination, resolution; 12.02.02.05 Counsel, advice
rǣdfæstnes 06.02.06.03 Persuasion, prompting; 12.03.02 Advice, admonition
rǣdfindende 12.02.02.04 Counsel, deliberation
rǣdgasram 01.02.01.01.02 Star
rǣdgeþeaht 12.02.02.05 Counsel, advice
rǣdgifa 12.02.02.02 A counsellor, advisor; 12.02.02.03 Terms for classical world
rǣdgift 12.02.02.03 Terms for classical world
rǣdhors 02.06.02.01.06 Horse
rǣdhycgende 06.01.05.02.01.01 Sagacity
rǣdic 02.07.09.02.02.01 Edible root/bulb
rǣding 06.01.06.02.03.03.01 An act of reading; 12.01.01.01 Rule, domination, direction; 12.02.02.04

Counsel, deliberation; 16.02.04.03.02 Parts of service
geræding 12.02.02.05 Counsel, advice
rædingbōc 16.02.05.10.02 A lectionary
rædinggrād 16.02.05.05.04 A lectern
rædingscamol 16.02.05.05.04 A lectern
rædistre 06.01.06.02.03.03.01 An act of reading
rædlēas 06.01.05.03.01.01 Dullness, folly, stupidity; 06.01.05.03.03.01 Unreasonableness, foolishness, imprudence; 08.01.03.06 Adversity, affliction
rædlic 11.07.01.01 Desirability, expediency
rædlīce 06.01.05.02.01.01.01 Reason, sense, discretion, prudence; 06.02.06 Mind, purpose; 11.04.02 Skill, skilfulness; 11.07.01.01 Desirability, expediency
gerædlīce 06.01.05.01.01 Clear to the understanding, plain
rædmægen 12 Power, might
(ge)rædnes 14.04.02 A stipulation
gerædnes 07 Judgement, forming of opinion; 14.01 Law, body of rules; 14.01.06 A rule, order, precept, tenet, principle; 14.04.01 A deed, contract, agreement; 16.02.01.09.01 Canon law
gerædod 04.02.05.06.05.03 Harness, trappings
rædsnottor 06.01.05.02.01.01 Sagacity
rædþeahtende 12.02.02.04 Counsel, deliberation
rædþeahtere 12.02.02.02 A counsellor, advisor
rædþeahtung 12.02.02.05 Counsel, advice
rædwita 12.02.02.02 A counsellor, advisor

geræf 14.03.03.09.01 Unfavourable judgement, condemnation
(ge)ræfnan 11.01.05 Accomplishment, fulfilment
(ge)ræfn(i)an 08.01.03.07.03 Suffering, torment, pain
ræfter 04.05.02.07 A beam, rafter
ræge 02.06.03.01.08 Goat
rægerēose 02.04.05.05 Muscle
ræghār 02.07.06 Lichen; 03.01.14.10 Grey-coated one
ræpan 05.05.03 Binding, fastening
(ge)ræpan 14.05.07 Binding, fastening with bonds
ræpling 14.02 Lawlessness
ræp(l)ing 14.05.08 Captivity
ræplingweard 14.05.08.01 Prison, confinement, durance
(ge)ræptan 14.05.07 Binding, fastening with bonds
rǣran 04.05 Building, construction; 05.05.01 An author, source, originator; 05.12.05.12.02 To raise, lift up, elevate; 06.02.06.03.03 Incitement; 08.01.01.01.03 An incitement, cause of strong feeling; 11.01.05.02 Furtherance, promotion
rǣs 01.01.03.04 Current, rush of water; 05.12.02.06.01 To push, drive; 05.12.03.01.01 Quick movement or movements; 13.02.03.01 An attack, assault
(ge)rǣsan 05.12.03.01 Swiftness, velocity; 05.12.03.01.01 Quick movement or movements
(ge)rǣsan on 11.02.04 Heedlessness
(ge)rǣsan on/wiþ 13.02.03.01 An attack, assault
rǣsbora 12.01.01.04 A leader, ruler; 12.02.02.02 A counsellor, advisor

ræsc 01.03.01.06.02 Rain
ræscan 03.01.12.01 Glittering, effulgence
ræscettan 03.01.12.01 Glittering, effulgence
ræscet(t)ung 01.03.01.03.01.02 Lightning
ræsn 04.05.02.07 A beam, rafter
ræswa 12.02.02.02 A counsellor, advisor
(ge)ræswa 12.01.01.04 A leader, ruler
geræswa 12.01.01.06.08 A person of rank, elder, great man
ræsw(i)an 06.01.01.01.01.01 Consideration, rumination; 06.01.03.02 Dialectics, logic; 06.01.08.03.02.01 Suspicion
ræswung 06.01.03.02 Dialectics, logic
ræt 02.06.03.01.13 Rodents
rætten 04.06.02.02 Foul, filthy, squalid
ræw 02.07.03.04.03 A hedge/border; 03.05.02 An arrangement, order, succession
geræwed 03.01.14.11 Medley/variety of colour; 13.02.07.02 Order (of troops), array
raggig 02.06.01.06 Skin, hide
ragu 02.07.06 Lichen
ragufinc 02.06.08.05 Forest bird, wild-fowl
rāhdēor 02.06.03.01.06 Deer, hart
rāhhege 04.02.05.06.09 An enclosure for wild animals
ramgealla 02.07.11 Plants/flowers (alphabetical order)
ramm 01.02.01.01.02.01.01 The Zodiac; 02.06.02.01.08 Sheep; 13.02.08.04.05 A warlike engine
rān 05.10.05.04.11.01 A bound, limit; 14.02.01.02.01 Open robbery, rapine, pillage
ranc 02.01.04.02 To grow, grow up; 06.02.07.06.02 Boldness; 07.06.01.01 Proud, arrogant; 07.06.04.01 Ostentation, showiness
ranclīce 06.02.07.06 Courage, boldness, valour; 07.06.04.01 Ostentation, showiness
rancstrǣt 05.12.01.03.01 A means of access
rand 05.10.05.04.11.01 A bound, limit; 13.02.08.03.01.06 A shield
randbēag 13.02.08.03.01.06 A shield
randbēah 13.02.08.03.01.06 A shield
randburg 01.01.03.01.02.05 Wave; 13.02.06.01 Stronghold, fort/fortified town
randgebeorh 01.01.03.01.02.05 Wave
randhæbbend 13.02.10.01 A man, warrior
randwiga 13.02.10.01 A man, warrior
randwīgend 13.02.10.01 A man, warrior
rāp 17.03.10 Supports and fastenings
rāpgenga 18.02.05 Buffoonery, speech of buffoon/actor
rāpincel 02.03.02.03 Ancestry, descent
rāplic 17.04.04 Fibrous materials
gerār 02.05.10.15.06 A roar, howl, etc.
rāradumbla 02.06.08.06 Water bird
rārian 02.05.10.15.06 A roar, howl, etc.; 08.01.03.04.01 Complaint, lamentation
rārigende 08.01.03.04.01 Complaint, lamentation
rārung 02.05.10.15.06 A roar, howl, etc.
rāsettan 03.01.09.02 Fire, flame
rāsian 09.05.01 Inspection, examination
rapost þinga 05.11.08.01.02 (Untimely) earliness
gerāwan 03.05.02 An arrangement, order, succession
raxan 05.10.05.02 Extension, stretching

1260

rēad 02.04.06.08.01 Blood; 03.01.09.02 Fire, flame; 03.01.14.05 Red/redness; 16.02.05.11 The cross (as Christian image)
rēada 02.04.06.05.01 Tonsil
rēadbasu 03.01.14.05 Red/redness
rēade 03.01.14.05 Red/redness
rēade clǣfre 02.07.11 Plants/flowers (alphabetical order)
rēadfāh 03.01.14.05 Red/redness
rēadgoldlæfer 17.02.05.02 Goldsmith's art
rēadian 03.01.14.05 Red/redness
rēadlēaf 02.07.02.06 A leaf
rēadlesc 04.04.06 Undressed condition (of hide)
rēadnes 03.01.14.05 Red/redness
rēadstalede 02.07.02.03 A stalk, stem
rēadung 03.01.14.05 Red/redness
rēaf 04.04.07 Trappings, equipment, garb; 13.02.05.01.02.02 Booty, spoils
rēafere 14.02.01.02.01 Open robbery, rapine, pillage
rēafgend 14.02.01.02.01 Open robbery, rapine, pillage
rēafian 04.04.07 Trappings, equipment, garb
(ge)rēafian 05.06.01 Devastation, laying waste; 14.02.01.02.01 Open robbery, rapine, pillage
(ge)rēafian (on) 14.02.01.02 Wrongful taking, theft
gerēafian 05.10.05.04.13 A removal of that which obscures or conceals
rēafigende 06.02.05.02 Greed, importunate desire, rapacity
rēaflāc 13.02.05.01.02.02 Booty, spoils; 14.02.01.02.01 Open robbery, rapine, pillage

rēafol 06.02.05.02 Greed, importunate desire, rapacity
rēafolnes 06.02.05.02 Greed, importunate desire, rapacity
rēafung 14.02.01.02.01 Open robbery, rapine, pillage
reahtigan 09.07 Dispute, debate
rēam 04.01.02.01.02.09.05 Cream
rēamwīn 04.01.03.05.01.01 Wine
rec 05.12.01.09.03.01.01 Kind of ship
gerec 09.04.03 Exposition, making clear by explanation; 12.01.01.01 Rule, domination, direction; 14.01.06 A rule, order, precept, tenet, principle
rēc 03.01.09.02.01.04 Smoke
recan 05.12.02.01 To fetch, bring, bear, conduct
(ge)recan 05.12.03.01 Swiftness, velocity
gerecan 05.12.01 To go, progress, travel (usually on land)
rēcan 03.01.09.02.01.04 Smoke; 04.01.02.02.02 To smoke food; 06.01.08.06.05 Wariness, carefulness; 06.02.05.01 Strong liking for, devotion to; 11.02.02.02 Care, mindfulness, attention; 16.02.04.18.02 Burning of incense
rēcan (be) 08.01.02.02 Love, affection, care
(ge)rēcan 02.08.12.02.05.04 To cleanse, clean away
reccan 05.12.05.01 To go astray; 09.04.03 Exposition, making clear by explanation; 09.04.03.01 A translation; 11.03.01.01.01 Proof, demonstration
(ge)reccan 03.05.01 Arranging, ordering, disposition; 05.10.05.02.02 Greater, bigger; 09.04.03 Exposition, making clear by explanation; 09.06.02.01 To tell, make known, declare, relate,

announce; 10.03 Giving; 12.01.01.01 Rule, domination, direction; 12.03 Direction, guidance; 12.08.02.02.01 Reform, correction

gereccan 06.01.06.02.03.04.03 To teach, instruct; 07.05.01 Censure, reproof, rebuke; 09.01.03 To address, speak to; 09.06.02 A saying, speech, statement; 10.03.07.01 To allot, assign; 11.03.01.01.01 Proof, demonstration; 14.01.06 A rule, order, precept, tenet, principle; 15.01.02 Gift, transfer of property

gereccan (on) 14.03.03.01 Accusation

gereccan tō 07.01 Appraisal, appraising

reccend 12.01.01.04 A leader, ruler; 16.01.01.01.01 The Almighty

reccendōm/recedōm 12.01.01.01 Rule, domination, direction

reccenes 09.04.03 Exposition, making clear by explanation

reccere 09.01.02 Fluency in speech; 09.04.03.03 A commentary, exposition; 16.02.03.02.07 A priest, cleric

reccing 09.06.01 To relate, recount, tell

reced 04.05.03.02.01 A building, house, hall, palace, etc.

recedlic 04.05.03.02.02.06.01 A hall building

(ge)rece(d)nes 09.06.01 To relate, recount, tell

gerecednes 09.04.03 Exposition, making clear by explanation; 09.06.01.01 A tradition, ordinance handed down

gerec(ed)nes 12.08.02.02 Righteousness, rectitude

rēcelēas 11.02.04.01 Rashness, madness; 11.06.01.01 Negligence, carelessness, heedlessness; 12.08.07.01.01 Wantonness, sensuality, lasciviousness

rēcelēasian 11.06.01.01 Negligence, carelessness, heedlessness

rēcelēaslīce 11.06.01.01 Negligence, carelessness, heedlessness

rēcelēasnes 11.06.01.01 Negligence, carelessness, heedlessness

rēcelēast 11.06.01.01 Negligence, carelessness, heedlessness

rēcel(s) 16.02.05.09.02 Incense

rēcelsbūc 16.02.05.05.07 A thurible, censer

rēcelsfæt 16.02.05.05.07 A thurible, censer

rēcelsian 02.05.08.02 Pleasant smell, fragrance, perfume

rēcelsrēoce 16.02.04.18.02 Burning of incense

recen 05.12.03.01 Swiftness, velocity; 06.01.08.06.03.01 Causing dread, terrifying; 11.02.01 Energy, vigour, vigorous action

recene 05.12.03.01 Swiftness, velocity

gerecenes 05.12.05.02.02 To come together, meet; 11.03.01.01.01 Proof, demonstration

recenian 15.02.04 Spending, disbursement

gerecenian 03.05 Order, arrangement, disposition; 09.04.03 Exposition, making clear by explanation

recenlīce 05.11.07.01 Contemporary, coeval

gerecennes 05.12.05.03.03 To depart, leave, set out

gereclic 14.03.03.03 Witness, testimony, attestation

gereclīce 03.05 Order, arrangement, disposition; 05.12.04 Absence of movement, stillness

recondlic 03.03.04.01.02 A great number, multitude
gerec(u) 08.01.01.03.01 Freedom from trouble, comfort, security
rēdestān 03.01.14.05 Red/redness
geredian 05.12.05.02.03 To arrive; 11.01.05 Accomplishment, fulfilment; 11.03.01.03 Finding, discovery
redlingas 02.03.03.06.07.01 African
(ge)rēfa 12.01.01.05 A leader, administrator; 12.01.01.06.08 A person of rank, elder, great man
gerēfa 12.01.01.08.01 A servant, attendant; 13.02.10.01.01 A commander, officer
gerēfærn 14.03.01 Judicial body, authority
(ge)rēfland 15.01.01 Landed property
gerēflang 12.01.01.08.01 A servant, attendant
gerēfmǣd 15.01.01 Landed property
gerēfmann 12.01.01.05 A leader, administrator
gerēfscipe 12.02 A public office; 12.02.02.03 Terms for classical world
gerēfscīre 12.02 A public office
gerēfscīr(e) 12.02.02.03 Terms for classical world
regallic 07.02.04.03 Nobleness, excellence, nobility, magnificence
regn 01.03.01.06.02 Rain
regnheard 03.01.03 Hardness, callosity, hard material
regnian 01.03.01.06.02 Rain; 05.12.05.13.03 To fall
geregnian 17.05.04 To kindle, set alight (fire, lamp)
regnþēof 14.02.01.02 Wrongful taking, theft

regol 03.05.03 A list, tale, series; 09.03.07.06.03 A ruler; 11.05.02.01 A standard, norm, ethos; 14.01.06 A rule, order, precept, tenet, principle; 16.02.01.09.01 Canon law; 16.02.03.03 A religious; 16.02.05.10.07 A rule
regolbryce 12.01.01.12.02 Disobedience; 16.02.03.03 A religious
regolfæst 16.02.03.03 A religious
regolian 09.03.07.06.03 A ruler
regollagu 16.02.03.03 A religious
regollic 16.02.01.09.01 Canon law; 16.02.03.03 A religious
regollīce 16.02.01.09.01 Canon law
regollīf 16.02.03.03 A religious
regolsticca 09.03.07.06.03 A ruler
regolþēaw 11.05 Natural/proper way/manner/mode of action; 16.02.03.03 A religious
regolweard 09.03.07.07.03.03 A writer, author; 12.01.01.04 A leader, ruler; 16.02.03.03.01.03 A prior
regulares 05.11.06.02.02 A calculated space of time
relicgang 16.02.05.02.04 A shrine; 16.02.05.05.10 Relics, a collection of relics
reliquias 16.02.05.05.10 Relics, a collection of relics
reliquias rǣran 16.02.05.05.10 Relics, a collection of relics
reliquiasōcn 16.02.05.02.04 A shrine; 16.02.05.05.10 Relics, a collection of relics
remian 17.04.04 Fibrous materials
rēmisc 02.03.03.06.04 Italians
rempan 05.12.03.01.02 Haste, hurry; 11.02.04 Heedlessness
gerēn 17.03 Implements, tools, etc.
rēnboga 01.03.01.06.02 Rain

renc 07.06.04 Pride, ostentation
rendan 05.06.02.02 A tearing apart
gerendrian 05.10.05.04.13 A removal of that which obscures or conceals
rēndropa 01.03.01.06.02 Rain
gerēne 04.05.02 A building, edifice, structure
gerēn(e) 17.02.05.01 Ornamental object; 07.10.03 An adornment, decoration, ornament
renge 02.06.09.02.10 Spider
rengwyrm 02.08.08.04.03 Intestinal worm
(ge)rēnian 05.10.04 Place, room; 06.02.06.02 A proposal, proposition, suggestion; 07.10.03 An adornment, decoration, ornament; 11.01.03 Preparation
gerēnian 04.03.02 A snare, trap, noose
rēnig 01.03.01.06.02 Rain
rēnlic 01.03.01.06.02 Rain
rēnscūr 01.03.01.06.02 Rain
rēnsnægl 02.06.09.02.09 Snail
gerēnung 11.01.03 Preparation
rēnwæter 03.01.16.02 Water, liquid
renweard 11.10.02.02 Watchful care, keeping guard
rēnwyrm 02.06.09.02.11 Worm
rēoc 05.08.02.01 (Of living creatures) fierceness, roughness
rēocan 02.05.08.01 Foul smell, stench, stink; 03.01.09.02.01.04 Smoke
(ge)rēocan 03.01.09.02.01.04 Smoke
rēocende 02.05.08.01 Foul smell, stench, stink; 03.01.09.02.01.04 Smoke
rēod 02.04.04.03.02 Colour of hair; 03.01.14.05 Red/redness
rēodan 02.02.04.03 To kill, slay; 03.01.14.05 Red/redness; 04.06.02.03 Stain, smear

reodian 09.05.01 Inspection, examination
rēodmūþa 02.06.08.07 Exotic bird
rēof 14.02.01 An offence
(ge)rēofan 05.06.02.02 A tearing apart
reohha 02.06.06.03.01.06 Ray
rēoma 02.04.05.03 Membrane
rēon 08.01.03.04.01 Complaint, lamentation
(ge)rēonian 12.01.01.12.04.02 Conspiracy
rēonig 03.01.13 Darkness, obscurity; 08.01.03.04 Grief
rēonigmōd 02.05.03.02 Weariness
rēonung 09.02.03.01 Murmur, whispering; 16.01.04.06.01 Astrology
(ge)rēonung 12.01.01.12.04.02 Conspiracy
(ge)reopa 04.02.04.04.04 Stack, rick
(ge)reord 02.05.10.15 Voice, cry (of living creature); 04.01.02.04.01 Meal; 04.01.02.04.02 Feast; 09 Speech, vocal utterance; 09.03 A language
gereord 04.01.02.01 Food/sustenance; 18.02.07.02.02.02 A trumpet
gereordan 04.01.01 Eating; 16.02.01.12 Spirituality
reordberend 02.03.01 People
gereorddæg 16.02.04.04.02 A feast-day, holy day
reordglēawnes 18.02.07.01 Singing, song
gereordglēawnes 09.03.05 Art of poetry
reordhūs 04.01.01.08 Eating place
(ge)reord(i)an 04.01.02.04.03.01 To feed/nourish
gereordnes 04.01.01 Eating; 04.01.01.05 Satiety (of food); 04.01.02.04.01 Meal; 04.01.02.04.03 Feeding, nourishing; 04.01.02.04.05 Entertainment with food; 16.02.01.12 Spirituality

(ge)reordung 04.01.02.04.01 Meal
gereordung 16.02.01.12 Spirituality
gereordunghūs 04.01.01.08 Eating place
gereordungtīd 04.01.02.04.01.01.01 Meal time
reosan 02.07.09.02.02.02 Other vegetables (alphabetical order)
rēost 04.02.04.06.07 Ploughing equipment
rēotan 01.03.01.06.02 Rain; 02.05.10.02 Noise, din; 08.01.03.04.01 Complaint, lamentation
rēotig 08.01.03.04 Grief
rēotu 08.01.01.03 Good feeling, joy, happiness
rēowe 04.04.08 A covering, curtain, veil, garment, etc.
repan 04.02.04.04.02.02 To gather fruits, crops, etc.
repel 13.02.08.04 Weapons, arms
reps 16.02.04.03.02 Parts of service
repsan 07.05.01 Censure, reproof, rebuke
repsung 05.11.04.02 Night, night time; 05.11.04.02.01 Sunset; 07.05.01 Censure, reproof, rebuke
rēsele 09.04.03 Exposition, making clear by explanation
geresp 14.03.03.09.01 Unfavourable judgement, condemnation
respons 16.02.04.03.02 Parts of service
rest 02.02.05.01.01 A grave, burial place, sepulchre; 02.05.04 Sleepiness, drowsiness, sleep; 05.10.04 Place, room; 05.12.04 Absence of movement, stillness; 18.01 Rest, quiet, freedom from toil
(ge)rest 04.05.04.05 A bed, bedstead
geresta 12.09 Marriage, state of marriage
(ge)restan 02.02.05 A burial, burying; 02.05.04 Sleepiness, drowsiness, sleep; 08.01.01.03.01 Freedom from trouble, comfort, security; 11.06 Disinclination to act, listlessness
(ge)restan in 06.02.07.03 Perseverance
gerestan 02.02.03.02 State of being dead; 02.08.13 Recovery, growing better; 05.10.05.04.02.03.02 Reclining, rest; 18.01 Rest, quiet, freedom from toil
restbedd 04.05.04.05 A bed, bedstead
gerested bēon/wesan 04.05.03.03 A lodging-house, inn
(ge)reste(n)dæg 16.02.01.08.04 Jewish seasons/feasts
restengēar 16.02.04.04.02 A feast-day, holy day; 18.01 Rest, quiet, freedom from toil
restgemāna 02.01.03.03 Sex, generation
resthūs 04.05.03.04 A closet, chamber, room
restlēas 02.05.02 Consciousness
gerestscipe 02.01.03.03 Sex, generation
(ge)rētan 02.08.12.02.05.02 Salves, ointments; 08.01.01.03.09.03 To make glad; 08.01.03.07.04.02 Relief, alleviation
rētend 08.01.03.07.04.02.01 Comfort, consolation
reþe 12.07.04 Truth, righteousness, justice, equity
rēþe 02.06 Animal; 05.08.02.01 (Of living creatures) fierceness, roughness; 08.01.03.09.10 Wrath, sternness, displeasure; 08.01.03.09.11 Hardheartedness, cruelty, severity
reþehygdig 12.08.02.02 Righteousness, rectitude
reþeman 15.04.01 Lending of money
rēþemōd 08.01.03.09.01 Fierceness; 08.01.03.09.10 Wrath, sternness, displeasure

rēþian 08.01.03.05.02 Anger
rēþig 08.01.03.09.11 Hardheartedness, cruelty, severity
rēþigmōd 08.01.03.09.01 Fierceness
rēþlic 08.01.03.09.11 Hardheartedness, cruelty, severity
rēþlīce 05.08.02 Violence, force
rēþnes 01.03.01.03.01 Storm, tempest; 05.08.02.01 (Of living creatures) fierceness, roughness; 08.01.03.07.04 Severity, harshness; 08.01.03.09.11 Hardheartedness, cruelty, severity
rēþra 05.12.01.09.03 A voyage
gerēþre 06.02.07.02 Constancy
(ge)rēþru 05.12.01.09.03.01.03 Part of ship
rēþscipe 08.01.03.05.02 Anger
rēwet 05.12.01.09.01 To row; 05.12.01.09.03.01.01 Kind of ship
rex 12.01.01.04.01 A royal leader
ribb 02.04.05.04.05.03 Rib
ribbe 02.07.11 Plants/flowers (alphabetical order)
ribbspācan 02.04.05.04.05.03 Rib
ric 01.01.02.01.01 Tract of land; 01.01.03.01 Body of water; 05.10.02 Narrowness, scantiness of space
rīca 12.01.01.04 A leader, ruler
rīce 02.03.03.03 A nation, people; 05.11.03 Period of time, era, epoch; 12 Power, might; 12.01.01 Authority; 12.06 A province, country, territory; 15.01.05 Possession of wealth; 16.01.02.01 Heavenly dwelling place; 16.02.03.02.05 A bishop
rīcedōm 12.01.01 Authority
rīcehealdend 12.01.01.04.01 A royal leader
rīcelīce 12 Power, might

rīceter(e) 06.02.05.04.01 Ambition; 12 Power, might; 12.05.06.02.01 Tyranny; 05.08.02 Violence, force; 07.06.01 Pride, arrogance
rīclic 07.06.05 Pomp, splendour, magnificence
rīclīce 07.06.05 Pomp, splendour, magnificence
rīcsere 12.01.01.04 A leader, ruler
rīcsian 12.05.06 Grasp, power, control, mastery; 12.05.06.02.01 Tyranny
(ge)rīcsian 12.01.01.01 Rule, domination, direction
rīcsiend 12.01.01.04 A leader, ruler
rīcsung 12.01.01.01 Rule, domination, direction
gerid 05.12.01.03.01.05 Types of road/path; 05.12.01.05 To ride (on horse, etc.)
rida 05.12.01.03.01.05 Types of road/path
rīdan 05.12.01 To go, progress, travel (usually on land); 05.12.01.07.01 To hang; 05.12.01.09 To travel on water; 14.05.08 Captivity
rīdan on 05.12.01.06 Vehicle
(ge)rīdan 05.12.01.05 To ride (on horse, etc.)
gerīdan 05.12.01.05.01 Modes of riding; 15.01 Property
ridda 05.12.01.05 To ride (on horse, etc.); 13.02.10.01.02.02.02 Branch of army
rīdehere 13.02.10.01.02.02.02 Branch of army
rīdend 05.12.01.05 To ride (on horse, etc.)
rīdere 13.02.10.01.02.02.02 Branch of army
ridesoht 02.08.10 Fever
rīdusende 05.12.01.07.01 To hang; 05.12.05.05 To shake, quake, wag

rīdwiga 13.02.10.01.02.02.02 Branch of army
gerif 03.03.04.01.02.01 A heap, mass, accumulation
rīf 05.08.02.01 (Of living creatures) fierceness, roughness
gerīf 04.04.07 Trappings, equipment, garb
rīfe 03.03.04.02.01 Abundance
(ge)rifeled 02.04.04 Skin
rifelede 05.10.06.05.01 A wrinkle
rifeling 02.04.04 Skin; 04.04.07.15 Footwear, covering for the feet; 05.10.06.05.01 A wrinkle
geriflian 05.10.06.05.01 A wrinkle
rīfnes 08.01.03.09.01 Fierceness
gerifod 02.04.04 Skin
rift 04.04.07.07 A long outer garment, covering, cloak, etc.; 04.04.08.01 Curtain, wall-hanging, etc.
riftere 04.02.04.04.02.01 Reaper, mower; 04.02.04.06.12 A scythe, sickle
riht 03.06.03.04 What is fitting/seemly/appropriate/decent; 05.10.05.04.02.04.01 Uprightness, straightness; 06.01.07 Truth, conformity with absolute standard; 06.01.07.01 Correct, right, free from error; 12.07.02.02 Truth, faithfulness, good faith, sincerity; 12.07.04 Truth, righteousness, justice, equity; 12.08.02.02 Righteousness, rectitude; 14.01.02 A law, statute; 15.02.03 An account; 16.02.01.04 Orthodoxy; 16.02.01.09.01 Canon law; 17.03.11 Other implements, etc.
riht āgildan 15.02.03 An account
riht cyning 12.01.01.04.01.01 Kings and queens
riht dōm 14.03.03.09 A sentence, judgement, ruling

(ge)riht 05.10.05.04.05 Straight, direct; 12.07.01 One's due, natural place or position; 14.01.05 Service, obligation, duty; 14.01.06 A rule, order, precept, tenet, principle; 14.03.03.09 A sentence, judgement, ruling
geriht 14.03.03 Law, action of the courts; 16.02.01.09.01 Canon law
rihtæþelcwēn 12.09 Marriage, state of marriage
rihtæþelo 12.08.01 Magnanimity, greatness of soul
rihtǣw 12.09 Marriage, state of marriage
rihtan 09.01.03 To address, speak to; 12.01.01.01 Rule, domination, direction; 14.01.04.01 A special right, right peculiar to a class
(ge)rihtan 03.05.01 Arranging, ordering, disposition; 11.12.02.02 Amendment, setting right, reparation; 12.03.01.01 Control, direction, regulation; 12.08.02.02 Righteousness, rectitude
gerihtan 05.10.05.04.05 Straight, direct; 07.05.01 Censure, reproof, rebuke; 09.04.03 Exposition, making clear by explanation; 10.03.07.01 To allot, assign; 12.08.02.02.01 Reform, correction
rihtāndaga 05.11.02 A time, particular time, occasion
rihtandswaru 07.05.01 Censure, reproof, rebuke
rihtbred 03.03.03.01 Arithmetic
rihtcynecynn 12.01.01.06.08 A person of rank, elder, great man
rihtcynn 12.01.01.06.08 A person of rank, elder, great man
rihtdōnde 12.08.02.02 Righteousness, rectitude

rihte 03.06.03.04 What is fitting/seemly/appropriate/decent; 05.10.05.04.05 Straight, direct; 05.11.07.01 Contemporary, coeval; 06.01.07.01 Correct, right, free from error; 12.07.04 Truth, righteousness, justice, equity; 15.01.01.01 Holding of land
geriht(e) 16.02.04.03.01 A rite, ceremony
rihtebegitan 15.05 Trade, traffic, commerce
rihtend 12.01.01.04 A leader, ruler; 12.03 Direction, guidance
rihtendebyrdnes 03.05 Order, arrangement, disposition
rihtere 12.01.01.04 A leader, ruler
rihtes 05.10.05.04.05 Straight, direct
rihtēþel 12.06.04 Native land
rihtfædrencynn 02.03.02.03.01 Ancestry, paternal kinship
rihtfæsten 04.01.01.06.01 Abstinence from food, fast; 16.02.04.04.02.02 A fast, act of fasting
rihtfæstendæg 04.01.01.06.01 Abstinence from food, fast; 16.02.04.04.02.02 A fast, act of fasting
rihtfæstentīd 04.01.01.06.01 Abstinence from food, fast; 16.02.04.04.02.02 A fast, act of fasting
rihtfremmende 12.08.02.02 Righteousness, rectitude
rihtful 12.08.02.02 Righteousness, rectitude
rihtgebrōþru 02.03.02.02.05.01 Brother
rihtgefēg 03.03.06.01 A whole formed by joining
rihtgefremed 12.08.02.02 Righteousness, rectitude

rihtgegylda 12.02.03 A society, guild, association
rihtgehātan 14.03.03.03 Witness, testimony, attestation
rihtgehīwan 12.09 Marriage, state of marriage
rihtgelēafa 16.02.01.04 Orthodoxy
rihtgelēafful 16.02.01.04 Orthodoxy
rihtgelēaffulnes 16.02.01.04 Orthodoxy
rihtgelēaflīce 16.02.01.04 Orthodoxy
rihtgelȳfed 16.02.01.04 Orthodoxy
riht(ge)lȳfende 16.02.01.04 Orthodoxy
rihtgemæcca 12.09 Marriage, state of marriage
rihtgemǣre 05.10.05.04.11.01 A bound, limit
rihtgemet 03.03 Measurement, determination of amount
rihtgesamhīwan 12.09 Marriage, state of marriage
rihtgescēad 06.01.05.01 Understanding
rihtgeset 16.02.01.09.01 Canon law
rihtgesetednes 16.02.03.03 A religious
rihtgesetnes 17.02.03 A task, service, duty
riht(ge)sinscipe 12.09 Marriage, state of marriage
gerihtgeswinc 17 Work, doings, actions, labour
rihtgeþancod 12.08.02.02 Righteousness, rectitude
rihtgeþwǣrlǣcan 03.06.03.01 Compatible
rihtgewitt 02.08.11.01 Sound mind
rihtgewittelic 06.01.03 Faculty of reason
rihtgewittig 02.08.11.01 Sound mind
rihtgifu 15.01.02 Gift, transfer of property
rihthǣmed 12.09 Marriage, state of marriage
rihthāmscyld 14.01.03.01 Sanctuary

rihthāmsōcn 14.02.01.02 Wrongful taking, theft
rihthand 02.04.03.04.01.01 Hand
rihthanddǣda 14.02 Lawlessness
rihtheort 12.08.02.02 Righteousness, rectitude
rihthīwa 12.09 Marriage, state of marriage
rihthlāford 12.01.01.04.02 A lord, master; 12.09 Marriage, state of marriage
rihthlāforddōm 12.01.01 Authority
rihthlāfordhyldo 12.01.01.12 Loyalty
rihthycgende 16.02.01.04 Orthodoxy
rihting 05.11.06.02.02 A calculated space of time; 07.05.01 Censure, reproof, rebuke; 11.12.02.02 Amendment, setting right, reparation; 12.03 Direction, guidance; 14.01.04 A legal right
rihtinge 05.11.06.02.02 A calculated space of time
(ge)rihtlǣcan 12.03.01.01 Control, direction, regulation; 12.08.02.02 Righteousness, rectitude; 12.08.02.02.01 Reform, correction
gerihtlǣcan 05.10.05.04.05 Straight, direct; 05.12.05.08.01 To go before and guide
rihtlǣce 02.08.12.02.01 A physician
rihtlǣcung 12.08.02.02.01 Reform, correction
rihtlagu 12.07.04 Truth, righteousness, justice, equity; 14.01 Law, body of rules
rihtlandgemǣre 05.10.05.04.11.01 A bound, limit
rihtlic 03.06.03 Congruity, fitness, suitability; 06.01.03.01 Argument, reasoning; 12.07.01 One's due, natural place or position; 12.07.04 Truth, righteousness, justice, equity; 12.08.02.02 Righteousness, rectitude; 14.01.04 A legal right
rihtlīce 03.06.03 Congruity, fitness, suitability; 05.10.05.04.05 Straight, direct; 06.01.07.01 Correct, right, free from error; 11.05.02.01 A standard, norm, ethos; 12.07.04 Truth, righteousness, justice, equity; 12.08.02.03.01 Honourable conduct, dignity; 16.02.01.04 Orthodoxy
rihtlīcettere 06.01.07.04.04.02.01 Hypocrisy
rihtlīf 12.09 Marriage, state of marriage
rihtlīflād 11.05.02 Mode, manner, way, method, fashion, course; 12.08.02.01 Goodness, excellence, virtue
rihtlīþlic 09 Speech, vocal utterance
rihtmēdrencynn 02.03.02.03.02 Maternal descent
rihtmēterfers 09.03.05.01.02 Art of verse composition
rihtmunuc 16.02.03.03.02 A monk
rihtnama 09.06.02.01.07 A name, appellation
rihtnes 05.10.05.04.02.04.01 Uprightness, straightness; 12.07.04 Truth, righteousness, justice, equity; 15.02.03 An account
gerihtnes 12.08.02.02.01 Reform, correction
rihtnorþanwind 01.03.01.05.01 Winds from particular points
rihtraciend 09.04.03.03 A commentary, exposition
rihtracu 06.01.03.01 Argument, reasoning; 06.01.07 Truth, conformity with absolute standard

gerihtreccan 11.03.01.01.01 Proof, demonstration
rihtregol 14.01.06 A rule, order, precept, tenet, principle; 16.02.03.03 A religious
rihtryne 01.01.03.01.01.01 River; 05.12.01.03 Expanse over which something travels
rihtscilling 15.01.04 Coinage, money
rihtscīr 12.06.02 District, province; 16.02.05.01 Land
rihtscrīfend 14.03.02 A legislator
rihtscriftscīr 12.06.02 District, province; 16.02.03.02.09 A confessor; 16.02.05.01 Land
rihtscytte 11.04.01 An aptitude, bodily skill
rihtsmēaung 06.01.03.01 Argument, reasoning
rihtspell 09.03.04.02.02 Eloquence, elegance in language
rihtstefn 09 Speech, vocal utterance
rihttīd 05.11.02 A time, particular time, occasion
rihttīma 05.11.02 A time, particular time, occasion
rihtþēowa 12.01.01.09 Bondage, slavery
gerihtu 16.02.04.07.06.01 Last rites
rihtung 14.01.06 A rule, order, precept, tenet, principle
rihtungþrēd 17.03.11 Other implements, etc.
rihtweg 12.08.02.01 Goodness, excellence, virtue
rihtwer 12.09 Marriage, state of marriage; 14.03.03.09.02 Atonement
rihtwestende 01.01.01.04 West
rihtwīf 12.09 Marriage, state of marriage
rihtwillende 12.08.02.02 Righteousness, rectitude
rihtwīs 12.07.04.01 Justification; 12.08.02.02 Righteousness, rectitude; 16.01.01.02.06 God as judge; 16.02.01.12.03 Righteousness
rihtwīsend 16.02.01.09.02 Knowledge of Jewish law
rihtwīsian 12.01.01.01 Rule, domination, direction
(ge)rihtwīsian 12.07.04.01 Justification
gerihtwīsian 14.03.03.08 Justification
rihtwīslic 12.07.04.01 Justification
rihtwīslīce 06.01.03.01 Argument, reasoning
rihtwīsnes 06.01.03.01 Argument, reasoning; 12.07.04 Truth, righteousness, justice, equity; 12.08.02.02 Righteousness, rectitude; 16.02.01.12.03 Righteousness
gerihtwīsung 14.03.03.08 Justification
rihtwrītere 09.03.07.03 A scribe, copyist
rihtwuldriende 16.02.01.04 Orthodoxy
rihtwyrþe 07.02.01 Right, virtue; 12.08.02.03.01 Honourable conduct, dignity
rihtymbren 16.02.04.04.02.02.01 Ember-tide, Ember-days
rihtymbrendagas 16.02.04.04.02.02.01 Ember-tide, Ember-days
rīm 03.03.03 Number
(ge)rīm 03.03.03 Number; 03.03.03.02 A number (mark/symbol); 03.04 Form, kind, nature, character
gerīm 05.11.06.02 Reckoning/computation of time; 05.11.06.02.01 A calendar; 05.11.06.02.02 A calculated space of time; 16.02.05.10.12 A computus and calendar
rima 05.10.05.04.11.01 A bound, limit

rīman 03.03.03 Number; 07.01 Appraisal, appraising
(ge)rīman 03.03.03 Number; 03.05.03 A list, tale, series
rīmāþ 14.03.03.04 Oath-swearing
gerīmbōc 05.11.06.02.01 A calendar; 16.02.05.10.12 A computus and calendar
rīmcræft 05.11.06.02.01 A calendar
(ge)rīmcræft 03.03.03.01 Arithmetic; 05.11.06.02.01 A calendar
rīmcræftig 03.03.03.01 Arithmetic; 06.01.06.02.02.01 Learning, science (secular knowledge)
rīmcræftiga 03.03.03.01 Arithmetic
rīmere 03.03.03.01 Arithmetic
gerīmes 03.03.03 Number
rīmgetæl 03.03.03 Number
gerīmian 03.03.03 Number
(ge)rīmtæl 03.03.03 Number
rimuc 05.10.05.04.11.01 A bound, limit
(ge)rīnan 01.03.01.06.02 Rain; 05.12.05.13.03 To fall
rinc 06.02.07.06 Courage, boldness, valour
rincgetæl 12.04.02 A crowding together, assembly
rind 01.01.02.01.02.02.01 Hill
rind(e) 03.03.07 A part, division, portion; 02.07.03.03.01 Wood (as substance)
rindeclifer 02.06.08.05 Forest bird, wild-fowl
rinden 02.07.03.03.01 Wood (as substance)
rindlēas 02.07.03 A tree; 05.10.05.04.13 A removal of that which obscures or conceals
rinnan 01.01.03.03 Flow/flowing
gerinnan 03.03.06.01.01 Mixing, mingling, preparation

rinnelle/rynel 01.01.03.01.01.03 Stream
gerinning 02.08.05.02.01 Matter, purulence, pus
(ge)rīp 04.02.04.04 Harvest, crop; 04.02.04.04.02 Harvesting
(ge)rīpan 04.02.04.04.02.02 To gather fruits, crops, etc.; 05.06.01 Devastation, laying waste; 14.02.01.02.01 Open robbery, rapine, pillage
rīpe 04.02.04.04.01 To ripen
gerīped 07.02.03 Perfection
rīpemann 04.02.04.04.02.01 Reaper, mower
rīpere 04.02.04.04.02.01 Reaper, mower; 14.02.01.02.01 Open robbery, rapine, pillage
(ge)rīpian 04.02.04.04.01 To ripen
rīpīsern 04.02.04.06.12 A scythe, sickle
rīpnes 02.01.04.02 To grow, grow up; 04.02.04.04 Harvest, crop
ripp 05.10.05.04.11.01 A bound, limit
rippel 02.07.03.04.01 A small wood, coppice, copse
rīptīma 04.02.04.04.02 Harvesting; 05.11.03.01.02.03 Autumn
rīpþ 04.02.04.04 Harvest, crop
rīpung 02.01.04.02 To grow, grow up; 04.02.04.04.01 To ripen; 04.02.04.04.02 Harvesting; 14.02.01.02.01 Open robbery, rapine, pillage
gerīs 08.01.03.05.02 Anger
(ge)rīsan 03.06.03 Congruity, fitness, suitability; 10.04.03 To take away, remove
gerīsan 05.12.05.12 To go up, ascend
riscbedd 02.07.08 Grasses, reeds, etc.
riscbrōc 01.01.03.01.01.03 Stream
risc(e) 02.07.08 Grasses, reeds, etc.

riscen 04.05.01.02.04 Made of rushes
riscene wēoce 17.05.03 Sources of fire/light
riscett 02.07.08 Grasses, reeds, etc.
rischealh 02.07.08 Grasses, reeds, etc.
risciht 02.07.08 Grasses, reeds, etc.
riscleac 02.07.09.02.02.01 Edible root/bulb
riscrīþig 01.01.03.01.01.03 Stream
riscþȳfel 02.07.08 Grasses, reeds, etc.
gerisen 10.04.02.02 To seize, take, grasp, lay hold on
rīsende 06.02.05.02 Greed, importunate desire, rapacity
(ge)ris(e)ne 03.06.03.04 What is fitting/seemly/appropriate/decent
geris(e)ne 07.08.02 Honour, glory; 12.08.02.03.01 Honourable conduct, dignity
gerisenlic 03.06.03 Congruity, fitness, suitability; 07.04.04.02 Laudable, praiseworthy; 12.07.01 One's due, natural place or position
gerisenlīce 03.06.03 Congruity, fitness, suitability; 07.04.03 Reverence, respect; 07.04.04.02 Laudable, praiseworthy
gerislīc 03.06.01 Similitude, likeness
(ge)risne 03.06.03.04 What is fitting/seemly/appropriate/decent
gerisnes 03.06.03 Congruity, fitness, suitability
gerisnian 03.06.03.01 Compatible
risoda 02.04.06.05.07.02 Mucus, phlegm, rheum
rispe 02.07.03.01 A bush
rispett 02.07.03.01 A bush
(ge)rīþ(e) 01.01.03.01.01.03 Stream
rīþig 01.01.03.01.01.03 Stream

rocc 04.04.07.07 A long outer garment, covering, cloak, etc.; 16.02.05.06.01 Outer garments
roc(c)ettan 05.12.05.03.04.01 To burst forth, break out
roccian 02.05.04.01 To make heavy with weariness/sleep
rocettan 09.01.02.01 Excessive fluency, loquacity
rod 04.02.03.01.02 Cleared land
rōd 04.02.03.03 A measure of land; 05.10.05.03 A measure of distance; 14.05.05.01.01 Crucifixion, death on cross; 14.05.06 Means/implement of torture; 16.02.04.18.01 Sign of the cross; 16.02.05.11 The cross (as Christian image)
rōdbīgenga 16.02.04 Worship, honour, praise
rōdbora 16.02.04.16 Martyrdom
rodd 14.05.06 Means/implement of torture
rōde tācen 16.02.04.18.01 Sign of the cross; 16.02.05.11 The cross (as Christian image)
rōdehengen 14.05.05.01.01 Crucifixion, death on cross; 16.01.01.04.02.02 Events associated with Christ
rōdestān 16.02.05.11 The cross (as Christian image)
rōdewyrþe 12.08.06.02.03 (Of persons) wicked, evil-doing
gerōdfæstnian 02.02.04.04.03 Putting to death; 14.05.05.01.01 Crucifixion, death on cross
rodor 01.02 Firmament; 16.01.02 The heavens, sky
rodorbeorht 03.01.12 Brightness, light
rodorcyning 16.01.01.01.01 The Almighty

rodorlic 01.02 Firmament; 16.01.02 The heavens, sky
rodorlīhtung 05.11.04.01.01 Dawn, daybreak, sunrise
rodorstōl 12.01.01.02 Seat of authority; 16.01.02.01 Heavenly dwelling place
rodortorht 03.01.12 Brightness, light
rodortungol 01.02.01.01.02 Star
rōdwurþiend 16.02.04 Worship, honour, praise
rōf 03.03.03 Number; 06.02.07.06 Courage, boldness, valour
rogian 02.01.03 Fruitfulness, fertility
rōm 12.06.02.01 A township
rōmāne 02.03.03.06.04 Italians
rōmānisc 02.03.03.06.04 Italians
rōmānisc fōstorcild 02.03.03.04.05 Populace of a town/city
rōmeburg 12.06.02.01 A township
rōmfeoh 16.02.04.20 Church due/requirement
rōm(ge)sceot 16.02.04.20 Church due/requirement
rōmigan 11.03 Endeavour
rōmpenig 16.02.04.20 Church due/requirement
rōmwalh 02.03.03.06.04 Italians
rōmware/-an 02.03.03.06.04 Italians
rop 04.01.02.01.07.01 Soup/pottage
rōp 10.03.08 Bountifulness, munificence
rōpnes 10.03.08 Bountifulness, munificence
ropp 02.04.06.03.02.04 Intestines
ropwærc 02.08.08.04.01 Gripe, colic
rōsbedd 02.07.09.02 Particular fruits (alphabetical order); 04.02.04.05.01 A garden-plot
geroscian 03.01.18 Dryness (not wetness)
rōse 02.07.09.02 Particular fruits (alphabetical order)

rōsen 02.07.09.02 Particular fruits (alphabetical order); 03.01.14.05 Red/redness
gerōsod 02.05.08.02 Pleasant smell, fragrance, perfume; 04.01.02.02.04.04 Flavoured with rose-leaves
rōsrēad 03.01.14.05 Red/redness
rōt 02.07.02.01 Root; 07.02.04.03 Nobleness, excellence, nobility, magnificence; 08.01.01.03.04 Gladness, cheerfulness
rōtfæst 05.12.04.01 Stability, firmness
rōthwīl 05.11.11.02 Let up, intermission, cessation
rotian 02.08.05.02.01 Matter, purulence, pus
(ge)rotian 03.02.01.01 Decay, corruption, rottenness
rōtlīce 08.01.01.03.04 Gladness, cheerfulness
rōtnes 08.01.01.03.04 Gladness, cheerfulness; 11.10.01.02 Refuge, help, shelter
(ge)rōtsian 08.01.01.03.09.03 To make glad
rōtsung 11.10.01.02 Refuge, help, shelter
rotung 02.08.05.02 Particular inflammation/swelling; 03.02.01.01 Decay, corruption, rottenness
roþ 04.02.03.01.02 Cleared land
roþer 04.02.03.01.02 Cleared land
rōþer 05.12.01.09.03 A voyage
roþhund 02.06.02.01.04 Dog; 04.03.01 Tracking
rōþor 05.12.01.09.03.01.03 Part of ship
rōw 05.09.02 Mildness, moderate quality; 05.12.04 Absence of movement, stillness
rōwan 05.12.01.08.01 To swim

(ge)rōwan 05.12.01.09 To travel on water; 05.12.01.09.01 To row
rōwend 05.12.01.09.03 A voyage
rōwett 05.12.01.09.01 To row
rōwing 05.12.01.09.01 To row
rōwnes 05.12.01.09.01 To row
rudduc 02.06.08.05 Forest bird, wild-fowl
rūde 02.07.11 Plants/flowers (alphabetical order); 02.08.05.02.02 Scab, roughness of skin
rudian 03.01.14.05 Red/redness
rudig 02.04.04.01 Having a certain complexion; 03.01.14.05 Red/redness
rudu 02.04.04.01 Having a certain complexion; 03.01.14.05 Red/redness; 04.06.01.08 Face powder
rugern 05.11.03.01.03.01 Specific months
rūh 01.01.02.01 Ground; 02.04.04.03.01 Texture of hair; 02.07.03.04.03 A hedge/border; 03.01.05 Roughness; 04.01.02.02.05 Cooking; 04.04.05.01 Coarse, rough (of cloth); 04.04.06 Undressed condition (of hide)
ruhha 02.06.06.03.01.06 Ray
ruine 05.12.05.13.03 To fall
rūm 03.03.04.02 A sufficiency, sufficient supply; 04.02.03.01.02 Cleared land; 05.10.01 Amplitude, spaciousness, vastness; 05.10.05.02 Extension, stretching; 05.11 A time, period of time; 05.11.01.01 Long duration, long space; 05.11.08 A suitable time, opportunity; 06.01.05.02 Intelligence; 11.12.01 Absence of restraint, freedom; 12.08.01 Magnanimity, greatness of soul; 12.08.07.01 Laxity, indulgence; 18 Quiet, leisure, rest
(ge)rūm 05.10 Space, extent; 07.08.08 Nobleness, honour, glory
rūma/ruina 11.11.02 A hindrance
gerūma 05.10.04 Place, room
rūme 03.03.04.02.01 Abundance; 03.03.06 Wholeness; 05.10.01 Amplitude, spaciousness, vastness; 09.05.05.01 Showing, manifestation, display; 10.03.08 Bountifulness, munificence
(ge)rūme 08.01.01.03.01 Freedom from trouble, comfort, security
rūmgāl 08.01.01.03.06 Exultation, joy
rūmgallīce 05.10.01 Amplitude, spaciousness, vastness
rūmgifa 10.03.08 Bountifulness, munificence
rūmgifol 10.03.08 Bountifulness, munificence
rūmgiful 03.03.04.02.01 Abundance
rūmgifulnes 03.03.04.02.01 Abundance; 10.03.08 Bountifulness, munificence
rūmheort 08.01.01.03.01 Freedom from trouble, comfort, security; 08.01.02.01 Favour, kindness, grace; 10.03.08 Bountifulness, munificence
rūmheortlīce 10.03.08 Bountifulness, munificence
rūmheortnes 10.03.08 Bountifulness, munificence
rūmian 03.03.08 Emptiness
rūmlic 03.03.04.02.01 Abundance; 08.01.02.01 Favour, kindness, grace
rūmlīce 03.03.06 Wholeness; 08.01.02.01 Favour, kindness, grace; 10.03.08 Bountifulness, munificence
(ge)rūmlīcor 05.10.05 A space, span
rūmmōd 03.03.04.02.01 Abundance; 10.03.08 Bountifulness, munificence; 10.03.08.01 Overliberality, waste of money

rūmmōdlic 10.03.08 Bountifulness, munificence
rūmmōdlīce 08.01.02.01 Favour, kindness, grace; 10.03.08 Bountifulness, munificence
rummōdnes 08.01.02.01 Favour, kindness, grace
rūmmōdnes 10.03.08 Bountifulness, munificence
rūmnes 03.03.04.02.01 Abundance; 05.10.01 Amplitude, spaciousness, vastness
rūmor 05.10.05 A space, span
gerumpen 02.06.01.02 Head
rūmwelle 05.10.01 Amplitude, spaciousness, vastness
rūn 09.03.07 Writing; 09.03.07.01.01 A runic letter; 09.04.02.01 A secret, mystery; 12.02.02.04 Counsel, deliberation
gerūna 12.02.02.02 A counsellor, advisor
rūncofa 08.01 Heart, spirit, mood, disposition
rūncræftig 16.01.04.06 Divination, augury
rūne healdan 09.05.04 A secret
rūnere 07.05.03.01 Falseness in speech, detraction
rūnian 07.05.03.01 Falseness in speech, detraction
rūniende 07.05.03.01 Falseness in speech, detraction
rūning 07.07.03 Flattery
runl 02.05.08.01 Foul smell, stench, stink
gerunnen 03.01.17.01 A coagulating, mixing
gerunnen tōgædere 03.03.06.01.01 Mixing, mingling, preparation
gerunnenes 03.01.17.01 A coagulating, mixing

rūnstæf 09.03.07.01.01 A runic letter
rūnung 12.02.02.04 Counsel, deliberation
rūnwita 06.01.06.02.01 A wise man, man of understanding or learning; 12.02.02.02 A counsellor, advisor
rūst 03.02.01.04 Rust; 12.08.06 Moral evil, depravity
rūstig 03.02.01.04 Rust
rūwa 04.04.08 A covering, curtain, veil, garment, etc.
ryd 04.02.03.01.02 Cleared land
geryddan 04.02.04.01 To occupy and cultivate land
gerȳde 02.05.05.04 Sensual pleasure
ryden 02.07.11.02 Unidentified plants (alphabetical order)
ryding/-en 04.02.03.01.02 Cleared land
rȳfe 05.11.09.02 Frequent, of common occurrence
ryft 04.04.08 A covering, curtain, veil, garment, etc.
ryge 04.01.02.01.03.04 Rye; 04.02.04.03.02.01.04 Rye
rygen 04.01.02.01.03.04 Rye
rȳhe 04.04.08 A covering, curtain, veil, garment, etc.
ryhtum gerisnum 03.06.03.04 What is fitting/seemly/appropriate/decent
rȳhþ 01.01.02.01 Ground
(ge)rȳman 05.10.04.04 Absence; 05.10.05.02.02 Greater, bigger; 05.10.05.04.14 An opening, aperture; 05.12.01.03.01 A means of access; 11.12.01 Absence of restraint, freedom
gerȳman 04.02.01 Farmstead
rȳmet 05.10 Space, extent; 05.10.04 Place, room; 05.10.05.02 Extension, stretching; 08.01.01.03.08 Happiness, well-being, prosperity

rȳmetlēast 08.01.02.04 Hospitality
rȳmþ 05.10.01 Amplitude, spaciousness, vastness
rȳn 02.05.10.15.06 A roar, howl, etc.
rȳnan 02.05.10.15.06 A roar, howl, etc.
ryne 01.01.03.01.01.01 River; 02.01.04 Age; 02.08.08.12 Disease of bowels; 05.11.06 Course/cycle of time; 05.12.01 To go, progress, travel (usually on land); 05.12.01.03 Expanse over which something travels; 05.12.01.06 Vehicle; 05.12.05.04 To rotate, turn round, revolve; 11.03.02 Advancement, progress
(ge)rȳne 09.03.04.02.01 A figure
gerȳne 06.01.06.02.02.01 Learning, science (secular knowledge); 09.04.02 Depth of meaning, mystery; 09.04.02.01 A secret, mystery; 16.01.04.06.04 Prophecy, divine speech; 16.02.04.03.01 A rite, ceremony; 16.02.04.07 A sacrament; 16.02.05.09.01 Eucharistic elements
rynegiest 01.03.01.03.01.02 Lightning
rynel 09.06.02.01.06.01 A messenger
(ge)rȳn(e)lic 16.02.01.12.01 Revelation, illumination, inspiration
gerȳn(e)lic 09.03.04.02.01 A figure; 09.05.04 A secret
gerȳnelic 16.02.04.07 A sacrament
rynelīce 05.12.03.01 Swiftness, velocity
(ge)rȳn(e)līce 16.02.01.12.01 Revelation, illumination, inspiration
gerȳnelīce 09.04.02.01 A secret, mystery
rȳnemann 16.01.04.06 Divination, augury
rynestrang 05.12.03.01 Swiftness, velocity
ryneswift 05.12.03.01 Swiftness, velocity

ryneþrāg 05.11 A time, period of time
rynewæn 05.12.01.06 Vehicle
rȳnig 12.02.02.05 Counsel, advice
ryniga 03.01.16 Liquid, a liquid
rȳnisc 06.01.08.05.01.01 Wondrous, glorious, marvellous
(ge)rȳnlic 09.04.02 Depth of meaning, mystery
rynning 04.01.02.01.02.09.06 Rennet
gerȳpan 04.02.04.04.04 Stack, rick
ryplen 17.04.04 Fibrous materials
rysel 02.04.06.03.01 Cavities of internal organs; 03.01.17.06 Resin, tar, gum; 04.01.02.01.02.05.05 Fat/suet/lard
ryselwærc 02.08.08.04 Pain in stomach
ryt 04.06.02.04 Refuse, litter, rubbish
(ge)ryþer 04.02.03.01.02 Cleared land
ryþþa 02.06.02.01.04 Dog; 04.03.01 Tracking
sā 04.01.03.05.04.02 A barrel, tun, vat, cask
saban 04.05.04.05.01 Bedding (e.g. of straw)
sabbat 16.02.01.08.04 Jewish seasons/feasts
sac (ge)twǣman 13.01.02 Reconciliation
gesaca 12.05.02 Hostility, contention, opposition; 14.03.03.01 Accusation
sacan 09.07.03.02 Refusal, denial; 12.05.03.01 Quarrel, contentiousness, strife; 12.05.04.01 Fighting, contention, warfare, strife; 14.03.03 Law, action of the courts; 14.03.03.01 Accusation
sacc 17.03.12 A receptacle, container
sācerd 16.02.03.02.07 A priest, cleric; 16.02.03.02.07.01 A priest of a church or minster
sācerdbana 02.02.04.04 Manslaughter, homicide

sǣd

sācerdgerisne 16.02.03.02.07 A priest, cleric
sācerdhād 16.02.03.02.07 A priest, cleric
sācerdland 16.02.05.01 Land
sācerdlic 16.02.03.02.07 A priest, cleric
sacful 12.05.03.01 Quarrel, contentiousness, strife; 14.03.03 Law, action of the courts
sacian 12.05.04.01.01 Fighting, a fight
saclēas 11.10 Safety, safeness; 14.03.03 Law, action of the courts; 14.03.03.08 Justification
sacramentor(i)um 16.02.05.10.01 Service books
sacu 07.05.01 Censure, reproof, rebuke; 08.01.03.06 Adversity, affliction; 12.05.03.01 Quarrel, contentiousness, strife; 12.08.09 Guiltiness, guilt; 14.02.01 An offence; 14.03.03 Law, action of the courts
sacu and sōcn 14.03 Right of holding court, jurisdiction
sāda 04.03.02 A snare, trap, noose; 17.03.10 Supports and fastenings
(ge)sadelian 04.02.05.06.05.03.04 Saddle
gesadelod 04.02.05.06.05.03.04 Saddle
sadian 04.01.01.05 Satiety (of food)
(ge)sadian 06.02.05.03 Satisfaction, repletion
sadol 04.02.05.06.05.03.04 Saddle
sadolbeorht 04.02.05.06.05.03.04 Saddle
sadolboga 04.02.05.06.05.03.04 Saddle
sadolfæt 04.02.05.06.05.03 Harness, trappings
sadolfelg 04.02.05.06.05.03.04 Saddle
sadolgearwe 04.02.05.06.05.03 Harness, trappings
sadolgerǣdu 04.02.05.05.02 Harness of draught animal
saducēas 02.03.03.06.07.05 Jews

saducēisc 02.03.03.06.07.05 Jews
sǣ 01.01.03.01.03 Lake; 01.01.03.01.02 Sea/ocean; 01.01.03 Water
sǣ and eorþe 01 Earth, world; 01.01 Surface of the earth
sǣ ostre 04.01.02.01.02.07 Fish
sǣæbbung 01.01.03.04 Current, rush of water
sǣæl 02.06.06.02.01.02 Eel
sǣælfen 16.01.03.04 Elfin race
sǣbāt 05.12.01.09.03.01 A ship, boat
sǣbeorg 01.01.02.01.02.02.04 Cliff; 01.01.03.01.02.05 Wave
sǣbrōga 06.01.08.06.03 Cause of fear, terror, horror
sǣburg 12.06.02.01 A township
sæc 05.08.02 Violence, force; 08.01.03.09.04 Hatred; 12.08.09 Guiltiness, guilt; 14.03.03.09.01 Unfavourable judgement, condemnation
sæcc 04.04.05.01 Coarse, rough (of cloth); 04.04.07.01 Mode of dressing, fashion; 13.02.02 Battle; 16.02.05.06 Ritual clothing
sæccing 04.05.04.05 A bed, bedstead
sǣceaster 12.06.02.01 A township
sǣceosol 01.01.02.02.02.01 Sand, gravel
sǣcir 01.01.03.06.01 Retreat (of Red Sea)
sǣclif 01.01.02.01.02.02.04 Cliff
sǣcocc 02.06.06.04.01.01 Cockle, whelk
sǣcol 17.04.03.04 Gems collectively
sǣcyning 12.01.01.04.01.01 Kings and queens
sæd 04.01.01.05 Satiety (of food); 06.02.05.03 Satisfaction, repletion
sǣd 02.01.03.03.04 Offspring, race, breed, family, children; 02.04.06.06.09 Semen; 02.07.02.04 Seed, kind of seed; 04.02.04.02.03

1277

sædberende

Sowing; 04.02.04.03.01 Seed; 05.03 Source, origin
sædberende 02.07.02.04 Seed, kind of seed; 05.03 Source, origin
sædcynn 02.07.02.04 Seed, kind of seed
sǣdēor 02.06.10.01.05 Sea-monster
sædere 04.02.04.02.03 Sowing
sædian 04.02.04.02.03 Sowing
sǣdlēap 04.02.04.06.09 A sower's basket
sǣdlic 02.07.02.04 Seed, kind of seed; 05.03 Source, origin
sædnaþ 04.02.04.02.03 Sowing
sædnes 06.02.05.03 Satisfaction, repletion
sǣdraca 02.06.10.01.05 Sea-monster
sǣdsworn 02.01.03.03.04 Offspring, race, breed, family, children
sǣdtīma 04.02.04.02.03 Sowing; 05.11.03.01.02 A season of the year
sǣearm 01.01.02.01.01.03.02 Inlet in river/sea
sǣfǣreld 05.12.01.01 To go on a journey/expedition, travel
sǣfæsten 01.01.03.01.02 Sea/ocean
sǣfaroþ 01.01.02.01.01.03 Shore, bank
sǣfern 01.01.03.01.01.01 River
sǣfisc 02.06.06 Fish
sǣflōd 01.01.03.01.02 Sea/ocean; 01.01.03.01.02.02 Sea-channel; 01.01.03.03 Flow/flowing; 01.01.03.04 Current, rush of water; 01.01.03.06 Flood
sǣflota 05.12.01.09.03.01 A ship, boat
sǣfōr 05.12.01.09.03 A voyage
sǣgan 05.12.05.13 To go down, descend
gesǣgan 05.06.01 Devastation, laying waste; 08.01.03.04 Grief
sǣge 01.01.02.01.04.01 Marsh, bog, swamp

sǣgēap 05.12.01.09.03.01.02 Of/concerning a ship, naval
sægednes 16.02.04.12 Sacrifice, a sacrifice
gesægednes 06.01.06.02.02.01 Learning, science (secular knowledge)
sǣgemǣre 01.01.02.01.01.03 Shore, bank
sǣgenga 05.12.01.09.03 A voyage; 05.12.01.09.03.01 A ship, boat
sǣgeset 01.01.02.01.01.03 Shore, bank
sǣgrund 01.01.03.01.02.01 Region of sea/ocean
sǣhealf 01.01.02.01.01.03 Shore, bank
sǣhengest 02.06.04.01.04 Hippopotamus; 05.12.01.09.03.01 A ship, boat
sǣhete 01.01.03.01.02.06 Surging, rolling, heaving of waves
sǣholm 01.01.03.01.02 Sea/ocean
sǣhund 16.01.06.02 Classical gods
sæl 04.05.03.02.01 A building, house, hall, palace, etc.
sǣl 05.02.01 Condition, state of affairs, situation; 05.11.02 A time, particular time, occasion; 05.11.08 A suitable time, opportunity; 08.01.01.03.08 Happiness, well-being, prosperity
sǣlāc 10.03 Giving
sǣlād 01.01.03.01.02.01 Region of sea/ocean
sǣlāf 05.12.01.01 To go on a journey/expedition, travel
(ge)sǣlan 05.03.02.01.01 An event, occurrence; 12.05.06.01 Restraint, check, curb, control; 14.05.07 Binding, fastening with bonds
gesǣlan 05 Aught, anything, something; 11.03.02.01 Efficacy, success
sǣland 01.01.02.01.01.03 Shore, bank
sælen 02.07.03.05 Particular trees/shrubs (alphabetical order)

1278

sǣlēoþ 18.02.07.01.01 A song, a poem to be sung or recited
sǣlic 01.01.03.01.02 Sea/ocean
sǣlida 05.12.01.09.03 A voyage; 05.12.01.09.03.03 Piracy
(ge)sǣlig 16.01.02.02 Glory/majesty of heaven; 16.02.01.10 Holiness
gesǣlig 05.03.02.01 Chance, hap, event; 08.01.01.03 Good feeling, joy, happiness; 08.01.01.03.03 Happiness, blessedness; 08.01.01.03.08.02 Good fortune, success; 13.02.10 The military, soldiers; 15.01.05 Possession of wealth; 16.02.01.10.02.01 A blessing, invocation of divine favour
gesǣlige 08.01.01.03 Good feeling, joy, happiness
gesǣliglic 08.01.01.03.08.02 Good fortune, success; 08.01.01.03.08.03 A favour, blessing
gesǣliglīce 08.01.01.03 Good feeling, joy, happiness; 08.01.01.03.08.03 A favour, blessing
gesǣlignes 02.01.03.01 Fertility, plenty; 05.03.02.01 Chance, hap, event; 05.04 Fate, lot, fortune, destiny; 08.01.01.03 Good feeling, joy, happiness; 08.01.01.03.08 Happiness, well-being, prosperity; 16.01.02.02 Glory/majesty of heaven
sǣlīþend 05.12.01.09.03 A voyage; 05.12.01.09.03.01 A ship, boat
sǣlīþende 05.12.01.09.03 A voyage
sǣlmerige 03.01.16.02 Water, liquid
gesǣlnes 05.03.02.01 Chance, hap, event
sǣltna 02.06.08.05 Forest bird, wild-fowl
sǣlþ 04.05.03 A dwelling-place, abode, habitation
(ge)sǣlþ 08.01.01.03.03 Happiness, blessedness; 08.01.01.03.08 Happiness, well-being, prosperity; 16.01.02.02 Glory/majesty of heaven
gesǣlþ 05.03.02.01 Chance, hap, event
sǣlwāg 04.05.03.02.02.06.01 A hall building
sǣlwang 01.01.02.01.04 Open (level) land
sǣmann 05.12.01.09.03 A voyage; 05.12.01.09.03.03 Piracy
sǣmearh 05.12.01.09.03.01 A ship, boat
sǣmest 03.03.05.01.03 Inferior
sǣmēþe 02.05.03.02 Weariness
sǣminte 02.07.10.01 Particular herbs/spices (alphabetical order)
sǣmra 03.03.05.01.03 Inferior
sǣn 01.01.03.01.02 Sea/ocean
sǣnaca 05.12.01.09.03.01 A ship, boat
sǣnæs 01.01.02.01.01.03.01 Promontory, headland, cape
sǣne 05.12.03.02 Slowness
sǣne/sēne 11.06 Disinclination to act, listlessness
sǣnet 04.03.05 Fishing
sǣnig 01.01.03.01.02 Sea/ocean
sǣostre 02.06.06.04.01.05 Oyster
sǣp 03.01.17.02 Sap, juice
sǣpig 03.01.17.02 Sap, juice
sǣppe 02.07.03.05 Particular trees/shrubs (alphabetical order)
sǣpspōn 03.03.07 A part, division, portion
sǣrima 01.01.02.01.01.03 Shore, bank
sǣrinc 05.12.01.09.03 A voyage
sǣrōf 05.12.01.09.03 A voyage
sǣrȳric 01.01.02.01.01.02 Island
sǣsceaþa 05.12.01.09.03.03 Piracy
sǣsīþ 05.12.01.09.03 A voyage
sǣsnægl 02.06.06.04.01.06 Sea-snail
sǣstæþ 01.01.02.01.01.03 Shore, bank
sǣstān 01.01.02.02.01 Rock, stone

sǣsteorra 16.01.02.05.02.01 Mary, queen of heaven
sǣstrand 01.01.02.01.01.03 Shore, bank
sǣstrēam 01.01.03.01.02.02 Sea-channel; 01.01.03.04 Current, rush of water
sǣswalwe 02.06.08.06 Water bird
sǣswelg 01.01.03.05 Whirlpool
gesæt 05.12.05.13.02.02 To sit down
sǣt 11.09.01.01 Ambush, lying in wait
sǣta 15.01.01.01 Holding of land
sǣte 04.05.03.02.01 A building, house, hall, palace, etc.
gesǣte 06.01.07.04.02.01 Deception, deceit, snare, wile; 11.09.01.01 Ambush, lying in wait
sæterdæg 05.11.03.01.05.01 Specific days
sǣtere 11.09.01 Stealthiness, a stealthy act; 16.01.05.02.01 The devil
sæterndæg 05.11.03.01.05.01 Specific days
sæter(ne)sdæg 05.11.03.01.05.01 Specific days
sæterniht 05.11.03.01.05.01 Specific days
sǣtian 06.01.07.04.02.01 Deception, deceit, snare, wile
sǣt(i)an 11.09.01.01 Ambush, lying in wait
sǣtnere 12.01.01.12.03 Rebellion, sedition
sǣt(n)ere 14.02.01.02 Wrongful taking, theft
gesǣtnian 06.01.07.04.02.01 Deception, deceit, snare, wile
sǣt(n)ung 06.01.07.04.02.01 Deception, deceit, snare, wile
sǣtnung 11.09.01.01 Ambush, lying in wait; 12.01.01.12.03 Rebellion, sedition

sǣwǣg 01.01.03.01.02.05 Wave
sǣwæter 03.01.16.02 Water, liquid
sǣwār 02.07.11.01 Seaweed
sǣwaroþ 01.01.02.01.01.03 Shore, bank
sǣweall 01.01.02.01.02.02.04 Cliff; 01.01.03.01.02.05 Wave
sǣweard 11.10.02.02 Watchful care, keeping guard
sǣweg 01.01.03.01.02 Sea/ocean; 01.01.03.01.02.01 Region of sea/ocean
sǣwērig 02.05.03.02 Weariness
sǣwet 04.02.04.02.03 Sowing
sǣwīcing 05.12.01.01 To go on a journey/expedition, travel
sǣwiht 02.06.05 Marine animal
sǣwinewincle 02.06.06.04.01.07 Winkle
sǣwong 01.01.02.01.01.03 Shore, bank
sǣwudu 05.12.01.09.03.01 A ship, boat
sǣwylm 01.01.03.01.02.05 Wave
sǣȳþ 01.01.03.01.02.05 Wave
safene 02.07.03.05 Particular trees/shrubs (alphabetical order)
saftriende 02.08.08.02 Lung disease
sāg 05.12.05.13 To go down, descend
sāgol 13.02.08.04 Weapons, arms; 17.03.09 A post, rod, stick, etc.
sagu 06.01.08.04.01 Premonition, prophecy; 09.06.01.02 A saying, saw, proverb, maxim; 09.06.02 A saying, speech, statement; 14.03.03.03 Witness, testimony, attestation; 17.03.03 A cutting tool
(ge)sagu 09.06.01 To relate, recount, tell
sāl 04.02.05.06.05.03.03 Reins; 04.04.10.01 A ring (for finger, arm, neck); 04.05.02.12 Gate/doorway of a building; 17.03 Implements, tools, etc.; 17.03.10 Supports and fastenings
sala 15.05 Trade, traffic, commerce

salfie 02.07.10.01 Particular herbs/spices (alphabetical order)
saliht 02.07.03.05 Particular trees/shrubs (alphabetical order)
salletan 16.02.04.03.03.02 A psalm; 18.02.07.01 Singing, song
sālnes 05.11.04.02 Night, night time
saltbrōc 01.01.03.01.01.03 Stream
saltere 16.02.01.08.01.01 Books of the Old Testament; 18.02.07.02.03.02 Psaltery
saltere/psaltere 16.02.05.10.04 Choir books, etc.
salthaga 02.06.08.05 Forest bird, wild-fowl
saltwelle 01.01.03.01.01.03 Stream
salu 02.04.04.01 Having a certain complexion; 03.01.14.04 Black/blackness
salubrūn 03.01.14.04 Black/blackness
saluneb 02.04.04.01 Having a certain complexion
salupād 02.06.08.01 Part of bird
salwed 03.01.14.04 Black/blackness
salwigfeþera 02.06.08.01 Part of bird
salwigpād 02.06.08.01 Part of bird
sam ... sam 05.03.01.03 Reason, cause
sam ge ... sam ge 05.03.01.03 Reason, cause
sam þe ... sam (þe) 05.03.01.03 Reason, cause
sāmbærned 03.01.09.02.01 Fire, burning
sāmboren 05.11.08.01 Untimeliness
sāmbryce 14.02 Lawlessness
sāmcwic 02.02.03.01 In process of dying
samen 03.03.06.01 A whole formed by joining
sāmgrēne 04.02.04.04.01 To ripen
sāmgung 02.01.04.01 Youth

sāmhāl 02.08.02 Disease, infirmity, sickness
samheort 13 Peace, tranquillity
samhīwan 02.03.03 A family, household
gesamhīwan 12.02.03 A society, guild, association; 12.09 Marriage, state of marriage
samhwilc 03.04.03.01 Someone/something
sāmlǣred 06.01.06.02.03.04.04 Under instruction, being taught
samlīce 03.03.06.01 A whole formed by joining
samlinga 05.11.07.01 Contemporary, coeval
sāmlocen 02.04.03.04.01.01 Hand
sammǣle 09.07.04.01 Confirmation, agreement
sāmmelt 04.01 Digestion
samnian 04.02.04.04.02.04 To glean; 09.03.07.07.03 Composition, arrangement, writing
(ge)samnian 03.03.04.01.02.01 A heap, mass, accumulation; 03.03.06.01 A whole formed by joining; 12.04.02 A crowding together, assembly
(ge)samnian (in) 04.02.04.04.02.02 To gather fruits, crops, etc.
gesamnian 05.05 Constitution, founding (e.g. of world); 12.04 Fellowship, union, association; 12.09.02 Marriage ceremony
gesamnian ingeþanc 06.01.01.01 Thinking about, minding, heeding
(ge)samnung 03.03.04.01.02 A great number, multitude; 12.02.02 An assembly, meeting; 12.04.02 A crowding together, assembly
gesamnung 03.03.04.01.02.01 A heap, mass, accumulation; 03.03.06.01 A whole formed by joining;

05.12.05.02.02 To come together, meet; 12.09 Marriage, state of marriage; 16.02.03 The church (as temporal/spiritual body)
samnunga 05.11.07.01 Contemporary, coeval
samnungcwide 16.02.04.03.02 Parts of service
samod 03.03.04.03 Growth, increase; 03.03.06.01 A whole formed by joining; 03.03.06.02 Fullness; 05.11.07.01 Contemporary, coeval; 05.11.11.01 A not ceasing, persistence, recurrence
samod ætgædere 03.03.06.01 A whole formed by joining
samod anlīce 03.06.01 Similitude, likeness
samod anlīce ... swā swā 03.06.01 Similitude, likeness
samod mid 03.03.06.01 A whole formed by joining
samod sīþian 12.04.01.02 A fellow traveller, companion
samodcumende 05.12.05.02.02 To come together, meet
samodeard 04.05.03.01 Habitation, sojourn; 12.06.04 Native land
samodēce 16.01.01.04 The Trinity
samodfæst 03.03.06.01 A whole formed by joining
samodgang 03.05.02 An arrangement, order, succession; 05.11.11 Continuity
samodgeflit 12.05.04.01 Fighting, contention, warfare, strife
samodgesīþ 12.04.01 A fellow, companion, associate, comrade
samodgieddung 18.02.07 Music
samodherian 16.02.04.01 Shared worship
samodherigendlic 16.02.04.01 Shared worship
samodhering 16.02.04.01 Shared worship
gesamodlǣcan 03.03.04.01.02.01 A heap, mass, accumulation
samodlīce 03.03.06.01 A whole formed by joining
samodrynelas 05.11.06.02.02 A calculated space of time
samodsprǣc 09.01.04 Conversation, discussion
samodswēgende 09 Speech, vocal utterance
samodtang 05.11.11 Continuity
samodþyrlic 13 Peace, tranquillity
samodwellung 05.01 Growth, increase, what springs up
samodwist 05 Aught, anything, something
samodwunung 04.05.03.01 Habitation, sojourn
samodwyrcende 12.04 Fellowship, union, association
samrād 13 Peace, tranquillity
samrǣden 12.09 Marriage, state of marriage
sāmsoden 04.01.02.02.05 Cooking
sāmstorfen 02.02.03.01 In process of dying
sāmswǣled 03.01.09.02.01 Fire, burning
samswēge 18.02.07 Music
samtinges 05.11.07.01 Contemporary, coeval
sāmweaxen 02.01.04.01 Youth
samwinnende 12.05.04.01 Fighting, contention, warfare, strife
sāmwīs 06.01.05.03.01.01 Dullness, folly, stupidity

sāmwīslīce 06.01.05.03.01.01 Dullness, folly, stupidity
samwist 05 Aught, anything, something; 12.09 Marriage, state of marriage; 12.09.06 Cohabitation
sāmworht 11.06.02 Suffering (not acting)
samwrædnes 03.03.06.01 A whole formed by joining
sāmwyrcan 11.06.02 Suffering (not acting)
sanct 16.01.02.05.02 A saint
sand 01.01.02.01.01.03 Shore, bank; 01.01.02.02.02.01 Sand, gravel; 04.01.02.04 Abundance of food; 05.12.02.03 To send; 09.06.02.01.06 A message, announcement by a messenger; 09.06.02.01.06.01 A messenger; 11.01.02 An undertaking; 12.02.01 A substitute, representative
sandbeorg 01.01.02.01.02.02.01 Hill
sandceosol 01.01.02.02.02.01 Sand, gravel
sandcorn 01.01.02.02.02.01 Sand, gravel
sandful 01.01.02.02.02.01 Sand, gravel
sandgeweorp 01.01.02.01.04.01 Marsh, bog, swamp
sandgewyrpe 01.01.02.01.02.02.01 Hill
sandgrot 01.01.02.02.02.01 Sand, gravel
sandhliþ 01.01.02.01.02.02.03 Slope
sandhof 02.02.05.01.01 A grave, burial place, sepulchre
sandhricg 01.01.02.01.01.02 Island
sandhrycg 01.01.02.01.02.01 Rising ground, eminence
sandhyll 01.01.02.01.02.02.01 Hill
sandig 01.01.02.02.02.01 Sand, gravel
sandiht 01.01.02.02.02.01 Sand, gravel
sandland 01.01.02.01.01.03 Shore, bank
sandpytt 17.04.01 Sources of materials
sandrid 01.01.02.01.04.01 Marsh, bog, swamp
sandsēaþ 17.04.01 Sources of materials
sang 02.05.10.01 Thing heard; 02.05.10.15 Voice, cry (of living creature); 02.05.10.15.07 Voice, note (of a bird); 09.03.05.01.01 Poetry; 16.01.04.01 Sorcery using incantation; 16.02.01.08.01.01 Books of the Old Testament; 16.02.04.03.03 Singing, church singing; 16.02.04.03.03.02 A psalm; 16.02.04.07.04.01 The service of the mass; 18.02.07.01 Singing, song; 18.02.07.01.01 A song, a poem to be sung or recited; 18.02.07.02.03.01 A harp, lyre
sang secgan 18.02.07.01 Singing, song
sangbōc 16.02.05.10.04 Choir books, etc.; 18.02.07.01.01 A song, a poem to be sung or recited
sangcræft 09.03.05 Art of poetry; 18.02.07 Music
sangdrēam 18.02.07.01 Singing, song
sangere 09.03.05 Art of poetry; 16.02.03.02.13 A church singer, singer in choir; 18.02.07.01 Singing, song
sangestre 18.02.07.01 Singing, song
sangpīpe 18.02.07.02.02.01 Pipe/flute
sāp/-e 03.01.17.07 Salves, ointments, etc.
sāpbox 04.06.01.04 What is used in washing, an ointment
sāpe 04.06.01.04 What is used in washing, an ointment
sāpere 15.05.01 Goods, stock, merchandise
sār 02.08.03 Pain, bodily discomfort; 02.08.05.02 Particular inflammation/swelling; 08.01.03 Bad feeling, sadness; 08.01.03.04 Grief; 08.01.03.06 Adversity, affliction
(ge)sār 02.08.03 Pain, bodily discomfort

sar(a)cene 02.03.03.06.07.02 Arab
saracenisc 02.03.03.06.07.02 Arab
sārbenn 02.08.05.02 Particular inflammation/swelling
sārbōt 14.03.03.09.02 Atonement
sārclāþ 02.08.12.02.06.01 A bandage, binding
sārcrene 02.08.08.04 Pain in stomach
sārcwide 08.01.03.04.01 Complaint, lamentation; 08.01.03.09.01.03 Sharpness (of speech)
sāre 08.01.03.07.03 Suffering, torment, pain; 08.01.03.09.01.03 Sharpness (of speech); 08.01.03.09.11 Hardheartedness, cruelty, severity
sārettan 08.01.03.04 Grief
sārferhþ 08.01.03 Bad feeling, sadness
sārga 18.02.07.02.02.02 A trumpet
(ge)sārgian 08.01.03.04 Grief; 08.01.03.07.02.01 Injury, offence
gesārgian 02.08.04.01 A wound
sārgung 08.01.03 Bad feeling, sadness; 08.01.03.04.01 Complaint, lamentation
sārian 02.08.03 Pain, bodily discomfort; 08.01.02.05 Compassion; 08.01.03.03 Anxiety
sārig 08.01.03 Bad feeling, sadness; 08.01.03.04.01 Complaint, lamentation; 08.01.03.06 Adversity, affliction
sārigcierm 08.01.03.04.01 Complaint, lamentation
sārigferhþ 08.01.03 Bad feeling, sadness
sāriglic 08.01.03.06 Adversity, affliction
sārigmōd 08.01.03 Bad feeling, sadness
sārignes 08.01.03 Bad feeling, sadness
sārlic 08.01.03.04 Grief; 08.01.03.04.01 Complaint, lamentation; 08.01.03.07.04 Severity, harshness
sārlic sang 18.02.06 Theatricals
sārlīce 08.01.03.03 Anxiety; 08.01.03.04 Grief; 08.01.03.04.01 Complaint, lamentation; 08.01.03.07.03 Suffering, torment, pain; 08.01.03.09.11 Hardheartedness, cruelty, severity
sārnes 02.08.03 Pain, bodily discomfort; 08.01.03.03 Anxiety
sārseofung 08.01.03.04.01 Complaint, lamentation
sārslege 05.06.09 Act of striking
sārspell 08.01.03.04.01 Complaint, lamentation
sārstæf 07.05.03.03 Scorn, insult, abuse
sārwracu 12.05.06.02.03 Trouble, disturbance
sārwylm 02.08.03 Pain, bodily discomfort
saturege 02.07.11 Plants/flowers (alphabetical order)
(ge)sāwan 04.02.04.02.03 Sowing; 05.05.01 An author, source, originator
gesāwelod 02.01.02.01 That lives, living; 06 Spirit, soul, heart
gesāwen 04.02.03.02.02 Sown part of field
sāwend 04.02.04.02.03 Sowing
sāwere 04.02.04.02.03 Sowing
sāwlian 02.02.03 To die, perish
sāwlung 02.02 Death
sāwol 02.01.01.01 Soul, spirit; 06 Spirit, soul, heart; 16.01.03.01 Soul of a deceased person
sāwolberend 02.03.01 People
sāwolcund 16.02.01.12 Spirituality
sāwoldrēor 02.04.06.08.01 Blood
sāwolgedāl 02.02 Death
sāwol(ge)scot 16.02.04.20 Church due/requirement

sāwolhord 02.01.01.01 Soul, spirit; 06 Spirit, soul, heart
sāwolhūs 06 Spirit, soul, heart
sāwollēas 02.02.03.02 State of being dead; 06 Spirit, soul, heart
sāwolsceat 16.02.04.20 Church due/requirement
sāwolþearf 06.02.04.01 Want, need; 16.02.01.12 Spirituality
scāda 02.04.03.01.01 Top of head
scæc 14.05.07 Binding, fastening with bonds
scægan 07.05.04 Mockery, derision, scorn
scǣnan 05.10.05.04.14 An opening, aperture
(ge)scǣnan 05.06.03 A dashing together, breaking, shattering
gescǣned 13.02.08.04.03.01.01 Hilt of sword
gescǣningnes 05.06.03 A dashing together, breaking, shattering
(ge)scafan 05.06.06 A scraping, scarifying
scāffōt 02.08.04.02 Blemish, disfigurement
scaldhūlas 02.07.08 Grasses, reeds, etc.
gesca(l)dwyrt 02.07.11 Plants/flowers (alphabetical order)
scamfæst 12.08.03.03.01.01 Chastity
scamfæstnes 12.08.03.03.01.01 Chastity
scamful 12.08.03.03.01.01 Chastity
(ge)scamian 07.09 Shame, disgrace
scamigendlican 02.04.06.04 Reproductive organs
scamlēas 07.06.01.01 Proud, arrogant; 12.08.07.01.04 Shamelessness, lasciviousness
scamlēaslic 12.08.07.01.04 Shamelessness, lasciviousness

scamlēaslīce 07.06.01.02 Proudly, arrogantly
scamlēast 12.08.07.01.04 Shamelessness, lasciviousness
scamlic 07.09 Shame, disgrace; 12.08.03.03.01.01 Chastity
scamlīce 07.09.02 Disgrace, shaming, humiliation
scamlim 02.04.06.04.01 Male genitalia
scamm 05.10.05.03.02 Shortness
scamol 04.05.04.01 A bench, seat
scamu 02.04.06.04 Reproductive organs; 07.09 Shame, disgrace; 07.09.01 Shame, confusion; 12.08.03.03.01.01 Chastity
scamu dōn 08.01.03.07.02.01 Injury, offence
scamung 07.09.02 Disgrace, shaming, humiliation
scanca 02.04.03.04.02 Leg; 02.04.03.04.02.03 Lower leg; 02.04.05.04.07 Bone of leg; 04.01.02.01.02.05.01 Edible part of animal
scancbend 04.04.07.09 Breeches
scancforad 02.08.04.04.01 Mutilation/injury to limbs
scancgebeorg 13.02.08.03.01.05 Greaves
scancgegirela 04.04.07.09 Breeches
scanclīra 02.04.03.04.02.03 Lower leg
scand 07.09 Shame, disgrace; 07.09.03 Infamy, ignominy, shame; 12.08.06.02.06 Deceit, evil, wickedness; 12.08.08.01.02.01.01 An adulterer/-ess, whore, prostitute
scandful 07.03.05 Infamy, shame, wickedness
scandhūs 12.08.08.01.02.01.01 An adulterer/-ess, whore, prostitute

scandlic 07.03.01.01 Abominable, detestable; 07.03.05 Infamy, shame, wickedness; 07.09 Shame, disgrace
scandlīce 07.05.03.03.01 Contumelious, scornful; 07.09.03 Infamy, ignominy, shame
scandlicnes 07.09.03 Infamy, ignominy, shame
scandlufiende 12.08.07.01.04 Shamelessness, lasciviousness
scandword 16.02.04.14.02.01 Cursing, imprecation
scandwyrde 07.05.03.02 Calumny, slander, insult
scapulare 04.04.07.07 A long outer garment, covering, cloak, etc.
sceabb 02.08.05.02.02 Scab, roughness of skin
sceabbede 02.08.05.02.02 Scab, roughness of skin
sceacan 04.04 Weaving; 05.12.02 To move, set in motion; 05.12.05.03.03 To depart, leave, set out; 05.12.05.05 To shake, quake, wag
sceacdōm 05.12.05.03.03 To depart, leave, set out
scēacere 14.02.01.02 Wrongful taking, theft
sceacga 02.04.04.03 Hair; 02.04.04.03.03 Hair of head
sceacgede 02.04.04.03.01 Texture of hair
sceacol 14.05.07 Binding, fastening with bonds; 18.02.07.02.03 Stringed instruments
scead 03.01.13.03 Overshadowing; 11.10.01 Protection, safekeeping
gescēad 03.03.07 A part, division, portion; 03.05 Order, arrangement, disposition; 03.06.02 Difference, diversity, dissimilarity; 05.03.01.03 Reason, cause; 06.01.03 Faculty of reason; 06.01.03.01 Argument, reasoning; 06.01.05.02.01.01.01 Reason, sense, discretion, prudence; 06.01.06.02.02.01 Learning, science (secular knowledge); 07.01.01.01 Discrimination, faculty of distinguishing; 09.06.02 A saying, speech, statement; 11.05.02 Mode, manner, way, method, fashion, course; 15.02 Worth, value; 15.02.03 An account
gescēad āgildan 15.02.03 An account
scēadan 03.06.02 Difference, diversity, dissimilarity; 05.10.04 Place, room
(ge)scēadan 03.03.07.01 Division, partition, separation; 03.06.02 Difference, diversity, dissimilarity; 05.10.05 A space, span; 05.10.05.02.01 Diffusion, effusion, spreading; 07 Judgement, forming of opinion
gescēadan 09.03.07.07.03.01 A description, writing down; 09.04.03 Exposition, making clear by explanation; 10.04.03.01 To take away, deprive of; 14.01.06 A rule, order, precept, tenet, principle
sceadd 02.06.06.03.01.10 Shad
sceaddgenge 04.03.05 Fishing; 05.11.03.01.02 A season of the year
gescēadenlīce 03.03.07.01 Division, partition, separation
scēadenmǣl 13.02.08.04.03 A sword
scēadesealf 02.08.12.02.07 Remedies for specific parts (head to toe)
sceadiht 03.01.13.03 Overshadowing
sceadlic 03.01.13.03 Overshadowing

gescēadlic 03.06.03 Congruity, fitness, suitability; 06.01.03.01 Argument, reasoning
gescēadlīce 03.06.03 Congruity, fitness, suitability; 06.01.03.01 Argument, reasoning; 07.01.01.01 Discrimination, faculty of distinguishing
gescēadnes 14.01.06 A rule, order, precept, tenet, principle
sceadu 03.01.13.03 Overshadowing; 05.03.01.02.01 A destructive influence; 05.07 Ending of existence, end of world; 11.10.01 Protection, safekeeping
sceadugeard 03.01.13.03 Overshadowing
sceadugenga 16.01.03.03 A doomed spirit
sceaduhelm 03.01.13.03 Overshadowing
sceadwian 11.10.01 Protection, safekeeping
sceadwig 03.01.13.03 Overshadowing
(ge)scēadwīs 07.01.01.01 Discrimination, faculty of distinguishing
gescēadwīs 06.01.05 Understanding, intellect; 06.01.05.02.01.01.01 Reason, sense, discretion, prudence
gescēadwīslic 06.01.03.01 Argument, reasoning; 06.01.05 Understanding, intellect
(ge)scēadwīslīce 06.01.05.02.01.01.01 Reason, sense, discretion, prudence
gescēadwīslīce 03.06.03.01 Compatible; 06.01.03.01 Argument, reasoning; 09.05.05.01 Showing, manifestation, display
(ge)scēadwīsnes 06.01.03 Faculty of reason
gescēadwīsnes 03.03.03 Number; 06.01.03.01 Argument, reasoning; 06.01.05.02.01.01.01 Reason, sense, discretion, prudence; 07.01.01.01 Discrimination, faculty of distinguishing
sceadwung 03.01.13.03 Overshadowing
gesceaf 03.03.07 A part, division, portion
scēaf 03.03.04.01.02.01 A heap, mass, accumulation; 04.02.04.04.04 Stack, rick
sceafa 17.03.04 Tools for smoothing/scraping/grinding
gesceafen 05.06.06 A scraping, scarifying
scēafmǣlum 03.03.04.01.02.01 A heap, mass, accumulation; 04.02.04.04.04 Stack, rick
sceaf(o)þa 03.03.07 A part, division, portion
sceaft 13.02.08.04 Weapons, arms; 13.02.08.04.01 A spear; 13.02.08.04.04.01 An arrow, dart, bolt; 17.03.09 A post, rod, stick, etc.; 17.05.03 Sources of fire/light
gesceaft 01 Earth, world; 02 Creation; 02.01.03.03 Sex, generation; 03 Material, matter, substance; 03.05 Order, arrangement, disposition; 05.02 State, condition; 05.03.02.01.01 An event, occurrence; 05.04 Fate, lot, fortune, destiny
sceafta mund 05.10.05.03 A measure of distance
sceaftlō 13.02.08.04.01 A spear
sceaftriht(e) 05.10.05.04.05 Straight, direct
sceafttog 13.02.08.04.01 A spear
sceaga 02.07.03.04.01 A small wood, coppice, copse
sceal 05.04 Fate, lot, fortune, destiny; 06.02.04 Necessity, inevitability; 06.02.04.01 Want, need; 06.02.07

Will, determination, resolution;
12.03.02 Advice, admonition; 12.07
An obligation, bounden duty; 14.01.05
Service, obligation, duty
scealc 05.12.01.09.03 A voyage; 11.08.04
Vanity, idleness, frivolity; 12.01.01.07
A follower; 12.08.06.02.06 Deceit,
evil, wickedness; 13.02.10.01 A man,
warrior
sceald 05.10.05.03.05 Shallow
scealdþȳfel 02.07.03.04.02 A thicket
scealfor/-ra 02.06.08.06 Water bird
scealga 02.06.06.02.01.07 Roach, rudd
sceallan 02.04.06.04.01 Male genitalia
scealu 03.03.02 Measurement by
weighing; 04.01.02.02.06.05.04
Cup/bowl/basin; 04.02.04.03.02.01
Grain crops; 05.10.05.03.05 Shallow
scēam 02.06.02.01.06 Horse
(ge)sceap 02.04.06.04 Reproductive
organs
gesceap 02 Creation; 02.01.03.03 Sex,
generation; 02.01.03.03.01 To beget;
03.05 Order, arrangement, disposition;
05.02 State, condition; 05.02.02
Nature, established order of things;
05.03.02.01.01 An event, occurrence;
05.04 Fate, lot, fortune, destiny; 05.05
Constitution, founding (e.g. of world);
05.10.06 Form, shape; 17.02.04.02.01
Cutting, hewing, shaping
scēap 02.06.02.01.08 Sheep;
16.02.03.03.05 A layman
scēapǣtere 02.06.02.01.08 Sheep
scēapen 02.06.02.01.08 Sheep
(ge)sceapennes 05.05 Constitution,
founding (e.g. of world)
gesceapennes 03.05.01 Arranging,
ordering, disposition
scēaphām 04.02.05.06.02.01 A sheepfold
scēapheord 02.06.02.01.08 Sheep
scēapheorden 04.02.05.06.02.01 A
sheepfold
gesceaphwīl 05.04.01 Fortune, Fate
(personification)
scēaphyrde 04.02.05.06.02 A shepherd
scēaplic 02.06.02.01.08 Sheep
gesceaplīce 03.06.03 Congruity, fitness,
suitability
scēapscearu 04.02.05.06.02.03
Sheep-shearing
gesceapþēote 02.06.01.03 Barrel, body of
animal
scēapwæsce 04.02.05.06.02.02 Dip,
washing-place
scēapwīc 04.02.05.06.02.01 A sheepfold
scear 04.02.04.06.07 Ploughing
equipment; 17.03.03 A cutting tool
scearbēam 04.02.04.06.07 Ploughing
equipment
sceard 02.08.04.01 A wound;
02.08.04.02.01 A maimed man;
05.06.04 Damage, injury, defect, hurt,
loss; 05.10.03 A gap, cleft;
10.04.03.01 To take away, deprive of;
17.03.12.02 A potter
(ge)scearfian 05.06.02 Cleaving,
splitting, cutting
scearflian 05.06.06 A scraping, scarifying
scearfung 05.06.06 A scraping, scarifying
gescearian 10.03.03 Granting
scearn 02.04.06.06.06 Faeces
scearnbudda 02.06.09.02.03 Beetle
scearnig 04.06.02.01 Dirty, unclean
scearnwibba 02.06.09.02.03 Beetle
scearp 02.05.07.01 Strong taste, acidity,
pungency; 02.05.09.01 To open the
eyes/be awake; 02.08.02 Disease,
infirmity, sickness; 02.08.12.02.05
Pharmacy, curing with salves;

03.01.05 Roughness; 03.01.12 Brightness, light; 04.01.02.01.01.04 (Of food/wine) sharp; 04.01.03.05.01.01 Wine; 05.08.01 Vigour, activity, force; 05.10.06.03.01 A point, spike, prickle; 06.01.05.02 Intelligence; 08.01.03.07.04 Severity, harshness; 08.01.03.09.01.03 Sharpness (of speech)

scearpe 02.05.09.01 To open the eyes/be awake; 02.08.12.02.06 Surgical; 05.06.06 A scraping, scarifying; 05.10.06.03.01 A point, spike, prickle; 06.01.01.02 Care, attention, observation

scearpecgede 05.10.06.03.01 A point, spike, prickle

scearpian 05.06.06 A scraping, scarifying

scearplic 06.01.05.02 Intelligence; 11.03.02.01 Efficacy, success

scearplīce 05.12.03.01 Swiftness, velocity; 06.01.01.02 Care, attention, observation; 08.01.03.07.03 Suffering, torment, pain; 11.03.02.01 Efficacy, success

scearpnes 02.05.07.01 Strong taste, acidity, pungency; 02.05.09.01 To open the eyes/be awake; 03.01.05 Roughness; 06.01.05.02 Intelligence; 07.06.01 Pride, arrogance; 08.01.03.09.01.03 Sharpness (of speech); 11.03.02.01 Efficacy, success

scearpnumol 02.08.12.02.05 Pharmacy, curing with salves

scearpsīene 02.05.09.01 To open the eyes/be awake

scearpsmēawung 09.07.01 Contention, argument, strife of words

scearpþancfullīce 11.03.02.01 Efficacy, success

scearpþanclīce 11.03.02.01 Efficacy, success

scearpþancol 06.01.05.02 Intelligence

scearpung 02.08.12.02.06 Surgical; 05.06.06 A scraping, scarifying

scearseax 17.03.03 A cutting tool

scearu 02.04.04.03.05 Haircutting, tonsure; 02.04.05.04.05.05 Share-bone; 04.02.05.06.02.03 Sheep-shearing; 16.02.04.13.03 Tonsure, haircutting, shaving

scearwund 02.08.04.01 A wound

scēat 01.01 Surface of the earth; 01.01.02.01 Ground; 01.01.02.01.01.03.01 Promontory, headland, cape; 01.01.02.01.01.03.02 Inlet in river/sea; 01.01.03.01.02.01 Region of sea/ocean; 02.04.03.03.05 Chest, breast, bosom; 02.04.03.03.07 Lap; 04.04.07 Trappings, equipment, garb; 04.04.08 A covering, curtain, veil, garment, etc.; 04.05.04.05.01 Bedding (e.g. of straw); 05.10.04.02 A region, zone; 09.05.04.01 Concealment, obscurity; 11.10.02.02.01 Care, interest in

scēata 01.01.02.01 Ground; 04.04.08 A covering, curtain, veil, garment, etc.; 05.10.06.04 A corner, bend, angle; 05.12.01.09.03.01.03 Part of ship

scēatlīne 05.12.01.09.03.01.03 Part of ship

sceatt 10.01.03 A sharing, participation; 15.01 Property; 15.01.04 Coinage, money; 15.02 Worth, value; 15.02.04.01 Payment for temporary use, rent, hire; 15.03 Exaction of tax/tribute

scēatt 05.10.04.02 A region, zone

sceattas 15.01.04 Coinage, money

sceattcod 04.01.02.02.06.03 Food receptacle, basket

gesceatwyrpan 12.09.01 Pledging, betrothal; 15.02.04 Spending, disbursement

scēaþ 13.02.08.04.03.01.02 Sheath for sword

sceaþa 08.01.03.07.02.01 Injury, offence; 08.01.03.09.05 Enmity; 13.02.10.01 A man, warrior; 14.02.01.02.01 Open robbery, rapine, pillage; 16.01.05.02 Species of devil, hellish race

sceaþel 04.04.03 A spinning-house or chamber

sceaþful 07.03.02 Ill, harm, hurt

sceaþian 14.02.01.02.01 Open robbery, rapine, pillage

(ge)sceaþian 07.03.02 Ill, harm, hurt

sceaþig 07.03.02 Ill, harm, hurt

sceaþþig 12.08.09 Guiltiness, guilt

sceaþþignes 07.03.02 Ill, harm, hurt

sceaþung 02.08.04 Hurt, injury, damage

scēawendspræc 18.02.05 Buffoonery, speech of buffoon/actor

scēawendwīse 18.02.05 Buffoonery, speech of buffoon/actor

scēawere 02.05.09.05 To watch, observe, survey; 02.05.09.10 Look-out place; 02.05.09.11 Mirror; 09.05.01 Inspection, examination; 11.09.01 Stealthiness, a stealthy act; 11.10.02.02 Watchful care, keeping guard; 18.02.05 Buffoonery, speech of buffoon/actor

scēawian 07.01.01 Choice, election; 09.03.07.07.03.01 A description, writing down; 13.02.07.02 Order (of troops), array

(ge)scēawian 02.05.09.04 To see, look upon, behold; 02.05.09.05 To watch, observe, survey; 06.01.01.01 Thinking about, minding, heeding; 06.01.01.02 Care, attention, observation; 07.04 Consideration, esteem; 09.05.05.01 Showing, manifestation, display

scēawigend 02.05.09.05 To watch, observe, survey

scēawung 02.05.09.05 To watch, observe, survey; 02.05.09.07 Form, appearance, aspect; 06.01.01.01 Thinking about, minding, heeding; 06.01.07.04.04.02 Pretence, feigning, dissimulation; 06.01.08.05.01.01.01 An exercise of power, mighty work, miracle; 07.04.03 Reverence, respect; 15.03.01 Toll

gescēawung 06.01.01.01 Thinking about, minding, heeding

scēawungstōw 02.05.09.10 Look-out place; 16.01.02.04 Paradise

scegþ 05.12.01.09.03.01 A ship, boat

scegþmann 02.03.03.05.06 Viking(s); 05.12.01.09.03.03 Piracy

scēla 04.05.03.02.02.08 A lowly dwelling, cottage, hut

scele 07.01.01.01 Discrimination, faculty of distinguishing

scelfan 05.12.04.01.01 Unstable

scelle 03.03.07.01 Division, partition, separation

scenc 04.01.03 Drinking; 04.01.03.05.04 Drinking vessel

(ge)scencan 04.01.03 Drinking

scencel/scencen 02.06.02.01.07 Pig, swine

scencingcuppe 04.01.03.05.04 Drinking vessel

(ge)scendan 07.05.01 Censure, reproof, rebuke; 07.09 Shame, disgrace;

12.08.06.01.04.01 To mislead, seduce, lead astray
gescendan 02.08.04 Hurt, injury, damage; 06.01.05.03.01.01 Dullness, folly, stupidity; 09.07.02 Contradiction; 13.02.05.01.01 To overcome, conquer
scending 07.05.03.03 Scorn, insult, abuse; 08.01.03.07.02.01 Injury, offence
scendle 07.05.03.03 Scorn, insult, abuse
gescendnes 07.09.01 Shame, confusion; 09.07.02 Contradiction
gescendþ 07.09.01 Shame, confusion
scenn 13.02.08.04.03.01.01 Hilt of sword; 17.02.04.03 Metal worker
gescentu 07.09.01 Shame, confusion; 08.01.03.07.02.01 Injury, offence
scēo 01.03.01.06 Cloud; 11.10.01.02 Refuge, help, shelter
scēoh 06.01.08.06.06 Timidity; 12.08.07.01.01 Wantonness, sensuality, lasciviousness
scēohmōd 06.01.08.06 Fear
sceol 02.08.07.02 Disorders of the eye
sceolhē(a)gede 02.08.07.02 Disorders of the eye
sceolhēge 02.08.07.02 Disorders of the eye
scēon 05.12.03.01 Swiftness, velocity
(ge)scēon 05.03.02.01.01 An event, occurrence
sceoppa 15.01.03 Treasure, riches, wealth
sceorf 02.04.04 Skin; 02.08.05.02.02 Scab, roughness of skin; 02.08.06 Skin disease, erysipelas
gesceorf 02.08.08.04.02 (Of stomach) disordered
sceorfan 05.06.06 A scraping, scarifying; 05.06.06.01 A tearing, laceration; 08.01.03.07.02.01 Injury, offence
sceorfe(n)de 02.08.07.07 Disorders of the body
sceorp 04.04.07 Trappings, equipment, garb
sceorpan 08.01.03.07.02.01 Injury, offence
gesceorpan 05.06.06 A scraping, scarifying
sceortwyrplic 02.08.13 Recovery, growing better
(ge)scēot 11.02.01.01 Active, nimble
sceota 02.06.06.02.01.09 Trout
scēotan 02.08.03 Pain, bodily discomfort; 05.06.09 Act of striking; 05.10.04 Place, room; 05.12.02.06 To push, impel, thrust; 15.02.04 Spending, disbursement
scēotan of 05.12.05.03.04.01 To burst forth, break out
(ge)scēotan 05.12.02.06 To push, impel, thrust; 05.12.03.01.01 Quick movement or movements; 13.02.08.04.02 A shot, missile, dart, spear, javelin, etc.; 14.03.03 Law, action of the courts
gescēotan 05.03.02.01.01 An event, occurrence; 10.03.07.01 To allot, assign; 15.01 Property; 17.02.04 Trade, calling, craft, aptitude
scēotend 13.02.10.01 A man, warrior
scēotere 13.02.10.01.02 An armed man
sceppe 03.03.01.02 Dry measures
scericge 18.02.05 Buffoonery, speech of buffoon/actor
sceþdǣd 12.08.06.02.05 Misdeed, sin
sceþ(e)nes 02.08.04 Hurt, injury, damage
(ge)sceþþan 05.06.04 Damage, injury, defect, hurt, loss; 05.09 Weakness
gesceþþan 08.01.03.09.05 Enmity

sceþþend 12.05.02 Hostility, contention, opposition
gesceþþendlic 07.03.02 Ill, harm, hurt
sceþþu 02.08.04 Hurt, injury, damage
sceþwræc 08.01.03.07.02 Misery, trouble, affliction
scīa 02.04.03.04.02.03 Lower leg
sciccel(s) 04.04.07.07 A long outer garment, covering, cloak, etc.
sciccing 04.04.07.07 A long outer garment, covering, cloak, etc.
scīd 17.05.01 Fuel, tinder
scīdhrēac 17.05.01 Fuel, tinder
scīdweall 04.05.01.02.07 A fence, hedge
scield 02.06.08.01 Part of bird; 11.10.01 Protection, safekeeping; 13.02.08.03.01.06 A shield
scieldan 12.03.04.02 Speech on behalf of, advocacy
scieldan ongēan 11.10.02.02 Watchful care, keeping guard
(ge)scieldan 11.10.01 Protection, safekeeping; 13.02.04 Defence, guard, protection
scieldhrēoþa 13.02.08.03.01.06 A shield
gescieldod 13.02.08.03.01.06 A shield
sciell 02.05.10.04 To resound; 02.06.06.01 Part of fish; 02.06.06.04 Shellfish; 02.06.08.01 Part of bird; 04.01.02.02.06.05.03 Plate/platter/bowl/dish
sciellfisc 02.06.06.04 Shellfish
scielliht 02.06.06.04 Shellfish
scīene 03.01.12 Brightness, light; 07.10 Beauty, fairness
scīenes 06.02.06.03.02 Instigation
(ge)scieppan 05.04.01 Fortune, Fate (personification); 05.05 Constitution, founding (e.g. of world); 16.01.01.02.01 Creator; 17.02.04 Trade, calling, craft, aptitude
(ge)scieppan (tō) 05.04 Fate, lot, fortune, destiny
scieppend 05.05.01 An author, source, originator
(ge)scieppend 16.01.01.02.01 Creator
scieran 04.02.05.06.02.03 Sheep-shearing; 16.02.04.13.03 Tonsure, haircutting, shaving
(ge)scieran 02.04.04.03.05 Haircutting, tonsure; 04.06.01.07 Hair-care; 05.06.02 Cleaving, splitting, cutting
gescieran 05.06.02.01 A cleft, split
scierden 17.03.12.02 A potter
sciering 16.02.04.13.03 Tonsure, haircutting, shaving
scierpan 05.08.02 Violence, force
(ge)scierpan 04.04.07 Trappings, equipment, garb; 17.02.04.03.02 Filings
gescierpan 02.05.09.03 To give light, restore to sight; 05.08 Strength; 05.10.05.04.12 The condition of being covered; 06.02.07.01 Strength, fortitude; 10.03.04 Provision, supply
gescierpla 04.04.07 Trappings, equipment, garb
scīete 02.02.05.02 To prepare for burial; 04.04.08 A covering, curtain, veil, garment, etc.
(ge)sciftan 10.03.07 Distribution; 14.01.06 A rule, order, precept, tenet, principle; 17.02.02 An office, function, employment
gesciftan 03.05.01 Arranging, ordering, disposition
scildburh 11.10.01.02 Refuge, help, shelter; 13.02.07.02 Order (of troops), array
scilden 11.10.01 Protection, safekeeping

(ge)scildend 16.01.01.02.04 Protector, defender
scildere 16.01.01.02.04 Protector, defender
scildfreca 13.02.10.01 A man, warrior
scildhete 12.05.04 Strife, hostility
scildhrēoþa 13.02.07.02 Order (of troops), array
(ge)scildnes 11.10.01 Protection, safekeeping
scildtruma 13.02.07.02 Order (of troops), array; 13.02.10.01.02.01 An armed force/band
scildung 11.10.01 Protection, safekeeping
scildweall 13.02.07.02 Order (of troops), array
scildwiga 13.02.10.01 A man, warrior
scildwyrhta 13.02.08.03.01.06 A shield
scilfe 04.05.02.10 Flooring, a floor
scilfor 03.01.12.01 Glittering, effulgence; 03.01.14.07 Yellow/yellowness
scilfrig 03.01.12.01 Glittering, effulgence
scilling 04.04.10.01 A ring (for finger, arm, neck); 15.01.04 Coinage, money
scillingrīm 15.02.03 An account
scīma 03.01.12 Brightness, light; 05.11.04.02.01 Sunset
scimerian 03.01.12.01 Glittering, effulgence
scīmian 03.01.12.01 Glittering, effulgence
scīmiende 03.01.12.01 Glittering, effulgence
scimriende 03.01.12.01 Glittering, effulgence
scīn/scinn 16.01.03 A spectre, ghost, demon, goblin
scīnan 02.05.09.06 Thing seen, sight, vision; 03.01.12.01 Glittering, effulgence; 07.10 Beauty, fairness

(ge)scīnan 03.01.12 Brightness, light
gescīnan 03.01.12.02 A beam of light
scinbān 02.04.05.04.07 Bone of leg
gescincio 02.04.05.02 Fat
scindel 04.05.01.02.02 A shingle
scīnefrian 03.01.12.01 Glittering, effulgence
scīnende 03.01.12 Brightness, light; 07.08.07 Glory, splendour, magnificence
scīnendlic 03.01.12 Brightness, light
scīnere 18.02.06 Theatricals
scīnfeld 16.01.02.04 Paradise
scingal 04.05.01.02.02 A shingle
scinhosu 13.02.08.03.01.05 Greaves
scinn/scynn 02.06.01.06 Skin, hide
scinncræft 16.01.04 Sorcery, magic, witchcraft; 16.01.04.03 Sorcery involving deceptive appearances; 16.01.04.04 A magical apparatus
scinncræfta 16.01.04.03 Sorcery involving deceptive appearances
scinncræftig 16.01.04 Sorcery, magic, witchcraft
scin(n)cræftig 16.01.05.02.02 Other terms for devils
scinncræftiga 16.01.04.03 Sorcery involving deceptive appearances
scinnere 16.01.04.03 Sorcery involving deceptive appearances
scīnnes 03.01.12 Brightness, light
scinn(ge)lāc 16.01.04 Sorcery, magic, witchcraft
scinnhīw 16.01.03 A spectre, ghost, demon, goblin
scinnlāc 02.08.11.02.01.01 Paroxysm of madness, folly; 16.01.03 A spectre, ghost, demon, goblin; 16.01.04 Sorcery, magic, witchcraft;

16.01.04.05 Necromancy; 16.02.01.05
Heresy, error, wrong belief
scinnlǣca 16.01.04.03 Sorcery involving
deceptive appearances
scinnlǣce 16.01.04.03 Sorcery involving
deceptive appearances
scinnlic 16.01.04.03 Sorcery involving
deceptive appearances
scinnsēoc 16.01.04.03 Sorcery involving
deceptive appearances
scinu 02.04.03.04.02.03 Lower leg;
02.04.05.04.07 Bone of leg
scip 05.12.01.09.03.01 A ship, boat
scipāc 05.12.01.09.03.01.04 Equipping of
ships
scipberende 05.12.01.09.03 A voyage
scipbroc 05.12.01.09.03.02 Hardship on
board
scipbrucol 05.06 Destruction,
dissolution, loss, breaking;
05.12.01.09.03.02 Hardship on board
scipbryce 14.01.04.02 Rights involving
property
scipbȳme 18.02.07.02.02.02 A trumpet
scipcræft 13.02.10.03.01 A fleet
scipdrincende 05.12.01.09.03.02
Hardship on board
scipe 12.01.01.06 Condition, rank,
standing; 15.02.04 Spending,
disbursement
gescipe 05.04 Fate, lot, fortune, destiny
scipen 04.02.05.06.01.01 A cattle
pen/cowshed
scipere 05.12.01.09.03 A voyage
scipfæreld 05.12.01.09.03 A voyage
scipfæt 16.02.05.05.06 A vessel for use in
services
scipfarend 05.12.01.09.03 A voyage
scipfērend 05.12.01.09.03 A voyage
scipfierd 13.02.10.03.01 A fleet

scipflota 05.12.01.09.03 A voyage
scipforþung 05.12.01.09.03.01.04
Equipping of ships
scipfultum 13.02.10.03.01 A fleet
scipfylleþ 14.03 Right of holding court,
jurisdiction
scipfyrdung 13.02.01 A military
expedition
scipfyrþ(r)ung 05.12.01.09.03.01.04
Equipping of ships
scipgebroc 05.12.01.09.03.02 Hardship
on board
scipgefær 05.12.01.09.03 A voyage
scipgefeoht 13.02.02 Battle
scipgesceot 15.03.02 A tax
scipgetāwu 05.12.01.09.03.01.03 Part of
ship
scipgyld 15.03.02 A tax
sciphamor 05.12.01.09.03.01.03 Part of
ship
sciphere 13.02.10.03 Crew/men of a ship;
13.02.10.03.01 A fleet
scipherelic 13.02.10.03.01 A fleet
sciphlǣder 05.12.01.09.03.01.03 Part of
ship
sciphlæst 05.12.01.09.03.01.01 Kind of
ship; 13.02.10.03 Crew/men of a ship
sciphlāford 05.12.01.09.03 A voyage
(ge)scipian 05.12.01.09 To travel on
water; 05.12.01.09.03.01.04
Equipping of ships
scipincel 05.12.01.09.03.01.01 Kind of
ship
sciplād 05.12.01.09.03 A voyage
sciplic 05.12.01.09.03.01.02
Of/concerning a ship, naval;
13.02.10.03.01 A fleet
scipliþ 13.02.10.03.01 A fleet
sciplīþend 05.12.01.09.03 A voyage
sciplīþende 05.12.01.09.03 A voyage

scipmærls 05.12.01.09.03.01.03 Part of ship
scipmann 05.12.01.09.03 A voyage; 13.02.10.03 Crew/men of a ship
sciprāp 05.12.01.09.03.01.03 Part of ship
sciprēþra 05.12.01.09.03 A voyage
sciprēþru 05.12.01.09.03.01.03 Part of ship
sciprōþor 05.12.01.09.03.01.03 Part of ship
sciprōwend 05.12.01.09.03 A voyage
scipryne 05.12.01.09.03.06 A channel for shipping
scipsetl 05.12.01.09.03.01.03 Part of ship
scipsōcn 14.03 Right of holding court, jurisdiction
scipsteall 05.12.01.09.03.04 A harbour
scipstēora 05.12.01.09.03 A voyage
scipsteorra 01.02.01.01.02 Star
sciptāwu 05.12.01.09.03.01.03 Part of ship
sciptearo 03.01.17.06.01 Bitumen, pitch
sciptoll 15.02 Worth, value
scipwealh 05.12.01.09.03 A voyage
scipweard 05.12.01.09.03 A voyage
scipwered 05.12.01.09.03 A voyage
scipwyrhta 05.12.01.09.03.01.04 Equipping of ships
scīr 02.03.03.03.01 A native people; 02.03.03.04.03 People of a shire; 03.01.12 Brightness, light; 03.01.12.03 Clear, transparent; 03.01.14 A colour; 03.01.14.03 White/whiteness; 07.02.04.03 Nobleness, excellence, nobility, magnificence; 12.01.01 Authority; 12.06.02 District, province; 12.08.04 Purity, moral cleanness; 14.03.03 Law, action of the courts; 16.02.03.02.05 A bishop; 18.02.07 Music
(ge)scīr 17.02.02 An office, function, employment
gescīr 05.02.02.02 (One's) own person
scīran 07.01.01.01 Discrimination, faculty of distinguishing; 09.06.02.01 To tell, make known, declare, relate, announce; 12.07.03 Abstinence/exemption (from); 14.03.03.01 Accusation
gescīran 12.02 A public office
scīrbasu 03.01.14.05 Red/redness
scīrbisceop 16.02.03.02.05 A bishop
scīre 03.01.12 Brightness, light; 05.08 Strength; 05.10.05.04.11 A circle, circuit, circumference; 18.02.07 Music
scīrecg 03.01.12 Brightness, light; 05.10.06.03.01 A point, spike, prickle
scirfemūs 02.06.03.01.13 Rodents
scīrgemōt 12.02.02 An assembly, meeting
scīrgerēfa 12.02.02 An assembly, meeting
scīrham 13.02.08.03.01 Body armour, war gear
(ge)scirian 03.03.07.01 Division, partition, separation; 05.04 Fate, lot, fortune, destiny; 10.03.03 Granting; 14.01.06 A rule, order, precept, tenet, principle
gescirian 03.03.03 Number
sciriendlic 03.03.07.01 Division, partition, separation
scīrlett 01.01.02.01.01 Tract of land
scīrmǣled 13.02.08.04.03 A sword
scīrmann 02.03.03.04.03 People of a shire; 12.02.02 An assembly, meeting
scīrnes 09.04.03 Exposition, making clear by explanation
(ge)scirpan 11.01.03 Preparation

scirpen 08.01.03.07.04 Severity, harshness
gescirpendlīce 03.06.03 Congruity, fitness, suitability
gescirpt 09 Speech, vocal utterance
scirte 01.01.02.01.01 Tract of land
scīrþegn 12.01.01.06.08 A person of rank, elder, great man
scirung 12.05.07.01 Separation, dismissal, rejection
scirwæter 01.01.03.01 Body of water
scīrwered 03.01.12 Brightness, light
scīrwita 12.01.01.05 A leader, administrator
scitere 04.05.03.05.01 A cess-pool, midden, sewer
scitol 02.08.12.02.07.01 Purgative
scitte 02.08.08.12 Disease of bowels; 04.02.05.02.01 (Of cattle) seized with disease
sclidd 01.01.02.01.04.01 Marsh, bog, swamp
scocha 06.02.06.03.04 Allurement
scōcnyll 02.05.10.13.01.01 Stroke/sound of a bell; 04.04.07.15 Footwear, covering for the feet; 16.02.05.05.02 A church/monastery bell
gescōd 04.04.07.15 Footwear, covering for the feet
scōere 04.04.07.15 Footwear, covering for the feet
scofettan 05.12.02.06.01 To push, drive
scofl 04.02.04.06.01 A spade; 17.03.07 Tools for digging/grasping/pulling
(ge)scōgan 04.04.07.15 Footwear, covering for the feet
scōh 04.04.07.15 Footwear, covering for the feet
scōhnægl 04.04.07.15 Footwear, covering for the feet
scōhþēn 04.04.07.15 Footwear, covering for the feet; 12.01.01.08.01 A servant, attendant
scōhþwang 04.04.07.15 Footwear, covering for the feet
scōhwyrhta 04.04.06 Undressed condition (of hide); 04.04.07.15 Footwear, covering for the feet
scōl 06.01.06.02.03.04.01 A school
gescola 12.04.01 A fellow, companion, associate, comrade; 15.04 A debt, due
scōlere 06.01.06.02.03.01 A pupil, disciple, scholar
scōlmann 06.01.06.02.03.01 A pupil, disciple, scholar; 12.01.01.07 A follower; 12.04.01 A fellow, companion, associate, comrade
scolu 02.06.06 Fish; 06.01.06.02.03.04.01 A school; 12.04.01.01 A company of people, fellowship, society
scomhylte 02.07.03.04.02 A thicket
scop 09.03.05 Art of poetry; 09.03.07.07.03.03 A writer, author; 16.01.04.06 Divination, augury; 18.02.06 Theatricals
scopcræft 09.03.05 Art of poetry
scopgereord 09.03.05.01 Poetical language
scoplēoþ 09.03.05.01.01 Poetry
scoplic 09.03.05.01 Poetical language; 09.03.05.01.01 Poetry
scora 01.01.02.01.01.03 Shore, bank; 04.04.07 Trappings, equipment, garb
scoren 05.06.02.01 A cleft, split
scorian 05.10.06.03 Projection, head, extremity (of anything); 09.07.03.02 Refusal, denial
scort 02.04.02.03.02 Short; 05.10.05.03.02 Shortness; 05.11.01.02 Shortness/brevity in time;

05.11.01.02.01 Swift movement of time; 09 Speech, vocal utterance; 09.03.07.07.03.02.01 An epitome, short account
scortian 05.11.03.01.05 A day
(ge)scortian 03.03.04.05 Insufficiency, lack, want
scortigende 05.11.03.01.05 A day
scortlic 05.11.01.02 Shortness/brevity in time
scortlīce 05.11.07.04.01 Nearness, approach, imminence; 09.03.04.05 To put briefly
scortnes 05.10.05.03.02 Shortness; 05.11.01.02 Shortness/brevity in time; 09.03.07.07.03.02.01 An epitome, short account
scoru 03.03.03.04.20 Twenty
scot 05.12.03.01.01 Quick movement or movements
(ge)scot 13.02.08.04.02 A shot, missile, dart, spear, javelin, etc.; 15.03 Exaction of tax/tribute
gescot 05.12.03.01.01 Quick movement or movements; 16.02.05.03.03 Chancel
gescota 13.02.10 The military, soldiers
gescotfeoht 13.02.02 Battle
scotfrēo 14.01.03.02 Freedom from punishment or fine
scotian 05.12.02.06 To push, impel, thrust; 05.12.03.01 Swiftness, velocity; 05.12.03.01.01 Quick movement or movements
(ge)scotian 13.02.08.04.02 A shot, missile, dart, spear, javelin, etc.
scotlīra 02.04.03.04.02.03 Lower leg
scotspere 13.02.08.04.02 A shot, missile, dart, spear, javelin, etc.
scottas 02.03.03.05.03 The Scots; 02.03.03.05.04 The Irish
scotung 13.02.08.04.02 A shot, missile, dart, spear, javelin, etc.
scōung 04.04.07.15 Footwear, covering for the feet
scræb 02.06.08.06 Water bird
scræf 01.01.02.01.03 Hollow/depression in land; 01.01.02.01.03.01 Cave; 04.05.03.02.02.01 Dwellings in particular places; 04.05.03.02.02.03 Disagreeable dwellings; 04.05.03.05.01 A cess-pool, midden, sewer
gescræf 04.05.03.02.02.01 Dwellings in particular places; 09.05.04.01 Concealment, obscurity
scræfen 01.01.02.01.03.01 Cave
scrǣman 02.05.10.15.01 To raise (the voice), raise up (noise)
scrætte 12.08.08.01.02.01.01 An adulterer/-ess, whore, prostitute
scrallettan 02.05.10.04 To resound
scrapian 02.05.06.02 Stroking, caressing; 05.06.06 A scraping, scarifying
scrēad(e) 03.03.07 A part, division, portion
scrēadian 05.10.05.04.13 A removal of that which obscures or conceals
(ge)scrēadian 04.02.04.05.04.01.01 Pruning/lopping
scrēadung 03.03.07 A part, division, portion; 04.01.02.01.01.08 Leftover food; 04.02.04.05.04.01.01 Pruning/lopping
scrēadungīsen 04.02.04.05.04.01.01 Pruning/lopping
scrēawa 02.06.03.01.13 Rodents
scremman 11.11.01 A physical difficulty, strait

(ge)screncan 11.11.01 A physical difficulty, strait
gescrencan 03.01.18 Dryness (not wetness)
scrence 03.01.18 Dryness (not wetness)
gescrence 02.08.04.04.03 Withered
gescrencednes 11.11.02 A hindrance
screpan 05.06.06 A scraping, scarifying; 05.06.08 A plucking, taking away
scrēpan 03.01.18 Dryness (not wetness)
(ge)scrēpe 03.06.03 Congruity, fitness, suitability
gescrēpe 11.07.02 Utility, advantage, convenience
gescrēpelīce 03.06.03 Congruity, fitness, suitability; 11.07.02 Utility, advantage, convenience
gescrēpnes 11.07.02 Utility, advantage, convenience
screpu 04.02.05.06.05.03.10 A curry-comb
scrīc 02.06.08.05 Forest bird, wild-fowl
scriccettan 02.05.10.05 Roaring, raging
scrid 05.12.01.06 Vehicle; 05.12.03.01 Swiftness, velocity
scridwǣn 05.12.01.06 Vehicle
scridwīsa 05.12.01.06 Vehicle; 13.02.10.01.02.02.02 Branch of army
gescrif 11.05 Natural/proper way/manner/mode of action; 14.01.06 A rule, order, precept, tenet, principle
scrīfan 06.01.01.02 Care, attention, observation; 07 Judgement, forming of opinion
(ge)scrīfan 05.04 Fate, lot, fortune, destiny; 05.04.01 Fortune, Fate (personification); 14.03.03.09 A sentence, judgement, ruling; 16.02.04.07.02 Confession

gescrīfan 12.05.06.03 Necessity, constraint
gescrifen 05.04.01 Fortune, Fate (personification)
scrift 14.03.02 A legislator; 14.05.04 A penalty, punishment; 16.02.03.02.09 A confessor; 16.02.04.07.02 Confession; 16.02.04.07.02.02 Absolution, forgiveness, remission; 16.02.04.07.02.03 Penance, an act/instance of penance
scriftæcer 16.02.05.01 Land
scriftbōc 16.02.04.07.02.03 Penance, an act/instance of penance; 16.02.05.10.09 A penitential
scriftscīr 16.02.03.02.09 A confessor
scriftsp(r)ǣc 16.02.04.07.02 Confession
scrimman 03.02.01 Decay, decline, corruption; 05.10.05.02.03 To reduce, make thin(ner)
scrīn 04.05.04.03 A box, case, chest, container; 14.05.08.01 Prison, confinement, durance; 16.02.05.02.04 A shrine; 16.02.05.05.01 Ark of the covenant
scrincan 02.08.02 Disease, infirmity, sickness
(ge)scrincan 03.02.01 Decay, decline, corruption; 03.02.01.05.01 Blight (causing leaves to look burned); 05.10.05.02.03 To reduce, make thin(ner)
scrind 05.12.03.01 Swiftness, velocity
scrippa 01.01.02.01 Ground
scritta 02.01.03.03.06 Sex, kind
scrīþan 05.11 A time, period of time; 05.12.01.02 To wander; 05.12.05.02 To go/travel towards, come, approach; 05.12.05.06.01 To travel smoothly, slide, glide

scriþe 05.12.01.03 Expanse over which something travels; 05.12.05.04 To rotate, turn round, revolve
scrofel 02.08.06 Skin disease, erysipelas
scrūd 04.04.07 Trappings, equipment, garb
scrūdelshūs 16.02.05.03.09 A vestry/sacristy
scrūdfeoh 15.01.02 Gift, transfer of property; 15.02.04 Spending, disbursement
scrūdfultum 15.01.02 Gift, transfer of property
scrūdland 16.02.05.01 Land
scrūdnere 09.05.01 Inspection, examination
scrūdwaru 04.04.07 Trappings, equipment, garb
gescruncen 02.08.04.04.03 Withered; 03.01.18 Dryness (not wetness)
scrūtnian 09.05.01 Inspection, examination
scrūtnung 09.05.01 Inspection, examination
scrybb 02.07.03.04.02 A thicket
scrȳdan 04.04.07 Trappings, equipment, garb; 05.12.01.09.03.01.04 Equipping of ships
gescrȳdan 03.01.13.03 Overshadowing
gescrȳdan (mid) 04.04.07 Trappings, equipment, garb
scrynce 02.08.04.04.03 Withered; 03.01.18 Dryness (not wetness)
scūa 03.01.13.03 Overshadowing; 05.07 Ending of existence, end of world; 11.10.01 Protection, safekeeping; 12.08.06.02.06 Deceit, evil, wickedness
scucca 16.01.03 A spectre, ghost, demon, goblin; 16.01.05.02.01 The devil
scuccen 16.01.05.02.02 Other terms for devils
scuccgyld 16.02.01.06.01.01.01 An image, idol
scūdan 05.12.03.01.02 Haste, hurry
scūfan 05.12.01 To go, progress, travel (usually on land); 05.12.05.09 To go forward, proceed; 11.12.02 Aid, help, succour
(ge)scūfan 05.12.02.04 To cast out, drive away; 05.12.02.06 To push, impel, thrust; 05.12.02.06.01 To push, drive; 06.02.06.03.03 Incitement
scufhrægl 04.04.08.01 Curtain, wall-hanging, etc.
sculan 06.02.04 Necessity, inevitability; 15.04 A debt, due
sculdor 02.04.03.03.02 Shoulder
sculdorhrægl 04.04.07.07 A long outer garment, covering, cloak, etc.
sculdorwærc 02.08.07.07 Disorders of the body
scunian 06.01.08.06 Fear; 07.03.01.03 To loathe, hate, abhor; 11.06.06 Turning
scunung 08.01.03.09.04 Hatred
scūr 01.03.01.03.01 Storm, tempest; 05.06.09.03 A shower of blows (?hammer on weapon); 05.08.02 Violence, force; 13.02.08.04.02 A shot, missile, dart, spear, javelin, etc.; 13.02.08.04.04.01 An arrow, dart, bolt
scūr(a) 01.03.01.06.02 Rain
scūrbeorg 11.10.01.02 Refuge, help, shelter
scūrboga 01.03.01.06.02 Rain
scūrfāh 01.03.01.03.01 Storm, tempest
scūrheard 05.08 Strength
scūrsceadu 11.10.01.02 Refuge, help, shelter

scutel 03.03.02 Measurement by weighing; 04.01.02.02.06.05.03 Plate/platter/bowl/dish; 13.02.08.04.04.01 An arrow, dart, bolt

gescȳ 04.04.07.15 Footwear, covering for the feet

scȳan 06.02.06.03 Persuasion, prompting

scydd 01.01.02.01.01 Tract of land

scyfe 05.12.02.06 To push, impel, thrust; 05.12.03.01.01 Quick movement or movements; 06.02.06.03.02.01 Prompting, instigation (pejorative); 11.01.05.02 Furtherance, promotion; 11.09 Peril, danger

scyfel(e) 04.04.07.11 A headcloth, covering for the head

goscȳgean 04.04.07.15 Footwear, covering for the feet

scyhtan 06.02.06.03.03 Incitement

scylcen 12.08.08.01.02.01.01 An adulterer/-ess, whore, prostitute

scyld 14.01.05 Service, obligation, duty; 16.02.01.13 Evil-doing, transgression, sin

gescyldan 14.03.03.01 Accusation

scyldfrecu 06.02.05.02 Greed, importunate desire, rapacity

scyldful 12.08.09 Guiltiness, guilt; 12.08.09.01 Blameableness, blameworthiness

scyldhǣta 12.01.01.08.01 A servant, attendant

scyldhata 08.01.03.09.05 Enmity

scyldig 10.02.01.01 Loss, forfeiture; 12.08.06.02.05.03 Guilty, sinful, criminal; 14.01.05 Service, obligation, duty; 14.03.03.01 Accusation; 14.03.03.09.01 Unfavourable judgement, condemnation

(ge)scyldigian 16.02.01.13 Evil-doing, transgression, sin

gescyldigian 14.03.03.09 A sentence, judgement, ruling

scyldignes 12.08.09 Guiltiness, guilt

scyldlēas 12.08.05 Innocence

gescyldru 02.04.03.03.02 Shoulder

scyldwīte 14.05.04.01 A fine

scyldwreccende 12.05.04.02 Vengeance, revenge

scyldwyrcende 12.08.06.02.05.03 Guilty, sinful, criminal

scylf 01.01.02.01.02.02.05 Crag, rock, stone; 04.05.02.08 Top of a building; 04.05.03.04 A closet, chamber, room

scylfig 01.01.02.01.02.02.05 Crag, rock, stone

scylfrung 03.01.12.01 Glittering, effulgence

scylian (of) 03.03.07.01 Division, partition, separation

scylian of māle 12.05.07.01 Separation, dismissal, rejection

scyllan 02.05.10.04 To resound

scyltumend 11.12.02 Aid, help, succour

scȳn 11.06.05 Hesitation, scruple

(ge)scyndan 05.12.03.01.02 Haste, hurry; 06.02.06.03.03.01 Incitement, prompting, exhortation

gescyndan 05.12.02.06.01 To push, drive

scyndel 12.08.06.02.06 Deceit, evil, wickedness

scyndendlīce 05.12.03.01.02 Haste, hurry

scyndnes 06.02.06.03 Persuasion, prompting

scyp 04.04.05.06 To sew, stitch

scypian 05.01 Growth, increase, what springs up

scȳr 04.05.03.02.02.08 A lowly dwelling, cottage, hut

scyrdan 08.01.03.07.02.01 Injury, offence

gescyrdan 05.06.02 Cleaving, splitting, cutting
scyrft 05.06.06 A scraping, scarifying
scȳrmǣlum 01.03.01.03.01 Storm, tempest
(ge)scyrtan 05.11.01.02 Shortness/brevity in time
gescyrtan 03.03.04.05 Insufficiency, lack, want; 09.03.04.05 To put briefly
scyrte 04.04.07.08 A short garment, skirt, kirtle
scyrting 09.03.07.07.03.02.01 An epitome, short account
scyte 01.01.02.01.02.02 Hill, mountain; 02.08.04 Hurt, injury, damage; 05.10.05 A space, span; 13.02.08.04.02 A shot, missile, dart, spear, javelin, etc.
scȳte 04.04.05 Woven material, fabric; 04.04.05.04 Linen, linen cloth; 04.05.04.05.01 Bedding (e.g. of straw)
scyteheald 05.10.05.04.04.01 Steep
scyteheald(en) 05.10.05.04.04 A descent, slope, incline
scytel 02.04.06.06.06 Faeces
scyte(l)finger 02.04.03.04.01.01.01 Finger
scyterǣs 05.12.03.01.01 Quick movement or movements; 05.12.05.13 To go down, descend
scytere 01.01.03.01.01.05 Torrent; 13.02.10.01.02 An armed man
scytta 13.02.10.01.02 An armed man
scyttan 05.10.05.04.15.01 A bar, bolt; 15.04 A debt, due
scyttel(s) 17.03.10.01 A bolt, lock, bar
scyttisc 02.03.03.05.03 The Scots; 02.03.03.05.04 The Irish; 09.03.01 Particular languages

scyþþisc 02.03.03.06.07.07 Other (alphabetical order)
se æftera lȳþa 05.11.03.01.03.01 Specific months
se æftera gēola 05.11.03.01.03.01 Specific months
se æftera stefn 05.12.01.09.03.01.03 Part of ship
se ǣrra lȳþa 05.11.03.01.03.01 Specific months
se ǣrra gēola 05.11.03.01.03.01 Specific months
se atola ēþel 16.01.05 Hell, lower world, abode of the dead
se blēdenda fīc 02.08.08.12 Disease of bowels
se drihtenlica ēasterdæg 16.02.04.04.02.01.03 Holy Week
se ēasterlica frēolsdæg 16.02.01.08.04 Jewish seasons/feasts
se ēca 16.01.01.01 Attributes of God
se forma ēasterdæg 16.02.04.04.02.01.03 Holy Week
se fulla mōna 01.02.01.01.04 Moon
se hālga gāst 16.01.01.04.03 The Holy Spirit
se hāra steorra 01.02.01.01.02 Star
se hearda dæg 16.02.01.08.03 The New Testament
se here 13.02.10.01.02.02.01 Types of army
se innra man 06 Spirit, soul, heart
se lǣsta finger 02.04.03.04.01.01.01 Finger
se licgende 02.02.03.02 State of being dead
se lȳtla finger 02.04.03.04.01.01.01 Finger
se mǣsta dæg 16.02.01.08.03 The New Testament

se micla dæg 16.02.01.08.03 The New Testament
se midlesta finger 02.04.03.04.01.01.01 Finger
se morgenlica dæg 05.11.07.04.01.01 (To)morrow
se gemyndiga 05.11.07.03.02.02 The aforesaid
se nimenda dǽl 09.03.02.02.01.02 A verb
sealdnes 10.03 Giving
(ge)sealdnes 10.03.03 Granting
sealegn 02.07.03.05 Particular trees/shrubs (alphabetical order)
sealf 02.08.12.02.05.02 Salves, ointments
sealfbox 04.05.04.03 A box, case, chest, container
sealfcynn 03.01.17.07 Salves, ointments, etc.
sealfian 03.01.17.07.01 An anointing, greasing
sealflǽc(n)ung 02.08.12.02.05 Pharmacy, curing with salves
sealh 02.07.03.05 Particular trees/shrubs (alphabetical order)
sealhangra 04.02.03.04.01.01 Water meadow
sealhrind 02.07.03.05 Particular trees/shrubs (alphabetical order)
sealhyrst 02.07.03.05 Particular trees/shrubs (alphabetical order)
sealm 16.02.01.08.01.01 Books of the Old Testament; 16.02.04.03.03.01 A hymn, song of praise, canticle; 16.02.04.03.03.02 A psalm
sealma 04.05.04.05 A bed, bedstead
sealmas 16.02.01.08.01.01 Books of the Old Testament; 16.02.04.03.03.02 A psalm
sealmbōc 16.02.05.10.05 A bible
sealmcwide 16.02.01.08.01.01 Books of the Old Testament; 16.02.04.03.03.02 A psalm
sealmfæt 18.02.07.02.03.02 Psaltery
sealmgetæl 16.02.04.03.03.02 A psalm
sealmglīg 16.02.04.03.03.02 A psalm; 18.02.07.02.03.02 Psaltery
sealmian 16.02.04.03.03 Singing, church singing; 16.02.04.03.03.02 A psalm; 18.02.07.02.03.01 A harp, lyre
sealmlēoþ 16.02.01.08.01.01 Books of the Old Testament; 16.02.04.03.03.02 A psalm
sealmlof 16.02.01.08.01.01 Books of the Old Testament; 16.02.04.03.03.02 A psalm
sealmlofian 16.02.04.03.03 Singing, church singing; 16.02.04.03.03.02 A psalm
sealmsang 16.02.01.08.01.01 Books of the Old Testament; 16.02.04.03.03.02 A psalm; 16.02.04.05 Canonical hour, service
sealmsangere 16.02.04.03.03.02 A psalm
sealmsangmǽrsung 16.02.04.03.03.02 A psalm
sealmscop 16.02.04.03.03.02 A psalm
sealmtraht 16.02.04.03.03.02 A psalm
sealmwyrhta 16.02.04.03.03.02 A psalm
sealt 01.01.02.02.03.01 Types of metals/minerals; 02.05.07 Faculty of taste; 02.05.07.01 Strong taste, acidity, pungency; 03.01.16.02 Water, liquid; 04.01.02.01.05.01 Salt; 04.01.02.02.04.01 To salt; 07.04.01 (Of persons) worth/value, worthiness
sealt mersc 01.01.02.01.04.01 Marsh, bog, swamp
(ge)sealt 04.01.02.01.01.02 Cooked food

sealtærnsteall 17.04.01 Sources of materials
sealtan 04.01.02.02.04.01 To salt
sealtere 04.01.02.02.10 Saltworks
sealtern 04.01.02.02.10 Saltworks; 17.04.01 Sources of materials
sealtfæt 04.01.02.02.06.03 Food receptacle, basket
sealthālgung 16.02.01.10.02 Consecration
sealtherpaþ 05.12.01.03.01.05 Types of road/path
sealthūs 04.01.02.02.10 Saltworks; 17.04.01 Sources of materials
sealtian 18.02.04 Dancing
sealticge 18.02.04 Dancing
sealting 18.02.04 Dancing
sealtlēap 04.01.02.02.06.03 Food receptacle, basket
sealtmere 01.01.03.01.03.01 Pool
sealtnes 02.01.03.02.01 Barrenness, aridity
sealtrod 05.12.01.03.01.01 A path, track
sealtsǣleþa 02.01.03.02.01 Barrenness, aridity
sealtsēaþ 01.01.03.01.01.07 Spring, fountain, well
sealtstān 01.01.02.02.03.01 Types of metals/minerals
sealtstrǣt 05.12.01.03.01.05 Types of road/path
sealtwīc 15.05.01 Goods, stock, merchandise
sealtwilling 01.01.03.01.01.07 Spring, fountain, well
sealtwylle 01.01.03.01.01.07 Spring, fountain, well
sealtȳþ 01.01.03.01.02.05 Wave
sēam 02.04.05.04.08 Joint; 03.03.06.01 A whole formed by joining; 04.02.05.05.02 Harness of draught animal; 04.02.05.06.05.03 Harness, trappings; 04.04.05.06 To sew, stitch; 14.01.05 Service, obligation, duty; 17.02.04.02.03 Carrying, carriage (of materials); 17.03.12 A receptacle, container
sēamere 02.06.02.01.01 Ass; 04.04.05.06 To sew, stitch
sēamestre 04.04.05.06 To sew, stitch
sēamhors 02.06.02.01.06 Horse
sēampending 15.03.01 Toll
sēamsadol 04.02.05.06.05.03.04 Saddle
sēamsticca 04.04.03 A spinning-house or chamber
sēamtoln 15.03.01 Toll
sēar 02.07.01 To grow; 03.01.18 Dryness (not wetness)
sēarian 02.08.02 Disease, infirmity, sickness; 03.02.01.05.01 Blight (causing leaves to look burned)
searo 11.04.02.01 Art, skill, contrivance, cunning; 11.04.02.01.01 Cunning, craft, craftiness, guile, wile; 12.01.01.12.04 Treachery; 13.02.08.03.01 Body armour, war gear; 17.03 Implements, tools, etc.
searobend 17.03.10 Supports and fastenings
searobunden 03.03.06.01 A whole formed by joining
searocǣg 02.08.02.01.02 Onset, attack of illness
searocēap 17.03 Implements, tools, etc.
searocēne 06.02.07.06.02 Boldness
searocræft 11.04.02.01 Art, skill, contrivance, cunning; 11.04.02.01.01 Cunning, craft, craftiness, guile, wile; 17.02.04 Trade, calling, craft, aptitude; 17.03 Implements, tools, etc.

searocræftig 11.04.02.01 Art, skill, contrivance, cunning; 11.04.02.01.01 Cunning, craft, craftiness, guile, wile

searofāh 03.01.14.11 Medley/variety of colour; 13.02.08.03.01.04 Coat of mail/corselet

searogeþræc 15.01.03 Treasure, riches, wealth

searogim 17.04.03.04 Gems collectively

searogrim 08.01.03.09.10 Wrath, sternness, displeasure; 13.02.08.04 Weapons, arms

searohæbbend 13.02.10.01 A man, warrior

searohwīt 03.01.14.03 White/whiteness

searolic 06.01.08.05.01.01 Wondrous, glorious, marvellous; 11.04.02.01 Art, skill, contrivance, cunning

searolīce 11.04.02.01 Art, skill, contrivance, cunning

searomete 04.01.02.01.07.05 Delicacy/dainty/titbit

searonet 06.01.07.04.02.01 Deception, deceit, snare, wile; 13.02.08.03.01.04 Coat of mail/corselet

searonīþ 12.01.01.12.04 Treachery; 13.02.02 Battle

searopīl 17.03.05 An awl, borer, gimlet, etc.

searorūn 09.04.02.01 A secret, mystery

searosæled 03.03.06.01 A whole formed by joining

searoþanc 06.01.07.04.02 Fraud, deceit, trick, trickery; 11.04.02.01.01 Cunning, craft, craftiness, guile, wile

searoþancol 06.01.05.02.01.01 Sagacity

searoþancum 06.01.05.02.01.01.01 Reason, sense, discretion, prudence; 11.04.02.01.01 Cunning, craft, craftiness, guile, wile

searowrenc 11.04.02.01.01 Cunning, craft, craftiness, guile, wile

searowundor 06.01.08.05.01.01.01 An exercise of power, mighty work, miracle

searwian 06.01.07.04 Deception; 06.01.07.04.04.02 Pretence, feigning, dissimulation

searwigende 06.01.07.04.04.03 Deceit, fraud, treachery

searwum 11.04.02.01 Art, skill, contrivance, cunning

sēaþ 01.01.02.01.03 Hollow/depression in land; 01.01.03.01.03 Lake; 01.01.03.01.03.01 Pool; 02.06.01.08 A lair, den; 04.05.03.05.01 A cess-pool, midden, sewer; 17.02.04.02.04 Leading/conducting of water

sēaþa 02.08.08.03 Heart disease

sēaw 03.01.17.02 Sap, juice

gesēaw 02.07.02.03 A stalk, stem; 03.01.16.06 A soaking, steeping

seax 13.02.08.04.03 A sword; 17.03.03 A cutting tool

seaxan 02.03.03.05.01.10 Saxons

seaxbenn 02.08.04.01 A wound

seaxclāþ 02.08.12.02.06.01 A bandage, binding

seaxe 02.03.03.05.01.10 Saxons

seaxland 12.06.01.01 England

sēcan 09.05.02 A question, inquiry, questioning

sēcan on mūþe 09.05.02 A question, inquiry, questioning

(ge)sēcan 05.10.04.03.01 Visiting/seeking of a place; 05.12.05.02 To go/travel towards, come, approach; 05.12.05.02.03 To arrive; 05.12.05.10 To go behind, follow; 06.02.06.01 An end, goal; 08.01.02.04.01 Visiting; 11.03 Endeavour; 11.03.01.02 To seek, seek for; 11.10.01 Protection, safekeeping; 12.03.04 A request, prayer; 12.04.01.02 A fellow traveller, companion; 13.02.03 To seek with active intent, attack; 14.03.03 Law, action of the courts

(ge)sēcan God 16.02.04.08 Prayer

gesēcan 05.04 Fate, lot, fortune, destiny; 05.12.05.02.01 To come upon, meet with; 10.01.02 Acquisition

secg 01.01.03.01.02 Sea/ocean; 02.07.08 Grasses, reeds, etc.; 06.02.07.06 Courage, boldness, valour; 13.02.08.04.03 A sword

secga 09.06.02.01.01 To make known, cause to know, inform

secgan 09.01 To speak, exercise faculty of speech; 09.03.07.07.03.02 To write, state/say in writing; 09.04 Sense, purport, meaning

secgan andsware 09.05.03 An answer, reply

secgan on 14.03.03.01 Accusation

(ge)secgan 09.06.01 To relate, recount, tell; 09.06.02.01 To tell, make known, declare, relate, announce; 09.06.02.01.04 A confession, declaration

(ge)secgan þancas 08.01.02.04.02 Thanks, gratitude

gesecgan 09.04.03 Exposition, making clear by explanation

secge 09.01 To speak, exercise faculty of speech

secgend 09.01 To speak, exercise faculty of speech

secgihtig 02.07.08 Grasses, reeds, etc.

secglēac 02.07.09.02.02.01 Edible root/bulb

secgplega 13.02.02 Battle

secgrōf 12.04.02 A crowding together, assembly

secgscāra 02.06.08.03 Game-bird; 02.06.08.05 Forest bird, wild-fowl

sēcnes 11.03.01.02 To seek, seek for

gesēdan 06.02.05.03 Satisfaction, repletion

sefa 06.01 The head (as seat of thought); 06.01.05.01 Understanding

sēfte 02.05.04 Sleepiness, drowsiness, sleep; 02.05.05.04 Sensual pleasure; 05.09.02 Mildness, moderate quality; 05.12.04 Absence of movement, stillness; 08.01.02.01.02 Gentleness; 12.08.07.01 Laxity, indulgence

gesēfte 11.12 Easiness

sēftēadig 08.01.01.03.08 Happiness, well-being, prosperity

sēftlic 08.01.01.03.08 Happiness, well-being, prosperity

sēftnes 05.12.04 Absence of movement, stillness

gesegen 06.01.08.04.01 Premonition, prophecy; 09.01 To speak, exercise faculty of speech; 09.01.04 Conversation, discussion; 09.06.01 To relate, recount, tell

segl 04.04.08 A covering, curtain, veil, garment, etc.; 05.12.01.09.03.01.03 Part of ship

seglbōsm 05.12.01.09.03.01.03 Part of ship

seglgerǣde 05.12.01.09.03.01.03 Part of ship

seglgyrd 05.12.01.09.03.01.03 Part of ship; 17.03.02 Item providing support

(ge)segl(i)an 05.12.01.09 To travel on water

geseglian 05.12.01.09.03.01.04 Equipping of ships
segling 05.12.01.09.02 To sail; 05.12.01.09.03 A voyage
seglrād 01.01.03.01.02 Sea/ocean
seglrōd 05.12.01.09.03.01.03 Part of ship
segn 09.04.01 Signal, signalling; 13.02.08.02 A standard, banner, ensign
segnberend 13.02.10.01 A man, warrior
segnbora 13.02.10 The military, soldiers
segncyning 12.01.01.04.01.01 Kings and queens
segne 04.03.05 Fishing
gesegnes 09.01 To speak, exercise faculty of speech
(ge)segnian 16.02.01.10.02 Consecration; 16.02.04.18.01 Sign of the cross
segnung 16.02.01.10.02 Consecration
seht 13 Peace, tranquillity; 14.04 Making of terms, agreement, convention; 14.04.04 An agreement, arrangement of dispute
sehtan 13.01.02.01 An appeasing, pacifying
(ge)seht(i)an 13.01.02 Reconciliation; 14.04.04 An agreement, arrangement of dispute
(ge)sehtlian 13.01.02.01 An appeasing, pacifying; 14.04.04 An agreement, arrangement of dispute
(ge)sehtnes 13 Peace, tranquillity; 13.01.02 Reconciliation
sehþe 02.05.09.04 To see, look upon, behold
(ge)sehþe 06.01.08.05.01 Amazement, astonishment, wonder, admiration
seim 03.01.17.03 Fat, grease
seint 16.01.02.05.02 A saint
sēl 02.08.01 Sound physical condition; 07.02 Goodness; 07.02.04.01 Excellence, virtue, goodness; 08.01.01.03.08.03 A favour, blessing; 11.04.02 Skill, skilfulness; 11.07.03 Use, advantage, profit; 12.08.02.01 Goodness, excellence, virtue; 12.08.02.03.01 Honourable conduct, dignity; 15.02.01 High/steep price
seld/setl 04.05.03.02.02.06 A royal/noble palace; 12.01.01.02 Seat of authority
geselda/gesetla 12.04.01 A fellow, companion, associate, comrade
seldan 05.11.09.04 Seldom, rarely
seldcūþ 03.04.02 A diversity; 06.01.08.05.01.01 Wondrous, glorious, marvellous
seldcyme 08.01.02.04.01 Visiting
selde 04.05.02.12.01 A porch, covered entrance
selden 03.03.04.04.01 Paucity, fewness, scarcity
seldguma 12.01.01.07 A follower
seldhwanne 05.11.09.04 Seldom, rarely
seldlic 06.01.08.05.01.01 Wondrous, glorious, marvellous; 07.02.04.03.01 Peculiar excellence
seldlīce 06.01.08.05.01.01 Wondrous, glorious, marvellous; 07.02.04.03 Nobleness, excellence, nobility, magnificence
seldsīene 06.01.08.05.01.01 Wondrous, glorious, marvellous
sele 04.05.03 A dwelling-place, abode, habitation; 04.05.03.02.01 A building, house, hall, palace, etc.; 04.05.03.03 A lodging-house, inn
gesele 16.01.02.04 Paradise
seledrēam 04.01.01.07 Feasting; 18.02 Amusement, revelry, festivity
seleful 04.01.03.05.04 Drinking vessel

selegesceot 02.04 Body; 04.05.03 A dwelling-place, abode, habitation; 16.01.02.04 Paradise
sele(ge)scot 16.02.05.02.01 A temple
selegyst 12.04.03 A stranger
selen 10.03.03 Granting; 10.03.08 Bountifulness, munificence; 15.01.02 Gift, transfer of property; 15.03.02 A tax
(ge)selenes 10.03 Giving; 11.05 Natural/proper way/manner/mode of action
selerædend 12.02.02.02 A counsellor, advisor
seleræst 04.05.04.05 A bed, bedstead
selescot 04.05.03 A dwelling-place, abode, habitation
selesecg 12.01.01.07 A follower
sēlest 11.03.02 Advancement, progress; 12.01.01.06.02.01 (High) rank, status, degree
seleþegn 12.01.01.08.01 A servant, attendant
seleweard 11.10.02.02 Watchful care, keeping guard; 13.02.10.01.02.02.03 Part of an army
self 03.04.01 Singularity, peculiarity; 03.06.01.02 Equality
selfǣta 04.01.01 Eating
selfǣte 02.07.11 Plants/flowers (alphabetical order)
selfbana 02.02.04.04.02 Suicide
selfcwala 02.02.04.04.02 Suicide
selfcwalu 02.02.04.04.02 Suicide
selfdēma 16.02.03.03.02 A monk
selfdēmende 16.02.03.03.02 A monk
selfdēmere 16.02.03.03.02 A monk
selfgewealdes 06.02.01 Freewill, own will
selfhǣle 02.07.11 Plants/flowers (alphabetical order)
selflic 06.02.01 Freewill, own will
selflīce 07.06.01 Pride, arrogance; 07.06.02 Arrogance, vainglory, vanity
selfmyrþra 02.02.04.04.02 Suicide
selfmyrþrung 02.02.04.04.02 Suicide
selfsceafte 05 Aught, anything, something
selfswēgend 09 Speech, vocal utterance
selfwealdlīce 06.02.02 Will, disposition
selfwill 06.02.01 Freewill, own will
selfwille 06.02.01 Freewill, own will
selfwillende 06.02.01 Freewill, own will
selfwillendlīce 06.02.02 Will, disposition
selfwilles 06.02.01 Freewill, own will
gesell 04.05.03.02.02.08 A lowly dwelling, cottage, hut
sella/sylla 10.03 Giving
sellan wītes clom 14.05 Punishment
(ge)sellan 04.01.02.03 To serve (food/drink); 09.01.02.01 Excessive fluency, loquacity; 10.02 Want, lack; 10.03 Giving; 10.03.03 Granting; 10.03.04 Provision, supply; 10.03.07.01 To allot, assign; 11.06.06.01 Abandonment (of principle); 11.10.02.02.01 Care, interest in; 12.01.01.12.04.01 Betrayal; 12.02 A public office; 12.09.01 Pledging, betrothal; 15.01.02 Gift, transfer of property; 15.02.04 Spending, disbursement; 15.04.01 Lending of money; 15.05 Trade, traffic, commerce
(ge)sellan tō/wiþ 15.05 Trade, traffic, commerce
gesellan 10.03.02 Presenting, offering
gesellan stefn 02.05.10.01 Thing heard
gesellan wedd 14.03.03.07 Security, pledge, bail
sellend 10.03 Giving; 12.01.01.12.04.01 Betrayal

sellendlic 10.03 Giving
sēl(or) 07.01.01.02 To prefer; 11.03.02 Advancement, progress; 02.08.13 Recovery, growing better
gesēm 13.01.02 Reconciliation
sēma 13.01.02.01 An appeasing, pacifying; 14.04.04 An agreement, arrangement of dispute
(ge)sēman 06.01.07.07.03 Certainty; 13.01.02 Reconciliation; 13.01.02.01 An appeasing, pacifying; 14.04.04 An agreement, arrangement of dispute
sēmend 13.01.02.01 An appeasing, pacifying; 14.04.04 An agreement, arrangement of dispute
semnendlic 05.11.08.01.01 Suddenness
semnendlīce 05.03.02.01 Chance, hap, event
semninga 05.11.07.01 Contemporary, coeval
(ge)sencan 02.02.04.03 To kill, slay; 03.01.16.06 A soaking, steeping; 05.12.05.02.04.03 To plunge (something into something)
send 10.03 Giving
sendan 05.03.01 A cause (of anything); 10.03 Giving
(ge)sendan 05.10.04 Place, room; 05.12.02.03 To send; 05.12.02.07 To throw, cast, toss; 09.01.02.01 Excessive fluency, loquacity; 11.01.02 An undertaking; 12.05.07.01 Separation, dismissal, rejection; 13.02.08.04.02 A shot, missile, dart, spear, javelin, etc.
(ge)sendan (æfter, tō) 09.06.02.01.06 A message, announcement by a messenger
sende 01.01.02.01 Ground
sendlic 05.12.02.03 To send
sendnes 16.02.04.07.04.01 The service of the mass
senep 02.07.10.01 Particular herbs/spices (alphabetical order); 04.01.02.01.05.05.02 Mustard
senepsǣd 02.07.10.01 Particular herbs/spices (alphabetical order)
sengan 04.01.02.02.02.01 To singe; 08.01.03.07.02.01 Injury, offence
sengel 03.03.04.01.02.01 A heap, mass, accumulation
senget 04.02.03.01.02 Cleared land
sēo æftere ǣ 16.02.01.08.01.01 Books of the Old Testament
sēo ealde ǣgesetnes 16.02.01.08.01 The Old Testament
sēo ealde hlǣfdige 12.01.01.06.08 A person of rank, elder, great man
sēo ealde lagu 16.02.01.08.01 The Old Testament
sēo grēate bānwyrt 02.07.11.02 Unidentified plants (alphabetical order)
sēo hærfæstlice efenniht 05.11.03.01.02.03 Autumn
sēo hālge gesegen 16.02.01.08 Scripture, the scriptures
sēo hundseofontige gefadung 16.02.01.08.01 The Old Testament
sēo lenctenlic efenniht 05.11.03.01.02.01 Spring
sēo lȳtle culmille 02.07.11 Plants/flowers (alphabetical order)
sēo lȳtle curmealle 02.07.11 Plants/flowers (alphabetical order)
sēo micle ādl 02.08.06 Skin disease, erysipelas
sēo nīwe ǣ 16.02.01.08.03 The New Testament

sēo nīwe gewitnes 16.02.01.08.03 The New Testament
sēo geolwe ādl 02.08.08.06 Disease of liver
sēo rēade netele 02.07.11 Plants/flowers (alphabetical order)
sēoc 02.08.02 Disease, infirmity, sickness; 02.08.04.01 A wound; 05.09 Weakness; 08.01.03 Bad feeling, sadness; 12.08.06.01.02 Lacking moral good
sēoca 02.08.02.01.04 A sick person, invalid
sēocian 02.08.02 Disease, infirmity, sickness
sēocmōd 02.08.11.02 Mental weakness
sēocnes 02.08.02 Disease, infirmity, sickness; 02.08.02.01 An illness, ailment, disorder
sēod 17.03.12 A receptacle, container
seofian 08.01.03.04.01 Complaint, lamentation; 08.01.03.05 Murmuring, complaint
seofon 03.03.03.04.07 Seven
seofonfeald 03.03.03.04.07 Seven
seofonfealdlīce 03.03.03.04.07 Seven
seofongetæl 03.03.03.04.07 Seven
seofonhīwe 05.10.06 Form, shape
seofonhundwintre 02.01.04 Age
seofonlēafe 02.07.11 Plants/flowers (alphabetical order)
seofonnihte 05.11.04.02 Night, night time; 05.11.06.03.01.04 (Of lunar cycle) so many nights old
seofontēoþa 03.03.03.04.17 Seventeen
seofontīene 03.03.03.04.17 Seventeen
seofontīenenihte 05.11.06.03.01.04 (Of lunar cycle) so many nights old
seofontīenewintre 02.01.04 Age
seofontig 03.03.03.04.25 Seventy

seofonwintre 02.01.04 Age
seofoþa 03.03.03.04.07 Seven
seofoþe 03.03.03.04.07 Seven
seofung 08.01.03.04.01 Complaint, lamentation
seohhe 04.06.01.10 To separate objects already connected, unmix
seohhian/sēon 05.12.05.03.04.02 To flow out, well up, erupt
(ge)seohhian/sēon 04.06.01.10 To separate objects already connected, unmix
seohter(e) 04.02.04.02.01.02 To irrigate (plants, land)/channel (water)
seohtra 04.05.03.05.03.01 A ditch, dike
seolc 04.04.04 A thread (of wool, etc.), fibre; 04.04.05.05 Fine woven material from silk, cotton or linen
seolcen 04.04.05.05 Fine woven material from silk, cotton or linen
seolcwyrm 02.06.09.02.11 Worm
seolfor 01.01.02.02.03.01 Types of metals/minerals; 15.01.04 Coinage, money; 17.04.02.08 Silver
seolforfæt 04.01.02.02.06.05 Vessel/utensil/cup
seolforgewiht 03.03.02 Measurement by weighing
seolforhammen 17.02.05.03 A silversmith
seolforhilt(ed) 13.02.08.04.03.01.01 Hilt of sword
seolforsmiþ 17.02.04.03 Metal worker; 17.02.05.03 A silversmith
seolforstycce 15.01.04 Coinage, money
seolfren 01.01.02.02.03.01 Types of metals/minerals; 17.04.02.08 Silver
seolfring 15.01.04 Coinage, money
seolh 02.06.05.01.02 Seal
seolhbæþ 01.01.03.01.02 Sea/ocean

seolhpæþ 01.01.03.01.02 Sea/ocean
seoluc 04.05.03.05 A drain
seomian 01.03.01.06 Cloud;
05.10.05.04.02.03.02 Reclining, rest;
05.12.01.07.01 To hang; 05.12.04
Absence of movement, stillness;
11.09.01.01 Ambush, lying in wait
sēon 02.05.09 Faculty of sight;
02.08.05.02.01 Matter, purulence, pus
sēo(n) 02.04.06.01 Sight organ
(ge)sēon 02.05.09.04 To see, look upon, behold; 05.12.05.02.03 To arrive; 06.01.06.01.01.02 To know, recognize; 08.01.01 A feeling, what is felt; 08.01.02.04.01 Visiting
gesēon 02.01.02.02 To come to life, have life; 02.05.09.05 To watch, observe, survey; 06.01.02 The imaginative faculty; 06.01.06.01.01 Knowledge; 07.01 Appraisal, appraising; 09.04.02.01 A secret, mystery; 10.03.04 Provision, supply; 11.02.02.02 Care, mindfulness, attention; 11.03.01.02 To seek, seek for
sēonian 02.08.02 Disease, infirmity, sickness
seono 02.04.05.06 Sinew/tendon/ligament
seonobenn 02.08.07.07 Disorders of the body
seonubend 14.05.07 Binding, fastening with bonds
seonudolg 02.08.07.07 Disorders of the body
seorþan 12.08.08.01.01 Rape
sēoslig 02.08.02 Disease, infirmity, sickness
sēoþan 08.01.03.01 Despondency;
08.01.03.05.02 Anger;
08.01.03.07.02.01 Injury, offence;
12.08.04 Purity, moral cleanness
(ge)sēoþan 04.01.02.02.05 Cooking;
04.01.02.02.05.02 To boil;
04.06.01.09 To cleanse, remove impurity from (an object)
sēowan 04.04.05.06 To sew, stitch;
13.02.08.03.01.01 Mail, iron-rings
gesēowod 04.04.05.06 To sew, stitch
sēpan 06.01.06.02.03.04.05 Edification, instruction
september 05.11.03.01.03.01 Specific months
sepulcer 02.02.05.01.01 A grave, burial place, sepulchre
seraphīn 16.01.02.05.01 An angel
serc 13.02.08.03.01.04 Coat of mail/corselet
serc(e) 04.04.07.08 A short garment, skirt, kirtle
sēremōnaþ 05.11.03.01.03.01 Specific months
seruian 12.01.01.08 Service
sescle 03.03.03.03 Fractions
sess 04.05.04.01 A bench, seat
sessian 01.01.03.01.02.04 State of sea;
05.12.04 Absence of movement, stillness
sester 03.03.01.02 Dry measures
set 01.02.01.01.03 Sun; 04.02.03.04.02 Pasture/pasturage; 04.02.05.03.01 A pen, fold, enclosure; 04.02.05.03.02 A byre, stall, sty, shed; 13.02.07.04 A camp, encampment
geset 04.05.03 A dwelling-place, abode, habitation
(ge)set(ed)nes 14.01.02 A law, statute
gesetednes 02.08.12.02.03 A medicine, prescription; 05.05 Constitution, founding (e.g. of world)

geset(ed)nes 05.11.07.03.03 Old, not new; 09.06.01.01 A tradition, ordinance handed down; 09.06.01.02 A saying, saw, proverb, maxim

gesetednes 11.05 Natural/proper way/manner/mode of action

seten 04.02.03 Cultivatable land/farmland; 04.02.04.03 A plant; 04.02.04.05 Garden

geseten 04.02.01 Farmstead; 04.05.03.01 Habitation, sojourn; 12.06.03 A site, settlement

gesetenes 05.12.05.13.02.02 To sit down

sethrægl 04.04.08 A covering, curtain, veil, garment, etc.

setl 01.02.01.01.03 Sun; 02.04.03.03.03 Buttock(s), back parts; 04.02.05.03.02 A byre, stall, sty, shed; 04.05.03 A dwelling-place, abode, habitation; 05.02.01.01 The course of human affairs; 05.12.05.13 To go down, descend; 05.12.05.13.02.02 To sit down; 12.06.03.02 Living, dwelling, residence (in); 13.02.03.01.02 To beset, surround; 14.01.04 A legal right; 14.03.01 Judicial body, authority; 16.02.03.02.05 A bishop

(ge)setl/seld 04.05.04.01 A bench, seat

gesetl 12.02.02 An assembly, meeting

gesetla 14.03.02 A legislator

setlan 01.02.01.01.03 Sun; 05.10.04 Place, room; 05.12.04 Absence of movement, stillness

setlgang 01.01.01.04 West; 01.02.01.01.03 Sun; 05.11.04.02.01 Sunset

setlgangende 01.02.01.01.03 Sun

setlrād 05.11.04.02.01 Sunset

setlung 01.02.01.01.03 Sun; 05.11.04.02.01 Sunset; 05.12.05.13 To go down, descend; 05.12.05.13.02.02 To sit down; 12.02.02 An assembly, meeting

(ge)setnes 05.05 Constitution, founding (e.g. of world); 11.05 Natural/proper way/manner/mode of action; 12.03.01.01 Control, direction, regulation; 14.01.02 A law, statute

gesetnes 05.04 Fate, lot, fortune, destiny; 05.10.04 Place, room; 06.02.06 Mind, purpose; 09.03.02.02 Vocabulary; 09.03.04.01 Mode of speech; 09.03.04.02.01 A figure; 09.03.07.07.02 A written work, book, treatise; 09.03.07.07.03.01 A description, writing down; 12.03.03 A command, bidding, order; 15.01.02 Gift, transfer of property

gesett 04.02.03 Cultivatable land/farmland; 04.02.03.02.02 Sown part of field

settan 05.12.05.03.03 To depart, leave, set out; 09.06.02.01.07.01 A title, label

settan of 05.10.04.04.02 Removal, taking away

settan on mūþe 09.06.02 A saying, speech, statement

settan to gafole 15.01.01.01.01 Hiring, letting out of property/land

settan ūt 05.12.01.01 To go on a journey/expedition, travel; 05.12.01.09 To travel on water

(ge)settan 03.03.06 Wholeness; 03.05 Order, arrangement, disposition; 04.02.04.02.04 Planting; 04.05 Building, construction; 05.05.01 An author, source, originator; 05.10.04 Place, room; 05.11.02 A time, particular time, occasion; 05.12.04 Absence of movement, stillness;

05.13.06.01 Firm, stable, steady; 09.03.07.07.03 Composition, arrangement, writing; 10.03.07.01 To allot, assign; 12.06.03 A site, settlement; 13.01.02 Reconciliation; 14.01.06 A rule, order, precept, tenet, principle

(ge)settan (in/on) 12.02 A public office

(ge)settan ongēan/wiþ 03.06 Comparison

gesettan 02.02.05 A burial, burying; 05.03.01.02 To work upon, influence; 05.10.04.03 Presence; 05.12.05.02.04.01 To insert into (a hole); 07 Judgement, forming of opinion; 10 Having, owning, possession; 13.02.03.01.03 To occupy a conquered land; 13.02.04 Defence, guard, protection; 16.02.04.07.05.01.01 Going into a monastery, admission; 17.02.04 Trade, calling, craft, aptitude

gesettan for 05.13.04 Exchange, commutation

gesettan morgendrenc 03.03.06.01.01 Mixing, mingling, preparation

gesettan tō 05.03.01 A cause (of anything)

gesettan ūt 12.02 A public office

settend 16.01.01.02.01 Creator

gesettendlic 16.02.01.09.01 Canon law

settung 11.09.01.01 Ambush, lying in wait; 13.02.07.01 A stratagem

setþorn 02.07.03.05 Particular trees/shrubs (alphabetical order)

(ge)sēþan 09.07.04 Assertion, affirmation; 11.03.01.01.01 Proof, demonstration; 14.03.03.03 Witness, testimony, attestation

gesēþedlic 11.03.01.01.01 Proof, demonstration

(ge)sēþend 14.03.03.03 Witness, testimony, attestation

sēþende 09.03.02.02.01.03 An adverb

gesēþnes 09.07.04 Assertion, affirmation

(ge)sēþung 09.07.04 Assertion, affirmation

gesewen 02.05.09.09 Visible

gesewenlic 02.05.09.09 Visible

gesewenlīce 02.05.09.09 Visible

sibæþeling 12.01.01.06.08 A person of rank, elder, great man

sibb 02.03.02.03.06 Kinship, relationship; 02.03.02.05 Spiritual relationships; 05.12.04 Absence of movement, stillness; 08.01.01.03.01 Freedom from trouble, comfort, security; 08.01.02.03 Friendliness, affection; 08.01.02.03.02 Friendly, amiable; 13 Peace, tranquillity; 13.01.01 Peace (not war); 14 Law, custom, covenant; 16.02.04.07.01 Baptism, baptizing (and anointing)

sibb niman 13.01.01.01 Cessation of hostilities

(ge)sibb 02.03.02.03.06 Kinship, relationship

gesibb 02.03.02.03.06.01 Kinsman, relative; 03.06.01 Similitude, likeness

sibbecos 16.02.04.03.02 Parts of service

(ge)sibbian 13.01.02 Reconciliation

gesibbian 12.04 Fellowship, union, association

sibcwide 08.01.02.03 Friendliness, affection

sibfæc 02.03.02.03.06.02 Close relationship

sibgebyrd 02.03.02.03.06 Kinship, relationship

sibgedryht 02.03.03.01 Body of retainers, household; 16.01.02.05.02 A saint

sib(ge)leger 12.08.08.01.02.01.03 Unnatural sexual behaviour
sibgemāgas 02.03.02.03.06.02 Close relationship
sibgeornes 08.01.02.02.04 Love, caritas
sibgesihþ 16.01.02.01 Heavenly dwelling place
siblāc 14.03.03.07 Security, pledge, bail
siblic 03.06.01 Similitude, likeness; 13 Peace, tranquillity
siblic coss 16.02.04.03.02 Parts of service
gesiblīce 13 Peace, tranquillity
(ge)sibling 02.03.02.03.06.01 Kinsman, relative
siblufu 08.01.02.03 Friendliness, affection; 16.02.01.12.04 A cardinal virtue
gesibnes 02.03.02.03.06 Kinship, relationship
sibrēden 02.03.02.03.06 Kinship, relationship
(ge)sibsum 13 Peace, tranquillity
gesibsum 13.01.01 Peace (not war); 13.01.01.01 Cessation of hostilities
gesibsumgend 13.01.02 Reconciliation
gesibsumian 13.01.02 Reconciliation
(ge)sibsumlīce 13 Peace, tranquillity
sibsumnes 08.01.02.02 Love, affection, care
(ge)sibsumnes 13 Peace, tranquillity
gesibsumung 13.01.02 Reconciliation
sīc 01.01.03.01.01.03 Stream
sīcan 02.04.06.07.06 A sigh; 08.01.03.04.04.01 Sighing, groaning
sīcan æfter 08.01.03.04 Grief
sice 02.04.06.07.06 A sigh; 08.01.03.04.04.01 Sighing, groaning
sīc(e) 01.01.03.01.01.03 Stream
sīcel 01.01.03.01.01.03 Stream
sicera 04.01.03.05.01 Intoxicating liquor

sicerian 03.01.16.03 A drop of liquid; 05.12.05.03.04.02 To flow out, well up, erupt
sicettan 02.05.10.15.03 Groaning; 08.01.03.04 Grief
sicettung 02.04.06.07.06 A sigh; 08.01.03.04.04 Sighing
sīcian 08.01.03.04.04 Sighing
sicilia (land) 12.06.01.03 The Continent
sicilie 02.03.03.06.04 Italians
sicilisc 02.03.03.06.04 Italians
sīcing 08.01.03.04.04 Sighing
sīcle 02.08.02 Disease, infirmity, sickness
(ge)sīclian 02.08.02 Disease, infirmity, sickness
sicol 04.02.04.06.12 A scythe, sickle
sicomorus 02.07.03.05 Particular trees/shrubs (alphabetical order)
sicor 11.10 Safety, safeness; 12.07.02.02 Truth, faithfulness, good faith, sincerity
sicorlīce 06.01.07.07.03 Certainty
sicornes 06.01.07.07.03 Certainty
sīd 03.03.04.01.01 Greatness, bigness, size; 04.04.07.01 Mode of dressing, fashion; 05.10.01 Amplitude, spaciousness, vastness; 05.10.05.02 Extension, stretching; 05.10.05.02.01 Diffusion, effusion, spreading; 06.01.05.02 Intelligence
sīdādl 02.08.08.02 Lung disease
sīde 01.01.02.01.02.02 Hill, mountain; 02.03.02.03 Ancestry, descent; 02.04.03.03.04 Side; 04.04.04 A thread (of wool, etc.), fibre; 04.04.05.05 Fine woven material from silk, cotton or linen; 05.10.05 A space, span; 05.10.05.04.09 Side, quarter, direction
sīdece 02.08.07.07 Disorders of the body

sideful 12.08.02.01 Goodness, excellence, virtue; 12.08.03.03 Moral restraint, modesty, sobriety
sidefullīce 12.08.02.01 Goodness, excellence, virtue
sidefulnes 12.08.02.01 Goodness, excellence, virtue
sidelic 12.08.03.03 Moral restraint, modesty, sobriety
sidelīce 03.06.03.04 What is fitting/seemly/appropriate/decent
sīden 04.04.05.05 Fine woven material from silk, cotton or linen
sīdewāre 02.07.11 Plants/flowers (alphabetical order)
sīdfæþme(d) 05.12.01.09.03.01.02 Of/concerning a ship, naval
sīdfeaxe 02.04.04.03.03 Hair of head
sīdfolc 02.03.03.03 A nation, people; 12.04.02 A crowding together, assembly
sīdhealf 05.10.01 Amplitude, spaciousness, vastness
(ge)sidian 03.05.01 Arranging, ordering, disposition
sīdian 05.10.05.02 Extension, stretching
sīdland 12.06 A province, country, territory
sīdling 01.01.02.01.01 Tract of land
sīdlingweg 05.12.01.03.01.05 Types of road/path
sīdrand 13.02.08.03.01.06 A shield
sidu 11.05 Natural/proper way/manner/mode of action; 12.08.02.01 Goodness, excellence, virtue; 16.02.04.03.01 A rite, ceremony
sidung 14.01.06 A rule, order, precept, tenet, principle
sīdung 03.03.04.03 Growth, increase

sīdwærc 02.08.08.02 Lung disease
sīdweg 05.12.01.03.01 A means of access
sīdwegas 05.10.05 A space, span
sīdwyrm 02.06.09.02.11 Worm
(ge)sīeman 17.02.04.02.03 Carrying, carriage (of materials)
sīen 02.04.03.01.03.02 Eye; 02.05.09 Faculty of sight
gesīene 02.05.09.09 Visible; 06.01.05.01.01 Clear to the understanding, plain; 09.05.05.01 Showing, manifestation, display
gesīenelic 02.05.09.09 Visible
gesīenelīce 02.05.09.09 Visible
sīere 02.07.01 To grow; 03.01.18 Dryness (not wetness)
sierwan 06.02.06.02 A proposal, proposition, suggestion; 11.09.01.01 Ambush, lying in wait
sierwan ongēan/ymbe 12.01.01.12.04.02 Conspiracy
(ge)sierwan 11.04.02.01.01 Cunning, craft, craftiness, guile, wile; 12.01.01.12.04.02 Conspiracy; 13.02.08.03.01 Body armour, war gear
gesierwan 13.02.08 Military equipment
gesierwed 13.02.08.03.01 Body armour, war gear
sierwet 06.01.07.04.02.01 Deception, deceit, snare, wile
sierwiende 11.04.02.01.01 Cunning, craft, craftiness, guile, wile
gesierwod 13.02.08 Military equipment
sierwung 11.04.02.01.01 Cunning, craft, craftiness, guile, wile
siex 03.03.03.04.06 Six
siexfeald 03.03.03.04.06 Six
siexhund 03.03.03.04.31 Six hundred
siexhundred 03.03.03.04.31 Six hundred
siexta 03.03.03.04.06 Six

siexte 03.03.03.04.06 Six
siextig 03.03.03.04.24 Sixty
sife 17.03.11 Other implements, etc.
sifeþ 03.03.01.02 Dry measures
sifeþa 04.01.02.01.03.06 Bran; 04.02.04.04 Harvest, crop; 04.02.04.04.05.02 Chaff
(ge)siftan 04.06.01.10 To separate objects already connected, unmix
sig 13.02.05.01 Victory
sīgan 05.12.05.02 To go/travel towards, come, approach
sīgan ūt 05.12.05.03.04 To come/go out from; 05.12.05.03.04.02 To flow out, well up, erupt
(ge)sīgan 05.11.10.02 End, completion; 05.12.05.02.04.03 To plunge (something into something); 05.12.05.13 To go down, descend; 11.06.03.01 Ill fortune, bad success
(ge)sīgan ūt 03.01.16.03 A drop of liquid
gesīgan 05.12.01.09 To travel on water
sigbēag 12.01.01.03 Symbols of power
sige 05.12.05.13 To go down, descend; 08.01.01.03.08.02 Good fortune, success; 13.02.05.01 Victory
sige niman 13.02.05.01 Victory
sigebēacen 13.02.08.02 A standard, banner, ensign
sigebēacn 13.02.05.01 Victory; 16.02.05.11 The cross (as Christian image)
sigebēah 16.01.02.03 Reward of heaven
sigebēam 16.02.05.11 The cross (as Christian image)
sigebearn 16.01.01.04.02 The Son, Christ
sigebeorht 03.01.12 Brightness, light; 13.02.05.01 Victory
sigebeorn 13.02.10.02 A victor/conqueror
sigebrōþor 13.02.10.02 A victor/conqueror
sigebȳme 13.02.08.01 Battle-horn; 18.02.07.02.02.02 A trumpet
sigecempa 13.02.10.02 A victor/conqueror
sigecwēn 12.01.01.04.01.01 Kings and queens
sigedēma 16.01.01.02.06 God as judge
sigedryhten 13.02.10.02 A victor/conqueror; 16.01.01 God, the Lord
sigeēadig 13.02.05.01 Victory
sigefæst 13.02.05.01 Victory
(ge)sigefæstan 13.02.05.01 Victory
gesigefæstan 07.08.04 An ornament, honour, glory
gesigefæsted 13.02.05.01 Victory
sigefæstnes 13.02.05.01 Victory
sigefolc 02.03.03.03 A nation, people; 13.02.10.02 A victor/conqueror
sigegealdor 16.01.04.01 Sorcery using incantation
sigegefeoht 13.02.05.01 Victory
sigegyrd 16.01.04.04 A magical apparatus
sigehrēmig 08.01.01.03.06 Exultation, joy; 13.02.05.01 Victory
sigehrēþ 07.08.10 Fame of courage, valour
sigehrēþig 13.02.05.01 Victory; 16.01.01.01.01.01 Mightiness
sigehwīl 13.02.05.01 Victory
sigel 01.02.01.01.03 Sun; 09.03.07.01.01 A runic letter
sigelaþung 16.02.03 The church (as temporal/spiritual body)
sigelbeorht 01.03.01.01 Hot, fine weather; 03.01.12 Brightness, light
sigelēan 13.02.05.01 Victory
sigelēas 13.02.05.02 Defeat

sigelēoþ 09.03.05.01.01 Poetry;
  13.02.07.03 A war song;
  18.02.07.01.01 A song, a poem to be sung or recited
sigelhearwa 02.03.03.06.07.01 African
sigelhearwen 02.03.03.06.07.01 African
sigelhweorfa 02.07.11 Plants/flowers (alphabetical order)
sigelic 13.02.05.01 Victory
sigeltorht 01.03.01.01 Hot, fine weather; 03.01.12 Brightness, light
sigelwaras 02.03.03.06.07.01 African
sigemēce 13.02.08.04.03 A sword
sīgend 01.01.03.01.02.05 Wave
sīgende 05.12.05.02.04 To go in, enter
siger/sīr 02.07.11 Plants/flowers (alphabetical order)
sīgere 04.01.01.04 Gluttony, overeating, greediness
sigerēaf 04.04.07.01 Mode of dressing, fashion
sigerian 04.01.01.04 Gluttony, overeating, greediness
sigerīce 13.02.05.01 Victory; 16.01.01.01.01.01 Mightiness
sigerōf 13.02.05.01 Victory; 16.01.01.01.01.01 Mightiness
sigesceorp 04.04.07.01 Mode of dressing, fashion
sigesīþ 13.02.05.01 Victory
sigespēd 11.03.02.01 Efficacy, success
sigetācen 09.04.01 Signal, signalling
sigetīber 16.02.04.12 Sacrifice, a sacrifice
sigetorht 03.01.12 Brightness, light; 16.01.01.01.01.01 Mightiness
sigetūdor 02.03 Humankind
sigeþēod 02.03.03.03 A nation, people; 13.02.10.02 A victor/conqueror
sigeþrēat 13.02.10.02 A victor/conqueror

sigeþūf 13.02.08.02 A standard, banner, ensign
sigewǣpen 13.02.08.04 Weapons, arms
sigewang 13.02.02 Battle
sigewīf 16.01.04 Sorcery, magic, witchcraft
gesigfæstnian 13.02.05.01 Victory
sigil 04.04.10 Ornaments, trappings, accoutrements; 04.04.10.02 A button, brooch
gesiglan 05.12.01.09 To travel on water; 05.12.01.09.02 To sail
sigle 04.01.02.01.03.04 Rye; 04.02.04.03.02.01.04 Rye; 04.04.10.01 A ring (for finger, arm, neck)
sigor 13.02.05.01 Victory
sigorbēacn 16.02.05.11 The cross (as Christian image)
sigorbeorht 03.01.12 Brightness, light; 16.01.01.01.01.01 Mightiness
sigorcynn 16.01.02.05.01 An angel
sigorēadig 13.02.05.01 Victory
sigorfæst 06.02.07.01 Strength, fortitude; 13.02.05.01 Victory; 16.01.01.01.01.01 Mightiness; 16.01.02.05.01 An angel
sigorfæstnes 13.02.05.01 Victory
sigorian 13.02.05.01 Victory
sigorlēan 16.01.02.03 Reward of heaven
sigorlic 13.02.05.01 Victory
sigorspēd 13.02.05 Luck in war
sigortācen 09.04.01 Signal, signalling
sigortīfer 16.02.04.12 Sacrifice, a sacrifice
sigorweorc 13.02.05.01 Victory
sigorwuldor 16.01.01.01.01.02 Glory
sigriend 13.02.10.02 A victor/conqueror
sigsonte 02.07.11.02 Unidentified plants (alphabetical order)
siht 04.05.03.05.03 Drainage

gesiht 02.05.09 Faculty of sight; 02.05.09.04 To see, look upon, behold; 02.05.09.06 Thing seen, sight, vision; 06.01.02.01.01 A vision, apparition
gesiht/gesihþ 02.04.06.01 Sight organ
(ge)sihþ 02.05.09.04 To see, look upon, behold; 02.05.09.06 Thing seen, sight, vision; 06.01.02.01.01 A vision, apparition
gesihþ 02.05.09 Faculty of sight
sihþe 06.01.08.05.01 Amazement, astonishment, wonder, admiration
gesihþnes 06.01.02.01.01 A vision, apparition
silet 02.07.03.05 Particular trees/shrubs (alphabetical order)
silte 17.04.01 Sources of materials
sīma 17.03.10 Supports and fastenings
simbelfarende 05.12.01.02 To wander
simfeld/sunfeld 16.01.02.04 Paradise
sinbyrnende 03.01.09.02.01 Fire, burning
sinc 15.01.03 Treasure, riches, wealth
sincaldu 01.03.01.04 Wintry weather, cold
sincan 01.01.03.06 Flood
(ge)sincan 05.12.05.02.04.03 To plunge (something into something)
sincbrytta 12.01.01.04 A leader, ruler
sinceald 03.01.11 Coldness, coolness
sincende 04.01.02.01.01 Edibility
sinces brytta 12.01.01.04 A leader, ruler
sinces hyrde 12.01.01.04.01 A royal leader
sincfæt 15.01.03 Treasure, riches, wealth; 17.02.05.01 Ornamental object
sincfāg 17.02.05.01 Ornamental object
sincgestrēon 15.01.03 Treasure, riches, wealth
sincgewæge 15.01.03 Treasure, riches, wealth

sincgiefa 12.01.01.04 A leader, ruler
sincgifu 10.03 Giving
sincgim 17.04.03.04 Gems collectively
sinchroden 17.02.05.01 Ornamental object
sincmāþþum 15.01.03 Treasure, riches, wealth
sincstān 17.04.03.04 Gems collectively
sincþego 10.01.01 Acceptance, receiving
sincweorþung 10.03 Giving
sinder 17.04.02.06 Dross, slag
sinderhǣwe 03.01.14.10 Grey-coated one
sinderōm 03.02.01.04 Rust
sindolh 02.08.04.01 A wound
sindonisc 04.04.05.04 Linen, linen cloth
sindrēam 08.01.01.03 Good feeling, joy, happiness
sineht 02.04.05.06 Sinew/tendon/ligament
sinewealt 04.05.02.08 Top of a building; 05.10.06.02 Rotundity, roundness; 05.10.06.02.01 A hemisphere
sinewealtian 05.12.04.01.01 Unstable
sinewealtnes 05.10.06.02 Rotundity, roundness
sinfrēa 12.09 Marriage, state of marriage
sinfulle 02.07.09.02.02.01 Edible root/bulb
singal 02.08.02.01 An illness, ailment, disorder; 05.11.03.01.05 A day; 05.11.11 Continuity; 05.11.11.01 A not ceasing, persistence, recurrence; 06.02.07.03 Perseverance
singala 05.11.11 Continuity
singales 05.11.11 Continuity
singalflōwende 01.01.03.03 Flow/flowing
gesingalian 05.11.11 Continuity
singallic 05.11.11 Continuity
singallīce 05.11.11 Continuity
gesingallician 05.11.11 Continuity

singalnes 06.02.07.03 Perseverance
singalrene 01.01.03.03 Flow/flowing
singan 09.03.05 Art of poetry;
  09.03.05.01.02 Art of verse composition; 16.01.04.01 Sorcery using incantation
(ge)singan 02.05.10.13 Sound of bell/musical instrument;
  02.05.10.15.07 Voice, note (of a bird); 09.03.05 Art of poetry; 16.02.04.03.03 Singing, church singing; 18.02.07.01 Singing, song
(ge)singan be/mid 18.02.07.02 A musical instrument
gesinge 12.09 Marriage, state of marriage
singendlic 18.02.07.01 Singing, song
singrēne 02.07.03 A tree;
  02.07.09.02.02.01 Edible root/bulb; 04.01.02.02.05 Cooking
singrim 08.01.03.09.01 Fierceness
sinhere 13.02.10.01.02.02.01 Types of army
(ge)sinhīwan 12.09 Marriage, state of marriage
gesinhīwen 12.09 Marriage, state of marriage
sinhīwscipe 12.09 Marriage, state of marriage
sinhwyrfel 05.10.06.02 Rotundity, roundness
sinhwyrfende 05.10.06.02 Rotundity, roundness
gesinīg 12.09 Marriage, state of marriage
gesinīg(i)an 12.09.02 Marriage ceremony
(ge)sinlīce 05.11.11 Continuity
gesinlīce 11.02.02.01 Diligence, studious care
sinnan 06.01.01.02 Care, attention, observation

sinnihte 05.11.04.02.01 Sunset; 16.01.05 Hell, lower world, abode of the dead
sinnīþ 08.01.03.06 Adversity, affliction
sinoþ 12.02.02 An assembly, meeting; 12.04.02 A crowding together, assembly; 16.02.03.01 Ecclesiastical authority
sinoþ/þing gehēgan 12.02.02 An assembly, meeting
sinoþbōc 16.02.05.10.08 A book of canons/decrees
sinoþdōm 16.02.01.09.01 Canon law
sinoþstōw 16.02.03.01 Ecclesiastical authority
sinrǣden 12.09 Marriage, state of marriage
(ge)sinscipe 12.09 Marriage, state of marriage
gesinsciplic 12.09 Marriage, state of marriage
gesinscippend 12.09 Marriage, state of marriage
sinsnǣdum 03.03.07 A part, division, portion
sinsorg 08.01.03.04 Grief
sinsorgna gedræg 08.01.03 Bad feeling, sadness
sintre(n)dende 05.10.06.02 Rotundity, roundness
sintryndel 05.10.06.02 Rotundity, roundness
sinþyrstende 02.05.05 Desire, appetite
sinulīra 02.04.05.05 Muscle
sinwrǣnnes 12.08.08.01 Eager, unseemly desire
sioloþ 01.01.03.01.02 Sea/ocean
sion 02.07.11.02 Unidentified plants (alphabetical order)
sīon 16.01.02.04 Paradise; 16.02.05.02.03 A church, place of worship

sīonbeorg 16.02.05.02.03 A church, place of worship

sīonbeorge 16.01.02.04 Paradise

sīpian 02.08.02 Disease, infirmity, sickness

sisemūs 02.06.03.01.13 Rodents

sittan 05.13.06 Constancy, unchangeableness; 12.05.06.02 Oppression

sittan cynestōl 12.01.01.02 Seat of authority

sittan on 05.12.01.05 To ride (on horse, etc.)

(ge)sittan 05.10.04 Place, room; 05.12.05.13.02.02 To sit down; 12.01.01.02 Seat of authority; 13.02.07.04 A camp, encampment

gesittan 04.05.03.01 Habitation, sojourn; 04.05.03.02.02.09 A tent, pavilion; 10 Having, owning, possession; 12.02 A public office; 12.06.03.02 Living, dwelling, residence (in); 13.02.03.01.03 To occupy a conquered land; 15.01.01.01 Holding of land; 18.01 Rest, quiet, freedom from toil

gesittan ūp 05.12.05.12.01 To reach up

gesittan wiþ 05.10.05.04.02.03.02 Reclining, rest

(ge)sittende 05.12.05.13.02.02 To sit down

sitting 05.12.05.13.02.02 To sit down

sīþ 02.02 Death; 05.04 Fate, lot, fortune, destiny; 05.11.02 A time, particular time, occasion; 05.11.07.04.02 (Of time) later/latter; 05.12.01 To go, progress, travel (usually on land); 05.12.01.01 To go on a journey/expedition, travel; 05.12.01.03 Expanse over which something travels; 05.12.01.03.01.01 A path, track; 05.12.05.02.03 To arrive; 11.05.02 Mode, manner, way, method, fashion, course

sīþ and ǣr 05.11.09.01 Always

sīþ āsettan 05.12.01.01 To go on a journey/expedition, travel

sīþ oþþe ǣr/ǣfre 05.11.02 A time, particular time, occasion

sīþ þām 05.11.07.04.02 (Of time) later/latter

gesīþ 02.03.03.01 Body of retainers, household; 12.01.01.06.08 A person of rank, elder, great man; 12.01.01.07 A follower; 12.01.01.08.01 A servant, attendant; 12.04.01 A fellow, companion, associate, comrade; 12.04.01.01 A company of people, fellowship, society; 13.02.10 The military, soldiers

gesīþa 02.03.03.01 Body of retainers, household; 12.01.01.08.01 A servant, attendant; 12.04.01 A fellow, companion, associate, comrade; 13.02.10 The military, soldiers

sīþberend 04.02.04.04.02.01 Reaper, mower

sīþboc 05.12.01.01 To go on a journey/expedition, travel

sīþboda 05.12.05.03.03 To depart, leave, set out; 12.03 Direction, guidance

sīþboren 02.01.03.03.03 Birth

gesīþcund 12.01.01.06.06 Gentle birth, nobility; 12.01.01.06.08 A person of rank, elder, great man

gesīþcundlic 08.01.02.03.02 Friendly, amiable; 12.08.08 Carnal nature, sensual appetites

sīþdagas 05.11.07.04 Future, time to come

sīþe 04.02.04.06.12 A scythe, sickle

sīþemest 05.11.08.01.03 Late
sīþ(e)mest 05.11.10.02 End, completion
sīþest 05.11.08.01.03 Late; 05.11.10.02 End, completion
sīþet 05.11.07.04.02 (Of time) later/latter
sīþfæt 05.02.01.01 The course of human affairs; 05.12.01 To go, progress, travel (usually on land); 05.12.01.01 To go on a journey/expedition, travel; 05.12.01.03 Expanse over which something travels; 05.12.01.03.01 A means of access
sīþfrom 06.02.07.06.02 Boldness
sīþgearu 05.12.01 To go, progress, travel (usually on land); 11.02.01.01 Active, nimble
sīþgēomor 02.05.03.02 Weariness
(ge)sīþian 05.12.01.01 To go on a journey/expedition, travel
sīþlic 05.11.08.01.03 Late
gesīþlic 08.01.02.03.02 Friendly, amiable
sīþlīce 05.11.07.03.01 Time within remembrance; 05.11.07.04.02 (Of time) later/latter
gesīþmǣgen 12.04.01.01 A company of people, fellowship, society
sīþmann 12.04.01 A fellow, companion, associate, comrade
gesīþmann 02.03.03.01 Body of retainers, household; 12.01.01.06.08 A person of rank, elder, great man; 12.01.01.08.01 A servant, attendant
sīþor 05.11.07.04.02 (Of time) later/latter
sīþra 05.11.08.01.03 Late
gesīþrǣden 13.02.10.01.02.01 An armed force/band
(ge)sīþscipe 12.04.01.01 A company of people, fellowship, society
gesīþscipe 12.04 Fellowship, union, association

sīþstapel 05.12.01.04.01 Manner of going, gait
sibþa 05.11.07.04.02 (Of time) later/latter
sibþan 05.11.07.04.02 (Of time) later/latter
sīþweg 05.12.01.03.01 A means of access
sīþwerod 13.02.10.01.02.02.03 Part of an army
(ge)sīþwīf 12.01.01.06.08 A person of rank, elder, great man
gesīwed 04.04.05.06 To sew, stitch
siwenīge 02.08.07.02 Disorders of the eye
(ge)sīwian 04.04.05.06 To sew, stitch
sixecge(bǣre) 05.10.06.04 A corner, bend, angle
sixecgede 05.10.06.04 A corner, bend, angle
sixfēte 09.03.05.01.02 Art of verse composition
sixgylde 14.03.03.09.02 Atonement
sixhynde 12.01.01.06.08 A person of rank, elder, great man
sixhynde man 12.01.01.06.08 A person of rank, elder, great man
sixhyrnede 05.10.06.04 A corner, bend, angle
sixnihte 05.11.06.03.01.04 (Of lunar cycle) so many nights old
sixteogoþa 03.03.03.04.24 Sixty
sixtēoþa 03.03.03.04.16 Sixteen
sixtigǣre 05.12.01.09.03.01.01 Kind of ship
sixtigfeald 03.03.03.04.24 Sixty
sixtigwintre 02.01.04 Age
sixtȳne 03.03.03.04.16 Sixteen
sixtȳnenihte 05.11.06.03.01.04 (Of lunar cycle) so many nights old
sixtȳnewintre 02.01.04 Age
slacful/slæcful 11.06 Disinclination to act, listlessness

geslæccan 10.04.02.02 To seize, take, grasp, lay hold on
slæcnes 05.12.03.02 Slowness; 06.01.05.03.01 Mental inertness
slæd 01.01.02.01.03.03 Valley; 01.01.02.01.04.01 Marsh, bog, swamp
slæf 01.01.02.01.04.01 Marsh, bog, swamp
slæget 04.02.03.04.02.01.02 Sheep pasture
slægu 11.06 Disinclination to act, listlessness
slæhtan 02.02.04.03 To kill, slay
slæp 01.01.02.01.04.01 Marsh, bog, swamp
slæp 02.02.03.02 State of being dead; 02.05.04 Sleepiness, drowsiness, sleep
slæpan 02.01.03.03 Sex, generation; 02.02.03.02 State of being dead; 02.08.04.03 Paralysis
(ge)slæpan 02.05.04 Sleepiness, drowsiness, sleep
slæpbǣre 02.05.04.01 To make heavy with weariness/sleep
slæpdrenc 02.05.04.01 To make heavy with weariness/sleep; 02.08.12.02.05 Pharmacy, curing with salves
slæpe 03.01.06 Smoothness
slæpe tōbregdan 02.05.02 Consciousness
slæpere 02.05.04 Sleepiness, drowsiness, sleep
slæpern 04.05.03.04 A closet, chamber, room
slæping 02.05.04 Sleepiness, drowsiness, sleep
slæplēas 02.05.02 Consciousness
slæplēast 02.05.02 Consciousness
slæpnes 02.05.04 Sleepiness, drowsiness, sleep
slæpor 02.05.04 Sleepiness, drowsiness, sleep
slæpwērig 02.05.04 Sleepiness, drowsiness, sleep
slǣtan 04.03 Hunting, the chase
slǣting 14.01.04.02 Rights involving property
slǣwþ 11.06 Disinclination to act, listlessness
slaga 02.02.04.04 Manslaughter, homicide; 14.05.05.01 Capital punishment
slāh 02.07.09.02 Particular fruits (alphabetical order)
slāhþorn 02.07.03.05 Particular trees/shrubs (alphabetical order)
slāhþornragu 02.07.06 Lichen
slāhþornrind 02.07.03.05 Particular trees/shrubs (alphabetical order)
slāpan 11.06 Disinclination to act, listlessness
slāpende 02.08.04.03 Paralysis
slāpian 02.05.04 Sleepiness, drowsiness, sleep
slāpol 11.06 Disinclination to act, listlessness
slāpolnes 11.06 Disinclination to act, listlessness
slāpornes 11.06 Disinclination to act, listlessness
slarege 02.07.11 Plants/flowers (alphabetical order)
slāw 11.06 Disinclination to act, listlessness
slāwa 11.06 Disinclination to act, listlessness
slāwian 05.12.03.02 Slowness; 11.06 Disinclination to act, listlessness
slāwlīce 05.12.03.02 Slowness
slāwyrm 02.06.07.03 Lizard, newt

slēa 01.01.02.01.02.02 Hill, mountain; 04.04.03 A spinning-house or chamber

sleac 02.08.02 Disease, infirmity, sickness; 05.12.03.02 Slowness; 11.06 Disinclination to act, listlessness; 11.06.01.01 Negligence, carelessness, heedlessness; 11.12 Easiness; 12.08.07.01 Laxity, indulgence

sleacian 05.12.03.02 Slowness; 11.11.02 A hindrance

sleaclic 11.06 Disinclination to act, listlessness

sleaclīce 05.12.03.02 Slowness

sleacmōdnes 11.06 Disinclination to act, listlessness

sleacnes 11.06 Disinclination to act, listlessness; 11.06.01.01 Negligence, carelessness, heedlessness

sleacornes 11.06.01.01 Negligence, carelessness, heedlessness

slēan 02.05.10.12 An audible signal; 05.12.02.06.01 To push, drive; 05.12.03.01.01 Quick movement or movements; 17.05.04 To kindle, set alight (fire, lamp); 18.02.07.02.03.01 A harp, lyre

slēan on racentan 14.05.07 Binding, fastening with bonds

slēan wedd 14.04 Making of terms, agreement, convention

(ge)slēan 02.02.04.03 To kill, slay; 02.08.03.02 Itch, irritation; 04.05.01.02.07 A fence, hedge; 05.06.09 Act of striking; 08.01 Heart, spirit, mood, disposition; 08.01.03.07.02.01 Injury, offence; 17.02.04.03 Metal worker

(ge)slēan of 05.06.09 Act of striking

geslēan 05.06.03 A dashing together, breaking, shattering; 13.02.05.01.02 To gain by fighting

gesleccan 05.09 Weakness

slecg 17.03.08 A hammer, mallet

slecgettan 05.12.05.05 To shake, quake, wag

slecgwyrhta 17.02.04.03 Metal worker

slēfan 04.04.07 Trappings, equipment, garb

geslēfed 04.04.07.03 Part of garment

slēfescōh 04.04.07.15 Footwear, covering for the feet

slege 01.03.01.03.01.01 Thundering, thunder; 02.02.04 Killing, violent death, destruction; 02.08.03.02 Itch, irritation; 02.08.10.03.01 Plague, pestilence; 04.04.03 A spinning-house or chamber; 05.06.09 Act of striking; 05.12.02.06.01 To push, drive; 13.02.05.02 Defeat; 14.05.05 Physical punishments; 14.05.06 Means/implement of torture; 15.01.04 Coinage, money; 17.03 Implements, tools, etc.; 18.02.07.02.03 Stringed instruments

slegebȳtl 17.03.08 A hammer, mallet

slegefæge 02.02.03.01 In process of dying

slegel 18.02.07.02.03 Stringed instruments

geslegen 02.08.02.01.04 A sick person, invalid; 17.02.04.03 Metal worker

sleghrȳþer 02.06.02.01.03 Cattle; 04.01.02.01.02.01 Cattle for slaughter

slegnēat 02.06.02.01.03 Cattle; 04.01.02.01.02.01 Cattle for slaughter

slic 17.03.08 A hammer, mallet

slica 03.01.06 Smoothness

slid 03.01.06 Smoothness

slīdan 05.07 Ending of existence, end of world; 05.12.01.04.01.04 To stumble,

trip, strike (with the foot);
05.12.05.06.01 To travel smoothly, slide, glide; 06.01.07.05 Error, being astray; 08.01.03.06.01 Affliction, misfortune, calamity
slide 05.12.05.13.03 To fall; 06.01.07.05 Error, being astray; 08.01.03.06.01 Affliction, misfortune, calamity
slidor 01.01.02.01.04.01 Marsh, bog, swamp; 03.01.06 Smoothness; 05.12.01.09.03.04 A harbour
slidornes 01.01.02.01.04.01 Marsh, bog, swamp
slidrian 05.12.01.04.01.04 To stumble, trip, strike (with the foot)
slīefe 04.04.07.03 Part of garment
slīeflēas 04.04.07.03 Part of garment
slieht 01.03.01.03.01.02 Lightning; 02.02.04 Killing, violent death, destruction; 02.06.02 Domestic animals, livestock; 02.08.02.01.02 Onset, attack of illness; 04.01.02.01.02 Animal(s) for food
geslieht 13.02.02 Battle
sliehtswȳn 02.06.02.01.07 Pig, swine; 04.01.02.01.02.03 Pig killed for food
slifer 03.01.06 Smoothness
slīm 01.01.02.01.04.01 Marsh, bog, swamp
slincan 05.12.05.03 To travel away (from); 11.09.01 Stealthiness, a stealthy act; 11.10.05.01 Evasion, escape from threat
slincend 02.06.07.01 Reptile (serpent, snake)
slincende 11.09.01 Stealthiness, a stealthy act
slind 01.01.02.01.02.02 Hill, mountain

slingan 05.10.06.02.03 A circular fold, coil; 05.12.05.04.01 (Of wheel, etc.) to roll, trundle
slinu 01.01.02.01.02.02 Hill, mountain
slipeg 03.01.17 Thickness, viscosity
slipor 03.01.06 Smoothness; 04.06.02.02 Foul, filthy, squalid; 05.12.01.04.01.04 To stumble, trip, strike (with the foot)
slipornes 04.06.02.02 Foul, filthy, squalid
geslit 02.08.03.02 Itch, irritation; 04.01.02.01.04.03 Prey to be torn or rent; 05.06.06.01 A tearing, laceration; 07.05.03 Calumny, backbiting
slītan 02.08.03.02 Itch, irritation; 02.08.12.02.05 Pharmacy, curing with salves; 05.06.02.01 A cleft, split; 05.06.02.02 A tearing apart; 05.06.06.01 A tearing, laceration; 07.05.03 Calumny, backbiting; 08.01.03.07.02.01 Injury, offence
(ge)slītan 05.06.01 Devastation, laying waste
slitcwealm 02.02.04.04.03 Putting to death
slite 02.06.07.01.01 Part of snake; 02.07.11 Plants/flowers (alphabetical order); 02.08.03.02 Itch, irritation; 05.06.02.02 A tearing apart
sliten 16.02.01.05 Heresy, error, wrong belief
slītendlic 04.01.01.04 Gluttony, overeating, greediness
slītere 04.01.01.04 Gluttony, overeating, greediness; 05.06 Destruction, dissolution, loss, breaking
geslitglīw 08.01.01.03.07.04 Scoffing, mockery
slītnes 05.06.06.01 A tearing, laceration
slītung 05.06.06.01 A tearing, laceration
slīþan 05.06 Destruction, dissolution, loss, breaking

slīþe 05.08.02.01 (Of living creatures) fierceness, roughness
slīþelic 07.03.01.01 Abominable, detestable
slīþen 05.08.02.01 (Of living creatures) fierceness, roughness
slīþful 08.01.03.09.04 Hatred
slīþheard 08.01.03.09.11 Hardheartedness, cruelty, severity
slīþhende 02.06.01.04 Leg
slīþnes 08.01.03.09.11 Hardheartedness, cruelty, severity; 16.02.01.06.01.01.01 An image, idol
slīw 02.06.06.02.01.08 Tench, mullet
slōh 01.01.02.01.04.01 Marsh, bog, swamp
slōhtre 01.01.02.01.04.01 Marsh, bog, swamp
slota 03.03.07 A part, division, portion
slūma 02.05.04 Sleepiness, drowsiness, sleep
slūmere 02.05.04 Sleepiness, drowsiness, sleep
slūpan 05.12.05.06.01 To travel smoothly, slide, glide
slypa 03.01.17 Thickness, viscosity
slȳpan 04.04.07 Trappings, equipment, garb
slȳpescōh 04.04.07.15 Footwear, covering for the feet
slyppe 03.01.17 Thickness, viscosity
slypræsn 04.05.02.06 A buttress, support
(ge)smacian 02.05.06.02 Stroking, caressing
smæc 02.05.07 Faculty of taste; 02.05.08 Faculty of smell
gesmæccan 02.05.07 Faculty of taste
smæl 02.04.02.02 Lean, thin, slender; 02.05.10.16 Quiet, soft, faint; 03.01.02 Thinness, slightness of density; 03.03.04.04 Littleness, smallness; 05.06.09.01 A slap with the hand, blow; 05.10.05.03.01.01 Breadth, width across
smælþearmas 02.04.06.03.02.04 Intestines
smælþearme 02.04.06.03.01 Cavities of internal organs
smǣr(-e) 02.04.03.01.03.06 Mouth
smǣte 04.06.01.09 To cleanse, remove impurity from (an object)
smǣte gold 01.01.02.02.03.01 Types of metals/minerals
smǣtegylden 01.01.02.02.03.01 Types of metals/minerals
smale 02.05.10.16 Quiet, soft, faint; 05.06.05 A grinding, pounding
smale clāte 02.07.11 Plants/flowers (alphabetical order)
smale clife 02.07.11 Plants/flowers (alphabetical order)
smale netel 02.07.11 Plants/flowers (alphabetical order)
smalian 02.04.02.02 Lean, thin, slender
smalum 03.03.07 A part, division, portion
smalung 02.04.02.02 Lean, thin, slender
smēa 04.01.02.01.07.05 Delicacy/dainty/titbit
smēagan 06.01.07.06.01 To accept as the result of enquiry, suppose
smēa(ga)n 12.01.01.12.04.02 Conspiracy
(ge)smēa(ga)n 09.05.01 Inspection, examination
(ge)smēa(ga)n be/on/ymbe 06.01.01.01.01 Thought, cogitation, meditation
smēagelegen 06.01.03.02 Dialectics, logic
smēagend 09.05.01 Inspection, examination

smēagendlic 06.01.01.01.01 Thought, cogitation, meditation
smēagendlīce 06.01.07.01.01 Strictness, exactness
smēa(g)ung 06.01.01.01.01 Thought, cogitation, meditation; 06.02.06 Mind, purpose; 09.04.03 Exposition, making clear by explanation; 09.05.01 Inspection, examination; 12.01.01.12.04.02 Conspiracy
smēah 11.04.02.01.01 Cunning, craft, craftiness, guile, wile; 11.09.01 Stealthiness, a stealthy act
gesmēah 12.01.01.12.04.02 Conspiracy
smēalic 06.01.01.01.01.01 Consideration, rumination; 07.10.01 Elegance, beauty, comeliness; 09.05.01 Inspection, examination
smēalīce 05.05.03 Binding, fastening; 06.01.01.01.01.01 Consideration, rumination; 06.01.07.01.01 Strictness, exactness; 09.05.01 Inspection, examination
smēalicnes 11.04.02.01.01 Cunning, craft, craftiness, guile, wile
smēamete 04.01.02.01.07.05 Delicacy/dainty/titbit
smearcian 08.01.01.03.07.01 Laughter
smeart 08.01.03.07.04 Severity, harshness
smēaþ 06.01.01.01.01 Thought, cogitation, meditation
smēaþanclīce 06.01.07.01.01 Strictness, exactness
smēaþancol 06.01.01.01.01.01 Consideration, rumination
smēaþancole 06.01.07.01.01 Strictness, exactness
smēaþancollic 11.04.02.01 Art, skill, contrivance, cunning
smēaþancollīce 06.01.07.01.01 Strictness, exactness; 11.04.02.01 Art, skill, contrivance, cunning
smēaþancolnes 06.01.07.01.01 Strictness, exactness
smēawrenc 11.04.02.01.01 Cunning, craft, craftiness, guile, wile
smēawyrhta 17.02.04 Trade, calling, craft, aptitude
smēawyrm 02.08.08.04.03 Intestinal worm
smedma 04.01.02.01.03.08 Fine flour
smedmen 04.01.02.01.03.08 Fine flour
smelt 02.06.06.03.01.08 Sardine
smelting 17.04.03.01 Amber
smēocan 02.08.12.02.05.04 To cleanse, clean away; 03.01.09.02.01.04 Smoke
smeortan 02.08.03.02 Itch, irritation
smeortung 02.08.03.02 Itch, irritation
smeoru 03.01.17.03 Fat, grease
smeorumangestre 15.05.01 Goods, stock, merchandise
smeorusealf 02.08.12.02.05.02 Salves, ointments
smeoruþearm 02.04.06.03.02.04 Intestines
smeoruwig 03.01.17.03 Fat, grease
smeoruwyrt 02.07.11 Plants/flowers (alphabetical order)
smerenes 02.08.12.02.05.02 Salves, ointments
smerian 07.05.04 Mockery, derision, scorn
smeru 04.01.02.01.02.05.05 Fat/suet/lard
smēþan 02.08.12.02.05.02 Salves, ointments
gesmēþan 03.01.06 Smoothness; 05.09.02 Mildness, moderate quality
smēþe 03.01.06 Smoothness; 05.09.02 Mildness, moderate quality; 05.12.04

Absence of movement, stillness; 09.03.04.02.02 Eloquence, elegance in language; 11.05.02.02 Humanity, courtesy, civility; 18.02.07 Music
smēþett 01.01.02.01.04 Open (level) land
smēþian 03.01.06 Smoothness
(ge)smēþian 03.01.06 Smoothness
smēþnes 01.01.02.01.04 Open (level) land; 03.01.06 Smoothness
smīc 03.01.15 Vapour, air
smīcan 03.01.09.02.01.04 Smoke; 04.01.02.02.02 To smoke food
smicer 07.10.01 Elegance, beauty, comeliness; 09.03.04.02.02 Eloquence, elegance in language; 18.02.07 Music
smicere 07.10.01 Elegance, beauty, comeliness; 18.02.07 Music
(ge)smicerian 07.10.03 An adornment, decoration, ornament
smicernes 09.03.04.02.02 Eloquence, elegance in language
smierwan 02.08.12.02.05.02 Salves, ointments
(ge)smierwan 03.01.17.07.01 An anointing, greasing
gesmired 03.01.17.07.01 An anointing, greasing
smirels 03.01.17.07 Salves, ointments, etc.; 03.01.17.07.01 An anointing, greasing; 16.02.05.09.03 Holy oil
smirenes 03.01.17.07 Salves, ointments, etc.
smiringele 16.02.05.09.03 Holy oil
smirung 02.08.12.02.05.02 Salves, ointments; 16.02.04.07.06 Unction, anointing with holy oil
(ge)smirwan/smirian 16.02.04.07.06 Unction, anointing with holy oil

smir(w)ung 03.01.17.07.01 An anointing, greasing
smītan 04.06.02.02 Foul, filthy, squalid
(ge)smītan (mid/on) 03.01.17.07.01 An anointing, greasing
smite 01.01.03.01.01.03 Stream
smitte 04.06.02.02 Foul, filthy, squalid; 04.06.02.03 Stain, smear
smittian 02.08.02.01.01 An infectious disease
(ge)smittian 04.06.02.02 Foul, filthy, squalid; 04.06.02.03 Stain, smear
smiþ 17.02.04 Trade, calling, craft, aptitude
smiþbelg 17.05.02 A hearth, fireplace
smiþcræft 17.02.04 Trade, calling, craft, aptitude
smiþcræftiga 17.02.04 Trade, calling, craft, aptitude; 17.02.04.03 Metal worker
(ge)smiþian 17.02.04.03 Metal worker
smiþlīce 11.04.01 An aptitude, bodily skill
smiþþe 17.02.04 Trade, calling, craft, aptitude
smoc 04.04.07.08 A short garment, skirt, kirtle
smoca 03.01.09.02.01.04 Smoke
smocian 02.08.12.02.05.04 To cleanse, clean away; 03.01.09.02.01.04 Smoke
smolt 03.01.17.03 Fat, grease; 05.12.04 Absence of movement, stillness
smoltlīce 01.01.03.03 Flow/flowing; 02.05.05.04 Sensual pleasure
smorian 02.02.04.03 To kill, slay
smōþ 08.01.02.01.02.02 Gentleness, meekness, composure
smūgan 05.12.03.02 Slowness; 11.09.01 Stealthiness, a stealthy act
smūgendlic 11.09.01 Stealthiness, a stealthy act

smugge 09.05.04.01 Concealment, obscurity
smygel(s) 11.10.01.02 Refuge, help, shelter
smyllende 02.05.10.07 A crashing, noise
(ge)smyltan 01.01.03.01.02.04 State of sea
gesmyltan 05.12.04 Absence of movement, stillness
smylte 01.03.01.01 Hot, fine weather; 01.03.01.05 Wind; 05.12.04 Absence of movement, stillness; 08.01.01.03.08.03 A favour, blessing; 08.01.02.01.02.02 Gentleness, meekness, composure
smyltlic 01.03.01.01 Hot, fine weather
smyltnes 02.05.10.17 Absence of noise or disturbance; 05.11.04.02 Night, night time; 05.12.04 Absence of movement, stillness; 08.01.02.01.02.02 Gentleness, meekness, composure; 13 Peace, tranquillity
snaca 02.06.07.01 Reptile (serpent, snake)
snacc 05.12.01.09.03.01.01 Kind of ship
snæd 04.01.02.04 Abundance of food; 04.02.04.05.04 A detached area of woodland; 04.02.04.06.12 A scythe, sickle
snædan 04.01.01 Eating; 04.02.04.05.04.01.01 Pruning/lopping; 04.05.01.01 Masonry, building in stone; 17.02.04.02.01 Cutting, hewing, shaping
gesnædan 05.06.02 Cleaving, splitting, cutting
snædelþearm 02.04.06.03.02.04 Intestines
snæding 04.01.02.04.01 Meal

snædinghūs 04.01.01.08 Eating place
snædingscēap 02.06.02.01.08 Sheep; 04.01.02.01.02.02 Sheep killed for food
snædmælum 03.03.07 A part, division, portion
snægl 02.06.09.02.09 Snail
snæp 01.01.02.01.04.01 Marsh, bog, swamp
snæsan 05.06.07 Pricking, a prick, puncture
snæþfeld 04.02.03.04.02 Pasture/pasturage; 04.02.04.05.04 A detached area of woodland
snās 03.03.01.02 Dry measures; 04.01.02.02.06 Kitchen
snāw 01.03.01.06.04 Snow
snāw(a) 01.03.01.06.04 Snow
snāwceald 03.01.11 Coldness, coolness
snāwgebland 01.03.01.06.04 Snow
snāwhwīt 03.01.14.03 White/whiteness
snāwig 01.03.01.06.04 Snow
snāwlic 01.03.01.06.04 Snow
sneare 04.03.02 A snare, trap, noose
snell 05.12.03.01 Swiftness, velocity; 06.02.07.06.02 Boldness
snellic 05.12.03.01 Swiftness, velocity; 06.02.07.06.02 Boldness
snellīce 05.12.03.01 Swiftness, velocity
snellscipe 06.02.07.06 Courage, boldness, valour
snelnes 05.12.03.01 Swiftness, velocity; 11.02.01 Energy, vigour, vigorous action
snēome 05.11.07.01 Contemporary, coeval; 05.12.03.01 Swiftness, velocity
gesneorcan 03.02.01 Decay, decline, corruption; 05.10.05.02.03 To reduce, make thin(ner)

snēowan 05.12.03.01 Swiftness, velocity; 05.12.03.01.02 Haste, hurry
snēr 18.02.07.02.03 Stringed instruments
(ge)snīcan 11.09.01 Stealthiness, a stealthy act
snid 03.03.07 A part, division, portion; 17.03.03 A cutting tool
gesnid 02.02.04 Killing, violent death, destruction; 02.08.12.02.06 Surgical
snide 02.02.04 Killing, violent death, destruction; 05.06.02 Cleaving, splitting, cutting
snidīsen 02.08.12.02.06 Surgical
snīte 02.06.08.03 Game-bird
snīþan 02.02.04.04.04 To slaughter (an animal); 02.04.04.03.05 Haircutting, tonsure
(ge)snīþan 04.02.04.04.02.02 To gather fruits, crops, etc.; 04.05.01.01 Masonry, building in stone; 05.06.02 Cleaving, splitting, cutting; 17.02.04.02.01 Cutting, hewing, shaping
gesnīþan 02.08.12.02.06 Surgical
snīþstrēo 02.07.11 Plants/flowers (alphabetical order)
snīþung 02.02.04 Killing, violent death, destruction; 02.08.04.01 A wound
snīwan 01.03.01.06.04 Snow
snōca 01.01.02.01.01.03.01 Promontory, headland, cape
snōd 04.04.07.11 A headcloth, covering for the head
snoffa 02.08.08.04.02 (Of stomach) disordered
snofl 02.04.06.05.07.02 Mucus, phlegm, rheum
snoflig 02.04.06.05.07.02 Mucus, phlegm, rheum

snoru 02.03.02.03.06.02.06 In-law relationships
gesnot 02.04.06.05.07.02 Mucus, phlegm, rheum
snotor 06.01.05.02.01.01 Sagacity
snotorlic 06.01.05.02.01.01 Sagacity
snotorlīce 06.01.05.02.01.01.01 Reason, sense, discretion, prudence; 06.01.06.02 Knowledge, learning, erudition
snotornes 06.01.05.02.01.01 Sagacity
snotorscipe 06.01.05.02.01.01.01 Reason, sense, discretion, prudence
snotorwyrde 06.01.07.04.04.02 Pretence, feigning, dissimulation
snūd 05.11.07.04.01 Nearness, approach, imminence; 05.12.03.01 Swiftness, velocity
snūde 05.11.07.01 Contemporary, coeval
snyflung 02.04.06.05.07.02 Mucus, phlegm, rheum
snyrian 05.12.03.01.02 Haste, hurry
snȳtan 02.04.06.06.03 Action of clearing nose
snȳting 02.04.06.06.03 Action of clearing nose
snytre 06.01.05.02.01.01 Sagacity
snytrian 06.01.05.02.01.01 Sagacity
snyttru 06.01.05.02.01.01 Sagacity
snyttrucræft 06.01.05.02.01.01 Sagacity
snyttruhūs 16.01.02.04 Paradise
snyttrum 06.01.05.02.01.01.01 Reason, sense, discretion, prudence
snyþian 05.12.05.09 To go forward, proceed
soc 04.05.03.05.03 Drainage
(ge)soc 04.01.01.02 Act/action of sucking
socc 04.04.07.15 Footwear, covering for the feet
socian 03.01.16.01 Moisture; 03.01.16.06 A soaking, steeping

sōcn 05.10.04.03.01 Visiting/seeking of a place; 09.05.02 A question, inquiry, questioning; 12.06.02 District, province; 13:02.03.01 An attack, assault; 14.01.03.01 Sanctuary; 15.03 Exaction of tax/tribute

sōcnmann 15.01.01.01 Holding of land

gesod 04.01.02.02.05 Cooking; 17.02.04.03.03 Smelting, heating, scorification

soden 02.08.03.01 Extreme pain, torture, torment

gesoden 04.01.02.02.05 Cooking; 04.01.02.02.05.02 To boil

sodomisc 02.03.03.06.07.07 Other (alphabetical order); 12.08.08.01.02.01.03 Unnatural sexual behaviour; 16.02.01.13.01 Kinds of sin

sodomitisc 02.03.03.06.07.07 Other (alphabetical order); 12.08.08.01.02.01.03 Unnatural sexual behaviour; 16.02.01.13.01 Kinds of sin

sōfte 02.05.04 Sleepiness, drowsiness, sleep; 02.05.05.04 Sensual pleasure; 02.05.05.04.01 Luxuries, dainties, good things; 08.01.02.01.02 Gentleness; 08.01.02.01.02.01 Mildness, leniency, indulgence; 11.12 Easiness; 13 Peace, tranquillity

sōftnes 12.08.07.01 Laxity, indulgence

sogeþa 02.04.06.05.07.07 Secretion from spleen; 02.08.08.04.02 (Of stomach) disordered

sohþa 04.01.02.01.07.01 Soup/pottage; 04.01.03.05 A drink/beverage

sol 01.01.02.01.04.01 Marsh, bog, swamp; 04.02.05.05.02 Harness of draught animal; 04.06.02.02 Foul, filthy, squalid

sōl 01.02.01.01.03 Sun

sōlate 02.07.11 Plants/flowers (alphabetical order)

gesolcen 02.05.03.02 Weariness

solcennes 11.06 Disinclination to act, listlessness

solian 04.06.02.01 Dirty, unclean

sōlmerca 05.11.05 A dial, horloge

solmōnaþ 05.11.03.01.03.01 Specific months

solor 04.05.02.10 Flooring, a floor; 04.05.03.02.01 A building, house, hall, palace, etc.; 04.05.03.04 A closet, chamber, room

sōlsēce 02.07.11 Plants/flowers (alphabetical order)

solu 04.04.07.15 Footwear, covering for the feet

sōm 13 Peace, tranquillity; 13.01.02 Reconciliation; 14.04.04 An agreement, arrangement of dispute

gesōm 13 Peace, tranquillity

sōn 18.02.07 Music

sōna 05.11.07.01 Contemporary, coeval; 05.11.07.04.01 Nearness, approach, imminence

sōna æfter 05.11.07.01 Contemporary, coeval

sōna eft 05.11.07.01 Contemporary, coeval

sōna swā 05.11.07.01 Contemporary, coeval

sōncræft 18.02.07 Music

song 02.07.09.02 Particular fruits (alphabetical order); 04.05.04.05 A bed, bedstead

sopa 04.01.03 Drinking

sopcuppe 04.01.02.02.06.05.04 Cup/bowl/basin

sopp 04.01.02.01.07.03.03 Piece of bread
soppian 03.01.16.06 A soaking, steeping
sorg 08.01.03 Bad feeling, sadness; 08.01.03.03 Anxiety
sorgbyrþen 08.01.03 Bad feeling, sadness
sorgcearig 08.01.03.03 Anxiety
sorgcearu 08.01.03 Bad feeling, sadness
sorgful 08.01.03 Bad feeling, sadness; 08.01.03.03 Anxiety; 08.01.03.04 Grief
sorgian 08.01.03.03 Anxiety
sorgian ymb 08.01.03.03 Anxiety
sorgian ymbe/on/for 08.01.03.04 Grief
(ge)sorgian 08.01.03.04 Grief
sorgiende 08.01.03.04 Grief
sorglēas 08.01.01.03 Good feeling, joy, happiness; 11.10 Safety, safeness
sorglēast 11.10 Safety, safeness
sorglēoþ 09.03.05.01.01 Poetry
sorglic 08.01.03.04 Grief
sorglīce 08.01.03.04 Grief; 08.01.03.04.01 Complaint, lamentation
sorglufu 08.01.02.02 Love, affection, care
sorgstafas 08.01.03.03 Anxiety
sorgung 08.01.03 Bad feeling, sadness
sorgwīte 08.01.03.07.03 Suffering, torment, pain
sorgword 08.01.03.04.01 Complaint, lamentation
sorgwylm 08.01.03.04 Grief
sorig 08.01.03 Bad feeling, sadness
sōt 03.01.14.04 Black/blackness; 04.06.02.05 Dust, powder
sōtig 04.06.02.01 Dirty, unclean
sotman 06.01.05.03.02 Foolish, silly, stupid
sotscipe 06.01.05.03.01.01 Dullness, folly, stupidity
sott 06.01.05.03.01.01 Dullness, folly, stupidity; 06.01.05.03.02 Foolish, silly, stupid
sottian 06.01.05.03.02 Foolish, silly, stupid
sōþ 06.01.07 Truth, conformity with absolute standard; 06.01.07.02 Certainty, truth, what really is; 09.07.04 Assertion, affirmation; 12.07.02.02 Truth, faithfulness, good faith, sincerity; 12.07.04 Truth, righteousness, justice, equity
sōþ hweþere 03.06 Comparison
sōþbora 16.01.04.06 Divination, augury
sōþcwed 06.01.07.03 Truth of speech or thought, veracity
sōþcweden 06.01.07.03 Truth of speech or thought, veracity
sōþcwide 06.01.07.03 Truth of speech or thought, veracity; 09.06.01.02 A saying, saw, proverb, maxim; 16.02.01.09 The law
sōþcyning 16.01.01.01.01 The Almighty
sōþe 06.01.07 Truth, conformity with absolute standard; 06.01.07.01 Correct, right, free from error; 12.07.02.02 Truth, faithfulness, good faith, sincerity
sōþfæder 16.01.01.04.01 God the Father
sōþfæst 06.01.07.03 Truth of speech or thought, veracity; 12.07.02.02 Truth, faithfulness, good faith, sincerity; 12.07.04 Truth, righteousness, justice, equity; 12.08.02.02 Righteousness, rectitude; 12.08.02.03 Goodness, probity; 16.02.01.12.03 Righteousness
(ge)sōþfæstian 12.07.04.01 Justification
sōþfæstlic 06.01.07 Truth, conformity with absolute standard

sōþfæstlīce 06.01.07.03 Truth of speech or thought, veracity
sōþfæstnes 06.01.07.03 Truth of speech or thought, veracity; 12.07.02.02 Truth, faithfulness, good faith, sincerity; 12.07.04 Truth, righteousness, justice, equity
sōþgiedd 09.06.01 To relate, recount, tell
sōþian 11.03.01.01.01 Proof, demonstration
gesōþian 14.03.03.03 Witness, testimony, attestation
gesōþian on ānum 14.03.03.09.01 Unfavourable judgement, condemnation
sōþlic 06.01.07 Truth, conformity with absolute standard
sōþlīce 06.01.07.01 Correct, right, free from error
sōþlufu 08.01.02.01 Favour, kindness, grace; 16.02.01.12.04 A cardinal virtue
sōþnes 06.01.07.01 Correct, right, free from error
sōþsagol 06.01.07.03 Truth of speech or thought, veracity
sōþsagu 06.01.07.03 Truth of speech or thought, veracity; 09.06.01.01 A tradition, ordinance handed down
sōþsecgan 06.01.07.03 Truth of speech or thought, veracity
sōþsecgende 06.01.07.03 Truth of speech or thought, veracity
sōþsecgendlīce 06.01.07.01 Correct, right, free from error
sōþsegen 06.01.07 Truth, conformity with absolute standard; 06.01.07.03 Truth of speech or thought, veracity
sōþspell 09.06.01.01 A tradition, ordinance handed down

sōþspræc 09.06.01.02 A saying, saw, proverb, maxim
sōþspræce 06.01.07.03 Truth of speech or thought, veracity
sōþtācen 06.01.08.05.01.01.01 An exercise of power, mighty work, miracle
sōþword 14.01.06 A rule, order, precept, tenet, principle
sōþwundor 06.01.08.05.01.01.01 An exercise of power, mighty work, miracle
spāca 02.04.05.04.06 Bone of arm; 17.03.01 A wheel
spadu 04.02.04.06.01 A spade; 17.03.07 Tools for digging/grasping/pulling
spæcehēow 09.03.04.01 Mode of speech
spæclēas 09.02.02 Dumbness, lack of speech
spær 10.03.09 Moderation in expenditure
spæren 04.05.01.03 Gypsum, chalk
spærhende 10.03.09 Moderation in expenditure
spærlic 10.03.09 Moderation in expenditure
spærlīce 10.03.09 Moderation in expenditure
spærlīra 02.04.03.04.02.03 Lower leg
spærlīred 02.04.03.04.02.03 Lower leg
spærnes 10.03.09 Moderation in expenditure
spærstān 01.01.02.02.02.03 Limestone, chalk; 04.05.01.03 Gypsum, chalk; 17.04.02.04 Gypsum, chalk
spætan 02.04.06.06.04 Spittle
gespætan 02.08.12.02.05.04 To cleanse, clean away
spætl(i)an 02.04.06.06.04 Spittle
spætung 02.04.06.06.04 Spittle

spala 12.02.01 A substitute, representative
spald 04.05.03.05.03.01 A ditch, dike
spaldur 02.08.12.02.05.02 Salves, ointments
(ge)span 03.03.06.01 A whole formed by joining; 04.04.10.02 A button, brooch
gespan 06.02.06.03.04 Allurement; 12.05.06.01 Restraint, check, curb, control
(ge)spanan 06.02.06.03.04 Allurement
spane 02.04.06.05.06 Mammary gland, breast
spanere 06.02.06.03.04 Allurement
spane(-u) 02.04.03.03.05 Chest, breast, bosom
(ge)spang 17.03.10 Supports and fastenings
spann 05.10.05.03 A measure of distance
spannan 04.02.05.05.03 A yoke; 12.05.06.04 A trampling upon, subjection
(ge)spannan 03.03.06.01 A whole formed by joining; 06.02.06.03.04 Allurement; 12.09.02 Marriage ceremony
spannung 05.10.05 A space, span
sparian 08.01.02.06 Mercy, pity; 15.01.05 Possession of wealth
(ge)sparian 11.06.04 Abstention, abstaining from
gesparian 10.03.09 Moderation in expenditure
gesparrian 05.10.05.04.15.01 A bar, bolt
spātan 02.04.06.06.04 Spittle
spātl/spold 02.04.06.06.04 Spittle
spātlian 02.04.06.06.04 Spittle
spātlung 02.04.06.06.04 Spittle
spearca 03.01.09.02 Fire, flame; 06.01.02 The imaginative faculty

spearcian 03.01.12.01 Glittering, effulgence
spearhafoc 02.06.08.04 Bird of prey
spearnlian 05.06.09.02 Act of kicking
spearwa 02.04.03.04.02.03 Lower leg; 02.06.08.05 Forest bird, wild-fowl
specca 02.08.05.02 Particular inflammation/swelling; 04.06.02.03 Stain, smear
specfāh 04.06.02.03 Stain, smear
sped 02.04.06.05.07.02 Mucus, phlegm, rheum
spēd 03.03.04.02.01 Abundance; 08.01.01.03.08.02 Good fortune, success; 11.04 Ability, capacity, power; 11.07.02 Utility, advantage, convenience
(ge)spēdan 11.03.02.01 Efficacy, success
spēddropa 09.03.07.06.02 Ink
spediende 02.08.08.02 Lung disease
spēdig 03.03.04.02.01 Abundance; 08.01.01.03.08.02 Good fortune, success; 12 Power, might; 15.01.05 Possession of wealth
gespēdiglīce 08.01.01.03.08 Happiness, well-being, prosperity
spēdignes 15.01.05 Possession of wealth
spēdlīce 05.03.02 Event, issue, result; 11.03.02.01 Efficacy, success
gespēdsumian 08.01.01.03.08 Happiness, well-being, prosperity
spēdum 03.03.04.02.01 Abundance; 05.12.03.01 Swiftness, velocity
spelc 02.08.12.02.06.01 A bandage, binding
spelcan 02.08.12.02.06.01 A bandage, binding
speld 17.05.03 Sources of fire/light
gespelia 12.02.01 A substitute, representative

spelian 12.02.01 A substitute, representative
speliend 12.02.01 A substitute, representative
speling 12.02.01 A substitute, representative
spell 06.01.03.02 Dialectics, logic; 06.01.07.04.03 Untruth, falsehood; 09.01.01 A speech, what is said, words; 09.06.01 To relate, recount, tell; 09.06.01.01 A tradition, ordinance handed down; 09.06.02.01.06 A message, announcement by a messenger; 16.02.04.03.02 Parts of service; 16.02.04.10 Preaching
spellbōc 16.02.04.10 Preaching; 16.02.05.10.03 A homiliary
spellboda 09.01.02 Fluency in speech; 09.06.02.01.06.01 A messenger
spellcwide 09.06.01.01 A tradition, ordinance handed down
spellian 12.01.01.12.04.02 Conspiracy
(ge)spellian 09.01 To speak, exercise faculty of speech; 09.01.04 Conversation, discussion
spellstōw 09.06.02.01.05 Proclamation, spreading abroad
spellung 09.01.04 Conversation, discussion; 09.06.01 To relate, recount, tell
spelt 04.01.02.01.03 Corn; 04.02.04.03.02.01 Grain crops; 09.03.07.07 A book
spendung 15.02.04 Spending, disbursement
spennels 04.04.10.01 A ring (for finger, arm, neck)
spennestre 06.02.06.03.04.01 Temptation
gespeoftian 02.04.06.06.04 Spittle

speoft(on) 02.04.06.06.04 Spittle
speoht 02.06.08.05 Forest bird, wild-fowl
spēonisc 02.03.03.06.06 Spanish
spere 02.08.03 Pain, bodily discomfort; 13.02.08.04.01 A spear
sperebrōga 06.01.08.06.03 Cause of fear, terror, horror
sperehand 02.03.02.03.01 Ancestry, paternal kinship
sperehealf 02.03.02.03.01 Ancestry, paternal kinship
sperelēas 13.02.08.04.01 A spear
sperenīþ 13.02.02 Battle
speresceaft 13.02.08.04.01 A spear
sperewriþ 13.02.08.04.01 A spear
sperewyrt 02.07.11 Plants/flowers (alphabetical order)
gesperod 13.02.08.04.01 A spear
spic 02.07.03.01 A bush; 04.01.02.01.02.05.02 Pork; 04.01.02.01.02.05.05 Fat/suet/lard
spīce/spīca 04.01.02.01.05.05 Spice
spichūs 04.01.02.02.06.02 Larder, pantry
spicmāse 02.06.08.05 Forest bird, wild-fowl
spīcung 17.03.10.02 A pin, peg, nail
spigettan 02.04.06.06.04 Spittle
spilæg 02.06.09 Insect/small creature
spild 05.06 Destruction, dissolution, loss, breaking
spildan 02.02.04.04.02 Suicide; 05.06 Destruction, dissolution, loss, breaking
spildsīþ 05.06 Destruction, dissolution, loss, breaking
spilere 18.02.05 Buffoonery, speech of buffoon/actor
spilian 18.02.02 Play, (athletic) sport
spillan 02.02.04.03 To kill, slay

(ge)spillan 05.06 Destruction, dissolution, loss, breaking; 10.03.08.01 Overliberality, waste of money
spillend 18.02.05 Buffoonery, speech of buffoon/actor
spilling 10.03.08.01 Overliberality, waste of money
spind 03.01.17.03 Fat, grease; 04.01.02.01.02.05.05 Fat/suet/lard
spinel 04.04.03 A spinning-house or chamber; 04.04.04 A thread (of wool, etc.), fibre
spinelhealf 02.03.02.03.02 Maternal descent
spinnan 05.10.06.02.03 A circular fold, coil; 05.12.05.04.01 (Of wheel, etc.) to roll, trundle
(ge)spinnan 04.04.03 A spinning-house or chamber
spīr 02.07.02.05 A shoot, sprout, tendril
spircan 03.01.12.01 Glittering, effulgence
spircende 03.01.12.01 Glittering, effulgence
spircing 03.01.12.01 Glittering, effulgence
spite/-u 04.01.02.02.06 Kitchen
spitel 04.02.04.06.01 A spade
spittan 04.02.04.02.02 To dig up the ground
(ge)spittan 02.04.06.06.04 Spittle
spīþra 02.06.09.02.10 Spider
spīwan 02.08.08.04.02 (Of stomach) disordered
spiwdrenc 02.08.12.02.07.01 Purgative
spiwe 02.08.08.04.02 (Of stomach) disordered
spīwere 02.08.08.04.02 (Of stomach) disordered
spiw(i)an 02.08.08.04.02 (Of stomach) disordered
spīwing 02.08.08.04.02 (Of stomach) disordered
spiwol 02.08.12.02.07.01 Purgative
spiwþa 02.08.08.04.02 (Of stomach) disordered
splātan 05.06.02.01 A cleft, split
splott 03.01.14.11 Medley/variety of colour; 04.02.03.01 Plot of land
gesplotted 03.01.14.11 Medley/variety of colour
spōn 03.03.07 A part, division, portion
spong 02.08.05.02 Particular inflammation/swelling
sponge 17.03.11 Other implements, etc.
spor 02.08.04.01 A wound; 04.03.01 Tracking; 05.12.01.03.01.01 A path, track
sporettan 05.06.09.02 Act of kicking
sporetung 05.06.09.02 Act of kicking
spornettan 05.06.09.02 Act of kicking
sporning 11.11.02 A hindrance
sporwrecel 14.02.01.02 Wrongful taking, theft
spot 03.03.04.04 Littleness, smallness
spōwan 11.07.03 Use, advantage, profit
(ge)spōwan 11.03.02.01 Efficacy, success
spōwende 08.01.01.03.08.02 Good fortune, success
spōwendlīce 08.01.01.03.08 Happiness, well-being, prosperity
spracen 02.07.03.05 Particular trees/shrubs (alphabetical order)
sp(r)æc 02.07.02.05 A shoot, sprout, tendril; 02.07.03.03.01 Wood (as substance)
spræc 09 Speech, vocal utterance; 09.03.04.01 Mode of speech; 09.03.04.02.02 Eloquence, elegance in language; 09.05.02 A question, inquiry, questioning; 09.06 To take

matter for discourse;
09.06.02.01.05.01 To spread, make known, proclaim, celebrate; 12.02.02.03 Terms for classical world
sp(r)æc 14.03.03 Law, action of the courts
spræc 14.03.03.09 A sentence, judgement, ruling; 16.02.05.02.03 A church, place of worship
(ge)spræc 09 Speech, vocal utterance; 09.01.01 A speech, what is said, words; 09.01.04 Conversation, discussion; 09.03 A language
gespræc 16.01.04.06.04 Prophecy, divine speech
spræccynn 09.03.04.01 Mode of speech
spræce 09.01.01 A speech, what is said, words
sp(r)æce drīfan 14.03.03 Law, action of the courts
gespræce 08.01.02.01 Favour, kindness, grace; 09.01.02 Fluency in speech
gespræcelic 09.03.02.02.01.05 Minor parts of speech, etc.
spræcful 09.01.02.01 Excessive fluency, loquacity
spræchūs 06.01.06.02.03.04.01 A school; 14.03.01 Judicial body, authority; 16.02.05.04.01 Parts of monastery
gesprædan 05.10.05.02 Extension, stretching
sprædung 05.10.05.02.01 Diffusion, effusion, spreading
spræg 02.07.03.01 A bush
spranca 02.07.03.03.01 Wood (as substance)
sprangettan 05.12.05.05 To shake, quake, wag
sprēawlian 05.12.05.05 To shake, quake, wag

(ge)sp(r)eca 09.01.04 Conversation, discussion; 12.02.02.02 A counsellor, advisor
sp(r)ecan æfter/on/ymb 14.03.03 Law, action of the courts
(ge)sprecan 09 Speech, vocal utterance; 09.01 To speak, exercise faculty of speech; 09.01.03 To address, speak to; 09.01.04 Conversation, discussion
gesprecan 13 Peace, tranquillity
gesprecendlic 09.01 To speak, exercise faculty of speech
sprēcern 14.03.01 Judicial body, authority
sprecolnes 09.01.02.01 Excessive fluency, loquacity
sprecul 09.01.02.01 Excessive fluency, loquacity
sprengan 04.02.04.02.03 Sowing; 05.12.02.08 To give a different direction to, turn
sprengan (on) 02.08.12.02.07.01 Purgative
(ge)sprengan 03.01.16.05 A sprinkling
sprenging 03.01.16.05 A sprinkling
sprēot 13.02.08.04.01 A spear; 17.03.09 A post, rod, stick, etc.
sprincel 04.03.05 Fishing
sprind 06.01.05.02 Intelligence
sprindlīce 05.08.01 Vigour, activity, force
spring 01.01.03.01.01.07 Spring, fountain, well; 02.08.05.02 Particular inflammation/swelling; 02.08.08.12 Disease of bowels; 02.08.12.02.05.04 To cleanse, clean away
springan 02.07.01 To grow; 05.12.05.11.01 To return; 05.12.05.12.01 To reach up
springan fram 06.02.04.01.01 Need, distress, straits, difficulty

(ge)springan 05.10.05.02.01 Diffusion, effusion, spreading; 05.12.05.03.04.01 To burst forth, break out
gespringan 05.12.02.03 To send; 08.01.03.09.02 Harsh, unfriendly, unkind; 09.01.02 Fluency in speech
sprin(g)d 05.08.01 Vigour, activity, force
springwyrt 02.07.11 Plants/flowers (alphabetical order)
sprota 02.07.03.03.01 Wood (as substance); 17.03.10.02 A pin, peg, nail
sprott 02.06.06.03.01.11 Sprat
sprot(t) 02.07.08 Grasses, reeds, etc.
sprytle 02.07.03.03.01 Wood (as substance)
spryttan 02.07.01 To grow; 06.02.06.03.03 Incitement
sprytting 02.07.02.05 A shoot, sprout, tendril; 03.03.04.03 Growth, increase
spura 04.02.05.06.05.03.09 A spur
spure 02.04.03.04.02.05.01 Heel
spurleþer 04.02.05.06.05.03.09 A spur
spurnan 05.06.09.02 Act of kicking; 05.12.01.04.01.03 To amble, stagger; 05.12.01.04.01.04 To stumble, trip, strike (with the foot)
(ge)spurnan 05.12.01.04.01.02 To tread upon, trample; 12.05.07 Casting out, rejection
gespurnan 01.03.01.05 Wind
spurnere 04.04.01 Fulling
spurul 05.06.09.02 Act of kicking
spynge 17.03.11 Other implements, etc.
spyrd 05.10.05.03 A measure of distance; 18.02.03.01.02 Racing
spyremann 04.03.01 Tracking
spyrian 05.12.05.02 To go/travel towards, come, approach; 09.05.01 Inspection, examination
spyrian æfter 04.03.01 Tracking
(ge)spyrian 04.03.01 Tracking
(ge)spyrian æfter 09.05.02 A question, inquiry, questioning
spyrigend 09.05.01 Inspection, examination
spyrran 12.05.04.01.01 Fighting, a fight
spyrring 05.06.09 Act of striking
spyrte 17.03.12.01 A basket
spyrung 09.05.02 A question, inquiry, questioning
staca 04.05.01.02.06 A log, stake, etc.; 05.10.05.04.11.01.01 Object placed as point to be reached, a mark; 05.10.06.03.01 A point, spike, prickle; 17.03.10.01 A bolt, lock, bar
stacan 04.01.02.02.05.03 Frying/roasting
stacing 05.10.05.04.11 A circle, circuit, circumference
stacung 05.06.07 Pricking, a prick, puncture
stæf 05.12.01.09.03.01.03 Part of ship; 06.01.07.01.01 Strictness, exactness; 09.03.07.01 A written character, letter; 09.03.07.04.01 To punctuate, divide; 12.01.01.03 Symbols of power; 16.02.05.05.08 A staff, wand of authority; 16.02.05.10.12 A computus and calendar; 17.03.09 A post, rod, stick, etc.
stæfcræft 09.03.02 Art of grammar
stæfcræftas 06.01.06.02.02.01 Learning, science (secular knowledge)
stæfcræftig 06.01.06.02 Knowledge, learning, erudition
stæfcyst 06.01.06.02.02.01 Learning, science (secular knowledge)
stæfer 05.10.05.04.11.01.01 Object placed as point to be reached, a mark

stæfgefēg 09.03.07 Writing; 09.03.07.01.02 A word
gestæflǣred 06.01.06.02 Knowledge, learning, erudition
stæfleahtor 09.03.02.04 A slip of the tongue, solecism
stæfleornere 06.01.06.02.01 A wise man, man of understanding or learning; 09.03.07.07.03.03 A writer, author
stæflic 09.03.04.01 Mode of speech; 09.03.04.03 Plain, simple
stæfliþere 13.02.08.04.05 A warlike engine
stæfplega 06.01.06.02.03.04 Teaching, instruction
stæfrǣw 09.03.07 Writing; 09.03.07.01 A written character, letter
stæfrōf 09.03.07.01 A written character, letter
stæfsweord 13.02.08.04.03 A sword
stæfwīs 06.01.06.02 Knowledge, learning, erudition
stæfwrītere 09.03.02 Art of grammar
stæg 01.01.03.01.03.01 Pool; 05.12.01.09.03.01.03 Part of ship
stǣgel 05.10.05.03.03 Height, loftiness, sublimity
stǣger 04.05.02.11 A staircase
stæl 05.10.04 Place, room
stæl/steall 05.02.01 Condition, state of affairs, situation
stǣlan 12.08.09 Guiltiness, guilt
(ge)stǣlan (on/ongēan) 14.03.03.01 Accusation
stælgiest 02.06.09 Insect/small creature
stælhere 13.02.10.01.02.02.01 Types of army
stælhrān 02.06.03.01.06 Deer, hart; 04.03.01 Tracking
gestællan 04.02.05.06.05.02.01 A stable

stæltihtle 14.03.03.01 Accusation
stælþing 14.02.01.02 Wrongful taking, theft
stælwyrt 02.07.11 Plants/flowers (alphabetical order)
stǣna/-e 04.01.02.02.06.05 Vessel/utensil/cup; 04.01.03.05.04 Drinking vessel
stǣnan 17.02.05.01 Ornamental object
(ge)stǣnan 05.06.09.04 Stoning, casting of stones
stǣne 01.01.02.01 Ground
stǣnen 01.01.02.01 Ground; 04.05.01.01 Masonry, building in stone; 06.02.07 Will, determination, resolution; 08.01.03.09.10 Wrath, sternness, displeasure
stǣner 01.01.02.01 Ground
stǣnilic 01.01.02.02.01 Rock, stone
stǣning 05.06.09.04 Stoning, casting of stones
stæpe 03.03.05.01 Rank, position, degree; 04.05.02.05 A pedestal, socket; 04.05.02.11 A staircase; 04.05.04.04 A ladder, set of steps; 05.10.05.03 A measure of distance; 05.12.01.03.01.01 A path, track; 05.12.01.04 To go, proceed on foot; 05.12.01.04.01 Manner of going, gait
stæpegong 05.12.01.04 To go, proceed on foot
stæpmǣlum 03.03.07 A part, division, portion; 05.12.03.02 Slowness
(ge)stæppan 05.12.01 To go, progress, travel (usually on land); 05.12.01.04 To go, proceed on foot
stæppescōh 04.04.07.15 Footwear, covering for the feet
stær 02.06.08.05 Forest bird, wild-fowl
stær 09.06.01 To relate, recount, tell

stærblind 02.08.07.02.01 Defective vision
stærleornere 06.01.06.02.01 A wise man, man of understanding or learning; 09.03.07.07.03.03 A writer, author
stǣrlīce 05.11.07.03 Former times, days of old
stærling 02.06.08.05 Forest bird, wild-fowl
stǣrtractere 09.03.07.07.03.03 A writer, author
stǣrwrītere 09.03.07.07.03.03 A writer, author
stæþ 01.01.02.01.01.03 Shore, bank
stæþfæst 05.12.04.01 Stability, firmness
stæþhlȳpe 01.01.02.01.02.02.04 Cliff
stæþhlȳplīce 05.10.05.04.04.01 Steep
stæþswealwe 02.06.08.06 Water bird
stæþþan 05.12.04.01 Stability, firmness
stæþþig 05.12.04.01 Stability, firmness
(ge)stæþþig 11.05.02.01 A standard, norm, ethos
gestæþþig 16.01.01.01 Attributes of God
(ge)stæþþignes 11.05.02.01 A standard, norm, ethos
gestæþþignes 11.05.02 Mode, manner, way, method, fashion, course
stæþweall 01.01.02.01.02.02.04 Cliff
stæþwierþe 11.07.01 Utility, usefulness
stæþwyrt 02.07.11.02 Unidentified plants (alphabetical order)
stafas 06.01.06.02.02.01 Learning, science (secular knowledge); 09.03.07 Writing; 09.03.07.07.03.02.02 A letter
stafian 06.01.06.02.03.03.01 An act of reading
stafod 03.01.14.11 Medley/variety of colour
stagga 02.06.03.01.06 Deer, hart

gestāl 07.05.01 Censure, reproof, rebuke; 14.03.03.01 Accusation
gestala 14.02 Lawlessness
stālern 14.03.01 Judicial body, authority
stalgong 11.09.01 Stealthiness, a stealthy act
stalian 11.09.01 Stealthiness, a stealthy act
(ge)stalian 14.02.01.02 Wrongful taking, theft
stālian 14.03.03.01 Accusation
stalu 11.09.01 Stealthiness, a stealthy act; 14.02.01.02 Wrongful taking, theft; 14.05.04.01 A fine
stalung 14.02.01.02 Wrongful taking, theft
stam 09.02.03.02 Stammering
stamera 09.02.03.02 Stammering
stamerian 09.02.03.02 Stammering
stammetan 09.02.03.02 Stammering
stamor 09.02.03.02 Stammering
stān 01.01.02.01.02.02.05 Crag, rock, stone; 01.01.02.02.01 Rock, stone; 01.01.02.02.03 Minerals and metals; 02.08.08 Internal disease; 04.05.01.01 Masonry, building in stone; 05.13.06.01 Firm, stable, steady; 16.02.01.06.01.01.01 An image, idol; 17.04.03.04 Gems collectively
stānæx 17.03.03 A cutting tool
stānbæþ 02.08.12.02.05.04 To cleanse, clean away
stānbeorg 01.01.02.01.02.02.01 Hill
stānberende 01.01.02.01 Ground; 01.01.02.02.01 Rock, stone
stānbill 17.03.03 A cutting tool
stānboga 01.01.02.01.03.01 Cave
stānbryce 04.05.01.01 Masonry, building in stone
stānbrycg 05.12.01.03.04 A bridge
stānbucca 02.06.03.01.08 Goat

stānburg 13.02.06.01 Stronghold, fort/fortified town
stanc 03.01.16.05 A sprinkling
stāncarr 01.01.02.02.01 Rock, stone
stānceastel 01.01.02.01.02.01 Rising ground, eminence
stānceosel 01.01.02.02.02.01 Sand, gravel
stānclif 01.01.02.01.02.02.04 Cliff
stānclūd 01.01.02.02.01 Rock, stone
stāncnoll 01.01.02.01.02.01 Rising ground, eminence; 01.01.02.01.02.02.05 Crag, rock, stone
stāncræftiga 04.05.01.01 Masonry, building in stone; 17.02.04.02.01 Cutting, hewing, shaping
stancrian 03.01.16.05 A sprinkling
stāncrop 02.07.11 Plants/flowers (alphabetical order)
stāncynn 01.01.02.02.01 Rock, stone
stāncyst(en) 02.07.03.05 Particular trees/shrubs (alphabetical order)
stand 05.10.04 Place, room; 05.11.08.01.03.01 Delay
standan 03.01.17.01 A coagulating, mixing; 05.11.02 A time, particular time, occasion; 06.02.07 Will, determination, resolution; 07.02.01 Right, virtue; 14.03.03.03 Witness, testimony, attestation
standan āstreht 05.11.11 Continuity
standan on 11.02 Occupation, activity, business
standan ūp āstreht 05.10.05.03.03 Height, loftiness, sublimity
(ge)standan 05.02 State, condition; 05.10.04 Place, room; 05.10.04.01 Position, stance; 05.10.05.04.02.04.01 Uprightness, straightness; 05.11.11 Continuity; 05.12.04 Absence of movement, stillness; 05.13.06 Constancy, unchangeableness; 14.01.06 A rule, order, precept, tenet, principle
gestandan 02.08.02.01.01 An infectious disease; 05.12.05.12.01 To reach up; 07.05.01 Censure, reproof, rebuke; 13.02.03.01 An attack, assault
gestandan mæssan 16.02.04.07.04.01 The service of the mass
gestandan mid miclum welum 08.01.01.03.08 Happiness, well-being, prosperity
standende 01.01.03.01 Body of water; 12.06.03.02 Living, dwelling, residence (in)
stāndenu 01.01.02.01.03.03 Valley
stānfæt 04.01.02.02.06.05 Vessel/utensil/cup; 13.02.08.04.03.01.02 Sheath for sword
stānfāh 04.05.02.10 Flooring, a floor
stānflōr 04.05.02.10 Flooring, a floor
stānford 05.12.01.03.03 A fordable place
stāngaderung 04.05.02.02 A wall
stāngeat 01.01.02.01.02.02.05 Crag, rock, stone; 05.10.03 A gap, cleft
stāngedelf 17.04.01 Sources of materials
stāngefeall 01.01.02.01.02.01 Rising ground, eminence
stāngefōg 04.05.01.01 Masonry, building in stone
stāngella 02.06.08.07 Exotic bird
stāngetimbre 04.05.01.01 Masonry, building in stone
stān(ge)weorc 04.05.01.01 Masonry, building in stone
stāngræf 17.04.01 Sources of materials
stāngripe 03.03.04.01.02.01 A heap, mass, accumulation

1339

stānhege 04.05.02.02 A wall
stānhenge 04.05.02.04 A column, pillar
stānhlinc 01.01.02.01.02.01 Rising ground, eminence
stānhliþ 01.01.02.01.02.02.04 Cliff; 04.05.02 A building, edifice, structure
stānhof 04.05.02 A building, edifice, structure
stānhol 01.01.02.01.03.01 Cave
stānhricg 01.01.02.01.02.01 Rising ground, eminence
stānhȳpe 01.01.02.01.02.01 Rising ground, eminence
stānhȳwet 17.04.01 Sources of materials
stānig 01.01.02.01 Ground; 01.01.02.02.01 Rock, stone
stāniht 01.01.02.01 Ground; 01.01.02.02.01 Rock, stone
stānincel 01.01.02.02.01 Rock, stone
stānlesung 04.05.01.01 Masonry, building in stone
stānlīm 04.05.01.03 Gypsum, chalk
stānmerce 02.07.10.01 Particular herbs/spices (alphabetical order)
stānrocc 01.01.02.01.02.02.05 Crag, rock, stone; 04.05.02.04 A column, pillar
stānscalu 01.01.02.02.02.02 Clay, loam
stānscræf 01.01.02.01.03.01 Cave
stānscylf 01.01.02.01.02.02.04 Cliff
stānscylig 01.01.02.01 Ground; 01.01.02.02.02.02 Clay, loam
stānsticce 03.03.07 A part, division, portion
stānstrǣt 05.12.01.03.01.03 A highway
stāntorr 01.01.02.01.02.02.05 Crag, rock, stone; 04.05.03.02.02.07 A tower
stānwalu 01.01.02.01.02.01 Rising ground, eminence
stānweall 04.05.02.02 A wall

stānweg 05.12.01.03.01.03 A highway
stānweorc 04.05.02 A building, edifice, structure
stānwong 01.01.02.01.04 Open (level) land
stānwurma 03.01.14 A colour
stānwurþung 16.02.01.06.01 Belief/practice of heathen people
stānwyrht 04.05.02 A building, edifice, structure
stānwyrhta 04.05.01.01 Masonry, building in stone; 17.02.04.02.01 Cutting, hewing, shaping
stapa 02.06.09.02.05 Cricket, grasshopper, locust
stapel(a) 04.05.01.02.06 A log, stake, etc.
stapol 04.05.02.04 A column, pillar; 04.05.02.11 A staircase
stapolweg 05.12.01.03.01.03 A highway
(ge)starian (on, tō) 02.05.09.04 To see, look upon, behold
staþol 01.02 Firmament; 04.02 Farm; 04.02.03.04 Grassland; 04.05.02.01 A foundation; 05.10.04 Place, room; 05.12.04.01 Stability, firmness; 05.13.06.01 Firm, stable, steady
staþolǣht 15.01.01 Landed property
staþolfæst 05.12.04.01 Stability, firmness; 06.02.07.02 Constancy
gestaþolfæst(i)an 05.10.04.03 Presence; 05.12.04.01 Stability, firmness; 05.13.06.01 Firm, stable, steady
staþolfæstlic 05.13.06.01 Firm, stable, steady
staþolfæstlīce 05.12.04.01 Stability, firmness; 06.02.07.02 Constancy
staþolfæstnes 05.12.04.01 Stability, firmness; 06.02.07.02 Constancy
gestaþolfæst(n)ian 11.01.05.01 Furtherance, making effectual

gestaþolfæstnian 11.10 Safety, safeness
staþolfæstnung 05.13.06.01 Firm, stable, steady
(ge)staþolian 04.05 Building, construction; 05.05 Constitution, founding (e.g. of world); 05.05.01 An author, source, originator; 05.13.06.01 Firm, stable, steady; 06.02.07 Will, determination, resolution; 16.01.01.02.01 Creator
gestaþolian 02.08.12 Healing, curing; 03.05.01 Arranging, ordering, disposition; 05.10.04.03 Presence; 05.11.07.04.03.01 Renewal, restoration; 07 Judgement, forming of opinion; 11.01.05.01 Furtherance, making effectual; 13.02.04 Defence, guard, protection
gestaþoliend 05.05.01 An author, source, originator
staþolnes 01.02 Firmament
staþolung 05.13.06.01 Firm, stable, steady
(ge)staþolung 03.05.01 Arranging, ordering, disposition
staþolwang 12.06.03 A site, settlement
gesteal 05.10.06 Form, shape
stealc 01.01.02.01.02.02.04 Cliff
stealcung 11.09.01 Stealthiness, a stealthy act
gesteald 04.05.03 A dwelling-place, abode, habitation
stealdan 10 Having, owning, possession
steall 01.01.03.01.01.01 River; 04.02.05.03.02 A byre, stall, sty, shed; 05.10.04 Place, room; 05.10.05.04.02.04.01 Uprightness, straightness
gesteall 17.03 Implements, tools, etc.

steallere 12.01.01.05 A leader, administrator
stēam 02.04.06.06 Discharge, emanation; 03.01.15 Vapour, air
stēap 01.01.02.01.02.02.02 Mountain; 01.01.02.01.02.02.04 Cliff; 02.04.03.01.03.02 Eye; 03.01.12 Brightness, light; 04.01.03.05.04.01 A flask, flagon, bottle; 05.10.05.03.03 Height, loftiness, sublimity; 05.10.06.03 Projection, head, extremity (of anything)
stēapheah 05.10.05.03.03 Height, loftiness, sublimity
stearc 01.01.03.04 Current, rush of water; 01.03.01.03 Bad weather; 03.01.03.02 Strength, power; 05.08.02 Violence, force; 06.02.07.01 Strength, fortitude; 06.02.07.04 Obstinacy; 08.01.03.09.10 Wrath, sternness, displeasure; 11.11.01 A physical difficulty, strait; 12.08.03.02 Strictness, austerity, severity
stearcferþ 08.01.03.09.10 Wrath, sternness, displeasure
stearcheard 05.08.02 Violence, force
stearcheort 06.02.07.06.02 Boldness
stearcian 03.01.03 Hardness, callosity, hard material
stearclīce 05.08.02 Violence, force; 12.08.03.02 Strictness, austerity, severity
stearcmōd 06.02.07.04 Obstinacy
stearn 02.06.08.06 Water bird
steartlian 05.06.09.02 Act of kicking
stēda 02.06.02.01.06 Horse; 02.06.04.01.02 Camel
stede 02.04.03 Part of body; 02.08.08.12 Disease of bowels; 05.02 State, condition; 05.10.04 Place, room; 05.10.04.01 Position, stance; 05.12.04

stedefæst

Absence of movement, stillness; 05.13.06 Constancy, unchangeableness; 11.02 Occupation, activity, business; 12.01.01.06 Condition, rank, standing
stedefæst 06.02.07 Will, determination, resolution
stedefæstnes 06.02.07.02 Constancy
stedeheard 03.01.03 Hardness, callosity, hard material; 13.02.08.04.03 A sword
stedelēas 05.12.04.01.01 Unstable
stedenægel 02.06.01.06 Skin, hide
stedewang 01.01.02.01.04 Open (level) land
stedewist 06.02.07.02 Constancy
gestēdhors 02.06.02.01.06 Horse
stedig 02.01.03.02 Barrenness, sterility
gestedigan 05.12.04 Absence of movement, stillness
stedignes 06.01.05.03.01 Mental inertness
stedinglīne 05.12.01.09.03.01.03 Part of ship
stefn 02.05.10.01 Thing heard; 02.05.10.13 Sound of bell/musical instrument; 02.05.10.15 Voice, cry (of living creature); 02.07.03.03.01 Wood (as substance); 05.11.02 A time, particular time, occasion; 05.12.01.09.03.01.03 Part of ship; 05.13.06.01 Firm, stable, steady; 09 Speech, vocal utterance; 09.03.02.02.01.05 Minor parts of speech, etc.; 13.02.09.01 Military service; 13.02.10.01.02.02 Armed forces; 18.02.07.02 A musical instrument
stefna 05.12.01.09.03.01.03 Part of ship
stefnan 05.13.03 Regular alternation; 12.03.01.01 Control, direction, regulation

gestefnan 05.05 Constitution, founding (e.g. of world); 16.01.01.02.01 Creator
stefnbyrd 12.03.01.01 Control, direction, regulation
stefne lof 16.02.04 Worship, honour, praise
(ge)stefned 04.04.09 A fringe, border, hem
stefnettan 06.02.07 Will, determination, resolution
stefnhlōw 09 Speech, vocal utterance
stefnian 14.03.03.01 Accusation
gestefnian 12.03.03.01 Summons, a call, summoning
stefning 04.04.09 A fringe, border, hem; 13.02.09.01 Military service
stefnmǣlum 05.13.03 Regular alternation
stela 02.07.02.03 A stalk, stem; 05.10.05.04.02.04.02 Support, maintenance
(ge)stelan 14.02.01.02 Wrongful taking, theft
gestelled bēon/wesan mid 02.08.02.01.01 An infectious disease
stelmēle 04.01.03.05.04 Drinking vessel
stempan 17.03.04 Tools for smoothing/scraping/grinding
stempingīsern 17.03.06 Tools for marking
gesten 02.05.10.15.03 Groaning
stenan 02.05.10.15.03 Groaning
stenc 02.05.08 Faculty of smell; 02.05.08.01 Foul smell, stench, stink; 02.05.08.02 Pleasant smell, fragrance, perfume
(ge)stenc 02.05.08 Faculty of smell
stencan 02.05.08.01 Foul smell, stench, stink; 04.02.04.02.03 Sowing

1342

stencbǣre 02.05.08.01 Foul smell, stench, stink
stencbrengende 02.05.08.02 Pleasant smell, fragrance, perfume
gestence 02.05.08.02 Pleasant smell, fragrance, perfume
stencfæt 02.05.08.02 Pleasant smell, fragrance, perfume
(ge)stencnes 02.05.08 Faculty of smell
stenecian 02.04.06.07.05 To breathe
steng 04.05.01.02.06 A log, stake, etc.; 13.02.08.04 Weapons, arms; 17.03.10.01 A bolt, lock, bar
stenian 02.04.06.07.05 To breathe
stēopbearn 02.03.02.02 Child, offspring
stēopcild 02.03.02.02 Child, offspring; 12.04.04 Solitude
stēopdohtor 02.03.02.03.06.02.05 Step relationships
stēopfæder 02.03.02.03.06.02.05 Step relationships
stēopmōdor 02.03.02.03.06.02.05 Step relationships
stēopsunu 02.03.02.03.06.02.05 Step relationships
stēor 02.06.02.01.03 Cattle; 12.03 Direction, guidance; 12.05.06.01 Restraint, check, curb, control; 14.05.01 Correction, discipline; 14.05.04 A penalty, punishment; 14.05.04.01 A fine
stēora 05.12.01.09.03 A voyage; 12.03 Direction, guidance
(ge)stēoran/(ge)stīeran 11.11.03 Impeding of progress, prevention
steorbǣre 01.02.01.01.02 Star
stēorbord 05.12.01.09.03.01.03 Part of ship
stēordalc 05.12.01.09.03.01.03 Part of ship
stēor(e) 14.01.06 A rule, order, precept, tenet, principle
stēorend 12.03 Direction, guidance; 14.05.01 Correction, discipline
stēorere 05.12.01.09.03 A voyage
stēoresmann 05.12.01.09.03 A voyage
steorf 04.02.03.04.02.01 Types of pasture
steorfa 02.06.01.01 Flesh of dead animal; 02.08.10.03.01 Plague, pestilence
steorfan 02.02.03 To die, perish
steorglēaw 06.01.06.02.02.01 Learning, science (secular knowledge); 16.01.04.06.01 Astrology
stēorlēas 06.01.06.04.02 Ignorance, uninstructedness; 11.12.01 Absence of restraint, freedom; 12.01.01.12.02 Disobedience; 12.08.06.01.02 Lacking moral good
stēorlēaslic 12.01.01.12.02 Disobedience
stēormann 05.12.01.09.03 A voyage
stēornægl 05.12.01.09.03.01.03 Part of ship
steornede 02.06.01.02 Head
stēoroxa 02.06.02.01.03 Cattle
steorra 01.02.01.01.02 Star
steorrēonung 16.01.04.06.01 Astrology
stēorrēþra 05.12.01.09.03 A voyage
stēorrōþor 05.12.01.09.03.01.03 Part of ship; 12.03 Direction, guidance
steorscēawere 16.01.04.06.01 Astrology
stēorscofel 05.12.01.09.03.01.03 Part of ship
stēorsetl 05.12.01.09.03.01.03 Part of ship
stēorsprǣc 07.05.01 Censure, reproof, rebuke
stēorstefn 05.12.01.09.03.01.03 Part of ship

steort 01.01.02.01.01.03.01 Promontory, headland, cape; 02.06.01.05 Tail; 04.02.04.06.07 Ploughing equipment
stēorweorþ/stēorwierþe 12.08.09.01 Blameableness, blameworthiness
steorwigle 16.01.04.06.01 Astrology
steorwiglere 16.01.04.06.01 Astrology
steorwiglung 16.01.04.06.01 Astrology
stēpan 07.08.06 Exaltation
(ge)stēpan 04.05 Building, construction; 05.05.01 An author, source, originator
gestēpan 11.12.02 Aid, help, succour
stēran 02.05.08.02 Pleasant smell, fragrance, perfume; 02.08.12.02.05.04 To cleanse, clean away; 16.02.04.18.02 Burning of incense
stercedferhþ 06.02.07.06.02 Boldness; 08.01.03.09.11 Hardheartedness, cruelty, severity
stēring 16.02.05.09.02 Incense
stermelda 14.03.03.01 Accusation
sticādl 02.08.07.07 Disorders of the body
sticca 03.03.01.02 Dry measures; 04.01.02.02.06.05.05 Ladle/scoop; 17.03.10.02 A pin, peg, nail; 17.03.11 Other implements, etc.
sticce 03.01.17 Thickness, viscosity
stice 05.06.07 Pricking, a prick, puncture
(ge)stice 02.08.03 Pain, bodily discomfort
sticel 05.10.06.03.01 A point, spike, prickle
sticels 05.10.06.03.01 A point, spike, prickle; 06.02.06.03.03 Incitement
sticel(s) 04.02.05.05.01 A goad
sticfōdder 17.03.12.01 A basket
stician 02.02.04.03 To kill, slay; 05.10.04 Place, room; 05.10.06.03 Projection, head, extremity (of anything); 05.13.06 Constancy, unchangeableness; 11.11.03 Impeding of progress, prevention
stician on 05.02.02 Nature, established order of things; 11.09.01.01 Ambush, lying in wait
stician (on) 02.08.11.02.01.01 Paroxysm of madness, folly
stician ūt 05.06.08 A plucking, taking away
(ge)stician 05.06.07 Pricking, a prick, puncture
sticol 01.01.02.01.02.02.02 Mountain; 02.05.07.01 Strong taste, acidity, pungency; 03.01.05 Roughness; 05.10.05.03.03 Height, loftiness, sublimity; 11.11.01 A physical difficulty, strait
sticolnes 05.10.05.03.03 Height, loftiness, sublimity
stictǣnel 17.03.12.01 A basket
sticung 02.02.04.04.04 To slaughter (an animal); 05.06.07 Pricking, a prick, puncture
sticwærc 02.08.07.07 Disorders of the body
sticwyrt 02.07.11 Plants/flowers (alphabetical order)
stiell 05.12.05.12.01 To reach up
stiellan 04.02.05.03.02 A byre, stall, sty, shed
(ge)stiellan 05.12.03.01.01 Quick movement or movements; 05.12.05.12.01 To reach up
stīeman 03.01.09.02.01.04 Smoke
stīeme 02.07.11.02 Unidentified plants (alphabetical order)
stīemende 02.05.08.02 Pleasant smell, fragrance, perfume
stīeming 02.05.08.02 Pleasant smell, fragrance, perfume

stīeran 05.12.01.09 To travel on water; 12.03.06 Prohibition
(ge)stīeran 07.05.01 Censure, reproof, rebuke; 12.03 Direction, guidance; 12.08.02.02.01 Reform, correction; 14.05.01 Correction, discipline
stīernes 14.05.01 Correction, discipline
stīf 03.01.03.01 Stiffness, hardness; 03.01.03.02 Strength, power; 06.02.07 Will, determination, resolution
stīfearh 02.06.02.01.07 Pig, swine
stīfian 02.08.02 Disease, infirmity, sickness
stificweg 05.12.01.03.01.05 Types of road/path
stīfig 01.01.02.01.02.02.04 Cliff
stig 04.02.05.03.02 A byre, stall, sty, shed; 04.05.03.02.02.06.01 A hall building
stīg 05.12.01.03.01.01 A path, track
stīga 05.12.01.03.01.01 A path, track
stīgan 11.03.02 Advancement, progress
stīgan on scip 05.12.01.09 To travel on water
(ge)stīgan 05.12.01 To go, progress, travel (usually on land); 05.12.05.12 To go up, ascend
(ge)stīgan (ādūne/niþer) 05.12.05.13 To go down, descend
(ge)stīgan (ūp) 05.12.05.12 To go up, ascend
gestīgan 05.12.05.02.03 To arrive; 05.12.05.13 To go down, descend
stige 05.12.05.12 To go up, ascend; 05.12.05.13 To go down, descend
stigel 05.10.05.04.14.02 An opening/space in an enclosure
stigelhamm 05.10.05.04.11 A circle, circuit, circumference

stīgend 02.08.07.02 Disorders of the eye; 05.12.01.05 To ride (on horse, etc.); 05.12.01.09.03 A voyage
stigian 04.02.05.03.02 A byre, stall, sty, shed
stīgnes 05.12.05.13 To go down, descend
stigrāp 04.02.05.06.05.03.08 A stirrup
gestiht 12.03.01.01 Control, direction, regulation
stihtan 06.02.06.03.02 Instigation; 12.01.01.01 Rule, domination, direction
(ge)stihtan 12.03.01.01 Control, direction, regulation
gestihtan 06.02.06.02 A proposal, proposition, suggestion; 06.02.06.02.01 To devise a plan, arrange, settle; 14.01.06 A rule, order, precept, tenet, principle
stihtend 12.03 Direction, guidance
stihtere 12.03 Direction, guidance; 15.01.03 Treasure, riches, wealth
(ge)stihtung 12.03.01.01 Control, direction, regulation
stillan 02.05.10.17 Absence of noise or disturbance
(ge)stillan 05.09.03 Mitigation, lightening, alleviation; 05.09.04 Abatement, reduction, checking; 05.12.04 Absence of movement, stillness
gestillan 02.05.10.17 Absence of noise or disturbance; 05.07 Ending of existence, end of world; 08.01.01.02.01 Want of interest or concern, indifference; 09.02 Silence, refraining from speech; 11.11.03 Impeding of progress, prevention; 12.05.06.01 Restraint, check, curb, control

stille 02.05.10.16 Quiet, soft, faint; 02.05.10.17 Absence of noise or disturbance; 03.01.17 Thickness, viscosity; 05.12.04 Absence of movement, stillness; 05.13.06 Constancy, unchangeableness; 08.01.02.01.02 Gentleness; 12.07.03 Abstinence/exemption (from)

stillīce 02.05.10.16 Quiet, soft, faint; 02.05.10.17 Absence of noise or disturbance; 09.02 Silence, refraining from speech

stil(l)nes 02.05.10.17 Absence of noise or disturbance

stillnes 06.02.05.03 Satisfaction, repletion

stil(l)nes 12.07.03 Abstinence/exemption (from)

stillnes 13 Peace, tranquillity

stilnes 05.12.04 Absence of movement, stillness

stincan 02.05.08 Faculty of smell; 02.05.08.01 Foul smell, stench, stink; 05.12.03.01.01 Quick movement or movements

gestincan 02.05.08 Faculty of smell

stincende 02.05.08.01 Foul smell, stench, stink

sting 02.08.03.02 Itch, irritation; 02.08.04.01 A wound

stingan on 15.01.01.01 Holding of land

(ge)stingan 05.06.07 Pricking, a prick, puncture

stint 02.06.08.06 Water bird

stīp 05.06.01 Devastation, laying waste

stīpel 04.05.03.02.02.07 A tower

stīpere 04.05.02.04 A column, pillar

stīþ 03.01.03.02 Strength, power; 03.01.17 Thickness, viscosity; 06.02.07 Will, determination, resolution; 06.02.07.04 Obstinacy; 08.01.03.09.01.03 Sharpness (of speech); 08.01.03.09.10 Wrath, sternness, displeasure; 08.01.03.09.11 Hardheartedness, cruelty, severity; 12.08.03.02 Strictness, austerity, severity

stīþe 02.07.11.02 Unidentified plants (alphabetical order); 05.08 Strength; 08.01.03.09.10 Wrath, sternness, displeasure

stīþecg 13.02.08.04.03 A sword

stīþferhþ 06.02.07 Will, determination, resolution; 16.01.01.01 Attributes of God

stīþhycgende 06.02.07 Will, determination, resolution; 06.02.07.04 Obstinacy; 08.01.03.09.10 Wrath, sternness, displeasure

stīþhȳdig 06.02.07 Will, determination, resolution

stīþhygd 06.02.07 Will, determination, resolution

gestīþian 05.08 Strength

stīþlic 05.12.04.01 Stability, firmness; 08.01.03.09.01.03 Sharpness (of speech); 08.01.03.09.10 Wrath, sternness, displeasure; 12.08.03.02 Strictness, austerity, severity

stīþlīce 03.06.03.02 Order, decorum, discretion; 05.08.02 Violence, force; 08.01.03.09.10 Wrath, sternness, displeasure; 11.02.01 Energy, vigour, vigorous action

stīþmægen 12 Power, might

stīþmōd 06.02.07 Will, determination, resolution; 06.02.07.04 Obstinacy; 08.01.03.09.11 Hardheartedness, cruelty, severity; 16.01.01.01 Attributes of God

stīþnes 03.01.03.01 Stiffness, hardness; 06.02.07.02 Constancy; 12.08.03.02 Strictness, austerity, severity
gestīþod bēon/wesan 02.01.04.02 To grow, grow up
stīþweg 05.12.01.03.01 A means of access
stīweard 11.10.02.02 Watchful care, keeping guard; 12.01.01.08.01 A servant, attendant
stīwita 04.05.03.02 A human habitation
stoc 04.05.03.02.01 A building, house, hall, palace, etc.; 16.02.01.06.01.01.01 An image, idol
stocc 14.05.07 Binding, fastening with bonds; 17.03.09 A post, rod, stick, etc.; 18.02.07.02.02.02 A trumpet
stoccen 04.05.01.02.06 A log, stake, etc.
stoccett 01.01.02.01.01 Tract of land
stoccgemǣre 05.10.05.04.11.01 A bound, limit
stocett 04.02.03.01.02 Cleared land
stoclīf 12.06.02.01 A township
stocweard 02.03.03.04.05 Populace of a town/city
stocwīc 04.05.03 A dwelling-place, abode, habitation
stod 04.05.02.04 A column, pillar
stōd 02.06.02.01.06 Horse; 04.02.05.06.05 Stud/herd of horses
stōdfald 04.02.05.06.05.02 A paddock
stōdhors 02.06.02.01.06 Horse
stodla 04.04.03 A spinning-house or chamber
stōdmyre 02.06.02.01.06 Horse
stōdþēof 14.02.01.02 Wrongful taking, theft
stofa 04.06.01.02 A bathing place
stofbæþ 04.06.01.03 A bath

stofn 02.01.03.03.04 Offspring, race, breed, family, children; 02.07.02.05 A shoot, sprout, tendril; 02.07.03.03.01 Wood (as substance); 05.13.06.01 Firm, stable, steady
stōl 04.05.04.01 A bench, seat; 12.01.01.02 Seat of authority; 16.02.03.02.05 A bishop
stole 04.04.07.07 A long outer garment, covering, cloak, etc.
stōpel 05.12.01.04.01 Manner of going, gait
stoppa 04.01.03.05.04.03 A bucket, pail
stōr 05.08.02.01 (Of living creatures) fierceness, roughness; 16.02.05.09.02 Incense
storc 02.06.08.06 Water bird
storcille 16.02.05.05.07 A thurible, censer
storfæt 16.02.05.05.07 A thurible, censer
storm 01.03.01.03.01 Storm, tempest; 02.05.10.03 Noise, tumult, uproar; 05.08.02 Violence, force; 13.02.03.01 An attack, assault; 13.02.08.04.04.01 An arrow, dart, bolt
stormig 01.03.01.03.01 Storm, tempest
stormsǣ 01.01.03.01.02.04 State of sea
storsæp 03.01.17.06 Resin, tar, gum
storsticca 16.02.05.05.07 A thurible, censer
stot 02.06.02.01.06 Horse
stōw 03.05.02 An arrangement, order, succession; 04.05.03 A dwelling-place, abode, habitation; 05.02.01.01 The course of human affairs; 05.10.04 Place, room; 09.03.07.07.02.01.04 A passage in a book; 16.02.05.02 A holy place or sanctuary
stōwigian 12.05.06.01 Restraint, check, curb, control

stōwlic 05.10.04 Place, room;
  09.03.02.03.01.01.01 Case
stōwlīce 05.10.04 Place, room
straca 01.01.02.01.01 Tract of land
strācian 02.05.06.02 Stroking, caressing
strācung 02.05.06.02 Stroking, caressing
stræc 05.08.02 Violence, force;
  06.02.07.04.01 Obduracy; 12.08.03.02 Strictness, austerity, severity
stræclic 12.08.03.02 Strictness, austerity, severity
stræclīce 05.08.02 Violence, force;
  08.01.03.09.10 Wrath, sternness, displeasure
stræcnes 06.02.07.03 Perseverance;
  06.02.07.04.01 Obduracy;
  08.01.03.07.04 Severity, harshness
stræde 05.10.05.03 A measure of distance
strægdnes 03.01.16.05 A sprinkling
stræl 04.05.04.05.01 Bedding (e.g. of straw); 13.02.08.04.04.01 An arrow, dart, bolt
strælbora 13.02.10.01.02 An armed man
strælian 13.02.08.04.04.01 An arrow, dart, bolt
st(r)ælwyrt 02.07.11.02 Unidentified plants (alphabetical order)
strǣt 05.12.01.03.01 A means of access;
  05.12.01.03.01.03 A highway
strǣtlanu 05.12.01.03.01.04 A lane, street
strǣtweard 17.02.04.01 Repairing, renewing
strand 01.01.02.01.01.03 Shore, bank
strang 01.01.03.04 Current, rush of water; 05.08.01 Vigour, activity, force;
  05.08.02.01 (Of living creatures) fierceness, roughness; 05.12.04.01 Stability, firmness; 06.01.07.07.03 Certainty; 06.02.07 Will, determination, resolution;
  08.01.01.01.04 Depth of feeling, zeal;
  08.01.03.09.10 Wrath, sternness, displeasure; 12 Power, might
strange 01.01.03.01.02.04 State of sea;
  08.01.03.09.10 Wrath, sternness, displeasure
stranghynde 05.08 Strength
strangian 05.08.01 Vigour, activity, force; 12.05.06 Grasp, power, control, mastery
(ge)strangian 05.08 Strength;
  06.02.07.01 Strength, fortitude
gestrangian 02.08.12 Healing, curing;
  05.11.09.02 Frequent, of common occurrence; 12 Power, might; 13.02.06 A fortification
stranglic 05.08 Strength; 05.08.01 Vigour, activity, force; 05.12.04.01 Stability, firmness; 08.01.03.09.10 Wrath, sternness, displeasure
stranglīce 05.08 Strength; 05.08.01 Vigour, activity, force; 05.08.02 Violence, force; 06.02.07.01 Strength, fortitude; 06.02.07.06 Courage, boldness, valour; 08.01.03.09.10 Wrath, sternness, displeasure
strangmōd 06.02.07 Will, determination, resolution
strangnes 05.08.02 Violence, force;
  06.02.07.01 Strength, fortitude
strangung 02.01.02 Gift of life;
  04.01.02.04.03 Feeding, nourishing;
  05.08.01 Vigour, activity, force;
  11.12.02.01 Strengthening, confirmation
(ge)strangung 05.08 Strength
strapulas 04.04.07.09 Breeches
strēam 01.01.03.01.01.01 River

strēamas 01.01.03 Water; 01.01.03.01.02 Sea/ocean
strēamfaru 01.01.03.04 Current, rush of water
strēamgewinn 01.01.03.01.02.06 Surging, rolling, heaving of waves
strēamlic 03.01.16.02 Water, liquid
strēamracu 01.01.03.01.01.04 Watercourse/channel
strēamrād 01.01.03.01.02.01 Region of sea/ocean
strēamrynes 01.01.03.03 Flow/flowing
strēamstæþ 01.01.02.01.01.03 Shore, bank
strēamweall 01.01.02.01.01.03 Shore, bank
strēamwelm 01.01.03.01.02.06 Surging, rolling, heaving of waves
strēaw 04.01.02.01.04 Animal food, fodder; 04.02.04.03.02.03 Hay
strēawberian wīse 02.07.09.02 Particular fruits (alphabetical order)
strēawberige 02.07.09.02 Particular fruits (alphabetical order)
strecca 01.01.02.01.01 Tract of land
streccan 05.10.05.02 Extension, stretching
(ge)streccan 05.10.05.04.12 The condition of being covered; 05.12.05.13.02 To bow, bend down
streccanmōd 06.02.07.03 Perseverance
streccednes 04.05.04.05 A bed, bedstead
(ge)strēgan 05.12.02.07.01 To throw, scatter
stregdan 03.01.16.05 A sprinkling; 05.10.04.04.01 Dispersion
(ge)stregdan 05.12.02.07.01 To throw, scatter
gestregdan 04.01.02.02.04 To season; 04.05.04.05.01 Bedding (e.g. of straw)
gestreht 04.05.04.05.01 Bedding (e.g. of straw)
streng 02.03.02.03 Ancestry, descent; 02.04.05.06 Sinew/tendon/ligament; 05.12.01.09.03.01.03 Part of ship; 13.02.08.04.04 A bow; 17.03.10 Supports and fastenings; 18.02.07.02.03 Stringed instruments
gestrengan 06.02.07.06.01 Emboldening, encouragement
strenge 08.01.03.09.10 Wrath, sternness, displeasure
gestrenged 17.02.04 Trade, calling, craft, aptitude
strengel 12.01.01.04 A leader, ruler
strenglic 05.12.04.01 Stability, firmness
strenglīce 06.02.07 Will, determination, resolution
strengþu 05.08.02 Violence, force; 12 Power, might
strengþ(u) 03.01.03.02 Strength, power; 02.01.04.02 To grow, grow up; 05.08.01 Vigour, activity, force; 06.02.07.01 Strength, fortitude; 02.08.12.02.05 Pharmacy, curing with salves
strengu 05.08 Strength; 06.01.05.02 Intelligence; 12 Power, might
(ge)strēon 02.01.03.03.01 To beget; 10.01.02 Acquisition; 15.01 Property; 15.01.03 Treasure, riches, wealth
gestrēon 14.02.01.02.01 Open robbery, rapine, pillage; 15.04.01 Lending of money; 15.05 Trade, traffic, commerce
gestrēonful 07.02.02 Good, what is beneficial, advantageous, etc.; 08.01.01.03.08 Happiness, well-being, prosperity; 15.02.01 High/steep price

strēowen 04.05.04.05 A bed, bedstead; 05.10.04 Place, room; 05.12.04 Absence of movement, stillness
strēownes 04.05.04.05.01 Bedding (e.g. of straw)
(ge)strewian 05.10.05.04.12.01 To bespread, cover with
strewung 04.05.04.05.01 Bedding (e.g. of straw)
stric 02.08.10.03.01 Plague, pestilence
gestric 12.01.01.12.03 Rebellion, sedition
strica 09.03.07 Writing
strīcan 04.06.01 Clean; 05.06.09 Act of striking; 05.12.01 To go, progress, travel (usually on land)
(ge)strīcan 02.05.06.02 Stroking, caressing
gestrīcan 09.03.07 Writing
stricel 02.04.03.03.05 Chest, breast, bosom; 02.04.06.05.06 Mammary gland, breast; 04.02.04.06.14.04 Part of a corn measure
strīchrægl 04.06.01.05 ?A cloth for wiping
gestrician 17.04.04 Fibrous materials
strīdan 05.12.01.04.01.01 To stride; 14.02.01.02.01 Open robbery, rapine, pillage
strīdan (ūp on) 05.12.01.05 To ride (on horse, etc.)
stride 05.10.05.03 A measure of distance
(ge)strīenan 02.01.03.03.01 To beget; 10.01.02 Acquisition
gestrīenan 15.01.05 Possession of wealth
gestrīenendlic 02.01.03.03.01 To beget; 09.03.02.03.01.01.01 Case
strīman 12.05.05 Resistance, repulsing
strīna 10.01.02 Acquisition
strīnend 10.01.02 Acquisition
stripligan 10.04.02.01 To pluck, gather

strīþ 09.07.01 Contention, argument, strife of words; 12.05.04.01 Fighting, contention, warfare, strife
stroccian 02.05.06.02 Stroking, caressing
gestrod 14.02.01.02 Wrongful taking, theft; 14.02.01.02.01 Open robbery, rapine, pillage; 14.05.04 A penalty, punishment
strōd 01.01.02.01.04.01 Marsh, bog, swamp
strōdett 01.01.02.01.04.01 Marsh, bog, swamp
strogdnes 03.01.16.05 A sprinkling
strop 05.12.01.09.03.01.03 Part of ship
(ge)strūdan 05.06.01 Devastation, laying waste
gestrūdan 14.02.01.02.01 Open robbery, rapine, pillage
strūdend 14.02.01.02.01 Open robbery, rapine, pillage; 15.04.01 Lending of money
strūdere 14.02.01.02.01 Open robbery, rapine, pillage
strūdgendlīce 06.02.05.02 Greed, importunate desire, rapacity
(ge)strūdian 14.02.01.02.01 Open robbery, rapine, pillage
strūdung 14.02.01.02.01 Open robbery, rapine, pillage
strump 02.07.03.03.01 Wood (as substance)
strūtian 05.10.05.04.02.04.01 Uprightness, straightness
(ge)strȳdan 14.02.01.02 Wrongful taking, theft
strȳdere 10.03.08.01 Overliberality, waste of money
gestrȳnd 02.03.03.02 A race, tribe
strȳndan 10.03.08.01 Overliberality, waste of money

stryndere 10.03.08.01 Overliberality, waste of money
gestrynge 18.02.03.01 A combatant, athlete
strȳta 02.06.08.07 Exotic bird
stubbig 02.07.03.03.01 Wood (as substance)
stūc 03.03.04.01.02.01 A heap, mass, accumulation
stūce 02.07.03.03.01 Wood (as substance)
studdian 11.02.02.02 Care, mindfulness, attention
studding 11.02.02.02 Care, mindfulness, attention
studu 04.05.02.04 A column, pillar
stulor 11.09.01 Stealthiness, a stealthy act; 14.02.01.02 Wrongful taking, theft
stulorlīce 11.09.01 Stealthiness, a stealthy act
stumbel 02.07.03.03.01 Wood (as substance)
stumblett 01.01.02.01.01 Tract of land; 04.02.03.01.02 Cleared land
gestun 01.03.01.03.01 Storm, tempest; 02.05.10.07 A crashing, noise
stund 02.05.10.12 An audible signal; 05.11.02 A time, particular time, occasion; 08.01.03.06 Adversity, affliction
stunde 05.11.07.01 Contemporary, coeval
stundmǣlum 03.03.07 A part, division, portion; 05.11.09.03 At times, sometimes; 05.12.03.02 Slowness
stundum 03.03.05 Extent, degree; 05.08.02 Violence, force; 05.11.09.03 At times, sometimes; 08.01.01.01.04 Depth of feeling, zeal; 17.01 Strenuous effort, hard work

stunian 02.05.10.07 A crashing, noise; 05.12.02.06.01 To push, drive
stunt 06.01.05.03.01.01 Dullness, folly, stupidity
stuntlic 06.01.05.03.02 Foolish, silly, stupid
stuntlīce 06.01.05.03.01.01 Dullness, folly, stupidity
stuntnes 06.01.05.03.01.01 Dullness, folly, stupidity
stuntscipe 06.01.05.03.01.01 Dullness, folly, stupidity
stuntsprǣc 06.01.05.03.02 Foolish, silly, stupid
stuntsprǣce 06.01.05.03.02 Foolish, silly, stupid
stuntwyrde 06.01.05.03.02 Foolish, silly, stupid
stūpian 05.10.05.04.04 A descent, slope, incline; 05.12.05.13.02 To bow, bend down
stūt 01.01.02.01.02.01 Rising ground, eminence; 02.06.09.02.08 Gnat, midge
stuþansceaft 04.05.02.04 A column, pillar
stybb 02.07.03.03.01 Wood (as substance)
stycce 03.03.07 A part, division, portion; 05.11.01.02 Shortness/brevity in time; 15.01.04 Coinage, money
styccemǣlum 03.03.07 A part, division, portion; 05.10.04.03 Presence; 05.12.03.02 Slowness
stȳcing 04.02.03.01.02 Cleared land
styfic 02.07.03.03.01 Wood (as substance)
styfician 05.06.08 A plucking, taking away
styficlēah 04.02.03.01.02 Cleared land
styficung 04.02.03.01.02 Cleared land
stȳle 17.04.02.05 Iron

stȳlecg 13.02.08.04.03 A sword
stȳled 13.02.08.04.03 A sword
stȳlen 17.04.02.05 Iron
(ge)styltan 06.01.08.05.01 Amazement, astonishment, wonder, admiration
stynt 05.10.05.04.11.01 A bound, limit
styntan 06.01.05.03.01 Mental inertness
gestyntan 05.09.01 Slow, inactive
gestynþo 12.05.06.02 Oppression
styrenes 01.01.03.01.01 Moving water; 05.08.02 Violence, force; 05.12 To move, be in motion; 05.12.02 To move, set in motion
(ge)styrenes 08.01.03.07.02 Misery, trouble, affliction
styrfig 02.02.03.02 State of being dead
styrian 02.05.10.01 Thing heard; 05.12 To move, be in motion; 09.03.04 Rhetoric, art of exposition; 18.02.07.02.03.01 A harp, lyre
(ge)styrian 05.12.02 To move, set in motion; 06.02.06.03.03 Incitement; 08.01.01.01.03 An incitement, cause of strong feeling
gestyrian 05.10.04.04.02 Removal, taking away
styri(g)a 02.06.06.03.01.13 Sturgeon
styrigendlic 05.12 To move, be in motion
styrman 01.03.01.03.01 Storm, tempest; 02.05.10.15.01 To raise (the voice), raise up (noise)
styrne 08.01.03.09.10 Wrath, sternness, displeasure
styrnenga 08.01.03.09.10 Wrath, sternness, displeasure
styrnlic 01.03.01.03 Bad weather; 08.01.03.09.10 Wrath, sternness, displeasure
styrnlīce 06.02.07.04.01 Obduracy; 08.01.03.09.10 Wrath, sternness, displeasure
styrnmōd 06.02.07 Will, determination, resolution
styrtan 05.12.05.12.01 To reach up
styrung 05.08.02 Violence, force; 05.12 To move, be in motion; 05.12.02 To move, set in motion; 05.12.05.05 To shake, quake, wag; 08.01.01 A feeling, what is felt; 08.01.03.07.02 Misery, trouble, affliction; 11.01.01 Practice, exercise, doing
sū/sugu 02.06.02.01.07 Pig, swine
subdīacon 16.02.03.02.11 A deacon, minister of the church
sūcan 04.01.01.02 Act/action of sucking; 05.12.05.03.04.02 To flow out, well up, erupt
succa 02.06.08.05 Forest bird, wild-fowl
sūcende 04.01.01.02 Act/action of sucking
sucga 01.01.02.01.04.01 Marsh, bog, swamp
sufel 04.01.02.01.05.05.07 Relish taken with bread
gesufel 04.01.02.02.04.07 Provided with a relish
suflmete 04.01.02.01.07.05 Delicacy/dainty/titbit
sūgan 02.08.08.04.02 (Of stomach) disordered; 04.01.01.02 Act/action of sucking; 05.12.05.03.04.02 To flow out, well up, erupt
sugesweard 02.08.06 Skin disease, erysipelas
sugga 02.06.08.05 Forest bird, wild-fowl
gesugian 09.02 Silence, refraining from speech
suht 02.08.02 Disease, infirmity, sickness
suhterga 02.03.02.03.06.02.03 Child of brother/sister

suhtergefæderan 02.03.02.03.06.02.03 Child of brother/sister
suhtorfædran 02.03.02.03.06.02.03 Child of brother/sister
sūlerēost 04.02.04.06.07 Ploughing equipment
sulh 04.02.03.03 A measure of land; 05.12.01.03.01.02 A cutting, pass
sulh/sūl 04.02.04.06.07 Ploughing equipment
sulhæcer 04.02.03.02.01 A strip for ploughing
sulhælmesse 16.02.04.20 Church due/requirement
sūlhandla 04.02.04.06.07 Ploughing equipment
sulhbēam 04.02.04.06.07 Ploughing equipment
sulhgang 04.02.03.03.01 A ploughland
sulhgesīdu 04.02.04.06.07 Ploughing equipment
sulhgetēog 04.02.04.06.07 Ploughing equipment
sulhgeweorc 04.02.04.06.07 Ploughing equipment
sulhhæbbere 04.02.04.02.02.02 Ploughing, tilling
sulhhandla 04.02.04.02.02.02 Ploughing, tilling
sulhmann 04.02.04.02.02.02 Ploughing, tilling
sulig 04.02.05.06.04.01 A piggery
sūlincel 04.02.03.02.01.01 A furrow
sūlung 12.06.02 District, province
sum 03 Material, matter, substance; 03.03.07 A part, division, portion; 03.04.01 Singularity, peculiarity; 03.04.03.01 Someone/something; 03.06 Comparison
sum dǣl 03.03.07 A part, division, portion
sum on dǣle 03.03.04.04 Littleness, smallness
sumdǣl 03.03.04.04 Littleness, smallness
sume dæge 05.11.02 A time, particular time, occasion
sume dǣle 03.03.04.04 Littleness, smallness; 03.03.07 A part, division, portion
sumerbōc 16.02.05.10.02 A lectionary
sumerrǣdingbōc 16.02.05.10.02 A lectionary
sumes 03.03.04.04 Littleness, smallness
sumhwænne 05.11.02 A time, particular time, occasion
sumhwilc 03.04.01 Singularity, peculiarity
sūmnes 05.11.08.01.03.01 Delay
sumor 05.11.03.01.02.02 Summer
sumorhǣte 01.03.01.01 Hot, fine weather
sumorhāt 01.03.01.01 Hot, fine weather
sumorhūs 04.05.03.02.02 Types of dwelling
sumorlǣcan 05.11.03.01.02.02 Summer
sumorlang 05.11.03.01.02.02 Summer
sumorlic 05.11.03.01.02.02 Summer
sumorlida 13.02.10.01.02.02.01 Types of army
sumorloda 02.07.02.05 A shoot, sprout, tendril
sumormæsse 05.11.03.01.02.02 Summer; 16.02.04.07.04.01 The service of the mass
sumorselde 04.05.03.02.02 Types of dwelling
sumorswegel 01.03.01.01 Hot, fine weather
sumpt 01.01.02.01.04.01 Marsh, bog, swamp
sumsende 01.03.01.06.02 Rain

sunbēam 01.03.01.01 Hot, fine weather
sunbearu 02.07.03.04.01 A small wood, coppice, copse
sunbeorht 03.01.12 Brightness, light
sunboga 01.02.01.01.03 Sun
sunbryne 02.08.10.02 Sunstroke
sund 01.01.03 Water; 01.01.03.01.02 Sea/ocean; 05.12.01.08.01 To swim
gesund 02.08.01 Sound physical condition; 07.02.03.01 Uninjured, unhurt, unharmed; 08.01.01.03.08.03 A favour, blessing; 11.10 Safety, safeness; 12.08.02 Integrity, absence of moral flaw
gesund bēon/wesan 11.05.02.02.01 Greetings, courteous terms of address
gesund faran 11.05.02.02.01.03 To bid farewell
sundampre 02.07.11 Plants/flowers (alphabetical order)
sundbūende 02.03.03.04.02 Dwellers by the sea
sundcorn 02.07.11 Plants/flowers (alphabetical order)
sunddēaw 02.07.10.01 Particular herbs/spices (alphabetical order)
sunderanweald 12.01.01 Authority
sunderboren 02.03.02.02.05 Having the same parents; 03.03.07.01 Division, partition, separation
sunderfolgoþ 17.02.02 An office, function, employment
sunderfrēodōm 14.01.03 Special law, privilege, law for an individual
sunderfrēols 14.01.03 Special law, privilege, law for an individual
sundermǣd 04.02.03.04.01 Meadow land/meadow
gesundful 02.08.01 Sound physical condition; 07.02.03 Perfection; 08.01.01.03.08.02 Good fortune, success
(ge)sundfullian 08.01.01.03.08 Happiness, well-being, prosperity
gesundfullic 12.08.02 Integrity, absence of moral flaw
gesundfullīce 08.01.01.03.08 Happiness, well-being, prosperity; 11.10 Safety, safeness
(ge)sundfulnes 02.08.01 Sound physical condition; 08.01.01.03.08 Happiness, well-being, prosperity
gesundfulnes 03.03.04.02.01 Abundance
sundgebland 01.01.03.01.02.06 Surging, rolling, heaving of waves
sundgyrd 05.12.01.09.03.01.03 Part of ship
sundhelm 01.01.03.01.02 Sea/ocean
sundhengest 05.12.01.09.03.01 A ship, boat
sundhwæt 05.12.01.08.01 To swim
gesundig 05.11.08 A suitable time, opportunity
gesundig/-syndig 01.03.01.05 Wind
gesundiglic 01.03.01.05 Wind; 05.11.08 A suitable time, opportunity
gesundiglic/gesyndelic 08.01.01.03.08.03 A favour, blessing
gesundlic 02.08.01 Sound physical condition; 11.10 Safety, safeness
gesundlic/gesyndlic 08.01.01.03.08.03 A favour, blessing
gesundlīce 08.01.01.03.08 Happiness, well-being, prosperity; 11.10 Safety, safeness
sundlīne 05.12.01.09.03.01.03 Part of ship
sundmere 01.01.03.01.03.01 Pool
sundnytt 05.12.01.08.01 To swim

sundor 03.03.07.01 Division, partition, separation; 03.06.02 Difference, diversity, dissimilarity; 05.10.04.04 Absence
sundorcræft 11.04 Ability, capacity, power
sundorcræftiglīce 11.04.02 Skill, skilfulness
sundorcȳþþu 08.01.02.03 Friendliness, affection
sundorfeoh 15.01.01 Landed property
sundorgecynd 05.02.02 Nature, established order of things
sundorgenga 02.06 Animal
sundorgerēfland 12.06.02 District, province
sundorgifu 10.03.01 Grace, favour; 14.01.03 Special law, privilege, law for an individual
sundorhālga 16.02.01.09.02 Knowledge of Jewish law
sundorland 15.01.01 Landed property
sundorlic 03.04.01 Singularity, peculiarity
sundorlīce 03.03.07.01 Division, partition, separation
sundorlīf 16.02.03.03.04 A solitary (anchorite, hermit)
sundorlīpes 03.03.07.01 Division, partition, separation
sundormǣlum 03.04.01 Singularity, peculiarity
sundormæsse 16.02.04.07.04.01 The service of the mass
sundornotu 17.02.02 An office, function, employment
sundornytt 17.02.02 An office, function, employment
sundorriht 14.01.04.01 A special right, right peculiar to a class
sundorrūnung 12.02.02 An assembly, meeting
sundorsetl 12.01.01.02 Seat of authority; 16.02.05.04.02 A hermitage, hermit's cell
sundorsprǣc 09.01.04 Conversation, discussion; 12.02.02 An assembly, meeting
sundorstōw 05.10.04 Place, room
sundorweorþmynt 14.01.03 Special law, privilege, law for an individual
sundorweorþung 14.01.03 Special law, privilege, law for an individual
sundorwīc 04.05.03.02.02 Types of dwelling
sundorwine 08.01.02.03.01 An acquaintance, friend, associate
sundorwīs 06.01.05.02.01.01 Sagacity
sundorwundor 06.01.08.05.01.01.01 An exercise of power, mighty work, miracle
sundoryrfe 15.01.02.01 Inherited property
sundplega 05.12.01.08 To move in/on water
sundrāp 05.12.01.09.03.01.03 Part of ship
sundreced 05.12.01.09.03.01.01 Kind of ship
sundwudu 05.12.01.09.03.01 A ship, boat
sunfolgend 02.07.11 Plants/flowers (alphabetical order)
sunganges 01.01.01.04 West
sungīhte 05.11.06.01 Cycle of the year
sunhāt 03.01.09 Heat
sunlic 01.02.01.01.03 Sun
sunna 01.02.01.01.03 Sun
sunnan lēoma 01.03.01.01 Hot, fine weather

sunnan scīma 01.03.01.01 Hot, fine weather
sunnan setlgang 05.11.04.02.01 Sunset
sunnanǣfen 05.11.03.01.05.01 Specific days
sun(nan)corn 02.07.11 Plants/flowers (alphabetical order)
sunnandæg 05.11.03.01.05.01 Specific days; 16.02.01.08.04 Jewish seasons/feasts; 16.02.04.04.01 The day of rest, sabbath
sunnanmergen 05.11.03.01.05.01 Specific days
sunnanniht 05.11.03.01.05.01 Specific days
sunnanūhta 05.11.03.01.05.01 Specific days; 16.02.04.05.02 The hour or service of Matins
sunnhǣte 03.01.09 Heat
sunnstede 05.11.06.01 Cycle of the year
sunor 02.06.02.01.07 Pig, swine
sunsceadu 04.04.08 A covering, curtain, veil, garment, etc.
sunscīene 03.01.12 Brightness, light; 07.10 Beauty, fairness
sunscīn 02.05.09.11 Mirror
sunset 01.01.01.04 West; 01.02.01.01.03 Sun
sunsunu 02.03.02.03.05 Descendant
sunu 02.03.02.02.03 A son; 02.06 Animal; 16.01.01.04.02 The Son, Christ
sunucennicge 02.01.03.03.03.01 Child-bearing, childbirth; 02.03.02.01 Parent
sunwlitig 01.03.01.01 Hot, fine weather
sūpan 04.01.01 Eating
(ge)sūpan 04 Consumption of food/drink; 04.01.03 Drinking

sūr 02.05.07.01 Strong taste, acidity, pungency; 04.01.02.01.01.04 (Of food/wine) sharp; 04.01.02.02.04.03 Fermented/soured
sūrappuldre rind 02.07.09.02 Particular fruits (alphabetical order)
sūrapuldre 02.07.09.02 Particular fruits (alphabetical order)
sūre 02.07.11 Plants/flowers (alphabetical order)
sūrēagede 02.08.07.02 Disorders of the eye
sūrmilsc 02.05.07.03 Sweetness; 02.07.09.02 Particular fruits (alphabetical order)
sūrmilsc apulder 02.07.09.02 Particular fruits (alphabetical order)
sūrnes 02.05.07.01 Strong taste, acidity, pungency
sūsl 08.01.03.07.03 Suffering, torment, pain
sūslbana 16.01.05.02.02 Other terms for devils
sūslcwalu 02.02.01 Particular mode of death
sūslhof 16.01.05.01 Damnation, perdition, reprobation
sūslstede 16.01.05.01 Damnation, perdition, reprobation
sūtere 04.04.07.15 Footwear, covering for the feet
sūþ 01.01.01.02 South
sūþan 01.01.01.02 South
sūþanēastan 01.01.01.02.01 South-east
sūþanēastanwind 01.03.01.05.01 Winds from particular points
sūþanēasterne 01.01.01.02.01 South-east
sūþanhymbre 02.03.03.05.01.06 Mercians
sūþanwestan 01.01.01.02.02 South-west

sūþanwesterne 01.01.01.02.02 South-west
sūþanwestwind(a) 01.03.01.05.01 Winds from particular points
sūþ(an)wind 01.03.01.05.01 Winds from particular points
sūþcroft 04.02 Farm
sūþdǣl 01.01.01.02 South
sūþduru 04.05.02.12 Gate/doorway of a building
sūþēast 01.01.01.02.01 South-east
sūþēastende 01.01.01.02.01 South-east
sūþēasterne 01.01.01.02.01 South-east
sūþēasterne wind 01.03.01.05.01 Winds from particular points
sūþēasthealf 01.01.01.02.01 South-east
sūþecg 01.01.01.02 South
sūþende 01.01.01.02 South
sūþengle 02.03.03.05.01.01 Angles
sūþerige 02.07.03.05 Particular trees/shrubs (alphabetical order); 02.07.11.02 Unidentified plants (alphabetical order)
sūþerne 01.01.01.02 South; 17.02.04 Trade, calling, craft, aptitude
sūþerne wermōd 02.07.11 Plants/flowers (alphabetical order)
sūþernewudu 02.07.11 Plants/flowers (alphabetical order)
sūþeweard 01.01.01.02 South
sūþfolc 02.03.03.04 An inhabitant; 12.06.01.01 England
sūþfōr 16.02.04.11 Pilgrimage
sūþgārsecg 01.01.03.01.02.03 Sea in particular area
sūþgemǣre 05.10.05.04.11.01 A bound, limit
sūþheald 01.01.01.02 South
sūþhealf 01.01.01.02 South
sūþhymbre 02.03.03.05.01.06 Mercians
sūþland 01.01.01.02 South
sūþmǣgþ 01.01.01.02 South
sūþmann 02.03.03.04 An inhabitant
sūþmearc 05.10.05.04.11.01 A bound, limit
sūþmest 01.01.01.02 South
sūþmyrce 02.03.03.05.01.06 Mercians
sūþportic 04.05.02.12.01 A porch, covered entrance
sūþrihte 01.01.01.02 South
sūþrima 01.01.02.01.01.03 Shore, bank
sūþrodor 01.02.01 Heaven(s), sky
sūþsǣ 01.01.03.01.02.02 Sea-channel
sūþseaxe (-an) 02.03.03.05.01.10 Saxons
sūþstæþ 01.01.02.01.01.03 Shore, bank
sūþwāg 04.05.02.02 A wall
sūþweall 04.05.02.02 A wall
sūþweard 01.01.01.02 South
sūþweardes 01.01.01.02 South
sūþweg 05.12.01.03.01 A means of access
sūþwest 01.01.01.02.02 South-west
sūþwesterne 01.01.01.02.02 South-west
swā forþ swā 03.03.05 Extent, degree
swā hraþe swā 05.11.07.01 Contemporary, coeval
swā hwā (swā) 03.04 Form, kind, nature, character
swā hwæt (swā) 03.04 Form, kind, nature, character
swā hwæþer (swā) 03.06 Comparison
swā hwider ymb 05.10.04.03 Presence
swā hwilc swā 03.04 Form, kind, nature, character
swā lange (oþ) þæt 05.11.07.03.02 Earlier, antecedent
swā gelīce 03.06.01 Similitude, likeness
swā gelīc 03.06.01 Similitude, likeness
swā gelīc swā 03.06.01 Similitude, likeness

swā gerād 03.04 Form, kind, nature, character
swā same (swā) 03.06.01 Similitude, likeness
swā sweart swā col 03.01.14.04 Black/blackness
swā þēah 03.06 Comparison
swā þēah hwæþre 03.06 Comparison
swæc 02.05.07 Faculty of taste; 02.05.08 Faculty of smell
geswæccan 02.05.07 Faculty of taste; 02.05.08 Faculty of smell
(ge)swǣlan 03.01.09.02.01 Fire, burning
geswǣled 03.01.09.02.01 Fire, burning
swǣlednes 03.01.09.02.01 Fire, burning
swǣlende 03.01.09.02.01 Fire, burning
swǣm 11.06 Disinclination to act, listlessness; 11.08.04 Vanity, idleness, frivolity
swǣp 06.02.06.03.04 Allurement
(ge)swǣpa 04.06.02.04 Refuse, litter, rubbish
swǣpels(e) 04.04.07 Trappings, equipment, garb
swǣpig 06.01.07.04.04 Deceitfulness, falseness, duplicity
swǣr 02.05.04 Sleepiness, drowsiness, sleep; 03.01.07 Weight, heaviness; 05.09 Weakness; 08.01.03 Bad feeling, sadness; 08.01.03.06 Adversity, affliction; 08.01.03.07.04 Severity, harshness; 11.06 Disinclination to act, listlessness; 12.08.06.02.04 Darkness, evil
swǣrbyrd 02.01.03.03.03.01 Child-bearing, childbirth
swǣre 08.01.03.07.03 Suffering, torment, pain
geswǣred 08.01.03.01 Despondency
swǣrig 08.01.03.07.02 Misery, trouble, affliction
swǣrlic 08.01.03.07.04 Severity, harshness
swǣrlīce 02.05.04 Sleepiness, drowsiness, sleep; 08.01.03.07.03 Suffering, torment, pain
swǣrmōd 11.06 Disinclination to act, listlessness
swǣrmōdnes 06.01.05.03.01.01 Dullness, folly, stupidity
swǣrnes 03.01.07 Weight, heaviness; 11.06 Disinclination to act, listlessness
swǣs 02.03.02.03.06.02 Close relationship; 02.05.07.03 Sweetness; 10 Having, owning, possession
(ge)swǣs 08.01.01.03.09.01 Pleasant, agreeable; 11.05.02.02 Humanity, courtesy, civility
geswǣs 06.02.06.03 Persuasion, prompting
geswǣse 08.01.01.03.09.02 Pleasantly, agreeably
swǣsenddagas 05.11.06.01 Cycle of the year
swǣsende 04.01.02.01 Food/sustenance; 07.07.03 Flattery
swǣsingdagas 05.11.06.01 Cycle of the year
(ge)swǣslǣcan 07.07.03 Flattery
swǣslic 08.01.01.03.09.01 Pleasant, agreeable
geswǣslic 06.02.06.03.04 Allurement
swǣslīce 06.02.06.03 Persuasion, prompting; 08.01.01.03.09.02 Pleasantly, agreeably; 10 Having, owning, possession; 11.05.02.02 Humanity, courtesy, civility
swǣsnes 07.07.03 Flattery
geswǣsscipe 12.04 Fellowship, union, association

swǣsung 02.08.12.02.05.02 Salves, ointments
swǣswyrde 09.03.04.02.02 Eloquence, elegance in language
swǣtan 02.04.06.08.01 Blood; 02.08.08.12 Disease of bowels; 17.01 Strenuous effort, hard work
(ge)swǣtan 02.04.06.06.01 Sweat
geswǣtan 17.02.01 Management of work; 17.02.04.03.03 Smelting, heating, scorification
swæþ 05.12.01.03.01.01 A path, track
swæþer 07.01.01 Choice, election
swæþer...swā...swā 07.01.01 Choice, election
geswæþian 09.05.01 Inspection, examination
swæþlǣcan 08.01.02.04.01 Visiting
swalg 01.01.02.01.03 Hollow/depression in land
swāmian 03.01.13.02 A growing dark, darkening
swamm 02.07.05 Fungus; 04.06.01.04 What is used in washing, an ointment
swan 02.06.08.06 Water bird
swān 04.02.05.01.02 To tend, herd; 04.02.05.06.04 A swineherd; 13.02.10.01 A man, warrior
swancor 02.06.02.01.06 Horse; 03.01.04.01 Power of bending, flexibility; 05.09 Weakness
swancornes 11.06 Disinclination to act, listlessness
swāngerēfa 12.01.01.08.01 A servant, attendant
swangettung 05.12 To move, be in motion; 05.12.05.05 To shake, quake, wag
swangor 11.06 Disinclination to act, listlessness

swānrād 01.01.03.01.02 Sea/ocean
swānriht 14.01.01 Law(s) of particular scope
swānsteorra 01.02.01.01.02 Star
swāpan 04.06.01 Clean; 05.12.05.04.01 (Of wheel, etc.) to roll, trundle
geswāpan 10.01.02 Acquisition
swāt 02.04.06.06.01 Sweat; 02.04.06.06.04 Spittle; 02.04.06.08.01 Blood; 03.01.16.01 Moisture; 04.01.02.01.02.05.05 Fat/suet/lard; 17.01 Strenuous effort, hard work
geswāt 02.04.06.06.01 Sweat
swatan (pl) 04.01.03.05.01.02 Broth
swātclāþ 04.06.01.05 ?A cloth for wiping
swātfāh 02.04.06.08.01 Blood; 13.02.02 Battle
swātig 02.04.06.06.01 Sweat; 02.04.06.08.01 Blood
swātighlēor 02.04.06.06.01 Sweat
swātlīn 04.06.01.05 ?A cloth for wiping
swātswaþu 05.12.01.03.01.01 A path, track
swātþyrel 02.04.04 Skin; 02.04.06.06.01 Sweat
swaþe weardian 05.10.05.04.09.02 Hinder part, rear
swaþian 05.10.05.04.12 The condition of being covered
swaþu 02.08.04.01 A wound; 05.12.01.03.01.01 A path, track
swaþul 03.01.09.02 Fire, flame
swealwe 02.06.08.05 Forest bird, wild-fowl
swearcian 03.01.13.02 A growing dark, darkening; 08.01.03.03 Anxiety
swearcmōdnes 06.02.07.07 Cowardice, pusillanimity
swearcung 03.01.13 Darkness, obscurity

sweard 02.04.04 Skin; 02.06.01.06 Skin, hide
swearm 02.06.09.02.02 Bee, hornet, wasp; 03.03.04.01.02 A great number, multitude
sweart 03.01.13 Darkness, obscurity; 03.01.14.04 Black/blackness; 12.08.06.02.04 Darkness, evil
swearte 12.08.06.02.04 Darkness, evil
swearthǣwen 03.01.14.05 Red/redness
(ge)sweartian 03.01.14.04 Black/blackness
sweartlāst 09.03.07.06.02 Ink
sweartnes 03.01.14.04 Black/blackness
sweartung 03.01.13 Darkness, obscurity
(ge)swebban 02.02.04.03 To kill, slay; 02.05.04.01 To make heavy with weariness/sleep
geswebban 05.09.03 Mitigation, lightening, alleviation
swefan 02.02.03.02 State of being dead; 02.05.04 Sleepiness, drowsiness, sleep; 11.06.01 Neglect; 11.06.04 Abstention, abstaining from
swefecere 02.05.04 Sleepiness, drowsiness, sleep
swefecung 02.05.04 Sleepiness, drowsiness, sleep
swefel 03.01.09.02.01.03 Sulphur, brimstone
swefelrēc 03.01.09.02.01.03 Sulphur, brimstone
sweflen 03.01.09.02.01.03 Sulphur, brimstone
sweflenes 03.01.09.02.01.03 Sulphur, brimstone
sweflsweart 03.01.13 Darkness, obscurity
sweflþrosm 03.01.09.02.01.03 Sulphur, brimstone

swefn 02.05.04 Sleepiness, drowsiness, sleep; 02.05.04.02 A dream; 06.01.02.01.01.01 A dream, vision
swefnes wōma 06.01.02.01.01.01 A dream, vision
swefnian 02.05.04.02 A dream; 06.01.02.01.01.01 A dream, vision
geswefnian 02.05.04.02 A dream; 06.01.02.01.01.01 A dream, vision
swefnigend 02.05.04.02 A dream; 06.01.02.01.01.01 A dream, vision
swefnracu 16.01.04.06.03 Interpretation of dreams
swefnreccere 16.01.04.06.03 Interpretation of dreams
swēg 02.03.01 People; 02.05.10.02 Noise, din; 02.05.10.15 Voice, cry (of living creature); 02.05.10.15.07 Voice, note (of a bird); 18.02.07.02 A musical instrument
swēgan 02.05.10.01 Thing heard; 02.05.10.07 A crashing, noise; 05.12.03.01.01 Quick movement or movements; 09.04 Sense, purport, meaning
swēgcræft 18.02.07 Music
swēgdynn 02.05.10.04 To resound
(ge)swēge 18.02.07 Music
swēgendlic 09 Speech, vocal utterance
sweger 02.03.02.02.03.06.02.06 In-law relationships
swēghlēoþor 02.05.10.01 Thing heard; 02.05.10.15 Voice, cry (of living creature); 18.02.07 Music
swēging 02.05.10.01 Thing heard
swegl 01.02.01 Heaven(s), sky; 01.02.01.01.03 Sun; 16.01.02 The heavens, sky; 18.02.07 Music
sweglbeorht 03.01.12 Brightness, light
sweglbōsm(as) 01.02.01 Heaven(s), sky
sweglcandel 01.02.01.01.03 Sun

sweglcyning 16.01.01.01.01 The Almighty
swegldrēam 08.01.01.03 Good feeling, joy, happiness
swegle 03.01.12 Brightness, light; 07.02.04.03 Nobleness, excellence, nobility, magnificence; 16.01.02 The heavens, sky
sweglhorn 18.02.07.02.02.02 A trumpet
swēglic 02.05.10.15 Voice, cry (of living creature)
sweglrād 18.02.07 Music
swegltorht 03.01.12 Brightness, light
sweglwered 03.01.12 Brightness, light
sweglwuldor 16.01.02.02 Glory/majesty of heaven
sweglwundor 18.02.07 Music
swēgnes 02.05.10.01 Thing heard
geswēgsumlīce 09.07.04.01.03 Unanimity
swelan 02.02.03 To die, perish; 03.01.09 Heat
swelc/swā ... swilce 03.06.01 Similitude, likeness
swelca 02.08.05.01 Swelling
geswelg 01.01.02.01.03.02 Abyss, chasm; 01.01.03.05 Whirlpool
swelgan 03.01.16.01 Moisture; 04 Consumption of food/drink; 06.01.06.02.03.03 To study, apply oneself to learning
(ge)swelgan 05.06.01 Devastation, laying waste
swelgend 01.01.03.05 Whirlpool; 12.08.07.01.01 Wantonness, sensuality, lasciviousness
swelgendnes 01.01.03.05 Whirlpool
swelgere 04.01.01.04 Gluttony, overeating, greediness
swelgnes 01.01.03.05 Whirlpool
geswell 02.08.05.01 Swelling

(ge)swellan 02.08.05.01 Swelling
swelle 01.01.02.01.02.02.01 Hill
swellende 02.08.05 Inflammation
swelling 05.12.01.09.02 To sail
sweltan 02.02.03 To die, perish
sweltendlic 02.02.03.01 In process of dying
(ge)swenc 06.02.06.03.04.01 Temptation; 08.01.03.06 Adversity, affliction
swencan 17.01 Strenuous effort, hard work
(ge)swencan 08.01.03.07.02 Misery, trouble, affliction; 12.05.06.02.03 Trouble, disturbance; 14.05.01 Correction, discipline
geswencan 02.05.03.02 Weariness
(ge)swencednes 08.01.03.06 Adversity, affliction
geswencnes 08.01.03.06 Adversity, affliction
sweng 05.06.09 Act of striking; 13.02.08.04.03.02.01 Striking/attack with sword
swengan 05.06.04 Damage, injury, defect, hurt, loss
swengan on 05.12.03.01.01 Quick movement or movements
sweofot 02.05.04 Sleepiness, drowsiness, sleep
swēoland 12.06.01.03 The Continent
sweoloþ(a) 03.01.09 Heat
sweoloþhāt 03.01.09 Heat
sweolung 02.08.05 Inflammation
swēon 02.03.03.06.05 Scandinavian
swēor 02.03.02.03.06.02.06 In-law relationships; 04.05.02.04 A column, pillar; 17.03.10.01 A bolt, lock, bar
(ge)swēor 02.03.02.03.06.02.04 Cousin
swēora 01.01.02.01.01.03.01 Promontory, headland, cape; 01.01.02.01.03

Hollow/depression in land;
01.01.03.01.02.02 Sea-channel;
02.04.03.02 Neck
swēorbān 02.04.05.04.03 Neck-bone
swēorbēag 04.04.10.01 A ring (for finger, arm, neck)
gesweorc 01.03.01.06.01 Cloud, mist
sweorcan 08.01.03.04 Grief
(ge)sweorcan 03.01.13.02 A growing dark, darkening; 03.01.14.04 Black/blackness; 08.01.03 Bad feeling, sadness
gesweorcan 02.08.11.02 Mental weakness; 08.01.03.05.02 Anger
sweorcendferhþ 08.01.03.01 Despondency
gesweorcenes 08.01.03.01 Despondency
gesweorcian 06.01.08.06 Fear
swēorclāþ 04.04.07.12 A collar, neck-cloth
swēorcops 14.05.06 Means/implement of torture
swēorcoþu 02.08.07.04.04 Respiratory disease
sweord 13.02.08.04.03 A sword
sweordbealo 02.02.04 Killing, violent death, destruction; 02.08.03 Pain, bodily discomfort
sweordberende 13.02.08.04.03.02 Armed with a sword
sweordbite 02.08.04.01 A wound
sweordbora 13.02.02.01 Single combat; 13.02.10.01.02 An armed man
sweordfætels 13.02.08.04.03.01.01 Hilt of sword
sweordfreca 13.02.10.01.02 An armed man
sweordgenīþla 08.01.03.09.05 Enmity
sweordgeswing 13.02.08.04.03.02.01 Striking/attack with sword

sweordgifu 10.03 Giving
sweordgripe 13.02.08.04.03.02.01 Striking/attack with sword
sweordhwīta 13.02.08.03.01 Body armour, war gear
sweordlēoma 03.01.12.01 Glittering, effulgence
gesweordod 13.02.08.04.03.02 Armed with a sword
sweordplega 13.02.02 Battle
sweordrǣs 13.02.03.01 An attack, assault
sweordslege 13.02.08.04.03.02.01 Striking/attack with sword
sweordtige 13.02.08.04.03.02 Armed with a sword
sweordwegend 13.02.10.01.02 An armed man
sweordwīgend 13.02.10.01.02 An armed man
sweordwund 02.08.04.01 A wound
sweordwyrhta 13.02.08.04.03 A sword
gesweorf 17.02.04.03.02 Filings
sweorfan 04.06.01 Clean; 05.06.05.02 A filing, rubbing with file
swēorhnitu 02.06.09.01 Parasite
swēorīce 12.06.01.03 The Continent
swēorracentēh 04.04.10.01 A ring (for finger, arm, neck)
swēorrōd 16.02.05.06.02 Garb for neck and shoulders
swēorscacul 14.05.06 Means/implement of torture
swēortēag 04.04.07.12 A collar, neck-cloth
geswēoru 01.01.02.01.02.02.01 Hill
swēorwærc 02.08.07.06 Disorders of the neck
gesweosternu bearn 02.03.02.03.06.02.04 Cousin

sweostor 02.03.02.02.05.02 Sister; 16.02.03.03.03 A nun
gesweostor 02.03.02.02.05.02 Sister
sweostorbearn 02.03.02.03.06.02.03 Child of brother/sister
sweostorsunu 02.03.02.03.06.02.03 Child of brother/sister
swēot 12.04.02 A crowding together, assembly; 13.02.10.01.02.01 An armed force/band
sweota 02.04.06.04.01 Male genitalia
sweotol 02.05.07 Faculty of taste; 02.05.09.09 Visible; 02.05.10.01 Thing heard; 06.01.05.01.01 Clear to the understanding, plain; 09.05.05.01 Showing, manifestation, display
sweotole 02.05.09.01 To open the eyes/be awake; 06.01.05.02 Intelligence; 09.05.05.01 Showing, manifestation, display
sweotolian 09.05.05.01 Showing, manifestation, display
(ge)sweotolian 09.04.03 Exposition, making clear by explanation; 09.06.02.01 To tell, make known, declare, relate, announce
gesweotolian 09.04.01 Signal, signalling; 09.05.05 Exposure, revealing, revelation; 09.05.05.01 Showing, manifestation, display
sweotollic 06.01.05.01.01 Clear to the understanding, plain
sweotollīce 06.01.05.02 Intelligence; 09.05.05.01 Showing, manifestation, display
sweotolung 02.05.09.12 To show; 09.03.07.07.03.04.01 A document, deed; 09.04.03 Exposition, making clear by explanation; 09.05.05.01 Showing, manifestation, display;

14.03.03.03 Witness, testimony, attestation
(ge)sweotolung 09.04.03 Exposition, making clear by explanation
gesweotolung 09.06.02.01.07.01 A title, label
(ge)sweotolungdæg 16.02.04.04.02.01.01 Around the Nativity
swēotum 03.03.04.01.02.01 A heap, mass, accumulation
swēoþēod 02.03.03.06.05 Scandinavian
sweoþol 03.01.09 Heat
(ge)swerian 12.07.02.01.01.01 A promise, oath
geswerian 14.03.03.04 Oath-swearing
swer(ig)endlic 09.03.02.02.01.03 An adverb
swertling 02.06.08.05 Forest bird, wild-fowl
swēt 08.01.01.03.09 Pleasantness, agreeableness
geswēt 02.05.07.03 Sweetness
(ge)swētan 04.01.02.02.04.06 To sweeten; 08.01.01.03.09.03 To make glad
swēte 02.05.07.03 Sweetness; 02.05.08.02 Pleasant smell, fragrance, perfume; 03.01.16.02 Water, liquid; 04.01.02.01.01.01 Good/palatable food; 04.06 Salubrity; 08.01.01.03.09.01 Pleasant, agreeable; 08.01.02.02.01 A favourite, loved one; 11.05.02.02 Humanity, courtesy, civility; 18.02.07 Music
geswēted 02.05.07.03 Sweetness
swētian 08.01.01.03.09.03 To make glad
geswētlæht 02.05.07.03 Sweetness
swētlīce 08.01.01.03.09.02 Pleasantly, agreeably

swētmete

swētmete 04.01.02.01.07.05 Delicacy/dainty/titbit
swētnes 02.05.07.03 Sweetness; 02.05.08.02 Pleasant smell, fragrance, perfume; 08.01.01.03.09 Pleasantness, agreeableness; 11.05.02.02 Humanity, courtesy, civility
swētswēge 18.02.07 Music
swētwyrde 09.03.04.02.02 Eloquence, elegance in language; 11.05.02.02 Humanity, courtesy, civility
sweþel 04.04.07 Trappings, equipment, garb
sweþolian 08.01.02.01.02 Gentleness; 08.01.02.06.02 Forgiveness, remission, clemency
(ge)sweþrian 05.09 Weakness
(ge)sweþrung 05.09.05 Ceasing, decline, fall off
sweþung 02.08.12.02.05.03 A poultice
swic 06.01.02.01 An imaginary form, fancy; 06.01.07.04.04.03 Deceit, fraud, treachery
geswic 04.03.02 A snare, trap, noose; 05.11.10.02 End, completion; 12.08.06.02.05.01 Transgression, trespass
swica 06.01.07.04 Deception; 12.01.01.12.04 Treachery
swīcan 05.12.01.02 To wander; 05.12.05.03.01 To part ways, separate from, depart; 06:01.07.04 Deception
swīcan (fram) 12.01.01.12.03 Rebellion, sedition
swīcan ūt 05.12.05.03.04 To come/go out from
(ge)swīcan 12.01.01.12.04 Treachery
(ge)swīcan (fram) 05.12.05.11 To turn back, retreat; 11.06.04 Abstention, abstaining from; 11.06.06.01 Abandonment (of principle)
geswīcan 05.11.10.02 End, completion; 11.06.04 Abstention, abstaining from
swiccræft 06.01.07.04.04.03 Deceit, fraud, treachery
swicdōm 06.01.07.04.02 Fraud, deceit, trick, trickery; 12.01.01.12.04 Treachery; 12.08.06.02.05.01 Transgression, trespass
swice 05.03.02 Event, issue, result; 05.12.05.03.03 To depart, leave, set out; 06.01.07.04.04 Deceitfulness, falseness, duplicity; 06.01.07.04.04.03 Deceit, fraud, treachery; 11.10.05.01 Evasion, escape from threat; 12.01.01.12.04 Treachery; 12.08.06.02.05.01 Transgression, trespass
swīcend 06.01.07.04.04.03 Deceit, fraud, treachery
geswicennes 05.11.10.02 End, completion; 08.01.03.02.01 Compunction, remorse, contrition; 11.06.04 Abstention, abstaining from; 16.02.04.07.02.01 Penitence
swicful 06.01.07.04 Deception
swician 05.12.01.02 To wander; 08.01.03.07.02.01 Injury, offence; 16.02.04.14.01 Blasphemy
swician (fram) 05.12.05.03.03 To depart, leave, set out
swician (on/ymb) 06.01.07.04 Deception
geswicing 05.11.11.02 Let up, intermission, cessation
swicn 14.03.03.08 Justification
geswīcnan 14.03.03.08 Justification
swicol 06.01.07.04 Deception; 06.01.07.04.04 Deceitfulness, falseness, duplicity; 07.03.01.01 Abominable, detestable

swicollic 06.01.07.04.04 Deceitfulness, falseness, duplicity; 07.03.01.01 Abominable, detestable
swicollīce 06.01.07.04 Deception
swicolnes 06.01.07.04.04.03 Deceit, fraud, treachery
geswicu 05.11.10.02 End, completion
swicung 12.08.06.02.05.01 Transgression, trespass
swīcung 06.01.07.04.04 Deceitfulness, falseness, duplicity
swīfan 05.12.05 To move and change direction, turn; 05.12.05.04.01 (Of wheel, etc.) to roll, trundle; 11.02 Occupation, activity, business
swift 01.01.02.01.02.02.04 Cliff; 05.12.03.01 Swiftness, velocity
swiftlēre 04.04.07.15 Footwear, covering for the feet
swiftlīce 05.12.03.01 Swiftness, velocity
swiftnes 05.12.03.01 Swiftness, velocity
swiftu 05.12.03.01 Swiftness, velocity
(ge)swīgan 06.01.08.05.01 Amazement, astonishment, wonder, admiration; 09.05.04 A secret
geswīgan 09.02 Silence, refraining from speech
swīgdagas 16.02.04.04.02.01.03 Holy Week
swīge 02.05.10.17 Absence of noise or disturbance; 05.11.08.01.03.01 Delay; 06.01.08.05.01 Amazement, astonishment, wonder, admiration; 09.02 Silence, refraining from speech; 09.02.01 Silent, taciturn
swīgen 09.02 Silence, refraining from speech
swīgenihte 16.02.04.04.02.01.03 Holy Week
swīg(i)an 02.05.10.17 Absence of noise or disturbance
swīgian 06.01.08.05.01 Amazement, astonishment, wonder, admiration
(ge)swīgian 09.05.04 A secret
geswīg(i)an 09.02 Silence, refraining from speech
swigiendlīce 02.05.10.17 Absence of noise or disturbance
swīglīce 02.05.10.17 Absence of noise or disturbance
swīglunga 02.05.10.17 Absence of noise or disturbance
swīgmæsse 16.02.04.07.04.01 The service of the mass
swīgnes 05.11.04.02 Night, night time
geswīgra 02.03.02.03.06.02.04 Cousin
swīgtīma 05.11.04.02 Night, night time
swīgūhte 16.02.04.04.02.01.03 Holy Week
swīgung 02.05.10.17 Absence of noise or disturbance; 05.11.04.02 Night, night time; 05.11.08.01.03.01 Delay; 06.01.08.05.01 Amazement, astonishment, wonder, admiration
(ge)swīgung 09.02 Silence, refraining from speech
swilc 03.04 Form, kind, nature, character; 03.06.01 Similitude, likeness; 03.06.01.02 Equality
swilc...swilc 03.04 Form, kind, nature, character
swilce 03.06 Comparison; 03.06.01 Similitude, likeness; 11.01.04 A doing, accomplishing (of something)
swilchwugu 03.06.01 Similitude, likeness
swilcnes 05.02.02 Nature, established order of things
swilian 02.08.12.02.07 Remedies for specific parts (head to toe)
geswilian 03.01.16.01 Moisture

swille 04.06.02.04 Refuse, litter, rubbish
swil(l)ing 02.08.12.02.07 Remedies for specific parts (head to toe)
swīma 02.05.03 Exhaustion, faintness, weariness; 02.08.11.02 Mental weakness
swimman 05.12.01.08 To move in/on water; 05.12.01.09 To travel on water
(ge)swimman 05.12.01.08.01 To swim
swimmendlic 05.12.01.08.01 To swim
swin 01.01.03.01.01.04 Watercourse/channel; 18.02.07 Music
geswin 18.02.07 Music
swīn 02.06.02.01.07 Pig, swine; 04.01.02.01.02.05.02 Pork; 13.02.08.03.01.02.01 Parts of a helmet
swīna sceadu 04.02.05.06.04.01 A piggery
(ge)swinc 08.01.03.06 Adversity, affliction; 17.01 Strenuous effort, hard work
geswinc 02.05.03.02 Weariness; 17.02.04 Trade, calling, craft, aptitude
swincan 02.07.01 To grow
swincan æfter/for/on 17 Work, doings, actions, labour
(ge)swincan 08.01.03.06 Adversity, affliction; 17.01 Strenuous effort, hard work
geswincdæg 08.01.03.06 Adversity, affliction
(ge)swincful 08.01.03.06 Adversity, affliction; 17.01 Strenuous effort, hard work
geswincful 11.02.01 Energy, vigour, vigorous action; 17 Work, doings, actions, labour
geswincfulnes 08.01.03.06 Adversity, affliction

(ge)swinclēas 18.01 Rest, quiet, freedom from toil
swinclic 17.01 Strenuous effort, hard work
(ge)swincnes 08.01.03.06 Adversity, affliction
swindan 02.08.02 Disease, infirmity, sickness
swīnen 02.06.02.01.07 Pig, swine
swīnflǣsc 04.01.02.01.02.05.02 Pork
geswing 01.01.03.01.02.06 Surging, rolling, heaving of waves
swingan 04.01.02.02.08 Churn; 05.06.09.01 A slap with the hand, blow; 05.12.01.07 To fly (with wings); 18.02.02 Play, (athletic) sport
swingan on twā 05.06.02.01 A cleft, split
(ge)swingan 12.05.06.02.03 Trouble, disturbance; 14.05.05 Physical punishments
swinge 12.05.06.02.03 Trouble, disturbance; 14.05.05 Physical punishments
swingel 04.02.04.06.13 A stick to beat flax; 05.06.09 Act of striking; 12.05.06.02.03 Trouble, disturbance; 14.05.05 Physical punishments; 14.05.06 Means/implement of torture
swingere 14.05.05 Physical punishments
swinglung 02.08.11.02 Mental weakness
swīnhaga 04.02.05.06.04.01 A piggery
swīnhege 04.02.05.06.04.01 A piggery
swīnhyrde 04.02.05.06.04 A swineherd
swīnland 04.02.03.04.02.01.03 Swine pasture
swīnlic 02.06.02.01.07 Pig, swine
swīnlīc 13.02.08.03.01.02.01 Parts of a helmet
swīnnes 04.01.02.01.02.05.02 Pork
swīnsceadu 15.02.04.01 Payment for temporary use, rent, hire

swinsian 18.02.07 Music
swinsung 02.05.10.01 Thing heard; 18.02.07 Music
swinsungcræft 18.02.07 Music
swinswēg 18.02.07 Music
swipian 14.05.05 Physical punishments
(ge)swipor 06.01.07.04.04 Deceitfulness, falseness, duplicity; 11.04.02.01.01 Cunning, craft, craftiness, guile, wile
geswipore 11.04.02.01.01 Cunning, craft, craftiness, guile, wile
geswiporlīce 11.04.02.01.01 Cunning, craft, craftiness, guile, wile
(ge)swipornes 11.04.02.01.01 Cunning, craft, craftiness, guile, wile
swippan 14.05.05 Physical punishments
swipu 12.05.06.02.03 Trouble, disturbance; 14.05.06 Means/implement of torture
swirman 02.06.09.02.02 Bee, hornet, wasp
swīþ 01.03.01.03 Bad weather; 03.01.03.02 Strength, power; 05.08 Strength; 05.08.01 Vigour, activity, force
swīþan 12.05.06 Grasp, power, control, mastery
swīþe 02.05.10.02 Noise, din; 03.03.04.01 Much; 03.03.04.02.02 Excess; 03.03.05 Extent, degree; 03.03.06 Wholeness; 05.13.06.01 Firm, stable, steady; 08.01.03.09.11 Hardheartedness, cruelty, severity; 10.03.08 Bountifulness, munificence
swīþe swīþe 05.08 Strength
swīþfæstnes 06.01.01.01 Thinking about, minding, heeding
swīþfeorm 01.03.01.03 Bad weather; 02.01.03 Fruitfulness, fertility; 02.01.03.01 Fertility, plenty

swīþfeormende 05.08.02 Violence, force
swīþferhþ 06.02.07.01 Strength, fortitude; 11.02.04.01 Rashness, madness
swīþfrom 16.01.01.01.01.01 Mightiness
swīþfromlīce 11.02.01 Energy, vigour, vigorous action
swīþhrēownes 08.01.03.04 Grief
swīþhwæt 05.08.01 Vigour, activity, force
swīþhycgende 06.02.07 Will, determination, resolution
swīþian 05.12.04.01 Stability, firmness; 12 Power, might; 12.05.06 Grasp, power, control, mastery
(ge)swīþ(i)an 06.02.07.01 Strength, fortitude
(ge)swīþian 12 Power, might
swīþlæt 05.12.03.02 Slowness
swīþlic 01.03.01.03 Bad weather; 02.05 Sensation, perception, feeling; 03.03.04.01.01 Greatness, bigness, size; 05.08.02.01 (Of living creatures) fierceness, roughness; 08.01.01.01 Ardour, fervour, strong feeling; 12 Power, might; 12.08.03.02 Strictness, austerity, severity
swīþlīce 03.03.05 Extent, degree; 05.08.01 Vigour, activity, force; 08.01.03.09.10 Wrath, sternness, displeasure
swīþlicnes 03.03.04.02.02 Excess
swīþmihtig 12 Power, might
swīþmōd 06.02.07 Will, determination, resolution; 07.06.01.01 Proud, arrogant; 12.08.01 Magnanimity, greatness of soul
swīþmōdnes 12.08.01 Magnanimity, greatness of soul
swīþnes 05.08.02 Violence, force

swīþor 03.03.04.03 Growth, increase; 05.08.02 Violence, force
swīþor þonne 07.01.01.02 To prefer
swīþost 03.03.06 Wholeness; 12.05.06.02 Oppression; 17.01 Strenuous effort, hard work
swīþra 02.04.03.04.01.01 Hand
swīþrian 11.07.03 Use, advantage, profit; 12.05.06 Grasp, power, control, mastery
(ge)swīþrian 05.08 Strength
swīþsnel 05.12.03.01 Swiftness, velocity
swīþspecende 09.01.02.01 Excessive fluency, loquacity
swīþsprecol 09.03.04.02.02 Eloquence, elegance in language
swīþstincende 02.05.08 Faculty of smell
swīþstrēme 01.01.03.04 Current, rush of water
swīþswēge 09.03.05.01.01 Poetry; 18.02.07 Music
swīþswōge 18.02.07 Music
swodrian 02.05.04 Sleepiness, drowsiness, sleep
swōgan 05.12.03.01.01 Quick movement or movements
geswogen 02.02.03.02 State of being dead; 02.05.03 Exhaustion, faintness, weariness
geswōgung 02.05.03 Exhaustion, faintness, weariness
swol 02.08.10 Fever; 03.01.09 Heat
swolgettan 02.08.12.02.07 Remedies for specific parts (head to toe)
swolig 01.03.01.05 Wind
geswollen 02.08.05.01 Swelling
geswōpe 04.06.02.04 Refuse, litter, rubbish
swōretendlic 02.04.06.07.04 Breathing
swōrettan 02.04.06.07.06 A sigh; 08.01.03.04 Grief
swōret(t)ung 02.04.06.07.04 Breathing; 02.04.06.07.06 A sigh; 08.01.03.04.04 Sighing
sworfen 17.02.04.03.02 Filings
swōrian 02.04.06.07.06 A sigh
swornian 03.01.17.01 A coagulating, mixing
swōt 02.05.08.02 Pleasant smell, fragrance, perfume
swōte 02.05.08.02 Pleasant smell, fragrance, perfume
swōtlic 02.05.07 Faculty of taste; 02.05.07.03 Sweetness
swōtlīce 08.01.02.02 Love, affection, care
swōtmete 04.01.02.01.07.05 Delicacy/dainty/titbit
swōtnes 02.05.08.02 Pleasant smell, fragrance, perfume
swōtstence 02.05.08.02 Pleasant smell, fragrance, perfume
swōtstencende 02.05.08.02 Pleasant smell, fragrance, perfume
swūrplætt 05.06.09 Act of striking
swylce ēac 03.03.04.03 Growth, increase
swyle 02.08.05 Inflammation; 02.08.05.01 Swelling
swylt 02.02 Death; 02.02.03.04 Spiritual death
swyltcwalu 02.02.01 Particular mode of death
swyltdæg 02.02.02 Liability to death, mortality
swyltdēaþ 02.02 Death
swylthwīl 02.02.02 Liability to death, mortality
swȳrige 08.01.03.07.04 Severity, harshness
(ge)sȳcan 04.01.01.02 Act/action of sucking

syce 04.01.01.02 Act/action of sucking
(ge)sȳced 04.01.01.02 Act/action of sucking
sycomer 02.07.03.05 Particular trees/shrubs (alphabetical order)
gesyd 01.01.02.01.04.01 Marsh, bog, swamp
syde 02.08.12.02.05 Pharmacy, curing with salves
sȳferǣte 04.01.01.06 Moderation in eating
sȳferlic 12.08.03.03 Moral restraint, modesty, sobriety
sȳferlīce 12.08.03 Restraint, temperance; 12.08.03.03 Moral restraint, modesty, sobriety; 12.08.04 Purity, moral cleanness
sȳferlicnes 12.08.04 Purity, moral cleanness
sȳfernes 12.08.03 Restraint, temperance; 12.08.03.03 Moral restraint, modesty, sobriety
gesyfled 04.01.02.02.04.07 Provided with a relish
syflige/syfling 04.01.02.01.05 Seasoning/flavouring
sȳfre 04.01.03.03 Sober; 12.08.03 Restraint, temperance; 12.08.04 Purity, moral cleanness
syge 06.02.06.01 An end, goal
sȳl 04.05.02.04 A column, pillar
sȳla 04.02.04.02.02.02 Ploughing, tilling
sȳlæx 04.02.04.06.07 Ploughing equipment
syle 01.01.02.01.04.01 Marsh, bog, swamp
sylfes willum 06.02.01 Freewill, own will
(ge)sylhþ(e) 04.02.05.06 Animals yoked together
sylian 04.06.02.02 Foul, filthy, squalid

syll 04.05.02.04 A column, pillar
syllestre 10.03 Giving
(ge)syltan 04.01.02.02.04.01 To salt
sylting 04.01.02.01.05 Seasoning/flavouring
symbel 04.01.02.04.02 Feast; 16.02.04.04.02 A feast-day, holy day
symbelbrēad 04.01.02.01.01.07 Water and loaf in desert (as a feast)
symbelcalic 16.02.05.05.06 A vessel for use in services
symbelcennes 16.02.04.04.02.01.01 Around the Nativity
symbeldæg 04.01.01.07 Feasting; 04.01.02.04.02 Feast; 16.02.01.08.04 Jewish seasons/feasts; 16.02.04.04.01 The day of rest, sabbath; 16.02.04.04.02 A feast-day, holy day
symbelgāl 04.01.03.02 To drink heavily, get drunk
symbelgefēra 12.04.01 A fellow, companion, associate, comrade
symbelgemaca 02.06.01.07 Breeding, hatching
symbelgereord 04.01.02.04.02 Feast
symbelgifa 16.01.01.02.02 A giving (by Deity)
symbelhūs 04.01.01.08 Eating place
symbellic 16.02.04.03.01 A rite, ceremony; 16.02.04.04.02 A feast-day, holy day
symbellīce 16.02.04.03.01 A rite, ceremony
symbelmōnaþlic 02.08.09.02 Epilepsy; 16.02.04.04.02 A feast-day, holy day
symbelnes 04.01.01.07 Feasting; 07.06.05 Pomp, splendour, magnificence; 16.02.04.04.02 A feast-day, holy day

symbeltīd 16.02.04.04.02 A feast-day, holy day
symbelwērig 02.05.03.02 Weariness
symbelwlonc 04.01.03.02 To drink heavily, get drunk
symbelwynn 04.01.01.07 Feasting
symblan 04.01.01.07 Feasting
symblian 04.01.01.07 Feasting
symbliend 04.01.01.07 Feasting
symeringwyrt 02.07.11 Plants/flowers (alphabetical order)
symle 05.11.09.02 Frequent, of common occurrence; 05.11.11 Continuity; 05.11.11.01 A not ceasing, persistence, recurrence
symles 05.11.11 Continuity
symling(a) 05.11.11 Continuity
synbend 16.02.01.13 Evil-doing, transgression, sin
synbōt 16.02.04.07.02.03 Penance, an act/instance of penance
synbryne 02.05.05.03 Sexual appetite, lust
synbyrþen 16.02.01.13 Evil-doing, transgression, sin
synbysig 12.08.09 Guiltiness, guilt
syndǣd 16.02.01.13 Evil-doing, transgression, sin
synderǣ 14.01.03 Special law, privilege, law for an individual
synderlic 07.02.04.03.01 Peculiar excellence
synderlicnes 03.04.01 Singularity, peculiarity; 07.02.04.03.01 Peculiar excellence
synderlīpe 03.04.01 Singularity, peculiarity
synderlīpes 03.03.03.04.01 One
gesyndgian 08.01.01.03.08.03 A favour, blessing

syndig 05.12.01.08.01 To swim
syndolh 02.02.04.01 Cause/occasion of death
syndonisc 02.03.03.06.07.04 Indian
syndorlic 05.10.05 A space, span; 05.11.03.01.05 A day
syndorlīce 03.03.05 Extent, degree; 03.03.05.01.01 Principal/chief (of its class or type); 03.04.01 Singularity, peculiarity
(ge)syndrian 03.03.07.01 Division, partition, separation; 03.06.02 Difference, diversity, dissimilarity
syndrig 03.03.07.01 Division, partition, separation; 03.04.01 Singularity, peculiarity; 05.10.05 A space, span; 06.01.08.05.01.01 Wondrous, glorious, marvellous; 10 Having, owning, possession
syndrige 03.03.03.04.01 One
syndrigendlic 09.03.02.02.01.03 An adverb
syndriglic 03.04.01 Singularity, peculiarity
syndriglīce 03.03.03.04.01 One; 03.03.05.01.01 Principal/chief (of its class or type)
gesyndrod 03.03.07.01 Division, partition, separation
synfāh 16.02.01.13 Evil-doing, transgression, sin
synfull 12.08.06.02.05.02 A sinner, transgressor
(ge)syngian 06.01.07.05 Error, being astray; 12.08.08.01.02.01 Fornication, adultery
(ge)syngian (wiþ) 16.02.01.13 Evil-doing, transgression, sin
syngiend/synnigiend 12.08.06.02.05.02 A sinner, transgressor

syngrin 16.02.01.13 Evil-doing, transgression, sin
syngung 16.02.01.13 Evil-doing, transgression, sin
synhrēoflig 02.08.06 Skin disease, erysipelas
synleahtor 16.02.01.13 Evil-doing, transgression, sin
synlēas 12.08.04 Purity, moral cleanness
synlic 16.02.01.13 Evil-doing, transgression, sin
synlīce 12.08.06.02.05.04 Sinfully, wickedly
synn 08.01.03.09.05 Enmity; 12.08.06.02.05 Misdeed, sin; 16.02.01.13 Evil-doing, transgression, sin
synne (ge)dōn 12.08.06.02.05.05 To sin (against), do wrong
synne stǣlan 12.05.03 Disagreement, discord, dissension
synnecge 12.08.08.01.02.01.01 An adulterer/-ess, whore, prostitute
synneþōht 12.08.06.01 Error, wrong conduct, erroneous practice
synnful 16.02.01.13 Evil-doing, transgression, sin
synnfull 16.02.01.13 Evil-doing, transgression, sin
synnig 12.08.09 Guiltiness, guilt; 14.03.03.09.01 Unfavourable judgement, condemnation; 16.02.01.13 Evil-doing, transgression, sin
synnigend 16.02.01.13 Evil-doing, transgression, sin
synnlēaw 12.08.06.01.01 Pollution, impairment
synnlust 16.02.01.13 Evil-doing, transgression, sin

synoþlic 16.02.03.01 Ecclesiastical authority
synrǣs 16.02.01.13 Evil-doing, transgression, sin
synrūst 16.02.01.13 Evil-doing, transgression, sin
synsceaþa 12.08.06.02.05.02 A sinner, transgressor
synscyldig 16.02.01.13 Evil-doing, transgression, sin
gesyntlǣcan 08.01.01.03.08.03 A favour, blessing
(ge)synto 11.10 Safety, safeness
gesynto 02.08 Mental/spiritual health; 03.03.06 Wholeness; 08.01.01.03.08 Happiness, well-being, prosperity
synwracu 14.05.03 Retribution, requital
synwund 12.08.06.01.01 Pollution, impairment
synwyrcende 16.02.01.13 Evil-doing, transgression, sin
sype 03.01.16.06 A soaking, steeping
sypian 03.01.16.01 Moisture
syretung 11.09.01.01 Ambush, lying in wait
syrfe 02.07.03.05 Particular trees/shrubs (alphabetical order)
syrftrēow 02.07.03.05 Particular trees/shrubs (alphabetical order)
sȳring 04.01.02.01.02.09.07 Buttermilk
syrisc 02.03.03.06.07.02 Arab
syrware 02.03.03.06.07.02 Arab
sȳþerra 01.01.01.02 South
tā 02.04.03.04.02.05.04 Toe
tabule 02.05.10.12 An audible signal; 09.03.07.06.04 A writing-tablet; 16.02.05.03.04 Part of temple containing altar/idol; 18.02.02.01 Gaming, playing at dice
tacan 10.04 To take

tacan on 02.05.06 Sense of touch
tācen 01.02.01.01.02.01.01 The Zodiac; 02.08.02.01.03 A symptom; 05.10.05.04.11.01.01 Object placed as point to be reached, a mark; 06.01.04.02 Living, remembered; 06.01.08.04.01 Premonition, prophecy; 06.01.08.05.01.01.01 An exercise of power, mighty work, miracle; 09.03.03 A gesture, action, gesticulation; 09.04.01 Signal, signalling; 11.03.01.01.01 Proof, demonstration
tācencircol 05.11.06 Course/cycle of time; 05.11.06.03 Lunar cycle of nineteen years
tācnberend 13.02.10 The military, soldiers
tācnbora 05.12.05.08.01 To go before and guide; 12.03 Direction, guidance; 13.02.10 The military, soldiers
(ge)tācnian 06.01.08.04.01 Premonition, prophecy; 09.03.04.02.01 A figure; 09.05.05.01 Showing, manifestation, display
getācnian 09.04 Sense, purport, meaning; 09.04.01 Signal, signalling; 14.04.01 A deed, contract, agreement
tācni(g)endlic 09.03.04.02.01 A figure
getācni(g)endlic 09.04.01 Signal, signalling
getācnigendlīce 09.03.04.02.01 A figure
tācnung 01.02.01.01.02.01.01 The Zodiac; 03.05.01 Arranging, ordering, disposition; 06.01.08.04.01 Premonition, prophecy; 09.03.03 A gesture, action, gesticulation; 09.04.01 Signal, signalling; 11.03.01.01.01 Proof, demonstration

(ge)tācnung 09.03.04.02.01 A figure; 09.04 Sense, purport, meaning
getācnung 01.02.01.01.02.01 Constellation; 09.04.01 Signal, signalling; 11.09.02 A reminder, warning
tācor 02.03.02.03.06.02.06 In-law relationships
tād(ig)e 02.06.07.02 Frog, toad
tæbere 04.04.03 A spinning-house or chamber
tæcan 09.04.01 Signal, signalling
tæcan fram 12.05.07.01 Separation, dismissal, rejection
(ge)tæcan 06.01.06.02.03.04.03 To teach, instruct; 09.05.05.01 Showing, manifestation, display; 12.03 Direction, guidance; 14.01.06 A rule, order, precept, tenet, principle
getæcan 06.01.01.01 Thinking about, minding, heeding; 06.02.06.03 Persuasion, prompting; 09.05.05 Exposure, revealing, revelation; 10.03.07.01 To allot, assign; 11.01.04 A doing, accomplishing (of something)
tæcels 05.10.05.04.11.01 A bound, limit
tæcend 06.01.06.02.03.04.02 A teacher
tæcing 06.01.06.02.03.04 Teaching, instruction; 14.01.06 A rule, order, precept, tenet, principle; 16.02.01.01 Creed, statement of faith
tæcnan 05.12.05.08.01 To go before and guide; 14.01.06 A rule, order, precept, tenet, principle
(ge)tæcnan 09.05.05.01 Showing, manifestation, display; 12.03 Direction, guidance
tæcnend 02.04.03.04.01.01.01 Finger
tæcnian 11.03.01.01.01 Proof, demonstration

tæcning 11.03.01.01.01 Proof, demonstration
tæfl 18.02.02.01 Gaming, playing at dice
tæfle 18.02.02.01 Gaming, playing at dice
tæflere 18.02.02.01 Gaming, playing at dice
tæfl(i)an 18.02.02.01 Gaming, playing at dice
tæflstān 18.02.02.01 Gaming, playing at dice
tæflung 18.02.02.01 Gaming, playing at dice
tæg tæg 08.01.01.03.07.01 Laughter
tægel 02.06.01.05 Tail
tæglhǣr 02.06.01.06 Skin, hide
(ge)tæl 03.03.06 Wholeness
getæl 03.03.03 Number; 03.03.03.02 A number (mark/symbol); 03.03.04.01.02.01 A heap, mass, accumulation; 03.04 Form, kind, nature, character; 05.11.06.02.02 A calculated space of time; 09.01.02 Fluency in speech; 09.03.02.03.01.01.02 Number; 09.03.07.07.03.04.02 A register, catalogue; 09.06.01 To relate, recount, tell; 11.04.02 Skill, skilfulness
tǣl 07.05.03.03 Scorn, insult, abuse; 07.09 Shame, disgrace; 16.02.04.14.01 Blasphemy
(ge)tǣlan 07.05 Disrespect, irreverence; 07.05.03.03.02 To reproach, revile, abuse; 07.05.04 Mockery, derision, scorn
getælcircul 05.11.06.02 Reckoning/computation of time
(ge)tælcræft 03.03.03.01 Arithmetic
tǣlend 07.05.01 Censure, reproof, rebuke; 07.05.03 Calumny, backbiting; 07.05.04 Mockery, derision, scorn
tǣlende 07.05.01 Censure, reproof, rebuke; 07.05.03 Calumny, backbiting
tǣlere 07.05.04 Mockery, derision, scorn
getælfæst 03.03.03 Number
getælfers 09.03.05.01.02 Art of verse composition
getælful 03.03.04.01.02 A great number, multitude
tǣlful 12.08.09.01 Blameableness, blameworthiness
tǣlhleahtor 07.05.04 Mockery, derision, scorn
tǣling 07.05.01 Censure, reproof, rebuke; 07.05.03.02 Calumny, slander, insult; 07.05.04 Mockery, derision, scorn
tǣllēas 12.08.05.01 Blameless
tǣllēaslīce 12.08.05.01 Blameless
tǣllic 12.08.09.01 Blameableness, blameworthiness; 16.02.04.14.01 Blasphemy
tǣllīce 07.03.05 Infamy, shame, wickedness; 12.08.09.01 Blameableness, blameworthiness
tælmearc 05.11.06.02 Reckoning/computation of time
tælmet 03.03 Measurement, determination of amount; 03.03.03 Number
tǣlnes 07.05.01 Censure, reproof, rebuke; 07.05.03.02 Calumny, slander, insult
getælrīm 03.05.02 An arrangement, order, succession
(ge)tælsum 18.02.07 Music
tǣlwierþe 12.08.09.01 Blameableness, blameworthiness
tǣlwierþlic 12.08.09.01 Blameableness, blameworthiness
tǣlwierþlicnes 12.08.09.01 Blameableness, blameworthiness

getælwīs 03.03.03.01 Arithmetic; 06.01.06.02.02.01 Learning, science (secular knowledge)
tæmespīle 04.06.01.10 To separate objects already connected, unmix; 17.03.11 Other implements, etc.
tænel 17.03.12.01 A basket
tænen 17.04.04 Fibrous materials
tæppa 17.03.11 Other implements, etc.
tæppe 04.04.09 A fringe, border, hem
tæpped 04.04.07.12 A collar, neck-cloth
tæpped/tæppet 04.04.08.02 Figured cloth, tapestry, carpet
tæppelbred 04.05.04.01 A bench, seat
tæppere 04.01.03.05.03 Tavern
tæppestre 04.01.03.05.03 Tavern
tæppian 17.03.11 Other implements, etc.
tæsan 02.08.04.01 A wound
(ge)tǣsan 04.04.01 Fulling
getǣsan 08.01 Heart, spirit, mood, disposition
(ge)tǣse 08.01.01.03.09.01 Pleasant, agreeable
getǣse 11.07.02 Utility, advantage, convenience; 11.07.03 Use, advantage, profit
tǣslic 11.07.02 Utility, advantage, convenience
(ge)tǣslīce 11.07.02 Utility, advantage, convenience
getǣslīce 02.05.05.04 Sensual pleasure
getǣsnes 11.07.02 Utility, advantage, convenience; 11.07.03 Use, advantage, profit
getǣsu 11.07.03 Use, advantage, profit
tǣtan 08.01.01.03.09.03 To make glad
tætteca 15.01.06 Poverty, indigence
tagga/tegga 02.06.02.01.08 Sheep
getāh 06.01.06.02.03.04 Teaching, instruction
tāhspura 02.04.03.04.02.05.04 Toe
talente 15.01.04 Coinage, money
(ge)talian 03.03.03 Number; 07.01 Appraisal, appraising; 14.03.03.01 Accusation
getalian 10.03.07.01 To allot, assign
getalscipe 03.03.04.01.02 A great number, multitude
talu 03.05.03 A list, tale, series; 09.06.01 To relate, recount, tell; 12.05.03.01 Quarrel, contentiousness, strife; 12.07.03.02 An excuse; 14.03.03 Law, action of the courts
tam 04.02.05.04 To tame, break in (animals); 08.01.02.01.02 Gentleness
tam getēagan 04.02.05.04 To tame, break in (animals)
tama 04.02.05.04 To tame, break in (animals)
(ge)tamcian 04.02.05.04 To tame, break in (animals)
tān 02.07.03.03.01 Wood (as substance); 04.05.01.02.06 A log, stake, etc.; 16.01.04.06.02 Prognostication by casting lots
tānede 02.08.07.08.03 Diseased in the toes
tang 17.05.02 A hearth, fireplace
getang 05.10.05.01 A little way, no great distance
getange 05.10.05.01 A little way, no great distance
getanglīce 05.10.05.01 A little way, no great distance
tānhlyta 16.01.04.06.02 Prognostication by casting lots
tānhlytere 16.01.04.06.02 Prognostication by casting lots
getanned 04.04.06 Undressed condition (of hide)

tannere 04.04.06 Undressed condition (of hide)
tansīþe 02.07.11 Plants/flowers (alphabetical order)
taperæx 13.02.08.04 Weapons, arms
tapor 03.01.12.02 A beam of light; 17.05.03 Sources of fire/light
taporberend 16.02.03.02.12 Cleric in minor orders
targa 13.02.08.03.01.06 A shield
getarged 13.02.08.03.01.06 A shield
taru 05.06.02.02 A tearing apart
(ge)tāwian (tō bysmore) 12.05.06.02.03 Trouble, disturbance
getāwian 02.08.02.01.01 An infectious disease; 07.09.03 Infamy, ignominy, shame; 11.01.03 Preparation
getāwu 02.04.06.04 Reproductive organs; 17.03 Implements, tools, etc.
te deum 16.02.04.03.03.01 A hymn, song of praise, canticle
tēafor 02.08.12.02.05.02 Salves, ointments; 03.01.14.05 Red/redness; 09.03.07.06.02 Ink
tēaforgēapa 04.05.02.03 An arch, vault
tēag 04.02.05.03 A park, enclosure for animals; 04.05.04.03 A box, case, chest, container; 17.03.10 Supports and fastenings
(ge)tēagan 04.02.04.02.01 To prepare land/soil
tēah 04.02.03.01.01 Enclosed land/field
tealt 05.11.01.02 Shortness/brevity in time; 05.12.04.01.01 Unstable
tealt(r)ian 05.12.01.04.01.03 To amble, stagger; 05.12.04.01.01 Unstable
tealtrian 06.01.07.05 Error, being astray
tealt(r)iende 05.12.01.04.01.03 To amble, stagger
tealtriende 05.12.04.01.01 Unstable

tēam 02.01.03.03.03.01 Child-bearing, childbirth; 02.01.03.03.04 Offspring, race, breed, family, children; 02.06 Animal; 04.02.05.06 Animals yoked together; 05.03.02 Event, issue, result; 14.03 Right of holding court, jurisdiction; 14.04.03 Confirmation, ratification
getēama 14.03.02 A legislator
tēamful 02.01.03 Fruitfulness, fertility
tēampōl 04.02.05.06.07 A fish-pond
tēar 02.04.06.06.02 Tear; 03.01.16.03 A drop of liquid; 08.01.03.04.02 Shedding of tears
tēara gegot 08.01.03.04.02 Shedding of tears
tēara gyte 08.01.03.04.02 Shedding of tears
tēaras 08.01.03.04 Grief
tearflian 05.12.05.04.01 (Of wheel, etc.) to roll, trundle
tēargēotende 08.01.03.04.02 Shedding of tears
(ge)tēarian 08.01.03.04.02 Shedding of tears
tēarig 02.08.07.02 Disorders of the eye; 08.01.03.04.02 Shedding of tears
tēarighlēor 08.01.03.04.02 Shedding of tears
tearn 02.06.08.06 Water bird
teart 05.10.06.03.01 A point, spike, prickle; 08.01.03.07.04 Severity, harshness; 08.01.03.09.01.02 Bitterness, acrimony
teartlic 08.01.03.07.04 Severity, harshness
teartlīce 08.01.03.07.04 Severity, harshness
teartnes 08.01.03.07.04 Severity, harshness

teartnumol 02.08.12.02.05 Pharmacy, curing with salves
tēfrung 17.02.05.06 A painting, picture, representation
tela 02.08.01 Sound physical condition; 03.03.04.01 Much; 03.03.06 Wholeness; 07.02.01 Right, virtue; 07.04.04 Praise, acclamation, applause; 08.01.01.03.08 Happiness, well-being, prosperity
(ge)teld 04.05.03.02.02.09 A tent, pavilion
geteld slēan 04.05.03.02.02.09 A tent, pavilion
telde 04.05.03.02.02.09 A tent, pavilion
(ge)teldgehlīwung 04.05.03.02.02.09 A tent, pavilion
teldian 04.03.03 Net, drag-net, hunting net; 04.05.03.02.02.09 A tent, pavilion; 05.10.05.02.01 Diffusion, effusion, spreading
teldsticca 04.05.03.02.02.09 A tent, pavilion
geteldung 04.05.03 A dwelling-place, abode, habitation
geteldwurþung 16.02.01.08.04 Jewish seasons/feasts
teldwyrhta 04.05.03.02.02.09 A tent, pavilion
telg 03.01.14.01 Dyeing
telga 02.07.03.03.01 Wood (as substance); 04.05.01.02.06 A log, stake, etc.
telgberend 03.01.14.01 Dyeing
telge 17.03.09 A post, rod, stick, etc.
getelged 03.01.14.01 Dyeing
telgestre 03.01.14.01 Dyeing
telgett 04.02.04.05.04 A detached area of woodland
telgian 02.07.01 To grow

(ge)telg(i)an 03.01.14.01 Dyeing
telgor 02.07.03.03.01 Wood (as substance)
telgung 03.01.14.01 Dyeing
(ge)tellan 03.03.03 Number; 03.03.05.01 Rank, position, degree; 03.04 Form, kind, nature, character; 07.01 Appraisal, appraising; 09.06.01 To relate, recount, tell; 09.06.02.01 To tell, make known, declare, relate, announce; 14.03.03.01 Accusation
(ge)tellan gelīc 03.06 Comparison
(ge)tellan tō 03.04 Form, kind, nature, character
getellan 12.02 A public office
getellan wiþ 03.06 Comparison
teltrē 04.05.03.02.02.09 A tent, pavilion
tēmbyrst 14.03.03.03 Witness, testimony, attestation
getemed 04.02.05.04 To tame, break in (animals)
temes 04.06.01.10 To separate objects already connected, unmix
temes(e) 01.01.03.01.01.01 River
(ge)temesed 04.01.02.02.09 A mill
(ge)temesian 04.01.02.02.09 A mill
(ge)temian 04.02.05.04 To tame, break in (animals); 08.01.01.02.01 Want of interest or concern, indifference
getemian 12.03.05 Permission
tempel 16.02.05.02.01 A temple
tempelgeat 16.02.05.03.01 Door or gate of church
tempelgeweorc 16.02.05.02.01 A temple
tempelhūs 16.02.05.02.01 A temple
templhālgung 16.02.01.10.02 Consecration
templic 16.02.05.02.01 A temple
temprian 03.03.06.01.01 Mixing, mingling, preparation

(ge)temprian 05.09.03 Mitigation, lightening, alleviation
getemprian 02.08.12.01 Medical care, treatment; 03.06.03 Congruity, fitness, suitability; 11.01.03 Preparation; 12.08.03 Restraint, temperance
temprung 05.09.03 Mitigation, lightening, alleviation
tend(l)ing 02.08.03.02 Itch, irritation
tengan on 13.02.03.01 An attack, assault
(ge)tengan 05.12.03.01.02 Haste, hurry; 11.02 Occupation, activity, business
getenge 05.10.05.01 A little way, no great distance; 08.01.03.07.04 Severity, harshness
tennan 06.02.06.03.04 Allurement
tēo 05.10.05.04.11.01 A bound, limit
teofenian 03.03.06.01 A whole formed by joining
tēofrian 10.03.07.01 To allot, assign
teogoþian 03.03.03.03 Fractions; 15.01 Property
(ge)teogoþian 16.02.04.20 Church due/requirement
teoh 02.03.03.02 A race, tribe; 12.04.01.01 A company of people, fellowship, society
getēoh 03 Material, matter, substance
(ge)teohhian 06.01.07.06.01 To accept as the result of enquiry, suppose; 06.02.06 Mind, purpose; 10.03.07.01 To allot, assign
geteohhung 14.01.06 A rule, order, precept, tenet, principle
teolþyrel 04.02.05.06.08.01 A beehive; 04.05.02.13 A window-space
tēon 03.03.02 Measurement by weighing; 05.12.01.01 To go on a journey/expedition, travel; 05.12.01.09.01 To row; 05.12.02.01 To fetch, bring, bear, conduct; 05.12.02.05 To pull, drag, draw; 10.03.04 Provision, supply; 11.03.02.01 Efficacy, success; 14.03.03.01 Accusation
tēon tō 05.12.05.02 To go/travel towards, come, approach
tēon (tō) 15.01.01.01 Holding of land
tēon ūp 05.12.05.12.02 To raise, lift up, elevate
tēon ūt 05.12.05.03.04 To come/go out from
(ge)tēon 05.04 Fate, lot, fortune, destiny; 05.05 Constitution, founding (e.g. of world); 05.10.04 Place, room; 05.12.02.05 To pull, drag, draw; 05.12.05.08.01 To go before and guide; 06.01.06.02.03.04.03 To teach, instruct; 06.02.06.03.04 Allurement; 07 Judgement, forming of opinion
(ge)tēon (forþ) 09.05.05.01 Showing, manifestation, display
(ge)tēon on/tō 10.04 To take
(ge)tēon tō 05.03.01.02 To work upon, influence
(ge)tēon (ūt) 13.02.08.04.03.02 Armed with a sword
getēon 03.03.06.01 A whole formed by joining; 10.03 Giving; 12.04 Fellowship, union, association; 12.05.03.01 Quarrel, contentiousness, strife; 12.05.06.01 Restraint, check, curb, control; 18.02.07.02.03.01 A harp, lyre
getēon oroþ 02.04.06.07.05 To breathe
getēon tō 05.03.01 A cause (of anything)
tēona 08.01.03.07.02 Misery, trouble, affliction; 08.01.03.07.02.01 Injury, offence; 08.01.03.09.05 Enmity; 12.08.06.02 Wickedness, evil

tēona/tēone 07.05.03.02 Calumny, slander, insult
tēoncwide 07.05.03.02 Calumny, slander, insult
tēoncwidian 07.05.03.02 Calumny, slander, insult
tēond 05.12.02.05 To pull, drag, draw; 14.03.03.01 Accusation
tēonere 07.05.03.02 Calumny, slander, insult
tēonful 07.03.02 Ill, harm, hurt; 07.05.03.02 Calumny, slander, insult; 08.01.03.05.03 Exasperation, irritation; 08.01.03.07.04 Severity, harshness
tēonfullic 07.05.03.03.01 Contumelious, scornful
tēonhete 08.01.03.09.04 Hatred
tēonian 07.05.03.02 Calumny, slander, insult; 08.01.03.05.03 Exasperation, irritation
tēonlēas 08.01.01.03.01 Freedom from trouble, comfort, security
tēonlēg 03.01.09.02.01.01 A kind of fire
tēonlīce 07.09.03 Infamy, ignominy, shame; 08.01.03.07.04 Severity, harshness
tēonrǣden 08.01.03.07.02.01 Injury, offence
tēonsmiþ 12.08.06.02.02 A bad man, inhuman person
tēonword 07.05.03.02 Calumny, slander, insult
tēorian 05.09.01 Slow, inactive
(ge)tēorian 05.07 Ending of existence, end of world
getēorian 02.05.03.02 Weariness; 11.06.04 Abstention, abstaining from
getēorigende 02.08.07.02 Disorders of the eye

(ge)tēorigendlic 07.03.03 Mediocrity, insignificance
getēorodnes 02.05.03.02 Weariness
teors 02.04.06.04.01 Male genitalia
teoru 02.04.06.05.07.04 Secretions of ear; 03.01.17.06 Resin, tar, gum
(ge)tēorung 02.05.03 Exhaustion, faintness, weariness
teosel 18.02.02.01 Gaming, playing at dice
teosu 07.03.02 Ill, harm, hurt; 12.08.06.02.05.01 Transgression, trespass
teosusprǣc 07.05.03.03 Scorn, insult, abuse
teosuword 07.05.03.03 Scorn, insult, abuse
teoswian 07.03.02 Ill, harm, hurt
tēoþa 03.03.03.04.10 Ten
tēoþa æcer 16.02.05.01 Land
tēoþa dǣl 03.03.03.03 Fractions
tēoþa sceatta 16.02.04.20 Church due/requirement
tēoþe 03.03.03.04.10 Ten
tēoþingealdor 16.02.03.03.01.04 A dean (in charge of ten religious)
tēoþingmann 12.01.01.05 A leader, administrator; 12.02.02 An assembly, meeting
tēoþung 04.02.03.03.02 A hide; 16.02.04.20 Church due/requirement
tēoþungcēap 16.02.04.20 Church due/requirement
tēoþunggeorn 11.02.02 Diligence; 16.02.04.20 Church due/requirement
tēoþungland 16.02.05.01 Land
tēoþungsceatt 16.02.04.20 Church due/requirement

geter 05.06.02.02 A tearing apart; 12.05.03 Disagreement, discord, dissension
teran 02.05.07.01 Strong taste, acidity, pungency; 05.06.02.02 A tearing apart; 07.05.03 Calumny, backbiting
(ge)teran 05.06.02.02 A tearing apart; 05.06.06.01 A tearing, laceration
terfinnas 02.03.03.06.05 Scandinavian
termen 05.11.06.02.02 A calculated space of time; 05.11.10.02 End, completion
teter 02.08.06 Skin disease, erysipelas
getēþed 02.06.01.02 Head
getēwian 07.10.03 An adornment, decoration, ornament
thila 01.01.01.01 North
tiber 16.02.04.12 Sacrifice, a sacrifice
tībernes 05.06.01 Devastation, laying waste
ticcen 02.06.02.01.05 Goat
ticgende 07.10.03 An adornment, decoration, ornament
ticia 02.06.09.01 Parasite
tictator 12.01.01.05 A leader, administrator
tīd 05.11 A time, period of time; 05.11.02 A time, particular time, occasion; 05.11.02.01.01 An anniversary; 05.11.02.01.02 A time of celebration; 05.11.03 Period of time, era, epoch; 05.11.03.01.02 A season of the year; 05.11.03.01.06 An hour; 05.11.08 A suitable time, opportunity; 09.03.02.03.01.02.03 Tense; 16.02.04.05 Canonical hour, service
(ge)tīdan 05.03.02.01.01 An event, occurrence; 05.04.01 Fortune, Fate (personification)
tīddæg 02.01.04 Age
tīde 05.11.03 Period of time, era, epoch

tīdfara 02.02.03.03 Appointed death, doom
tīdgenge 05.11.06.03 Lunar cycle of nineteen years
tīdlic 05.11.01.02 Shortness/brevity in time; 05.11.08 A suitable time, opportunity; 09.03.02.03.01.02.03 Tense
tīdlīce 05.11.01.02 Shortness/brevity in time; 05.11.01.03 Mutability; 05.11.08 A suitable time, opportunity; 05.11.08.01.02 (Untimely) earliness
tīdlicnes 05.11.08 A suitable time, opportunity
tīdrēn 01.03.01.06.02 Rain
(ge)tīdrian 02.08.02 Disease, infirmity, sickness; 03.02.01 Decay, decline, corruption
tīdriende 02.08.02 Disease, infirmity, sickness
tīdsang 16.02.04.05 Canonical hour, service
tīdscēawere 16.01.04.06.01 Astrology
tīdscriptor 09.03.07.07.03.03 A writer, author
tīdþēnung 16.02.04.05 Canonical hour, service
tīdum 05.11.09.03 At times, sometimes
tīdung 09.06.02.01.06 A message, announcement by a messenger
tīdwrītere 09.03.07.07.03.03 A writer, author
tīdwurþung 16.02.04.05 Canonical hour, service
tīdymbwlātend 16.01.04.06.01 Astrology
tīederlic 02.08.02 Disease, infirmity, sickness
tīedernes 02.08.02 Disease, infirmity, sickness; 05.09 Weakness; 06.02.07.05.02 Moral weakness

tīedre 02.08.02 Disease, infirmity, sickness; 03.01.03.01 Stiffness, hardness; 05.09 Weakness; 05.11.01.02.01 Swift movement of time; 06.01.08.06.06 Timidity; 06.02.07.07 Cowardice, pusillanimity
(ge)tīegan 03.03.06.01 A whole formed by joining; 05.05.03 Binding, fastening
getīeged 04.02.05.05.04 Rope, rein
tīeman 02.01.03.03 Sex, generation; 02.01.03.03.02 To bring forth, produce; 11.03.01.01.01 Proof, demonstration; 14.04.03 Confirmation, ratification
tīeman be 02.01.03.03.02 To bring forth, produce
getīeme 03.06.03 Congruity, fitness, suitability; 04.02.05.06 Animals yoked together
tīen 03.03.03.04.10 Ten
tīen bebodu 16.02.01.08.01 The Old Testament
tīenambre 03.03.01.02 Dry measures
tīenfeald 03.03.03.04.10 Ten
tīengewintred 02.01.04 Age
tīennihte 05.11.06.03.01.04 (Of lunar cycle) so many nights old
tīenstrenge 18.02.07.02.03 Stringed instruments
tīenstrenged 18.02.07.02.03 Stringed instruments
tīenwintre 02.01.04 Age; 05.11.03.01 A year
tīer 03.01.16.01 Moisture
tife 02.06.02.01.04 Dog
tigelærne 17.05.02 A hearth, fireplace
tigel(e) 04.01.02.02.06.04 Pot, vessel, crock; 17.03.12.02 A potter; 09.03.07.06.04 A writing-tablet; 04.05.01.04 A tile, brick; 04.05.02.08 Top of a building
tigelen 17.03.12.02 A potter
tigelfāg 03.01.14.11 Medley/variety of colour
tigelgetel 04.05.01.05 Brickmaking
tigelgeweorc 04.05.01.05 Brickmaking
tigellēah 04.05.01.05 Brickmaking
tigelstān 04.05.01.04 A tile, brick
tigelwyrhta 04.05.01.05 Brickmaking
tiger 02.06.04.01.12 Tiger
tiging 09.03.02.03 Composition (inflectional or compounding)
tiglere 04.05.01.05 Brickmaking
tigrisc 02.06.04.01.12 Tiger
tiht 14.02.01 An offence; 14.03.03.01 Accusation
tihtan 14.03.03.01 Accusation
tihtbysig 14.03.03.01 Accusation
tihtle 14.03.03.01 Accusation
tihtlian 14.03.03.01 Accusation
getihtlod 14.03.03.01 Accusation
til 03.06.03 Congruity, fitness, suitability; 07.02.04.03 Nobleness, excellence, nobility, magnificence; 08.01.02.01 Favour, kindness, grace; 11.04 Ability, capacity, power; 11.07.01 Utility, usefulness; 11.07.02 Utility, advantage, convenience; 12.08.02.02 Righteousness, rectitude
tilen 11.03 Endeavour
tilfremmende 08.01.02.01 Favour, kindness, grace
tilia 04.02.02 Farmer, cultivator; 04.02.04.02 Cultivation/tillage
tilian 04.02.04.02 Cultivation/tillage; 15.05 Trade, traffic, commerce
(ge)tilian 10.01.02 Acquisition; 11.02.02.02 Care, mindfulness, attention; 11.03 Endeavour

getilian 02.08.12.01 Medical care, treatment; 10.03.04 Provision, supply
till 05.10.04 Place, room
(ge)tillan 05.12.05.02.03 To arrive
getillan 02.05.06 Sense of touch
tillic 11.04 Ability, capacity, power
tillīce 08.01.02.01 Favour, kindness, grace
tilman 04.02.02 Farmer, cultivator; 04.02.04.02 Cultivation/tillage
tilmōdig 08.01.02.01 Favour, kindness, grace
tilþ(e) 17.02 Work, occupation, employment; 04.02.04.03.02 Crop/crops; 10.01.02 Acquisition; 04.02.04.02 Cultivation/tillage
(ge)tilþe 15.05 Trade, traffic, commerce
tilung 02.08.12.01 Medical care, treatment; 04.02.04 Agriculture; 10.01.02 Acquisition; 11.03 Endeavour; 17.02 Work, occupation, employment
tīma 02.01.03.03.01 To beget; 05.02.01 Condition, state of affairs, situation; 05.11 A time, period of time; 05.11.02 A time, particular time, occasion; 05.11.03 Period of time, era, epoch; 05.11.03.01.02 A season of the year; 05.11.08 A suitable time, opportunity; 09 Speech, vocal utterance
timber 02.07.03.04 A wood, trees; 03 Material, matter, substance; 04.05 Building, construction
timbergeweorc 14.01.04.02 Rights involving property
getimberhālgung 16.02.01.08.04 Jewish seasons/feasts
timberhrycg 01.01.02.01.02.01 Rising ground, eminence
timberland 04.02.04.05.04 A detached area of woodland

getimbernes 06.01.06.02.03.04.05 Edification, instruction
timbor 17.03.05 An awl, borer, gimlet, etc.
(ge)timbran 06.01.06.02.03.04.05 Edification, instruction; 11.01.04 A doing, accomplishing (of something)
getimbre 04.05 Building, construction
timbrian 04.02.04.05.04.01 A forester, woodman
(ge)timbr(i)an 04.05 Building, construction; 05.05 Constitution, founding (e.g. of world)
(ge)timbrian 05.05.01 An author, source, originator
(ge)timbr(i)an 16.01.01.02.01 Creator
getimbr(i)an 13.02.06 A fortification
timbr(i)end 04.05 Building, construction
timbriend 17.02.04 Trade, calling, craft, aptitude
(ge)timbrung 04.05 Building, construction; 05.05 Constitution, founding (e.g. of world); 06.01.06.02.03.04.05 Edification, instruction
getimbrung 09.04.03 Exposition, making clear by explanation
getīmian 05.03.02.01.01 An event, occurrence
tīmlic 05.11.08 A suitable time, opportunity
tīmlīce 05.11.08 A suitable time, opportunity; 05.11.08.01.02 (Untimely) earliness
timpana 18.02.07.02.01 Percussion instruments
timpestre 18.02.07.02.01 Percussion instruments
timple 04.04.03 A spinning-house or chamber

tin 01.01.02.02.03.01 Types of metals/minerals; 17.04.02.09 Tin
tinclian 02.05.06.01 To touch and press
tincligende 08.01.01.01 Ardour, fervour, strong feeling
tind 17.03 Implements, tools, etc.
tindig 05.10.06.03.01 A point, spike, prickle
tindiht 05.10.06.03.01 A point, spike, prickle
tinen 01.01.02.02.03.01 Types of metals/minerals; 17.04.02.09 Tin
geting 05.02.01 Condition, state of affairs, situation
getingan 12.04.02 A crowding together, assembly
getingcræft 09.03.04 Rhetoric, art of exposition; 17.02.04 Trade, calling, craft, aptitude
tinn 04.05.02.07 A beam, rafter
tinnan 05.10.05.02 Extension, stretching; 13.02.08.04.04 A bow
tintreg(a) 14.05.02 Torment, punishment
tintregan ēa 16.01.05 Hell, lower world, abode of the dead
tintreganlic 16.01.05 Hell, lower world, abode of the dead
tintregend 14.05.02 Torment, punishment
(ge)tintregian 08.01.03.07.02 Misery, trouble, affliction; 14.05.02 Torment, punishment
tintreglic 16.01.05 Hell, lower world, abode of the dead
tintregstōw 16.01.05.01 Damnation, perdition, reprobation
tintregþegn 14.05.02 Torment, punishment
tintregung 14.05.02 Torment, punishment
tīr 01.02.01.01.01 Planet; 07.08.09 Renown, fame, glory; 09.03.07.01.01 A runic letter; 16.01.06.01 Northern gods
tīrēadig 07.08.09 Renown, fame, glory; 16.01.01.01.01.02 Glory
tīrfæst 07.08.09 Renown, fame, glory; 16.01.01.01.01.02 Glory
tīrfruma 16.01.01 God, the Lord
(ge)tirgan 07.05.03.03.02 To reproach, revile, abuse; 08.01.03.07.02 Misery, trouble, affliction
tirgung 07.05.03.03 Scorn, insult, abuse
tirisc 02.03.03.06.07.07 Other (alphabetical order); 04.04.05.05 Fine woven material from silk, cotton or linen
tīrlēas 07.09.03 Infamy, ignominy, shame
tīrmeahtig 16.01.01.01.01.01 Mightiness
tīrwine 07.08.09 Renown, fame, glory
getītelian 05.03.01.03 Reason, cause; 09.03.07.04 To make a symbol, mark
getītelian tō 12.02 A public office
getītelod 09.03.07.04 To make a symbol, mark
tītelung 09.03.07.07.02.01.01 A heading, title, superscription
tītolōse 02.07.11 Plants/flowers (alphabetical order)
titt 02.04.03.03.05 Chest, breast, bosom; 02.04.06.05.06 Mammary gland, breast
tittstrycel 02.04.03.03.05 Chest, breast, bosom; 02.04.06.05.06 Mammary gland, breast
tītul 09.03.07.07.02.01.01 A heading, title, superscription
tīþ 10.03.03 Granting; 12.03.05 Permission
tīþa bēon/weorþan 15.01.02 Gift, transfer of property
tīþe fremian 15.01 Property

(ge)tīþian 10.03.03 Granting; 12.03.05 Permission
getīung 06.01.02.01.01 A vision, apparition
tīw 09.03.07.01.01 A runic letter; 16.01.06.01 Northern gods; 16.01.06.02 Classical gods
tīwesdæg 05.11.03.01.05.01 Specific days
tīwesniht 05.11.03.01.05.01 Specific days
tō 03.03.04.03 Growth, increase; 05.10.05.01 A little way, no great distance; 03.03.04.02.02 Excess
tō ... foran 05.10.04.03 Presence
tō ... weard(-es/-e) 05.12.05.02 To go/travel towards, come, approach
tō ǣfen 05.11.04.02 Night, night time
tō ǣr 05.11.08.01.02 (Untimely) earliness
tō āhte 03.06 Comparison
tō ānes dæges 05.11.03.01.05 A day
tō gēare 05.11.03.01 A year
tō ātēon 06.02.06.03.04 Allurement
tō beflōwan 05.12.05.02 To go/travel towards, come, approach
tō begietan 15.05 Trade, traffic, commerce
tō bismere 07.09 Shame, disgrace
tō bismere gerēnian 07.09.02 Disgrace, shaming, humiliation
tō cūþan 06.01.07.07.03 Certainty
tō cyrcan werd 16.02.04.06 Attendance at church, church-going
tō dæg(e) 05.11.03.01.05 A day; 05.11.07.02 The present (time)
tō dēaþ gedōn 02.02.04.03 To kill, slay
tō dōn 03.03.04.03 Growth, increase
tō (ge)dōn 05.03.01 A cause (of anything)
tō gedrēog gān 02.04.06.06.07 Urine
tō drȳgum 03.03.06 Wholeness
tō ēac 03.03.04.03 Growth, increase
tō ēacan 03.03.04.03 Growth, increase

tō ealdre 05.11.01.01.01 Eternity
tō ēcum þingum 05.11.01.01.01 Eternity
tō geefnan 12.04 Fellowship, union, association
tō emnes 05.10.05.04.09.04 Opposite (av)
tō geflites 11.02.01 Energy, vigour, vigorous action
tō fulluhte (ge)būgan 16.02.04.10.01 Conversion
tō gifes 15.02.02 Cheap
tō gife(s) 10.03.08 Bountifulness, munificence; 10.03 Giving
tō gōde (ge)dōn 12.08.02.02 Righteousness, rectitude
tō handa 05.10.05.01 A little way, no great distance; 10 Having, owning, possession; 12.02.01 A substitute, representative; 14.05.08.01 Prison, confinement, durance
tō handa (ge)healdan 15.01.01.01 Holding of land
tō handa gerīdan 15.01 Property
tō handa weorpan 11.06.06.01 Abandonment (of principle); 12.05.07 Casting out, rejection
tō hlāfe gān 04.01.01 Eating; 16.02.04.07.04 Communion/eucharist
tō huntian 04.03 Hunting, the chase
tō hūsle gān/gangan 16.02.04.07.04 Communion/eucharist
tō hūsle gehālgian 16.02.04.07.04 Communion/eucharist
tō hwǣm 05.03.01 A cause (of anything)
tō hwæs 05.10.04.03 Presence
tō hwān 05.03.01 A cause (of anything)
tō hwȳ 05.03.01 A cause (of anything)
tō lāfe 03.03.07.02 What is left, remnant, remains
tō langre hwīle 05.11.01.01 Long duration, long space

tō langum fyrste 05.11.01.01 Long duration, long space
tō gelēafsuman 16.02.01 Faith
tō lēanes 10.03.05 Recompense, reward
tō leornunge oþfæst 06.01.06.02.03.04.04 Under instruction, being taught
tō lore 05.06 Destruction, dissolution, loss, breaking
tō lose 05.06 Destruction, dissolution, loss, breaking
tō lȳt 03.03.04.05 Insufficiency, lack, want; 05.07 Ending of existence, end of world
tō gemānan 10.01.03 A sharing, participation
tō mannum cuman 05.03.02.01.01 An event, occurrence
tō mēdes 10.03.05 Recompense, reward
tō mergen 05.11.07.04.01.01 (To)morrow
tō middes dæges 05.11.04.01.03 Mid-day, noon
tō middes mergenes 05.11.04.01.02 Morning
tō midre nihte 05.11.04.02.02 Midnight
tō morgen 05.11.07.04.01.01 (To)morrow
tō nōnes 05.11.04.01.03 Mid-day, noon
tō rǣde niman 06.02.06 Mind, purpose
tō rǣde þyncan 11.07.01.01 Desirability, expediency
tō rihtes tīman 05.11.08 A suitable time, opportunity
tō sǣles 05.11.08 A suitable time, opportunity
tō scande 07.03.05 Infamy, shame, wickedness
tō scrifte gān 16.02.04.07.02 Confession
tō sīþ 05.11.08.01.03 Late
tō somnian 03.03.04.01.02.01 A heap, mass, accumulation

tō sōþan 06.01.07.01 Correct, right, free from error
tō sōþan þingon 06.01.07.01 Correct, right, free from error
tō sōþe 06.01.07.01 Correct, right, free from error
tō sōþum 06.01.07.01 Correct, right, free from error
tō swīþe scortre hwīle 05.11.01.02 Shortness/brevity in time
tō tīman 05.11.07.01 Contemporary, coeval; 05.11.08 A suitable time, opportunity
tō twēon weorþan 06.01.07.07.03.01 Unknown, uncertain
tō þæs gemearces þe 05.12.05.02 To go/travel towards, come, approach
tō þæs (þæt) 03.03.05 Extent, degree
tō þæs þe 05.10.04.03 Presence
tō þām 05.03.01.03 Reason, cause
tō þām ǣrdæge 05.11.04.01 Day (not night)
tō þām gerāde þe 14.04.02 A stipulation
tō þām þæt 05.03.02 Event, issue, result
tō þance 11.12.02 Aid, help, succour
tō þearfe 06.02.04.01 Want, need
tō þises 05.11.07.02 The present (time)
tō þon 03.03.05 Extent, degree
tō þon þæt 05.03.02 Event, issue, result; 05.11.07.03.02 Earlier, antecedent
tō þon þætte 05.03.02 Event, issue, result
tō þȳ ... þæt 06.02.06.01 An end, goal
tō þȳ (þæt) 03.03.05 Extent, degree
tō ūhtes 05.11.04.01 Day (not night)
tō underne(s) 05.11.04.01.02 Morning
tō wel 03.03.06 Wholeness
tō wīdan ealdre 05.11.01.01.01 Eternity
tō wīdan fēore 05.11.01.01.01 Eternity

tō gewissan 06.01.07.02 Certainty, truth, what really is; 06.01.07.07.03 Certainty
tō gewisse 06.01.07.07.03 Certainty
tō worulde 05.11.01.01.01 Eternity
tō gewunan niman 11.01.01 Practice, exercise, doing
tō wundre 06.01.08.05.01.01 Wondrous, glorious, marvellous
tōætēacnian 03.03.04.03 Growth, increase
tōætȳcan 03.03.04.03 Growth, increase
tōætȳcnes 03.03.04.03 Growth, increase
tōāmearcian 07.01.01 Choice, election
tōāwrītan 09.03.07.07.03 Composition, arrangement, writing
tōbǣdan 16.02.04 Worship, honour, praise
tōbǣden 05.12.05.12.02 To raise, lift up, elevate; 07.02.04 Excellence
tōbeatan 05.06.05.03 Bruising, crushing
tōbeaten 05.06.05.03 Bruising, crushing
tōbefealdan 05.10.06.05 A fold, plait, wrinkle
tōbeflōwan 01.01.03.03 Flow/flowing
tōbelimpan 12.07 An obligation, bounden duty
tōberan 05.10.05 A space, span; 05.12.02.02 To carry off, remove; 05.12.05.03.01 To part ways, separate from, depart
tōberan wiþ 12.05.03 Disagreement, discord, dissension
tōberennes 03.06.02 Difference, diversity, dissimilarity
tōberstan 02.08.05.02 Particular inflammation/swelling; 05.06.03 A dashing together, breaking, shattering; 05.12.05.03.04.01 To burst forth, break out

tōberstung 02.08.05.01 Swelling
tōbesettan 03.03.04.03 Growth, increase
tōbīcnan 09.05.05.01 Showing, manifestation, display
tōbīgende 05.12.04.01.01 Unstable
tōblǣdan 03.01.15.01 Inspiration, inbreathing; 05.10.05.02.02 Greater, bigger
tōblāwan 03.01.15.01 Inspiration, inbreathing; 08.01 Heart, spirit, mood, disposition
tōblāwennes 02.08.05.01 Swelling
tōborsten 02.08.05.02 Particular inflammation/swelling; 05.06.03 A dashing together, breaking, shattering
tōborstennes 02.08.05.02 Particular inflammation/swelling
tōbrǣdan 05.10.05.02.01 Diffusion, effusion, spreading; 05.10.05.02.02 Greater, bigger
tōbrǣd(ed)nes 05.10.01 Amplitude, spaciousness, vastness
tōbrecan 05.06 Destruction, dissolution, loss, breaking; 05.06.03 A dashing together, breaking, shattering; 05.07 Ending of existence, end of world; 05.10.05.04.12.01 To bespread, cover with; 05.11.11.02 Let up, intermission, cessation; 13.02.03.01 An attack, assault; 13.02.05.01.01 To overcome, conquer; 14.02 Lawlessness
tōbregdan 05.06.02.02 A tearing apart; 08.01.03.07.02 Misery, trouble, affliction
tōbrengnes 16.02.04.12 Sacrifice, a sacrifice
tōbringan 10.03.02 Presenting, offering
tōbrocen 05.06.03 A dashing together, breaking, shattering

tōbrocenlic 03.01.03.01 Stiffness, hardness; 03.02.01 Decay, decline, corruption

tōbrȳs(i)an 05.06.05.03 Bruising, crushing

tōbrȳtan 05.06 Destruction, dissolution, loss, breaking; 05.06.05.03 Bruising, crushing; 08.01.03.07.02.01 Injury, offence

tōbrȳtednes 02.08.04 Hurt, injury, damage; 08.01.03.02.01 Compunction, remorse, contrition

tōbrȳtendlic 03.01.03.01 Stiffness, hardness

tōbrȳting 05.06 Destruction, dissolution, loss, breaking

tōbrȳtt 08.01.03.02.01 Compunction, remorse, contrition

tōceorfan 05.06.02 Cleaving, splitting, cutting

tōcēowan 04.01.01.01 Chewing

tōcīnan 05.06.02.01.01 A crack

tōcirhūs 04.01.02.04.05.01.01 Quartering of officials; 04.05.03.03 A lodging-house, inn

tōclæfan 05.06.02.01 A cleft, split

tōclēofan 05.06.02 Cleaving, splitting, cutting; 05.06.02.01 A cleft, split

tōclifian 03.01.17 Thickness, viscosity; 06.02.07.03 Perseverance

tōclifrian 05.06.06.01 A tearing, laceration

tōclypigendlic 09.03.02.03.01.01.01 Case

tōclypung 09.01.03 To address, speak to

tōcnāwan 06.01.06 Understanding, knowledge, cognizance

tōcnāw(en)nes 06.01.06 Understanding, knowledge, cognizance

tōcnyccan 03.03.06.01 A whole formed by joining

tōcnyssan 05.06.05.03 Bruising, crushing

tōcuman 05.12.05.02.03 To arrive

tōcumende 12.06.05 A foreign country

tōcwæscednes 05.06 Destruction, dissolution, loss, breaking

tōcwæstednes 05.06 Destruction, dissolution, loss, breaking

tōcweþan 12.03.06 Prohibition

tōcwylman 14.05.02 Torment, punishment

tōcwȳsan 05.06.05.03 Bruising, crushing

tōcwȳsednes 05.06.01 Devastation, laying waste

tōcyme 05.12.05.02 To go/travel towards, come, approach; 05.12.05.02.03 To arrive; 16.01.01.04.02.02 Events associated with Christ; 16.02.04.04.02.01.01 Around the Nativity

tōcyrran 05.12.05.03.01 To part ways, separate from, depart

tōdǣlan 03.03.03.01 Arithmetic; 03.03.07.01 Division, partition, separation; 03.06.02 Difference, diversity, dissimilarity; 05.06 Destruction, dissolution, loss, breaking; 05.10.04.04.01 Dispersion; 07.01.01.01 Discrimination, faculty of distinguishing; 09.01 To speak, exercise faculty of speech; 09.03.07.04.01 To punctuate, divide; 10.03.07 Distribution; 12.05.03 Disagreement, discord, dissension

tōdǣled 03.03.07 A part, division, portion; 03.06.02 Difference, diversity, dissimilarity

tōdǣledlīce 03.03.07.01 Division, partition, separation

tōdǣlednes 03.03.07 A part, division, portion; 03.03.07.01 Division,

partition, separation; 03.06.02 Difference, diversity, dissimilarity; 05.11.11.02 Let up, intermission, cessation; 07.01.01.01 Discrimination, faculty of distinguishing
tōdǣlendlic 03.03.07.01 Division, partition, separation
tōdǣlendlīce 03.06.02 Difference, diversity, dissimilarity
tōdǣlnes 03.03.07 A part, division, portion
tōdāl 03.03.07 A part, division, portion; 03.03.07.01 Division, partition, separation; 03.06.02 Difference, diversity, dissimilarity; 05.10.04.04.01 Dispersion; 07.01.01.01 Discrimination, faculty of distinguishing; 09.03.07.04.01 To punctuate, divide; 10.03.07 Distribution; 12.05.03 Disagreement, discord, dissension
tōdēman 07.01.01.01 Discrimination, faculty of distinguishing
tōdihtnian 03.05 Order, arrangement, disposition
tōdōn 03.03.07.01 Division, partition, separation; 03.06.02 Difference, diversity, dissimilarity; 05.05.04 That loosens, loosening
tōdrǣfan 05.10.04.04.01 Dispersion; 05.12.02.04 To cast out, drive away
tōdrǣfednes 05.12.02.04 To cast out, drive away
tōdrǣfnes 09.07.03 Disagreement, dissent; 12.05.03 Disagreement, discord, dissension
tōdrēosan 03.02.01 Decay, decline, corruption
tōdrīfan 03.03.07.01 Division, partition, separation; 05.06 Destruction, dissolution, loss, breaking; 05.07 Ending of existence, end of world; 05.10.04.04.01 Dispersion; 05.12.02.04 To cast out, drive away
tōdrifen 05.10.05.02.01 Diffusion, effusion, spreading; 12.06.05.01 State of exile, banishment
tōdwǣscan 03.01.13.02 A growing dark, darkening
tōecnes 03.03.04.03 Growth, increase
tōemnes 05.10.05.04.09 Side, quarter, direction
tōendebyrdnes 03.05.02 An arrangement, order, succession
tōēþian 02.04.06.07.05 To breathe; 03.01.15.01 Inspiration, inbreathing
tof 05.12.03.02 Slowness
tōfær 02.02 Death
tōfaran 05.07 Ending of existence, end of world; 05.10.04.04.01 Dispersion; 05.12.05.03.01 To part ways, separate from, depart
tōfealdan 05.12.01.09 To travel on water
tōfeallan 03.02.01 Decay, decline, corruption; 05.06.01 Devastation, laying waste; 05.12.05.13.03 To fall
tōfeng 10.04.02.02 To seize, take, grasp, lay hold on
tōfēran 05.10.04.04.01 Dispersion; 05.12.05.03.01 To part ways, separate from, depart
tōferian 04.01 Digestion; 05.06.02.02 A tearing apart; 05.10.04.04.02 Removal, taking away; 05.11.08.01.03.01 Delay
tōfēsian 05.10.04.04.01 Dispersion
tōflēam 11.10.01.02 Refuge, help, shelter
tōflēogan 05.10.04.04.01 Dispersion
tōflēon 01.01.03.03 Flow/flowing
tōflēotan 01.01.03.06 Flood

tōflogen 02.08.05.02 Particular inflammation/swelling
tōflōwan 03.02.01.01 Decay, corruption, rottenness; 05.07 Ending of existence, end of world; 05.10.04.04.01 Dispersion; 05.10.05.02.01 Diffusion, effusion, spreading; 06.01.05.03.01.01 Dullness, folly, stupidity
tōflōwednes 03.01.16 Liquid, a liquid
tōflōwende 05.12.05.02.02 To come together, meet; 15.01.05 Possession of wealth
tōflōwendnes 01.01.03.03 Flow/flowing; 03.01.16 Liquid, a liquid
tōflōwennes 03.01.16 Liquid, a liquid
tōforan 03.03.05 Extent, degree; 03.03.05.01.01 Principal/chief (of its class or type); 05.03 Source, origin; 05.10.05.04.09.01 Front; 05.11.07.03.02 Earlier, antecedent; 07.01.01.02 To prefer
tōforlǣtan 12.05.07.01 Separation, dismissal, rejection; 15.01.02.01 Inherited property
tōforlǣtennes 05.11.11.02 Let up, intermission, cessation
toft 04.02.03 Cultivatable land/farmland
tōfyllan 05.06.03 A dashing together, breaking, shattering
tog 12.05.04.01 Fighting, contention, warfare, strife
getog 02.08.07.06 Disorders of the neck
tōgǣd(e)re 03.03.06.01 A whole formed by joining
tōgǣdere 05.11.11.01 A not ceasing, persistence, recurrence
tōgǣdere gāras beran 13.02.02 Battle
tōgǣdere lǣtan 02.08.13 Recovery, growing better
tōgǣdereweard 05.12.05.02 To go/travel towards, come, approach
tōgǣlan 16.02.04.14 Sacrilege
tōgǣnan 09.07.04 Assertion, affirmation
tōgān 01.01.03.03 Flow/flowing; 03.03.07.01 Division, partition, separation; 05.12.05.03.01 To part ways, separate from, depart
tōgang 05.12.05.02 To go/travel towards, come, approach
tōgangan 05.07 Ending of existence, end of world; 05.12.05.03.01 To part ways, separate from, depart
getoge 04.02.05.05.02 Harness of draught animal
tōgēan 05.12.05.02 To go/travel towards, come, approach
tōgēanes 03.06 Comparison; 05.11.07.04 Future, time to come; 05.11.09.06 Frequency, repetition; 05.12.05.02 To go/travel towards, come, approach; 05.13.04 Exchange, commutation; 11.01.03 Preparation; 12.05 Contradiction, opposition
tōgearwian 11.01.03 Preparation
tōgecīgan 09.01.03 To address, speak to
tōgecorennes 07.01.01 Choice, election
tōgedēgled 09.05.04.01 Concealment, obscurity
tōgegrīpan 10.04.02 To grasp, take hold of
tōgehlytto 12.04 Fellowship, union, association
tō(ge)īecan 03.03.04.03 Growth, increase
tōgeīecendlic 09.03.02.02.01.04 Adjectival
tōgeīht 03.03.04.03 Growth, increase
tōgeīhtnes 03.03.04.03 Growth, increase
tō(ge)lǣdan 05.12.05.08.01 To go before and guide

tōgelǣstan 12.04.01.02 A fellow traveller, companion
tōgelan 01.01.03.03 Flow/flowing
tōgelaþian 08.01.02.04 Hospitality
tōgelaþung 12.04.02 A crowding together, assembly
tōgelicgende 10.01 Fact of belonging, possession by
getogen 06.01.06.02.03.04.04 Under instruction, being taught; 09 Speech, vocal utterance; 11.04.02 Skill, skilfulness
tōgengan 05.12.05.03.01 To part ways, separate from, depart
tōgēotan 05.10.05.02.01 Diffusion, effusion, spreading
tōgescēadan 09.04.03 Exposition, making clear by explanation
tō(ge)settan 03.03.04.03 Growth, increase
tōgetēon 03.03.04.01.02.01 A heap, mass, accumulation; 06.02.06.03.04 Allurement
tō(ge)tēon 02.04.06.07.05 To breathe
togettan 05.12.05.05 To shake, quake, wag
tōgeþēodan 03.03.06.01 A whole formed by joining; 06.02.07.03 Perseverance
tōgeþeodd 05.10.05.01 A little way, no great distance
tōgewegen 05.11.11 Continuity
tōgewunod 11.05 Natural/proper way/manner/mode of action
togian 05.12.02.05 To pull, drag, draw
tōgīnan 05.10.05.04.14.01 A yawning, gaping opening
tōglīdan 01.01.03.03 Flow/flowing; 03.01.09.02.01.04 Smoke; 05.06.01 Devastation, laying waste; 05.12.05.03.04 To come/go out from

tōgliden 05.06.01 Devastation, laying waste
tōgotennes 05.10.05.02.01 Diffusion, effusion, spreading
togung 02.08.08.04.01 Gripe, colic
tōh 03.01.04.01 Power of bending, flexibility; 03.01.17 Thickness, viscosity
tōhaccian 05.06.02 Cleaving, splitting, cutting
tōhǣlan 05.09 Weakness
tōhāwiend 02.05.09.05 To watch, observe, survey
tōheald 05.10.05.04.04 A descent, slope, incline
tōhēawan 05.06.02 Cleaving, splitting, cutting
tōhelpan 11.12.02 Aid, help, succour
tōhīgung 05.03.02 Event, issue, result
tōhladan 05.10.04.04.01 Dispersion
tōhlēotan 10.03.07 Distribution; 18.02.02.01 Gaming, playing at dice
tōhlīce 03.01.17 Thickness, viscosity
tōhlīdan 05.06.02.01 A cleft, split; 05.10.05.04.14.01 A yawning, gaping opening
tohlīne 17.03.07 Tools for digging/grasping/pulling
tōhlystend 02.05.10 Faculty of hearing
tōhnescan 02.08.12.02.05.02 Salves, ointments
tōhopa 06.01.08 Expectation; 06.01.08.02 Hope, expectation
tōhopung 06.01.08.02 Hope, expectation
tōhrēosan 05.06.01 Devastation, laying waste
tōhrēran 05.06.04 Damage, injury, defect, hurt, loss
tōhrēred 05.06 Destruction, dissolution, loss, breaking

tōhrīcod 03.03.07 A part, division, portion
tōhroren 03.02.01.01 Decay, corruption, rottenness; 05.06 Destruction, dissolution, loss, breaking; 05.06.01 Devastation, laying waste
getoht 13.02.02 Battle
tohte 13.02.02 Battle
tōhwega 03.03.04.04 Littleness, smallness
tōhweorfan 05.10.04.04.01 Dispersion; 05.12.05.03.01 To part ways, separate from, depart
tōhwyrfan 05.06 Destruction, dissolution, loss, breaking
tōhyht 06.01.08.02 Hope, expectation
tōiernan 05.12.03.01 Swiftness, velocity
tōiernende 05.12.05.02.02 To come together, meet
tōirnan/tōrinnan 05.12.05 To move and change direction, turn
tōl 17.03 Implements, tools, etc.
tōlǣtan 02.08.08.12 Disease of bowels; 02.08.13 Recovery, growing better; 05.10.04.04.01 Dispersion; 08.01.03.07.04.02 Relief, alleviation
tōlǣten 02.05.04 Sleepiness, drowsiness, sleep
tōlǣtennes 08.01.03.01 Despondency
tolcendlīce 12.08.07.01.01 Wantonness, sensuality, lasciviousness
tolcettende 09.01.02.01 Excessive fluency, loquacity; 12.08.07.01.01 Wantonness, sensuality, lasciviousness
tolcetung 02.05.05.03 Sexual appetite, lust
tolfrēo 14.01.03.02 Freedom from punishment or fine
tōlicgan 05.10.04 Place, room
tōlīhtan 03.01.12.02 A beam of light

tōliþian 05.06.02.01 A cleft, split; 08.01.03.07.04.02 Relief, alleviation; 15.04 A debt, due
tōliþod 08.01.03.07.04.02 Relief, alleviation
toll 14.01.04.03 Rights involving money; 15.02 Worth, value; 15.02.04.01 Payment for temporary use, rent, hire; 15.03 Exaction of tax/tribute; 15.03.01 Toll
tollere 15.03 Exaction of tax/tribute
tollsceamol 15.03 Exaction of tax/tribute
tollscīr 12.06.02 District, province
toln 15.03.01 Toll
tolnere 15.03 Exaction of tax/tribute
tōlōcian 10.01 Fact of belonging, possession by
tolsetl 15.03 Exaction of tax/tribute
tōlūcan 05.06 Destruction, dissolution, loss, breaking
tōlūtan 05.10.05.04.04 A descent, slope, incline
tōlynnan 10.04.03 To take away, remove
tōlȳsan 03.03.07.01 Division, partition, separation; 05.05.04 That loosens, loosening; 05.06.01 Devastation, laying waste; 05.07 Ending of existence, end of world; 05.09 Weakness; 08.01.03.07.04.02 Relief, alleviation; 11.10.03 Salvation/deliverance from; 15.04 A debt, due
tōlȳsed 05.06.03 A dashing together, breaking, shattering
tōlȳsednes 05.06 Destruction, dissolution, loss, breaking; 05.10.04.04.01 Dispersion
tōlȳsend 05.06 Destruction, dissolution, loss, breaking; 05.06.01 Devastation, laying waste

tōlȳsendlic 05.06 Destruction, dissolution, loss, breaking
tōlȳsing 05.06.01 Devastation, laying waste; 11.10.03 Salvation/deliverance from
tōlȳsnes 02.02 Death; 05.06.01 Devastation, laying waste
tōm 03.03.08 Emptiness
tōmældan 07.05.03 Calumny, backbiting
tōmearcian 03.03.03 Number; 05.03.01.03 Reason, cause
tōmearcodnes 03.03.03 Number
tōmerigen 05.11.07.04.01.01 (To)morrow
tōmetan 10.03.07 Distribution
tōmiddes 05.10.05.04.01.01 The middle; 05.10.05.04.10 Among
tōnama 09.06.02.01.07 A name, appellation
getōnamian 09.06.02.01.07 A name, appellation
tōnēalǣcan 05.12.05.02 To go/travel towards, come, approach
tōnemnan 09.06.02.01.07.02 A categorizing name
tonian 01.03.01.03.01.01 Thundering, thunder
tōniman 05.06.02.01 A cleft, split; 10.04.03 To take away, remove
top 01.01.02.01.02.02 Hill, mountain; 18.02.02 Play, (athletic) sport
topazion 17.04.03.04 Gems collectively
topazius 17.04.03.04 Gems collectively
toppa 04.04.09 A fringe, border, hem
tōrǣcan 03.03.04.03 Growth, increase; 10.03.02 Presenting, offering
tōrbegete 11.11 Difficulty
torcul 04.01.03.05.01.01.01 Wine-press
torcyrre 06.02.07.04 Obstinacy
tord 02.04.06.06.06 Faeces; 04.06.02.02 Foul, filthy, squalid

tordwifel 02.06.09.02.03 Beetle
tōrendan 05.06.03 A dashing together, breaking, shattering
torenēage 02.08.07.02 Disorders of the eye
torfian 05.12.02.07 To throw, cast, toss
(ge)torfian 05.06.09.04 Stoning, casting of stones; 05.12.02.07.01 To throw, scatter; 05.12.05.05.01 To wave, undulate
torfung 14.05.05 Physical punishments
torht 02.05.09.01 To open the eyes/be awake; 03.01.12 Brightness, light; 07.02.04.03 Nobleness, excellence, nobility, magnificence; 07.10 Beauty, fairness; 18.02.07 Music
torhte 07.10 Beauty, fairness; 18.02.07 Music
torhtian 09.05.05.01 Showing, manifestation, display
torhtlic 07.10 Beauty, fairness
torhtlīce 07.10 Beauty, fairness
torhtmōd 07.08.07 Glory, splendour, magnificence; 16.01.01.01.01.02 Glory
torhtnes 03.01.12 Brightness, light; 07.08.09 Renown, fame, glory
torn 08.01.03.04 Grief; 08.01.03.05.02 Anger; 08.01.03.07.04 Severity, harshness
torncwide 07.05.03.03 Scorn, insult, abuse
torne 08.01.03.07.04 Severity, harshness
torngemōt 13.02.03.01 An attack, assault
torngenīþla 08.01.03.09.05 Enmity
tornlic 08.01.03.07.04 Severity, harshness
tornmōd 08.01.03.05.02 Anger
tornsorg 08.01.03.03 Anxiety
tornword 07.05.03.03 Scorn, insult, abuse

tornwracu 12.05.04.02 Vengeance, revenge
tornwyrdan 07.05.03.03.02 To reproach, revile, abuse
toroc 02.06.09.02.03 Beetle
torr 01.01.02.01.02.02.05 Crag, rock, stone; 04.05.03.02.02.07 A tower; 13.02.06.01 Stronghold, fort/fortified town
torrian 05.10.05.03.03 Height, loftiness, sublimity
tōryne 12.05.04 Strife, hostility
tōrȳpan 05.06.06.01 A tearing, laceration
tōsǣlan 06.02.04.01.01 Need, distress, straits, difficulty; 11.06.03.01 Ill fortune, bad success
tōsāwan 04.02.04.02.03 Sowing; 05.12.02.07.01 To throw, scatter
tosca 02.06.07.02 Frog, toad
tōscǣnan 05.06.03 A dashing together, breaking, shattering
toscanlēac 02.07.11.02 Unidentified plants (alphabetical order)
tōsceacan 05.10.04.04.01 Dispersion; 05.12.02 To move, set in motion
tōscēacerian 05.10.04.04.01 Dispersion
tōscēad 03.03.07.01 Division, partition, separation; 03.06.02 Difference, diversity, dissimilarity; 07.01.01.01 Discrimination, faculty of distinguishing
tōscēadan 03.03.07.01 Division, partition, separation; 03.05 Order, arrangement, disposition; 03.06.02 Difference, diversity, dissimilarity; 05.10.04.04.01 Dispersion; 06.01.06 Understanding, knowledge, cognizance; 07 Judgement, forming of opinion; 09.01 To speak, exercise faculty of speech; 09.04.03 Exposition, making clear by explanation; 09.07 Dispute, debate; 12.05.03 Disagreement, discord, dissension
tōscēadednes 03.03.07.01 Division, partition, separation
tōscēadend 03.03.07.01 Division, partition, separation; 07.01.01.01 Discrimination, faculty of distinguishing
tōscēadennes 03.06.02 Difference, diversity, dissimilarity
tōscearian 05.10.04.04.01 Dispersion
tōscecgan 03.06.02 Difference, diversity, dissimilarity
tōscendan 05.06 Destruction, dissolution, loss, breaking
tōscēotan 05.12.05.03.03 To depart, leave, set out
tōscirian 03.03.07.01 Division, partition, separation; 03.06.02 Difference, diversity, dissimilarity; 09.03.07.04 To make a symbol, mark; 10.03.07 Distribution
tōscrīpan 01.01.03.03 Flow/flowing
tōscūfan 05.10.04.04.01 Dispersion; 05.12.02.02 To carry off, remove; 06.02.06.03.03 Incitement
tōscyftan 10.03.07 Distribution
tōscylian/tōscyllan 03.03.07.01 Division, partition, separation
tōsendan 05.10.04.04.01 Dispersion
tōsēoþan 03.01.09.01.01 (Of liquids) boiling
tōsetednes 08.01 Heart, spirit, mood, disposition
tōsett 02.04.06.03.02.01.01 Tooth/teeth
tōsettan 03.03.07.01 Division, partition, separation; 03.05 Order, arrangement, disposition
tōsēþan 11.03.01.01 Trial, probation

tōsīgan 03.02.01.02 Decay from age
tōsittan 05.10.05 A space, span
tōslacian 11.06.01.01 Negligence, carelessness, heedlessness
tōslǣfan 05.06.02 Cleaving, splitting, cutting
tōslēan 05.06.02.01 A cleft, split; 05.06.03 A dashing together, breaking, shattering; 05.12.02.04 To cast out, drive away
tōslīfan 05.06.02 Cleaving, splitting, cutting
tōslītan 02.08.03.02 Itch, irritation; 03.06.02 Difference, diversity, dissimilarity; 05.06.02.01 A cleft, split; 05.06.02.02 A tearing apart; 05.06.04 Damage, injury, defect, hurt, loss; 05.06.06.01 A tearing, laceration; 05.07 Ending of existence, end of world; 05.11.11.02 Let up, intermission, cessation; 08.01.03.07.02 Misery, trouble, affliction
tōslite 02.08.04.01 A wound
tōsliten 05.06.02 Cleaving, splitting, cutting
tōslītere 16.02.01.05 Heresy, error, wrong belief
tōslitnes 05.06.06.01 A tearing, laceration; 09.07.03 Disagreement, dissent; 12.05.03 Disagreement, discord, dissension; 16.02.01.05 Heresy, error, wrong belief
tōslopen 02.05.04 Sleepiness, drowsiness, sleep; 05.05.04 That loosens, loosening; 11.06.01.01 Negligence, carelessness, heedlessness
tōslūpan 02.08.02 Disease, infirmity, sickness; 02.08.08.12 Disease of bowels; 02.08.13 Recovery, growing better; 05.05.04 That loosens, loosening; 05.06.01 Devastation, laying waste; 05.07 Ending of existence, end of world; 06.01.08.06.01 A shuddering with fear, nervousness; 12.08.07.01 Laxity, indulgence
tōslūping 03.03.07.01 Division, partition, separation
tōsmēagan 09.05.01 Inspection, examination
tōsnǣdan 05.06.02 Cleaving, splitting, cutting
tōsniden 05.06.02 Cleaving, splitting, cutting
tōsnīþan 05.06.02 Cleaving, splitting, cutting
tōsōcn 08.01.02.04.01 Visiting
tōsōcnes 05.12.05.10 To go behind, follow
tōsōcnung 05.12.05.10 To go behind, follow
tōsomne 03.03.06.01 A whole formed by joining; 05.10.05.01 A little way, no great distance; 05.11.07.01 Contemporary, coeval; 05.11.11.01 A not ceasing, persistence, recurrence; 05.12.05.02 To go/travel towards, come, approach
tōsomne gedōn 12.09.02 Marriage ceremony
tōsomne geþēodan 12.09.02 Marriage ceremony
tōspillan 05.06 Destruction, dissolution, loss, breaking
tōsprǣc 09.01.01 A speech, what is said, words
tōsprǣd 02.04.04.03.03 Hair of head; 05.10.05.02 Extension, stretching

tōsprǣdan 05.10.05.02.02 Greater, bigger
tōspringan 05.06.02.01.01 A crack; 05.06.03 A dashing together, breaking, shattering; 05.10.05.04.14 An opening, aperture
tōsprytting 06.02.06.03.02 Instigation
tōspurnan 12.05.07 Casting out, rejection
tōstandan 03.06.02 Difference, diversity, dissimilarity; 05.10.05 A space, span; 15.02.04 Spending, disbursement
tōstencan 02.02.03 To die, perish; 05.06 Destruction, dissolution, loss, breaking; 05.10.04.04.01 Dispersion
tōstenced 05.06 Destruction, dissolution, loss, breaking
tōstencednes 05.06 Destruction, dissolution, loss, breaking
tōstenc(ed)nes 05.10.04.04.01 Dispersion
tōstencend 10.03.08.01 Overliberality, waste of money
tōstician 05.06.04 Damage, injury, defect, hurt, loss
tōstiht(i)an 03.05 Order, arrangement, disposition
tōstincan 02.05.08 Faculty of smell
tōstingan 05.06.07 Pricking, a prick, puncture
tōstregdan 05.06 Destruction, dissolution, loss, breaking; 05.10.04.04.01 Dispersion; 06.01.05.03.01.01 Dullness, folly, stupidity
tōstrogden 05.10.05.02.01 Diffusion, effusion, spreading
tōsundrian 03.03.07.01 Division, partition, separation
tōswāpan 05.12.02.06 To push, impel, thrust
tōswellan 03.03.04.03 Growth, increase
tōswengan 05.06.03 A dashing together, breaking, shattering
tōsweorcan 03.01.13.02 A growing dark, darkening
tōswīfan 05.12.05.03.01 To part ways, separate from, depart
tōswollen 02.08.05.01 Swelling
tōswung 05.12.02.07 To throw, cast, toss; 18.02.02 Play, (athletic) sport
tōsyndrian 05.10.05 A space, span; 07.01.01.01 Discrimination, faculty of distinguishing
getot 07.06.04.01 Ostentation, showiness
tōtalu 07.08 Reputation, fame
tōtellan 03.03.03 Number
tōtēon 05.06.02.02 A tearing apart; 05.12.02.05 To pull, drag, draw; 14.03.03 Law, action of the courts
tōteran 05.06.02.02 A tearing apart; 08.01.03.07.02.01 Injury, offence
tōthyll 02.05.09.10 Look-out place
tōtian 05.10.06.03 Projection, head, extremity (of anything)
tōtian ūt 02.05.09.06 Thing seen, sight, vision
tōtihting 06.02.06.03.02 Instigation
tōtorfian 05.06.09.04 Stoning, casting of stones; 05.12.02.07 To throw, cast, toss
tōtrǣglian 05.06.02.02 A tearing apart
tōtredan 05.06.04 Damage, injury, defect, hurt, loss; 05.12.01.04.01.02 To tread upon, trample
totrida 05.12.01.07.01 To hang
tōtwǣman 03.03.07.01 Division, partition, separation; 05.10.04 Place, room; 05.10.04.04.01 Dispersion; 05.10.05 A space, span; 05.11.08.01.03.01 Delay; 05.12.02.02 To carry off, remove; 07.01.01.01

Discrimination, faculty of distinguishing
tōtwǣmednes 12.05.03 Disagreement, discord, dissension
tōþ 02.04.06.03.02.01.01 Tooth/teeth
tōþ onforan hēafde 02.04.06.03.02.01.01 Tooth/teeth
tōþa gebitt 08.01.03.03 Anxiety
tōþa gristbītung 08.01.03.03 Anxiety
tōþa gristlung 08.01.03.03 Anxiety
tōþa gehēaw 08.01.03.03 Anxiety
tōþece 02.08.07.04.01 Mouth disease
tōþenednes 05.10.05.02 Extension, stretching
tōþēnian 12.01.01.08 Service
tōþening 05.10.05.02 Extension, stretching
tōþerscan 05.06.03 A dashing together, breaking, shattering
tōþgār 04.06.01.06 A toothpick
tōþindan 03.03.04.03 Growth, increase; 07.06.01.03 To be proud/arrogant
tōþlēas 02.04.06.03.02.01.01 Tooth/teeth
tōþmægen 05.08 Strength
tōþrǣstan 05.06.05.03 Bruising, crushing
tōþrima 02.04.06.03.02.01 Mouth
tōþringan 05.10.04.04.01 Dispersion
tōþsealf 02.08.12.02.07 Remedies for specific parts (head to toe)
tōþsticca 04.06.01.06 A toothpick
tōþum ontȳnan 09.01 To speak, exercise faculty of speech
tōþunden 02.08.05.01 Swelling; 07.06.01.01 Proud, arrogant
tōþundenes 07.06.01 Pride, arrogance
tōþundenlīce 07.06.01.02 Proudly, arrogantly
tōþundennes 02.08.05.01 Swelling
tōþuniende 06.01.08.05.01 Amazement, astonishment, wonder, admiration
tōþwærc 02.08.07.04.01 Mouth disease
tōþwīnan 02.05.09.14 To vanish, disappear
tōþwyrm 02.08.07.04.01 Mouth disease
towcræft 04.04 Weaving
tōweard 05.10.05.04.09.01 Front; 05.11.07.04 Future, time to come; 05.11.07.04.01 Nearness, approach, imminence; 05.12.05.02 To go/travel towards, come, approach
tōwe(a)rd 09.03.02.03.01.02.03 Tense
tōweardes 05.12.05.02 To go/travel towards, come, approach
tōweardlic 05.11.07.04 Future, time to come
tōweardlīce 05.11.07.04 Future, time to come
tōweardnes 05.11.07.04 Future, time to come; 05.11.07.04.01 Nearness, approach, imminence; 16.01.01.04.02.02 Events associated with Christ; 16.01.02.01 Heavenly dwelling place
tōweaxan 02.07.01 To grow
tōweccan 06.02.06.03.03 Incitement; 12.08.07.01.01 Wantonness, sensuality, lasciviousness
tōwegan 05.10.04.04.01 Dispersion
tōwendan 05.06 Destruction, dissolution, loss, breaking; 14.01.06 A rule, order, precept, tenet, principle
tōweorpan 05.06 Destruction, dissolution, loss, breaking; 05.06.01 Devastation, laying waste; 05.06.02.02 A tearing apart; 05.07 Ending of existence, end of world; 05.10.04.04.01 Dispersion
tōweorpan (ūt) 05.12.02.07 To throw, cast, toss

tōweorþian 16.02.04 Worship, honour, praise
tōwesan 05.10.04.03 Presence
tōwesnes 03.03.07.01 Division, partition, separation; 12.05.03 Disagreement, discord, dissension
towettan 12.04 Fellowship, union, association
towhūs 04.04.03 A spinning-house or chamber
tōwieltan 05.12.05.04.01 (Of wheel, etc.) to roll, trundle
tōwītan 05.12.05.03.01 To part ways, separate from, depart
tōwiþere 09.05.03 An answer, reply
tōwiþre 12.05.02 Hostility, contention, opposition
towlic 04.04 Weaving
towlic weorc 04.04.04 A thread (of wool, etc.), fibre
towmȳderce 04.04.03 A spinning-house or chamber
tōworpednes 05.06 Destruction, dissolution, loss, breaking
tōworpen 05.06 Destruction, dissolution, loss, breaking
tōworpennes 05.06 Destruction, dissolution, loss, breaking
tōworpnes 05.06 Destruction, dissolution, loss, breaking; 05.10.04.04.01 Dispersion; 05.12.02.04 To cast out, drive away
tōwrecan 05.10.04.04.01 Dispersion
tōwrītan 05.03.01.03 Reason, cause; 09.03.07.07.03.01 A description, writing down
tōwritennes 09.03.07.07.03.01 A description, writing down
tōwrīþan 05.10.05.04.08.01 A bend

towtōl 04.04.03 A spinning-house or chamber
tōwundorlic 06.01.08.05.01.01 Wondrous, glorious, marvellous
tōwyrd 05.11.08 A suitable time, opportunity
tōwyrpendlic 05.06 Destruction, dissolution, loss, breaking
tracter 17.02.04.02.04 Leading/conducting of water
træf 04.05.02 A building, edifice, structure; 04.05.03.02.02.09 A tent, pavilion
træglian 05.06 Destruction, dissolution, loss, breaking
trāg 07.03 Evil; 08.01.03.07.02 Misery, trouble, affliction
trāge 08.01.03.07.04 Severity, harshness
traht 09.03.07.07.02.01.04 A passage in a book; 09.04.03.03 A commentary, exposition; 09.06 To take matter for discourse
trahtaþ 09.04.03.03 A commentary, exposition
trahtbōc 09.04.03.03 A commentary, exposition
trahtian 09.03.07.07.03 Composition, arrangement, writing
traht(n)ere 09.04.03.03 A commentary, exposition
trahtnian be 09.04.03 Exposition, making clear by explanation
trahtnian be/ymbe 09.06 To take matter for discourse
(ge)traht(n)ian 06.01.01.01 Thinking about, minding, heeding; 09.04.03 Exposition, making clear by explanation
getraht(n)ian 09.04.03.01 A translation
traht(n)ung 09.04.03.03 A commentary, exposition

trāisc 08.01.03.04 Grief
tramet 09.03.07.07 A book
treaflīce 08.01.03.07.03 Suffering, torment, pain
(ge)trēagian 04.04.05.06 To sew, stitch
getrēagod 04.04.05.06 To sew, stitch
getred 12.04.02 A crowding together, assembly
tredan 05.12.01.04.01.02 To tread upon, trample; 07.03.01.03 To loathe, hate, abhor; 12.05.06.02 Oppression
(ge)tredan 05.06.09.02 Act of kicking; 05.12.01.04.01.02 To tread upon, trample
treddan 05.12.01.04.01.02 To tread upon, trample; 09.05.01 Inspection, examination
tredde 04.01.02.02.07 Press; 04.01.03.05.01.01.01 Wine-press
treddian 05.12.01.04 To go, proceed on foot
trede 05.12.04.01 Stability, firmness
tredel 02.04.03.04.02.05.02 Sole; 04.05.02.11 A staircase
tredend 05.12.01.04.01.02 To tread upon, trample
trefet 17.03.02 Item providing support
trega 08.01.03.07.02 Misery, trouble, affliction
(ge)tregian 08.01.03.07.02 Misery, trouble, affliction
getregian 07.05.02 Contempt
trendan 05.12.05.04.01 (Of wheel, etc.) to roll, trundle
trendel 03.03.03.01 Arithmetic; 05.10.06.02 Rotundity, roundness; 05.11.06 Course/cycle of time; 18.02.03 A spectacle, display
trendeled 05.10.06.02 Rotundity, roundness
trendelnes 05.12.01.03 Expanse over which something travels
trēow 02.07.03 A tree; 02.07.03.04 A wood, trees; 04.02.04.05.04.01 A forester, woodman; 04.05.01.02.06 A log, stake, etc.; 04.05.02.07 A beam, rafter; 08.01.02.01 Favour, kindness, grace; 12.01.01.12 Loyalty; 12.07.02.01 Covenant, assurance of faith, promise; 13.02.08.04 Weapons, arms; 16.02.05.11 The cross (as Christian image)
(ge)trēow 06.01.08.03 Trust, faith, confidence; 12.07.02.02 Truth, faithfulness, good faith, sincerity
getrēowan 06.01.07.07.01 Likelihood, probability, chance
trēowbicen 04.01.02.01.05.04 Honey
trēowcynn 02.07.03 A tree
trēowe geniman tō 12.07.02.01 Covenant, assurance of faith, promise
(ge)trēowe/trīwe 12.07.02.02 Truth, faithfulness, good faith, sincerity
(ge)trēow(e) 12.01.01.12 Loyalty
getrēowe 14.03.03.03 Witness, testimony, attestation
trēowen 02.07.03 A tree; 04.05.01.02 Timber for building
(ge)trēowfæst 12.07.02.02 Truth, faithfulness, good faith, sincerity
getrēowfæstnian 06.01.08.03.01 Belief, trust, faithfulness; 12.07.02.02 Truth, faithfulness, good faith, sincerity
trēowfēging 04.05.01.02.01 Boarding, planking, floor
trēowfugol 02.06.08.05 Forest bird, wild-fowl
getrēowful 06.01.08.03 Trust, faith, confidence; 12.07.02.02 Truth, faithfulness, good faith, sincerity;

14.03.03.03 Witness, testimony, attestation; 16.02.01 Faith
getrēowfullīce 06.01.08.03 Trust, faith, confidence
getrēowfulnes 16.02.01 Faith
trēowgeþofta 12.04.01 A fellow, companion, associate, comrade
trēowgeweorc 04.05 Building, construction
trēowgewrid 02.07.03.04.02 A thicket
(ge)trēow(i)an 06.01.08.03 Trust, faith, confidence
(ge)trēowian 12.01.01.12 Loyalty
(ge)trēow(i)an 14.03.03.08 Justification
getrēowian 06.02.06.03 Persuasion, prompting; 12.04 Fellowship, union, association
(ge)trēowlēas 12.01.01.12.04 Treachery; 16.02.01.03 Unbelief, want of belief
trēowlēasnes 16.02.01.05 Heresy, error, wrong belief
(ge)trēowlēasnes 12.01.01.12.04 Treachery
trēowlic 11.10 Safety, safeness
getrēowlic 06.01.08.03.01 Belief, trust, faithfulness
trēowlīce 12.01.01.12 Loyalty
(ge)trēowlīce 12.07.02.02 Truth, faithfulness, good faith, sincerity
getrēowlīce 06.01.07.03 Truth of speech or thought, veracity; 06.01.08.03 Trust, faith, confidence; 06.01.08.03.01 Belief, trust, faithfulness
trēowloga 12.01.01.12.03 Rebellion, sedition
trēowlufu 08.01.02.02 Love, affection, care
getrēownes 06.01.08.03.01 Belief, trust, faithfulness
trēowrǣden 06.01.08.03.01 Belief, trust, faithfulness; 12.07.02.02 Truth, faithfulness, good faith, sincerity
(ge)trēowsian 12.07.02.01 Covenant, assurance of faith, promise; 14.03.03.08 Justification
getrēowsian 06.01.08.03.01 Belief, trust, faithfulness
trēowsteall 04.02.04.05.04 A detached area of woodland
trēowstede 04.02.04.05.04 A detached area of woodland
trēowteru 03.01.17.06 Resin, tar, gum
(ge)trēowþ 12.01.01.12 Loyalty; 12.07.02.01 Covenant, assurance of faith, promise; 12.07.02.02 Truth, faithfulness, good faith, sincerity
trēowþrāg 12.07.02.02 Truth, faithfulness, good faith, sincerity
trēowwæstm 02.07.01.01 Fruit of the earth
trēowweorþung 16.02.01.06.01 Belief/practice of heathen people
trēowwyrhta 17.02.04.02.01 Cutting, hewing, shaping
trēowwyrm 02.06.09.02.04 Butterfly, moth
treppan 05.12.01.04 To go, proceed on foot
treppe 04.03.02 A snare, trap, noose
getricce 08.01.01.03.02 Pleasure, satisfaction
getridwet 13.02.08.04.01 A spear
trifelung 05.06.05 A grinding, pounding
trifet 15.03.02 A tax
(ge)trifulian 05.06.05 A grinding, pounding
trīg 04.01.02.02.06.05.02 Tray
trīnan 02.05.06 Sense of touch
trinda 05.10.06.02 Rotundity, roundness

trindhyrst 02.07.03.04.01 A small wood, coppice, copse
trindle 05.10.06.02 Rotundity, roundness
getrīwe 06.01.08.03 Trust, faith, confidence
trod 05.12.01.03.01.01 A path, track
trog 04.01.03.05.04.02 A barrel, tun, vat, cask; 05.12.01.09.03.01.01 Kind of ship; 17.03.12 A receptacle, container
troghrycg 01.01.02.01.02.01 Rising ground, eminence
trogscip 05.12.01.09.03.01.01 Kind of ship
trondende 01.01.02.01.02.02.04 Cliff
tropere 16.02.05.10.04 Choir books, etc.
trucian 03.03.04.05 Insufficiency, lack, want; 05.07 Ending of existence, end of world; 11.06.01 Neglect; 11.06.03 Failing, failure
trūht 02.06.06.02.01.09 Trout; 04.01.02.01.02.07 Fish
trum 05.08 Strength; 05.12.04.01 Stability, firmness; 05.13.06.01 Firm, stable, steady; 06.02.07.02 Constancy; 12.07.02.02 Truth, faithfulness, good faith, sincerity
getrum 13.02.10.01.02.02 Armed forces
truma 13.02.07.02 Order (of troops), array
(ge)truma 13.02.10.01.02.01 An armed force/band
trumian 06.02.07 Will, determination, resolution; 06.02.07.06.01 Emboldening, encouragement
getrumian 02.08.13 Recovery, growing better; 05.08 Strength
trumlic 05.08 Strength; 05.12.04.01 Stability, firmness; 06.02.06.03.03.01 Incitement, prompting, exhortation
trumlīce 03.03.04.01 Much; 05.08 Strength; 06.02.07.01 Strength, fortitude
trumnaþ 05.08 Strength
trumnes 02.08.01 Sound physical condition
trumnes/trymnes 01.02 Firmament; 06.01.07.07.03 Certainty
trūs 17.05.01 Fuel, tinder
trusen 02.07.03.01 A bush
trūþ 18.02.05 Buffoonery, speech of buffoon/actor
trūþhorn 18.02.07.02.02.02 A trumpet
trūwa 11.10.02.02.01 Care, interest in; 12.07.02.01 Covenant, assurance of faith, promise; 12.07.02.02 Truth, faithfulness, good faith, sincerity
(ge)trūwa 06.01.08.03 Trust, faith, confidence
(ge)trūwian 06.01.08.02 Hope, expectation
(ge)trūwian (be/on/tō) 06.01.08.03 Trust, faith, confidence
getrūwian 06.02.06.03 Persuasion, prompting; 14.03.03.08 Justification; 14.04 Making of terms, agreement, convention
getrūwod 06.01.08.03 Trust, faith, confidence
getrūwung 06.01.08.03.01 Belief, trust, faithfulness
getryccan 06.01.08.03 Trust, faith, confidence
getrym 01.02 Firmament
getrymednes 05.10.05.04.02.04.02 Support, maintenance
trymes 03.03.02.01 A weight, definite amount; 15.01.04 Coinage, money
(ge)trymman/(ge)trymian 05.08 Strength

trymman 02.08.13 Recovery, growing better; 13.02.07.02 Order (of troops), array; 14.03.03.07 Security, pledge, bail

(ge)trymman 02.08.12 Healing, curing; 04.05 Building, construction; 05.08 Strength; 06.02.06.03.03.01 Incitement, prompting, exhortation; 06.02.07 Will, determination, resolution; 06.02.07.01 Strength, fortitude; 09.07.04 Assertion, affirmation; 11.03.01.01.01 Proof, demonstration; 13.02.07.02 Order (of troops), array; 14.01.06 A rule, order, precept, tenet, principle

getrymman 05.04 Fate, lot, fortune, destiny; 05.13.06.01 Firm, stable, steady; 12.07.02.01 Covenant, assurance of faith, promise

getrymmed 13.02.07.02 Order (of troops), array

trymmend 09.07.04.01 Confirmation, agreement; 11.12.02 Aid, help, succour

trymmendlic 06.02.06.03.03.01 Incitement, prompting, exhortation

trymming 05.08 Strength; 05.13.06.01 Firm, stable, steady; 06.01.06.02.02 That which is taught, doctrine or teaching; 06.01.06.02.03.04.05 Edification, instruction; 09.07.04.01 Confirmation, agreement

(ge)trymming 11.12.02.01 Strengthening, confirmation

getrymming 11.10.01 Protection, safekeeping; 13.02.06.01 Stronghold, fort/fortified town

trymnes 06.01.06.02.03.04.05 Edification, instruction; 09.07.04.01 Confirmation, agreement; 11.12.02.01 Strengthening, confirmation

(ge)trymnes 05.10.05.04.02.04.02 Support, maintenance

getrymnes 06.01.08.02.01 Encouragement, comfort

trymþ 05.08 Strength

tū swā lang(e) 05.10.05.03.01 Length

(ge)tūcian 08.01.03.07.02.01 Injury, offence; 14.05 Punishment

(ge)tūcian (tō bysmore/yfle) 12.05.06.02.03 Trouble, disturbance

getūcod 07.10.03 An adornment, decoration, ornament

tūddorfōstor 04.01.02.04.03.02 Bringing-up, fostering

tūddorful 02.01.03 Fruitfulness, fertility

tūddorspēd 02.01.03 Fruitfulness, fertility

tūddortēonde 02.01.03.03.02 To bring forth, produce

tudenard 13.02.08.03.01.06 A shield

tūdor 02.01.03.03.02 To bring forth, produce; 02.01.03.03.04 Offspring, race, breed, family, children; 02.03.02.02 Child, offspring; 02.06 Animal; 05.03.02 Event, issue, result

tūdorfæst 02.01.03 Fruitfulness, fertility

tulge 05.08 Strength

tumbere 18.02.04 Dancing

tumbian 18.02.04 Dancing

tumbing 18.02.04 Dancing

tūn 04.02 Farm; 04.02.03.01.01 Enclosed land/field; 04.05.03 A dwelling-place, abode, habitation; 04.05.03.02 A human habitation; 12.06.02.01 A township

tūncærse 02.07.09.02.02.02 Other vegetables (alphabetical order)

tunece 04.04.07.08 A short garment, skirt, kirtle

getunecod 04.04.07.01 Mode of dressing, fashion
tūnesman 02.03.03.04.04 Inhabitant(s) of a 'tūn'
tunge 02.04.06.03.02.01 Mouth; 05.10.06.03 Projection, head, extremity (of anything); 09.03 A language
tūngebūr 02.03.03.04.04 Inhabitant(s) of a 'tūn'; 04.05.03.01 Habitation, sojourn
tungellic 01.02.01 Heaven(s), sky
tūngerēfa 12.01.01.05 A leader, administrator; 12.01.01.08.01 A servant, attendant
tungeþrum 02.04.05.06 Sinew/tendon/ligament
tungful 09.01.02.01 Excessive fluency, loquacity
tunggelælle 09.01.02.01 Excessive fluency, loquacity
tunglen 01.02.01.01.02 Star
tunglere 16.01.04.06.01 Astrology
tungol 01.02.01.01 Heavenly body; 01.02.01.01.01 Planet; 01.02.01.01.02 Star; 01.02.01.01.02.01 Constellation
tungolæ 16.01.04.06.01 Astrology
tungolbære 01.02.01.01.02 Star
tungolcræft 16.01.04.06.01 Astrology
tungolcræft(i)ga 16.01.04.06.01 Astrology
tungolcræftwīse 16.01.04.06.01 Astrology
tungolgescēad 16.01.04.06.01 Astrology
tungolgim 01.02.01.01.02 Star
tungolspræc 16.01.04.06.01 Astrology
tungolwītega 16.01.04.06.01 Astrology
tungwōd 08.01.03.09.01.03 Sharpness (of speech)
tūnhōfe 02.07.11 Plants/flowers (alphabetical order)
tūnincel 04.02 Farm; 04.05.03.02 A human habitation
tūnkirke 16.02.05.02.03 A church, place of worship
tūnland 04.02.03 Cultivatable land/farmland
tūnlic 12.06.02.01.01 Country (not town)
tūnman 02.03.03.04.04 Inhabitant(s) of a 'tūn'
tūnmelde 02.07.11 Plants/flowers (alphabetical order)
tunne 04.01.03.05.04.02 A barrel, tun, vat, cask
tunnebotm 18.02.07.02.01 Percussion instruments
tūnprēost 16.02.03.02.07.01 A priest of a church or minster
tūnræd 12.02.02 An assembly, meeting
tūnscipe 02.03.03.04.04 Inhabitant(s) of a 'tūn'
tūnscīr 12.02 A public office
tunsingwyrt 02.07.11 Plants/flowers (alphabetical order)
tūnsōcn 14.03 Right of holding court, jurisdiction
tūnsteall 04.02.01 Farmstead
tūnstede 04.02.01 Farmstead
tūnweg 05.12.01.03.01.05 Types of road/path
tūr 04.05.03.02.02.07 A tower; 13.02.06.01 Stronghold, fort/fortified town
turf 01.01.02.01.05 Covered with vegetation; 04.02.03.04 Grassland
turfgret 17.04.01 Sources of materials
turfhacce 04.02.04.06.01 A spade
turfhaga 04.02.03.04 Grassland

turfhleow 04.05.03.02.02.08 A lowly dwelling, cottage, hut; 11.10.01.02 Refuge, help, shelter
turfung 13.02.08.04.02 A shot, missile, dart, spear, javelin, etc.
turl 04.01.02.02.06.05.05 Ladle/scoop
turnian 02.08.07.01 Pain in head/neck; 05.12.05 To move and change direction, turn; 05.12.05.04 To rotate, turn round, revolve
turniende 05.12.05.04 To rotate, turn round, revolve
turnigendlic 05.12.05.04 To rotate, turn round, revolve
turnung 05.12.05 To move and change direction, turn
turtla 02.06.08.02.01.04 Pigeon, dove, culver
turtle 02.06.08.02.01.04 Pigeon, dove, culver
turtur 02.06.08.02.01.04 Pigeon, dove, culver
turture 02.06.08.02.01.04 Pigeon, dove, culver
tūsc 02.04.06.03.02.01.01 Tooth/teeth
tūxl 02.04.06.03.02.01.01 Tooth/teeth
twā 03.03.03.03 Fractions; 03.03.03.04.02 Two
twā swā 03.03.03.04.02 Two
twā swā micel 03.03.03.04.02 Two
twædding 07.07.03 Flattery
twǣde 03.03.03.03 Fractions
getwǣfan 05.07 Ending of existence, end of world; 10.04.03.01 To take away, deprive of
twǣman 12.05.03 Disagreement, discord, dissension
(ge)twǣman 03.03.07.01 Division, partition, separation
twǣmendlīce 03.03.07.01 Division, partition, separation
twǣming 03.03.07.01 Division, partition, separation; 03.06.02 Difference, diversity, dissimilarity
twām and twām 03.03.03.04.02 Two
getwanc 06.01.07.04.04 Deceitfulness, falseness, duplicity
twānihte 05.11.06.03.01.04 (Of lunar cycle) so many nights old
twēgen 03.03.03.04.02 Two
twēgen and twēgen 03.03.03.04.02 Two
twelf 03.03.03.04.12 Twelve
twelffeald 03.03.03.04.12 Twelve
twelfgylde 14.03.03.09.02 Atonement
twelfhund 03.03.03.04.33 Twelve hundred
twelfhundred 03.03.03.04.33 Twelve hundred
twelfhynde 12.01.01.06.08 A person of rank, elder, great man
twelfhynde mann 12.01.01.06.08 A person of rank, elder, great man
twelfmōnaþ 05.11.03.01 A year
twelfnihta 05.11.06.03.01.04 (Of lunar cycle) so many nights old
twelfta 03.03.03.04.12 Twelve
twelfta ǣfen 16.02.04.04.02.01.01 Around the Nativity
twelfta dæg 16.02.04.04.02.01.01 Around the Nativity
twelfta mæssǣfen 16.02.04.04.02.01.01 Around the Nativity
twelfte 03.03.03.04.12 Twelve
twelfte niht 16.02.04.04.02.01.01 Around the Nativity
twelfwintre 02.01.04 Age
twengan 05.10.05.02.03 To reduce, make thin(ner)
twēntig 03.03.03.04.20 Twenty

twēntiges nihte 05.11.06.03.01.04 (Of lunar cycle) so many nights old
twēntigfeald 03.03.03.04.20 Twenty
twēntiggēare 02.01.04 Age
twēntigoþa 03.03.03.04.20 Twenty
twēntigum 03.03.03.04.20 Twenty
twēntigwintre 02.01.04 Age
twēo 06.01.07.06.02.01 Doubt, uncertainty; 11.06.05 Hesitation, scruple
(ge)twēo 06.01.07.06.02.01 Doubt, uncertainty
twēogende 06.01.07.06.02.01 Doubt, uncertainty
twēogendlic 06.01.07.06.02.01 Doubt, uncertainty
twēoglīce 06.01.07.06.02.01 Doubt, uncertainty
twēo(g)ung 06.01.07.06.02.01 Doubt, uncertainty
twēolic 06.01.07.06.02.01 Doubt, uncertainty; 09.04.02.02 Dubiety, ambiguity
twēolīce 09.04.02.02 Dubiety, ambiguity
(ge)twēon 06.01.07.06.02.01 Doubt, uncertainty; 06.02.03 Unwilling, loath; 11.06.05 Hesitation, scruple
twēona 06.01.07.06.02.01 Doubt, uncertainty
twēondlic gewrit 16.02.01.08.02 Apocrypha
twēonelēoht 05.11.04.02.01 Sunset
twēonian 06.01.07.06.02.01 Doubt, uncertainty
(ge)twēonian 06.01.07.06.02.01 Doubt, uncertainty
twēonigend 06.01.07.06.02.01 Doubt, uncertainty
twēonigendlic 06.01.07.06.02.01 Doubt, uncertainty

twēonol 06.01.07.06.02.01 Doubt, uncertainty
twēonung 06.01.07.06.02 Unbelief; 06.01.07.06.02.01 Doubt, uncertainty; 09.04.02.02 Dubiety, ambiguity
twēowmann 02.06.10.01.03 Half of another kind
twībēte 14.03.03.09.02 Atonement
twībil 17.03.03 A cutting tool
twībille 05.10.06.03.01 A point, spike, prickle
twīblēo 05.10.06 Form, shape
twīblēoh 03.01.14.01 Dyeing
twībōte 14.03.03.09.02 Atonement
twībrowen 04.01.03.05.01.02 Broth; 04.01.03.05.02 Brewing
twībrowen ealoþ 04.01.03.05.01.02 Broth
twiccere 16.02.03.03.02.01 Monastic functionaries
twiccian 10.04.01 To hold, have; 10.04.02.01 To pluck, gather
twicele 01.01.03.01.01.02 Tributary
twicen 05.12.01.03.01.04 A lane, street
twicen(e) 05.12.01.03.01 A means of access
twīdæglic 05.11.03.01.05 A day
twīdǣl 03.03.03.03 Fractions
twīdǣlan 03.03.03.01 Arithmetic; 03.06.02 Difference, diversity, dissimilarity
twīdēagod 03.01.14.01 Dyeing
twīecge(de) 05.10.06.03.01 A point, spike, prickle
twīendlīce 06.01.07.06.02 Unbelief
twīfeald 03.03.03.04.02 Two; 03.04.02 A diversity; 06.01.07.04.04 Deceitfulness, falseness, duplicity; 06.02.07.05 Irresolution

(ge)twīfealdian/(ge)twīfildan 03.03.03.04.02 Two
twīfealdlic 03.03.03.04.02 Two
twīfealdlīce 03.03.03.04.02 Two
twīfealdnes 06.01.07.04.02.01 Deception, deceit, snare, wile; 06.01.07.04.04 Deceitfulness, falseness, duplicity; 06.02.07.05 Irresolution
twīfēre 05.12.01.03.01 A means of access
twīfērlǣcan 03.03.07.01 Division, partition, separation
twīfēte 02.04.03.04.02.05 Foot
twīfeþerede 02.06.10 Monster, strange creature
twīfingre 05.10.05.03 A measure of distance
twīfyrclian 05.06.02.01 A cleft, split; 05.10.05.04.07 A fork (in river, road, etc.)
twīfȳrede 04.02.03.02.01.01 A furrow
twīgǣrede 02.06.01.04 Leg
twīgilde 14.03.03.09.02 Atonement
twig(u) 02.07.03.03.01 Wood (as substance)
twīhǣmed 12.09 Marriage, state of marriage
twīhēafdede 02.06.10 Monster, strange creature
twīheolor 03.03.02 Measurement by weighing
twīhīw(ed)e 03.01.14.11 Medley/variety of colour; 05.10.06 Form, shape
twīhīwian 06.01.07.04.04.02 Pretence, feigning, dissimulation
twīhlidede 05.10.05.04.14 An opening, aperture
twīhwēole 05.12.01.06 Vehicle
twīhwyrft 05.11.06 Course/cycle of time
twīhynde 12.01.01.11 The common people

twīhynde man 12.01.01.11 The common people
twīhynde wer 14.03.03.09.02 Atonement
twīlæpped 04.04.07.03 Part of garment
twīlafte 05.10.06.03.01 A point, spike, prickle
twīlēafa 02.07.11.02 Unidentified plants (alphabetical order)
twīlībrocen 04.04.05 Woven material, fabric
twīlic 03.03.03.04.02 Two; 04.04.05 Woven material, fabric
twīmylte 03.01.16 Liquid, a liquid
twīn 04.04.05.04 Linen, linen cloth
twinclian 03.01.12.01 Glittering, effulgence
twīnebbe 02.06.10 Monster, strange creature
twīnen 04.04.05.04 Linen, linen cloth
twīnihte 05.11.06.03.01.04 (Of lunar cycle) so many nights old
(ge)twinn 03.03.03.04.02 Two
getwinn 02.03.02.02.01 Twins
getwinnas 02.03.02.02.01 Twins; 02.03.02.02.02 Triplets
getwinnes 09.03.04 Rhetoric, art of exposition
twīnwyrm 02.06.09 Insect/small creature
twīrǣde 06.02.07.05 Irresolution; 12.05.03 Disagreement, discord, dissension
twīrǣdnes 12.05.03 Disagreement, discord, dissension; 12.05.03.01 Quarrel, contentiousness, strife
getwis 02.03.02.02.05 Having the same parents
getwisa 02.03.02.02.01 Twins
twīsceatte 15.02.04 Spending, disbursement
twīscyldig 14.03.03.09.02 Atonement

twīseht 12.05.03 Disagreement, discord, dissension
twīsehtan 12.05.03 Disagreement, discord, dissension
twīsehtnes 12.05.03 Disagreement, discord, dissension
twiseltōþ 02.04.06.03.02.01.01 Tooth/teeth
twīsestre 03.03.01.02 Dry measures
twisla 01.01.03.01.01.02 Tributary; 05.10.05.04.07 A fork (in river, road, etc.)
twisled 05.10.05.04.07 A fork (in river, road, etc.)
twislian 05.10.05.04.07 A fork (in river, road, etc.)
twisliht 05.10.05.04.07 A fork (in river, road, etc.)
twislung 03.03.07.01 Division, partition, separation; 03.06.02 Difference, diversity, dissimilarity
twīsnæcce 02.06.01.04 Leg
twīsnēse 02.06.01.04 Leg
twīsp(r)ǣc 07.05.03.01 Falseness in speech, detraction
twīsprǣc 09.01.02.02 Dissembling speech
twīsprǣce 06.01.07.04.03 Untruth, falsehood; 06.01.07.04.04.02.01 Hypocrisy
twīsp(r)ǣce 07.05.03.01 Falseness in speech, detraction
twīsprǣce 09.03 A language
twīsprǣcnes 07.05.03.01 Falseness in speech, detraction
twīsprecan 07.05.03.01 Falseness in speech, detraction
twīspunnen 04.04.04 A thread (of wool, etc.), fibre

twīstrenge 18.02.07.02.03 Stringed instruments
twītælged 03.01.14.01 Dyeing
twīþrāwen 05.10.06.02.03 A circular fold, coil
twīwǣg 03.03.02 Measurement by weighing
twīweg 05.12.01.03.01 A means of access
twīwintre 02.01.04 Age
twīwyrdig 09.04.02.02 Dubiety, ambiguity
getȳd 06.01.06.02 Knowledge, learning, erudition
tȳdernes 02.01.03.03.01 To beget; 02.07.02.05 A shoot, sprout, tendril
getȳdnes 06.01.06.02 Knowledge, learning, erudition; 06.01.06.02.03.04.05 Edification, instruction
tȳdred 02.01.03 Fruitfulness, fertility
tȳdr(i)an 02.01.03 Fruitfulness, fertility
(ge)tȳdr(i)an 05.05 Constitution, founding (e.g. of world)
tȳdriend 05.05.02 Productivity, bringing forth
tȳdrung 02.01.03.02 Barrenness, sterility; 02.01.03.03 Sex, generation; 02.07.03.03.01 Wood (as substance)
tyge 04.01.03 Drinking; 05.12.02.05 To pull, drag, draw; 06.01.03.02 Dialectics, logic; 17.02.04.02.04 Leading/conducting of water
tygehōc 17.03.07 Tools for digging/grasping/pulling
tygehorn 02.08.12.02.06 Surgical
tygel 04.02.05.05.04 Rope, rein; 17.03.07 Tools for digging/grasping/pulling
tygle 02.06.06.03.01.04 Mullet
tyht 11.05.02 Mode, manner, way, method, fashion, course

tyhtan 06.01.01.01 Thinking about, minding, heeding; 06.02.06.03.04 Allurement
(ge)tyhtan 06.01.06.02.03.04.03 To teach, instruct; 06.02.06.03 Persuasion, prompting
getyhtan 06.02.06.03.04 Allurement
tyhten 06.02.06.03.04 Allurement
tyhtend 06.02.06.03.02 Instigation
tyhtendlic 06.02.06.03.03.01 Incitement, prompting, exhortation
tyhtere 06.02.06.03.04 Allurement
tyhting 06.02.06.03.04 Allurement
tyhtnes 06.02.06.03.02 Instigation
tyldsyle 04.05.03.02.02.09 A tent, pavilion
tyllan 15.03 Exaction of tax/tribute
getȳme oxena 04.02.05.06 Animals yoked together
(ge)tȳn 06.01.06.02.03.04.05 Edification, instruction
tȳnan 05.10.05.04.15 Closure, being closed; 05.11.10.02 End, completion; 07.05.03.03.02 To reproach, revile, abuse; 08.01.03.07.02 Misery, trouble, affliction
(ge)tȳnan 04.05.01.02.07 A fence, hedge; 05.10.05.04.15 Closure, being closed
getȳnan 09.05.04.01 Concealment, obscurity
tyncen 04.01.03.05.04.02 A barrel, tun, vat, cask
tynder 17.03.06 Tools for marking; 17.05.01 Fuel, tinder
tyndercynn 17.05.01 Fuel, tinder
getȳne 04.05.02.12.02 A vestibule, entrance, courtyard
tȳnende 07.05.03.02 Calumny, slander, insult

getynge 09.01.02 Fluency in speech; 09.01.02.01 Excessive fluency, loquacity; 09.03.04 Rhetoric, art of exposition; 11.04.02 Skill, skilfulness
(ge)tyng(e)lic 09.01.02 Fluency in speech
getyngelic 09.03.04 Rhetoric, art of exposition
getyngelīce 09.01.02 Fluency in speech
getyngnes 09.01.01 A speech, what is said, words; 09.03.04.02.02 Eloquence, elegance in language; 09.06.01.02 A saying, saw, proverb, maxim; 11.04.02 Skill, skilfulness
tȳnum 03.03.03.04.10 Ten
tȳran 02.08.07.02 Disorders of the eye; 08.01.03.04.02 Shedding of tears
tyrd(e)lu 02.04.06.06.06 Faeces
tȳrende 02.08.07.02 Disorders of the eye
getyrfan 05.06.09 Act of striking
tyrfhaga 04.02.04.06.01 A spade
tȳriāca 02.08.12.02.05 Pharmacy, curing with salves
tyrnan 05.12.02.08 To give a different direction to, turn; 05.12.05 To move and change direction, turn; 05.12.05.04 To rotate, turn round, revolve
tyrnende 05.12.05 To move and change direction, turn
tyrngeat 05.10.05.04.14.02 An opening/space in an enclosure
tyrning 05.10.06.02 Rotundity, roundness; 05.12.05 To move and change direction, turn; 06.01.07.04.04 Deceitfulness, falseness, duplicity
tyrrenisc 02.03.03.06.07.07 Other (alphabetical order)
tyrwa(-e) 03.01.17.06 Resin, tar, gum
tyrwen 03.01.17.06 Resin, tar, gum
getyrw(i)an 03.01.17 Thickness, viscosity

tysca 02.06.08.04 Bird of prey
tyslian 04.04.07 Trappings, equipment, garb
tyslung 04.04.07.01 Mode of dressing, fashion
tysse 04.04.05.01 Coarse, rough (of cloth)
tȳtan 03.01.12.01 Glittering, effulgence
þā 05.03.01.03 Reason, cause; 05.11.07.04.02 (Of time) later/latter; 05.11.02 A time, particular time, occasion
þā ... þā 05.03.02 Event, issue, result
þā bebodu 16.02.01.08.01 The Old Testament
þā cālendas 05.11.06.01 Cycle of the year
þā clypunga 05.11.06.01 Cycle of the year
þā deniscan 02.03.03.06.05 Scandinavian
þā gīet 03.03.04.03 Growth, increase
þā grēatan netlan 02.07.11 Plants/flowers (alphabetical order)
þā hwīle 05.11 A time, period of time
þā gēo 05.11.07.03.02 Earlier, antecedent
þā pleglican plegan 18.02.06 Theatricals
þā twelfan apostolas 16.02.01.08.03.01 New Testament persons
þaca 04.05.02.08 Top of a building
(ge)þaca 05.10.05.04.12 The condition of being covered
þaccian 03.03.04.03 Growth, increase; 05.06.09 Act of striking
(ge)þaccian 02.05.06.02 Stroking, caressing
þacian 04.05.02.08.01 Thatch
þæc 04.05.02.08 Top of a building; 04.05.02.08.01 Thatch
þæcele 08.01.01.01 Ardour, fervour, strong feeling; 17.05.03 Sources of fire/light

þæctigile 04.05.01.04 A tile, brick; 04.05.02.08 Top of a building
(ge)þæf 08.01.01.03.02 Pleasure, satisfaction
geþæf 09.07.04.01 Confirmation, agreement
geþæf bēon/wesan 09.07.04.01.01 Acknowledgement
þǣnan 03.01.16.01 Moisture
(ge)þǣnan 03.01.16.01 Moisture
geþǣnan 16.02.01.12 Spirituality
þǣr 05.03.01 A cause (of anything); 05.03.01.03 Reason, cause; 05.10.04.03 Presence; 05.10.04.04 Absence; 05.11.02 A time, particular time, occasion
þǣr nēhst 05.11.07.04.02.01 Succession
þǣr on ufenan 05.10.05.04.02 Face, surface
þǣr onbūtan 05.10.05.04.11 A circle, circuit, circumference
þǣr onemn 05.10.05.04.09 Side, quarter, direction
þǣr tō ēacan 03.03.04.03 Growth, increase
þǣr þǣr 05.10.04.03 Presence
þǣr under 05.10.05.04.02.02 Under, beneath
þǣr ūp 05.10.05.04.02 Face, surface
þǣr wiþinnan 05.10.05.04.01 Inside, interior
þǣr ymbūtan 05.10.05.04.11 A circle, circuit, circumference
þǣrābūtan 05.10.04.03 Presence
þǣræfter 05.11.07.04.02 (Of time) later/latter
þǣræt 05.10.04.03 Presence
þǣran 03.01.18 Dryness (not wetness)
þǣrbig 11.01.04 A doing, accomplishing (of something)

þærbinnan 05.10.05.04.01 Inside, interior
þærbufan 03.03.04.03 Growth, increase
þære sunnan gēar 05.11.06.01 Cycle of the year
þærforan 05.10.05.04.09.01 Front
þærfore 05.03 Source, origin
þærgemang 05.13.03 Regular alternation
þærin 05.10.05.04.01 Inside, interior
þærinne 05.10.05.04.01 Inside, interior
þærmid 05.11.07.01 Contemporary, coeval; 05.11.07.02 The present (time)
þærnian 10.02.01 Loss, deprivation
þærof 05.03 Source, origin
þærofer 05.10.05.04.02 Face, surface
þæron 05.03 Source, origin; 05.10.05.04.01 Inside, interior; 05.10.05.04.02 Face, surface
þærongēan 12.05 Contradiction, opposition
þærongēn 03.06.02.01 Contrariety, diversity
þæroninnan 05.10.04.03 Presence
þæronuppan 05.10.05.04.02 Face, surface
þærrihte 05.11.07.01 Contemporary, coeval
þærrihtes 05.11.07.01 Contemporary, coeval
þærtō 06.02.06.01 An end, goal; 03.03.04.03 Growth, increase; 05.03 Source, origin; 05.11.07.04.02.01 Succession; 05.10.04.03 Presence
þærtōgēanes 03.06.02.01 Contrariety, diversity; 05.10.05.04.09.04 Opposite (av); 05.13.04 Exchange, commutation
þæruppan 05.10.05.04.02 Face, surface
þæruppe 05.10.05.04.02 Face, surface

þærūt(e) 05.10.05.04.02.01 Exterior, outside of
þærwiþ 05.03 Source, origin; 05.10.05.04.09 Side, quarter, direction; 05.13.04 Exchange, commutation
þærymbe 05.03 Source, origin
þæs 03.06 Comparison; 05.03.01 A cause (of anything)
þæs mōnan gēar 05.11.03.01 A year; 05.11.06.03 Lunar cycle of nineteen years
þæs þe 05.03 Source, origin
þæs (þe) 05.11.07.04.02 (Of time) later/latter
þæs ymb 05.11.07.03.02 Earlier, antecedent
þæs ymb(e) 05.11.07.03 Former times, days of old
(ge)þæslǣcan 03.06.03.01 Compatible
þæslic 03.06.03.01 Compatible; 05.11.08 A suitable time, opportunity; 07.10.01 Elegance, beauty, comeliness
(ge)þæslic 03.06.03 Congruity, fitness, suitability; 03.06.03.04 What is fitting/seemly/appropriate/decent
þæslīce 11.01.04 A doing, accomplishing (of something)
(ge)þæslīce 03.06.03.04 What is fitting/seemly/appropriate/decent
þæslicnes 03.06.03 Congruity, fitness, suitability
þæsma 04.01.02.01.06 Leaven/yeast
þæt 05.03.01 A cause (of anything); 05.03.02 Event, issue, result
þæt ēce fȳr 16.01.05 Hell, lower world, abode of the dead
þæt hwerfende hwēol 05.04.01 Fortune, Fate (personification)
þæt māre land 01.01.02.01.01.01 Mainland

þæt þe 05.03.02 Event, issue, result
þætte 05.03.02 Event, issue, result
geþafa 09.07.04 Assertion, affirmation;
    09.07.04.01 Confirmation, agreement
þafetere 09.07.04.01 Confirmation,
    agreement
geþafettan 09.07.04.01.02 Consent
(ge)þafian 08.01.03.07.03 Suffering,
    torment, pain; 09.07.04.01
    Confirmation, agreement; 12.03.05
    Permission; 12.05.06.04.01
    Submission to action, toleration
geþafsum 09.07.04.01 Confirmation,
    agreement
geþafsumnes 09.07.04.01.02 Consent
(ge)þafung 09.07.04.01.02 Consent;
    12.03.05 Permission
geþafung 12.05.06.04.01 Submission to
    action, toleration
þām gelīce 03.06.01 Similitude, likeness
þām mycle mā 03.03.05 Extent, degree
þān 03.01.16.01 Moisture; 04.02.03.02
    Arable/ploughed land
þanc 08.01.01.03.02 Pleasure,
    satisfaction; 08.01.02.01 Favour,
    kindness, grace; 08.01.02.04.02
    Thanks, gratitude
þanc cunnan 08.01.02.04.02 Thanks,
    gratitude
geþanc 06.01 The head (as seat of
    thought); 06.01.01 Thought, the
    faculty of thinking, mind; 06.02.06
    Mind, purpose; 11.03.01.03.01
    Discovery, invention
þances 06.02.01 Freewill, own will;
    06.02.02 Will, disposition;
    08.01.02.04.02 Thanks, gratitude
þancful 06.01.01.01.01 Thought,
    cogitation, meditation; 08.01.03.02
    Pleasure, satisfaction;
    08.01.01.03.09.01 Pleasant, agreeable;
    08.01.02.04.02 Thanks, gratitude;
    11.04 Ability, capacity, power
(ge)þancful 08.01.01.01 Ardour, fervour,
    strong feeling
þancfullīce 08.01.02.01 Favour, kindness,
    grace; 08.01.02.04.02 Thanks,
    gratitude
þanchycgende 06.01.01.01.01 Thought,
    cogitation, meditation
(ge)þancian 08.01.01.03.06 Exultation,
    joy; 08.01.02.04.02 Thanks, gratitude
þancmet(eg)ung 06.01.01.01.01.01
    Consideration, rumination
geþancmetian 06.01.01.01.01 Thought,
    cogitation, meditation
þancol 06.01.05.02.01.01 Sagacity
geþancol 02.05.05 Desire, appetite;
    06.01.04 Faculty of memory;
    08.01.02.04.02 Thanks, gratitude;
    11.02.03 Forethought, care; 12.03.04
    A request, prayer
þancolmōd 06.01.05.02.01.01 Sagacity
þancsnot(t)or 06.01.05.02.01.01 Sagacity
þancung 08.01.02.04.02 Thanks,
    gratitude
þancweorþ 07.04.04.02 Laudable,
    praiseworthy
þancweorþ/-wurþe/-wirþe 06.01.04.02
    Living, remembered
þancweorþlīce 06.02.02.01 Will, wish,
    pleasure; 08.01.02.04.02 Thanks,
    gratitude
þancword 08.01.02.04.02 Thanks,
    gratitude
þanēcan þe 05.11.09.02 Frequent, of
    common occurrence
geþang 03.03.04.03 Growth, increase
þānian 03.01.16.01 Moisture

þanon 05.03 Source, origin; 05.03.01.03 Reason, cause; 05.10.04.03 Presence; 05.11.07.04.02 (Of time) later/latter
þanonforþ 05.11.07.04.02 (Of time) later/latter
þanonsīþ 05.12.05.03.03 To depart, leave, set out
þanonweard 05.10.04.03 Presence
þās sweartan mistas 16.01.05 Hell, lower world, abode of the dead
þāwian 03.01.16 Liquid, a liquid
þe 03.06 Comparison; 05.13.04 Exchange, commutation
þē mā þe 03.03.05 Extent, degree
þē swīþost micle 03.03.05 Extent, degree
þēah 03.06 Comparison; 05.03.01.03 Reason, cause
þēah hwæþere 03.06 Comparison
þēah (þe) ... hwæþere 03.06 Comparison
(ge)þeaht 06.01.01.01.01.01 Consideration, rumination; 12.02.02.05 Counsel, advice
geþeaht 06.01.05.02.01.01 Sagacity; 06.02.06.02 A proposal, proposition, suggestion; 12.02.02 An assembly, meeting
geþeahta 12.02.02.02 A counsellor, advisor
geþeahtend 12.02.02.02 A counsellor, advisor
geþeahtendlic 06.01.01.01.01.01 Consideration, rumination
geþeahtere 12.01.01.05 A leader, administrator; 12.02.02.02 A counsellor, advisor
(ge)þeahtian 12.02.02.04 Counsel, deliberation
þeahtung 12.02.02.05 Counsel, advice
geþeahtung 06.01.01.01.01.01 Consideration, rumination

þēana 03.06 Comparison
þearf 06.02.04 Necessity, inevitability; 06.02.04.01 Want, need; 06.02.04.01.01 Need, distress, straits, difficulty; 11.07.03 Use, advantage, profit; 11.11.01 A physical difficulty, strait; 12.07 An obligation, bounden duty; 14.01.05 Service, obligation, duty
þearfa 06.02.04.01.01 Need, distress, straits, difficulty; 15.01.06 Poverty, indigence
þearfan 15.01.06 Poverty, indigence
(ge)þearfan 06.02.04.01 Want, need
þearfednes 15.01.06 Poverty, indigence
þearfende 15.01.06 Poverty, indigence
þearfendlic 03.03.04.05 Insufficiency, lack, want; 15.01.06 Poverty, indigence
þearfendlīce 08.01.03.06.01 Affliction, misfortune, calamity; 15.01.06 Poverty, indigence
geþearfian 12.05.06.03 Necessity, constraint
þearf(ig)end 08.01.03.06 Adversity, affliction; 15.01.06 Poverty, indigence
þearflēas 05.03.01.01 Without need or cause
þearflēase 05.03.01.01 Without need or cause
þearflic 06.02.04 Necessity, inevitability; 11.07.03 Use, advantage, profit; 15.01.06 Poverty, indigence
þearflīce 11.07.01 Utility, usefulness
þearflicnes 15.01.06 Poverty, indigence
þearl 03.03.04.01.03 An immense quantity, immensity, immense number; 08.01.03.07.04 Severity, harshness; 08.01.03.09.10 Wrath, sternness, displeasure

1410

þearle 03.03.05 Extent, degree; 07.03 Evil
þearlic 08.01.03.07.04.01 Unbearableness
þearllīce 05.08.02 Violence, force; 06.01.07.01.01 Strictness, exactness; 08.01.03.09.10 Wrath, sternness, displeasure
þearlmōd 08.01.03.09.11 Hardheartedness, cruelty, severity; 12.08.03.02 Strictness, austerity, severity
þearlwīs 08.01.03.09.10 Wrath, sternness, displeasure
þearlwīslic 08.01.03.09.10 Wrath, sternness, displeasure
þearlwīslīce 08.01.03.09.10 Wrath, sternness, displeasure
þearlwīsnes 12.08.03.02 Strictness, austerity, severity
þearm 02.04.06.03.02.04 Intestines
þearm(ge)wind 02.04.06.07.01 Wind-pipe
þearmgyrd 04.02.05.06.05.03.05 A girth
þēater 18.02.06 Theatricals
þēaw 11.05 Natural/proper way/manner/mode of action; 11.05.02 Mode, manner, way, method, fashion, course; 16.02.04.03 Ritual, rite, service; 16.02.04.03.01 A rite, ceremony
geþēawe 11.05 Natural/proper way/manner/mode of action
þēawfæst 11.05.02.02 Humanity, courtesy, civility; 12.08.02.01 Goodness, excellence, virtue
þēawfæstlīce 11.05.02.01 A standard, norm, ethos
þēawfæstnes 12.01.01.12.01 Obedience, service
þēawful 12.08.02.01 Goodness, excellence, virtue
geþēawian 06.01.06.02.03.04.03 To teach, instruct
þēawlēas 11.05.02.03 Indecorum, impropriety, unseemliness
þēawlic 09.03.04.02.01 A figure; 11.05 Natural/proper way/manner/mode of action; 12.08.02.01 Goodness, excellence, virtue
þēawlīce 11.05.02.01 A standard, norm, ethos
geþēawod 11.05 Natural/proper way/manner/mode of action; 11.05.02 Mode, manner, way, method, fashion, course
þēawum 11.05 Natural/proper way/manner/mode of action; 12.08.02.01 Goodness, excellence, virtue
þeccan 05.10.05.04.12 The condition of being covered; 09.05.04.01 Concealment, obscurity
(ge)þeccan 05.10.05.04.12.01 To bespread, cover with
þeccbryce 04.05.01.04 A tile, brick
þeccend 11.10.01 Protection, safekeeping
þecen 04.05.02.08 Top of a building; 04.05.02.08.01 Thatch; 04.05.03.02.01 A building, house, hall, palace, etc.
þecge 17.03.12 A receptacle, container
þefian 02.04.06.07.05 To breathe
þegn 06.01.06.02.03.02 Discipleship; 12.01.01.05 A leader, administrator; 12.01.01.06.08 A person of rank, elder, great man; 12.01.01.07 A follower; 12.01.01.08.01 A servant, attendant; 13.02.10 The military,

soldiers; 13.02.10.01 A man, warrior; 16.01.01.04.02 The Son, Christ
þegnboren 12.01.01.06.06 Gentle birth, nobility
þegngyld 14.03.03.09.02 Atonement
þegnhyse 02.03.03.01 Body of retainers, household
þegnian 10.03.04 Provision, supply; 17.02.02 An office, function, employment
(ge)þegnian 12.01.01.08 Service
þegnlagu 14.01.04.01 A special right, right peculiar to a class
þegnland 15.01.01 Landed property
þegnlic 12.01.01.06.05 Nobility, noble condition
þegnlīce 06.02.07.06 Courage, boldness, valour
þegnrǣden 12.01.01.08 Service
þegnriht 14.01.04.01 A special right, right peculiar to a class
þegnscipe 06.02.07.06 Courage, boldness, valour; 11.04 Ability, capacity, power; 12.01.01.06.08 A person of rank, elder, great man; 12.01.01.07 A follower; 12.01.01.08 Service
þegnscolu 12.01.01.07 A follower
þegnsorh 08.01.03 Bad feeling, sadness
þegnweorud 12.01.01.07 A follower; 16.01.02.05 Inhabitants of heaven
þegnwer 14.03.03.09.02 Atonement
þel 04.05.01.02.01 Boarding, planking, floor
þelbrycg 05.12.01.03.04 A bridge
þellfæsten 05.12.01.09.03.01.01 Kind of ship
þelma 04.03.02 A snare, trap, noose
þelneþung 02.07.11.02 Unidentified plants (alphabetical order)

þencan 06.01 The head (as seat of thought); 06.01.08 Expectation; 11.03.01.02 To seek, seek for
(ge)þencan 06.01.01 Thought, the faculty of thinking, mind; 06.01.01.01.01 Thought, cogitation, meditation; 06.01.07.06.01 To accept as the result of enquiry, suppose; 06.02.06 Mind, purpose; 12.02.02.04 Counsel, deliberation
(ge)þencan mid 10.03 Giving
geþencan 06.01.04 Faculty of memory; 06.01.06.02.03.03 To study, apply oneself to learning; 06.02.06.02 A proposal, proposition, suggestion
þencendlic 06.01.01.01.01 Thought, cogitation, meditation
þenden 05.11 A time, period of time
þende(n) 05.11 A time, period of time
þēnest 11.05.02.02 Humanity, courtesy, civility
þēnestmann 12.01.01.07 A follower
þēnestre 12.01.01.08.01 A servant, attendant
þengel 12.01.01.04 A leader, ruler
þēningfæt 04.01.02.02.06.05.01 Dish for food/serving-dish
þēninggāst 16.01.02.05 Inhabitants of heaven
þēninghus 17.02.01 Management of work
þēningmann 12.01.01.06.08 A person of rank, elder, great man
þēni(n)gmann 12.01.01.07 A follower
þēningmann 12.01.01.08.01 A servant, attendant
þēnisc 16.02.04.03 Ritual, rite, service
þennan 05.06.01 Devastation, laying waste; 05.10.06.02.02 Curvature, bend, twist; 07.08 Reputation, fame; 11.03 Endeavour

(ge)þennan 05.10.05.02 Extension, stretching; 05.10.05.02.01 Diffusion, effusion, spreading
þenning 05.10.05.02 Extension, stretching
geþēnsum 11.07.01 Utility, usefulness; 11.12.02 Aid, help, succour
þēnung 04.01.02.04.01 Meal; 08.01.02.01 Favour, kindness, grace; 11.07 Use (made of things), service; 11.07.01 Utility, usefulness; 12.01.01.07 A follower; 12.01.01.08 Service; 12.01.01.12.01 Obedience, service; 12.02 A public office; 16.02.04.03.01 A rite, ceremony; 16.02.04.05 Canonical hour, service
þēnungbōc 16.02.01.08.01.01 Books of the Old Testament; 16.02.05.10.01 Service books
þēnungwerod 12.01.01.08.01 A servant, attendant
þēod 02.03.01 People; 02.03.03.03 A nation, people; 02.03.03.06.07.05.01 Gentiles; 03.04 Form, kind, nature, character; 09.03 A language; 12.04.02 A crowding together, assembly; 12.06 A province, country, territory; 13.02.10.01.02.01.01 Military followers (of household)
geþēod 12.04 Fellowship, union, association
(ge)þēodan 03.03.06.01 A whole formed by joining; 08.01.02.03.04 To show gladness, be friendly; 11.01.02 An undertaking; 12.04 Fellowship, union, association
(ge)þēodan fram 03.03.07.01 Division, partition, separation
(ge)þēodan tō 12.01.01.07 A follower

geþēodan 03.01.17 Thickness, viscosity; 03.03.04.03 Growth, increase; 05.02.02.03 A connexion, association; 05.10.05.01 A little way, no great distance; 05.12.05.02.03 To arrive; 06.02.07.03 Perseverance; 09.04.03.01 A translation; 11.07 Use (made of things), service; 12.09.06 Cohabitation
geþēodan in 03.03.06.01 A whole formed by joining; 05.12.05.02.04.01 To insert into (a hole); 11.02 Occupation, activity, business
þēodbealu 08.01.03.06 Adversity, affliction
þēodbūende 02.03.01 People
þēodcwēn 12.01.01.04.01 A royal leader
þēodcyning 12.01.01.04.01 A royal leader; 16.01.01.01.01 The Almighty
þēodcynn 02.03.03.02 A race, tribe
geþēode 02.03.03.03 A nation, people; 09.03 A language; 09.04.03.01 A translation
þēodegesa 06.01.08.06.02 Great fear, terror, horror
þēoden 12.01.01.04 A leader, ruler; 12.01.01.04.01 A royal leader; 16.01.01 God, the Lord
þēodenbealu 07.03 Evil
þēodend 09.04.03.01 A translation
þēodendlic 09.03.02.02.01.05 Minor parts of speech, etc.
þēodengedāl 02.02 Death
þēodenhold 12.01.01.12 Loyalty
þēodenlēas 10.02 Want, lack; 12.04.04 Solitude
þēodenmāþm 10.03 Giving
þēodenstōl 12.01.01.02 Seat of authority
þēodeorþe 01 Earth, world
þēodfēond 16.01.05.02.01 The devil
þēodfruma 12.01.01.04.01 A royal leader

þēodgestrēon 15.01.03 Treasure, riches, wealth
þēodguma 12.01.01.07 A follower
þēodhere 13.02.10.01.02.02 Armed forces
þēodisc 02.03.03.06.07.05.01 Gentiles; 09.03 A language
geþēodlǣcan 06.02.07.03 Perseverance
þēodland 05.10.04.02 A region, zone; 12.06.01.03 The Continent
þēodlārēow 06.01.06.02.03.04.02 A teacher
þēodlic 02.03.03.03 A nation, people
geþēodlic 12.04 Fellowship, union, association
þēodlīcetere 16.01.05.02.01 The devil
þēodloga 06.01.07.04 Deception
þēodmægen 02.03.03.01 Body of retainers, household
(ge)þēodnes 03.03.06.01 A whole formed by joining
geþēodnes 02.04.05.04.08 Joint; 09.03.02.02.01.05 Minor parts of speech, etc.; 09.03.02.03.01.02 A conjugation; 09.04.03.01 A translation; 12.04.01.01 A company of people, fellowship, society
(ge)þēodrǣden 08.01.02.03 Friendliness, affection; 16.02.01.02 Communion, fellowship
geþēodrǣden 02.04.05.04.08 Joint
þēodsceaþa 02.06.10.01.01 Dragon; 04.01.01.03 Hunger; 14.02 Lawlessness; 16.01.05.02.01 The devil
þēodscipe 02.03.03.03 A nation, people; 05.02.02.03 A connexion, association; 06.01.06.02 Knowledge, learning, erudition; 06.01.06.02.03.04 Teaching, instruction; 08.01.02.03 Friendliness, affection; 11.05 Natural/proper way/manner/mode of action; 11.05.02.01 A standard, norm, ethos; 12.05.06.01 Restraint, check, curb, control; 14.01 Law, body of rules; 14.01.06 A rule, order, precept, tenet, principle; 14.03.03.03 Witness, testimony, attestation; 16.02.03.03 A religious
þēodstefn 02.03.03.03 A nation, people
geþēodsumnes 09.07.04.01.02 Consent
þēodþrēa 08.01.03.06 Adversity, affliction
þēodwiga 13.02.10.01 A man, warrior
þēodwita 06.01.05.02.01.01 Sagacity; 06.01.06.02.01 A wise man, man of understanding or learning; 12.02.02.02 A counsellor, advisor
þēodwundor 06.01.08.05.01.01.01 An exercise of power, mighty work, miracle
þēof 14.02.01.02 Wrongful taking, theft
þēofa cot 04.05.03.02.02.01 Dwellings in particular places; 09.05.04.01 Concealment, obscurity
þēofdenn 04.05.03.02.02.01 Dwellings in particular places; 09.05.04.01 Concealment, obscurity
þēofend 14.02.01.02 Wrongful taking, theft
þēoffeng 14.01.04.03 Rights involving money; 14.01.05 Service, obligation, duty
þēofgyld 14.05.04.01 A fine
(ge)þēofian 14.02.01.02 Wrongful taking, theft
þēofmann 14.02.01.02 Wrongful taking, theft
þēofsceaþa 14.02.01.02 Wrongful taking, theft

þeofscip 05.12.01.09.03.01.01 Kind of ship
þeofscolu 14.02.01.02 Wrongful taking, theft
þeofscyldig 14.03.03.09.01 Unfavourable judgement, condemnation
þeofslege 02.02.04.04 Manslaughter, homicide
þeofsliht 02.02.04.04 Manslaughter, homicide
þeofstolen 14.02.01.02 Wrongful taking, theft
þeofung 14.02.01.02 Wrongful taking, theft
þeofwracu 14.05 Punishment
þeoging 03.03.04.03 Growth, increase; 11.03.02 Advancement, progress
þeoh 02.04.03.04.02.01 Thigh
þeohece 02.08.07.07 Disorders of the body
þeohgelǣte 02.04.05.04.08 Joint
þeohgeweald 02.04.06.04 Reproductive organs
þeohhweorfa 02.04.05.04.07 Bone of leg
þeohscanca 02.04.03.04.02.01 Thigh; 02.04.05.04.07 Bone of leg
þeohseax 13.02.08.04.03 A sword
þeohwræc 02.08.07.07 Disorders of the body
þeon 05.11.01.01 Long duration, long space
(ge)þeon 02.01.04.02 To grow, grow up; 03.03.04.01.02 A great number, multitude; 03.03.04.03 Growth, increase; 11.01 Action, doing, performance; 16.02.01.12 Spirituality
(ge)þeon (tō) 05 Aught, anything, something
geþeon 02.07.01 To grow; 08.01.01.03.08 Happiness, well-being, prosperity; 10.01.01.01 Receiving, gaining, getting; 10.01.02 Acquisition; 15.05 Trade, traffic, commerce
geþeon tō 08.01.01.03.08 Happiness, well-being, prosperity
þeor 02.08.05 Inflammation
þeorādl 02.08.05 Inflammation
þeordrenc 02.08.12.02.05 Pharmacy, curing with salves
þeorf 04.01.02.01.02.09 Milk; 04.01.02.01.07.03.01 Unleavened bread
þeorfdagas 16.02.01.08.04 Jewish seasons/feasts
þeorfhlāf 04.01.02.01.07.03.01 Unleavened bread
þeorfling 04.01.02.01.07.03.01 Unleavened bread
þeorfnes 12.08.04 Purity, moral cleanness
þeorfsymbel 16.02.01.08.04 Jewish seasons/feasts
þeorgerid 02.08.05 Inflammation
þeorwærc 02.08.05 Inflammation
þeorwenn 02.08.05.02 Particular inflammation/swelling
þeorwyrm 02.08.05 Inflammation
þeorwyrt 02.07.11.02 Unidentified plants (alphabetical order)
þeostor 03.01.13 Darkness, obscurity; 08.01.03 Bad feeling, sadness
þeostor/-re 06.01.05.03 Want of understanding
þeostorcofa 09.05.04.01 Concealment, obscurity
þeostorful 03.01.13 Darkness, obscurity
þeostorfulnes 03.01.13 Darkness, obscurity
þeostorlic 03.01.13 Darkness, obscurity
þeostorloca 02.02.05.01.01 A grave, burial place, sepulchre

þēostornes 03.01.13 Darkness, obscurity
þēostre/-tru 02.08.07.02.01 Defective
vision
þēostrian 02.05.09.02 Inability to see
(because of darkness); 02.08.07.02.01
Defective vision
(ge)þēostrian 03.01.13.02 A growing
dark, darkening
geþēostrian 06.01.07.04.01 Deception, a
leading astray
þēostrig 03.01.13 Darkness, obscurity;
06.01.05.03 Want of understanding
þēostru 03.01.13 Darkness, obscurity
þēostru/-e 06.01.05.03 Want of
understanding
þēostrung 03.01.13 Darkness, obscurity
(ge)þēot 02.05.10.15.01 To raise (the
voice), raise up (noise)
geþēot 02.05.10.15.06 A roar, howl, etc.
þēotan 02.05.10.04 To resound;
02.05.10.14 Sound of water;
02.05.10.15.06 A roar, howl, etc.;
08.01.03.05 Murmuring, complaint
þēote 01.01.03.01.01.06 Waterfall;
17.02.04.02.04 Leading/conducting of
water
þēow 12.01.01.08.01 A servant, attendant;
12.01.01.09 Bondage, slavery
þēowa 12.01.01.08.01 A servant,
attendant; 12.01.01.09 Bondage,
slavery
þēow(a) 16.02.03.03.02 A monk
þēowan 05.06.07 Pricking, a prick,
puncture; 05.12.02.06.01 To push,
drive
(ge)þēowan 02.05.06.01 To touch and
press; 05.10.05.02.03 To reduce, make
thin(ner); 07.05.01 Censure, reproof,
rebuke; 08.01.03.09.07 Threat,
threatening, menace; 12.05.06.04 A
trampling upon, subjection
geþēowan 12.05.06.03 Necessity,
constraint; 17.02.04 Trade, calling,
craft, aptitude
þēowberde 12.01.01.09 Bondage, slavery
þēowboren 12.01.01.09 Bondage, slavery
þēowcnapa 12.01.01.09 Bondage, slavery
þēowdōm 12.01.01.08 Service;
12.01.01.09 Bondage, slavery;
16.02.04.03.01 A rite, ceremony
þēowdōmhād 12.01.01.08 Service
þēowe 12.01.01.08.01 A servant,
attendant; 12.01.01.09 Bondage,
slavery
þēowhād 12.01.01.08 Service
þēowian 11.07.01 Utility, usefulness;
12.01.01.08 Service; 12.01.01.09
Bondage, slavery; 16.02.04.03.01 A
rite, ceremony; 17 Work, doings,
actions, labour; 17.02.03 A task,
service, duty
(ge)þēowian 12.01.01.08 Service;
12.01.01.09 Bondage, slavery
þēowincel 12.01.01.08.01 A servant,
attendant
þēowing 07.05.01 Censure, reproof,
rebuke
þēowlic 12.01.01.08 Service
þēowmann 12.01.01.08.01 A servant,
attendant
þēownȳd 12.01.01.09 Bondage, slavery
þēowot 12.01.01.08 Service; 12.01.01.09
Bondage, slavery
þēowotdōm 12.01.01.08 Service
þēowracian 08.01.03.09.07 Threat,
threatening, menace
geþēowtian 12.05.06.04 A trampling
upon, subjection
þēowtlic 12.01.01.08 Service

þēowtling 12.01.01.08.01 A servant, attendant
þēowtscipe 12.01.01.08 Service
þēowweorc 17 Work, doings, actions, labour
þēowwracu 08.01.03.09.07 Threat, threatening, menace
þeox 04.03 Hunting, the chase; 13.02.08.04.01 A spear
þeran 05.12.03.01.01 Quick movement or movements
geþersc 14.05.05 Physical punishments
þerscan 04.02.04.04.05 To thresh (corn); 05.06.05 A grinding, pounding
(ge)þerscan 05.06.09 Act of striking
þerscel 04.02.04.06.14 A flail for threshing corn
geþerscing 14.05.05 Physical punishments
þerscold 04.05.02.12.02 A vestibule, entrance, courtyard; 05.10.05.04.11.01 A bound, limit
þicce 02.04.04.03.01 Texture of hair; 02.07.01 To grow; 03.01.01 Thick, close-textured, dense; 03.01.17 Thickness, viscosity; 03.03.04.01.02 A great number, multitude; 03.03.04.02.01 Abundance; 04.04.05 Woven material, fabric; 05.10.05.03.01.01 Breadth, width across; 05.11.09.02 Frequent, of common occurrence
þicce meolc 04.01.02.01.02.09.04 Beestings (colostrum)
þiccet 02.07.03.04.02 A thicket
þiccian 03.01.17 Thickness, viscosity; 03.03.04.01.02 A great number, multitude
þiccol 02.04.02.01 Fat/plump

þicfeald 12.04.02 A crowding together, assembly
geþicfyldan 03.03.04.01.02.01 A heap, mass, accumulation
(ge)þicgan 04 Consumption of food/drink; 10.04 To take
þiclīce 03.03.04.01.02 A great number, multitude
þicnes 02.07.03.04.02 A thicket; 03.01.13 Darkness, obscurity; 03.01.17 Thickness, viscosity; 05.10.05.03.01.01 Breadth, width across
þider 05.10.04.03 Presence
þider geond 05.10.04.03 Presence
þidercyme 05.12.05.02 To go/travel towards, come, approach; 05.12.05.02.03 To arrive
þideres 05.10.04.03 Presence
þiderinn 05.03 Source, origin; 05.10.05.04.01 Inside, interior
þiderlēodisc 02.03.03.03.01 A native people
þiderweard 05.10.04.03 Presence
þiderweardes 05.10.04.03 Presence
þīefefeoh 14.02.01.02 Wrongful taking, theft
þīefþ 14.02.01.02 Wrongful taking, theft
þigen 04 Consumption of food/drink; 04.01.02.01 Food/sustenance; 16.02.04.07.04 Communion/eucharist
þilian 04.05.01.02.01 Boarding, planking, floor
þiling 04.05.01.02.01 Boarding, planking, floor; 04.05.04.02 A table
þille 04.05.02.10 Flooring, a floor
þimiama 16.02.05.09.02 Incense
þīn brōþorlicnes 11.05.02.02.01.01 Courteous forms of address
þīnan 03.01.16.01 Moisture
geþind 02.08.05.01 Swelling

þindan 02.08.05.01 Swelling; 08.01.03.05.02 Anger
þīnen 02.01.03.03.03.01 Child-bearing, childbirth; 12.01.01.08.01 A servant, attendant
þing 02 Creation; 03 Material, matter, substance; 05.02.01 Condition, state of affairs, situation; 05.03.01.03 Reason, cause; 05.03.02.01.01 An event, occurrence; 06.02.06.01 An end, goal; 08.01.03.06 Adversity, affliction; 09.06 To take matter for discourse; 11.01.01 Practice, exercise, doing; 11.02 Occupation, activity, business; 11.05.02 Mode, manner, way, method, fashion, course; 14.03.01 Judicial body, authority; 14.03.03.01 Accusation; 15.01 Property
(ge)þing 05.02 State, condition; 12.02.02 An assembly, meeting
geþing 05.03.02 Event, issue, result; 13.01.03 Intercession, pleading, mediation
geþingan 08.01.01.03.08 Happiness, well-being, prosperity
(ge)þinge 14.04.02 A stipulation
geþinge 14.04 Making of terms, agreement, convention; 14.04.04 An agreement, arrangement of dispute
þingere 12.03.04.02 Speech on behalf of, advocacy; 13.01.03 Intercession, pleading, mediation; 14.04.04.01 Intercession, mediation; 16.02.03.02.07 A priest, cleric
þingestre 16.01.02.05.02.01 Mary, queen of heaven
þinggemearc 05.11 A time, period of time

þingian 09.01 To speak, exercise faculty of speech
þing(i)an (ongēan/wiþ) 09.01.03 To address, speak to
(ge)þingian 06.02.07 Will, determination, resolution; 07 Judgement, forming of opinion; 09.07.04.01 Confirmation, agreement; 12.03.04.02 Speech on behalf of, advocacy; 13.01.02 Reconciliation; 13.01.03 Intercession, pleading, mediation; 14.04 Making of terms, agreement, convention; 14.04.04 An agreement, arrangement of dispute; 14.04.04.01 Intercession, mediation
(ge)þingian (mid/tō/wiþ) 14.04.04.01 Intercession, mediation
geþingian 06.02.06.02 A proposal, proposition, suggestion; 06.02.06.02.01 To devise a plan, arrange, settle; 10.01.02 Acquisition; 10.04 To take; 16.02.04.07.02.03 Penance, an act/instance of penance
þinglēas 12.07.03 Abstinence/exemption (from)
þingrǣden 13.01.03 Intercession, pleading, mediation; 14.04.04.01 Intercession, mediation
geþingsceat 10.03.05.01.01 A bribe, gift, payment
þingstede 12.02.02.01 Place of conference or assembly
(ge)þingstōw 12.02.02.01 Place of conference or assembly
geþingþ 13.01.03 Intercession, pleading, mediation; 14.03.01 Judicial body, authority; 14.04 Making of terms, agreement, convention
þingum 06.02.06 Mind, purpose
þingung 14.04.04.01 Intercession, mediation

(ge)þingung 13.01.03 Intercession, pleading, mediation
þīr 12.01.01.08.01 A servant, attendant
þīsl 04.05.01.02.06 A log, stake, etc.; 05.12.01.06 Vehicle; 13.02.08.04 Weapons, arms
þism 03.01.09.02.01.04 Smoke
þistel 02.07.11 Plants/flowers (alphabetical order)
þistelgeblǣd 02.08.05.02 Particular inflammation/swelling
þistellēag 04.02.03.04.01.02 Thistle-covered meadow
þisteltwige 02.06.08.05 Forest bird, wild-fowl
þistles blōstm 02.07.11 Plants/flowers (alphabetical order)
þīstra 04.02.05.05.02 Harness of draught animal
þō/þōhe 01.01.02.02.02.02 Clay, loam
þocerian 05.12.03.01 Swiftness, velocity
þoddettan 05.06.09 Act of striking
þoden 01.01.03.05 Whirlpool; 01.03.01.05 Wind
geþofta 12.01.01.07 A follower; 12.04.01 A fellow, companion, associate, comrade
þoft(e) 05.12.01.09.03.01.03 Part of ship
geþoftian 12.04 Fellowship, union, association
(ge)þoftrǣden 12.04 Fellowship, union, association
geþoftrǣden 02.01.03.03 Sex, generation; 09.01.04 Conversation, discussion
(ge)þoftscipe 12.04 Fellowship, union, association; 12.04.01.01 A company of people, fellowship, society
geþoftscipe 02.01.03.03 Sex, generation

geþogen 02.01.04.02 To grow, grow up; 08.01.01.03.08.02 Good fortune, success; 11.04 Ability, capacity, power
(ge)þōht 06.01.01 Thought, the faculty of thinking, mind
geþōht 06.01 The head (as seat of thought); 06.02.06 Mind, purpose; 06.02.06.02 A proposal, proposition, suggestion; 08.01.02.05 Compassion; 11.03.01.03.01 Discovery, invention; 12.02.02.04 Counsel, deliberation; 12.02.02.05 Counsel, advice; 14.01.06 A rule, order, precept, tenet, principle
geþōhtung 12.02.02.04 Counsel, deliberation
þōiht 01.01.02.02.02.02 Clay, loam
þol 05.12.01.09.03.01.03 Part of ship
þolebyrde 08.01.03.08 Patience
þolebyrdnes 08.01.03.08 Patience
þol(e)mōd 08.01.03.08 Patience
þolian hȳde 14.05.05 Physical punishments
(ge)þolian 06.02.07.01 Strength, fortitude; 08.01.03.07.03 Suffering, torment, pain; 10.02.01 Loss, deprivation; 12.05.06.04.01 Submission to action, toleration
geþolian 03.03.07.02 What is left, remnant, remains; 05.12.04 Absence of movement, stillness
þolle 04.01.02.02.06.01 Cooking vessel/pot; 14.05.06 Means/implement of torture
þolmōd 08.01.03.08 Patience
þolmōdnes 08.01.03.08 Patience
þolung 08.01.03.07.03 Suffering, torment, pain; 16.02.04.16 Martyrdom
þon 05.11.07.04.02 (Of time) later/latter
þon ǣr 05.11.08.01.02 (Untimely) earliness
þon mā 03.03.05 Extent, degree

þon mā þe 03.03.05 Extent, degree
þone micclan hād 16.02.03.02.02 The pope
þonne 03.03.04.03 Growth, increase; 03.06 Comparison; 05.03.01 A cause (of anything); 05.03.01.03 Reason, cause; 05.03.02 Event, issue, result; 05.11.07.01 Contemporary, coeval; 05.11.07.04.02 (Of time) later/latter; 05.11.07.04.02.01 Succession; 05.11.11.02 Let up, intermission, cessation
þon(ne) 05.11.02 A time, particular time, occasion
þonne gīet 03.03.04.03 Growth, increase
þonne gȳt 05.11.07.03.02 Earlier, antecedent
þonne hwæþere 03.06 Comparison
þonne (þe) 05.11.07.03.02 Earlier, antecedent
þōr 16.01.06.01 Northern gods
þorfæst 11.07.01 Utility, usefulness
þorfnian 10.02.01 Loss, deprivation
þorlēas 11.08 Uselessness
þorn 02.07.02.05 A shoot, sprout, tendril; 02.07.03.05 Particular trees/shrubs (alphabetical order); 09.03.07.01.01 A runic letter
þornegn 02.07.03.05 Particular trees/shrubs (alphabetical order)
þorneht 05.10.06.03.01 A point, spike, prickle
þornett 02.07.03.05 Particular trees/shrubs (alphabetical order)
þorngeblǣd 02.08.05.02 Particular inflammation/swelling
þorngrǣfe 02.07.03.05 Particular trees/shrubs (alphabetical order)
þornig 02.07.03.05 Particular trees/shrubs (alphabetical order); 05.10.06.03.01 A point, spike, prickle
þorniht(e)/-eht(e) 02.07.03.05 Particular trees/shrubs (alphabetical order)
þorning 02.07.03.05 Particular trees/shrubs (alphabetical order)
þornrǣw 02.07.03.05 Particular trees/shrubs (alphabetical order)
þornrind 02.07.03.05 Particular trees/shrubs (alphabetical order)
þornstybb 02.07.03.05 Particular trees/shrubs (alphabetical order)
þornþȳfel 02.07.03.05 Particular trees/shrubs (alphabetical order)
þorp 04.02 Farm; 12.06.02.01 A township
þost 02.04.06.06.06 Faeces
þoterian 02.05.10.15.03 Groaning
þoterung 02.05.10.15.03 Groaning
þōþor 05.10.06.02 Rotundity, roundness; 18.02.02 Play, (athletic) sport
geþracen 05.08 Strength
þracian 06.01.08.06.02 Great fear, terror, horror
þracu 05.08.01 Vigour, activity, force; 05.08.02 Violence, force; 12 Power, might
geþræc 03.03.04.01.02.01 A heap, mass, accumulation; 05.08.02 Violence, force; 17.03 Implements, tools, etc.
þræcful 06.02.07.06 Courage, boldness, valour
þræcheard 06.02.07.06 Courage, boldness, valour
þræchwīl 11.06.03.01 Ill fortune, bad success
þræcrōf 06.02.07.06 Courage, boldness, valour
þræcwīg 13.02.02 Battle
þræcwudu 13.02.08.04.01 A spear

þrǣd 04.04.04 A thread (of wool, etc.), fibre; 17.03.10 Supports and fastenings
geþrǣf 12.05.06.03.01 Pressure, compulsion
geþrǣf 09.07.04.01.03 Unanimity
þrǣft 12.05.03.01 Quarrel, contentiousness, strife
þrǣgan 05.12.05.02 To go/travel towards, come, approach
þrǣl 12.01.01.08.01 A servant, attendant; 12.01.01.09 Bondage, slavery
þrǣlriht 14.01.04.01 A special right, right peculiar to a class
þrǣs 04.04.09 A fringe, border, hem
þrǣstan 05.10.06.02.03 A circular fold, coil
(ge)þrǣstan 02.08.03.01 Extreme pain, torture, torment; 08.01.03.07.02 Misery, trouble, affliction; 12.05.06.01 Restraint, check, curb, control
geþrǣstan 05.06 Destruction, dissolution, loss, breaking; 05.06.05.03 Bruising, crushing; 05.12.05.04.01 (Of wheel, etc.) to roll, trundle
geþrǣsted 08.01.03.02.01 Compunction, remorse, contrition; 16.02.04.07.02.01 Penitence
geþrǣstednes 05.06.05.03 Bruising, crushing
geþrǣst(ed)nes 08.01.03.02.01 Compunction, remorse, contrition; 16.02.04.07.02.01 Penitence
þrǣstung 02.08.03.01 Extreme pain, torture, torment
þrafian 07.05.01 Censure, reproof, rebuke
(ge)þrafian 06.02.06.03.03 Incitement
(ge)þrafian (æfter/for) 12.03.04 A request, prayer

þrafung 07.05.01 Censure, reproof, rebuke
þrāg 02.08.08.04.01 Gripe, colic; 05.11 A time, period of time; 05.11.02 A time, particular time, occasion
þrāgbysig 05.11.11 Continuity
þrāge 05.11.01 Length/duration in time
þrāge þe 05.11 A time, period of time
þrāglic 05.11.11 Continuity
þrāgmǣl 08.01.03.06 Adversity, affliction
þrāgmǣlum 05.11.09.03 At times, sometimes
þrāgum 05.11.09.03 At times, sometimes
geþrang 12.04.02 A crowding together, assembly
þrāwan 05.12.05.04 To rotate, turn round, revolve; 14.05.05 Physical punishments
(ge)þrāwan 04.06.01.07 Hair-care
geþrāwan 05.12.05 To move and change direction, turn
þrāwere 06.02.07.04.02 Perversity
þrāwingspinl 04.06.01.07 Hair-care
þrēa 07.05.01 Censure, reproof, rebuke; 08.01.03.06.01 Affliction, misfortune, calamity; 08.01.03.09.07 Threat, threatening, menace; 14.05.01 Correction, discipline
þrēagan/þrēawian 08.01.03.09.07 Threat, threatening, menace
(ge)þrēagan 08.01.03.07.02 Misery, trouble, affliction; 08.01.03.07.02.01 Injury, offence; 14.05.01 Correction, discipline
geþrēagan/geþrēawian 05.06.04 Damage, injury, defect, hurt, loss; 12.05.06.03 Necessity, constraint
(ge)þrēagan(-wian) 07.05.01 Censure, reproof, rebuke

þrēagend 07.05.01 Censure, reproof, rebuke
þrēagung 07.05.01 Censure, reproof, rebuke; 08.01.03.09.07 Threat, threatening, menace; 14.05.01 Correction, discipline
þrēal 07.05.01 Censure, reproof, rebuke; 14.05.01 Correction, discipline
þrēalic 08.01.03.06 Adversity, affliction
þrēam 08.01.03.09.10 Wrath, sternness, displeasure
þrēanīed 08.01.03.06.01 Affliction, misfortune, calamity
þrēanīedla 12.05.06.02 Oppression
þrēanīedlic 08.01.03.07.04 Severity, harshness
þrēap 12.04.01.01 A company of people, fellowship, society
þrēapian 07.05.01 Censure, reproof, rebuke
þrēapung 07.05.01 Censure, reproof, rebuke
þrēaswinge 14.05.06 Means/implement of torture
þrēat 08.01.03.07.02 Misery, trouble, affliction; 08.01.03.09.07 Threat, threatening, menace; 12.04.02 A crowding together, assembly; 13.02.10.01.02.01 An armed force/band
(ge)þrēat 05.08.02 Violence, force
þrēatend 12.05.06.02 Oppression
geþrēatian 12.05.06.01 Restraint, check, curb, control
þrēatmǣlum 03.03.04.01.02.01 A heap, mass, accumulation
þrēatnes 08.01.03.06 Adversity, affliction
þrēat(n)ian 07.05.01 Censure, reproof, rebuke
(ge)þrēat(n)ian 12.05.06.02 Oppression; 12.05.06.03 Necessity, constraint; 14.05.01 Correction, discipline
þrēatung 05.08.02 Violence, force; 07.05.01 Censure, reproof, rebuke; 08.01.03.07.02 Misery, trouble, affliction; 08.01.03.09.07 Threat, threatening, menace; 14.05.01 Correction, discipline
þrēaweorc 08.01.03.07.03 Suffering, torment, pain
þreax 03.02.01.01 Decay, corruption, rottenness
þrece 02.05.03.02 Weariness; 12.05.06.02 Oppression
þreclic 06.01.08.06.03.01 Causing dread, terrifying
þrefe 03.03.01.02 Dry measures
þrēodǣglic 05.11.03.01.05 A day
þreodian 06.01.01.01.01 Thought, cogitation, meditation; 11.06.05 Hesitation, scruple
geþreodian 06.02.07 Will, determination, resolution
þreodung 06.01.01.01.01.01 Consideration, rumination; 11.06.05 Hesitation, scruple
þrēohund 03.03.03.04.29 Three hundred
þrēohundred 03.03.03.04.29 Three hundred
þrēohundwintre 02.01.04 Age
þrēoniht 05.11.03.01.05 A day
þreotan 08.01.03.07.02 Misery, trouble, affliction
þrēotēoþa 03.03.03.04.13 Thirteen
þrēotīene 03.03.03.04.13 Thirteen
þrēotīnegēare 02.01.04 Age
þrepel 14.05.06 Means/implement of torture
þrīdægþern 05.11.03.01.05 A day
þrīdǣled 05.10.06 Form, shape

þridda 03.03.03.03 Fractions; 03.03.03.04.03 Three
þridda fæder 02.03.02.03.04 (Of degrees of descent) great-, grand-
þridda sunu 02.03.02.03.05 Descendant
þriddan dǣl 03.03.03.03 Fractions
þridde dohtor 02.03.02.03.05 Descendant
þridde healf 03.03.03.04.02.01 Two and a half
þridde mōdor 02.03.02.03.04 (Of degrees of descent) great-, grand-
þrīe 03.03.03.04.03 Three
þrīetan 02.05.03.02 Weariness; 12.05.06.03.01 Pressure, compulsion
þrīfeald 03.03.03.04.03 Three
þrīfealdlīce 03.03.03.04.03 Three
þrīfēte 05.10.06.03 Projection, head, extremity (of anything)
þrīfeþor 05.10.06.04 A corner, bend, angle
þrīfingre 05.10.05.03 A measure of distance
þrīflēre 04.05.02 A building, edifice, structure
þrīfōted 05.10.06.03 Projection, head, extremity (of anything)
þrīfyldan 03.03.03.04.03 Three
þrīfyrclede 05.10.06.03.01 A point, spike, prickle
þrīfyrede 04.02.03.02.01.01 A furrow
þrīgǣrede 05.10.06.03.01 A point, spike, prickle
þrīgēare 02.01.04 Age; 05.11.06 Course/cycle of time
þrīgylde 15.02.04 Spending, disbursement
þrīhǣmed 12.09 Marriage, state of marriage
þrīhēafede 05.10.06.03 Projection, head, extremity (of anything)
þrīhīwede 05.10.06 Form, shape
þrīhlidede 05.10.05.04.14 An opening, aperture
þrīhyrne(de) 05.10.06.04 A corner, bend, angle
þrīlēfe 02.07.02.06 A leaf; 02.07.11.02 Unidentified plants (alphabetical order)
þrīlen 04.04.05 Woven material, fabric
þrīlic 03.03.03.04.03 Three
þrīli(g) 04.04.05 Woven material, fabric
þrīlīþe 05.11.06.02.02.01 Adjustment in calculation
þrimen 03.03.03.03 Fractions
þrīmeolce 05.11.03.01.03.01 Specific months
þrīmilcemōnaþ 05.11.03.01.03.01 Specific months
þrīnes 03.03.03.04.03 Three
geþring 05.08.02 Violence, force; 12.04.02 A crowding together, assembly
þringan 05.12.03.01.02 Haste, hurry; 12.04.02 A crowding together, assembly
(ge)þringan 05.12.05.09 To go forward, proceed
geþringan 05.10.05.02.03 To reduce, make thin(ner); 10.04.02.02 To seize, take, grasp, lay hold on; 12.05.06.04 A trampling upon, subjection
þrīnihte 05.11.06.03.01.04 (Of lunar cycle) so many nights old
þrinlic 03.03.03.04.03 Three; 16.01.01.04 The Trinity
þrinna 03.03.03.04.03 Three
þrinnes 16.01.01.04 The Trinity
þrintan 03.03.04.03 Growth, increase

þīrēþre 05.12.01.09.03.01.01 Kind of ship; 05.12.01.09.03.01.02 Of/concerning a ship, naval
þrīrēþrecēol 05.12.01.09.03.01.01 Kind of ship
þrīscȳte 05.10.06.04 A corner, bend, angle
þrīslite tunge 02.06.07.01.01 Part of snake
þrīsnæcce tunge 02.06.07.01.01 Part of snake
þrīste 06.02.07.06.02.02 Boldness, daring; 06.02.07.06.02.03 Presumption; 08.01.03.07.04 Severity, harshness; 08.01.03.09.11 Hardheartedness, cruelty, severity; 12.08.07.01.04 Shamelessness, lasciviousness
þrīst(e) 06.02.07.06 Courage, boldness, valour
þrīstful 06.02.07.06.02.03 Presumption
þrīsthycgende 06.02.07 Will, determination, resolution
þrīsthȳdig 06.02.07 Will, determination, resolution
geþrīstian 07.06.01.03 To be proud/arrogant
þrīstiglic 06.02.07.06.02.02 Boldness, daring
þrīstiglīce 06.02.07.06.02.02 Boldness, daring
(ge)þrīstlǣcan 07.06.01.03 To be proud/arrogant
þrīstlǣcnes 06.02.07.06.02.03 Presumption
geþrīstlǣcung 06.02.07.06.02.03 Presumption
þrīstlic 06.02.07.06.02 Boldness
þrīstlīce 06.02.07.06.02.02 Boldness, daring; 07.06.01.02 Proudly, arrogantly; 11.02.04.01 Rashness, madness
þrīstling 02.06.08.05 Forest bird, wild-fowl
þrīstlong 05.10.05.03.01 Length
þrīstnes 07.06.01 Pride, arrogance
þrīstrenge 18.02.07.02.03 Stringed instruments
þrīsumer 02.01.04 Age
þrītig 03.03.03.04.21 Thirty
þrītigfeald 03.03.03.04.21 Thirty
þrītigoþa 03.03.03.04.21 Thirty
þrītigwintre 02.01.04 Age
þrīþing 12.06.02 District, province
þrīþinggerēfa 12.01.01.05 A leader, administrator
þriwa 03.03.03.04.03 Three
þrīwintre 02.01.04 Age
þroc 04.02.04.06.07 Ploughing equipment; 04.05.04.02 A table
þrocen 02.07.03.04 A wood, trees
þrōh 08.01.03.09.01.02 Bitterness, acrimony
þroht 08.01.03.07.02 Misery, trouble, affliction
þrohtheard 06.02.07.01 Strength, fortitude; 17.01 Strenuous effort, hard work
þrohtig 06.02.07.03 Perseverance
þrosm 03.01.09.02.01.04 Smoke; 03.01.13 Darkness, obscurity
þrosmig 03.01.09.02.01.04 Smoke
þrostle 02.06.08.05 Forest bird, wild-fowl
þrotbolla 02.04.06.07.01 Wind-pipe
þrotbolle 02.04.06.03.02.02 Throat/gullet
þrote 02.04.06.03.02.02 Throat/gullet
þrōwad bēon/wesan 08.01.03.07.02.01 Injury, offence; 16.01.01.04.02.02 Events associated with Christ

geþrōwad 02.08.03.01 Extreme pain, torture, torment
þrōwend 02.06.10.01.06 Serpent, scorpion, basilisk
þrōwendlic 09.03.02.03.01.02.02 Voice
þrōwendlic dēaþ 02.08.09.01 Apoplexy
þrōwere 02.08.02.01.04 A sick person, invalid; 16.02.04.16 Martyrdom
þrōwerhād 08.01.03.07.03 Suffering, torment, pain; 16.02.04.16 Martyrdom
þrōwestre 16.02.04.16 Martyrdom
þrōwethād 08.01.03.07.03 Suffering, torment, pain; 16.02.04.16 Martyrdom
þrōwian 11.06.02 Suffering (not acting)
(ge)þrōwian 02.02.01 Particular mode of death; 02.08.03 Pain, bodily discomfort; 16.02.04.07.02.03 Penance, an act/instance of penance; 16.02.04.16 Martyrdom
geþrōwian 03.06.03.01 Compatible; 08.01.02.05 Compassion
þrōw(i)endhād 08.01.03.07.03 Suffering, torment, pain; 16.02.04.16 Martyrdom
þrōwiendlic 08.01.03.07.03 Suffering, torment, pain
þrōwingrǣding 16.02.04.16 Martyrdom
þrōwingtīma 08.01.03.06 Adversity, affliction
þrōwung 02.02.01 Particular mode of death; 02.08.02.01.03 A symptom; 02.08.03 Pain, bodily discomfort; 08.01.01.01 Ardour, fervour, strong feeling; 08.01.03.07.03 Suffering, torment, pain; 11.06.02 Suffering (not acting); 16.01.01.04.02.02 Events associated with Christ; 16.02.04.04.02 A feast-day, holy day; 16.02.04.16 Martyrdom
þrōwungdæg 16.02.04.04.02 A feast-day, holy day; 16.02.04.16 Martyrdom

þrōwungtīd 16.02.04.04.02 A feast-day, holy day; 16.02.04.16 Martyrdom
þrūh 02.02.05.01.01 A grave, burial place, sepulchre; 17.02.04.02.04 Leading/conducting of water
þrūstfell 02.08.06 Skin disease, erysipelas
þrūtigende 07.06.02 Arrogance, vainglory, vanity; 08.01.03.09.07 Threat, threatening, menace
þrūtung 08.01.03.09.07 Threat, threatening, menace
(ge)þryccan 12.05.06.01 Restraint, check, curb, control; 12.05.06.02 Oppression
geþryccan 02.05.06.01 To touch and press; 08.01 Heart, spirit, mood, disposition; 09.06.02 A saying, speech, statement
geþryccednes 08.01.03.06 Adversity, affliction
þrycnes 08.01.03.06 Adversity, affliction
þrȳfeald āþ 14.03.03.04 Oath-swearing
geþrȳl 12.04.02 A crowding together, assembly
þrymcyme 05.12.05.02 To go/travel towards, come, approach
þrymcyning 16.01.01.01.01 The Almighty
þrymdōm 07.08.05 Glorifying, making great, glorification; 16.02.01.08.03 The New Testament
þrymfæst 07.08.09 Renown, fame, glory
þrymful 07.02.04.03 Nobleness, excellence, nobility, magnificence
þrymlic 07.02.04.03 Nobleness, excellence, nobility, magnificence; 12 Power, might
þrymlīce 06.01.08.05.01.01 Wondrous, glorious, marvellous

þrymm 01.01.03.01 Body of water; 07.02.04.03 Nobleness, excellence, nobility, magnificence; 07.08.07 Glory, splendour, magnificence; 12 Power, might; 12.01.01 Authority; 12.04.02 A crowding together, assembly; 13.02.10.01.02.02 Armed forces; 16.01.01.01.01 The Almighty
þrymma 06.02.07.06 Courage, boldness, valour
þrymme 05.08.02 Violence, force; 12 Power, might
þrymmum 05.08.02 Violence, force; 12 Power, might
þrymrīce 16.01.02.01 Heavenly dwelling place
þrymseld 14.03.01 Judicial body, authority
þrymseld/-setl 12.01.01.02 Seat of authority
þrymsetl 16.01.02.05.01 An angel
þrymsittende 16.01.01.01.01.02 Glory; 16.01.02.05 Inhabitants of heaven
þrymwealdend 16.01.01.01.01 The Almighty; 16.01.01.01.01 Mightiness
geþrȳn 05.05.03 Binding, fastening; 09.03.07.07 A book; 09.06.02 A saying, speech, statement; 12.05.06.04 A trampling upon, subjection
þryng 01.01.03.01.01.04 Watercourse/channel
geþryscan 12.05.06.02 Oppression
þrysce 02.06.08.05 Forest bird, wild-fowl
þrysman 12.05.06.04 A trampling upon, subjection
þrȳþ 12 Power, might
þrȳþærn 04.05.03.02.02.06 A royal/noble palace
þrȳþbearn 02.01.04.01 Youth

þrȳþbord 13.02.08.03.01.06 A shield
þrȳþcyning 16.01.01.01.01 The Almighty
geþrȳþed 12 Power, might
þrȳþful 07.02.04.03 Nobleness, excellence, nobility, magnificence; 12 Power, might
þrȳþgesteald 04.05.03.02.02.06 A royal/noble palace
þrȳþig 12 Power, might
þrȳþlic 12 Power, might
þrȳþlīce 12 Power, might
þrȳþswȳþ 12 Power, might
þrȳþu 03.03.04.01.02 A great number, multitude
þrȳþum 05.08.02 Violence, force; 12 Power, might
þrȳþweorc 17.02.04 Trade, calling, craft, aptitude
þrȳþword 09.03.04.02.02 Eloquence, elegance in language
þūf 02.07.02.06 A leaf; 13.02.08.02 A standard, banner, ensign
geþūf 02.07.02.06 A leaf; 02.07.03.04 A wood, trees
þūfbǣre 02.07.02.06 A leaf
þūfian 02.07.01 To grow
þūfig 02.07.02.06 A leaf
þūft 02.07.03.04.02 A thicket
(ge)þuhsian 01.03.01.06 Cloud
geþuhtsum 03.03.04.02.01 Abundance
þūma 02.04.03.04.01.01.01 Finger
þūman nægl 02.04.04.02 Nail
þumle 02.04.06.03.02.04 Intestines
geþun 02.05.10.02 Noise, din
þung 02.07.11.02 Unidentified plants (alphabetical order); 04.06.02.06 Poison
geþungen 02.01.04.02 To grow, grow up; 03.06.03 Congruity, fitness, suitability; 06.01.06.02 Knowledge,

learning, erudition; 07.02.04.02 Nobleness, nobility, dignity; 07.04.04.02 Laudable, praiseworthy; 11.07.04 Superiority, pre-eminence, primacy

geþungenlīce 12.08.02.01 Goodness, excellence, virtue; 12.08.03.03 Moral restraint, modesty, sobriety

(ge)þungennes 07.02.04.02 Nobleness, nobility, dignity; 11.07.04 Superiority, pre-eminence, primacy

geþungennes 02.01.04.02 To grow, grow up; 11.03.02 Advancement, progress; 12.08.03.03.01.01 Chastity

þunian 02.05.10.03 Noise, tumult, uproar; 05.10.06.03 Projection, head, extremity (of anything); 07.06.01.03 To be proud/arrogant

þunor 01.03.01.03.01.01 Thundering, thunder; 16.01.06.01 Northern gods; 16.01.06.02 Classical gods

þunorbodu 02.06.06.03.01.09 Sea bream

þunorclǣfre 02.07.11 Plants/flowers (alphabetical order)

þunorlic 01.03.01.03.01.01 Thundering, thunder; 02.05.10.03 Noise, tumult, uproar

þunorrād 01.03.01.03.01.01 Thundering, thunder

þunorrādlic 02.05.10.03 Noise, tumult, uproar

þunorrādstefn 02.05.10.03 Noise, tumult, uproar

þunorslege 01.03.01.03.01.01 Thundering, thunder

þunorsliht 01.03.01.03.01.01 Thundering, thunder

þunorwyrt 02.07.09.02.02.01 Edible root/bulb

þunresǣfen 05.11.03.01.05.01 Specific days

þunresdæg 05.11.03.01.05.01 Specific days

þunresniht 05.11.03.01.05.01 Specific days

(ge)þunrian 01.03.01.03.01.01 Thundering, thunder

þunring 01.03.01.03.01.01 Thundering, thunder

þunung 02.05.10.07 A crashing, noise

þunwang(e) 02.04.03.01.03.01 Forehead

þurfan 05.04 Fate, lot, fortune, destiny; 06.02.04 Necessity, inevitability; 06.02.04.01 Want, need; 15.01.06 Poverty, indigence; 15.04 A debt, due

(ge)þurfan 06.02.04.01 Want, need

þurh 05.03.01 A cause (of anything); 05.10.04.03 Presence; 05.10.05.04.10.02 Through (into and out); 05.11 A time, period of time; 06.02.06.01 An end, goal; 11.01.04 A doing, accomplishing (of something); 12.07.01 One's due, natural place or position

þurh ǣlc þing 03.04.03.01 Someone/something

þurh ǣnig þing 11.01.04 A doing, accomplishing (of something)

þurh sōþ 06.01.07.01 Correct, right, free from error

þurh getācnunge 09.03.04.02.01 A figure

þurh ūt 03.03.06 Wholeness

þurh ūtlīce 03.03.06 Wholeness

þurhbeorht 03.01.12 Brightness, light; 06.01.05.01.01 Clear to the understanding, plain; 07.10 Beauty, fairness

þurhbiter 08.01.03.05.03 Exasperation, irritation

þurhblāwan 02.01.02 Gift of life

þurhborian 05.06.07 Pricking, a prick, puncture
þurhbrecan 05.12.05.03.04.01 To burst forth, break out
þurhbregdan 05.12.02 To move, set in motion
þurhbrengan 05.12.02.01 To fetch, bring, bear, conduct
þurhbrūcan 02.05.05.04.01 Luxuries, dainties, good things
þurhburnen 03.01.09.02.01 Fire, burning
þurhclǣnsian 04.06.01 Clean
þurhcrēopan 05.12.03.02 Slowness
þurhdelfan 05.06.07 Pricking, a prick, puncture
þurhdōn 11.01.05 Accomplishment, fulfilment
þurhdrencan 03.01.16.06 A soaking, steeping
þurhdrēogan 05.11 A time, period of time; 11.01.05 Accomplishment, fulfilment
þurhdrīfan 05.06.07 Pricking, a prick, puncture; 05.12.05.02.04 To go in, enter; 05.12.05.06.02 To force a way through
þurhdūfan 05.12.05.02.04.03 To plunge (something into something)
þurhendian 11.01.05 Accomplishment, fulfilment
þurhetan 03.02.01.04 Rust; 04.01.01 Eating; 05.06.01 Devastation, laying waste
þurhfǣr 09.05.04.01 Concealment, obscurity
þurhfǣreld 05.12.05.03.03 To depart, leave, set out
þurhfæstnian 05.06.07 Pricking, a prick, puncture

þurhfaran 05.06.07 Pricking, a prick, puncture; 05.12.05.02.04 To go in, enter; 05.12.05.06 To travel over/through/along, traverse; 05.12.05.06.02 To force a way through; 05.12.05.07 To go beyond, pass; 08.01 Heart, spirit, mood, disposition
þurhfarennes 04.05.03.04 A closet, chamber, room
þurhfēran 05.12.05.02.04 To go in, enter; 05.12.05.06 To travel over/through/along, traverse; 05.12.05.06.02 To force a way through; 06.01.05.01 Understanding
þurhfēre 04.05.03.04 A closet, chamber, room; 05.12.01.03.01 A means of access; 11.12.01 Absence of restraint, freedom
þurhflēon 05.12.01.07 To fly (with wings)
þurhfōn 05.06.07 Pricking, a prick, puncture
þurhfrignan 09.05.02 A question, inquiry, questioning
þurhgān 05.06.07 Pricking, a prick, puncture; 05.12.05.02.04 To go in, enter; 05.12.05.06 To travel over/through/along, traverse; 05.12.05.06.02 To force a way through; 06.01.05.01 Understanding
þurhgangan 05.12.05.06 To travel over/through/along, traverse
þurhgeendad 11.01.06 End, completion (of action), fulfilment
þurhgefeht 13.02 War
þurhgēotan 03.01.16.06 A soaking, steeping; 05.12.05.02.04 To go in, enter; 08.01 Heart, spirit, mood, disposition

þurhgēotan on gescyndnesse 07.09.01.01 Reddening with shame, confusion
þurhglēdan 03.01.09.01 Warmth, heat
þurhhǣlan 02.08.12 Healing, curing
þurhhālig 16.02.01.10 Holiness
þurhhefig 08.01.03.07.02 Misery, trouble, affliction
þurhholod 05.06.07 Pricking, a prick, puncture
þurhhwīt 03.01.14.03 White/whiteness
þurhiernan 05.06.07 Pricking, a prick, puncture; 05.12.05.06 To travel over/through/along, traverse
þurhlǣdan 05.12.05.08.01 To go before and guide
þurhlǣran 06.02.06.03 Persuasion, prompting
þurhlǣred 06.01.06.02 Knowledge, learning, erudition
þurhlāþ 07.03.01.01 Abominable, detestable
þurhlēor(i)an 05.12.05.06 To travel over/through/along, traverse; 05.12.05.06.02 To force a way through
þurhleornian 06.01.06.02.03.03 To study, apply oneself to learning
þurhlōcung 09.03.07.07.02.01.02 A prologue, preface
þurhlonge 05.11 A time, period of time
þurhrǣdan 06.01.06.02.03.03.01 An act of reading
þurhrǣsan 05.12.05.06 To travel over/through/along, traverse
þurhscēotan 05.06.07 Pricking, a prick, puncture
þurhscīnan 03.01.12.03 Clear, transparent
þurhscīnendlic 03.01.12 Brightness, light; 07.10 Beauty, fairness
þurhscrīpan 05.12.05.06 To travel over/through/along, traverse; 05.12.05.06.01 To travel smoothly, slide, glide; 09.05.01 Inspection, examination
þurhscyldig 12.08.09 Guiltiness, guilt
þurhscȳne 03.01.12.03 Clear, transparent
þurhsēcan 09.05.01 Inspection, examination; 11.03.01.02 To seek, seek for
þurhsēon 02.05.09.05 To watch, observe, survey; 05.12.05.02.04 To go in, enter; 06.01.05.01 Understanding
þurhslēan 02.08.03 Pain, bodily discomfort; 05.06.07 Pricking, a prick, puncture; 05.06.09 Act of striking
þurhsmēagan 09.05.01 Inspection, examination
þurhsmūgan 05.12.03.02 Slowness; 09.05.01 Inspection, examination
þurhsmyrian 16.02.04.07.06 Unction, anointing with holy oil
þurhspēdig 15.01.05 Possession of wealth
þurhstandan 05.12.05.09 To go forward, proceed
þurhsticcian 05.06.07 Pricking, a prick, puncture
þurhstingan 05.06.07 Pricking, a prick, puncture
þurhstrang 05.08 Strength
þurhswerian 14.03.03.06 False witness
þurhswimman 05.12.01.08.01 To swim
þurhswīpan 06.02.07.01 Strength, fortitude
þurhswōgan 05.12.05.02.01 To come upon, meet with; 05.12.05.02.04 To go in, enter
þurhsȳne 03.01.12.03 Clear, transparent

þurhtēon 05.12.05.09 To go forward, proceed; 06.02.06.03.04 Allurement; 06.02.07.01 Strength, fortitude; 11.01.04 A doing, accomplishing (of something); 11.01.05 Accomplishment, fulfilment; 11.01.06 End, completion (of action), fulfilment; 15.05 Trade, traffic, commerce

þurhtogennes 16.02.04.03.02 Parts of service

þurhtrymman 09.07.04 Assertion, affirmation

þurhþrāwan 01.01.03.03 Flow/flowing

þurhþyddan 05.06.07 Pricking, a prick, puncture

þurhþȳn/-þēowan 05.06.07 Pricking, a prick, puncture

þurhþyrel 05.06.07 Pricking, a prick, puncture

þurhþyr(e)lian 05.06.07 Pricking, a prick, puncture

þurhunrōt 08.01.03 Bad feeling, sadness

þurhwacian 16.02.04.07.06.02 A vigil

þurhwacol 02.05.02 Consciousness; 11.10.02.01 Vigilance

þurhwadan 05.06.07 Pricking, a prick, puncture; 05.12.05.06 To travel over/through/along, traverse; 05.12.05.06.02 To force a way through

þurhwæccan 16.02.04.07.06.02 A vigil

þurhwæccendlic 11.10.02.01 Vigilance; 16.02.04.07.06.02 A vigil

þurhwǣt 03.01.16.01 Moisture

þurhwerod 02.05.07.03 Sweetness

þurhwlītan 02.05.09.05 To watch, observe, survey

þurhwrecan 05.06.07 Pricking, a prick, puncture

þurhwundian 02.08.04.01 A wound

þurhwunenes 06.02.07.03 Perseverance

þurhwunian 04.05.03.01 Habitation, sojourn; 05.11.11 Continuity; 05.13.06 Constancy, unchangeableness; 06.02.07.03 Perseverance

þurhwunigendlic 06.02.07.03 Perseverance

þurhwunigendlīce 06.02.07.03 Perseverance

þurhwunol 05.11.11 Continuity

þurhwunung 06.02.07.03 Perseverance; 12.06.03.02 Living, dwelling, residence (in)

þurhwunungnes 06.02.07.03 Perseverance

þurruc 05.12.01.09.03.01.03 Part of ship

þurst 02.05.05 Desire, appetite; 04.01.03.01 Thirst; 06.02.05 Will, desire, wish

þurstig 04.01.03.01 Thirst; 06.02.05.02 Greed, importunate desire, rapacity

(ge)þurstig 02.05.05 Desire, appetite

þus 03.03.05 Extent, degree; 11.01.04 A doing, accomplishing (of something)

þus gerād 03.04 Form, kind, nature, character

þūsend 03.03.03.04.32 Thousand; 15.01.01 Landed property

þūsendealdor 13.02.10.01.01 A commander, officer

þūsendealdormann 13.02.10.01.01 A commander, officer

þūsendfeald 03.03.03.04.32 Thousand

þūsendfealdgetel 03.03.03.04.32 Thousand

þūsendgerīm 03.03.03.04.32 Thousand

þūsendgetel 03.03.03.04.32 Thousand

þūsendhīwe 03.04.02 A diversity

þūsendlic 03.03.03.04.32 Thousand

þūsendmǣle 03.03.03.04.32 Thousand
þūsendmǣlum 03.03.03.04.32 Thousand
þūsendmann 13.02.10.01.01 A commander, officer
þūsendrīca 13.02.10.01.01 A commander, officer
þūþistle 02.07.11 Plants/flowers (alphabetical order)
þwǣle 04.04.07.11 A headcloth, covering for the head
(ge)þwǣnan 03.01.04 Softness
(ge)þwǣre 13 Peace, tranquillity
geþwǣre 03.06.03.01 Compatible; 05.12.04 Absence of movement, stillness; 08.01.01.03.02 Pleasure, satisfaction; 12.01.01.12.01 Obedience, service; 12.04 Fellowship, union, association
(ge)þwǣrian 13.01.02 Reconciliation
geþwǣrian 03.06.03.01 Compatible; 09.07.04.01 Confirmation, agreement
(ge)þwǣrlǣcan 09.07.04.01 Confirmation, agreement; 13.01.02 Reconciliation
geþwǣrlǣcan 03.06.03.01 Compatible; 11.05.02 Mode, manner, way, method, fashion, course; 12.04 Fellowship, union, association; 14.04.04 An agreement, arrangement of dispute
geþwǣrlic 03.06.03.01 Compatible; 05.10.06 Form, shape
geþwǣrlīce 03.06.03.01 Compatible; 07.07.01 Simplicity, mildness; 09.07.04.01.03 Unanimity
(ge)þwǣrnes 13 Peace, tranquillity
geþwǣrnes 08.01.02.01.02 Gentleness
geþwǣrung 09.07.04.01.02 Consent
þwang 04.04.07.15 Footwear, covering for the feet; 17.04.04.02 Skin, hide (as material)

þwāstrian 09.02.03.01 Murmur, whispering
þwēal 04.06.01.01 Cleansing, washing; 04.06.01.04 What is used in washing, an ointment
(ge)þwēan 04.06.01.01 Cleansing, washing; 16.02.04.07.01 Baptism, baptizing (and anointing)
þwearm 17.03.03 A cutting tool
þwēora 12.08.06.01 Error, wrong conduct, erroneous practice
þwēor(a) 08.01.03.05.03 Exasperation, irritation
þwēores 05.10.05.04.06 Cross, transverse, bent, crooked; 05.10.05.04.09 Side, quarter, direction; 12.08.06.01.03 Evilly, badly
þweorh 05.10.05.04.06 Cross, transverse, bent, crooked; 07.06.01.01 Proud, arrogant; 08.01.03.07.02 Misery, trouble, affliction; 08.01.03.09.01.02 Bitterness, acrimony; 12.05.02 Hostility, contention, opposition; 12.08.06.01.02 Lacking moral good
þweorhfero 04.02.03.02.01.01 A furrow
þweorhlic 12.05.02 Hostility, contention, opposition; 12.08.06.01.02 Lacking moral good
þweorhtīeme 12.08.06.01.02 Lacking moral good
þweorhtimber 06.02.07 Will, determination, resolution
þweorian 03.06.02 Difference, diversity, dissimilarity; 12.05.02 Hostility, contention, opposition
þwēorlic 03.06.02.01 Contrariety, diversity
þwēorlīce 03.05 Order, arrangement, disposition; 06.02.07.04 Obstinacy;

07.06.01.02 Proudly, arrogantly; 12.08.06.01.03 Evilly, badly
þwēornes 06.01.07.04.04 Deceitfulness, falseness, duplicity; 06.02.07.04 Obstinacy
(ge)þwēornes 12.08.06.01 Error, wrong conduct, erroneous practice
þwēorscipe 12.08.06.01 Error, wrong conduct, erroneous practice
þwēortīeme 12.05.03.01 Quarrel, contentiousness, strife
geþweran 03.03.06.01.01 Mixing, mingling, preparation; 17.02.04.03 Metal worker
þwēre 17.03.04 Tools for smoothing/scraping/grinding
geþwerian 12.04 Fellowship, union, association
þwīnan 02.08.05.01 Swelling
geþwinglod 04.06.01.07 Hair-care
þwiril 04.01.02.02.08 Churn
geþwit 03.03.07 A part, division, portion
þwītan 05.06.02 Cleaving, splitting, cutting
þȳ 05.03.01.03 Reason, cause; 05.03.01 A cause (of anything); 03.06 Comparison
þȳ ǣr 05.11.08.01.02 (Untimely) earliness
þȳ hraþor 03.03.05 Extent, degree; 05.11.08.01.02 (Untimely) earliness
þȳ lǣs (þe) 05.03.01.03 Reason, cause
þȳ mā 03.03.05 Extent, degree
þyddan 05.06.07 Pricking, a prick, puncture; 05.12.02.06 To push, impel, thrust
geþȳde 11.01.02 An undertaking
þȳfel 02.07.03.01 A bush; 02.07.03.04.02 A thicket; 02.07.11.02 Unidentified plants (alphabetical order)

þȳfelett 02.07.03.04.02 A thicket
þȳfeþorn 02.07.03.05 Particular trees/shrubs (alphabetical order)
þȳflig 02.07.03.05 Particular trees/shrubs (alphabetical order)
þyften 12.01.01.08.01 A servant, attendant
geþyht 11.07.01 Utility, usefulness
þyhtig 05.08 Strength
þylcræft 09.03.04 Rhetoric, art of exposition
geþyldan 12.05.06.04.02 Submission, subjection, obedience
(ge)þyldelic 08.01.03.08 Patience
þyldelīce 08.01.03.08 Patience
geþyldian 06.01.08.01 Expectation, waiting
geþyld(i)an 08.01.03.08 Patience
(ge)þyldig 08.01.03.08 Patience
geþyld(ig)līce 08.01.03.08 Patience
geþyldmōd 08.01.03.08 Patience
geþyldmōdnes 08.01.03.08 Patience
(ge)þyld(-u/-o) 08.01.03.08 Patience
geþyldum 08.01.03.08 Patience
þyle 09.01.02 Fluency in speech; 12.02.02.02 A counsellor, advisor
geþyll 01.03.01.05 Wind
þyllan 05.09.03 Mitigation, lightening, alleviation
þyllic 03.04 Form, kind, nature, character
geþyllic 03.01.01 Thick, close-textured, dense
geþylmed 07.09.02 Disgrace, shaming, humiliation
þȳmel 02.08.12.02.06.01 A bandage, binding; 04.04.07.14 A glove
þȳmele 05.10.05.03 A measure of distance
(ge)þyncan 02.05.09.08 To seem, appear to be; 11.07.03 Use, advantage, profit

(ge)þyncþo 03.03.05.01 Rank, position, degree

geþyncþo 07.08.02 Honour, glory; 12.01.01.06.02.01 (High) rank, status, degree; 12.08.02.01 Goodness, excellence, virtue

geþynge 11.01.05.02 Furtherance, promotion

þynhlǣne 02.08.04.04.03 Withered; 03.01.18 Dryness (not wetness)

geþynnan 05.10.05.02.03 To reduce, make thin(ner)

þynne 02.04.02.02 Lean, thin, slender; 02.08.02 Disease, infirmity, sickness; 03.01.02 Thinness, slightness of density; 05.10.05.03.01.01 Breadth, width across; 06.01.05.02 Intelligence

þynnes 02.08.07.02.01 Defective vision; 03.01.02 Thinness, slightness of density

þynnian 05.09.05 Ceasing, decline, fall off

(ge)þynnian 02.04.02.02 Lean, thin, slender

geþynnian 02.08.07.02.01 Defective vision

þynnol 02.04.02.02 Lean, thin, slender

þynnung 02.04.02.02 Lean, thin, slender

þynwefen 04.04.05 Woven material, fabric

þyrel 04.05.02.13 A window-space; 05.06.07 Pricking, a prick, puncture

þyrelhūs 17.02.04.02.01 Cutting, hewing, shaping

þyrelung 05.06.07 Pricking, a prick, puncture

þyrelwamb 05.06.07 Pricking, a prick, puncture

þyrlian 05.06.07 Pricking, a prick, puncture; 17.02.04.02.02 Digging

þyrncin 02.07.03.05 Particular trees/shrubs (alphabetical order)

þyrne 02.07.03.05 Particular trees/shrubs (alphabetical order)

þyrnen 05.10.06.03.01 A point, spike, prickle

þyrnet 02.07.03.05 Particular trees/shrubs (alphabetical order)

þyrniht 05.10.06.03.01 A point, spike, prickle

þyrniht(e) 02.07.02.05 A shoot, sprout, tendril

þyrran 03.01.18 Dryness (not wetness)

þyrre 01.01.02.01.06 Wild/uncultivated land; 02.07.01 To grow; 03.01.18 Dryness (not wetness)

þyrs 02.03.01.11 Giant; 16.01.03 A spectre, ghost, demon, goblin; 16.01.04.01 Sorcery using incantation

þyrsce(l)flōr 04.02.04.04.05 To thresh (corn)

þyrst 02.05.05 Desire, appetite

geþyrst 04.01.03.01 Thirst

þyrstan 02.05.05 Desire, appetite

(ge)þyrstan 04.01.03.01 Thirst; 06.02.05.02 Greed, importunate desire, rapacity

þyrste (ge)þecgan 04.01.03.01 Thirst

þys(ge)lic 03.04 Form, kind, nature, character

geþȳwe 11.05 Natural/proper way/manner/mode of action

u 09.03.07.01 A written character, letter

ualeriane 02.07.11 Plants/flowers (alphabetical order)

ūder 02.04.03.03.05 Chest, breast, bosom; 02.04.06.05.06 Mammary gland, breast

ūf 02.04.05.06 Sinew/tendon/ligament; 02.06.08.04 Bird of prey; 02.06.08.05

Forest bird, wild-fowl; 02.08.07.04.02 Tumour affecting epiglottis
ufan on þæt 03.03.04.03 Growth, increase
ufan rihte 05.10.05.03.03 Height, loftiness, sublimity
ufancumende 05.12.05.13 To go down, descend
ufancund 16.01.02 The heavens, sky
ufane 16.01.02 The heavens, sky
ufan(e) 05.10.05.03.03 Height, loftiness, sublimity
ufan(-e) 05.10.05.04.02.03 Laid below
ufanmearcung 09.03.07.05 To cover with writing, inscribe
ufanweard 05.10.05.04.02 Face, surface
ufemest 05.10.05.03.03 Height, loftiness, sublimity
ufenan 03.03.04.03 Growth, increase; 03.06.04 Incongruity, absurdity; 05.10.05.04.02.03 Laid below
(ge)uferian 05.10.05.04.02.04 Above; 05.11.08.01.03.01 Delay; 05.12.05.12.02 To raise, lift up, elevate
geuferian 02.05.10.15.01 To raise (the voice), raise up (noise); 07.08.06 Exaltation
geuferod 05.12.05.12.02 To raise, lift up, elevate; 07.02.04 Excellence
uferor 05.10.05.03.03 Height, loftiness, sublimity
uferra 04.04.07.07 A long outer garment, covering, cloak, etc.; 05.10.05.03.03 Height, loftiness, sublimity; 05.11.07.04.02 (Of time) later/latter
uferra lippa 02.04.03.01.03.06 Mouth
uferung 05.11.08.01.03.01 Delay

ufeweard 05.10.05.03.03 Height, loftiness, sublimity; 05.11.07.04.02 (Of time) later/latter
ufeweard ēare 02.04.03.01.03.03 Ear
ufor 05.10.05 A space, span; 05.10.05.03.03 Height, loftiness, sublimity; 05.11.07.04.02 (Of time) later/latter; 07.08.06 Exaltation; 11.07.04 Superiority, pre-eminence, primacy
ūhta(n)tīd 05.11.04.01 Day (not night)
ūhtantīma 05.11.04.01 Day (not night); 16.02.04.05.01 The hour or service of Nocturns
ūhtcearu 08.01.03 Bad feeling, sadness
ūhte 05.11.04.02.03 Last hour of the night, just before daybreak; 16.02.04.05.01 The hour or service of Nocturns
ūhternlic 05.11.04.01.02 Morning
ūhtfloga 02.06.10.01.01 Dragon
ūhtgebed 16.02.04.05.02 The hour or service of Matins
ūhthlem 02.05.10.03 Noise, tumult, uproar
ūhtlic 05.11.04.01 Day (not night); 16.02.04.05.02 The hour or service of Matins
ūhtsang 16.02.04.05.02 The hour or service of Matins
ūhtsanglic 16.02.04.05.02 The hour or service of Matins
ūhtsceaþa 02.06.10.01.01 Dragon
ūhttīd 05.11.04.01 Day (not night)
ūhtþegnung 16.02.04.05.02 The hour or service of Matins
ūhtwæcce 16.02.04.07.06.02 A vigil
uīpere 07.05.03.03 Scorn, insult, abuse
ūle 02.06.08.05 Forest bird, wild-fowl
ulmtrēow 02.07.03.05 Particular trees/shrubs (alphabetical order)
ultur 02.06.08.04 Bird of prey

uma 02.07.11.02 Unidentified plants (alphabetical order)
ūma 04.04.03 A spinning-house or chamber
umbor 02.03.01.04 Child
umborwesende 02.01.04.01 Youth
unābeden 09.05.02 A question, inquiry, questioning
unāberendlic 08.01.03.07.04.01 Unbearableness
unāberendlīce 08.01.03.07.04.01 Unbearableness
unāberiende 08.01.03.07.04.01 Unbearableness
unābindendlic 05.05.03 Binding, fastening
unāblinn 05.11.11 Continuity; 05.11.11.01 A not ceasing, persistence, recurrence
unāblinnende 05.11.11.01 A not ceasing, persistence, recurrence
unāblinnendlic 05.11.11.01 A not ceasing, persistence, recurrence
unāblinnendlīce 05.11.11.01 A not ceasing, persistence, recurrence
unābrecendlic 05.05.03 Binding, fastening
unābȳgendlic 03.01.03.01 Stiffness, hardness; 06.02.07.04.01 Obduracy
unācenned 05 Aught, anything, something; 16.01.01.04.01 God the Father
unācnycendlic 05.05.03 Binding, fastening
unācumen(d)lic 06.01.07.07.02 Impossible
unācumendlic 08.01.03.07.04.01 Unbearableness
unācumendlicnes 08.01.03.07.04.01 Unbearableness

unācwencedlic 03.01.09.02 Fire, flame
unādrūgod 03.01.03 Hardness, callosity, hard material
unādrysnende 03.01.09.02 Fire, flame
unādrysnendlic 03.01.09.02 Fire, flame
unādwæsced 03.01.09.02 Fire, flame
unādwæsce(n)dlic 03.01.09.02 Fire, flame
unādwæscendlīce 03.01.09.02 Fire, flame
unæm(et)ta 11.02 Occupation, activity, business
unæmtigian 18 Quiet, leisure, rest
unæt 04.01.01.04 Gluttony, overeating, greediness
unætnessa gebīdan 02.02.03 To die, perish
unætspornen 11.12.01 Absence of restraint, freedom
unæþelboren 12.01.01.11 The common people
unæþele 07.03.05.01 Ignobility; 12.01.01.11 The common people
unæþelian 07.03.03.02 To degrade, debase
unæþelīce 07.03.05.01 Ignobility
unæþelnes 07.03.05.01 Ignobility
unæwfæstlīce 14.02 Lawlessness; 16.02.01.11.02 Impiety, lack of piety
unæwisc 12.08.07.01.04 Shamelessness, lasciviousness
unāfandod 11.06.02 Suffering (not acting)
unāfeohtendlic 06.01.07.07.03 Certainty
unāfīled 04.06.02.01 Dirty, unclean
unāfūliende 05.11.01.04 Incorruption, incorruptibility; 12.08.04 Purity, moral cleanness
unāfunden 11.03.01.03 Finding, discovery; 11.06.02 Suffering (not acting)

unāfylledlic 06.02.05.03 Satisfaction, repletion
unāfyllendlic 06.02.05.03 Satisfaction, repletion
unāfyllendlīce 06.02.05.03 Satisfaction, repletion
unāga 15.01.06 Poverty, indigence
unāgæledlīce 05.11.11.01 A not ceasing, persistence, recurrence
unāgān 15.01.01.01 Holding of land
unāgen 10.02 Want, lack
unāgifen 15.02.04 Spending, disbursement
unāgunnen 05 Aught, anything, something; 16.01.01.04.02 The Son, Christ
unāhefendlic 08.01.03.07.04.01 Unbearableness
unāhladen 03.03.07.02 What is left, remnant, remains
unālogen 06.01.07 Truth, conformity with absolute standard
unālȳfed 12.03.06 Prohibition; 14.02 Lawlessness
unālȳfedlic 14.02 Lawlessness
unālȳfedlīce 12.07.05 Wrong, injustice; 14.02 Lawlessness
unālȳfednes 12.08.07.01.01 Wantonness, sensuality, lasciviousness
unālȳsendlic 12.08.09 Guiltiness, guilt
unāmælt 03.01.16 Liquid, a liquid
unāmansumod 16.02.02 Christianity, the Christian faith
unāmeten 03.03.04.01.03 An immense quantity, immensity, immense number; 16.01.01.01 Attributes of God
unāmeten(d)lic 16.01.01.01 Attributes of God

unāmetgod 16.01.01.01 Attributes of God
unāmyrred 07.02.03.01 Uninjured, unhurt, unharmed
unanbindendlic 05.05.03 Binding, fastening
unandcȳþignes 06.01.06.04 Ignorance
unandergilde 07.04.01 (Of persons) worth/value, worthiness
unandett 16.02.01.13.01 Kinds of sin
unandgitfull 06.01.05.03 Want of understanding; 06.01.05.03.02 Foolish, silly, stupid
unandgittol 06.01.05.03 Want of understanding
unandhēfe 08.01.03.07.04.01 Unbearableness
unandweard 05.10.04.04 Absence
unandwendlic 05.13.06 Constancy, unchangeableness
unandwīs 06.01.06.03.01 Inexperienced
unānrǣdnes 06.02.07.05.01 Inconstancy
unāpīnedlīce 12.07.03.01 Impunity
unār 07.09.03 Infamy, ignominy, shame
unāræf(n)ed 08.01.03.07.04.01 Unbearableness
unāræfnedlīce 08.01.03.07.04.01 Unbearableness
unāræfne(n)dlic 08.01.03.07.04.01 Unbearableness
unāreccendlic 06.01.08.05.01.01 Wondrous, glorious, marvellous
unāreht 09.07 Dispute, debate
geunārian 07.09.03 Infamy, ignominy, shame
unārīmed 03.03.04.01.03 An immense quantity, immensity, immense number
unārīme(n)dlic 03.03.04.01.03 An immense quantity, immensity, immense number

unarīmendlīce 05.11.09.02 Frequent, of common occurrence
unārlic 07.09.03 Infamy, ignominy, shame
unārlīce 07.09 Shame, disgrace; 08.01.03.09.12 Pitilessness
unarodscipe 11.06 Disinclination to act, listlessness
unārwurþian 07.09.03 Infamy, ignominy, shame
unārwurþlic 07.09.03 Infamy, ignominy, shame
unārwyrþnes 07.05 Disrespect, irreverence
unāscended 07.02.03.01 Uninjured, unhurt, unharmed
unāscruncen 07.02.03.01 Uninjured, unhurt, unharmed
unāscyrigendlīce 16.01.01.04 The Trinity
unāscyrod 03.03.06.03 Unity/oneness
unāsecgende 06.01.08.05.01.01 Wondrous, glorious, marvellous
unāsecgendlic 06.01.08.05.01.01 Wondrous, glorious, marvellous; 12.08.08.01.02 Unchastity, incontinence; 16.01.01.01 Attributes of God
unāsecgendlīce 06.01.08.05.01.01 Wondrous, glorious, marvellous
unāsedd 03.03.04.05 Insufficiency, lack, want
unāsēþen(d)lic 06.02.05.03 Satisfaction, repletion
unāsīwod 04.04.05.06 To sew, stitch
unāsmēagendlic 09.04.02.01 A secret, mystery
unāsolcenlīce 05.08.01 Vigour, activity, force
unāspringende 05.13.06 Constancy, unchangeableness
unāspringen(d)lic 05.13.06 Constancy, unchangeableness
unāspyriendlic 09.04.02.01 A secret, mystery
unāstīþod 03.01.04.01 Power of bending, flexibility
unāstyred 05.12.04 Absence of movement, stillness
unāstyriende 05.13.06 Constancy, unchangeableness
unāstyriendlic 05.12.04 Absence of movement, stillness
unāsundrodlic 03.03.06.03 Unity/oneness; 16.01.01.01 Attributes of God
unāswundenlīce 05.12.03.01 Swiftness, velocity
unātalodlic 03.03.04.01.03 An immense quantity, immensity, immense number
unāteald 03.03.04.01.03 An immense quantity, immensity, immense number
unātellendlic 03.03.04.01.03 An immense quantity, immensity, immense number
unātemed 12.06.05 A foreign country
unātemedlic 05.08.02.01 (Of living creatures) fierceness, roughness
unātēoriende 11.02.01.02 Unwearied
unātēorigende 06.02.07.01 Strength, fortitude
unātēorigendlic 05.13.06 Constancy, unchangeableness; 11.02.01.02 Unwearied
unātēorigendlīce 05.11.11.01 A not ceasing, persistence, recurrence; 11.02.01.02 Unwearied
unātēorod 05.11.11.01 A not ceasing, persistence, recurrence
unātwēogendlīce 06.01.07.07.03 Certainty

unāþrēotend 05.11.11.01 A not ceasing, persistence, recurrence
unāþroten 11.02.01.02 Unwearied
unāþrotenlīce 05.11.11.01 A not ceasing, persistence, recurrence; 11.02.01.02 Unwearied
unāwægendlic 05.13.06 Constancy, unchangeableness
unāwæscen 04.06.02.01 Dirty, unclean
unāwemmed 12.08.04 Purity, moral cleanness
unāwemmedlic 12.08.04 Purity, moral cleanness
unāwemmednes 07.02.03.01 Uninjured, unhurt, unharmed
unāwemmende 12.08.04 Purity, moral cleanness
unāwend(ed) 05.13.06 Constancy, unchangeableness
unāwendedlic 05.12.04.01 Stability, firmness; 16.01.01.01 Attributes of God
unāwendende 05.13.06 Constancy, unchangeableness
unāwenden(d)lic 05.13.06 Constancy, unchangeableness
unāwendendlic 16.01.01.01 Attributes of God
unāwendendlīce 05.13.06 Constancy, unchangeableness
unāwerded 07.02.03.01 Uninjured, unhurt, unharmed
unāwīdlod 12.08.04 Purity, moral cleanness
unāwrēon 05.10.05.04.13 A removal of that which obscures or conceals
unāwriten 09.03.07.07.03.02 To write, state/say in writing
unbealaful 12.08.05 Innocence
unbeald 06.01.08.06.06 Timidity

unbealu 12.08.05 Innocence
unbeboht 15.05 Trade, traffic, commerce
unbebyriged 02.02.05 A burial, burying
unbecēas 14.03.03 Law, action of the courts
unbecrafod 14.03.03 Law, action of the courts
unbecweden 14.03.03 Law, action of the courts; 15.01.02.01 Inherited property
unbeden 12.03.03.01 Summons, a call, summoning
unbefangenlic 09.04.02.01 A secret, mystery; 16.01.01.01 Attributes of God
unbefliten 14.03.03 Law, action of the courts
unbefohten 13.02 War
unbefōndlic 09.04.02.01 A secret, mystery
unbegān 01.01.02.01.06 Wild/uncultivated land; 07.10.03.01 Unornamented, unadorned
unbegripendlic 16.01.01.01 Attributes of God
unbegrīpendlic 09.04.02.01 A secret, mystery
unbegunnen 05 Aught, anything, something; 16.01.01.01 Attributes of God; 16.01.01.04.01 God the Father
unbegunnen and ungeendod 16.01.01.04 The Trinity
unbehēafod 02.02.04.04.03 Putting to death
unbehēfe 11.08.02 Inconvenience, unfitness
unbehelendlīce 09.05.05.01 Showing, manifestation, display
unbehelod 04.04.07.02.01 Nakedness

1438

unbehrēowsigende 08.01.03.02.01 Compunction, remorse, contrition; 16.02.04.07.02.01 Penitence
unbelimp 08.01.03.06.01 Affliction, misfortune, calamity
unbeorhte 03.01.13.01 Not shining, dim
unberēafigendlic 15.01.01.01 Holding of land
unberende 02.01.03.02 Barrenness, sterility
unberendlic 08.01.03.07.04.01 Unbearableness
unberendnes 02.01.03.02 Barrenness, sterility
unbermed 04.01.02.01.07.03.01 Unleavened bread
unbesacen 14.03.03 Law, action of the courts
unbescēawod 11.06.01.01 Negligence, carelessness, heedlessness
unbescēawodlīce 11.06.01.01 Negligence, carelessness, heedlessness
unbescoren 16.02.04.13.03 Tonsure, haircutting, shaving
unbesenged 03.01.09.02.01 Fire, burning
unbesmiten 04.06.02.01 Dirty, unclean; 12.08.04 Purity, moral cleanness
unbesorh 11.06.01 Neglect
unbesprecen 14.03.03 Law, action of the courts
unbēted 16.02.01.13.01 Kinds of sin
unbeþōht 06.01.01.01.01.02 Forethought, consideration; 06.01.08.05 Unexpected
unbeþōhte 11.06.01.01 Negligence, carelessness, heedlessness
unbeweddod 12.09.03 Unmarried state
unbewelled 03.01.09.01.01 (Of liquids) boiling

unbiddende 16.02.04.08 Prayer
unbieldo 06.01.08.06.06 Timidity
unbilewit 05.08.02.01 (Of living creatures) fierceness, roughness
unbindan 05.05.04 That loosens, loosening; 11.10.03 Salvation/deliverance from; 16.02.04.07.02 Confession
unbiscopod 16.02.04.07.03 Confirmation
unbiþyrfe 11.08.03 Needless, useless, unprofitable
unblēoh 03.01.14.03 White/whiteness
unbletsung 16.02.04.19 Excommunication
unblinnendlīce 05.11.11.01 A not ceasing, persistence, recurrence
unbliss 08.01.03 Bad feeling, sadness
geunblissian 08.01.03.04 Grief
unblīþe 08.01.03 Bad feeling, sadness; 08.01.03.09.10 Wrath, sternness, displeasure; 12.05.02.01 Lack of peacefulness
unblīþemēde 08.01.03 Bad feeling, sadness
unblōdig 13.02.02 Battle
unblonden 03.03.06.03 Unity/oneness
unboht 15.02.02 Cheap
unboren 02.01.03.03.03 Birth
unbrād 05.10.05.03.01.01 Breadth, width across
unbræce 03.03.06 Wholeness
unbrocheard 05.09.02 Mildness, moderate quality
unbrosnodlīce 05.11.01.04 Incorruption, incorruptibility
unbryce 03.03.06 Wholeness
unbrȳce 11.08.01 Uselessness, unserviceableness
unbrȳde 12.08.02.03 Goodness, probity

unbȳed 12.06.03.01 Waste land, deserted place
unbȳeng 12.04.04 Solitude
unbyrged 02.02.05 A burial, burying
unbyrnende 03.01.09.02 Fire, flame
uncāfscipe 11.06 Disinclination to act, listlessness
uncamprōf 06.01.08.06.06 Timidity
uncapitulod 09.03.07.07.02.01.01 A heading, title, superscription
uncēap 15.02.02 Cheap
uncēaped 15.02.02 Cheap
uncēapunga 15.02.02 Cheap
uncēas(t)es āþ 14.03.03.04 Oath-swearing
unclǣmod 03.01.05 Roughness
unclǣne 04.01.02.01.01 Edibility; 04.06.02.01 Dirty, unclean; 12.08.08.01.02 Unchastity, incontinence; 16.02.04.13 Ceremonial cleanness
unclǣnlic 12.08.08.01.02 Unchastity, incontinence
unclǣnlīce 12.08.08.01.02 Unchastity, incontinence
unclǣnnes 04.06.02.01 Dirty, unclean; 12.08.08.01.02 Unchastity, incontinence
unclǣno 12.08.08.01.02 Unchastity, incontinence
(ge)unclǣnsian 04.06.02.02 Foul, filthy, squalid
geunclǣnsian 12.08.08.01.02 Unchastity, incontinence
uncnyttan 05.05.04 That loosens, loosening
uncoþa (-u/-e) 02.08.10.03.01 Plague, pestilence
uncoþe/-u 02.08.10.03.01 Plague, pestilence

uncræft 12.08.06.01 Error, wrong conduct, erroneous practice
uncræftig 05.09 Weakness
uncrafod 14.03.03 Law, action of the courts
uncristen 16.02.02 Christianity, the Christian faith
uncumlīþe 08.01.03.09.02 Harsh, unfriendly, unkind
uncūþ 06.01.06.04.01 What is uncertain/unknown; 06.01.07.07.03.01 Unknown, uncertain; 06.01.08.05.01.01 Wondrous, glorious, marvellous; 08.01.03.09.02 Harsh, unfriendly, unkind; 12.04.03 A stranger; 12.06.05 A foreign country
uncūþa 12.04.03 A stranger
uncūþlic 06.01.08.05.01.01 Wondrous, glorious, marvellous
uncūþlīce 08.01.03.09.02 Harsh, unfriendly, unkind
uncūþnes 05.11.07.04.03 Newness, novelty
uncwaciende 05.12.04.01 Stability, firmness
uncweden 14.01.06 A rule, order, precept, tenet, principle
uncweþende 09.02.02 Dumbness, lack of speech
uncwisse 09.02.02 Dumbness, lack of speech
uncwyd(d) 14.03.03 Law, action of the courts
uncyme 03.03.05.01.03 Inferior
uncynlic 11.08.02 Inconvenience, unfitness
uncynn 11.08.02 Inconvenience, unfitness
uncȳpe 15.02.02 Cheap
uncyst 02.08.02.01 An illness, ailment, disorder; 09.03.02.04 A slip of the

tongue, solecism; 10.03.09.01.01
    Covetousness, avarice; 12.08.06
    Moral evil, depravity
uncystig 10.03.09 Moderation in
    expenditure; 10.03.09.01 Parsimony,
    niggardliness
uncȳþig 06.01.06.04 Ignorance
uncȳþþu 12.06.05 A foreign country
uncȳþþ(u) 06.01.06.04 Ignorance
undǣd 12.08.06.02.05 Misdeed, sin
undǣled 03.03.06.03 Unity/oneness
undǣledlīce 16.01.01.04 The Trinity
undēaded 02.07.01 To grow
undēadlic 05.11.01.04 Incorruption,
    incorruptibility; 16.01.01.01
    Attributes of God
undearnunga 09.05.05.01 Showing,
    manifestation, display
undēaþlic 05.11.01.04 Incorruption,
    incorruptibility; 16.01.01.01
    Attributes of God
undēaþlīce 16.01.02.03 Reward of
    heaven
undēaþlicnes 05.11.01.01.01 Eternity;
    16.01.02.03 Reward of heaven
undēaw 01.03.01.02 Dry weather
undeclīnigendlic 09.03.02.03.01.01
    Declension
undēogollīce 09.05.05.01 Showing,
    manifestation, display
undēop 05.10.05.03.05 Shallow;
    06.01.05.03.02.01 Foolishness,
    lightmindedness
undēopþancol 06.01.05.03.02.01
    Foolishness, lightmindedness
undēore 15.02.02 Cheap
under 03.03.05.01 Rank, position,
    degree; 04.01 Digestion;
    05.10.05.04.02.02 Under, beneath;
    05.10.05.04.10 Among;
    05.10.05.04.12 The condition of being
    covered; 11.01.04 A doing,
    accomplishing (of something);
    12.05.06.04 A trampling upon,
    subjection
under ... neoþan 05.10.05.04.02.02
    Under, beneath
under hand 12.05.06.04 A trampling
    upon, subjection
under sunnan 01 Earth, world
under wolcna hrōfe 01 Earth, world
under wolcnum 01 Earth, world
underandfōnd 10.01.01.01 Receiving,
    gaining, getting
underbæc 05.12.05.11 To turn back,
    retreat
underbæcling 05.12.05.11 To turn back,
    retreat
underberan 05.10.05.04.02.04.02
    Support, maintenance; 06.02.07.01
    Strength, fortitude
underbeþēodan 12.05.06.04 A trampling
    upon, subjection
underbīegan 12.05.06.04 A trampling
    upon, subjection
underbregdan 05.10.05.04.02.03 Laid
    below
underbūgan 12.05.06.04.02 Submission,
    subjection, obedience
underburg 12.06.02.01 A township
underburhware 02.03.03.04.05 Populace
    of a town/city
undercerran 11.11.04 Subversion,
    change
undercrammian 03.03.06.02 Fullness
undercrēopan 11.09.01 Stealthiness, a
    stealthy act
undercuman 11.12.02 Aid, help, succour
undercyning 12.01.01.04.01.01 Kings
    and queens

1441

underdelf 11.11.04 Subversion, change
underdelfan 12.05.06 Grasp, power, control, mastery; 17.02.04.02.02 Digging
underdīacon 16.02.03.02.11 A deacon, minister of the church
underdōn 05.10.05.04.02.02 Under, beneath
underdrencan 02.02.03 To die, perish
underdrifennes 12.05.06.04 A trampling upon, subjection
underetan 05.09.01 Slow, inactive
underfang 10.01.01 Acceptance, receiving
underfangen 16.02.04.10.01 Conversion
underfangennes 10.01.01 Acceptance, receiving
underfeng 10.01.01 Acceptance, receiving
underflōwan 01.01.03.03 Flow/flowing
underfolgoþ 17.02.02 An office, function, employment
underfōn 05.10.05.04.01.02 Contents, what is included; 05.12.05.02.04 To go in, enter; 06.01.01 Thought, the faculty of thinking, mind; 08.01.02.04 Hospitality; 08.01.03.07.03 Suffering, torment, pain; 09.07.04.01 Confirmation, agreement; 10.01.01 Acceptance, receiving; 11.01.02 An undertaking; 11.10.02.02.01 Care, interest in; 12.05.06.04.02 Submission, subjection, obedience; 14.02.01.02 Wrongful taking, theft
underfōnd 10.01.01.01 Receiving, gaining, getting
underfōnlic 10.01.01 Acceptance, receiving
underfyl(i)gan 05.12.05.10 To go behind, follow

undergān 12.08.06.01.04.01 To mislead, seduce, lead astray
undergangan 12.05.06.04.01 Submission to action, toleration
undergeoc 04.02.05.04 To tame, break in (animals)
undergerēfa 12.02.02.03 Terms for classical world
under(ge)sett 05.10.05.04.02.03 Laid below
undergestandan 05.10.05.04.02.02 Under, beneath
under(ge)þēodan 12.05.06.04 A trampling upon, subjection
under(ge)þēoded 12.05.06.04 A trampling upon, subjection
undergietan 06.01.05.01 Understanding; 06.01.06.01.01.02 To know, recognize
undergietende 06.01.05.01 Understanding
underginnan 05.03 Source, origin; 11.01.02 An undertaking
undergrīpan 08.01 Heart, spirit, mood, disposition
underhebban 05.10.05.04.02.04.02 Support, maintenance
underhlystan 09.03.07.02 To make a mistake in writing
underhlystung 09.03.07.02 To make a mistake in writing
underhnīgan 05.03.02 Event, issue, result; 05.12.05.13.01 To descend beneath, go lower than (a place); 08.01.03.07.03 Suffering, torment, pain
underhwītel 04.04.07.04 An undergarment
underīecan 03.03.04.03 Growth, increase
underiende 12.08.05 Innocence
underiendlic 04.06 Salubrity

underiernan 05.12.05.13.01 To descend beneath, go lower than (a place)
underlātēow 12.01.01.05 A leader, administrator
underlecgan 05.10.05.04.02.02 Under, beneath; 05.10.05.04.02.04.02 Support, maintenance
underlēd 05.10.05.04.02.03 Laid below
underlicgan 12.05.06.04.02 Submission, subjection, obedience
underlīhtan 08.01.03.07.04.02 Relief, alleviation
underling 12.05.06.04 A trampling upon, subjection
underlūtan 05.12.05.12.02 To raise, lift up, elevate
undern 05.11.04.01.02 Morning; 16.02.04.05.05 The hour or service of Tierce
underneoþan 05.10.05.04.02.02 Under, beneath
underngereord 04.01.02.04.01.01 Meal at particular time of day
underngeweorc 04.01.02.04.01.01 Meal at particular time of day
underngiefl 04.01.02.04.01.01 Meal at particular time of day
underniman 06.01.05.01 Understanding; 08.01.03.05.05 Indignation; 10.01.02 Acquisition; 14.02.01.02 Wrongful taking, theft
underniþemest 05.10.05.04.02.03.01 A low position, the bottom
undernmǣl 05.11.04.01.02 Morning
undernmete 04.01.02.04.01.01 Meal at particular time of day
undernrest 02.05.04 Sleepiness, drowsiness, sleep
undernsang 16.02.04.05.05 The hour or service of Tierce
undernswǣsendu 04.01.02.04.01.01 Meal at particular time of day
underntīd 05.11.04.01.02 Morning; 16.02.04.05.05 The hour or service of Tierce
underntīma 05.11.04.01.02 Morning
underplantian 12.05.06.04 A trampling upon, subjection
underrīm 03.03.03.02 A number (mark/symbol)
underscēotan 05.12.05.13.01 To descend beneath, go lower than (a place); 11.12.02.01 Strengthening, confirmation
underscyte 05.12.05.13.01 To descend beneath, go lower than (a place); 11.11.01 A physical difficulty, strait; 17.03.07 Tools for digging/grasping/pulling
undersēcan 09.05.01 Inspection, examination
undersingan 18.02.07.01 Singing, song
underslīcende 05.12.05.13.01 To descend beneath, go lower than (a place)
undersmūgan 06.01.08.05 Unexpected
understandan 06.01.01.02 Care, attention, observation; 06.01.06 Understanding, knowledge, cognizance
understandan be 06.01 The head (as seat of thought); 09.07.04.01 Confirmation, agreement
understandan (ymbe) 06.01.05.01 Understanding
understanding 06.01.05 Understanding, intellect
understapplian 11.11.04 Subversion, change
understingan 11.12.02.01 Strengthening, confirmation

understregdan 05.12.02.07.01 To throw, scatter
understrēowod 04.05.04.05.01 Bedding (e.g. of straw); 05.12.02.07.01 To throw, scatter
undersyrc 04.04.07.04 An undergarment
undertōdāl 09.03.07.07.02.01 A main division
undertunge 02.04.05.06 Sinew/tendon/ligament
undertungeþrum 02.04.05.06 Sinew/tendon/ligament
underþencan 06.01.01.01.01 Thought, cogitation, meditation
underþēnian 12.01.01.08 Service
underþēod 12.05.06.04 A trampling upon, subjection; 16.02.03.02.05 A bishop
underþēodan 03.03.04.03 Growth, increase; 05.10.05.04.02.04.02 Support, maintenance; 14.05 Punishment
underþēoden(d)lic 09.03.02.03.01.02.01 Mood
underþēodnes 12.05.06.04.02 Submission, subjection, obedience
underþēow 12.01.01.09 Bondage, slavery
underwedd 14.03.03.07 Security, pledge, bail
underwrǣdel 04.04.07.03 Part of garment
underwreþian 05.10.05.04.02.04.02 Support, maintenance
underwreþung 11.12.02.01 Strengthening, confirmation
underwrītan 09.03.07.01.02.01 Handwriting, autograph, signature
underwyrtwalian 11.11.04 Subversion, change

undierne 09.05.05.01 Showing, manifestation, display
undīgle 09.05.05.01 Showing, manifestation, display
undīlegod 03.03.07.02 What is left, remnant, remains
undolfen 01.01.02.01.06 Wild/uncultivated land
undōm 12.07.05 Wrong, injustice
undōmlīce 12.07.05 Wrong, injustice
undōn 05.05.04 That loosens, loosening; 05.06 Destruction, dissolution, loss, breaking; 05.07 Ending of existence, end of world; 05.10.05.04.14 An opening, aperture; 11.10.03 Salvation/deliverance from; 14.03.03.08 Justification
undōnnes 11.06.02 Suffering (not acting)
undrēfed 01.01.03.01 Body of water
undrifen 05.12.01.09.03.02 Hardship on board; 06.02.01 Freewill, own will
undruncen 04.01.03.03 Sober
undrysnende 03.01.09.02 Fire, flame
unēacen 02.01.03.02 Barrenness, sterility
unēacniendlic 02.01.03.02 Barrenness, sterility
unearfoþlīce 11.11 Difficulty
unearg 06.02.07.06.02.01 Fearlessness
unearhlic 06.02.07.06.02.01 Fearlessness
unēaþe 03.06 Comparison; 06.02.03 Unwilling, loath; 08.01.03.07 Unpleasantness; 08.01.03.07.04 Severity, harshness; 08.01.03.07.04.01 Unbearableness; 11.11 Difficulty
unēaþelic 11.11 Difficulty
unēaþelīce 11.11 Difficulty
unēaþelicnes 11.11 Difficulty
unēaþlācne 02.08.12 Healing, curing
unēaþmylte 04.01.02.01.01 Edibility

unēaþnes 08.01.03.07.02 Misery, trouble, affliction; 08.01.03.07.04 Severity, harshness
unefen 03.06.02 Difference, diversity, dissimilarity
unefenlic 03.06.02 Difference, diversity, dissimilarity
unefesung 14.02.01.01 Types of crime; 16.02.04.13.03 Tonsure, haircutting, shaving
unefn 09.03.02.03.01.02 A conjugation
unefne 03.06.02 Difference, diversity, dissimilarity
unendebyrdlīce 11.05.02.03 Indecorum, impropriety, unseemliness
unered 01.01.02.01.06 Wild/uncultivated land
unēstful 11.05.02.03 Indecorum, impropriety, unseemliness
unfǣcne 12.08.02.03 Goodness, probity
unfæderlīce 08.01.03.09.02 Harsh, unfriendly, unkind
unfǣge 02.02.03.01 In process of dying
unfǣger 07.10.02 Ugliness
unfǣgernes 07.10.02 Ugliness
unfǣglic 06.01.08.02.01 Encouragement, comfort
unfægre 08.01.03.09.10 Wrath, sternness, displeasure
unfǣhþ 13.01 Peace, state of law and order
unfǣle 07.03 Evil
unfæst 02.08.11.02 Mental weakness; 05.13.05 Changeability
unfæstende 04.01.01.06.01 Abstinence from food, fast; 16.02.04.04.02.02 A fast, act of fasting
unfæstlīce 06.02.07.05.01 Inconstancy
unfæstnian 05.05.04 That loosens, loosening

unfæstrǣd 06.02.07.05.01 Inconstancy
unfæstrǣdnes 06.02.07.05.01 Inconstancy
unfāh 14.01.03.02 Freedom from punishment or fine
unfealdan 05.05.04 That loosens, loosening; 09.04.03 Exposition, making clear by explanation
unfēferig 02.08.10 Fever
unfēlende 02.05.01 Without feeling, insensible
unfenge 08.01.03.07 Unpleasantness
unfeor 05.10.05.01 A little way, no great distance
unfeor ... (fram) 05.10.05.01 A little way, no great distance
unfeor (þanon) 05.10.05.01 A little way, no great distance
unfeormigende 16.02.01.13.01 Kinds of sin
unfēre 02.08.04.04 State of being crippled
unfērnes 05.09 Weakness
unflitme 09.07.04.01 Confirmation, agreement
unflycge 02.06.08 Bird
unforbærned 03.01.09.02.01 Fire, burning
unforboden 12.03.05 Permission
unforbodene 09.07.04.01 Confirmation, agreement
unforbūgendlic 06.02.04 Necessity, inevitability
unforbūgendlīce 06.02.07.01 Strength, fortitude
unforburnen 03.01.09.02.01 Fire, burning
unforcumen 13.02.05.01 Victory
unforcūþ 07.02.04 Excellence

1445

unforcūþlīce 07.02.04.03 Nobleness, excellence, nobility, magnificence
unfordytt 06.02.07.04 Obstinacy
unforebyrdig 08.01.03.08.01 Impatience
unfored 03.03.06 Wholeness
unforedlic 03.03.06 Wholeness; 05.05.03 Binding, fastening
unforescēawod 06.01.05.03.03 Indiscretion; 11.06.01.01 Negligence, carelessness, heedlessness
unforescēawodlic 06.01.05.03.03 Indiscretion; 11.06.01.01 Negligence, carelessness, heedlessness
unforfeored 03.03.06 Wholeness
unforgifen 12.09.03 Unmarried state; 16.02.04.07.02.02 Absolution, forgiveness, remission
unforgifende 08.01.03.09.12 Pitilessness
unforgitende 06.01.04 Faculty of memory
unforgolden 10.03.05 Recompense, reward
unforgrīpendlic 16.02.01.09 The law
unforhæfednes 12.08.08.01.02 Unchastity, incontinence
unforhladen 05.11.11.01 A not ceasing, persistence, recurrence
unforht 06.01.08.06.02 Great fear, terror, horror; 06.02.07.06.02.01 Fearlessness
unforhte 06.02.07.06.02.01 Fearlessness
unforhtigende 06.02.07.06.02.01 Fearlessness
unforhtlēasnes 06.01.08.06.06 Timidity
unforhtlīce 06.02.07.06.02.01 Fearlessness
unforhtmōd 06.02.07.06.02.01 Fearlessness
unforlǣten 02.01.03.03.01 To beget; 15.01.02.01 Inherited property

unformolsnod 03.02.01.01 Decay, corruption, rottenness
unformolten 04.01 Digestion
unforrotedlic 05.11.01.04 Incorruption, incorruptibility
unforrotenlic 05.11.01.04 Incorruption, incorruptibility
unforroteslic 05.11.01.04 Incorruption, incorruptibility
unforrotigendlic 05.11.01.04 Incorruption, incorruptibility
unforscēawodlīce 06.01.05.03.03 Indiscretion; 06.01.08.05 Unexpected; 11.06.01.01 Negligence, carelessness, heedlessness
unforsewen 06.01.08.05 Unexpected
unforsporned 11.12.01 Absence of restraint, freedom
unforspornen 11.12.01 Absence of restraint, freedom
unforswǣled 03.01.09.02.01 Fire, burning
unforswīgod 06.01.01.02 Care, attention, observation
unforswȳþed 13.02.05.01 Victory
unfortredde 02.07.08 Grasses, reeds, etc.
unfortreden wyrt 02.07.08 Grasses, reeds, etc.
unforþōht 06.01.08.05 Unexpected
unforwandigendlīce 06.02.07.06.02.01 Fearlessness
unforwandodlic 06.02.07.06.02.01 Fearlessness
unforwandodlīce 05.10.05.04.05 Straight, direct; 06.01.08.05 Unexpected; 06.02.07.06.02.01 Fearlessness; 11.02.04 Heedlessness
unforwealwod 02.07.01 To grow
unforwordenlic 03.02.01.01 Decay, corruption, rottenness
unforworht 14.03.03.08 Justification

unforwyrded 02.07.01 To grow
unforwyrht 15.01.01 Landed property
unfracodlīce 12.08.02.03.01 Honourable conduct, dignity
unfrætewod 07.10.03.01 Unornamented, unadorned
unfram 05.09 Weakness
unfremful 11.08.01 Uselessness, unserviceableness
unfremu 05.06.04 Damage, injury, defect, hurt, loss
unfrēondlīce 08.01.03.09.02 Harsh, unfriendly, unkind
unfricgende 06.01.08.03 Trust, faith, confidence; 09.05 Curiosity
unfriþ 13.02 War; 14 Law, custom, covenant
unfriþflota 13.02.10.03.01 A fleet
unfriþhere 13.02.10.01.02.02.01 Types of army
unfriþland 05.10.04.02 A region, zone
unfriþmann 08.01.03.09.05 Enmity
unfriþscip 05.12.01.09.03.01.01 Kind of ship
unfrōd 06.01.06.03.01 Inexperienced
unfrōdnes 06.01.06.04 Ignorance
unfrōforlīce 09.07.04.01 Confirmation, agreement
unfulfremed 07.03.03 Mediocrity, insignificance; 09.03.02.03.01.02.04 Aspect
unfulfremednes 07.03.03 Mediocrity, insignificance
unfulfremmung 07.03.03 Mediocrity, insignificance
unfūliende 05.11.01.04 Incorruption, incorruptibility
unfūliendlic 05.11.01.04 Incorruption, incorruptibility

unfūliendrelic 05.11.01.04 Incorruption, incorruptibility
unfullod 16.02.04.07.01 Baptism, baptizing (and anointing)
unfulworht 11.06.02 Suffering (not acting)
unfyrn 05.11.07.03.01 Time within remembrance
ungænge 11.08.04 Vanity, idleness, frivolity
ungeǣsce 06.01.08.05.01.01 Wondrous, glorious, marvellous
ungeǣwed 12.09.03 Unmarried state
ungeandet 16.02.04.07.02 Confession
un(ge)andett 16.02.04.07.02.02 Absolution, forgiveness, remission
ungēaplīce 06.01.05.03.03 Indiscretion; 11.06.01.01 Negligence, carelessness, heedlessness
ungēara 05.11.07.03.01 Time within remembrance; 05.11.07.04.01 Nearness, approach, imminence
ungearo 06.01.08.05 Unexpected; 11.01.03 Preparation
ungearu 01.01.02.01.06 Wild/uncultivated land; 11.06 Disinclination to act, listlessness
ungearuwitolnes 06.01.05.03.01 Mental inertness
ungeāxod 09.05.02 A question, inquiry, questioning
ungebēaten 17.02.04.02.01 Cutting, hewing, shaping
ungebeorhlīce 12.08.07 Immoderation, excess
ungebēt 14.03.03.09.01 Unfavourable judgement, condemnation
un(ge)bēt(ed) 16.02.04.07.02.03 Penance, an act/instance of penance
ungebēt(ed) 16.02.01.13.01 Kinds of sin

ungebierde 02.04.04.03.03.01 Beard, whisker
ungebīged 05.10.05.04.05 Straight, direct
ungebīgendlic 05.10.05.04.05 Straight, direct; 09.03.02.03.01.01 Declension
ungeblēoh 03.01.14.11 Medley/variety of colour
ungebletsod 16.02.01.10.02.02 Not blessed, unconsecrated
ungeblȳged 06.02.07.06.02.01 Fearlessness
ungeboden 12.03.03.01 Summons, a call, summoning
ungeboht 10.03.05.01.01 A bribe, gift, payment
un(ge)boren 05.11.07.04 Future, time to come
ungebrocen 03.03.06 Wholeness
ungebrocod 07.02.03.01 Uninjured, unhurt, unharmed
un(ge)brosn(ig)endlic 05.11.01.04 Incorruption, incorruptibility
ungebrosnod 07.02.03.01 Uninjured, unhurt, unharmed
un(ge)brosnung 05.11.01.04 Incorruption, incorruptibility
un(ge)bunden 11.10.03 Salvation/deliverance from
ungebunden 09.03.02.03 Composition (inflectional or compounding)
ungebyrde 05.02.02 Nature, established order of things
ungebyrded 07.02.03.01 Uninjured, unhurt, unharmed
un(ge)clǣnsod 12.08.08.01.02 Unchastity, incontinence
ungecnāwen 06.01.06.04.01 What is uncertain/unknown
ungecnyrdnes 11.06.01.01 Negligence, carelessness, heedlessness
ungecōplic 11.05.02.03 Indecorum, impropriety, unseemliness
ungecōplīce 05.11.08.01 Untimeliness
un(ge)coren 16.02.01.13.02 Evil, reprobate, damned
ungecoren āþ 14.03.03.04 Oath-swearing
ungecost 16.02.01.13.02 Evil, reprobate, damned
ungecristnod 16.02.04.07.01 Baptism, baptizing (and anointing)
un(ge)cwēme 08.01.03.07 Unpleasantness
ungecȳd 09.06.02.01.02 Not said, undeclared, unsaid
un(ge)cynde 05.02.02 Nature, established order of things
ungecynde 02.03.02.03.06 Kinship, relationship
ungecyndelic 05.02.02 Nature, established order of things; 06.01.08.05.01.01 Wondrous, glorious, marvellous
ungecyndelīce 05.02.02 Nature, established order of things
ungecyrred 16.02.04.10.01 Conversion
ungedæftlīce 05.11.08.01 Untimeliness
ungedæftnes 05.11.08.01 Untimeliness
ungedafeniendlic 03.06.04 Incongruity, absurdity
ungedafenlic 03.06.04 Incongruity, absurdity; 11.05.02.03 Indecorum, impropriety, unseemliness
ungedafenlīce 03.06.04 Incongruity, absurdity; 05.11.08.01 Untimeliness; 11.05.02.03 Indecorum, impropriety, unseemliness; 12.08.07 Immoderation, excess
ungedafenlicnes 11.08.02 Inconvenience, unfitness

ungedāllic 03.03.04.01.03 An immense quantity, immensity, immense number
ungedēfe 08.01.03.07 Unpleasantness; 11.05.02.03 Indecorum, impropriety, unseemliness
ungedēfelīce 03.06.04 Incongruity, absurdity
ungedēflic 11.05.02.03 Indecorum, impropriety, unseemliness
ungedered 07.02.03.01 Uninjured, unhurt, unharmed
ungedōn 11.06.02 Suffering (not acting)
ungedrehtlīce 11.02.01.02 Unwearied
ungedrȳme 18.02.07 Music
ungedwimorlīce 06.01.05.01.01 Clear to the understanding, plain
ungedyrstig 06.01.08.06.06 Timidity
ungeeahtendlic 06.01.08.05.01.01 Wondrous, glorious, marvellous
ungeearned 07.04.02 Merit, desert(s)
ungeendigendlic 09.03.02.02.01.02 A verb
ungeendod 03.03.04.01.03 An immense quantity, immensity, immense number; 05.11.01.01.01 Eternity; 16.01.01.01 Attributes of God
ungeendodlic 03.03.04.01.03 An immense quantity, immensity, immense number; 05.11.01.01.01 Eternity
ungefæd 06.01.05.03.03 Indiscretion
ungefandod 11.03.01 Experience, trial, experiment
ungefaren 11.11.01 A physical difficulty, strait
ungefēa 08.01.03 Bad feeling, sadness
ungefēalīce 08.01.03 Bad feeling, sadness
ungefēge 03.06.04 Incongruity, absurdity
ungefēle(d) 02.05.01 Without feeling, insensible

ungefēre 05.12.01.03.02 Impasse, want of a road; 06.02.07.04.01 Obduracy; 09.04.02.01 A secret, mystery
ungefēred 05.12.01.03.02 Impasse, want of a road
ungefērenlic 11.11.01 A physical difficulty, strait
ungefērlic 13.02 War; 13.02.03.01.02 To beset, surround
ungefērlīce 13.02 War
ungefērne 05.12.01.03.02 Impasse, want of a road
ungefeþered 02.06.08 Bird
ungefōg 03.03.04.01.01 Greatness, bigness, size; 03.03.04.02.02 Excess; 12.08.07 Immoderation, excess
ungefōge 03.03.04.02.02 Excess
ungefōglic 02.05.10.02 Noise, din; 03.03.04.01.01 Greatness, bigness, size
ungefōglīce 03.03.04.02.02 Excess
ungefrǣge 06.01.08.05.01.01 Wondrous, glorious, marvellous
ungefrǣglīce 06.01.08.05.01.01 Wondrous, glorious, marvellous
ungefrætwod 07.10.03.01 Unornamented, unadorned
ungefrēdelīce 08.01.01.02 Lacking in feeling, insensitive
ungefremmed 11.06.02 Suffering (not acting)
ungefremmung 07.03.03 Mediocrity, insignificance
ungefullod 11.06.02 Suffering (not acting)
ungefulwod 16.02.04.07.01 Baptism, baptizing (and anointing)
ungefylled 06.02.05.03 Satisfaction, repletion

ungefylle(n)dlic 06.02.05.03 Satisfaction, repletion
ungefynde 04.02.04.04.01 To ripen
un(ge)fyrn 05.11.07.04.01 Nearness, approach, imminence
ungegearwod 04.04.07.02 Not dressed, unclothed
ungegerad 04.04.07.02 Not dressed, unclothed
ungeglenged 07.10.03.01 Unornamented, unadorned
ungegrēt 11.05.02.02.01.03 To bid farewell
un(ge)hādod 16.02.04.07.05.01 Ordination
ungehǣle(n)dlic 02.08.12 Healing, curing
un(ge)hǣmed 12.09.03 Unmarried state
ungehǣplic 03.06.04 Incongruity, absurdity
un(ge)hālgod 16.02.01.10.02.02 Not blessed, unconsecrated
ungehāten 12.07.02.01.01 A promise
ungehēafdod 02.08.12 Healing, curing
ungehealdsum 12.08.08.01.02 Unchastity, incontinence
ungehealdsumlīce 12.08.08.01.02 Unchastity, incontinence
ungehealdsumnes 12.08.08.01.02 Unchastity, incontinence
ungehefegod 02.01.03.02 Barrenness, sterility
ungehende 05.10.05 A space, span
ungehendnes 05.10.05 A space, span
ungeheort 06.02.07.07 Cowardice, pusillanimity
un(ge)hīersum 12.01.01.12.02 Disobedience
un(ge)hīrsumnes 12.01.01.12.02 Disobedience
ungehīrsumod 12.01.01.12.02 Disobedience
ungehīw 03.01.14.11 Medley/variety of colour
ungehīwod 06.01.07 Truth, conformity with absolute standard
un(ge)hīwod 05.10.06.01 Not formed, without form
ungehīwodlic 05.10.06.01 Not formed, without form
ungehlēoþor 18.02.07 Music
ungehrepod 02.05.06 Sense of touch; 07.02.03.01 Uninjured, unhurt, unharmed
ungehrinen 07.02.03.01 Uninjured, unhurt, unharmed
ungehwǣde 03.03.04.01.01 Greatness, bigness, size
ungehȳred 06.01.06.04.01 What is uncertain/unknown
ungehȳrnes 02.08.07.03.01 Deafness
ungehyrt 06.01.08.06 Fear; 06.02.07.07 Cowardice, pusillanimity
ungel 04.01.02.01.02.05.05 Fat/suet/lard
ungelācnod 02.08.12 Healing, curing
ungelādod 12.08.09 Guiltiness, guilt; 14.03.03.09.01 Unfavourable judgement, condemnation
ungelǣccendlic 12.08.05.01 Blameless
un(ge)lǣred 06.01.06.04.02 Ignorance, uninstructedness
ungelǣredlic 06.01.06.02.03.04.04 Under instruction, being taught
ungelǣredlīce 06.01.06.04.02 Ignorance, uninstructedness; 11.05.02.03 Indecorum, impropriety, unseemliness
ungelǣrednes 06.01.06.04.02 Ignorance, uninstructedness
un(ge)laþod 08.01.02.04.01 Visiting
ungelēaf 06.01.07.06.02 Unbelief

ungelēafa 06.01.07.06.02 Unbelief
ungelēafful 06.01.07.06.02 Unbelief; 16.02.01.03 Unbelief, want of belief
ungelēaffullic 06.01.07.06.02 Unbelief
ungelēaflic 06.01.07.06.02 Unbelief
ungelēafsum 06.01.07.06.02 Unbelief; 16.02.01.03 Unbelief, want of belief
ungelēafsumnes 16.02.01.06 Paganism, a false religion
ungelēafullic 06.01.07.06.02 Unbelief
ungelēafullīce 06.01.07.06.02 Unbelief
ungelēafulnes 06.01.07.06.02 Unbelief
ungelīc 03.06.02 Difference, diversity, dissimilarity
ungelīca 03.06.02 Difference, diversity, dissimilarity
ungelīce 03.06.02 Difference, diversity, dissimilarity
ungelīcian 08.01.03.07 Unpleasantness
ungelīclic 11.05.02.03 Indecorum, impropriety, unseemliness
ungelīclīce 11.05.02.03 Indecorum, impropriety, unseemliness
ungelīcnes 03.06.02 Difference, diversity, dissimilarity
ungelīefe(n)dlic 06.01.07.06.02 Unbelief
ungelīfed 12.03.06 Prohibition; 16.02.01.03 Unbelief, want of belief
ungelīfe(n)d 16.02.01.03 Unbelief, want of belief
ungelīfnes 06.01.07.06.02 Unbelief
un(ge)limp 08.01.03.06.01 Affliction, misfortune, calamity
ungelimplic 05.03.02.01.01 An event, occurrence; 08.01.03.06 Adversity, affliction
ungelimplīce 08.01.03.06.01 Affliction, misfortune, calamity
ungelustfullung 12.08.08.01 Eager, unseemly desire

ungelygen 06.01.07 Truth, conformity with absolute standard
ungemaca 03.06.02 Difference, diversity, dissimilarity
ungemæc 03.06.02 Difference, diversity, dissimilarity
ungemæcca 03.06.02 Difference, diversity, dissimilarity
ungemǣte 03.03.04.01.03 An immense quantity, immensity, immense number
un(ge)mǣtlic 03.03.04.01.03 An immense quantity, immensity, immense number
ungemedemad 03.03.04.01.03 An immense quantity, immensity, immense number
ungemēdnes 08.01.03.06.01 Affliction, misfortune, calamity
ungemeltnes 02.08.08.04.02 (Of stomach) disordered
ungemenged 03.03.06.03 Unity/oneness
ungemet 03.03.04.01.01 Greatness, bigness, size; 03.03.04.01.03 An immense quantity, immensity, immense number; 03.03.04.02.02 Excess
ungemēt 06.01.06.03.01 Inexperienced
ungemetceald 01.03.01.04 Wintry weather, cold; 03.01.11 Coldness, coolness
ungemete/-es/-um 03.03.04.02.02 Excess
ungemetfæst 02.08.08.04.02 (Of stomach) disordered; 03.03.04.02.02 Excess; 05.12.04.01 Stability, firmness; 12.08.07 Immoderation, excess
ungemetfæstlic 02.08.08.04.02 (Of stomach) disordered
ungemetfæstnes 12.08.07 Immoderation, excess

ungemetgod 03.03.04.02.02 Excess; 06.01.03.03 Absence of reason; 12.08.07 Immoderation, excess
ungemetgung 12.08.07 Immoderation, excess
ungemethleahtor 08.01.01.03.07.01 Laughter
ungemetigende 12.08.07 Immoderation, excess
ungemetlic 03.03.04.01.03 An immense quantity, immensity, immense number; 03.03.04.02.02 Excess; 03.06.02 Difference, diversity, dissimilarity
ungemetlīce 03.03.04.02.02 Excess
ungemetlicnes 12.08.07 Immoderation, excess
ungemetnes 03.03.04.02.02 Excess
ungemīdlod 04.02.05.06.05.03.01 Bridle/halter/curb/muzzle
un(ge)mīdlod 08.01.03.09.01.03 Sharpness (of speech); 12.05.06.01 Restraint, check, curb, control
ungemiht 05.09 Weakness
ungemōd 12.05.03.01 Quarrel, contentiousness, strife
ungemōdignes 12.05.03.01 Quarrel, contentiousness, strife
ungemōdnes 12.05.03.01 Quarrel, contentiousness, strife
ungemolsnod 03.02.01.01 Decay, corruption, rottenness
un(ge)munecod 16.02.04.07.05.01.01 Going into a monastery, admission
ungemylt 04.01 Digestion; 04.01.02.01.01 Edibility
ungemynd 02.08.11.02.01.02 Madness, frenzy, folly
ungemyndig 06.01.04.03 Forgetfulness
ungenæmnendlic 06.01.06.04.01 What is uncertain/unknown
ungenīdd 11.12.01 Absence of restraint, freedom
ungenīwiendlic 03.02.01 Decay, decline, corruption
ungenyhtsumnes 03.03.04.05 Insufficiency, lack, want
ungeocian 05.05.04 That loosens, loosening
ungeorne 06.02.03 Unwilling, loath; 11.06.01.01 Negligence, carelessness, heedlessness
ungeornful 11.06.01.01 Negligence, carelessness, heedlessness
ungeorwyrd 07.08 Reputation, fame
ungerād 06.01.05.03.01 Mental inertness; 06.01.05.03.01.01 Dullness, folly, stupidity; 06.01.06.04.02 Ignorance, uninstructedness; 11.05.02.03 Indecorum, impropriety, unseemliness; 12.05.03 Disagreement, discord, dissension; 12.06.05 A foreign country; 18.02.07 Music
ungerǣd 06.01.05.03.01.01 Dullness, folly, stupidity
ungerǣdelīce 11.05.02.03 Indecorum, impropriety, unseemliness
ungerǣdlic 06.01.06.04.02 Ignorance, uninstructedness
ungerǣdnes 12.05.03 Disagreement, discord, dissension
ungerǣdod 04.02.05.06.05.03 Harness, trappings
ungerec 05.08.02 Violence, force
ungereccan 14.03.03.08 Justification
ungereclic 12.08.07 Immoderation, excess
ungereclīce 05.08.02 Violence, force
ungerēnod 07.10.03.01 Unornamented, unadorned

ungereord 12.06.05 A foreign country
ungereordod 04.01.01.03 Hunger; 04.01.02.04.03.01.01 Fed/nourished
ungeriht 12.08.02.02.01 Reform, correction
un(ge)rīm 03.03.04.01.03 An immense quantity, immensity, immense number
ungerīmed 03.03.04.01.03 An immense quantity, immensity, immense number
un(ge)rīmedlic 03.03.04.01.03 An immense quantity, immensity, immense number
ungerīmlic 03.03.04.01.03 An immense quantity, immensity, immense number
ungerīped 05.11.08.01.02 (Untimely) earliness
ungerīsende 12.08.07.01.04.01 Impropriety, disgrace
ungerisene 03.06.04 Incongruity, absurdity; 12.08.07.01.04.01 Impropriety, disgrace
ungerisenlic 12.08.07.01.04.01 Impropriety, disgrace
ungerisenlīce 07.09 Shame, disgrace
ungerisnes 12.08.07.01.04.01 Impropriety, disgrace
ungerisnu 03.06.04 Incongruity, absurdity; 12.08.07.01.04.01 Impropriety, disgrace
un(ge)rōtsod 08.01.03 Bad feeling, sadness
ungerȳde 01.01.02.01 Ground; 05.08.02.01 (Of living creatures) fierceness, roughness
ungerȳdelic 04.04.05.01 Coarse, rough (of cloth); 05.08.02.01 (Of living creatures) fierceness, roughness
ungerȳdelīce 04.04.07.01 Mode of dressing, fashion; 05.08.02 Violence, force

ungerȳdnes 05.08.02 Violence, force
un(ge)sadelod 04.02.05.06.05.03.04 Saddle
ungesǣlig 07.03.03.01 Empty, useless, worthless; 08.01.03.06 Adversity, affliction; 12.08.06.01.02 Lacking moral good
un(ge)sǣlig 08.01.03.06.01 Affliction, misfortune, calamity
ungesǣliglīce 08.01.03.06.01 Affliction, misfortune, calamity
ungesǣl(ig)līce 12.08.06.02.03.01 Wickedly
ungesǣlignes 08.01.03.06.01 Affliction, misfortune, calamity
ungesǣlþ 12.08.06 Moral evil, depravity
un(ge)sǣlþ 08.01.03.06.01 Affliction, misfortune, calamity
ungescæþfulnes 12.08.05 Innocence
un(ge)scæþþignes 12.08.05 Innocence
ungescēad 03.03.04.01.03 An immense quantity, immensity, immense number; 03.03.05 Extent, degree; 06.01.03.03 Absence of reason
un(ge)scēad(e)līce 06.01.05.03.03.01 Unreasonableness, foolishness, imprudence
ungescēadlic 06.01.03.03 Absence of reason
ungescēadlīce 03.03.04.02.02 Excess; 06.01.03.03 Absence of reason
ungescēadwīs 06.01.03.03 Absence of reason; 06.01.05.03.03.01 Unreasonableness, foolishness, imprudence
un(ge)scēadwīslic 06.01.05.03.03.01 Unreasonableness, foolishness, imprudence

ungescēadwīslīce 06.01.05.03.03.01 Unreasonableness, foolishness, imprudence
ungescēadwīsnes 06.01.05.03.03.01 Unreasonableness, foolishness, imprudence
ungesceapen 16.01.01.01 Attributes of God
un(ge)sce(a)pen 05.10.06.01 Not formed, without form
ungescended 07.02.03.01 Uninjured, unhurt, unharmed
ungesceþþed 07.02.03.01 Uninjured, unhurt, unharmed
ungescrēpe 11.08.02 Inconvenience, unfitness
ungescrēpnes 02.08.03 Pain, bodily discomfort
un(ge)seht 12.05.03 Disagreement, discord, dissension
ungesēnod 16.02.01.10.02.02 Not blessed, unconsecrated
ungesēonde 02.08.07.02.01 Defective vision
ungesewen 02.05.09.13 Invisible
un(ge)sewenlic 02.05.09.13 Invisible
ungesewenlīce 02.05.09.13 Invisible
ungesibb 02.03.02.03.06.02 Close relationship
un(ge)sibb 12.05.03 Disagreement, discord, dissension
ungesibsum 12.05.03.01 Quarrel, contentiousness, strife
ungesibsumnes 12.05.03.01 Quarrel, contentiousness, strife
ungesilt 04.01.02.02.04.01 To salt
un(ge)soden 04.01.02.02.05 Cooking
ungesōm 12.05.03 Disagreement, discord, dissension
un(ge)stæþþig 12.08.07.01.03 Wantonness, levity, frivolity
ungestæþþiglīce 05.13.05 Changeability
un(ge)stæþþignes 12.08.07.01.03 Wantonness, levity, frivolity
ungestrēon 15.01.03 Treasure, riches, wealth
ungestroden 15.01.01 Landed property
ungesund 07.03 Evil
ungesundlīce 03.03.04.02.02 Excess
ungeswēge 18.02.07 Music
ungeswenced 11.02.01.02 Unwearied
ungeswencedlic 11.02.01.02 Unwearied
ungeswīcendlīce 06.02.07.03 Perseverance
ungeswuncen 11.06.02 Suffering (not acting)
ungesȳne 02.05.09.13 Invisible
ungesȳnelic 02.05.09.13 Invisible
ungetǣse 12.08.03.02 Strictness, austerity, severity
ungetǣslīce 11.08.02 Inconvenience, unfitness
ungetǣsnes 11.08.02 Inconvenience, unfitness
ungetel 03.03.04.01.03 An immense quantity, immensity, immense number
un(ge)temed 05.08.02.01 (Of living creatures) fierceness, roughness
ungetemprung 01.03.01.03 Bad weather
ungetēorede 11.02.01.02 Unwearied
ungetēori(g)endlic 05.11.11.01 A not ceasing, persistence, recurrence
ungetēorigendlīce 05.11.11.01 A not ceasing, persistence, recurrence
ungetēorod 03.03.04.02.01 Abundance
un(ge)tīmu 08.01.03.06.01 Affliction, misfortune, calamity
ungetinge 09.01.02 Fluency in speech
ungetingful 09.01.02 Fluency in speech

ungetowen 06.01.06.04.02 Ignorance, uninstructedness
un(ge)trēowe 12.01.01.12.04 Treachery; 16.02.01.03 Unbelief, want of belief
ungetrēownes 12.01.01.12.04 Treachery; 16.02.01.03 Unbelief, want of belief; 16.02.01.12.06 Unfaithfulness, undutifulness
un(ge)trēowþ 12.01.01.12.04 Treachery
un(ge)trum 05.09 Weakness
un(ge)twēogendlīce 06.01.07.07.03 Certainty
un(ge)tȳd 06.01.06.04.02 Ignorance, uninstructedness
ungeþanc 12.08.06.02 Wickedness, evil
un(ge)þancful 08.01.03.09.09 Ingratitude, displeasure expressed in words
ungeþeaht 12.02.02.05 Counsel, advice
ungeþeahtendlīce 11.06.01.01 Negligence, carelessness, heedlessness
ungeþēawe 11.05.01.01 Unfamiliarity
ungeþēawfæst 12.08.06.01.02 Lacking moral good
ungeþēod 03.03.07.01 Division, partition, separation
un(ge)þinged 06.01.08.05 Unexpected
un(ge)þingod 16.02.01.13.01 Kinds of sin
ungeþungen 07.03.05 Infamy, shame, wickedness
ungeþwǣre 02.08.03 Pain, bodily discomfort; 08.01.03.07 Unpleasantness; 09.07.03 Disagreement, dissent; 12.05.02.01 Lack of peacefulness; 12.05.03.01 Quarrel, contentiousness, strife
un(ge)þwǣre 12.05.03 Disagreement, discord, dissension
ungeþwǣrian 09.07.03 Disagreement, dissent; 12.05.03 Disagreement, discord, dissension
ungeþwǣrlic 12.05.03 Disagreement, discord, dissension
ungeþwǣrlīce 08.01.03.05.04 Irritability
ungeþwǣrnes 08.01.03.06 Adversity, affliction; 08.01.03.09.11 Hardheartedness, cruelty, severity
un(ge)þwǣrnes 12.05.03 Disagreement, discord, dissension; 12.05.03.01 Quarrel, contentiousness, strife
ungeþyld 08.01.03.08.01 Impatience
ungeþyldelīce 08.01.03.08.01 Impatience
ungeþyldig 08.01.03.08.01 Impatience
ungeþyre 09.07.03 Disagreement, dissent
ungewǣpnod 13.02.08 Military equipment
ungewealden 02.08.08.04.02 (Of stomach) disordered; 06.02.03 Unwilling, loath
ungewealdes 06.02.03 Unwilling, loath
ungeweaxen 02.01.04.01 Youth
un(ge)weder 01.03.01.03.01 Storm, tempest
un(ge)wemmed 03.03.06 Wholeness; 12.08.04 Purity, moral cleanness
ungewemmedlic 07.02.03.01 Uninjured, unhurt, unharmed
ungewemmedlīce 12.08.04 Purity, moral cleanness
un(ge)wem(med)nes 12.08.04 Purity, moral cleanness
ungewendendlic 02.08.02.01 An illness, ailment, disorder; 02.08.12 Healing, curing
ungewendnes 05.13.05 Changeability
ungewēned 06.01.08.05 Unexpected
ungewēnedlic 03.03.04.01.03 An immense quantity, immensity,

immense number; 06.01.08.05 Unexpected
ungewērgod 11.02.01.02 Unwearied
un(ge)widere 01.03.01.03 Bad weather; 01.03.01.03.01 Storm, tempest
ungewiderung 01.03.01.03 Bad weather
ungewilde 12.01.01.10 Freedom, being free
ungewildelic 06.02.07.04.01 Obduracy
ungewildendlic 08.01.03.08.01 Impatience
ungewill 08.01.03.07 Unpleasantness
ungewilles 06.02.03 Unwilling, loath
ungewintred 02.01.04.01 Youth
ungewīslic 06.01.06.04.01 What is uncertain/unknown
ungewīsnes 06.01.06.04 Ignorance
ungewiss 06.01.06.04 Ignorance; 06.01.06.04.01 What is uncertain/unknown; 06.01.07.07.03.01 Unknown, uncertain; 07.09 Shame, disgrace; 09.04.02.01 A secret, mystery
ungewisses 06.01.06.04 Ignorance
ungewītendlic 05.11.01.04 Incorruption, incorruptibility
ungewītendlīce 05.11.01.01.01 Eternity
ungewitfæstnes 02.08.11.02.01.02 Madness, frenzy, folly
ungewitful 02.08.11.02.01 Insanity, madness; 06.01.05.03.01.01 Dullness, folly, stupidity
ungewitfulnes 02.08.11.02.01 Insanity, madness
ungewitlic 06.01.05.03.01.01 Dullness, folly, stupidity
ungewitnes 06.01.06.04.03 Ignorance, folly
ungewītnigendlīce 12.07.03.01 Impunity
un(ge)wītnod 12.07.03.01 Impunity

ungewitt 02.08.11.02.01 Insanity, madness; 06.01.05.03.01.01 Dullness, folly, stupidity
ungewittig 02.08.11.02.01 Insanity, madness; 06.01.03.03 Absence of reason; 06.01.05.03 Want of understanding
un(ge)wittig 12.08.05 Innocence
ungewittiglīce 02.08.11.02.01.02 Madness, frenzy, folly
ungewittignes 02.08.11.02.01 Insanity, madness; 02.08.11.02.01.02 Madness, frenzy, folly; 06.01.05.03.03.01 Unreasonableness, foolishness, imprudence
un(ge)wlitegian 07.10.02.01 Deformed, ugly
un(ge)wlitig 03.01.13.01 Not shining, dim
ungeworht 11.06.02 Suffering (not acting); 16.01.01.01 Attributes of God
ungewriten 09.03.07.07.03.02 To write, state/say in writing
ungewuna 11.05.01.01 Unfamiliarity; 12.08.06 Moral evil, depravity
ungewunelic 11.05.01.01 Unfamiliarity; 12.06.03.01 Waste land, deserted place
ungewunelīce 11.05.01.01 Unfamiliarity
un(ge)wuniendlic 12.06.03.01 Waste land, deserted place
un(ge)wyrd 08.01.03.06.01 Affliction, misfortune, calamity
ungewyrded 03.03.06 Wholeness
ungierw(i)an 05.10.05.04.13 A removal of that which obscures or conceals
ungifre 07.03.02 Ill, harm, hurt
ungifu 12.08.06.01.01 Pollution, impairment
unginne 03.03.04.04 Littleness, smallness

unglæd 08.01.03.06 Adversity, affliction
unglædlic 08.01.03.06 Adversity, affliction; 08.01.03.09.10 Wrath, sternness, displeasure
ungléaw 05.10.06.03.01 A point, spike, prickle; 06.01.05.03 Want of understanding; 06.01.06.04.02 Ignorance, uninstructedness
ungléawlīce 06.01.05.03 Want of understanding
ungléawnes 06.01.05.03 Want of understanding
ungléawscipe 06.01.05.03 Want of understanding
ungnīþelīce 07.02.04.03 Nobleness, excellence, nobility, magnificence
ungnȳþe 10.03.08 Bountifulness, munificence
ungōd 07.03 Evil
ungrǣdiglīce 10.03.08 Bountifulness, munificence
ungrāpigende 02.05.06 Sense of touch
ungrēne 02.07.01 To grow
ungrīpendlic 16.02.01.09 The law
ungrund 03.03.04.01.03 An immense quantity, immensity, immense number
ungrynde 05.10.05.03.04 Depth, deepness
ungyfeþe 10.03.03 Granting
ungylda 12.02.03 A society, guild, association
ungylde 14.03.03.09.02 Atonement
ungyld(e) 15.03.02 A tax
ungyltig 12.08.05 Innocence
ungȳmen 11.06.01.01 Negligence, carelessness, heedlessness
ungȳmende 11.06.01.01 Negligence, carelessness, heedlessness
ungystlīþe 08.01.03.09.02 Harsh, unfriendly, unkind

unhādian 16.02.04.07.05.01.02 Unfrocking
unhādung 16.02.04.07.05.01.02 Unfrocking
geunhǣlan 02.08.02 Disease, infirmity, sickness
unhǣlþ 02.08.02 Disease, infirmity, sickness
unhǣlu 02.08.02 Disease, infirmity, sickness; 04.02.05.02 Animal diseases; 08.01.03.06.01 Affliction, misfortune, calamity
unhāl 02.08.02 Disease, infirmity, sickness; 04.02.05.02 Animal diseases
unhālian 02.08.02 Disease, infirmity, sickness
unhālig 16.02.01.10.01 Unholy
unhālwende 02.08.12 Healing, curing; 08.01.03.06 Adversity, affliction
unhālwendlic 02.08.12 Healing, curing
unhandworht 06.01.08.05.01.01 Wondrous, glorious, marvellous
unhār 02.04.04.03.02 Colour of hair
unhēah 05.10.05.04.02.03.01 A low position, the bottom
unhēanlīce 06.02.07.06 Courage, boldness, valour; 07.02.04.03 Nobleness, excellence, nobility, magnificence
unhearmgeorn 07.07 Humility
unhelian 09.05.05 Exposure, revealing, revelation
unhered 07.04.04 Praise, acclamation, applause
unherigendlic 07.04.04 Praise, acclamation, applause
unhetol 13 Peace, tranquillity
unhīere 05.08.02.01 (Of living creatures) fierceness, roughness; 06.01.08.06.03.01 Causing dread,

terrifying; 07.03.02 Ill, harm, hurt; 08.01.03.09.01.01 Savage; 08.01.03.09.11 Hardheartedness, cruelty, severity
unhīerlic 05.08.02.01 (Of living creatures) fierceness, roughness; 08.01.03.06 Adversity, affliction
unhīerlīce 08.01.03.09.01.01 Savage
unhīersumlīce 12.01.01.12.02 Disobedience
unhierwan 07.05.03.02 Calumny, slander, insult
unhīredwist 11.05.01.01 Unfamiliarity
unhīwe 05.10.06.01 Not formed, without form
unhīwed 06.01.07 Truth, conformity with absolute standard
unhlēow 08.01.03.09.06 Hostility
unhlidian 05.10.05.04.13 A removal of that which obscures or conceals
unhlīsa/unliss 07.09.03 Infamy, ignominy, shame
unhlīsbǣre 07.09.03 Infamy, ignominy, shame
unhlīse 07.03.05.01 Ignobility
unhlīsēadig 07.09.03 Infamy, ignominy, shame
unhlīsful 07.09.03 Infamy, ignominy, shame
unhlīsig 07.09.03 Infamy, ignominy, shame
unhlitme 08.01.03.06.01 Affliction, misfortune, calamity
unhlūd 02.05.10.16 Quiet, soft, faint
unhnēaw 10.03.08 Bountifulness, munificence
unhoga 06.01.05.03.02.01 Foolishness, lightmindedness
unhold 08.01.03.09.06 Hostility; 12.01.01.12.04 Treachery

unholda 16.01.05.02 Species of devil, hellish race
unhrædspǣce 09.02.01 Silent, taciturn
unhrēoflig 02.08.06 Skin disease, erysipelas
unhrōr 05.12.04 Absence of movement, stillness
unhūfed 02.04.04.03.04 Bald, shaven
unhwearfiende 05.13.06 Constancy, unchangeableness
unhwīlen 05.11.01.01.01 Eternity
unhȳdig 06.01.05.03.02 Foolish, silly, stupid
unhyldo 08.01.03.09.05 Enmity
unhȳþig 08.01.03.06.01 Affliction, misfortune, calamity
unīeþe 11.11 Difficulty
uninseglian 05.10.05.04.15.01 A bar, bolt
unlācnigendlic 02.08.12 Healing, curing
unlācnod 02.08.12 Healing, curing
unlǣce 02.08.12.02.01 A physician
unlǣde 04.02.05.06.01 A cowherd
unlǣd(e) 07.03.04 A wretch, poor creature; 08.01.03.06.01 Affliction, misfortune, calamity; 12.08.06.02.03 (Of persons) wicked, evil-doing
unlǣdlic 08.01.03.06.01 Affliction, misfortune, calamity
unlǣdlīce 08.01.03.06 Adversity, affliction
unlǣdu 08.01.03.06 Adversity, affliction
unlǣne 05.11.01.01.01 Eternity
unlǣt 11.02.01.02 Unwearied
unlǣttu 16.02.01.13 Evil-doing, transgression, sin
unlāf 02.03.02.02 Child, offspring
unlagu 14.02 Lawlessness
unland 01.01.02.01.06 Wild/uncultivated land; 06.01.07.04.04.02 Pretence, feigning, dissimulation

unlandāgende 15.01.01.01 Holding of land
unlār 12.08.06.02.01 Wrong, evil-doing
unleahtorwyrþe 12.08.05.01 Blameless
unlēanod 15.02.04 Spending, disbursement
unlēas 06.01.07 Truth, conformity with absolute standard; 06.01.07.03 Truth of speech or thought, veracity
unlēaslīce 06.01.07 Truth, conformity with absolute standard
unlēof 07.03.01.01 Abominable, detestable
unleoþuwāc 06.02.07.04.01 Obduracy
unleoþuwācnes 06.02.07.04.01 Obduracy
unlīchamlic 16.01.02.05.01 An angel
unlīcwyrþe 08.01.03.07 Unpleasantness
unlīefed 14.02 Lawlessness
unlīesan 09.04.03 Exposition, making clear by explanation; 11.10.03 Salvation/deliverance from
unlīf 02.02.03.04 Spiritual death
unlīfes 02.02.03.01 In process of dying
unlifi(g)ende 02.02.03.02 State of being dead
unlīþe 07.03.02 Ill, harm, hurt
unlofod 07.04.04 Praise, acclamation, applause
unlūcan 05.06.08 A plucking, taking away; 05.10.05.04.14 An opening, aperture
unlust 02.05.05.03 Sexual appetite, lust; 04.01.01.03 Hunger; 08.01.03.01 Despondency; 11.06 Disinclination to act, listlessness
geunlustian 07.03.01.03 To loathe, hate, abhor
unlybba 04.06.02.06 Poison; 16.01.04 Sorcery, magic, witchcraft
unlybwyrhta 16.01.04 Sorcery, magic, witchcraft
unlȳfendlic 14.02 Lawlessness
unlyft 02.08.10.01 Malaria
unlygen 06.01.07.03 Truth of speech or thought, veracity; 14.03.03 Law, action of the courts
unlȳsan 05.05.04 That loosens, loosening
unlȳt 03.03.04.01 Much
unlȳtel 03.03.04.01 Much; 03.03.04.01.01 Greatness, bigness, size; 11.07.04 Superiority, pre-eminence, primacy
unmǣg 02.03.02.03.06.01 Kinsman, relative
unmǣge 02.03.02.03.06.02 Close relationship
unmægnes 11.06 Disinclination to act, listlessness
unmǣle 07.02.03.01 Uninjured, unhurt, unharmed; 12.08.04 Purity, moral cleanness
unmǣne 03.04.01 Singularity, peculiarity; 12.08.04 Purity, moral cleanness; 14.03.03.06 False witness
unmǣre 07.09.03 Infamy, ignominy, shame
unmǣrlic 07.09.03 Infamy, ignominy, shame
unmǣte 03.03.04.01.01 Greatness, bigness, size; 03.03.04.01.03 An immense quantity, immensity, immense number
unmǣtlic 03.03.04.01.01 Greatness, bigness, size
unmǣtnes 03.03.04.01.03 An immense quantity, immensity, immense number; 05.08.02 Violence, force
unmǣþ 16.02.01.13 Evil-doing, transgression, sin

1459

unmǣþful 12.08.07 Immoderation, excess
unmǣþlic 12.08.07 Immoderation, excess
unmǣþlīce 08.01.03.09.12 Pitilessness; 12.08.07 Immoderation, excess
unmaga 12.01.01.07 A follower; 15.01.06 Poverty, indigence
unmanig 03.03.04.04.01 Paucity, fewness, scarcity
unmann 06.02.07.06 Courage, boldness, valour; 12.08.06.02.02 A bad man, inhuman person
unmeagol 02.05.07.02 Insipid; 05.09 Weakness
unmedome 11.04.03 (Of ability) low, mean, of less worth; 11.08.04 Vanity, idleness, frivolity
unmedomlīce 11.05.02.03 Indecorum, impropriety, unseemliness; 11.06.01.01 Negligence, carelessness, heedlessness
unmeltung 02.08.08.04.02 (Of stomach) disordered
unmenged 03.03.06.03 Unity/oneness
unmennisclic 08.01.01.02 Lacking in feeling, insensitive
unmethāt 03.01.09 Heat
unmicel 03.03.04.04 Littleness, smallness
unmiht 02.08.02 Disease, infirmity, sickness; 05.09 Weakness; 06.01.07.07.02 Impossible
geunmihtan 05.09 Weakness
unmiht(e)lic 06.01.07.07.02 Impossible
unmihtig 05.09 Weakness; 06.01.07.07.02 Impossible
unmihtiglic 02.08.02 Disease, infirmity, sickness
unmihtiglicnes 05.09 Weakness
unmihtignes 02.08.02 Disease, infirmity, sickness; 05.09 Weakness

unmilde 08.01.03.09.12 Pitilessness
unmildheort 08.01.03.09.12 Pitilessness
unmilts 08.01.03.09.10 Wrath, sternness, displeasure
unmiltsigendlic 16.02.01.13.01 Kinds of sin
unmiltsung 08.01.03.09.12 Pitilessness; 16.02.01.11.02 Impiety, lack of piety
unmōd 08.01.03.01 Despondency
unmōdig 06.02.07.07 Cowardice, pusillanimity; 07.07 Humility
unmōdnes 07.06 Pride
unmolsniendlic 03.02.01.01 Decay, corruption, rottenness
unmurn 08.01.01.03.01 Freedom from trouble, comfort, security
unmurnlīce 08.01.01.03 Good feeling, joy, happiness; 08.01.03.09.12 Pitilessness
unmynd(l)inga 06.01.08.05 Unexpected
unmyndlinga 06.02.03 Unwilling, loath
unmynegian 11.06.04 Abstention, abstaining from
unmyrge 08.01.03.07 Unpleasantness
unmyrhþ 08.01.03.06 Adversity, affliction
unnan 06.02.05 Will, desire, wish; 08.01.01.03.05 Pleasure, delight
(ge)unnan 10.03.03 Granting; 15.01.02 Gift, transfer of property
geunnan 12.03.05 Permission
unne 06.02.02.01 Will, wish, pleasure; 08.01.02.01 Favour, kindness, grace; 10.03.03 Granting; 12.03.05 Permission; 15.01.02 Gift, transfer of property
unnēah 05.10.05 A space, span
unnend 10.03.03 Granting
unnende 06.02.02.01 Will, wish, pleasure
unnīedige 06.02.01 Freewill, own will

1460

unnīedunga 06.02.01 Freewill, own will
unnīþing 12.08.02.03 Goodness, probity
unnyt 03.03.04.02.02.01 Superabundance, excess; 11.08.01 Uselessness, unserviceableness; 11.08.04 Vanity, idleness, frivolity; 12.08.06.02.01 Wrong, evil-doing
unnytlic 11.08.01 Uselessness, unserviceableness
unnytlīce 11.08.03 Needless, useless, unprofitable; 12.08.06.02.03.01 Wickedly
unnytlicnes 11.08.01 Uselessness, unserviceableness
unnytnes 06.01.05.03.02.01 Foolishness, lightmindedness; 11.08 Uselessness
unnytwurþlīce 11.08.03 Needless, useless, unprofitable
unnytwyrþe 11.08.01 Uselessness, unserviceableness
unnȳþnes 13 Peace, tranquillity
unofercumen 13.02.05.01 Victory
unoferfēre 05.12.01.03.02 Impasse, want of a road
unoferhrēfed 04.05.02.08 Top of a building
unoferswīþed 13.02.05.01 Victory
unoferswīþende 13.02.05.01 Victory
unoferswīþe(n)dlic 13.02.05.01 Victory
unoferwinnendlic 13.02.05.01 Victory
unoferwinnene 13.02.05.01 Victory
unoferwrigen 05.10.05.04.13 A removal of that which obscures or conceals
unoferwunnen 13.02.05.01 Victory
unoflinnendlīce 11.02.01.02 Unwearied
unofslegen 02.02.04 Killing, violent death, destruction
unongunnen 05 Aught, anything, something; 16.01.01.01 Attributes of God

unonlȳsendlic 16.02.01.13.01 Kinds of sin
unorne 12.01.01.11 The common people
unornlic 04.04.07.01 Mode of dressing, fashion; 07.10.03.01 Unornamented, unadorned
unplēolic 11.10 Safety, safeness
unrād 13.02.01 A military expedition
unrǣd 05.06.04 Damage, injury, defect, hurt, loss; 06.01.05.03.03.01 Unreasonableness, foolishness, imprudence; 12.01.01.12.04 Treachery
unrǣden 06.01.05.03.03.01 Unreasonableness, foolishness, imprudence
unrǣdfæst 06.01.05.03.03.01 Unreasonableness, foolishness, imprudence
unrǣdfæstlīce 06.01.05.03.03.01 Unreasonableness, foolishness, imprudence
unrǣdlic 06.01.05.03.03.01 Unreasonableness, foolishness, imprudence
unrǣdlīce 06.01.05.03.03.01 Unreasonableness, foolishness, imprudence
unrǣdsīþ 06.01.05.03.03.01 Unreasonableness, foolishness, imprudence
unræfniendlic 08.01.03.07.04.01 Unbearableness
unreclīce 12.08.07 Immoderation, excess
unrēnod 07.10.03.01 Unornamented, unadorned
unrēone 08.01.03 Bad feeling, sadness
unreordedlic 06.02.05.03 Satisfaction, repletion
unreordlic 06.02.05.03 Satisfaction, repletion

(ge)unrētan 08.01.03.02 Discontent; 08.01.03.04 Grief
unrētu 08.01.03.03 Anxiety
unrēþe 05.09.02 Mildness, moderate quality
unrīce 12.01.01.11 The common people; 15.01.06 Poverty, indigence
unriht 12.05.06.02 Oppression; 12.07.05 Wrong, injustice; 12.08.06 Moral evil, depravity; 12.08.06.02 Wickedness, evil; 12.08.06.02.01 Wrong, evil-doing; 12.08.06.02.03 (Of persons) wicked, evil-doing; 14.02 Lawlessness
unriht gewil 06.02.02 Will, disposition
unrihtcræfing 14.03.03 Law, action of the courts
unrihtcyst 12.08.06 Moral evil, depravity
unrihtdǣd 12.08.06.02.01 Wrong, evil-doing
unrihtdǣda 12.08.06.02.02 A bad man, inhuman person
unrihtdēma 14.03.02 A legislator
unrihtdōend 12.08.06.02.02 A bad man, inhuman person
unrihtdōm 12.07.05 Wrong, injustice
unrihte 12.07.05 Wrong, injustice
unrihtfēoung 08.01.03.09.04 Hatred
unrihtful 12.08.06.02.03 (Of persons) wicked, evil-doing
unrihtgafol 15.04.01 Lending of money
unrihtgestrēon 15.04.01 Lending of money
unrihtgestrod 14.02.01.02 Wrongful taking, theft
unrihtgewilnung 06.02.02 Will, disposition
unrihtgilp 07.06.02 Arrogance, vainglory, vanity
unrihtgītsung 10.03.09.01.01 Covetousness, avarice
unrihthād 11.05.02.03 Indecorum, impropriety, unseemliness
unrihthǣman 12.08.08.01.02.01 Fornication, adultery
unrihthǣmdere 12.08.08.01.02.01 Fornication, adultery
unrihthǣmed 12.08.08.01.02.01 Fornication, adultery; 12.08.08.01.02.01.03 Unnatural sexual behaviour
unrihthǣmedfremmere 12.08.08.01.02.01 Fornication, adultery
unrihthǣmend 12.08.08.01.02.01 Fornication, adultery
unrihthǣmere 12.08.08.01.02.01 Fornication, adultery
unrihthǣming 12.08.08.01.02.01 Fornication, adultery
unrihtlic 12.07.05 Wrong, injustice; 12.08.06.02.03 (Of persons) wicked, evil-doing
unrihtlīce 12.07.05 Wrong, injustice; 12.08.06.02.03.01 Wickedly; 16.02.01.11.02 Impiety, lack of piety
unrihtlust 12.08.08.01 Eager, unseemly desire
unrihtlyblāc 16.01.04 Sorcery, magic, witchcraft
unrihtnes 12.07.05 Wrong, injustice; 12.08.06.02 Wickedness, evil
unrihttīd 16.02.01.13 Evil-doing, transgression, sin
unrihtweorc 12.08.06.02.01 Wrong, evil-doing; 16.02.04.04.01 The day of rest, sabbath
unrihtwīf 12.08.08.01.02.01.01 An adulterer/-ess, whore, prostitute

unrihtwīfung 12.08.08.01.02.01 Fornication, adultery
unrihtwilla 12.08.06.01 Error, wrong conduct, erroneous practice
unrihtwillend 12.08.06.02.02 A bad man, inhuman person
unrihtwillnung 06.02.05.01 Strong liking for, devotion to
unrihtwīs 12.07.05 Wrong, injustice; 12.08.06.02.03 (Of persons) wicked, evil-doing; 16.02.01.11.02 Impiety, lack of piety
unrihtwīslīce 12.08.06.02.03.01 Wickedly
unrihtwīsnes 12.08.06.02 Wickedness, evil
unrihtwīsu 12.08.06.02 Wickedness, evil
unrihtwrīgels 06.01.07.05 Error, being astray
unrihtwyrcend 12.08.06.02.02 A bad man, inhuman person
unrihtwyrhta 12.08.06.02.02 A bad man, inhuman person
unrīme 03.03.04.01.03 An immense quantity, immensity, immense number
unrīmfolc 12.04.02 A crowding together, assembly
unrīmgōd 07.02 Goodness; 12.08.02.02 Righteousness, rectitude
unrīpe 05.11.08.01.02 (Untimely) earliness
unrōt 08.01.03.01 Despondency; 08.01.03.09.10 Wrath, sternness, displeasure
geunrōtian 08.01.03.04 Grief
unrōtlic 08.01.03 Bad feeling, sadness
unrōtlīce 08.01.03 Bad feeling, sadness
unrōtmōd 08.01.03 Bad feeling, sadness
(ge)unrōtsian 08.01.03 Bad feeling, sadness; 08.01.03.04 Grief

unrūh 03.01.06 Smoothness
unrūm 05.10.02 Narrowness, scantiness of space
unsac 14.03.03.08 Justification
unsæd 06.02.05.03 Satisfaction, repletion
unsǣd 09.06.02.01.02 Not said, undeclared, unsaid; 12.08.06.01.01 Pollution, impairment
unsǣl 08.01.03.06.01 Affliction, misfortune, calamity
unsǣlan 05.05.04 That loosens, loosening
unsǣlig 08.01.03.04 Grief; 12.08.06.02.03 (Of persons) wicked, evil-doing
unsæpig 02.07.01 To grow; 03.01.18 Dryness (not wetness)
unsamwrǣde 13.02 War
unsang 02.05.10.17 Absence of noise or disturbance
unsār 02.08.01 Sound physical condition
unsāwen 04.02.03.02.02 Sown part of field
unscæþful 12.08.05 Innocence
unscæþfullīce 12.08.05 Innocence
unscæþfulnes 12.08.05 Innocence
unscæþþig 05.09.02 Mildness, moderate quality; 12.08.05 Innocence
unscæþþ(ig)ende 12.08.05 Innocence
unscamfæst 07.06.01.01 Proud, arrogant; 12.08.07.01.04 Shamelessness, lasciviousness
unscamfulnes 12.08.07.01.04 Shamelessness, lasciviousness; 12.08.08.01.02 Unchastity, incontinence
unscamiende 12.08.07.01.04 Shamelessness, lasciviousness
unscamig 12.08.07.01.04 Shamelessness, lasciviousness

unscamlic 12.08.07.01.04 Shamelessness, lasciviousness
unscamlīce 12.08.07.01.04 Shamelessness, lasciviousness
unsceaft 02.06.10 Monster, strange creature
unsceandlīce 12.08.07.01.04 Shamelessness, lasciviousness
unscearp 04.01.03.05.01.01 Wine
unscearpnes 06.01.05.03.01 Mental inertness
unscearpsȳne 02.08.07.02.01 Defective vision
unscēaþian 13.02.08.04.03.02 Armed with a sword
unscelleht 02.06.06.04 Shellfish
unscellīce 06.01.06.04.03 Ignorance, folly
unscende 07.08.02 Honour, glory
unscended 03.03.06 Wholeness
unscendende 12.08.05 Innocence
unscennan 04.02.05.05.03 A yoke
unsceþþiglīce 12.08.05 Innocence
unscirped 04.04.07.02 Not dressed, unclothed
unscōd 04.04.07.15 Footwear, covering for the feet
unscōgan 04.04.07.15 Footwear, covering for the feet
unscoren 04.06.01.07 Hair-care
unscortende 03.03.04.02.01 Abundance
unscrȳdan 05.10.05.04.13 A removal of that which obscures or conceals
unscrȳdd 04.04.07.02.01 Nakedness
unscyld 12.08.05 Innocence; 12.08.06.02.05.01 Transgression, trespass
unscyldgung 12.08.05 Innocence
unscyldig 12.07.03 Abstinence/exemption (from); 12.08.05 Innocence

unscyldiglic 12.07.03.02 An excuse
unscyldiglīce 12.08.05 Innocence
unscyldignes 12.08.05 Innocence
unscyttan 05.10.05.04.15.01 A bar, bolt
unseald 10.03 Giving
unsealt 02.05.07.02 Insipid
unsefful 06.01.03.03 Absence of reason
unseglian 05.10.05.04.15.01 A bar, bolt
unseht 12.05.03 Disagreement, discord, dissension; 12.05.03.01 Quarrel, contentiousness, strife
unsehtnes 12.05.03.01 Quarrel, contentiousness, strife
unseldan 05.11.09.02 Frequent, of common occurrence
unseofiende 08.01.01.03.04 Gladness, cheerfulness
unsettan 05.10.04.04.02 Removal, taking away
unsibb 08.01.03.09.05 Enmity; 12.05.03 Disagreement, discord, dissension; 13.02 War
unsibbian 12.05.03 Disagreement, discord, dissension
unsibsumnes 08.01.03.03 Anxiety
unsideful 12.08.08.01.02 Unchastity, incontinence
unsidefullnes 12.08.08.01.02 Unchastity, incontinence
unsidelīce 11.05.02.03 Indecorum, impropriety, unseemliness; 12.08.08.01.02 Unchastity, incontinence
unsidu 11.05.02.03 Indecorum, impropriety, unseemliness; 12.08.06 Moral evil, depravity
unsigefæst 13.02.05.02 Defeat
unsīþ 05.12.01.01 To go on a journey/expedition, travel;

08.01.03.06.01 Affliction, misfortune, calamity
unslæpig 02.05.02 Consciousness
unslāw 11.02.01.01 Active, nimble
unslāwlīce 11.02.01 Energy, vigour, vigorous action
unsleac 11.02.01 Energy, vigour, vigorous action
unsleaclīce 11.02.01 Energy, vigour, vigorous action
unslit 02.05.07.02 Insipid
unsliten 03.03.06 Wholeness
unslopen 05.05.04 That loosens, loosening
unslȳped 09.02.02 Dumbness, lack of speech
unsmeoruwig 04.01.02.01.01.01 Good/palatable food
unsmēþe 02.08.06 Skin disease, erysipelas; 03.01.05 Roughness
unsmēþnes 03.01.05 Roughness
unsmōþe 03.01.05 Roughness
unsmyltnes 01.03.01.03.01 Storm, tempest
unsnotorlīce 06.01.05.03.03.01 Unreasonableness, foolishness, imprudence
unsnotornes 06.01.05.03.01.01 Dullness, folly, stupidity; 12.08.06.02 Wickedness, evil
unsnottor 06.01.06.04.03 Ignorance, folly
unsnyttru 06.01.06.04.03 Ignorance, folly
unsnyttrum 06.01.06.04.03 Ignorance, folly
unsōfte 02.08.03 Pain, bodily discomfort; 05.08.02.01 (Of living creatures) fierceness, roughness; 11.11 Difficulty

unsōftlīce 05.08.02.01 (Of living creatures) fierceness, roughness
unsōm 12.05.03 Disagreement, discord, dissension
unsorh 08.01.01.03.01 Freedom from trouble, comfort, security
unsōþ 06.01.07.04.03 Untruth, falsehood
unsōþfæst 06.01.07.04.03 Untruth, falsehood; 12.07.05 Wrong, injustice
unsōþfæstnes 12.07.05 Wrong, injustice
geunsōþian 11.03.01.01.01 Proof, demonstration
unsōþsagol 06.01.07.04.03 Untruth, falsehood
unspannan 05.05.04 That loosens, loosening
unspēd 15.01.06 Poverty, indigence
unspēdig 02.01.03.02 Barrenness, sterility; 15.01.06 Poverty, indigence
unspiwol 02.08.12.02.07.01 Purgative
unsp(r)ecende 09.02.02 Dumbness, lack of speech
unstæfwīs 06.01.06.04.02 Ignorance, uninstructedness
unstæþþig 05.12.02 To move, set in motion; 05.13.05 Changeability; 06.02.07.05.01 Inconstancy; 12.08.07.01.03 Wantonness, levity, frivolity
unstæþþignes 06.02.07.05.01 Inconstancy
unstaþolfæst 05.13.05 Changeability; 06.02.07.05 Irresolution; 06.02.07.05.01 Inconstancy
unstaþolfæstnes 05.13.05 Changeability; 06.02.07.05.01 Inconstancy
unstedefæst 05.13.05 Changeability
unstedeful 16.02.01.07 Apostasy
unstille 05.12 To move, be in motion; 08.01.03.03 Anxiety; 12.05.02.01 Lack of peacefulness

(ge)unstill(i)an 08.01.03.07.02 Misery, trouble, affliction; 12.05.02.01 Lack of peacefulness
unstil(l)nes 02.05.10.03 Noise, tumult, uproar; 05.12 To move, be in motion; 08.01.03.03 Anxiety
unstillnes 12.05.02.01 Lack of peacefulness
unstil(l)nes 14.02.01.01 Types of crime
unstrang 02.08.02 Disease, infirmity, sickness; 05.09 Weakness
unstrenge 05.09 Weakness
unstydfullnes 06.02.07.05.01 Inconstancy
unstyrendlic 08.01.03.07.04.01 Unbearableness
unstyriende 05.12.04.01 Stability, firmness
unsūr 02.05.07.03 Sweetness
unswǣs 08.01.03.07 Unpleasantness
unswǣslic 08.01.03.09.10 Wrath, sternness, displeasure
unswefn 02.05.04.02 A dream
unsweotol 02.05.09.13 Invisible
unswēte 02.05.07.01 Strong taste, acidity, pungency; 02.05.08.01 Foul smell, stench, stink
unswētian 08.01.03.09.01.02 Bitterness, acrimony
unswicen 11.10 Safety, safeness
unswic(i)ende 12.01.01.12 Loyalty
unswicol 12.07.02.02 Truth, faithfulness, good faith, sincerity
unswīþ 04.01.03.05.01 Intoxicating liquor
unswīþe 05.09 Weakness; 05.12.03.02 Slowness
unsȳferlic 12.08.08.01.02 Unchastity, incontinence
unsȳfernes 02.08.05.02.01 Matter, purulence, pus; 04.06.02.02 Foul, filthy, squalid; 12.08.08.01.02 Unchastity, incontinence
unsȳfre 02.08.05.02.01 Matter, purulence, pus; 04.06.02.02 Foul, filthy, squalid; 12.08.08.01.02 Unchastity, incontinence
unsyngian 14.03.03.08 Justification
unsynnig 07.04.02 Merit, desert(s); 12.08.05 Innocence
unsynnum 12.08.05.01 Blameless
untǣle 12.08.05.01 Blameless
untǣled 12.08.05.01 Blameless
untǣllic 12.08.05.01 Blameless
untǣllīce 12.08.05.01 Blameless
untǣlwierþe 07.04.04.02 Laudable, praiseworthy; 12.08.05.01 Blameless
untǣlwierþlīce 07.04.04.02 Laudable, praiseworthy
untamcul 04.02.05.04 To tame, break in (animals)
unteald 03.03.04.01.03 An immense quantity, immensity, immense number
untealt 05.13.06.01 Firm, stable, steady
untela 07.03 Evil; 12.07.05 Wrong, injustice
untellendlic 06.01.08.05.01.01 Wondrous, glorious, marvellous
unteogoþad 16.02.04.20 Church due/requirement
untēorig 05.11.11.01 A not ceasing, persistence, recurrence
untīdǣt 04.01.01.04 Gluttony, overeating, greediness
untīdfyl 04.01.01.04 Gluttony, overeating, greediness
untīdgewidere 01.03.01 Weather, condition of atmosphere
untīdlic 05.11.01.01.01 Eternity; 05.11.08.01 Untimeliness
untīdlīce 05.11.08.01 Untimeliness

untīdspǣc 05.11.08.01 Untimeliness
untīdweorc 16.02.04.04.01 The day of rest, sabbath
untīgan 05.05.04 That loosens, loosening
untilad 11.01.03 Preparation
untīma 05.11.08.01 Untimeliness; 08.01.03.06 Adversity, affliction
untīmaǣt 04.01.01.04 Gluttony, overeating, greediness
untimber 11.08.04 Vanity, idleness, frivolity
untīme 08.01.03.06.01 Affliction, misfortune, calamity
untīmnes 08.01.03.06 Adversity, affliction
untōbrocen 03.03.06 Wholeness
untōclofen 02.06.01.04 Leg
untōdǣled 03.03.06.03 Unity/oneness; 03.03.07 A part, division, portion; 16.01.01.01 Attributes of God; 16.01.01.04 The Trinity
untōdǣl(ed)lic 03.03.06.03 Unity/oneness
untōdǣledlic 16.01.01.04 The Trinity
untōdǣledlīce 03.03.06.03 Unity/oneness
untōdǣlednes 03.03.06.03 Unity/oneness
untōdǣlendlic 03.03.06.03 Unity/oneness
untōdǣle(n)dlic 16.01.01.01 Attributes of God
untōdǣlendlic 16.01.01.04 The Trinity
untōdǣlendlīce 07.01.01.03 Confusion
untogen 05.05.04 That loosens, loosening
untōlǣtendlīce 05.11.11.01 A not ceasing, persistence, recurrence
untōlēsende 05.05.03 Binding, fastening
untōlȳsendlic 05.05.03 Binding, fastening; 16.02.01.13.01 Kinds of sin
untōsceacen 05.13.06 Constancy, unchangeableness

untōslegen 03.03.06 Wholeness
untōsliten 03.03.06 Wholeness
untōslopen 03.03.06 Wholeness
untōsprecendlic 16.01.01.01 Attributes of God
untōtwǣmed 03.03.06.03 Unity/oneness; 16.01.01.04 The Trinity
untōworpenlic 03.03.06 Wholeness
untrāglīce 06.01.07.03 Truth of speech or thought, veracity
untrēowfæst 12.01.01.12.04 Treachery
untrēowlīce 12.01.01.12.04 Treachery
untrēowsian 06.01.07.04 Deception
(ge)untrēowsian 08.01.03.07.02.01 Injury, offence
untrīwe 16.02.01.11 Firmness in the law, piety, devoutness
untrum 02.08.02 Disease, infirmity, sickness
untrumhād 02.08.02 Disease, infirmity, sickness
untrumian 05.09 Weakness
(ge)untrumian 02.08.02 Disease, infirmity, sickness
untrumlic 05.09 Weakness
untrumnes 02.08.11.02 Mental weakness; 05.09 Weakness
untrumnes/untrymnes 02.08.02 Disease, infirmity, sickness
untrymed 16.02.04.07.03 Confirmation
untrymigan 02.08.02 Disease, infirmity, sickness
untrym(m)ig 02.08.02 Disease, infirmity, sickness
untrymmigo 02.08.02 Disease, infirmity, sickness
untrymþ 02.08.02 Disease, infirmity, sickness
untwēo 06.01.07.07.03 Certainty
untwēod 06.01.07.07.03 Certainty

untwēogende 06.01.07.07.03 Certainty
untwēogendlic 06.01.07.07.03 Certainty
untwēogendlīce 06.01.07.02 Certainty, truth, what really is
untwēolic 06.01.07.07.03 Certainty
untwēolīce 06.01.07.07.03 Certainty
untwēonigende 06.01.07.07.03 Certainty
untwīfeald 03.03.06.03 Unity/oneness; 12.08.04 Purity, moral cleanness
untȳdre 02.06.10 Monster, strange creature; 06.02.07 Will, determination, resolution
untȳdrende 02.01.03.02 Barrenness, sterility
untygþa 11.06.03.01 Ill fortune, bad success
untȳmende 02.01.03.02 Barrenness, sterility
untȳned 05.10.05.04.14 An opening, aperture
unþærfeþing 11.08.03 Needless, useless, unprofitable
unþæslic 03.06.04 Incongruity, absurdity; 05.11.08.01 Untimeliness; 11.05.02.03 Indecorum, impropriety, unseemliness
unþæslīce 03.06.04 Incongruity, absurdity; 11.05.02.03 Indecorum, impropriety, unseemliness
unþæslicnes 11.05.02.03 Indecorum, impropriety, unseemliness
unþæslicu 03.06.04 Incongruity, absurdity
unþanc 08.01.03.07.02.01 Injury, offence; 08.01.03.09.09 Ingratitude, displeasure expressed in words; 08.01.03.09.10 Wrath, sternness, displeasure
unþances 06.02.03 Unwilling, loath

unþancol 08.01.03.09.09 Ingratitude, displeasure expressed in words
unþancwurþe 08.01.03.07 Unpleasantness; 08.01.03.09.09 Ingratitude, displeasure expressed in words
unþancwyrþlīce 08.01.03.09.09 Ingratitude, displeasure expressed in words
unþearf 07.03.02 Ill, harm, hurt
unþearfes 11.08.03 Needless, useless, unprofitable
unþēaw 12.08.06 Moral evil, depravity
unþēawfæst 11.05.02.03 Indecorum, impropriety, unseemliness
unþēawful 12.05.06.01 Restraint, check, curb, control
unþeccan 05.10.05.04.13 A removal of that which obscures or conceals
unþingod 16.02.04.07.02.03 Penance, an act/instance of penance
unþolemōdnes 08.01.03.08.01 Impatience
unþoligendlic 08.01.03.07.04.01 Unbearableness
unþorfæst 11.08.03 Needless, useless, unprofitable
unþrīste 06.01.08.06.06 Timidity
unþrōwendlicnes 02.05.01 Without feeling, insensible
unþrōwigendlic 02.05.01 Without feeling, insensible
unþurhfēre 05.12.01.03.02 Impasse, want of a road
unþurhscēotendlic 05.12.01.03.02 Impasse, want of a road
unþurhtogen 11.06.02 Suffering (not acting)
geunþwǣrian 09.07.03 Disagreement, dissent
unþwogen 04.06.02.01 Dirty, unclean

unþyhtig 02.08.07.02.01 Defective vision
unþyldlicnes 11.11 Difficulty
unwāclic 07.02.04.03 Nobleness, excellence, nobility, magnificence
unwāclīce 06.02.07 Will, determination, resolution; 07.02.04.03 Nobleness, excellence, nobility, magnificence
unwǣded 04.04.07.02 Not dressed, unclothed
unwǣlgrim 08.01.02.01.02 Gentleness
unwǣr 06.01.08.05 Unexpected; 11.02.04 Heedlessness; 11.09 Peril, danger
unwǣres 06.01.08.05 Unexpected
unwǣrlic 11.02.04 Heedlessness
unwǣrlīce 11.02.04 Heedlessness
unwǣrnes 11.02.04 Heedlessness
unwǣrscipe 11.02.04 Heedlessness
unwǣscen 04.06.02.01 Dirty, unclean
unwǣstm 02.07 A plant; 04.02.04.04 Harvest, crop
unwǣstmbǣre 02.01.03.02 Barrenness, sterility
unwǣstmbǣrnes 02.01.03.02 Barrenness, sterility
unwǣstmberendlic 02.01.03.02 Barrenness, sterility
unwǣstmberendnes 02.01.03.02 Barrenness, sterility
unwǣstmfæst 02.01.03.02 Barrenness, sterility
unwǣstmfæstnes 02.01.03.02 Barrenness, sterility
unwæterig 03.01.18 Dryness (not wetness)
unwandiende 11.02.01.03 Unhesitating
unwarnod 11.09 Peril, danger
unwealden 06.02.03 Unwilling, loath
unwealt 05.12.01.09.03.01.02 Of/concerning a ship, naval

unwearnum 11.12.01 Absence of restraint, freedom
unweaxen 02.01.04.01 Youth
unwederlīce 01.03.01.03.01 Storm, tempest
unwegen 03.03.02.01 A weight, definite amount
unwemlic 12.08.04 Purity, moral cleanness
unwemme 07.02.03.01 Uninjured, unhurt, unharmed; 12.08.04 Purity, moral cleanness; 12.09.03 Unmarried state
unwemme(d) 07.02.03.01 Uninjured, unhurt, unharmed
unwemmend 12.08.05 Innocence
unwemming 05.11.01.04 Incorruption, incorruptibility
unwemmu 05.11.01.04 Incorruption, incorruptibility
unwēne 06.01.08.05 Unexpected; 06.01.08.06.07 Despair
unwēned 06.01.08.05 Unexpected
unwēnlic 06.01.08.06.07 Despair
unwēnlīce 06.01.08.05 Unexpected
unwēnunga 06.01.08.05 Unexpected
unwēod 02.07 A plant; 16.02.01.13 Evil-doing, transgression, sin
unweorcheard 02.08.02 Disease, infirmity, sickness
unweorclic 05.11.08.01 Untimeliness
unweorþ 07.03.03.01 Empty, useless, worthless; 07.09 Shame, disgrace; 11.08.04 Vanity, idleness, frivolity; 12.01.01.11 The common people; 15.02.02 Cheap
unweorþe 07.09.03 Infamy, ignominy, shame
unweorþian 07.09.03 Infamy, ignominy, shame

unweorþlic 07.03.05.01 Ignobility; 11.08.04 Vanity, idleness, frivolity
unweorþlīce 07.09.03 Infamy, ignominy, shame; 08.01.03.05.05 Indignation; 11.08.04 Vanity, idleness, frivolity
unweorþnes 07.09.03 Infamy, ignominy, shame
unweorþscipe 07.09.03 Infamy, ignominy, shame; 08.01.03.05.05 Indignation
unweorþung 07.09.02 Disgrace, shaming, humiliation; 07.09.03 Infamy, ignominy, shame; 08.01.03.05.05 Indignation
unwered 11.09 Peril, danger; 15.01.01 Landed property
unwērig 02.08.13 Recovery, growing better; 11.02.01.02 Unwearied
unwerod 02.05.07.01 Strong taste, acidity, pungency; 02.05.07.01.01 (Of food, etc.) bad, tainted, rancid
unwīd 05.10.02 Narrowness, scantiness of space
unwīdlod 16.02.01.10 Holiness
unwilla 08.01.03.07 Unpleasantness
unwillende 06.02.03 Unwilling, loath
unwilles 06.02.03 Unwilling, loath
unwillum 06.02.03 Unwilling, loath
unwilsumlīce 06.02.03 Unwilling, loath
unwindan 05.05.04 That loosens, loosening
unwine 08.01.03.09.05 Enmity
unwīs 02.08.11.02.01 Insanity, madness; 06.01.06.04 Ignorance; 06.01.06.04.03 Ignorance, folly
unwīsdom 06.01.05.03.01.01 Dullness, folly, stupidity
unwīsdōm 06.01.06.04 Ignorance
unwīslic 06.01.06.04.03 Ignorance, folly
unwīslīce 06.01.06.04.03 Ignorance, folly

unwīsnes 06.01.06.04 Ignorance; 12.08.06.02 Wickedness, evil
unwita 06.01.05.03.02 Foolish, silly, stupid
unwitende 06.01.06.04 Ignorance
unwītnigendlīce 12.07.03.01 Impunity
unwītnung 12.07.03.01 Impunity
unwitod 06.01.07.07.03.01 Unknown, uncertain
unwittig 06.01.06.04.03 Ignorance, folly
unwittol 06.01.06.04 Ignorance
unwiþerweard 08.01.02.03.02 Friendly, amiable
unwiþerweardlic 09.07.04.01 Confirmation, agreement
unwiþmeten(d)līce 03.06.02.02 Incomparability
unwiþmetenes 03.06.02.02 Incomparability
unwiþmetenlic 03.06.02.02 Incomparability
unwlite 07.09.03 Infamy, ignominy, shame
unwlitegian 07.10.02 Ugliness
unwlitegung 07.10.02.01 Deformed, ugly
unwlitig 02.08.04.02 Blemish, disfigurement; 07.10.02 Ugliness
unwlitignes 07.10.02.01 Deformed, ugly
unword 07.05.03.02 Calumny, slander, insult
unwrǣne 02.05.05.03 Sexual appetite, lust
unwrǣst(e) 08.01.03.06.01 Affliction, misfortune, calamity; 05.09 Weakness
unwrǣstlīce 06.01.07.05 Error, being astray
unwrecen 12.05.04.02 Vengeance, revenge; 14.03.03.09.01 Unfavourable judgement, condemnation

unwrenc 12.08.06 Moral evil, depravity; 12.08.06.02.06 Deceit, evil, wickedness
unwrēon 05.10.05.04.13 A removal of that which obscures or conceals; 09.05.05 Exposure, revealing, revelation; 09.05.05.01 Showing, manifestation, display
unwrigednes 09.05.05 Exposure, revealing, revelation
unwrigen 09.05.05.01 Showing, manifestation, display
unwriten 09.03.07.07.03.02 To write, state/say in writing
unwrītere 09.03.07.03 A scribe, copyist
unwrīþan 05.05.04 That loosens, loosening
unwunden gearn 04.04.04 A thread (of wool, etc.), fibre
unwundod 02.08.04.01 A wound
(ge)unwurþian 07.09.03 Infamy, ignominy, shame
unwynsum 08.01.03.07 Unpleasantness
unwynsumnes 08.01.03.07 Unpleasantness
unwyrcan 05.06 Destruction, dissolution, loss, breaking
unwyrht 12.08.06.01 Error, wrong conduct, erroneous practice
unwyrtrumian 05.06.08 A plucking, taking away
unymbfangen 16.01.01.02.06 God as judge
unymbfangenlic 16.01.01.02.06 God as judge
unymbwendedlic 05.13.06 Constancy, unchangeableness
unymbwriten 16.01.01.02.06 God as judge
unȳþgian 08.01.03.07.02 Misery, trouble, affliction
ūp 01.01.02 Land; 01.01.03.01.01.01 River
ūp āblāwan 05.12.05.03.04.02 To flow out, well up, erupt
ūp ābrecan 05.12.05.03.04.01 To burst forth, break out
ūp ābregdan 05.12.05.12.02 To raise, lift up, elevate
ūp ādelfan 05.06.08 A plucking, taking away
ūp ādōn 05.10.04.04.02 Removal, taking away
ūp āgān 05.10.06.03 Projection, head, extremity (of anything)
ūp āhebban 05.03.01 A cause (of anything); 07.04.04 Praise, acclamation, applause; 07.06.01.03 To be proud/arrogant; 07.08.06 Exaltation
ūp āhebban handa 12.05.05 Resistance, repulsing
ūp āhōn 02.02.04.04.03 Putting to death; 05.12.01.07.01 To hang; 14.05.05.01.01 Crucifixion, death on cross
ūp āhwylfan 05.06.08 A plucking, taking away
ūp ālipod 05.06.08 A plucking, taking away
ūp ālocen 05.06.08 A plucking, taking away
ūp ālūcan 05.06.08 A plucking, taking away
ūp ālȳman 03.01.12.02 A beam of light; 07.08.07 Glory, splendour, magnificence
ūp āmȳlan 02.05.09.06 Thing seen, sight, vision
ūp ārǣman 05.12.05.12.01 To reach up

ūp ārǣran 05.12.05.12.02 To raise, lift up, elevate; 08.01.01.01.03 An incitement, cause of strong feeling
ūp āreccan 05.12.05.12.02 To raise, lift up, elevate
ūp ārengan 05.12.05.12.02 To raise, lift up, elevate
ūp ārīsan 05.03.02.01.01 An event, occurrence
ūp āscēotan 05.12.05.03.04.01 To burst forth, break out
ūp āsettan 05.12.05.03.03 To depart, leave, set out
ūp āsittan 05.12.05.12.01 To reach up
ūp āspringan 02.07.01 To grow
ūp āspryttan 02.07.01 To grow
ūp āstandan 05.10.05.04.02.04.01 Uprightness, straightness
ūp āstreccan 05.12.05.12.02 To raise, lift up, elevate
ūp ātēon 05.06.08 A plucking, taking away; 05.12.02.05 To pull, drag, draw
ūp āþenian 05.12.05.12.02 To raise, lift up, elevate
ūp āweallan 05.01 Growth, increase, what springs up
ūp ēþian 03.01.09.02.01.04 Smoke
ūp flēogan 05.12.01.07 To fly (with wings)
ūp gān 05.10.04 Place, room
ūp iernan 02.07.01 To grow
ūp gelǣded 05.12.05.08.01 To go before and guide
ūp lǣtan 05.12.01.09 To travel on water
ūp on gerihte 05.10.05.04.02.04.01 Uprightness, straightness
ūp springan 02.07.01 To grow; 05.12.05.11.01 To return
ūp weallan 01.01.03.01.01.01 River

ūpābregdan 05.10.05.02.02 Greater, bigger
ūpāfangnes 16.01.01.04.02.02 Events associated with Christ
ūpāhafen 05.12.05.12.02 To raise, lift up, elevate; 07.08.06 Exaltation
ūpāhafenlīce 07.06.01.02 Proudly, arrogantly
ūpāhafennes 05.12.05.12.02 To raise, lift up, elevate; 08.01.01.03.06 Exultation, joy
ūpāhafennes/ūpāhefednes 07.06.01 Pride, arrogance; 07.08.06 Exaltation
ūpāhafu 05.12.05.12.02 To raise, lift up, elevate
ūpāhebban 05.12.05.12.01 To reach up
ūpāhebbendlic 05.12.05.12.02 To raise, lift up, elevate
ūpāhefedlīce 07.06.01.02 Proudly, arrogantly
ūpāhefednes 05.12.05.12.02 To raise, lift up, elevate; 08.01.01.03.06 Exultation, joy
ūpārǣran 09.06 To take matter for discourse
ūpārīsan 05.12.05.12 To go up, ascend
ūpārīsnes 16.01.01.02.09 Resurrection
ūpāspringan 05.12.05.12 To go up, ascend
ūpāspringnes 05.12.05.12 To go up, ascend
ūpāsprungennes 05.11.10.01.01 Origin
ūpāsprungnes 05.03 Source, origin
ūpāspryttan 05.03 Source, origin
ūpāstīgan 05.12.05.12 To go up, ascend
ūpāstigennes 05.12.05.12 To go up, ascend
ūpāstīgnes 05.12.05.12 To go up, ascend; 16.01.01.04.02.02 Events associated with Christ; 16.02.04.04.02.01.03 Holy Week

ūpāstīgnestīd 16.02.04.04.02.01.03 Holy Week
ūpāstreht 05.12.05.12.02 To raise, lift up, elevate
ūpātēon 05.12.05.12.02 To raise, lift up, elevate
ūpāweallan 03.01.16.01 Moisture
ūpāwegan 05.10.05.04.02.04.02 Support, maintenance
ūpāwend 05.10.05.04.02.04.01 Uprightness, straightness; 05.12.05.12.02 To raise, lift up, elevate
ūpcuman 05.12.05.12 To go up, ascend
ūpcund 16.01.02 The heavens, sky
ūpcyme 05.12.05.03.04.02 To flow out, well up, erupt; 05.12.05.12 To go up, ascend
ūpeard 16.01.02.01 Heavenly dwelling place
ūpende 05.10.05.04.11.01 A bound, limit
ūpengel 16.01.02.05.01 An angel
ūpfǣreld 05.12.05.12 To go up, ascend
ūpfeax 02.04.04.03.01 Texture of hair
ūpfēgan 04.05 Building, construction
ūpfēran 05.12.05.03.04.02 To flow out, well up, erupt
ūpflēring 04.05.02.09 A storey; 04.05.02.10 Flooring, a floor
ūpflor 16.02.05.03.06 Triforium
ūpflōr(e) 04.05.02.09 A storey
ūpgān 05.12.05.12 To go up, ascend; 05.12.05.12.02 To raise, lift up, elevate
ūpgang 01.01.03.03 Flow/flowing; 05.12.01.09 To travel on water; 05.12.05.02.01 To come upon, meet with; 05.12.05.12 To go up, ascend
ūpgange 05.12.01.09 To travel on water

ūp(ge)brēdan 07.05.03.03.02 To reproach, revile, abuse
ūp(ge)bregdan 14.03.03.01 Accusation
ūpgemynd 16.02.01.12 Spirituality
ūpgodu 16.01.06 A god (of any faith)
ūphēafod 05.10.05.04.11.01 A bound, limit
ūphēah 05.10.05.03.03 Height, loftiness, sublimity; 05.10.05.04.02.04.01 Uprightness, straightness; 07.02.04.03 Nobleness, excellence, nobility, magnificence
ūpheald 05.10.05.04.02.04.02 Support, maintenance
ūphebbing 05.12.05.12 To go up, ascend
ūphef(en)nes 05.12.05.12.02 To raise, lift up, elevate
ūphefnes 08.01.01.03.06 Exultation, joy
ūpheofon 16.01.02 The heavens, sky
ūphūs 04.05.03.04 A closet, chamber, room
ūplǣdende 05.10.05.03.03 Height, loftiness, sublimity
ūplang 05.10.05.03.03 Height, loftiness, sublimity; 05.10.05.04.02.04.01 Uprightness, straightness
ūplegen 04.04.10 Ornaments, trappings, accoutrements
ūplendisc 12.06.02.01.01 Country (not town)
ūplic 05.10.05.04.02.04 Above; 16.01.01 God, the Lord; 16.01.02 The heavens, sky
ūplyft 01.03 Air surrounding earth, atmosphere; 16.01.02 The heavens, sky
ūpnes 05.10.05.03.03 Height, loftiness, sublimity
ūpniman 05.12.05.12.02 To raise, lift up, elevate

uppeland 12.06.02.01.01 Country (not town)
uppeornende 01.02.01.01.03 Sun
uppian 01.01.03.01.02.06 Surging, rolling, heaving of waves
ūprǣcan 05.12.05.12.01 To reach up
ūprǣran 05.12.05.12.02 To raise, lift up, elevate
ūpreccan 05.12.05.12.02 To raise, lift up, elevate
ūpriht 05.10.05.04.02.04.01 Uprightness, straightness; 05.12.05.12.01 To reach up
ūprihte 05.10.05.04.02.04 Above; 05.10.05.04.02.04.01 Uprightness, straightness; 05.10.05.04.05 Straight, direct
ūprist 16.01.01.02.09 Resurrection
ūprocettan 05.12.05.03.04.01 To burst forth, break out
ūprodor 01.02.01 Heaven(s), sky; 16.01.02 The heavens, sky
ūpryne 05.12.05.12 To go up, ascend
ūpscīnan 03.01.12.02 A beam of light
ūpspring 01.01.03.01.01.07 Spring, fountain, well; 02.01.03.03.03 Birth; 05.01 Growth, increase, what springs up; 05.12.05.12 To go up, ascend
ūpspringan 05.12.05.12 To go up, ascend
ūpsprungen 01.02.01.01.03 Sun; 05.12.05.12 To go up, ascend
ūpsprungennes 01.02.01.01.07 An eclipse
ūpstandende 05.12.05.12.01 To reach up
ūpstīgan 03.03.04.03 Growth, increase; 05.12.05.12 To go up, ascend
ūpstīgan (on) 05.12.01.05 To ride (on horse, etc.)
ūpstige 05.12.05.12 To go up, ascend
ūpstīge 16.01.01.04.02.02 Events associated with Christ
ūpstīgend 05.12.01.05 To ride (on horse, etc.); 05.12.05.12 To go up, ascend
ūpþyddan 03.03.04.03 Growth, increase
ūpwæstm 02.04.02.03 Height, stature or form
ūpware 16.01.02.05 Inhabitants of heaven
ūpweard 05.10.05.04.02.04 Above; 05.11.06.02.02.01 Adjustment in calculation
ūpweardes 05.10.05.04.02.04 Above; 05.10.05.04.02.04.01 Uprightness, straightness
ūpweg 05.12.05.12 To go up, ascend
ūpwill 01.01.03.01.01.07 Spring, fountain, well
ūr 02.06.03.01.04 Bison; 09.03.07.01.01 A runic letter
ūrelendisc 02.03.03.03.01 A native people; 12.06.04 Native land
ūrigfeþere 02.06.08.01 Part of bird
ūriglāst 05.12.01.03.01.01 A path, track
url 04.04.09 A fringe, border, hem
ūt 05.10.05.04.02.01 Exterior, outside of; 05.12.05.03.04 To come/go out from; 12.06.05 A foreign country
ūt ābēodan 12.03.03.01 Summons, a call, summoning
ūt āblāwan 02.04.06.07.05 To breathe
ūt ābrecan 05.12.05.03.04.01 To burst forth, break out
ūt ābūtan 05.10.05.04.02.01 Exterior, outside of
ūt ādelfan 05.06.08 A plucking, taking away
ūt ādōn 05.06.08 A plucking, taking away; 05.12.02.05 To pull, drag, draw; 05.12.05.03.04 To come/go out from
ūt ādrǣfan 05.12.02.04 To cast out, drive away

ūt ādrīfan 05.12.02.04 To cast out, drive away
ūt ætbregdan 05.12.05.03.03 To depart, leave, set out
ūt ætswimman 11.10.05 Escape
ūt æþmian 02.04.06.07.05 To breathe
ūt āfaran 05.12.05.03.03 To depart, leave, set out
ūt āfeohtan 05.12.05.03.04.01 To burst forth, break out
ūt āgān 05.12.05.03.03 To depart, leave, set out
ūt ālǣdan 05.05 Constitution, founding (e.g. of world)
ūt ālocen 05.06.08 A plucking, taking away
ūt ālūcan 03.04.01 Singularity, peculiarity; 05.06.08 A plucking, taking away; 05.12.02.05 To pull, drag, draw
ūt āmǣr(i)an 05.06.01 Devastation, laying waste; 05.12.05.03.04 To come/go out from
ūt ānȳdan 05.12.05.03.04 To come/go out from
ūt āpyffan 02.04.06.07.05 To breathe
ūt āpȳtan 05.06.08 A plucking, taking away
ūt āscēotan 05.06.07 Pricking, a prick, puncture; 05.12.05.03 To travel away (from); 05.12.05.03.04.01 To burst forth, break out
ūt āscūfan 05.12.01.09 To travel on water; 05.12.02.04 To cast out, drive away; 05.12.05.03.04 To come/go out from
ūt āscyndan 05.12.05.03.04 To come/go out from
ūt āsellan 15.01.02 Gift, transfer of property

ūt āsittan 13.02.03.01.02 To beset, surround
ūt āslēan 05.12.05.03.04 To come/go out from; 05.12.05.03.04.01 To burst forth, break out
ūt āspringan 02.07.01 To grow
ūt āstingan 05.06.08 A plucking, taking away
ūt āsundr(i)an 03.04.01 Singularity, peculiarity
ūt āþringan 05.12.05.03.04 To come/go out from; 17.02.05.05.01 Graven, embossed, chased
ūt āþȳdan 05.12.05.03.04 To come/go out from
ūt āþȳwan 03.01.16.03 A drop of liquid; 05.12.02.06 To push, impel, thrust; 05.12.05.03.04 To come/go out from
ūt āwegan 05.12.02.02 To carry off, remove
ūt āweorpan 05.12.02.04 To cast out, drive away
ūt āwindan 05.12.05.03 To travel away (from)
ūt āwyrtrumian 05.06.08 A plucking, taking away
ūt brecan 05.12.05.03.03 To depart, leave, set out
ūt cȳþan 09.06.02.01.05 Proclamation, spreading abroad
ūt gedōn 11.10.03 Salvation/deliverance from
ūt drīfan 05.12.02.04 To cast out, drive away; 05.12.05.03.04 To come/go out from
ūt fēolan 05.12.05.03.04 To come/go out from
ūt forlǣtan 05.12.02.03 To send

ūt gangan 02.04.06.06.06 Faeces; 11.06.06.01 Abandonment (of principle)
ūt (ge)gān 02.04.06.06.06 Faeces
ūt iernan 02.04.06.06 Discharge, emanation
ūt lǣtan 05.12.01.09 To travel on water
ūt mǣran 09.06.02.01.05 Proclamation, spreading abroad
ūt niman 11.10.03 Salvation/deliverance from
ūt ofgān 05.12.05.03.04 To come/go out from
ūt oþbregdan 11.10.03 Salvation/deliverance from
ūt rǣsan 05.12.05.03.04.01 To burst forth, break out
ūt scēotan 05.10.05.01 A little way, no great distance; 11.12.02 Aid, help, succour
ūt scūfan 05.12.02.04 To cast out, drive away
ūt sīon 05.12.05.03.04.02 To flow out, well up, erupt
ūt yrnan 02.08.08.12 Disease of bowels
ūtāberstan 05.12.05.03.04.01 To burst forth, break out
ūtāblegned 02.08.05.02 Particular inflammation/swelling
ūtācnyssan 05.12.05.03.04 To come/go out from
ūtācuman 05.12.05.03.04 To come/go out from
ūtācumen 12.06.05 A foreign country
ūtacund 12.06.05 A foreign country
ūtacunda 12.04.03 A stranger
ūt(ā)gān 05.12.05.03.04 To come/go out from
ūtagecælced 03.01.14.03 White/whiteness

ūtālǣdan 05.12.05.08.01 To go before and guide
ūtālēoran 05.12.05.03.03 To depart, leave, set out
ūtan 05.10.05.04.02.01 Exterior, outside of; 05.10.05.04.11 A circle, circuit, circumference
ūtan befaran 05.12.05.04 To rotate, turn round, revolve
ūtan begān 13.02.03.01.02 To beset, surround
ūtan behringan 05.10.05.04.11 A circle, circuit, circumference
ūtan bordes 12.06.05 A foreign country
ūtan landes 12.06.05 A foreign country
ūtan ymbfōn 05.10.05.04.12 The condition of being covered
ūtanburhware 02.03.03.04.05 Populace of a town/city
ūtancumen 05.12.05.01 To go astray; 12.06.05 A foreign country
ūtane 05.10.05.04.02.01 Exterior, outside of
ūtan(e) 05.10.05.04.02.01 Exterior, outside of
ūtanweard 05.10.05.04.02.01 Exterior, outside of
ūtanymbstandnes 05.10.05.04.11 A circle, circuit, circumference
ūtāsliden 05.12.05.03.04 To come/go out from
ūtāspīwan 02.08.08.04.02 (Of stomach) disordered
ūtāwinden 05.12.05.03.04 To come/go out from
ūtcwealm 05.06.01 Devastation, laying waste
ūtdrǣf 05.12.02.04 To cast out, drive away

ūtdrǣfere 05.12.02.04 To cast out, drive away
ūte 05.10.04.04 Absence; 05.10.05.04.02.01 Exterior, outside of; 12.06.03.01 Waste land, deserted place; 12.06.05 A foreign country
ūte betȳnan 05.12.05.03.04 To come/go out from
ūtera 05.10.05.04.02.01 Exterior, outside of; 12.06.05 A foreign country
ūtera/ȳtera 05.10.05 A space, span; 05.10.05.04.02.01 Exterior, outside of
ūterlic 05 Aught, anything, something; 05.10.05.04.02.01 Exterior, outside of
ūtermere 01.01.03.01.02 Sea/ocean
ūteweard 05.10.05.04.02.01 Exterior, outside of; 05.11.10.02 End, completion
ūtfær 05.12.05.03.03 To depart, leave, set out; 05.12.05.03.04 To come/go out from
ūtfæreld 05.12.05.03.04 To come/go out from
ūtfangeneþēof 14.03 Right of holding court, jurisdiction
ūtfaran 05.12.05.03.04 To come/go out from
ūtfaru 05.12.05.03.04 To come/go out from
ūtflōwan 05.10.04.04.01 Dispersion; 05.12.05.03.04.02 To flow out, well up, erupt
ūtfōr 02.04.06.06 Discharge, emanation
ūtfūs 05.12.05.03 To travel away (from)
ūtgang 02.04.06.03.02.04 Intestines; 02.04.06.06 Discharge, emanation; 02.04.06.06.06 Faeces; 04.05.03.05.02 A privy; 05.12.01.03.01 A means of access; 05.12.05.03.04 To come/go out from; 12.03.05 Permission

ūtgangende 05.12.05.03.03 To depart, leave, set out
ūtgārsecg 01.01.03.01.02 Sea/ocean
ūt(ge)feoht 13.02 War
ūtgemǣre 05.10.05.04.11.01 A bound, limit
ūtgeng(a) 05.12.01.03.01 A means of access
ūthealf 05.10.05.04.09 Side, quarter, direction
ūthere 13.02.10.01.02.02.01 Types of army
ūthlēap 14.05.04.01 A fine
ūthwīt 03.01.14.03 White/whiteness
(ge)ūtian 05.12.05.03.04 To come/go out from; 15.01.02 Gift, transfer of property
ūtirnende 02.08.08.12 Disease of bowels; 02.08.12.02.07.01 Purgative
ūtirning 02.08.08.12 Disease of bowels
ūtlād 15.03.01 Toll
ūtlǣs 04.02.03.04.02.01 Types of pasture
ūtlaga 14.03.03.09.03 Outlawry
(ge)ūtlagian 14.03.03.09.03 Outlawry
ūtlagu 14.03.03.09.03 Outlawry
ūtlah 14.03.03.09.03 Outlawry
ūtland 12.06.05 A foreign country; 15.01.01 Landed property
ūtlenda 12.06.05 A foreign country
ūtlende 12.06.05 A foreign country
ūtlendisc 12.06.05 A foreign country
ūtlēoriende 05.12.05.03.03 To depart, leave, set out
ūtlic 05.10.05 A space, span; 12.06.05 A foreign country
ūtlīce 03.03.06 Wholeness
ūtmest/ȳt(e)mest 05.10.05 A space, span
ūtrīdan 05.12.01.05.01 Modes of riding
ūtroccettan 02.08.08.04.02 (Of stomach) disordered

ūtroccian 02.08.08.04.02 (Of stomach) disordered
ūtryne 05.12.01.03.01 A means of access; 05.12.05.03.04 To come/go out from; 05.12.05.03.04.02 To flow out, well up, erupt
ūtscyte 05.10.05.04.07 A fork (in river, road, etc.)
ūtscytling 12.06.05 A foreign country
ūtsihtādl 02.08.08.12 Disease of bowels
ūtsiht(e) 02.08.08.12 Disease of bowels
ūtsīþ 02.02 Death; 05.12.05.03.04 To come/go out from
ūttor 03.03.06 Wholeness; 05.10.05 A space, span
ūtwǣpnedmann 12.04.03 A stranger
ūtwærc 02.08.08.12 Disease of bowels
ūtwald 02.07.03.04 A wood, trees
ūtwaru 14.01.05 Service, obligation, duty
ūtweallan 03.01.16.01 Moisture
ūtweard 05.10.05.04.02.01 Exterior, outside of; 05.12.05.03 To travel away (from)
ūtweardes 05.10.05.04.02.01 Exterior, outside of
ūtwīcing 05.12.01.09.03.03 Piracy
ūþgende 05.11.01.02 Shortness/brevity in time
ūþgenge 05.11.01.02 Shortness/brevity in time; 05.12.05.03.03 To depart, leave, set out
ūþmǣte 03.03.04.01.01 Greatness, bigness, size
ūþwita 06.01.06.02.02.01.01 Philosophy
ūþwitegung 06.01.06.02.02.01.01 Philosophy
ūþwitian 06.01.06.02.02.01.01 Philosophy
ūþwitlic 06.01.06.02.02.01.01 Philosophy

wā 08.01.03.04.01 Complaint, lamentation
wā (lā) wā 08.01.03.05.02 Anger
wā lā (wā) 08.01.03.04.01 Complaint, lamentation
wā lā (wā)/wei lā wei 08.01.03.04.01 Complaint, lamentation
wāc 03.01.04.01 Power of bending, flexibility; 03.03.05.01.03 Inferior; 05.09 Weakness; 06.01.05.03 Want of understanding; 06.02.07.07 Cowardice, pusillanimity; 07.03.04 A wretch, poor creature
wacan 02.01.03.03.03 Birth
wāce 06.02.07.07 Cowardice, pusillanimity; 11.06.01.01 Negligence, carelessness, heedlessness
wacen 02.05.02 Consciousness; 05.11 A time, period of time; 06.02.06.03.03 Incitement; 11.10.02.02 Watchful care, keeping guard; 16.02.04.07.06.02 A vigil
wacian 02.05.02 Consciousness; 02.05.09.01 To open the eyes/be awake; 11.09.01.01 Ambush, lying in wait; 11.10.02.01 Vigilance; 16.02.04.07.06.02 A vigil
wacian ofer 11.10.02.02 Watchful care, keeping guard
wācian 03.03.05.01.03 Inferior; 06.02.07.07 Cowardice, pusillanimity
(ge)wācian 03.02.01 Decay, decline, corruption; 05.09 Weakness
waciende 11.10.02.01 Vigilance
wāclic 03.03.05.01.03 Inferior
wāclīce 03.03.05.01.03 Inferior; 05.09 Weakness
wācmōd 06.02.07.05.02 Moral weakness; 06.02.07.07 Cowardice, pusillanimity

wācmōdnes 02.08.02 Disease, infirmity, sickness; 06.02.07.05.02 Moral weakness; 06.02.07.07 Cowardice, pusillanimity; 11.06.01.01 Negligence, carelessness, heedlessness
wācnes 12.01.01.06.04 Inferiority of status, lowest place
wacol 11.10.02.01 Vigilance
wacollīce 11.10.02.01 Vigilance
wacor 11.10.02.01 Vigilance
wacorlīce 11.10.02.01 Vigilance
wācscipe 11.06.01.01 Negligence, carelessness, heedlessness
wacung 11.10.02.01 Vigilance
wād 02.07.11 Plants/flowers (alphabetical order); 03.01.14.08 A blue dye, woad
(ge)wadan 05.12.01 To go, progress, travel (usually on land)
gewadan 05.12.05.02.04 To go in, enter
wādsǣd 02.07.11 Plants/flowers (alphabetical order)
wādspitl 04.02.04.06.08 A dibble
wadu 04.03.03 Net, drag-net, hunting net
wadung 05.12.01 To go, progress, travel (usually on land)
(ge)wǣcan 05.09 Weakness; 05.09.04 Abatement, reduction, checking; 12.05.06.02 Oppression
gewǣcan 02.05.03.02 Weariness; 11.08.04 Vanity, idleness, frivolity
(ge)wæccan 11.10.02.01 Vigilance
wæcce 05.11 A time, period of time; 16.02.04.07.06.02 A vigil
wæcc(e) 16.02.04.07.06.02 A vigil; 02.05.02 Consciousness
wæccende 11.10.02.01 Vigilance
wæccendlīce 11.10.02.01 Vigilance
gewǣcednes 06.02.07.05.02 Moral weakness

wæcnan 02.01.03.03.03 Birth; 05.01 Growth, increase, what springs up
wæd 01.01.03.01.02 Sea/ocean
(ge)wæd 01.01.03.01 Body of water; 05.12.01.03.03 A fordable place
wǣd 04.04.07 Trappings, equipment, garb
wǣdbrēc 04.04.07.09 Breeches
wǣde 05.12.01.09.03.01.03 Part of ship
wǣd(e) 16.02.05.11 The cross (as Christian image); 04.05.04.05.01 Bedding (e.g. of straw); 02.06.08.01 Part of bird
gewǣde 04.04.07 Trappings, equipment, garb; 04.04.07.01 Mode of dressing, fashion
gewǣd(e) 02.02.05.02 To prepare for burial
wǣdelnes 15.01.06 Poverty, indigence
wǣden 03.01.14.08 A blue dye, woad
wǣderāp 05.12.01.09.03.01.03 Part of ship
wǣderāpas 05.12.01.09.03.01.03 Part of ship
gewǣdian 04.04.07 Trappings, equipment, garb; 05.12.01.09.03.01.04 Equipping of ships
wǣdl 02.01.03.02 Barrenness, sterility; 15.01.06 Poverty, indigence
wǣdla 03.03.04.05 Insufficiency, lack, want; 15.01.06 Poverty, indigence; 15.01.06.01 Begging
wǣdlian 03.03.04.05 Insufficiency, lack, want; 15.01.06 Poverty, indigence; 15.01.06.01 Begging
wǣdlig 15.01.06 Poverty, indigence
wǣdligend 15.01.06 Poverty, indigence
wǣdling 15.01.06 Poverty, indigence
wǣdlung 15.01.06 Poverty, indigence; 15.01.06.01 Begging

wæfan 04.04.07 Trappings, equipment, garb
wæfels 04.04.07.07 A long outer garment, covering, cloak, etc.
wæfergange 02.06.09.02.10 Spider
wæfergeornnes 06.02.05.04 Desire, eagerness
wæferhūs 18.02.03 A spectacle, display
wæferlic 18.02.06 Theatricals
wæfernes 02.05.09.12 To show
wæfersolor 18.02.06 Theatricals
wæferstōw 18.02.03 A spectacle, display
wæfersȳn 02.05.09.12 To show; 18.02.03 A spectacle, display
wæflian 06.01.05.03.02 Foolish, silly, stupid
wæfre 03.01.12.01 Glittering, effulgence; 11.02.01.01 Active, nimble; 11.06 Disinclination to act, listlessness
wæfþ/wæft 02.05.09.12 To show
wæg 01.01.03.01.02.05 Wave; 03.01.16.02 Water, liquid; 05.12.01 To go, progress, travel (usually on land); 05.12.05.05.01 To wave, undulate; 11.11.02 A hindrance
wǣgan 06.01.07.04.01 Deception, a leading astray
(ge)wǣgan 12.05.06.02 Oppression
gewǣgan 06.01.07.04.01 Deception, a leading astray
wǣgbora 02.06.10.01.05 Sea-monster
wǣgbord 05.12.01.09.03.01 A ship, boat
wǣgdēor 02.06.10.01.05 Sea-monster
wǣgdropa 08.01.03.04.02 Shedding of tears
wǣge 03.03.02 Measurement by weighing; 04.01.03.05.04 Drinking vessel
(ge)wǣge 03.03.02 Measurement by weighing; 03.03.02.01 A weight, definite amount
wǣgende 06.01.07.04.03 Untruth, falsehood
wǣgetunge 03.03.02 Measurement by weighing; 17.03.11 Other implements, etc.
wǣgfær 05.12.01.09.03 A voyage
wǣgfæt 01.03.01.06 Cloud
wǣgfaru 05.12.01.09.03 A voyage
wǣgflota 05.12.01.09.03.01 A ship, boat
wǣghengest 05.12.01.09.03.01 A ship, boat
wǣgholm 01.01.03.01.02 Sea/ocean
wǣglīþend 05.12.01.09.03 A voyage
wǣglīþende 05.12.01.09.03 A voyage
wægn 05.12.01.06 Vehicle
wægnere 05.12.01.06 Vehicle
wægnere 06.01.07.04 Deception
wægnfaru 05.12.01.06 Vehicle
wægngehrado 05.12.01.06 Vehicle
wægngerēfa 05.12.01.06 Vehicle
wægngewǣde 05.12.01.06 Vehicle
gewǣgnian 06.01.07.04.01 Deception, a leading astray; 14.03.03.09.01 Unfavourable judgement, condemnation
wægnscilling 15.03.01 Toll
wægntrēow 15.02.04 Spending, disbursement
wægnweg 05.12.01.03.01.05 Types of road/path
wægnwyrhta 17.02.04.02.01 Cutting, hewing, shaping
wǣgpundern 03.03.02 Measurement by weighing
wǣgrāp 01.03.01.04.02 Ice
wǣgscalu 03.03.02 Measurement by weighing
wǣgstæþ 01.01.02.01.01.03 Shore, bank

wǣgstrēam 01.01.03.04 Current, rush of water
wǣgsweord 13.02.08.04.03 A sword
wǣgþel 05.12.01.09.03.01 A ship, boat
wǣgþrēa 11.09 Peril, danger
wǣgþrēat 01.01.03.06 Flood
wǣhþoll 13.02.08.04.05 A warlike engine
wæl 01.01.03.01.02 Sea/ocean; 02.02.04 Killing, violent death, destruction; 02.04.01 Dead body; 05.06.01 Devastation, laying waste
wæl geslēan 02.02.04.03 To kill, slay
wæl 01.01.03.01 Body of water; 01.01.03.01.01.01 River; 01.01.03.01.02.01 Region of sea/ocean; 01.01.03.05 Whirlpool
(ge)wǣlan 12.05.06.02.03 Trouble, disturbance
wælbedd 02.02.04 Killing, violent death, destruction
wælbend 02.02.04.01 Cause/occasion of death
wælbenn 02.02.04.01 Cause/occasion of death
wælblēat 02.02.04.01 Cause/occasion of death
wælceald 03.01.11 Coldness, coolness
wælcēasega 02.06.08.04 Bird of prey
wælclomm 02.02.04.01 Cause/occasion of death
wælcræft 02.02.04.01 Cause/occasion of death
wælcwealm 02.02.01 Particular mode of death
wælcyrige 16.01.04 Sorcery, magic, witchcraft; 16.01.06.02 Classical gods
wældēaþ 02.02.01 Particular mode of death
wældrēor 02.04.06.08.01 Blood
wælfǣhþ 08.01.03.09.05 Enmity

wælfæþm 02.02.04.01 Cause/occasion of death
wælfāg 08.01.03.09.11 Hardheartedness, cruelty, severity
wælfel 02.02.04.02 Murderous, bloodthirsty
wælfeld 13.02.02 Battle
wælfill 02.02.04 Killing, violent death, destruction
wælfūs 02.02.03.01 In process of dying
wælfyllu 02.02.04 Killing, violent death, destruction
wælfyr 02.02.04.01 Cause/occasion of death; 02.02.05.01.01 A grave, burial place, sepulchre
wælgǣst 16.01.03.02 A demonic apparition
wælgār 13.02.08.04.01 A spear
wǣlgenga 02.06.10.01.05 Sea-monster
wælgīfre 02.02.04.02 Murderous, bloodthirsty
wælgim 13.02.08.04.03.01.02 Sheath for sword
wǣlgrǣdig 02.02.04.02 Murderous, bloodthirsty
wælgrim 02.02.04.02 Murderous, bloodthirsty; 05.06 Destruction, dissolution, loss, breaking
wælgrimlīce 08.01.03.09.01.02 Bitterness, acrimony
wælgrimnes 08.01.03.09.11 Hardheartedness, cruelty, severity
wælgryre 06.01.08.06.03 Cause of fear, terror, horror
wælhere 13.02.10.01.02.02.01 Types of army
wælhlem 02.02.04.01 Cause/occasion of death
wælhlence 13.02.08.04.01 A spear

wælhrēow 08.01.03.09.11 Hardheartedness, cruelty, severity
wælhrēowlic 08.01.03.09.11 Hardheartedness, cruelty, severity
wælhrēowlīce 08.01.03.07.04 Severity, harshness; 08.01.03.09.11 Hardheartedness, cruelty, severity
wælhrēownes 08.01.03.09.11 Hardheartedness, cruelty, severity
wælhwelp 02.06.02.01.04 Dog; 04.03.01 Tracking
wælkyrging 16.01.06.02 Classical gods
wælmist 01.03.01.06.01 Cloud, mist
wælnett 13.02.08.03.01.04 Coat of mail/corselet
wælnīþ 08.01.03.09.05 Enmity
wælnōt 16.01.04.04 A magical apparatus
wælpīl 02.08.02.01.02 Onset, attack of illness
wælrǣs 13.02.03.01 An attack, assault
wælrēaf 13.02.05.01.02.02 Booty, spoils; 14.02.01.02.01 Open robbery, rapine, pillage
wælrēc 03.01.09.02.01.04 Smoke
wælregn 01.03.01.06.02 Rain
wælrest 02.02.05.01.01 A grave, burial place, sepulchre
wælrūn 09.05.04 A secret
wælsceaft 13.02.08.04.01 A spear
wælscel 02.02.04 Killing, violent death, destruction
wælseax 13.02.08.04.03 A sword
wælsliht 02.02.04 Killing, violent death, destruction; 13.02.02 Battle
wælslihta 02.02.04.03.01 A killer
wælslītende 02.02.04.02 Murderous, bloodthirsty
wælspere 13.02.08.04.01 A spear
wælsteng 13.02.08.04.01 A spear
wælstōw 02.02.04 Killing, violent death, destruction; 13.02.02 Battle
wælstrǣl 02.08.02.01.02 Onset, attack of illness
wælstrēam 01.01.03.06 Flood
wælsweng 02.02.04.01 Cause/occasion of death
wælt 02.04.05.06 Sinew/tendon/ligament
wælwang 13.02.02 Battle
wælweg 02.02 Death
wælwulf 04.01.01 Eating; 13.02.10.01 A man, warrior
wælwyrte more 02.07.09.02.02.01 Edible root/bulb
wæmbede 02.04.03.03.06 Belly/abdomen
wænere 13.02.10.01.02.02.02 Branch of army
wænes þīsl(a) 01.02.01.01.02.01 Constellation
wǣpen 02.04.06.04.01 Male genitalia; 13.02.08.04 Weapons, arms; 13.02.08.04.03 A sword
wǣpenbǣre 13.02.08 Military equipment
wǣpenberend 13.02.10.01.02 An armed man
wǣpenberende 13.02.08 Military equipment
wǣpenbora 13.02.10.01 A man, warrior
wǣpen(ge)tæc 12.06.02 District, province
wǣpengeþræc 13.02.02 Battle
wǣpengewrixl(e) 13.02.02 Battle
wǣpenhete 08.01.03.09.04 Hatred
wǣpenhūs 13.02.08 Military equipment
wǣpenlēas 13.02.08 Military equipment
wǣpenlic 02.03.01.01 Male person, man
wǣp(en)mann 02.03.01.01 Male person, man
wǣpenstrǣl 13.02.08.04.04.01 An arrow, dart, bolt
wǣpenþracu 13.02.08.04 Weapons, arms

wǣpenþrǣge 13.02.08 Military equipment
wǣpenwiga 13.02.10.01.02 An armed man
wǣpna lāf 13.02.10.02.01 Survivors of a battle
wǣpned 02.03.01.01 Male person, man
wǣpnedbearn 02.03.01.04 Child
wǣpnedcild 02.03.01.04 Child
wǣpnedcynn 02.01.03.03.06 Sex, kind
wǣpnedhād 02.01.03.03.06 Sex, kind
wǣpnedhand 02.03.02.03.01 Ancestry, paternal kinship
wǣpnedhealf 02.03.02.03.01 Ancestry, paternal kinship
wǣpnedmann 02.03.01.01 Male person, man
wǣpnedwīfestre 02.01.03.03.06 Sex, kind
(ge)wǣpnian 13.02.08 Military equipment
gewǣpnod 13.02.08 Military equipment
gewǣpnu 13.02.08.04 Weapons, arms
(ge)wǣpnung 13.02.08 Military equipment
wæps 02.06.09.02.02 Bee, hornet, wasp
wær 01.01.03.01.02 Sea/ocean; 06.01.06 Understanding, knowledge, cognizance; 06.01.08.06.05 Wariness, carefulness; 11.10.02.01 Vigilance
wǣr 06.01.07 Truth, conformity with absolute standard; 08.01.02.03 Friendliness, affection; 11.10.01 Protection, safekeeping; 12.01.01.12 Loyalty; 14.04 Making of terms, agreement, convention
wærc 02.08.03 Pain, bodily discomfort
wærcan 02.08.03 Pain, bodily discomfort
wærcsār 02.08.03 Pain, bodily discomfort

wǣre geniman (wiþ) 14.04 Making of terms, agreement, convention
wǣrfæst 06.02.07.02 Constancy; 12.01.01.12 Loyalty; 16.01.01.01 Attributes of God
wǣrgēapnes 11.04.02.01.01 Cunning, craft, craftiness, guile, wile
wǣrgenga 12.07.02.02 Truth, faithfulness, good faith, sincerity
gewǣrlǣcan 11.09.02.01 An admonition, warning, exhortation
(ge)wǣrlan 05.12.05.07.01 To pass by
wǣrlēas 12.01.01.12.04 Treachery; 16.01.05.02.02 Other terms for devils
wǣrlic 06.01.08.06.05 Wariness, carefulness
wǣrlīce 06.01.08.06.05 Wariness, carefulness; 11.02.03 Forethought, care; 11.10 Safety, safeness
wǣrlīce 06.01.07 Truth, conformity with absolute standard
wǣrlicnes 06.01.08.06.05 Wariness, carefulness
wǣrloga 06.01.07.04.04.03 Deceit, fraud, treachery; 14.04 Making of terms, agreement, convention; 16.01.05.02.02 Other terms for devils
wǣrlot 11.04.02.01.01 Cunning, craft, craftiness, guile, wile
wærnes 06.01.08.06.05 Wariness, carefulness; 11.05.02.02 Humanity, courtesy, civility
wǣrsagol 06.01.08.06.05 Wariness, carefulness
wǣrscip 06.01.08.06.05 Wariness, carefulness
wǣrscipe 11.04.02.01.01 Cunning, craft, craftiness, guile, wile
wǣrword 11.09.02 A reminder, warning
wǣrwyrde 06.01.08.06.05 Wariness, carefulness

wæsc 04.06.01.01 Cleansing, washing
gewæsc 01.01.03.06 Flood
wæscærn 04.06.01.02 A bathing place
wæscels 04.06.01.03 A bath
wæscestre 04.06.01.02 A bathing place
wæschūs 04.06.01.02 A bathing place
wæscing 04.02.05.06.02.02 Dip, washing-place
wǣsend 02.04.06.03.02.02 Throat/gullet
wæsse 01.01.02.01.04.01 Marsh, bog, swamp
wæstling 04.05.04.05.01 Bedding (e.g. of straw)
wæstm 02.01.03 Fruitfulness, fertility; 02.01.03.03.04 Offspring, race, breed, family, children; 02.04.02.03 Height, stature or form; 02.07.01 To grow; 02.07.01.01 Fruit of the earth; 03.03.04.03 Growth, increase; 04.02.04.03.02 Crop/crops; 05.03.02 Event, issue, result; 11.07.03 Use, advantage, profit; 15.04.01 Lending of money
wæstma seten 04.02.04.02.04 Planting
wæstmbǣre 02.01.03 Fruitfulness, fertility
gewæstmbǣrian 02.01.03 Fruitfulness, fertility
wæstmbǣrnes 02.01.03 Fruitfulness, fertility
wæstmbǣro 02.01.03 Fruitfulness, fertility
wæstmberende 02.01.03 Fruitfulness, fertility
wæstmberendnes 02.01.03 Fruitfulness, fertility
wæstmfæst 02.01.03 Fruitfulness, fertility
wæstmian 02.01.03 Fruitfulness, fertility

wæstmlēas 02.01.03.02 Barrenness, sterility
wæstmlic 02.01.03 Fruitfulness, fertility
wæstmsceatt 15.04.01 Lending of money
wǣt 01.03.01.06.02 Rain; 02.04.06.05.07.01 Humours; 03.01.16.01 Moisture; 04.01.03.05 A drink/beverage
wǣta 02.04.06.05.07.01 Humours; 02.04.06.06.07 Urine; 02.07.02.03 A stalk, stem; 03.01.16 Liquid, a liquid; 03.01.16.01 Moisture; 04.01.03.05 A drink/beverage
(ge)wǣtan 03.01.16.01 Moisture
wæter 01.01.03.01 Body of water; 01.03.01.06.02 Rain; 03 Material, matter, substance; 03.01.16.02 Water, liquid; 04.01.03.04 Water
wætera þrȳþe 01.01.03.04 Current, rush of water
wæterādl 02.08.05.01 Swelling
wæterǣd(d)re 01.01.03.01.01.07 Spring, fountain, well
wæterælfādl 02.08.05.01 Swelling
wæterælfen 16.01.03.04 Elfin race
wæteras 01.01.03.01 Body of water
wæterberend 15.05.01 Goods, stock, merchandise
wæterberere 15.05.01 Goods, stock, merchandise
wæterbōh 02.07.02.05 A shoot, sprout, tendril
wæterbolla 02.08.05.01 Swelling
wæterbrōga 06.01.08.06.03 Cause of fear, terror, horror
wæterbūc 04.01.03.05.04 Drinking vessel
wæterbucca 02.06.09.02.10 Spider
wæterburne 01.01.03.01.01.03 Stream
wæterbyden 04.01.03.05.04.02 A barrel, tun, vat, cask

wæterclāþ 04.06.01.05 ?A cloth for wiping
wætercrōg 04.01.03.05.04 Drinking vessel
wætercrūce 04.01.03.05.04 Drinking vessel
wætercynn 03.01.16.02 Water, liquid
wæterdrync 04.01.03.04 Water
wæteregesa 06.01.08.06.03 Cause of fear, terror, horror
wæterfæsten 11.10.01.02.01 A naturally secure place, fastness
wæterfæt 04.01.03.05.04 Drinking vessel
wæterflaxe 04.01.03.05.04 Drinking vessel
wæterflōd 01.01.03.01.02.04 State of sea; 01.01.03.06 Flood
wæterfrocga 02.06.07.02 Frog, toad
wæterful 02.08.05.01 Swelling
wæterfyrhtnes 06.01.08.06 Fear
wætergāt 02.06.09.02.10 Spider
wætergeblǣd 02.08.05.02 Particular inflammation/swelling
wætergefeall 01.01.03.01.01.06 Waterfall
wætergelād 01.01.03.01.01.04 Watercourse/channel
wætergelæt 01.01.03.01.01.04 Watercourse/channel
wætergesceaft 01.01.03 Water
wætergewæsc 01.01.02.01.01 Tract of land
wætergrund 01.01.03.01.02.01 Region of sea/ocean
wætergyte 01.02.01.01.02.01.01 The Zodiac
wæterhæfern 02.06.06.04.01.02 Crab
wæterhālgung 16.02.01.10.02 Consecration
wæterian 04.02.05.01.01 To feed/fatten animals

(ge)wæterian 03.01.16.06 A soaking, steeping; 04.01.03.04 Water
gewæterian 04.02.04.02.01.02 To irrigate (plants, land)/channel (water); 11.12.02.01 Strengthening, confirmation
wæterig 03.01.16.02 Water, liquid; 03.01.16.06 A soaking, steeping
wæterlēas 03.01.18 Dryness (not wetness)
wæterlēast 04.01.03.01 Thirst
wæterlēod 02.06.06 Fish
wæterlic 02.06 Animal
wæterlist 04.01.03.01 Thirst
wætermēle 04.01.03.05.04 Drinking vessel
wæternǣdre 02.06.07.01.02.02 Watersnake
wæterordāl 14.03.03.05 Ordeal
wæterpund 03.03.01.01 Liquid measures
wæterpytt 01.01.03.01.01.07 Spring, fountain, well
wæterrīþe 01.01.03.01.01.03 Stream
wætersċēat 04.06.01.05 ?A cloth for wiping
wæterscipe 01.01.03.01 Body of water; 01.01.03.01.01.04 Watercourse/channel
wæterscȳte 04.06.01.05 ?A cloth for wiping
wætersēaþ 01.01.03.01.03.01 Pool; 17.02.04.02.04 Leading/conducting of water
wætersēoc 02.08.05.01 Swelling
wætersēocnes 02.08.05.01 Swelling
wæterslæd 01.01.02.01.03.03 Valley
wætersol 01.01.03.01.03.01 Pool
wæterspring 01.01.03.01.01.07 Spring, fountain, well
wætersteall 01.01.03.01.03.01 Pool

wæterstefn 02.05.10.14 Sound of water
wæterstoppa 04.01.03.05.04.03 A bucket, pail
wæterstrēam 01.01.03.01.01.01 River
wætertīge 01.01.03.01.01.04 Watercourse/channel
wæterþēote 01.01.03.01.01.05 Torrent; 01.01.03.01.01.06 Waterfall
wæterþīsa 02.06.05.01.04 Whale
wæterþruh 01.01.03.04 Current, rush of water
wæterþrūh 17.02.04.02.04 Leading/conducting of water
wæterþrȳþ 01.01.03.04 Current, rush of water
wæterþyssa 05.12.01.09.03.01 A ship, boat
wæterung 04.01.03.04 Water; 04.02.04.02.01.02 To irrigate (plants, land)/channel (water)
wæterwǣdlnes 04.01.03.01 Thirst
wæterweg 01.01.03.01.01.04 Watercourse/channel
wæterwrīte 05.11.05 A dial, horloge
wæterwyll 01.01.03.01.01.07 Spring, fountain, well
wæterwyrt 02.07.11 Plants/flowers (alphabetical order)
wæterȳþ 01.01.03.01.02.05 Wave
wǣtian 03.01.16.01 Moisture
wætla 02.08.12.02.06.01 A bandage, binding
wǣtnes 03.01.16.01 Moisture
gewǣtte 03.01.16.01 Moisture
wǣtung 03.01.16.01 Moisture
wæþ 05.12.01.03.03 A fordable place
wǣþan 04.03 Hunting, the chase; 05.12.01.02 To wander
wǣþeburne 01.01.03.01.01.03 Stream

wǣwærþlic 11.07.04 Superiority, pre-eminence, primacy
wǣwærþlīce 11.03.02.01 Efficacy, success
wæxæppel 03.01.17.05 Wax
wafian 09.03.03 A gesture, action, gesticulation
wāfian 06.01.08.05.01 Amazement, astonishment, wonder, admiration; 11.06.05 Hesitation, scruple
wāfiende 06.01.08.05.01 Amazement, astonishment, wonder, admiration; 18.02.03 A spectacle, display
wāfung 06.01.08.05.01 Amazement, astonishment, wonder, admiration; 18.02.03 A spectacle, display
wāfungstede 18.02.03 A spectacle, display
wāfungstōw 18.02.03 A spectacle, display
wāg 04.05.02.02 A wall; 05.10.05.04.15.02 A wall
wagge/wagen 01.01.02.01.04.01 Marsh, bog, swamp
wāghrægl 04.04.08.01 Curtain, wall-hanging, etc.
wagian 02.08.07.04.01 Mouth disease; 05.12.04.01.01 Unstable; 05.12.05.05 To shake, quake, wag
wāgrift 04.04.08.01 Curtain, wall-hanging, etc.
wāgþeorl 04.05.02.12 Gate/doorway of a building; 05.10.05.04.14.02 An opening/space in an enclosure
wāgþyling 04.05.02.02 A wall
wagung 02.08.07.04.01 Mouth disease
wāh 04.01.02.01.03.07 Meal
waldenīge 02.04.03.01.03.02 Eye
waled 03.01.14.11 Medley/variety of colour; 05.10.06.03 Projection, head, extremity (of anything)

wālic 08.01.03.04 Grief
walu 01.01.02.01.02.01 Rising ground, eminence; 02.08.04 Hurt, injury, damage; 13.02.08.03.01.02.01 Parts of a helmet
wamb 01.01.02.01.03 Hollow/depression in land; 02.04.06.03.01 Cavities of internal organs; 02.04.06.03.02.03 Stomach/belly; 02.04.06.03.02.04 Intestines; 02.04.06.04.02 Female reproductive organs; 05.10.05.04.01 Inside, interior
wambādl 02.08.08.04 Pain in stomach
wambe coþu 02.08.08.04 Pain in stomach
wambe gicþa 02.08.08.04 Pain in stomach
wambe wyrm 02.08.08.04.03 Intestinal worm
wambhord 05.10.05.04.01.02 Contents, what is included
wambscyldig 04.01.01.04 Gluttony, overeating, greediness
wambsēoc 02.08.08.04 Pain in stomach
wamcwide 07.05.03.03.01 Contumelious, scornful
wamdǣd 12.08.06.02.05.01 Transgression, trespass
wamfreht 16.01.04.06 Divination, augury
wamful 12.08.06.02.05.03 Guilty, sinful, criminal
wamlust 06.02.06.03.04 Allurement
wamm 04.06.02.03 Stain, smear; 07.03.01.01 Abominable, detestable; 07.09 Shame, disgrace; 12.08.06.02.03 (Of persons) wicked, evil-doing; 12.08.06.02.05 Misdeed, sin; 12.08.08.01.02 Unchastity, incontinence
wamsceaþa 16.01.05.02.02 Other terms for devils
wamscyldig 12.08.06.02.05.03 Guilty, sinful, criminal
wamwlite 02.08.07.01 Pain in head/neck
wamwyrcende 16.02.01.13 Evil-doing, transgression, sin
wan 10.02 Want, lack
wana 03.03.04.05 Insufficiency, lack, want; 10.02 Want, lack; 10.02.01 Loss, deprivation
wan(a) 03.03.04.05 Insufficiency, lack, want
wana bēon/wesan 03.03.04.05 Insufficiency, lack, want
(ge)wana 10.02 Want, lack
wanǣht 15.01.06 Poverty, indigence
wananbēam 02.07.03.05 Particular trees/shrubs (alphabetical order)
wancian 06.02.07.05 Irresolution
wancol 06.02.07.05.01 Inconstancy
wand 02.06.03.01.11 Mole
gewand 03.06.02 Difference, diversity, dissimilarity; 06.01.08.06 Fear; 06.01.08.06.01 A shuddering with fear, nervousness
wandeweorpe 02.06.03.01.11 Mole
wandian 11.02.02.02 Care, mindfulness, attention; 11.06.04 Abstention, abstaining from; 11.06.05 Hesitation, scruple; 11.06.06 Turning
wandlung 05.13.05 Changeability
wandrian 05.12.01.02 To wander; 05.12.05.01 To go astray; 06.01.07.05 Error, being astray; 12.08.06.01.04 To lead a bad life
wandung 07.04.03 Reverence, respect; 11.06.06 Turning
wanfāh 03.01.14.04 Black/blackness
wanfeax 02.04.04.03.02 Colour of hair
wanfōta 02.06.08.07 Exotic bird
wanfȳr 03.01.09.02 Fire, flame

wang 01.01 Surface of the earth; 01.01.02.01.04 Open (level) land; 01.01.02.01.05 Covered with vegetation; 05.10.05.04.02 Face, surface
wangbeard 02.04.04.03.03.01 Beard, whisker
wange 02.04.03.01.03.05 Cheek
wangere 04.05.04.05.01 Bedding (e.g. of straw)
wangstede 05.10.04 Place, room
wangtōþ 02.04.06.03.02.01.01 Tooth/teeth
wangturf 04.02.03.04 Grassland
gewanhǣlan 05.09 Weakness
wanhǣle 02.08.02 Disease, infirmity, sickness
wanhǣlþ 02.08.02 Disease, infirmity, sickness
wanhǣw 03.01.14.08 A blue dye, woad
wanhafa 15.01.06 Poverty, indigence
wanhaf(e)nes 15.01.06 Poverty, indigence
wanhafol 15.01.06 Poverty, indigence
wanhafolnes 15.01.06 Poverty, indigence
wanhāl 02.08.02 Disease, infirmity, sickness
wanhālian 05.09 Weakness
gewanhālian 02.08.02 Disease, infirmity, sickness
wanhālnes 02.08.02 Disease, infirmity, sickness
wanhlyte 06.02.04.01.01 Need, distress, straits, difficulty
wanhoga 06.01.05.03.02 Foolish, silly, stupid
wanhygd 06.01.05.03.03.01 Unreasonableness, foolishness, imprudence; 11.02.04.01 Rashness, madness
wanhygdig 06.01.05.03.03.01 Unreasonableness, foolishness, imprudence; 11.02.04.01 Rashness, madness
wanian 02.08.02 Disease, infirmity, sickness; 03.02.01 Decay, decline, corruption; 03.03.04.06 Diminution; 05.07 Ending of existence, end of world; 05.09 Weakness; 05.09.05 Ceasing, decline, fall off; 05.11.06.03.01.02 Waning of the moon
(ge)wanian 03.03.04.06 Diminution; 05.09.04 Abatement, reduction, checking; 07.09.02 Disgrace, shaming, humiliation
gewanian 03.03.04.05 Insufficiency, lack, want; 15.01.01.01 Holding of land
(ge)wānian 08.01.03.04.01 Complaint, lamentation
waniendlic 09.03.02.03 Composition (inflectional or compounding)
wanigend 14.02.01.02.01 Open robbery, rapine, pillage
wanigende 01.02.01.01.04 Moon
wann 02.08.04 Hurt, injury, damage; 03.01.13 Darkness, obscurity; 03.01.13.01 Not shining, dim; 03.01.14.04 Black/blackness
wannian 03.01.13 Darkness, obscurity; 03.01.14.04 Black/blackness
wanniht 03.01.14.02 Pallor, absence of colour; 03.01.14.04 Black/blackness
wansǣlig 07.03.04 A wretch, poor creature; 08.01.03.06 Adversity, affliction
wansceaft 08.01.03.07.02 Misery, trouble, affliction
wansceafta/-e 02.08.02.01 An illness, ailment, disorder

wanscrȳd 04.04.07.01 Mode of dressing, fashion
wansēoc 02.08.11.02.01 Insanity, madness
wansian 03.03.04.06 Diminution
wanspēd 15.01.06 Poverty, indigence
wanspēdig 15.01.06 Poverty, indigence
wanspēdignes 15.01.06 Poverty, indigence
wanung 03.02.01 Decay, decline, corruption; 03.03.04.05 Insufficiency, lack, want; 03.03.04.06 Diminution; 05.06.04 Damage, injury, defect, hurt, loss; 05.09 Weakness; 05.09.04 Abatement, reduction, checking; 05.11.06.03.01.02 Waning of the moon
wānung 08.01.03.04.01 Complaint, lamentation
wanwegende 05.11.06.03.01.02 Waning of the moon
wanwilla 06.02.07.06.02.03 Presumption
wāpe 04.06.01.05 ?A cloth for wiping
wapelian 03.01.16.04 Foam, froth
wapul 03.01.16.04 Foam, froth
wār 01.01.02.01.01.03 Shore, bank; 01.01.02.02.02.01 Sand, gravel; 02.07.11.01 Seaweed
(ge)waran 02.03.01 People
ware niman 06.01.08.06.05 Wariness, carefulness
warian 06.01 The head (as seat of thought); 06.01.08.06.05 Wariness, carefulness; 12.05.05 Resistance, repulsing; 12.06.03.02 Living, dwelling, residence (in); 14.04 Making of terms, agreement, convention
warian (wiþ) 11.10.02.01 Vigilance
(ge)warian 11.09.02 A reminder, warning

gewarian 11.10.01 Protection, safekeeping
wārig 04.06.02.03 Stain, smear
wāriht 02.07.11.01 Seaweed
warnian 11.06.04 Abstention, abstaining from
(ge)warnian 11.02.02.02 Care, mindfulness, attention; 11.09.02 A reminder, warning; 11.10.02.01 Vigilance; 12.05.05 Resistance, repulsing
(ge)warnian (wiþ) 13.02.04 Defence, guard, protection
warnung 06.01.08.06.05 Wariness, carefulness; 11.09.02.01 An admonition, warning, exhortation
waroþ 01.01.02.01.01.03 Shore, bank
wāroþ 02.07.11.01 Seaweed
waroþa geweorp 01.01.02.01.01.03 Shore, bank
waroþfaruþ 01.01.03.01.02.05 Wave
waroþgewinn 01.01.03.01.02.05 Wave
waru 06.01.08.06.05 Wariness, carefulness; 11.10.01 Protection, safekeeping; 11.10.02.02.01 Care, interest in; 12.07.02 Observance, keeping; 13.02.04 Defence, guard, protection; 15.05.01 Goods, stock, merchandise
(ge)wascan 04.06.01.01 Cleansing, washing
wāse 01.01.02.01.04.01 Marsh, bog, swamp
wāsend 02.04.06.07.01 Wind-pipe
wāsescite 02.06.06.03.01.12 Squid, cuttlefish
wassen 12.01.01.07 A follower
wāt 06.01.03.01 Argument, reasoning
watel 04.05.01.02.03 Wattle; 04.05.02.08.01 Thatch

wāþ 04.03 Hunting, the chase;
    05.12.01.02 To wander
wāþol 05.12.01.02 To wander
waþum(a) 01.01.03.01.02.05 Wave
wāwa 08.01.03.04 Grief; 08.01.03.06
    Adversity, affliction
wāwan 01.03.01.05 Wind
wēa 08.01.03.04 Grief; 08.01.03.06
    Adversity, affliction; 12.08.06.02
    Wickedness, evil
wēadǣd 12.08.06.02.01 Wrong,
    evil-doing
wēagesīþ 12.08.06.02.02 A bad man,
    inhuman person
wēalāf 11.10.05 Escape
wēalas 02.03.03.05.02 The
    British/Welsh/Bretons; 12.06.01.02
    Britain
wealc 04.04.01 Fulling
gewealc 01.01.03.01.02.06 Surging,
    rolling, heaving of waves; 12.05.04.01
    Fighting, contention, warfare, strife;
    13.02.01 A military expedition
wealca 01.01.03.01.02.05 Wave; 04.04.07
    Trappings, equipment, garb
wealcan 05.12.02.07 To throw, cast, toss;
    09.01 To speak, exercise faculty of
    speech
wealcan (ymbe) 06.01.01.01.01 Thought,
    cogitation, meditation
(ge)wealcan 01.01.03.01.02.06 Surging,
    rolling, heaving of waves; 05.12.05.06
    To travel over/through/along, traverse
gewealcan 05.06.05 A grinding,
    pounding; 05.10.06.05 A fold, plait,
    wrinkle
wealcere 04.04.01 Fulling
wealcian 04.04.07 Trappings, equipment,
    garb
gewealcian 04.06.01.07 Hair-care

wealcol 01.01.03.01.02.06 Surging,
    rolling, heaving of waves;
    05.12.05.04.01 (Of wheel, etc.) to roll,
    trundle
wealcspinl 04.06.01.07 Hair-care
weald 01.01.02.01.02 High land;
    01.01.02.01.05 Covered with
    vegetation; 02.07.03.04.02 A thicket;
    12 Power, might
weald þēah 06.01.07.07.01 Likelihood,
    probability, chance
(ge)weald 02.04.03.03.08 Groin/crotch;
    04.02.05.06.05.03.01
    Bridle/halter/curb/muzzle
geweald 02.04.05.05 Muscle; 02.04.06.04
    Reproductive organs; 05.10.05.04.12
    The condition of being covered;
    06.02.06 Mind, purpose; 11.04
    Ability, capacity, power; 11.10.01
    Protection, safekeeping; 12 Power,
    might; 12.01 Power, control, sway;
    12.05.06.01 Restraint, check, curb,
    control; 12.05.06.04 A trampling
    upon, subjection; 12.06 A province,
    country, territory
wealdan 07 Judgement, forming of
    opinion; 11.04 Ability, capacity,
    power; 12 Power, might
(ge)wealdan 10 Having, owning,
    possession; 12.01 Power, control,
    sway; 12.01.01.01 Rule, domination,
    direction; 13.02.08 Military
    equipment
gewealdan 11.01 Action, doing,
    performance
wealdbǣr 04.02.03.04.02.01.03 Swine
    pasture
gewealden 03.03.05.01.03 Inferior;
    05.09.02 Mildness, moderate quality;

12.05.06.04 A trampling upon, subjection
wealdend 10 Having, owning, possession; 12.01.01.04 A leader, ruler; 12.03 Direction, guidance; 16.01.01.01.01 The Almighty
wealdende 12.01 Power, control, sway
(ge)wealdende 16.01.01.01.01.01 Mightiness
wealdendgod 16.01.01.01.01 The Almighty
gewealdendlīce 12 Power, might
wealdendwyrhta 15.01 Property
gewealdenmōd 12.05.06.01 Restraint, check, curb, control
(ge)wealdes 06.02.06 Mind, purpose
wealdgenga 14.02.01.02 Wrongful taking, theft
(ge)wealdleþer 04.02.05.06.05.03.03 Reins
wealdnes 12.01.01.01 Rule, domination, direction
wealdstapa 02.06.09.02.05 Cricket, grasshopper, locust
wealdswaþu 05.12.01.03.01 A means of access
wealdweaxe 02.04.05.06 Sinew/tendon/ligament
wealg 02.05.07.01.01 (Of food, etc.) bad, tainted, rancid
wealh 02.03.03.05.02 The British/Welsh/Bretons; 02.03.03.06.04 Italians; 04.02.04.06.06 Harrowing equipment; 12.01.01.09 Bondage, slavery; 12.06.05 A foreign country; 17.03.07 Tools for digging/grasping/pulling
wealhāt 03.01.09 Heat
wealhbaso 03.01.14.05 Red/redness
wealhcynn 02.03.03.05.02 The British/Welsh/Bretons
wealhfæreld 13.02.10.01.02.02.03 Part of an army
wealhgerēfa 12.01.01.05 A leader, administrator
wealhhafoc 02.06.08.04 Bird of prey
wealhmoru 02.07.09.02.02.01 Edible root/bulb
wealhnutu 02.07.09.02.01.01 Particular nuts (alphabetical order)
wealhsāda 05.05.03 Binding, fastening
wealhstod 09.04.03.01 A translation; 09.04.03.03 A commentary, exposition; 13.01.03 Intercession, pleading, mediation
wealhþēod 02.03.03.05.02 The British/Welsh/Bretons
wealian 12.05.05 Resistance, repulsing
wēalic 08.01.03 Bad feeling, sadness
weall 01.01.02.01.02.02.04 Cliff; 04.05.02.02 A wall; 05.10.05.04.15.02 A wall; 08.01.01.01 Ardour, fervour, strong feeling
weallan 01.01.03.01.01.07 Spring, fountain, well; 01.01.03.01.02.06 Surging, rolling, heaving of waves; 03.01.09.02 Fire, flame; 03.03.04.01.02 A great number, multitude; 03.03.04.02.01 Abundance; 05.12.05.03.04.02 To flow out, well up, erupt
(ge)weallan 01.01.03.01.01 Moving water; 03.01.09.01.01 (Of liquids) boiling; 08.01.01.01 Ardour, fervour, strong feeling
wēalland 12.06.01.03 The Continent; 12.06.05 A foreign country
weallclif 01.01.02.01.02.02.04 Cliff
wealldīc 04.05.03.05.03.01 A ditch, dike

wealldor 04.05.02.12 Gate/doorway of a building; 05.03 Source, origin
weallende 01.01.03.01.02.06 Surging, rolling, heaving of waves; 01.01.03.03 Flow/flowing; 03.01.09 Heat; 03.01.09.01.01 (Of liquids) boiling; 03.03.04.02.01 Abundance; 08.01.01.01 Ardour, fervour, strong feeling
weallfæsten 13.02.06 A fortification
weallgeat 13.02.06.01 Stronghold, fort/fortified town
weallgebrec 13.02.03.01.01 Inroad, attack
weallgeweorc 13.02.03.01.01 Inroad, attack
weall(ge)weorc 04.05.01.01 Masonry, building in stone; 04.05.02.02 A wall
weallian 05.12.01.02 To wander; 16.02.04.11 Pilgrimage
weallīm 04.05.01.03 Gypsum, chalk
geweallod 13.02.06.01 Stronghold, fort/fortified town
weallstān 04.05.01.01 Masonry, building in stone
weallstaþol 09.04.03.01 A translation
weallsteall 04.05.02.01 A foundation
weallstēap 05.10.05.04.04.01 Steep
weallstilling 17.02.04.01 Repairing, renewing
weallþrǣd 17.03.11 Other implements, etc.
weallung 05.12.05.05 To shake, quake, wag; 08.01.01.01.04 Depth of feeling, zeal
weallwala 04.05.02.02 A wall
weallweg 05.12.01.03.01.03 A highway
weallwyrhta 04.05.01.01 Masonry, building in stone; 17.02.04.02.01 Cutting, hewing, shaping

wealsāda 14.05.07 Binding, fastening with bonds
wealte 04.03.02 A snare, trap, noose; 05.10.06.02 Rotundity, roundness; 14.05.07 Binding, fastening with bonds
wealwian 05.09.05 Ceasing, decline, fall off; 05.12.05.04.01 (Of wheel, etc.) to roll, trundle
wealword 07.05.03.03 Scorn, insult, abuse
wealwyrt 02.07.11 Plants/flowers (alphabetical order)
wēamēt(tō) 08.01.03.05.02 Anger
wēamōd 08.01.03.05.02 Anger
wēamōdnes 08.01.03.05.02 Anger
weard 11.09.01.01 Ambush, lying in wait; 11.10.02 Watching, guard, watch; 11.10.02.02 Watchful care, keeping guard; 11.10.02.02.01 Care, interest in; 12.01.01.04 A leader, ruler; 16.01.01.02.04 Protector, defender
weardgerēfa 13.02.10.01.02.02.03 Part of an army
weardian 04.05.03.01 Habitation, sojourn; 11.10 Safety, safeness; 11.10.01 Protection, safekeeping; 11.10.02 Watching, guard, watch; 12.01.01.01 Rule, domination, direction; 13.02.04 Defence, guard, protection; 13.02.06 A fortification; 16.02.04.07.06.02 A vigil
weardmann 11.10.02.02 Watchful care, keeping guard
weardpening 15.03.02 A tax
weardseld 11.10.02.02 Watchful care, keeping guard; 13.02.06.01 Stronghold, fort/fortified town
weardsteall 02.05.09.10 Look-out place
weardstōw 02.05.09.10 Look-out place
weardwīte 14.05.04.01 A fine

wearg 12.08.06.02.03 (Of persons) wicked, evil-doing; 14.02 Lawlessness; 16.01.03 A spectre, ghost, demon, goblin; 16.01.05.02.02 Other terms for devils
weargbeorg 01.01.02.01.02.02.01 Hill
weargberende 12.08.06.02.03 (Of persons) wicked, evil-doing
weargbrǣde 02.08.06 Skin disease, erysipelas
weargcwedol/wyrgcwedol 16.02.04.14.02.01 Cursing, imprecation
weargcwedolnes/wyrgcwedolnes 16.02.04.14.02.01 Cursing, imprecation
weargcweþan/wyrgcweþan 16.02.04.14.02.01 Cursing, imprecation
wearglic 07.03.04 A wretch, poor creature
wearglīce 07.03.04 A wretch, poor creature
weargnes 07.03 Evil
weargol 02.07.09.02 Particular fruits (alphabetical order)
weargolnes 16.02.04.14.02.01 Cursing, imprecation
weargrōd 14.05.06 Means/implement of torture
weargtrafu 16.01.05 Hell, lower world, abode of the dead
weargtrēow 14.05.06 Means/implement of torture
weargung 08.01.03.06 Adversity, affliction
wearm 03.01.09.01 Warmth, heat
wearme 03.01.09.01 Warmth, heat
(ge)wearmian 03.01.09.01 Warmth, heat
wearmlic 03.01.09.01 Warmth, heat

wearmnes 03.01.09.01 Warmth, heat
wearn 03.03.04.01 Much; 07.05.03.03 Scorn, insult, abuse; 09.07.03.02 Refusal, denial; 11.11.01 A physical difficulty, strait
wearnmǣlum 03.03.04.01.02.01 A heap, mass, accumulation
wearnwīslīce 11.11 Difficulty
wearp 04.04.05 Woven material, fabric; 17.04.04 Fibrous materials
wearpfæt 17.03.12.01 A basket
wearr 02.08.05.02.02 Scab, roughness of skin; 04.01.02.02.06.05.04 Cup/bowl/basin; 04.01.03.05.04 Drinking vessel
wearrig 02.08.05.02.02 Scab, roughness of skin
wearriht 02.07.03 A tree; 02.08.06 Skin disease, erysipelas
wearrihtnes 02.08.05.02.02 Scab, roughness of skin; 03.01.05 Roughness
weart(e) 02.08.05.02 Particular inflammation/swelling
weartere 02.03.03.04 An inhabitant; 04.05.03.01 Habitation, sojourn
wēas 05.03.02.01 Chance, hap, event
wēasgelimp 05.03.02.01 Chance, hap, event
wēaspell 09.06.02.01.06.03 Ill tidings
wēatācen 06.01.08.04.01 Premonition, prophecy
wēaþearf 15.01.06 Poverty, indigence
weax 03.01.17.05 Wax
weaxan 02.01.03 Fruitfulness, fertility; 04.02.05.01.01 To feed/fatten animals
(ge)weaxan 02.01.04.02 To grow, grow up; 02.07.01 To grow; 03.03.04.03 Growth, increase; 05.01 Growth, increase, what springs up;

08.01.01.03.08 Happiness, well-being, prosperity
geweaxan 02.01.03.03.02 To bring forth, produce; 04.02.04.03 A plant; 08.01.01.03.08.03 A favour, blessing
weaxbred 09.03.07.06.04 A writing-tablet
weaxcandel 17.05.03 Sources of fire/light
weaxen 03.01.17.05 Wax
geweaxen 02.01.04.02 To grow, grow up
weaxgeorn 06.02.05.02 Greed, importunate desire, rapacity
weaxgescot 16.02.04.20 Church due/requirement
weaxhlāf 03.01.17.05 Wax
weaxhlāfsealf 02.08.12.02.05.02 Salves, ointments
weaxiende 01.02.01.01.04 Moon
weaxnes 03.03.04.03 Growth, increase
geweaxnes 15.04.01 Lending of money
weaxung 03.03.04.03 Growth, increase; 08.01.01.03.08 Happiness, well-being, prosperity
webb 04.04.05 Woven material, fabric; 04.04.08.02 Figured cloth, tapestry, carpet
webba 04.04 Weaving
webbēam 04.04.03 A spinning-house or chamber
webbestre 04.04 Weaving
webbgeweorc 04.04 Weaving
webbian 12.01.01.12.04.02 Conspiracy
webbung 12.01.01.12.04.02 Conspiracy; 18.02.03 A spectacle, display
webgerēþru 04.04.03 A spinning-house or chamber
webgerod 04.04.03 A spinning-house or chamber
webhōc 04.04.03 A spinning-house or chamber
weblic 04.04 Weaving
websceaft 04.04.03 A spinning-house or chamber
webtāwa 04.04.04 A thread (of wool, etc.), fibre
webtēag 04.04.04 A thread (of wool, etc.), fibre
webwyrhta 04.04 Weaving
weccan 02.05.02 Consciousness; 05.03 Source, origin; 05.12.02 To move, set in motion
(ge)weccan 02.05.02 Consciousness; 08.01.01.01.03 An incitement, cause of strong feeling
geweccan 02.08.12 Healing, curing
weccend 06.02.06.03.02 Instigation
wecedrenc 02.08.12.02.07.01 Purgative
wecg 15.01.04 Coinage, money; 17.02.04.03 Metal worker; 17.04.02 Ore, unwrought metal
wecgan 05.12.05.05 To shake, quake, wag
gewēd 02.08.11.02.01.02 Madness, frenzy, folly; 05.10.05.04.08 Crookedness, a crooked place
wēdan 02.08.11.02.01 Insanity, madness; 02.08.11.02.01.02 Madness, frenzy, folly
wēdberge 02.07.11 Plants/flowers (alphabetical order)
wedbrōþor 14.03.03.07 Security, pledge, bail
wedbryce 12.01.01.12.04 Treachery
wedd 12.07.02.01 Covenant, assurance of faith, promise; 12.09.01 Pledging, betrothal; 14.03.03.07 Security, pledge, bail
weddian 12.09.02 Marriage ceremony; 14.03.03.07 Security, pledge, bail
(ge)weddian 12.09.02 Marriage ceremony

(ge)weddod 12.09.01 Pledging, betrothal
weddung 12.09.01 Pledging, betrothal
wēde 02.08.11.02.01 Insanity, madness; 12.03.04.03 Importunity, persistence
wēdehund 02.06.02.01.04 Dog
wēdende 02.08.11.02.01 Insanity, madness; 02.08.11.02.01.02 Madness, frenzy, folly
wēden(d)sēoc 02.08.11.02.01.02 Madness, frenzy, folly
wēdenheort 02.08.11.02.01 Insanity, madness; 02.08.11.02.01.02 Madness, frenzy, folly
wēdenheortnes 02.08.11.02.01.02 Madness, frenzy, folly
weder 01.03.01 Weather, condition of atmosphere; 01.03.01.05 Wind
wederāwendednes 01.03.01 Weather, condition of atmosphere
wederblāc 03.01.14.03 White/whiteness
wederburg 12.06.02.01 A township
wedercandel 01.02.01.01.03 Sun
wederdæg 01.03.01.01 Hot, fine weather
wederfæst 01.03.01.03 Bad weather
wederian 01.03.01 Weather, condition of atmosphere
wedertācn 01.02.01.01.03 Sun
wederung 01.03.01 Weather, condition of atmosphere
wederwolcen 01.03.01.06 Cloud
gewedfæst 12.09.01 Pledging, betrothal
(ge)wedfæstan 14.03.03.07 Security, pledge, bail
wedgifu 12.09.01 Pledging, betrothal
wēding 02.08.11.02.01.02 Madness, frenzy, folly
wedlāc 12.09.01 Pledging, betrothal; 14.03.03.07 Security, pledge, bail

wedloga 06.01.07.04.04.03 Deceit, fraud, treachery; 14.04 Making of terms, agreement, convention
gewef 04.04.05 Woven material, fabric; 09.06 To take matter for discourse
wefan 05.05 Constitution, founding (e.g. of world); 06.02.06.02 A proposal, proposition, suggestion
(ge)wefan 04.04 Weaving
wefl 04.04.03 A spinning-house or chamber; 04.04.05 Woven material, fabric
weft(a) 04.04.05 Woven material, fabric
wefung 04.04 Weaving
weg 05.12.01.03 Expanse over which something travels; 05.12.01.03.01 A means of access; 11.05.02 Mode, manner, way, method, fashion, course
wega (ge)lǣte 05.12.01.03.01 A means of access
wega gemȳþe 05.12.01.03.01 A means of access
wegan 04.04.07 Trappings, equipment, garb; 05.03.01 A cause (of anything); 05.10.05.04.02.04.02 Support, maintenance; 08.01.03.07.03 Suffering, torment, pain; 09.06.02.01.01 To make known, cause to know, inform
(ge)wegan 03.03.02 Measurement by weighing; 05.12.01 To go, progress, travel (usually on land); 05.12.02.01 To fetch, bring, bear, conduct; 08.01.01 A feeling, what is felt
gewegan wiþ 12.05.04.01 Fighting, contention, warfare, strife
wegbrǣde 02.07.11 Plants/flowers (alphabetical order)
wegend 05.12.02.01 To fetch, bring, bear, conduct
wegfarende 05.12.01.01 To go on a journey/expedition, travel

wegfērend 05.12.01.01 To go on a journey/expedition, travel
wegfērende 05.10.04.03 Presence; 05.12.01.01 To go on a journey/expedition, travel
wegfōr 05.12.05.03.03 To depart, leave, set out
weggedāl 05.12.01.03.01 A means of access
weggelǣte 05.12.01.03.01 A means of access
weggesīþa 12.04.01.02 A fellow traveller, companion
weggewit 02.08.11.02 Mental weakness
weglā 08.01.03.04.01 Complaint, lamentation
weglēas 05.12.01.03.02 Impasse, want of a road; 06.01.07.07.02 Impossible
weglēast 05.12.01.03.02 Impasse, want of a road
wegnest 04.01.02.04 Abundance of food; 16.02.04.07.06.01 Last rites
wegrēaf 14.02.01.02.01 Open robbery, rapine, pillage
wegtwislung 05.12.01.03.01 A means of access
wegu 05.12.01.06 Vehicle
wel 03.03.04.01 Much; 03.03.06 Wholeness; 07.02 Goodness; 08.01.01.03.08 Happiness, well-being, prosperity; 08.01.01.03.09.02 Pleasantly, agreeably; 11.03.02 Advancement, progress; 11.07.03 Use, advantage, profit; 11.12.01 Absence of restraint, freedom
wel bescēawod 11.02.03 Forethought, care
wel hwā 03.04.03.01 Someone/something
wel hwæt 03.04.03.01 Someone/something

wel lā (wel) 08.01.03.04.01 Complaint, lamentation
wel līcian 03.03.04.02 A sufficiency, sufficient supply
wel (ge)līcian 08.01.01.03.05 Pleasure, delight
wel līciendlīce 08.01.01.03.09.02 Pleasantly, agreeably
wel on hand gān 08.01.01.03.08 Happiness, well-being, prosperity
wel gesund 11.05.02.02.01 Greetings, courteous terms of address
wel swēgende 18.02.07 Music
wel wīde 05.10.04.03 Presence
wela 03.03.04.02.01 Abundance; 08.01.01.03.08 Happiness, well-being, prosperity; 15.01.03 Treasure, riches, wealth
welan (ge)gadrian 15.01.05 Possession of wealth
wēland 16.01.06.01 Northern gods
welboren 12.01.01.06.06 Gentle birth, nobility
welcweþan 08.01.02.01 Favour, kindness, grace
weldǣd 08.01.02.01 Favour, kindness, grace; 11.07 Use (made of things), service
weldōn 08.01.01.03.09.03 To make glad
weldōnd 08.01.02.01 Favour, kindness, grace
weldōnde 12.08.02.02 Righteousness, rectitude
weldōnnes 08.01.02.01 Favour, kindness, grace
weler 02.04.03.01.03.06 Mouth; 03 Material, matter, substance
weleþig 15.01.05 Possession of wealth
welfremmend 08.01.02.01 Favour, kindness, grace

welfremming 08.01.02.01 Favour, kindness, grace
welfremnes 08.01.02.01 Favour, kindness, grace
welga 11.05.02.02.01 Greetings, courteous terms of address
welgecwēme 08.01.01.03.09.01 Pleasant, agreeable
welgecwēmedlic 08.01.01.03.09.01 Pleasant, agreeable
welgecwēmnes 08.01.01.03.09 Pleasantness, agreeableness
wel(ge)dōn 08.01.02.01 Favour, kindness, grace
welgedōn 12.08.02.02 Righteousness, rectitude
wel(ge)hwǣr 05.10.04.03 Presence
welgelǣred 06.01.06.02.03.04.04 Under instruction, being taught
wel(ge)līcod 08.01.01.03.09.01 Pleasant, agreeable
wel(ge)līcwirþe 08.01.01.03.09.01 Pleasant, agreeable
welgelīcwirþnes 08.01.01.03.09 Pleasantness, agreeableness
welgestemned 18.02.07.01 Singing, song
welgetȳd 06.01.06.02.03.04.04 Under instruction, being taught
wel(ge)þungen 07.08.01 Nobility (of character, rank, etc.)
welgewende 08.01.01.03.08.02 Good fortune, success
welhǣwen 03.01.14 A colour
welhold 12.01.01.12 Loyalty
(ge)welhwǣr 05.10.04.03 Presence
welhwæs 03.03.06.02 Fullness
(ge)welhwilc 03.04.03.01 Someone/something
welig 02.01.03.01 Fertility, plenty; 02.07.03.05 Particular trees/shrubs (alphabetical order); 15.01.05 Possession of wealth
weligian 03.03.04.02.01 Abundance
(ge)weligian 03.03.04.02.01 Abundance; 10.03.08 Bountifulness, munificence; 15.01.05 Possession of wealth
geweligian 07.08.08 Nobleness, honour, glory
weligstedende 03.03.04.02.01 Abundance
wellibbende 12.08.02.01 Goodness, excellence, virtue
wellīcian 08.01.01.03.09.03 To make glad
wellīcung 08.01.01.03.09 Pleasantness, agreeableness
wellwill 01.01.03.01.01.07 Spring, fountain, well
welmanig 03.03.04.01.02 A great number, multitude
welrūmlīce 08.01.02.01 Favour, kindness, grace
welrūmmōd 08.01.02.01 Favour, kindness, grace
welstincende 02.05.08.02 Pleasant smell, fragrance, perfume
welung 05.12.05.04 To rotate, turn round, revolve
welweorþe 07.08.01 Nobility (of character, rank, etc.)
welwillende 08.01.02.01 Favour, kindness, grace; 12.07.04 Truth, righteousness, justice, equity
welwillendlīce 08.01.02.01 Favour, kindness, grace
welwille(n)dnes 08.01.02.01 Favour, kindness, grace
welwilnes 08.01.02.01 Favour, kindness, grace
welwyrcend 12.08.02.02 Righteousness, rectitude

welwyrcende 12.08.02.02 Righteousness, rectitude
wēman 09.06.02.01.05 Proclamation, spreading abroad
(ge)wēman 06.02.06.03.04 Allurement
(ge)wēman fram 06.02.06.03.01 To dissuade (from)
wēmend 09.06.02.01.06.01 A messenger
wēmere 12.08.08.01.02.01.01 An adulterer/-ess, whore, prostitute
(ge)wemman 07.03.02 Ill, harm, hurt; 12.08.06.01.04.01 To mislead, seduce, lead astray; 16.02.04.14 Sacrilege
gewemman 02.08.04.02.01 A maimed man; 05.06 Destruction, dissolution, loss, breaking; 05.09.05 Ceasing, decline, fall off; 12.08.08.01.02.01 Fornication, adultery
gewemmedlic 12.08.06.01.02 Lacking moral good
gewemmedlīce 12.08.08.01.02 Unchastity, incontinence
gewemmednes 02.08.04.02 Blemish, disfigurement; 03.02.01.01 Decay, corruption, rottenness; 12.08.06.01 Error, wrong conduct, erroneous practice; 12.08.06.01.01 Pollution, impairment; 12.08.08.01.02 Unchastity, incontinence
wemmend 12.08.08.01.02 Unchastity, incontinence
(ge)wemmend 12.08.08.01.02.01 Fornication, adultery
gewemmend 12.08.08.01.02.01.03 Unnatural sexual behaviour
gewemmende 12.08.08.01.02 Unchastity, incontinence
gewemme(n)dlic 03.02.01.01 Decay, corruption, rottenness
gewemmendlic 12.08.06.01.02 Lacking moral good; 12.08.08.01.02 Unchastity, incontinence
wemming 12.08.06.01.01 Pollution, impairment
(ge)wemming 12.08.08.01.02 Unchastity, incontinence
gewemming 12.08.06.01.01 Pollution, impairment; 16.02.04.14 Sacrilege
wemnes 12.08.06.01.01 Pollution, impairment
wēn 06.01.07.06.01 To accept as the result of enquiry, suppose; 06.01.07.07.01 Likelihood, probability, chance; 06.01.08.02 Hope, expectation; 07.01 Appraisal, appraising
wēn is þæt 06.01.07.07.01 Likelihood, probability, chance
gewēn 05.10.05.04.08 Crookedness, a crooked place
wēna 06.01.07.06.01 To accept as the result of enquiry, suppose; 06.01.08.02 Hope, expectation
wēnan 06.01.08 Expectation; 06.01.08.05.01 Amazement, astonishment, wonder, admiration
wēnan tō 06.01.08 Expectation
(ge)wēnan 06.01.07.06.01 To accept as the result of enquiry, suppose; 07.01 Appraisal, appraising
gewēnan 06.01.08.02 Hope, expectation
wenbȳl 02.08.05.01 Swelling
wencel 02.03.01.04 Child; 12.01.01.09 Bondage, slavery
wend 05.02.01 Condition, state of affairs, situation
wendan 05.03.02.01.01 An event, occurrence
wendan on 12.05.04 Strife, hostility
(ge)wendan 05.12.01 To go, progress, travel (usually on land); 05.12.02 To

move, set in motion; 05.12.02.08 To give a different direction to, turn; 05.12.05 To move and change direction, turn; 05.12.05.03 To travel away (from); 05.12.05.03.03 To depart, leave, set out; 05.13 Changeableness, change; 09.04.03.01 A translation

(ge)wendan tō 06.01.01.02 Care, attention, observation

gewendan 02.07.01 To grow; 05.12.05.11.01 To return; 11.01.05 Accomplishment, fulfilment

gewendan tō 05.13 Changeableness, change

wende 05.10.06.02.02 Curvature, bend, twist

wendedlic 05.13 Changeableness, change

(ge)wend(ed)nes 05.13 Changeableness, change

wendelsǣ 01.01.03.01.02.03 Sea in particular area

wendend 05.12.05.04 To rotate, turn round, revolve

wendende 05.12.05.04 To rotate, turn round, revolve

wendere 09.04.03.01 A translation

wendlas/-e 02.03.03.06.05 Scandinavian

wendsum 05.10.06.02.02 Curvature, bend, twist

wendung 02.08.08.04 Pain in stomach; 05.12.05.04 To rotate, turn round, revolve; 05.13 Changeableness, change

gewēne 06.01.07.07.01 Likelihood, probability, chance

wēnendlic 06.01.08.02 Hope, expectation

wenian mid wynnum 10.03.08 Bountifulness, munificence

wenian tō wiste 04.01.02.04.05 Entertainment with food

(ge)wenian 04.01.01.02 Act/action of sucking; 05.12.02.02 To carry off, remove; 06.01.06.02.03.04.03 To teach, instruct; 06.02.06.03.04 Allurement

gewenian 11.05 Natural/proper way/manner/mode of action

gewenian tam 04.02.05.04 To tame, break in (animals)

wēnlic 03.06.03 Congruity, fitness, suitability; 07.10.01 Elegance, beauty, comeliness

wēnlīce 07.10.01 Elegance, beauty, comeliness

wenn 02.08.05.01 Swelling

wenncīcen 02.08.05.02 Particular inflammation/swelling

wennsealf 02.08.12.02.07 Remedies for specific parts (head to toe)

wenspryng 02.08.05.02 Particular inflammation/swelling

wentas 02.03.03.05.01.07 People of Monmouthshire

wēnum 06.01.08.02 Hope, expectation

wēnung 05.03.02.01 Chance, hap, event; 06.01.07.06.02.01 Doubt, uncertainty; 06.01.08.02 Hope, expectation

wēnunga/-e 06.01.07.07.01 Likelihood, probability, chance

wenwyrt 02.07.11 Plants/flowers (alphabetical order)

wēoce 17.05.03 Sources of fire/light

wēod 02.07 A plant

wēodhōc 04.02.04.06.05 A hoe

wēodian 04.02.04.02.01 To prepare land/soil

wēodmōnaþ 05.11.03.01.03.01 Specific months

wēodung 04.02.04.02.01 To prepare land/soil
wēofod 16.02.05.03.04 Part of temple containing altar/idol
wēofodbōt 14.05.04.01 A fine
wēofodheorþ 16.02.05.03.04 Part of temple containing altar/idol
wēofodhrægl 16.02.05.05.09 Cloths
wēofodscēat(a) 16.02.05.05.09 Cloths
wēofodsteall 16.02.05.03.04 Part of temple containing altar/idol
wēofodþegn 16.02.03.02.07.01 A priest of a church or minster
wēofodþēnung 16.02.04.03.01 A rite, ceremony
wēofodwiglere 16.01.04.06 Divination, augury
weofung 04.04 Weaving
wēohsteall 16.02.05.03.04 Part of temple containing altar/idol
weolme 07.02.04 Excellence
weoloc 02.06.06.04.01.01 Cockle, whelk; 03.01.14.05 Red/redness; 04.01.02.01.02.07 Fish
weolocbasu 03.01.14.05 Red/redness
weolocrēad 03.01.14.05 Red/redness
weolocscyll 02.06.06.04.01.01 Cockle, whelk
weoloctælg 03.01.14.05 Red/redness
weorc 08.01.03.07.03 Suffering, torment, pain; 11.01 Action, doing, performance; 17.02 Work, occupation, employment
(ge)weorc 05.03.02 Event, issue, result; 11 Action, operation; 11.01 Action, doing, performance; 11.01.01 Practice, exercise, doing; 11.03 Endeavour; 11.04.02 Skill, skilfulness; 13.02.06 A fortification; 17 Work, doings, actions, labour; 17.02.04 Trade, calling, craft, aptitude
weorccræft 11.04.01 An aptitude, bodily skill
weorcdǣd 11.01 Action, doing, performance
weorcdæg 05.11.03.01.05 A day
weorce 11.11 Difficulty
weorce wesan 08.01.03.07.02.01 Injury, offence
weorcful 11.02.01 Energy, vigour, vigorous action; 17 Work, doings, actions, labour
weorcgerēfa 17.02.01 Management of work
weorchūs 17.02.01 Management of work
weorcland 15.01.01 Landed property
weorcmann 17.02.01 Management of work
weorcnȳten 02.06.02.01.03 Cattle
weorcrǣden 14.01.05 Service, obligation, duty
weorcsige 08.01.01.03.08.02 Good fortune, success
weorcstān 04.05.01.01 Masonry, building in stone
weorcsum 04.06.02.06 Poison
weorcþēow 12.01.01.09 Bondage, slavery
weorcūhta 16.02.04.05.02 The hour or service of Matins
weorcum 06.01.07.01 Correct, right, free from error
weorcwisung 17.02.01 Management of work
weorcwyrþe 02.08.01 Sound physical condition
weorf 02.06.02 Domestic animals, livestock; 02.06.02.01.01 Ass
weorftord 02.06.02.01.03 Cattle
(ge)weornian 05.09 Weakness
weorp 18.02.02 Play, (athletic) sport

weorp/wyrp 05.12.02.07 To throw, cast, toss
geweorp 05.12.02.07 To throw, cast, toss
weorpan 03.01.16.05 A sprinkling
weorpan on 14.03.03.01 Accusation
weorpan tō handa 05.12.02 To move, set in motion
weorpan ūp 05.10.05.04.14 An opening, aperture
(ge)weorpan 05.06.09 Act of striking; 05.12.02.07 To throw, cast, toss
(ge)weorpan in 05.12.02.07 To throw, cast, toss
(ge)weorpan in/on 05.12.02.07 To throw, cast, toss
(ge)weorpan of/ūt 05.12.02.04 To cast out, drive away
geweorpan 05.10.04 Place, room; 05.11 A time, period of time
geweorpan handa on 10.04.01 To hold, have
geweorpan mid grīne 05.12.02.07 To throw, cast, toss
weorpere 18.02.03.01 A combatant, athlete
weorpetung 07.06.01 Pride, arrogance
weorpian 05.09 Weakness
weorþ 07.04 Consideration, esteem; 07.04.01 (Of persons) worth/value, worthiness; 07.04.02 Merit, desert(s); 07.08.02 Honour, glory; 12.01.01.06.05 Nobility, noble condition; 12.07 An obligation, bounden duty; 12.07.01 One's due, natural place or position; 14.01.04 A legal right; 14.03.03.09.02 Atonement; 15.02 Worth, value
(ge)weorþ 15.02 Worth, value
weorþan æfterweard 05.12.05.10 To go behind, follow
weorþan behworfen 05.03.02 Event, issue, result
weorþan genge 05.11.07.02 The present (time)
weorþan tō nāuhte 05.07 Ending of existence, end of world
weorþan gewær 06.01.06 Understanding, knowledge, cognizance
(ge)weorþan 05 Aught, anything, something; 05.12.05.02 To go/travel towards, come, approach
(ge)weorþan of 05.03.02 Event, issue, result
(ge)weorþan on 11.01.02 An undertaking
(ge)weorþan (on/tō) 05 Aught, anything, something
(ge)weorþan (on) 05 Aught, anything, something
(ge)weorþan tō 05.02.02 Nature, established order of things; 05.03.02 Event, issue, result
geweorþan 03.06.03 Congruity, fitness, suitability; 05.03.02.01.01 An event, occurrence; 09.07.04.01 Confirmation, agreement; 10.01 Fact of belonging, possession by
geweorþan be 05.03.02 Event, issue, result
weorþere 16.02.04 Worship, honour, praise
weorþful 07.02.04.03 Nobleness, excellence, nobility, magnificence; 07.04 Consideration, esteem; 07.08.02 Honour, glory; 12.01.01.06.05 Nobility, noble condition; 12.07.01 One's due, natural place or position
weorþfullic 07.02.04.03 Nobleness, excellence, nobility, magnificence
weorþfullīce 07.02.04.03 Nobleness, excellence, nobility, magnificence;

07.04 Consideration, esteem; 07.08.02 Honour, glory; 12.07.01 One's due, natural place or position

weorþfulnes 07.02.04.03 Nobleness, excellence, nobility, magnificence

weorþgeorn 07.08.01 Nobility (of character, rank, etc.)

weorþian 06.01.01.02 Care, attention, observation; 07.07.03 Flattery; 07.08.03 Honour, veneration; 07.08.05 Glorifying, making great, glorification; 11.02.02.02.01 Attention, cultivation; 15.04.01 Lending of money; 16.02.04.03.01 A rite, ceremony; 17 Work, doings, actions, labour

(ge)weorþian 07.08.02 Honour, glory; 15.02 Worth, value; 16.02.04 Worship, honour, praise; 16.02.04.03.03 Singing, church singing; 16.02.04.04.02 A feast-day, holy day

geweorþian 07.04 Consideration, esteem; 07.08.06 Exaltation; 07.10.03 An adornment, decoration, ornament; 14.01.04 A legal right

weorþlic 07.02.04.03 Nobleness, excellence, nobility, magnificence; 12.07.01 One's due, natural place or position; 15.02.01 High/steep price

weorþlīce 07.02.04.03 Nobleness, excellence, nobility, magnificence; 07.04 Consideration, esteem; 12.07.01 One's due, natural place or position

weorþmetednes 06.01.08.05.01.01.01 An exercise of power, mighty work, miracle

weorþmynd 07.06.05 Pomp, splendour, magnificence; 07.08.02 Honour, glory; 07.08.05 Glorifying, making great, glorification; 07.08.09 Renown, fame, glory; 07.10.03 An adornment, decoration, ornament; 12.02 A public office

weorþnes 07.02.04.03 Nobleness, excellence, nobility, magnificence; 07.06.05 Pomp, splendour, magnificence; 07.08.01 Nobility (of character, rank, etc.); 07.08.02 Honour, glory; 12.01.01.06.05 Nobility, noble condition; 12.02 A public office

geweorþod 07.10.03 An adornment, decoration, ornament

weorþscipe 07.02.04.03 Nobleness, excellence, nobility, magnificence; 07.04.01 (Of persons) worth/value, worthiness; 07.06.05 Pomp, splendour, magnificence; 07.08.02 Honour, glory; 12.01.01.05 A leader, administrator; 12.02 A public office; 13.02.05.01 Victory; 16.01.01.01.01.02 Glory

weorþþearfa 15.01.06 Poverty, indigence

weorþung 07.08.03 Honour, veneration; 07.08.07 Glory, splendour, magnificence; 13.02.05.01 Victory; 16.02.04 Worship, honour, praise; 16.02.04.03 Ritual, rite, service; 16.02.04.07.06.03 Commemoration, festival

weorþungdæg 05.11.02.01.02 A time of celebration; 16.02.04.04.02 A feast-day, holy day

weorþungstōw 16.02.05.02 A holy place or sanctuary

weoruda drihten (/ealdor/helm, etc.) 16.01.01.01.01 The Almighty

weoxian 04.06.01 Clean

wēpan 08.01.03.04 Grief; 08.01.03.04.01 Complaint, lamentation

(ge)wēpan 08.01.03.04 Grief; 08.01.03.04.01 Complaint, lamentation; 08.01.03.04.02 Shedding of tears
wēpende 08.01.03.04.01 Complaint, lamentation; 08.01.03.04.02 Shedding of tears
wēpendlic 08.01.03.04 Grief
wēpendlīce 08.01.03.04.01 Complaint, lamentation
wer 01.01.03.01.03.02 Weir; 02.01.03.03.06 Sex, kind; 02.03.01.01 Male person, man; 02.03.01.08 Adult male; 06.02.07.06 Courage, boldness, valour; 09.03.02.03.01.01.03 Gender; 12.04.01.01 A company of people, fellowship, society; 12.09 Marriage, state of marriage; 14.03.03.09.02 Atonement; 15.02 Worth, value
weras 02.03.01 People
werbǣr 04.02.03.04.02.01 Types of pasture
wērbēam 04.05.02.04 A column, pillar
werbold 14.01.05 Service, obligation, duty
werborg 14.03.03.07 Security, pledge, bail
wercyn 02.03 Humankind
gewered in/mid 04.04.07 Trappings, equipment, garb
gewered mid 02.07.01 To grow
werednys 04.01.02.01.05.05 Spice
wereþ 01.01.02.01.04.01 Marsh, bog, swamp
werewulf 16.01.05.02 Species of devil, hellish race
werfǣhþ 14.02.01.01 Types of crime
(ge)wērgian 02.05.03.02 Weariness
wergild 14.03.03.09.02 Atonement; 14.05.04.01 A fine; 15.02 Worth, value
wergildþēof 14.02.01.02 Wrongful taking, theft
gewērgod 02.05.03.02 Weariness
wergulu 02.07.09.02 Particular fruits (alphabetical order)
werhād 02.01.03.03.06 Sex, kind
werian 02.04.04.03.03.01 Beard, whisker; 04.04.07 Trappings, equipment, garb; 05.12.02.08 To give a different direction to, turn; 11.10.01.01 Preservation from injury/destruction; 11.11.02 A hindrance; 11.11.03 Impeding of progress, prevention; 13.02.04 Defence, guard, protection; 13.02.08.03.01 Body armour, war gear
werian land 15.01.01.01 Holding of land
(ge)werian 04.02.04.02.01.02 To irrigate (plants, land)/channel (water); 10 Having, owning, possession; 14.03.03.01.01 Defence, reply
(ge)werian (wiþ) 13.02.04 Defence, guard, protection
gewerian 05.10.05.04.12 The condition of being covered; 14.04 Making of terms, agreement, convention
weriend 11.10.01 Protection, safekeeping
wērig 02.05.03.02 Weariness; 08.01.03.01 Despondency; 08.01.03.04 Grief; 08.01.03.07.01 Tedium
wērigferhþ 08.01.03.01 Despondency
wērigmōd 08.01.03.01 Despondency
wērignes 02.05.03 Exhaustion, faintness, weariness
wērigu 08.01.03.01 Despondency
wering 01.01.03.01.03.02 Weir
werlād 14.03.03.04 Oath-swearing
werlēas 12.09.03 Unmarried state

werlic 02.01.04.02 To grow, grow up; 02.03.01.01 Male person, man; 12.09 Marriage, state of marriage
werlīce 02.03.01.01 Male person, man; 06.02.07.01 Strength, fortitude
wermǣgþ 02.03.03.03 A nation, people
wermet 02.04.02.03 Height, stature or form
wermōd 02.07.11 Plants/flowers (alphabetical order); 04.01.03.05 A drink/beverage; 04.06.02.06 Poison
wernægel 02.08.05.02 Particular inflammation/swelling
werod 02.03.03.01 Body of retainers, household; 02.03.03.03 A nation, people; 02.05.07.03 Sweetness; 05.12.01.09.03 A voyage; 12.02.02 An assembly, meeting; 12.04.02 A crowding together, assembly; 13.02.10.01.02.02 Armed forces
werodian 02.05.07.03 Sweetness
gewerodlǣcan 04.01.02.02.04.06 To sweeten
werodlēst 13.02.10.01.02.02 Armed forces
werodlīce 18.02.07 Music
werodnes 02.05.05.04.01 Luxuries, dainties, good things; 02.05.07.03 Sweetness
werrēaf 04.04.07.01 Mode of dressing, fashion
werstede 01.01.03.01.03.02 Weir
wertihtle 02.02.04.04 Manslaughter, homicide; 14.02.01.01 Types of crime; 14.03.03.01 Accusation
werþēod 02.03.03.03 A nation, people
werþēode 02.03.01 People
wēsa 04.01.03.02 To drink heavily, get drunk

wesan 02 Creation; 02.01 Existence, life; 05.03.02 Event, issue, result; 10.01 Fact of belonging, possession by
wesan fornumen 05.06.01 Devastation, laying waste; 05.11 A time, period of time
gewesan ymbe 09.07.01 Contention, argument, strife of words
wēsan 02.08.05.02.01 Matter, purulence, pus
(ge)wēsan 03.01.16.06 A soaking, steeping
gewēsan 03.01.14.01 Dyeing
wēse 03.01.16.06 A soaking, steeping
wesend 02.06.03.01.04 Bison
wesendhorn 02.06.03.01.04 Bison
wesendlīce 02.01 Existence, life
wēsing 03.01.16.06 A soaking, steeping
wesle 02.06.03.01.14 Weasel
gewesnes 12.05.03.01 Quarrel, contentiousness, strife
west 01.01.01.04 West
westan 01.01.01.04 West
(ge)wēstan 05.06.01 Devastation, laying waste
westane 01.01.01.04 West
westannorþan 01.01.01.01.02 North-west
westansūþanwind 01.03.01.05.01 Winds from particular points
westanweard 01.01.01.04 West
west(an)wind 01.03.01.05.01 Winds from particular points
westcentingas 02.03.03.05.01.03 Kentish people
westdǣl 01.01.01.04 West
westdene 02.03.03.06.05 Scandinavian
wēste 01.01.02.01.06 Wild/uncultivated land; 02.01.03.02 Barrenness, sterility; 03.03.08 Emptiness; 05.06.01 Devastation, laying waste

wēste land 01.01.02.01.06 Wild/uncultivated land

wēsten 01.01.02.01.06 Wild/uncultivated land; 12.06.03.01 Waste land, deserted place

wēstend 05.06.01 Devastation, laying waste

westende 01.01.01.04 West

wēstengryre 06.01.08.06.03 Cause of fear, terror, horror

wēstensetla 16.02.03.03.04 A solitary (anchorite, hermit)

wēstenstaþol 01.01.02.01.06 Wild/uncultivated land; 12.06.03.01 Waste land, deserted place

wester 01.01.01.04 West

westerne 01.01.01.04 West

wēste(r)nlic 16.02.03.03.04 A solitary (anchorite, hermit)

west(e)weard 01.01.01.04 West

westhealf 01.01.01.04 West

wēstig 01.01.02.01.06 Wild/uncultivated land; 12.06.03.01 Waste land, deserted place

westlang 01.01.01.04 West

westmearc 05.10.05.04.11.01 A bound, limit

westmest 01.01.01.04 West

wēstnes 01.01.02.01.06 Wild/uncultivated land; 12.06.03.01 Waste land, deserted place

westnorþ 01.01.01.01.02 North-west

westnorþlang 01.01.01.01.02 North-west

westnorþwind 01.03.01.05.01 Winds from particular points

westrīce 12.06 A province, country, territory

westrihte(s) 01.01.01.04 West

westrodor 01.02.01 Heaven(s), sky

westsǣ 01.01.03.01.02.03 Sea in particular area

westseaxe 12.06.01.01 England

westseaxe (-an) 02.03.03.05.01.10 Saxons

westseaxena land/rīce 12.06.01.01 England

westsūþende 01.01.01.02.02 South-west

westsūþwind 01.03.01.05.01 Winds from particular points

westwēalas 02.03.03.05.02 The British/Welsh/Bretons

westweard 01.01.01.04 West

westweg 05.12.01.03.01 A means of access

westwegas 01.01.01.04 West

wēþan 05.12.04 Absence of movement, stillness

wēþe 02.05.05.04 Sensual pleasure; 08.01.02.01 Favour, kindness, grace; 18.02.07 Music

weþer 02.06.02.01.08 Sheep

gewēþnes 08.01.02.01.02 Gentleness

wibba 02.06.09.02.03 Beetle

wībora 13.02.10 The military, soldiers

wīc 01.01.02.01.01.03.02 Inlet in river/sea; 04.05.03 A dwelling-place, abode, habitation; 05.10.04 Place, room; 05.12.01.03.01.04 A lane, street; 12.06.02.01 A township; 13.02.06 A fortification; 13.02.07.04 A camp, encampment; 17.04.01 Sources of materials

(ge)wīcan 05.09.05 Ceasing, decline, fall off

gewīcan 05.12.05.03.03 To depart, leave, set out

wicca 16.01.04 Sorcery, magic, witchcraft

wicce 16.01.04 Sorcery, magic, witchcraft

wiccecræft 16.01.04 Sorcery, magic, witchcraft

wiccedōm 16.01.04 Sorcery, magic, witchcraft
wiccian 16.01.04 Sorcery, magic, witchcraft
wiccræft 11.04.01 An aptitude, bodily skill
wiccung 16.01.04 Sorcery, magic, witchcraft
wiccungdōm 16.01.04 Sorcery, magic, witchcraft
wicdæg 05.11.03.01.05 A day
wice 02.07.03.05 Particular trees/shrubs (alphabetical order)
wīce 12.01.01.05 A leader, administrator; 17.02.02 An office, function, employment
wīceard 04.05.03 A dwelling-place, abode, habitation
wīcfreoþu 13 Peace, tranquillity
wicg 02.06.02.01.06 Horse
wicga 02.06.09.02.03 Beetle
wīcgerēfa 12.01.01.05 A leader, administrator; 15.03 Exaction of tax/tribute
wīcherpaþ 05.12.01.03.01.05 Types of road/path
wīcian 05.12.01.09 To travel on water
(ge)wīcian 04.05.03.01 Habitation, sojourn; 04.05.03.02.02.09 A tent, pavilion; 13.02.07.04 A camp, encampment
wīcing 02.03.03.05.06 Viking(s); 05.12.01.09.03.03 Piracy
wīcingsceaþa 05.12.01.09.03.03 Piracy
wīcingsceaþe 05.12.01.09.03.03 Piracy
wīcnere 12.01.01.05 A leader, administrator
wīcnian 04.05.03.01 Habitation, sojourn; 12.01.01.08 Service

(ge)wīcnian 17.02.02 An office, function, employment
wīcnung 17.02.02 An office, function, employment
wīcscēawere 05.11.07.03.02.01 A precursor, one who goes before; 05.12.05.08 To go before, precede
wīcsteall 04.05.03.02.02.09 A tent, pavilion; 05.10.04 Place, room; 13.02.07.04 A camp, encampment
wīcstede 04.05.03 A dwelling-place, abode, habitation
wīcstōw 04.05.03 A dwelling-place, abode, habitation; 13.02.07.04 A camp, encampment
wīctūn 04.05.02.12.02 A vestibule, entrance, courtyard
wicþēnestre 12.01.01.08.01 A servant, attendant
wīcung 04.05.03 A dwelling-place, abode, habitation
wīd 03.03.04.01.01 Greatness, bigness, size; 05.10.01 Amplitude, spaciousness, vastness; 05.10.05 A space, span; 05.10.05.02.01 Diffusion, effusion, spreading; 05.10.05.03.01.01 Breadth, width across; 05.10.05.04.14 An opening, aperture; 12 Power, might
wīdan 05.10.05 A space, span
wīdan and sīdan 05.10.05 A space, span
wīdan fēore 05.11.01.01.01 Eternity
wīdan feorh 05.11.01.01.01 Eternity
wīdan ferhþ 05.11.01.01.01 Eternity
wīdbrād 05.10.01 Amplitude, spaciousness, vastness; 05.10.05.02 Extension, stretching
wīdcūþ 06.01.06.01.01 Knowledge; 12.01.01.06.05 Nobility, noble condition
wīde 03.03.05 Extent, degree; 05.10.01 Amplitude, spaciousness, vastness;

05.10.05 A space, span;
05.10.05.02.01 Diffusion, effusion, spreading
wīde and sīde 05.10.05 A space, span
wīde drēogan 05.12.01.02 To wander
wīdefeorh 05.11.01 Length/duration in time; 05.11.01.01.01 Eternity
wīdefeorhlic 05.11.01.01.01 Eternity
wīdeferhþ 05.11.01 Length/duration in time; 05.11.01.01.01 Eternity
gewidere 01.03.01 Weather, condition of atmosphere
gewiderian 01.03.01.01 Hot, fine weather
wīdfæþme 03.03.04.01.01 Greatness, bigness, size; 05.12.01.09.03.01.02 Of/concerning a ship, naval
wīdfarend 05.12.01.02 To wander
wīdfērende 05.12.01.01 To go on a journey/expedition, travel
wīdfloga 02.06.10.01.01 Dragon
wīdfolc 02.03.03.03 A nation, people
wīdgangol 05.12.01.02 To wander
wīdgenge 05.12.01.02 To wander
wīdgil 05.10.01 Amplitude, spaciousness, vastness; 05.12.01.02 To wander
wīdgilnes 05.10.01 Amplitude, spaciousness, vastness; 09.03.04.04 Discursiveness
wīdhergan 07.04.04 Praise, acclamation, applause
wīdian 05.10.05.02.02 Greater, bigger
wīdl 04.06.02.02 Foul, filthy, squalid
wīdlǣste 05.10.05 A space, span
wīdland 01.01 Surface of the earth; 12.06 A province, country, territory
wīdlāst 05.10.05 A space, span; 05.12.01.01 To go on a journey/expedition, travel; 05.12.01.02 To wander

wīdlian 12.08.06.01.04.01 To mislead, seduce, lead astray
(ge)wīdlian 04.06.02.02 Foul, filthy, squalid; 16.02.04.14 Sacrilege
gewīdlod 04.06.02.01 Dirty, unclean
wīdmǣre 07.03.05.01 Ignobility; 07.08.09 Renown, fame, glory; 07.09.03 Infamy, ignominy, shame
(ge)wīdmǣr(i)an 09.06.02.01.05.01 To spread, make known, proclaim, celebrate
(ge)wīdmǣrsian 07.08 Reputation, fame; 09.05.05 Exposure, revealing, revelation; 09.06.02.01.05.01 To spread, make known, proclaim, celebrate
(ge)wīdmǣrs(i)an 16.02.04 Worship, honour, praise
gewīdmǣrsian 07.04.04 Praise, acclamation, applause
gewīdmǣrsod 09.05.05.01 Showing, manifestation, display
wīdmǣrsung 09.06.02.01.05 Proclamation, spreading abroad
wīdnes 05.10.05.03.01.01 Breadth, width across
wīdnett 18.02.03.01 A combatant, athlete
wīdor 03.03.05 Extent, degree
gewidora bīdan 01.03.01.05 Wind
wīdrynig 01.01.03.03 Flow/flowing
wīdsǣ 01.01.03.01.02 Sea/ocean
wīdsceop 05.10.05.02.01 Diffusion, effusion, spreading
wīdscofen 05.10.05.02.01 Diffusion, effusion, spreading
wīdscriþol 05.12.01.02 To wander; 05.12.05.01 To go astray
wīdsīþ 05.12.01.01 To go on a journey/expedition, travel
wīdu/wīde 05.10.05.03.01.01 Breadth, width across

wīdwegas 05.10.05 A space, span
gewield 12.01 Power, control, sway
(ge)wieldan 12.05.06 Grasp, power, control, mastery; 12.05.06.01 Restraint, check, curb, control; 12.05.06.04 A trampling upon, subjection; 13.02.05.01.01 To overcome, conquer
(ge)wieldan tō 12.05.06.04 A trampling upon, subjection
gewieldan 04.02.05.04 To tame, break in (animals); 05.09 Weakness; 12.05.06.03 Necessity, constraint
(ge)wielde 12 Power, might
gewielde 12.05.06.04 A trampling upon, subjection
gewieldend 12.05.06.04 A trampling upon, subjection
wielding 12.01.01.01 Rule, domination, direction
wielincel 12.01.01.09 Bondage, slavery
wielisc 02.03.03.05.02 The British/Welsh/Bretons; 12.01.01.09 Bondage, slavery; 12.06.05 A foreign country
wiell(-a/-e) 01.01.03.01.01.07 Spring, fountain, well; 05.03 Source, origin
wielm 01.01.03.01.01 Moving water; 01.01.03.01.01.07 Spring, fountain, well; 01.01.03.01.02.06 Surging, rolling, heaving of waves; 02.08.05 Inflammation; 03.01.09 Heat; 03.01.09.02.01 Fire, burning; 05.08.02 Violence, force; 08.01.01.01 Ardour, fervour, strong feeling; 08.01.03.05.02 Anger
wielma 02.08.05 Inflammation
wielmfȳr 03.01.09.02 Fire, flame
wielmhāt 03.01.09 Heat

wierdan 11.11.02 A hindrance; 12.05.06.02.03 Trouble, disturbance; 14.02 Lawlessness
(ge)wierdan 02.08.04 Hurt, injury, damage; 08.01.03.07.02 Misery, trouble, affliction
wierdend 12.08.06.02.05.02 A sinner, transgressor
wierding 02.08.04 Hurt, injury, damage; 02.08.04.02 Blemish, disfigurement
wierdnes 08.01.03.07.02.01 Injury, offence; 12.08.06 Moral evil, depravity
wiergan 12.08.06.02.03.02 To do evil; 16.02.04.14.01 Blasphemy
wiernan 10.03.06 Withholding, keeping back; 12.03.06 Prohibition
(ge)wierpan 02.08.13 Recovery, growing better
wierping 12.05.07 Casting out, rejection
wiers 03.02.01 Decay, decline, corruption; 03.03.05.01.03 Inferior; 08.01.03.06 Adversity, affliction; 08.01.03.07.04 Severity, harshness; 12.08.06.01.03 Evilly, badly
wiersa 07.03 Evil
wierst 03.02.01 Decay, decline, corruption; 03.03.05.01.03 Inferior; 07.03 Evil; 08.01.03.06 Adversity, affliction; 12.08.06.01.03 Evilly, badly
gewif 02.08.07.02 Disorders of the eye; 05.04 Fate, lot, fortune, destiny
wīf 02.01.03.03.06 Sex, kind; 02.03.01.02 Female person, woman; 09.03.02.03.01.01.03 Gender; 12.09 Marriage, state of marriage
wīf begietan 12.09.02 Marriage ceremony
wīf habban 12.09.02 Marriage ceremony
wīf lǣdan 12.09.02 Marriage ceremony
wīf niman 12.09.02 Marriage ceremony
wīf onfōn 12.09.02 Marriage ceremony

wīfa wuldor/wynn 16.01.02.05.02.01 Mary, queen of heaven
wīfcild 02.03.01.04 Child
wīfcynd 12.08.08.01.02.01 Fornication, adultery
wīfcynn 02.01.03.03.06 Sex, kind; 02.03.01.02 Female person, woman
wīfcȳþþu 02.01.03.03 Sex, generation
wifel 02.06.09.02.03 Beetle
wifer 13.02.08.04.02 A shot, missile, dart, spear, javelin, etc.
wiffæst 12.09 Marriage, state of marriage
wīffæst wer 12.09 Marriage, state of marriage
wiffex 02.04.04.03 Hair
wiffrēond 08.01.02.03.01 An acquaintance, friend, associate
wīfgāl 12.08.07.01.01 Wantonness, sensuality, lasciviousness
wīfgehrine 02.01.03.03 Sex, generation
wīfgemǣdla 08.01.03.05.02 Anger
wīfgemāna 02.01.03.03 Sex, generation
wīfgeornes 12.08.08.01.02.01 Fornication, adultery
wīfgifta 12.09.02 Marriage ceremony
wīfhād 02.01.03.03.06 Sex, kind; 02.03.01.02 Female person, woman
wīfhand 02.03.02.03.02 Maternal descent
wīfhealf 02.03.02.03.02 Maternal descent
wīfhearpe 18.02.07.02.01 Percussion instruments
wīfhīred 16.02.03.03 A religious
wīfhrægel 04.04.07.01 Mode of dressing, fashion
(ge)wīfian (on) 12.09.02 Marriage ceremony
wīflāc 02.01.03.03 Sex, generation
wīflēas 12.09.03 Unmarried state
wīflēast 03.03.04.05 Insufficiency, lack, want

wīflic 02.03.01.02 Female person, woman; 09.03.02.03.01.01.03 Gender
wīflīce 02.03.01.02 Female person, woman
wīflufu 08.01.02.02.03 A loving relationship
wīfmann 02.03.01.02 Female person, woman; 02.07 A plant; 12.01.01.08.01 A servant, attendant
wīfmyne 08.01.02.02.03 A loving relationship
wifrian 05.12.05.05 To shake, quake, wag
wīfscrūd 04.04.07.01 Mode of dressing, fashion
wīfþegn 12.08.08.01.02.01.01 An adulterer/-ess, whore, prostitute
wīfþing 02.01.03.03 Sex, generation; 12.09 Marriage, state of marriage
wīfung 12.09.02 Marriage ceremony
wīg 05.06.01 Devastation, laying waste; 06.02.07.06 Courage, boldness, valour; 13.02.02 Battle; 13.02.10.01.02.02 Armed forces
wiga 05.06 Destruction, dissolution, loss, breaking; 13.02.10.01 A man, warrior; 13.02.10.01.01 A commander, officer
(ge)wīgan 13.02 War
wīgbǣre 13.02 War
wīgbealu 13.02 War
wīgbill 13.02.08.04.03 A sword
wīgblāc 03.01.12 Brightness, light; 13.02.08 Military equipment
wīgblēd 13.02.05 Luck in war
wīgbora 13.02.10.01 A man, warrior
wīgbord 13.02.08.03.01.06 A shield
wīgcræft 13.02.07 War-craft, art of war; 13.02.08.04.05 A warlike engine; 13.02.10.01.02.01 An armed force/band
wīgcræftig 13.02.08.04.03 A sword

wīgcyrm 02.05.10.03 Noise, tumult, uproar; 13.02.02 Battle
wīgend 13.02.10.01 A man, warrior
wīgende 13.02.02 Battle
wīgendra hlēo 12.01.01.04 A leader, ruler; 16.01.01.02.04 Protector, defender
wīgfreca 13.02.10.01 A man, warrior
wīgfruma 13.02.10.01.01 A commander, officer
wīggār 13.02.08.04.01 A spear
wīggetāwe 13.02.08 Military equipment
wīggild 16.02.01.06.01.01.01 An image, idol
wīggryre 06.01.08.06.03 Cause of fear, terror, horror
wīghaga 13.02.07.02 Order (of troops), array
wīgheafola 13.02.08.03.01.02 A helmet
wīghēap 13.02.10.01.02.01 An armed force/band
wīgheard 06.02.07.06 Courage, boldness, valour
wīghete 08.01.03.09.04 Hatred
wīghryre 02.02.04 Killing, violent death, destruction
wīghūs 13.02.06.01 Stronghold, fort/fortified town
wīghyrst 13.02.08 Military equipment
wīgian 12.05.04.01.01 Fighting, a fight
wigle 16.01.04.06 Divination, augury; 16.02.01.06.01.01 Pagan worship, idolatrous practice(s)
wīglēoþ 13.02.07.03 A war song
wiglere 16.01.04.06 Divination, augury
(ge)wiglian 16.01.04.06 Divination, augury
wīglic 13.02 War
wīglice tōl 13.02.08.04 Weapons, arms
wīglīce 13.02 War

wiglung 16.01.04.06 Divination, augury
wīgmann 13.02.10.01 A man, warrior
wīgnoþ 13.02 War
wigol 16.01.04.06 Divination, augury
wīgplega 13.02.02 Battle
wīgrād 05.12.01.03.01.03 A highway
wīgrǣden 13.02.02 Battle
wīgsigor 13.02.05.01 Victory
wīgsīþ 13.02.01 A military expedition
wīgsmiþ 13.02.10.01 A man, warrior; 16.02.01.06.01.01.01 An image, idol
wīgspēd 13.02.05.01 Victory
wīgspere 13.02.08.04.01 A spear
wīgsteall 13.02.06.01 Stronghold, fort/fortified town
wīgstrǣt 05.12.01.03.01.03 A highway
wīgstrang 13.02 War
wīgtrod 05.12.01.03.01.03 A highway
wīgþracu 13.02.02 Battle; 13.02.03.01 An attack, assault
wīgþrīst 06.02.07.06.02 Boldness
wīgwǣgn 05.12.01.06 Vehicle; 13.02.08.04.06 A chariot
wīgwǣpen 13.02.08.04 Weapons, arms
wīgweorþung 16.02.01.06.01.01 Pagan worship, idolatrous practice(s)
wīh 16.02.01.06.01.01.01 An image, idol
wiht 02 Creation; 05.10.06.02.02 Curvature, bend, twist; 12.06.01.01 England
gewiht 03.03.02 Measurement by weighing; 03.03.02.01 A weight, definite amount
wihte 06.01.07.07.02 Impossible
wihtland 12.06.01.01 England
wihtmearc 17.03.11 Other implements, etc.
wihtsǣtan 02.03.03.05.01.03 Kentish people

wihtware 02.03.03.05.01.03 Kentish people
(ge)wil 06.02.02.01 Will, wish, pleasure
wīl 11.04.02.01.01 Cunning, craft, craftiness, guile, wile
wīlbec 08.01.03.04.02 Shedding of tears
gewilbod 12.03.03 A command, bidding, order
wilboda 16.01.02.05.01 An angel
gewilc 01.01.03.01.02.06 Surging, rolling, heaving of waves
gewilcþ 01.01.03.01.02.06 Surging, rolling, heaving of waves
wilcuma 08.01.02.04.01 Visiting
wilcume 11.05.02.02.01 Greetings, courteous terms of address
(ge)wilcumian 11.05.02.02.01 Greetings, courteous terms of address
wildæg 08.01.01.03.08 Happiness, well-being, prosperity
wilddēor 02.06 Animal; 02.06.03.01.06 Deer, hart
wilddēoren 02.06 Animal
wilde 01.01.02.01.06 Wild/uncultivated land; 02.06 Animal; 02.07 A plant; 04.02.05.04 To tame, break in (animals); 05.08.02.01 (Of living creatures) fierceness, roughness; 12.01.01.12.02 Disobedience
wilde cyrfet 02.07.11 Plants/flowers (alphabetical order)
wilde nǣp 02.07.09.02.02.01 Edible root/bulb
wildecynn 02.06 Animal
wildefȳr 01.03.01.03.01.02 Lightning; 02.08.06 Skin disease, erysipelas
wildēor 02.06 Animal
wildēorcyn 02.06 Animal
wildēorlic 08.01.03.09.01.01 Savage
wildēorlīce 08.01.03.09.01.01 Savage

wildeswīn 02.06.03.01.05 Boar
wildgōs 02.06.08.06 Water bird
wilfægn 06.02.02.01 Will, wish, pleasure
wilfullīce 06.02.02 Will, disposition
wilgæst 08.01.02.04.01 Visiting
wilgedryht 08.01.02.03.01 An acquaintance, friend, associate
wilgehlēþa 08.01.02.03.01 An acquaintance, friend, associate
wilgesīþ 08.01.02.03.01 An acquaintance, friend, associate
wilgeþofta 08.01.02.03.01 An acquaintance, friend, associate
wilgiefa 12.01.01.04 A leader, ruler; 16.01.01.02.02 A giving (by Deity)
wilh/wiel 12.01.01.09 Bondage, slavery
wilhrēmig 08.01.01.03.06 Exultation, joy
wilhrēþig 08.01.01.03.06 Exultation, joy
(ge)wilian 05.05.03 Binding, fastening
wilige 17.03.12.01 A basket
wiligwīse 17.04.04 Fibrous materials
wiliht 02.07.03.05 Particular trees/shrubs (alphabetical order)
wil(l) 08.01.01.03.09 Pleasantness, agreeableness
willa 02.05.05.04 Sensual pleasure; 06.02 Will, the faculty of willing; 06.02.02 Will, disposition; 06.02.02.01 Will, wish, pleasure; 06.02.05 Will, desire, wish; 06.02.06 Mind, purpose; 06.02.07 Will, determination, resolution; 08.01.01.03.05 Pleasure, delight; 08.01.01.03.09 Pleasantness, agreeableness; 08.01.02.01 Favour, kindness, grace; 12.03.03 A command, bidding, order; 12.08.08.01 Eager, unseemly desire; 14.04.01 A deed, contract, agreement; 15.01.02.01 Inherited property

willan 05.02.02.01 Inclination; 05.11.07.04 Future, time to come; 06.02 Will, the faculty of willing; 06.02.02 Will, disposition; 06.02.05 Will, desire, wish; 06.02.06 Mind, purpose; 11.05 Natural/proper way/manner/mode of action; 12.03.03 A command, bidding, order; 12.03.05 Permission; 12.07.02.01 Covenant, assurance of faith, promise

willan habban 06.01.07.03 Truth of speech or thought, veracity; 09.06.02 A saying, speech, statement

willen 06.02.05.01 Strong liking for, devotion to

willende 02.05.05 Desire, appetite; 06.02.02 Will, disposition

willendlīce 06.02.02 Will, disposition

willes 06.02.01 Freewill, own will

willflōd 01.01.03.06 Flood

willgebrōþor 02.03.02.02.05.01 Brother

willgesteald 15.01.03 Treasure, riches, wealth

willgesweostor 02.03.02.02.05.02 Sister

willian 12.03.05 Permission

(ge)willian 02.05.05 Desire, appetite

willic 01.01.03.01.01.07 Spring, fountain, well

willīce 06.02.01 Freewill, own will

willodlīce 06.02.02 Will, disposition

willsele 04.05.03.02.02.02 Agreeable dwellings

willspell 09.06.02.01.06.02 Good tidings

gewillung 02.05.05 Desire, appetite

willwong 01 Earth, world

willwyrdan 07.07.03 Flattery

wiln 12.01.01.09 Bondage, slavery

gewilnes 06.02.02 Will, disposition

wilnian 05.02.02.01 Inclination

(ge)wilnian 02.05.05 Desire, appetite; 06.02.05.01 Strong liking for, devotion to; 08.01.03.09.08 Envy, jealousy; 12.03.04.01 Entreaty, solemn appeal

(ge)wilnian (tō) 06.02.05.04 Desire, eagerness

gewilniendlic 02.05.05 Desire, appetite; 02.05.05.01 Object of desire; 12.08.08.01 Eager, unseemly desire

wilnincel 12.01.01.08.01 A servant, attendant

wilnung 06.02.04.01 Want, need

(ge)wilnung 02.05.05 Desire, appetite; 08.01.02.02.03 A loving relationship; 12.08.08.01 Eager, unseemly desire

gewilnung 02.05.05.01 Object of desire; 04.01.01.04 Gluttony, overeating, greediness; 06.02.06 Mind, purpose

gewilsælig 08.01.01.03.08.02 Good fortune, success

wilsǣte (-an) 02.03.03.05.01.04 People of Wiltshire

wilsīþ 05.12.01.01 To go on a journey/expedition, travel

wilsum 08.01.01.03.09.01 Pleasant, agreeable

(ge)wilsum 06.02.01 Freewill, own will

(ge)wilsumlic 06.02.01 Freewill, own will

wilsumlīce 06.02.01 Freewill, own will; 16.02.01.11 Firmness in the law, piety, devoutness

wilsumnes 06.02.01 Freewill, own will; 16.02.01.11 Firmness in the law, piety, devoutness; 16.02.04.15 A vow

wiltīþe 08.01.01.03.04 Gladness, cheerfulness

wilþegu 04.01.02.01.01.01 Good/palatable food

wilweg 05.12.01.03.01 A means of access

wimpel 04.04.07.11 A headcloth, covering for the head
gewin drēogan 13.02 War
wīn 04.01.03.05.01.01 Wine; 16.02.05.09.01 Eucharistic elements
wīnærn 04.01.01.08 Eating place; 04.01.03.05.03 Tavern; 04.05.03.04 A closet, chamber, room
wīnbēam 02.07.09.02 Particular fruits (alphabetical order)
wīnbeger 02.07.09.02 Particular fruits (alphabetical order)
wīnbelg 04.01.02.02.06.05.04 Cup/bowl/basin
wīnberge 02.07.09.02 Particular fruits (alphabetical order)
wīnber(i)ge 02.07.09.02 Particular fruits (alphabetical order)
wīnbōh 02.07.09.02 Particular fruits (alphabetical order)
wīnbrytta 04.01.03.05.03 Tavern
wīnburg 12.06.02.01 A township
wīnburh 04.02.04.05.03 A wine-growing country
wīnbyrele 04.01.03.05.03 Tavern
wince 17.03.07 Tools for digging/grasping/pulling
wincel 05.10.06.04 A corner, bend, angle
wincettan 02.05.09.01 To open the eyes/be awake
wincian 02.05.09.01 To open the eyes/be awake; 09.03.03 A gesture, action, gesticulation
winclian 02.05.09.01 To open the eyes/be awake
wīnclyster 02.07.09.02 Particular fruits (alphabetical order)
wīncolc 04.01.03.05.04.02 A barrel, tun, vat, cask
wīncynn 04.01.03.05.01.01 Wine

wind 01.03.01.05 Wind; 02.04.06.07.03 Breath; 02.08.08.04.02 (Of stomach) disordered
gewind 02.07.09.02 Particular fruits (alphabetical order); 04.04.05 Woven material, fabric; 04.04.07 Trappings, equipment, garb; 05.12.01.03.01.01 A path, track
windǣddre 02.04.06.07.01 Wind-pipe
windan 01.01.03.01.02.06 Surging, rolling, heaving of waves; 05.10.06.02.03 A circular fold, coil; 05.12.03.01.01 Quick movement or movements; 05.12.05.04.01 (Of wheel, etc.) to roll, trundle; 05.12.05.05 To shake, quake, wag; 05.12.05.05.01 To wave, undulate; 06.02.07.05 Irresolution; 11.06.05 Hesitation, scruple; 17.02.04.01 Repairing, renewing
(ge)windan 05.05.03 Binding, fastening; 05.12.02.08 To give a different direction to, turn; 05.12.05.04.01 (Of wheel, etc.) to roll, trundle; 17.04.04 Fibrous materials
gewindan of 05.05.04 That loosens, loosening
gewindan ymbe 11.02 Occupation, activity, business
windbǣre 01.03.01.05 Wind
windbland 01.03.01.05 Wind
gewinde 01.03.01.05 Wind
windel 17.03.12.01 A basket
windelocc 02.04.04.03.03 Hair of head
windelstān 04.05.03.02.02.07 A tower
windelstrēaw 02.07.03.05 Particular trees/shrubs (alphabetical order)
windeltrēow 02.07.03.05 Particular trees/shrubs (alphabetical order)

windfylled 01.03.01.05 Wind; 05.06.01 Devastation, laying waste
windgeard 01.01.03.01.02 Sea/ocean
windgeat 05.10.03 A gap, cleft
wind(ge)fona 04.02.04.06.14.01 A winnowing fan
windgereste 04.05.03.02.02 Types of dwelling
windhladen 01.03.01.05 Wind
windig 01.03.01.05 Wind; 02.08.08.04.02 (Of stomach) disordered; 08.01.03.07.02 Misery, trouble, affliction
windrǣs 01.03.01.03.01 Storm, tempest
wīndred 04.01.03.05.01.01 Wine
wīndrenc 04.01.03 Drinking; 04.01.03.05.01.01 Wine
wīndrend 04.01.03.05.01.01 Wine
wīndruncen 04.01.03.02 To drink heavily, get drunk
windscofl 04.02.04.06.14.01 A winnowing fan
windsele 04.05.03.02.02 Types of dwelling
windswingel 04.02.04.06.14.01 A winnowing fan
windumǣr 02.05.10.04 To resound
windung 04.02.04.04.05.02 Chaff; 04.05.01.02.05 A hurdle
windwian 04.02.04.04.05.01 To winnow; 09.05.01 Inspection, examination
(ge)windwian 03.01.15.01 Inspiration, inbreathing
windwigceaf 04.02.04.04.05.02 Chaff
windwigsyfe 04.02.04.06.14.02 A winnowing sieve
wine 08.01.02.02.03 A loving relationship; 08.01.02.03.01 An acquaintance, friend, associate; 11.10.02.02.01 Care, interest in; 12.01.01.07 A follower
winedryhten 12.01.01.04.02 A lord, master; 16.01.01.02.04 Protector, defender
winegēomor 08.01.03 Bad feeling, sadness
winelēas 12.04.04 Solitude
winemǣg 08.01.02.03.01 An acquaintance, friend, associate
winescype 08.01.02.03 Friendliness, affection
winetrēow 12.09 Marriage, state of marriage
wineþearfende 12.04.04 Solitude
winewincle 02.06.06.04.01.07 Winkle
wīnfæt 04.01.03.05.04.02 A barrel, tun, vat, cask
gewinful 08.01.03.06 Adversity, affliction; 17.01 Strenuous effort, hard work
gewinfullic 17.01 Strenuous effort, hard work
gewinfullīce 17.01 Strenuous effort, hard work
wīngāl 04.01.03.02 To drink heavily, get drunk
wīngeard 02.07.09.02 Particular fruits (alphabetical order); 04.02.04.05.03 A wine-growing country
wīngeardbōg 02.07.09.02 Particular fruits (alphabetical order)
wīngeardhōc 02.07.09.02 Particular fruits (alphabetical order)
wīngeardhring 02.07.09.02 Particular fruits (alphabetical order)
wīngeardseax 04.02.04.05.03 A wine-growing country
wīngeardwealh 04.02.04.05.03 A wine-growing country

wīn(ge)drinc 04.01.03 Drinking; 04.01.03.05.01.01 Wine
wīngemang 04.01.03.05.01.01 Wine
wīnhāte 04.01.03.05.03 Tavern
wīnhorn 04.01.03.05.04 Drinking vessel
wīnhrēafetian 04.02.04.05.03 A wine-growing country
wīnhūs 04.01.03.05.03 Tavern
wīnian 04.02.04.05.03 A wine-growing country
wining 04.04.07.09 Breeches
wīnland 04.02.04.05.03 A wine-growing country
wīnlēaf 02.07.09.02 Particular fruits (alphabetical order)
wīnlic 04.01.03.05.01.01 Wine
wīnmere 04.01.03.05.04.02 A barrel, tun, vat, cask
winn 04.02.03.04.01 Meadow land/meadow
(ge)winn 12.05.03.01 Quarrel, contentiousness, strife; 12.05.04.01 Fighting, contention, warfare, strife; 13.02 War; 13.02.02 Battle
gewinn 01.01.03.01.02.04 State of sea; 02.08.03 Pain, bodily discomfort; 05.12 To move, be in motion; 08.01.03.03 Anxiety; 10.01.02 Acquisition; 11.02.02.02 Care, mindfulness, attention; 17.01 Strenuous effort, hard work
(ge)winna 12.05.04 Strife, hostility
gewinna 03.06.02.01 Contrariety, diversity; 08.01.03.09.05 Enmity; 12.05.01 Rivalry, contest
winnan 02.08.02 Disease, infirmity, sickness; 05.12.05.02 To go/travel towards, come, approach; 08.01.03.06 Adversity, affliction; 17 Work, doings, actions, labour; 17.01 Strenuous effort, hard work
winnan æfter/be 11.03 Endeavour
(ge)winnan 05.12.05.05 To shake, quake, wag; 08.01.03.07.03 Suffering, torment, pain; 10.01.02 Acquisition; 12.05.04.01 Fighting, contention, warfare, strife; 13.02 War; 13.02.05.01.01 To overcome, conquer; 13.02.05.01.02 To gain by fighting
(ge)winnan ongēan/wiþ 12.05.04.01 Fighting, contention, warfare, strife; 12.05.05 Resistance, repulsing
gewinnan 14.02.01.02.01 Open robbery, rapine, pillage; 17.01 Strenuous effort, hard work
(ge)winndæg 08.01.03.06 Adversity, affliction
gewinndæg 13.02.02 Battle
winnend 13.02.10.01 A man, warrior
winnende 08.01.03.03 Anxiety; 17 Work, doings, actions, labour
winnendlic 13.02.02 Battle
gewinnesful 17.01 Strenuous effort, hard work
gewinnesfullīce 17.01 Strenuous effort, hard work
(ge)winnstōw 18.02.03 A spectacle, display
wīnreced 04.01.01.08 Eating place
wīnreopan 04.02.04.05.03 A wine-growing country
wīnsæd 04.01.03.02 To drink heavily, get drunk
wīnsæl 04.01.01.08 Eating place
wīnsele 04.01.01.08 Eating place
wīnsester 04.01.02.02.06.05.04 Cup/bowl/basin
winstra 02.04.03.04.01.01 Hand
winstre 02.04.03.04.01.01 Hand
wīntæppere 04.01.03.05.03 Tavern

winter 01.03.01.04 Wintry weather, cold; 05.11.03.01 A year; 05.11.03.01.02.04 Winter
winterbiter 01.03.01.04 Wintry weather, cold; 03.01.11 Coldness, coolness
winterburna 01.01.03.01.01.03 Stream
winterceald 01.03.01.04 Wintry weather, cold
wintercearig 08.01.03 Bad feeling, sadness
winterdæg 05.11.03.01.05 A day
winterdūn 01.01.02.01.02.02.01 Hill; 04.02.03.04.02.01.02 Sheep pasture
winterfeorm 04.01.02.04.02 Feast
winterfylledmōnaþ 05.11.03.01.03.01 Specific months
winterfylleþ 05.11.03.01.03.01 Specific months
wintergegong 05.04 Fate, lot, fortune, destiny
winter(ge)rīm 05.11.06.02 Reckoning/computation of time; 05.11.06.02.02 A calculated space of time
wintergetæl 05.11.06.02.02 A calculated space of time
wintergewǣde 01.03.01.06.04 Snow
wintergeweorp 01.03.01.03.01 Storm, tempest
winterhām 04.05.03.03.01 Lodgings, quarters; 13.02.07.04 A camp, encampment
winterhūs 04.05.03.02.02 Types of dwelling
winterlǣcan 05.11.03.01.02.04 Winter
winterlic 05.11.03.01.02.04 Winter
winterrǣdingbōc 16.02.05.10.02 A lectionary
winterscūr 01.03.01.06.02 Rain

wintersetl 04.05.03.03.01 Lodgings, quarters; 13.02.07.04 A camp, encampment
wintersteal 02.06.02.01.06 Horse
winterstund 05.11.03.01.06 An hour
wintersufel 04.01.02.04 Abundance of food
wintertīd 05.11.03.01.02.04 Winter
winterwille 01.01.03.01.01.07 Spring, fountain, well
wīntīber 16.02.04.12 Sacrifice, a sacrifice
gewintīd 08.01.03.06 Adversity, affliction
gewintred 02.01.04.02 To grow, grow up; 02.01.04.03 Aging, growing old
wīntredde 04.01.02.02.07 Press; 04.01.03.05.01.01.01 Wine-press
wīntrēow 02.07.09.02 Particular fruits (alphabetical order)
wīntrēowig 02.07.09.02 Particular fruits (alphabetical order)
wintrig 01.03.01.04 Wintry weather, cold
wīntrog 04.01.03.05.01.01.01 Wine-press
wintru 05.11.03.01 A year
wīntunne 04.01.03.05.04.02 A barrel, tun, vat, cask
wīntwig 02.07.09.02 Particular fruits (alphabetical order)
wīnþegu 04.01.02.04.02 Feast
wīnwircend 04.02.04.05.03 A wine-growing country
gewinworuld 08.01.03.06 Adversity, affliction
wīnwringe 04.01.03.05.01.01.01 Wine-press
wiorþegend 16.02.04 Worship, honour, praise
wīpian 04.06.01 Clean
wīr 02.07.03.05 Particular trees/shrubs (alphabetical order); 04.04.04 A thread (of wool, etc.), fibre; 17.02.05.01 Ornamental object

wīrboga 17.02.05.01 Ornamental object
gewīred 17.02.05.01 Ornamental object
wīrgrǣfe 02.07.03.05 Particular trees/shrubs (alphabetical order)
wirgunggalere 16.01.04.01 Sorcery using incantation
wirnung 09.07.03.02 Refusal, denial
wirpels 05.12.01.03.01.01 A path, track
wīrrind 02.07.03.05 Particular trees/shrubs (alphabetical order)
wīrtrēow 02.07.03.05 Particular trees/shrubs (alphabetical order)
wīrtrēowen 02.07.03.05 Particular trees/shrubs (alphabetical order)
wīs 06.01.05.02.01.01 Sagacity; 06.01.06.01.01.02 To know, recognize; 11.04.02 Skill, skilfulness; 11.04.02.01.01 Cunning, craft, craftiness, guile, wile
wīsa 06.01.05.02.01.01 Sagacity; 06.01.06.02.01 A wise man, man of understanding or learning
(ge)wīsa 12.03 Direction, guidance
wīsbōc 09.03.07.07.03.04.02 A register, catalogue
wisce 04.02.03.04.01.01 Water meadow
wischere 16.01.04.06 Divination, augury
wīsdōm 06.01.05.02.01.01 Sagacity; 06.01.06.01 Knowledge, cognizance, knowing; 06.01.06.02 Knowledge, learning, erudition; 06.01.06.02.02.01.01 Philosophy; 16.01.01.01 Attributes of God
wise 04.02.03.04.01.01 Water meadow
wīse 02 Creation; 02.07.02.05 A shoot, sprout, tendril; 05.02.01 Condition, state of affairs, situation; 05.03.01.03 Reason, cause; 06.01.05.02.01.01 Reason, sense, discretion, prudence; 06.01.06.02.03.04 Teaching, instruction; 09.01.01 A speech, what is said, words; 11.05.02 Mode, manner, way, method, fashion, course; 12.03.01.01 Control, direction, regulation; 14.04.01 A deed, contract, agreement; 15.01.02.01 Inherited property; 18.02.07 Music
wīsfæst 06.01.05 Understanding, intellect; 06.01.05.02.01.01 Sagacity; 06.01.06.02 Knowledge, learning, erudition; 12.08.02 Integrity, absence of moral flaw
wīsfæstlic 06.01.05.02.01.01 Sagacity
gewīsfullīce 06.01.06.01.01 Knowledge
wīshycgende 06.01.05.02.01.01 Sagacity
wīshȳdig 06.01.05.02.01.01 Sagacity
(ge)wīsian 05.12.05.08.01 To go before and guide
gewislic 06.01.07.07.03 Certainty
wīslic 06.01.05.02.01.01 Sagacity
gewislīce 06.01.05.01.01 Clear to the understanding, plain; 06.01.05.02 Intelligence; 06.01.07.01 Correct, right, free from error; 06.01.07.02 Certainty, truth, what really is; 06.01.07.07.03 Certainty
wīslīce 11.04.02.01 Art, skill, contrivance, cunning
(ge)wīslīce 06.01.05.02.01.01.01 Reason, sense, discretion, prudence
gewīslīce 06.01.06.01.01 Knowledge
wīsnes 06.01.05.02.01.01 Sagacity
gewīsnes 06.01.05.01 Understanding; 06.01.06.02.03.04 Teaching, instruction
wisnian 03.01.18 Dryness (not wetness)
wisoc 04.02.03.04.01.01 Water meadow
gewiss 03.04.01 Singularity, peculiarity; 05.10.05.04.05 Straight, direct; 06.01.06.01 Knowledge, cognizance,

knowing; 06.01.07.01 Correct, right, free from error; 06.01.07.02 Certainty, truth, what really is; 06.01.07.07.03 Certainty; 09.03.07.07.03.04.01 A document, deed; 12.07.02.02 Truth, faithfulness, good faith, sincerity
gewisse 06.01.07.02 Certainty, truth, what really is
wīssefa 06.01.05.02.01.01 Sagacity
(ge)wissian 05.12.05.08.01 To go before and guide; 09.06.02.01.01 To make known, cause to know, inform; 12.03 Direction, guidance
gewissian 06.01.06.02.03.04.03 To teach, instruct; 14.01.06 A rule, order, precept, tenet, principle
wissigend 05.12.01.06 Vehicle
wissi(g)end 05.12.05.08.01 To go before and guide; 12.03 Direction, guidance
(ge)wissigend 14.01.06 A rule, order, precept, tenet, principle
wissung 05.12.05.08.01 To go before and guide; 12.01.01.01 Rule, domination, direction; 12.03 Direction, guidance
(ge)wissung 06.01.06.02.03.04 Teaching, instruction
gewissung 06.01.06.01.01 Knowledge; 06.01.07.07.03 Certainty
wist 02.01 Existence, life; 04.01.01.07 Feasting; 04.01.02.01 Food/sustenance; 04.01.02.04.02 Feast
wistful 02.01.03 Fruitfulness, fertility
wistfulgend 04.01.01.07 Feasting
(ge)wistfullian 04.01.01.07 Feasting
wistfullīce 02.05.05.04.01 Luxuries, dainties, good things
wistfullnes 04.01.01.07 Feasting
wistfullung 04.01.01.07 Feasting
wistfyllo 04.01.02.04 Abundance of food

wistgifende 02.01.03 Fruitfulness, fertility
gewistian 04.01.01.07 Feasting
gewistlǣcan 04.01.01.07 Feasting
wistmete 04.01.02.01 Food/sustenance
wīswylle 06.01.05.02.01.01 Sagacity
wīswyrdan 06.01.05.02.01.01 Sagacity
wīswyrde 06.01.05.02.01.01 Sagacity
gewit 06.01.05 Understanding, intellect
wita 06.01.05.02.01.01 Sagacity; 06.01.06.02.01 A wise man, man of understanding or learning; 06.01.06.02.03.02 Discipleship; 12.01.01.06.08 A person of rank, elder, great man; 12.02.02.02 A counsellor, advisor; 16.01.04 Sorcery, magic, witchcraft
(ge)wita 06.01.06.01.01 Knowledge; 11.03.01.01.01 Proof, demonstration; 14.03.03.03 Witness, testimony, attestation
gewita 02.05.09.05 To watch, observe, survey; 11.05.02.01 A standard, norm, ethos; 12.04.01 A fellow, companion, associate, comrade; 14.02 Lawlessness
witan 11.10.02.02 Watchful care, keeping guard
(ge)witan 08.01.01 A feeling, what is felt
(ge)witan (be) 06.01.06.01.01 Knowledge
gewitan 06.01.06.01 Knowledge, cognizance, knowing
wītan 02.02.03 To die, perish; 12.07 An obligation, bounden duty; 14.03.03.01 Accusation
(ge)wītan 05.12.05.03 To travel away (from); 05.12.05.03.03 To depart, leave, set out
gewītan 05.07 Ending of existence, end of world; 05.13 Changeableness,

change; 11.02.02.02 Care, mindfulness, attention; 11.06.03.01 Ill fortune, bad success; 11.06.06.01 Abandonment (of principle)
gewītan fram 15.01.02 Gift, transfer of property
gewītan (fram/of) 11.06.04 Abstention, abstaining from
gewītan of līce 02.02.03 To die, perish
wīte 02.08.03 Pain, bodily discomfort; 02.08.10.03.01 Plague, pestilence; 08.01.03.07.02 Misery, trouble, affliction; 14.05.02 Torment, punishment; 14.05.04.01 A fine; 14.05.06 Means/implement of torture; 16.01.05.01 Damnation, perdition, reprobation
(ge)wīte 14.05.02 Torment, punishment
wīteærn 14.05.08.01 Prison, confinement, durance
wītebend 14.05.06 Means/implement of torture
wītebendum belecgan 14.05.07 Binding, fastening with bonds
wītebrōga 06.01.08.06.02 Great fear, terror, horror
wītecyll 14.05.06 Means/implement of torture
wītedōmlic 06.01.08.04.01 Premonition, prophecy
wītefæst 12.01.01.09 Bondage, slavery
wītega 06.01.05.02.01.01 Sagacity; 06.01.06.02.01 A wise man, man of understanding or learning; 06.01.08.04.01 Premonition, prophecy; 16.01.04.06 Divination, augury; 16.01.04.06.04 Prophecy, divine speech; 16.02.01.12.01.01 Prophecy

wītegdōm 06.01.08.04 Foreseeing; 06.01.08.04.01 Premonition, prophecy
wītege 16.02.01.12.01.01 Prophecy
wītegeard 18.02.03 A spectacle, display
wītegestre 16.01.04.06 Divination, augury; 16.02.01.12.01.01 Prophecy
(ge)wītegian 06.01.08.04.01 Premonition, prophecy; 16.02.01.12.01.01 Prophecy
gewītegian 09.06.02.01 To tell, make known, declare, relate, announce
wītegiende 06.01.08.04.01 Premonition, prophecy
wītegung 06.01.08.04 Foreseeing; 06.01.08.04.01 Premonition, prophecy; 16.02.01.12.01.01 Prophecy
wītegungbōc 16.02.01.12.01.01 Prophecy
wītehrægl 04.04.07.01 Mode of dressing, fashion; 16.02.05.06 Ritual clothing
wītehūs 14.05.08.01 Prison, confinement, durance; 16.01.05.01 Damnation, perdition, reprobation; 16.02.04.16 Martyrdom; 18.02.03 A spectacle, display
wītelāc 14.05.02 Torment, punishment
wītelēas 14.01.03.02 Freedom from punishment or fine
wītelēaslīce 12.07.03.01 Impunity
wītelēast 14.01.03.02 Freedom from punishment or fine
wītelic 08.01.03.07.04 Severity, harshness
witena gemōt 12.02.02 An assembly, meeting
witende 06.01.06.01 Knowledge, cognizance, knowing
(ge)wītende 05.11.01.03.01 Mortal state, this life
(ge)wīten(d)lic 05.11.01.02 Shortness/brevity in time
gewitendnes 02.02 Death

gewitennes 05.11.02.01.01 An anniversary; 16.02.04.07.06.03 Commemoration, festival
wīteræden 14.05 Punishment; 14.05.04.01 A fine
gewiterian 09.06.02.01.01 To make known, cause to know, inform
wītescræf 16.01.05.01 Damnation, perdition, reprobation
wīt(e)steng 14.05.06 Means/implement of torture
wītestōw 16.01.05.01 Damnation, perdition, reprobation
wīteswinge 14.05.05 Physical punishments
wīteþēow 12.01.01.09 Bondage, slavery
wītewyrþe 14.03.03.09.01 Unfavourable judgement, condemnation
gewitfæst 02.08.11.01 Sound mind
wītigendlic 06.01.08.04.01 Premonition, prophecy
wītiglic/wītelic 14.05 Punishment
(ge)witlēas 02.08.11.02.01 Insanity, madness
gewitlēas 06.01.05.03.01.01 Dullness, folly, stupidity
witlēasnes 06.01.05.03 Want of understanding
(ge)witlēast 02.08.11.02.01 Insanity, madness
gewitlēast 06.01.05.03.01.01 Dullness, folly, stupidity; 06.01.05.03.03.01 Unreasonableness, foolishness, imprudence
gewitloca 06.01 The head (as seat of thought)
witmǣreswyrt 02.07.11.02 Unidentified plants (alphabetical order)
wītnere 14.05.02 Torment, punishment
witnes 06.01.06.02 Knowledge, learning, erudition
(ge)witnes 02.05.09.05 To watch, observe, survey; 06.01.06.01 Knowledge, cognizance, knowing; 14.03.03.03 Witness, testimony, attestation
witnesman 14.03.03.03 Witness, testimony, attestation
gewitnian 09.06.02.01.04 A confession, declaration
(ge)wītnian 14.05 Punishment; 14.05.01 Correction, discipline
wītnigend 14.05 Punishment
wītnigende 14.05 Punishment
wītnigendlic 14.03.03.09.01 Unfavourable judgement, condemnation; 14.05.02 Torment, punishment
(ge)wītnung 14.05.02 Torment, punishment
wīt(n)ungstōw 16.01.05.01 Damnation, perdition, reprobation
witod 06.01.07.01 Correct, right, free from error; 06.01.07.07.03 Certainty
(ge)witod 06.01.07.07.03 Certainty
witodlic 06.01.07.07.03 Certainty
witodlīce 06.01.07.07.03 Certainty
(ge)witodlīce 06.01.07.01 Correct, right, free from error
witolnes 06.01.05.02.01.01 Sagacity
(ge)witscipe 02.05.09.05 To watch, observe, survey
gewitscipe 14.03.03.03 Witness, testimony, attestation
(ge)witsēoc 02.08.11.02.01 Insanity, madness
(ge)witt 02.08.11.01 Sound mind
gewitt 02.05 Sensation, perception, feeling; 06.01 The head (as seat of thought); 06.01.05 Understanding,

intellect; 06.01.05.02 Intelligence; 06.01.05.02.01.01 Sagacity; 06.01.06.01 Knowledge, cognizance, knowing; 08.01.01 A feeling, what is felt; 12.07 An obligation, bounden duty
witter 06.01.05.02.01.01 Sagacity
wittig 16.01.01.01 Attributes of God
(ge)wittig 02.08.11.01 Sound mind; 06.01.05.02.01 Intelligent, sensible
gewittig 11.04.02 Skill, skilfulness
gewittiglīce 02.08.11.01 Sound mind; 06.01.03.01 Argument, reasoning
wittignes 06.01.05.02 Intelligence
wituma 15.02 Worth, value
witumbora 12.09.02 Marriage ceremony
witword 14.03.03.03 Witness, testimony, attestation
wiþ 03.03.06.01 A whole formed by joining; 05.10.05.04.02 Face, surface; 05.10.05.04.09 Side, quarter, direction; 05.10.05.04.09.04 Opposite (av); 05.13.04 Exchange, commutation; 06.02.06.01 An end, goal; 11.11.01 A physical difficulty, strait; 12.05.02 Hostility, contention, opposition
wiþ ... foran 05.10.05.04.09.01 Front
wiþ ælce hand 05.10.04.03 Presence
wiþ ēastan 01.01.01.03 East
wiþ sūþan 01.01.01.02 South
wiþ tacan 05.12.05.02.04 To go in, enter
wiþ þingian 09.01.04 Conversation, discussion; 09.07.02 Contradiction; 13.01.02 Reconciliation
wiþ westan 01.01.01.04 West
wiþæftan 05.10.05.04.09.02 Hinder part, rear
wiþblāwan 05.12.02.06.01 To push, drive

wiþbregdan 10.04.03 To take away, remove; 12.05.06.01 Restraint, check, curb, control
wiþcēosan 07.05.01 Censure, reproof, rebuke
wiþcoren 16.02.01.13.02 Evil, reprobate, damned
wiþcostian 07.05.01 Censure, reproof, rebuke
wiþcwedennes 09.07.02 Contradiction
wiþcweþan 09.05.03 An answer, reply; 09.07.02 Contradiction; 09.07.03.02 Refusal, denial; 12.05 Contradiction, opposition
wiþdrīfan 05.12.02.08 To give a different direction to, turn
wiþer 12.05.02 Hostility, contention, opposition
wiþerbersta 12.05.02 Hostility, contention, opposition
wiþerbreca 12.05.02 Hostility, contention, opposition; 16.01.05.02 Species of devil, hellish race; 16.01.05.02.01 The devil
wiþerbreca(-broca) 06.02.07.04 Obstinacy
wiþerbroca 12.05.02 Hostility, contention, opposition
wiþerbrocian 12.05.02 Hostility, contention, opposition
wiþerbrōga 16.01.05.02 Species of devil, hellish race
wiþercora 12.05.02 Hostility, contention, opposition; 12.08.06.02.05.02 A sinner, transgressor; 16.02.01.13 Evil-doing, transgression, sin
wiþercoren 12.08.06.02.03 (Of persons) wicked, evil-doing; 16.02.01.13.02 Evil, reprobate, damned
wiþercorennes 16.01.05.01 Damnation, perdition, reprobation

wiþercwedolnes 09.07.02 Contradiction
wiþercwedung 09.07.02 Contradiction
wiþercweþan 09.07.02 Contradiction
wiþercweþnes 09.07.02 Contradiction
wiþercweþol 09.07.02 Contradiction
wiþercwida 12.05 Contradiction, opposition
wiþercwiddian 08.01.03.05 Murmuring, complaint
wiþercwide 01.01.03.01.01.01 River; 05.12.02.06.01 To push, drive; 09.07.01 Contention, argument, strife of words; 12.05 Contradiction, opposition
wiþercwidennes 09.07.02 Contradiction
wiþercyr 05.13.02 A reversal
wiþerdūne 01.01.02.01.02.02.04 Cliff
wiþerflita 09.07.01 Contention, argument, strife of words
wiþerhabban 12.05.05 Resistance, repulsing
wiþerhliniende 05.10.05.04.04 A descent, slope, incline
wiþerhycgende 12.08.06.02.03 (Of persons) wicked, evil-doing
wiþerhȳdig 08.01.03.09.06 Hostility
wiþerian 08.01.03.05.02 Anger; 08.01.03.09.06 Hostility; 09.07.01 Contention, argument, strife of words; 09.07.02 Contradiction; 12.05.02 Hostility, contention, opposition
wiþerlǣcan 10.04.03.01 To take away, deprive of
wiþerlēan 10.03.05 Recompense, reward; 14.05.03 Retribution, requital
wiþerling 08.01.03.09.05 Enmity
wiþermāl 14.03.03.01.01 Defence, reply
wiþermēda 16.01.05.02.01 The devil
wiþermēde 12.08.06.01.02 Lacking moral good; 12.08.06.02.02 A bad man, inhuman person
wiþermēdnes 08.01.03.06 Adversity, affliction; 12.08.06.01 Error, wrong conduct, erroneous practice
wiþermēdo 08.01.03.06 Adversity, affliction; 08.01.03.09.05 Enmity; 12.08.06.01 Error, wrong conduct, erroneous practice
wiþermetan 03.06 Comparison
wiþermōd 12.05.02 Hostility, contention, opposition
wiþermōdnes 08.01.03.06.01 Affliction, misfortune, calamity
wiþerrǣde 03.06.02.01 Contrariety, diversity; 07.03.01.01 Abominable, detestable; 08.01.03.06 Adversity, affliction; 08.01.03.09.06 Hostility; 12.01.01.12.03 Rebellion, sedition
wiþerrǣdlic 09.03.02.02.01.03 An adverb
wiþerrǣdlīce 06.02.07.04.02 Perversity
wiþerrǣdnes 03.06.02.01 Contrariety, diversity; 08.01.03.06 Adversity, affliction; 08.01.03.09.06 Hostility
wiþerrǣhtes 05.10.05.04.09.04 Opposite (av)
wiþerriht 14.05.03 Retribution, requital
wiþersaca 08.01.03.09.05 Enmity; 12.01.01.12.03 Rebellion, sedition; 14.03.03.01 Accusation; 16.02.01.07 Apostasy
wiþersacend 16.02.04.14.01 Blasphemy
wiþersacian 16.02.01.07 Apostasy; 16.02.04.14.01 Blasphemy
wiþersacung 16.02.01.07 Apostasy; 16.02.04.14.01 Blasphemy
wiþersǣc 01.01.03.01.01.01 River; 05.12.02.06.01 To push, drive; 08.01.03.06 Adversity, affliction; 09.07.03.01 A denial; 12.05

Contradiction, opposition; 16.02.01.07 Apostasy
wiþersprecend 12.05 Contradiction, opposition
wiþerstǣger 05.10.05.04.04.01 Steep
wiþerstandan 12.05.05 Resistance, repulsing
wiþersteall 12.05.05 Resistance, repulsing
wiþerstede 05.13.04 Exchange, commutation
wiþersȳnes 05.12.05.11 To turn back, retreat
wiþertalu 14.03.03.01.01 Defence, reply
wiþertihtle 14.03.03.01.01 Defence, reply
wiþertrod 05.12.05.11 To turn back, retreat
wiþertȳme 03.06.02.01 Contrariety, diversity; 08.01.03.07.04 Severity, harshness
wiþerung 06.02.07.04 Obstinacy
wiþerweard 03.06.02.01 Contrariety, diversity; 05.12.05 To move and change direction, turn; 06.02.07.04.02 Perversity; 08.01.03.06 Adversity, affliction; 08.01.03.07 Unpleasantness; 08.01.03.09.05 Enmity; 08.01.03.09.06 Hostility; 12.01.01.12.03 Rebellion, sedition; 12.08.06.01.02 Lacking moral good; 16.02.01.05 Heresy, error, wrong belief
wiþerwearda 16.01.05.02.01 The devil
wiþerweardian 12.05.02 Hostility, contention, opposition
wiþerweardlic 08.01.03.06 Adversity, affliction
wiþerweardlīce 08.01.03.06.01 Affliction, misfortune, calamity; 12.05.06.02.03 Trouble, disturbance
wiþerweardnes 03.06.02.01 Contrariety, diversity; 07.06.01 Pride, arrogance; 08.01.03.06 Adversity, affliction; 12.05.02 Hostility, contention, opposition; 12.08.06.01 Error, wrong conduct, erroneous practice
wiþerwengel 12.05.02 Hostility, contention, opposition
wiþerwenning 12.05.03.01 Quarrel, contentiousness, strife
wiþerwinn 12.05.01 Rivalry, contest
wiþerwinna 08.01.03.09.05 Enmity; 12.05.01 Rivalry, contest
wiþerwinnan 12.01.01.12.03 Rebellion, sedition
wiþfaran 11.10.05 Escape
wiþfeohtan 13.02 War
wiþfeohtend 12.05.04 Strife, hostility
wiþfēolan 11.01.02 An undertaking
wiþferian 11.10.03 Salvation/deliverance from
wiþflītan 12.05.04.01 Fighting, contention, warfare, strife
wiþfōn 10.04.02 To grasp, take hold of
wiþforan 05.10.05.04.09.01 Front; 05.11.07.03.02 Earlier, antecedent
wiþgān 14.02 Lawlessness
wiþgangan 03.02.01 Decay, decline, corruption; 12.05.05 Resistance, repulsing
wiþgehæftan 13.02 War
wiþgemetnes 03.06 Comparison
wiþgeondan 05.10.04.04 Absence
wiþgrīpan 10.04.02 To grasp, take hold of
wiþgȳnan 09.05.03 An answer, reply
wiþhabban 11.11.02 A hindrance; 12.05.05 Resistance, repulsing
wiþhæftan 11.11.02 A hindrance

wiþheardian 08.01.03.09.10 Wrath, sternness, displeasure
wiþhindan 05.10.05.04.09.02 Hinder part, rear
wiþhogian 07.05 Disrespect, irreverence
wīþig 02.07.03.05 Particular trees/shrubs (alphabetical order)
wīþigett 02.07.03.05 Particular trees/shrubs (alphabetical order)
wīþigrǣw 02.07.03.04.03 A hedge/border
wīþigrind 02.07.03.05 Particular trees/shrubs (alphabetical order)
wīþigstybb 02.07.03.05 Particular trees/shrubs (alphabetical order)
wiþinnan 05.10.05.04.01 Inside, interior
wiþlǣdan 10.04.03 To take away, remove
wiþlǣdnes 14.02.01.02.01 Open robbery, rapine, pillage
wiþlicgan 12.05.05 Resistance, repulsing
wiþmetan 03.06 Comparison
wiþmētednes 06.02.06.02 A proposal, proposition, suggestion
wiþmeten(d)lic 09.03.02.03.01.01.05 Comparative
wiþmetennes 03.06 Comparison
wiþmeting 03.06 Comparison
wiþneoþan 05.10.05.04.02.02 Under, beneath
wiþobān 02.04.05.04.05.01 Collar-bone
wiþobend 02.07.11 Plants/flowers (alphabetical order)
wiþowinde 02.07.11 Plants/flowers (alphabetical order)
wiþre 12.05.05 Resistance, repulsing
wiþrēotan 08.01.03.05 Murmuring, complaint
wiþriend 08.01.03.09.05 Enmity
wiþsacan 09.07.03.01 A denial; 09.07.03.02 Refusal, denial; 10.03.06 Withholding, keeping back; 12.05.04.01 Fighting, contention, warfare, strife; 12.05.07 Casting out, rejection; 14.01.06 A rule, order, precept, tenet, principle
wiþsacendlic 09.03.02.02.01.03 An adverb
wiþsacung 12.08.03.01 Abstinence (from)
wiþsceorian 09.07.03.02 Refusal, denial
wiþscūfan 05.12.02.04 To cast out, drive away; 09.07.02 Contradiction
wiþsecgan 12.05.07 Casting out, rejection
wiþsēon 12.01.01.12.03 Rebellion, sedition
wiþsetnes 12.05.05 Resistance, repulsing
wiþsettan 12.05.05 Resistance, repulsing; 14.03.03.09.01 Unfavourable judgement, condemnation
wiþslēan 05.07 Ending of existence, end of world; 11.06.03 Failing, failure
wiþsprecan 07.05.03.02 Calumny, slander, insult; 09.01.04 Conversation, discussion
wiþsp(r)ecan 09.07.02 Contradiction
wiþspurnan 05.12.02.06.01 To push, drive
wiþstæppan 05.12.01.04 To go, proceed on foot
wiþstandan 05.10.04.01 Position, stance; 08.01.03.09.06 Hostility; 11.03.02.01 Efficacy, success; 11.11.02 A hindrance; 12.05.05 Resistance, repulsing; 15.02.04 Spending, disbursement
wiþstunian 05.12.02.06.01 To push, drive
wiþstyllan 05.12.05.11 To turn back, retreat
wiþstyltan 06.01.07.06.02.01 Doubt, uncertainty

wiþtēon 02.04.06.07.05 To breathe; 05.12.05.02 To go/travel towards, come, approach; 05.12.05.11 To turn back, retreat; 10.04.03 To take away, remove; 12.05.06.01 Restraint, check, curb, control

wiþtremman 05.12.05.11 To turn back, retreat

wiþþe 14.05.07 Binding, fastening with bonds; 17.03.10 Supports and fastenings

wiþþyddan 05.12.02.06 To push, impel, thrust

wiþufan 05.10.05.04.02.04 Above; 05.11.07.03.02 Earlier, antecedent

wiþuppon 05.10.05.04.02.04 Above

wiþūtan 03.03.08 Emptiness; 03.04.01 Singularity, peculiarity; 05.10.05.04.02.01 Exterior, outside of

wiþweorpan 12.05.07 Casting out, rejection

wiþwinnan 13.02 War

wiþwiþerian 12.05.05 Resistance, repulsing

gewixlan 05.13 Changeableness, change

wlacian 03.01.10 Tepidity, lukewarmness

(ge)wlacian 03.01.10 Tepidity, lukewarmness

wlaco 08.01.01.02.01 Want of interest or concern, indifference

wlacu/wlæc 03.01.10 Tepidity, lukewarmness

wlæc 03.01.10 Tepidity, lukewarmness

wlæclīce 08.01.01.02.01 Want of interest or concern, indifference

wlæcnes 03.01.10 Tepidity, lukewarmness

wlæffetere 09.02.03.02 Stammering

wlæffian 09.02.03.02 Stammering

gewlǣt 12.08.06.01.02 Lacking moral good

wlǣtlic 04.06.02.02 Foul, filthy, squalid

wlǣtta 02.08.04.02 Blemish, disfigurement; 08.01.03.09.04 Hatred

wlǣtung 02.08.04.02 Blemish, disfigurement; 02.08.08.04.02 (Of stomach) disordered

wlanc 06.02.07.06 Courage, boldness, valour; 07.06 Pride; 07.06.01.01 Proud, arrogant; 07.08.07 Glory, splendour, magnificence; 12.08.01 Magnanimity, greatness of soul

wlancian 07.06 Pride; 07.06.01.03 To be proud/arrogant

wlanclīce 07.06.01.02 Proudly, arrogantly

wlātere 02.05.09.05 To watch, observe, survey

wlātian 02.05.09.04 To see, look upon, behold; 07.03.01.03 To loathe, hate, abhor

wlātung 02.05.09.12 To show

(ge)wleccan 03.01.10 Tepidity, lukewarmness

gewlecced 03.01.10 Tepidity, lukewarmness

gewlenced 07.08.07 Glory, splendour, magnificence; 07.10.03 An adornment, decoration, ornament

wlenc(o) 08.01.01.03.08 Happiness, well-being, prosperity; 07.08.07 Glory, splendour, magnificence; 07.06.01 Pride, arrogance; 07.06 Pride

wlenc(u) 06.02.07.06.02.02 Boldness, daring

wlisp 09.02.03.03 Lisping

wlita 02.04.03.01.03 Face

wlītan 02.05.09.04 To see, look upon, behold

wlite 02.05.09.07 Form, appearance, aspect; 03.01.12 Brightness, light;

07.10 Beauty, fairness; 07.10.03 An adornment, decoration, ornament
wliteandet 09.06.02.01.04 A confession, declaration
wlitebeorht 03.01.12 Brightness, light; 07.10 Beauty, fairness
wliteful 07.10 Beauty, fairness
wlitelēas 07.10.02 Ugliness
wlitelīce 07.10.01 Elegance, beauty, comeliness
wlitescēawung 16.01.02.04 Paradise
wlitescīne 03.01.12 Brightness, light; 07.10 Beauty, fairness
wlitesēon 02.05.09.12 To show
wlitetorht 03.01.12 Brightness, light
wlitewamm 02.08.04.02 Blemish, disfigurement
wliteweorþ 14.03.03.09.02 Atonement
wlitig 07.02.04.03 Nobleness, excellence, nobility, magnificence; 07.10 Beauty, fairness
wlitige 07.10 Beauty, fairness
wlitigfæst 07.10 Beauty, fairness
wlitigian 07.10 Beauty, fairness
(ge)wlitigian 07.10 Beauty, fairness
gewlitigian 07.08.02 Honour, glory; 07.10.03 An adornment, decoration, ornament; 17.02.04 Trade, calling, craft, aptitude
wlitiglīce 07.10 Beauty, fairness
wlitignes 07.08.05 Glorifying, making great, glorification; 07.10 Beauty, fairness
wlōh 03.03.04.04 Littleness, smallness; 04.04.09 A fringe, border, hem
gewlōh 05.10.05.04.12 The condition of being covered
wlott 02.08.04.02 Blemish, disfigurement
wōci(g)e 04.03.02 A snare, trap, noose

wōcor 02.01.03.03.04 Offspring, race, breed, family, children; 05.01 Growth, increase, what springs up
wōd 02.08.11.02.01 Insanity, madness; 05.08.02 Violence, force; 08.01.03.05.02 Anger; 16.02.04.14.01 Blasphemy
wōda 02.08.11.02.01 Insanity, madness; 05.08.02 Violence, force
woddor 02.04.06.03.02.02 Throat/gullet
wōddrēam 16.01.05.02 Species of devil, hellish race
wōden 16.01.06.01 Northern gods; 16.01.06.02 Classical gods
wōdendrēam 02.08.11.02.01.02 Madness, frenzy, folly
wōdewistle 02.07.11 Plants/flowers (alphabetical order)
wōdfrec 04.01.01.03 Hunger
wōdheortnes 02.08.11.02.01.02 Madness, frenzy, folly
wōdlic 02.08.11.02.01.02 Madness, frenzy, folly
wōdlīce 02.08.11.02.01.02 Madness, frenzy, folly; 16.02.04.14.01 Blasphemy
wōdnes 02.08.11.02.01.02 Madness, frenzy, folly; 16.02.04.14.01 Blasphemy
wōdnesdæg 05.11.03.01.05.01 Specific days
wōdnesniht 05.11.03.01.05.01 Specific days
wōdscinn 02.08.11.02.01.01 Paroxysm of madness, folly; 06.01.07.04.02 Fraud, deceit, trick, trickery
wōdscipe 02.08.11.02.01 Insanity, madness
wōdsēoc 02.08.11.02.01.02 Madness, frenzy, folly

wōdþrāg 02.08.11.02.01.01 Paroxysm of madness, folly
woffian 08.01.03.05.02 Anger; 16.02.04.14.01 Blasphemy
woffung 02.08.11.02.01 Insanity, madness; 16.02.04.14.01 Blasphemy
wōgere 08.01.02.02.03.01 Wooing; 12.09.01 Pledging, betrothal
wōgerlic 08.01.02.02.03 A loving relationship
wōgian 08.01.02.02.03.01 Wooing
wōgung 08.01.02.02.03.01 Wooing
wōh 03.01.05 Roughness; 03.03.02 Measurement by weighing; 05.10.05.04.08 Crookedness, a crooked place; 06.01.07.05 Error, being astray; 12.07.05 Wrong, injustice; 12.08.06.01.02 Lacking moral good; 12.08.06.02 Wickedness, evil
wōh drīfan 12.07.05 Wrong, injustice
wōhbogen 02.08.04.02 Blemish, disfigurement
wōhcēapung 14.05.04.01 A fine
wōhdǣd 12.08.06.02.05 Misdeed, sin
wōhdōm 12.07.05 Wrong, injustice
wōhfōted 02.08.04.02 Blemish, disfigurement
wōhfremmend 12.08.06.02.02 A bad man, inhuman person
wōhful 12.08.06.02.03 (Of persons) wicked, evil-doing
wōhfulnes 12.08.06.02 Wickedness, evil
wōhgeorn 12.08.06.02.03 (Of persons) wicked, evil-doing
wōhgestrēon 08.01.01.03.08 Happiness, well-being, prosperity
wōhgod 16.01.06 A god (of any faith)
wōhhǣmed 12.08.08.01.02.01 Fornication, adultery
wōhhǣmend 12.08.08.01.02.01 Fornication, adultery
wōhhǣmere 12.08.08.01.02.01 Fornication, adultery
wōhhandede 02.08.04.02 Blemish, disfigurement
wōhhian 02.08.11.02.01 Insanity, madness
wōhlic 12.07.05 Wrong, injustice; 12.08.06.02.03 (Of persons) wicked, evil-doing
wōhlīce 12.07.05 Wrong, injustice; 12.08.06.02.03.01 Wickedly
wōhnes 05.10.05.04.08 Crookedness, a crooked place; 12.08.06.02.01 Wrong, evil-doing
wōhsum 12.08.06.02.03 (Of persons) wicked, evil-doing
wōl 02.08.10.03.01 Plague, pestilence; 07.03.02 Ill, harm, hurt
wōlbǣrnes 02.08.10.03 Pestiferousness, pest, bane
wōlberende 02.08.10.03.01 Plague, pestilence; 07.03.02 Ill, harm, hurt
wōlberendlic 02.08.10.03.01 Plague, pestilence
wōlbryne 02.08.10.03.01 Plague, pestilence
wolcen 01.03.01.06 Cloud; 06.01.07.05 Error, being astray
wolcenfaru 01.03.01.06 Cloud
wolcengehnāst 01.03.01.03.01 Storm, tempest
wolcenwyrcende 01.03.01.06 Cloud
wolcnu 01.02.01 Heaven(s), sky
wōldæg 08.01.03.06 Adversity, affliction
wōlgewinn 13.02 War
wollentēare 08.01.03.04.02 Shedding of tears

wōma 02.05.10.03 Noise, tumult, uproar; 06.01.08.06.02 Great fear, terror, horror
woman 14.02 Lawlessness
gewoman 10.04.03.01 To take away, deprive of
wōp 08.01.03.04.01 Complaint, lamentation; 08.01.03.04.02 Shedding of tears
wōpdropa 08.01.03.04.02 Shedding of tears
wōperian 08.01.03.04.01 Complaint, lamentation
wōpig 08.01.03.04.01 Complaint, lamentation
wōplēoþ 09.03.05.01.01 Poetry
wōplic 08.01.02.06.01 Pity; 08.01.03.04.01 Complaint, lamentation
wōplīce 08.01.03.04.01 Complaint, lamentation
wōpstōw 02.02.05.03 To attend the dead
word 02.07.03.01 A bush; 06.01.07.06.01 To accept as the result of enquiry, suppose; 06.02.06 Mind, purpose; 07.08 Reputation, fame; 09 Speech, vocal utterance; 09.01.01 A speech, what is said, words; 09.03.02.02 Vocabulary; 09.03.02.02.01.02 A verb; 09.03.04.01 Mode of speech; 09.03.07.01.02 A word; 09.06.01 To relate, recount, tell; 09.06.01.02 A saying, saw, proverb, maxim; 09.06.02.01.06 A message, announcement by a messenger; 12.03.03 A command, bidding, order; 12.07.02.01 Covenant, assurance of faith, promise; 12.07.02.01.01.01 A promise, oath; 16.01.01.04.02.01 Incarnation; 16.02.01.08.03 The New Testament
word indrīfan 09.01.02.01 Excessive fluency, loquacity
worda gong 09.01.02.01 Excessive fluency, loquacity
wordbebod 12.03.03 A command, bidding, order
wordbēotung 12.07.02.01.01 A promise
wordcennend 16.01.01.04.01 God the Father
wordclipinde 09.01 To speak, exercise faculty of speech
wordcræft 09.03.04.02.02 Eloquence, elegance in language
wordcwide 09 Speech, vocal utterance; 09.01.01 A speech, what is said, words
wordes 09.01 To speak, exercise faculty of speech
wordes gefēra 09.03.02.02.01.03 An adverb
wordfæst 12.07.02.02 Truth, faithfulness, good faith, sincerity
wordful 09.01.02.01 Excessive fluency, loquacity
wordgaldor 16.01.04.01 Sorcery using incantation
word(ge)bēot 12.07.02.01.01 A promise
wordgecwide 14.04 Making of terms, agreement, convention
wordgemearc 14.04.03 Confirmation, ratification
wordgerȳne 09.04.02.01 A secret, mystery
wordglēaw 09.01.02 Fluency in speech
wordgydd 09.03.05.01.01 Poetry
wordhlēoþor 09 Speech, vocal utterance
wordhord 09.03.02.02 Vocabulary
wordig 09.01.02.01 Excessive fluency, loquacity

wordig gehlȳd 09.01.02.01 Excessive fluency, loquacity
wordlāc 09.01.01 A speech, what is said, words
wordlār 06.01.06.02.03.04 Teaching, instruction
wordlatu 05.11.08.01.03.01 Delay
wordlaþu 09.01.02 Fluency in speech
wordlēan 18.02.07.01.01 A song, a poem to be sung or recited
wordlian 09.01.04 Conversation, discussion; 12.01.01.12.04.02 Conspiracy
wordliend 09.01 To speak, exercise faculty of speech
wordloca 09.03.02.02 Vocabulary
wordlof 07.04.04 Praise, acclamation, applause
wordloga 06.01.07.04 Deception
wordlung 09.01.02.01 Excessive fluency, loquacity; 09.01.04 Conversation, discussion
wordmittung 16.02.04.03.02 Parts of service
wordprēdicung 16.02.04.03.02 Parts of service; 16.02.04.10 Preaching
wordriht 14.01 Law, body of rules; 14.01.02 A law, statute
wordsāwere 09.03.04 Rhetoric, art of exposition
wordsige 08.01.01.03.08.02 Good fortune, success
wordsnoter 09.01.02 Fluency in speech
wordsnoterlic 06.01.06.02.02.01.01 Philosophy
wordsnoterung 06.01.06.02.02.01.01 Philosophy
wordsomnere 03.05.03 A list, tale, series
wordsomnung 16.02.04.03.02 Parts of service
wordsprecende 09.01 To speak, exercise faculty of speech
wordum befōn 09.06.01 To relate, recount, tell
wordum wrixlan 09.01.04 Conversation, discussion
wordwīsa 06.01.06.02.02.01.01 Philosophy
wordwynsum 11.05.02.02 Humanity, courtesy, civility
wōrhana 02.06.08.03 Game-bird
wōrhenn 02.06.08.03 Game-bird
geworht 04.02.03 Cultivatable land/farmland; 06.02.06 Mind, purpose; 07.10.03 An adornment, decoration, ornament; 11.01.03 Preparation; 17.02.05.01 Ornamental object
wōrian 05.06.01 Devastation, laying waste; 12.08.06.01.04 To lead a bad life
wōriend 05.12.01.02 To wander; 12.06.05.01 State of exile, banishment
wōriende 01.02.01.01.01 Planet; 05.12.01.02 To wander; 12.08.06.01.02 Lacking moral good
wōri(g)an 05.12.01.02 To wander
worms 02.08.05.02.01 Matter, purulence, pus
wormsgemang 02.08.05.02.01 Matter, purulence, pus
worn 03.03.04.01 Much; 03.03.04.01.02.01 A heap, mass, accumulation
worngehāt 02.01.03 Fruitfulness, fertility; 12.07.02.01.01 A promise
worpian 05.06.09 Act of striking
(ge)worpian 05.12.02.07 To throw, cast, toss
worþ 04.02.03.01.01 Enclosed land/field

worþ(ig) 05.12.01.03.01.04 A lane, street; 04.05.03.02.02.06.01 A hall building; 04.02.01 Farmstead

worþ(ig)cærse 02.07.09.02.02.02 Other vegetables (alphabetical order)

worþignetele 02.07.11 Plants/flowers (alphabetical order)

worþlēas 15.02.02 Cheap

woruld 01 Earth, world; 02 Creation; 02.01.02.02.01 Condition of life; 02.01.02.02.02 Lifetime; 02.03 Humankind; 05.02.01.01 The course of human affairs; 05.11.01.03 Mutability; 05.11.01.03.01 Mortal state, this life; 05.11.03 Period of time, era, epoch; 05.11.07.02 The present (time); 05.11.07.04 Future, time to come; 16.02.01.12.05 The world (i.e. unspirituality, worldliness)

woruldǣht 15.01 Property

woruldafol 12.01 Power, control, sway

woruldār 07.08.02 Honour, glory; 15.01 Property

woruldbearn 02.03.01 People

woruldbebod 14.01.06 A rule, order, precept, tenet, principle

woruldbisgu 11.02 Occupation, activity, business

woruldbisgung 08.01.03.03 Anxiety; 11.02 Occupation, activity, business

woruldbismer 07.05.03.03 Scorn, insult, abuse

woruldblis 08.01.01.03 Good feeling, joy, happiness

woruldbōt 14.03.03.09.02 Atonement

woruldbroc 08.01.03.06 Adversity, affliction; 11.07 Use (made of things), service

woruldbūende 02.03.01 People

woruldcamp 13.02 War

woruldcandel 01.02.01.01.03 Sun

woruldcearu 08.01.03.03 Anxiety

woruldcempa 13.02.10.01 A man, warrior

woruldcræft 11.04 Ability, capacity, power; 17.02.04 Trade, calling, craft, aptitude

woruldcræftig 11.04.02 Skill, skilfulness

woruldcræft(ig)a 17.02.01 Management of work

woruldcund 01 Earth, world; 16.02.01.12.05 The world (i.e. unspirituality, worldliness); 16.02.03.03.05 A layman

woruldcundlīce 16.02.01.12.05 The world (i.e. unspirituality, worldliness)

woruldcyning 12.01.01.04.01 A royal leader; 12.01.01.04.01.01 Kings and queens

worulddǣd 11.02 Occupation, activity, business

worulddēma 14.03.02 A legislator

worulddōm 14.03.03.09 A sentence, judgement, ruling

worulddrēam 08.01.01.03 Good feeling, joy, happiness

worulddrihten 16.01.01.02.01 Creator

worulduguþ 15.01.03 Treasure, riches, wealth

woruldēad 02.02.03.02 State of being dead

woruldearfoþ 08.01.03.06 Adversity, affliction

woruldege 06.01.08.06.03 Cause of fear, terror, horror

woruldende 05.07 Ending of existence, end of world

woruldfægernes 07.10 Beauty, fairness

woruldfeoh 15.01.03 Treasure, riches, wealth

woruldfolgaþ 17.02 Work, occupation, employment
woruldfrætwung 07.10.03 An adornment, decoration, ornament
woruldfrēond 08.01.02.03.01 An acquaintance, friend, associate
woruldfriþ 13.01 Peace, state of law and order
woruldfruma 07.08.01 Nobility (of character, rank, etc.)
woruldgālnes 06.02.05.01 Strong liking for, devotion to
woruldgebyrd 02.03.02.03 Ancestry, descent
woruldgedāl 02.02 Death
woruldgefeoht 12.05.04.01 Fighting, contention, warfare, strife
woruldgeflit 14.03.03 Law, action of the courts
woruldgerǣdnes 14.01.06 A rule, order, precept, tenet, principle
woruld(ge)riht 14.01 Law, body of rules
woruldgerysne 11.05.02.01 A standard, norm, ethos
woruldgesǣlig 08.01.01.03.08 Happiness, well-being, prosperity
woruld(ge)sælþa 08.01.01.03.08 Happiness, well-being, prosperity
woruldgesceaft 01 Earth, world; 02 Creation
woruldgestrēon 15.01.03 Treasure, riches, wealth
woruldgeswinc 17.01 Strenuous effort, hard work
woruldgeþincþ 07.08.02 Honour, glory
woruldgeþingu 11.02 Occupation, activity, business
woruldgeþōht 06.01.01 Thought, the faculty of thinking, mind;

16.02.01.12.05 The world (i.e. unspirituality, worldliness)
woruldgewin 13.02 War
woruldgewritu 09.03.07.07.03.04 Chronicle, annals, history
woruldgewuna 14.01 Law, body of rules
woruldgielp 07.08.07 Glory, splendour, magnificence
woruldgifu 10.03 Giving
woruldgītsere 06.02.05.01 Strong liking for, devotion to
woruldgītsung 06.02.05.01 Strong liking for, devotion to
woruldglenge 07.06.05 Pomp, splendour, magnificence
woruldgōd 15.01 Property
woruldgyrla 04.04.07.01 Mode of dressing, fashion; 16.02.05.08 Lay clothing
woruldhād 16.02.03.03.05 A layman
woruldhlāford 12.01.01.04.02 A lord, master
woruldhlīsa 07.08.09 Renown, fame, glory
woruldhogu 08.01.03.03 Anxiety
woruldhremming 11.11.02 A hindrance
woruldhyht 08.01.01.03 Good feeling, joy, happiness
woruldlǣce 02.08.12.02.01 A physician
woruldlagu 14.01 Law, body of rules
woruldlēan 10.03.05 Recompense, reward
woruldlic 01 Earth, world; 16.02.01.12.05 The world (i.e. unspirituality, worldliness); 16.02.03.03.05 A layman
woruldlīce 11.05 Natural/proper way/manner/mode of action; 16.02.01.12.05 The world (i.e. unspirituality, worldliness)

woruldlīf 02.01.02.02.01 Condition of life; 05.11.03 Period of time, era, epoch; 16.02.03.03.05 A layman
woruldlufu 08.01.01.03.05 Pleasure, delight
woruldlust 08.01.01.03.05 Pleasure, delight
woruldmǣg 02.03.02.03.06.01 Kinsman, relative
woruldman 02.03.01 People; 11.02 Occupation, activity, business
woruldmann 16.02.03.03.05 A layman
woruldmēd 10.03.05 Recompense, reward
woruldnēod 06.02.04.01 Want, need
woruldnytt 11.07.03 Use, advantage, profit
woruldprȳdo 07.06 Pride
woruldrǣden 11.05 Natural/proper way/manner/mode of action
woruldrīca 08.01.01.03.08 Happiness, well-being, prosperity
woruldrīce 01 Earth, world; 12.01 Power, control, sway; 12.06 A province, country, territory
woruldrīcetere 12.01 Power, control, sway
woruldriht 16.02.01.08.01 The Old Testament
woruldsacu 12.05.04.01 Fighting, contention, warfare, strife
woruldscamu 07.09 Shame, disgrace
woruldsceaft 02 Creation
woruldscēat 05.10.04.02 A region, zone
woruldscēawung 02.05.09.12 To show
woruldscipe 11.02 Occupation, activity, business
woruldscīr 17.02 Work, occupation, employment
woruldscrift 16.02.03.02.09 A confessor
woruldsnotor 06.01.05.02.01.01 Sagacity
woruldsorg 08.01.03.03 Anxiety
woruldspēd 08.01.01.03.08.02 Good fortune, success; 15.01.03 Treasure, riches, wealth
woruldspēdig 15.01.05 Possession of wealth
woruldsprǣc 09.01.04 Conversation, discussion
woruldstēor 14.05.04 A penalty, punishment
woruldstrang 12.01 Power, control, sway
woruldstrengu 05.08 Strength
woruldstrūdere 14.02.01.02.01 Open robbery, rapine, pillage
woruldstund 02.01.04 Age
woruldþearf 06.02.04.01 Want, need
woruldþearfa 15.01.06 Poverty, indigence
woruldþearfende 15.01.06 Poverty, indigence
woruldþēaw 11.05.02 Mode, manner, way, method, fashion, course
woruldþegn 12.01.01.06.08 A person of rank, elder, great man
woruldþēnung 17.02 Work, occupation, employment
woruldþēowdōm 12.01.01.08 Service; 17.02 Work, occupation, employment
woruldþing 11.02 Occupation, activity, business; 15.01.03 Treasure, riches, wealth
woruldþrymm 07.08.07 Glory, splendour, magnificence
woruldwǣpen 13.02.08.04 Weapons, arms
woruldwæter 01.01.03.01.02 Sea/ocean
woruldwela 15.01.03 Treasure, riches, wealth

woruldwelig 15.01.05 Possession of wealth
woruldweorc 17.02 Work, occupation, employment; 17.02.04 Trade, calling, craft, aptitude
woruldweorþscipe 07.08.02 Honour, glory
woruldwīdl 04.06.02.01 Dirty, unclean; 12.08.08.01.02 Unchastity, incontinence
woruldwīg 12.05.04.01 Fighting, contention, warfare, strife
woruldwilla 15.01 Property
woruldwilnung 06.02.05.01 Strong liking for, devotion to
woruldwīs 06.01.05.02.01.01 Sagacity; 06.01.06.02.02.01 Learning, science (secular knowledge)
woruldwīsdōm 06.01.06.02.02.01 Learning, science (secular knowledge)
woruldwīse 11.05 Natural/proper way/manner/mode of action
woruldwita 06.01.06.02.01 A wise man, man of understanding or learning
woruldwīte 14.05.04.01 A fine
woruldwlenco 07.06.05 Pomp, splendour, magnificence
woruldwrenc 11.04.02.01.01 Cunning, craft, craftiness, guile, wile
woruldwuldor 07.08.07 Glory, splendour, magnificence
woruldwuniende 02.03.01 People; 04.05.03.01 Habitation, sojourn
woruldyrmþu 08.01.03.06 Adversity, affliction
wōrung 05.12.01.02 To wander
wōs 02.07.02.03 A stalk, stem
gewosa 09.01.04 Conversation, discussion
wōsig 02.07.02.03 A stalk, stem

wōþ 02.05.10.01 Thing heard; 09.01.02 Fluency in speech; 18.02.07.01 Singing, song
wōþbora 09.03.05 Art of poetry; 18.02.07.01 Singing, song
wōþcræft 09.03.05 Art of poetry; 18.02.07.01 Singing, song
wōþgifu 09.03.05 Art of poetry
wōþsong 18.02.07.01 Singing, song
wrace dōn 12.05.04.02 Vengeance, revenge
wracian 11.01 Action, doing, performance; 12.06.05.01 State of exile, banishment
wracnian 12.06.05.01 State of exile, banishment
wracu 08.01.03.07.03 Suffering, torment, pain; 08.01.03.09.05 Enmity; 12.05.04.02 Vengeance, revenge; 12.06.05.01 State of exile, banishment; 14.03.03.09.03 Outlawry; 14.05.02 Torment, punishment; 14.05.03 Retribution, requital
wræc 05.12.01.09.03.01.01 Kind of ship; 08.01.03.07.03 Suffering, torment, pain; 12.06.05.01 State of exile, banishment; 14.03.03.09.03 Outlawry; 14.05.02 Torment, punishment
wræcca 08.01.03.06 Adversity, affliction; 12.04.04 Solitude; 12.06.05.01 State of exile, banishment; 12.08.06.02.02 A bad man, inhuman person
wræcfæc 08.01.03.06 Adversity, affliction
wræcful 08.01.03.06 Adversity, affliction
wræchwīl 08.01.03.06 Adversity, affliction
wræclāst 12.06.05.01 State of exile, banishment
wræclāstas wunian 12.06.05.01 State of exile, banishment

wrǣclāstian 05.12.02.04 To cast out, drive away; 05.12.05.03.04 To come/go out from
wrǣclic 06.01.08.05.01.01 Wondrous, glorious, marvellous; 08.01.03.06 Adversity, affliction
wrǣclīce 06.01.08.05.01.01 Wondrous, glorious, marvellous; 12.06.05 A foreign country
wrǣcmæcg 08.01.03.06 Adversity, affliction
wrǣcmæcga 16.01.05.02.01 The devil
wrǣcmæcg(a) 16.01.05.02.02 Other terms for devils
wrǣcmon 12.06.05.01 State of exile, banishment
wrǣcscipe 12.06.05.01 State of exile, banishment
wrǣcsetl 12.06.05.01 State of exile, banishment
wrǣcsīþ 08.01.03.06 Adversity, affliction; 12.06.05.01 State of exile, banishment; 16.02.04.11 Pilgrimage
wrǣcsīþian 16.02.04.11 Pilgrimage
wrǣcstōw 08.01.03.06 Adversity, affliction; 12.06.05.01 State of exile, banishment
wrǣcwīte 14.05 Punishment
wrǣcworuld 08.01.03.06 Adversity, affliction
wrǣd 02.08.12.02.06.01 A bandage, binding; 03.03.04.01.02.01 A heap, mass, accumulation; 04.04.07.11 A headcloth, covering for the head
wrǣdmǣlum 03.03.04.01.02.01 A heap, mass, accumulation
wrǣne 12.08.07.01.01 Wantonness, sensuality, lasciviousness
wrǣnnes 12.08.07.01.01 Wantonness, sensuality, lasciviousness
wrǣnsa 12.08.07.01.01 Wantonness, sensuality, lasciviousness
wrǣnscipe 12.08.07.01.01 Wantonness, sensuality, lasciviousness
wrǣnsian 12.08.07.01.01 Wantonness, sensuality, lasciviousness
wrǣsl 05.10.05.04.08 Crookedness, a crooked place
wrǣst 05.10.05.04.08 Crookedness, a crooked place; 07.02.04.03 Nobleness, excellence, nobility, magnificence; 07.10.01 Elegance, beauty, comeliness
wrǣstan 05.10.05.04.08.01 A bend; 07.10.01 Elegance, beauty, comeliness; 18.02.07.02.03.01 A harp, lyre
gewrǣstan 05.05.03 Binding, fastening
wrǣste 07.10.01 Elegance, beauty, comeliness
wrǣstlere 18.02.03.01.01 Wrestling, contending, striving
wrǣstlic 07.10.01 Elegance, beauty, comeliness; 18.02.03.01.01 Wrestling, contending, striving
wrǣstliend 18.02.03.01.01 Wrestling, contending, striving
wrǣstlung 18.02.03.01.01 Wrestling, contending, striving
wrǣtbasu 03.01.14.05 Red/redness
wrǣterēad 03.01.14.05 Red/redness
wrǣtlic 06.01.08.05.01.01 Wondrous, glorious, marvellous; 07.10 Beauty, fairness
wrǣtlīce 06.01.08.05.01.01 Wondrous, glorious, marvellous; 07.10.01 Elegance, beauty, comeliness
wrǣtt 07.10.03 An adornment, decoration, ornament; 17.04.03.04 Gems collectively

wrætt(e) 02.07.11.02 Unidentified plants (alphabetical order)
(ge)wræþan 08.01.03.05.02 Anger
gewræþan 12.05.04.01.01 Fighting, a fight
wræþstudu 04.05.02.04 A column, pillar
wræþþo 08.01.03.05.02 Anger
wræþþu 16.01.01.01 Attributes of God
wrang 03.01.05 Roughness; 12.07.05 Wrong, injustice
wranga 05.12.01.09.03.01.03 Part of ship
wrangwīs 03.01.05 Roughness
wrāsen 17.03.10 Supports and fastenings
wrāþ 08.01.03.05.02 Anger; 08.01.03.06 Adversity, affliction; 08.01.03.07.04 Severity, harshness; 08.01.03.09.11 Hardheartedness, cruelty, severity; 16.01.01.01 Attributes of God
wrāþe 08.01.03.05.02 Anger; 08.01.03.07.04 Severity, harshness; 08.01.03.09.11 Hardheartedness, cruelty, severity; 12.08.06.02.03.01 Wickedly
wrāþian 08.01.03.05.02 Anger
(ge)wrāþian 08.01.03.05.02 Anger
wrāþlic 08.01.03.07.04 Severity, harshness
wrāþlīce 08.01.03.09.11 Hardheartedness, cruelty, severity
wrāþmōd 08.01.03.05.02 Anger; 16.01.01.01 Attributes of God
wrāþscræf 16.01.05 Hell, lower world, abode of the dead
wrāþu 04.05.02.04 A column, pillar; 11.12.02 Aid, help, succour
gewraxl 18.02.03.01.01 Wrestling, contending, striving
wraxlere 18.02.03.01.01 Wrestling, contending, striving
wraxlian 18.02.03.01.01 Wrestling, contending, striving
wraxliende 18.02.03.01.01 Wrestling, contending, striving
wraxlung 18.02.03.01.01 Wrestling, contending, striving
wrecan 05.12.02.06 To push, impel, thrust; 05.12.02.06.01 To push, drive; 05.12.05.09 To go forward, proceed; 09.01 To speak, exercise faculty of speech
wrecan (of) 05.12.02.04 To cast out, drive away
(ge)wrecan 11.01.04 A doing, accomplishing (of something); 12.05.04.02 Vengeance, revenge; 14.05 Punishment
(ge)wrecan torn/yrre 08.01.03.05.02 Anger
wreccan 02.05.02 Consciousness; 05.12.05.12.02 To raise, lift up, elevate; 11.01.02 An undertaking
wrecend 12.05.04.02 Vengeance, revenge
wrecnes 12.05.04.02 Vengeance, revenge; 12.08.06.02 Wickedness, evil
wrecscip 04.05.03.01 Habitation, sojourn
wrēgan 14.03.03.01 Accusation
(ge)wrēgan 01.01.03.01.02.04 State of sea; 14.03.03.01 Accusation
gewrēgednes 14.03.03.01 Accusation
wrēgend 14.03.03.01 Accusation
wrēgendlic 09.03.02.03.01.01.01 Case
wrēgere 14.03.03.01 Accusation
wrēgistre 14.03.03.01 Accusation
wrēgung 14.03.03.01 Accusation
wrehtend 06.02.06.03.02 Instigation
wrēhtend 14.03.03.01 Accusation
wrenc 11.04.02.01.01 Cunning, craft, craftiness, guile, wile; 13.02.07.01 A stratagem; 18.02.07.01 Singing, song

wrencan 05.10.06.02.03 A circular fold, coil; 05.12.05.04.01 (Of wheel, etc.) to roll, trundle; 11.04.02.01.01 Cunning, craft, craftiness, guile, wile
wrengel 05.10.05.04.08 Crookedness, a crooked place
wrenna 02.06.08.05 Forest bird, wild-fowl
wrēo 05.10.05.04.07 A fork (in river, road, etc.)
wrēon 05.10.05.04.12.01 To bespread, cover with; 09.03.07.07 A book; 09.05.04.01 Concealment, obscurity; 11.10.01 Protection, safekeeping; 11.10.01.02 Refuge, help, shelter
(ge)wrēon 04.04.07 Trappings, equipment, garb; 05.10.05.04.12 The condition of being covered
wreoþenhilt 13.02.08.04.03.01.01 Hilt of sword
wreþian 04.05.02.06 A buttress, support
wrid 02.07 A plant
gewrid 02.07.03.04.02 A thicket; 04.02.04.03.02.01 Grain crops
wrīdan 02.01.03 Fruitfulness, fertility
wride 05.10.06.02.02 Curvature, bend, twist
wridels 02.07.03.04.02 A thicket
wrīdende 02.01.03 Fruitfulness, fertility
(ge)wrīdian 02.01.03 Fruitfulness, fertility
wrigelnes 05.10.05.04.12 The condition of being covered
wrigels 04.04.07.10 A veil; 05.10.05.04.12 The condition of being covered
wrigennes 05.10.05.04.12 The condition of being covered
wrigian 05.12.01 To go, progress, travel (usually on land)

gewrinclod 05.10.05.04.08.01 A bend; 05.10.06.05.01 A wrinkle
gewring 04.01.03.05 A drink/beverage
wringan 04.01.02.02.07 Press; 05.06.08 A plucking, taking away
(ge)wringan 03.01.16.03 A drop of liquid
gewringan 17.02.04 Trade, calling, craft, aptitude
wringe 04.01.02.02.07 Press
wringhwǣg 04.01.02.01.02.09.08 Whey
wrist 02.04.03.04.01 Arm
(ge)writ 09.03.07 Writing; 16.02.01.08 Scripture, the scriptures
gewrit 03.05.03 A list, tale, series; 09.03.07.07.02 A written work, book, treatise; 09.03.07.07.02.01.04 A passage in a book; 09.03.07.07.03.02.02 A letter; 09.03.07.07.03.04.01 A document, deed
wrītan 09.03.07.04.02 A diagram; 09.03.07.07.03 Composition, arrangement, writing; 09.03.07.07.03.02 To write, state/say in writing; 09.03.07.07.03.02.02 A letter; 17.02.05.05 A carving, graving; 17.02.05.06 A painting, picture, representation
wrītan be/ymbe 09.03.07.07.03.01 A description, writing down
(ge)wrītan 09.03.07 Writing; 15.01.02 Gift, transfer of property
writbred 09.03.07.06.04 A writing-tablet
wrītere 09.03.07.07.03.03 A writer, author; 16.02.01.09.02 Knowledge of Jewish law; 17.02.05.06 A painting, picture, representation
(ge)wrītere 09.03.07.03 A scribe, copyist
writian 02.05.10.15.07 Voice, note (of a bird); 17.02.05.05 A carving, graving

wrīting 09.03.07 Writing
wrītingfeþer 09.03.07.06.01 A writing instrument
wrītingīsen 09.03.07.06.01 A writing instrument
writīren 09.03.07.06.01 A writing instrument
writīsen 09.03.07.06.01 A writing instrument
writol 03.01.16.02 Water, liquid
gewritrǣden 14.04.01 A deed, contract, agreement
writseax 09.03.07.06.01 A writing instrument
gewritu 16.02.01.08 Scripture, the scriptures
gewriþ 17.03.10 Supports and fastenings
wriþa 04.04.07.03 Part of garment; 05.10.06.02 Rotundity, roundness; 17.03.10 Supports and fastenings
wrīþan 05.10.06.02.03 A circular fold, coil
(ge)wrīþan 03.03.06.01 A whole formed by joining; 05.05.03 Binding, fastening; 14.05.07 Binding, fastening with bonds
gewrīþan 02.08.12.02.06.01 A bandage, binding; 05.10.05.04.12 The condition of being covered; 06.01.04 Faculty of memory; 08.01.03.07.02 Misery, trouble, affliction; 12.05.06.01 Restraint, check, curb, control; 12.05.06.03 Necessity, constraint
gewriþelian 05.05.03 Binding, fastening
wriþels 04.04.07.11 A headcloth, covering for the head
wriþen 13.02.08.03.01.01 Mail, iron-rings
(ge)wriþen 05.05.03 Binding, fastening

gewriþen 12.07 An obligation, bounden duty
wrīþende 05.05.03 Binding, fastening
gewriþennes 05.05.03 Binding, fastening
gewrīþing 05.05.03 Binding, fastening
wrix(i)endlic 05.13.04 Exchange, commutation
wrix(i)endlīce 05.13.03 Regular alternation
wrixl 05.13.04 Exchange, commutation; 15.04.01 Lending of money
(ge)wrixl 05.13 Changeableness, change; 08.01.03.06.01 Affliction, misfortune, calamity; 11.01.01 Practice, exercise, doing; 12.05.04.02.01 Retribution, requital
gewrixl 05.12 To move, be in motion; 05.13.03 Regular alternation; 05.13.04 Exchange, commutation; 12.02 A public office; 12.02.01 A substitute, representative; 15.02.04 Spending, disbursement
wrixlan 15.04.01 Lending of money
(ge)wrixlan 05.13 Changeableness, change; 15.05 Trade, traffic, commerce
(ge)wrixlian 05.13 Changeableness, change
gewrixlian 10.01.02 Acquisition; 10.03.03 Granting; 12.05.04.02.01 Retribution, requital
gewrixlic 05.13.03 Regular alternation
wrixliende 05.13.03 Regular alternation
wrixlung 15.04.01 Lending of money
(ge)wrixlung 05.13 Changeableness, change
wrōc 02.06.08.04 Bird of prey
wrōht 05.06.04 Damage, injury, defect, hurt, loss; 07.05.03.02 Calumny, slander, insult; 09.06.02.01.01 To make known, cause to know, inform;

12.05.03.01 Quarrel, contentiousness, strife; 12.08.06.02.05.01 Transgression, trespass; 14.03.03.01 Accusation
wrōht ālecgan 12.05.06.02.03 Trouble, disturbance
wrōhtberend 14.03.03.01 Accusation
wrōhtbora 14.03.03.01 Accusation; 14.03.03.06 False witness; 16.01.05.02.01 The devil
wrōhtdropa 14.02.01.01 Types of crime
wrōhtgeorn 12.05.03.01 Quarrel, contentiousness, strife
wrōhtgetīma 12.08.06.02.05.01 Transgression, trespass
wrōhtian 07.03.02 Ill, harm, hurt
wrōhtlāc 07.05.03.02 Calumny, slander, insult
wrōhtsāwere 12.08.06.02.02 A bad man, inhuman person
wrōhtscipe 12.08.06.02.05.01 Transgression, trespass
wrōhtsmiþ 12.08.06.02.02 A bad man, inhuman person
wrōhtspitel 07.05.03.02 Calumny, slander, insult
wrōhtstæf 14.03.03.01 Accusation
wrōhtstæpe 05.06.04 Damage, injury, defect, hurt, loss
wrōt 02.06.01.02 Head
wrōtan 05.06.08 A plucking, taking away
wucþegn 16.02.03.03.02.01 Monastic functionaries
wucþēnung 16.02.03.03.02.01 Monastic functionaries
wucu 05.11.03.01.04 A week; 05.11.03.01.05 A day
wucubōt 16.02.04.07.02.03 Penance, an act/instance of penance
wucweorc 17 Work, doings, actions, labour
wudere 04.02.04.05.04.01 A forester, woodman
wudian 04.02.04.05.04.01 A forester, woodman
wudig 01.01.02.01.05 Covered with vegetation; 02.07.03.04 A wood, trees
wudiht 02.07.03.04 A wood, trees
wudu 01.01.02.01.05 Covered with vegetation; 02.07.03 A tree; 02.07.03.03.01 Wood (as substance); 02.07.03.04 A wood, trees; 04.05.01.02 Timber for building; 16.02.05.11 The cross (as Christian image); 17.02.04 Trade, calling, craft, aptitude
wuduælfen 16.01.03.04 Elfin race
wuduæppel 02.07.09.02 Particular fruits (alphabetical order)
wudubǣr 04.02.03.04.02.01 Types of pasture
wudubǣre 02.07.03.04 A wood, trees
wudubærnett 14.02.01.01 Types of crime
wudubāt 05.12.01.09.03.01 A ship, boat
wudubēam 02.07.03 A tree
wudubearo 02.07.03.04 A wood, trees
wudubill 17.03.03 A cutting tool
wudubind(l)e 02.07.11 Plants/flowers (alphabetical order)
wudubior 04.02.04.05.04.01 A forester, woodman
wudublǣd 02.07.02.07 Blossom, flower(s)
wudubrycg 05.12.01.03.04 A bridge
wudubucca 02.06.03.01.08 Goat
wudubyrþa 04.02.04.05.04.01 A forester, woodman
wuducerfille 02.07.11 Plants/flowers (alphabetical order)

wuduclæfre 02.07.11 Plants/flowers (alphabetical order)
wuduclāte 02.07.11.02 Unidentified plants (alphabetical order)
wuducocc 02.06.08.03 Game-bird
wuducroft 04.02 Farm
wuduculfre 02.06.08.03 Game-bird
wuducunelle 02.07.10.01 Particular herbs/spices (alphabetical order)
wuducynn 02.07.03 A tree
wududocce 02.07.11 Plants/flowers (alphabetical order)
wudufæsten 05.12.01.09.03.01.01 Kind of ship; 11.10.01.02.01 A naturally secure place, fastness
wudufald 01.01.02.01.05 Covered with vegetation
wudufeld 01.01.02.01.04 Open (level) land; 01.01.02.01.05 Covered with vegetation
wudufeoh 15.03.02 A tax
wudufille 02.07.10.01 Particular herbs/spices (alphabetical order)
wudufīn 17.05.01 Fuel, tinder
wudufugol 02.06.08.05 Forest bird, wild-fowl
wudugāt 02.06.03.01.08 Goat
wudugehæg 04.02.03.04.02.01 Types of pasture
wuduhætt 02.07.02.06 A leaf; 02.07.03.03.02 Tree top
wuduhēawere 04.02.04.05.04.01 A forester, woodman
wuduherpaþ 05.12.01.03.01.05 Types of road/path
wuduhīewet 14.02.01.01 Types of crime; 14.05.04.01 A fine
wuduholt 02.07.03.04 A wood, trees
wuduhona 02.06.08.03 Game-bird
wuduhunig 04.01.02.01.05.04 Honey

wudulād 17.02.04.02.03 Carrying, carriage (of materials)
wudulǣs 04.02.03.04.02.01 Types of pasture
wuduland 01.01.02.01.05 Covered with vegetation; 02.07.03.04 A wood, trees
wuduleahtric 02.07.11 Plants/flowers (alphabetical order)
wudulic 02.07 A plant; 02.07.03.04 A wood, trees
wudumær 02.05.10.04 To resound; 16.01.03.04 Elfin race
wudumann 04.02.04.05.04.01 A forester, woodman
wudumerce 02.07.11 Plants/flowers (alphabetical order)
wudung 04.02.04.05.04.01 A forester, woodman; 14.01.04.02 Rights involving property
wudurǣden 14.01.04.02 Rights involving property
wudurēc 02.02.05.01.01 A grave, burial place, sepulchre; 03.01.09.02.01.04 Smoke
wudurima 05.10.05.04.11.01 A bound, limit
wudurofe 02.07.11 Plants/flowers (alphabetical order)
wudurōse 02.07.09.02 Particular fruits (alphabetical order)
wudusnīte 02.06.08.03 Game-bird
wudusūræppel 02.07.09.02 Particular fruits (alphabetical order)
wudusūre 02.07.11 Plants/flowers (alphabetical order)
wudutelga 02.07.03.03.01 Wood (as substance)
wudutrēow 02.07.03 A tree
wuduþistle 02.07.11 Plants/flowers (alphabetical order)

wuduwa 12.09.05 State of woman whose husband has died
wuduwald 02.07.03.04 A wood, trees
wuduwanhād 12.09.05 State of woman whose husband has died
wuduwāsa 16.01.03.04 Elfin race
wuduwe 12.09.05 State of woman whose husband has died
wuduweard 04.02.04.05.04.01 A forester, woodman
wuduweax(e) 02.07.11 Plants/flowers (alphabetical order)
wuduwēsten 02.07.03.04 A wood, trees
wuduwinde 02.07.11 Plants/flowers (alphabetical order)
wuduwyrt 02.07 A plant
wuhhung 02.08.11.02.01.02 Madness, frenzy, folly
wuhhunge 16.01.06.02 Classical gods
wuldor 07.06.02 Arrogance, vainglory, vanity; 07.08.07 Glory, splendour, magnificence; 08.01.02.04.02 Thanks, gratitude; 16.01.01.01.01 The Almighty; 16.01.01.01.01.02 Glory; 16.01.02.02 Glory/majesty of heaven; 16.02.04 Worship, honour, praise
wuldorbēacn 16.01.02.03 Reward of heaven
wuldorbēag 02.04.06.01 Sight organ; 16.01.02.03 Reward of heaven
(ge)wuldorbēagian 07.08.04 An ornament, honour, glory
wuldorblǣd 16.01.02.02 Glory/majesty of heaven
wuldorcyning 16.01.01.01.01 The Almighty
wuldordrēam 16.01.02.02 Glory/majesty of heaven
wuldorfæder 16.01.01.04.01 God the Father
wuldorfæst 03.01.12 Brightness, light; 07.08.09 Renown, fame, glory; 16.01.01.01.01.02 Glory; 16.01.02.02 Glory/majesty of heaven
wuldorfæstlīce 06.01.08.05.01.01 Wondrous, glorious, marvellous
wuldorfæstlicnes 16.01.02.02 Glory/majesty of heaven
wuldorful 07.06.02 Arrogance, vainglory, vanity; 07.08.07 Glory, splendour, magnificence; 16.01.01.01.01.02 Glory
(ge)wuldorfullian 07.08.05 Glorifying, making great, glorification
wuldorfullīce 06.01.08.05.01.01 Wondrous, glorious, marvellous
wuldorgāst 16.01.02.05.01 An angel
wuldorgeflogena 16.01.05.02.02 Other terms for devils
wuldorgesteald 15.01.03 Treasure, riches, wealth; 16.01.02.01 Heavenly dwelling place
wuldorgeweorc 06.01.08.05.01.01.01 An exercise of power, mighty work, miracle
wuldorgifa 16.01.01.02.02 A giving (by Deity)
wuldorgifu 16.01.01.01 Attributes of God
wuldorgim 01.02.01.01.03 Sun
wuldorgod 16.01.01.01.01 The Almighty
wuldorhama 04.04.07.01 Mode of dressing, fashion
wuldorhēap 16.01.02.05.01 An angel
wuldorhelm 16.01.02.03 Reward of heaven
wuldorlēan 16.01.02.03 Reward of heaven
wuldorlic 06.01.08.05.01.01 Wondrous, glorious, marvellous; 16.02.01.04 Orthodoxy

wuldorlīce 07.08.07 Glory, splendour, magnificence
wuldormago 16.01.02.05.02 A saint
wuldormicel 07.02.04.03 Nobleness, excellence, nobility, magnificence
wuldornytting 11.07 Use (made of things), service
wuldorsang 18.02.07.01.01 A song, a poem to be sung or recited
wuldorspēd 03.03.04.02.01 Abundance
wuldorspēdig 07.08.07 Glory, splendour, magnificence
wuldortān 16.01.04.04 A magical apparatus
wuldortorht 03.01.12 Brightness, light
wuldorþrymm 16.01.02.02 Glory/majesty of heaven
wuldorweorud 16.01.02.05 Inhabitants of heaven
wuldorword 16.02.01.12.01 Revelation, illumination, inspiration
wuldrian 07.06.03 Boastfulness, arrogance; 07.08.08 Nobleness, honour, glory
(ge)wuldrian 07.08.05 Glorifying, making great, glorification; 16.02.04 Worship, honour, praise
(ge)wuldrian in/on 08.01.01.03.06 Exultation, joy
gewuldrian 16.02.04.09 Almsgiving, charitableness
wuldrig 06.01.08.05.01.01 Wondrous, glorious, marvellous
gewuldrod 16.01.01.01.01.02 Glory
wuldrung 07.08.05 Glorifying, making great, glorification; 08.01.01.03.06 Exultation, joy
wulf 02.06.03.01.15 Wolf; 08.01.03.09.11 Hardheartedness, cruelty, severity

wulfes camb 02.07.11 Plants/flowers (alphabetical order)
wulfes hēafod 02.06.03.01.15 Wolf; 12.06.05.01 State of exile, banishment
wulfes tæsel 02.07.11 Plants/flowers (alphabetical order)
wulfhaga 04.02.05.03 A park, enclosure for animals
wulfhēafodtrēo 14.05.06 Means/implement of torture
wulfheort 08.01.03.09.11 Hardheartedness, cruelty, severity
wulfhliþ 01.01.02.01.02.02.01 Hill
wulfhol 02.06.01.08 A lair, den
wulflȳs 02.06.02.01.08 Sheep
wulfpytt 04.03.02 A snare, trap, noose
wulfsēaþ 04.03.02 A snare, trap, noose
wulfslæd 01.01.02.01.03.03 Valley
wull 04.04.04 A thread (of wool, etc.), fibre
wullcamb 04.04.01 Fulling
wullcnoppa 04.04.04 A thread (of wool, etc.), fibre
wullmod 04.04.03 A spinning-house or chamber
wulltewestre 04.04.03 A spinning-house or chamber
wulluc 05.10.05.04.12 The condition of being covered
wullwǣga 03.03.02 Measurement by weighing
gewuna 03.05 Order, arrangement, disposition; 11.05 Natural/proper way/manner/mode of action; 11.05.02 Mode, manner, way, method, fashion, course; 16.02.04.03 Ritual, rite, service
wund 02.08.04.01 A wound; 02.08.05.02 Particular inflammation/swelling; 08.01.03.06 Adversity, affliction; 08.01.03.07.02.01 Injury, offence

wundel 02.08.05.02 Particular inflammation/swelling; 08.01.03.07.02.01 Injury, offence
wundel/wyndle 02.08.04.01 A wound
(ge)wunden 05.10.06.02.03 A circular fold, coil; 17.04.04 Fibrous materials
gewunden 04.04.04 A thread (of wool, etc.), fibre
wundenfeax 02.06.01.06 Skin, hide
wundenhals 05.12.01.09.03.01.02 Of/concerning a ship, naval
wundenlocc 02.04.04.03.03 Hair of head
wundenmæl 13.02.08.04.03 A sword
wundenstefna 05.12.01.09.03.01.01 Kind of ship
wunderseon 02.05.09.12 To show
(ge)wundian 02.08.04.01 A wound; 02.08.12.02.06 Surgical; 08.01.03.07.02.01 Injury, offence
wundiend 05.06 Destruction, dissolution, loss, breaking
wundig/wundiht 02.08.05.02 Particular inflammation/swelling
wundlic 07.03.02 Ill, harm, hurt
wundor 02.06.10 Monster, strange creature; 06.01.08.05.01 Amazement, astonishment, wonder, admiration; 06.01.08.05.01.01.01 An exercise of power, mighty work, miracle; 16.01.01.02.03 A wonder, miracle
wundor āgræfen 17.02.05.05 A carving, graving
wundorbēacen 06.01.08.05.01.01.01 An exercise of power, mighty work, miracle
wundorbebod 12.03.03 A command, bidding, order
wundorblēo 03.01.14 A colour
wundorclam 17.03.10 Supports and fastenings

wundorcræft 06.01.08.05.01.01.01 An exercise of power, mighty work, miracle; 17.02.04 Trade, calling, craft, aptitude
wundorcræftiglīce 11.04.02 Skill, skilfulness
wundorcyning 16.01.01.01.01 The Almighty
wundordǣd 11.01 Action, doing, performance
wundordēaþ 02.02.01 Particular mode of death
wundoreardung 04.05.03.02.02.02 Agreeable dwellings
wundorfæt 04.01.02.02.06.05 Vessel/utensil/cup
wundorful 06.01.08.05.01.01 Wondrous, glorious, marvellous
wundorfullīce 06.01.08.05.01.01 Wondrous, glorious, marvellous
wundorgehwyrft 05.12.05 To move and change direction, turn
wundorgewyrd 06.01.08.05.01.01.01 An exercise of power, mighty work, miracle
wundorgiefu 11.04 Ability, capacity, power
wundorhǣlo 16.01.01.02.03 A wonder, miracle
wundorhūs 04.05.03.04 A closet, chamber, room
gewundorlǣcan 16.02.04 Worship, honour, praise
wundorlic 06.01.08.05.01.01 Wondrous, glorious, marvellous; 16.01.01.01.01.02 Glory
wundorlīce 06.01.08.05.01.01 Wondrous, glorious, marvellous
wundormāþm 15.01.03 Treasure, riches, wealth

wundorsēon 06.01.08.05.01.01.01 An exercise of power, mighty work, miracle
wundorsmiþ 17.02.04.03 Metal worker
wundortācen 06.01.08.05.01.01.01 An exercise of power, mighty work, miracle
wundorweorc 06.01.08.05.01.01.01 An exercise of power, mighty work, miracle
wundorworuld 01 Earth, world
wundrian (æfter/fram) 06.01.08.05.01 Amazement, astonishment, wonder, admiration
(ge)wundrian 07.08.05 Glorifying, making great, glorification; 16.02.04 Worship, honour, praise
wundrigendlic 06.01.08.05.01 Amazement, astonishment, wonder, admiration
wundrum 06.01.08.05.01.01 Wondrous, glorious, marvellous
wundrung 02.05.09.12 To show; 06.01.08.05.01 Amazement, astonishment, wonder, admiration; 06.01.08.05.01.01.01 An exercise of power, mighty work, miracle
wundspring 02.08.05.02 Particular inflammation/swelling
wundswaþu 02.08.04.01 A wound
wundwāco 02.08.04.01 A wound
wundwīte 14.03.03.09.02 Atonement
(ge)wunelic 11.05 Natural/proper way/manner/mode of action
gewunelic 03.04.03 Generality; 03.06.03 Congruity, fitness, suitability; 05.11.09.02 Frequent, of common occurrence
gewunelīce 03.04.03 Generality; 06.02.07.03 Perseverance; 11.05 Natural/proper way/manner/mode of action; 11.05.02.01 A standard, norm, ethos; 16.02.04.03.01 A rite, ceremony
wunenes 04.05.03 A dwelling-place, abode, habitation; 06.02.07.03 Perseverance
wunian 02.01.02.02.02 Lifetime; 05 Aught, anything, something
(ge)wunian 03.03.07.02 What is left, remnant, remains; 04.05.03.01 Habitation, sojourn; 05.10.04 Place, room; 05.11.11 Continuity; 08.01.02.03.04 To show gladness, be friendly; 11.05 Natural/proper way/manner/mode of action; 12.06.03.02 Living, dwelling, residence (in)
gewunian 04.01 Digestion; 05.12.04 Absence of movement, stillness
wuniendlīce 05.11.11 Continuity
wunigend 02.03.03.04 An inhabitant; 04.05.03.01 Habitation, sojourn
wunung 02.01 Existence, life; 04.05.03 A dwelling-place, abode, habitation; 12.06.03.02 Living, dwelling, residence (in)
wunungstōw 04.05.03 A dwelling-place, abode, habitation
(ge)wurdlian 09.03.04 Rhetoric, art of exposition
wurma 03.01.14.01 Dyeing; 03.01.14.05 Red/redness
wurma(-e) 02.07.11.02 Unidentified plants (alphabetical order); 02.06.06.04 Shellfish
wurmille 02.07.10.01 Particular herbs/spices (alphabetical order)
wurpol 05.06 Destruction, dissolution, loss, breaking

wūscbearn 02.03.01.04 Child
wylf 02.06.03.01.15 Wolf
wylfen 02.06.03.01.15 Wolf; 08.01.03.09.11 Hardheartedness, cruelty, severity; 16.01.06.02 Classical gods
wylisc eala (-o) 04.01.03.05.01.02 Broth
wyll 04.04.04 A thread (of wool, etc.), fibre
wyllan 04.01.02.02.05.02 To boil
(ge)wyllan 03.01.09.01.01 (Of liquids) boiling
wylleburne 01.01.03.01.01.07 Spring, fountain, well
wyllecærse 02.07.09.02.02.02 Other vegetables (alphabetical order)
gewylled 04.01.03.05.01.01 Wine
wyllen 04.04.05.03 Woollen stuff
wyllere 04.01.02.02.10 Saltworks
wyllestrēam 01.01.03.01.01 Moving water; 01.01.03.01.01.03 Stream
wyllewæter 03.01.16.02 Water, liquid
wylleweg 05.12.01.03.01.05 Types of road/path
wyll(ge)spring 01.01.03.01.01.07 Spring, fountain, well
wyllspring 05.03 Source, origin
wyllung 01.01.03.01.01.07 Spring, fountain, well
(ge)wyltan 05.12.05.04.01 (Of wheel, etc.) to roll, trundle
wylw(i)an 05.05 Constitution, founding (e.g. of world)
(ge)wylw(i)an 05.12.05.04.01 (Of wheel, etc.) to roll, trundle
wynbēam 16.02.05.11 The cross (as Christian image)
wynburh 12.06.02.01 A township
wyncandel 01.02.01.01.03 Sun

wyndæg 08.01.01.03.08 Happiness, well-being, prosperity
gewynde 04.04 Weaving
wyndecræft 04.04 Weaving
wyndrēam 08.01.01.03.07 Joyous sound, mirth
wyndrēamnes 08.01.01.03.07 Joyous sound, mirth
wynele 03.01.17.07 Salves, ointments, etc.
wynfæst 08.01.01.03 Good feeling, joy, happiness
wyngesīþ 12.04.01 A fellow, companion, associate, comrade
wyngrāf 02.07.03.04.01 A small wood, coppice, copse
wynland 16.01.02.01 Heavenly dwelling place; 16.01.02.04 Paradise
wynlēas 08.01.03.06 Adversity, affliction
wynlic 08.01.01.03.09.01 Pleasant, agreeable
wynlīce 08.01.01.03.09.02 Pleasantly, agreeably
wynlust 12.08.08.01 Eager, unseemly desire
wynmǣg 02.03.01.07 Girl
wynn 07.02.04 Excellence; 08.01.01.03.05 Pleasure, delight; 08.01.01.03.09 Pleasantness, agreeableness; 09.03.07.01.01 A runic letter; 16.01.01.01 Attributes of God
wynnum 08.01.01.03.09.02 Pleasantly, agreeably
wynpsalterium 16.02.04.03.03.02 A psalm
wynrōd 16.02.05.11 The cross (as Christian image)
wynsang 18.02.07.01.01 A song, a poem to be sung or recited
wynstaþol 08.01.01.03.05 Pleasure, delight

wynsum 08.01.01.03 Good feeling, joy, happiness; 08.01.02.01 Favour, kindness, grace
(ge)wynsum 08.01.01.03.09.01 Pleasant, agreeable
(ge)wynsumian 08.01.01.03.06 Exultation, joy; 08.01.01.03.09.03 To make glad
(ge)wynsumlic 08.01.01.03.09.01 Pleasant, agreeable
wynsumlīce 08.01.01.03.04 Gladness, cheerfulness; 08.01.01.03.09.02 Pleasantly, agreeably; 08.01.02.01 Favour, kindness, grace
wynsummung 08.01.01.03 Good feeling, joy, happiness
wynsumnes 08.01.01.03.06 Exultation, joy; 08.01.01.03.09 Pleasantness, agreeableness; 11.05.02.02 Humanity, courtesy, civility; 16.02.01.11 Firmness in the law, piety, devoutness
wynwerod 12.04.02 A crowding together, assembly
wynwyrt 02.07 A plant
wyrcan 04.02.04.02 Cultivation/tillage; 17 Work, doings, actions, labour
wyrcan tō wīte 14.05 Punishment
(ge)wyrcan 04.05 Building, construction; 05.03 Source, origin; 05.05 Constitution, founding (e.g. of world); 07.04.02 Merit, desert(s); 11.01 Action, doing, performance; 11.01.04 A doing, accomplishing (of something); 16.02.04.04.02 A feast-day, holy day; 17.02.04 Trade, calling, craft, aptitude
gewyrcan 02.07.01 To grow; 05.03.01 A cause (of anything); 05.03.01.02 To work upon, influence; 09.03.07.07.03 Composition, arrangement, writing; 11 Action, operation; 14.05 Punishment
gewyrcan ǣ 14.01.06 A rule, order, precept, tenet, principle
gewyrcan on 17.02.05.05.02 To make a mark/cut by striking
gewyrce 10.01.02 Acquisition; 17.02.04 Trade, calling, craft, aptitude
wyrcend 11.01.04 A doing, accomplishing (of something); 16.01.01.02.01 Creator
wyrcing 11.01 Action, doing, performance
wyrcnes 11 Action, operation; 17 Work, doings, actions, labour
wyrd 02.02.03.03 Appointed death, doom; 05.03.02.01 Chance, hap, event
(ge)wyrd 05.03.02 Event, issue, result; 05.03.02.01.01 An event, occurrence; 05.04 Fate, lot, fortune, destiny; 05.04.01 Fortune, Fate (personification); 16.01.06.02 Classical gods
gewyrd 06.02.02.01 Will, wish, pleasure; 09.03.04.04 Discursiveness; 11.01 Action, doing, performance; 14.01.06 A rule, order, precept, tenet, principle; 14.04.02 A stipulation
wyrde 05.04.01 Fortune, Fate (personification)
gewyrde 09.07.04.01.01 Acknowledgement
gewyrdelic 05.03.02.01 Chance, hap, event; 09.03.07.07.03.04 Chronicle, annals, history
gewyrdelīce 06.01.05.02.01.01.01 Reason, sense, discretion, prudence; 09.03.04.02.02 Eloquence, elegance in language; 09.03.07.07.03.04 Chronicle, annals, history

gewyrdelicnes 09.03.04.02.02 Eloquence, elegance in language
wyrdgesceapum 05.03.02.01 Chance, hap, event
gewyrdignes 09.03.04.02.02 Eloquence, elegance in language
wyrdnes 05.02 State, condition
wyrdstæf 05.04 Fate, lot, fortune, destiny
(ge)wyrdwrītere 09.03.07.07.03.03 A writer, author
wyrgan 05.06.04 Damage, injury, defect, hurt, loss; 16.02.04.14.02.01 Cursing, imprecation
wyrgcwedolian 16.02.04.14.02.01 Cursing, imprecation
wyrged 16.01.05.02.02 Other terms for devils
wyrgend 12.08.06.02.02 A bad man, inhuman person; 16.02.04.14.02.01 Cursing, imprecation
wyrgende 16.02.04.14.02.01 Cursing, imprecation
wyrgnes 16.02.04.14.02.01 Cursing, imprecation
wyrgþu 08.01.03.07.03 Suffering, torment, pain; 12.08.06.02 Wickedness, evil; 14.05 Punishment; 16.01.05.01 Damnation, perdition, reprobation; 16.02.04.14.02.01 Cursing, imprecation
wyrgung 16.02.04.14.02.01 Cursing, imprecation
wyrhta 05.05 Constitution, founding (e.g. of world); 16.01.01.02.01 Creator; 17.02.01 Management of work; 17.02.04 Trade, calling, craft, aptitude
(ge)wyrhta 11.01.04 A doing, accomplishing (of something)
gewyrhta 12.04.01 A fellow, companion, associate, comrade; 14.02 Lawlessness
gewyrht(o) āgan 07.04.02 Merit, desert(s)
gewyrhtu 11.01 Action, doing, performance
gewyrht(u) 07.04.02 Merit, desert(s); 12.08.06.02.05.01 Transgression, trespass
wyrm 02.06.07 Reptile (serpent, snake, dragon); 02.06.09.02.11 Worm; 02.08.08.04.03 Intestinal worm; 07.03.04 A wretch, poor creature
wyrmǣte 03.02.01.03 Worm-eaten state
(ge)wyrman 03.01.09.01 Warmth, heat
wyrmbasu 03.01.14.05 Red/redness
wyrmcynn 02.06.07 Reptile (serpent, snake, dragon)
wyrmfāh 13.02.08.04.03 A sword
wyrmgaldere 16.01.04.01 Sorcery using incantation
wyrmgalere 16.01.04.01 Sorcery using incantation
wyrmgealdor 16.01.04.01 Sorcery using incantation
wyrmgeard 02.06.01.08 A lair, den
wyrmgeblǣd 02.08.05.02 Particular inflammation/swelling
wyrmhǣlsere 16.01.04.06 Divination, augury
wyrmhīw 17.02.05.04 An image, figure
wyrmhord 15.01.03 Treasure, riches, wealth
wyrming 03.01.09.01 Warmth, heat
wyrmlīc 07.03.04 A wretch, poor creature; 17.02.05.04 An image, figure
wyrmmelu 04.06.02.05 Dust, powder
wyrmrēad 03.01.14.05 Red/redness
wyrms 02.08.05.02.01 Matter, purulence, pus; 12.08.06.01.01 Pollution, impairment

(ge)wyrmsan 02.08.05.02.01 Matter, purulence, pus
gewyrms(ed) 02.08.05.02.01 Matter, purulence, pus
wyrmsele 16.01.05 Hell, lower world, abode of the dead
wyrmshrǣcing 02.04.06.06.04 Spittle
(ge)wyrmsig 02.08.05.02.01 Matter, purulence, pus
wyrmslite 02.08.03.02 Itch, irritation
wyrmsspīung 02.04.06.06.04 Spittle
wyrmsteall 04.02.05.06.01.01 A cattle pen/cowshed
wyrmwort 02.07.11 Plants/flowers (alphabetical order)
wyrp 02.08.04 Hurt, injury, damage; 05.09.03 Mitigation, lightening, alleviation; 05.10.05 A space, span; 11.12.02.02 Amendment, setting right, reparation; 13.02.08.04.02 A shot, missile, dart, spear, javelin, etc.; 18.02.02 Play, (athletic) sport
wyrpe 02.08.13 Recovery, growing better
gewyrpe 01.01.02.01.02.01 Rising ground, eminence
wyrpel 04.02.05.05.04 Rope, rein
wyrpendlic 05.12.02.07 To throw, cast, toss
wyrsian 02.08.02 Disease, infirmity, sickness
wyrslic 07.03.04 A wretch, poor creature
wyrt 02.07 A plant; 02.07.02.01 Root; 02.07.10 (Garden) herb/spice; 04.01.03.05.02 Brewing
wyrtbedd 04.02.04.05.01 A garden-plot
gewyrtbox 02.05.08.02 Pleasant smell, fragrance, perfume
wyrtbrǣþ 02.05.08.02 Pleasant smell, fragrance, perfume
wyrtcynn 02.07 A plant

wyrtcynren 02.07 A plant
wyrtdrenc 02.08.12.02.05.01 A herb with medicinal properties; 04.01.03.05 A drink/beverage
wyrtecedrenc 02.08.12.02.05.01 A herb with medicinal properties
gewyrten 05.06.01 Devastation, laying waste
wyrtfæt 02.05.08.02 Pleasant smell, fragrance, perfume
wyrtforbor 02.08.08.12 Disease of bowels
wyrtgælstre 16.01.04.02 Sorcery involving drugs or potions
wyrtgeard 04.02.04.05 Garden
wyrtgemang 02.05.08.02 Pleasant smell, fragrance, perfume
wyrtgemengnes 02.05.08.02 Pleasant smell, fragrance, perfume
(ge)wyrtian 04.01.02.02.04 To season
gewyrtian 02.05.08.02 Pleasant smell, fragrance, perfume
wyrtig 04.02.04.05 Garden
wyrtmete 04.01.02.01.07.01 Soup/pottage
gewyrtod 04.01.02.02.04 To season
wyrtrum 02.04.06.03.02.01.01 Tooth/teeth
wyrtruma 01.01.02.01.02.02 Hill, mountain; 02.07.02.01 Root; 05.03 Source, origin
wyrttruma 02.03.03.02 A race, tribe
wyrttrumian 02.07.01 To grow
(ge)wyrt(t)rumian 05.12.04.01 Stability, firmness
gewyrt(t)rumian 05.06.08 A plucking, taking away
(ge)wyrttūn 04.02.04.05 Garden
wyrttūnhege 04.02.04.05 Garden
wyrtung 04.01.02.01.07.01 Soup/pottage

wyrtwala 02.07.02.01 Root
wyrtwalian 04.02.04.02.04 Planting; 05.06.08 A plucking, taking away
wyrtwalu 01.01.02.01.02.02 Hill, mountain; 05.03 Source, origin; 05.13.06.01 Firm, stable, steady
wyrtweard 04.02.04.05 Garden
wyrþan 04.02.04.02.01.02 To irrigate (plants, land)/channel (water)
gewyrþan 07.01 Appraisal, appraising
gewyrþe 03.03.04 Quantity
wyrþig 07.04.02 Merit, desert(s)
wyrþing 04.02.03 Cultivatable land/farmland
wȳsc 07.01.01 Choice, election
(ge)wȳscan 06.02.05.01 Strong liking for, devotion to
gewȳscan 02.03.02.04 Adoption
gewȳsced 06.02.05 Will, desire, wish
gewȳscednes 02.03.02.04 Adoption
gewȳscendlic 02.03.02.04 Adoption; 02.05.05.01 Object of desire; 09.03.02.03.01.02.01 Mood
gewȳscendlīce 02.03.02.04 Adoption
gewȳscing 02.03.02.04 Adoption
wytuma 12.09.02 Marriage ceremony
ȳce 02.06.07.02 Frog, toad
ȳddisc 15.01 Property
yfel 02.08.02.01 An illness, ailment, disorder; 04.06.02 Insalubrious, injurious to health; 07.03 Evil; 07.03.02 Ill, harm, hurt; 07.05.03.03 Scorn, insult, abuse; 12.08.06.02 Wickedness, evil; 12.08.06.02.06 Deceit, evil, wickedness
yfelādl 02.08.08.02 Lung disease
yfelberende 09.06.02.01.06.03 Ill tidings
yfelcund 07.03.02 Ill, harm, hurt
yfelcwedolian 16.02.04.14.02.01 Cursing, imprecation
yfelcweþan 16.02.04.14.02.01 Cursing, imprecation
yfelcweþelgiende 07.05.03.03.01 Contumelious, scornful
yfeldǣd 08.01.03.07.02.01 Injury, offence; 16.02.01.13 Evil-doing, transgression, sin
yfeldǣda 12.08.06.02.02 A bad man, inhuman person
yfeldǣde 12.08.06.02.03 (Of persons) wicked, evil-doing
yfeldēma 14.03.02 A legislator
yfeldōnd 12.08.06.02.02 A bad man, inhuman person
yfeldōnde 12.08.06.02.03 (Of persons) wicked, evil-doing
yfeldysig 12.08.06.01.02 Lacking moral good
yfelful 12.08.06.02.03 (Of persons) wicked, evil-doing
yfelgiornes 12.08.06.02 Wickedness, evil
yfelhæbbende 02.08.02 Disease, infirmity, sickness
yfelian 03.02.01 Decay, decline, corruption
(ge)yfelian 02.08.02 Disease, infirmity, sickness; 02.08.04 Hurt, injury, damage
yfellǣrende 06.02.06.03 Persuasion, prompting
yfellibbende 12.08.06.01.02 Lacking moral good
yfellic 04.06.02.02 Foul, filthy, squalid
yfel(l)ic 07.03.04 A wretch, poor creature; 12.08.06.02.03 (Of persons) wicked, evil-doing
yfellīce 07.03 Evil; 07.03.04 A wretch, poor creature
yfelmynnan 08.01.03.05.04 Irritability; 12.08.06.02.03.02 To do evil

yfelnes 08.01.03.06.01 Affliction, misfortune, calamity; 08.01.03.09.11 Hardheartedness, cruelty, severity; 12.08.06.02 Wickedness, evil
yfelonbecweþende 06.02.06.03 Persuasion, prompting
yfelsacend 16.02.04.14.01 Blasphemy
(ge)yfelsacian 16.02.04.14.01 Blasphemy
yfelsacung 07.05.03.02 Calumny, slander, insult; 16.02.04.14.01 Blasphemy
yfelsæc 16.02.04.14.01 Blasphemy
(ge)yfelsian 16.02.04.14.01 Blasphemy
yfelsōþ 06.01.07 Truth, conformity with absolute standard
yfelspræce 07.05.03.03.01 Contumelious, scornful
yfelspræcende 07.05.03.03.01 Contumelious, scornful
yfelsung 16.02.04.14.01 Blasphemy
yfeltihtend 06.02.06.03.02.01 Prompting, instigation (pejorative)
yfeltihtende 06.02.06.03.02.01 Prompting, instigation (pejorative)
yfelweorc 16.01.04 Sorcery, magic, witchcraft
yfelwiht 16.01.03 A spectre, ghost, demon, goblin
yfelwille 08.01.03.09.03 Malevolence, malice
yfelwillende 08.01.03.09.03 Malevolence, malice
yfelwillendnes 12.08.06.02 Wickedness, evil
yfelwilnian 08.01.03.09.03 Malevolence, malice
yfelwyrcende 07.03.02 Ill, harm, hurt; 12.08.06.02.03 (Of persons) wicked, evil-doing
yfelwyrde 07.05.03.03.01 Contumelious, scornful

yfemest 05.10.05.03.03 Height, loftiness, sublimity; 11.07.04 Superiority, pre-eminence, primacy; 12.01.01.06.02.01 (High) rank, status, degree
yfera 05.10.05.03.03 Height, loftiness, sublimity; 05.11.07.04.02 (Of time) later/latter; 11.07.04 Superiority, pre-eminence, primacy
geyferian 07.08.06 Exaltation
yfesdrop 04.05.02.08 Top of a building
yfle 02.08.02 Disease, infirmity, sickness; 07.03 Evil; 08.01.03.09.03 Malevolence, malice; 08.01.03.09.11 Hardheartedness, cruelty, severity; 11.06.03.01 Ill fortune, bad success; 12.08.06.01.03 Evilly, badly
yfle habban 12.05.06.02.03 Trouble, disturbance
yflung 02.08.04 Hurt, injury, damage
ȳfre 01.01.02.01.02.01 Rising ground, eminence
ylfig 02.08.11.02.01 Insanity, madness
ylp 02.06.04.01.03 Elephant
ymb 03.06 Comparison
ymb ... ūtan(e) 05.10.05.04.02.01 Exterior, outside of
ymb handa 05.10.05.01 A little way, no great distance
ymb stefn 05.13.03 Regular alternation
ymb stycce 05.11.11.02 Let up, intermission, cessation
ymb ūtan 05.10.05.04.11 A circle, circuit, circumference
ymbærnan 05.12.05.06 To travel over/through/along, traverse
ymb(be)bīgnes 05.10.06.02.02 Curvature, bend, twist
ymbberan 05.12.05.04 To rotate, turn round, revolve

ymbbindan 05.05.03 Binding, fastening
ymbcæfian 04.04.05.07 Embroidery
ymbceorfan 16.02.04.13.04 Circumcision
ymbceorfnes 16.02.04.13.04 Circumcision
ymbcerr 01.01.03.01.01 Moving water; 05.12 To move, be in motion; 05.12.05.03.04 To come/go out from; 06.01.07.04.04.03 Deceit, fraud, treachery
ymbcirran 05.12.05 To move and change direction, turn
ymbclyccan 05.10.05.04.11 A circle, circuit, circumference; 08.01.02.02.02 An embrace
ymbclyppan 05.10.05.04.11 A circle, circuit, circumference
ymbclyppung 08.01.02.02.02 An embrace
ymbcyme 12.02.02 An assembly, meeting
ymbcyrran 05.12 To move, be in motion; 05.12.05.04 To rotate, turn round, revolve; 05.13 Changeableness, change
ymbcyrran fram 05.12.02.08 To give a different direction to, turn
ymbe 02.06.09.02.02 Bee, hornet, wasp
ymb(e) ... þæs þe 05.11.07.04.02 (Of time) later/latter
ymb(e) 05.10.05.04.11 A circle, circuit, circumference; 05.11.07.04.02 (Of time) later/latter; 05.10.05.04.11 A circle, circuit, circumference; 05.11.07.03 Former times, days of old; 03.03.06.01 A whole formed by joining; 05.03 Source, origin; 05.10.05.04.09 Side, quarter, direction; 05.11.07.02 The present (time)

ymbe hand 05.11.07.01 Contemporary, coeval
ymbe wucstemne 05.11.03.01.04 A week
ymb(e)... (ūtan) 05.10.05.04.11 A circle, circuit, circumference
ymbeaht 16.02.04.03.02 Parts of service
ymbeardiende 04.05.03.01 Habitation, sojourn
ymbeardung 04.05.03.01 Habitation, sojourn
ymbebǣtan 12.05.06.01 Restraint, check, curb, control
ymb(e)fōn 10.04.02 To grasp, take hold of
ymb(e)sprǣc 09.01.04 Conversation, discussion
ymb(e)þanc(a) 06.01.01.01 Thinking about, minding, heeding
ymb(e)þridian 06.01.01.01.01 Thought, cogitation, meditation
ymbfær 05.12.05.04 To rotate, turn round, revolve
ymbfæreld 05.12.05.04 To rotate, turn round, revolve
ymbfæstnes 05.10.05.04.11 A circle, circuit, circumference
ymbfæstnung 02.02.05.01.01 A grave, burial place, sepulchre
ymbfæþmian 05.10.05.04.11 A circle, circuit, circumference
ymbfaran 05.12.05.06 To travel over/through/along, traverse
ymbfaran (... ūtan) 05.12.05.04 To rotate, turn round, revolve
ymbfaru 05.12.05.04 To rotate, turn round, revolve
ymbfeng 05.10.05.04.12 The condition of being covered
ymbfēran 05.12.05.04 To rotate, turn round, revolve

ymbfōn 05.10.05.04.11 A circle, circuit, circumference; 05.10.05.04.12 The condition of being covered; 06.01.05.01 Understanding

ymbgān 05.12.05.04 To rotate, turn round, revolve; 05.12.05.06 To travel over/through/along, traverse

ymbgang 05.10.06.02.02 Curvature, bend, twist; 05.12.01.03 Expanse over which something travels; 05.12.05.04 To rotate, turn round, revolve; 11.01.01 Practice, exercise, doing

ymbgangan 05.12.05.04 To rotate, turn round, revolve; 05.12.05.06 To travel over/through/along, traverse

ymbgearwian 04.04.07 Trappings, equipment, garb

ymbgedelf 17.02.04.02.02 Digging

ymb(ge)frætwian 07.10.03 An adornment, decoration, ornament

ymbgerēnian 07.10.03 An adornment, decoration, ornament

ymb(ge)sett 05.10.05.01 A little way, no great distance

ymbgyrd 11.01.03 Preparation

ymbgyrdan 04.04.07 Trappings, equipment, garb; 05.10.05.04.11 A circle, circuit, circumference

ymbgyrdan...lendena 11.02.01 Energy, vigour, vigorous action

ymbhabban 05.10.05.04.01.02 Contents, what is included; 05.10.05.04.11 A circle, circuit, circumference; 12.05.06.01 Restraint, check, curb, control

ymbhaga 04.02.05.06.08.01 A beehive

ymbhammen 05.10.05.04.12 The condition of being covered

ymbhealdan 05.10.05.04.11 A circle, circuit, circumference

ymbhēapian 05.12.05.04 To rotate, turn round, revolve

ymbhegian 05.10.05.04.11 A circle, circuit, circumference

ymbhlennan 05.10.05.04.11 A circle, circuit, circumference

ymbhoga 06.01.08.06.04 Care, anxiety, solicitude; 08.01.03.03 Anxiety

ymbhogian 06.01.08.06.04 Care, anxiety, solicitude; 11.10.02.02.01 Care, interest in

ymbhōn 04.04.07 Trappings, equipment, garb

ymbhringan 05.05.03 Binding, fastening; 05.10.05.04.11 A circle, circuit, circumference

ymbhringend 02.03.03.01 Body of retainers, household

ymbhweorfan 05.12.02.08 To give a different direction to, turn; 05.12.05.04 To rotate, turn round, revolve; 05.12.05.06 To travel over/through/along, traverse; 11.02.02.02.01 Attention, cultivation

ymbhweorfnes 11.11.04 Subversion, change

ymbhwyrft 01 Earth, world; 05.10 Space, extent; 05.10.04.02 A region, zone; 05.10.06.02 Rotundity, roundness; 05.10.06.02.02 Curvature, bend, twist; 05.12.05.04 To rotate, turn round, revolve; 11.02.02.02.01 Attention, cultivation

ymbhȳdig 06.01.08.06 Fear; 06.01.08.06.04 Care, anxiety, solicitude; 08.01.03.03 Anxiety

ymbhȳdiglic 06.01.08.06.04 Care, anxiety, solicitude

ymbhȳdiglīce 06.01.08.06.04 Care, anxiety, solicitude

ymbhȳdignes 06.01.08.06.01 A shuddering with fear, nervousness; 06.01.08.06.04 Care, anxiety, solicitude
ymbhygd 06.01.08.06.04 Care, anxiety, solicitude
ymbhȳpan 13.02.03.01.02 To beset, surround
ymbhȳwung 16.02.04.13.04 Circumcision
ymbiernan 05.12.05.04 To rotate, turn round, revolve; 05.12.05.06 To travel over/through/along, traverse
ymblǣdan 12.04.01.02 A fellow traveller, companion
ymblǣrgod 04.04.09 A fringe, border, hem
ymblicgan 05.10.05.04.11 A circle, circuit, circumference; 05.12.05.04 To rotate, turn round, revolve
ymblīpan 05.12.01.09 To travel on water
ymblōcian 02.05.09.04 To see, look upon, behold
ymblofian 16.02.04 Worship, honour, praise
ymblyt 05.10.05.04.11 A circle, circuit, circumference
ymbren 16.02.04.04.02.02.01 Ember-tide, Ember-days
ymbrendæg 16.02.04.04.02.02.01 Ember-tide, Ember-days
ymbrendagas 16.02.04.04.02.02.01 Ember-tide, Ember-days
ymbrenfæsten 16.02.04.04.02.02.01 Ember-tide, Ember-days
ymbrenwucu 16.02.04.04.02.02.01 Ember-tide, Ember-days
ymbryne 05.11.06 Course/cycle of time; 05.12.05.04 To rotate, turn round, revolve
ymbsǣlan 05.05.03 Binding, fastening
ymbscēawian 02.05.09.04 To see, look upon, behold
ymbscēawiendlīce 11.02.03 Forethought, care
ymbscēawung 02.05.09.04 To see, look upon, behold
ymbscīnan 03.01.12.02 A beam of light
ymbscrīpan 05.12.05.04 To rotate, turn round, revolve
ymbscrȳdan 04.04.07 Trappings, equipment, garb
ymbscūwan 09.05.04.01 Concealment, obscurity
ymbsellan 04.04.07 Trappings, equipment, garb; 05.10.05.04.11 A circle, circuit, circumference; 13.02.03.01.02 To beset, surround
ymbsēon 02.05.09.04 To see, look upon, behold; 02.05.09.05 To watch, observe, survey
ymbset 13.02.03.01.02 To beset, surround
ymbsetennes 13.02.03.01.02 To beset, surround
ymbsetl 13.02.03.01.02 To beset, surround
ymbsetnung 12.01.01.12.03 Rebellion, sedition; 13.02.03.01.02 To beset, surround
ymbsettan 04.02.04.02.04 Planting; 05.10.05.04.11 A circle, circuit, circumference
ymbsewen 11.02.03 Forethought, care
ymbsi(e)rwan 06.01.07.04.02.01 Deception, deceit, snare, wile
ymbsierwan 12.01.01.12.04.02 Conspiracy
ymbsittan 04.01.01 Eating; 05.10.05.01 A little way, no great distance; 12.02.02 An assembly, meeting;

13.02.03.01 An attack, assault; 13.02.03.01.02 To beset, surround
ymbsittend 04.01.01.07 Feasting; 12.06.03.03 A neighbour
ymbsmēagung 06.01.01.01 Thinking about, minding, heeding
ymbsnidennes 16.02.04.13.04 Circumcision
ymbsnīþan 16.02.04.13.04 Circumcision
ymbspænning 06.02.06.03.04 Allurement
ymbspannan 10.04.02 To grasp, take hold of
ymbsprăce 06.01.06.01.01 Knowledge
ymbsprecan 09.01 To speak, exercise faculty of speech
ymbsprecende 09.03.04.04 Discursiveness
ymbstandan 05.10.05.04.11 A circle, circuit, circumference
ymbstandednes 05.10.05.04.11 A circle, circuit, circumference
ymbstandend 02.05.09.05 To watch, observe, survey; 05.10.04.03 Presence; 12.06.03.03 A neighbour
ymbstand(en)nes 05.10.05.04.11 A circle, circuit, circumference
ymbstocc 04.02.05.06.08.01 A beehive
ymbstrīcan 03.01.06 Smoothness
ymbstyrian 05.06.01 Devastation, laying waste
ymbswăpe 05.12.01.03 Expanse over which something travels
ymbswāpan 01.01.03.01.02.06 Surging, rolling, heaving of waves; 04.04.07 Trappings, equipment, garb
ymbswīfan 05.12.05.04 To rotate, turn round, revolve

ymbtrymman 05.12.05.04 To rotate, turn round, revolve; 11.10.01 Protection, safekeeping
ymbtrymming 13.02.06 A fortification
ymbtȳnan 05.10.05.04.11 A circle, circuit, circumference
ymbtyrnan 05.10.05.04.11 A circle, circuit, circumference; 05.12.05 To move and change direction, turn
ymbþeahtian 06.01.01.01.01 Thought, cogitation, meditation
ymbþencan 06.01.01.01.01 Thought, cogitation, meditation
ymbþreodung 06.01.01.01.01.01 Consideration, rumination
ymbþringan 05.12.05.04 To rotate, turn round, revolve
ymbūtan 05.03 Source, origin; 05.10.05.04.11 A circle, circuit, circumference
ymbwăfan 04.04.07 Trappings, equipment, garb
ymbwærlan 05.12.05 To move and change direction, turn
ymbweaxan 05.10.05.04.11 A circle, circuit, circumference
ymbwendan 05.12.05 To move and change direction, turn
ymbwendan fram 05.12.02.08 To give a different direction to, turn
ymbwendung 02.08.13 Recovery, growing better; 11.05.02 Mode, manner, way, method, fashion, course
ymbweorpan 05.10.05.04.11 A circle, circuit, circumference
ymbwesan 11.02 Occupation, activity, business
ymbwīcigan 13.02.07.04 A camp, encampment
ymbwindan 05.05.03 Binding, fastening; 05.10.05.04.11 A circle, circuit,

circumference; 14.05.07 Binding, fastening with bonds
ymbwlātend 02.05.09.05 To watch, observe, survey
ymbwlātian 02.05.09.05 To watch, observe, survey
ymbwlātung 02.05.09.05 To watch, observe, survey
ymbwrēon 05.10.05.04.12 The condition of being covered
ymbwrītan 05.06.06 A scraping, scarifying
ymbwyrcan 05.10.05.04.11 A circle, circuit, circumference; 17.04.04 Fibrous materials
ymel 02.06.09.02.03 Beetle
ym(e)le 09.03.07.06.06 Membrane, vellum
ymen 16.02.04.03.03.01 A hymn, song of praise, canticle
ymenbōc 16.02.05.10.04 Choir books, etc.
ymensang 16.02.04.03.03.01 A hymn, song of praise, canticle
ymesēne 02.08.07.02.01 Defective vision
ymnensingende 16.02.04.03.03 Singing, church singing
ymnere/hymnere 16.02.05.10.04 Choir books, etc.
ynce 05.10.05.03 A measure of distance
yndse 03.03.02.01 A weight, definite amount; 15.01.04 Coinage, money
ynnelēac 02.07.09.02.02.01 Edible root/bulb
(ge)yppan 05.10.05.04.02.01 Exterior, outside of; 09.05.05.01 Showing, manifestation, display; 11.03.01.01.01 Proof, demonstration
geyppan 09.01 To speak, exercise faculty of speech; 09.05.05 Exposure, revealing, revelation; 14.03.03.01 Accusation
yppe 02.05.09.10 Look-out place; 04.05.02.10 Flooring, a floor; 04.05.03.04 A closet, chamber, room; 06.01.06.02.03.04.01 A school; 09.05.05.01 Showing, manifestation, display
ypping 02.05.09.12 To show; 09.05.05.01 Showing, manifestation, display
yppingīren 17.03.07 Tools for digging/grasping/pulling
ypplen 01.01.02.01.02.02 Hill, mountain
ȳr 09.03.07.01.01 A runic letter; 13.02.08.04 Weapons, arms
ȳre 15.01.04 Coinage, money
yrfan 04.01.02.04.05 Entertainment with food; 15.01.02.01 Inherited property
yrfcwealm 04.02.05.02.01 (Of cattle) seized with disease
yrfe 04.02.05 Livestock
yrfebēc 15.01.02.01 Inherited property
yrfebinn 04.02.05.03.02 A byre, stall, sty, shed
yrfebōc 14.04.01 A deed, contract, agreement
yrfefyrst 14.03.03 Law, action of the courts
yrfegedāl 15.01.02.01 Inherited property
yrfegeflit 09.07.01 Contention, argument, strife of words; 15.01.02.01 Inherited property
yrfegewrit 14.04.01 A deed, contract, agreement; 15.01.02.01 Inherited property
yrfehand 15.01.02.01 Inherited property
yrfelāf 15.01.02.01 Inherited property
yrfeland 15.01.02.01 Inherited property

yrfelēas 04.02.03.04.02 Pasture/pasturage; 15.01.01 Landed property
yrfenuma 02.03.02.03.05 Descendant; 15.01.02.01 Inherited property
yrfestōl 04.05.03.02.02.05 A paternal dwelling
yrf(e)weard 02.03.02.02.03 A son; 15.01.02.01 Inherited property
(ge)yrfeweardian 15.01.02.01 Inherited property
yrfeweardnes 15.01.02.01 Inherited property
yrfeweardwrītere 15.01.02.01 Inherited property
yrfewrītend 15.01.02.01 Inherited property
yrmen 05.10.05.02 Extension, stretching; 05.10.05.03.01.01 Breadth, width across
yrþ 04.02.03.02 Arable/ploughed land; 04.02.04.02.02.02 Ploughing, tilling; 04.02.04.03.02 Crop/crops
yrþland 04.02.03.02 Arable/ploughed land
yrþling 02.06.08.05 Forest bird, wild-fowl; 04.02.04.02 Cultivation/tillage
yrþmearc 05.10.05.04.11.01 A bound, limit
ysl(e) 03.01.09.02 Fire, flame
yslende 03.01.09.02 Fire, flame
ysope 02.07.11 Plants/flowers (alphabetical order)
ȳst 01.03.01.03.01 Storm, tempest
ȳstan 01.03.01.03.01 Storm, tempest
ȳstig 01.03.01.03.01 Storm, tempest
ȳtan 14.05.04 A penalty, punishment
(ge)ȳtan (ūt) 05.12.02.04 To cast out, drive away
ȳt(e)mest 05.11.10.02 End, completion
ȳtend 05.06.01 Devastation, laying waste
ȳtera 03.03.05.01.03 Inferior
yteren 04.04.06 Undressed condition (of hide)
ȳting 05.12.01.01 To go on a journey/expedition, travel
ȳtmest 03.03.05.01.03 Inferior
ȳþ 01.01.03.01.02 Sea/ocean; 01.01.03.01.02.05 Wave; 03.01.16 Liquid, a liquid
ȳþa ful 01.01.03.01.02 Sea/ocean
ȳþbord 05.12.01.09.03.01.03 Part of ship
ȳþfaru 01.01.03.01.02 Sea/ocean
ȳþgebland 01.01.03.01.02.06 Surging, rolling, heaving of waves
ȳþgewinn 01.01.03.01.02 Sea/ocean
ȳþ(g)ian 01.01.03.01.02.05 Wave; 01.01.03.06 Flood
ȳþgian 05.12.05.05.01 To wave, undulate
ȳþ(g)ian (mid) 03.03.04.02.02.01 Superabundance, excess
ȳþ(g)ung 05.08.02 Violence, force
ȳþhengest 05.12.01.09.03.01 A ship, boat
ȳþhof 05.12.01.09.03.01 A ship, boat
ȳþig 05.11.01.02.01 Swift movement of time
ȳþ(ig)ende 05.11.01.02.01 Swift movement of time
ȳþlād 05.12.01.09.03 A voyage
ȳþlāf 01.01.02.01.01.03 Shore, bank
ȳþlid 05.12.01.09.03.01 A ship, boat
ȳþlida 05.12.01.09.03.01 A ship, boat
ȳþmearh 05.12.01.09.03.01 A ship, boat
ȳþmere 01.01.03.01.02 Sea/ocean
ȳþung 01.01.03.06 Flood
ȳþwōrigende 02.06.06 Fish

KING'S COLLEGE LONDON MEDIEVAL STUDIES

I: James E. Cross, *Cambridge Pembroke College MS 25: a Carolingian sermonary used by Anglo-Saxon preachers.* viii + 252 pp., 1987. ISBN 0 9513085 0 5.

II: *The Sacred Nectar of the Greeks: the study of Greek in the West in the Early Middle Ages*, edited by Michael W. Herren in collaboration with Shirley Ann Brown. (10) + xii + 313 pp., 24 plates, 1988. ISBN 0 9513085 1 3.

III: *Cultures in Contact in Medieval Spain: historical and literary essays presented to L. P. Harvey*, edited by David Hook and Barry Taylor. xvi + 216 pp., 1990. ISBN 0 9513085 2 1.

IV: *Eleven Old English Rogationtide Homilies*, edited by Joyce Bazire and James E. Cross. xxxii + 143 pp., 1989. ISBN 0 9513085 3 X.

V: *Chaucer and Fifteenth-century Poetry*, edited by Julia Boffey and Janet Cowen. x + 174 pp., 1991. ISBN 0 9513085 4 8.

VI: Lynne Grundy, *Books and Grace: Ælfric's theology.* viii + 290 pp., 1991. ISBN 0 9513085 5 6.

VII: *Richard Cœur de Lion in History and Myth*, edited by Janet L. Nelson. xiv + 165 pp., 1992. ISBN 0 9513085 6 4.

VIII: Frank W. Chandler, *A Catalogue of Names of Persons in the German Court Epics. An examination of the literary sources and dissemination together with notes on the etymologies of the more important names*, edited by Martin H. Jones. 1992. ISBN 0 9513085 7 2.

IX: *Evangelista's 'Libro de cetrería': a fifteenth-century satire of falconry books*, edited by José Manuel Fradejas Rueda. liv + 87 pp., 1992. ISBN 0 9513085 8 0.

X: *Kings and Kingship in Medieval Europe*, edited by Anne J. Duggan. xv + 440 pp., 17 plates, 1993. ISBN 0 9513085 9 9.

XI: Jane Roberts and Christian Kay, with Lynne Grundy, *A Thesaurus of Old English*, in two volumes: Volume I - Introduction and Thesaurus; Volume II - Index. xxxv + 1555 pp., 1995. ISBN 0 9522119 0 4; vol. I: 0 9522119 2 0; vol. II 0 9522119 3 9.